The **Rough Guide** to

Ireland

written and researched by

Paul Gray and Geoff Wallis

NEW YORK • LONDON • DELHI

www.roughguides.com

Contents

◀◀ Benchoona, Connemara ◀ Powerscourt Estate

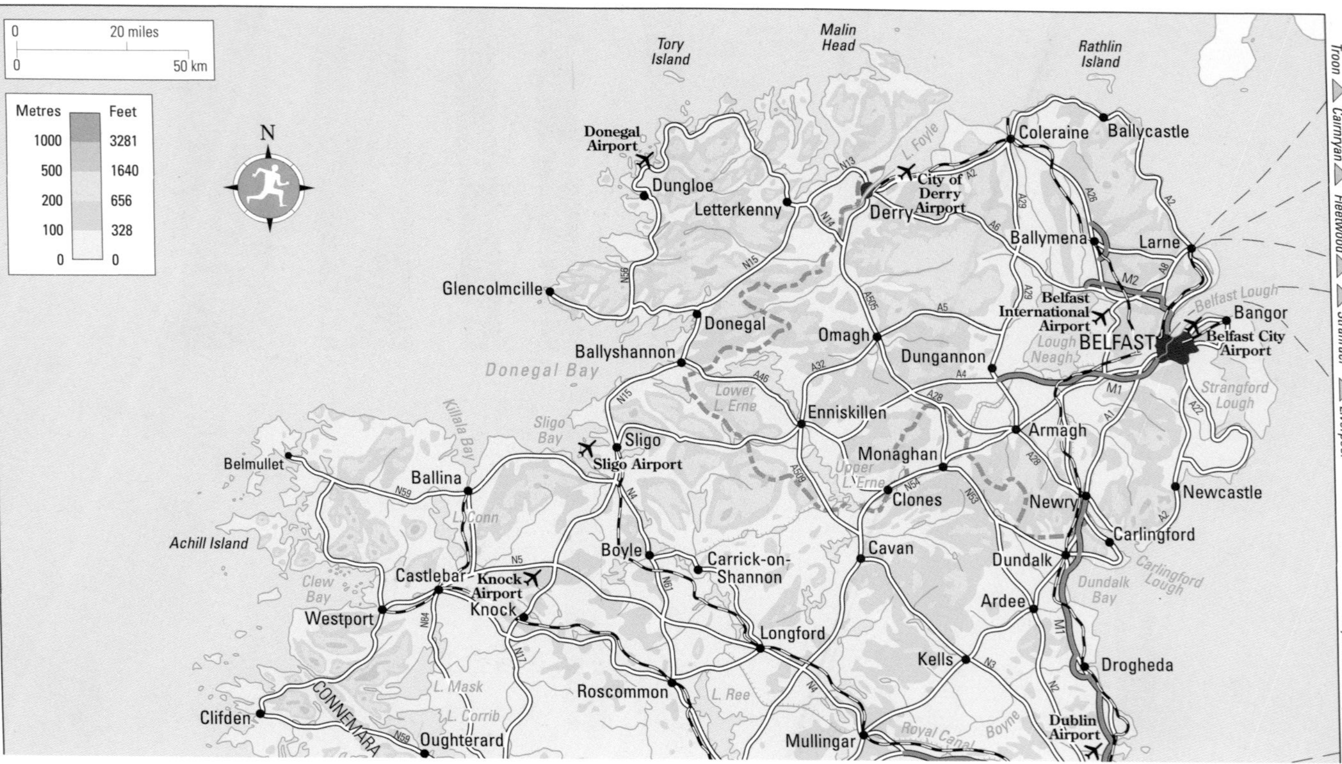
0 20 miles
0 50 km
Metres Feet
1000 3281
500 1640
200 656
100 328
0 0
N
Troon
Cairnryan
Fleetwood
Stranraer
Liverpool
Holyhead & Liverpool
Malin Head
Tory Island
Rathlin Island
Donegal Airport
Dungloe
Letterkenny
L. Foyle
City of Derry Airport
Derry
Coleraine
Ballycastle
Ballymena
Larne
Belfast Lough
Bangor
Belfast International Airport
Belfast City Airport
BELFAST
Lough Neagh
Strangford Lough
Glencolmcille
Donegal
Omagh
Dungannon
Ballyshannon
Donegal Bay
Lower L. Erne
Enniskillen
Armagh
Killala Bay
Sligo Bay
Sligo
Sligo Airport
Monaghan
Upper L. Erne
Clones
Newry
Newcastle
Belmullet
Ballina
L. Conn
Carlingford
Carlingford Lough
Achill Island
Boyle
Carrick-on-Shannon
Cavan
Dundalk
Dundalk Bay
Clew Bay
Castlebar
Knock Airport
Knock
Westport
Ardee
Longford
Kells
Drogheda
L. Mask
Roscommon
L. Ree
CONNEMARA
L. Corrib
Clifden
Oughterard
Mullingar
Royal Canal
Boyne
Dublin Airport
A2
A26
A29
A6
M2
A8
A5
A505
A4
M1
A1
A22
A28
A32
A46
N13
N14
N15
N56
N59
N4
N5
N61
N84
N17
A509
N54
N53
N3
N2

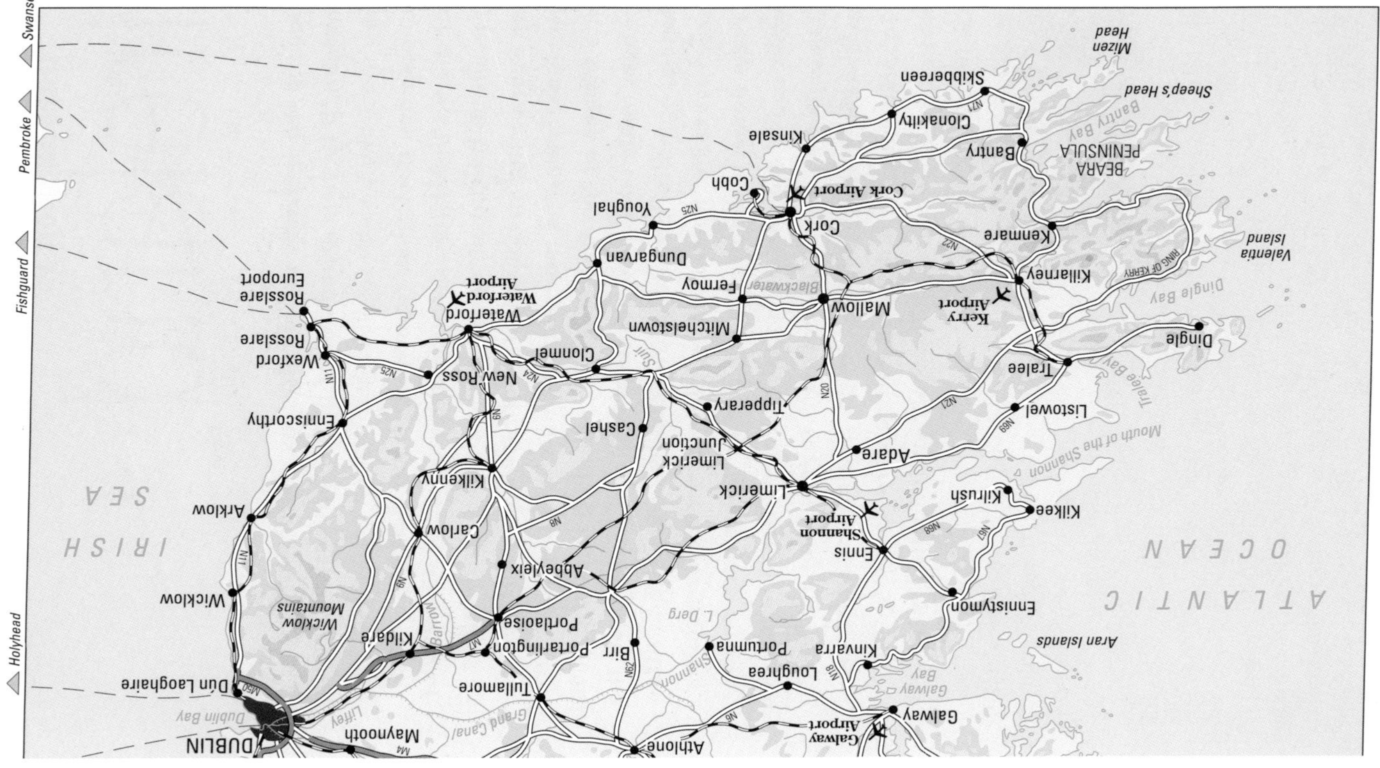
Holyhead
Fishguard
Pembroke
Swansea
IRISH SEA
ATLANTIC OCEAN
DUBLIN
Dublin Bay
Dún Laoghaire
Maynooth
Liffey
Wicklow
Wicklow Mountains
Arklow
Enniscorthy
Wexford
Rosslare
Rosslare Europort
Kildare
Barrow
Carlow
Kilkenny
New Ross
Waterford
Waterford Airport
Tullamore
Grand Canal
Portarlington
Portlaoise
Abbeyleix
Clonmel
Dungarvan
Youghal
Birr
Cashel
Suir
Athlone
Shannon
L. Derg
Limerick Junction
Mitchelstown
Fermoy
Blackwater
Portumna
Tipperary
Cobh
Loughrea
Limerick
Kinsale
Galway Airport
Shannon Airport
Mallow
Cork
Cork Airport
Kinvarra
Ennis
Adare
Galway
Galway Bay
Clonakilty
Skibbereen
Kerry Airport
Ennistymon
Kilrush
Bantry
Kilkee
Tralee
Kenmare
Listowel
Mouth of the Shannon
Killarney
BEARA PENINSULA
Bantry Bay
Aran Islands
Tralee Bay
RING OF KERRY
Mizen Head
Sheep's Head
Dingle
Dingle Bay
Valentia Island
M4
M50
N11
N9
N7
N25
N24
N8
N62
N6
N18
N20
N21
N22
N68
N67
N69
N71

Introduction to Ireland

Among the romantic preconceptions visitors bring to Ireland, it is their expectations of the landscape that are most likely to be fulfilled and indeed surpassed. An uncommon geological richness and the warming effect of the North Atlantic produce an astonishing diversity of terrain on this small island, accompanied overhead by an ever-changing canvas of wind-blown cloud effects. Ancient, crumpled mountains tumble into the ocean at the fringes of the land, which is splashed throughout with green, misty lakes and primeval bogland. In the east, the lonely, beautiful granite of the Wicklow Hills sits in utter contrast to the horse-grazing plain of the Curragh just a few dozen kilometres away, and in Connemara on the west coast, the ancient poets' "many-coloured land", you can walk from beach to mountain to fen, from seaweed-strewn inlet to lily-covered lough, in a matter of hours. Coupled with the unhurried nature of rural living, this scenic array encourages leisurely investigation, especially on foot or by bicycle.

With the richest store of **mythological traditions** in northern Europe, Ireland adds further interest to the landscape through the sacred associations of so many of its physical features – few counties do not shelter a pile of stones called "Diarmuid and Gráinne's Bed", where the star-crossed lovers are said to have slept together on their flight from the great warrior-seer Fionn Mac Cumhaill. But there's much more than the resonance of place names to this treasure chest of myths, which still has a life of its own in the tradition of storytelling. The great body of Irish **literature**, though much of it concerns the dysfunction of real life, is often spiked with wild, fantastical imaginings, from Swift, Sterne and Wilde through to Joyce, Flann O'Brien and Seamus

Heaney. And unlikely stories and surreal comedy are integral elements of the *craic*, the talking therapy of Ireland's pubs. Meanwhile, in the rich culture of **traditional music**, the two forms that are most likely to enrapture an audience – whether singing along or in silent appreciation – are ballads and *sean-nós* ("old-style" Irish-language singing), which recount tales of love, history and humour.

Many of Ireland's mythical deities were reinvented by the Church after the tenth century as historical personages, which can make interpretation of the country's abundance of **historic sites** more difficult, especially its enigmatic but awe-inspiring prehistoric tombs, stone circles and hill forts. There are few remnants of the Church itself from the

▲ Doheny and Nesbitt pub, Dublin

Fact file

- Ireland's landmass has a total area of 84,412 square kilometres, with its coastline stretching for 3152km. Its longest river is the Shannon (358km), largest lake Lough Neagh (387 square kilometres) and its highest point is Carrauntoohil in Kerry (1038m).
- Since 1921 the country has been divided into what's now called the Republic of Ireland, consisting of 26 counties, and Northern Ireland, subject to devolved British rule, which comprises 6 counties. The Republic's population is roughly 4.2 million, with 1.2 million residing in the Greater Dublin area, while Northern Ireland's population is approximately 1.7 million, with some 350,000 occupying the Greater Belfast area.
- The UK's 2001 Census reported that 44 percent of Northern Ireland's population is from a Catholic background and 53 percent from a Protestant background, while the Republic's 2006 Census revealed that 88 percent of its population is Catholic. Irish is the national language of the Republic, according to the constitution, with English recognized as a second official language. However, only around fifteen percent of the population has proficiency in Irish.
- Ireland divides into four provinces, loosely corresponding to ancient kingdoms: Leinster (covering counties Carlow, Dublin, Kildare, Kilkenny, Laois, Longford, Louth, Meath, Offaly, Westmeath, Wexford and Wicklow); Munster (Clare, Cork, Kerry, Limerick, Tipperary and Waterford); Connacht (Galway, Leitrim, Mayo, Roscommon and Sligo); and Ulster (Antrim, Armagh, Derry, Down, Fermanagh and Tyrone in Northern Ireland, plus Cavan, Donegal and Monaghan in the Republic). They do not have a political role but crop up in everything from Gaelic games to weather forecasts.

Hurling and Gaelic football

Ireland has two hugely popular, indigenous amateur sports, **hurling** and **Gaelic football** (see also p.47), which occupy a special place in the country's social fabric as ancient games whose renaissance was entwined with the struggle for independence. The **Gaelic Athletic Association (GAA)** was founded in 1884, coinciding both with moves to codify the rules of other sports in England and the US and with a growing nationalist awareness – indeed the GAA was dominated for a short period in its early years by the revolutionary Irish Republican Brotherhood. The first county championships were held in 1887, and the GAA went on to foster a network of local clubs – "a field in every parish", promised William P. Clifford, the GAA's 1926 president – which are still the heart and soul of many communities, with around 300,000 members. "One of the most important mass movements in European history," according to distinguished writer and politician Conor Cruise O'Brien, the GAA still requires that its top intercounty stars also play for their clubs back in their own parishes.

When played at the highest level, Gaelic football is a fast, skilful and muscular sport, in which the strongest rivalry is between old adversaries Dublin and Kerry. It's more widespread, though more recently developed, than hurling, which is said to have descended from a game played by the legendary warrior Cúchulainn. With its heartland extending in a rough, low-lying arc from Wexford to southeast Galway, hurling is an exciting, intricately skilled stick-and-ball game that's said to be the fastest team-sport in the world. If you can't get to a match yourself, the best place to get a flavour of these passionately supported games is the **Croke Park GAA Museum** in Dublin (see p.117).

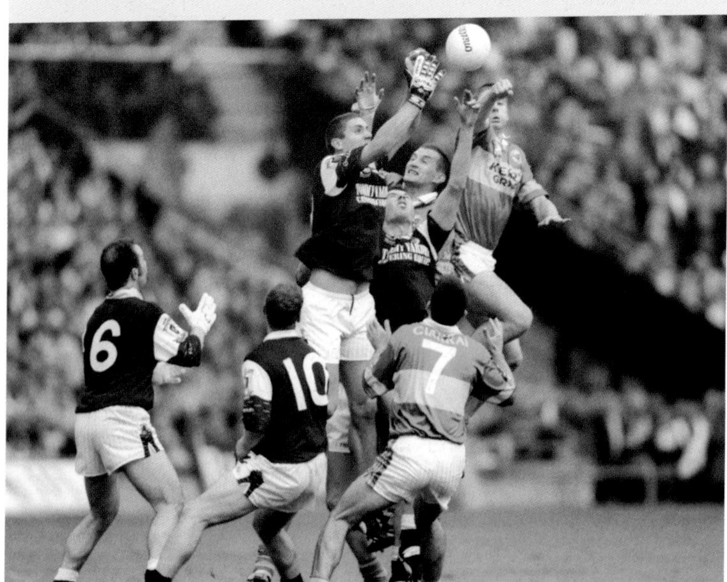

Stone crosses, Skellig Michael

so-called "Dark Ages", when the monasteries of Ireland clung on as great centres of learning, but their elaborate craftsmanship is evident in surviving illuminated manuscripts. Stone began to be used for religious buildings only in the ninth century, and the country is strewn with fine churches, distinctive round-towers and high crosses from later periods. Doughty castles and tower houses are reminders of the unrest and oppression that followed the twelfth-century Anglo-Norman invasion, while numerous stately homes from the eighteenth and nineteenth centuries attest to the power of the Protestant Ascendancy, alongside Neoclassical institutions in the cities and Dublin's extensive Georgian areas.

There is little vernacular architecture of note, however, thanks to centuries of oppression as the laboratory for British colonialism. The poverty experienced by ordinary Irish people under foreign rule was not immediately righted by Independence in 1921, and for most of the twentieth century the economy continued to stagnate. The last fifteen years, however, have seen a remarkable **rejuvenation** of Ireland's fortunes. The North, though still blighted by sectarianism and gangsterism, has received massive British and European investment and has achieved far greater stability since the 1998 Good Friday Agreement. So rapid was the Republic's economic growth during the 1990s – now somewhat abated – that it acquired the nickname of the Celtic Tiger. And, for the first time since the Great Famine of the 1840s, immigration began to outstrip emigration. Many Irish people have returned from abroad, bringing fresh ideas and

Many Irish people have returned from abroad, bringing fresh ideas and vibrancy to commerce and culture

▲ Millennium Footbridge, Dublin

vibrancy to commerce and culture, after the authoritarianism that followed Independence.

Greater prosperity has necessitated an influx of migrant workers, too, mostly from Eastern Europe and Africa. This has presented new challenges on both sides of the border, but in time may bring diversity to the South's Catholic homogeneity and the rigid duality of the North. At the same time, Ireland has one of the youngest populations in Europe, energizing the burgeoning bar, café and restaurant scenes in Dublin, Belfast, Cork and Galway. And the recent development of a modern Irish cuisine, using local ingredients and giving traditional recipes a global twist, is a telling sign of a new self-confidence. Meanwhile, an ever-expanding network of relationships with Europe and the US – where forty million people claim Irish descent – and between the two parts of the island, can only continue to have a constructive effect.

Where to go

Dublin is the Republic's main entry-point, a confident capital whose raw, modern energy is ever set beside rich cultural traditions, and which boasts outstanding **medieval monuments** and the richly varied exhibits of the **National Gallery** and **National Museum**. South of the city, the desolate **Wicklow Mountains** offer a breathtaking contrast to the urban flurry.

If you arrive on the **west coast** at Shannon Airport in County Clare, Ireland's most spectacular landscapes lie within easy reach. **Clare**'s coastline itself rises to a head at the vertiginous **Cliffs of Moher**, while inland lies **The Burren**, a barren limestone plateau at odds with the lush greenery characteristic of much of Ireland. To Clare's south, Limerick's **Hunt Museum** houses one of Ireland's most diverse and fascinating collections.

County Kerry, south of Limerick, features dazzling scenery, an intoxicating brew of invigorating seascapes, looming mountains and sparkling lakes. Though the craggy coastline traversed by the **Ring of Kerry** is a

Prehistoric tombs

Ireland is sprinkled with an extraordinary number of megalithic tombs, of which more than 1500 examples have been identified, and many are in remarkably fine condition.

The oldest tomb-form, dating from around 4000 BC, is the **passage grave**, consisting of a rounded mound or cairn with a stone-lined passage leading from the perimeter to a central chamber. Of the three hundred-plus surviving examples, mostly found in Ireland's north and east, **Newgrange** (see p.178) is the most renowned, remarkable not just because of its intricate construction – and the site's sheer scale – but also for its implicit associations with magic and ritual.

Dating from before 3000 BC, **court tombs** feature an open area beside the entrance, probably used for religious ceremonies. The majority are found in the country's north, **Creevykeel** in County Sligo being the best known (see p.485).

Portal tombs (known as **dolmens**), from around 2500–2000 BC, are the most easily recognizable form, consisting of three or more sturdy upright boulders, dragged into position, on which an often bigger capstone was placed. This tripod-like structure would then have a gallery tomb excavated beneath. Found in the north, west and southeast, a particularly fine example is at **Kilclooney** in County Donegal (see p.520).

Lastly, **wedge tombs** date from the early Bronze Age (around 2000–1500 BC), and are so termed because their burial chamber narrows and decreases in height as one moves inwards. More than a quarter of the recorded four hundred examples are located in **The Burren** in County Clare (see p.401).

major tourist attraction, it's still relatively easy to find seclusion. In County Galway, to Clare's north, lies enthralling **Connemara**, untamed bogland set between sprawling beaches and a muddle of quartz-gleaming mountains; in contrast, university cities such as Galway and Limerick possess an enticing vibrancy. Further north, **Donegal** offers a dramatic mix of rugged peninsulas and mountains, glistening beaches and magical lakes.

Dotted around the west coast are numerous **islands**, providing a glimpse of the harsh way of life endured by remote Irish-speaking communities. The **Arans** are the most famous – windswept expanses of limestone supporting extraordinary prehistoric sites – but the savagely beautiful landscape of the **Blasket Islands**, off Kerry's coast, is equally worth exploration.

Geological richness and the warming effect of the North Atlantic produce an astonishing diversity of terrain on this small island

On Ireland's southern coast, **Cork**'s shoreline is punctuated by secluded estuaries, rolling headlands and historic harbours, while **Cork city** itself is the region's hub, with a vibrant cultural scene and nightlife. To Cork's east, **Waterford city** houses the wondrous Viking and medieval collections of **Waterford Treasures**, while, in Ireland's southeastern corner, **Wexford**'s seashore features broad estuaries teeming with bird life and expansive dune-backed beaches.

▲ Book of Kells

Inland the Republic's scenery is less enchanting, its **Midland** counties characterized by fertile if somewhat drab agricultural land, as well as broad expanses of **peat bog**, home to endangered species of rare plants. However, there is gentle appeal in Ireland's great watercourse, the **Shannon**, with its succession of vast loughs, and the quaint river valleys of the southeast.

Numerous **historic** and **archeological sites** provide fine alternative attractions. The prehistoric tomb at Meath's **Newgrange** and the fortress of **Dun Aengus** on

▲ Barley Cove, County Cork

Inishmore are utterly mesmerizing; County Cork features many **stone circles**; and there's a multitude of **tombs** and **ring forts** across the west coast counties. Stunning early **Christian monuments** abound, too, including those located on **Skellig Michael** and the **Rock of Cashel** and atmospheric sites at **Clonmacnois**, **Glendalough** and **Monasterboice**. Of more recent origin, the Anglo-Irish nobility's planned **estates**, developed during the eighteenth and nineteenth centuries around impressive Neoclassical mansions, are visible across Ireland.

Much of **Northern Ireland**'s countryside is intensely beautiful and unspoilt, though most of the major attractions lie around its fringes. To the north are the green **Glens of Antrim** and a coastline as scenic as anywhere in Ireland, with, as its centrepiece, the bizarre basalt geometry

▲ Connemara, Country Galway

of the **Giant's Causeway**. In the southeast, **Down** offers the contrasting beauties of serene **Strangford Lough** and the brooding presence of the **Mourne Mountains**, while, to the west, **Fermanagh** has the peerless lake scenery of **Lough Erne**, a fabulous place for watersports, fishing and exploring island monastic remains. Evidence of the plantation is also provided by planned towns and various grand **mansions**, often set in sprawling, landscaped grounds.

To get to grips with the North's history, a visit to its **cities** is essential: **Belfast**, with its grand public buildings, was built on the profits ofVictorian industry; **Derry** has grown around the well-preserved walls of its medieval antecedent; and the cathedral town of **Armagh** is where St Patrick established Christianity in Ireland. Further insights are provided by tremendous museums, including Derry's **Tower Museum** and Down's **Ulster Folk and Transport Museum**.

When to go

Whenever you visit Ireland it's wise to come prepared for wet and/or windy conditions, especially along the Atlantic (west) coast. However, most years see weeks of gorgeous weather, though predicting their occurrence is often well nigh impossible. Generally, the sunniest months are May and June, while July and August are the warmest. Overall, the southeast gets the best of the sunshine.

Ireland is renowned as a **rainy** country and, on average, it rains on around 150 days a year along the east and southeast coasts, and up to as many as 225 days a year in parts of the west and southwest. April is the driest time, while December and January are the wettest. Whatever the case, the weather rolling in from the Atlantic is very volatile and you'll often find a soggy morning rapidly replaced by brilliant sunshine in the afternoon.

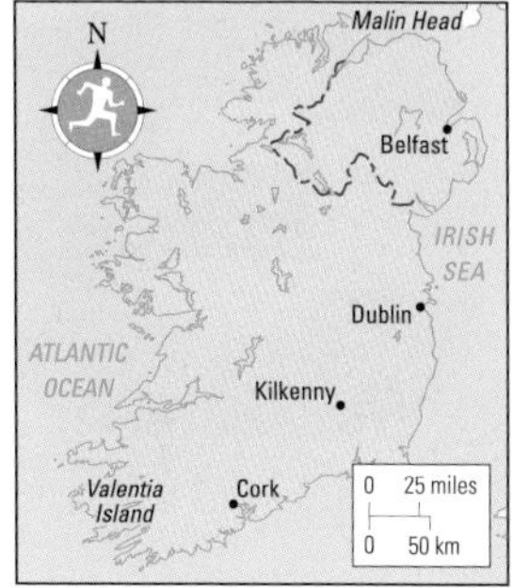

Average maximum and minimum daily temperatures (°C/°F) and monthly rainfall (mm)

	Feb	April	June	Aug	Oct	Dec
Belfast						
max	7/45	10/50	15/59	17/63	11/52	7/45
min	5/41	6/43	11/52	12/54	8/46	5/41
rainfall	77	66	72	101	106	106
Cork						
max	9/48	13/55	19/66	20/68	14/57	9/48
min	3/37	5/41	10/50	12/54	7/45	3/37
rainfall	79	57	57	71	99	122
Dublin						
max	8/46	13/55	18/64	19/66	14/57	8/46
min	2/36	4/39	9/48	11/52	6/43	3/37
rainfall	55	45	57	74	70	74
Kilkenny						
max	8/46	12/54	18/64	20/68	14/57	8/46
min	2/36	3/37	8/46	10/50	6/43	2/36
rainfall	66	51	51	69	85	89
Malin Head						
max	8/46	10/50	15/59	17/63	13/55	8/46
min	3/37	5/41	10/50	11/52	8/46	4/39
rainfall	76	58	64	91	118	103
Valentia Island						
max	23/73	17/63	11/52	12/54	17/63	21/70
min	11/52	8/46	6/43	4/39	7/45	10/50
rainfall	74	234	550	328	127	104

33 things not to miss

It's not possible to see everything that Ireland has to offer in one trip – and we don't suggest you try. What follows is a selective taste of the country's highlights: natural wonders and outstanding sites, plus the best activities and experiences. They're arranged in five colour-coded categories, which you can browse through to find the very best things to see and do. All highlights have a page reference to take you straight into the Guide, where you can find out more.

01 **Surfing** Page **50** • Thunderous waves roll in at great locations such as Brandon Bay, Easkey and Portrush.

02 Oysters see **Irish food and drink *colour section*** • Sample the shellfish at numerous great places along Ireland's coast or try your hand at an oyster-opening competition.

04 The Spike Page **105** • This tapering, 120-metre-high stainless-steel needle towers over Dublin's O'Connell Street, and is easily the most striking of the city's modern landmarks.

03 Georgian Dublin Pages **91–95** • Elegant squares and boulevards from the city's architectural heyday.

05 Ulster Folk and Transport Museum Page **630** • A massive and enthralling collection of galleries, re-creating Irish rural village life and celebrating Irish engineering, including exhibits on the ill-fated *Titanic*.

06 Brú na Bóinne Page 177 • One of Europe's finest prehistoric sites, an extraordinary ritual landscape.

07 Dun Aengus Page 435 • Spectacular cliff-edge fort, the Iron Age capital of the Aran Islands.

08 Ór in the National Museum, Dublin Page 89 • Lavish gold ornaments, preserved by the peat bogs since prehistoric times.

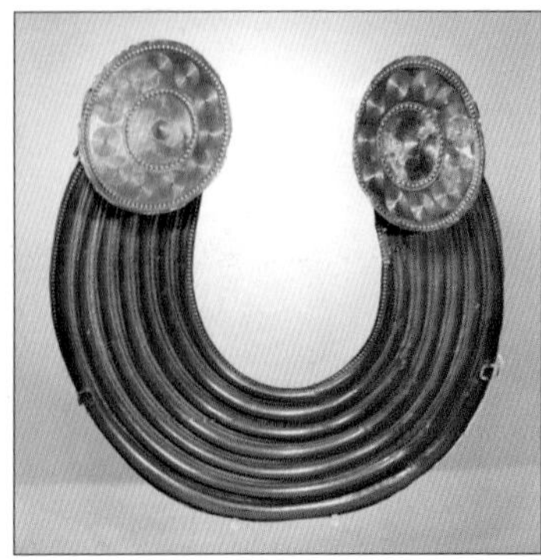

09 Dublin bars Page 125 • Feel the heartbeat of the city's social life, with over seven hundred venues to choose from.

10 Croagh Patrick Page **458** • It's a stiff climb, but the fine views and the mountain's religious and historical connotations make it all worthwhile.

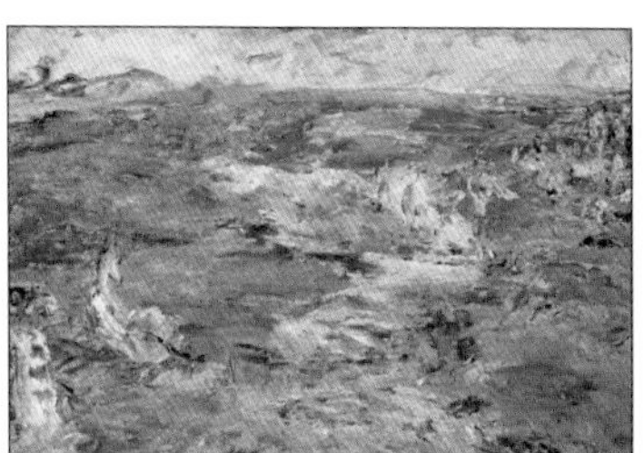

11 The Jack B. Yeats Collection in the National Gallery Page **90** • A room devoted to Ireland's greatest twentieth-century painter, bursting with raw energy and colour.

12 Traditional music Page **711** • All across Ireland, many a bar hosts exciting traditional-music sessions, with *Hughes's* in Dublin (see p.129), *McCollam's* in Cushendall (see p.591), and *Ciarán's Bar* in Ennis (see p.391) providing some of the best.

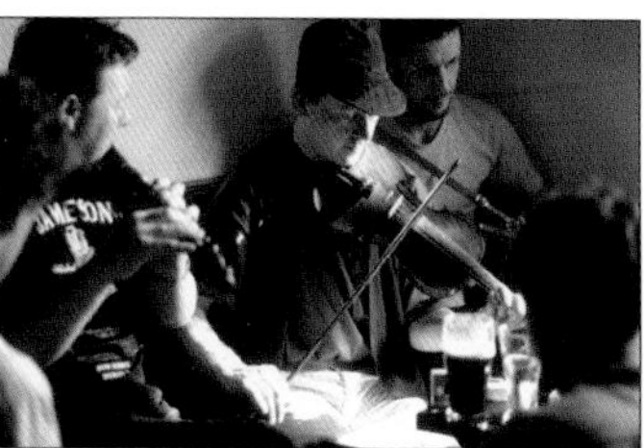

13 Horn Head Page **533** • Possibly the most breathtaking of County Donegal's numerous rugged peninsulas, with plenty of exhilarating cliff-top walks.

14 The Rock of Cashel Page **258** • Rising high above the Golden Vale, the Rock features an entrancing group of early ecclesiastical remains.

15 Kinsale Page **302** • Explore the imposing forts and sample some of Ireland's finest cuisine, in a glorious bay-side setting.

16 Connemara Page **440** • A varied landscape of mountains, lakes and beaches that's great for walking, with some pretty villages to base yourself in.

17 Horse racing Page **48** • Take a trip to one of Ireland's many racing festivals, savour the banter, pick up some tips and have a flutter.

18 Garinish Island Page **323** • Sail across from Glengarriff to these magical, otherworldly gardens.

19 Guinness see ***Irish food and drink colour section*** • The black stuff really does taste better in its own country, especially in its home town, Dublin.

20 The Giant's Causeway Page **596** • Marvel at the eerie but entirely natural basalt formation of the Causeway.

21 Kilmainham Gaol Page **115** • A grim encounter with the spartan prison regime experienced by Ireland's freedom fighters, with superb displays on the country's political and penal history.

22 Strangford Lough Page **633** • Breathtaking scenery, numerous ecclesiastical and historic sites combine in perfect harmony to make this one of Northern Ireland's major lures.

23 Political murals Pages **570, 609 & 610** • Politics and art combine in Northern Ireland's renowned political murals.

24 Killarney National Park Page **334** • The grandeur of the lakes and mountains has been drawing visitors to Killarney for over three centuries.

25 Festivals see **Festive Ireland *colour section*** • Festivals abound throughout Ireland, not least on March 17 when the whole country celebrates St Patrick's Day.

26 Bloomsday Page **110** • Don an appropriate costume and follow in the footsteps of characters from *Ulysses*, James Joyce's masterwork, each June 16.

27 Horse riding Page **49** • Enjoy an invigorating hack along the beach or trek through the mountains on a pony.

28 Glendalough Page **151** • This wonderfully remote and beautiful mountain valley shelters an atmospheric monastery.

29 Bantry House Page **321** • A magnificent setting for some lavish artworks, among formal gardens overlooking Bantry Bay.

30 Walking Page **49** • Whether it's a breezy seaside stroll or a more arduous long-distance path, one of the best ways to enjoy Ireland's magnificent land- and seascapes is on foot.

31 Skellig Michael Page **344** • A remarkable and inspiring early Christian hermitage clinging to a mountain summit on a wild, bleak island.

32 The Burren Page **401** • A barren expanse of cracked limestone terraces, stretching out towards the Atlantic and peppered with a multitude of fascinating megalithic remains.

33 Chester Beatty Library, Dublin Page **99** • An astonishing collection of manuscripts and artworks from around the world.

Basics

Basics

Getting there

Dublin is the Republic of Ireland's main point of arrival, Belfast that of the North, while Shannon, near Limerick city in County Clare, is the major airport providing direct access to the west coast. There's an ever-growing route map of flights between Britain and Ireland, on which you should try to book as early as you can to get the best price. Train–ferry and bus–ferry combinations are kinder to the environment and generally cheaper, though of course they take longer; on some routes, however, if you take a train and a catamaran (same price as a train–ferry combination), the journey times are surprisingly short. For those bringing their own car, there's a wide range of ferry routes from southwest Scotland, northwest England and Wales to Northern Ireland, Dublin and Wexford. North American visitors can fly direct to Shannon, Dublin, Knock or Belfast, but those from South Africa, Australia and New Zealand have to travel via Britain or Europe. Transport to Ireland is generally busiest, and fares at their highest, from June to September, especially in July and August, and over the Christmas and New Year period. If you're thinking of booking an organized tour, there are plenty of interesting options based in Ireland which have an online presence.

Flying from Britain

It's never been easier or cheaper to fly from Britain to Ireland. There are dozens of **routes** available, as detailed below, with new destinations regularly appearing (and unsuccessful routes sometimes being phased out). With so much competition, **prices** can be ridiculously cheap, especially if you book online (note that some of the airlines listed below do not accept telephone bookings at all). The secret is to book as early as possible: the biggest carrier, Ryanair, for example, offers fares of under £5 one-way if booked well in advance, but these can rise to around £140 one-way if left till the last minute. On top of these quoted fares, you'll be charged £20–30 each way in taxes, fees and charges. Flight time between London, for example, and Ireland is between one hour and one hour thirty minutes.

Airlines and routes

Aer Arann ⓣ0870 876 7676, ⓦwww.aerarann.com. Bristol, Cardiff, Edinburgh, Jersey, Leeds Bradford and Southampton to Cork; Glasgow to Donegal; Cardiff, Inverness and Isle of Man to Dublin; Bristol, Cardiff, Edinburgh, Leeds Bradford, London, Manchester and Newcastle to Galway; Manchester to Kerry; Manchester to Sligo; and Birmingham, London and Manchester to Waterford.

Aer Lingus ⓣ0870 876 5000, ⓦwww.aerlingus.com. London to Belfast; Birmingham, London and Manchester to Cork; and Birmingham, Edinburgh, Glasgow, London, Manchester and Newcastle to Dublin.

Air Berlin ⓣ0871 500 0737, ⓦwww.airberlin.com. London to Belfast.

Air Southwest ⓣ0870 241 8202, ⓦwww.airsouthwest.com. Newquay to Cork and Dublin.

BMI Baby ⓣ0871 224 0224, ⓦwww.bmibaby.com. Birmingham, Cardiff, East Midlands and Manchester to Belfast; Birmingham and Manchester to Cork; and Birmingham and Manchester to Knock.

British Airways ⓣ0870 850 9850, ⓦwww.ba.com. London to Dublin; and Glasgow to Derry.

Cityjet ⓣ0870 142 4343, ⓦwww.cityjet.com. London to Belfast and Dublin.

easyJet ⓣ0871 244 2366 or 0905 821 0905, ⓦwww.easyjet.com. Bristol, Edinburgh, Glasgow, Liverpool, London and Newcastle to Belfast.

Euromanx ⓣ0870 787 7879, ⓦwww.euromanx.com. Isle of Man to Belfast.

Flybe ⓣ0871 522 6100, ⓦwww.flybe.com. Aberdeen, Birmingham, Cardiff, Doncaster, Edinburgh, Exeter, Glasgow, Inverness, Jersey, Leeds Bradford, London, Manchester, Newcastle, Newquay and Southampton to Belfast; Exeter, Norwich and Southampton to Dublin; and Birmingham and Southampton to Galway.

Fly less – stay longer! Travel and climate change

Climate change is the single biggest issue facing our planet. It is caused by a build-up in the atmosphere of carbon dioxide and other greenhouse gases, which are emitted by many sources – including planes. Already, flights account for around 3–4 percent of human-induced global warming: that figure may sound small, but it is rising year on year and threatens to counteract the progress made by reducing greenhouse emissions in other areas.

Rough Guides regard travel, overall, as a global benefit, and feel strongly that the advantages to developing economies are important, as are the opportunities for greater contact and awareness among peoples. But we all have a responsibility to limit our personal "carbon footprint". That means giving thought to how often we fly and what we can do to redress the harm our trips create.

Flying and climate change

Pretty much every form of motorized travel generates CO_2, but planes are particularly bad offenders, releasing large volumes of greenhouse gases at altitudes where their impact is far more harmful. Flying also allows us to travel much further than we would contemplate doing by road or rail, so the emissions attributable to each passenger become truly shocking. For example, one person taking a return flight between Europe and California produces the equivalent impact of 2.5 tonnes of CO_2 – similar to the yearly output of the average UK car.

Less harmful planes may evolve but it will be decades before they replace the current fleet – which could be too late for avoiding climate chaos. In the meantime, there are limited options for concerned travellers: to reduce the amount we travel by air (take fewer trips, stay longer!), to avoid night flights (when plane contrails trap heat from Earth but can't reflect sunlight back to space), and to make the trips we do take "climate neutral" via a carbon offset scheme.

Carbon offset schemes

Offset schemes run by **climatecare.org**, **carbonneutral.com** and others allow you to "neutralize" the greenhouse gases that you are responsible for releasing. Their websites have simple calculators that let you work out the impact of any flight. Once that's done, you can pay to fund projects that will reduce future carbon emissions by an equivalent amount (such as the distribution of low-energy light bulbs and cooking stoves in developing countries). Please take the time to visit our website and make your trip climate-neutral.

Ⓦ www.roughguides.com/climatechange

Jet2.com Ⓣ 0871 226 1737, Ⓦ www.jet2.com. Blackpool and Leeds Bradford to Belfast; and Newcastle to Cork.

Luxair Ⓣ 0800 389 9443, Ⓦ www.luxair.lu. Manchester to Dublin.

Manx2 Ⓣ 0871 200 0440, Ⓦ www.manx2.com. Blackpool and Isle of Man to Belfast.

Ryanair Ⓦ www.ryanair.com. East Midlands, Glasgow and Liverpool to Belfast; Liverpool and London to Cork; Bristol, East Midlands, Glasgow, Liverpool and London to Derry; Aberdeen, Birmingham, Blackpool, Bournemouth, Bristol, Doncaster, Durham Tees Valley, East Midlands, Edinburgh, Glasgow, Leeds Bradford, Liverpool, London, Manchester and Newcastle to Dublin; London to Kerry; Bristol, East Midlands and London to Knock; and Birmingham, Bournemouth, Bristol, East Midlands, Edinburgh, Glasgow, Leeds Bradford, Liverpool, London and Manchester to Shannon.

By ferry from Britain

Ferry **routes** to Ireland are detailed below, along with the length of each voyage. High-speed catamarans operate on some of these routes, as noted below, though some don't run in the winter and in bad weather they're more likely to be cancelled than regular ferries. At the time of writing, Swansea Cork Ferries (Ⓣ 01792/456116, Ⓦ www.swanseacorkferries.com) were not operating on the ten-hour, usually overnight, route from Swansea to Cork, but were planning to buy a new boat to enter service in 2008.

Prices vary hugely according to the time of year, and even the day and hour you travel. Most ferry companies have peak seasons of July and August and may charge higher fares around public holidays; generally, it's cheaper to travel midweek, and to book online and in advance. As an example of prices, Stena Line's single fares for a car and driver from Holyhead to Dublin Port cost from £75 off-peak (Mon–Thurs) to £150 peak season (Sat); additional passengers cost £18 per adult, £6 per child, while foot passengers are charged £23 per adult, £15 per child.

Ferry companies and routes

Irish Ferries ⓣ0870 517 1717, ⓦwww.irishferries.com. Holyhead to Dublin Port (3hr 15min, catamaran 1hr 50min); and Pembroke to Rosslare (3hr 45min).
Norfolkline ⓣ0870 600 4321, ⓦwww.norfolkline-ferries.co.uk. Liverpool to Belfast (8hr) and Dublin Port (7hr).
P&O Irish Sea ⓣ0870 242 4777, ⓦwww.poirishsea.com. Cairnryan to Larne (1hr 45min; catamaran 1hr); Troon to Larne (catamaran 1hr 50min); Liverpool to Dublin (8hr).
Stena Line ⓣ0870 570 7070, ⓦwww.stenaline.com. Fishguard to Rosslare (3hr 30min, catamaran 2hr); Fleetwood to Larne (8hr); Holyhead to Dublin Port (3hr 15min) and Dún Laoghaire (catamaran 1hr 40min); and Stranraer to Belfast (3hr 15min, catamaran 1hr 45min).

By train from Britain

Combined train and boat journeys from Britain generally use one of three **routes** across the Irish Sea: Stranraer to Belfast, Holyhead to Dublin/Dún Laoghaire or Fishguard to Rosslare. Journey times are considerably quicker than by coach: London to Dublin, for example, can take as little as six hours thirty minutes, Glasgow to Belfast as little as four hours.

Ticket **prices** have recently been simplified on a zonal basis, and reduced: Manchester to Dublin, for example, including the cost of any of the boats from Holyhead, is a set fare of £23 single, London to Dublin £26; add £16 one-way if you're continuing by train to Cork, for example. It's not currently possible to **book** train–boat tickets online, but you can do it in person at most railway stations in Britain, or by phoning Stena Line (Stena Line sailings only), Sailrail or Virgin Trains.

Rail contacts

The Man in Seat 61 ⓦwww.seat61.com.
National Rail UK ⓣ0845 748 4950, ⓦwww.nationalrail.co.uk.
Sailrail ⓣ0845 0755 755, ⓦwww.sailrail.co.uk.
Stena Line ⓣ0870 545 5455, ⓦwww.stenaline.com.
Virgin Trains ⓣ0845 722 2333, ⓦwww.virgintrains.co.uk.

By bus from Britain

The main bus services to Ireland are provided by National Express and Bus Éireann, under the brand name **Eurolines**, crossing the Irish Sea via Stranraer, Holyhead and Fishguard. They're generally cheaper than travelling by train, but take far longer. The roughly twice-daily through service from London to Dublin, for example, takes around eleven hours or more and **costs** £43 for a standard return; a variety of promotional fares are available if you book seven, fifteen or thirty days in advance. Direct coaches also run between other major cities in Britain and Ireland; a standard return ticket from London to Cork costs £50, for example. Cheap advance offers, known as "funfares", can be accessed online, and reductions are also available for anyone under 26 or over 59. Tickets can be **booked** at any National Express agent, by phoning ⓣ0870 580 8080, or online at ⓦwww.nationalexpress.com/eurolines.

Flying from the US and Canada

Ireland is easily accessible **from the US**, with several airlines offering nonstop flights to Dublin and Shannon, the major gateway to the west of Ireland; Continental also operates a flight from Newark to Belfast, and Flyglobespan runs summertime services from New York and Boston to Knock in County Mayo. Flying time to Dublin, for example, is around six hours thirty minutes from New York and ten hours from Los Angeles. Aer Lingus, the national airline of the Republic, offers the widest choice of routes, including nonstop flights from Boston, Chicago and New York to both Shannon and Dublin, and from Los Angeles, Orlando, San Francisco and Washington to Dublin. If booked well in advance, their low-season fares from New York (JFK) to Dublin are around US$450–550 return (including taxes), and from Los Angeles around US$600–750. In high season fares rise to around US$750 from New York, US$1050–1300 from Los Angeles.

From Canada, Air Canada flies from Toronto nonstop to Dublin during the summer; Air Transat has summertime flights from Toronto to Dublin and Belfast; and Zoom Airlines flies to Belfast from Toronto and Vancouver year-round, from Halifax in the summer. Flight times are around six hours thirty minutes from Toronto, nine hours from Vancouver. If booked well in advance, Air Canada's fares are around Can$1000–1050 return (including taxes), while Vancouver to Belfast with Zoom Airlines, for example, can cost as little as Can$700.

Airlines

Aer Lingus ⓣ1-800/IRISH-AIR, ⓦwww.aerlingus.com.
Air Canada ⓣ1-888/247-2262, ⓦwww.aircanada.com.
Air Transat ⓣ1-866/847-1112, ⓦwww.airtransat.ca.
American Airlines ⓣ1-800/433-7300, ⓦwww.aa.com.
Continental Airlines ⓣ1-800/231-0856, ⓦwww.continental.com.
Delta Air Lines ⓣ1-800/221-1212, ⓦwww.delta.com.
Flyglobespan ⓣ0044 131 466 7612 (in the UK), ⓦwww.flyglobespan.com.
US Airways ⓣ1-800/428-4322, ⓦwww.usair.com.
Zoom Airlines ⓣ1-866/359-9666, ⓦwww.flyzoom.com.

Flying from Australia, New Zealand and South Africa

Travel from Australia, New Zealand and South Africa is generally via London, or one of the other European cities such as Frankfurt which have nonstop flights to Ireland. From Australia and New Zealand, it takes over twenty hours to reach Ireland, from South Africa at least thirteen hours. **Fares** from Sydney to Dublin start at around A$1900 (including taxes), from Auckland around NZ$2000 plus NZ$100–200 tax, and from Johannesburg around R7000 (including taxes).

Airlines

Air New Zealand Australia ⓣ13 24 76, New Zealand ⓣ0800 737000; ⓦwww.airnz.co.nz.
British Airways Australia ⓣ1300 767177, New Zealand ⓣ09/966 9777, South Africa ⓣ11/411 8600; ⓦwww.ba.com.
Cathay Pacific Australia ⓣ13 17 47, New Zealand ⓣ09/379 0861; ⓦwww.cathaypacific.com.
Emirates Australia ⓣ03/9940 7807, New Zealand ⓣ05/0836 4728; ⓦwww.emirates.com.
Lufthansa Australia ⓣ1300 655727, New Zealand 0800 945220, South Africa ⓣ0861 842538; ⓦwww.lufthansa.com.
Qantas Australia ⓣ13 13 13, New Zealand ⓣ0800 808767 or 09/357 8900; ⓦwww.qantas.com.
Singapore Airlines Australia ⓣ13 10 11, New Zealand ⓣ0800 808909; ⓦwww.singaporeair.com.
South African Airways South Africa ⓣ11/978 1111, ⓦwww.flysaa.com.
Virgin Atlantic Airways Australia ⓣ1300 727340, South Africa ⓣ11/340 3400; ⓦwww.virgin-atlantic.com.

Agents and operators worldwide

Travel agents and tour operators

Access Ireland Holidays Australia ⓣ1800 336676, ⓦwww.accessirelandholidays.com. Ireland specialists who offer walking and cycling tours, car rental and fly-drive, accommodation, coach and rail tours.
Celtic Trails Republic of Ireland ⓣ086 265 6258, ⓦwww.celtictrails.com. Well-organized and -equipped guided cycle tours along the west coast, with cycles, accommodation and luggage transfer covered.
Claddah Travel UK ⓣ0845 658 9007, ⓦwww.claddahtravel.co.uk. Birmingham-based agents that handle ferry, hotel, B&B, self-catering, coach-tour and car-rental bookings.
Clissmann Republic of Ireland ⓣ0404/48188, ⓦwww.clissmann.com/wicklow (Carrigmore,

Wicklow); **Into the West 2000** ⓣ090/974 5211, ⓦwww.kylebrack.net (Loughrea, Galway); **Kilvahan** ⓣ057/873 5178, ⓦwww.horsedrawncaravans.com (Coolrain, Laois); **Mayo Horsedrawn Caravans** ⓣ094/903 2054, ⓦwww.horsedrawn.mayonet.com (Castlebar, Mayo). These four companies offer horse-drawn caravan holidays in their local areas, driving and sleeping in traditional, wooden covered wagons.

ebookers UK ⓣ0800 082 3000, Republic of Ireland ⓣ01/488 3507; ⓦwww.ebookers.com. Low fares on an extensive selection of scheduled flights and package deals.

Euro-Bike & Walking Tours US ⓣ1-800-321-6060, ⓦwww.eurobike.com. Seven-day walking tours on the Ring of Kerry, and eleven-day cycling trips in west Cork and Kerry.

Go Ireland Republic of Ireland ⓣ066/976 2094, ⓦwww.govisitireland.com. Small-group, customized and self-guided walking and cycling tours on the west coast, as well as horse-riding and yoga holidays.

Inland Waterways Association of Ireland ⓦwww.iwai.ie. Umbrella association of companies who rent out barges and cruisers for holidays on the country's many lakes, canals and rivers.

Inroads Ireland US ⓣ1-888/220-7711, ⓦwww.inroadsireland.com. Irish-American company offering seven-day small-group tours of either the northern or southern half of Ireland, staying in B&Bs and taking in out-of-the-way places such as Inishmaan and Loughcrew Cairns as well as the major sights.

Irish Cycling Safaris Republic of Ireland ⓣ01/260 0749, ⓦwww.cyclingsafaris.com. Long-established and well-regarded company, offering guided and self-led tours, lasting a week, a weekend or customized, with cycles, accommodation and luggage transfer covered; also walking tours in Connemara.

Irish Ways Republic of Ireland ⓣ01/260 0340, ⓦwww.irishways.com. Long-standing organizer of guided hill and mountain walking tours throughout Ireland, which also offers self-guided trips on waymarked ways.

Leisurebreaks UK ⓣ0845 458 5200, ⓦwww.irelandbreaks.co.uk. Long-standing Ireland specialist, offering all manner of tailor-made breaks, encompassing ferries, fly-drives and city breaks, cruising, hotel and self-catering accommodation.

Naturetrek UK ⓣ01962/733051, ⓦwww.naturetrek.co.uk. Wildlife specialist offering five-day birdwatching trips to Mayo, and four-day botanical tours of the Burren.

North South Travel UK ⓣ01245/608291, ⓦwww.northsouthtravel.co.uk. Friendly, competitive travel agency, offering discounted fares worldwide. Profits are used to support projects in the developing world, especially the promotion of sustainable tourism.

Pat Falvey's Irish and Worldwide Adventures Republic of Ireland ⓣ064/44181, ⓦwww.patfalvey.com. Walking and mountaineering holidays and courses, mostly in the Macgillycuddy's Reeks, from the Kerry base of one of Ireland's leading explorers, as well as holistic and de-stress activities and island tours.

Shamrock Travel Australia ⓣ03/9602 3700, ⓦwww.irishtravel.com.au. Air tickets, accommodation, car rental and coach tours from Irish specialists.

South West Walks Ireland Republic of Ireland ⓣ066/712 8733, ⓦwww.southwestwalksireland.com. Guided and self-guided walking holidays on the west coast, in Antrim and in Wicklow.

STA Travel US ⓣ1-800/781-4040, UK ⓣ0871 230 0040, Australia ⓣ134 STA, New Zealand ⓣ0800 474400, SA ⓣ0861 781781; ⓦwww.statravel.com. Worldwide specialists in independent travel; also student IDs, travel insurance, car rental, rail passes and more. Good discounts for students and under-26s.

Trailfinders UK ⓣ0845 058 5858, Republic of Ireland ⓣ01/677 7888, Australia ⓣ1300 780212; ⓦwww.trailfinders.com. One of the best-informed and most efficient agents for independent travellers.

Online booking

ⓦ**www.expedia.co.uk** (in UK), ⓦ**www.expedia.com** (in US) ⓦ**www.expedia.ca** (in Canada)
ⓦ**www.lastminute.com** (in UK)
ⓦ**www.opodo.co.uk** (in UK)
ⓦ**www.orbitz.com** (in US)
ⓦ**www.travelocity.co.uk** (in UK), ⓦ**www.travelocity.com** (in US), ⓦ**www.travelocity.ca** (in Canada)
ⓦ**www.zuji.com.au** (in Australia),
ⓦ**www.zuji.co.nz** (in New Zealand)

Getting around

It's relatively easy to travel between the Republic's larger towns and cities, by means of the state-funded bus and rail companies Bus Éireann and Iarnród Éireann (Irish Rail) and a network of private buses. However, away from the major routes, timetabled services can be infrequent and it's common for many small towns and villages to have just one or two buses a week, often geared towards local market days. Transport in Northern Ireland is equally sparse in rural areas, with just a few train lines across the region, though the Ulsterbus network is pretty comprehensive. Renting a car is perhaps the easiest way to explore Ireland's rural and remote areas, though increasingly busy traffic means that many major routes can be clogged during rush-hour periods. Picturesque areas are particularly enjoyable on a bike, though you may need to bring your own or rent one in a major centre as the number of local outlets has diminished significantly of late because of the rising cost of insurance. If you want to travel quickly from Dublin or Belfast to outlying areas, it's also worth considering the internal flights available.

By rail

Ireland's topography was never amenable to the railway pioneers, and many branch lines closed for economic reasons during the middle decades of the last century. All that remains is a rather sketchy network that takes Dublin and Belfast as the main hubs, though work has begun to open what has become known as the Western Rail Corridor, County Clare to County Sligo (and trains are expected to run from Ennis to Athenry in 2009, though the entire route will not be open until 2014). Train services in the **Republic** are operated by Iarnród Éireann (Irish Rail; ⓣ01/836 6222, ⓦwww.irishrail.ie). Prices are usually higher than taking a coach, though journeys are often much quicker – for example, the train from Dublin to Killarney can take at least two and a half hours less than the bus. The main lines fan out from Dublin towards the southern and western coasts, but there are few links between them, and some counties (such as Donegal and Cavan) have no rail links at all.

Tickets come in a variety of formats – single, day return, five-day return, monthly return, family day and monthly returns. However, bear in mind that sometimes a single can cost almost as much as a return ticket – for example, a single to Killarney is €59, a five-day return €62 – and note also that the price of travelling on the lines from Dublin to Sligo, Ballina/Westport, Galway, Waterford and Rosslare is higher on Fridays and Sundays. It's always worth checking if any special deals are available, especially via the website.

The **North**'s rail service is operated by Translink (ⓣ028/9066 6630, ⓦwww.translink.co.uk) and restricted to just a few lines running out of Belfast. Services are generally efficient and the rolling stock has been recently updated. Fares are pretty reasonable – for example, travelling from Belfast to Derry costs £9.80 single and £13 return – and often comparable with bus services. The only line operating **between the Republic and the North** is the Dublin–Belfast Enterprise service (€34.50/£24 single, €50/£35 return).

For information on **transporting bikes** on trains, see p.37.

Rail passes

Although rail passes for travel within Ireland represent reasonably good value, a combined bus and rail pass is probably more useful owing to the limitations of the rail network. Passes are available at all major train and bus stations.

– An **Irish Rover** rail pass, covering both the Republic and Northern Ireland, costs €171,

with travel allowed on five days out of the fifteen for which it is valid. The **Irish Explorer** rail pass, covering only the Republic, is €138 for the same period, though you can extend this to cover bus travel in the Republic on Bus Éireann and Dublin Bus's station link services; this combined pass costs €210 and covers eight days' travel out of fifteen. The **Emerald Card** allows travel on all scheduled bus and rail services in the Republic and Northern Ireland and costs €236 for eight consecutive days or €406 for fifteen. If you're only visiting the North, it's worth acquiring a **Freedom of Northern Ireland pass**, offering unlimited travel on trains, Ulsterbus and Belfast Metro bus services – passes are available for one day (£14), three days out of eight (£34) and seven consecutive days (£50).

If your visit to Ireland is just part of a grander European trip, it's well worth investigating the range of different passes on offer, such as Inter-Rail (Ⓦwww.interrail.com) and Eurail (Ⓦwww.eurail.com). Details of these are provided by **Rail Europe** (Ⓦwww.raileurope.co.uk or Ⓦwww.raileurope.com), the umbrella company for all European national and international rail purchases, which also sells passes online and Inter-Rail.

Distance chart

Km/miles

	Athlone	Belfast	Cork	Derry	Dublin	Enniskillen	Galway
Athlone	-	227	219	209	126	142	93
	-	141	136	130	78	88	58
Belfast	227	-	424	117	167	138	306
	141	-	264	73	104	86	190
Cork	219	424	-	428	257	360	209
	136	264	-	266	160	224	130
Derry	209	117	428	-	237	98	272
	130	73	266	-	147	61	169
Dublin	126	167	257	237	-	184	219
	78	104	160	147	-	109	136
Enniskillen	142	138	360	98	184	-	183
	88	86	224	61	109	-	114
Galway	93	306	209	272	219	183	-
	58	190	130	169	136	114	-
Kilkenny	126	284	148	335	117	232	172
	78	177	82	208	73	144	107
Killarney	232	436	87	441	309	364	193
	144	271	54	274	192	226	120
Limerick	121	323	105	328	198	262	105
	75	201	65	204	123	163	65
Rosslare	209	330	208	397	163	312	274
Europort	130	205	129	247	101	170	170
Shannon	134	346	129	351	222	260	92
Airport	83	215	80	218	138	161	57
Sligo	117	206	336	135	217	68	138
	73	128	209	84	135	42	86
Waterford	174	333	126	383	158	260	220
	108	207	78	238	98	174	137

By bus

Bus Éireann (Ⓣ01/836 6111, Ⓦwww.buseireann.ie) runs **express coach** and slower **local services** throughout the Republic. Services between major towns are usually fast and direct, though you might experience delays if you have to wait for connections. Ticket prices are generally far more reasonable than trains and Bus Éireann regularly offers some extraordinarily good-value deals, especially between Dublin and Cork. Timetables and fares for the major routes can be found on the website, which is particularly worth checking for special deals, and on the Aertel teletext service provided by RTÉ (see p.43). The majority of buses show destinations in both Irish and English, but some in rural areas may only display the former.

Bus Éireann offers two different bus-only travel passes (for combined bus–rail passes see p.33). The **Open Road** pass can be purchased in a variety of combinations covering from three to fifteen days' travel during periods of double your chosen length. So, for example, a pass allowing travel for three days out of six costs €47, five days out of ten is €74, ten out of twenty €141.50 and fifteen out of thirty €209. The **Irish Rover** pass covers travel on services in both the Republic and Northern Ireland and costs €73 for three days travel out of eight, €165 for eight out of fifteen and €245 for fifteen out of thirty.

A vast number of **private bus companies** also operate in the Republic, running services on major routes, as well as areas not covered by the Bus Éireann network (especially County Donegal). The names, contact details and routes of these companies are listed at the end of each Guide chapter, where applicable. These can sometimes be cheaper and quicker than Bus Éireann, but are usually very

Kilkenny	Killarney	Limerick	Rosslare Europort	Shannon Airport	Sligo	Waterford
126	**232**	**121**	**209**	**134**	**117**	**174**
78	144	75	130	83	73	108
284	**436**	**323**	**330**	**346**	**206**	**333**
177	271	201	205	215	128	207
148	**87**	**105**	**208**	**129**	**336**	**126**
82	54	65	129	80	209	78
335	**441**	**328**	**397**	**351**	**135**	**383**
208	274	204	247	218	84	238
117	**309**	**198**	**163**	**222**	**217**	**158**
73	192	123	101	138	135	98
232	**364**	**262**	**312**	**260**	**68**	**260**
144	226	163	195	161	42	174
172	**193**	**105**	**274**	**92**	**138**	**220**
107	120	65	170	57	86	137
-	**198**	**113**	**100**	**137**	**245**	**48**
-	123	70	62	85	152	30
198	**-**	**111**	**275**	**135**	**343**	**193**
123	-	69	171	84	213	120
113	**111**	**-**	**211**	**24**	**232**	**129**
70	69	-	131	15	144	80
100	**275**	**211**	**-**	**235**	**327**	**82**
62	171	131	-	146	203	51
137	**135**	**24**	**235**	**-**	**219**	**153**
85	84	15	146	-	136	95
245	**343**	**232**	**327**	**219**	**-**	**293**
152	213	144	203	136	-	182
48	**193**	**129**	**82**	**153**	**293**	**-**
30	120	80	51	95	182	-

busy at weekends, when advance booking is advisable.

In **Northern Ireland**, **Ulsterbus**, part of Translink (see p.32), runs a pretty comprehensive network of regular and reliable services across the six counties. For details of its combined bus–rail pass, see p.33.

Each chapter in the Guide includes information on the most useful bus services in its closing "Travel details" section. For information on transporting bikes on buses, see p.37.

By car and motorcycle

Travelling by **car** or **motorbike** is the ideal way to explore some of the best of Ireland's landscape, especially in remote areas, though traffic has become increasingly busy in recent years, particularly during rush hour in major centres. If you bring your own vehicle, it's essential to carry its registration document and certificate of **insurance** – and make sure that your existing policy covers you for driving in Ireland. Whether bringing your own vehicle or renting one on arrival, you'll need to be in possession of a valid **driving licence** (and should bring it with you – a photocopy is insufficient). A licence from any EU country is acceptable, but visitors from outside the EU must acquire an International Driving Permit, which can be obtained from motoring organizations before leaving for Ireland.

The fundamental rule of the road in Ireland, both North and South, is to **drive on the left**. Wearing **seat belts** is compulsory for drivers and passengers, as is the wearing of helmets for motorcyclists and their pillion riders. The Republic's **speed limits** are 50kph in built-up urban areas, 80kph on rural roads (denoted by the letter "R" on maps and signposts), 100kph on national roads (denoted by an "N") and 120kph on motorways ("M" roads). Maximum speeds in

Northern Ireland are 20–40mph in built-up areas, 70mph on motorways and 60mph on most other main roads. Minor rural roads in the Republic are generally poor in quality, often potholed and sometimes rutted – a situation notably different from the North where the overwhelming majority of roads, of all categories, are well maintained. **Signposts** in the Republic generally provide place names in both Irish and English, though in the Gaeltacht you'll generally only encounter signposts in Irish. Virtually all signposts in the Republic provide distance information in kilometres; in the North distances are given in miles.

Throughout Ireland many town centres require payment for on-street **parking**, either using ticket machines or a disc or card parking scheme (discs or cards can be purchased in adjacent shops). If you don't display a ticket or disc you may end up with a parking fine or, particularly in Dublin, Cork and Galway, your car being clamped or towed away. Some Dublin streets still have parking meters, but since the city suffers from high rates of **theft** and vandalism, it's always advisable to use a secure car park.

In the Republic, unleaded **petrol** costs around €1.18 a litre – cheaper than the North where the equivalent price is 98p – so filling up before you cross the border from the South will save money.

Car rental

Outlets of multinational **car rental companies**, such as Avis and Hertz, can be found at airports, in the cities and in some tourist hotspots. Rental charges are high – expect to pay around €30/£22 per day plus insurance – though prices are often much cheaper in the Republic than in the North, with the best offers garnered if you book well in advance, especially via the Internet. Sometimes smaller local firms can undercut the big names.

In all cases, to secure your rental, you must be 23 or over (though some may accept drivers aged 21 or 22 with a hefty price hike) and able to produce a full and valid driving licence, with no endorsements incurred during the previous two years. Considering the nature of Ireland's roads and all the attendant risks, it's always advisable to take up the collision damage waiver (CDW) offered when picking up your car. The daily rate for this is usually around €9/£6, but it guarantees that you won't be liable for a hefty bill if you suffer an accident or any other damage. If you're planning to cross the border, ensure that your rental agreement provides full insurance; in some cases, you may need to pay extra.

Booking a car prior to your journey saves time when you arrive in Ireland and provides the chance to shop around on the Web for the best deals. We've listed the main brokers and agencies below.

Rental brokers

The following brokers all provide online car-rental booking from anywhere in the world and some offer fly–drive or train–sail–drive options.

5th Gear Ⓦwww.car-rental-hire.co.uk.
Auto Europe Ⓦwww.autoeurope.com.
Autos Abroad Ⓦwww.autosabroad.com.
Go Ireland Ⓦwww.goireland.com.
Holiday Autos Ⓦwww.holidayautos.com.

Rental agencies

Contact numbers are for the Republic of Ireland unless stated otherwise.

Argus Ⓣ01/499 9658, UK Ⓣ0207/300 3787; Ⓦwww.argusrentals.com.
Atlas Ⓣ01/844 4859, Ⓦwww.atlascarhire.com.
Avis Ⓣ1/605 7500, Ⓦwww.avis.ie; in Northern Ireland Ⓣ028/9024 0404, Ⓦwww.avis.co.uk.
Budget Ⓣ090/662 7711, Ⓦwww.budgetcarrental.ie.
County Ⓣ01/235 2030, Ⓦwww.countycar.ie.
Dan Dooley Ⓣ062/53103, Ⓦwww.dan-dooley.ie.
Europcar Ⓣ01/614 2888, Ⓦwww.europcar.ie.
Hertz Ⓣ01/709 3060; in Northern Ireland Ⓣ028/9073 2451; Ⓦwww.hertz.com.
Nova Ⓣ066/979 1818 or 1800 200115; from the UK Ⓣ0800 018 6682; from the USA Ⓣ1-866-NOVACAR.
SIXT (Irish Car Rentals) Ⓣ1850 206088; from Europe and the UK Ⓣ0800 4747 4227; from the USA Ⓣ1-877-347 3227; Ⓦwww.irishcarrentals.ie.
Thrifty Ⓣ1/844 1944 or Ⓣ1800 515800; in Northern Ireland Ⓣ028/9445 2565; in Britain Ⓣ0800 783 0405; from the USA & Canada Ⓣ1-800/229 0984; Ⓦwww.thrifty.ie.

Cycling

Apart from some steep ascents, occasional poor road surfaces and an unpredictable climate, Ireland provides ideal territory for **cycling**, one of the most enjoyable ways to explore the country's often stunning scenery. There are a number of waymarked **trails** (see p.48). Tourist offices (see p.56) can supply information on organized cycling **tours**, or contact a specialist cycling-tour operator (see p.30). The Northern Ireland Tourist Board's free *Cycling Holidays guide*, available at tourist offices, describes various routes and accommodation packages available.

If you plan to **bring your own bike**, note that some airlines will transport bicycles for free as long as you keep within your weight allowance, but it's always worth checking with them well in advance.

Thanks to a rise in insurance premiums, far fewer places in the Republic now **rent out bikes**, and there are still just a small number of outlets in the North, meaning that it's always wise to book your wheels well ahead. Eurotrek Raleigh (ⓣ01/465 9659, ⓦwww.raleigh.ie) is the largest distributor of bikes in Ireland and its website lists a number of its agents offering rental. It's best to contact one of these directly, and bear in mind that local dealers, including some hostels, may often be cheaper. Rental rates are generally around €20 per day, €80 per week and rising to €100 a week if you want to leave the bike at another agency, with an extra charge of €5 per day or €20 per week for hiring panniers, though a helmet is usually included gratis. A deposit of anything from €100 to €200 is also required. When collecting your bike, check that its brakes and tyres are in good condition, and make sure that it comes equipped with a pump and repair kit. If you're planning on cycling in upland areas it makes sense to rent a bike with at least sixteen gears and preferably 24.

Across the island, minor roads in rural areas generally see little traffic, but major roads are well worth avoiding due to heavy traffic. Bikes are easy to **transport** over long distances by train, but less so by bus though note that you can only take folding bikes, which must be covered, on DART and commuter services in the **Republic**. Bikes cannot be taken on some Intercity trains (such as the Dublin–Sligo service) though on those where conveyance is possible the cost ranges between €3 and €15 depending upon the length of the journey. Folding bicycles incur no charge. Taking your bike with you on Bus Éireann costs an additional €11 single, however long your journey, though drivers are not obliged to take a bike and may in any case only have room for one. Private bus companies will sometimes allow bikes to be carried, though usually only if booked at the same time as your seat; prices vary according to the company. In the **North** carrying a bike is free on both Ulsterbus services (provided that a boot and space is available – folding bikes can be taken on board) and the railways (as long as room is available and, in the case of commuter routes, it's after 9.30am).

By air

Easily the quickest way to reach outlying areas is to take a scheduled flight from Dublin or Belfast to one of the **regional airports** dotted around the country. Aer Arann operates the largest network. Prices are not cheap (singles range from around €30 to €80, depending on season and demand) and there's often little to be saved by booking a return ticket. However, much time can be gained; for instance, the flight from Dublin to Donegal takes only an hour, compared with at least four hours on the bus.

Airlines and routes

Aer Arann ⓣ0818/210210, ⓦwww.aerarann.com. Belfast City to Cork; Cork to Galway; Dublin to Cork, Donegal, Galway, Kerry and Sligo.
Aer Lingus ⓣ0818/365000, ⓦwww.aerlingus.com. Dublin to Shannon.
British Airways ⓣ0870/850 9850 (UK), ⓦwww.britishairways.com. Dublin to Derry.
Flybe ⓣ0871/522 6100 (UK), ⓦwww.flybe.com. Belfast City to Galway.
Ryanair ⓣ0818/303030, ⓦwww.ryanair.com. Dublin to Cork.

Accommodation

There's a huge variety of accommodation across Ireland, ranging from the luxurious to the very basic. At the top of the range are swish modern hotels, usually found in the cities and major tourist spots, and castles, often in glorious locations, which have opened their doors to paying guests. Below these in price come elegant, often historic country houses, followed by well-furnished and very comfortable guesthouses. Then there's an abundance of places offering bed and breakfast (B&Bs), whether run as a year-round business or a family home taking guests during the school summer holidays or at festival time. There are also more than two hundred hostels, which vary tremendously in quality and atmosphere, but all provide a bed and often a kitchen; plenty offer a good deal more. Finally, there are numerous well-run campsites and, if you're feeling hardy, the chance to pitch a tent in a farmer's field or on common land.

You'll need to book your accommodation well in advance over **St Patrick's Day**, **Easter**, summer **public holidays** (see p.55), and during all of **July** and **August**. Accommodation is at a premium in Dublin throughout the year, especially at weekends, and in places such as the **Aran Islands**, **Belfast**, **Cork**, **Derry**, **Dingle**, **Galway city**, **Kilkenny** and **Killarney**, and during major festivals elsewhere (see p.44). Many establishments close over the Christmas period.

Booking accommodation

Unless you know the specific place you want to stay, the easiest way to book accommodation (including tourist-board-approved hostels) is via the officially approved agency **Gulliver Ireland** (freephone: in the Republic ⓣ1800 3698 7412; from Britain and Northern Ireland ⓣ800 783 8359 or 783 5740; from the USA ⓣ1-888/827-3028; from other countries insert the international freephone code, where available, before 800 6686 6866; the payphone number from any country is ⓣ+00353/66 979 2030; ⓦwww.gulliver.ie and ⓦwww.goireland.com). Each hotel, B&B or hostel reservation costs €4, though you can reserve subsequent nights in other establishments for an additional €1.50 per booking as part of the same transaction. To reserve self-catering accommodation costs €7. Usually a non-refundable deposit of ten percent is also charged to your card, deducted from the price of your first night's stay, though if booking self-catering accommodation less than two weeks in advance, you will be asked to pay the full amount. The system can also be accessed via the website of the two Irish tourist boards (ⓦwww.discoverireland.ie and ⓦwww.discovernorthernireland.com). Accommodation endorsed by the tourist boards demands certain service standards, so if your approved hotel or B&B is below par, then complaints should be addressed to the local tourist office.

In addition to Gulliver Ireland, a number of **accommodation associations** produce their own brochures or have sites offering online reservations. In the **Republic** one very useful publication is the annual *Ireland Accommodation Guide*, produced by Tourism Accommodation Approvals (ⓦwww.taaireland.com; €5), which covers all registered establishments except hotels and details of their facilities though does not provide descriptions. In the **North**, the Northern Ireland Tourist Board (ⓦwww.discovernorthernireland.com) produces free annual accommodation guides covering B&Bs and guesthouses, hotels, and budget options (including hostels), available from its website or local tourist offices.

All Fáilte Ireland and NITB **tourist offices** (see p.56) can help find accommodation, as can many other local tourism initiatives (listed in the Guide). When there's no office available, finding somewhere to stay is often still relatively simple – just pop into a local shop or pub and ask for advice.

Accommodation associations

Adams & Butler ⓦwww.irishluxury.com. A selection of rural and historic family-run guesthouses and inns across Ireland, as well as self-catering in a variety of settings.
Family Homes of Ireland ⓦwww.familyhomes.ie. B&B association whose website lists numerous pleasant options for the budget conscious.
Hidden Ireland ⓦwww.hiddenireland.com. Over thirty private homes, mainly in the Republic, most of which are selected for their historic nature or architectural merit.
Ireland's Blue Book ⓦwww.irelandsbluebook.com. Upmarket country houses and restaurants, both North and South.
Irish Farmhouse Holidays ⓦwww.irishfarmholidays.com. More than 300 farmhouse B&Bs, some in exquisite rural locations.
The Irish Hotels Federation ⓦwww.irelandhotels.com. Covering numerous hotels and guesthouses across Ireland, the federation's comprehensive *Be My Guest* brochure (€10) is well worth acquiring.
Manor House Hotels ⓦwww.cmvhotels.com. Around 30 luxury and boutique hotels in the Republic.
Northern Ireland Hotels Federation ⓦwww.nihf.co.uk. Smaller than its equivalent in the Republic, but still offering an extensive range of more than one hundred hotels and guesthouses.
The Northern Ireland Self Catering Holidays Association ⓦwww.nischa.com. Covers everything from thatched cottages to castles and luxury apartments.
Self Catering Ireland ⓦwww.selfcatering-ireland.com. A good starting-point for finding your preferred holiday home, with more than 2500 listed.
Town and County Homes ⓦwww.townandcountry.ie. The major B&B association in the Republic (plus a few members in the North); produces a valuable annual guide (€10), describing all its tourist-board-approved accommodation.

B&Bs, guesthouses and hotels

The quality of accommodation on offer in the multitude of **B&Bs** and **guesthouses** across Ireland very much reflects a combination of the personality of their owners and the nature of the premises. The overwhelming majority are welcoming family homes, sometimes furnished in the appropriate period of the building's origin, and provide clean and well-heated accommodation, usually with en-suite facilities.

Most B&Bs and guesthouses offer mammoth **breakfasts**, known as the "full Irish" in the Republic or the "Ulster fry" in the North. Many also serve **afternoon tea**, usually costing around €6/£4, while some, especially the classier establishments, also offer **dinner** to residents, though the price here very much depends on the menu and the place's reputation.

The majority of B&Bs in the Republic, and virtually all in Northern Ireland, are **registered** with the official tourist board, but many other places also open their doors during local festivals or high season. Registration is usually a guarantee of well-maintained standards and good service, though non-registered places are not necessarily of lower quality.

In most areas **hotels** are usually the most expensive option, and prices can veer towards the astronomical in cities such as Dublin, Galway and Belfast. Elsewhere, though, it's still often possible to find real bargains in family-run establishments away from the tourist areas. All come equipped with a range of facilities – at the very least, these will include a bar and breakfast room, with more upmarket options also providing plush restaurants and all manner of leisure facilities. Most hotels in the Republic offer reductions mid-week and sometimes business rates (carrying a briefcase or business-style shoulder bag can be useful). In the North, however, especially in Belfast or Derry, you're far more likely to get a good deal at the weekend.

Hostels

A plethora of well-run, good-quality **hostels** can be found across all of Ireland, including many off the beaten track, and often in very scenic locations. With just a few exceptions to the rule, the austere rigours of yore are long gone and you'll encounter a very broad range of accommodation – with both dormitories and private rooms – sometimes in stylish modern constructions. Meals, bike rental and other facilities are also

Accommodation price codes

Throughout this book, prices of hotels, guesthouses, B&Bs and, where appropriate, hostels have been graded with the **codes** below, according to how much you can expect to pay for a double room in high season.

❶ under €60/£40	❹ €120–150/£80–100	❼ €250–300/£170–200
❷ €60–90/£40–60	❺ €150–200/£100–140	❽ €300–400/£200–270
❸ €90–120/£60–80	❻ €200–250/£140–170	❾ over €400/£270

When applied to B&Bs, the ❶ rating indicates somewhere providing a decently furnished room, usually en suite, often with a TV and tea- and coffee-making facilities; when applied to hostels, it may just mean a room with either a double or twin beds and just occasionally en suite. ❷ and ❸ are a slight cut above and usually apply to places styling themselves as guesthouses or B&Bs, set in very attractive locations or renowned for the standard of their breakfasts, though in major cities they are likely to be more basic; some decent, well-run hotels in small towns or off the tourist trail also fall into this category. ❹–❻ generally refers to very comfortable en-suite rooms, sometimes luxurious in quality, in plush guesthouses, inns or hotels outside the major cities. Additionally, there are modern hotel developments, sometimes called "inns" or "travel lodges", veering towards the functional rather than opulent, which fall into this category. ❼–❾ normally applies to very sumptuous country houses, mansions and castles, often in astonishingly scenic locations; evening meals of gourmet quality are also usually provided. The range also includes deluxe hotels in cities and major tourist areas, with facilities usually including bars and at least one estimable restaurant, and amenities such as a gym, indoor heated pool, sauna and Jacuzzi. However, prices do vary enormously around the country and you might only pay a ❼ rate for a top-notch hotel in Derry, for example, when the equivalent in Dublin would be ❾.

Some establishments provide **single rooms**, but, in the vast majority of cases, single travellers will occupy a double room and pay a steep supplement for doing so; usually the rate is around 25 to 40 percent higher than the cost of a double per person.

often provided, as detailed within the Guide. Booking ahead is advisable, especially in Dublin and Galway at all times, and elsewhere during high season or local festivals.

Independent hostels

There are more than two hundred **independently run hostels** across Ireland, most of which belong to either the Independent Holiday Hostels of Ireland association (IHH; ⓣ01/836 4700, ⓦwww.hostels-ireland.com) or the Independent Hostel Owners organization (IHO; ⓣ074/973 0130, ⓦwww.independenthostelsireland.com) and sometimes both. All IHH hostels are approved by either Fáilte Ireland or the NITB, meaning that their facilities meet certain standards. Many IHO hostels are also approved, but even those that aren't are usually equally well kept and provide equivalent facilities. The majority of hostels offer dorms of varying sizes, as well as smaller private and family rooms; some of the newer city hostels have facilities comparable with a good-quality B&B. Most independent hostels are open year-round. Note that HI membership (see opposite) does not cover independent hostels, apart from a few that are affiliated to An Óige.

The character of independent hostels varies enormously. Some are set in incredibly beautiful countryside, while others are located on busy city streets. Though most hostels are efficiently run, there's generally a relaxed atmosphere, often with no curfews. In the most popular tourist areas, however, they can be crammed to the rafters at busy times. The vast majority provide bedding free of charge, but some may charge a fee for a sheet sleeping-bag, with costs varying considerably. In high season expect to pay €18–30 for a dorm bed in Dublin, and around €15–25 elsewhere; in Northern Ireland you'll usually pay £8–15. If you're on a tight budget, it's worth acquiring the hostel listings brochures produced by the IHH and IHO before you depart.

An Óige and HINI hostels

The Republic's Youth Hostel Association, **An Óige** (☎01/830 4555, Ⓦwww.irelandyha.org; annual membership €20, under-18s €10, family €40), has closed many of its remoter hostels and its remaining network of just 25 or so is concentrated mainly on popular tourist spots. Some are also only open for limited periods during the year (details are given in the Guide chapters) and a few may be closed during the daytime and/or have an evening curfew. Most offer smaller dorms or private rooms, usually with very good facilities, especially in some of the recently refurbished town-centre hostels or the newly built hostels at Errigal in Donegal and Knockree in Wicklow. Rates are around €13–25 per night depending on the season and room. **Hostelling International Northern Ireland** (HINI; ☎028/9032 4733, Ⓦwww.hini.org.uk; annual membership £15, under-25s £10, family £25, one-adult family £15) has just six hostels, most of which are recently built or refurbished. Prices are around £8.50–13 per night.

You don't have to be a member of either organization or the umbrella **Hostelling International** (HI) to stay in an An Óige or HINI hostel. However, membership provides numerous **discounts**, ranging from travel to entry to attractions, and nonmembers pay a supplementary fee of €2/£1.50 for each night spent in a hostel. In other words, if you're planning to use the An Óige/HINI network it's well worth joining or signing up with your own country's HI-affiliated association in advance.

Hostelling International affiliated associations

Hostelling International USA (HI-USA) ☎1-301/495 1240, Ⓦwww.hiayh.org.
Hostelling International/Canadian Hostelling Association (HI-Canada) ☎1-800/663-5777, Ⓦwww.hihostels.ca.
Scottish Youth Hostel Association (SYHA) ☎01786/891400, Ⓦwww.syha.org.uk.
YHA Australia ☎02/9565 1699, Ⓦwww.yha.com.au.
YHA New Zealand ☎0800 278299, Ⓦwww.yha.co.nz.
Youth Hostel Association (YHA) England and Wales ☎0870 870 8808, Ⓦwww.yha.org.uk.

Camping

Most tourist offices in the Republic stock the booklet of caravan and camping parks produced yearly by the **Irish Caravan and Camping Council** (Ⓦwww.camping-ireland.ie; €4). The price of a night's stay at an organized campsite depends on the popularity of the area, the facilities on offer, tent size and your party's number. Usually it will cost around €8–12 to pitch a tent and €2–4 per person on top of that, though some campsites may charge an all-in flat rate of €10–15. Some hostels also allow camping on their land for around €5–8 per person per night, with use of a kitchen and showers. In the **North**, NITB produces an annual free leaflet listing campsites, with prices around £7–12 per tent.

Camping rough is possible in many parts of Ireland, though the likelihood of rain coupled with the lack of proper campsite facilities may prove a deterrent. Some of the terrain in the west of Ireland, often boggy or rocky, may make pitching a tent difficult too. Off the beaten track, many farmers in the Republic will allow camping in one of their fields, usually for a few euros. It's permissible to camp in some state forests in the North, but not in the Republic.

Food and drink

Like Britain, Ireland doesn't have a strong tradition of eating out, and few visitors come here just for the food (though plenty come to drink). However, the quality and choice on offer have improved markedly in the last twenty years, with chefs, backed up by artisan producers, finding renewed confidence in local, seasonal, often organic ingredients. The highlights of what you can expect to tuck into are covered in the "Irish food and drink" colour insert, while this section deals with the nuts and bolts of where to eat.

The widest array of **restaurants** is naturally concentrated in the big cities, where, alongside Dublin and Belfast, Cork has a particularly vibrant scene, but good spots can be found all over the country, sometimes in quite unexpected places, as detailed throughout the Guide. Off the beaten track, it's usually worth phoning ahead, as opening hours can be erratic and, in winter, some establishments in tourist areas close down entirely. There's no getting away from the fact that dining out in Ireland is expensive, particularly when you factor in the high price of wine, but many fine restaurants offer cheaper, simpler menus at lunchtime, and plenty also lay on good-value **early-bird menus** in the evening – two or three courses for a set price, usually available until 7 or 7.30pm, though often not at weekends. Found in small towns across the country, though sometimes takeaway only, the most widespread ethnic restaurants are Chinese, Indian and Italian, followed by Thai; reflecting recent immigration patterns, you'll find Eastern European delis everywhere and restaurants occasionally.

Most **pubs** across the country will be able to rustle you up a simple sandwich or toastie and a cup of tea or coffee, and many offer full-blown lunch. This is often based around a carvery, serving slices of roast meat, potatoes and veg, as well as sandwiches and salads – which regularly feature crab and other seafood in coastal areas – and hot staples such as Irish stew and soups. An increasing number of Irish pubs now also serve meals in the evening. Similar fare is also available in traditional daytime **cafés**, alongside cakes and scones, which are now augmented in some towns by deli-cafés, offering a more interesting array of food. To end with what comes first, big **breakfasts** are an Irish tradition and invariably included in the price at hotels and B&Bs. The "full Irish" or "Ulster fry" typically consists of bacon, sausage, eggs and tomatoes, sometimes stretching to mushrooms, black pudding and white pudding, though many establishments now offer less heart-stopping alternatives such as smoked salmon and fruit salad.

The media

The Republic of Ireland has a flourishing national press, as well as many local, usually county-based newspapers, while the North has its own daily and local newspapers. The choices for Ireland-based TV are more limited both sides of the border, but there's an abundance of local radio stations, together with several national stations in the Republic.

Newspapers and magazines

The Republic's most popular middlebrow **newspapers** are the *Irish Times* and the more populist *Irish Independent*. Though generally liberal, if sometimes tinged by old-fashioned Ascendancy attitudes, the *Times* offers comprehensive news coverage of events both at home and abroad and often excellent features – its website ⓦwww.irishtimes.com also has plenty of listings. The *Independent* (ⓦwww.independent.ie) has a more right-of-centre outlook, while the *Irish Examiner* (formerly the *Cork Examiner*; ⓦwww.irishexaminer.com) has a Munster-based focus and generally less analytical coverage of news. Sundays see the publication the *Sunday Independent* (same Web address as its daily sister), the sometimes radical *Sunday Tribune*, and the *Sunday Business Post* which offers a wider selection of stories than its name implies. British newspapers are commonly available in Dublin and other cities and some produce Irish editions.

Every county has at least one weekly newspaper, often conservative and usually crammed with local stories of little interest to outsiders. However, some, such as the *Kerryman*, the *Kilkenny People* and the *Donegal Democrat* often provide good coverage of local events and very readable features. To delve deeper into the seamy world of Irish politics, turn to the monthly *Village* (ⓦwww.village.ie) or the satirical fortnightly **magazine** *Phoenix* (ⓦwww.phoenix-magazine.com).

The **North**'s two morning dailies, both **tabloids**, are the Nationalist *Irish News* (ⓦwww.irishnews.com) and the Unionist *News Letter* (ⓦwww.newsletter.co.uk), while Sunday sees the *Sunday World* (ⓦwww.sundayworld.com). The widest circulation however belongs to the evening **broadsheet** *Belfast Telegraph* (which now comes out around noon and has a very informative website (ⓦwww.belfasttelegraph.co.uk); its Unionist stance has become progressively more liberal over the years. Also worth purchasing is the biweekly *Derry Journal* (ⓦwww.derryjournal.com). All UK daily and Sunday papers are also available in the North.

Television and radio

In the **Republic**, the state-sponsored Radio Telefís Éireann (RTÉ; ⓦwww.rte.ie) operates three **TV channels**. As well as imported shows, the main news and current affairs channel, RTÉ 1, also features the popular home-grown Dublin-based soap, *Fair City*, and Friday's *Late Late Show*, a long-standing chat and entertainment institution. RTÉ 2 is a little more bubbly, with a smattering of locally produced programmes, though still swamped by imported tat. Some of the most innovative viewing is provided by the Irish-language channel TG4 (which provides English subtitles; ⓦwww.tg4.ie), including excellent traditional-music shows and often incisive features on the culture of Irish-speaking areas. The independent channel TV3 (ⓦwww.tv3.ie) churns out a dire mix of dated films and imported soaps and sitcoms. In most of the Republic, the four major British terrestrial TV channels are available on cable or satellite, as well as a vast number of other digital and freeview channels such as Sky, CNN and Eurosport. The Republic also has its own dedicated cable/satellite sports channel, Setanta, showing everything from major soccer matches to under-16s GAA events, as well as the somewhat lower than highbrow Channel 6, offering plenty of programmes you'll be very keen to miss.

RTÉ also operates four **radio stations**, three of which are English-language: the mainstream RTÉ Radio 1 (FM 88–89), whose morning shows are largely devoted to current affairs and chat; RTÉ 2FM (FM 90–92), which is more music- and youth-oriented; and Lyric FM (FM 96–99), which mixes popular classics with jazz and occasionally inspiring world-music shows. Raidió na Gaeltachta (FM 93) is the national Irish-language station, with broadcasts including much traditional music. The national commercial radio station, Today FM (FM 100–102), offers a largely bland schedule of MoR music shows. There are also numerous local radio stations across the Republic.

Northern Ireland receives television and radio programmes from the BBC (ⓦwww.bbc.co.uk/northernireland) and has a limited, if often keenly followed, number of locally produced current-affairs productions. On BBC Radio Ulster (FM 92.4–95.4), *Talkback* (daily noon–1.30pm) offers lively discussions on the North's political situation. The BBC's main commercial rival, Ulster Television (ⓦu.tv) relies on the standard ITV diet of soaps and drama. In most parts of the North you can also watch or listen to RTÉ programmes.

Festivals and events

Ireland has a plethora of annual festivals, ranging from small local affairs to major international occasions (see also *Festive Ireland* colour section) significant events in the sporting calendar and there is a host of opportunities for enjoyment. For more Dublin festivals, see the box on p.66.

March/April

St Patrick's Day March 17; ⓦwww.stpatricksday.ie. Almost every Irish town and village commemorates the national patron saint's day, though the most significant celebration is the week-long festival held in Dublin.

Irish Grand National ⓦwww.fairyhouseracecourse.ie. The biggest event of the National Hunt horse-racing season takes place at Fairyhouse, Co. Meath, on Easter Monday.

May

Wicklow Gardens Festival ⓦwww.wicklow.ie/tourism. A host of gardens, both large and small, on view across County Wicklow from the beginning of May to mid-August.

Cork International Choral Festival ⓦwww.corkchoral.ie. Featuring many choirs and the Fleischmann International Trophy competition over five days in early May.

North West 200 ⓦwww.northwest200.org. Major international motorcycle road-racing event held in Portstewart, Co. Derry, in the middle of the month.

Irish Open Golf Championship ⓦwww.irishopenatadaremanor.com. Traditionally the major golf tournament, this event will be held at Adare Manor, Co. Limerick, during mid-May in both 2008 and 2009.

Fleadh Nua ⓦwww.fleadhnua.com. One of the country's biggest traditional-music festivals, held in Ennis, Co. Clare, over more than a week in late May.

June

The Cat Laughs ⓦwww.thecatlaughs.com. Five-day fun-fest featuring an array of renowned and lesser-known comedians, staged in Kilkenny in early June.

Bloomsday ⓦwww.jamesjoyce.ie. A week of Dublin-based James Joyce-related events leading up to June 16, the day on which his masterwork *Ulysses* is set.

Irish Derby ⓦwww.curragh.ie. The major event in the Irish flat-racing season, held at the Curragh, Co. Kildare, late in the month.

July

Willie Clancy Summer School ⓦwww.setdancingnews.net/wcss. Hugely popular traditional-music event with a host of pub sessions and several concerts, hosted in Miltown Malbay, Co. Clare, in the second week of July.
Galway Film Fleadh ⓦwww.galwayfilmfleadh.com. New Irish and international releases shown in the city during six days in the middle of the month.
Orange Order Parades July 12. Unionists and Loyalists commemorate the Battle of the Boyne and close down much of Northern Ireland in the process.
Galway International Arts Festival ⓦwww.galwayartsfestival.com. Massive festival of music, drama and general revelry over the last two weeks in July.
Boyle Arts Festival ⓦwww.boylearts.com. Smaller but popular version of the Galway festival, staged in Co. Roscommon towards the end of the month.
Mary from Dungloe ⓦwww.maryfromdungloe.com. Ten days of entertainment in Co. Donegal, usually featuring Daniel O'Donnell and culminating in a beauty contest (where one of the prizes is normally a date with the man himself); runs from late July.
Galway Races ⓦwww.galwayraces.com. The west of Ireland's biggest horse-racing event, long celebrated in the song of the same name; starts at the end of the month.

August

Yeats International Summer School ⓦwww.yeats-sligo.com. Sligo-based mid-August literary festival focusing on the life of the poet.
Kilkenny Arts Festival ⓦwww.kilkennyarts.ie. All manner of musical and literary events, recitals and exhibitions staged in the city over ten days in mid-August.
Puck Fair ⓦwww.puckfair.ie. Three days of mayhem in Killorglin, Co. Kerry, culminating in the crowning of a goat as King Puck; takes place in the middle of the month.
Rose of Tralee International Festival ⓦwww.roseoftralee.ie. Tremendously popular event, focused on a beauty contest, but offering an enormous range of other entertainment; mid-August.
Fleadh Cheoil na hÉireann ⓦwww.comhaltas.com. Competitive traditional-music festival, drawing hundreds of participants and big crowds – different towns bid for the late-August event each year.

Ould Lammas Fair More than 400 years old, Ballycastle's traditional market fair remains a huge draw, featuring livestock sales, and bucket-loads of music, dancing and entertainment on the last Monday and Tuesday of the month.

September

All-Ireland Senior Hurling and Football Finals ⓦwww.gaa.ie. The zenith of the sporting year for Gaelic games with its two major finals, held on two Sundays a fortnight apart, in Dublin.
Open House Folk and Traditional Music Festival ⓦwww.openhousefestival.com. Major traditional-music festival running for five days or so in Belfast at the end of the month.
Lisdoonvarna Matchmaking Festival ⓦwww.matchmakerireland.com. A month-long date-athon which attracts hopeful suitors from all over the world, and there's plenty of traditional entertainment too.
Dublin Fringe Festival ⓦwww.fringefest.com. Lively programme of theatre, dance, performance arts and comedy, featuring more than 300 events spread over more than a fortnight.
Dublin Theatre Festival ⓦwww.dublintheatrefestival.com. Major drama festival encompassing around 30 productions, commencing late in the month.

October

Cork Film Festival ⓦwww.corkfilmfest.org. Established in 1956 and still going strong with a broad-ranging programme of big-budget and international cinema staged over a week mid-month.
Wexford Opera Festival ⓦwww.wexfordopera.com. Prestigious and massively popular international festival now lasting for more than a fortnight, commencing in mid-October.
Belfast Festival at Queen's ⓦwww.belfastfestival.com. Major arts festival, Ireland's equivalent to Edinburgh, nowadays complete with its very own Fringe and running for seventeen days from the middle of the month.
Cork Jazz Festival ⓦwww.corkjazzfestival.com. Four days of jazz in all its forms at the end of the month.
Derry Halloween Carnival ⓦwww.derrycity.gov.uk/halloween. Street theatre, music and mayhem, especially during the fireworks display on October 31.

November

Foyle Film Festival ⓦwww.foylefilmfestival.com. The best of new Irish and international film in Derry, over a week in mid-month.

Culture and etiquette

Ireland likes to describe itself as the land of Cead Míle Fáilte ("a hundred thousand welcomes"), which you'll often see inscribed on pubs, and that's essentially true for most visitors. In terms of general etiquette, wherever you go, you'll encounter the standard Irish greeting – an enquiry about your health (sometimes just abbreviated to "About you?" in parts of the North) and it's reasonable to return the compliment. Also, if someone buys you a pint in a pub, then an even-handed gesture is to pay for the next round.

Children

Children are very well received, though few places, including cafés, hotels and many key attractions, are actually designed with them in mind. Baby supplies are readily available and most B&Bs and hotels welcome children, though few have cots. It's usually fine to take a child into a pub during the daytime, though definitely not so in the Republic after 9pm.

Women

For **women** Ireland represents a mixed experience. Much of the country remains distinctly untouched by even the slightest move towards sexual equality and, both North and in the Republic, this often reveals itself in the form of outlandish sexist behaviour, ranging from the amusing to the sometimes absolutely intolerable. However, even the latter rarely transforms itself into physical intimidation and the vast majority of situations can be easily managed. Like any other country, though, Ireland has its own quota of dangerous people, so it's always wise to adopt a cautionary attitude when travelling and enjoying pubs and nightlife. In the rare case of experiencing a serious personal assault, it's always worth contacting either a rape crisis centre or Tourist Assistance Service (see p.51), as local police, though well intentioned, are generally not experienced in dealing with distressed women.

Racism

The last few years have witnessed a marked change in attitudes amongst the majority of the Irish people brought about via gradual changes in the make-up of Irish society and a widening experience of the world at large. Though overall the population remains remarkably conservative in many ways, the arrival of asylum seekers, refugees and, latterly, large numbers of migrant workers over the last decade or so has undoubtedly softened feelings in the Republic towards those from other cultures and had a significant affect upon the population's long-standing homogeneity.

However, that being said, it's still likely that black visitors will encounter **racist attitudes** at some point in their travels, especially in rural areas, but these are generally not threatening and usually the result of ignorance of other cultures, rather than an intention to cause deliberate offence.

The situation is far less optimistic in Northern Ireland where, especially in Belfast, Loyalist gangs have attempted to "cleanse" the city's ethnic population, targeting mainly the local Chinese community, and there have been several reported attacks on migrant workers across the region. Tourists, of whatever culture, are very rarely the victims of assaults.

Ireland also has its own recognized ethnic minority, the **travellers** (widely known across class and backgrounds by a range of insulting epithets) against whom discrimination remains widespread, both North and South.

Gays and lesbians

Attitudes towards **gays and lesbians** remain largely discriminatory, and the gay community in Ireland keeps a low profile, the only "scene" largely concentrated on the nightlife of Belfast and Dublin. Though private same-sex activity is legal across Ireland, public displays of affection may produce hostile verbal reactions, and many small-town and rural B&Bs will look askance at a pair of men wanting to share a bed for the night. Be aware that known cruising areas, such as Belfast's Cave Hill and Dublin's Phoenix Park, are often patrolled by the police.

Sports

Hurling and Gaelic football, Ireland's two home-grown sports, are among the fastest and most physical in the world, and well worth catching on your travels, whether on TV or, preferably, live. Rugby and soccer are also widely followed, while going to the races is a great day out, with less of the snobbery sometimes found in Britain.

Hurling and Gaelic football

Both Gaelic football and hurling (see also p.8), Ireland's two main indigenous sports, are played at a rollicking pace on huge pitches, 140m long and 80m wide, between teams of fifteen; goalposts are H-shaped, with three points awarded for a goal, when the ball goes under the crossbar, and a point when it goes over the crossbar. Over two thousand clubs in villages and parishes all over Ireland vie for the privilege of reaching the club finals, held on St Patrick's Day at 80,000-seater Croke Park in Dublin, one of the largest stadiums in Europe, while the more popular and prestigious intercounty seasons begin with provincial games in the early summer, reaching their climax in the All-Ireland County Finals in September, also at Croke Park. Details of all fixtures for hurling and Gaelic football can be obtained from the Gaelic Athletic Association (Ⓣ01/836 3222, Ⓦwww.gaa.ie), while there's always something of interest on Ⓦwww.anfearrua.ie, an independent fans' forum.

Hurling is played with a leather *sliothar*, similar in size to a hockey ball, and a hurley (or *camán*), a broad stick made of ash that is curved outwards at the end. The *sliothar* is belted prodigious distances, caught and carried on the flattened end of the player's hurley. It's a highly skilled game of constant movement and aggression that does not permit a defensive, reactive style of play. Cork, Kilkenny and Tipperary are the most successful counties, while Clare, Galway, Offaly and Wexford have emerged in the modern era. No county from the North has ever won an All-Ireland, though the sport is very popular in the Glens of Antrim and parts of the Ards Peninsula in County Down. **Camogie**, the women's version of hurling, is becoming increasingly popular, and is also well worth watching. Dublin has won the most All-Irelands, though the most successful teams in the modern era have been Cork, Kilkenny and Tipperary.

Gaelic football has similarities with both rugby and association football, but its closest relation is Australian Rules Football; indeed every autumn, Australia play Ireland in a series of "international rules" matches. The round Gaelic ball, which is slightly smaller than a soccer ball, can be both kicked and caught. However, running with the ball is only permitted if a player keeps control by tapping it from foot to hand or by bouncing it, and throwing is not allowed – the ball must be "hand-passed", volleyball-style. Whereas hurling's strongholds are in the southern counties of the island, footballing prowess is more widely spread – Kerry is the most successful county, followed by Dublin, then Galway, but there are plenty of strong teams in Ulster at the moment, notably Tyrone and Armagh.

Rugby union and soccer

Rugby union and **soccer** are very popular in Ireland and tickets for international matches, especially for rugby, can be hard to come by. The Republic's home soccer matches and Ireland's rugby matches are currently played at Dublin's Croke Park (see p.117), while Lansdowne Road Stadium undergoes a massive redevelopment that's not due to finish until late 2009. Northern Ireland's soccer matches are played at Windsor Park, Belfast (see p.578). For the international rugby team (Ⓣ01/647 3800, Ⓦwww.irishrugby.ie), which is a joint Republic–Northern Ireland side, the main event of the year is the Six Nations Championship, a series of international games played in February and March against England, France, Wales, Scotland and Italy. You're more likely to get tickets, however, for matches featuring the four provinces, Munster (which includes Irish rugby's natural heartland, Limerick), Leinster, Connacht and Ulster, in the Europe-wide Heineken Cup or the Celtic League.

Soccer is played semiprofessionally in both the North and the Republic, organized into the Irish League (Ⓣ028/9066 9458, Ⓦwww.irishfa.com) and the Eircom League (Ⓣ01/703 7500, Ⓦwww.fai.ie) respectively. Both international teams field most of their players from the English leagues; Manchester United and Liverpool are the most popular clubs among Irish fans. Glasgow Celtic are also popular both north and south, Rangers in the North, with support following Catholic and Protestant divisions, respectively.

Racing

Going to the **races** is a hugely popular and enjoyable day out in Ireland. A good place to get a sense of the Irish passion for horses is the National Stud in Kildare (see p.159), while for details of all meetings, contact Horse Racing Ireland (Ⓣ045/842800, Ⓦwww.goracing.ie). The Irish Grand National is run at Fairyhouse in County Meath on Easter Monday (see p.134), followed in April by the four-day Irish National Hunt Festival at Punchestown in County Kildare (see box, p.161); at the Curragh, the classic flat-race course in Kildare (see box, p.161), the Irish 1000 Guineas and 2000 Guineas are held in May, the Irish Derby in late June or early July, the Irish Oaks in July and the Irish St Leger in September. For details of Dublin's race course, Leopardstown, see p.134; notable local meetings, such as those at Galway and Listowel, are described in the Guide.

Outdoor activities

Despite the weather, Ireland is a great place for getting out and about. Cycling is one of the best ways to appreciate the quiet pleasures of the Irish countryside, while walkers can take advantage of generally free access across much of the countryside and a number of waymarked trails. With over 120 sailing and yacht clubs, plenty of lakes, rivers and sheltered coastline to explore and some great beaches for surfers, there are many opportunities for watersports enthusiasts, too.

Cycling

Signposted **cycling trails** in the Republic include the Beara Way (see p.322) and the Sheep's Head Cycling Route (see p.319) in Cork, the Kerry Way (p.339), and the epic, 610-kilometre Táin Trail, which links sites associated with the *Táin Bó Cúailnge* saga in a figure-of-eight that stretches from Carlingford in County Louth, via Kells in County Meath, to Rathcroghan in County Roscommon (map guides are available from local tourist offices). In the North, cycling trails come under the umbrella of the UK's ambitious National Cycle Network; for details, contact Cycle Northern Ireland in Belfast (Ⓣ028/9030 3930, Ⓦwww.ncn-ni.com) or go to Ⓦwww.sustrans.org.uk. They include the Kingfisher route (see p.680), which also stretches into Leitrim and Cavan; for information about this route, you can also contact Green Box in County Leitrim (Ⓣ071/985 6898; Ⓦwww.greenbox.ie or www.cycletours ireland.com). Bikes are available to rent all over the island, as detailed throughout the Guide (see also p.37), though the number of outlets has diminished in recent years.

Walking and mountain climbing

There are dozens of waymarked **walking trails** in the Republic, ranging from linear mountain routes, such as the Wicklow Way (see p.148) and the Western Way (p.441), to walks around entire peninsulas, like the Sheep's Head Way (p.319), the Beara Way (p.322), the Kerry Way (p.340) and the Dingle Way (p.351). Even though the walks are waymarked, you should get hold of the relevant Ordnance Survey map, whether you're doing the whole or just part of the route. In the North, the Ulster Way (see p.685) is the oldest and longest waymarked walking trail in the whole of Ireland, describing a 560-mile circuit of the province, with links to trails from Donegal and Cavan. For information on these trails in the Republic, go to Ⓦwww .walkireland.ie or phone Ⓣ01/860 8800, while some shorter loop walks are detailed on the tourist board's Ⓦwww.walking.ireland.ie; in the North, go to Ⓦwww.walkni.com or phone Ⓣ028/9030 3930; some councils and local tourist offices have produced helpful map guides for the main routes, too. Other walking highlights include the ascents of Croagh Patrick in County Mayo (see p.458) and of Carrauntoohil, for more experienced walkers, in County Kerry (see p.340), and just about anywhere in Connemara (see p.441). The Republic has no "rights of way" or "right to roam", but there is a tradition of relatively free access to privately owned countryside. In recent years, the growing numbers and occasional carelessness of walkers, as well as insurance worries, has led some farmers to bar access to their land, but all the same, the majority of landowners do not object to walkers crossing their property.

For detailed advice on **access**, including a Good Practice Guide, have a look at the compendious website of the Mountaineering Council of Ireland (Ⓣ01/625 1115, Ⓦwww .mountaineering.ie), an organization that covers hill-walking and rambling, as well as climbing, and also publishes a quarterly magazine, *Irish Mountain Log*. Particularly useful walking guidebooks are listed in Contexts, p.739. Other useful walking websites include Ⓦmountainviews.ie and Ⓦwww.simonstewart.ie, while Ⓦwww .climbing.ie is devoted to **rock climbing**. If you need help in a real emergency on the hills, phone Ⓣ999 or 112 and ask for **mountain rescue**.

Other land-based activities

With a wide variety of flocks, including a large number of rare species, visiting its shores, Ireland is a great place for **birdwatching**; the best contacts are Birdwatch Ireland in the Republic (Ⓣ01/281 9878, Ⓦwww .birdwatchireland.ie) and, in the North, the Royal Society for the Protection of Birds (Ⓣ028/9049 1547, Ⓦwww.rspb.org.uk).

Horse riding, whether over the hills or along the beaches, is also a popular pastime, for both novices and experienced riders. The Association of Irish Riding Establishments (Ⓣ01/281 0963, Ⓦwww.aire.ie) maintains standards among riding centres in the Republic and the North and publishes details on its website.

Golf, which was probably first brought to Ireland by the Ulster Scots, attracts huge numbers of visitors every year; the Golfing Union of Ireland, based in Kildare (Ⓣ01/505 4000, Ⓦwww.gui.ie), will provide details of over four hundred clubs, north and south.

Watersports and activities

Ireland's many **sailing** and yacht clubs Include the Royal Cork Yacht Club, established in Cobh in 1720, which is thought to be the oldest in the world. The most popular areas for sailing are the relatively sheltered waters of the east coast, especially in Dublin Bay and further south around Wexford; Cork Harbour and west Cork; Lough Swilly on the north coast of Donegal; Strangford Lough in County Down; and some of the larger lakes, such as Lough Derg in County Clare. For further information contact the Irish Sailing Association (Ⓣ01/280 0239, Ⓦwww.sailing.ie).

Inland waterways and sheltered coasts – notably in west Cork (see p.311) and Waterford (see p.274) – also offer **canoeing** and **kayaking** opportunities, ranging from day-trips and touring to rough- and white-water racing; the website of the Irish Canoe Union (Ⓣ01/625 1105, Ⓦwww.canoe.ie) provides advice and links to trip and training providers.

There are some superb beaches for **windsurfing** (Ⓦwww.windsurfing.ie) and **surfing** (Ⓦwww.isasurf.ie), and their various spin-offs. For the former, some of the best are: Rosslare, County Wexford; Coolmaine, near Kinsale in Cork; Brandon Bay, Kerry; Rusheen Bay, County Galway; Keel Strand, Achill and Elly Bay, Belmullet, in Mayo; and Lough Allen, Leitrim. Surfers head for: Long Strand, County Cork; Brandon Bay, Kerry; Lahinch, Clare; Easkey and Strandhill, County Sligo; Bundoran and Rossnowlagh, County Donegal; Portrush, Antrim; and Tramore, County Waterford.

Right in the path of the North Atlantic Drift, Ireland offers some of the best **scuba diving** in Europe, notably off the rocky west coast. The website of the Irish Underwater Council (Ⓣ01/284 4601, Ⓦwww.cft.ie) provides links to places to dive and to learn. There are also plenty of opportunities for sea **angling** and dozens of rivers and lakes for fly- and game-fishing. For information, the best places to start are the tourist-board websites, Ⓦwww.discoverireland.ie and Ⓦwww.discovernorthernireland.com.

Travel essentials

Contraceptives

Condoms can be purchased at supermarkets and pharmacies across Ireland, though the pill is only available on prescription.

Costs

Prices have risen dramatically in the **Republic** over the last few years, particularly for bus and train travel, eating out, accommodation and, thanks to deregulation, a pint of stout or beer, with the steepest hikes occurring in Dublin and popular tourist areas along the southern and western coasts.

Though it's still possible to get a decent, wholesome main **meal** in cafés and pubs for around €8, bear in mind that a three-course dinner in a restaurant will usually cost at least €30, with a bottle of wine setting you back €20–25, though some offer "early bird" special menus at reduced rates. The price of a pint in a pub is €3.40–4.50 and may be significantly higher in some city-centre clubs.

The cheapest **accommodation** is a hostel dorm bed, which will cost around €13–20, rising to as much as €30 at peak periods in Dublin. Alternatively, it's also possible to get a decent bed and breakfast from around €32 per person sharing or €40 in Dublin. Where single rooms are not available, single travellers will usually face supplements of 25–50 percent on the price per person of two people sharing a double, except in hostels.

So, even if you count the cents, you're likely to spend a daily minimum of around €35, and more than double this if you're eating out and staying in a B&B.

Prices in the **North** are roughly the same for drinking and eating out, though B&Bs

may be cheaper in rural areas, and the **cost of petrol** is around 25 per cent higher.

Crime and personal safety

Crime in Ireland is largely an urban affair and generally at a low level compared with other European countries. However, thieves do target popular tourist spots, both in the cities and rural areas, so don't leave anything of value visible in your car and take care of your bags while visiting bars and restaurants. It's sensible to seek advice from your accommodation provider about safety in the local area and take as much care as you would anywhere else.

Crimes against the person are extremely rare, except in certain inner-city areas, and seldom involve tourists. The **Republic**'s police force is An Garda Síochána (Ⓦwww.garda.ie), more commonly referred to as the guards or **Gardaí**, whom you'll find generally helpful when it comes to reporting a crime. The Irish Tourist Assistance Service (Ⓣ01/478 5295, Ⓦwww.itas.ie) offers support to tourist victims of crime. Rape crisis support is available from the Dublin Rape Crisis Centre (Ⓣ1800/778888), which can also direct you to similar agencies across Ireland.

Away from the sectarian hotspots, crime in **Northern Ireland** is very low. In the unlikely event that your person or property is targeted, contact the Police Service of Northern Ireland (Ⓣ028/9065 0222, Ⓦwww.psni.police.uk for details of the nearest police station). The presence of the British army has diminished almost to invisibility, though it is just possible you might encounter police or army security checks on the extremely rare occasion nowadays that a major incident has occurred.

Disabilities

Disabled travellers should glean as much information as possible before travelling since facilities in Ireland are generally poor. For example, older buildings may lack lifts and their entrances may not have been converted to allow easy wheelchair access.

The main **transport** companies (see pp.32–35), Iarnród Éireann (Irish Rail) and Bus Éireann in the Republic, and the joint organization Translink in the North have, however considerably improved their facilities for disabled travellers, with, for example, low-floor city buses and kneeling coaches on many routes.

Disabled drivers travelling with their cars from Britain can usually obtain reduced rates for ferry travel. Discounts vary according to the time of year and the ferry companies usually require membership of Mobilise – see below.

Contacts in Ireland

Citizens Information Board Ⓣ01/605 9000, Ⓦwww.citizensinformationboard.ie. The Republic's government support agency for social services provides information and advice, though is more geared up for disabled Irish citizens than for travellers to Ireland.

Disability Action Ⓣ028/9029 7880, Ⓦwww.disabilityaction.org. This Northern Irish campaign and information group is also better at addressing the needs of local disabled people, but its *A–Z Guide for People with Disabilities,* downloadable from Ⓦwww.dsdni.gov.uk/disabilitya_z.pdf, has plenty of useful contacts.

Irish Wheelchair Association Ⓣ01/818 6400, Ⓦwww.iwa.ie. Gives advice on accessible accommodation and other amenities in Ireland; the IWA hires out wheelchairs and its website provides contact details for companies and organizations offering similar services.

Contacts abroad

Access-Able US Ⓦwww.access-able.com. Online resource for travellers with disabilities.

e-Bility AUS Ⓦwww.e-bility.com. Information provider and Web portal which includes plenty of material on travelling abroad.

Holiday Care UK Ⓣ0845/124 9971, Ⓦwww.holidaycare.org.uk. Provides advice and information on travel and holidays, as well as publishing an information sheet on accessibility in Northern Ireland (£2.50).

Mobilise UK Ⓣ01508/489449, Ⓦwww.mobilise.info. Promotes and protects the welfare and personal mobility of all disabled people, drivers and non-drivers; members have access to a helpline and various concessions, and can receive a copy of the *Ferry Concessions* booklet. Annual membership £14; £18 for two persons at the same address.

RADAR (Royal Association for Disability and Rehabilitation) UK Ⓣ020/7250 3222, Ⓦwww.radar.org.uk. A good source of advice on holidays and travel in the UK and Ireland – its annual guide *Holidays in Britain and Ireland* costs £13.50 to buy in the UK, £16.75 from Europe and £20 from other overseas destinations (includes postage).

Society for Accessible Travel & Hospitality (SATH) US ⓣ212/447 7284, ⓦwww.sath.org. Nonprofit educational organization that has actively represented travellers with disabilities since 1976. Annual membership $49; $29 for students and seniors.

Discount cards

Visitors to historic sites and monuments run by the Republic's Office of Public Works can save a good deal of money by purchasing a **Heritage Card** (€21, senior citizens €16, children/students €8, family €55; ⓦwww.heritageireland.ie), which is valid for twelve months from the date of purchase and provides unlimited entry; attractions covered by the card are detailed throughout the Guide. It can be purchased at many of the sites themselves, some tourist offices and online.

Members of **An Óige** (see p.41) also receive discounts on entry to certain sites. A number of historic buildings and sites in the North are operated by the **National Trust**. Membership (£43.50; under-25s £19.50, family £77.50, one-adult family £58.50; ⓦwww.ntni.org.uk) provides free and unlimited entry to these and all National Trust–run sites in Britain too. More than eighty sites across Ireland are members of the independent **Heritage Island** organization (ⓦwww.heritageisland.com) whose booklet (€5.99) provides discounted admission prices. We've provided the adult entry price for all these sites, together with numerous other attractions in the Guide. The majority offer reduced rates for children (under-5s usually get in free), students and senior citizens.

Electricity

The standard **electricity** supply is 220V AC in the Republic and 240V AC in the North. Most sockets require three-pin plugs. To operate North American appliances you'll need to bring or buy a transformer and an adapter; only the latter is needed for equipment made in Australia or New Zealand.

Emergencies

Across Ireland, in the case of an **emergency** call either ⓣ999 or 112.

Entry requirements

The border between Northern Ireland and the Republic is an open one, with no passport or immigration controls. UK nationals do not need a passport to enter the Republic, but it's a good idea to carry one – note that airlines generally require some form of official **photo ID** on flights between Britain and Ireland. Under EU regulations, British passport holders are entitled to stay in the Republic for as long as they like.

Travellers from the US, Canada, Australia, New Zealand and South Africa are required to show a passport and can stay for up to three months in the **Republic**. If you want to stay beyond that, you must seek permission from the Garda National Immigration Bureau, 13–14 Burgh Quay, Dublin 2 (ⓣ01/666 9100), or from the immigration officer at your local Garda station; for further information, contact the Irish Naturalization and Immigration Service, also at 13–14 Burgh Quay, Dublin (ⓣ01/616 7700 or 1890 551500, ⓦwww.inis.gov.ie). A list of Irish consulates and embassies, along with comprehensive visa information, is available on the Department of Foreign Affairs website, ⓦwww.dfa.ie.

US, Canadian, Australian, South African and New Zealand citizens can enter **Northern Ireland** for up to six months with just a passport. A full list of British diplomatic representatives overseas is available on the British Foreign Office's website, ⓦwww.fco.gov.uk, while detailed visa information is available on ⓦwww.ukvisas.gov.uk. For further information on immigration once in the UK, contact the Border and Immigration Agency (ⓣ0870 606 7766, ⓦwww.bia.homeoffice.gov.uk).

Irish embassies abroad

Australia 20 Arkana St, Yarralumla, Canberra, ACT 2600 ⓣ02/6273 3022.

Canada 130 Albert St, Suite 1105, Ottawa, ON K1P 5G4 ⓣ613-233-6281.

New Zealand Handled by the embassy in Australia.

South Africa Southern Life Plaza, 1059 Schoeman Street, Arcadia 0083, Pretoria ⓣ012/342 5062, ⓦwww.embassyireland.org.za.
UK 17 Grosvenor Place, London SW1X 7HR ⓣ020/7235 2171.
US 2234 Massachusetts Ave NW, Washington, DC 20008 ⓣ202/462-3939, ⓦwww.irelandemb.org.

British embassies and high commissions abroad

Australia High Commission, Commonwealth Ave, Yarralumla, Canberra, ACT 2600 ⓣ02/6270 6666, ⓦwww.britaus.net.
Canada High Commission, 80 Elgin St, Ottawa, ON K1P 5K7 ⓣ613/237-1530, ⓦwww.britainincanada.org.
Ireland 29 Merrion Rd, Dublin 4 ⓣ01/205 3700, ⓦwww.britishembassy.ie.
New Zealand High Commission, 44 Hill St, PO Box 1812, Wellington ⓣ04/924 2888, ⓦwww.britain.org.nz.
South Africa High Commission, 255 Hill Street, Arcadia 0002, Pretoria ⓣ012/421 7500, ⓦwww.britain.org.za.
US 3100 Massachusetts Ave NW, Washington, DC 20008 ⓣ202/588-6500, ⓦwww.britainusa.com.

Insurance

Visitors from the UK are entitled to medical treatment in the Republic under the EU Reciprocal Medical Treatment arrangement, for which you'll need to get hold of a **European Health Insurance Card** (EHIC), the recent replacement for the E111 form. You can apply for an EHIC online (ⓦwww.ehic.org.uk), by phone (ⓣ0845 606 2030), or you can pick up an application form from a post office. This will give access only to state-provided medical treatment in the Republic, which covers emergency hospital treatment but not all GP's surgeries – check that the doctor you're planning to use is registered with the local Health Board Panel. Citizens of some other countries also enjoy reciprocal agreements – in Australia, for example, Medicare has such an arrangement with Ireland and Britain.

None of these arrangements cover all the medical costs you may incur or repatriation, so it's advisable for all travellers to take out some form of **travel insurance**. Most travel insurance policies exclude so-called dangerous sports unless an extra premium is paid; in Ireland this could mean, for example, horse riding, scuba diving, windsurfing, mountaineering and kayaking.

Rough Guides has teamed up with Columbus Direct to offer you travel insurance that can be tailored to suit your needs. Products include a low-cost **backpacker** option for long stays, a **short break** option for city getaways, a typical **holiday package** option, and others. There are also annual **multi-trip** policies for those who travel regularly. Different sports and activities (trekking, skiing, etc) can usually be covered if required. See our website (ⓦwww.roughguidesinsurance.com) for eligibility and purchasing options. Alternatively, UK residents should call ⓣ0870 033 9988, Australians should call ⓣ1300 669999 and New Zealanders should call ⓣ0800 559911. All other nationalities should call ⓣ+44 870 890 2843.

Internet

Most cities and major towns have **Internet** cafés, as detailed throughout the Guide, and prices vary according to the level of competition. In Dublin, for instance, several places offer access at the rate of €1–1.50 per hour, but elsewhere you're more likely to pay from €3–5/£2–3 for the same period.

Broadband has spread relatively slowly around Ireland and there are still many rural parts of the country with no or variable access. However, in parts that do have it, you'll find hotels, and some B&Bs and hostels, offering free wireless connection (if you've brought your laptop or Blackberry). Otherwise, many local library branches offer Internet access (usually from around €2/£1.50 per hour).

Maps

The **maps** in this guide will provide you with sufficient detail to navigate your way around cities, towns and counties, though, if you're visiting Dublin you might want to purchase the Rough Guides map of the city (£4.99/$8.95). The Rough Guide 1:350,000 scale *Ireland* map (same prices) is handy if you're touring the country or, alternatively, for more detail there's the Ordnance Survey of Ireland's (ⓦwww.osi.ie) four *Holiday* maps at 1:250,000 scale (£5.30/€7.99), dividing the country into quadrants, and its *Complete*

Road Atlas of Ireland (£8.25/€12.50) which is extremely useful if you're driving.

The majority of tourist offices will provide free local maps, but, if you're planning on walking or exploring a locality to the full, then the OSI's *Discovery* 1:50,000 scale series of maps (£5.80/€8.25 each) is the best bet for the Republic. The Ordnance Survey of Northern Ireland (ⓦwww.osni.gov.uk) produces a similar *Discoverer* series (same prices) which fulfils the same function.

If you're walking or cycling, the OSI/OSNI also produce special-interest 1:25,000-scale maps covering areas such as the Aran Islands, Brandon Mountain, Killarney National Park, Lough Erne, Macgillicuddy's Reeks, Slieve Croob, and the Mourne and Sperrin mountain ranges.

All of these maps can be purchased via the Internet, but, if you're visiting Dublin, the most comprehensive selection of maps in Ireland is provided by the National Map Centre, 34 Aungier Street (ⓣ01/476 0471, ⓦwww.irishmaps.ie).

Money and banks

The **currency** of the Republic is the euro (€), divided into 100 cents (c). Northern Ireland's currency is the pound sterling (£), though notes are printed by various local banks and are different from those found in Britain; however, standard British banknotes can still be used in Northern Ireland.

Exchange rates fluctuate but, at the time of writing, £1 sterling was equivalent to around €1.48, €1 was worth £0.67 and US$1.37. The best exchange rates are provided by banks, though it's easiest to use an ATM, for which your own bank or credit card company may charge a fixed-rate or percentile fee. Unless you're absolutely stuck, avoid changing money or Traveller's cheques in hotels, where the rates are often very poor. In areas around the border between the Republic and the North many businesses accept both currencies, and the euro can even be used in public telephones in Belfast.

Credit and debit cards

The handiest means of obtaining cash is to use a **debit or credit card**. ATMs are very common throughout Ireland except in remote rural areas, with most accepting Visa, MasterCard and Cirrus. Major credit cards, such as Visa, MasterCard and American Express and all cards bearing the Eurocard symbol, are widely accepted, though in rural areas, you'll find that they're not accepted by many B&Bs.

Traveller's cheques

Traveller's cheques are less commonly used in Ireland nowadays, though still widely accepted, and represent a secure alternative to plastic money, thanks to the possibility of reimbursement should your cheques be lost or stolen. Do keep a record of your transactions to facilitate the process. Traveller's cheques can be purchased from branches of American Express and Thomas Cook, the majority of banks and, in the UK, from post offices. In the majority of cases a small commission fee is charged.

If you're only planning to visit the Republic, you should ask for cheques in euros, but if you're also intending to visit Northern Ireland, you'll need cheques in pounds sterling. A small commission fee is levied when you cash each cheque, but not in the case of Amex or Thomas Cook cheques exchanged in those companies' own branches.

Banks

Banks are usually the best places to exchange money and Traveller's cheques, though when they're closed you'll need to visit a **bureau de change**, commonly found in city centres, some major tourist destinations and at international arrival points (listed in the Guide). Banks in large towns and cities of the Republic are open from Monday to Friday between 10am and 4pm, and until 5pm one day a week, usually Thursday; in the North, they open Monday to Friday 9.30am to 4.30pm, with some opening for longer hours and on Saturdays. Outside the cities and bigger towns, many bank branches in the Republic and some in the North close between 12.30pm and 1.30pm, and in some cases may only be open a few days a week.

Wiring money

Having **money wired** from home is never convenient or cheap, and should be considered as a last resort. Money wiring can be done online with **Travelers Express/ MoneyGram** (ⓦwww.moneygram.com) and **Western Union** (ⓦwww.westernunion.com) – the latter service is also available in larger post offices. It's also possible to have money wired directly from a bank in your home country to a bank in Ireland, although this is somewhat less reliable because it involves two separate institutions. If you choose this route, your home bank will need the address of the bank branch where you want to pick up the money and the address and telex number of the Dublin or Belfast head office, which will act as the clearing house. Money wired this way normally takes two working days to arrive, and costs around £25/$40 per transaction.

Opening hours and holidays

Opening hours for **shops and businesses** across Ireland are usually 9am to 5.30pm, Monday to Saturday. In most large towns shops open late (until 8pm or 9pm) one day a week, usually Thursdays, and some also open on Sundays from around noon until 6pm. Lunchtime closing still applies in many smaller towns, where you may also find businesses (except pubs) close for a half-day midweek. In rural areas opening times may be far more variable.

Throughout Ireland **cafés** tend to open from 8am or 9am until 6pm, Monday to Saturday. **Restaurants** are usually open from around noon until 3pm and from 6pm until 10pm daily, though, away from the major towns and popular tourist areas, many may be closed at lunchtimes or all day on certain days of the week (especially out of season). We've indicated significant variations from these hours for both cafés and restaurants in the Guide.

Pubs in the Republic open Monday to Thursday 10.30am to 11.30pm, Friday and Saturday 10.30am to 12.30am, Sunday 11.30am to 11pm; in the North the hours are Monday to Saturday 11.30am to 11pm and Sunday 12.30pm to 10pm. Across Ireland **clubs** have variable opening days, though the majority are open from Thursday to Sunday and hours tend to be from around 10pm to 2am (or later in the major cities).

Public holidays

Holiday	Republic	N Ireland
New Year's Day	√	√
St Patrick's Day – March 17	√	√
Good Friday	√	√
Easter Monday	√	√
May – first Mon	√	√
May – last Mon	×	√
June – first Mon	√	×
Orange Day – July 12	×	√
Aug – first Mon	√	×
Aug – last Mon	×	√
Oct – last Mon	√	×
Christmas Day	√	√
St.Stephen's Day /Boxing Day – Dec 26	√	√

On **public holidays**, away from the cities, most businesses will be closed, apart from pubs, newsagents, some supermarkets and grocers, and garages. If St Patrick's Day or Orange Day falls at the weekend, then the holiday is held on the following Monday.

The majority of churches and cathedrals, when still in use, are open from around 9am to 5pm. However, sometimes in rural areas they're locked after a service and you'll need to enquire locally about access.

Phones

Domestic calls from a **payphone** start at 50c in the Republic, 40p in the North. All calls, including overseas, are cheapest if dialled direct after 6pm or at the weekend. In the Republic, Eircom Talk Global cards, available for €10 at newsagents and post offices, offer savings on international calls over the standard rates; they can be used in payphones, as well as on hotel phones. Throughout Ireland, many phones will accept debit or credit cards, but at a premium. Similarly, calls from a hotel or the like are pricey, while the cheapest way of making international calls is via VoIP at an Internet café.

The international **dialling code** for the Republic is +353, and for Northern Ireland, as part of the UK, it's +44. If you're calling the North from the Republic, however, knock off the 028 area code and instead dial 048 followed by the eight-digit subscriber number.

Mobile phones

If you want to use your **mobile phone**, you'll need to check with your phone provider whether it will work in Ireland, and it's worth finding out what the call charges will be. Unless you have a tri-band phone, it is unlikely that a mobile bought for use in the US will work outside the States. GSM, the system most commonly found in other parts of the world, works well in Ireland, though it's still advisable to check with your provider before travelling. If you are coming from Britain your mobile phone should work in Northern Ireland, but making and receiving calls in the Republic requires international access.

Operator services

In the Republic:

Directory Enquiries within Ireland, including the North ⓣ11811
International Directory Enquiries ⓣ11818
Operator Assistance, including overseas ⓣ10

In the North:

British Telecom Operator ⓣ100
British Telecom Directory Enquiries ⓣ118500
British Telecom International Directory Enquiries ⓣ118505
British Telecom International Operator Services ⓣ155

Post

In the **Republic**, post is handled by An Post (the national postal service); allow three days (or more) for a letter to reach Britain, for example. Small letters and postcards to any destination overseas cost 78c. Main post offices are open Monday to Friday 9am to 5.30pm, Saturday 9am to 1pm (in cities and large towns until 5.30pm on Saturday). From **the North** with the Royal Mail, postcards and the smallest airmail letters cost 54p to destinations outside Europe. Post-office hours in the North are generally Monday, Tuesday, Thursday and Friday 9am to 5.30pm and Wednesday and Saturday 9am to 12.30pm – later on Wednesday and Saturday in large towns and cities.

Time

Ireland is on **GMT**, eight hours ahead of US Pacific Standard Time and five hours ahead of Eastern Standard Time. Clocks are advanced one hour at the end of March and back again at the end of October.

Tipping

Though discretionary, **tipping** restaurant staff or taxi drivers is the expected reward for satisfactory service; ten to fifteen percent of your tab will suffice.

Toilets

Public toilets are usually only found in the big towns in the Republic (especially in shopping malls), though in the North are much more common and generally well maintained. Toilet doors often bear the indicator *Fir* (men) and *Mná* (women).

Tourist information

A wealth of tourist information is published on Ireland, mostly free and obtainable before your departure. The Irish tourist development agency, **Fáilte Ireland** (ⓦwww.discoverireland.ie), and the **Northern Ireland Tourist Board** (NITB; ⓦwww.discovernorthernireland.com) both provide a wealth of area-specific information on their websites and the latter includes brochures which can also be ordered or downloaded. Abroad the two boards combine as **Tourism Ireland** (ⓦwww.discoverireland.com); offices are listed below. There are also plenty of local and regional tourism websites and we have listed the best of these in the relevant sections of the Guide.

Both Fáilte Ireland and the NITB provide an extensive network of **tourist offices**, covering every city, many major towns and almost all the popular tourist areas. Additionally, some local councils provide their own offices. The majority of offices offer plenty of information on local attractions, and can book accommodation (€4/£2 per reservation). Bear in mind though that Fáilte Ireland and NITB offices will usually only direct you towards approved accommodation, thus excluding some fine hostels and campsites and some private bus services, and that some tourist offices operate seasonal opening times, days and months.

Tourism Ireland offices abroad

Australia Level 5, 36 Carrington St, Sydney NSW 2000, ⓣ02/9299 6177.
Britain Nations House, 103 Wigmore St, London W1U 1QS, and James Miller House, 7th Floor, 98 West George St, Glasgow G2 1PJ; both ⓣ0800 039 7000.
Canada 2 Bloor St West, Suite 3403, Toronto, ON M4W ⓣ0416/925 6368.
New Zealand Level 7, Citigroup Building, 23 Customs St East, Auckland ⓣ09/977 2255.
South Africa c/o Development Promotions, Everite House, Level 7, 20 De Korte Street, Gauteng, Braamfontein 2001 ⓣ011/339 4865.
US 345 Park Ave, 17th Floor, New York, NY 10154 ⓣ212/418-0800.

Guide

Guide

Dublin

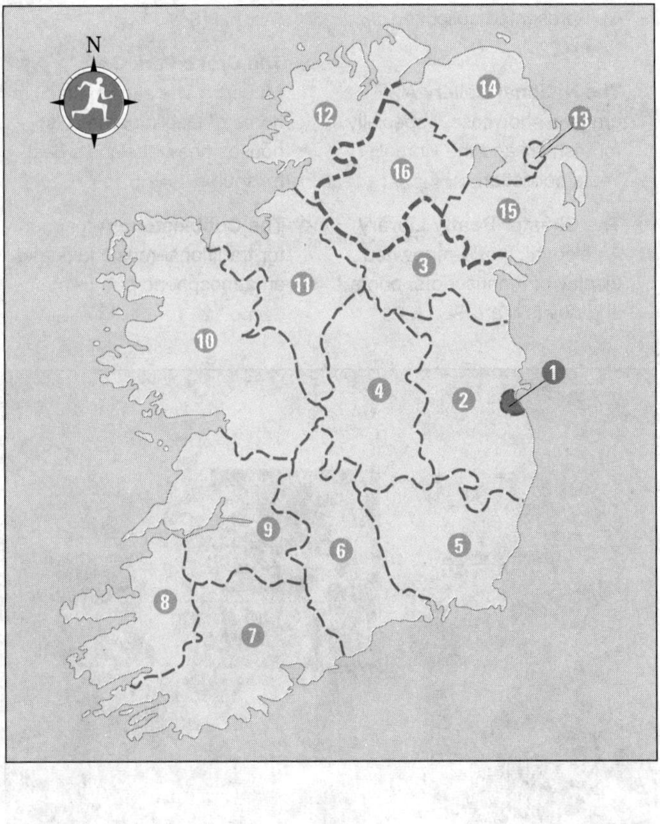

CHAPTER 1

Highlights

* **Trinity College** Admire the illuminated *Book of Kells* and the magnificent Long Room, or just enjoy the architecture. See p.84

* **The National Museum** Stunning prehistoric gold and Christian treasures are the highlights of this well-presented collection. See p.89

* **The National Gallery** A graceful showcase, especially for Irish art and the vibrant Yeats collection. See p.90

* **The Chester Beatty Library** An elegant, world-renowned display of manuscripts, prints and *objets d'art*. See p.99

* **Bloomsday** Follow Joyce's Dublin novel nonpareil on this annual pilgrimage on June 16. See p.110

* **Kilmainham Gaol** Tour the city's most historic prison and visit the museum for fascinating insights into Republican history. See p.115

* **The Croke Park GAA Museum** The superb stadium home of Gaelic games also houses one of Ireland's best museums. See p.117

* **The Cobblestone** A magnet for traditional-music fans and an atmospheric pub to boot. See p.129

▲ National Gallery

1

Dublin

Set beside the shores of curving Dublin Bay, Ireland's capital city, **DUBLIN**, is a thrusting, dynamic place, which despite its size remains utterly beguiling and an essential part of any visit to the country. Much of Dublin's centre has been redeveloped over the last few decades, leaving a wag to comment that "the city's only sights are building sites", as it built on Ireland's economic boom. So, alongside the city's historic buildings – its cathedrals and churches, Georgian squares and town houses, castles, monuments and pubs – you'll discover grand new hotels and shopping centres, stunning new street architecture and a state-of-the-art tramway system.

More than a quarter of the Republic of Ireland's population of almost four million lives within the Greater Dublin area. Intensely proud of their city, Dubliners seem to possess an innate sense of its heritage and powerful literary culture, and can at times exhibit a certain snobbishness towards those living in Ireland's rural backwaters (people often termed "culchies"). Locals are noted for their often caustic, but engaging, brand of humour, as shown in the numerous and sometimes bawdy nicknames given to many of the city's landmarks (the Millennium Spire, for instance, has all manner of sobriquets including "the eyeful tower" and "the stiffy by the Liffey"), but there is also a warmth in their welcome – it's easy to find yourself drawn into conversation or debates in bars and cafés (or, if you smoke, outside them). Dubliners are also increasingly style-conscious; where once the city looked inwards for inspiration, today it glances both east and west, to Europe and America, catching new trends and bringing a decidedly Irish slant to bear upon them.

Most of Dublin's attractions are contained within a relatively compact area, spreading either side of the many-bridged **River Liffey**, which divides the city between its **Northside** and **Southside**. These have very distinct characters, defined over the city's historical development: stereotypically, the south is viewed in terms of its gentility while the north is seen as brash and working class. Certainly, the Southside is regarded as more fashionable and fashion-conscious, thanks to its **Grafton Street** shopping area and the rejuvenated **Temple Bar** arts quarter, yet the north possesses Ireland's two most renowned theatres and its own increasingly lively nightlife. On either side of the river it's easy to escape the city's bustle, to relax or picnic in its numerous green spaces (especially expansive **Phoenix Park**); or visitors can head to the shoreline for seaside strolls and blustery cliff-top walks.

Some history

Dublin's origins date back to ninth-century **Viking** times when the Norsemen saw the strategic potential of Dublin Bay and established a trading post on the

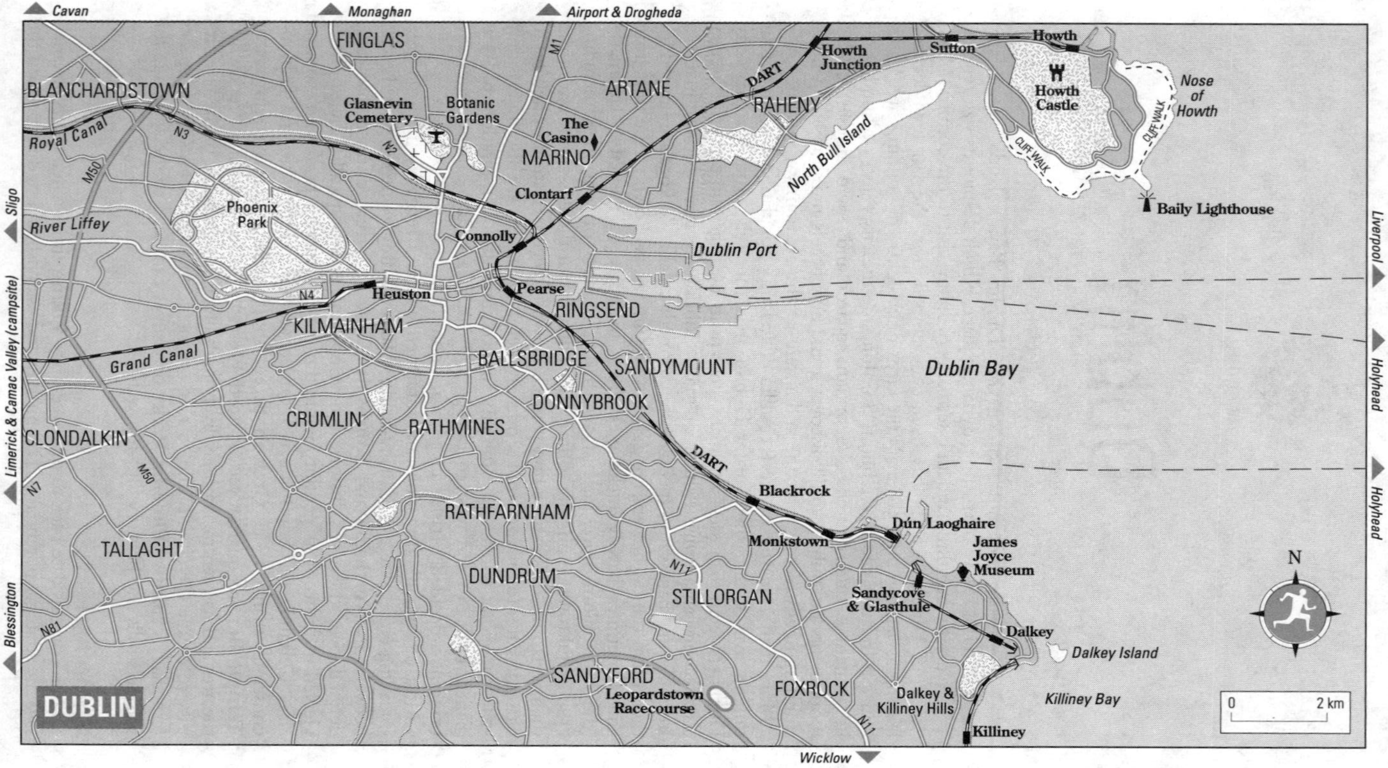

DUBLIN

Cavan
Monaghan
Airport & Drogheda
Sligo
Limerick & Camac Valley (campsite)
Blessington
Wicklow
Liverpool
Holyhead
Holyhead

FINGLAS
BLANCHARDSTOWN
Glasnevin Cemetery
Botanic Gardens
ARTANE
RAHENY
The Casino
MARINO
Clontarf
Connolly
Royal Canal
N3
N2
M1
M50
Phoenix Park
River Liffey
N4
Heuston
Pearse
RINGSEND
KILMAINHAM
Grand Canal
BALLSBRIDGE
SANDYMOUNT
DONNYBROOK
CRUMLIN
RATHMINES
CLONDALKIN
N7
M50
RATHFARNHAM
TALLAGHT
DUNDRUM
N11
STILLORGAN
N81
SANDYFORD
Leopardstown Racecourse
FOXROCK
N11
Howth Junction
DART
Sutton
Howth
Howth Castle
Nose of Howth
CLIFF WALK
CLIFF WALK
North Bull Island
Baily Lighthouse
Dublin Port
Dublin Bay
DART
Blackrock
Dún Laoghaire
Monkstown
James Joyce Museum
Sandycove & Glasthule
Dalkey
Dalkey Island
Dalkey & Killiney Hills
Killiney Bay
Killiney
N
0 2 km

Liffey's southern bank at the point where the ancient royal road from Tara to Wicklow forded the river. They adopted the location's Irish name, Dubh Linn ("dark pool"), for their new home, soon amalgamating with an Irish settlement on the northern bank called Baile Atha Cliath ("place of the hurdle ford"), which remains the Irish name for the city.

The twelfth century saw Dublin conquered by the **Anglo-Normans** when Dermot McMurrough, the deposed King of Leinster, sought help from Henry II to regain his crown. In return for Dermot's fealty, Henry sent Strongbow (see p.692) and a contingent of Welsh knights to restore MacMurrough's power. Strongbow conquered Dublin in the process and, concerned at this threat to his authority, Henry came over to Ireland to assert control, establishing Dublin as the focus for British sway over Ireland. This became the centre of the "English Pale" (from the Latin *palum*, meaning originally a "stake", though later a "defined territory"), ruling over the areas of Anglo-Norman settlement in Ireland; since Irish resistance to conquest was so strong in other parts of the country, the pejorative phrase "beyond the pale" evolved as a means of signifying (at least in English terms) a lack of civilized behaviour.

Only a few buildings have survived from before the seventeenth century, mainly in the area encompassing Dublin Castle and the two cathedrals, and much of the city's layout is essentially **Georgian**. During this period, Dublin's Anglo-Irish nobility and its increasingly wealthy mercantile class used their money (often, in the aristocracy's case derived from confiscated land granted as a reward for services to the Crown) to showcase their wealth in the form of grandiose houses, public buildings and wide new thoroughfares. Wealthy members of the elite revelled in their new-found opulence, filling their houses with works by the latest artists and craftsmen, and seeking to enhance their own cachet by patronizing the arts; Handel conducted the first performance of his *Messiah* in the city, for example. Increasing political freedom resulted in demands for self-government, inspired by the American and French revolutions. The legislative independence achieved during "Grattan's Parliament" in 1782 was to be short-lived, however, and the failure of the **1798 Rebellion** (see p.696), led largely by members of the Protestant Anglo-Irish Ascendancy, inevitably led to the 1801 **Act of Union** and the removal of Dublin's independent powers.

With Ireland now governed by a British vice-regent, Dublin sank into a period of **economic decline**, brought about by its inability to compete with Britain's flourishing industries. The city remained the focus of agitation for self-rule, and by the end of the nineteenth century had also become the centre for efforts to form a sense of Irish national consciousness via the foundation of the **Gaelic League** in 1893. This sought to revive both the Irish language and traditional culture, and set the scene for the **Celtic literary revival**, led by W.B. Yeats and Lady Gregory, who established the Abbey Theatre in 1904. The political struggle for independence remained a live issue and events came to a head with the **Easter Rising** of 1916 (see box, p.107). The city's streets saw violence again during the **civil war**, which followed the establishment of the Irish Free State in 1921.

Austerity and much **emigration** followed Independence and it was not until the 1950s that Dublin began to emerge from its colonial past. The city's infrastructure was ravaged by ill-conceived redevelopment in the 1960s which saw the demolition of many Georgian edifices, as well as the creation of poorly-planned "sink" estates to replace dilapidated tenements. A couple of decades later city planners began to address the issue of inner-city depopulation, constructing apartment blocks to house Dublin's wealthy middle classes, and the numerous cranes on the city's skyline demonstrate the continuing activity of the **regeneration** process, not least in the former docklands. The most obvious

Festivals and events

January

Temple Bar Trad Festival ⓣ01/677 2397, ⓦwww.templebartrad.com. Four days and nights of traditional-music pub sessions, concerts, instrument workshops and more in the heart of the city.

Feburary

Jameson Dublin International Film Festival ⓣ01/672 8861, ⓦwww.dubliniff.com. Held at cinemas and other venues across the city centre for ten days in mid-February. While screening the latest in new Irish cinema, the festival also has a decidedly international flavour and its hundred or so films include special themes and retrospectives.

RTÉ Living Music Festival ⓣ01/208 2617, ⓦwww.rte.ie/music. Three days of contemporary classical music concerts and events, featuring leading Irish and international figures held in mid-February at a variety of central venues.

March/April

Easter Rising Commemorations take place on Easter Sunday, featuring speeches and a march from the General Post Office to Glasnevin Cemetery.

St Patrick's Festival ⓣ01/676 3205, ⓦwww.stpatricksfestival.ie. Running for five days on and around St Patrick's Day (March 17), this city-wide festival includes a parade, light shows, concerts, funfair, films, exhibitions and a *céilí mór* (thousands of locals and visitors fill the streets in a traditional danceathon).

Poetry Now Festival ⓣ01/205 4873, ⓦwww.dircoco.ie/arts. A major three-day event, held over the first weekend in April at The Pavilion Theatre, Dún Laoghaire, the festival features readings by well-known Irish and international poets, master classes, exhibitions and children's events.

Handel's Messiah Festival ⓣ01/677 2255, ⓦwww.templebar.ie. A week-long festival in mid-April celebrating Handel's visit to Dublin in 1742, featuring free concerts, workshops and talks held in various venues around Temple Bar and the Old City.

Convergence Sustainable Living Festival ⓣ01/674 6396, ⓦwww.sustainable.ie/convergence. Run by the Sustainable Ireland Cooperative, and focusing on ecological and environmental matters, the festival takes place in Temple Bar over six days in late April and features a diverse range of events.

May

Heineken Green Energy ⓣ0818/719 300, ⓦwww.ticketmaster.ie. Major music acts play outdoors at Dublin Castle over the first weekend in May; previous performers have included The White Stripes, Lou Reed, Faithless and Kasablan.

International Dublin Gay Theatre Festival ⓣ01/677 8511, ⓦwww.gaytheatre.ie. Almost three weeks of drama, comedy, cabaret and musical theatre with international and Irish casts taking place at a variety of city-centre locations, plus a post-performance Festival Club at *The Dragon* (see p.132).

June

Diversions Temple Bar ⓣ01/677 2255, ⓦwww.templebar.ie. This series of free outdoor events runs from June to September in and around Meeting House Square

evidence of reinvigoration in the city centre is the Temple Bar area, though the original intention to develop a Parisian-style quarter of *ateliers* and arts centres soon fell foul of the moneygrubbers. Today, the arrival of **migrants**, particularly and includes film screenings, music performances, circus acts, family fun days and other entertainment.

Docklands Maritime Festival ⓣ01/818 3300, ⓦwww.ddda.ie. Tall ships open their decks to visitors over the first weekend in June at North Wall Quay, plus there's a market, street theatre, trips along the Liffey and a variety of events for children.

Dublin Writers Festival ⓣ01/222 7848, ⓦwww.dublinwritersfestival.com. Major Irish and international writers and poets take part in five days of readings, discussions and other events around the city centre in mid-June.

Bloomsday ⓣ01/878 8547, ⓦwww.jamesjoyce.ie. The James Joyce Centre organizes a week of events in mid-June, culminating in Bloomsday itself (June 16), the day on which Joyce's *Ulysses* is set.

July

Howth Peninsula Festival ⓦwww.howthpeninsula.com. A plethora of fun events, from tug-of-war competitions via a fun fair, various displays and a variety of music, held in the harbour area and other locations around the peninsula during the first weekend in July.

August

Look Out! ⓦwww.dlgff/ie. Dublin's Lesbian and Gay Film Festival takes place at the Irish Film Institute (see p.96) over four days in early August and features a strong programme of new feature and documentary works.

Dublin Horse Show ⓣ1850/882883, ⓦwww.dublinhorseshow.com. Five days of equestrian events in early August at the RDS arena in Ballsbridge, featuring major international showjumpers participating in the Nations Cup.

Dún Laoghaire Festival of World Cultures ⓣ01/230 1035, ⓦwww.festivalofworldcultures.com. The last weekend in August sees more than 150 (mostly free) events in over forty venues around the town, featuring major international acts and a host of lively outdoor activities.

September/October

All-Ireland Senior Hurling and Gaelic Football finals Two of Ireland's major sporting events are staged at Croke Park (see p.117) in September: the hurling final on the second Sunday and the football final on the fourth.

Dublin Fringe Festival ⓣ01/677 8511, ⓦwww.fringefest.com. Ireland's biggest performing-arts festival takes place over more than two weeks from during mid-September and features all manner of music, dance, street theatre, comedy and children's events.

Dublin Theatre Festival ⓣ01/677 8899, ⓦwww.dublintheatrefestival.com. A major celebration of theatre, held during the last few days of September and the first two weeks in October, this includes performances of new and classic drama at various city-centre venues.

Dublin City Marathon ⓣ01/623 2250, ⓦwww.dublincitymarathon.ie. Featuring 10,000 entrants, the race takes place on the last Monday in October and involves a roughly circular course starting from Kildare Street, crossing the Liffey and taking in Phoenix Park and the Grand Canal Basin before terminating at Merrion Square West.

from Africa and Eastern Europe, together with the city's longer-standing Chinese community, has seen Dublin gradually inch towards multiculturalism. The effects of these changes are most visible in the city's restaurants, shops and street markets, broadening native Dublin tastes and introducing locals to all manner of culinary and fashion delights.

Arrival

Dublin's train and bus stations are centrally located while efficient local transport makes the city centre easily accessible from the airport and ferry terminals.

By air

Dublin Airport (Ⓣ01/874 1111, Ⓦwww.dublinairport.com) is some 11km north of the centre. The arrivals hall contains a tourist office (daily 8am–10pm), a travel information desk (Mon–Sat 8am–1pm & 2–5pm, Sun 10.30am–1pm & 2–4.30pm), a branch of the Bank of Ireland (Mon–Fri 10am–4pm, Wed until 5pm), a bureau de change (daily 5.30am–9pm, closes Mon 8pm), several ATMs and a number of car-rental outlets.

Buses to the centre depart from outside the arrivals exit and the journey takes from around 30 minutes to one hour depending upon the service you choose and the time of day. The most direct are the **Airlink** bus #747 (every 10–15min Mon–Sat 5.45am–11.30pm, every 15–20min Sun 7.15am–11.30pm; €6 single, €10 return) which runs via O'Connell Street to Busáras, the central bus station; and #748 (every 30min Mon–Sat 6.50am–9.30pm, Sun 7am–10.05pm; same prices), which takes a similar route but continues to Heuston railway station. Alternatively, **Aircoach** (Ⓦwww.aircoach.ie) operates two services – the first runs into the centre via College Green and onwards to hotels in Donnybrook and Ballsbridge (daily every 10–20min 4.30am–midnight, hourly midnight–4.30am; €7 single, €12 return); the second also takes in the centre and Donnybrook before continuing onwards to Stillorgan and Leopardstown (daily every 10–20min 4am–midnight, hourly midnight–4am; same prices).

The slower but cheaper option (€1.90) is to take one of the regular **Dublin Bus** services such as the #16A to O'Connell Street and College Green (every 15–30min Mon–Fri 6.50am–11.10pm, every 20–50 min Sat 7.40am–10.20pm, every 25min–1hr Sun 8.30am–10.40pm) or #41 to Abbey Street Lower, just off O'Connell Street (every 15–30min Mon–Sat 6.20am–11.50pm, every 30min–1hr Sun 7.15am–11.35pm). Additionally, the #746 (every 30min–1hr 15min Mon–Fri 9.15am–9.45pm, hourly Sat 9.45am–9.45pm & Sun 10am–7pm) runs to the centre and thence to Dún Laoghaire.

The **taxi** rank is also outside the arrivals exit; a metered cab to the centre should cost around €30.

By bus

Busáras, Dublin's central bus station, is on Store Street behind the Custom House, some ten minutes' walk east of O'Connell Street. It serves Bus Éireann express coaches from all parts of Ireland (North and South) as well as the Airlink service and coaches from Britain. City buses run into the centre along Talbot Street, a block to the north, while there are LUAS Red Line (see p.74) stops outside the bus station's northern exit or to the west on Abbey Street Lower. Alternatively, a taxi can usually be hailed on Beresford Place just south of Busáras. There are left-luggage lockers in the station's basement (€6–10 depending on size).

Private coaches from the north and west usually operate from and terminate at Parnell Square and O'Connell Street while those from the south and southwest tend to terminate at Southside spots such as Nassau Street – check with the service operator for details.

By train

Services from Belfast, Sligo and Rosslare terminate at **Connolly Station**, fifteen minutes' walk east of O'Connell Street and connected to the centre by regular buses and LUAS trams – it's also on the DART line. Left-luggage lockers are available on the concourse (€4 or €6, depending on size). **Heuston Station**, 3km west of the centre, serves trains from Cork, Galway, Kerry, Kilkenny, Limerick, Mayo and Waterford, and is connected to the centre by LUAS and buses #90 and #92. Again left-luggage lockers are available on the concourse (€1.50 or €5). Two other Southside stations, **Tara Street** and **Pearse**, serve DART and suburban railways. **Information** on train services and timetables is available on ⓣ01/836 6222, ⓦwww.irishrail.ie.

By ferry

All services – except Stena Line's HSS (see below) – arrive at **Dublin Port,** two miles east of the centre. An unnumbered Dublin Bus service (€2.50 single) meets arrivals and runs directly to Busáras. The return service leaves Busáras daily at 6.45am (Sun 7am), 7.30am, 1.15pm and 8pm. Stena Line HSS ferries arrive at **Dún Laoghaire**, nine miles southeast of the city centre. The DART (see p.75) station is directly opposite the terminal and trains (€2) run every 20 minutes to the centre (including the central Pearse, Tara St and Connolly stations). Alternatively, bus #46A (Mon–Sat every 5–15min, Sun every 10–40min; €1.90) runs from outside the Crofton Road entrance to the station via Donnybrook to St Stephen's Green and O'Connell Street. The Dún Laoghaire ferry terminal has a tourist office (Mon–Sat 10am–1pm & 2–6pm).

Information, passes and tours

The main **Dublin Tourism Centre** (Mon–Sat 9am–5.30pm, July & Aug until 8pm, Sept until 7pm, Sun and public holidays 10.30am–3pm; ⓦwww.visitdublin.com) occupies the former St Andrew's Church on Suffolk Street, a short distance west of the Grafton Street junction with Nassau Street. A numbered-ticket queuing system operates for information and accommodation reservations (€4 per booking) and there are also desks for currency exchange, car rental and the purchase of tickets for events. Outside is a touch-screen information console that accepts credit-card accommodation bookings. Dublin Tourism's other offices are at the airport, Dún Laoghaire ferry terminal, 14 O'Connell St Upper (Mon–Sat 9am–5pm) and Baggott Street Bridge (Mon–Fri 9.30am–noon & 12.30–5pm). If you're planning to see the North, then it's worth visiting the **Northern Ireland Tourist Board** office, 16 Nassau St (Mon–Fri 9am–5.30pm, Sat 10am–5pm; ⓣ1850/230230, ⓦwww.discovernorthernireland.com).

The national daily *Irish Times* and the local daily *Evening Herald* are useful sources of information, notably for cinema and theatre **listings**, and the former also produces a weekly Friday listings supplement, *The Ticket*. Free listings magazines include the fortnightly *Event Guide* (ⓦwww.eventguide.ie) and *Mongrel* (monthly; free; ⓦwww.mongrel.ie), which also has articles

Aras na Uachtárain, Farmleigh & Phoenix Park Visitor Centre

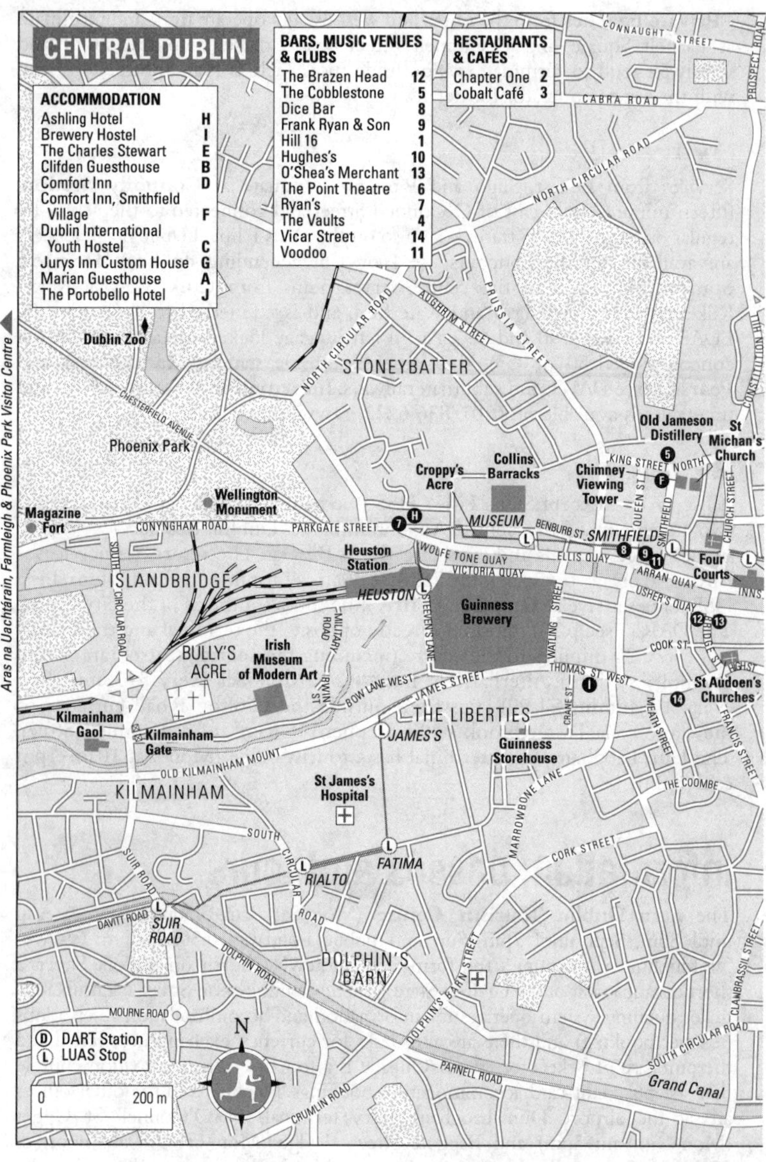

on the local arts scene, while *Connected* (monthly; free; Ⓦ www.connected.ie) is music-oriented and offers detailed listings coverage – all of these can be picked up in bars, cafés, CD shops and shopping malls. The O'Connell Street Lower branch of Eason's stocks just about every magazine published in Ireland, along with all Irish and UK daily and Sunday newspapers. For music listings, see p.128.

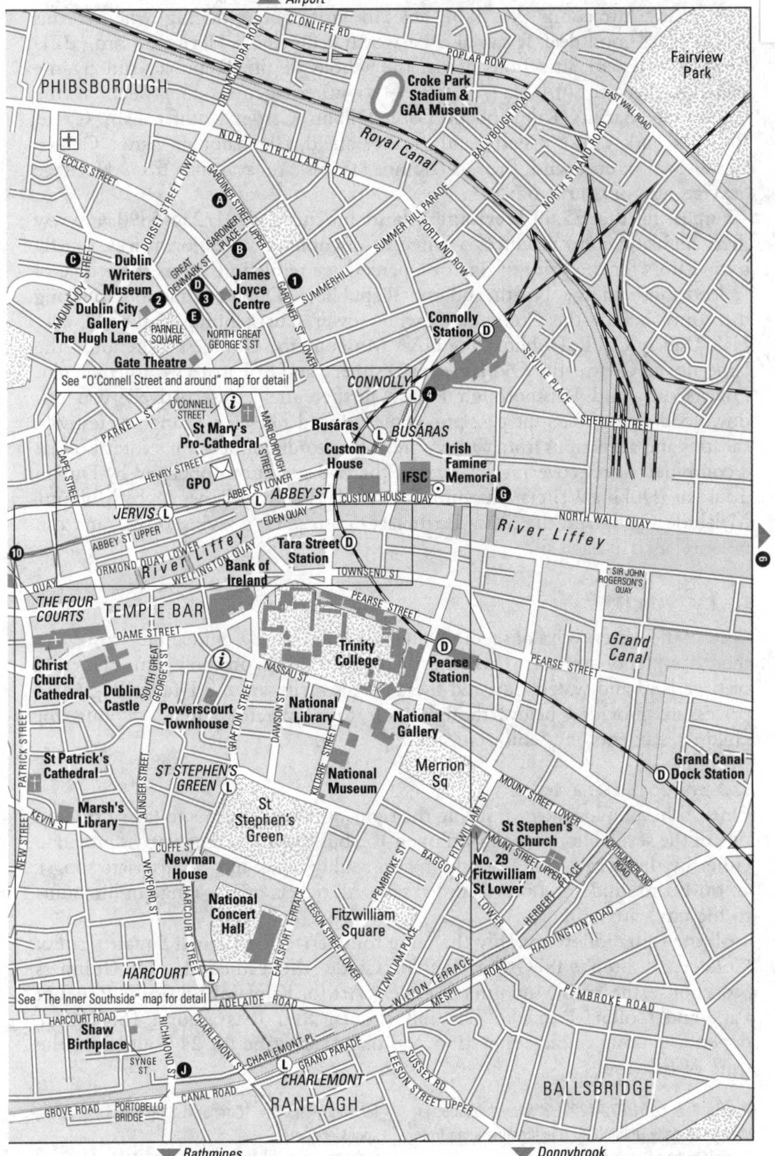

Tourist passes

Available at any tourist information office or online at Ⓦ www.dublinpass.com, the **Dublin Pass** provides free entry to more than thirty attractions as well as a range of other special offers and a one-way journey from the airport on the Aircoach service (see p.68). A one-day pass costs €31 with two-, three- and six-day passes at €49, €59 and €89 respectively – it's well worth checking just how many attractions you'll be able to visit when judging whether this represents a good deal. It can also be worth acquiring a Heritage Card (€21) for free entry to attractions across the whole of the Republic run by the Heritage Service (Ⓣ01/647 2453, Ⓦwww.heritageireland.ie), such as the Casino at Marino, Kilmainham Gaol, Dublin Castle, Rathfarnham Castle, Phoenix Park Visitor Centre and, further afield, Glendalough Visitor Centre, Castletown House and Brú na Boinne. Cards are available from Heritage Service sites or tourist offices.

Purchasing the €5.99 **Heritage Island** brochure (Ⓣ01/236 6890, Ⓦwww.heritageisland.com) produces a range of discounted admission prices, usually two visitors for the price of one or a percentage reduction, across the whole of Ireland, both in the North and the Republic – Dublin attractions offering discounts include the Chimney Viewing Tower, Christchurch Cathedral, City Hall, Dalkey Castle, Dublinia, the GAA Museum, the Guinness Storehouse, the James Joyce Centre, the Old Jameson Distillery, and St Patrick's Cathedral, plus Powerscourt and Russborough House further afield. Alternatively, you can download a free discount pass providing reduced rates for a range of festivals, theatres and attractions from Ⓦwww.irelandvisitordiscounts.com. Note also that a combined ticket covering any two of the five attractions operated by Dublin Tourism (Dublin Writers Museum, Fry Model Railway, James Joyce Museum, Malahide Castle and the Shaw Birthplace) costs €12, a saving of €2, and can be purchased at each site.

City tours

One of the easiest ways of seeing Dublin's attractions is a guided **city tour**, and there are plenty available – whether by open-top bus, on foot, along the river, or on a land and water tour; and there are also trips around Dublin Bay. Adult prices are provided below, though most tour operators offer discounts for children, students and senior citizens.

Open-top bus tours

One of the simplest ways of seeing the sights if time is short is to take a ride on one of the several hop-on-and-off open-top bus tours. Commentary is provided either by the driver (some of whom also readily break into appropriate songs), an on-board guide or a pre-recorded tape. All tickets offer a range of discounts to the city's attractions.

All the tours follow roughly the same route covering Parnell Square, Trinity College, St Stephen's Green, Dublin Castle, the cathedrals, the Guinness Storehouse, the Irish Museum of Modern Art (or Kilmainham Gaol), Phoenix Park and Collins Barracks. The full circular tour lasts around 1hr 15min, depending upon traffic congestion, and tickets are valid for 24 hours from the time of first use.

Dublin Bus Ⓣ01/873 4222, Ⓦwww.dublinbus.ie Offers the daily Dublin City Tour, commencing from Cathal Brugha St, off O'Connell St Upper (daily every 10min 9.30am–3pm, every 15min 3–5pm and also April–Oct every 30min 5–6.30pm). Tickets cost €14 and can be purchased from the Dublin Bus office (see p.74) or driver and from certain hotels. The company also operates a Ghost Bus Tour (Mon & Thurs 8pm, Fri 8pm & 8.30pm, Sat 7pm & 9.30pm; €25; not suitable for under-14s; 2hr 15mins) visiting the city's spookier spots.

Irish Tours Ⓣ01/605 7705 or 01/458 0054, Ⓦwww.irishcitytours.com. Operates a City Sightseeing Tour (daily every 10–15min; April–June 9.15am–5pm, July to Sept 9.15am–5.30pm, Oct to March 9.30am–4.30pm; €15). Tickets can be purchased from the driver, tourist information offices and some hotels. Tours commence from outside 14 O'Connell St Upper.

Land and water tour

The award-winning **Viking Splash** tour (64–65 Patrick St ⓣ01/707 6000, ⓦwww.vikingsplash.ie) uses reconditioned World War II amphibious vehicles known as Ducks and guides in Norse costume to provide a lively tour of the centre, culminating in a voyage from the Grand Canal Basin (daily: mid-Feb to mid-March & Nov 10am–4pm; mid-March to Oct 9.30am–5pm; 1hr 15min; call for times). Tours operate from both Bull Alley Street (next to St Patrick's Cathedral) and St Stephen's Green North and tickets (€20) can be purchased at the departure points or by telephone.

River cruises

A waterborne trip along the River Liffey is provided by **Liffey River Cruises** (ⓣ01/473 4082, ⓦwww.liffeyrivercruises.com). Sailings depart from Bachelors Walk (daily: March–Nov 11am, noon, 1.45pm & 2.45pm, also March–Oct 4pm & April–Sept 5pm) or you can leave from Custom House Quay (March–Nov 11.35am & 2.20pm, also April–Sept 4.35pm). The 45-minute tour includes guided commentary and costs €12.

Sea cruises

Two companies offer exhilarating trips around **Dublin Bay**, lasting 1hr 15min, taking in views of islands such as Ireland's Eye and possible sightings of seals and porpoises as well as a host of birdlife. **Sea Safari** (ⓣ01/855 7600, ⓦwww.seasafari.ie) runs two cruises in open rigid inflatable boats (waterproof clothing and lifejackets are provided) running from Dublin City Moorings, near the IFSC on Custom House Quay, or from Malahide harbour. Both tours cost €30 and are not suitable for children under 8.

Dublin Sea Tours (ⓣ01/492 5919, ⓦwww.dublinseatours.ie) operates from Poolbeg Marina, Seán Moore Road, Ringsend, just east of the East Link Bridge (buses #2 or #3 from O'Connell St) and Dún Laoghaire Harbour East Pier. Trips are in a covered, heated boat (no special clothing needed) and cost €35; children must be over 6 years of age.

Advance booking for all cruises is essential. Though there may be up to six cruises daily in high season their frequency is always subject to weather conditions.

Walking tours

Several general and specialist **walking tours** are also available, covering all manner of subjects from the city's history, and its physical and social fabric, to literature and music, all led by informative and entertaining guides. If you have an iPod, you can download one of a dozen or so free guided iWalks podcasts, providing a range of different walking tours with commentary provided by the notable local author and historian Pat Liddy (ⓦwww.visitdublin.com/multimedia/DublinPodcasts).

The 1916 Rebellion tour ⓣ086/858 3847, ⓦwww.1916rising.com. Describes events leading up to the Easter Rising, the rebellion itself and its aftermath. Commences inside the *International Bar*, Wicklow St (Nov to mid-March Sat 11.30am, Sun 1pm; mid-March to Oct Mon–Sat 11.30am, Sun 1pm; 2hr; €12).

Historical Insights ⓣ087/688 9412 or 087/830 3523, ⓦwww.historicalinsights.ie. A tour run by Trinity history graduates covering Dublin's development and major events, which starts from Trinity College's front gate (April & Oct daily 11am; May–Sept daily 11am & 3pm; Nov–March Fri–Sun 11am; 2hr; €12).

Jameson Dublin Literary Pub Crawl ⓣ01/670 5602, ⓦwww.dublinpubcrawl.com. Starts upstairs at *The Duke* on Duke St and involves actors performing extracts from major works in a number of pubs with literary connections (April–Nov daily 7.30pm, also Sun noon; Dec–March Thurs–Sun only; 2hr 15min; €12).

Traditional Irish Music Pub Crawl ⓣ01/475 3313, ⓦwww.discoverdublin.ie/musicalpubcrawl.html. Two musicians guide you on a tour of half a dozen pubs, performing songs and music while recounting Ireland's musical history. Tours begin upstairs at *Oliver St John Gogarty's*, Fleet St (daily April–Oct 7.30pm; Nov–March Thurs–Sat only; 2hr 30min; €12).

City transport

Though the best way to get to know Dublin is on foot, visiting the city's outlying attractions will entail use of the efficient and comprehensive **public transport** network.

Dublin Bus

Dublin Bus (ⓦwww.dublinbus.ie) operates a network of routes covering just about everywhere in the city and extending far beyond its boundaries into Dublin County, as well as counties Kildare, Meath and Wicklow. Most of its bus stops display route maps. A free guide to the services, timetables and an excellent, free visitors' map are available from the company's offices at 59 O'Connell St Upper (Mon 8.30am–5.30pm, Tues–Fri 9am–5.30pm, Sat 9am–2pm, Sun 9.30am–2pm), while travel information is also available from ⓣ01/873 4222. If your mobile is connected to an Irish network you can also send text message enquiries to ⓣ53503 – type "BUS" followed by the route number (such as "BUS46A") to receive details of the next three buses in each direction. You can also specify different times using the 24-hour clock (such as "BUS19 2100" or even "BUS15 0830 TOMORROW").

All bus fares are exact-change only and regular ticket prices range from €1 for a short ride to €1.90 for the longest journeys (child fares €0.70–0.90), though there's a flat €0.60 shopper's fare for short-hop journeys within the city centre. If you do not have the exact fare and pay more than required, you will receive a refund voucher from the bus driver; this and your bus ticket should be presented at the Dublin Bus office (see above) to obtain a refund.

Most services operate around 6.30am–11.30pm on weekdays, starting later and finishing earlier on Sundays. Special **Nitelink buses** run in the small hours (Tues–Fri 12.30am–2am, Sat & Sun 12.30–4.30am; every 30min). These buses run from College Street, D'Olier Street and Westmoreland Street, all routes carry the suffix "N" (e.g. 46N) and tickets cost a flat-fare rate of €4 for the shorter routes and €6 for longer journeys to places such as Ashbourne and Maynooth.

LUAS

LUAS (the Irish for "speed"; ⓦwww.luas.ie) currently operates two overground tramway routes (more are in the pipeline) which are much quicker than buses and avoid traffic congestion. The **Red Line** runs from Connolly Station along Abbey Street to Collins Barracks before crossing the river at Heuston Station then heads southwest to the suburb of Tallaght; while the **Green Line** commences at St Stephen's Green, then heads down Harcourt Street before cruising along to the southeastern suburbs of Dundrum and Sandyford. Trams run every 5–15 minutes (Mon–Fri 5.30am–12.30am, Sat 6.30am–12.30am, Sun 7am–11.30pm) and singles cost €1.40–2.10 and returns €2.70–4 (children €1 and €1.90 respectively). Tickets are bought from vending machines at the tramway stops.

▲Trams, O'Connell Street

DART and suburban trains

The trains of the Dublin Area Rapid Transit system or **DART** (Mon–Sat 6.20am–midnight, Sun 9.20am–11.40pm; ⓦwww.iarnrodeireann.ie/dart/home) link Howth and Malahide to the north of the city with Bray and Greystones to the south via places such as Blackrock, Dún Laoghaire and Dalkey. It's certainly the quickest option for visiting some of the outlying attractions. Single fares range from €1.20–3.70 with returns at €2.05–6.90 (children's fares €0.75–1.60 and €1.30–2.90), though buying a travel pass (see p.76) is a cheaper option. The **suburban train services** operated by Iarnród Éireann (ⓦwww.iarnrodeireann.ie/home) utilize the same tracks as the DART, but stop at fewer stations (Connolly, Tara St and Pearse in the centre, the new Docklands station just east of the centre, Dún Laoghaire and Bray to the south and Howth Junction to the north). The Northern Commuter line from Pearse Station via Tara Street and Connolly is the quickest means of making day-trips to Malahide and to Drogheda for Brú na Boinne.

Taxis

Dublin's **taxis** vary in shape and size from London-style black cabs and saloon cars to people carriers, though all are readily identifiable by an illuminated box on the roof displaying the driver's taxi licence number. Taxis can be hailed on the street, but it is often easier to head to one of the various ranks, such as at the northwest corner of St Stephen's Green, next to the Bank of Ireland on College Green, outside the *Westin Hotel* on Westmoreland Street, in front of the *Gresham Hotel* on O'Connell Street or on the western branch of Parnell Street.

Finding a taxi after 11pm can be arduous, especially at weekends in the city centre, so it's advisable to book one earlier. Conversely, if you're heading back to the centre from the suburbs, it can often be easy to hail a cab returning the same way. City Cabs (ⓣ01/872 7272), Satellite Taxis (Northside ⓣ01/836 5555, Southside ⓣ01/454 3333) and Eurocabs (ⓣ01/623 4100) are all

Travel passes

A bewildering range of **travel passes** is available from the Dublin Bus office (see p.74), newsagents and other shops displaying the Dublin Bus sign, and from DART and suburban railway stations. Bus-only Rambler passes are accepted on all routes except Airlink and Nitelink and cover one day (€5), three (€11), five (€17.30) and seven (€21) days. Alternatively, the Rambler Handy Pack (€18.30) consists of five one-day passes and is useful if you don't intend to travel every day, while the family one-day Rambler (€8.50) covers travel by two adults and up to four children. Additionally, there's the three-day Freedom ticket (€25) which includes travel to and from the airport on the Airlink service (so is best bought at the airport's travel information desk), all Dublin bus services (including Nitelink) and the company's hop-on-and off city tour (see p.72).

One-day passes for the LUAS service (see p.74) cost €4.80 and a seven-day pass is €17.20 when purchased from station vending machines, but they're cheaper (€4.50 and €15.50) when bought from shops bearing the LUAS sign (usually found near a station).

A combined one-day bus and LUAS pass is €6.50 and a seven-day pass is €25 (there is no reduction in price if buying from a LUAS agent).

The price of most DART railway/suburban rail passes depends on the starting and finishing points of your journey. A three-day pass ranges from €7.40–14.20 and a seven-day pass from €15.30–26. Alternatively, to roam more widely around the service, a one-day pass is €7.20 and a one-day family pass is €12.40, while a three-day adult pass is €15.30. A combined bus/DART/suburban rail one-day pass costs €8.80, rising to €17.30 for three days and €30 for seven, and a one-day family pass covering these services is €13.50. A one-day LUAS and rail pass is €8.20 (there is no family pass for this combination). All of these passes can only be used in the short-hop zone (the entire DART network and suburban rail services as far as Balbriggan to the north, Maynooth and Celbridge to the west and Kilcoole to the south).

generally reliable options. Eurocabs can also supply a wheelchair-accessible taxi if booked one hour or more in advance.

As for **fares**, a short hop will usually cost €6–9 while a trip from the centre to one of the closer suburbs, such as Clontarf or Ballsbridge will set you back €10–13. Metered taxis tend to be cheaper than the flat-fare variety and can use the city's bus lanes.

Cars and parking

Dublin's "rush-hour" covers the entire weekday periods from 7–10am and 4–7pm and some areas, such as The Quays and Dame Street, are best avoided at all times. As for **car parks**, a good Southside option is the Royal College of Surgeons multi-storey off the west side of St Stephen's Green. On-street spaces are hard to find, but Merrion Square and Fitzwilliam Square are usually sure bets.

Accommodation

The growth in visitor numbers over the last decade or so has had a positive effect on the variety of **accommodation** available in Dublin, and there is plenty to choose from for all budgets, with the Northside and suburbs generally cheaper than the centre. Hotels in the city centre tend to be expensive, though many offer discounts midweek or outside the high season, while B&Bs usually provide a very welcoming and comfortable alternative. If money is comparatively tight and you want to be near the action, hostels are the best option and almost all have private rooms. **Booking** in advance is always highly advisable, and essential around major festivals such as St Patrick's Day, in July and August, and on weekends all year round, especially when major concerts or sporting events are taking place. There is one campsite on Dublin's outskirts.

Hotels and B&Bs

Many of the city's top-range **hotels** also provide stylish luxury and excellent food. There is a concentration around Temple Bar and St Stephen's Green, though the Northside also has some chic options. Dublin has a staggering number of **B&Bs** and you'll find economically priced options on the Northside's Gardiner Street or in the pleasant Southside suburbs of Ballsbridge, Donnybrook and Rathmines, which are all within easy reach of the centre. All rooms listed provide en-suite bathrooms unless stated otherwise.

Temple Bar and the Inner Southside

Accommodation in this section is shown on the "Temple Bar" map (p.97) or the "Inner Southside" map (pp.82–83), except where noted.

Brooks Hotel Drury St ⓣ01/670 4000, ⓦwww.brookshotel.ie. Compact, four-star boutique hotel, on a quiet road that's handy for Temple Bar and Grafton St, with stylish bedrooms and public rooms, a small gym and sauna, and very friendly service. ❺

Buswells Hotel 23–27 Molesworth St ⓣ01/614 6500, ⓦwww.quinnhotels.com. Popular with politicians via its proximity to Leinster House, *Buswells* offers 67 pleasantly designed en-suite rooms in a converted Georgian townhouse. Ornate plasterwork and fireplaces testify to those origins and the hotel also has a splendid carvery/restaurant, its own bar and secure overnight parking. ❺

Central Hotel 1–5 Exchequer St ⓣ01/679 7302, ⓦwww.centralhotel.ie. Centrally located, as its name suggests, this hotel is one of the city's oldest, having been in business since 1887. Rooms are stylishly furnished, appointed and reasonably well soundproofed, though some can feel a little cramped, and the hotel's first-floor *Library Bar* is a popular spot for everything from morning coffee to pre-dinner drinks. All rooms are en suite. ❹

The Clarence 6–8 Wellington Quay ⓣ01/407 0800, ⓦwww.theclarence.ie. Formerly a bolt hole for priests and lawyers up from the country, *The Clarence* retains the distinctive light oak panelling of its former incarnation, but has been transformed into a hip, informal, luxury hotel. Owned by U2, it contains the *Tea Room* restaurant in the former ballroom and the stylish *Octagon Bar*, as well as a two-storey penthouse suite used by sundry rock stars. All 45 rooms come with a state-of-the-art multimedia system. At the time of writing plans were afoot to redevelop and expand the hotel, incorporating adjacent buildings on Wellington Quay. ❾

The Fitzwilliam Hotel St Stephen's Green ⓣ01/478 7000, ⓦwww.fitzwilliamhotel.com. With a grand and expansive foyer and luxurious rooms designed by Sir Terence Conran, the *Fitzwilliam* offers deluxe accommodation in a marvellous central location. The double-room rate ranges considerably depending on size and facilities (though all include free Internet access, a CD player and fresh flowers supplied daily), and there's also a beauty salon, roof garden, bars, secure parking and restaurant, and a new penthouse suite which includes its own private bar and grand piano. ❻–❽

Frankie's Guesthouse 8 Camden Place ⓣ01/478 3087, ⓦwww.frankiesguesthouse.com. By some distance the best gay- and lesbian-friendly guesthouse in Dublin, *Frankie's* occupies a fine mews location and proffers a dozen rooms, including standard singles and doubles as well as en-suite doubles and twins – though note that there's a minimum stay of two/three nights for respectively doubles/twins and singles at weekends. There's a glorious roof garden and a sumptuous breakfast included. ❷

Harding Hotel Copper Alley, Fishamble St ⓣ01/679 6500, ⓦwww.hardinghotel.ie. Massively popular due to its budget-conscious high-season room rate (breakfast is an additional €6.50–8.50) and roomy twins, doubles, triples and family accommodation, the *Harding* also includes the atmospheric *Darkey Kelly's* bar (taking its name from an eighteenth-century Copper Alley brothel-keeper), supplying good food and a regular programme of live entertainment. ❸

Harrington Hall 70 Harcourt St ⓣ01/475 3497, ⓦwww.harringtonhall.com. Occupying elegant Georgian premises and offering equally stylish interiors, this guesthouse just south of St Stephen's Green has 28 thoughtfully furnished and generously sized en-suite rooms, complete with secondary glazing and ceiling fans. Substantial discounts available in low season. ❻

Jurys Inn Christchurch Christchurch Place ⓣ01/454 0000, ⓦwww.jurysinn.com. Bang opposite the Cathedral (though don't compare the relative architectural merits), *Jurys* is a well-liked spot for families thanks to its low-cost room rate per night (breakfast is not included). Rooms are both restful and functional and the hotel offers a restaurant, café and bar. ❹

Kilronan House 70 Adelaide Rd ⓣ01/475 5266, ⓦwww.dublinn.com. It's hard to top the welcome at this fine Georgian townhouse which features elegant decoration, including Waterford crystal chandeliers, and orthopedic mattresses in all its rooms. It also has some standard budget rooms (❸). ❺

Leeson Inn Downtown 24 Leeson St Lower ⓣ01/662 2002, ⓦwww.leesoninndowntown.com. Some three hundred yards from the southeast corner of St Stephen's Green, the *Leeson*'s tastefully furnished and well-accoutred 28 en-suite rooms give respite from the city's hurly burly and at a reasonable price too. ❹

Longfields Hotel 9–10 Fitzwilliam St Lower ⓣ01/676 1367, ⓦwww.longfields.ie. *Longfields* fully proves the point that size isn't everything. Its 26 en-suite rooms are furnished and decorated to a high standard and include elegant drapes, prints and some four-poster beds. Run by a helpful team, and the facilities include a cosy lounge as well as an excellent breakfast. ❺

The Merrion Hotel Merrion St Upper ⓣ01/603 0600, ⓦwww.merrionhotel.com. The Duke of Wellington's dismissal of his Irish connections, "being born in a stable doesn't make one a horse", rings even hollower now that his birthplace at no. 24 is part of this very civilized luxury hotel. Four eighteenth-century townhouses have been elegantly redecorated in Georgian style and hung with a superb collection of Irish art, overlooking a private landscaped garden. Facilities include the luxurious Tethra Spa and *Restaurant Patrick Guilbaud*. (see p.124) Breakfast not included. ❾

Mont Clare Hotel Merrion St Lower ⓣ01/607 3800, ⓦwww.ocallaghanhotels.com. Just off Merrion Square the *Mont Clare* offers over seventy recently refurbished air-conditioned rooms, providing a degree of comfort for which you might pay double elsewhere, as well as an attractive location. Facilities include a bar and restaurant. ❹

The Morgan 10 Fleet St ⓣ01/643 7000, ⓦwww.themorgan.com. Sheer bliss in terms of the quality of its accommodation and crisply designed throughout, this establishment fully merits the term bijou. The hotel's 121 rooms vary in size and facilities, but none are anything less than extremely comfortable. ❺–❼

The Portobello Hotel 33 Richmond St South ⓣ01/475 2715, ⓦwww.portobellohotel.ie. Actually accessed by the canal-side Charlemont Mall (see map, p.70) and with reception on the first floor, this welcoming 24-room establishment has incredibly spacious and reasonably priced en-suite doubles. Most have views of the canal and to the Dublin mountains beyond and all also have baths as well as showers. ❷

River House Hotel 23–24 Eustace St ⓣ01/670 7655, ⓦwww.riverhousehotel.com. Tucked away on one of Temple Bar's quieter streets, the red-fronted *River House* is one of the few family-run establishments in the centre, with 29 thoughtfully decorated double rooms. Excellent breakfasts, especially the freshly baked scones, add to the attraction. ❹

The Shelbourne 27 St Stephen's Green ⓣ01/663 4500, ⓦwww.theshelbourne.ie. The *grande dame* of Dublin hotels has recently been gleamingly renovated and expanded by *Marriott*, under its "Renaissance" brand. Highlights of the new look are the gilded lobby, where the old lift has been removed to reveal the grand staircase, and the *Saddle Room* restaurant. The *Horseshoe Bar* (see p.127) and the *Lord Mayor's Lounge*, where you can tuck into traditional afternoon tea, accompanied by views of the Green and the tinkling of a piano, have been refurbished but, mercifully, not reconstructed. A spa, pool and gym are planned. Breakfast not included. ❼

Stauntons on the Green 83 St Stephen's Green ⓣ01/478 2300, ⓦwww.stauntonsonthegreen.ie. Set in an unbeatable location on the south side of the Green with its own private gardens, this is a luxurious guesthouse whose 30 en-suite rooms offer both comfort and style befitting this Georgian building. ❺

Stephen's Green Hotel St Stephen's Green ⓣ01/607 3600, ⓦwww.ocallaghanhotels.com Swish, classy, yet thoroughly modernist, this utterly enjoyable hotel occupies a spot overlooking the southwestern corner of the Green. As well as its lively bar and economically priced bistro, fitness centre, libraries and wireless Internet access, the hotel provides 68 spacious a/c double rooms equipped with fridges and power showers and a number of even more luxurious suites. ❹, suites ❾

Temple Bar Hotel 13–17 Fleet St ⓣ01/677 3333, ⓦwww.templebarhotel.com. Tastefully designed throughout, from its bright and airy lobby to its attractive, modern en-suite bedrooms, the *Temple Bar* has a high reputation for service, though some of its front-facing rooms can suffer from late-night street noise. The hotel's *Buskers* bar is a popular spot and there's reduced-rate secure car parking nearby. ❹

The Westbury Harry St, off Grafton St ⓣ01/679 1122, ⓦwww.jurysdoyle.com. The glossy lobby of this luxurious five-star hotel is an indicator of the treats that lie in store. Its bedrooms are not so much furnished as designed to pamper and the range of facilities on offer includes a fitness centre, a svelte bar specializing in champagne cocktails, and underground parking. High-season bargains without breakfast can be as low as €189 for a double. ❾

The Westin Dublin Westmoreland St ⓣ01/645 1000, ⓦwww.westin.com/dublin. Hiding behind the facade of the old Allied Irish Bank building just north of Trinity College, the *Westin* is a marvellously luxurious establishment. Its 163 bedrooms (all non-smoking) are designed with character and elegantly equipped, and some now feature personal workout facilities, while the bar is housed in the former bank's vaults, and the lounge has a stunning glass roof. Breakfast not included. ❻–❾

The Northside

Accommodation in this section is shown on "Central Dublin" map (pp.70–71), or the "O'Connell Street and around" map (p.105).

Academy Plaza Hotel Findlater Place, Cathal Brugha St ⓣ01/878 0666, ⓦwww.academy-hotel.ie. Tucked away behind O'Connell St, this well-appointed hotel has recently been massively redeveloped and now sports 285 tastefully furnished. a/c en-suite rooms and suites as well as a fine range of breakfasts and a friendly bar, plus free wireless Internet access. Early Internet bookings can be as low as €106 per room. ❸

Ashling Hotel Parkgate St ⓣ01/677 2324, ⓦwww.ashlinghotel.ie. Conveniently set near Heuston Station, this modern hotel offers 150 bedrooms providing tastefully designed comfort and plenty of space, as well as a pleasant bar and excellent breakfasts. ❹

The Charles Stewart 5–6 Parnell Square ⓣ01/878 0350, ⓦwww.charlesstewart.ie. Despite its busy location, most of this budget-friendly hotel's rooms are well secluded from street noise. Though en-suite doubles and triples are well kept, if somewhat basic, some singles can be tiny and plasterboard dividing walls do not prevent noise emanating from adjoining rooms. Nevertheless, there are plenty of bargains to be had, staff are both helpful and friendly, and a filling breakfast is served. ❷

Clifden Guesthouse 32 Gardiner Place ⓣ01/874 6364, ⓦwww.clifdenhouse.com. One of the North-side's most reliable options, this comfortable Georgian house is well maintained by very friendly hosts. Fifteen pleasant en-suite rooms include doubles as well as a triple and a family room. Off-street parking is available. ❸

Comfort Inn Great Denmark St ⓣ1850/266 3678, ⓦwww.comfortinndublin.com. The *Comfort*'s Georgian exterior encompasses a stylish modern hotel. Rooms are attractively furnished, bright and airy and the hotel's bar, *The Belvedere*, is becoming a popular meeting-place. Free broadband access is available in all rooms and the hotel is wheelchair accessible. Big discounts available in off-season. ❸

Comfort Inn Smithfield Village ⓣ01/485 0900, ⓦwww.comfortinnsmithfield.com. A great addition to the Smithfield area, this new-build hotel provides excellently equipped and furnished rooms, tastefully decorated using primary colours, and has a remarkably good-value restaurant. There's secure overnight parking nearby and it's handily placed for music at *The Cobblestone* (see p.129). ❸

The Gresham Hotel 23 O'Connell St Upper ⓣ01/874 6881, ⓦwww.gresham-hotels.com. The *Gresham* isn't just a splendidly equipped four-star hotel, but one of Dublin's landmarks, a place where you don't have to be a guest to enjoy afternoon tea in the opulent surroundings of its lobby or sample the meals in its restaurant. Rooms are stylish and spacious while the individually designed penthouse suites offer differing views of the city. ❹–❻

Hotel Isaacs Store St ⓣ01/813 4700, ⓦwww.isaacs.ie. Though its setting opposite Busáras isn't exactly auspicious, *Isaacs*' tastefully designed interior, friendly staff and 99 well-accoutred bedrooms more than compensate. The hotel has its own attached Italian restaurant, *Il Vignardo*, as well as a suitably cosmopolitan café-bar, *Le Monde*. ❸

Jurys Inn Custom House Custom House Quay ⓣ01/607 5000, ⓦwww.jurysinn.com. The riverside location really is hard to beat and the views of Dublin's developing docklands are staggering from rooms on the upper storeys. Facilities include a bar, café and restaurant. ❸

Marian Guest House 21 Gardiner St Upper ⓣ01/874 4129, ⓦwww.marianguesthouse.ie. Immensely popular due to its budget prices and warm welcome, the *Marian* offers five clean and comfortable en-suite double rooms as well as one standard, plus a filling breakfast. Off-street parking is available and buses #16 and #41 stop just around the corner on Dorset St Upper. ❷

The Morrison Ormond Quay Lower ⓣ01/887 2400, ⓦwww.morrisonhotel.ie. Black remains the new black as far as this swish temple of minimalism is concerned. While that colour dominates the lobby and ultra-cool bar (see p.128), the luxurious rooms also feature chocolate-and-cream decor using natural materials (fashion designer John Rocha was employed as consultant). The exclusive penthouse (€1100) offering lush furnishings and all manner of creature comforts has spectacular riverside views. ❺

Othello House 74 Gardiner St Lower ⓣ01/855 4271, ⓦwww.othellodublin.com. A good option on a busy street, this comfortable B&B provides 22 en-suite rooms, all equipped with TV, telephone and tea/coffee-making facilities, as well as an excellent Irish breakfast. Limited parking is available. ❷

The Townhouse 47–48 Gardiner St Lower ⓣ01/878 8808, ⓦwww.townhouseofdublin.com. This superbly converted Georgian house remains an oasis of calm in one of the city's busiest streets. Stylish twins, doubles, triples and a family room are thoughtfully decorated and include sizeable en-suite facilities. A buffet breakfast is served in an elegant dining room with a balcony and there are secure off-street parking spaces. ❸

Hostels

Dublin has numerous **hostels**, the majority of which offer both dormitory accommodation (€15–25 per person, depending on the season) and private rooms, usually sleeping between two and four people (€25–45 per person). Most rooms are en suite and the standard of private rooms is often as good as at B&Bs. Most hostels in Dublin belong to either the **IHH** though a few are members of the **IHO** (see p.40) – all those listed below are affiliated to IHH unless stated otherwise. Many hostels offer Internet access.

The Southside

Ashfield House 19–20 D'Olier St ⓣ01/679 7734, ⓦwww.ashfieldhouse.ie. One of the centre's most popular choices provides over 130 beds in a variety of bright and spacious rooms, all with en-suite facilities. Dorms come in a variety of sizes, most four- and six-bed (and there are comfortable doubles), as well as a kitchen and Internet access. Dorms €16, doubles ❷.

Avalon House 55 Aungier St ⓣ01/475 0001, ⓦwww.avalon-house.ie. 5min walk south of South Great George's Street, *Avalon House* occupies a former medical school and has a variety of accommodation available, including various-sized dorms, as well as twin-bedded rooms. It's a large hostel (281 beds) and has a café, kitchen, Internet access, TV and games rooms. Dorms €20, doubles ❶.

Barnacles Temple Bar House, 19 Temple Lane ⓣ01/671 6277, ⓦwww.barnacles.ie. This modern hostel's lobby is strangely reminiscent of a sub-post office, but don't be dissuaded because its en-suite rooms and facilities cover all essentials. Dorms €18.50, doubles ❷.

Brewery Hostel 22–23 Thomas St ⓣ01/453 8600, ⓦwww.irish-hostel.com. This IHO hostel's inauspicious location (see map, p.70) is certainly mitigated by the friendliness of its welcome and all-round cosiness. More like a country hostel than its Dublin cousins, the hostel offers 70 beds, including four private rooms. Facilities include a large lounge, a well-equipped kitchen and well-maintained showers, plus a courtyard for alfresco conviviality. Dorms €18, doubles ❷.

Kinlay House 2–12 Lord Edward St ⓣ01/679 6644, ⓦwww.kinlayhouse.ie. A very lively and busy hostel near Christ Church Cathedral, *Kinlay House* offers good-value private rooms as well as both small six-bed and much bigger 24-bed dorms. There's a large kitchen as well as a café, and residents qualify for reductions at *Darkey Kelly's* restaurant. Internet access is available. Dorms €19, doubles ❷.

Oliver St John Gogarty's 18–21 Anglesea St ⓣ01/671 1822, ⓦwww.gogartys.ie. Not to be recommended at weekends thanks to its popularity with British hen and stag parties, this well-equipped hostel has more than 100 beds in a range of accommodation, including standard and en-suite twins, up to eight- and ten-bed dorms as well as stylish one- to three-bed apartments. Kitchen and laundry facilities are available. Dorms €20, doubles ❷, apartments €135–300.

The Northside

Abbey Court 29 Bachelors Walk ⓣ01/878 0800, ⓦwww.abbey-court.com. Right next to O'Connell Bridge, this upmarket, well-designed hostel provides en-suite twins/doubles and dorms ranging from four to twelve beds. Very security conscious, access is via keycards and there are lockers in every room. Add to that a café, kitchen, laundry, two TV lounges, a conservatory and a barbecue area, plus Internet access. Dorms €22, doubles ❷.

Abraham House 82–83 Gardiner St Lower ⓣ01/855 0600, ⓦwww.abraham-house.ie One of the larger Northside hostels, *Abraham House* has both a friendly staff and atmosphere. En-suite rooms range in size from doubles and triples to four-, six-, eight-, ten- and sixteen-bed dorms. There's a good kitchen, lockers, Internet access and a small car park. The stop for bus #41 to and from the airport is adjacent. Dorms €21, doubles ❸.

Dublin International Youth Hostel Mountjoy St ⓣ01/830 1766, ⓦwww.anoige.ie. A gargantuan 293-bed establishment in a somewhat grim Northside area, just west of the Black Church and Dorset St Upper, this An Óige flagship is more homely than its forbidding exterior might suggest. Much of the accommodation is in largish dorms though there are some private and four-bedded rooms. Non–An Óige or International Youth Hostelling Association members are charged a supplement of €2. There's a reasonably priced restaurant and Internet access too. Dorms €21, doubles ❶.

Globetrotters 46 Gardiner St Lower ⓣ01/873 5893, ⓦwww.globetrottersdublin.com. Under the same excellent management as *The Townhouse*, this 94-bed hostel offers 6- to 12-bed dorms, equipped with some of the most comfortable bunks in Dublin. All are en suite and there's a good kitchen too, plus free Internet access. Dorms €24.

Isaacs Hostel 2–5 Frenchman's Lane ⓣ01/855 6125, ⓦwww.isaacs.ie. Dublin's oldest independent hostel is still one of its best and consists mostly of eight- and ten-bed dorms and some cosy twin-bedded private rooms, though none are en suite. Efficiently run and very welcoming; facilities include a high-quality kitchen, a café, a small garden hosting barbecues in summer, Internet access and live acoustic music on Fri. Dorms €16, twins ❷.

Jacobs Inn 21–28 Talbot Place ⓣ01/855 5660, ⓦwww.isaacs.ie. Recently refurbished, this is Dublin's largest independent hostel which, despite its size, remains one of the most convivial, with a ground-floor café and first-floor common room with pool table and big-screen TV. En-suite private rooms are large and well-furnished, and the twelve-bed dorms are en suite and comfortable too. Internet facilities are available and the hostel is wheelchair accessible. Dorms from €17, doubles ❷.

Litton Lane Hostel 2–4 Litton Lane ⓣ01/872 8389, ⓦwww.irish-hostel.com. Housed in a former recording studio in a quiet side-street off Bachelors Walk, this popular and efficient hostel offers eight- and ten-bed dorms as well as comfortable private rooms. There's a sizeable kitchen too, and a pool table. Some self-contained apartments, sleeping from two to four. Dorms €19, doubles ❷, apartments €90–120.

Camping

The only **campsite** within easy reach of the city centre is *Camac Valley Tourist Caravan & Camping Park*, Corkagh Regional Park, Naas Road, Clondalkin (ⓣ01/464 0644, ⓦwww.camacvalley.com), 8km southwest of Dublin. This well-equipped, family-oriented site offers excellent facilities, including 24-hour security, an Internet café and campers' kitchen, as well as fine views of the surrounding countryside. Take bus #69 from Aston Quay, or it's a five-minute drive from the Red Cow LUAS station.

The City

The **River Liffey** divides the city neatly into north and south sides, and polarizes attitudes on both banks. The generally wealthier and posher Southsiders mock their poor northerly cousins, supposedly blighted by unemployment and drugs. The current Taoiseach, Bertie Ahern, however, has his political

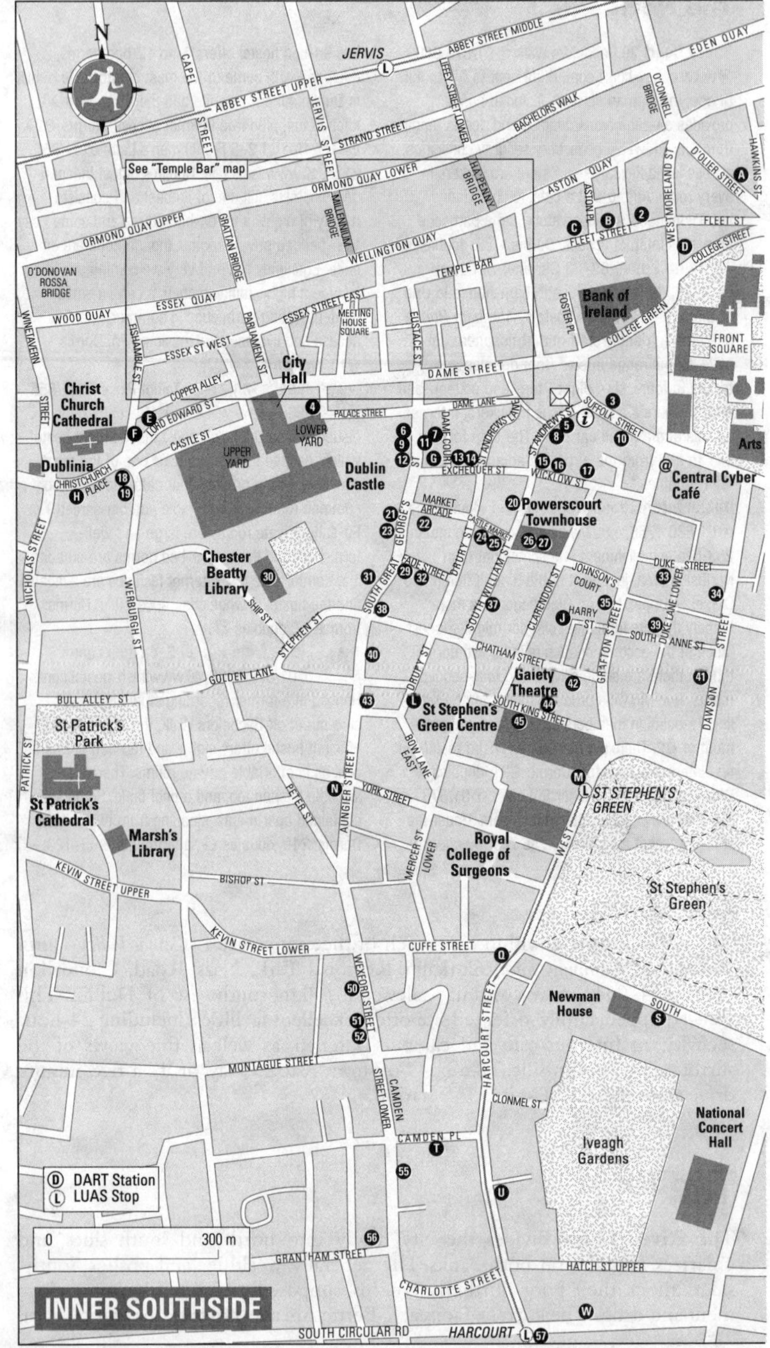
INNER SOUTHSIDE
See "Temple Bar" map
JERVIS
ABBEY STREET MIDDLE
EDEN QUAY
ABBEY STREET UPPER
CAPEL STREET
JERVIS STREET
LIFFEY STREET LOWER
O'CONNELL BRIDGE
STRAND STREET
BACHELORS WALK
D'OLIER STREET
HAWKINS ST
ORMOND QUAY LOWER
HA'PENNY BRIDGE
ASTON QUAY
ASTON PL
WESTMORELAND ST
FLEET ST
FLEET STREET
COLLEGE STREET
ORMOND QUAY UPPER
GRATTAN BRIDGE
MILLENNIUM BRIDGE
WELLINGTON QUAY
TEMPLE BAR
O'DONOVAN ROSSA BRIDGE
WOOD QUAY
ESSEX QUAY
ESSEX STREET EAST
MEETING HOUSE SQUARE
EUSTACE ST
FOSTER PL
Bank of Ireland
COLLEGE GREEN
FRONT SQUARE
WINETAVERN STREET
FISHAMBLE ST
ESSEX ST WEST
PARLIAMENT ST
City Hall
DAME STREET
Christ Church Cathedral
COPPER ALLEY
LORD EDWARD ST
DAME LANE
PALACE STREET
DAME COURT
ST ANDREWS LANE
ST ANDREW'S ST
SUFFOLK STREET
Arts
CASTLE ST
LOWER YARD
UPPER YARD
Dublin Castle
EXCHEQUER ST
WICKLOW ST
Central Cyber Café
Dublinia
CHRISTCHURCH PLACE
Powerscourt Townhouse
MARKET ARCADE
CASTLE MARKET
SOUTH GREAT GEORGE'S ST
DRURY ST
SOUTH WILLIAM ST
NICHOLAS STREET
Chester Beatty Library
FADE STREET
JOHNSON'S COURT
DUKE STREET
DUKE LANE LOWER
WERBURGH ST
SHIP ST
STEPHEN ST
CLARENDON ST
HARRY ST
GRAFTON STREET
SOUTH ANNE ST
DAWSON STREET
CHATHAM STREET
GOLDEN LANE
Gaiety Theatre
BULL ALLEY ST
St Stephen's Green Centre
SOUTH KING STREET
St Patrick's Park
PATRICK ST
BOW LANE EAST
AUNGIER STREET
PETER ST
YORK STREET
ST STEPHEN'S GREEN
St Patrick's Cathedral
Marsh's Library
MERCER ST LOWER
Royal College of Surgeons
WEST
KEVIN STREET UPPER
BISHOP ST
St Stephen's Green
KEVIN STREET LOWER
CUFFE STREET
WEXFORD STREET
HARCOURT STREET
Newman House
SOUTH
MONTAGUE STREET
CAMDEN STREET LOWER
CLONMEL ST
National Concert Hall
CAMDEN PL
Iveagh Gardens
DART Station
LUAS Stop
0
300 m
GRANTHAM STREET
HATCH ST UPPER
CHARLOTTE STREET
SOUTH CIRCULAR RD
HARCOURT

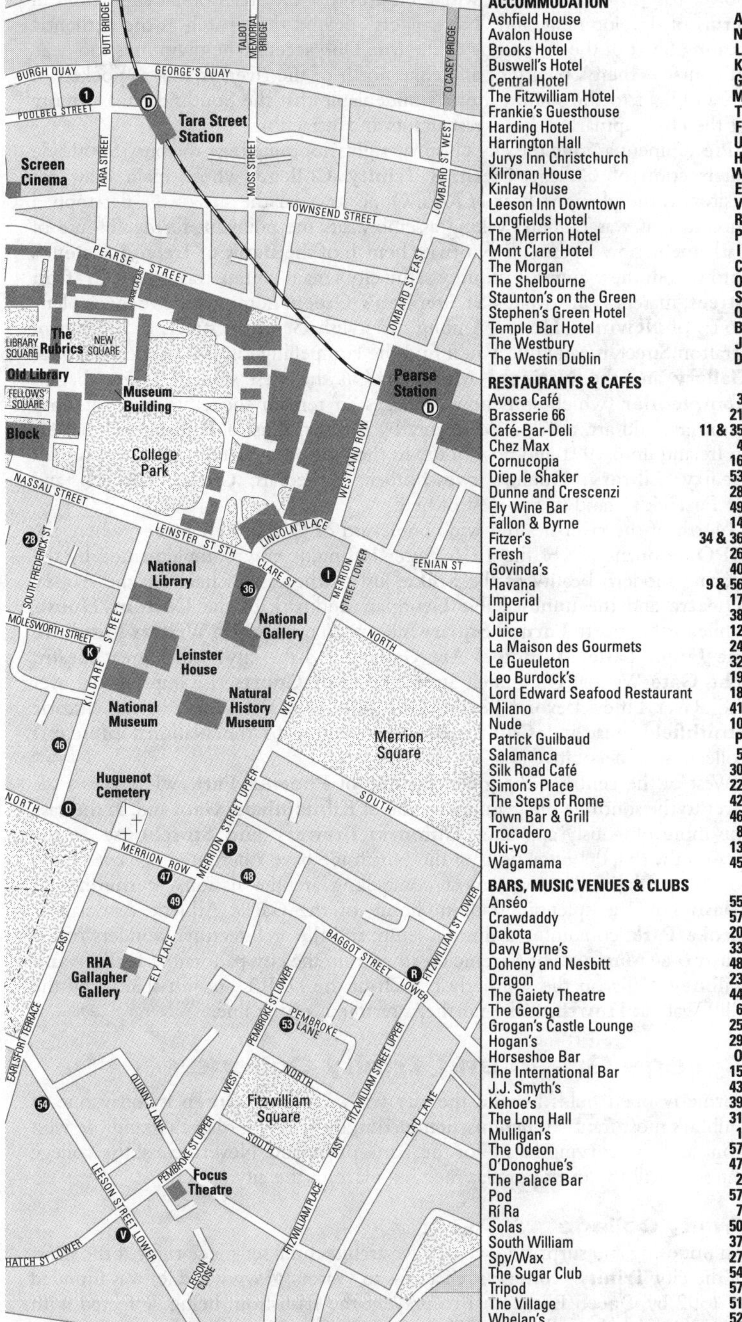
ACCOMMODATION
Ashfield House A
Avalon House N
Brooks Hotel L
Buswell's Hotel K
Central Hotel G
The Fitzwilliam Hotel M
Frankie's Guesthouse T
Harding Hotel F
Harrington Hall U
Jurys Inn Christchurch H
Kilronan House W
Kinlay House E
Leeson Inn Downtown V
Longfields Hotel R
The Merrion Hotel P
Mont Clare Hotel I
The Morgan C
The Shelbourne O
Staunton's on the Green S
Stephen's Green Hotel Q
Temple Bar Hotel B
The Westbury J
The Westin Dublin D
RESTAURANTS & CAFÉS
Avoca Café 3
Brasserie 66 21
Café-Bar-Deli 11 & 35
Chez Max 4
Cornucopia 16
Diep le Shaker 53
Dunne and Crescenzi 28
Ely Wine Bar 49
Fallon & Byrne 14
Fitzer's 34 & 36
Fresh 26
Govinda's 40
Havana 9 & 56
Imperial 17
Jaipur 38
Juice 12
La Maison des Gourmets 24
Le Gueuleton 32
Leo Burdock's 19
Lord Edward Seafood Restaurant 18
Milano 41
Nude 10
Patrick Guilbaud P
Salamanca 5
Silk Road Café 30
Simon's Place 22
The Steps of Rome 42
Town Bar & Grill 46
Trocadero 8
Uki-yo 13
Wagamama 45
BARS, MUSIC VENUES & CLUBS
Anséo 55
Crawdaddy 57
Dakota 20
Davy Byrne's 33
Doheny and Nesbitt 48
Dragon 23
The Gaiety Theatre 44
The George 6
Grogan's Castle Lounge 25
Hogan's 29
Horseshoe Bar O
The International Bar 15
J.J. Smyth's 43
Kehoe's 39
The Long Hall 31
Mulligan's 1
The Odeon 57
O'Donoghue's 47
The Palace Bar 2
Pod 57
Rí Ra 7
Solas 50
South William 37
Spy/Wax 27
The Sugar Club 54
Tripod 57
The Village 51
Whelan's 52
BUTT BRIDGE
TALBOT MEMORIAL BRIDGE
O CASEY BRIDGE
BURGH QUAY
GEORGE'S QUAY
POOLBEG STREET
Tara Street Station
Screen Cinema
TARA STREET
MOSS STREET
LOMBARD ST WEST
TOWNSEND STREET
PEARSE STREET
PARK LA EAST
LOMBARD ST EAST
The Rubrics
LIBRARY SQUARE
NEW SQUARE
Old Library
FELLOWS' SQUARE
Museum Building
Block
College Park
Pearse Station
WESTLAND ROW
NASSAU STREET
LEINSTER ST STH
LINCOLN PLACE
CLARE ST
FENIAN ST
MERRION STREET LOWER
SOUTH FREDERICK ST
National Library
National Gallery
MOLESWORTH STREET
KILDARE STREET
Leinster House
NORTH
Natural History Museum
National Museum
WEST
Merrion Square
Huguenot Cemetery
SOUTH
MERRION STREET UPPER
MERRION ROW
EAST
ELY PLACE
BAGGOT STREET LOWER
FITZWILLIAM ST LOWER
RHA Gallagher Gallery
EARLSFORT TERRACE
PEMBROKE ST LOWER
PEMBROKE LANE
FITZWILLIAM ST UPPER
QUINN'S LANE
Fitzwilliam Square
LAD LANE
PEMBROKE ST UPPER
Focus Theatre
LEESON STREET LOWER
FITZWILLIAM PLACE
HATCH ST LOWER
LEESON CLOSE

power base in north Dublin, which ensures that the area doesn't lag behind in terms of development, and "Nortsoiders" defend their patch as the authentic beating heart of the city, home of the true Dub accent. The division is too neat, of course – there's plenty of affluence north of the river, as well as pockets of urban blight to the south – but it's undeniable that the Southside boasts more of the city's upmarket shops, restaurants and attractions.

Pre-eminent among the city's historic sights, looming over the busy, Southside intersection of College Green, is **Trinity College**, whose main draw for visitors is the glorious *Book of Kells*. Opposite, near the site of the flat-topped mound that was Dublin's Viking assembly, sits the poignant former House of Parliament, now a particularly ornate branch of the **Bank of Ireland**. A stone's throw from these august institutions, the city's main commercial street, **Grafton Street**, marches off towards **St Stephen's Green**, home to the rococo splendours of **Newman House**. Among the stylish Georgian streets to the east of Grafton Street, meanwhile, you'll find the compelling displays of the **National Gallery** and the **National Museum**. On the west side of Trinity begins **Temple Bar**, which somehow manages to remain the city's hub for both carousing and art, overlooked sternly by **Dublin Castle**, British headquarters in Ireland until 1921 and now home to the glorious collections of the **Chester Beatty Library**. Dublin's two historic cathedrals, **Christ Church** and **St Patrick's**, stand to the west of here.

North of the river lies the wide boulevard of **O'Connell Street**, where the **GPO**, resonant site of the 1916 Easter Rising, is now complemented by the soaring modern beauty of the **Spike**. Just to the east of here are the **Abbey Theatre** and the unmistakable Georgian landmark of the **Custom House**, while further north **Parnell Square** is home to the **Dublin Writers Museum**, **the Hugh Lane Municipal Art Gallery** and the city's other great theatre, **The Gate**. West of O'Connell Street, the **Four Courts** rise impressively over the River Liffey. Beyond lie the **Old Jameson Distillery**, in the historic **Smithfield** area, and **Collins Barracks**, home to the National Museum's collection of decorative arts.

West of the centre is the green expanse of **Phoenix Park**, while across the river to the south lie the grim memorial of **Kilmainham Gaol** and, to the east, the more obviously appealing **Guinness Brewery and Storehouse**. In the city's **suburbs**, the attractions of the Northside have a definite edge over those to the south of the river: most compelling are the national **cemetery at Glasnevin**; the splendid stadium home of the Gaelic Athletic Association, **Croke Park**, containing a fine museum; and the architectural wonders of the **Casino at Marino**. For a scenic breather from the city, panoramic **Dalkey and Killiney Hills** on the southerly branch of the DART are just shaded by the Cliff Walk at **Howth**, at the northern terminus of the line.

College Green and Trinity College

Formerly open fields beyond the city walls, **College Green** is today one of Dublin's most frantic junctions, hemmed in by Trinity College's grandiose west front and the curving facade of the Bank of Ireland. Nevertheless, the college gates are still the most popular meeting place in the city.

Trinity College

An imposing and surprisingly extensive architectural set-piece right at the heart of the city, **Trinity College** (free access to visitors; Ⓦ www.tcd.ie) was founded in 1592 by Queen Elizabeth I to prevent the Irish from being "infected with popery and other ill qualities" at French, Spanish and Italian universities.

▲ The Long Room, Trinity College

Catholics were duly admitted until 1637, when restrictions were imposed that lasted until the Catholic Relief Act of 1793; the Catholic Church, however, banned its flock from studying here until 1970 because of the college's Anglican orientation. Famous alumni range from politicians Edward Carson and Douglas Hyde, through philosopher George Berkeley and Nobel Prize–winning physicist Ernest Walton, to writers such as Swift, Wilde and Beckett. Today seventy percent of the students are Catholic, and Trinity, though it also calls itself Dublin University, is actually just one of three universities in the capital: its main rival, University College Dublin (UCD), part of the National University of Ireland, is based at Belfield in the southern suburbs; while Dublin City University is in Glasnevin.

Inside the imposing main gates, eighteenth-century **Front Square** is flanked, with appealing symmetry, by the Chapel and the Examination Hall, which is the elegant, stuccoed setting for occasional concerts. On the east side of adjoining Library Square is the college's oldest surviving building, the **Rubrics**, a red-brick student dormitory dating from around 1701, though much altered in the nineteenth century. In New Square beyond, the School of Engineering occupies the old **Museum Building** (1852), designed in extravagant Venetian Gothic style by Benjamin Woodward under the influence of his friend, John Ruskin, and awash with decorative stone-carving of animals and floral patterns. In Fellows' Square, on the south side of Library Square, the modern Arts Block by the college's Nassau Street entrance is home to the Douglas Hyde Gallery, one of Ireland's most important galleries of modern art, hosting top-notch temporary shows by Irish and international artists (Mon–Wed & Fri 11am–6pm, Thurs 11am–7pm, Sat 11am–4.45pm; free; free guided tours of the current exhibitions Tues 1.15pm & Sat 2pm; ⓣ01/896 1116, ⓦwww.douglashydegallery.com). From mid-May to September, Trinity students lead thirty-minute **walking tours** of the college from the main gate (Mon–Sat 9 daily, Sun 7 daily; €5, or €10 including admission to the Old Library).

The Old Library and the Book of Kells

Trinity's most compelling tourist attraction – sometimes with half-hour queues in June, July and August – is the **Book of Kells**, kept in the eighteenth-century **Old Library**, which is entered from Fellows' Square to the south of Library Square (May–Sept Mon–Sat 9.30am–5pm, Sun 9.30am–4.30pm; Oct–April Mon–Sat 9.30am–5pm, Sun noon–4.30pm; closed for 10 days over Christmas and New Year; €8; Heritage Island). On the library's ground floor, beautiful pages are displayed not just from the *Book of Kells* (around 800 AD), but also the *Book of Armagh* (early ninth century) and the *Book of Mulling* (late eighth century), preceded by a fascinating exhibition, **Turning Darkness into Light**, which sets Irish illuminated manuscripts in context – ranging from ogham (the earlier, Celtic writing system of lines carved on standing stones) to Ethiopian books of devotions.

Pre-eminent for the scale, variety and colour of its decoration, the *Book of Kells* probably originated at the monastery on Iona off the west coast of Scotland, which had been founded around 561 by the great Irish scholar, bard and ruler St Colmcille (St Columba in English). After a Viking raid in 806 the Columbines moved to the monastery of Kells in County Meath (see p.173), and around 1653 the manuscript was moved to Dublin for safekeeping during the Cromwellian Wars. The 340 calfskin folios of the *Book of Kells* contain the four New Testament gospels along with preliminary texts, all in Latin. It's thought that three artists created the book's lavish decoration, which shows Pictish, Germanic and Mediterranean, as well as Celtic influences. Not only are there full-page illustrations of Christ and the Virgin and Child, but an elaborate decorative scheme of animals and spiral, roundel and interlace patterns is employed throughout the text, on the initials at the beginning of each Gospel and on full-length "carpet pages".

Upstairs is the library's magnificent, barrel-vaulted **Long Room**, built by Thomas Burgh between 1712 and 1732 and enlarged, with a barrel-vaulted ceiling, in 1860. As a copyright library, Trinity has had the right to claim a free copy of all British and Irish publications since 1801; of its current stock of three million titles, 200,000 of the oldest are stored in the Long Room's oak bookcases. Besides interesting temporary exhibitions of books and prints from the library's collection, the Long Room also displays a gnarled fifteenth-century harp, the oldest to survive from Ireland, and a highly rare original printing of the 1916 Proclamation of the Irish Republic, made on Easter Sunday in Dublin's Liberty Hall.

The Bank of Ireland

The Neoclassical granite **Bank of Ireland**, opposite Trinity on College Green, was built in 1729 by Sir Edward Pearce – himself an MP – as the **House of Parliament**. An Irish parliament had existed in one limited form or another since the thirteenth century, but achieved its greatest flowering here in 1782, when "Grattan's Parliament" (so named after the prime mover behind the constitutional reform) was granted legislative independence from the British Parliament. Catholics were still barred from sitting, but many signs of Irish sovereignty were established during this period, including the founding of the Bank of Ireland itself. Around this time, the Lords deemed it necessary to build themselves a separate entrance on Westmoreland Street, designed in 1785 by James Gandon in the Corinthian style in order to distinguish it from the Ionic colonnade of what is still the main entrance. After the Rebellion of 1798, however, the Irish House was persuaded and bribed to vote itself out of existence, and with the 1801 Act of Union Ireland became part of the United Kingdom, governed from Westminster. The Bank of Ireland bought the building for £40,000 in 1802, and the Commons chamber was demolished to remove a highly charged symbol of independence.

The barrel-vaulted **House of Lords** was also meant to be knocked down, but survives to this day to host high-level state functions and as the main attraction for visitors (Mon, Tues & Fri 10am–4pm, Wed 10.30am–4pm, Thurs 10am–5pm; guided tours Tues 10.30am, 11.30am & 1.45pm; free). Here you'll find one or two exhibits such as the Lord Chancellor's richly embroidered purse, used to carry the Great Seal of Ireland, and tapestries showing William of Orange's victories over James II and his Catholic supporters, the *Siege of Derry* and the *Battle of the Boyne*. It's also planned to put the mace used in the former House of Commons on display here. Sold on by the descendants of the last Speaker, the mace was bought at Christie's of London by the bank in 1937 for £3100. The richly stuccoed **Cash Hall** – an elegant spot to do any banking chores you may have – used to be the Parliament's Hall of Requests, where constituents would petition their representatives.

Grafton Street and around

Running from College Green to St Stephen's Green, the city's main commercial drag, **Grafton Street**, gets off to an inauspicious start with "the tart with the cart", a gaggingly kitsch bronze, complete with wheelbarrow of cockles and mussels, of Molly Malone, who was immortalized – though it's unlikely that she ever existed – in the popular nineteenth-century song. For those who hate crowds, pedestrianized Grafton Street won't get any better; for people-watchers, however, it's a must, noted especially for its buskers, who range from string quartets to street poets. Shoppers will be drawn here, too, in particular to the city's flagship department store, **Brown Thomas** (see p.133). The street's other major landmark, **Bewley's Oriental Café**, owes its beautiful mosaic facade to the mania for all things Egyptian that followed the discovery of Tutenkhamun's tomb in 1922. Founded by the Quaker Bewley family as a teetotal bulwark against the demon drink, the café was forced to close down in 2004 in the face of escalating ground rents that have made Grafton Street one of the world's five most expensive shopping streets on which to trade. The ornate premises, however, have recently reopened, incorporating a much-reduced Bewley's café and a branch of *Café-Bar-Deli* (see p.123).

Powerscourt Townhouse

A short detour west off Grafton Street will bring you to the Clarendon Street entrance of **Powerscourt Townhouse**, a stylish shopping centre which incorporates the eighteenth-century Palladian mansion of Lord Powerscourt (see p.149). The house's main door across on South William Street gives straight onto the trompe l'oeil stone floor of the entrance hall and, beyond, the central mahogany staircase, with its flighty rococo plasterwork and what are thought to be the most elaborately carved balusters in Ireland. More geometrical, Neo-classical stucco work can be seen in two commercial outlets upstairs, the Solomon Gallery and The Town Bride. The café-bar in the atrium is notable for its location – bathed in light on sunny days – in what was once the mansion's inner courtyard. On Saturdays (11am–1pm & 2–5pm), you can arrange a free guided tour of the townhouse at the nearby information desk.

Kildare Street and Merrion Square

Ireland's political and cultural establishments have their power bases in the tight confines of **Kildare Street** and **Merrion Square**. Leinster House, home of Ireland's parliament, straddles the two locations, surrounded by the unmissable treasures of the National Museum, the National Library and its impressive literary exhibitions, the National Gallery's treasure-trove of European art and the charmingly unreconstructed displays of the Natural History Museum. Former residences of a *Who's Who* of Ireland, from O'Connell to the Wildes, Merrion Square's Georgian terraces are now occupied by such diverse organizations as the Arts Council and the Football Association of Ireland, while its quiet, tree-shaded lawns lighten the heavy, stately feel.

Leinster House

Now the seat of the **Oireachtas** (Irish Parliament; ⓣ01/618 3781, ⓦwww.oireachtas.ie), **Leinster House** was built in 1745 as a mansion on the edge of town for James Fitzgerald, Earl of Kildare (later the Duke of Leinster). The architect, Richard Castle, designed the impressive pedimented frontage to be viewed along Molesworth Street, and employed the Swiss Lafranchini brothers to adorn the ceilings with baroque stuccowork. The house was sold to the Royal Dublin Society in 1815 as their headquarters, around which grew a dense concentration of national cultural institutions in the second half of the nineteenth century. After the establishment of the Irish Free State, Leinster House was chosen as the seat of parliament in 1922, because it was considered easier to defend during the civil war than the Bank of Ireland, the former Grattan Parliament (see p.87). Kevin O'Higgins, the Minister for Home Affairs who was later assassinated by the IRA, memorably described the provisional government as "eight young men standing amidst the ruins of one administration with the foundation of another not yet laid, and with wild men screaming through the keyhole".

The Oireachtas has two chambers: elected by proportional representation, the **Dáil** (or House of Representatives, members of which are known as *teachtaí Dála* or TDs) sits in the nineteenth-century former lecture theatre of the Royal Dublin Society; members of the **Seanad** (Senate), who are either nominated by the Taoiseach (prime minister), or elected from various panels or by the universities, meet in a semicircular eighteenth-century room that was the mansion's picture gallery. Parliament usually sits from mid-January to early July (breaking for Easter), and October until Christmas, on Tuesday afternoons, Wednesdays and Thursdays. Overseas visitors wishing to arrange a free guided **tour** need to be sponsored by their embassy in Dublin (see p.134); visits are possible year-round (indeed, you're likely to see more of the building itself when the Oireachtas isn't in session), and tend to be busiest in May and June.

The National Museum

The **National Museum** on Kildare Street (Tues–Sat 10am–5pm, Sun 2–5pm; free; ⓣ01/677 7444, ⓦwww.museum.ie) is the finest of a portfolio of jointly run museums – including the Natural History Museum (see p.91), Collins Barracks (see p.112), which focuses on the decorative arts, and the National Museum of Country Life in Castlebar (see p.463) – and a must-see for visitors to Dublin. Undoubted stars of the show here are a stunning hoard of prehistoric gold and a thousand years' worth of ornate ecclesiastical treasures, but the whole collection builds up a fascinating and accessible story of Irish archeology and history. The shop in the beautiful entrance rotunda sells a range of high-quality crafts inspired by works in the museum, and there's a small café. **Guided tours** (40min; €2) are organized from Tuesday to Saturday at 3.30pm, on Sunday at 2.30pm, and at other variable times, which are posted up in the entrance rotunda each day.

Prehistoric gold, much of it discovered during peat-cutting, takes pride of place on the ground floor of the main hall. From the Earlier Bronze Age (c. 2500–1500 BC) come *lunulae*, thin sheets of gold formed into crescent-moon collars. After around 1200 BC, when new sources of the metal were apparently found, goldsmiths could be more extravagant, fashioning chunky torcs, such as the spectacular Gleninsheen Collar and the Tumna Hoard of nine large gold balls, which are perforated, suggesting that when joined together they formed a huge necklace. Further prehistoric material is arrayed around the walls of the main hall, including the fifteen-metre-long Lurgan Logboat, dating from around 2500 BC, which was unearthed in a Galway bog in 1902.

The adjacent **Treasury** holds most of the museum's better-known ecclesiastical exhibits, notably the ornate, eighth-century Ardagh Chalice and the Tara Brooch, decorated with beautiful knot designs. Also on the ground floor is Kingship and Sacrifice, showcasing the leathery bodies of four Iron Age noblemen that were preserved and discovered in various bogs around Ireland.

Upstairs, **Viking-age Ireland** (c. 800–1150) features models of a house and the layout of Dublin's Fishamble Street, while an adjoining room displays some famous Christian objects from the same period, notably the beautiful Crozier of St Tola and the Cross of Cong, created to enshrine a fragment of the True Cross given to the King of Connacht by the Pope in 1123. The next exhibit moves on to **Medieval Ireland** (1150–1550), to cover the first English colonists, their withdrawal to the fortified area around Dublin known as "the Pale" after 1300, and the hybrid culture that developed all the while – you can listen to recordings of poetry written in Ireland in Middle Irish, Middle English and Norman French. Unmissable here is a host of strange, ornate portable shrines, made to hold holy relics or texts, including examples for all three of

Ireland's patron saints: the Shrine of St Patrick's Tooth, the Shrine of St Brigid's Shoe (see p.158) and the Shrine of the Cathach, containing a manuscript written by St Colmcille (St Columba), legendary bard, scholar, ruler and evangelizer of Scotland.

The National Library

The **National Library** (Mon–Wed 10am–9pm, Thurs & Fri 10am–5pm, Sat 10am–1pm; free; Ⓦ www.nli.ie) was opened on Kildare Street in 1890, shortly after the National Museum, whose design it mirrors across the courtyard of Leinster House. Its main draws are its long-term temporary exhibitions on subjects such as W.B. Yeats, which are mounted in a beautiful, new, high-tech space on the lower ground floor. Visitors are also allowed up to the hushed domed **Reading Room** on the first floor, decorated with ornate bookcases and an incongruously playful frieze of cherubs. It is in the office here that Stephen Dedalus engages the librarians – who appear under their real names – in literary talk in the "Scylla and Charybdis" episode of *Ulysses*. On the way up, on the mezzanine landing, look out for the curious stone plaques representing, from left to right, Asia, Europe, America and Africa. In the **Genealogy Room** (Mon–Fri 10am–4.45pm, Sat 10am–12.30pm; free), professional genealogists can give advice to anyone researching their family history on how to access the records here and elsewhere in Dublin, as well as in Belfast. The library's ground floor shelters a very attractive café and a small bookshop.

The National Gallery

The **National Gallery** (Mon–Sat 9.30am–5.30pm, Thurs until 8.30pm, Sun noon–5.30pm; free, €3 donation suggested; Ⓣ 01/661 5133, Ⓦ www.nationalgallery.ie) hosts a fine collection of Western European art dating from the Middle Ages to the twentieth century, which will happily engage you for several hours. The gallery's old building, divided into Beit, Milltown and Dargan wings and entered from Merrion Square West, has now been joined by the **Millennium Wing**, giving access from Clare Street, which hosts major temporary exhibitions around its striking, sky-lit atrium. The resulting layout of the gallery, however, can be confusing, so the first thing to do when you go in is pick up a free floor-plan leaflet. Free **guided tours** (Sat 3pm, Sun 2pm, 3pm & 4pm) begin in the Shaw Room on Level 1 of the Dargan Wing, near the Merrion Square entrance. In a prime location under the Millennium Wing's glass roof, there's a good self-service, lunchtime restaurant and an all-day café upstairs. The gallery also offers classical and contemporary concerts, lectures and workshops, which are detailed in the monthly *Gallery News* (available in the foyer).

Level 1 is chiefly given over to **Irish art** from the seventeenth century onwards, including a large gallery in the Millennium Wing devoted to the twentieth century. The real stand-out in the Irish collection, however, is the **Yeats Museum** (in the Dargan Wing below the National Portrait Gallery), which traces the development of Jack B. Yeats (1871–1957), younger brother of the writer W.B. Yeats, from an unsentimental illustrator of everyday scenes to an expressive painter in abstract, unmixed colours. In the mezzanine **Print Gallery**, as well as temporary exhibitions throughout the year, watercolours by Turner are exhibited every January, when the light is low enough for these delicate works.

Highlights of Level 2 include *Kitchen Maid with the Supper at Emmaus*, the earliest known picture by **Velázquez** (c. 1617–18), in Room 33 of the Beit Wing, while in Room 29 beyond there's a haunting **Mantegna**, *Judith with the Head of Holofernes*, painted in monochrome to simulate a marble relief.

Room 25 covers "Art in Rome in the eighteenth century", with plenty of local interest. Among some diverting views of Rome and various Irish gentlemen who had themselves immortalized in the Eternal City, don't miss **Reynolds**' fascinating *Parody of Raphael's "School of Athens"*, which purveys some familiar Irish stereotypes to ridicule the Grand Tourists. Nearby in Room 42 is **Caravaggio**'s dynamic *The Taking of Christ*, in which the artist portrayed himself as a passive spectator on the right of the picture, holding a lamp. You'll find the highlight of the Dutch collection next door in Room 40: **Vermeer**'s *Woman Writing a Letter, with her Maid*, one of only 35 accepted works by the artist, with his characteristic use of white light from the window accentuating the woman's heated emotions. At the top of the Dargan Wing, there's an excellent survey of **French art** from Poussin to the Cubists, featuring works by Millet, Monet and Picasso.

Merrion Square

Begun in 1762, **Merrion Square** represents Georgian town planning at its grandest. Its long, graceful terraces of red-brown brick sport elaborate doors, knockers and fanlights, as well as wrought-iron balconies (added in the early nineteenth century) and tall windows on the first floor, where the main reception rooms would have been; the north side of the square was built first and displays the widest variety of design.

The broad, manicured lawns of the square's gardens themselves are a joy, quieter than St Stephen's Green, and especially agreeable for picnics on fine days. Revolutionary politician Michael Collins is commemorated with a bronze bust on the gardens' south side, near a slightly hapless stone bust of Henry Grattan (see p.695), while writer, artist and mystic George Russell ("AE") stands gravely near the southwest corner and his former home at no. 74. But the square's most remarkable and controversial statue is at the northwest corner, where **Oscar Wilde** reclines on a rock facing his childhood home at no. 1 (now the American College Dublin), in a wry, languid pose that has earned the figure the nickname "the fag on the crag". In front of him, a male torso and his wife Constance, pregnant with their second child, stand on plinths inscribed with Wildean witticisms: "This suspense is terrible. I hope it will last," "I drink to keep body and soul apart." Nearby on the railings around the square's gardens, dozens of artists hang their paintings for sale every Sunday (and some Saturdays, depending on the weather).

The Merrion Square South terrace has the greatest concentration of famous former residents, giving a vivid sense of the history of the place: politician Daniel O'Connell bought no. 58 in 1809; the Nobel Prize-winning Austrian physicist, Erwin Schrödinger, occupied no. 65; and Gothic novelist Joseph Sheridan Le Fanu died at no. 70, which is now the Arts Council. At no. 39 stood the British Embassy, burnt down by a crowd protesting against the Bloody Sunday massacre in Derry in 1972.

The Natural History Museum

Billing itself "a museum of a museum", the **Natural History Museum** on Merrion Square West (currently closed long-term due to structural problems; Ⓦ www.museum.ie) has evolved remarkably little since its inauguration in 1856. The tone is set on the lawn outside, by a heroic Victorian bronze of Surgeon-Major T.H. Parke with his foot planted on an animal skull and a rifle in his hands – born in Roscommon, Parke went with Stanley on his 1887 expedition to the Congo River and was the first Irishman to cross Africa. The museum's display of around ten thousand animals, out of a holding of two million specimens, would be impressive in any age, however.

Guarding the ground-floor **Irish Room** stand three skeletons of giant Irish deer which, despite intimidating rivals and impressing females with the largest antler span – three metres – of any deer ever, became extinct around 9000 BC. Upstairs, the **World Collection** concentrates on the zoology of Africa and Asia, but includes the Barrington Collection of birds, many of which were hapless enough to crash into Irish lighthouses. The lower gallery here, the last resting place of a dodo skeleton, is the best spot to view the skeletons of two whales stranded on Irish shores, one of them a twenty-metre fin whale. The upper gallery deals with invertebrates, including the **Blaschka Collection**, beautiful nineteenth-century glass models of marine creatures; look out also for a pair of cosy golden gloves, knitted from threads secreted by the fan mussel.

No. 29 Fitzwilliam Street Lower

This **townhouse** at the southeast corner of Merrion Square (Tues–Sat 10am–5pm, Sun 1–5pm, closed last three weeks of Dec; €5; ⓦwww.esb.ie/no29) has been carefully reconstructed in the style of a middle-class home of the period 1790–1820 by the Electricity Supply Board, using furniture from the National Museum's collection. The ESB may sound like a strange curator for such a venture, but the house was rebuilt as an act of homage after the Board had knocked down 26 Georgian houses here to build its adjoining offices in the 1960s. Entertaining guided tours bring to life the details of bourgeois Georgian life, both below stairs and in the elegant living rooms upstairs, which benefited from such gadgets as a lead-lined wine cooler and a belly-warmer for soothing gastric complaints. From this corner of the square there's a fine view down Mount Street Upper of the "peppercanister" church of **St Stephen's**, a Greek Revival work dating from 1824.

St Stephen's Green and beyond

As well as being a major landmark and transport hub for buses, taxis and the LUAS, St Stephen's Green is central Dublin's largest and most varied park, whose statuary provides a poignant history lesson in stone, wood and bronze. The main sightseeing draws in the area date from the Georgian period: the splendid stuccowork of Newman House and the elegant streets and squares to the east of the Green, which are also home to some fine, upmarket eateries.

The Green

Central Dublin's main square, **St Stephen's Green** (Mon–Sat 8am–dusk, Sun 10am–dusk) preserves its distinctive Victorian character with a small lake, bandstand, arboretum and well-tended flower displays. It was originally open common land, a notoriously dirty and dangerous spot and the site of public hangings until the eighteenth century. In 1880, however, it was turned into a public park with funding from the brewer Lord Ardilaun (Sir Arthur Guinness), who now boasts the grandest of the Green's many statues, seated at his leisure on the far western side. Over-anxious locals make exaggerated complaints that drunks and ne'er-do-wells are returning the Green to its former unsavoury nature, but it's actually a pleasant, popular spot to take a break in the very heart of the city centre. From the Green's northwest corner, by the top of Grafton Street, you can hire a **horse and carriage**, either as a grandiose taxi or for a tour of the sights, which will typically set you back €50 for thirty minutes.

Termed in the eighteenth century "Beau Walk", **St Stephen's Green North** is still the most fashionable side of the square. The **Shelbourne Hotel** here claims to have been "the best address in Dublin" since its establishment in 1824

A monumental tour of St Stephen's Green

A short stroll around the **monuments** of St Stephen's Green will give you a vivid sense of the city's history, of diverse episodes and characters that are each firmly rooted in their location; maps at the main entrances help you find your way. Probably the most striking of the statues is a piercing bronze bust of **James Joyce**, gazing intently over his bony hand towards his alma mater, just across the road on St Stephen's Green South, Newman House. At the southeast corner, the **Three Fates** fountain was presented to Dublin by the German government in recognition of the help given to refugee children after World War II.

An uninspiring bust on the south side of the central floral display does scant justice to the remarkable **Countess Markiewicz**, dynamic socialist and feminist, who was second-in-command of the insurgents at St Stephen's Green during the Easter Rising of 1916. On the west side of the flower display, a tiny plaque inlaid in a wooden park bench commemorates the so-called "fallen women" – mostly unmarried mothers or abused girls – who were forced to live and work in severe conditions in Ireland's **Magdalen laundries**; the last of them, in Dublin, wasn't closed down until 1996. Just beyond on a small rise, *Knife Edge*, a bronze memorial by Henry Moore to **W.B. Yeats**, is more spiritually uplifting. On the far west side of the Green, an animated bronze of **Robert Emmet**, leader of the 1803 Rebellion, looks proudly across towards the site of his birthplace, now demolished.

Facing Grafton Street from the northwest corner, **Fusiliers' Arch**, which remembers Royal Dublin Fusiliers killed in the Boer War, is still known to some as "Traitors' Gate". Humour resurfaces at the northeast corner, where a row of granite monoliths in honour of eighteenth-century nationalist **Wolfe Tone** is nicknamed "Tonehenge". Behind it stands a moving commemoration of the **Great Famine**.

(see p.78). Beyond the hotel at the start of Merrion Row, the tiny, tree-shaded **Huguenot Cemetery** was opened in 1693 for Protestant refugees fleeing religious persecution in France. A large plaque inside the gates gives a roll call of Huguenot Dubliners, among whom the most famous have been writers Dion Boucicault and Sheridan Le Fanu.

Newman House

Newman House at 85–86 St Stephen's Green South boasts probably the finest Georgian interiors in Dublin, noted especially for their decorative plasterwork (guided tours only: June–Aug Tues–Fri 2pm, 3pm & 4pm; €5). The place is named after John Henry Newman, the famous British convert from Anglicanism, who was invited to found the Catholic University of Ireland here in 1854 as an alternative to Anglican Trinity College and the recently established "godless" Queen's Colleges in Belfast, Cork and Galway. James Joyce and Éamon de Valera were educated at what became University College Dublin (UCD), which now occupies a large campus in the southern suburbs.

Newman House began life as two houses. **No. 85** is a Palladian mansion built by Richard Castle in 1738 and adorned with superb baroque stuccowork by the Swiss Lafranchini brothers, notably in the ground-floor **Apollo Room**, where the god himself appears majestically over the fireplace, attended by the nine muses on the surrounding walls. The much larger **no. 86**, with flowing rococo plasterwork by Robert West, the notable Dublin-born imitator of the Lafranchinis, was added in 1765. On the top floor of the latter are a lecture room, done out as in Joyce's student days (1899–1902), and the bedroom of the English poet **Gerard Manley Hopkins**. Having converted from Anglicanism, Hopkins became a Jesuit priest and then Professor of Classics here in 1884; after

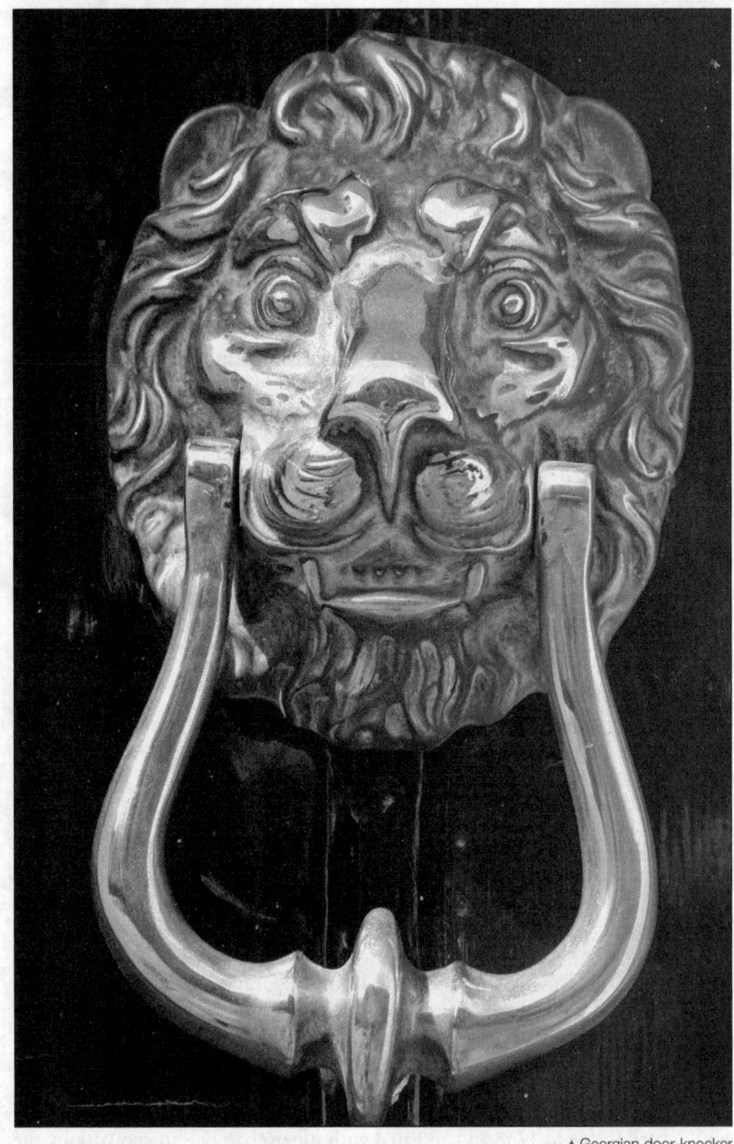
▲ Georgian door-knocker

five wretched years in Dublin, he died of typhoid and was buried in an unmarked grave in Glasnevin Cemetery.

East of St Stephen's Green

The area to the east of St Stephen's Green is the best in the city for a Georgian architectural tour, where an aimless wander will reveal plenty of wrought-iron balconies and much-photographed doorways sporting elegant knockers and fanlights. At its centre lie the still-private lawns of the small but well-preserved **Fitzwilliam Square** (1825), where, at no. 42, W.B. Yeats lived from 1928 to 1932. His brother, the painter Jack B., had a house and studio round the corner at no. 18 Fitzwilliam Place, which together with its continuation Fitzwilliam Street forms a – now much-interrupted – kilometre-long terrace of Georgian houses, marching off towards the magnificent backdrop of the Wicklow Mountains.

Nearby on Ely Place, the **Royal Hibernian Academy of Arts Gallagher Gallery** is one of the country's leading contemporary-art venues, hosting major temporary shows by Irish and international artists (Tues, Wed, Fri & Sat 11am–5pm, Thurs 11am–8pm, Sun 2–5pm; free; free 45min guided tours of the current exhibition Wed 1.15pm; ⓣ01/661 2558, ⓦwww.royalhibernianacademy.com). Where once stood the home of Oliver St John Gogarty, wit, writer and the model for Buck Mulligan in *Ulysses*, this discreet 1970s building now lies at the end of a quiet Georgian cul-de-sac. Its well-designed viewing spaces are home to the RHA Annual Exhibition, usually in May and June, and include the ground-floor Ashford Gallery, devoted to introducing emerging, mostly Irish artists.

The Shaw Birthplace

Just west of Wexford Street, at 33 Synge St, is the unpretentious terraced house where the acclaimed playwright George Bernard Shaw (see p.96) was born. His family, having fallen on hard times, stayed here for ten years before moving to Harcourt Street. Open to the public as the **Shaw Birthplace** (May–Sept Mon, Tues, Thurs & Fri 10am–1pm & 2–5pm; Sat, Sun & public holidays 2–5pm; €6.50), the house has been kitted out with appropriate period furniture, decor and plenty of Shaw memorabilia. The basement kitchen is where the young GBS often sought solace away from, in his own words, the "loveless" atmosphere of his parents' upstairs domain, while upstairs are the family bedrooms – Shaw's is tiny – and a remarkably claustrophobic parlour, all chintz and red velvet. On the top floor is the more expansive reception room equipped with a period pianoforte where Shaw's mother held her musical soirées.

Temple Bar

Sandwiched between the busy thoroughfare of Dame Street and the Liffey, **Temple Bar** is marketed, with a fair dose of artistic licence, as Dublin's "Left Bank" (inconveniently, it's on the right bank as you face downstream). Its transformation into the city's main cultural and entertainment district came about after a 1960s plan for a new central bus terminal here was abandoned after much procrastination. Instead, the area's narrow cobbled streets and old warehouses, by now occupied by short-lease studios, workshops and boutiques, began to be sensitively redeveloped as an artistic quarter in the 1980s. Nowadays, as well as more galleries and arts centres than you can shake a paintbrush at – plus its own, friendly **information centre** on Essex Street East (Mon–Fri 9am–5.30pm, Sat 10am–5.30/6pm, Sun noon–3pm; ⓣ01/677 2255, ⓦwww.templebar.ie) – Temple Bar shelters a huge number of restaurants, pubs and clubs, engendering a notoriously raucous nightlife scene that attracts more outsiders than Dubliners.

The heart of Temple Bar

Most people get into Temple Bar from Dame Street, past the unusual and highly controversial 1970s **Central Bank**, whose floors are suspended from the roof

George Bernard Shaw

Born in Dublin in 1856, **George Bernard Shaw** grew up among a Protestant family fallen on hard times. His father was an unsuccessful grain merchant and alcoholic – prompting Shaw to become a lifelong abstainer – and there was no money to pay for his education. At 15 he started work as a junior clerk for a land agency, but five years later went to London to join his mother who had moved there to further the musical career of one of his sisters. Reliant on what little income his mother earned as a music teacher, Shaw set about educating himself by spending his afternoons in the reading room of the British Museum. He hoped to become a novelist, but, following the rejection of no fewer than five novels, turned his hand to journalism instead, contributing music and drama criticism to London newspapers.

Shaw was a devout socialist, joining the Fabian Society in 1884, writing pamphlets and gaining a reputation as a natural orator. He espoused numerous causes, including electoral reform, vegetarianism and the abolition of private property. His **theatrical career** began in the 1890s when, influenced by Ibsen, he began to compose plays focusing on social and moral matters, rather than the romantic and personal subjects which then dominated British theatre.

In 1898 he married the heiress Charlotte Payne-Townshend and the same year saw the production of his first successful play, *Candida*. A stream of equally lauded comedy-dramas followed – including *The Devil's Disciple*, *Arms and the Man*, *Major Barbara* and *Pygmalion* – though he later turned to more serious drama, such as *Heartbreak House* and *Saint Joan*. Simultaneously, he maintained an active career as a **critic**, journalist and essayist; his often bitterly ironic wit ("England and America are two countries separated by a common language") becoming legendary. In 1925 he was awarded the Nobel Prize for Literature, but initially rejected the honour before relenting and giving his prize money to a newly established Anglo-Swedish Literary Foundation.

Shaw's attitude to Ireland was ever ambivalent – he once commented "I am a typical Irishman; my family came from Yorkshire" – and, though he remained interested in Irish affairs and became a personal friend of Michael Collins, his brand of democratic socialism would have been antipathetic to the austere Catholic and anti-British state that emerged post-independence. Shaw died in 1950 at Ayot St Lawrence, Hertfordshire.

by external cables. The main access from the Northside is the cast-iron **Ha'penny Bridge**, Dublin's oldest and most renowned pedestrian river crossing, with great views of the river along the quays in both directions. It began life in 1816 as the Wellington Bridge but soon acquired its nickname thanks to a halfpenny toll, levied until 1919. Whether you arrive via the bank or the bridge, you'll come to the central **Temple Bar Square**, which hosts a small book market on Saturdays and Sundays and, at its northwest corner, **Temple Bar Gallery and Studios** (Tues–Sat 11am–6pm, Thurs until 7pm; ⓣ01/671 0073, ⓦwww.templebargallery.com). This publicly funded gallery, purpose-built in the 1990s with thirty artists' studios attached, exhibits cutting-edge Irish and international artists working in a wide range of media.

Turning left into Eustace Street to the west of here will bring you to Europe's first custom-built cultural centre for children, **The Ark** (ⓣ01/670 7788 or ⓦwww.ark.ie for details of its plays, exhibitions, workshops, festivals, concerts and multimedia programmes). In a converted eighteenth-century Quaker meeting-house further up Eustace Street, the **Irish Film Institute** is principally an art-house cinema (see p.131), but has evolved into a stylish and sociable all-round venue, whose bar-restaurant (see p.122) is a fashionable meeting-place.

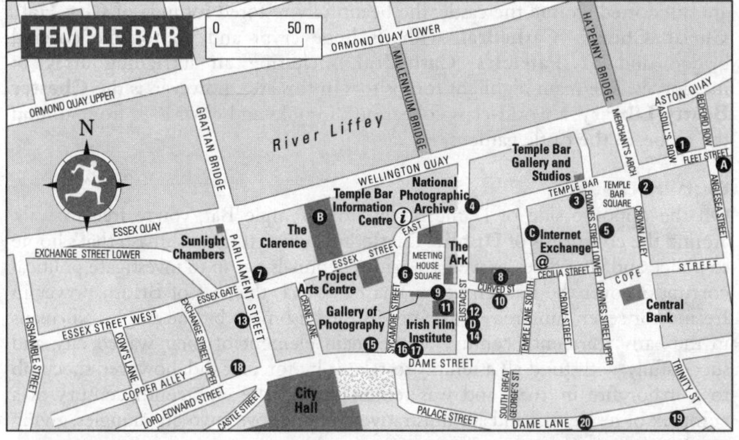

ACCOMMODATION		RESTAURANTS & CAFÉS				BARS, MUSIC VENUES & CLUBS			
Barnacles Temple Bar House	C	Café Irie	5	Irish Film Institute	11	4 Dame Lane	19	Temple Bar Music Centre	8
The Clarence	B	Curved St Café	10	The Mermaid Café	16	Eamonn Doran's	2		
Oliver St. John Gogarty's	A	Eden	6	Milano	4	The Front Lounge	13		
River House Hotel	D	Elephant & Castle	1	Monty's of Kathmandu	14	The Mezz	12		
		Fitzer's	3	Queen of Tarts	18	Olympia Theatre	15		
		Gruel	17			The Porterhouse	7		
		Il Baccaro	9			The Stag's Head	20		

Down the alley at the side of the Ark, **Meeting House Square** hosts many of the free outdoor cultural events of the summertime Diversions festival (contact the Temple Bar Information Centre for details), as well as an excellent food market on Saturdays (see p.133). It's well worth checking out the **Gallery of Photography** on the south side of the square (Tues–Sat 11am–6pm, Sun 1–6pm; free; ⓣ01/671 4654, ⓦwww.irish-photography.com), which stages some great shows of contemporary photographs from Ireland and around the world in smart, well-lit rooms above a good photographic bookshop. Across the square, the **National Photographic Archive** (Mon–Fri 10am–5pm, Sat 10am–2pm; free; ⓣ01/603 0374, ⓦwww.nli.ie) mounts a series of often fascinating temporary exhibitions, mostly on Irish historical subjects, from the photographic collections of the National Library.

Out on Essex Street East stands the bright-blue flagship of the Dublin contemporary-arts scene, **Project Arts Centre** (ⓣ01/881 9613 or 881 9614, ⓦwww.project.ie), which hosts theatre, dance, film and live music as well as challenging visual and performance art. Beyond, at the bottom of Parliament Street, are the **Sunlight Chambers**, whose curious facade merits a short detour. Built in the early twentieth century in the style of an Italian Renaissance palace by the Sunlight soap company, the Chambers' exterior sports colourful ceramic friezes on the theme of hygiene; underneath the soot you can make out farmers and builders getting their clothes dirty on the upper tier, and women washing them below.

Dublin Castle and around

On a ridge above the Liffey, where previously the Vikings had established themselves, the Anglo-Norman invaders rebuilt Dublin in the thirteenth century around a doughty **castle**. Several other remnants of British hegemony are still dotted around the castle: the beautifully restored rotunda of **City Hall**; **Christ Church Cathedral**, with its huge crypt and photogenic covered bridge; and **St Patrick's Cathedral**, sheltering an intriguing array of memorials. The main highlight for visitors in this area, however, is the **Chester Beatty Library**, a world-class collection of books and *objets d'art* from around the globe, in the castle gardens.

Dublin Castle

On the opposite side of Dame Street from Temple Bar, you're free to walk around the courtyards of **Dublin Castle**, an architectural mishmash that's home to police and tax offices, as well as various tribunals set up to investigate political corruption over the last ten years. The castle was the seat of British power in Ireland for seven hundred years, after its establishment by the Anglo-Normans in the early thirteenth century as the main element of their walled city, and successfully withstood all attempts to take it by force. It did, however, succumb to a major fire in 1684 and was rebuilt during the eighteenth century as a complex of residential and administrative buildings over two quadrangles, giving a sedate collegiate appearance.

Looming over the Lower Yard, the **Record Tower** was built in 1258 but heavily renovated and Gothicized in the early nineteenth century; it was originally a prison and now, fittingly but not at all compellingly, hosts the Garda Síochána Museum, stuffed with musty memorabilia of the Irish police force. If it's open (at the time of writing, it was closed for repairs due to subsidence), it's well worth looking in on the adjacent **Chapel Royal**, an ornate Gothic Revival gem; note especially the viceroys' coats of arms carved on the balcony rail and around the altar. The **Upper Yard** follows the outline of the medieval castle. Above its original main gate, the Cork Hill State Entrance, stands a statue of *Justice*, wearing no blindfold and turning her back on the city – a fitting symbol of British rule, locals reckon.

Built as the residence of the English viceroy and entered from the Upper Yard, the **State Apartments** now host major Irish state occasions – including the signing of the ground-breaking Anglo-Irish Agreement by Taoiseach Garrett Fitzgerald and Prime Minister Margaret Thatcher in 1985 – as well as 50-minute guided tours for the public (Mon–Fri 10am–4.45pm, Sat & Sun 2–4.45pm; €4.50; Heritage Card; ⓣ01/645 8813, ⓦwww.dublincastle.ie). It's advisable to ring ahead, however, as the tours don't run during big occasions, when a tour of the Undercroft and the Chapel Royal or courtyards may be substituted. Places on the timed tours are allocated on a first-come, first-served basis, so it's worth arriving early and, if necessary, booking a place for later in the day.

Inside the apartments, the Grand Staircase leads up to the east wing of bedrooms and drawing rooms, which had to be refurbished after a major fire in 1941, and were restored to their eighteenth- and nineteenth-century style. The bedrooms served as a Red Cross hospital during World War I; here, the wounded James Connolly, one of the leaders of the 1916 Easter Rising, was treated before being carted off to a firing squad at Kilmainham Gaol. The tour's artistic highlight is *The Countess of Southampton* by Van Dyck, a keenly wrought, restrained – apart from the shimmering dress – portrait of the 17-year-old Elizabeth Leigh, painted for her wedding.

The brass chandelier in the Throne Room, with its shamrock, rose and thistle emblems, commemorates the 1801 Act of Union, while the Picture Gallery beyond is lined with viceroys, including – hiding ignominiously behind the door – the First Marquis of Cornwallis, who not only lost the American colonies, but also faced rebellions as viceroy, first of India, then of Ireland (1798).

St Patrick's Hall, formerly a ballroom that hosted investitures of the Knights of St Patrick, is now used for the inaugurations and funerals of Irish presidents. Its overblown, late eighteenth-century ceiling paintings show St Patrick converting the Irish, Henry II receiving the submission of the Irish chieftains, and George III's coronation.

The tour finishes at the excavations of the **Undercroft** beneath the Lower Yard, which have revealed the base of the gunpowder tower of the medieval castle and steps leading down to the moat, fed by the old River Poddle on its way down to the Liffey, as well as part of the original Viking ramparts.

The Chester Beatty Library

Behind the Record Tower and Chapel Royal lies the pretty **castle garden**; now adorned with a swirling motif taken from the passage grave at Newgrange, it marks the site of the "black pool" (*dubh linn*) from which the city derives its name. Overlooking the garden from the renovated eighteenth-century Clock Tower Building, the **Chester Beatty Library** preserves a dazzling collection of books, manuscripts, prints and *objets d'art* from around the world (Tues–Fri 10am–5pm, Sat 11am–5pm, Sun 1–5pm, plus May–Sept Mon 10am–5pm; free; free guided tours Wed 1pm & Sun 3pm & 4pm; ⓣ01/407 0750, ⓦwww.cbl.ie). Superlatives come thick and fast here: as well as one of the finest Islamic collections in existence, containing some of the earliest manuscripts from the ninth and tenth centuries, the library holds important Biblical papyri, including the earliest surviving examples in any language of Mark's and Luke's Gospels, St Paul's Letters and the Book of Revelations. Elegantly displayed in high-tech galleries, the artefacts are used to tell the story of religious and artistic traditions across the world with great ingenuity, a formula which justifiably won the CBL the European Museum of the Year award in 2002. It's well worth timing your visit to coincide with lunch at the excellent *Silk Road Café* (see p.122).

The collection was painstakingly put together by the remarkable **Sir Alfred Chester Beatty**, an American mining magnate who moved himself and his works to Dublin in the early 1950s, after cutting a deal with the Irish government on import taxes and estate duties. In 1957 he was made the first honorary citizen of Ireland and, when he died in 1968, he bequeathed his collection to the state and was given a state funeral.

Most of the CBL's vast holding is accessible only to scholars via the reference library, with less than two percent on show in the public galleries at any one time – though that's more than enough to keep you occupied for a few hours. It makes sense to start with the second-floor gallery, which covers "Sacred Traditions", while the first floor deals with "Artistic Traditions" (alongside a space for fascinating temporary exhibitions), with each divided into Western, Islamic and Eastern sections; exhibits range from sixteenth-century biblical engravings by Albrecht Dürer to books carved in jade for the Chinese emperors, and from gorgeously illustrated collections of Persian poetry to serene Burmese statues of the Buddha.

City Hall

In front of the castle on Dame Street stands the gleamingly restored rotunda of **City Hall** (Mon–Sat 10am–5.15pm, Sun 2–5pm; free; ⓦwww.dublincity.ie/cityhall), where creamy Portland-stone columns, interspersed with statues of notables, including Daniel O'Connell (the city's first Catholic Lord Mayor), bathe in wonderful natural light from the dome. The sumptuous Neoclassical building was constructed between 1769 and 1779 as the Royal Exchange, but fell into disuse after the Act of Union of 1801 passed governance of Ireland back to London; Dublin Corporation bought it in 1851, and it's still the venue for city council meetings. Among the Arts and Crafts murals under the dome that trace Dublin's history, look out for one depicting Lambert Simnel – 10-year-old pretender to Henry VII's throne, who ended up enslaved as his kitchen-scullion – being carried through the streets after his mock coronation in Christ Church Cathedral in 1487. The colourful floor mosaic shows the civic coat of arms, three castles topped by flames, which apparently represent the zeal of the citizens to defend Dublin – reinforced by the city motto *Obedientia Civium Urbis Felicitas* ("Happy the City whose Citizens Obey").

The vaults beneath City Hall now shelter **The Story of the Capital** (Mon–Sat 10am–5.15pm, Sun 2–5pm; €4; Heritage Island), a fascinating multimedia journey through Dublin's history and politics – with occasional hints of self-promotion for the exhibition's sponsors, the city council. The story is told through exhaustive display panels, slick interactive databases and a series of videos, complemented by an entertaining audioguide narrated by Irish actress Sinead Cusack with snippets from leading historians. There are few exhibits as such, though a notable exception is the intricate city seal and its strongbox, which was instituted after the seal was stolen in 1305 and required the presence of all six keyholders. To make up for the lack of hard evidence on show, however, the enterprising curators have commissioned a series of artworks, including *Utopian Column*, a stack of glass plates engraved with historical scenes and flooded with light.

Christ Church Cathedral

Though occupying the highest point of the old city, **Christ Church Cathedral** is now hemmed in by buildings and traffic and appears as an unexceptional Gothic Revival edifice (June–Aug daily 9am–6pm, Jan–May & Sept–Dec 9.45am–5/6pm; €5, discounted to €3.95 with a ticket for Dublinia – see opposite; Heritage Island; Choral Evensong Wed & Thurs 6pm, Sat 5pm, Sun 3.30pm, Sung Eucharist Sun 11am; ⓣ01/677 8099, ⓦwww.cccdub.ie). Inside, however, you'll find some fascinating remnants from its long history as the seat of the (now Anglican) Archbishop of Dublin and Glendalough. From as early as the seventh century, there may have been a small Celtic church on these grounds, and in about 1030, the recently converted Viking king of Dublin, Sitric Silkenbeard, built a wooden cathedral here. This in turn was replaced by the Normans, who between 1186 and 1240 erected a magnificent stone structure to mark their accession to power. Of this, the crypt, the transept (which retains a few eroded Romanesque carvings), the west end of the choir and the remarkable **leaning north wall** can still be seen – as the church had been built over a bog, the roof collapsed in 1562, bringing down the south wall and pulling the north side of the nave half a metre out of the

Dublin and the Messiah

Opposite the cathedral on Fishamble Street once stood **Neal's Music Hall**, where **Handel** conducted the combined choirs of Christ Church and St Patrick's cathedrals in the first performance of his *Messiah* in 1742. As the takings were going to charity, ladies were requested not to wear hoops in their crinolines, to get more bums on seats. Jonathan Swift exclaimed, "Oh, a German, a genius, a prodigy." In a private garden on the site, the composer's reward is a statue of himself conducting in the nude, perched on a set of organ pipes. Every April 13, on the anniversary of the first performance, Our Lady's Choral Society gives a singalong performance of excerpts from the *Messiah* here.

perpendicular. In the 1870s, distiller Henry Roe lavished the equivalent of €30 million on the heavy-handed restoration you can see today, and bankrupted himself.

Near the main entrance at the southwest corner you'll come across the strange **tomb of Strongbow**, the Norman leader who captured Dublin in 1170 and was buried here six years later. The original, around which the landlords of Dublin had gathered to collect rents, was destroyed by the sixteenth-century roof collapse, and had to be replaced with a fourteenth-century effigy of one of the earls of Drogheda so that business could proceed as usual. The small half-figure alongside is probably a fragment of the original tomb, though legend maintains that it's an effigy of Strongbow's son, hacked in two by his own father for cowardice in battle.

The nearby **State Pew** for the Irish president, still bearing the arms of the Stuart kings, and the **Civic Pew** opposite, for Dublin's Lord Mayor, are rarely used today. In the ambulatory, look out for a mummified cat and rat, which were frozen in hot pursuit in an organ pipe in the 1860s. The chapels off the choir show the Anglo-Normans celebrating their dual nationality. To the left stands the **Chapel of St Edmund**, the ninth-century king of East Anglia who was martyred by the Vikings, while on the right is the **Chapel of St Laud**, the sixth-century bishop of Coutances in Normandy. The floor tiles here are original – those in the rest of the cathedral are 1870s replicas – while on the wall you can see an iron box containing the embalmed heart of twelfth-century St Laurence O'Toole, Dublin's only canonized archbishop.

If you descend the stairs by the south transept, you'll reach the crypt, the least changed remnant of the twelfth-century cathedral; formerly a storehouse for the trade in alcohol and tobacco, it's one of the largest crypts in Britain and Ireland, extending under the entire cathedral for 55m. Here you'll find the **Treasures of Christ Church** exhibition (same ticket and hours as the rest of the cathedral, except in winter on Sun it closes after Choral Evensong), which includes an interesting twenty-minute audiovisual on the history of the cathedral, as well as a miscellany of manuscripts and church crockery. Look out for a ropey tabernacle and pair of candlesticks made for James II on his flight from England in 1689, when, for three months only, Latin Mass was again celebrated at Christ Church (the existing cathedral paraphernalia was hidden by quick-thinking Anglican officials under a bishop's coffin). In extravagant contrast is a chunky silver-gilt plate, around a metre wide, presented by King William III in thanksgiving for his victory at the Battle of the Boyne in 1690.

Dublinia & the Viking World

Housed in the former Synod Hall of the Church of Ireland, **Dublinia & the Viking World** (April–Sept daily 10am–5pm; Oct–March Mon–Fri 11am–4pm, Sat & Sun 10am–4pm; €6.25, children €3.75, family ticket €17; Heritage Island; Ⓣ01/679 4611, Ⓦwww.dublinia.ie) provides a lively, hands-on portrait of Viking and medieval Dublin that's especially good fun for kids (phone for details of special activities during the summer months). Themes such as the plague and the medieval fair are explored via walk-through tableaux of streets and houses, sound effects and lots of fun interactive possibilities, including throwing balls at a criminal in the stocks. The first floor's centrepiece is a fascinating model of Dublin in about 1500, showing the walled city dominated by Christ Church, while neighbouring rooms explore the excavations of the Viking and medieval settlements at nearby Wood Quay. On the second floor, the Great Hall, where the Anglican bishops met until 1982, is now the home of Viking World, which uses a near-life-size ship, audiovisuals on the sagas and the chance to try on slave chains to convey Viking life. Before crossing the graceful, much-photographed bridge over to Christ Church Cathedral, it's worth climbing **St Michael's Tower**, a remnant of the seventeenth-century Church of St Michael and All Angels, for fine views over the city.

St Audoen's

Just to the west of Dublinia, on the corner of Bridge Street, stand two churches dedicated to St Audoen (in French, Ouen, seventh-century bishop of Rouen and the patron saint of Normandy). The monumental but largely uninteresting nineteenth-century Catholic version overshadows its neighbour, **Protestant St Audoen's**, which was built around 1190 and is now an intriguing tourist site (June–Sept daily 9.30am–5.30pm, last admission 4.45pm; free). There are still services every Sunday, however, at 10.15am – the church has been continuously used for worship for over eight centuries, longer than any other in Dublin.

The most fascinating aspect of a visit is seeing the physical evidence of how the church's fortunes waxed and waned over the centuries. As it prospered through close association with the city's guilds, St Audoen's expanded in stages around its original single-naved church, including the addition, in 1431, of **St Anne's Guild Chapel**, making a two-aisled nave. The latter is now the main exhibition area, with informative displays on the parish and the guilds.

Until the Reformation, St Audoen's was the most prestigious parish church among Dublin's leading families. Afterwards, however, many members of the all-important Guild of St Anne refused to become Protestant and the congregation declined. By the nineteenth century St Audoen's had retreated to its original single nave, by the simple expediency of removing the roofs from the other parts of the church and letting them rot. You can now poke around the open-air **chancel** and **Portlester Chapel**, where, before the building was declared a national monument, locals would hang their washing out to dry.

Behind the Protestant church, steps descend to thirteenth-century **St Audoen's Arch**, the only remaining gate in the **Norman city walls** – a dramatic, though heavily restored remnant stretching for two hundred metres along Cook Street, 7m high and tipped with battlements.

St Patrick's Cathedral

A short stroll down Nicholas and Patrick streets from Dublinia will bring you to **St Patrick's Cathedral** (March–Oct daily 9am–6pm; Nov–Feb Mon–Fri 9am–6pm, Sat 9am–5pm, Sun 9am–3pm; €5; Heritage Island; Ⓣ01/475 4817, Ⓦwww.stpatrickscathedral.ie); note that visitors are not admitted, except for worship, during services, which include Choral Matins on weekdays at 9.40am (during school terms), Choral Evensong on weekdays at 5.45pm (except Wed in July & Aug) and on Sunday at 3.15pm, and Choral Eucharist/Matins on Sunday at 11.15am.

St Patrick's history is remarkably similar to that of its fellow-Anglican rival Christ Church up the road. It was built between 1220 and 1270 in Gothic style, but its roof collapsed in 1544, leading to a decline that included its use as a stable by Cromwell's army in 1649. Its Victorian restoration, however, by Sir Benjamin Guinness in the 1860s, was more sensitive than at Christ Church, and it has a more appealing, lived-in feel, thanks largely to its clutter of quirky funerary monuments. If you're wondering why Dublin should have two Church of Ireland cathedrals, the answer is (of course) shrouded in the mists of time, tradition and rivalry: in the 1190s, Archbishop John Comyn left the clergy of

Jonathan Swift

"Here is laid the body of Jonathan Swift . . . where fierce indignation can no longer rend the heart. Go, traveller, and imitate if you can this earnest and dedicated champion of liberty."

Swift's epitaph in St Patrick's Cathedral, penned by himself and translated here from the Latin, conveys not only his appetite for political satire and campaigning, but also perhaps a certain prescience about the longevity of his fame. Born in Dublin in 1667 and educated at Trinity College, Swift went to England in 1689 to work as secretary to the retired diplomat Sir William Temple. Here he met Esther Johnson, nicknamed **Stella**, the daughter of Temple's housekeeper, who became his close companion – whether platonic or sexual, no one knows – until her death in 1728. Swift was ordained in the Church of Ireland in 1695, and wrote his first major work, **A Tale of a Tub**, anonymously in 1704, satirizing the official churches and the unscrupulous "modern" writers of his day. Sent to London to lobby the government for the relief of church taxes, from 1710 he was at the centre of England's political and literary life, a friend of Tory ministers as well as of Alexander Pope and John Gay. When the Tories fell, however, instead of the English bishopric he had hoped for, he was made Dean of St Patrick's, in 1713. Here he turned his caustic wit on Irish injustices, writing a series of pamphlets in the 1720s and 1730s including **A Modest Proposal**, one of the most admired works of irony in the English language, which suggests that the Irish poor sell off their children to the rich as "a most delicious, nourishing and wholesome food". At this time, too, he wrote his most famous work, the gloriously imaginative satirical novel, **Gulliver's Travels** (1726). Swift's later years were blighted by a progressive mental illness causing dizziness, and when he died, in 1745, he left his estate to build St Patrick's on James's Street, the first psychiatric hospital in Ireland.

Christ Church and built his own palace and collegiate church (that is, a more secular church devoted to both worship and learning) here outside the city walls and therefore beyond the jurisdiction of the city provosts. St Patrick's is now the national cathedral of the Church of Ireland.

To the right of the entrance in the harmoniously proportioned nave are diverse memorials to **Jonathan Swift**, the cathedral's dean for 32 years, including his and his long-term partner Stella's graves, his pulpit and table, and a cast of his skull – both his and Stella's bodies were dug up by Victorian phrenologists, studying the skulls of the famous. In the south transept, look out for the marble **monument to Archbishop Marsh** (see p.104), the finest work by sculptor Grinling Gibbons in Ireland. The **Door of Reconciliation** by the north transept recalls a quarrel between the earls of Kildare and Ormond in 1492. Ormond fled and sought sanctuary in the cathedral's chapterhouse, but Kildare, eager to make peace, cut a hole in the door and stretched his arm through to shake Ormond's hand – so giving us the phrase "chancing your arm". Nearby in the north aisle of the choir, a simple black slab commemorates **Duke Frederick Schomberg**, who advised William of Orange to come to Ireland in 1686 but had the misfortune to be slain at the ensuing Battle of the Boyne. His family didn't bother to erect a memorial for him, so it was left to Dean Swift to do the honours here in 1731; in Swift's words, "The renown of his valour had greater power among strangers than had the ties of blood among his kith and kin."

In the northwest corner of the nave you'll find a slab carved with a Celtic cross that once marked the site of a well next to the cathedral, where St Patrick baptized converts in the fifth century. Back near the entrance, you can't miss the extravagant **Boyle monument**, which Richard Boyle, Earl of Cork, erected in 1632 in memory of his wife Katherine who had borne him fifteen children, including the famous chemist Robert Boyle (shown in the bottom-centre niche). Viceroy Wentworth, objecting to being forced to kneel before a Corkman, had the monument moved here from beside the altar, but Boyle exacted revenge in later years by engineering Wentworth's execution.

Marsh's Library

Behind St Patrick's Cathedral lies the oldest public library in Ireland, **Marsh's Library** (Mon & Wed–Fri 10am–1pm & 2–5pm, Sat 10.30am–1pm; €2.50; Ⓦwww.marshlibrary.ie), which has remained delightfully untouched since it was built by Sir William Robinson, the architect of Kilmainham Hospital, in 1701, and still functions as a research and conservation library. Its founder, Archbishop Narcissus Marsh, was particularly interested in science, mathematics and music, and oversaw the first translation of the Old Testament into Irish. His books form one of the library's four main collections, totalling 25,000 works, relating to the sixteenth, seventeenth and early eighteenth centuries. They're housed in beautiful rows of dark-oak bookcases, each with a carved and lettered gable (for cataloguing purposes) topped by a bishop's mitre, and three screened alcoves, or "cages", where readers were locked in with rare books. The library mounts regular exhibitions from its collections on subjects such as astronomy, and displays a death mask of its former governor, Jonathan Swift, as well as a cast of his companion Stella's skull.

O'Connell Street and around

Running due north from O'Connell Bridge, broader than it is long, to Parnell Square, **O'Connell Street** is the main artery of Dublin's Northside. Lined with numerous impressive memorials and the remarkable four-hundred-foot- high stainless steel "**Spike**" sculpture, this bustling thoroughfare was originally laid out in the fashion of the grand Parisian boulevards. Poorly redeveloped since the damage caused by the 1916 Easter Rising, nowadays the street is very much a mishmash of modern shop frontages, though glancing at the upper storeys reveals some of its former glory. The streets around, however, represent a consumer's paradise and, particularly on Liffey Street Lower and in the burgeoning **Italian quarter** centred on Bloom Lane (the result of a local developer's fascination with all things Tuscan), you'll find plenty of stylish bars and cafés. Notable cultural landmarks east of O'Connell Street include the **Abbey Theatre**, centre of the twentieth-century revival in Irish theatre, and, along The Quays, the opulent eighteenth-century **Custom House**.

O'Connell Street

There are few vestiges of O'Connell Street's one-time grandeur, but there remain a remarkable number of monuments, mostly positioned in its broad central reservation, as well as the historic GPO. Just north of O'Connell Bridge, you'll encounter first the imposing figure of the politician **Daniel O'Connell**, "The Liberator", who played a major role in nineteenth-century political campaigns to secure independence. The winged figures by his side represent O'Connell's bravery, patriotism, fidelity and eloquence, while the smaller female figure nearby symbolizes Ireland unchained. At the Abbey Street junction is a statue of the trade unionist **Jim Larkin**, caught in the act of addressing a crowd.

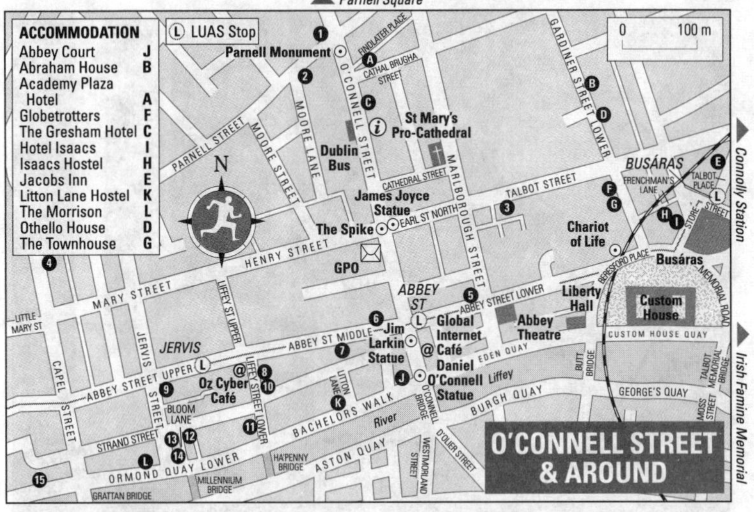

RESTAURANTS & CAFÉS	
101 Talbot	3
Caffe Cagliostro	12
The Epicurean Food Hall	8
Govinda's	6
Halo	L
Panem	14
Le Phare	9

BARS, MUSIC VENUES & CLUBS	
Ambassador Theatre	1
Bleu Note Café	4
Enoteca delle Langhe	13
The Flowing Tide	5
The Lotts	10
Morrison	L
Patrick Conway's	2
Pravda	11
Sin É	15
Spirit	7

Further up, by the junction with Earl Street North stands the Northside's most remarkable landmark on the spot where Nelson's Pillar stood until it was blown up by Republicans in 1966 – the frankly astonishing **Dublin Spire** or "Spike" as it's colloquially known. Designed by Ian Ritchie, this 120-metre-high stainless-steel needle, surmounted by a beacon, is easily the tallest structure in the city centre. Just over a metre wide at its base, it tapers to a mere fifteen centimetres at its summit. In the early morning or at dusk its surface takes on an ethereal blue colour while at night it seems to loom ominously over the city. What the ghost of **James Joyce**, whose adjacent and somewhat rakish statue stands just down Earl Street North, would make of it all is open to question.

Just to the left of the "Spike" stands one of O'Connell Street's few remaining buildings of major historical importance, the **General Post Office** (Mon–Sat 8am–8pm; free) whose significance lies in its role as the rebels' headquarters during the Easter Rising of 1916 (see box, p.107). The building was originally built in 1818 but only its Ionic portico survived the fighting – and still bears the marks of gunfire. Following restoration, the GPO reopened in 1929 and inside its marble halls you'll find Oliver Sheppard's intricately wrought bronze statue *The Death of Cúchulainn*, representing a key moment in the Irish legend *Táin Bó Cúailnge*.

At the very top of O'Connell Street stands an imposing statue of **Charles Stewart Parnell**, the leading late nineteenth-century advocate of Irish Home Rule. The plinth records his famous declaration:

No man has a right to fix the boundary to the march of a nation. No man has a right to say to his country, "Thus far shalt thou go and no further."

▲ James Joyce

The Abbey Theatre

Just east of O'Connell Street's southern end stands the **Abbey Theatre**, focal point for Ireland's twentieth-century cultural revival. It first opened its doors in December 1904 to present three plays, two by the poet and dramatist W.B. Yeats and the other by his patron Lady Gregory. The theatre's company turned professional in 1906 and Yeats and Gregory along with J.M. Synge became its first directors. The staging of Synge's own tragicomic *Playboy of the Western World*,

The Easter Rising

The initial impact of some historical events often runs counter to their long-term effects and such was the case with the **Easter Rising** of 1916. Truth be told, this inherently idealistic rebellion was a bungled affair from start to finish, and it was only the repressive response of the British Army, whose political overlords were unsurprisingly sidetracked by the seemingly more pressing affairs taking place in the fields of Flanders, that gave the event its pivotal role in attaining Ireland's independence.

The Rising was organized by the **Irish Republican Brethren** (IRB), a Republican grouping that had been founded in 1858, and was now led by educationalist and Gaelic cultural revivalist **Patrick Pearse** and Scots-born socialist and trades union activist **James Connolly**. Impelled by the continuing failure of democratic means to achieve the goal of independence, they concocted a plan to take over by force, aided by the much larger **Irish Volunteers**, a Nationalist corps founded in 1913, and using arms acquired from Germany. The armaments were however intercepted by the British, and though the Volunteers' leader withdrew his support, the rising still went ahead.

On the morning of Easter Monday, the rebels took control of a number of key buildings in the city centre and further afield (see p.701). They made the **General Post Office** on O'Connell Street their base, and it was from here that Pearse emerged to make his Proclamation of the Irish Republic. The British response was initially guarded, but a full-scale battle soon ensued, destroying much of the surrounding area and heavily damaging rebel-held buildings elsewhere in the city.

It took five days for the rebellion to be suppressed and its leaders captured. Dubliners decried the uprising at its outset, dismayed by the devastation ravaged upon their city by the fighting. Had the British simply imprisoned the IRB's leaders, it's extremely unlikely later political developments would have occurred as quickly as they did, but the draconian decision was made to execute all of them (with the exception of Éamon de Valera, who had US citizenship). In the process, the British created national martyrs, transforming the situation irrevocably and ultimately leading to a bitter war of independence.

with its frank language and suggestion that Irish peasants would condone a murder, provoked riots on its opening night while later, in 1926, Seán O'Casey's *The Plough and the Stars* incited bitter outrage, the audience regarding its view of the Easter Rising as derisive not least because the theatre had begun to receive state funding the previous year.

The original Abbey burnt to the ground in 1951 and its more modern, outwardly grim replacement opened in 1966. Informative guided tours – a must for anyone interested in the link between Ireland's culture and politics – take in both back- and front-stage areas and recount key moments in the Abbey's history (Tues & Thurs 2.30pm; €6; call ⓣ01/887 2223 to book). Its programme continues to include a range of drama, blending revivals of Irish classics with new works by established writers such as Hugh Leonard and Brian Friel, while the much smaller Peacock Theatre in the basement is devoted to new experimental works. In 2005, financial mismanagement almost saw the Abbey's closure, though it was bailed out by the Irish Government, and there are now plans afoot to relocate the theatre into a newly-built docklands development.

The Custom House and around

Opened in 1791, the imposing **Custom House** is one of several notable Dublin landmarks designed by the English architect James Gandon (others include the Four Courts and O'Connell Bridge). The Custom House cost the then unearthly sum of £500,000 sterling to construct, owing to its bulk and the intricacy of Gandon's architectural detail – and because it was constructed on a submerged mudflat which required covering by a layer of solid pine planks. Such cost proved even more extravagant when the Act of Union transferred customs and excise to London in 1800. The building's grandiose Neoclassical exterior, more than a hundred metres long, features heads sculpted by Gandon's contemporary Edward Smyth, with cattle heads symbolizing Ireland's beef trade and the others representing Ireland's rivers (including the Liffey above the main entrance). Its 35-metre-high-dome was based upon Christopher Wren's Greenwich Hospital.

After 1801, the Custom House became the administrative centre for the city's work on public hygiene and Poor Law relief, the latter demonstrated by an enormous Famine pot. The building suffered a major fire in 1833 and was completely gutted in 1921 after being set alight by the IRA. Subsequently restored, though with significant changes to its internal structure and facade, it housed various government departments and some of its more illustrious employees, including Brian O'Nolan, better known as the comic novelist Flann O'Brien, and the songwriter Percy French.

To the Custom House's east, and set between the looming presence of the International Financial Services Centre and the Liffey is the **Irish Famine Memorial**. These six, life-sized bronze figures were designed and cast by the Dublin sculptor Rowan Gillespie to mark the 150th anniversary of the worst year of the Great Famine (see p.697). That these stark, beseeching figures are staring eastwards towards Britain is not coincidental.

St Mary's Pro-Cathedral

To the east of O'Connell Street, Cathedral Street leads to **St Mary's Pro-Cathedral**, the city's principal Catholic church, which features a six-columned facade modelled on the Temple of Theseus in Athens. Its side-street position resulted from Protestant opposition to plans to site the building in a more central location on Sackville Street (now O'Connell Street), a spot instead occupied by the General Post Office. The Pro-Cathedral is best known for its male **Palestrina Choir**, founded in 1903 and named after the sixteenth-century Italian composer. The choir can be heard singing Latin Mass every Sunday at 11am from September to June, though during July and August its place is taken by visiting choirs.

Parnell Square and around

Parnell Square might lack the allure of its Southside Georgian equivalents, but it still has a certain grace. The Square's north side hosts one of Dublin's premier galleries, the **Hugh Lane**, as well as the **Dublin Writers Museum**, an excellent place to learn about the city's literary history, while nearby is a centre devoted to the works of the acclaimed writer **James Joyce**.

Dublin City Gallery – The Hugh Lane

The elegant, Georgian, stone-clad Charlemont House, with its curved outer and inner walls and Neoclassical interior has provided a permanent home for the **Hugh Lane** gallery since 1933 (Tues–Thurs 10am–6pm, Fri & Sat 10am–5pm, Sun 11am–5pm; free, but €2 donation suggested; Ⓦwww.hughlane.ie). Sir Hugh, a nephew of Lady Gregory (see p.424), wanted Dublin to house a major gallery of Irish and international art. He amassed a considerable collection by persuading native artists to contribute their work and purchasing many other paintings himself, particularly from the French Impressionist school and Italy.

The gallery holds around half of the Lane collection (the rest is in London's National Gallery) and only a fraction is on display here at any one time, though you're likely to see works by Renoir, Monet and Degas, as well as Pissarro and the Irish painters Jack B.Yeats, Roderic O'Connor and Louis le Brocquy, as well as stained-glass pieces by Evie Hone and Harry Clarke. Simultaneously, there are usually other temporary exhibitions of more modern artworks.

Part of the gallery is devoted to a re-creation of Dublin-born painter **Francis Bacon's studio**, transported from its original location at Reece Mews in South Kensington, London, where the artist lived and worked for the last thirty years of his life. After his death in 1992, his studio was donated to the gallery by his heir, John Edwards, and reconstructed here with astonishing precision – more than seven thousand individual items were catalogued and placed here with verisimilitude in the reconstruction. The studio can only be viewed through the window glass but amongst the apparent debris are an old Bush record-player, empty champagne boxes and huge tins of the type of matt vinyl favoured by Bacon, the fumes of which exacerbated his asthma. The surrounding rooms hold displays of memorabilia, such as photographs and correspondence, as well as a detailed database of every item found in the studio (accessible via touch-screen consoles) and large canvasses from the painter's last years.

The gallery runs guided **tours** of the exhibits (Tues 11am & Sun 1.30pm), a programme of **lectures and films** related to its current shows (Sun 3pm) and very popular classical-music **concerts** (Sun noon) – and all of these events are free.

Dublin Writers Museum

Almost next door to the gallery is the **Dublin Writers Museum** (Mon–Sat 10am–5pm, Sun & public hols 11am–5pm; July & Aug Mon–Fri open until 6pm; €7; Ⓦwww.writersmuseum.com), which aims to illuminate Ireland's literary history, featuring not just giants such as Wilde, Shaw, Joyce and Beckett, but also lesser-known figures like Sheridan Le Fanu and Oliver St John Gogarty. The ground floor contains a plethora of displays on particular writers or literary schools, and it is well worth picking up the free and entertaining guide-tape to receive background information on the authors.

The hall downstairs, hung with modern paintings of writers, leads to an outdoor Zen garden where you can contemplate works you've purchased in the museum's bookshop or, alternatively, head for the café at the rear. On the first floor is the Gallery of Writers, an elegant salon with plasterwork by Michael Stapleton, which features James Joyce's piano and more paintings, of which the most impressive is John B. Yeats's portrait of George Moore. Beside this is the Gorham Library, which features numerous rare editions. The museum's basement houses one of the Northside's best restaurants, *Chapter One* (see p.125).

The James Joyce Centre

A short hop to the east up North Great George's Street is the **James Joyce Centre** (Tues–Sat 10am–5pm; €5; Ⓣ01/878 8547, Ⓦwww.jamesjoyce.ie), occupying a grand eighteenth-century townhouse, restored in the 1980s. The centre aims to illuminate the work of perhaps Ireland's most imaginative yet most complex writer, who spent part of his life living in the inner Northside, and drew upon his experiences in the creation of his characters and the settings for his works. The building features decorative stucco mouldings by Michael Stapleton. The ground floor houses a small shop full of Joyceiana, such as books and prints, and an airy courtyard which includes the actual period door of

Bloomsday

Perhaps no other writer has so encapsulated the life, lore and mores of his native city as **James Joyce** so successfully achieved in his remarkable novels, most notably **Ulysses** (1922). So precise are the author's descriptions of the locales visited by the book's protagonists on the date of the book's setting, June 16, that it is possible to follow literally in their footsteps. This annual pilgrimage undertaken by Joycean aficionados across the city has become known as Bloomsday. Though you can undertake to cover the **Bloomsday** route independently (a *Ulysses* map is available from the Dublin Tourism Centre), guided walks are organized by the James Joyce Centre (see below). There are plenty of other associated events, including re-creations by actors of some of the book's central passages and concerts devoted to music referenced in the novel.

Strangely, for someone who documented his native city's life with such pride, Joyce came to loathe Dublin, once describing the place in a letter as a "city of failure, of rancour and of unhappiness", and concluding "I long to be out of it." Though his early works, such as the short-story collection **Dubliners** and the semi-autobiographical novel **A Portrait of the Artist as a Young Man**, draw heavily upon his upbringing, Catholic education and Dublin experiences, by the time of the latter's publication in 1916, Joyce had long abandoned Ireland. Not long after meeting a Connemara-born chambermaid, Nora Barnacle, having first dated her on June 16, 1904, the pair eloped to Europe. Other than two brief visits to Ireland, Joyce spent the rest of his life in exile living in cities across Europe – in Pola (now Pula) in Istria, Trieste, Zurich and, notably, Paris, where *Ulysses* was published in 1922 and he finally wed Nora in 1931. Joyce's only subsequent published work was the convoluted **Finnegans Wake** (1939). When he died in 1941, *Ulysses* was still unavailable in Ireland (though it never officially fell foul of Ireland's censorship laws, booksellers were loath to stock copies), and was not published in the country until the 1960s.

7 Eccles Street, the fictional home of Leopold and Molly Bloom, two of the main protagonists in *Ulysses*, as well as a somewhat enigmatic, modernist Joyce-inspired sculpture of a cow.

The building's upper floors house a re-creation of the tiny room occupied by Joyce in Trieste, featuring various books, pianola music-rolls and a splendid collection of hats, as well as photographs of people and places associated with *Ulysses*, and touchscreen consoles tracing the development of the novel's plot and its variety of characters. Three short documentary films on the writer's life can also be viewed. The centre's **walking tour** (Sat 11am & 2pm; €10; 1hr), which begins here, is well worth taking if you want to learn more about Joycean connections with the surrounding area.

The Four Courts and St Michan's Church

About a kilometre west along the Quays from O'Connell Bridge stands the imposing riverside structure of the **Four Courts**. Fronted by Corinthian columns and surmounted by an impressive dome, the building has seen many a legal hearing since it first opened its doors in 1802. Like the Custom House (see p.107) it was designed by James Gandon, and took some sixteen years to complete at a cost of £200,000 sterling. The Four Courts was seized by Republicans opposed to the Anglo-Irish Treaty in 1921, and heavily bombarded by Free State forces during the subsequent Civil War using, ironically, howitzers borrowed from the British. However, before the siege came to its inevitable end, the rebels accidentally set off explosives inside the building, destroying the Public Records Office and innumerable irreplaceable historic documents in the process. After rebuilding, the Four Courts reopened in 1931 and nowadays houses the High Court of Justice. To view a trial though, a better – and often more entertaining – bet is to visit the **District Court** (Oct–July Mon–Fri 11am–1pm & 2–4pm; free), entered via Chancery Place, which deals with less salubrious local matters.

Just north of Arran Quay on Church Street stands **St Michan's Church**, constructed in 1095 by the Vikings in honour of a Danish bishop, and substantially rebuilt some six hundred years later. Next to the church organ, reputedly once played by Handel, is the unusual Penitents' Pew, in which parishioners knelt facing the congregation to confess their errant ways. It is the church's **vaults**, however, that hold the most fascination. Guided **tours** (March–Oct Mon–Fri 10am–12.45pm & 2–4.45pm, Sat 10am–12.45pm; Nov–Feb Mon–Fri 12.30–3.30pm, Sat 10am–12.45pm; €3.50) descend an almost sheer staircase to view the contents of tiny crypts, which contain a dozen bodies, some dating back more than seven hundred years. These have been mummified by a process that involves two factors: the vaults' limestone walls, which absorb the air's natural moisture, and the methane produced by vegetation decaying below the floor. One of the mummies is believed to have been a Crusader, another a nun and a third, which lacks a hand, may have been a repentant thief. Another crypt contains John and Henry Sheares, executed for their role in the 1798 Rebellion, as well as the death mask of one of its leaders, Wolfe Tone. Two other rebels, Oliver Bond and the Reverend William Jackson, are buried in the church's graveyard, and some reckon an unmarked grave to the rear houses the body of Robert Emmet, leader of the 1803 rising.

Old Jameson Distillery and Smithfield

Northwest of St Michan's on Duck Lane are the buildings of the **Old Jameson Distillery** (daily 9.30am–6pm; last tour 5.30pm; €9.75; Ⓦwww.jamesonwhiskey.com), where John Jameson set up his whiskey company. They have long been turned over to a somewhat touristy shrine to "the hard stuff". Guided **tours** whirl visitors through the process itself, from milling and mashing to the essential distillation element; while the separation of water from alcohol only occurs once in bourbon and twice in Scotch, the production of *uisce beatha* (Irish for "water of life", anglicized to "whiskey") involves a three-stage process. The resulting liquid is diluted via the addition of water and then left in imported oak casks, formerly used for sherry, port or brandy, to mature for five to seven years, though some rare whiskeys are left 25 years before bottling. The tour ends with a tasting exercise in which testers are requested to sample four brands of whiskey, plus a bourbon and Scotch, before plumping for their favourite – if you want to take part, make sure to volunteer at the start of the tour, or you'll only receive the complimentary tot of Jameson's from the bar.

Next to the *Park Inn* hotel nearby stands the former chimney of the distillery company, now the **Chimney Viewing Tower** (June–Aug Mon–Sat 10am–5.30pm, Sun 11am–5.30pm; rest of the year call for times; €5 – tickets from the adjacent *Park Inn* hotel; Ⓣ01/817 3838, Ⓦwww.dublin.parkinn.ie). A lift attached to its side whisks passengers up to an enclosed platform, which gives panoramic views that vividly present the city in action. The tower is one of the features of an area christened **Smithfield Village** by developers. More an ongoing process of urban renewal than an identifiable community, its centrepiece is also the city's largest civic open space, cobbled **Smithfield** itself. Surrounded by rising blocks of executive flats and new shops and restaurants, Smithfield still manages to host one of the city's major sights – the 300-year-old **Dublin Horse**

Fair, which takes place from around 9am or so until noon on the first Sunday of each month and draws a fair number of traders and other horse-lovers from the city and outlying rural areas. From mid-November to early January, Smithfield also hosts a massive open-air ice-rink (Ⓦwww.smithfieldonice.ie).

Collins Barracks and around

West of Smithfield on Benburb Street is the **National Museum's Decorative Arts Collection**, housed in the eighteenth-century **Collins Barracks** (Tues–Sat 10am–5pm, Sun 2pm–5pm, free; guided tours daily at 3.30pm, €2; Ⓦwww.museum.ie), which surrounds Europe's largest regimental drilling square.

The buildings set around this quadrangle contain a wonderful series of galleries devoted to the fine arts of Ireland and selections from abroad. Unquestionably, the best of these is Curator's Choice, on the first floor of the west block, which is selected by museum curators from all over Ireland. Among its draws are a medieval oak carving of St Molaise; the extravagant cabinet presented by Oliver Cromwell to his daughter Bridget in 1652; and the remarkable fourteenth-century Chinese porcelain Fonthill Vase. The Out of Storage section is another highlight, bringing together everything from decorative glassware to a seventeenth-century suit of Samurai armour, while others focus on Celtic art, coinage, silverware, period furniture, costumes and scientific instruments, and there are usually plenty of temporary exhibits.

On the ground floor a recent addition is the chain of thematically interconnected galleries, Soldiers and Chiefs, devoted to almost five hundred years of Irish military history. Apart from an array of helmets and weaponry, there's the remarkable Stokes tapestry, created by one Stephen of that ilk, a British soldier who devoted his spare time to the depiction of contemporary garrison life and was honoured to have his work shown to Queen Victoria on a royal visit to Ireland in 1849. Other exhibits trace the Irish involvement in the US Civil War and World War I with later examples of tanks and a Havilland Vampire fighter plane while, contrastingly, there's the 200-year-old Bantry Boat, captured from the French frigate *La Résolue* during the abortive invasion of 1796.

Just south of the Barracks lies **Croppy's Acre**, where many of those executed for their part in the 1798 Rebellion are buried – a Wicklow-granite monument marks the precise location of their graves.

West of the centre

Unless you're a keen walker, you'll want to take a bus or LUAS tram to reach some of the city's western attractions. Highlights on the north side of the river include the vast grounds of **Phoenix Park**, with the dazzling interiors of **Farmleigh** mansion lying just beyond. Across the Liffey, the area west of the old city is dominated by the mammoth Guinness Brewery, whose wares are celebrated by the **Guinness Storehouse**. Further west lies the suburb of **Kilmainham**, home to the impressive **Irish Museum of Modern Art** and the forbidding **Kilmainham Gaol**, where the leaders of the 1916 Easter Rising were executed.

Phoenix Park

Europe's largest urban walled park, **Phoenix Park**'s undulating landscape sprawls across some 1750 acres. Originally intended as a deer park for Charles II (a small herd still ranges across its fields), the park takes its name from Phoenix House, the original residence of the British viceroys, whose title derived from the Irish *fionn uisce* ("clear water"). Much of the park is open space, sparsely dotted with trees, shrubs and wild flowers, though there are also areas of woodland and hawthorn. Overall it's an ideal place to escape the city's bustle, a popular venue for sports, and offers plenty of spots for a picnic.

By the park's Parkgate Street entrance lies the **People's Garden**, a pleasant area of formal flowerbeds and hedges. The nearby **Wellington Monument** took some 44 years to complete before it was finally unveiled in 1861. The obelisk – at some sixty metres the tallest of its kind in the British Isles – features bas-reliefs, using bronze from cannons captured at Waterloo, which depict scenes from the successful military campaigns of the "Iron Duke". West from here, alongside Military Road, is the derelict **Magazine Fort**, built on the site originally occupied by Phoenix House. It's an easy climb up the hill to take a trip around its walls and to take in some fine views.

Heading northwest from the People's Garden along Chesterfield Avenue will bring you to **Dublin Zoo** (Mon–Sat 9.30am–6.30pm, Sun 10.30am–6.30pm; Oct–Feb closes at dusk); €14, children under 16 €9.50, children under 3 free; Ⓦwww.dublinzoo.ie), spread over sixty acres, which focuses today on raising species threatened by extinction, such as Amur tigers and waldrapp ibis. Its other attractions include the "African Plains", featuring giraffes, rhinos and hippos, as well as aviaries and reptile houses, polar bears and gorillas. There is a city farm too for younger children.

Further northwest stands the impressive Palladian **Aras an Uachtaráin** (Sat 10.30am–4.30pm; free guided tours; tickets from Phoenix Park Visitor Centre only on the day), the home of Britain's viceroys from the 1780s until Ireland's independence and since 1938 the official residence of the President of Ireland. Tours start from the Phoenix Park Visitor Centre (minibus transport provided) and whisk you through a section of the grandly decorated house, including the State Reception Rooms and the Presidential Office.

At the park's centre on Chesterfield Avenue rises the **Phoenix Monument**, dating from 1747, which more resembles an eagle or falcon than the phoenix it supposedly represents. To its southwest, by the US Ambassador's Residence, is the thirty-metre-high stainless-steel **Papal Cross**, bearing testament to the spot where the late Pope John Paul II celebrated Mass in September 1979 before a congregation of around 1.25 million people.

Northwest of the Monument is the **Phoenix Park Visitor Centre** (mid- to end of March and Oct daily 10am–5.30pm; April–Sept daily 10am–6pm; Nov to mid-March Sat–Wed 10am–5pm; €2.90; Heritage Card), which recounts the history of the park through the ages, focusing on its wildlife and flora. Tickets include a tour of the adjacent **Ashtown Castle**, an early seventeenth-century tower house whose existence was only uncovered when the former residence of the Papal Nuncio, which had been constructed around it, was demolished in 1978.

Farmleigh

White's Gate on the park's northwestern fringe provides access to one of the most splendid buildings in the city, **Farmleigh** (early March–Dec Thurs–Sun & Bank Holiday Mondays 10.30am–5pm; free; call Ⓣ01/815 5981 for information on tours; Ⓦwww.farmleigh.ie), famed for its gorgeous interiors and set in equally impressive grounds (daily 10am–6pm; free). Constructed in 1752 for the Trench family, the building was later purchased by Edward Cecil Guinness, the first Earl of Iveagh, as a rustic residence offering easy access to his brewery. Extensions were made in the 1880s, and the Guinness family remained in residence until 1992. Farmleigh was then purchased by the Irish government for use as a state guesthouse and, consequently, tours may not be available if a visiting delegation is in residence. Tours commence in the dining room, whose unusual decorations include statues of Bacchus either side of the fireplace and a clock inlaid in its centre. The hall features Waterford-crystal chandeliers and a pair of debtors' chairs in which the paupers' legs would be trapped until they agreed to pay their debts, while the library contains four thousand items on loan from the Iveagh Collection, including a first edition of *Ulysses* and books dating back to the twelfth century. The Blue Room, dedicated to Ireland's Nobel Prize winners, has another strange fireplace – this one situated below a window. However, the real treat is the ballroom whose Irish oak floor was constructed of wood originally intended for Guinness barrels; the doors here, fringed with delicate linen portieres, lead you out to a massive, plant-stocked conservatory. Behind the house there's a tearoom in the stable block and an extremely pleasant walled garden.

Farmleigh hosts a number of free **cultural events** from July to September, ranging from ballet and brass bands in the gardens, to indoor concerts in the ballroom, though tickets for the latter are strictly limited and only available via the house's website, as well as garden tours and a food market.

The Guinness Storehouse

South of the Liffey, much of James Street, west of the old city, is centred around the colossal complex of the **Guinness Brewery**. Founded by Arthur Guinness in 1759, the Guinness Brewery initially manufactured ale, but in the 1770s started making porter, a drink so named because of its popularity with the porters of London's markets. Arthur's new brew, whose distinctive black colouring derived from the addition of roasted barley to the brewing process, found such favour that by 1796 it was being exported to London, and three years later ale production ceased altogether. From that point, Guinness and his successors never looked back and, at its peak in the middle of the twentieth century, their brewery produced some 2,500,000 pints of their now eponymous product a day.

The brewery is sadly not open to the public, but instead you can visit the seven-storey **Guinness Storehouse**, signposted from Crane Street (daily: July & Aug 9.30am–7pm; Sept–June 9.30am–5pm; €14; Ⓦwww.guinness-storehouse.com), a high-tech temple to the black stuff. Its self-guided tour kicks off with the brewing process – a whirl of water (not from the Liffey, despite the myth) and a reek of barley, hops and malt – before progressing to the storage and transportation areas. A huge barrel dominates the section on the lost art of coopering, and nearby there's an engine from the brewery's old railway system. The remainder of the tour consists of an array of marketing memorabilia, supported by plenty of facts and figures about the Guinness empire, and there's a gallery on John Gilroy, an esteemed painter who designed many of the company's advertisements. Right at the top of the tower is the *Gravity Bar*, where you can savour your complimentary pint of perhaps the best Guinness in Dublin while absorbing the superb panorama of the city and the countryside beyond.

Kilmainham

West of the Guinness Brewery lies the rather more salubrious area of Kilmainham where, just off Military Road, is the impressive **Royal Hospital**, part of which now houses the Irish Museum of Modern Art. Based on Les Invalides in Paris, the Hospital (entry by guided tour only: hourly July to mid-Sept Mon–Sat 11am–4pm, Sun 1–4pm; free; to book places call Ⓣ01/612 9967) was built between 1680 and 1684 to house war pensioners. Its interior features an impressive banqueting hall hung with seventeenth- and eighteenth-century portraits, and a baroque chapel with a reconstructed papier-maché ceiling and woodcarvings by the Huguenot designer James Tarbery.

The **Irish Museum of Modern Art** (IMMA; Tues–Sat 10am–5.30pm, Sun & public hols noon–5.30pm; free; guided tours of the exhibitions Wed, Fri & Sun 2.30pm, free; Ⓦ www.imma.ie) has a justifiable reputation for its imaginative exhibitions, covering both selections from its own permanent collection and loaned works. All shows are temporary and range from retrospectives of major international artists to new works by modern Irish painters and sculptors. Some of IMMA's most exciting exhibitions draw upon the museum's Outsider Art collection – works, largely paintings, by unschooled artists that explore the psyche – as well as the Madden Armholz collection of Old Master prints, drawing upon the works of Goya, Rembrandt and Hogarth. A small heritage exhibition in IMMA's south wing recounts the history of the Royal Hospital and includes an informative video.

Taking the tree-lined avenue from the Hospital's west wing will lead you past **Bully's Acre**, one of the city's oldest cemeteries, to **Kilmainham Gaol** (April–Sept daily 9.30am–5pm; Oct–March Mon–Sat 9.30am–4pm, Sun 10am–5pm; guided tours every 45min until 1hr 15min before closing; €5.30; Heritage Card). The jail has an iconic position in the history of Ireland's struggle for independence and came to symbolize both Irish political martyrdom and British oppression. Opened in 1796, it became the place of incarceration for captured revolutionaries, including the leaders of the 1916 Easter Rising, who were also executed here. Even after the War of Independence, Republicans continued to be imprisoned here, though it closed in July 1924 after the release of its last inmate, Éamon de Valera – later to become Ireland's Taoiseach and president. **Tours** of the jail provide a chilling impression of the prisoners' living conditions and spartan regime. Its single cells ensured that they were forced into solitary contemplation, and since the building was constructed on top of limestone, their health was often sorely affected by damp and severe cold in winter. Before embarking on the tour, it's well worth visiting the **exhibition galleries**. The ground floor display includes a mock-up of a cell and an early mug-shot camera, and there is a small side gallery showing paintings by Civil War internees and a huge self-portrait of Constance Gore-Booth (better known as the Countess Markiewicz, see p.484) as the Good Shepherd. The upstairs gallery provides an enthralling account of the struggle for independence with numerous mementos, old cinematic footage of Michael Collins and the letter ordering the release of Charles Stewart Parnell.

The northern suburbs

The northern suburbs of Dublin from Glasnevin across to the coast hold a wide variety of attractions, some of which can easily be combined on the same excursion. You'll want fine weather for a trip to the beautiful **Botanic Gardens** and the adjacent **Glasnevin Cemetery**, last resting-place for the major figures in Irish history since 1832, which is best appreciated on a guided tour. To the east lie **Croke Park**, a major sports arena and home to the innovative **GAA Museum**, the exquisite Georgian **Casino at Marino** and, at the end of the DART line, **Howth**, an attractive seaside village with a good concentration of places to eat and drink and a fine cliff-walk.

The National Botanic Gardens

The twenty-hectare **National Botanic Gardens** on the south bank of the River Tolka in Glasnevin (summer Mon–Sat 9am–6pm, Sun 10am–6pm; winter daily 10am–4.30pm; free; free guided tour Sun 2.30pm; ⓣ01/837 7596, ⓦwww.heritageireland.ie) are a great place to wander on a fine day, while their magnificent Victorian wrought-iron glasshouses (summer Mon–Fri 9am–5pm, Sat & Sun 10am–5.45pm; winter daily 10am–4.30pm) offer diversion and shelter whatever the weather. Laid out between 1795 and 1825 with a grant from the Irish parliament, the gardens were, in 1844, the first in the world to germinate orchids from seed successfully, and in August of the following year, the first to notice the potato blight that brought on the Great Famine. Nowadays, a total of around twenty thousand species and cultivated varieties flourish here, including an internationally important collection of cycads, primitive fern-like trees. Outdoor highlights include the rose garden, collections of heather and rhododendrons, the Chinese shrubbery and the arboretum. Among the beautifully restored glasshouses, the Curvilinear Range was built by Richard Turner, a Dublin ironfounder who also built the palm house at Kew Gardens in London, as well as the huge conservatories for the Great Exhibitions in London in 1851 and Dublin in 1853.

To **get there** from the centre, catch bus #13 from Merrion Square or O'Connell Street, or #19 or #19A from South Great George's Street or O'Connell Street. The only entrance is on Glasnevin Hill, off Botanic Road, where you'll find the visitor centre and a pleasant self-service café with picture windows.

Glasnevin Cemetery

Fifteen minutes' walk from the Botanic Gardens – down Botanic Road, then right into Prospect Way and Finglas Road – lies the entrance to **Glasnevin Cemetery** (aka Prospect Cemetery; Mon–Sat 8am–4.30pm or later, Sun 9am–4.30pm or later; free; ⓣ01/830 1133, ⓦwww.glasnevin-cemetery.ie). Founded as a burial place for Catholics by the nationalist political leader Daniel O'Connell in 1832, it's now the national cemetery, open to all denominations and groaning with Celtic crosses, harps and other patriotic emblems. It's well worth timing your visit to coincide with one of the fascinating ninety-minute guided **tours** (Wed & Fri 2.30pm; free); if you're coming here directly from the centre, take bus #40 or #40A/B/C from Parnell Street.

O'Connell himself is commemorated near the entrance by a fifty-metre-high round tower, which managed to survive a Loyalist bomb in the 1970s. His corpse was interred in the tower's crypt in 1869, having been brought home from Genoa where he died (in fact, not all of his body is here: his heart was buried in Rome).

To the left of the round tower, O'Connell's political descendant, Charles Stewart Parnell, who asked to be buried in a mass grave among the people of Ireland, is commemorated by a huge granite boulder from his estate at Avondale, County Wicklow. Other notable figures among the 1.2 million dead at Glasnevin – most of them gathered around O'Connell's tower – include Countess Markiewicz (see p.484), Éamon de Valera, prime minister, president and architect of modern Ireland, and his old rival Michael Collins, the most charismatic leader of the successful independence struggle; from the arts, there's Gerard Manley Hopkins (unmarked, in the Jesuit plot), W.B.Yeats's muse Maud Gonne MacBride, writer, drinker and Republican Brendan Behan, and Alfred Chester Beatty (see p.99). To the right of the tower is the Republican plot, with a memorial to hunger strikers, from Thomas Ashe who died in 1917 to Bobby Sands in 1981, while in front of the tower lie the recent graves of 18-year-old Kevin Barry and eight other Volunteers hanged by the British during the War of Independence; originally buried in Mountjoy Prison, their

▲ Glasnevin Cemetery

bodies were moved here with the full honours of a state funeral in October 2001. For refreshment after your visit, call in at nearby *Kavanagh's* (aka *The Gravediggers* – see p.128), a very characterful old pub.

Croke Park and the GAA Museum

Three kilometres northeast of O'Connell Street, **Croke Park** is the home of the **Gaelic Athletic Association** (GAA), a magnificent, much redeveloped and now very modern stadium whose capacity of 82,000-plus puts it amongst the largest in Europe. Situated under the Cusack Stand is one of Dublin's finest museums, the **GAA Museum** (Mon–Sat 9.30am–5pm, July & Aug until 6pm, Sun & public hols noon–5pm; €5.50; Ⓦwww.museum.gaa.ie), whose creatively designed exhibits provide an enthralling account of not only the sports of hurling and Gaelic football, but also lesser known games such as camogie (the women's version of hurling) and handball. Historical and political contexts are explored in a thoroughly engaging manner – since its foundation in 1884 the GAA has always been irrevocably linked with Irish Nationalism. Thus the museum does not shirk from recounting key, politically sensitive events such as the first Bloody Sunday, when British troops fired on the crowd attending a match in 1920, killing twelve people in the process. On a lighter note, upstairs you can have a go at whacking a hurling ball or test your balance and reactions via various simulations.

Taking the **stadium tour** (hourly: Mon–Sat 10am–4pm, Sun 1–4pm, Sept–June last tour 3pm; call Ⓣ01/819 2323 to check availability and note that there are no tours on match days; €9.50, including entry to the museum) is highly recommended, not just to view this remarkable arena at first hand, but to learn more about key events in its history – including, not least, the momentous decision in 2005 to suspend the GAA's constitution to allow professional Rugby Union and Association Football international matches to take place in the stadium while the Lansdowne Road stadium undergoes redevelopment; previously only games of Irish origin, played by amateurs, could be staged here.

The Casino at Marino

Sited in the now unpromising suburb of Marino, the **Casino** is probably the finest piece of Neoclassical architecture in Ireland (guided tours only: Jan–March, Nov & Dec Sat & Sun noon–4pm; April Sat & Sun noon–5pm; May & Oct daily 10am–5pm; June–Sept daily 10am–6pm; last admission 50min before closing; €2.90; Heritage Card; Ⓦwww.heritageireland.ie). It's located on Cherrymount Crescent, just off the Malahide Road; to get there from the centre catch bus #20B or #27B from Eden Quay, or #27 from Talbot Street, to the Malahide Road, or take the DART to Clontarf, which will leave a fifteen-minute walk.

The building was commissioned by **James Caulfield**, the first Earl of Charlemont (1728–99), shortly after returning from eight years on the Grand Tour (during which time he was the first to identify the Mausoleum of Halicarnassus at Bodrum in Turkey, one of the seven wonders of the ancient world). One of the leading intellectual figures of Georgian Dublin, Charlemont was the first president of the Royal Irish Academy and a committed opponent of legislative union, which he did not live to see pass in 1801. Seeking to re-create an Italianate park with a *casino* ("little house" in Italian) as its focus, emphasizing the fine views of Dublin Bay that his estate then enjoyed, Charlemont turned to Sir William Chambers, the architect of Somerset House in London, whom he had met in Rome (Chambers also designed the earl's new townhouse at around the same time, Charlemont House, now the Hugh Lane Gallery on Parnell Square – see p.108). Started in 1757, construction of the Casino lasted nearly twenty years and cost £20,000 (equivalent to about €5 million today), depleting the estate to such a degree that the second Earl was obliged to sell off his father's precious library and collection of art and antiquities.

The Casino's exterior is covered in exquisite and remarkably well-preserved carving in Portland stone, which reflects, notably in the ox skulls symbolizing animal sacrifice, the Enlightenment's preoccupation with pagan antiquity. To maintain the pristine Neoclassical appearance, Chambers disguised chimney pots as urns and used hollow Doric columns at the corners to act as drainpipes (with bronze chains inside to reduce the noise of the falling water). His most remarkable trick, however, was one of scale: from outside, the Casino appears to be a single-storey villa, but once inside you'll find three floors containing a total of sixteen rooms. To heighten the illusion, the main rooms have coffered ceilings, hidden doors and sky-blue domes to make them appear larger than they actually are. The standards of craftsmanship are as remarkable as on the exterior, with ornate plasterwork and beautiful wooden floors inlaid in geometric patterns. Nothing was allowed to mar the guests' views: the entrance doors convert into a window, and a series of tunnels were built under the surrounding land, including one that ran to the main house (now demolished) so that the servants wouldn't blot the landscape. On the top floor is the earl's extravagant state room, with a screen of gilded columns separating a reception area from the bed.

Howth

Clinging to the slopes of a rocky peninsula and overlooking an animated fishing harbour, the village of **Howth** (rhymes with "both"), at the end of the DART line, is a fine place to escape the rigours of the city centre. The windy walk along the harbour's east pier will blow away any Guinness-induced cobwebs and give you the chance to stare out at **Ireland's Eye**, an island seabird sanctuary that shelters a ruined sixth-century monastery and a Martello tower; during the summer, boats from the pier run across to the island when they have enough takers. To the west of the harbour, about ten minutes' walk beyond the DART station, **Howth Castle**, built in 1564 and now the oldest inhabited house in Ireland, is closed to the public, but a barn in the grounds has been turned into the **National Transport Museum** (June–Aug Mon–Fri 10am–5pm, Sat & Sun 2–5pm; Sept–May Sat & Sun 2–5pm; €3; Ⓦwww.nationaltransportmuseum.org), containing rustic tractors, a horse-drawn fire engine and an old Hill of Howth tram.

South along the coast

A ride on a DART train south along the coast, as well as giving access to **Sandycove**'s James Joyce Museum and the charming, historic neighbourhood

The Howth Cliff Walk

The best way to appreciate Howth – if the weather's fine – is to do the **Cliff Walk** around the peninsula, taking in great views south over the city to the Wicklow Mountains and north to the Boyne Valley. The footpath runs for some eight kilometres clockwise from the village round to the west-facing side of the peninsula, followed by a three-kilometre walk by the sea along Strand Road and Greenfield Road to Sutton DART station; allow at least three hours in total. (Bus #31B, serving Sutton and the city centre in one direction, Howth village in the other, runs roughly parallel but well above the path for much of the way, along Carrickbrack Road, so you can bail out of the walk if you feel like it.)

You first head out east along Balscadden Road to the **Nose of Howth**, before the path turns south, crossing the slopes above the cliffs, which are covered in colourful gorse and bell heather in season; for refreshment on this stretch, the area known as **The Summit**, just inland of the path, has a pub and a café. The southeast point is marked by the **Baily Lighthouse**, which until March 1997, was the last manned lighthouse on Ireland's coastline. The path along the south-facing coast of the peninsula is the most spectacular part of the walk, providing close-up views of cliffs, secluded beaches and rocky islands.

of **Dalkey**, is a scenic attraction in itself, displaying the great sweep of Dublin Bay before dramatically skirting Dalkey and Killiney hills and arrowing off towards Bray and Greystones (see p.144).

The James Joyce Museum

The diverting **James Joyce Museum** in Sandycove (March–Oct Mon–Sat 10am–1pm & 2–5pm, Sun 2–6pm; €7) is housed inside an impressive **Martello tower**, one of fifteen such towers erected along the coast between Dublin and Bray in 1804–06 against the threat of invasion by Napoleon. Built with 2.5-metre-thick, granite circular walls and an armoured door four metres off the ground as the only entrance, the towers never fired a shot in anger. Joyce stayed here for just a week, in September 1904, a month before he left the country for Italy with Nora Barnacle. At the time, his host, the writer and wit Oliver St John Gogarty, was renting the tower from the War Office for £8 a year as digs during his medical studies. Joyce immortalized the tower as the setting for the opening chapter of his masterpiece, *Ulysses* – and Gogarty as "stately, plump Buck Mulligan" – and it's now the focus for readings and celebrations every year on June 16, Bloomsday (see box, p.110). To get there, catch the DART to Sandycove & Glasthule station, from which it's a ten-minute walk down Islington Avenue then east along the seafront.

Opened in 1962 by Sylvia Beach, who first published *Ulysses* in Paris in 1922, the museum displays Joyce's guitar, waistcoat and walking stick, as well as one of two official death-masks (the other is in Zurich where he died in 1941). There are also copious letters, photos, and rare and first editions, notably one of *Ulysses* beautifully illustrated by Matisse. On the first floor, Gogarty's living quarters in the former guardroom have been re-created as Joyce described them, and you can climb up to the gun platform on the roof for panoramic views of Dublin Bay.

Dalkey

Around the coast from Sandycove, **Dalkey** (pronounced "Dawky") is a pretty seaside suburb set against the tree-clad slopes of Dalkey Hill. In medieval times, it prospered as a fortified settlement and the main port of Dublin, until the dredging of the River Liffey in the sixteenth century took away its business. Nowadays, with the building of the railway, Dalkey's characterful old houses and villas are much sought after by well-to-do commuters, as well as celebrities seeking privacy.

Just down Railway Road from Dalkey DART station, Castle Street boasts two fortified warehouses from Dalkey's medieval heyday. Goat Castle, across the road from Archibold's Castle, serves as an attractive and well-designed **Heritage Centre** (Mon–Fri 9.30am–5pm, Sat, Sun & public holidays 11am–5pm; €6; Ⓦwww.dalkeycastle.com). The detailed exhibition, with panels written by playwright and local resident Hugh Leonard, covers the town's history, especially its transport systems and literary associations, the latter including an exhibit on Joyce, who set the second chapter of *Ulysses* in Dalkey. The castle interior is impressive in itself, and fine views are to be had from the battlements. From May to October the entry price includes Living History theatre tours (every 30min: Mon–Fri 10am–4.30pm; Sat, Sun & public holidays 11.30am–4.30pm) in which suitably attired actors recount the lives and times of a selection of Dalkey's medieval residents.

The Heritage Centre regularly organizes interesting guided historical tours in the town (May–Aug Mon & Fri 11am, Wed 2pm; €4), and can also arrange guided literary walks of the town during the same period (and for the same price), but only for groups of six or more (call for details). The Centre also

Dalkey and Killiney hills

A walk up adjoining **Dalkey and Killiney hills**, before descending to Killiney DART station, offers panoramic views of the city and its environs, and can all be done in an hour and a half from Dalkey DART station at a moderate pace. From Dalkey, head southeast on Sorrento Road, and then either take the easier route to the right up Knocknacree and Torca roads, or continue along cliffside Vico Road, from where steps and a path ascend steeply. On Torca Road, Shaw fans might want to track down privately owned **Torca Cottage**, where GBS lived for several years as a boy and where he occasionally returned to write in later years. On the way to Dalkey Hill's summit, with its crenellated former telegraph station and fine views over Dublin Bay, you'll pass Dalkey quarry, which provided the granite blocks for the massive piers of Dún Laoghaire harbour below.

From here, follow the partly wooded ridge up to Killiney Hill, where a stone obelisk, built to provide work during the severe winter of 1741, enjoys even more glorious views, north to Howth and south to Killiney Bay and the Wicklow Mountains. From the obelisk, you can quickly descend to the park gate on Killiney Hill Road and refreshment at the cosy *Druid's Chair* pub directly opposite; from there it's a fifteen-minute walk down Victoria Road and Vico Road through the leafy and exclusive borough of Killiney, to the DART station by the beach.

participates in Bloomsday, re-enacting the Dalkey schoolroom scene in *Ulysses* and staging a special Joycean evening of entertainment.

If you want to take a trip out to tiny **Dalkey Island**, some 300 metres offshore, then your best bet is to pay a visit to Coliemore Harbour, down Coliemore Road from the southern end of the town, and negotiate a trip with one of the local fishermen (high season only). Once a Viking base, the island features the ruins of a seventh-century church, a Martello tower and gun battery from Napoleonic times, a herd of semi-wild goats, and views of seals and a variety of seabird species.

Eating

It's fair to say that no one comes to Dublin just for the cuisine, but the last twenty years has seen a remarkable growth in the variety of **places to eat**, from Lebanese to Nepalese. The consequent rise in both standards and expectations looks set to continue – especially in the area of **modern Irish cooking** – though prices across the board can sometimes be off-putting. Many restaurants, however, offer lunchtime or early-bird (typically before 7pm) **set menus** of two or three courses, sometimes for as little as half the cost of their regular evening fare. Some cafés and restaurants, catering to a crowd who have spent their money carousing late into Saturday night, also provide good-value **Sunday brunch**. In addition, plenty of pubs (see p.125) dish up decent, reasonably priced food, with menus based around hearty soups, Irish stew and carvery lunches.

Cafés and quick meals

Dublin has long had a thriving **café** scene, strongly supported by the widespread temperance movement and the churches. Nowadays you're almost as likely to find baklava as traditional brack, accompanied by a speciality tea or a frothy cappuccino. As well as cafés, we've listed below other good spots for a quick, tasty, inexpensive meal; the places reviewed here are open daytimes only, except where noted.

Temple Bar

Café Irie 11 Fownes St Lower. Grungy café offering a tempting variety of cheap sandwiches with copious fillings – "build your own" (one meat, one cheese, one veg) gives the flavour of it. Salads are available if that all sounds too starchy. Daily 9am–9pm.

Curved Street Café Filmbase, Curved St. This friendly spot in the first-floor atrium of a film-making centre sources ingredients from small Irish producers and transforms them into tasty soups and sandwiches; scrummy cakes and coffee, too. Mon & Tues 9.30am–6pm, Wed 9.30am–8.30pm, Thurs 9.30am–7.30pm, Sat noon–5.30pm.

Irish Film Institute 6 Eustace St. Great for an inexpensive lunch or dinner before the show, whether sitting in the cosy bar or the echoing atrium. Simple meals range from burgers and lasagne to fishcakes and goat's cheese salad, with lots of vegetarian options.

Queen of Tarts 4 Cork Hill, Lord Edward St. Small, laid-back patisserie-cum-café, offering bagels, veggie and meaty fry-ups and granola for breakfast; chicken, spinach and cheese tarts, Greek salad and all sorts of sandwiches for lunch; and yummy cakes baked fresh on the premises to keep you going betweentimes.

The rest of the Southside

Avoca Café 11 Suffolk St. The bright, buzzy café on the top floor of this department store (see p.133) dishes up everything from fisherman's pie to potted crabmeat with watercress and potato salad, as well as a tempting array of cakes, all beautifully presented and courteously served.

Cornucopia 19–21 Wicklow St. Small, friendly, buffet café serving an excellent range of vegetarian breakfasts, salads, soups and main courses, as well as cakes, breads, juices and organic wine. Mon–Wed, Fri & Sat 8.30am–8pm, Thurs 8.30am–9pm, Sun noon–7pm.

Dunne and Crescenzi 14 & 16 South Frederick St. A cosy, popular Italian café, with croissants and spot-on coffee, all manner of Italian sandwiches and excellent plates of *antipasti*, as well as salads and daily special main courses. Mon–Sat 8.30am–11pm, Sun 10am–9pm.

Fresh Second floor, Powerscourt Townhouse Centre. A great setting overlooking the glassed-in courtyard, and a marvellous vegetarian and vegan menu: soups, salads, sandwiches, pasta, veggie tarts, curries, pulse dishes and hotpots; various breads, cakes and desserts; and wines, fresh juices and smoothies. Closed Sun.

Govinda's 4 Aungier St. Excellent Hare Krishna-run vegetarian café, serving cheap and filling samosas, salads, pizzas and burgers, as well as daily specials such as pasta and vegetables au gratin. They also offer great juices and lassis, as well as cakes and other desserts. Mon–Sat noon–9pm.

La Maison des Gourmets 15 Castle Market. Chic *salon de thé* above a French patisserie, serving light meals such as smoked salmon and chive cream tartine, delicious cakes and coffee. Closed Sun.

Leo Burdock's 2 Werburgh St. Dublin's most famous fish-and-chipper (takeaway only, but the garden of Christ Church Cathedral is just over the road) is all gleaming surfaces and friendly service. The multi-award-winning menu now stretches to lemon sole goujons, but otherwise there are no surprises. Closed Sun lunchtime.

Nude 21 Suffolk St. Funky canteen-style café with a big open kitchen, serving up wraps, panini, salads, pastas, noodles, soups, juices and smoothies, to eat in or take away; ample choice for vegetarians. Mon–Wed 7.30am–9pm, Thurs & Fri 7.30am–midnight, Sat 8am–midnight, Sun 10am–8pm.

Silk Road Café Chester Beatty Library, Dublin Castle. Stylish and good-value museum café, spilling over into the library's sky-lit atrium. Mostly Middle Eastern food: Lebanese chicken, falafel, spinach and feta filo pie and very good salads, as well as great coffee and titbits such as Turkish delight and baklava. Same hours as museum (see p.99).

Simon's Place Market Arcade, South Great George's St. Funky, unpretentious spot with plain wooden furniture that's popular for its basic soups, salads, filling sandwiches and fine coffee. A good to place to check out what's on in the city, scattered with fliers and posters. Closed Sun.

The Northside

Caffè Cagliostro Bloom Lane. A splendid, tiny Italian café serving arguably the Northside's premier coffees, alongside delicious pastries, with newspapers for perusal.

Cobalt Café and Gallery 16 North Great George's St. A relaxing haven in an area with a dearth of cafés, offering a range of coffees as well as light snacks, all of which can be enjoyed while admiring the original artworks displayed on the walls. Closed Sun.

The Epicurean Food Hall 13–14 Liffey St Lower. You're spoilt for choice here in this food mall, wondering which of the dozen or so eateries (and a bar) to plump for.

The Gresham Hotel 23 O'Connell St Upper. Enjoy afternoon tea in the opulent surroundings of this grand hotel's lobby.

Le Phare 20 Capel St. Absolutely excellent and good-value café, offering breakfasts, soups, wraps and lunch specials, including a wonderfully herb-rich Irish stew. Closed Sun.

Panem 21 Ormond Quay Lower. Petite but perfectly formed, dishing up a worthy range of good-value snacks and savouries, including freshly-made soups, strikingly good focaccia and a variety of pasta dishes. Closed Sun.

Restaurants

The majority of Dublin's **restaurants** are on the south side of the river in the city centre, with a tight concentration in Temple Bar. The places listed below are open daily for lunch and dinner, except where noted; it's generally worth booking ahead if you can, especially in the evenings.

Restaurant **chains** worth mentioning are the reliable, moderately priced *Fitzer's*, which offers daily-changing menus and lots of choice for vegetarians from its branches on Temple Bar Square (☎01/679 0440), at 51 Dawson St (☎01/677 1155) and in the National Gallery (a self-service lunchtime restaurant and a café); *Jaipur*, which serves a wide range of excellent Indian food at 41 South Great George's St (☎01/677 0999; evenings only) and 21 Castle St, Dalkey (☎01/285 0552; closed Mon–Wed lunchtimes); and *Milano*, 19 Temple Bar (☎01/670 3384) and 61 Dawson St (☎01/670 7744), part of the British *Pizza Express* chain, which dishes up superior pizzas at affordable prices.

Temple Bar

Eden Sycamore St/Meeting House Square ☎01/670 5372. Stylish, upmarket but convivial restaurant – with much-coveted tables out on the square in summer – producing excellent modern Irish cuisine with a global twist. Cheaper menus at lunchtime (brunch on Sat & Sun) and in the early evening (Sun–Thurs).

Elephant & Castle 18 Temple Bar. Ever-popular, cosy, pine-furnished diner that opens for breakfast on weekdays and much-sought-after brunches on weekends. Later in the day, the choice stretches from omelettes and salads to more complex main courses such as venison with chestnut purée and wild mushrooms in a gin sauce. No bookings.

Gruel 67 Dame St. Wholesome, inexpensive food from an open kitchen, including "gruel awakening" breakfasts on weekdays. At lunchtime, soups, roast meat rolls, salads and pizza are prepared to eat in or take away. In the evening, it's a very good value restaurant with no frills, no bookings and just one house wine.

Il Baccaro Meeting House Square ☎01/671 4597. Friendly, reasonably priced trattoria, serving up good versions of Italian standards, in an atmospheric cellar. Closed lunchtimes (except Sat).

The Mermaid Café 69–70 Dame St ☎01/670 8236. Chic restaurant with unfussy modern decor, where the emphasis is on helpful service and great global-influenced food. Though expensive, it's more manageable at lunchtime when there are set menus Mon–Sat, and brunch on Sun.

Monty's of Kathmandu 28 Eustace St ☎01/670 4911. Excellent, authentic Nepalese restaurant serving delicious dishes such as spicy chicken *gorkhali*, cooked with yoghurt, chilli, coriander and ginger. Set early-bird (Mon–Thurs) and lunch menus. Closed Sun lunchtime.

The rest of the Southside

Brasserie 66 66 South Great George's St ☎01/400 5878. The epitome of the modern international bistro, with smart-casual decor and unpretentious, well-executed food, using carefully sourced ingredients. Breakfast is served on weekdays, brunch at the weekend.

Café-Bar-Deli 12–13 South Great George's St. A smartly updated former *Bewley's Café*, presenting a reasonably priced and justly popular menu of simple food well done, featuring starters, pastas, salads, pizzas and desserts. There's also a branch in *Bewley's* old flagship café on Grafton St.

Chez Max 1 Palace St ☎01/633 7215. Archetypal French bistro, offering a wide-ranging evening menu of classic dishes, supplemented by specialities from the owner's home region in southwest France. Lunch consists of simpler main courses, including a good-value *plat du jour*, while cold meat and cheese platters are available all day long. Simple French breakfast Mon–Fri, inexpensive early-bird menu Sun–Thurs.

Diep le Shaker 55 Pembroke Lane, off Pembroke St Lower ☎01/661 1829. Dublin's best and most expensive Thai restaurant, whose menu, strong on fish and seafood, offers imaginative takes on thoroughly authentic dishes. Closed Sat lunchtime & Sun.

Ely Wine Bar 22 Ely Place ☎01/676 8986. Popular, congenial and moderately priced wine bar that offers wholesome snacks and meals, using carefully sourced, mostly organic Irish ingredients, to accompany over ninety wines by the glass. Closed Sun.

Fallon and Byrne 11–17 Exchequer St ☎01/472 1000. Foodie heaven in a converted telephone exchange: a smart grocery store on the ground floor; a seductive, Parisian-style brasserie upstairs, offering everything from burgers to oysters and French-influenced dishes such as lamb rump with Puy lentils; and a wine bar and shop in the basement, serving cheaper food, though in much less appealing surroundings.

Havana South Great George's St ☎01/400 5990 (closed Sun lunchtime) & 3 Camden Market, Grantham St ☎01/476 0046 (closed Sun). Congenial, laid-back bar-restaurants where, surrounded by eccentric decor and cool Cuban sounds, you can graze on tasty and cheap tapas such as paella or lentil and chorizo stew.

Imperial 12A Wicklow St ☎01/677 2580. A thumbs-up from loyal Chinese customers, who generally rate it the best restaurant in the city centre. Excellent dim sum (served daily until 5.30pm) is especially popular on Sun.

Juice 73–83 South Great George's St ☎01/475 7856. Stylish, moderately priced vegetarian and vegan restaurant, rustling up dishes such as mushroom Wellington in the evening, and simpler, cheaper alternatives such as tabouleh and scrambled tofu at lunchtime; great-value early-bird menu Mon–Fri.

Le Gueuleton 1 Fade St. A recent instant hit on Dublin's restaurant scene, serving great French bistro food from an open kitchen at reasonable prices, accompanied by good-value French wine. No booking by phone, but if you turn up in person, you can put your name down for a table later in the evening. Closed Sun.

Lord Edward Seafood Restaurant 23 Christchurch Place ☎01/454 2420. Old-fashioned combination of simple, fresh seafood dishes – fish stew a speciality – traditional hospitality from bow-tied waiters, and manageable prices. The congenial bar and lounge of the eponymous pub below also serve decent food (Mon–Fri lunchtimes). Closed Sat lunchtime & Sun.

Patrick Guilbaud *Merrion Hotel*, 21 Merrion St Upper ☎01/676 4192. One of Dublin's finest and most expensive, a classic French restaurant that makes the most of Irish seasonal produce. Formal and showy in the evenings, "Paddy Giblets" loosens his collar just a little at lunchtime, when the €35 set menu (two courses plus coffee and petits fours) represents very good value. Closed Sun & Mon.

Salamanca 1 St Andrew's St ☎01/677 4799. A huge range of good-value tapas, including tasty and substantial paella, enhanced by friendly service and warm, simple decor.

The Steps of Rome 1 Chatham Court, Chatham St ☎01/670 5630. Tiny, basic restaurant, serving very cheap and excellent pizza (also to take away), alongside pasta, salads and a few meat dishes.

Town Bar & Grill 21 Kildare St ☎01/662 4724. Cavernous cellar, decorated simply and elegantly, where the very high standards of cooking – under a strong Italian influence – match the complex menu and extensive wine list. Expensive, but there's a good-value set menu at lunchtimes.

Trocadero 3 St Andrew's St ☎01/677 5545. A welcoming haven, done out with plush booths, signed photos of showbiz visitors and yards of red velvet. Excellent, though predictable, international food, whether à la carte or on the reasonably priced set menus, which include a good-value pre-theatre option (you must vacate the table by 7.45pm). Evenings only, closed Sun.

Uki-yo 7–9 Exchequer St ☎01/633 4071. Chic Korean and Japanese bar-restaurant, with a novel take on the Dublin snug: karaoke boxes out the back for €25 per hour. Out front, graze on appetizers such as tasty prawn and pork dumplings, or tuck into something more substantial, including chicken curry and noodle soup (cheap early-bird menu available). Open till 2.30am Thurs, Fri & Sat.

Wagamama South King St. Basement branch of the well-known, good-value chain, knocking out healthy Japanese meat and vegetarian dishes to punters sharing long bench tables. Best for noodle soups, dumplings and a wide variety of wholesome juices.

The Northside

101 Talbot 100–101 Talbot St ⓣ01/874 5011, ⓦwww.101talbot.com. Imaginative starters, including Vietnamese-style warm squid salad, are but a prelude to the delightful Mediteranean-influenced dishes, such as crispy lamb with Moroccan spices or roast red peppers stuffed with a blend of pistachio nuts and vegetables. It's worth taking advantage of the three-course early-bird menu (€21.50), served until 8pm. Closed Sun, Mon and lunchtimes Tues–Sat.

Chapter One 18–19 Parnell Square North ⓣ01/873 2266, ⓦwww.chapteronerestaurant.com. Housed in the cellars of the Dublin Writers Museum, this recently Michelin-starred culinary gem specializes in French-inspired modern Irish food, using an imaginative blend of herbs, spices and fruit to enhance a variety of fish and meat dishes, plus a selection of taste-bud-titillating desserts. The restaurant offers a pre-theatre special dinner (6–7pm, €35 for three courses). Closed Sat lunch, Sun & Mon.

Govinda's 84 Abbey St Middle. This breezy and inexpensive South Indian vegetarian restaurant has added some culinary variety to the Northside. Till 9pm Mon–Sat; closed Sun.

Halo *Morrison Hotel*, Ormond Quay Lower ⓣ01/887 2421, ⓦwww.morrisonhotel.ie. Briliantly designed modern decor married to faultless cuisine makes *Halo* a gourmet's dream. Starters include seared scallops with polenta or smoked haddock and potato soup; main courses cover fish and meat dishes, such as pan-fried pike fillet or loin of venison. Expect to pay around €50 (plus wine) for a three-course meal.

The suburbs

Caviston's 59 Glasthule Rd, Sandycove ⓣ01/280 9245, ⓦwww.cavistons.com. Near Sandycove and Glasthule DART station, this restaurant works to a basic but hugely successful formula – the day's freshest fish and seafood cooked simply. Booking is essential and there are a few outside tables in summer. 3 lunch sittings: Tues to Fri noon, 1.30pm & 3pm, Sat noon, 1.45pm and 3.15pm.

King Sitric's Fish Restaurant East Pier, Howth ⓣ01/832 5235. Excellent, plush restaurant with panoramic sea views, offering local fish and lobster, and plenty of other delicious seafood and game. Though it's expensive, the set menus at lunchtimes are very good value. Smart bedrooms are available (4) if you really want to push the boat out. Closed Sun.

Pubs and bars

Good puzzle would be cross Dublin without passing a pub

James Joyce, *Ulysses*

Not known for their understatement, Dubliners boast that their city possesses the finest **pubs** in the world. They're probably right too, but with over seven hundred watering holes to choose from, forming the backbone of the capital's social life, there's no harm in checking out their assertion. Along the way, you'll also be able to test out competing claims about the hometown drink, **Guinness**: that it tastes better here is not open to doubt, but locals argue about exactly which pub pours the best drop (is the travel-shy liquid better at *Ryan's*, just across the river from the brewery, than downstream at *Mulligan's*?). In general, the stout is best in the characterful and sociable historic pubs, many of which retain their cut-glass screens, ornate wood-carving and cosy snugs, often with a private hatch to the bar.

In recent years, a plethora of cosmopolitan, youth-oriented **bars** have come onto the scene, the best of which have forged a style and character of their own, be they cavernous microbrewery-pubs, studenty DJ bars or chic designer lounges. Plenty of these bars have **late licences**, as noted in the reviews below, which allow them to stay open until 2.30am or so, usually from Thursday to

Saturday. It's also worth knowing that most of the bars listed under "Traditional music pubs" (see p.129) are great for a drink in their own right. For details of Dublin's highly entertaining pub tours, see p.73; for gay bars, see p.132.

The Southside

4 Dame Lane 4 Dame Lane. Announced by burning braziers, this bar-club probably has the stylistic edge over its bare-brickwork-and-wood rivals. The tunes are good too, encompassing anything from techno to funk, with a DJ every night in the ground-floor bar, Fri & Sat in the upstairs room. Open till 1.30am Mon–Thurs & Sun, 3am Fri & Sat.

Anséo 18 Camden St. Unpretentious venue with plenty of velour banquettes to chill out on, but one of the bars of the moment for its easy-going atmosphere and nightly roster of DJs. Tues is open-mike night for singer-songwriters. The upstairs room hosts jazz on Wed, and more live music is planned.

▲ Palace Bar

Dakota 9 South William St. A stylish conversion, in chocolate and brick, of a fabric warehouse. Table service at the dark leather booths and armchairs and a wide array of food is aimed at pulling in a late-twenties and early-thirties crowd, who duly cram the place at weekends. Thurs till 2am, Fri & Sat till 2.30am.

Davy Byrne's 21 Duke St. After extensive redecoration as a lounge bar, you'll have your work cut out to imagine Davy Byrne's "moral pub" where Bloom takes a break for a gorgonzola sandwich and a glass of Burgundy in *Ulysses*. All the same, it's a good place for a quiet drink and perhaps a plate of oysters or shepherd's pie.

Doheny and Nesbitt 5 Baggot St Lower. Don't be dismayed if the tiny front bar, all dark wood and cut-glass partitions, is packed: there's a spacious back bar where the interior courtyard for smokers is almost as coveted these days as the atmospheric snug.

Grogan's Castle Lounge 15 South William St. Lively, eccentric traditional pub, popular with budding writers and artists, with quiet outdoor tables.

Hogan's 35 South Great George's St. A favourite of the cheery, beery under-thirties – especially hectic during weekend late-opening – this rambling, easy-going bar plays an eclectic range of music. Open till 1am Thurs, 2.30am Fri & Sat.

The Horseshoe Bar *Shelbourne Hotel*, 27 St Stephen's Green. In this renovated luxury hotel, the *Horseshoe*'s deep-red leather banquettes and white marble counter maintain a cosy pub feel. The recent cleaning of the cautionary, satirical prints by Hogarth above the bar has not deterred the city's politicos and journos, who still gather here to drink, swap tall tales and set the world to rights.

The International Bar 23 Wicklow St ⓣ01/677 9250. Old-fashioned pub decorated with stained glass and ornate woodcarving that heaves congenially at weekends. Just about every evening sees some form of entertainment on offer: comedy on Mon (improv) and Wed–Sun, singer-songwriters on Mon and jazz most Tuesdays.

Kehoe's 9 South Anne St. Characterful meeting place, sporting cosy snugs and a low mahogany bar, with an old-fashioned till and drawers, that used to double up as a grocery.

The Long Hall 51 South Great George's St. Old-time classic, sporting ornate plasterwork, mirrors and dark-wood panelling, a suitably long bar, friendly staff and a good pint of Guinness.

Mulligan's 8 Poolbeg St. A little off the beaten track, this large no-nonsense pub pours an excellent pint and remains a favoured watering hole for workers at the nearby *Irish Times*.

The Odeon Old Harcourt St Station, Harcourt St. Palatial and sophisticated bar sporting Art Deco fittings and plenty of outdoor tables under the portico of the old station. One of Dublin's few gastropubs, it's chilled out on Sat & Sun for brunch. Late opening with DJ Thurs (till 1.30am), Fri (2.30am) & Sat (2.30am, cover charge after 10pm).

The Palace Bar 21 Fleet St. Relaxing, sociable Victorian pub famed both for the quality of its pint and for its handsome decor. The overflow bar upstairs hosts sessions of traditional music on Wed, Thurs & Sun.

The Porterhouse 16 Parliament St. Excellent, rambling microbrewery-bar, where for €5 you can sample three different stouts. Live music every night, including traditional sessions on Sun, and good food. Open till 2am Thurs, 2.30am Fri & Sat.

Solas 31 Wexford St. Lively bar offering bright, comfy booths, good DJs nightly, and an appealing outdoor terrace on the first floor. The global-influenced food menu ranges from snacks to salads and hot meals.

South William 52 South William St. New DJ bar that's more informal and lively than its angular, contemporary look might suggest. On top of a wide range of beers and cocktails, it offers the ultimate comfort food, hot pies, with an eclectic choice of fillings. Open Thurs till 1am, Fri & Sat till 3am.

The Stag's Head 1 Dame Court. Pretty Victorian bar, all dark woods and stuffed, tiled and stained-glassed stags, that attracts a hugely varied crowd. Cheap unpretentious pub grub at lunchtime. Closed Sun.

The Northside

Dice Bar 78 Queen St. Low-lit and compact, the *Dice Bar* is an ultra-cool, New York–style joint that remains atmospheric without ever feeling too cramped. DJs play nightly, and there's late opening Fri & Sat until 2.30am.

Enoteca delle Langhe Bloom Lane. A focal part of Dublin's new Italian quarter, the *Enoteca* brings all the flavours of an Umbrian bar to the city, serving up an astonishingly wide range of wines and a small, but still intriguing menu of *antipasti* and other dishes.

The Flowing Tide 9 Abbey St Lower. Long connected with the Abbey Theatre opposite, this pub features tasteful stained-glass windows, a mural celebrating the theatre's history and a horseshoe-shaped bar.

Frank Ryan & Son 5 Queen St. Definitely a place for respite from the city's hurly-burly, this sociable, old-fashioned bar is cosiness incarnate. The friendly staff serve a grand pint of stout.

Hill 16 Gardiner St Middle. Named after Croke Park's most popular stand, the bar is a magnet for GAA devotees, particularly those who follow the fortunes of Dublin's Gaelic football team.

Kavanagh's (aka *The Gravediggers*). Prospect Square, Glasnevin. One of the city's finest old pubs, located just outside the old entrance to Glasnevin Cemetery, where it has consoled mourners (and changed little) since 1833. It's best reached from the present-day entrance by retracing your steps along Finglas Rd and taking the first small lane on the left along the cemetery walls.

The Lotts 9 Liffey St Lower. It's often standing-room-only at this friendly corner bar, which lays claim to being the Northside's smallest. It offers a tasty selection of Mediterranean-inspired meals in its fashionable café-bar next door.

Morrison *Morrison Hotel*, Ormond Quay Lower. Chic and stylishly modern, with good views of the river, this hotel bar is one of the city's mellowest places to pass the time. Don't be deterred by the apparent ultra-hip exterior for inside you'll find a broad mix of locals and guests enjoying their pints or sampling the range of tempting cocktails.

Patrick Conway's 70 Parnell St. Running since 1745 (when it was known as *Doyle's*), *Conway's* is the oldest pub on the Northside. It's also famous since Pádraig Pearse surrendered to the British on the corner outside after the Easter Rising. The pub offers filling bar meals, and *The Boom Boom Room* upstairs hosts a diverse range of live gigs.

Ryan's 28 Parkgate St. The longtime challenger to the reputation of *Mulligan's* (see p.127) for serving the best pint of Guinness in the city, based on its proximity to the brewery just across the river, also dishes up fine seafood in its upstairs restaurant.

Sin É 14–15 Ormond Quay Upper. This candlelit bar appeals to a lively cosmopolitan crowd because of its wide selection of brews and eclectic choice of nightly musical entertainment (sometimes live gigs, but mostly DJs).

Live music

Dublin's **music scene** is thriving but ever-changing, so it's always wise to check listings in the *Event Guide* or *The Ticket* (see p.69), or the fortnightly rock-and-style magazine *Hot Press*. Ticket prices are dependent on the venue's size and the performers' status, usually costing €10–30, although major gigs can be as much as €75. There are also a number of **open-air events** during the summer, commencing in early May with the rocking Heineken Green Energy Festival at Dublin Castle, followed later in the year by one-off gigs by major acts at places such as Croke Park and Marlay Park in Rathfarnham. **Traditional music** is flourishing in the city with a number of pubs offering sessions, usually commencing at around 9.30pm. Listings of these can be found in the monthly *Irish Music* magazine, or ask for advice in Claddagh Records (see p.133).

Live-music venues

The Ambassador Theatre O'Connell St Upper ⓣ0818/719 300, ⓦwww.mcd.ie. An old but well-regarded venue at the very northern end of O'Connell Street, the Ambassador's programme is decidedly eclectic, focusing very much on middle-ranking, left-field indie and rock bands.

The Bleu Note Café 61–63 Capel St ⓣ01/878 3371. The Northside's hippest place to catch live jazz and blues acts, featuring an attractive street-level bar and two music rooms – upstairs is usually free and operates Thurs–Sun, while downstairs sees admission prices for its Fri & Sat night gigs.

Crawdaddy Old Harcourt Street Station, Harcourt St ⓣ01/478 0166, ⓦwww.pod.ie. Named after a famed London blues club, this compact live venue offers an imaginative programme of mainly indie and alternative bands, but occasionally branches out into jazz, reggae and world music.

Eamonn Doran's 3A Crown Alley ⓣ01/679 9114. *Doran's* cemented its reputation as the place to catch both hopeless wannabes and potential contenders a long time ago, and its basement continues to host an eclectic range of bands and singers, plus regular club nights.

The International Bar 23 Wicklow St ☎01/677 9250. Old-fashioned pub decorated with stained glass and ornate woodcarving that heaves congenially at weekends. Upstairs is the lively venue for comedy (Mon, Thurs, Fri & Sat), jazz (Tues), and Lazybird, a club night with live bands on Sun.

J.J. Smyth's 12 Aungier St ☎01/475 2565. The best place on the Southside to catch blues and jazz-fusion bands (to whom Sunday and often Thursday nights are devoted), this pub's intimate upstairs room rocks most nights to the sound of the city's finest 12-bar and "let's try that again in 7/4 time" merchants.

The Mezz 23 Eustace St ☎01/670 7655, ⓦwww.thehubmezz.com. Raucous, grungy bar that lays on a very popular and eclectic nightly roster of live music and DJs. From Tues (sometimes Wed) to Sun you can go on to *The Hub* nightclub downstairs, which usually has a live band – anything from traditional Irish to punk – then a DJ.

Olympia Theatre Dame St ☎01/677 7744, ⓦwww.mcd.ie/venues/?c=olympiatheatre. An old and much-esteemed venue, the Olympia continues to stage a variety of musical events, featuring major Irish names such as Paul Brady and Luka Bloom, as well as international stars. For much of the summer it turns over to the Ragus traditional music and dance show.

The Point *Theatre* East Link Bridge Rd, North Wall Quay ☎0818/719 391, ⓦwww.thepoint.ie. Once a railway depot, the cavernous Point, a mile east of O'Connell Bridge, is Ireland's largest dedicated music venue with a capacity of 7500 (half of this for seated gigs). Unsurprisingly, it hosts major international names with high prices to boot.

Temple Bar Music Centre Curved St ☎01/670 9202, ⓦwww.tbmc.ie. Brash and determinedly modernist, TBMC's booking policy is decidedly left field, focussing mainly on art-house and indie bands. The bar area is often used for free concerts showcasing emerging acts and the place transforms itself into a late club (until 3am) at weekends – with a wide variety of differently themed events.

Tripod Old Harcourt Street Station, Harcourt St ☎01/478 0166, ⓦwww.pod.ie. A combination of live venue (one of the city's largest at 1300 capacity), bar and club, staging an eclectic range of genre-crossing gigs (from Hayseed Dixie to Lee "Scratch" Perry) and regular club nights such as the-often packed Heat (Wed).

Vicar Street 58–59 Thomas St West ☎01/454 5533, ⓦwww.vicarstreet.com. Arguably the city's premier small live music venue, this 300-seater has an estimable programme of live music, comedy and other events, featuring major names.

The Village 26 Wexford St ☎01/475 8555, ⓦwww.thevillagevenue.com. Startlingly successful since its arrival a couple of years back, *Whelan's* bigger sister has double the capacity (around 750) and consequently books bigger names while following its sibling's eclectic booking policy. DJs spin sounds in the hyper-cool bar nightly and *The Village* also operates late clubs (Thurs–Sat 11pm–late) with guests at the turntables.

Voodoo 39 Arran Quay ☎01/873 6013. Much larger than its exterior might suggest, *Voodoo* is the bigger sister to the *Dice Bar* (see p.127) and packs a similarly powerful punch, with nightly gigs showcasing the best of the local indie-band scene.

Whelan's 25 Wexford St ☎01/478 0766, ⓦwww.whelanslive.com. Featuring a popular front bar too, *Whelan's* has recently celebrated fifteen years as one of the city's most successful live venues, thanks to an extensive programme of the old and the new – a blend of traditional music, renowned folk acts, emerging talent and occasional one-off performances by major names.

Traditional-music pubs

The Brazen Head 20 Bridge St Lower ☎01/679 5186. Established in 1189 and laying claim to the title of Ireland's oldest pub, *The Brazen Head*'s many rooms feature all manner of music-related memorabilia on the walls and ramble round a large courtyard. Traditional musicians play every night (as well as Sun 1.30–4.30pm), though the quality of the sessions can be extremely variable.

The Cobblestone 77 King St North ☎01/872 1799. Arguably the best traditional-music venue in Dublin, this dark, cosy, wooden-floored bar is also a fine place to sample the hoppy products of the nearby Dublin Brewery Company. High-quality sessions take place nightly from around 9pm (from 7pm on Thurs), and on Sun afternoons, while the *Back Room* hosts a variety of gigs (see ⓦwww.musiclee.ie/ilistings.php).

Hughes's 19 Chancery St ☎01/872 6540. Tucked away behind The Four Courts, *Hughes's* attracts the cream of the city's traditional musicians to its nightly sessions (from around 10pm until closing time). Fri can draw a large crowd, so arrive early to grab a seat.

O'Donoghue's 15 Merrion Row ⓣ01/676 2807. The centre of the folk and traditional-music revival that began in the late 1950s, forever associated with ground-breaking balladeers The Dubliners. Nightly sessions from about 9pm draw a considerable crowd, partly because the pub is a landmark on the tourist trail.

O'Shea's Merchant 12 Bridge St Lower ⓣ01/679 3797. Opposite the more famous *Brazen Head*, the *Merchant* nurtures the atmosphere of a homely, good-natured country pub in the centre of the city, providing sanctuary for "culchies" from any county, but especially Kerrymen. Traditional sessions are hosted every night in high season from around 10pm, including set dancing on Mon & Wed, and it's a good place to watch a GAA game.

Clubs

It is best to check the latest listings in the *Event Guide*, *Mongrel* or *Connected* (see p.69) or *Hot Press* (see p.128), as Dublin's **club scene** is volatile. Clubs can be found in most areas of the city centre and prices vary considerably, depending on the venue, night of the week and whether a "name" DJ is spinning the turntables – expect to pay anything from €5 to €30.

Gaiety Theatre King St South ⓣ01/677 1717, ⓦwww.gaietytheatre.ie. The *Gaiety* transforms itself each Fri & Sat night from theatre into a three-level hotbed of dance, trance and, possibly, romance, claiming to be the latest-opening club in the city. With four bars, and up to four DJs spinning discs in different rooms, plus a variety of live acts, there's plenty to entice and invigorate.

POD Old Harcourt St Station, Harcourt St ⓣ01/478 0166, ⓦwww.pod.ie. Housed in the station's vaults, *POD* ("Place of Dance") has enjoyed many a makeover during its more than decade-long existence. It's currently sporting black granite walls, overhead amoebic inflatables and rich mandarin booths – all guaranteed to enhance the lighting, whose vibrancy matches the intense rhythms supplied by resident and international guest DJs. Its major draws are the Antics indie-night (Wed), plus Backbeat (Thurs) and Stereotonic (Fri) for hardcore dance fans.

Rí Rá 13 Dame Court ⓣ01/677 4835, ⓦwww.rira.ie. Though nowadays more institution than innovator, there's still plenty to thrill at split-level *Rí-Rá*, especially when the redoubtable Dandelion is unleashing the beat at Monday's longstanding Strictly Handbag – great sounds and a unique atmosphere. Friday night features guest DJs, often including major international names.

Spirit 57 Abbey St Middle ⓣ01/877 9999, ⓦwww.spiritdublin.com. Wed–Sun 10.30pm–5am. One of the city's largest clubbing venues, *Spirit*'s three floors are devoted to a variety of different club nights, including the popular Revelation (Fri) and Carnavale (Sat). Entry prices can be steep at weekends (around €20 for international guest DJs).

The Sugar Club 8 Leeson St Lower ⓣ01/679 7188, ⓦwww.thesugarclub.com. A lush and plush Southside venue, just off St Stephen's Green, *The Sugar Club* hosts a diverse and often left-field variety of entertainment (bands, torch-singers, comedy, cabaret) – some divine, others dreadful – but the atmosphere is always unquestionably on the button.

The Vaults Harbourmaster Place ⓣ01/605 4700, ⓦwww.thevaults.ie. Tucked away under Connolly Station, this spacious cellar bar hosts popular club nights at weekends (Fri & Sat 11pm–3am), with a house and funk focus.

Theatre and cinema

Drama played a pivotal role in Ireland's twentieth-century cultural revival and Dublin's theatres continue to act as a crucible for innovation, alongside staging a range of Irish classics. Highlights include the **Dublin Theatre Festival** (late Sept & early Oct) and the **Dublin Fringe Festival** (mid-Sept). Ticket prices vary, and you should expect to pay €10–20 per ticket for fringe shows, €15–30 for mainstream. Advance bookings can be made at the venues or through Ticketmaster (☎0818/719 300, Ⓦwww.ticketmaster.ie). If you're budget-conscious, it's worth enquiring about low-cost previews and occasional cut-price Monday- and Tuesday-night shows, while students (with ID) and OAPs can sometimes find good concessionary rates.

Mainstream **cinemas** include Cineworld, 17 Parnell St (☎1520/880444, Ⓦwww.cineworld.ie); Savoy, 17 O'Connell St (☎0818/776776, Ⓦwww.savoy.ie); and Screen, Townsend Street (☎01/672 5500, Ⓦwww.screencinema.ie) which often offers more innovative fare. Check the listings guides for details of what's on. For more interesting fare, the Irish Film Institute is the chief venue its outdoor summer screenings in Meeting House Square are also well worth checking out. All cinemas operate a policy of cheap seats daily before 5pm (6.30pm in some cases), during which time tickets cost around €5 – after this they cost €6–10. Student discounts are also often available.

The Abbey Theatre Abbey St Lower ☎01/878 7222, Ⓦwww.abbeytheatre.ie. The National Theatre of Ireland (see also p.106) tends to show international and Irish classics plus new offerings by contemporary playwrights.

Gaiety Theatre South King St ☎01/677 1717, Ⓦwww.gaietytheatre.net. An old-style playhouse with velvet curtains and gilded boxes, The Gaiety hosts everything from opera and Irish classics to musicals, concerts and other family entertainment. Late on Fri & Sat it becomes a nightclub (see opposite).

Gate Theatre 1 Cavendish Row, Parnell Square ☎01/874 4045 or 01/874 6042, Ⓦwww.gate-theatre.ie. Founded in the 1920s in an eighteenth-century building leased from the Rotunda Hospital, the Gate has a reputation for staging adventurous experimental drama as well as established classics in its small, elegant auditorium, and gave an early boost to the acting careers of James Mason and Orson Welles.

Irish Film Institute 6 Eustace St ☎01/679 3477, Ⓦwww.fii.ie. The focus for Irish cineastes provides a broad programme of international and new Irish films, as well being the hub of the Jameson International Film Festival in Feb (Ⓦwww.dubliniff.com) and the Look Out! gay and lesbian film festival in July (Ⓦwww.dlgff/ie). There's an excellent film-related bookshop as well as a good bar and café-restaurant (see p.122).

The Lambert Puppet Theatre 5 Clifton Lane, Monkstown ☎01/280 0974, Ⓦwww.lambertpuppettheatre.com. Dublin's only puppet theatre produces shows of very high quality every Sat & Sun at 3.30pm throughout the year and daily (call for times) in May & June. Great for kids, though there are also performances for adults during the International Puppet Festival in September. To get there, take the DART from Connolly, Tara St or Pearse stations.

New Theatre 43 Essex St East ☎01/670 3361, Ⓦwww.thenewtheatre.com. Recently reopened in rebuilt premises and staging a variety of classic, rarely performed and new drama.

Peacock Theatre 26 Abbey St Lower ☎01/878 7222, Ⓦwww.abbeytheatre.ie. Located in the Abbey's basement, the Peacock stages an innovative programme of new drama in both Irish and English.

Project Arts Centre 39 Essex St East ☎01/679 6622 or 1850 260027, Ⓦwww.project.ie. Renowned for its experimental and often controversial Irish and international theatre, this flagship of the contemporary art scene also hosts dance, film, music and performance art.

Gay and lesbian Dublin

As attitudes to homosexuality in Dublin have become increasingly liberal over the last decade, so the capital's **gay** community has grown in confidence, and a small but vibrant scene has established a niche in the city's social life. The latest **information** on gay events and venues in Dublin is provided by *Outhouse*, 105 Capel St (☎01/873 4932, Ⓦwww.outhouse.ie), a gay and lesbian resource centre with a café (Mon–Fri 1.30–5.30pm, Sat 1–5pm, also Tues 6.30–9.30pm, Thurs 7–10pm women only & Fri 7–10pm men only) and a small library, or from Gay Switchboard (Mon–Fri 7.30–9.30pm, Sat 3.30–6pm; ☎01/872 1055, www.gayswitchboard.ie). The free magazine *GCN* (*Gay Community News*) has detailed listings of upcoming events and can be found in the gay-friendly Books Upstairs, College Green, or in clubs and bars. Useful websites include www.queerid.com for events and news and www.gaire.com for information, message boards and online chat. There are few **accommodation** options specifically aimed at gay and lesbian travellers but *Frankie's* (see p.77) is the pick of them.

Dragon 64 South Great George's St. Expansive and extravagant gay bar in a former bank, decorated with botanical prints, Buddhas and dragons. As well as a dance floor, there are cosy booths and a large, first-floor courtyard to choose from. Popular drag show on Mon, DJs Thurs–Sat. Open till 2.30am Mon & Thurs–Sat.

The Front Lounge 33 Parliament St. A sophisticated decor of polished wood floors and comfy red armchairs plus contemporary art on the walls attracts a mixed crowd, but *The Front Lounge* has been a big hit with gay Dubliners, not least for its range of entertainment, including karaoke on Tues, cabaret on Wed and DJs at the weekend. Open till 2.30am Fri & Sat, 1am Sun.

The George 89 South Great George's St. Ireland's longest-established gay bar still draws huge crowds at weekends. There are two distinct sections: a lushly decorated main venue on two floors, and a quieter, more traditional pub to the right. Entertainment includes cabaret, quiz nights, DJs and Sunday-night bingo with drag queen, Shirley Temple-Bar. Open till 2.30am Wed–Sun.

Shopping

The Southside is the most fruitful hunting ground for shoppers, especially fashionistas: you can pick up Irish and global designer clothes on and around **Grafton Street**, notably at the major department store, Brown Thomas, and in the **Powerscourt Townhouse Centre**, and there are more alternative boutiques in the **Market Arcade** and **Temple Bar**. Also south of the river, you'll find an attractive and eclectic range of Irish artisan products gathered from around the country, from cheeses and whiskey through Aran sweaters to jewellery and ceramics. Despite a recent revamp, Dublin's most extensive shopping boulevard, **O'Connell Street**, is likely to hold little of interest for the visiting consumer, though the raucous Moore Street market, off Henry Street, is always entertaining. The city boasts some excellent book and CD shops too, the best of them specializing in Irish literature and music. The majority of shops in Dublin are open Monday to Saturday only; we've noted below those that also open on Sunday.

Arts, crafts and jewellery

Barry Doyle Jewellers Upstairs, 30 Market Arcade, South Great George's St. Stylish contemporary designs including many sophisticated silver necklaces, in all price ranges.

The Bridge Art Gallery 6 Ormond Quay Upper 01/872 9702. All manner of contemporary arts and crafts are on sale, ranging from ceramics and sculpture to paintings and prints, often at reasonable prices. The gallery at the rear also hosts exhibitions of innovative work.

Kilkenny 6 Nassau St. A varied collection of fine Irish crafts: Newbridge silver cutlery and jewellery; John Rocha's elegant collection for Waterford Crystal; Jerpoint glassware; and extensive ranges of ceramics and of women's clothes and accessories by contemporary designers. Open Sun.

Louis Mulcahy 46 Dawson St. Beautiful household objects, including vases, lights and crockery, by one of Ireland's most famous potters, plus a small selection of woollen items.

Books

Cathach Books 10 Duke St. The place to come for first editions by Irish writers, as well as rare Irish maps and prints of literary interest.

Chapters Bookstore Ivy Exchange, Parnell St. Claiming to be Dublin's largest bookshop, its ground floor features a massive range of fiction and fact, including impressive sections on Irish literature and history. Upstairs is devoted to the secondhand section which also includes bargain-priced CDs and DVDs. Open Sun.

Connolly Books 43 Essex St East, Temple Bar. Vibrant socialist bookshop that covers labour and Irish history, philosophy, politics, biography, as well as stocking left-wing newspapers, pamphlets and magazines. Diverse events, meetings and talks are held here.

Hodges Figgis 56–58 Dawson St. A Dublin institution since the eighteenth century, behind an ornate, Dutch-style facade. A huge range of books on and from Ireland are on the ground floor, with book bargains in the basement. Open Sun.

The Winding Stair 40 Ormond Quay Lower. This bookshop is chock-full of secondhand titles, and is especially good on Irish literature and biography.

Clothes

Cleo 18 Kildare St. Small shop specializing in traditional Irish designs and natural fibres, including hand-knit sweaters, linen shirts and woollen coats, scarves and other accessories.

Costume corner of Drury St & Castle Market. Stylish, upmarket boutique, selling everything from jumpers and coats to evening dresses, by less familiar international designers and on its own label.

Design Centre Top floor, Powerscourt Townhouse Centre. An extensive showcase for Irish designers of women's fashion, such as Louise Kennedy and John Rocha, as well as diverse international names.

Department stores and markets

Avoca 11 Suffolk St. Highly successful, small Irish department store, stocking its own clothing ranges for women and children, jewellery, beautiful rugs and throws woven at the original mill in Avoca, Co. Wicklow, plus toys, chic houseware and deli goods. Open Sun.

Blackrock Market 19A Main St, Blackrock. Hugely varied and popular weekend market, close to the DART station of this southern suburb. Antiques and bric-a-brac, books and CDs, crafts, jewellery, shoes and clothes. Sat 11am–5.30pm, Sun noon–5.30pm.

Brown Thomas 88–95 Grafton St. The city's flagship department store is sophisticated and pricey, featuring a long roll-call of Irish and international designer labels, and complemented by its trendier younger sibling, BT2, opposite. Open Sun.

Cow's Lane Market Off Essex St West. On a pedestrianized alley in Temple Bar stalls concentrate on contemporary women's clothes, bags and jewellery, generally sold by the designers themselves. Sat 10am–5.30pm, closed Jan & Feb.

The Market Arcade Between South Great George's St and Drury St. Laid-back indoor market with an alternative edge to it, offering secondhand books and records, upmarket and street clothing, jewellery and speciality foods. Some shops open Sun.

Moore St Market Moore St. This lively street market is a long-standing Dublin institution and much reflects the city's changing ethnicity. The traditional butchers, fishmongers and greengrocers are still present, though you're bound to see price tags in Cantonese too, and there are also a number of Afro-Caribbean stalls and shops offering a range of produce.

Food and drink

Celtic Whiskey Shop 27–28 Dawson St ⓦwww.celticwhiskeyshop.com. Probably the best selection of Irish whiskeys anywhere, including rare examples from distilleries that have now closed down. The well-informed staff always have bottles open to taste and will ship around the world. Open Sun.

Sheridan's Cheesemongers 11 South Anne St. Fantastic, pungent array of cheeses, mostly by Irish artisan producers, plus cold meats and other deli goods, sold by knowledgeable staff.

Temple Bar Food Market Meeting House Square. A magnet for Dublin's foodies, but also one of your best bets to grab Sat lunch, with stalls selling tapas, Mexican food, burgers, breads, cakes, a huge variety of cheeses, and a West Clare oyster bar. Sat 10am–5pm.

Music

Big Brother Records 4 Crow St, Temple Bar. Basement trove of vinyl and CDs, focusing on hip-hop, funk, soul, electronica and deep house; check out the noticeboard for the city's newest club nights.

Claddagh Records 2 Cecilia St, Temple Bar ⓦwww.claddaghrecords.com. Unquestionably the finest traditional-music emporium in Dublin, with helpful and knowledgeable staff, Claddagh also stocks contemporary Irish music, Scottish and English folk, world music, country and blues.

Freebird Records Downstairs, 1 Eden Quay. Crams an astonishing range of new and secondhand CDs into its racks covering numerous genres with an extensive section on Irish bands and singers.

Road Records 16B Fade St. Tucked away off South Great George's St, Road is the ultimate indie, alternative, electronica and alternative country specialist, stocking vinyl and CDs. Open Sun afternoon.

Walton's 69 South Great George's St. Dublin's leading music shop sells Irish traditional instruments, as well as teaching aids, sheet music and recordings. The attached music school (☎01/478 1884, Ⓦwww.newschool.ie) offers two-hour crash courses (minimum 5 students) for absolute beginners in the tin whistle and the *bodhrán*.

Listings

Airlines Aer Arann ☎01/844 7700 or 0818 210210, Ⓦwww.aerarann.ie; Aer Lingus ☎01/705 2222, Ⓦwww.aerlingus.com; Air France ☎01/605 0383, Ⓦwww.airfrance.com; BMI ☎01/407 3036, www.flybmi.com; British Airways ☎1890 626747, Ⓦwww.british-airways.com; Continental ☎1890 925252, Ⓦwww.continental.com; Delta ☎01/679 6756, Ⓦwww.delta.com; Iberia ☎01/407 3017, Ⓦwww.iberia.com; Lufthansa ☎01/844 5544, Ⓦwww.lufthansa.com; Qantas ☎01/407 3278, Ⓦwww.qantas.com.au; Ryanair ☎01/812 1327, Ⓦwww.ryanair.com; Virgin ☎01/435 0055, Ⓦwww.virgin.com.

Bicycle rental Cycle Ways, 185–186 Parnell St ☎01/873/4748, Ⓦwww.cycleways.com.

Car rental Argus at the airport and Dublin Tourism Centre, Suffolk St ☎01/499 9624, Ⓦwww.argusrentals.com; Atlas at the airport ☎01/864 4859, Ⓦwww.atlascarhire.com); Avis at the airport and 35–39 Old Kilmainham Rd ☎01/605 7500), Ⓦwww.avis.com; County at the airport (☎01/854 5689) and Dublin Tourism Centre, 14 O'Connell St Upper ☎01/874 6084, Ⓦwww.countycar.ie; Dan Dooley at the airport (☎01/844 5156) and 42 Westland Row (☎01/677 2723), Ⓦwww.dan-dooley.ie; Hertz at the airport (☎01/844 5466) and 151 South Circular Rd (☎01/709 3060), Ⓦwww.hertz.co.uk; Irish Car Rentals at the airport (☎01/844 4199, Ⓦwww.irishcarrentals.com).

Crime Dublin suffers from street crime, so watch your belongings in crowded or popular areas and in pubs, cafés and restaurants. Be particularly alert when withdrawing cash from ATMs, both for bogus card-reader attachments and for theft. If driving, do not leave anything valuable visible in the car or on a roof rack, and use secure car parks. The Irish Tourist Assistance Service (☎01/478 5295, Ⓦwww.itas.ie) offers support to tourist victims of crime.

Dentists For dental emergencies contact the Dublin Dental School and Hospital, Lincoln Place ☎01/812 7200, Ⓦwww.tcd.ie/dental_school.

Embassies Australia, 7th floor, Fitzwilton House, Wilton Terrace ☎01/664 5300; Canada, 65 St Stephen's Green ☎01/417 4100; South Africa, Alexandra House, Earlsfort Centre, Earlsfort Terrace ☎01/661 5553; UK, 29 Merrion Rd ☎205 3700; USA, 42 Elgin Rd ☎01/668 8777.

Emergencies Dial ☎112 or 999 for emergency medical assistance, fire services or the police.

Exchange Bureaux de change include Thomas Cook, 118 Grafton St (Mon–Sat 9am–5.30pm, Thurs until 8pm), and the Dublin Tourism Centre, Suffolk St (Mon–Sat 9am–5pm). Many banks also provide exchange facilities.

Ferry companies Irish Ferries ☎0818 300400, Ⓦwww.irishferries.com; Norfolkline ☎01/819 2999, Ⓦwww.norfolkline-ferries.co.uk; P & O ☎01/407 3434, Ⓦwww.poirishsea.com; Stena Line ☎01/204 7799, Ⓦwww.stenaline.ie.

Gaelic football and hurling Most of the season's major games are played at Croke Park (see p.117; ☎01/836 3222, Ⓦwww.gaa.ie). In football, the All-Ireland Final occurs on the third or fourth Sun in Sept and has been won by Dublin on 22 occasions (a record beaten only by Kerry). The Dubs have a poor record at hurling, so the crowd at the All-Ireland Final on the first or second Sun in Sept mainly consists of out-of-towners. You'll be hard pushed to get tickets for either of the finals, but you're quite likely to get in for a semi-final at "Croker" – expect to pay around €30 to stand, and sing, on the famous Hill 16, €45 to sit in the stands and less for earlier rounds.

Helplines Rape Crisis Centre ☎1800 778888; Samaritans ☎1850 609090.

Horse racing Dublin's nearest large racecourse is Leopardstown (☎01/289 0500, Ⓦwww.leopardstown.com), in the southern suburb of Foxrock (LUAS to Sandyford station then a 15min walk). Races are held at weekends at various points of the year and on Wed evenings during June and July, but the main events are the four-day Christmas Festival starting on St Stephen's Day (Dec 26), and the Hennessy Cognac Gold Cup in Feb. The Irish Grand National is held on Easter Mon at Fairyhouse (☎01/825 6167, Ⓦwww.fairyhouseracecourse.ie) in Ratoath, 24km northwest of Dublin, followed in April by the Irish National Hunt Festival at Punchestown (see box, p.161), 40km southwest of Dublin. Flat-racing classics are held at the Curragh, nearly 50km southwest of the capital – see box, p.161. Bus Éireann lays on race-day transport to Fairyhouse

Hospitals Those with accident and emergency departments include: Beaumont Hospital, Beaumont Rd ⓣ01/809 3000; Mater Misericordiae, Eccles St ⓣ01/803 2000; St James's, James St ⓣ01/410 3000; and St Vincent's, Elm Park ⓣ01/269 4533. In emergencies dial ⓣ999 or 112 for an ambulance.
Internet cafés Central Cyber Café, 6 Grafton St; Global Internet Café, 8 O'Connell St Lower; Internet Exchange, 3 Cecilia St, Temple Bar; and Oz Cyber Café, 39 Abbey St Upper.
Laundries Most launderettes are open Mon–Sat 8am–8pm, though central ones offer service washes only. These include All American, Wicklow Court, South Great George's St (ⓣ01/677 2779), and The Wash House, 12 Townsend St (ⓣ01/670 6530). Dry-cleaners include Excel, Moira House, Trinity St (ⓣ01/677 6878), and Grafton, 32 William St South (ⓣ01/679 4309).
Left luggage There are lockers at Busáras and at Connolly and Heuston railway stations.
Lost property Dublin Bus ⓣ01/703 1321; Bus Éireann ⓣ01/836 6111; Connolly Station ⓣ01/703 2362; Heuston Station ⓣ01/703 2102; airport ⓣ01/814 5555.
Pharmacies Branches of Hickey's at 55 O'Connell St Lower (open daily until 10pm) ⓣ01/873 0427 and 17 Westmoreland St ⓣ01/677 8440.
Police The main police station (Garda Síochána) is on Harcourt Terrace (ⓣ01/666 9500).
Post offices General Post Office, O'Connell St Lower (Mon–Sat 8am–8pm; ⓣ01/705 7000) or on St Andrew's St (by the Suffolk St Tourism Centre), Ormond Quay Upper or Clare St. For mail enquiries call ⓣ1850 575589. Many newsagents sell postage stamps.

Travel details

Services listed are for Mon–Sat; extra services may run on Mon and/or Fri, but fewer on Sun.

Trains

Dublin Connolly to: Belfast (8 Mon–Sat, 5 Sun; 2hr 10min); Boyle (5–6 Mon–Sat, 4 Sun; 2hr 30min); Carrick-on-Shannon (5–6 Mon–Sat, 4 Sun; 2hr 15min); Drogheda (29–32 Mon–Sat, 14 Sun; 30min–1hr); Dundalk (13–17 Mon–Sat, 8 Sun; 50min–1hr 20min); Enniscorthy (3 daily; 2hr–2hr 15min); Mullingar (6–10 daily; 1hr 10min); Newry (8 Mon–Sat, 5 Sun; 1hr 15min); Rosslare Europort (3 daily; 3hr); Sligo (5–6 Mon–Sat, 4 Sun; 3hr 10min); Wexford (3 daily; 2hr 35min); Wicklow (4–5 daily; 50min–1hr 10min).
Dublin Heuston to: Athlone (11 daily; 1hr 35min); Castlebar (3 daily; 3hr 10min–3hr 20min); Cork (hourly; 2hr 50min); Galway (7 daily; 2hr 20min–2hr 40min); Kildare (20–30 daily; 40min); Kilkenny (6 daily; 1hr 45min); Killarney (8 daily, most with a change at Mallow; 3hr 30min); Limerick (15 daily, some with a change at Limerick Junction; 2hr 15min–2hr 25min); Tralee (8 daily, most with a change at Mallow; 4hr 5min); Waterford (6 daily; 2hr 35min); Westport (3 daily; 3hr 40min).

Buses

Dublin Busáras to: Athlone (hourly; 2hr 15min); Belfast (20 daily; 2hr 30–2hr 55min); Cahir (6 daily; 3hr 5min); Carrick-on-Shannon (6–7 daily; 2hr 30min–3hr); Carrick-on-Suir (5–6 daily; 3hr 10min); Cashel (6 daily; 2hr 50min); Cavan (20–22 daily; 1hr 40min–2hr); Clonmel (5–7 daily; 3hr 30min); Cork (6 daily; 4hr 25min); Derry (9 daily; 4hr); Donegal town (6–7 daily; 3hr 30min–4hr 5min); Drogheda (36 daily; 1hr 15min); Enniscorthy (11–13 daily; 2hr 20min); Enniskillen (6–7 daily; 2hr 20min–3hr); Galway (hourly; 3hr 30min); Kildare (at least hourly; 1hr–1hr 30min); Kilkenny (6 daily; 2hr 10min–2hr 30min); Killarney (6 daily, change at Limerick; 6hr 10min); Limerick (hourly; 3hr 40min); Letterkenny (9–10 daily; 4hr); Monaghan (18–19 daily; 1hr 55min); Newry (21 daily; 1hr 40min); Omagh (9 daily; 2hr 55min); Rosslare Europort (13 daily; 3hr 20min); Sligo (5–6 daily; 3hr 30min–4hr); Tralee (7 daily, change at Limerick; 6hr 10min); Waterford (10 daily; 3hr); Westport (3 daily; 5hr–5hr 30min); Wexford (13 daily; 2hr 50min); Wicklow (7–11 daily; 1hr–1hr 30min).

For details of private bus services connecting Dublin to other parts of Ireland, refer to the "Travel details" sections of the relevant chapter.

2

Around Dublin: Wicklow, Kildare and Meath

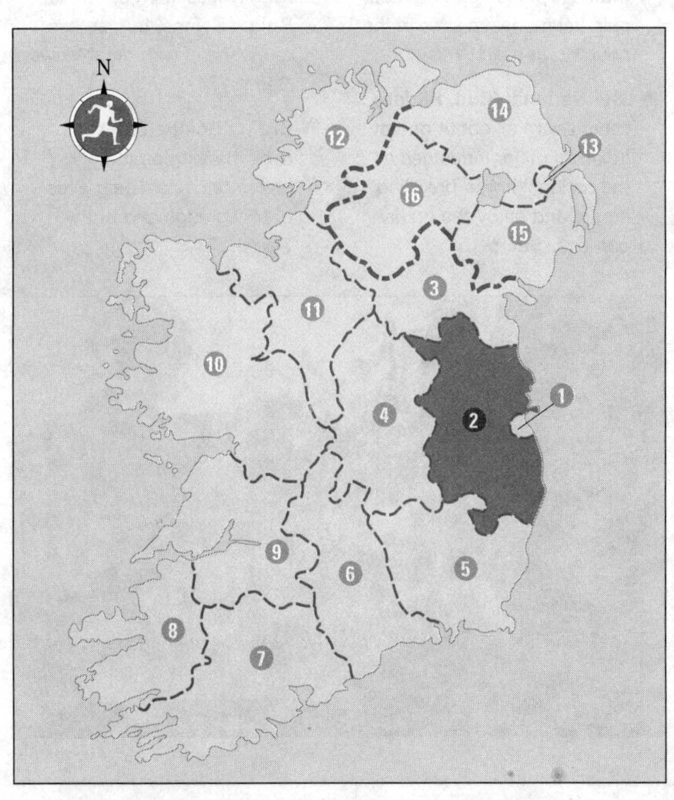

CHAPTER 2

Highlights

* **Powerscourt** Beautiful ornamental gardens and the highest waterfall in Ireland. See p.148
* **Walking in the Wicklow Mountains** Wild and desolate terrain, traversed by the Wicklow Way, within easy reach of Dublin. See p.148
* **Glendalough** Hidden deep in this remote valley lies one of the best-preserved and most spiritual monastic sites in the country. See p.151
* **The National Stud, Kildare town** Learn all about one of Ireland's major industries at the national horse-breeding centre and enjoy the quirky gardens. See p.159
* **Castletown** Just west of Dublin, a Palladian mansion of unrestrained extravagance. See p.164
* **Trim** A historic town boasting the largest Anglo-Norman castle in Ireland and other fine medieval remains. See p.167
* **Loughcrew Cairns** These Neolithic mounds are slightly less impressive than Brú na Bóinne, but far less touristy and with great views. See p.174
* **Brú na Bóinne** Don't miss the extraordinary prehistoric passage graves of Newgrange and Knowth. See p.177

▲Powerscourt

2

Around Dublin: Wicklow, Kildare and Meath

The modern counties of **Wicklow, Kildare** and **Meath** equate roughly – Wicklow's wild mountains were always something of a no-man's-land – with the **Pale**, the fortified area around Dublin to which the English colonists retreated after 1300. The colonists coined the expression "beyond the pale" and implanted the language, customs and government of lowland England in these "obedient shires", leaving today's visitors a rich architectural legacy of castles, abbeys and, from a later period, stately homes. Wicklow, Kildare and Meath are much sought after by modern-day settlers, too: unable to afford Dublin's astronomical property prices, thousands of the capital's workers have recently set up home in the hinterland, making these counties the fastest-growing in the Republic in terms of population.

This chapter sweeps clockwise, starting from the Wicklow coast south of Dublin and pulling up just short of Drogheda in County Louth to the north. If you have your own transport, this would make a very satisfying loop around the capital through diverse terrains, from the expansive, sandy beaches and spectacular granite mountains of County Wicklow, through the grassy, horse-rearing heath of the Curragh and the Bog of Allen in Kildare, to the lush, undulating farmland of Meath. The **highlights** detailed opposite would form a sound basic itinerary. If you have more time to spare, in County Wicklow, add in Parnell's home **Avondale House**, designed by James Wyatt and surrounded by forested parkland, and the Neoclassical marvels of **Russborough**; in County Kildare, the quirky, carefully restored **Larchill Arcadian Gardens**; and the atmospheric seat of the Celtic High Kings, the **Hill of Tara**, in Meath.

It wouldn't be possible to cover this same arc by **public transport**, which tends to run radially in and out of Dublin. Nearly all of the places described in this chapter, however, are accessible on a day-trip from the capital by bus or train, with organized **tours** also available in many cases (see box, p.142). A welcome effect of these counties' growing popularity with commuters has been an increase in the frequency of services between the capital and outlying towns

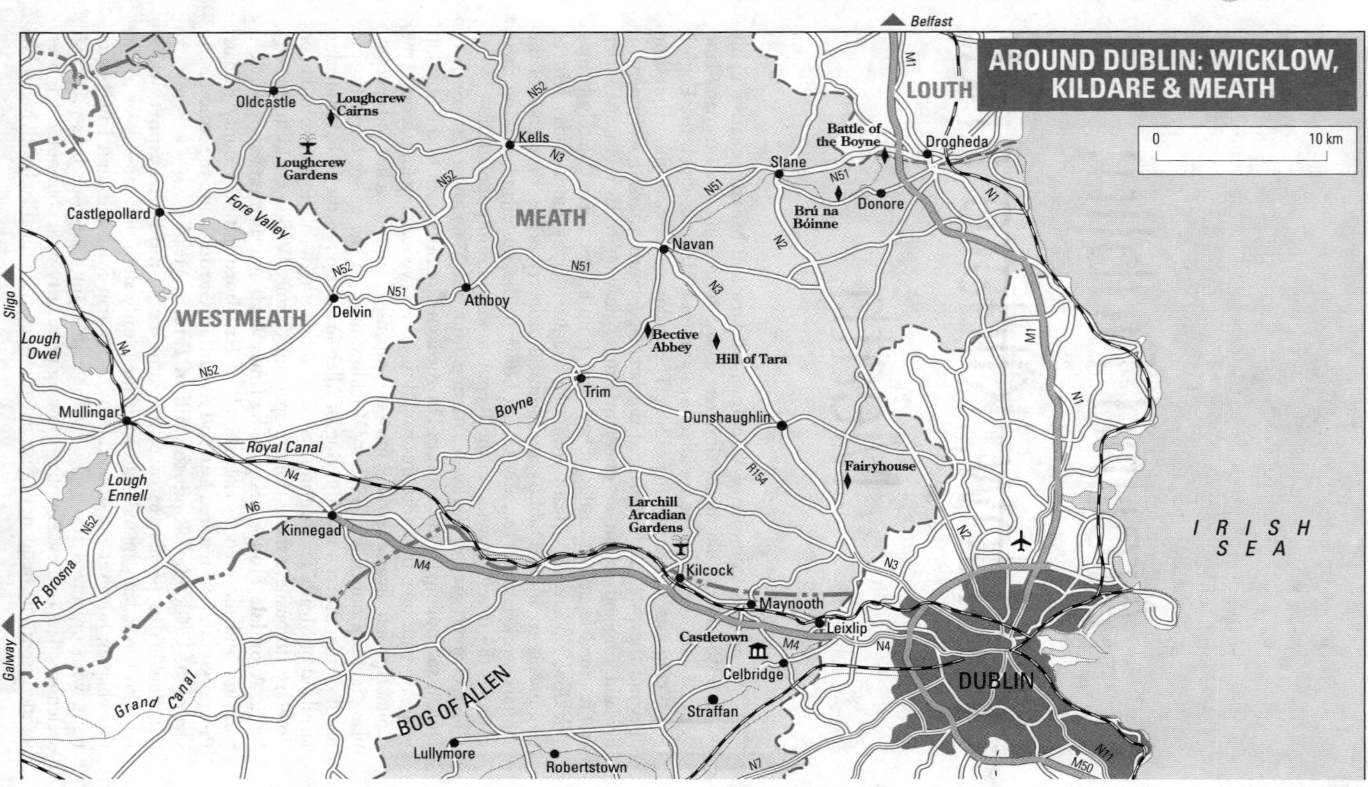
AROUND DUBLIN: WICKLOW, KILDARE & MEATH
0
10 km
Belfast
Sligo
Galway
LOUTH
MEATH
WESTMEATH
IRISH SEA
Drogheda
Battle of the Boyne
Slane
Donore
Brú na Bóinne
Oldcastle
Loughcrew Cairns
Loughcrew Gardens
Kells
Castlepollard
Fore Valley
Navan
Athboy
Delvin
Bective Abbey
Hill of Tara
Trim
Boyne
Dunshaughlin
Mullingar
Lough Owel
Lough Ennell
Royal Canal
Fairyhouse
Kinnegad
Larchill Arcadian Gardens
Kilcock
Maynooth
Leixlip
Castletown
Celbridge
Straffan
DUBLIN
R. Brosna
Grand Canal
BOG OF ALLEN
Lullymore
Robertstown
M1
N1
N2
N3
N4
N6
N7
N11
N51
N52
M4
M50
R154

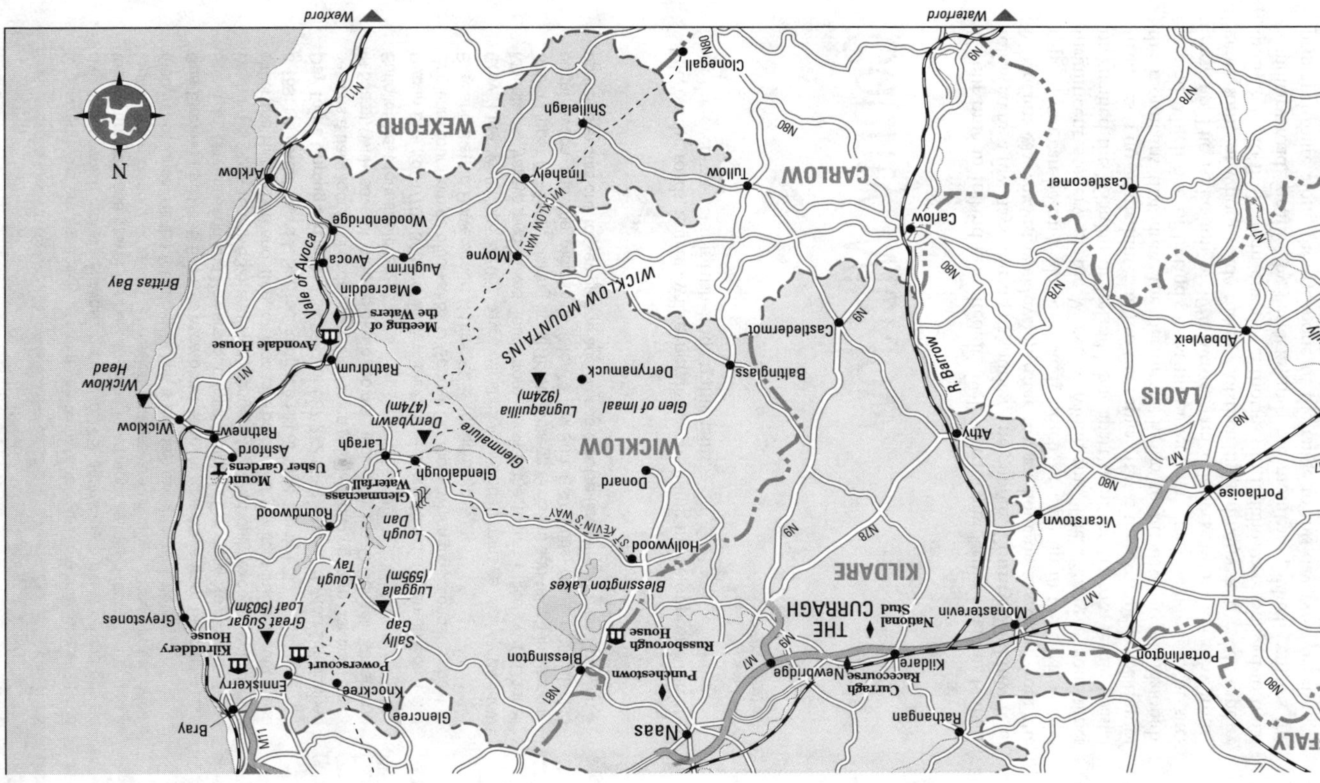
N
Bray
Kilruddery House
Greystones
Wicklow
Wicklow Head
Brittas Bay
M11
Enniskerry
Great Sugar Loaf (503m)
Mount Usher Gardens
Ashford
Rathnew
N11
Avondale House
Arklow
Powerscourt
Roundwood
Lough Tay
Knockree
Glencree
Sally Gap
Luggala (595m)
Lough Dan
Glenmacnass Waterfall
Laragh
Rathdrum
Vale of Avoca
Avoca
Woodenbridge
Wexford
Glendalough
Derrybawn (474m)
Meeting of the Waters
Macreddin
Aughrim
Glenmalure
WEXFORD
Blessington
N81
Blessington Lakes
Lugnaquillia (924m)
WICKLOW MOUNTAINS
Moyne
WICKLOW WAY
Tinahely
Shillelagh
Naas
Punchestown
Russborough House
Hollywood
ST KEVIN'S WAY
Donard
WICKLOW
Glen of Imaal
Derrynamuck
Clonegall
N80
M7
Newbridge
N9
THE CURRAGH
Baltinglass
Castledermot
Tullow
CARLOW
Curragh Racecourse
National Stud
KILDARE
N78
Rathangan
Kildare
Monasterevin
Athy
R. Barrow
Carlow
Waterford
Vicarstown
Castlecomer
Portarlington
LAOIS
Abbeyleix
N77
Portlaoise
N8
N7
OFFALY
R. Gully
Limerick
Cork

Day-tours from Dublin

Organized tours are especially useful if you want to take in more than one sight in a day; those which include Newgrange (see p.178) guarantee a place on the guided tour of the passage grave. It's best to book in advance, either directly or through a tourist office or your hotel. All admission charges are usually included in the price, though not lunch. All the tours below last a full day, except where noted.

Bus Éireann (☎01/836 6111, Ⓦwww.buseireann.ie) runs tours from Busáras, Store Street, to: Glendalough and Powerscourt (mid-March to Oct daily; Nov to mid-March Wed, Fri & Sun; 10am; €32) and Newgrange (May–Sept daily except Fri, including either the Hill of Tara and Trim, or Monasterboice and Mellifont in Co. Louth – see p.189; Nov–April Thurs & Sat, including the Hill of Tara; 10am; €32).

Day Tours Unplugged (☎01/834 0941 or 087 272 0764, Ⓦwww.daytoursunplugged.ie) runs a daily tour to Glendalough and Avoca (€26), departing from Gardiner Street (8.50am), with several other pick-up points, including the O'Connell Street and Suffolk Street tourist offices.

Dublin Bus (☎01/703 3028, Ⓦwww.dublinbus.ie) operates a daily "South Coast and Gardens" tour from its office at 59 O'Connell St Upper, which runs along the coast to Bray and then to Powerscourt (11am; €25; 4hr 30min).

Gray Line (☎01/605 7705, Ⓦwww.irishcitytours.com) runs a daily "Wicklow Mountains, Valleys and Lakes Tour" from outside the tourist office on O'Connell Street Upper (9.45am), picking up at Trinity College (9.55am) and taking in Glendalough, Avoca and the mountains (Mon & Fri–Sun €30, Tues–Thurs €25). It also operates excursions to Newgrange and Monasterboice (Easter–Oct Mon, Tues, Fri &

while, on the roads, tourists will generally be travelling in the opposite direction from the ever-worsening rush-hour traffic jams.

County Wicklow

If your time in Ireland is limited, it's well worth considering a stay in Dublin, followed by a few days touring its southern neighbour, **County Wicklow** (Cill Mhantáin; Ⓦwww.visitwicklow.ie). After just an hour or so's drive from the capital, you can be on a glorious, sandy beach, or high up in the fresh air and magnificent scenery of the Wicklow Mountains. The county is sometimes nicknamed the "Garden of Ireland", but apart from the narrow, fertile coastal strip, this is no gentle hinterland to the capital. It was the extreme desolation of the mountains that drew the hermit St Kevin to his cave at Glendalough, around which one of Ireland's most prominent and charismatic monastic sites grew up. The Rebellion of 1798 was sustained longest by its Wicklow insurgents, some of whom made the best of their upland fastness to evade capture until 1803. To flush them out, the authorities in Dublin were obliged to build a military road, fortified by barracks, into the mountains, which remains the principal route along the backbone of the range to this day. Not surprisingly,

Sat 10am; €32) and to Kildare's National Stud (late April–Oct Wed & Thurs 10am; €39), from the Suffolk Street tourist office; and a "Grand Wicklow Tour", including Glendalough, Avoca and Powerscourt (mid-March to mid-Nov Sun; €38), from outside the tourist office on O'Connell Street Upper (10am), picking up at Trinity College (10.10am).

Mary Gibbons Tours (ⓣ01/283 9973, ⓦwww.newgrangetours.com) takes in Newgrange, the Hill of Tara (seat of the Celtic High Kings of Ireland) and the Boyne Valley (Mon–Sat; €35), picking up at *Pizza Hut* beside the Suffolk Street tourist office at 10.15am, as well as several leading Dublin hotels.

Over the Top Tours (ⓣ1800 424252 or 01/860 0404, ⓦwww.overthetoptours.com) runs minibus trips to Glendalough and the Wicklow Mountains (€26) leaving from outside the *Gresham Hotel*, O'Connell Street Upper, at 9.20am, calling at the Suffolk Street tourist office at 9.45am; and to the Hill of Tara, Slane, Mellifont and Monasterboice from the Suffolk Street tourist office (Mon–Sat 9am, Sun 9.30am; €28).

Railtours (ⓣ01/856 0045, ⓦwww.railtoursireland.com) operates combined rail and coach tours, including the "Wicklow Mountaineer" (Mon–Sat 11.35am; €39), which visits Avoca and Glendalough. Tours depart from Connolly Station.

The Wild Wicklow Tour (ⓣ01/280 1899, ⓦwww.wildwicklow.ie) explores Glendalough and Avoca, and heads off the beaten track into the mountains (€28), departing from outside the *Shelbourne Hotel*, St Stephen's Green, at 8.50am daily, calling at the Suffolk Street tourist office at 9.10am and the *Gresham Hotel* at 9.20am.

wealthy English and Irish landowners built their great country houses around the edges of the mountains, of which fine examples at Powerscourt, Russborough and Avondale are now open to visitors. Wicklow is a great county to explore on foot or by bike; Wicklow Tourism produces a useful booklet, *The Wicklow Walking Guide* (available in tourist offices), which covers all manner of hiking, with route maps and descriptions. With such a variety of backdrops on Dublin's doorstep, Wicklow is also an attractive county for film-makers: *Braveheart*, *Excalibur* and many others have been shot here, and the county's film commission (ⓦwww.wicklowfilmcommission.com) produces a film-trails brochure for committed buffs.

The Wicklow coast

County Wicklow's main draw is without doubt the stunning scenery of the inland mountains, but the **coast** can offer some very attractive beaches, notably at **Brittas Bay**, south of Wicklow town, and is easily accessible from Dublin. The N11 runs the length of the county roughly parallel to the sea, while by **train**, the DART service runs as far as Bray and Greystones, and the Wexford mainline stops at Wicklow town. Keen to maintain its independence from Dublin, **Bray** is a lively, sometimes rowdy, resort and commuter town, which offers an expansive beach and the finest walk along this coast, across Bray Head to the village of **Greystones**. Halfway down the county's seaboard, **Wicklow** town enjoys a fine setting and a good choice of upmarket places to stay – if you have your own transport, this would make a good base for exploring the mountains.

Bray and around

Just south of the border with County Dublin, the formerly genteel Victorian resort of **BRAY** draws a great influx of day-tripping city-dwellers down the DART line on summer weekends, when the amusement arcades and fast-food outlets along the seafront go into overdrive. The attractive sand and shingle beach, however, dramatically set against the knobbly promontory of **Bray Head**, is long enough to soak up the crowds, and the enterprising town lays on a diverse roster of **festivals** to broaden its appeal, including the prestigious three-day Bray Jazz Festival in early May (Ⓦwww.brayjazz.com).

Further details of these events are available from the **tourist office**, in the nineteenth-century former courthouse on Main Street, a ten-minute walk inland from the DART station (June–Aug Mon–Fri 9am–1pm & 2–5pm, Sat 10am–3pm; Sept–May Mon–Fri 9.30am–1pm & 2–4.30pm, Sat 10am–3pm; Ⓣ01/286 6796, Ⓦwww.bray.ie). The attached **heritage centre** (same hours; €3) is devoted to local history, focusing on the achievements of Sir William Dargan, who built the Dublin–Kingstown (now Dún Laoghaire) railway, the world's first suburban line, in 1831–34, and helped to establish Dublin's National Gallery.

Bray's main attraction, however, especially popular with children, is the **National Sea Life Centre**, on the seafront (summer daily 10am–6pm; winter Mon–Fri 11am–5pm, Sat & Sun 10am–6pm; last admission 1hr before closing; €9.95, children €7.50; Ⓦwww.sealifeeurope.com). The aquarium is one of a Europe-wide chain of aquariums run by fishy enthusiasts, who lay on plenty of activities for kids, as well as informative display boards that'll keep adults interested. The full range of sea- and freshwater habitats is covered – including "probably the largest shoal of piranhas in Ireland" – with a strong emphasis on the need for conservation. Inevitably, the more exotic, far-flung creatures provide the big thrills, notably the blacktips in the tropical shark tank, and the scary giant Japanese spider crab, a species that can grow up to 4m from claw to claw.

Also on the seafront is *The Porterhouse*, a branch of the excellent Temple Bar microbrewery-**pub**, serving its own great stouts, lagers and ales, as well as good, basic **food** such as Irish stew, salads and burgers. There's a beer garden overlooking the esplanade, and on weekends DJs play till late. It's unlikely that you'll want to **stay** in Bray, but it might be worth knowing that *The Porterhouse* also offers chic, modern rooms, some with sea views (Ⓣ01/286 0668, Ⓦwww.porterhousebrewco.com; ❸).

Killruddery House and Gardens

Used as a film location on many occasions, including for *My Left Foot* and *Becoming Jane*, the **Killruddery** estate on the southern edge of Bray (gardens: April Sat & Sun 1–5pm; May–Sept daily 1–5pm; house: May, June & Sept daily 1–5pm; gardens €6, house and gardens €10; Ⓣ0404/46024, Ⓦwww.killruddery.com) is most notable for its **gardens**. Designed in the seventeenth century in early French formal style, and added to in the eighteenth and nineteenth, they're the oldest gardens in Ireland, featuring extensive walks flanked by hornbeam, beech and lime hedges, and an eighteenth-century "sylvan theatre" framed by a high bay hedge and terraced banks, where plays are still staged in the summer, especially during the house's three-day arts festival at the end of June. The two-hundred-metre-long twin ponds, once stocked with fish for the table, were designed as "water mirrors" in front of the main **house**. The latter, in Tudor Revival style, is still home to the Brabazon family (the earls of Meath), and boasts some fine plasterwork ceilings. When the house is open, you can get into the **Orangery**, which was built in the

1850s after the fashion of London's Crystal Palace and restored in 2000 – so styling itself "Ireland's Millennium Dome".

Killruddery features prominently in the **Wicklow Gardens Festival** from May to July every year, when a wide variety of privately owned gardens throw open their gates to the public (Ⓣ0404/20070). To **get to Killruddery**, catch bus #84, #184 or Finnegan's bus from Bray DART station, or set out on the twenty-minute walk there from the southern end of the seafront, via Putland Road, Newcourt Road, Vevay Road and Southern Cross Road.

A walk over Bray Head to Greystones

There's an excellent two- to three-hour **walk** from Bray seafront south across Bray Head to **GREYSTONES**, a small commuter town at the end of the DART line. You can follow the comparatively flat **cliff path** that runs above the rail tracks for most of the way, giving close-up views of rocky coves and slate pinnacles, lashed by magnificent waves on windy days. Alternatively, if you have more time, take on the steep climb over the top of **Bray Head** for great views of Killiney Bay and the cone-shaped hills inland known as Little Sugar Loaf and Great Sugar Loaf, with a distant backdrop of the Wicklow Mountains. The latter route ascends rapidly from the end of Bray seafront through pine woods and over gorse slopes to a large cross, 200m above sea level, which was erected to mark the Holy Year of 1950; from here a track winds across the ridge below the 240-metre summit of Bray Head, before you turn sharp left down to join the cliff path which will bring you into Greystones. The village supports several pubs serving food, as well as *The Hungry Monk* on Church Road (Ⓣ01/287 5759), a fine traditional **restaurant**, specializing in game in winter and seafood in summer, that's especially popular for Sunday lunch, served any time between 12.30 and 8pm. The restaurant is also open Wednesday to Saturday evenings, while the wine bar downstairs serves a cheaper, simpler menu every evening.

Wicklow and around

WICKLOW, 27km south of Bray, is a modest, easy-going county town, though change is under way now that it's within the ever-expanding range of Dublin commuters, as evidenced by new boutiques and galleries and the closure of several old pubs. Transport connections are less favourable for tourists than workers, however, as there are no buses from here into the heart of the Wicklow Mountains just to the west, but if you have a car, you could stay at one of several fine country hotels near the town that make good bases for jaunts into the uplands.

Built around a small port that busies itself with fishing, timber and yachts, the town is enlivened by its unusual setting: the Vartry River broadens into a lough here before flowing into the Irish Sea, cutting off a narrow strip of land, **the Murrough**, that's rich in bird life, notably wintering swans and geese. On a small rise above the harbour's south pier stand the meagre ruins of **Black Castle**, built by the Fitzgeralds around 1175 after they were granted land in the area by the Anglo-Norman invader, Strongbow; it's most notable now for its fine views of the coast, north to the Sugarloaf Mountains and south to Wicklow Head. The town's major tourist attraction is **Wicklow's Historic Gaol** (mid-March to Oct daily 10am–6pm, tours every 10min until 5pm; €7.30; Ⓦwww.wicklowshistoricgaol.com), dating from 1702, just up Kilmantin Hill from Market Square. Employing actors, mannequins and audiovisuals, a lively and imaginative picture of life in the prison is built up, fleshed out by sections on the 1798 Rebellion, the Great Famine and the transportation of almost 50,000 Irish convicts to Australia. On Friday evenings at 6.30pm, the gaol also runs scary, adults-only tours (€10, including a glass of wine).

Practicalities

The **train station** is fifteen minutes' walk northwest of the centre, off the Rathnew (Dublin) road, while **buses** stop either on Market Street, just east of Market Square, or opposite the *Grand Hotel*, just west of the centre. The **tourist office** (June–Aug Mon & Sat 9.30am–1pm & 2–5.15pm, Tues–Fri 9am–6pm; Sept–May Mon–Fri 9.30am–1pm & 2–5.15pm; ⓣ0404/69117) on Fitzwilliam Square, which is linked to Market Square to the east by Main Street, can provide details of the town's five-day **arts festival** in mid-May (or go to ⓦwww.wicklowartsfestival.ie). **Internet** access is available at Internet World on the Mall, Main Street, opposite the post office, while **horse riding** can be arranged at Devils' Glen (ⓣ0404/40637, ⓦwww.devilsglen.ie), 1.5km west of Ashford off the N11 (about 8km from Wicklow town). If you need a **taxi**, call Wicklow Taxis on ⓣ086 246 4332–3.

Your best bet for inexpensive **accommodation** in the town centre is *Kilmantin House*, right next door to Wicklow's Historic Gaol on Kilmantin Hill (ⓣ0404/67373, ⓔkilmantinhouse@eircom.net; closed Nov–March; ❷), a welcoming B&B with bright, airy rooms, all en suite with TV. Otherwise, if you have a little more money and your own transport, head out of town to one of the nearby country houses, each of which has its own fine restaurant. The cheapest of these is the furthest away, at Glenealy, about 8km southwest of town on the Rathdrum road: *Ballyknocken House* (ⓣ0404/44627, ⓦwww.ballyknocken.com; ❹), an elegant, ivy-clad 1850s farmhouse, furnished with antiques and set in an attractive garden, which offers cookery courses and walking programmes. *Hunter's Hotel*, about 3km from Wicklow on the R761 north of Rathnew (ⓣ0404/40106, ⓦwww.hunters.ie; ❻), is a creaky old coaching inn, very comfortable yet unpretentious and welcoming, with pretty riverside gardens. Closest to town, just over a kilometre out on the Rathnew road, lies *Tinakilly* (ⓣ0404/69274, ⓦwww.tinakilly.ie; ❼), a Victorian mansion covered in creepers and set in secluded gardens with fine views down to the sea, where some rooms have four-poster or half-tester beds. **Camping** is available at *Wolohan's* (ⓣ0404/69404, ⓦwww.wolohanssilverstrand.com), about 5km south of town by the beach at Silver Strand.

There are a number of decent **eating** possibilities in Wicklow. With tables out on Market Square, *Donelli's* (ⓣ0404/61333) is a bustling, modern, daytime deli-café that also opens Thursday to Saturday evenings. On offer are all manner of tasty sandwiches, soups, salads, cakes and a small range of global main courses such as Thai curries. Also recommended is *The Bakery*, Church Street, just off Fitzwilliam Square (ⓣ0404/66770), a smart, upmarket restaurant serving dishes such as Wicklow venison with wild mushrooms and red wine. Other choices include a welcoming, Italian-run restaurant, *Vesuvius*, behind the tourist office (ⓣ0404/64877; Tues–Sun evenings), serving good *antipasti*, meat and fish dishes, as well as tasty pasta, and the *Square Steakhouse* on Market Square (ⓣ0404/66422; closed Sat lunchtime, Sun & Mon), which specializes in steak and seafood. Among the town's remaining **pubs**, *Phil Healy's* on Fitzwilliam Square is a congenial place for a drink, while *The Bridge Tavern*, just off the square on Bridge Street, has live music every night.

Mount Usher Gardens and Brittas Bay

Five kilometres northwest of Wicklow, on the N11 just south of Ashford, lie **Mount Usher Gardens** (late April–Oct daily 10.30am–6pm; €7;

Ⓦwww.mount-usher-gardens.com), where a plethora of rare trees, shrubs and flowers, including the finest eucalyptus specimens in Europe, grow in an informal style in the woodlands and meadows. The gardens straddle the Vartry River, which is broken up here by a remarkable series of nineteenth-century weirs, watercourses and miniature suspension bridges.

Running south from Wicklow, off the R750 towards Arklow, are a series of fine, sandy **beaches** backed by rolling dunes, beginning at Silver Strand just 5km from town. **Brittas Bay**'s three-kilometre-long, Blue-Flag strand, around 8km further on, is especially attractive and popular with weekending Dubliners. If you want to get to Brittas Bay by public transport, any bus on the inland N11 to Arklow will put you off at Jack White's Crossroads, from where it's a half-hour walk to the beach.

The Wicklow Mountains

The **Wicklow Mountains**, so close to the capital that they're often called the Dublin Mountains – by Dubliners, at any rate – rise only to 924m at their highest point, Lugnaquillia. Nevertheless, this granite mass, which forms the largest area of continuous upland in Ireland, is wild, desolate and sparsely populated at its centre, and, despite the influx of outdoorsy city-dwellers at weekends, never feels crowded. The range has been heavily glaciated to form attractive valleys, lakes and corries, while an extensive covering of peat supports purple heather and yellow gorse in abundance. To protect this huge natural playground on Dublin's doorstep, part of the massif has been designated as a national park, and walkers are signposted onto the **Wicklow Way**, a managed, long-distance trail that bisects the mountains from north to south.

Public **transport** with Dublin Bus will get you to **Powerscourt**'s beautiful gardens and the neighbouring village of **Enniskerry**, and to **Blessington**, which is flanked by the fine stately home of **Russborough House**. Further

▲ Wicklow Mountains

The Wicklow Way

The Republic's oldest designated long-distance walk, opened in 1982, the **Wicklow Way** runs the length of the Wicklow Mountains from Dublin's southern suburbs, taking in wild uplands and picturesque valleys, as well as long stretches of conifer plantation. The trail cuts across the Glencree valley, passes Lough Tay and Lough Dan, and continues to Glendalough, before entering Glenmalure and skirting Lugnaquillia, the highest Wicklow peak; the walk finishes after 130km at Clonegall on the Wexford–Carlow border. The whole route is waymarked with yellow signs and can be walked in five to six days, though some people take as many as ten.

The Way begins at Marlay Park in Dublin's southern suburbs – take the #16 bus from O'Connell Street or South Great George's Street to get there. Its highlight – if you lack the time or inclination to complete the whole Way – is probably the 29-kilometre section from **Knockree to Glendalough**, which passes the Powerscourt waterfall and can be covered in one very long day – or preferably two, with a short detour to overnight at Roundwood.

Finding **accommodation** is not usually a problem, and some B&Bs will collect you from, or deliver you to, parts of the route, or ferry your bags to your next resting place, if given prior notice. Three An Óige hostels line the route – at Knockree (see p.150), Glendalough (see p.153) and Glenmalure (see p.154). Accommodation in Enniskerry, Roundwood, Laragh/Glendalough and Glenmalure is detailed in the text. An excellent **website**, Ⓦwww.wicklowway.com, gives full details of other accommodation along the route, as well as trail descriptions, maps and other useful advice.

Ordnance Survey **maps** nos. 56 and 62 cover almost the whole route at 1:50,000, with nos. 50 and 61 picking up the extremities. EastWest Mapping (Ⓦwww.eastwestmapping.ie) also produce *The Wicklow Way Map Guide*, a booklet of 1:50,000 maps with accompanying text and details of accommodation.

south, the dramatic monastic site of **Glendalough** and its service town **Laragh**, along with the lofty village of **Roundwood**, are all accessible from Dublin on the St Kevin's bus service and make good bases from which to explore the mountains. One or two buses a day on the Dublin–Arklow route (#133) detour inland from Wicklow to **Rathdrum** and the intensely pretty **Vale of Avoca**, on the southern edge of the mountains. The nearest village to the former home and estate of Charles Stewart Parnell, **Avondale House**, Rathdrum also has a station on the Dublin–Wexford rail line.

Of course, you'll get the most out of the mountains and their many opportunities for walking if you have your own transport, but otherwise it's worth considering one of the many tours on offer. As well as the day-trips from Dublin detailed on p.142, there are **guided walking tours** in the mountains by outfits such as Footfalls, Trooperstown, Roundwood (Ⓣ0404/45152, Ⓦwww.walkinghikingireland.com), and the Kippure Walking Centre, Manor Kilbride, near Blessington (Ⓣ01/458 2889, Ⓦwww.walkingwicklow.com).

Enniskerry and Powerscourt

In the northeastern foothills of the Wicklow Mountains, 19km south of Dublin and less than a kilometre beyond the village of **ENNISKERRY**, lies the massive **Powerscourt Estate**, where given fine weather you could easily pass a whole day (house and gardens daily 9.30am–5.30pm; gardens close at dusk in winter; €9; Ⓦwww.powerscourt.ie). Although the estate is now something of an all-round leisure complex, with a golf course, garden centre and craft shops, and a luxury *Ritz-Carlton* hotel under construction, the central attraction remains the formal gardens, whose spectacular design matches their superb setting facing Great Sugar Loaf Mountain.

In the late twelfth century, a castle was built on this strategic site by the Anglo-Norman le Poer (Power) family, from whom it takes its name. However, what you see today was the work of the dynasty of Sir Richard Wingfield, a successful general who was appointed Marshal of Ireland and granted these lands in 1603. In the early eighteenth century, his descendant, also Richard Wingfield, employed Richard Castle to build one of the largest Palladian mansions in Ireland. The new house was flanked by terraced gardens, which were further developed by another eponymous descendant and his son, Mervyn, in the nineteenth century.

Erected between 1731 and 1741, the **house** remains impressive from a distance, but most of its interior was destroyed by a fire in 1974 (on the eve of a party to celebrate major refurbishment). Parts have since been re-created, notably the colonnaded, double-height ballroom, though sadly without its original magnificent walnut parquetry or fireplace, which had been taken from a design in the Doge's Palace in Venice. The ballroom is accessible as part of an **exhibition**, which features displays on the house's former grandeur (including a model of Castle's ballroom) as well as short films on the estate's history and development.

The terraced **Italian Gardens** slope gracefully down from the back of the house. The uppermost terrace, with its winged figures of Fame and Victory flanking Apollo and Diana, was designed in 1843 by the gout-ridden Daniel Robertson, who used to be wheeled about the site in a barrow, cradling a bottle of sherry – the last of the sherry apparently meant the end of the day's work. A grand staircase leads down to a spirited pair of zinc winged horses, guarding the **Triton Lake**, whose central statue of the sea god (based on Bernini's fountain in the Piazza Barberini in Rome) fires a jet of water thirty metres skywards.

On the east side of the terraces are the curious **Pepper Pot Tower** (accurately modelled on the canister of the eighth Viscount Powerscourt's dinner set), surrounded by fine North American conifers, and a colourful **Japanese Garden** of maples, azaleas and fortune palms, laid out on reclaimed bogland. To the west of the Italian Gardens lies the **walled garden**, with its rose beds, herbaceous borders and fine ceremonial entrances: the Chorus Gate, decorated with beautiful golden trumpeters, and the Bamberg Gate, which originally belonged to Bamberg cathedral in Bavaria and features remarkable perspective arches as part of its gilded ironwork design.

The estate's final attraction is Ireland's highest **waterfall** (daily: Jan, Feb, Nov & Dec 10.30am–4pm; March, April, Sept & Oct 10.30am–5.30pm; May–Aug 9.30am–7pm; closed 2 weeks prior to Christmas; €5), which leaps and bounds diagonally down a 120-metre rock face to replenish the waters of the River Dargle in the valley below. It's 6km further down the road from the main gate, but well signposted.

Practicalities

Enniskerry is accessible from Dublin by taking the #44 **bus** from Townsend Street (Mon–Fri roughly every 30min, Sat & Sun at least hourly; 1hr), or the DART **train** to Bray followed by the #185 bus (Mon–Sat roughly every 30min, Sun roughly hourly; 30min), which continues to Powerscourt Estate several times a day. You may well want to push on further into the mountains for somewhere **to stay**, though Enniskerry does have a good B&B on the village square: *Ferndale* (ⓣ01/286 3518, ⓦwww.ferndalehouse.com; closed

Nov–March; ❷), an attractive, all-en-suite place, furnished in period style, in an early Victorian house set in pretty gardens.

By far your best bet for daytime **eating** is the self-service restaurant and café at Powerscourt House, run by Avoca (see p.122), whose terrace provides sumptuous views of the garden. In the evening, head for *Emilia's*, an Italian-run, first-floor restaurant overlooking the square in Enniskerrry (Ⓣ01/276 1834), which serves up mostly pasta and pizza, cooked in a wood-burning oven, all at very reasonable prices.

To Glencree and south through the mountains

KNOCKREE, 7km west of Enniskerry on the Wicklow Way, is home to an An Óige **hostel** with fine views of the lush valley of Glencree (Ⓣ01/286 4036, Ⓦwww.anoige.ie); at the time of writing, it was closed for refurbishment, but it's due to reopen in 2008 as a five-star hostel. Several times a day the #185 from Bray DART station continues from Enniskerry to Shop River, about 3km north of the hostel. At the head of the valley, the village of **GLENCREE** lies on the old military road from Dublin south into the mountains. In the village, there's a cemetery for German airmen who died in Ireland during the two world wars, and a reconciliation centre set up for people affected by the conflict in the North, containing a café and a visitor centre (daily 10am–5pm; Ⓦwww.glencree.ie), which displays contemporary art, photographs and diverse temporary exhibitions on the Troubles.

South of the village the military road climbs past the dramatic twin tarns of Lough Bray Lower and Upper (accessible by boggy paths opposite a car park) and then through ever wilder terrain towards one of the Wicklow Mountains' two main passes, the **Sally Gap**. From here the military road (R115) continues south through superb countryside, passing the beautiful **Glenmacnass Waterfall**, down to Laragh and Glendalough. If you fancy stretching your legs along the way, pull in at the car park 2.5km south of the Sally Gap, cross the road and follow the rough, boggy path for 45 minutes or so to the prominent summit of **Luggala**, or Fancy Mountain; from here, you'll be rewarded with precipitous views straight down to Lough Tay and a panorama to the south and west of Lough Dan and the major Wicklow peaks.

The R759 heading southeast of the Sally Gap winds its way past impressive **Lough Tay**, where scree slopes tumble headlong into the water from the summit of Luggala, down to Sraghmore, 3km north of Roundwood. Just to the south of Lough Tay, linked by the Cloghoge River with its gentler woodlands, is **Lough Dan**. This is private land, but visitors are normally allowed to descend through the pillared gates towards Lough Tay, turning left before reaching the lake onto a track that leads down to Lough Dan after about an hour. In the other direction you can walk from one of the car parks above Lough Tay north up the Wicklow Way for about fifteen minutes to the memorial to J.B. Malone (one of the pioneers of Irish hill-walking and of the Way itself) for the finest view of the ensemble, and on to the top of White Hill in another twenty minutes for further scenic delights.

Roundwood

From Dublin, the quicker route to Glendalough is along the N11 and R755 through **ROUNDWOOD**, which is accessible on the St Kevin's bus service (see opposite). This attractive village, which can also be reached from Sally Gap via the R759, claims to be the highest in Ireland, at 220m above sea level, and enjoys a gentle setting on the eastern flank of the range by the Vartry Reservoir – a good spot for an easy, flat, evening stroll. With a decent range of food and accommodation, Roundwood is a popular stop for hikers on the Wicklow Way, which is just 2.5km away.

Good central **B&Bs** include *Woodstock* (ⓣ01/281 8005, ⓔwoodstockjohn@hotmail.com; ❷) and *Riverbank* (ⓣ01/281 8117, ⓔriverbank1@eircom.net; March–Oct; ❶), which both offer luggage transfer and transport to the trail for walkers; the latter will also provide packed lunches. At the north end of the village is a large, smart, well-equipped **campsite** (ⓣ01/281 8163, ⓦwww.dublinwicklowcamping.com; May–Aug). Roundwood's best **eating** choice is *The Roundwood Inn*, a seventeenth-century coaching inn which serves great bar meals, ranging from local seafood to Irish stew, and fine, though more expensive food in its more formal restaurant (ⓣ01/281 8107).

Glendalough and Laragh

A deep glaciated valley in the heart of the Wicklow Mountains, **GLENDALOUGH** ("valley of the two lakes") provides a delightfully atmospheric location for some of the best-preserved monastic sites in Ireland. Despite the coach parties, enough of the valley's tranquillity remains for you to understand what drew monks and pilgrims here in the first place. The monastery was established in the sixth century by **St Kevin** (Caoimhín), who retreated to Glendalough to pray in solitude. His piety attracted many followers to the site, especially after his death in 618, and the monastic community here came to rival Clonmacnois (see p.215) for its learning. It was raided by the Vikings at least four times between the eighth and eleventh centuries, then by the English in the fourteenth, and was finally dissolved during the Reformation. Pilgrimages continued, however, as the pope declared that seven visits to Glendalough would earn the same indulgence as one to Rome, but the pilgrims' abstemious devotions on St Kevin's Day (June 3) were often followed by drink and debauchery, and in 1862 a local priest banned the gatherings.

The Glendalough visitor centre, its adjacent car park and the main monastic site are reached first, on the eastern side of the **Lower Lake**, while further west up the valley is the larger and more impressive **Upper Lake**, with its wooded cliffs and dramatic waterfall as well as more ruins, the national park information point and another car park. On the main road in, just over a mile to the east of the visitor centre, lies the small village of **LARAGH**, which has most of the area's amenities, notably accommodation. **Getting there** from Dublin is straightforward: St Kevin's bus service (ⓣ01/281 8119, ⓦwww.glendaloughbus.com) runs from opposite the Mansion House on Dawson Street, via Bray (Town Hall, Main St) and Roundwood, to Laragh and Glendalough on Monday to Saturday at 11.30am and 6pm (7pm on Sat and in July & Aug), Sunday at 11.30am and 7pm (€11 single, €18 return).

The Lower Lake sites

The **visitor centre** (daily: mid-March to mid-Oct 9.30am–6pm, mid-Oct to mid-March 9.30am–5pm; €2.90; Heritage Card; ⓦwww.heritageireland.ie) features photographic displays and a film on Glendalough's place within Ireland's monastic heritage as well as a model of how the monastery is thought to have looked at the height of its activity. All visitors are welcome to join the informative, forty-minute **guided tours** of the site (included in the entry price) that are laid on for large groups, including a regular slot at 2pm every day.

Once you've entered the **monastic site** (same hours; free), through a double stone archway that was once surmounted by a tower, you'll come to its largest structure, the roofless but impressive **cathedral**, begun in the early ninth century. Among the tombs outside stands **St Kevin's Cross**, one of the best remaining relics from the period, consisting of a granite monolith decorated with an eighth-century carving of a Celtic cross over a wheel; unusually, the quadrants of the cross have not been cut through, which suggests that it was left unfinished. Above the doorway of the nearby twelfth-century **Priests' House**, which may have been the site of Kevin's tomb-shrine, are faint carvings of figures believed to depict the saint and two (later) abbots. Downhill from here stands the two-storey **St Kevin's Church**, whose steeply pitched roof and bell turret so resemble a chimney that the building is also known as "St Kevin's Kitchen", although it was almost certainly an oratory. Glendalough's **Round Tower** rises to over thirty metres, its conical roof having been restored in 1876. Such tapering stone towers are found only in Ireland and probably had multiple functions, as belfries, watchtowers, treasuries and places of refuge from danger – the entrance is usually well above ground level, accessible by a ladder that could be removed if necessary. To the south of St Kevin's Church, a footbridge crosses the river to the **Deerstone**, so called after a legend that claims that a tame doe squirted milk into the hollowed-out stone to feed the twin orphaned babies of one of Kevin's followers.

The Upper Lake sites

You can drive to the Upper Lake car park along the north side of the valley, but it's far preferable to walk from the Deerstone along the signposted **Green Road** (part of the Wicklow Way), a scenic track that skirts the south side of the Lower Lake. After twenty minutes or so, this will bring you to the Upper Lake and the tiny, ruined **Reefert Church**, which dates from the late tenth century and whose small cemetery is thought to contain the graves of local chieftains. From here a path runs up to **St Kevin's Cell**, a typically Celtic, corbel-roofed, "beehive" hut on a promontory overlooking the lake. Further up the cliff, **St Kevin's Bed** is a small cave into which the saint reputedly moved to avoid the allures of an admirer called Caitlín; he's supposed to have offered the final resistance to her advances by chucking the poor woman into the lake.

Walks around Glendalough

At the eastern end of the Upper Lake, the **Wicklow Mountains National Park Information Office** (May–Sept daily 10am–5.30pm; Feb–April, Oct & Nov Sat & Sun 10am–6pm; Jan & Dec Sat & Sun 10am–4pm; plus extra days during school holidays; Ⓣ0404/45425, Ⓦwww.wicklownationalpark.ie) has details of local walking routes and conditions and sells a series of leaflets on the national park, including *The Walking Trails of Glendalough*, which suggests routes taking anything from 45 minutes to four hours; a couple of good hikes here are also covered by Joss Lynam's *Easy Walks near Dublin*. The visitor centre also runs free guided nature walks, such as bat walks on Thursday evenings in summer and rut walks to observe deer on some Sundays in the autumn.

The recently laid-out **St Kevin's Way** follows what was the main pilgrim path to Glendalough in medieval times. Waymarked with yellow pilgrim symbols, the 29-kilometre trail runs along country tracks and quiet roads from Hollywood, near the N81 south of Blessington, climbing to the **Wicklow Gap**, 470m above sea level in the shadow of Tonelagee (817m), before following the descent of the Glendasan River for 7km to the Glendalough visitor centre. *St Kevin's Way*, a booklet by Peter Harbison and Joss Lynam, covers the route with comprehensive 1:50,000 maps and text.

The easiest to follow and most satisfying short hike is on the south side of Glendalough valley, where it's possible to climb 474-metre **Derrybawn** in around an hour, for spectacular views. Follow the Wicklow Way south from the national park information point past the Poulanass Waterfall, before eventually peeling left off the waymarked forest track up a narrow path, which climbs steeply to the edge of the forest and then straight up to Derrybawn's ridge and summit cairn.

Practicalities

Horse riding can be arranged at the Glendalough Equestrian Centre (T0404/45569). **Accommodation** in the area encompasses a hostel and two hotels, with the greatest concentration of B&Bs in Laragh. **Places to eat** are limited, however. Unless you're staying at the hostel, the only spot in Glendalough itself is the hotel restaurant or bar. In Laragh, you can dine in the smart restaurant at *Lynham's Hotel*, or its popular bar with open fires in winter and outside tables by the river in summer. *The Wicklow Heather* (Ⓣ0404/45157), a cosy, wood-furnished restaurant nearby on the Glendalough road, serves everything from breakfast and morning coffee to upmarket dinners featuring, for example, Wicklow venison and lamb.

Accommodation

Carmel's Annamoe Ⓣ0404/45297, Ⓦhttp://homepage.eircom.net/~carmels. Hospitable, modern house, set back from the R755 about 3km northeast of Laragh, with a beautifully kept garden and bright, en-suite bedrooms. March–Oct. ❷

Derrymore Glendalough Ⓣ0404/45493, Ⓦhttp://homepage.eircom.net/~derrymore. Handily placed on the road between Laragh and Glendalough with views of the Lower Lake, this B&B offers comfortable, en-suite rooms furnished with antiques, good breakfasts including home-baked soda bread, and a warm welcome. Packed lunches available for walkers. April–Oct. ❷

Glendale Laragh Ⓣ0404/45410, Ⓦwww.glendale-glendalough.com. Welcoming, en-suite accommodation in a modern bungalow, 400m from the centre of the village on the R755 towards Roundwood. ❷

Glendaloch International Hostel Glendalough, on the road to the Upper Lake (An Óige) Ⓣ0404/45342, Ⓔglendaloughyh@ireland.com. Large, comfortable, recently refurbished hostel, offering en-suite and private rooms, breakfast, packed lunches and evening meals, drying room and laundry facilities, Internet access and exchange facilities. Dorms from €16, twins ❶.

Glendalough Hotel Glendalough Ⓣ0404/45135, Ⓦwww.glendaloughhotel.com. Recently extended, family-run Victorian hotel near the visitor centre, offering great views from many of the comfortable, en-suite bedrooms, some of which have balconies; good-value half-board deals available. Closed Jan. ❺

Lynham's Hotel Laragh Ⓣ0404/45345, Ⓦwww.lynhamsoflaragh.ie. Airy, tasteful, modern hotel overlooking the Glenmacnass River at the heart of the village; half-board deals offered. ❺

Riversdale Wicklow Gap road, just over a kilometre northwest of the Glendalough Visitor Centre Ⓣ0404/45858, Ⓦwww.glendalough.eu.com. Hospitable, well-run B&B in a tranquil location with great views. The en-suite rooms are simply and tastefully furnished, and breakfast is taken in the picturesque sun room overlooking the Glendasan River. Packed lunches available for walkers. March–Nov. ❷

Glenmalure and the Glen of Imaal

Arrowing down from the northwest around the Avonbeg River, **Glenmalure** is the next valley south of Glendalough. Besides the river, this peaceful, enclosed glen has room only for a thin strip of emerald fields and a narrow, gorse-flanked road between its steep slopes of scree and forestry. For drivers and cyclists, the military road offers a scenic route there, branching off the R755 just south of Laragh and continuing southwest; walkers can follow the Wicklow Way out of

Glendalough, skirting Derrybawn Mountain and 657-metre Mullacor before descending into the valley. At the point where the military road hits the glen stands a ruined barracks, used in the suppression of the 1798 Rebellion. Here too is *Glenmalure Lodge* (Ⓣ0404/46188, Ⓔglenmalurelodge@yahoo.com; ②), a quaint and welcoming whitewashed inn in a beautiful spot on the Wicklow Way, offering comfortable, en-suite **B&B**, decent food and a cosy bar with outdoor tables; its rooms are very popular at weekends with walkers, for whom luggage transfer and packed lunches can be arranged. Northwest of the *Lodge*, the valley road ends at a car park and footbridge over the river, where a track takes over, up to Glenmalure's An Óige **youth hostel** (book through An Óige's Dublin office Ⓣ01/830 4555; open July & Aug only; €15), which is very basic but holds interest as the house formerly owned by playwright J.M. Synge and by W.B. Yeats's muse, Maud Gonne McBride.

Wicklow's highest peak, wild and lonely **Lugnaquillia**, rises to 924m to the southwest of Glenmalure. On the mountain's west flank, the broad, green **Glen of Imaal** opens up, but note that the eastern part of the valley is used by the army as a shooting range – look out for the red flags to show when the range is in use and therefore off limits to visitors. Given the all-clear, walkers can follow the track further up Glenmalure from the youth hostel, then over Table Mountain before descending into Imaal; drivers are faced with a long haul either around the south side of the Lugnaquillia massif or to the north via Glendalough and the Wicklow Gap.

Near the southeast corner of the Glen of Imaal, at Derrynamuck, is the **Dwyer McAllister Cottage**, a traditional dwelling that's recently been re-thatched, whitewashed and opened as a folk museum (mid-June to mid-Sept daily 2–6pm, last admission 5.15pm; free; Ⓦwww.heritageireland.ie). Here Michael Dwyer, local leader of the 1798 Rebellion, was surrounded by the British, but made good his escape into the snow-covered mountains when his comrade Samuel McAllister ran out of the front of the cottage, drawing the Brits' fire and meeting his death. Dwyer was finally captured and deported to Australia in 1803, where he ended up as chief constable of Liverpool, near Sydney.

Avondale House, the Vale of Avoca and Macreddin

In the lush foothills at the southeastern edge of the Wicklow Mountains, the main settlement is peaceful **RATHDRUM**, its long main street and pretty village green perched high above the Avonmore River. There's a small **tourist office** in the market square (Mon–Fri 9am–1pm & 2–5pm, plus July & Aug Sat 2–5pm; Ⓣ0404/46262), and **bikes** can be rented from McGrath's on Main Street (Ⓣ0404/46172). Overlooking the Fairgreen, the *Old Presbytery* **hostel** (IHH; Ⓣ0404/46930, Ⓔtheoldpres@eircom.net) offers comfortable dorms (€17), en-suite twins (①) and family rooms, while **camping** is available down by the river at the attractive *Hidden Valley Caravan and Camping Park* (Ⓣ0404/46080, Ⓦwww.irelandholidaypark.com; June–Sept), who also have log cabins for rent by the week. For food and drink you need look no further than *Jacob's Well* on the main street, a welcoming and popular **pub** that dishes up well-prepared, hearty lunch and dinner and good Guinness.

About 2km south of the village stands **Avondale House** (mid-March, April, Sept & Oct daily except Mon 11am–6pm; May–Aug daily 11am–6pm; last admission 1hr before closing; €6; open access to grounds, though parking on-site costs €5), birthplace and home of **Charles Stewart Parnell**, the nineteenth-century campaigner for home rule. Completed in 1779 to a design by English architect James Wyatt, the house, which features an audiovisual on Parnell and the history of Avondale and an attractive basement café, is well worth a visit. Over the main door in the hall hangs a poignant banner, representing the arms of Ireland's four provinces in pastel colours; given to Parnell in the 1880s, when home rule seemed a racing certainty, it was vainly intended for display in the future Irish House of Commons. The beautiful, bright dining room nearby is adorned with delicate, foliate stuccowork in Wedgwood style by the Lafranchini brothers (who also decorated Dublin's Newman House). Upstairs, the highlight is the master bedroom where Parnell was born, with a bay of large windows overlooking the grounds. Stretching over five hundred acres, the **estate** is now owned by the Irish Forestry Board, Coillte, who have laid out several trails, which take between twenty minutes and three hours to cover, through the forested parkland, with its rare tree species and fine views of the Avonmore River.

The beautiful, thickly wooded **Vale of Avoca** (Ⓦwww.valeofavoca.com) begins 3km south of Avondale at the **Meeting of the Waters**, the confluence of the Avonmore and Avonbeg rivers, where *The Meetings* **pub** takes pride of place. Picturesquely located with its own gardens and picture windows, the pub offers decent food, en-suite accommodation and exchange facilities, and is known for its traditional-music sessions (year-round Sat & Sun, plus July & Aug Mon–Thurs evenings; Ⓣ0402/35226; ❷).

A few kilometres downstream, the pretty village of **AVOCA** still trades on its role as the location for the now-defunct BBC-TV series *Ballykissangel*. There's more to it than that though, most notably in the form of its famous eighteenth-century **mill** – original home of the now-nationwide Avoca shops – where you can watch the weavers at work (daily: summer 9am–6pm; winter 9.30am–5.30pm; free; Ⓦwww.avoca.ie). You can eat at the excellent **café** here and, of course, there's a shop selling the fruits of the looms as well as the other good-quality gifts the Avoca chain is known for. In the centre of the village, the small library in the old courthouse (Mon–Fri 9am–5pm, Sat 10am–2pm; Ⓣ0402/35022) provides **tourist information** and **Internet access**. There are plenty of **B&Bs** in the vicinity, notably *Keppels Farmhouse* (Ⓣ0402/35168, Ⓦwww.keppelsfarmhouse.com; June–Sept; ❷), a nineteenth-century dairy farm signposted 3km south of the village, with comfortable and relaxing en-suite accommodation; and *Sheepwalk House* (Ⓣ0402/35189, Ⓦwww.sheepwalk.com; ❸; self-catering cottages also available), offering tasteful rooms in a Georgian country house with views of the sea, 3km away off the Arklow road.

Venturing further afield, you might well be tempted to **stay** or **eat** at the *Brook Lodge and Wells Spa* at **MACREDDIN**, to the west of Avoca, 3km north of Aughrim (Ⓣ0402/36444, Ⓦwww.brooklodge.com; ❻). The enterprising owners have redeveloped this picturesque village, which had fallen into decline in the late nineteenth century, with a modern country-house-style hotel, a spa and swimming pool, the excellent and innovative *Strawberry Tree Restaurant*, which uses only organic, free-range or wild ingredients, a pub with its own microbrewery, an equestrian centre, and craft and organic-food stores. From March to October, the first Sunday of the month sees a big organic food fair in the afternoon, with barbecues and a jazz band.

Blessington and Russborough House

On the western edge of the Wicklow Mountains and close to the shining waters of the Blessington Lakes (aka Pollaphuca Reservoir), the village of

BLESSINGTON has lately been attracting scores of Dublin commuters to the burgeoning housing estates hereabouts. Three kilometres south of the village stands **Russborough House** (guided tours April & Oct Sun & public hols 10am–5pm; May–Sept daily 10am–5pm; €6; ⓣ045/865239, ⓔrussborough@eircom.net), a lavish Palladian country house designed by Richard Castle for Joseph Leeson, later Lord Russborough and the Earl of Milltown, whose family had made their money in the brewing trade. Castle died before the project was completed, leaving Francis Bindon to oversee the fulfilment of his grand design. Completed in 1751, the Wicklow-granite building's 200-metre frontage, with its curving colonnaded wings, is the longest of its kind in Ireland.

Russborough has gained widespread fame for its **art collections**, under both the Milltowns and latterly the Beits, who derived their fortune from the De Beers Diamond Mining Company and bought the house in 1952 (both families made substantial donations of artworks to the National Gallery in Dublin). Unfortunately, this fame has attracted the wrong kind of attention: the house has been **burgled** on no fewer than four occasions, though almost all of the stolen paintings have subsequently been recovered. The first burglary was in 1974, when nineteen paintings were stolen by Englishwoman Rose Dugdale in order to raise funds for the IRA. The house was again broken into in 1986, by "The General", aka Martin Cahill, one of Dublin's most notorious criminals (this episode featured prominently in John Boorman's 1997 film *The General*). Russborough was burgled again in 2001, possibly by an associate of Cahill's, when a Gainsborough portrait was stolen for the third time, along with a work by Bellotto. Both were recovered in September 2002, only days before a fourth break-in, which netted five pictures including two by Rubens. At the moment, because of conservation work, none of the paintings are on show; to compensate, the guided tour currently takes in the first-floor bedrooms as well as the main, ground floor. However, it's planned to rehang works by Murillo, Bellotto and Gainsborough among others; when that happens, there will probably be a choice of two guided tours: one of the ground floor and the paintings: the other, less frequently and less compellingly, of the first floor.

With or without the paintings, the **interior** of the house is sumptuous, featuring baroque plasterwork ceilings by the Lafranchini brothers, notably in the saloon, depicting the four seasons, and in the music room, where the ingenious geometrical design seems to add height to the room. Further beautiful stuccowork, representing hunting and garlands, adorns the cantilevered main staircase, which was ornately carved out of dark Cuban mahogany by Irish craftsmen in the eighteenth century. Other highlights include the Italian-marble fireplace in the dining room depicting Bacchus and vines, and a series of French clocks dating back as far as the fifteenth century, which are still wound every Tuesday. The house has a pleasant **café**, while in the **grounds** are a maze (June–Aug daily 10am–5pm; €2) and a 2km trail through the parkland, which will take you past a walled garden and a bog garden.

Practicalities

Blessington is about ninety minutes from central Dublin on the roughly hourly #65 **bus** from Eden Quay, College Green or South Great George's Street (six or seven times a day these buses continue southwest of Blessington, towards Ballymore Eustace, which will leave you much less of a walk to Russborough House). The central **tourist office** is set back from the main street opposite the church (Mon–Fri 9.30am–5pm, plus summer Sat roughly 11am–3pm; ⓣ045/865850).

The very welcoming *Haylands House*, on Dublin Road at the north end of town (Ⓣ045/865183, Ⓔhaylands@eircom.net; March–Nov; ❷), offers standard and en-suite **B&B** – with good single rates – in a spacious bungalow with an impressive garden. Several pubs serve **food**, but during the daytime pride of place goes to *Grangecon* (Ⓣ045/857892; closed Sun), in the old schoolhouse on Kilbride Road just off the main street, a relaxing setting for delicious versions of simple dishes such as shepherd's pie and sausage rolls, using organic ingredients and priced very keenly.

County Kildare

In contrast to the harsh landscape of the Wicklow Mountains to the east, **County Kildare** (Cill Dara; Ⓦwww.kildare.ie) is prosperous farming country, which was gladly seized and fortified by the English as part of the medieval Pale. Rich pasture for cattle and horses in the north of the county gives way to fertile ploughland in the south, the **Bog of Allen** in the northwest providing the only unproductive blot on the landscape. The county's main attractions for visitors are neatly concentrated in two areas. Servicing the bloodstock farms on **the Curragh's** lush heathland, **Kildare town** is generally a low-key affair, especially

The Grand and Royal canals

County Kildare is traversed by the **Royal and Grand canals**, which run from Dublin to the River Shannon. Reminders of Ireland's mercantile confidence in the eighteenth century, before the disenfranchisement of the Act of Union, they were built to service the mills, distilleries and breweries of a minor industrial revolution. Passenger boats on both canals were soon eclipsed by the railways and stopped running around 1850, but freight services continued until as late as 1960.

Completed in stages between 1779 and 1805, the **Grand Canal** heads out from south Dublin to Robertstown in County Kildare, where it splits into two branches. The fifty-kilometre southern branch (aka the Barrow Line), completed in 1791, meets the River Barrow at Athy in the south of the county, allowing passage as far south as Waterford; the main waterway runs west via Tullamore in County Offaly to Shannon Harbour, a total of 114km from Dublin.

The **Royal Canal**, a rival northern route opened between 1796 and 1816, was never quite as successful, though it managed to reach a peak tonnage of 112,000 in 1847. It runs along the northern border of County Kildare via Maynooth, before heading northwest to Mullingar and joining the Shannon, 144km from north Dublin, at Cloondara in County Longford.

The canals are flanked by a series of pleasantly undeveloped – and easy-to-follow – **trails**, the Royal Canal Way, the Grand Canal Way and the Barrow Way. Go to Ⓦwww.kildare.ie for full details and descriptions of the routes as they pass through Kildare. It's also possible to navigate the Grand Canal through the county and beyond (including the River Barrow) by **renting a narrowboat**, for €800–2200 per week depending on size and season, from Canalways, Rathangan (Ⓣ045/524646, Ⓦwww.canalways.ie), or from Barrowline Cruisers, Vicarstown, just across the border in Co. Laois (Ⓣ05786/26060, Ⓦwww.barrowline.ie).

now that the M7 bypass has opened. Here you can explore the monastery and church founded by St Brigid in the fifth century, and see what all the equine fuss is about at the fascinating **National Stud**. Hard by the university town of **Maynooth**, in the rapidly expanding commuter belt on the county's northern edge, lie the motley attractions of **Straffan** and **Larchill Arcadian Gardens**, as well as one of Ireland's finest stately homes, **Castletown**.

Many of the major routes out of Dublin traverse Kildare, so **transport** is generally easy. If you have a car, however, it's wise not to attempt to drive in or out of Dublin during rush hour – Friday afternoons coming out of the capital and Sunday or bank-holiday evenings returning are particularly bad. In the north of the county, Dublin city **buses** serve Castletown, Straffan and Maynooth, which is also on the N4 towards Galway and Sligo and the main **rail** line to the northwest. Buses between Dublin and Limerick stop in Kildare town, which is also on the rail line towards Waterford, the southwest and west.

Kildare town and around

In **KILDARE**'s quiet moments, of which there are many, you are keenly aware that the pre-eminent local business all takes place outside of town. For **the Curragh**, which stretches east from the town to the River Liffey, is Ireland's horse-racing centre. The underlying limestone of this five-thousand-acre plain, the largest area of semi-natural grassland in Europe, is good for a horse's bone formation, and the grass is said to be especially sweet. Consequently, the Curragh is home not only to a famous racecourse, but also to dozens of stud farms and stables, engaged in the multimillion-euro pursuit of breeding and training racehorses, one of the country's biggest sources of income – as vividly illustrated at the **National Stud** at Tully. To the north of Kildare, in stark contrast, stretches the **Bog of Allen**, whose development is traced at the nature centre in **Lullymore**.

The Town

Compactly arrayed around a triangular main square, which retains its central, nineteenth-century Market House, Kildare has fallen back into market-town sleepiness now that it's no longer a notorious bottleneck on the N7. The town does, however, hold one compelling point of interest, the huge Church of Ireland **Cathedral of St Brigid**, which overlooks the square. In the late fifth century, St Brigid is said to have founded a religious house here on a major pagan site, which became an important monastic centre of art, learning and culture – the *Book of Kildare*, for example, produced here in the seventh century but now lost, was, according to twelfth-century scholar Giraldus Cambrensis, dictated by an angel and as magnificent as the *Book of Kells*. Brigid herself, who may well have originated as the Celtic goddess Brigantia, has become Ireland's second most important saint after Patrick, with many holy wells that are thought to cure sterility dedicated to her.

The present church (May–Sept Mon–Sat 10am–1pm & 2–5pm, Sun 2–5pm) was originally constructed in the thirteenth century, but the north transept and choir were destroyed during the 1641 Rebellion, and the building was largely reconstructed in the nineteenth century. Its twelfth-century **round tower** (€4), the second highest in Ireland at 33m, is surmounted by mid-eighteenth-century battlements that replaced the original roof, and affords a fine panorama from the top – eastwards to the Curragh, and north to the Bog of Allen. On the north side of the church is the restored **fire temple** – Brigid had cannily preserved the pagan cult of fire, which her nuns observed here until the Reformation in the sixteenth century. A fire is lit here every year on **St Brigid's Day** (Feb 1), formerly the pagan festival of spring, Imbolc, when one of the few folkloric objects to persist into the modern era can be seen around Ireland: St Brigid's Cross, traditionally woven from rushes, but which can now be bought as a plastic replica in supermarkets, to be hung from your car windscreen.

Practicalities

Buses stop on the main square, while the **train station** is a ten-minute walk to the north. The **tourist office** (May–Sept Mon–Sat 9am–1pm & 2–5pm; Oct–April Mon–Fri 10am–1pm & 2–5pm; ⓣ045/530672) and its **heritage centre** (same hours; free), which contains mildly interesting display boards and a short audiovisual on the history of Kildare and the Curragh, are in the Market House in the centre of the square. Free but infrequent **shuttle buses** connect the train station, the tourist office, the National Stud and Kildare Village, a shopping centre on the southwest side of town. **Internet access** is available at the Internet Centre, just west of the square on the main street.

The best **accommodation** option in town is the comfortable, pristine-white *Singleton's B&B*, just north of the square at 1 Dara Park, Station Road (ⓣ045/521964; Feb–Nov; ❷), offering en-suite rooms at the lower end of this price code; otherwise try the en-suite rooms at the *Lord Edward*, behind – and owned by – the *Silken Thomas* pub on the square (ⓣ045/522232, ⓦwww.silkenthomas.com; ❶). It's also possible to stay at the Curragh Racecourse itself (see box, p.161), about 5km east of town, in the upmarket *Standhouse Hotel* (ⓣ045/436177, ⓦwww.carlton.ie; ❺), though this is not as atmospheric as you might expect: the building is right behind the main stand, which obscures any view of the famous course. Recently expanded from its original eighteenth-century building, the hotel now includes a leisure centre with a twenty-metre swimming pool and gym.

For **eating**, the *Silken Thomas* offers tempting lunches and dinners at the bar and has a smart, modern and popular evening restaurant, *Chapter 16*, whose menu stretches to global-influenced dishes such as steamed sea bass with lemongrass. The town's other good upmarket option is *Annamars*, 200m up Station Road (ⓣ045/522899; Wed–Sun evenings), where the French chef's inspiration runs to dishes such as duck fillet with fondue of red-cabbage marmalade. Just off the square on Claregate Street stands *Mahon's*, a smartly kept, old-time **pub** done out in cosy dark woods and green leather; or try *Nolan's*, beside the cathedral, a congenial place with welcoming snugs and regular live music. The *Silken Thomas* completes its role as the town's major hospitality complex with a weekend nightclub and an Irish theme bar, *Lil Flanagan's*, which hosts traditional music every Thursday, Friday and Sunday nights.

The National Stud

The **National Stud** (mid-Feb to mid-Nov daily 9.30am–6pm, last admission 5pm; mid-Nov to Christmas daily 10am–5pm, last admission 3.30pm; €10; ⓦwww.irish-national-stud.ie) shows the highly evolved business of horse breeding in action. Here, you can look round the stables themselves and stroll through two attractive on-site gardens (included in the admission price). Based at Tully on the south side of Kildare, it's a well-signposted 2km from the town centre (see above re shuttle buses); you should try to time your visit to coincide with one of the entertaining, free guided tours, which run at least three times

▲ Japanese Garden, The National Stud

daily from mid-February until mid-November, thereafter on request (☎045/522963 for details).

The stud farm was established here, by the mineral-rich River Tully, in 1900 by Colonel William Hall Walker, of the famous Scotch whisky family. Hall Walker's methods were highly successful, though eccentric: each newborn foal's horoscope was read, and those on whom the stars didn't shine were immediately sold, regardless of their lineage or physical characteristics. In

Horse racing in Kildare

Two of Ireland's major racecourses, where you're practically guaranteed a fun, boisterous day out, are just a short trot from Kildare. The major Irish flat-racing classics are held at the **Curragh Racecourse**, about 5km east of town (℡045/441205, Ⓦwww.curragh.ie): the Irish 1000 Guineas and 2000 Guineas in May, the Irish Derby in late June or early July, the Irish Oaks in July and the Irish St Leger in September. You can take special **bus** services to get to the Curragh from Busáras in Dublin on race days (contact Bus Éireann on ℡01/836 6111), and there are free shuttle buses from Kildare station to the course; on Derby day there are usually special train services from Heuston to the racecourse's own station (contact Iarnród Éireann on ℡01/836 6222, Ⓦwww.irishrail.ie).

About 20km east, just south of the town of Naas, **Punchestown Racecourse** (℡045/897704, Ⓦwww.punchestown.com) hosts the four-day Irish National Hunt Festival in April, a typically rural affair that attracts a lot of farmers. J.J. Kavanagh (℡056/883 1106) lays on race-day buses from Dublin airport via Naas.

1915, the colonel presented the farm to the British government – who promptly made him Lord Wavertree – on condition that it became the British National Stud. It was finally transferred to the Irish government in 1944 at an agreed valuation.

Within the attractive grounds, with their various yards, paddocks and stallion boxes, you can watch traditional saddlers and farriers at work. But the highlight of the tour has to be the horses themselves. They include fallabellas from Argentina, the smallest horses in the world (above pony height), as well as top stallions who command up to €75,000 for what's quaintly called a live cover and who jet as far afield as Australia to mate with local mares. From February until July, you should be able to see mares and their young foals in the paddocks.

The small, on-site **Irish Horse Museum** naturally focuses on Irish racing in its historical account of man's relationship with the horse. Its prize exhibit is the skeleton of Arkle, the greatest steeplechaser of all time, who was born and trained in Ireland and won the Cheltenham Gold Cup three years in a row in the 1960s. Much more of a draw is the beautiful and playful **Japanese Garden**, created by Colonel Hall Walker along with two Japanese gardeners on a reclaimed bog between 1906 and 1910. A product of the Edwardian obsession with the Orient, it symbolizes the life of man from oblivion to eternity. Over miniature hills, streams and waterfalls and past colourful flowers, shrubs and miniature trees, you follow from birth to death a delightful numbered trail, which yields a choice between bachelorhood and marriage, as well as a few false leads along the way.

The recently created **St Fiachra's Garden** close by is perhaps a little less compelling. St Fiachra was an Irish monk from a noble family who established a much-revered hermitage near Kilkenny town in the early seventh century. The hermitage became too popular for its own good, however, and the saint was forced to move to France, where he eventually founded another retreat near Meaux, 40km northeast of Paris, before his death in about 670. Fiachra always encouraged his disciples to cultivate gardens, from which they could distribute produce to the poor, and thus became the patron saint of gardeners – as well as of French taxi-drivers (after the cabs, known as *fiacres*, which used to take pilgrims from Paris to his shrine at Meaux). The garden comes across as a stylishly enhanced arboretum. A series of walkways leads you for spiritual reflection among a variety of trees and lakes, in one of which has been placed a group of 5000-year-old bog-oak trunks, branchless and blackened, suggesting not only death but also longevity. The miniature Waterford Crystal Garden, embedded in the floor of a stone monastic cell at the garden's heart, is rather twee, but in the nearby lake there's a dignified statue of St Fiachra sitting on a rock, examining a seed.

The Bog of Allen

To the north of Kildare lies the great **Bog of Allen**, Ireland's most famous peatland. Actually a complex of bogs that once covered two thousand square kilometres between the rivers Liffey, Barrow, Shannon and Boyne, it's now much diminished by drainage and stripping. The best place to get a handle on the bog is **LULLYMORE**, a tranquil parish and former monastic settlement on the road to nowhere 16km north of Kildare, which sits on an island of mineral soil, surrounded by peat.

Here you'll find the **Bog of Allen Nature Centre** (Mon–Fri 10am–5pm; €5; ⓣ045/860133, ⓦwww.ipcc.ie), run by the Irish Peatland Conservation Council, a charity whose aim is to ensure the conservation of a representative sample of Irish bogs. Informative exhibits at the centre, which is housed in the farm buildings of nineteenth-century Lullymore Lodge, trace the development of bogs, as well as their significance as habitats for rare animals and plants. The latter include species such as sundews, butterworts and pitcher plants, which have developed the capacity to eat insects, as the peat they grow on is deficient in nutrients; a small greenhouse in the centre's back garden displays carnivorous plants from Ireland and around the world, and their various methods of drugging, gluing or otherwise catching the poor critters. Also in the garden, miniature lake, fen and bog habitats have been reconstructed to show the stages

Bogs

Bogs once covered around one-sixth of Ireland's surface, a higher proportion than any other European country apart from Finland. They began to form around 9000 years ago after the last Ice Age, when retreating glaciers and ice sheets left central Ireland covered by myriad shallow lakes. Gradually the partly decomposed remnants of mosses, pondweeds, water lilies and reeds built up on many of the lake beds as layers of peat, reducing the area of open water and eventually forming **fens**.

Between 7500 and 1500 years ago, further changes occurred to most of Ireland's fens. As the fen peat became so thick that it filled up the lakes, its surface was colonized by sphagnum moss which, able to hold twenty times its own weight in water, accelerated the accumulation of peat. Thus, huge, sponge-like domes of water were formed above the level of the surrounding land, known as **raised bogs**, which have an average peat depth of 9–12 metres. Around 4000 years ago, a different kind of bog began to develop in areas of very high rainfall, either along the west coast or in the mountains. These **blanket bogs** carpet the land surface with a layer of black peat, 2–6m thick.

It's not surprising that, as such a prominent part of the environment, bogs occupy a significant place in Irish **folk history**, as evidenced by the many songs, poems and stories associated with the annual harvesting of the turf. They are also **habitats** of great ecological value, sheltering many rare and protected species of plant and animal. And, as well as being important to biologists and climatologists, bogs have produced some of the most spectacular finds of Irish **archeology**. The slow rate of organic decomposition that allowed the bogs to form in the first place has also in the Bog of Allen's development. Next to the centre, a hundred-metre boardwalk has been built over Lodge Bog, a small raised bog that's home to around 150 species of plants, including carnivorous round-leaved sundews, as well as mountain hares, foxes and over 70 species of butterflies and moths.

North Kildare

In the north of the county there's a tight cluster of attractions around the historic university town of **Maynooth**, each within day-tripping distance of Dublin, though it's not possible to combine them all if you're relying on **public transport**. There are no services at all to the beautifully restored gardens of **Larchill**, but frequent trains run to Maynooth from Dublin's Pearse, Tara Street and Connolly stations, as well as Dublin Bus's #66 from Pearse Street. Bus Éireann's #120 and #123, from either Busáras or Connolly LUAS station, connect Dublin with both the Palladian marvels of **Castletown** in Celbridge and **Straffan**, with its steam engines and butterflies.

Maynooth

Around 25km west of central Dublin, **MAYNOOTH** (pronounced "ma-nooth", with the stress on the second syllable) is the home of one of Ireland's most famous seminaries, **St Patrick's College**, which was founded in 1795 by the independent but short-lived Grattan Parliament in Dublin, and now also houses a branch of the National University of Ireland (ⓦwww.maynoothcollege.ie). Visitors are welcome to tour the college's forbidding grey quadrangles, leavened by Virginia creepers and ornamental gardens, and can buy a useful

preserved thousands of remarkable artefacts from the Neolithic period to the Middle Ages: ornaments and weapons, some of which were deliberately left in sacred bog pools as votive offerings during the Bronze Age; surprisingly intact human bodies, a few of which are now on display at Dublin's National Museum (see p.89); elaborate wooden roads from the Bronze and Iron ages, such as the Corlea Trackway (see p.214); and indeed, whole settlements that were engulfed by peat, as at Céide Fields (see p.467).

The bogs of Ireland, however, are under grave threat. Man has **exploited** the peatlands on a small scale for many centuries. Marl, the chalky soil found beneath the peat, is a lime-rich fertilizer; the peat itself has always been cut and dried for use as fuel; and the overlying mat of vegetation on the bog surface was once used as roof insulation. However, in the twentieth century, exploitation dramatically accelerated. Bord na Móna (the Irish Turf Board) introduced large-scale, mechanized extraction schemes, especially from raised bogs, producing fuel for power stations and domestic use, as well as horticultural peat. There have been further losses to forestry programmes and agricultural intensification, to the extent that only twenty percent or so of the original peatlands, around one-thirtieth of Ireland's landmass, remains intact. Under pressure from the Irish Peatland Conservation Council, however, the Irish government has committed itself to acquiring 500 square kilometres of raised and blanket bog, around a quarter of what remains, for conservation. For more information on bogs, go to the Irish Peatland Conservation Council's excellent website at ⓦwww.ipcc.ie.

guide (€4) at the visitor centre by the main entrance, which houses an exhibition on the history of the college (May–Sept Mon–Fri 11am–5pm, Sat & Sun 2–6pm; free). The Victorian-era second quad was designed in Gothic Revival style by Augustus Pugin, while the adjoining chapel is notable for its huge stained-glass rose window and finely carved oak choir stalls. The grandiosely titled **National Science Museum** (May–Sept Tues & Thurs 2–4pm, Sun 2–6pm; free) hosts a bizarre collection of bishops' copes, harps and induction coils, the latter invented by Nicholas Callan, who was professor of natural philosophy here in the early nineteenth century.

By the entrance to the college stand the substantial remains of **Maynooth Castle**'s doughty keep (June–Sept Mon–Fri 10am–6pm, Sat & Sun 1–6pm; Oct Sun 1–5pm; free; ⓦ www.heritageireland.ie), one of the largest of its kind in the country, which can be visited on forty-minute guided tours. Built in around 1200, the castle became the principal residence of the Anglo-Norman Fitzgeralds, later the Earls of Kildare, the most powerful family in Ireland between the late thirteenth and sixteenth centuries. Within the line of the castle's curtain wall stands St Mary's Chapel, a collegiate church that was the sixteenth-century forerunner of St Patrick's seminary.

It's unlikely that you'll want to stay in Maynooth, but it does boast a very good **restaurant**, *Lemongrass*, in the *Glenroyal Hotel*, Straffan Road (ⓣ 01/629 0915), which serves all manner of East and Southeast Asian food – including good-value lunchtime bento boxes containing a variety of taster dishes – in smart, modern surroundings.

Castletown

The oldest and largest Palladian country house in Ireland, **Castletown** (Easter–Sept Mon–Fri 10am–6pm, Sat & Sun 1–6pm; Oct Mon–Fri 10am–5pm, Sun 1–5pm; last admission 1hr before closing; €3.70; Heritage Card; ⓦ www.heritageireland.ie) is also one of the very finest. Its plain, grey but elegant facade, built in the style of a sixteenth-century Italian town palace, conceals a wealth of beautiful and fascinating interior detail. The house is accessed by gates and then a beautiful avenue of lime trees at the northern end of **CELBRIDGE**'s high street, around 6km southeast of Maynooth and 18km west of Dublin.

The house was built for William Conolly, son of a Donegal publican who, as legal adviser to William III, became the wealthiest man in Ireland from dealing in forfeited estates after the Battle of the Boyne, and was made Speaker of the Irish House of Commons in 1715. Though construction began in 1722, under first the Italian architect Alessandro Galilei and then his acquaintance, Edward Lovett Pearce, the interior was still unfinished at the time of Speaker Conolly's death seven years later. A second phase of work began in 1758, when great-nephew Tom Conolly married the 15-year-old Lady Louisa Lennox, who set about altering and redecorating the house to restrained, Neoclassical designs by Sir William Chambers, the architect of London's Somerset House.

The engaging hour-long guided tour begins in the **Entrance Hall**, decorated with gorgeous, three-dimensional baskets of flowers and fruit, which look like plasterwork but were actually carved in wood and painted white. To one side rises the **Grand Staircase**, its cantilevered Portland-stone steps and solid brass banisters weighing at least ten tonnes. Rococo stuccowork by the Swiss-Italian Lafranchini brothers, depicting Tom Conolly in high relief and personifications of the four seasons, swirls extravagantly over the walls here, but in such a huge, white space manages to appear delicate and restrained. The ground-floor **Brown Study** is the only room to retain its original, rich pine panelling and

▲ Castletown

narrow oak doors from the 1720s, and features a portrait of William III, donated to William Conolly by the king himself. Original furniture from the 1760s redesign can be found next door in the **Red Drawing Room**, including Lady Louisa's huge and impressively organized mahogany cabinet, which incorporates no fewer than 54 drawers and four secret compartments. Beyond the

Green Drawing Room, the principal reception room, with walls covered in gorgeous green silk, lies perhaps the most ostentatious display of wealth and fashion at Castletown. Over six years, at huge cost and with painstaking effort, Lady Louisa had the walls of the **Print Room** papered with black-and-white prints from London and Paris, portraying everything from landscapes and biblical scenes to royalty and famous actors of the day, complemented by decorative borders of swags, chains and masks; it must have looked fantastic in its original state, on a background of bright yellow paint.

The highlight upstairs is the **Long Gallery**, which was decorated by Lady Louisa with busts of Greek and Roman philosophers and murals of classical scenes of love and tragedy, in the style of the recently rediscovered Pompeii. It must have been a bit of a blow, however, to Lady Louisa when the extravagant glass chandeliers arrived from Murano in Venice and were found to be the wrong shade of blue for her newly decorated living room. From the gallery's windows you can make out the **Conolly Folly**, some 3km north, an arcane, fifty-metre-high edifice consisting of an obelisk perched shakily on top of a cascade of arches. Attributed to Richard Castle, it was built in 1740 as a monument to Speaker Conolly by his widow, and as a Famine relief scheme.

A recently opened **café** at the house serves up contemporary versions of Georgian fare, such as savoury pies, syllabubs and trifles, as well as soups, salads and pasta. Back in Celbridge, a hundred metres from the Castletown gates on Main Street, a handy watering-hole is the *Castletown Inn*, which serves exceptionally good, often gargantuan, bar **meals**.

Straffan

The village of **STRAFFAN**, about 6km southwest of Celbridge, is home to the varied attractions of **Lodge Park Heritage Centre** (June–Aug Wed–Sun 2–6pm, €7.50; Ⓦwww.steam-museum.com). Housed in the former Great Southern and Western Railway Church of St Jude, which has been brought here stone by stone from Inchicore in Dublin, the **Steam Museum** displays early model prototypes, as well as working steam engines from breweries, factories and ships throughout Ireland; Sunday is the day to catch them in action. In bucolic contrast is Lodge Park's recently restored eighteenth-century **walled garden**, which encloses such features as a salad vegetable parterre, an orchard, a topiary and a greenhouse containing an unusual collection of plants from around the world.

The nearby **Straffan Butterfly Farm** (June–Aug daily noon–5.30pm; €7; Ⓦwww.straffanbutterflyfarm.com) displays butterfly collections from all over the world. There's also a tropical greenhouse with live butterflies flying around, as well as some fiercer-looking inmates – including an assortment of reptiles, scorpions and tarantulas.

Larchill Arcadian Gardens

If you have your own transport, **Larchill Arcadian Gardens** (June–Aug daily except Mon noon–6pm; Sept Sat & Sun noon–6pm; €7.50, children €5.50, family ticket €27.50; Ⓣ01/628 7354, Ⓦwww.larchill.ie), 5km north of Kilcock and 11km from Maynooth, are well worth the short detour off the N4. Painstakingly restored, Larchill is the only complete surviving example in Europe of a *ferme ornée* ("ornamental farm"), the first type of garden to feature, under the influence of eighteenth-century Romanticism, elements of the natural landscape. Such gardens attained a degree of modishness among wealthy landowners during the latter half of the century, inspired by the influence of Versailles.

Beautiful parkland walks, along beech avenues and past ornate bridges, statuary and gazebos, link ten **follies**, in both Classical and Gothic style. These include **Gibraltar**, a lake island with a copy of the fortress on the Rock of Gibraltar, where mock naval battles were fought in the eighteenth century, and **Foxes' Earth**. This grassy mound, pierced with tunnels, was constructed for a reformed fox-hunter, who, believing that he was to be punished in the next life by being reborn as a fox, needed somewhere to get away from the hounds.

The ten-acre grounds are stocked with rare breeds of sheep and other farm animals, and there's a host of other attractions designed for kids, including an adventure playground and pets' corner, as well as regular family shows and events. An attractively restored eighteenth-century **walled garden** contains one of the follies, a tower decorated with shells, as well as a variety of unusual flowers, herb and vegetable gardens, and there's a pleasant **tearoom**.

County Meath

The rich limestone lowlands of **County Meath** (An Mhí; Ⓦwww.meathtourism.ie), cut across by the River Boyne and supporting ample cattle pasturage, have always attracted settlers and invaders. The valley's Neolithic people somehow found the resources and manpower to construct the huge, ornately decorated passage graves of **Newgrange**, **Knowth** and **Dowth**, part of the extraordinary landscape of ritual sites known as **Brú na Bóinne**, which is today one of the country's most famous and best organized visitor attractions. In contrast, the **Loughcrew Cairns**, a similarly extensive grouping of burial mounds in the far northwest corner of the county, have failed to garner present-day resources for excavation and tourist development, leaving you to explore this mysterious landscape unaided and usually in solitude. The **Hill of Tara** started out as a Stone Age cemetery, too, but evolved into one of Ireland's most important symbolic sites, the seat of the High Kings of the early Christian period. Meath also caught the eye of the Anglo-Norman invaders, who heavily fortified and held several parliaments at **Trim**, where you can visit the mighty castle and several other well-preserved medieval remnants.

The only useful **train** service here is to Drogheda on the Dublin–Belfast line, with buses onwards to Brú na Bóinne, but the main radial roads to the north of the capital – the R154 to Trim, the N3 via the Hill of Tara and Kells towards Cavan and the N2 via Slane towards Monaghan – are frequently served by **buses**.

Trim and around

Fifty kilometres northwest of Dublin, **TRIM** (Ⓦwww.trimtourism.com) is one of the most attractive towns within striking distance of the capital. Its imposing Anglo-Norman castle overlooks the curving, tree-flanked River Boyne and some picturesque ruins across on the north bank, while green meadows run downriver to the extensive remains of two medieval churches and a fine bridge.

Trim is also the easiest jumping-off point for the Cistercian abbey of **Bective**, set in lush countryside to the northeast.

The Town

The town's outstanding centrepiece is **Trim Castle** (Easter–Oct daily 10am–6pm; Nov–Easter Sat & Sun 10am–5pm; last admission and tour 1hr before closing; €3.70 for admission to the castle grounds plus 45min guided tour of the keep, €1.60 grounds only; Heritage Card; Ⓦwww.heritageireland.ie), which is intact enough to have been used as a location for Mel Gibson's 1995 film *Braveheart*. In 1172, Henry II, fearing that the adventurer Strongbow might try to establish his own Anglo-Norman kingdom in Ireland, granted the lordship of Meath to Hugh de Lacy, who along with his son Walter gradually built the most impressive castle in Ireland, the "keystone of the Pale", at this important ford over the Boyne. It's well worth taking the illuminating guided **tour** of the keep, and leaving yourself enough time to poke around the enclosure's assorted towers, ruined buildings and mighty curtain-wall.

The cruciform floor plan of the **keep** was a unique experiment in military architecture – the design increased possible angles of attack and thus was not emulated elsewhere. However, with walls up to five metres thick and over twenty metres high, which have survived to this day, the keep was obviously stout enough. The tour inside reveals a chapel, the former Great Hall, a bedroom with an early walk-in wardrobe and spectacular views of the town from the battlements.

The fording of the Boyne was defended by the castle's strongest tower, the **Magdalen Tower**, at the northern tip of the curtain wall, but during a period of greater stability and prosperity in the late thirteenth century, this was converted into private apartments, and a new **Great Hall** was built alongside. On the right-hand side of the hall, look out for a passage cut through the bedrock from the river gate, which allowed stores brought by boat from Drogheda on the coast to be delivered directly to the cellar.

▲ Trim Castle

The 450-metre **curtain wall**, with its ten D-shaped towers, is best appreciated from the south side of the keep. Low, marshy, easily defensible ground originally stood beyond this part of the enclosure, to which was added a deep, wide moat that could be flooded using weirs on the River Boyne. This sector is punctuated by the **Barbican Gate**, whose unusual but powerful design comprises a cylindrical tower linked by a heavily defended bridge over the moat to a forward square tower. The future King Henry V was imprisoned in this gate tower by Richard II, when his father, Henry of Bolingbroke, launched his ultimately successful coup d'etat in 1399.

Crossing the river by the footbridge under the castle walls, you can see the only surviving remnant of the fourteenth-century outer walls, the arched **Sheep Gate**. Nearby stands **Talbot's Castle** (privately owned), a beautiful tower house built in 1415 by Sir John Talbot, the Lord Lieutenant of Ireland. In the eighteenth century, Jonathan Swift (see p.103) bought the building and turned it into a Latin school, whose most famous alumnus was Arthur Wellesley, later the Duke of Wellington and MP for Trim. The tower house had been constructed on the site of an Augustinian abbey, St Mary's, which in turn had been built over one of the first monasteries in Ireland, dating from the fifth century. All that remains of St Mary's is the **Yellow Steeple**, a huge, half-ruined belfry that's so named because it glows in the evening sunlight.

About 1.5km east of the town centre on Lackanash Road, off the Dublin road, the beautiful remains of thirteenth-century **Newtontrim (SS Peter & Paul) Cathedral** stand in the meadows on the north bank of the river. The priory of Newtowntrim was founded here under the protective gaze of Trim Castle in 1202 by Simon de Rochfort, Bishop of Meath, and was soon elevated to become the seat of his diocese instead of Clonard. As a sign of Trim's pre-eminence, the largest and most sophisticated Gothic cathedral in Ireland was constructed here. Substantial parts of the nave and chancel can still be seen, alongside a ruined refectory.

Just across the river is another fine ruin, the **Priory of St John the Baptist**, also founded by Simon de Rochfort in the early thirteenth century. It was used as a hospital and guesthouse (with its own brewery) by the *Fratres Cruciferi*, the Crutched (or Cross-bearing) Friars, Augustinian monks who had attended the Crusaders. Between the cathedral and the priory, the Boyne is spanned by the wonderful Norman **St Peter's Bridge**, which is reckoned to be the second oldest bridge in the country.

Practicalities

Buses from Dublin currently stop on New Road, just north of the Dublin road, a few hundred metres east of Trim Castle, though the stop may be moved back into the centre in the future. On Castle Street by the main entrance to the castle, the helpful **tourist office** (Mon–Sat 9.30am–5.30pm, Sun noon–5.30pm; ⓣ046/943 7227) houses a coffee shop and an engaging audiovisual, *The Power and the Glory* (€3.20), on the medieval period in Trim. There's an **Internet** café on Market Street, which runs west off Castle Street.

Trim Castle Hotel (ⓣ046/948 3000, ⓦwww.trimcastlehotel.com; ❺) is a brand-new **hotel** opposite the castle, done out in a tasteful, contemporary style. Moving a little downmarket, and across the river, *Brogan's Bar & Guesthouse* on High Street (ⓣ046/943 1237, ⓦwww.brogans.ie; ❸) offers comfortable, well-equipped rooms, either in the main building, a nineteenth-century mill built with stone from the castle, or in the quieter stables at the back. **B&B** is available at the welcoming *Crannmor House* (ⓣ046/943 1635, ⓦwww.crannmor.com;

closed mid-Dec to early Feb; ❷), a Georgian country house with fine gardens, 1.5km north of town on the Dunderry road. Centrally placed just off Bridge Street on the north side of the river, Trim's **hostel**, *Bridge House* (IHH; ⓣ046/943 1848, ⓔsilvertrans@eircom.net), provides dorms (€20–25) and reasonably priced en-suite private rooms (❶).

Trim's best **restaurant** is *Franzini O'Brien's* (ⓣ046/943 1002), a spacious, modern but comfortable spot opposite the castle entrance on Frenches Lane, producing delicious dishes such as monkfish with lemon and orange *beurre blanc*. Just across the river on High Street, *The Bounty* is a characterful old **bar** that hosts sporadic traditional-music sessions.

Bective Abbey

In a beautiful setting by an old arched bridge on the west bank of the River Boyne, **Bective Abbey**, around 8km northeast of Trim, is a fine example of Cistercian architecture. To get there, take the Navan road from Trim, look out for a signposted right turn and then it's just over a kilometre on the left; continuing along these winding minor roads you could move on to Tara, 5km due east (see below).

Founded as a satellite of Mellifont (see p.189) in 1147, the abbey soon rose to prominence, its abbot holding a peer's seat in the Irish Parliament. The place was rebuilt in the thirteenth century, though only one wall of the nave remains from this phase. The majority of the extant building dates from the fifteenth century or later, remaining so remarkably intact because it was converted into a mansion house after Henry VIII's dissolution of the abbey in 1536. The sturdy and imposing fifteenth-century **tower** at the entrance is especially well preserved, and the south and west ranges of the **cloister** remain partly roofed – keep your eyes peeled for a carving of a monk near the southwest corner.

The Hill of Tara

Perhaps more than anywhere else in Ireland, the **Hill of Tara** is loaded with both historical and mythical significance. It's best known as the seat of the High Kings of Ireland in the early centuries after Christ, but had been a major ritual site since the late Stone Age, giving it plenty of time to accrue prehistoric legends. The aura of this long, grass-covered hill, covered with mostly circular mounds and ditches, is unmistakable, and the views of the surrounding countryside – which are said to take in thirteen counties – are magnificent.

The hill, which is just on the west side of the N3, stands at the centre of a widespread but interconnected complex of prehistoric ritual sites, many of which remain unexcavated. This is why you may well come across protesters at Tara and around Meath, objecting to the proposed route of the M3 motorway, which is slated to plough straight through the eastern side of the complex. For the moment, signposts off the current N3 bring you to a **visitor centre** (mid-May to mid-Sept daily 10am–6pm; €2.10; Heritage Card; ⓦwww.heritageireland.ie), where an impressive twenty-minute film provides historical and mythological background on Tara and shows some stunning views of the hill from the air; regular guided tours of the site leave from here, too. The centre occupies a nineteenth-century church, adorned with beautiful painted windows showing the Pentecost and the Apostles. Executed by Evie Hone in 1935, they commemorate the 1500th anniversary of St Patrick's mission to bring Christianity to Ireland.

There's a coffee shop by the car park, and if you want to stay near Tara, there's **B&B** in a modern bungalow with standard and en-suite rooms and fine views at *Seamróg*, right next to the site (Ⓣ046/902 5296; May–Sept; ❷), while *Bellinter House* (Ⓣ046/903 0900, Ⓦwww.bellinterhouse.com; ❻), a chic country-house **hotel** with a swimming pool, seaweed baths and other spa treatments, is just a few kilometres to the northwest off the N3.

Some history – and myth

It's likely that the site started out in the Neolithic period (c.3500 BC) as a place for burials and for ritual gatherings, with no resident population. Around sixty monuments, mostly barrows, have been discovered on the hill, the latest probably dating to the late Iron Age (c.400 AD). So much for the archeology, but mythology, literature and propaganda have imbued Tara with a far greater significance, as the ritual seat of kings – who did not have to be based here, but derived their authority from association with this revered place.

The earliest Irish sagas portray the hill as the home of the master-of-all-trades **Lug**, the greatest of the Celtic gods and the divine manifestation of Tara's kingship, and the goddess **Medb** (Maeve), who could also legitimize a king, sometimes by getting him drunk and sleeping with him – if she couldn't find a suitable candidate, Medb would rule herself. Of these legendary kings, the greatest were **Cormac Mac Airt** and **Conaire Mór**, semi-divine embodiments of peace, prosperity and righteousness. On somewhat firmer ground, seventh-century historical texts tell of recent struggles between the dynasties of Leinster, Ulster and the **Uí Néills** (pronounced "Ee-nails"; based in the northwest and the midlands) for the kingship of Tara. The Uí Néills came out on top, but while the title *rí Temrach* (king of Tara) would have given them special status over the other kings, territorial control over the whole island was not a possibility until the ninth century, when the island became less politically fragmented. In the eleventh century, however, geopolitical reality bit, and Tara lost out to the big city, Dublin.

Tara's significance continues into modern times: during the 1798 Rebellion some of the United Irishmen made a dramatic last stand on the hill, while in 1843 Daniel O'Connell harnessed the symbolic pull of the site to stage his biggest "monster meeting" here, attended by up to a million people, as part of his campaign to repeal the Union with England.

The site

Hard up against the wall of the church's graveyard, the first of the mounds you come to is the 83-metre-wide ring fort known as the **Rath of the Synods** (Ráith na Senad), so named as this was the reputed location of ecclesiastical synods in the sixth century. It's the untidiest of Tara's mounds: not only has it been partly destroyed by the church graveyard, but between 1899 and 1902 members of a cult, the British Israelites, dug up the rath, believing they would find the Ark of the Covenant. It's a particular shame that they kept no record of their efforts as this site went through many functions over the centuries: from early Bronze Age barrow, through palisaded ceremonial building, back to cemetery, and finally to ring fort. A Roman seal and lock have been found from this last phase, evidence of contact with the Roman world (probably Britain) in the fourth and fifth centuries AD.

The next tumulus to the south is the earliest on the site, the so-called **Mound of the Hostages** (Duma na nGiall). It takes its name from the primitive medieval peacekeeping practice of exchanging hostages with neighbouring kingdoms, who were supposedly imprisoned within the mound by Cormac Mac Airt. Built around 3000 BC, it's actually a Neolithic tomb with a four-metre-long passage that was reputed to have given entry to the other world. Access is no longer possible, but you can admire the typical concentric circles and zigzag patterns carved on one of the portal stones. No fewer than two hundred cremated late-Neolithic burials were found here, to which were added around forty from the Bronze Age, some cremated, some inhumed, the latter including a high-ranking teenage boy wearing a necklace of jet, amber, bronze and exotic faïence beads.

A kilometre-long circular bank, the **Royal Enclosure** (Ráith na Ríg), surrounds the Mound of the Hostages, and two larger, conjoined earthworks: the **Forrad**, a Bronze Age burial complex, and **Cormac's Residence** (Tech Cormaic), an Iron Age ring fort to the east. In the centre of the Forrad now stands the **Stone of Destiny** (the Lia Fail), a phallic standing stone used in the coronation of the High Kings, which was moved here from its original position near the Mound of the Hostages to commemorate those who died in 1798. Tradition states that the royal candidate had to drive his chariot wheel against the stone, and the gods, if they approved, would screech out his name. To the south of the Royal Enclosure lie the crescent-shaped remains of Ráith Lóegaire, the **Enclosure of King Laoghaire** (see p.176), who is said to be buried here standing upright and dressed in his armour, facing his enemies, the Leinstermen.

To the north of the church, the so-called **Banqueting Hall** (Tech Midchúarta) is actually two low banks of earth running parallel for over 200 metres. Though traditionally held to have been an enormous hall into which thousands of men from all over Ireland would have collected on ritual occasions, this was in fact probably Tara's ceremonial entrance avenue, aligned with the Mound of the Hostages and flanked by tombs and temples.

West of this avenue stands **Gráinne's Fort** (Ráith Gráinne), a burial mound surrounded by a circular ditch and bank. Like many ancient sites throughout Ireland, it has become associated with the tale of "The Pursuit of Diarmuid and Gráinne": the daughter of Cormac Mac Airt, Gráinne is betrothed to the king's elderly commander, Fionn Mac Cumhaill, but falls in love with one of his young warriors, Diarmuid, and elopes with him from Tara, with Fionn and his warriors in hot pursuit.

Beyond a line of trees to the west of Gráinne's Fort, two ring barrows known as the **Sloping Trenches** (Clóenfherta) cling to the hill's steep western slope, an unusual location that has given rise to a couple of legends. In one, the "trenches" are created when the palace of the bad king, Lugaid Mac Conn, collapses, after his judgments are shown to be false by a young Cormac Mac Airt. In the second, the site is explained as being the burial place of thirty princesses of Leinster slain by the king of Tara.

Kells and Loughcrew

Along the N3 northwest from Tara sits the unremarkable junction town of Navan, at the confluence of the Blackwater and Boyne rivers. Heading northeast along the N51 from here will bring you to Slane and the major sites of the Boyne valley (see p.175), while the N3 and the Blackwater lead 16km further northwest to **Kells**, a small market town and former monastic site with some decent options for bed and board. Another 20km northwest will take you to the

Loughcrew Cairns, one of Ireland's largest Neolithic cemeteries, in a dramatic, unspoilt hilltop setting. From Loughcrew, the Fore valley (see p.211) is only 15km or so to the south down the R195.

Kells

KELLS was founded in around 550 when St Colmcille (Columba) established a monastery here. After the Viking raids on Iona off the west coast of Scotland in around 806, the monks fled here, helping to create the leading Columbine house in Ireland. It's likely that the monks actually produced the great **Book of Kells**, now housed in Trinity College, Dublin (see p.86), on Iona, and brought it on their migration. Kells in its turn was plundered four times between 920 and 1019 by the Vikings, who looted the book's *cumdach* or metal shrine cover. The pagan Norsemen did not value the book itself, however, and despite spending some time buried underground and losing thirty folios, it survived here up to the seventeenth century when it was taken to Dublin for safekeeping. By this time, the Columbines' headquarters had long moved north to Derry, and the dissolution of 1551 had conclusively ended the monastery's slow decline.

A good place to start your explorations is the town's **heritage centre** on Navan Road (May–Sept Mon–Sat 10am–5.30pm, Sun 2–6pm; Oct–April Mon–Sat 10am–5pm; last admission 45min before closing; €4), located in the old courthouse designed in 1801 by Francis Johnston, architect of Dublin's GPO. There's a well-made audiovisual on the history of the town, as well as a facsimile of the *Book of Kells* and touch screens for accessing its pages on CD-ROM, plus a café. In front of the heritage centre stands the impressive **Market Cross**, a ninth-century High Cross that used to stand in the central market square. It was said to have been placed there by Jonathan Swift and was used as a gallows for 1798 rebels, but was damaged when the school bus driver ran into it and has recently been moved here.

Next, make for the modern bell tower of **St Columba's Church**, which stands on the site of the monastery. Another three **High Crosses** surround the church in the graveyard, carved with biblical scenes that are now heavily eroded – an exhibition in the church makes some sense of them, but it's only sporadically open in summer. The thirty-metre **Round Tower** in the corner of the cemetery is known to predate 1076, when it was the scene of the murder of Murchadh Mac Flainn, a claimant to the High Kingship of Tara.

The curious, beautifully preserved building known as **St Columcille's House**, with its very steeply pitched stone roof, now stands outside the church grounds, a short way up Church Lane. At least as old as the tenth century, it's actually an oratory, which may have been built to house the relics of St Columcille. To see inside, you'll need to call on the keeper of the keys, Miss Carpenter, at the orange-brown house just after the one-way sign on Church Lane (or ask the heritage centre to phone ahead). The oratory turns out to be barrel-vaulted, with three tiny chambers that may have been residential quarters high up in the roof space.

Practicalities

Kells' **tourist office** is in the heritage centre (same hours; ⓣ046/924 7840). The *Headfort Arms* (ⓣ046/924 0063, ⓦwww.headfortarms.ie; ❺) on Navan Road is a comfortable, family-run **hotel**, recently refurbished in crisp, modern style with the addition of a spa. Very good **B&B** accommodation is available at the friendly *Avalon*, with good rates for singles and children; it's just 100m from the heritage centre, from where it's signposted, in a quiet, modern house at 5

Headfort Park (Ⓣ046/924 1536, Ⓔavalonbb@gofree.indigo.ie; ❷). Kells' **hostel** (IHH & IHO; Ⓣ046/924 9995, Ⓦwww.kellshostel.com; March–Oct), at the top of Carrick Street (which becomes the N3 towards Cavan), offers four- or eight-bed dorms (€15–18) and en-suite private rooms (❶), as well as laundry and summer **camping** in the garden.

Havana, a café on Kenlis Place, which runs off Navan Road opposite the *Headfort Arms*, is a good, inexpensive option for daytime **eating**, offering everything from scones with jam and cream to panini and a few simple main courses. For dinner, choose between the chic surroundings of *Vanilla Pod* at the *Headfort Arms*, which serves well-prepared, sophisticated dishes such as wild mushroom risotto, and *The Ground Floor* on Bective Square on the south side of the centre (Ⓣ046/924 9688), a relaxing bistro serving salads, pasta, seafood and grilled meats.

The Loughcrew Cairns and Gardens, and Oldcastle

Sited on a row of four hills at the far northwestern tip of County Meath, the **Loughcrew Cairns** consist of more than thirty chambered mounds and over a hundred curiously carved stones. Local folklore has bestowed on the hills a colourful name, **Sliabh Na Caillighe** (as now marked on Ordnance Survey maps, meaning "Mountain of the Sorceress"), and foundation legend: the said witch, believing she would become mistress of all Ireland if she leapt from hill to hill carrying an apron full of rocks, performed the mighty jumps, shedding handfuls of stones on each peak, but fell at the last, breaking her neck (a cairn at the bottom of the easternmost hill is traditionally known as the witch's grave). The true story of the cairns' construction is only slightly less amazing: archeologists believe that between approximately 3500 and 3300 BC, Neolithic people travelled considerable distances to build these communal tombs, each of which may have taken anything from four to thirty years to complete. The alignment of the passage tombs and the elaborate carvings on their stone slabs display an association with sun worship, and it's obvious that this high-status ritual site was meant to be visible from afar. In reverse, the cairns afford a magnificent panorama over quiet lakes and gently undulating farmland, encompassing up to sixteen counties on a clear day.

Though on a smaller scale, the Loughcrew Cairns are contemporary with the more famous burial sites at Brú na Bóinne (see p.177), but, having never been comprehensively excavated, provide quite a different experience to the modern-day visitor. If you're going to visit both complexes, it makes sense to take the guided tours of the reconstructed mounds of Newgrange and Knowth first, before letting your imagination run wild on the unspoilt ritual landscape at Loughcrew. The majority of the tombs here are located on top of two hills, Carnbane East and Carnbane West, though unfortunately the latter is private land and currently inaccessible to visitors. To get to Carnbane East, follow the Oldcastle road for about 15km from Kells, before forking left towards Loughcrew Gardens; after 3km a right turn leads to the car park beneath the summit of Carnbane East after about a kilometre. To make the most of a visit, however, ignore this turn-off for the moment, and continue for a couple of kilometres to the café at Loughcrew Gardens, where you can pick up the **key to Cairn T** (€50 deposit), the site's most impressive passage tomb, and a torch.

Carnbane East

From the Carnbane East car park, it's a steep, ten-minute walk up to **Cairn T**, the focus of this summit and probably of the whole complex – most of the tombs on the other hills face towards it. The cairn's 113-metre circumference is reinforced by large kerbstones, behind which originally ran the thick layer of white quartz (as at Brú na Bóinne) that gave the hill its name: *carn bán* is Irish for "white cairn". On the north side is one of the largest kerbstones, known as the "Hag's Chair", where the witch of legend sat smoking her pipe (local lore adds that any wish you make while sitting here will come true). You can make out faint traces of carved Neolithic whorls on this stone, as well as a prominent cross, which strongly suggests that Masses (officially forbidden under the penal laws) were held in secret here during the eighteenth century.

The cairn's low, five-metre-long **passage**, aligned with the rising sun on the equinox days in March and September (just south of east), leads into a roughly circular chamber with three side recesses. Once your eyes become accustomed to the gloom, you'll start seeing wonderful, mysterious carvings – chevrons, whorls, waves, petals – on the large stones all around you. These incisions are especially ornate in the back recess, where a prominent sun pattern may have been specifically designed to catch the first rays of the equinox sun along the passage.

Another six kerbstoned mounds cluster around the central cairn, including **Cairn U** just to the northeast, which features further enigmatic carvings on its passage and chamber stones, now open to the elements.

Loughcrew Gardens and Oldcastle

While you're in the area, it's well worth visiting **Loughcrew Gardens** (April–Sept daily 12.30–6pm; Oct–March Sun & bank hols 1–5pm; €7; Ⓦwww.loughcrew.com), signposted on the southwestern side of Carnbane East. These painstakingly restored gardens encompass an impressive seventeenth-century avenue of grotesquely fluted yew trees and nineteenth-century lawns, herbaceous borders, ponds and a grotto, as well as signposted woodland walks and the family church of St Oliver Plunkett (see p.187), now roofless. The oldest part of the church was formerly a tower house, the seat of the Plunketts until the 1652 Act of Settlement, when Cromwell's surveyor, Sir William Petty, installed his brother-in-law, William Naper, at Loughcrew.

There's a **café** serving tea, coffee and light meals, and it's possible to **stay** in luxurious style in *Loughcrew House*, still the home of the Napers (Ⓣ049/854 1356; ⑤), where the grand, ornate bedrooms boast fine views of the estate. Though much reduced in size from its nineteenth-century heyday – three serious fires have done the damage – the house's enormous Neoclassical portico of four Ionic columns has been atmospherically re-erected as a ruined "Temple of the Rains". In the summer, the Napers host popular outdoor jazz and opera **festivals** in the gardens. Upmarket **B&B** is also available at *Knockbrack Grange* (Ⓣ049/854 1771, Ⓔkittybevan@eircom.net; closed Oct–April; ③), a welcoming, creeper-clad, 1820s rectory in an attractive garden, where fine dinners can also be arranged; it's about 1km west of Loughcrew Gardens along the same road, towards Millbrook.

Around 3km north in **OLDCASTLE**, a thriving village that sports several galleries and boutiques, there's a **tourist information** centre at *Kraft Kaffee*, a craft shop and café on Millbrook Road (Tues–Fri 10am–5.30pm, Sat 11am–5.30pm; Ⓣ049/854 2645). You can **stay** at the stylish, modern *Oldcastle House Hotel* (Ⓣ049/854 2400, Ⓦwww.oldcastlehousehotel.com; ⑤), while *Caffrey's*, an equally smart **pub** opposite, offers lunch and dinner, and live music at weekends.

The lower Boyne valley

A little over 20km due east of Kells, **Slane's** historic castle and monastery enjoy a picturesque setting on a steep, wooded hillside above the River Boyne.

Between here and Drogheda (see p.185), the river bends dramatically south around **Brú na Bóinne**, one of the world's most important archeological landscapes, now designated a UNESCO World Heritage site, where around forty Neolithic mounds have been discovered. This extraordinary ritual landscape was also the scene, some five thousand years later, of one of the most significant battles in Ireland's history, the **Battle of the Boyne**.

Slane

The village of **SLANE** grew up around **Slane Castle**, whose estate extends westwards from the large Gothic gate by the bridge over the River Boyne. The main entrance for visitors, however, is now round the back of the house, about a kilometre west of the village crossroads (early May to early Aug Mon–Thurs & Sun noon–5pm; €7; Ⓦwww.slanecastle.ie). The era's finest architects – Gandon, Wyatt and Johnston – constructed the castle, with its mock battlements and turrets, from 1785 onwards, while Capability Brown designed the grounds. A devastating fire struck in 1991, however, and it took until 2001 for the castle to open again, with its interior redesigned in largely contemporary style as a venue for conferences and society weddings. Consequently, the guided tour smacks a little of *Hello* magazine, though there are one or two points of architectural interest remaining, notably the lofty ballroom, with its ornate fan vaulting and an original carved wooden chandelier, which was built by Thomas Hopper for George IV's 1821 visit to his mistress, Lady Conyngham. The present Conyngham, Henry, Lord Mountcharles, is a friend of rock band U2, who lived here while recording *The Unforgettable Fire in 1984*, and mounts huge concerts in the grounds most summers.

From the main crossroads in the village, it's a fifteen-minute walk north up to the **Hill of Slane**, which affords views over rolling farmland to the Irish Sea at Drogheda and the Wicklow Mountains. Here, in 433, according to tradition, **St Patrick** lit the Paschal (Easter) Fire for the first time in Ireland, signalling the arrival of Christianity. In this he challenged the pagan *Bealtaine* fire on the Hill of Tara, 15km to the south, lit by the High King, Laoghaire, to celebrate the arrival of summer. Laoghaire was soon won over, however, and although the king did not take on the new religion himself, he allowed his subjects to be converted. These included St Earc, who became Patrick's great friend and follower and established a **monastery** here on the hill, which eventually evolved into a Franciscan house. Today you can see the extensive remains of its sixteenth-century church and fine bell tower, along with an associated college built around an open quadrangle.

Heading east out of Slane on the N51 towards Drogheda, you'll find the **Francis Ledwidge Museum** after just over a kilometre (Feb to Oct daily 10am–1pm & 2–5.30pm or dusk, if earlier; €2.50; Ⓦwww.francisledwidge.com). This simple stone cottage was the birthplace, in 1887, of the poet Francis Ledwidge, who left school at 13 to work on a farm, and later the roads. His poetry derived inspiration from the beautiful landscape around his home here, as well as from the history and myth of County Meath. The small museum includes re-creations of the kitchen and the poet's bedroom, some fascinating display boards and a pretty, shady garden out the back. Although a member of the Irish Volunteers, Ledwidge, like 150,000 other Irishmen, joined the British Army in World War I to protect the rights of small nations, to try to secure Home Rule after the end of the war and to fight "an enemy common to our civilization", as he put it. He survived the horrors of Gallipoli in 1915 – the year in which his only volume of poems, *Songs of the Fields*, was published – but was killed by a stray shell at the Third Battle of Ypres in 1917. Inscribed on a plaque by the cottage's front door are the lines written by Ledwidge about his poet friend, Thomas MacDonagh, who was executed by the British for his part in the 1916 Easter Rising:

He shall not hear the bittern cry
In the wild sky, where he is lain,
Nor voices of the sweeter birds
Above the wailing of the rain.

Practicalities

Comfortable, en-suite budget **accommodation** can be found in the converted coach house and stables of a working farm at the well-run *Slane Farm Hostel*, just over 2km west of the village beyond the castle (ⓣ041/988 4985, ⓦwww.slanefarmhostel.ie; IHH; Feb to mid-Dec; dorms €18, private rooms ❶); the hostel also offers **camping**, laundry facilities and Internet access. En-suite B&B accommodation, with a pleasant garden and good single rates, is offered at modern *Castle View House* (ⓣ041/982 4510, ⓔcastleview@oceanfree.net; March–Oct; ❷), just west of the village on the N51. Conveniently located in the centre of the village is the *Conyngham Arms Hotel* (ⓣ041/988 4444, ⓦwww.conynghamarms.com; ❹), which offers comfortable rooms, a pretty beer garden and good-value **food**. *George's Patisserie and Deli*, north of the crossroads on Chapel Street (ⓣ041/982 4493; closed Mon), serves fantastic cakes, sandwiches, salads and good coffees and teas; the owner is planning to open a restaurant, *The Poet's Rest*, next door, serving traditional European and Irish fare.

Brú na Bóinne

Between the River Boyne and the N51 to the north, **Brú na Bóinne** (the "palace of the Boyne"; ⓦwww.heritageireland.ie) encompasses the spectacular 5000-year-old **passage graves** of **Newgrange**, **Knowth** and **Dowth**, high round tumuli raised over stone passages and burial chambers. Entry is funnelled through the impressive **visitor centre** on the south side of the river, which provides detailed information on the significance of the sites, their construction and artwork, and the Neolithic society that created them, as well as housing a tourist information desk and café. A footbridge crosses from the centre to the north side of the river, where the compulsory minibuses shuttle you to Newgrange and Knowth, which have both been comprehensively excavated and reconstructed, for guided tours (for Dowth, see p.179).

Brú na Bóinne is one of Ireland's foremost attractions, and the **numbers** visiting each site daily are strictly limited. Booking by phone isn't possible, so it's advisable to arrive as early in the day as you can, especially at Easter or in summer, and book your places on the minibuses, which have timed departures. Sunday mornings are generally the quietest time of the week. There's no point in arriving late in the day, as it takes at least three hours to see Newgrange, Knowth and the visitor centre.

There are a couple of good **B&Bs**, both on working farms, if you want to **stay** in the immediate vicinity of Brú na Bóinne. *Roughgrange* is a comfortable seventeenth-century house with en-suite bedrooms, a kilometre or two west of the visitor centre on the Slane road (ⓣ041/982 3147; March–Oct; ❷), while *Rossnaree*, an Italianate Victorian country house about a kilometre further along the same road, offers considerably more luxury, as well as art and cookery courses (ⓣ041/982 0975, ⓦwww.rossnaree.ie; ❹). Opposite the Brú na Bóinne Visitor Centre, the new, purpose-built *Newgrange Lodge* offers a range of attractive and

Visiting Brú na Bóinne

Opening times and admission prices

The Brú na Bóinne Visitor Centre is open daily: March, April & Oct 9.30am–5.30pm; May & second half of Sept 9am–6.30pm; June to mid-Sept 9am–7pm; Nov–Feb 9.30am–5pm; last admission 45min before closing.

The last **minibuses** to Newgrange and to Knowth depart 1hr 45min before closing. Knowth is open Easter–Oct only.

The **tourist office** (ⓣ041/988 0305) closes around 40min before the rest of the visitor centre.

Admission prices: visitor centre €2.90; combined ticket with Newgrange €5.80; combined ticket with Knowth €4.50; all three €10.30. The Heritage Card is valid for all of these.

Transport

If you have your own transport, follow signs from the south side of the bridge in Slane or from the M1 motorway to the southwest of Drogheda (via Donore).

If you're relying on **public transport**, take Bus Éireann service #100 from Busáras to Drogheda (which is also served by suburban trains from Pearse, Tara Street or Connolly stations), and then the #163 bus to the visitor centre, which connects with the #100 5 or 6 times a day. Alternatively, a Newgrange shuttlebus operated by Over the Top Tours (see p.143; €18 return) leaves Suffolk Street tourist office daily at 8.45am & 11.15am, stopping outside the *Royal Dublin Hotel*, O'Connell Street Upper, at 9am & 11.30pm, and returns from the visitor centre at 1pm & 4pm (though return times may vary in peak season). The journey takes about 45min; tickets can be purchased on board but it's better to book your seat in advance at any tourist office.

comfortable, en-suite **budget accommodation** (ⓣ041/988 2478, ⓦwww.newgrangelodge.com; dorms from €15, private rooms ❷).

Newgrange

Newgrange is unquestionably the most striking of the Brú na Bóinne mounds, not least because its facade of white quartz stones and round granite boulders has been reassembled. The quartz originally came from Wicklow, the granite from the Mourne and Carlingford areas, exemplifying the mind-boggling levels of resources and organization lavished on this project, by these farmers who used nothing but simple tools of wood and stone. It has been estimated that the tumulus, which is over 75m in diameter, weighs 200,000 tonnes in total and would have taken around forty years to build. It was the final resting place of a high-status family within the Neolithic community – the cremated remains and grave goods of at least five people were recovered from the burial chamber during excavation – but seems also to have had a wider purpose as a ritual site or gathering place.

The **entrance stone** is one of the finest examples of the art of the tomb-builders, who carved spectacular but enigmatic spirals, chevrons, lozenges and other geometric designs onto many of the large stones around the mound and up the nineteen-metre passage. The tomb's pivotal feature, however, is a **roof-box** above the entrance whose slit was perfectly positioned to receive the first rays of the rising sun on the day of the **winter solstice** (December 21); the light first peeps into the cruciform burial chamber itself before spreading its rays along the length of the passage. The engaging guided tour provides an electrically powered simulation in the burial chamber, while tickets for the real thing are decided by lottery each year. To prehistoric farmers, this solstice marked the start of a new year, promising rebirth for their crops and perhaps new life for the spirits of the dead.

It seems probable that by around 2000 BC, in the Late Neolithic or Early Bronze Age, the mound had collapsed and fallen into disuse, but it still provided a powerful focal point for ritual. During this era, a huge religious enclosure known as the **pit circle** was constructed here, consisting of a double circle of wooden posts, within which animals were cremated and buried in pits. To this was added a circle of around 35 **standing stones**, which may have had an astronomical function; about a dozen of them remain upright.

Knowth

It's well worth signing up for the lively guided tour of **Knowth** too, which provides some telling contrasts with the more famous Newgrange – not least in interpretation: the archeologist in charge of this site, for example, thought the white quartz stones discovered around the main passage entrance were to reflect the sun, so left them as a shimmering carpet on the ground. The Knowth mound is pierced by two passages, each around twice the length of the Newgrange tunnel, aligned roughly with sunrise and sunset on the equinox days in March and September and leading to back-to-back burial chambers. Unfortunately, it's no longer possible to follow the passages themselves, but the tour takes you inside the mound to look along the eastern tunnel, and you can also climb on top of the mound for views of the Hill of Slane and the Wicklow Mountains.

Knowth is even richer in **Neolithic art** than Newgrange, with about 250 decorated stones discovered here – over half of all known Irish passage-tomb art. The mound is surrounded by over 120 huge kerbstones, one of which supports a carved pattern of crescents and lines that may represent the equinox; elsewhere, patterns of circular and serpentine incisions have been interpreted, perhaps with a nod to Australian Aboriginal art, as local maps, showing the River Boyne and the burial mounds. Hard by the main mound, you can poke around eighteen smaller or **satellite mounds**, at least two of which were built before the main tomb. The Knowth mound attracted habitation in various eras right up until the sixteenth century AD, and your guide will show you several **souterrains**, underground tunnels that were dug in the early Christian period for hiding, escape and possibly food preservation.

Dowth

The mound at **Dowth** has recently passed into state ownership, and although there's no entry to its two passage tombs, you can freely walk around the site by yourself and see some of its 115 kerbstones; it's on the north side of the Boyne, about a kilometre north of the visitor centre, where you can pick up a map of the local area. The grassy hummock, some 85m in diameter, has not received the same reconstruction treatment as Newgrange and Knowth, and is scarred by quarrying for road building on its western side and by a central crater resulting from excavations in the 1840s. The name Dowth may come from *dubh* ("darkness"), and it's thought that the main passage was deliberately aligned to catch sunset at the winter solstice, while the short secondary passage points southwest towards Newgrange.

The Battle of the Boyne site

On July 1, 1690 (July 11 according to our modern calendar, though it's celebrated by Northern Protestants on July 12, due to a mistaken recalculation following the eighteenth-century change to the Gregorian calendar), William III met his father-in-law, the deposed King James II, at the **Battle of the Boyne**. At stake were the English throne, now held by William with support from the pope and the Catholic king of Spain, and the dominance of Europe by the French, who backed the Catholic James. At the head of an army of 36,000, William took up position on the north side of the river just west of Drogheda, while on the opposite bank, James commanded 25,000 men, mostly Irish irregulars, but including 7000 well-armed French soldiers. To counter William's flanking movement, upriver and around the Knowth mound, James was drawn into sending a large part of his force westward, which allowed the main Williamite army to cross the river to Oldbridge and put the Jacobite centre to flight. The Irish and French regrouped to carry on fighting for another year, notably at Aughrim and Limerick, but James kept running, via Dublin and Kinsale, to France, never to return.

The Oldbridge **battle site** (Ⓣ041/988 9950, Ⓦwww.battleoftheboyne.ie), which is currently being developed with cross-border funding, can be reached from Brú na Bóinne by making for Donore, then heading north for 3km to the river, or from the Drogheda–Slane road (N51) by crossing the Obelisk Bridge. At the site, you'll find display boards and signposted battlefield walks, including a 40-minute circular trail past Oldbridge House, and in summer you can take a 45-minute guided tour (May–Sept daily 10am–6pm; free) and watch actors in period costume give "living history" displays (June–Sept Sun only). Future plans include a display and audiovisual in Oldbridge House, a peace garden and more extensive signposted walks.

Travel details

Trains

Dublin Connolly to: Maynooth (10–30 daily; 30min; some trains start at Pearse Station, via Tara St); Rathdrum (3–5 daily; 1hr 15min; via Tara St and Pearse); Wicklow (3–5 daily; 50min; via Tara St and Pearse).
Dublin Heuston to: Kildare (20–30 daily; 40min).

Buses

Bus Éireann

Dublin to: Ashford (6–10 daily; 1hr 20min); Avoca (1–2 daily; 2hr 5min); Celbridge (Mon–Sat roughly every 30min, Sun 6 daily; 30min); Kells (Mon–Sat every 30min, Sun hourly; 1hr 30min); Kildare (at least hourly; 1hr–1hr 30min); Meeting of the Waters (1–2 daily; 2hr); Rathdrum (1–2 daily; 1hr 50min); Slane (6–9 daily; 45min); Straffan (Mon–Sat roughly every 30min, Sun 6 daily; 40min); Trim (5–10 daily; 1hr 15min); Wicklow (7–11 daily; 1hr–1hr 30min).
Kells to: Oldcastle (Mon–Sat 1–3 daily; 45min).
Slane to: Drogheda (3–6 daily; 35min).
Wicklow to: Avoca (1–2 daily; 35min); Meeting of the Waters (1–2 daily; 30min); Rathdrum (1–2 daily; 20min).

Dublin Bus

Ⓣ01/873 4222, Ⓦwww.dublinbus.ie
Bray to: Enniskerry (#185 from the DART station; Mon–Sat roughly every 30min, Sun roughly hourly; 30min).
Dublin to: Blessington (#65 from Eden Quay, College Green or South Great George's St; roughly hourly; 90min); Enniskerry (#44 from Townsend St; Mon–Fri roughly every 30min; Sat & Sun at least hourly; 1hr); Maynooth (#66 from Pearse St; roughly every 30min; 1hr 10min).

St Kevin's Bus Service

Ⓣ01/281 8119, Ⓦwww.glendaloughbus.com
Dublin (Dawson St) to: Glendalough, via Bray, Roundwood and Laragh (2 daily; 1hr 30min).

3

Louth, Monaghan and Cavan

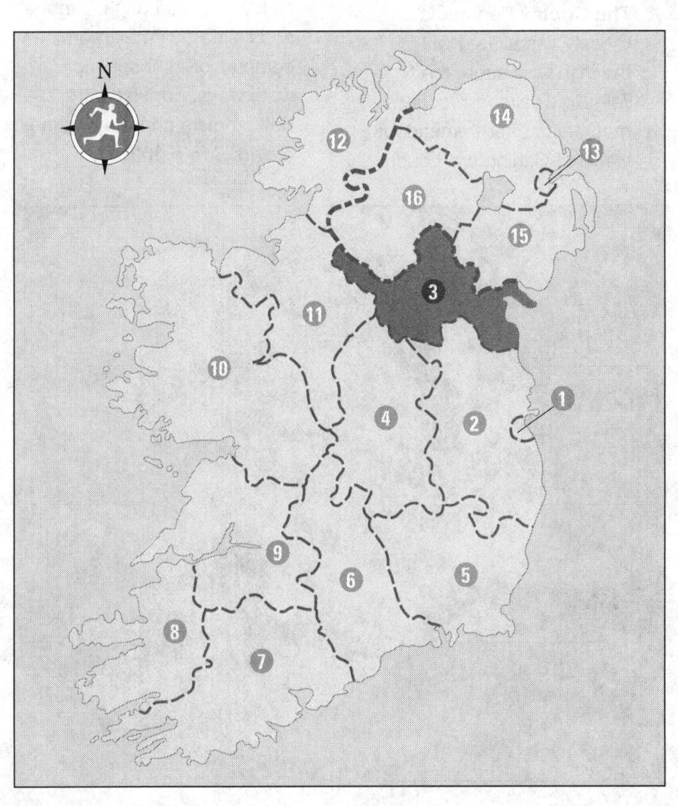

CHAPTER 3

Highlights

* **Drogheda** One of Ireland's liveliest towns, rich in antiquities and with atmospheric bars. See p.185
* **Monasterboice** Ecclesiastical relics here include Ireland's tallest round-tower and also two of the most splendid high-crosses in the whole of the country. See p.189
* **The Cooley Peninsula** Closely associated with the Irish epic saga, the *Táin Bó Cúailnge*, Cooley's mountains offer tremendous views of Carlingford Lough, while Carlingford itself has some terrific restaurants. See p.191
* **Inniskeen** The birthplace of one of the country's greatest poets, Patrick Kavanagh, celebrates its scion through an excellent and informative resource centre. See p.196
* **The Lakes of Cavan** Known collectively as Lough Oughter and linked by an extraordinary complex of atmospheric waterways, popular with both anglers and the boating crowd. See p.200

▲ High Cross at Monasterboice

3

Louth, Monaghan and Cavan

Louth, Monaghan and Cavan all share a border with Northern Ireland and, as throughout the North, still bear many signs of the Plantation in the form of "big houses" and planned towns. **Louth** is Ireland's smallest county and the most northerly in the Leinster province, and much of its activity is focused on the divergent towns of Drogheda and Dundalk. In its northeast the Cooley Peninsula provides somewhat dramatic relief from the county's otherwise drab coastline.

The topography of Monaghan and Cavan, both in the Ulster province, is markedly different. **Monaghan**'s landscape is characterized by eruptions of small hills, known as drumlins, while contrastingly, much of **Cavan** is defined by its many waterways and small lakes. Away from the major roads that pierce both counties, the countryside has an unhurried charm, though it's easy to get lost when navigating their tangled grid of lanes without a map or compass. However, the Shannon–Erne Waterway offers a readily navigable route through Cavan's lakes and cruisers can be hired in places such as **Belturbet** as a starting point for a waterways holiday.

Most of the attractions in Louth (which has rail links to Dublin and Belfast) and Monaghan are easily accessible by **public transport**, but bus services in Cavan are somewhat less frequent.

County Louth

County Louth is easily accessible from Dublin via the main N1/M1 road and Belfast railway line. Its most historic and intriguing town is **Drogheda**, bisected by the River Boyne, and forever associated with Cromwell's arrival in Ireland. His New Model Army besieged the town in 1649 and, once its walls were breached, zealously massacred not only the Royalist garrison, but

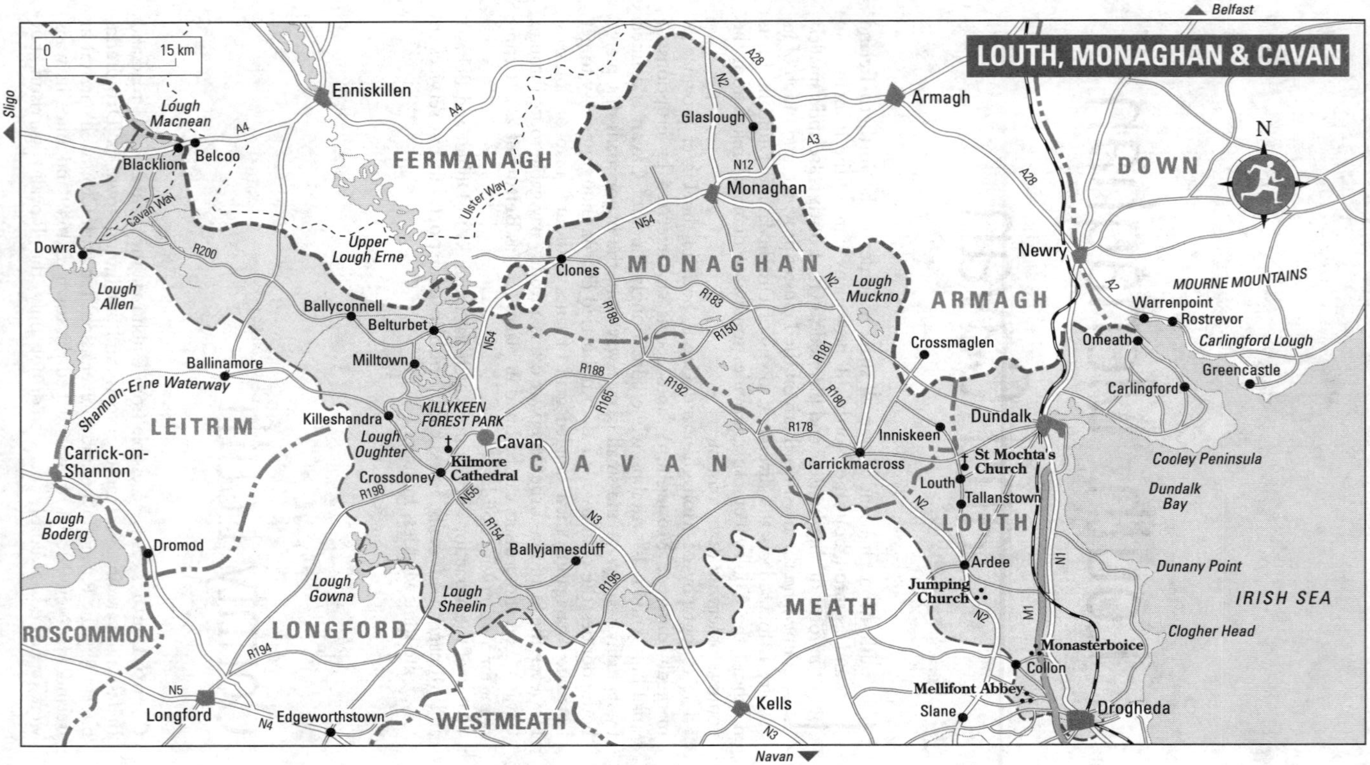

LOUTH, MONAGHAN & CAVAN

0 15 km
Sligo
Belfast
Navan
N
Enniskillen
Armagh
Lough Macnean
Blacklion
Belcoo
FERMANAGH
Ulster Way
Cavan Way
Glaslough
Monaghan
DOWN
Dowra
R200
Upper Lough Erne
Clones
MONAGHAN
Lough Muckno
ARMAGH
Newry
MOURNE MOUNTAINS
Warrenpoint
Rostrevor
Omeath
Carlingford Lough
Lough Allen
Ballyconnell
Belturbet
Milltown
Crossmaglen
Greencastle
Carlingford
Ballinamore
Shannon-Erne Waterway
KILLYKEEN FOREST PARK
Killeshandra
Lough Oughter
Cavan
Kilmore Cathedral
CAVAN
Dundalk
Inniskeen
Carrickmacross
St Mochta's Church
Louth
Tallanstown
Cooley Peninsula
Dundalk Bay
LEITRIM
Carrick-on-Shannon
Crossdoney
LOUTH
Lough Boderg
Dromod
Ballyjamesduff
Ardee
Dunany Point
Jumping Church
IRISH SEA
Lough Gowna
Lough Sheelin
MEATH
ROSCOMMON
LONGFORD
Clogher Head
Monasterboice
Collon
Mellifont Abbey
Longford
Edgeworthstown
WESTMEATH
Kells
Slane
Drogheda
A28
N2
A3
A4
N12
N54
A2
R183
R189
R150
R181
R188
R192
R165
R180
R178
R198
N55
R154
N3
R195
R194
N5
N4
M1
N1

numerous citizens as well. As well as being home to the most important megalithic remains in the whole country at Brú na Bóinne and site of the Battle of the Boyne (see p.177–180), the fertile **Boyne valley** also boasts major religious sites at **Monasterboice** and **Mellifont**. In the county's north the border town of **Dundalk** features one of the country's best local museums.

The countryside of Louth also plays a major role in the greatest of Irish mythological epics, the *Táin Bó Cúailnge* (Cattle Raid of Cooley), especially the **Cooley Peninsula**, where many of the saga's events took place.

Drogheda

DROGHEDA (pronounced "droch – as in loch – edda") was once two separate Viking settlements, huddled together on either side of the River Boyne. These developed into twin towns during the Anglo-Norman period, whose intermittent rivalry was quashed by a royal charter uniting the pair in 1412. Today, Drogheda is a thoroughly enjoyable place to visit, with a lively arts scene, and its old docks, once the focus for the numerous trades that developed here during the eighteenth and nineteenth centuries, are being redeveloped with vitality, not least in the shape of the huge new Scotch Hall shopping centre on the south side of the river.

Arrival and information

The **bus station** (ⓣ041/983 5023) is on Donore Road, just south of the river, and the train station is also on the southern side, just off Dublin Road to the east of town. The **tourist office** (Mon–Sat 9am–5pm; ⓣ041/983 7070, ⓦwww.drogheda.ie) lies on Mayoralty Street. **Walking tours** of the town (early July to Sept Mon–Fri 11am & 2pm daily; €3; ⓣ041/983 3097) depart from the Tony Byrne statue next to the Scotch Hall Shopping Centre on South Quay. **Bikes** can be rented from Quay Cycles, 11 North Quay (ⓣ041/983 4526).

Accommodation

Drogheda isn't exactly awash with **accommodation** options, but there's still enough to satisfy most budgets.

Boyne Valley Hotel and Country Club Dublin Rd ⓣ041/983 7737, ⓦwww.boyne-valley-hotel.ie. Just outside town, set in beautiful grounds, this pleasant hotel has its own leisure centre and tennis courts. ❺

The D Scotch Hall ⓣ041/987 7700, ⓦwww.thed.ie. Very style-conscious riverside establishment providing swish doubles, a great waterside bar, and an utterly *outré* penthouse suite (€1000 per night); plenty of off-season and early-booking bargains on offer. ❻

Green Door Hostel 47 John St ⓣ041/983 4422, ⓦwww.greendoorireland.com. A well-run and amenable IHH hostel, also affiliated to An Óige, offering a variety of private rooms and dorms. Dorms €18, doubles ❶.

Maple House 69 Maple Drive ⓣ041/983 3502, ⓕ983 2244. A relaxing B&B with en-suite facilities, five minutes east of the town centre. ❷

Orley House Bryanstown, Dublin Rd ⓣ041/983 6019, ⓦwww.orleyhouse.com. Spruce modern townhouse with en-suite rooms, just off the N1 near the train station. ❷

Scholars Townhouse Hotel King St ⓣ041/983 5410, ⓦwww.scholarshotel.com. Renovated former Christian Brothers residence whose opulence might have some of the CBs questioning their faith; excellently furnished rooms and a fine restaurant too. ❹

Westcourt Hotel West St ⓣ041/983 0965, ⓦwww.westcourt.ie. Right in the centre of town with secure parking, this is a very welcoming and comfortable establishment. ❹

ACCOMMODATION	
Boyne Valley Hotel and Country Club	G
The D Hotel	D
Green Door Hostel	E
Maple House	B
Orley House	F
Scholars Townhouse Hotel	A
Westcourt Hotel	C

EATING & DRINKING	
Bella Atina	9
The Boiled Onion	10
The Bru	12
Carberry's	1
Clarke and Sons	2
La Pizzeria	6
The Laurence Inn	8
Monk's Café	11
Moorland Café	5
New Central	7
Peter Matthews	4
Sarsfields	3

The Town

Drogheda's attractions lie both sides of the **River Boyne**. The walled town, which developed in the late medieval period, became one of Ireland's most important religious and political centres – the parliament would occasionally convene in Drogheda – and a few remnants from this time are still visible. The town incurred the most infamous onslaught of Cromwell's Irish campaign of 1649 when its defending garrison and many inhabitants were savagely massacred by the Lord Protector's army. Later constructions by the town's Protestant middle classes, such as the Tholsel and courthouse, reflect a burgeoning confidence enhanced by Drogheda's growing importance as a manufacturing town, thriving on the export of linen, shoes and alcohol.

The northside

Start your exploration of the northside at the junction of West Street and Shop Street by the eighteenth-century **Tholsel**, the former town hall, a solid limestone building topped by a domed tower which features a four-faced clock. A short distance east from here is **St Laurence Gate**, one of the few vestiges of the town's medieval walls. This imposing barbican, with its two tall rounded towers, once housed a portcullis protecting the toll gate just within. The interiors of the Tholsel and the Gate are not open to visitors.

Uphill from the Tholsel, Magdalene Street Lower passes **St Peter's Church** (Church of Ireland), a graceful mid-eighteenth century edifice whose porch and spire were added by the renowned Irish architect Francis Johnston in 1793. The church replaced the original thirteenth-century structure whose stone steeple was blown down by a violent storm in 1548 and subsequently refurbished with a wooden replacement. During the massacre that followed the 1649 siege of the town, many people sought sanctuary in the steeple but perished when Cromwell's troops set it ablaze.

Rising above the northside is the two-storey **Magdalene Tower**, the erstwhile belfry and only remnant of a large Dominican friary founded here around 1224 by the Archbishop of Armagh, Lucas de Netterville. A couple of notable historical events occurred here: within the friary's walls, in March 1394, the Ulster chiefs swore their obedience to Richard II; and, just outside, Thomas, Earl of Desmond, was beheaded in 1467 after being found guilty of treason.

Back downhill and along the main thoroughfare, West Street, stands the town's other **St Peter's Church** (Roman Catholic), a solidly Neogothic late nineteenth-century structure topped by an elegant spire and accessed via a sweeping stone stairway. Its interior is equally impressive, featuring stout granite pillars and walls of Bath stone, and just off its left-hand aisle is a small shrine devoted to **Oliver Plunkett**, Archbishop of Armagh and Primate of All Ireland from 1670. Towards the end of that decade, at a time of widespread anti-Catholic feeling in England, Titus Oates hatched a fabricated claim (which became known as the Popish Plot) that the pope was preparing to invade the country and that Plunkett was one of the main organizers of the papal army. Plunkett was arrested and put on trial in Dundalk, but, when the jury failed to convict him, was moved first to Dublin and then to Newgate prison in London. Found guilty of treason on July 1, 1681, he was hanged, drawn and quartered, and his remains were thrown onto a fire, but his head and other parts of his body were rescued. The head finally arrived back in Ireland around 1722, following a circuitous route via Rome, and is now contained in a silver-ornamented box within the shrine. The other parts of Plunkett's body on view in the church did not return until after his canonization in 1975. A booklet on sale in the church wonderfully recounts the whole story.

The southside

Once you've completed your northside explorations, cross the river and head for **Millmount Hill**, which rises above the Boyne's southern bank and is easily accessed via a stairway directly opposite **St Mary's Bridge**. The hill commands an unhindered view of the town, revealing its still largely extant, cramped medieval street pattern.

Millmount features strongly in Irish mythology, supposedly being the burial place of the Celtic poet Amergin, while the hill's strategic value was quickly recognized by the Anglo-Normans who constructed a motte here in the late twelfth century. Subsequently, a castle was erected which stood until 1808 when the fortifications were demolished and replaced by the barracks and **Martello tower** which stand here today. The old castle provided the fiercest resistance to Cromwell during the 1649 siege while the tower was severely damaged by shelling during the 1922 Civil War, though it has recently been restored.

The barracks square houses the **Millmount Museum** (Mon–Sat 9.30am–5.30pm, Sun & public holidays 2.30–5pm; museum only €3.50, tower only €3, combined ticket €5.50; Ⓦwww.millmount.net), one of those haphazardly organized places that offers plenty of intriguing displays alongside others that are bewilderingly esoteric. The best of the displays are contained within the **Industrial Room**, which focuses on Drogheda's manufacturing history – particularly the town's erstwhile role as a major producer of alcoholic beverages, with no fewer than fourteen breweries and sixteen distilleries. A well-equipped Victorian **kitchen** features numerous contemporary appliances, including an early example of a vacuum cleaner, while the **Religious** display concentrates on the life of Oliver Plunkett (see p.187). Access is also available to the fully restored Martello tower (same hours as museum), though there's little to see inside. However, a climb to the top does reveal a panoramic view of Drogheda and the surrounding area.

Eating

Drogheda might not be a culinary hotspot, but it has plenty of reasonably priced choices for **meals** throughout the day, including a surprising number of Italian restaurants and pizzerias.

Bella Atina The Mall Ⓣ041/984 4878. Immensely popular restaurant, serving a range of high-quality Italian specialities.
The Boiled Onion Shop St Ⓣ041/987 5566. Don't be deterred by the ghastly name – this is one of the town's more upmarket eateries, providing a range of modern Irish and European cuisine. Expect to pay around €25 plus wine.
The Bru Haymarket Ⓣ041/987 2785. Plush new riverside bar with a bistro offering a wide range of tasty treats.
La Pizzeria Peter St Ⓣ041/983 4208. Serving a delicious range of doughy delights, this place soon fills up, so arrive early or book ahead. Closed Wed.
The Laurence Inn Laurence St. Good-value bar meals served all day.
Monk's Café North Quay. Trendy spot for great coffee and a variety of snacks and meals.
Moorland Café 97 West St. Friendly and popular place for snacks, lunches and tea.

Pubs and entertainment

Drogheda has a tremendous number of pubs, including several very atmospheric spots. A few stage live music – for **listings** check the *Drogheda Independent*, published on Wednesdays. Besides the pubs there are few other **entertainment** options, but it's always worth investigating the programme of the Droichead Arts Centre (Ⓦdroicheadartscentre.com) in Stockwell Lane, which stages exhibitions, drama, comedy and musical events. St Peter's Church on West Street (Ⓣ041/987 6100) mounts a varied programme of monthly concerts. Drogheda's arts festival takes place over the May public holiday weekend (Ⓦwww.droghedaartsfestival.ie) and features a wealth of events around the town. Drogheda's two Omniplex **cinemas** (Ⓣ0818/719719, Ⓦwww.filminfo. net) are in the Abbey and Boyne shopping centres. The local association **football** team, Drogheda United (Ⓦwww.droghedaunited.ie), plays at United Park; the area is also one of the last bastions of **road bowling** (see p.656) and matches take place each Sunday morning at 11am along the Termonfeckin to Clougher head road.

Carberry's North Strand. Old-fashioned bar, well worth making the 10min walk from the centre for, with traditional-music sessions on Tues night and early afternoon on Sun, and a traditional-singing night on Wed.
Clarke and Sons Peter St. Characterful old shop-style bar, dark and woody with some very cosy snugs.
New Central Peter St. Once a commercial hotel, this revamped, big bar has walls bedecked by

some of Oscar Wilde's pithier epithets and live music most nights of the week.
Peter Matthews Laurence St. Also known as *McPhail's*, this lively place has a traditional front bar with snugs and a back room hosting live music (Thurs–Sun), plus a beer garden.

Sarsfields By St Laurence Gate. Inviting old bar featuring modern jazz on Mon and, on the first Fri of each month, a night of song and comedy.

Monasterboice, Mellifont and Ardee

Close to Drogheda to the north lie the remains of the monasteries of **Monasterboice** and **Mellifont**, two of Ireland's most significant ecclesiastical sites, the former including a superb high-cross and the latter providing ample evidence of its erstwhile power and importance. Monasterboice is the more easily accessed, via the regular Drogheda–Dundalk bus – ask to be set down at the *Monasterboice Inn*, from which it's an easy fifteen-minute signposted walk. Getting to Mellifont is more problematic: the infrequent Drogheda–Collon bus will stop at Monleek Cross, from where it's a three-kilometre walk. Further north there are two other intriguing sites a few kilometres either side of **Ardee**.

Monasterboice

Monasterboice (dawn to dusk; free), 6km north of Drogheda, has an idyllic rural setting and the remains of its monastic settlement – founded in either the eighth or ninth century – include not only one of Ireland's finest high-crosses, dating from the tenth century, but one of the best-preserved round towers in the country too. The stocky **St Muiredach's Cross**, just inside the churchyard, is the better preserved of the pair. Its elaborate series of carved panels depict a variety of biblical events, loosely arranged in supposed chronological order. The base of its **east face** begins in the Garden of Eden, before moving upwards to the stories of Cain and Abel, David and Goliath, Moses bringing water to the Israelites and the Magi bearing gifts for the newborn Christ. Above these, the cross's carved wheel depicts the **Last Judgment** and the risen multitudes pleading for entry into Heaven. The **west face** depicts events during the later life of **Christ**, ranging from his arrest at Gethsemane to the Ascension, though the hub of the cross's wheel shows Moses with the Ten Commandments. Unusually, both flanks of the cross are also decorated and feature the Flight of the Israelites and saints Anthony and Paul.

The taller **West Cross**, unfortunately chipped at its top, features another array of biblical scenes, though erosion makes most of them indecipherable without the assistance of the adjacent display board. Certainly, its **east face** features David and the lion, and the **west** includes the Resurrection, but much of the remainder is difficult to discern. Adjacent to this cross is what's reckoned to be the tallest **round tower** in Ireland, standing at some thirty metres, though it has long since lost its conical cap and cannot be entered for safety reasons. The two ruined **churches** within the enclosure, which date from the thirteenth century, probably had little connection with the, by then, defunct monastery.

Mellifont Abbey

Founded in 1142 by St Malachy, **Mellifont**, some 8km northwest of Drogheda (May–Sept daily 10am–6pm; €2.10; Heritage Card), was the first and subsequently most important Cistercian foundation in Ireland, eventually heading an affiliation of more than twenty monasteries. Set in a tranquil spot by the River Mattock, Mellifont must once have been a hugely impressive complex, though its scant ruins leave much to the imagination.

Before touring the remains, take in the small exhibition in the visitor centre (same hours; free) by the entrance, which details the foundation's history and provides a scale model of the abbey's layout. After the Reformation the abbey passed into the hands of Edward Moore, who converted its buildings into a fortified residence. Here in 1603, the great Irish chieftain **Hugh O'Neill** was besieged by Lord Mountjoy until starvation forced his surrender. During the Battle of the Boyne, William of Orange based himself at Mellifont, after which the property was abandoned and fell ultimately into dilapidation. It eventually passed into the hands of the Office of Public Works in the late twentieth century.

Entrance to the site is via the church's **north transept** which features the remains of two stone *piscinae*, sinks for cleaning sacred serving vessels. As the church was built on sloping ground the broad **nave** has an uncommon feature, a **crypt** constructed to ensure it remained level. Next to the south transept stood the **chapter house**, whose floor features medieval glazed tiles, though some of these have been brought here from other parts of the abbey.

The tallest and finest remnant of the abbey stands in its expansive cloister garth, a remarkable octagonal arched **lavabo**, with fountains and basins where the monks would wash. The remaining ruins rarely rise above knee-height and you'll need to consult the display-board map or buy the visitors' guide to interpret them. Behind the lavabo, the southern ruins included both the **calefactory** (or warming house), the only heated room in the entire complex, and the **refectory**.

Towards Monaghan

If you're heading north towards Monaghan, it's well worth taking a short detour a little way along a winding lane, signposted to the east about 7km up the N2 from Collon, to the well-known and long-ruined **Jumping Church** at Kildemock. The church's name derives from the curious position of its western wall, which leans inwards and has clearly shifted a metre inwards from its original foundations. The cause of this "jump" is either supernatural or meteorological, according to your preference. The former view asserts that the church took umbrage at the burial of a recently excommunicated local within its bounds and leapt inwards to exclude the blighter; the latter account involves a thunderous storm in 1715 which saw the wall struck and repositioned by lightning. If you're lucky, the farmer from across the road will appear to recount his own theory and sell you a copy of his pamphlet on the subject.

Further north off the N2, beyond the town of **Ardee** (the location for one of Ireland's most renowned ballads, *The Turfman from Ardee*), is the village of **LOUTH**, easily the smallest of the country's namesake county capitals; to get there take the R171 to Tallanstown and then follow the signposts. Just up the Inniskeen road stands **St Mochta's Church**, the only trace of a very early monastic settlement. Clearly early medieval in style, the church retains its original vaulted roof, which is accessible via a stairway. Be careful of the bulls in the adjacent field, though, before entering the churchyard.

Dundalk and the Cooley Peninsula

Northern County Louth is dominated by the strongly Republican border-town of **Dundalk**. To its northeast lies the **Cooley Peninsula**, a major focus for Irish mythology via its role in the *Táin* saga, offering a wealth of good walking country and spectacular views of **Carlingford Lough**.

Dundalk

DUNDALK is unquestionably a boomtown, built on industrial success dating back to the establishment of its docks and a variety of industries, from linen to brewing. Nowadays the focus is on food processing and computer components and the town has flourished so much that its much-clogged bypass actually needed another circumvention (the recently opened M1 extension). It's a hard-edged place, long associated with obdurate Republicanism – the Real IRA (see p.708) was based around here – but does have one or two places of interest. The foremost attraction is the **Louth County Museum**, on Jocelyn Street (Tues–Sat 10.30am–5.30pm, Sun & public holidays 2–6pm; also May–Sept Mon 10.30am–5.30pm; €3.80; Ⓦwww.dundalktown.ie/dundalktown/museo1.htm), one of the most successful local museums in the country. Spread over three floors, and often employing interactive technology, its exhibits provide fascinating accounts of the county's archeology, life in Louth over the ages and Dundalk's own rich industrial history. Ireland's biggest cigarette manufacturer, Carroll's, was once based here and, in the late 1950s, the Irish government bid successfully to take over the production of the German Heinkel bubble car. For a brief period the town produced these vehicles based on old fighter-bomber cockpits and a shining 1966 example is situated on the museum's first-floor landing. The cars were notorious because their single door opened frontwards and they did not have a reverse gear, so parking too close to another vehicle could result in a long wait. Dundalk's oldest building is **Kelly's Tower**, a four-storey Franciscan bell-tower, dating from the middle of the thirteenth century, on the corner of Mill Street and Castle Road. The tower was sacked in 1315 by Edward Bruce and again, in 1538, by Lord Deputy Grey.

Practicalities

Dundalk's **bus** station (Ⓣ042/933 4075) is on Long Walk, off Market Square, and the **train** station (Ⓣ042/933 5521) is 800m west of the town centre on Carrick Road. The **tourist office** is next door to the museum on Jocelyn Street (June to mid-Sept Mon–Sat 9am–1pm & 2–5.15pm; mid-Sept to May Mon–Fri 9.30am–1pm; Ⓣ042/933 5484, Ⓦwww.eastcoastmidlands.ie).

With Carlingford so close (see p.193) and the attractions of South Armagh and County Down not much further away, there really is no need to stay in Dundalk. However, should you be stuck here, the best central bets are the *Hotel Imperial*, Park Street (Ⓣ042/933 2241, Ⓔinfo@imperialhoteldundalk.com; ❹), with refurbished en-suite rooms, or, for **B&B**, *Krakow*, 190 Ard Easmuinn (Ⓣ042/933 7535, Ⓦwww.krakowbandb.com; ❷), a comfortable guesthouse off the road to Carrickmacross. For **food** look no further than *Quaglino's* (Ⓣ042/933 8567), above the *Century Bar* at 19 Roden Place, by the cathedral, which serves delicious meals using local produce, stylishly delivered – expect to pay around €45 plus wine. The best **bars** are on Seatown: *McManus's* pub has old-fashioned snugs while *Pádraig Ó Donngaile* is another cosy spot. Dundalk does have one very notable **music venue**, *The Spirit Store* (Ⓦwww.spiritstore.ie), down by the harbour on George's Quay, whose programme mixes Ireland's own rock and traditional stars with guests from further afield.

The Cooley Peninsula

East of Dundalk, the **Cooley Peninsula** is Louth's most hyped tourist destination – though all told it doesn't quite match up to the glories often claimed in

▲ Carlingford Lough

its name. It's true that the mountains and surrounding rich verdure offer great walking territory and many a stunning seascape, but the countryside lacks the raw, rugged and often downright exhilarating feel of the Mournes over the other side of Carlingford Lough. That said there's still plenty here to delight, even if **Carlingford** village itself has somewhat meretriciously cashed in on its waterside location. From Dundalk, off the N1 Newry road, the R173 skirts the southern slopes of the mountains, taking in flat, dull countryside on the way, while the approach from Newry on the same road, runs first beside the canal, before meeting the lough shore itself, with the peninsula's mountains ascending to the south.

If you start from Dundalk, look out for signs to the *Ballymascanlon Hotel*, a kilometre or so after the R173 turn-off from the N1. A footpath from the hotel's car park runs beside the golf course to the **Proleek Dolmen**, a regular photographic feature in tourist brochures. Perched on the points of three triangular stones, its massive capstone weighs a remarkable 46 tonnes and, having

Walks on the Cooley Peninsula

The varied terrain of the peninsula offers a range of opportunities for **walking**, whether in the hills, offering often sumptuous views across the lough to the Mournes, by the shore or along lush valleys. The longest waymarked walk is the 26-kilometre Táin Trail, which takes a circular route around Slieve Foye (587m), up to the west above Carlingford village and includes much of the higher ground. Undertaking this requires proper walking equipment and clothing, and supplies of food and drink, as well as Ordnance Survey of Ireland Discovery map #36. However, there are plenty of less arduous walks, some of which, such as the eight-kilometre round-trip to Maeve's Gap, are easily accessible from Carlingford village. For others you'll need to head northwest to Omeath or east to Greenore. *McKevitt's Village Hotel* publishes the very handy *Rambles*, which details ten walks on the peninsula, including maps, directions and comments on difficulty – the Carlingford tourist office has copies on sale.

Táin Bó Cúailnge (The Cattle Raid of Cooley)

The location of many an Irish legend is still immediately identifiable thanks to a wealth of extant place names, and perhaps no more so than in the case of the **Táin Bó Cúailnge**. Set around 500 BC, many of the events in perhaps the greatest of the Celtic epics clearly take place in the mountains of the Cooley Peninsula. The villainess of the tale is Medb, the great Queen of Connacht, who so envies her husband Aillil's White Bull (Finnbenach) that she determines to capture the Brown Bull of Cooley (Donn Cúailnge). Drawing Aillil into her campaign she begins a war against the east of Ireland, targeting Ulster in particular. All the Ulster men are rendered immobile by a curse except the tale's hero, Cúchullain, who is left to confront Medb's armies single-handedly. Much of the plot concerns his feats and victories, often achieved in bloodthirsty fashion, and the text is also brought to life by vivid topographical detail. The first known written version of the saga was included in the twelfth-century **Book of the Dun Cow**, and Thomas Kinsella's twentieth-century English translation encapsulates much of the vivacity of the Irish-language version (see p.735). In 1973 the legend formed the basis for one of Ireland's most successful concept albums, *The Táin*, by the traditional-rock pioneers Horslips.

inspected the scene, you'll probably spend the rest of the day wondering about the ingenuity of prehistoric hoisting engineers.

Carlingford

Set a short distance back from the lough's southern shore, the trim and charming former fishing village of **CARLINGFORD** is by far the best base for exploring the peninsula. Its tight and tortuous streets reflect its medieval origins and house a host of places where you can eat, drink and sleep. However, this is not a place for the light of purse or pocket: prices here are significantly higher than elsewhere in the county or across the water in Down.

Carlingford's name is Old Norse in origin, deriving from "Kerlingfjörthr" (the fjord of the hag-shaped rock), and indicating that this was once a Viking settlement. By the lough shore stands the ruin of **King John's Castle**, which served as an Anglo-Norman sentinel over the lough's entrance. The village itself contains some impressive later buildings, including the fifteenth-century **Mint**, a fortified townhouse just off the main square. To learn more about Carlingford's history, visit the **Heritage Centre** (Mon–Fri 10am–12.30pm & 2–4pm; €3), housed in the restored medieval Holy Trinity church, whose displays document the village's development from Norman times.

Practicalities

The **tourist office** (daily 10am–5pm, Nov–March closed Tues; ⓣ042/937 3033, ⓦwww.carlingford.ie), housed in a small building just back from the water, can book accommodation and provides advice on the many **walks** available in the hills above town, as well as having an extensive range of maps and related material on sale. **Walking tours** of the town (April–Sept 2pm daily; €6; ⓣ086/352 2732) leave from here. The Carlingford Adventure Centre on Tholsel Street (ⓦwww.carlingfordadventure.com) offers a range of activities on both land and water, either on a daily basis or as part of a package including accommodation.

For a village with a resident population of just over 600 people, Carlingford has an astonishing number of **places to stay**, though at busy times it's worth using the tourist office's €2 accommodation booking service. The most upmarket option is the modern *Four Seasons Hotel & Leisure Club* (ⓣ042/937 3530, ⓦwww.4seasonshotel.ie; ❻), many of whose plush, well-equipped rooms overlook the lough, and which also features an indoor pool, gym and sauna. Right in the village centre *McKevitt's Village Hotel*, Market Square (ⓣ042/937 3116, ⓦwww.mckevittshotel.com; ❺), has bright and airy modern rooms. **B&Bs** close to the lough shore include the superb *Ghan House* (ⓣ042/937 3682, ⓦwww.ghanhouse.com; ❺), a beautifully kept eighteenth-century building with an exceptionally good restaurant (see below). More modest but still very comfortable is the nearby *Shalom* (ⓣ042/937 3151, ⓦwww.jackiewoods.com; ❷). *The Foy Centre* on Dundalk Street (IHH; ⓣ042/938 3624, ⓦwww.carlingfordbeds.com; dorms €23) provides hostel accommodation in small dorms, but you may have to book up well in advance as it is very popular with groups.

The village has plenty of very good, if somewhat pricey, places to **eat**. The undoubted peach is *Ghan House* (Fri & Sat 7–9.30pm, Sun 12.30–4pm) which serves modern Irish cuisine (expect to pay around €50 plus wine), using ingredients from its own gardens, and has eight-course gourmet nights approximately once a month (€68 plus wine) as well as occasional Georgian evenings (€75) with appropriate period menus and entertainment. *The Oystercatcher Bistro* (ⓣ042 937 3989) in the centre of the village will please seafood lovers and serves locally sourced meat dishes too (around €40 plus wine). For delicious daytime snacks, soups and salads head to *Georgina's Bakehouse Tearooms*, Castle Hill. *O'Hare's* by the Mint is an old-fashioned grocery-cum-**bar** which has a traditional-music session on Tuesdays.

County Monaghan

"Miss Monaghan" is the title of a well-known Irish reel – and since the major roads running through the county encourage speedy driving it would be very easy to take this as a piece of travel advice. However, to do so would be to miss something topographically intriguing, for much of Monaghan's gently rolling landscape is configured by the stout, grassy hillocks and elongated ridges known as **drumlins**, which were originally formed at the end of the Ice Age as glaciers receded northwards. The word "drumlin" itself is thought to derive from the Irish word for "back" or "ridge", coupled with the Old English diminutive "-ling".

Greenery predominates with small fields fringed by low hedgerows, and the land is occasionally punctuated by tiny lakes. Such a landscape, however, means that much of the surrounding ground once supported little more than subsistence farming. The sense of life in this part of Ireland is encapsulated in much of the writing of **Patrick Kavanagh**; born in **Inniskeen**, his works, especially the autobiographical *The Green Fool*, fully depict the vicissitudes of rural life.

Monaghan's few towns offer little of interest, though the busy **county town** itself is attractively laid out, features a few buildings of note and is a major transport hub if you're travelling by bus. To its southwest, the hilltop market town of **Clones**, almost on the border with Fermanagh, was a former ecclesiastical centre and possesses several notable relics. To Monaghan town's north lies **Glaslough**, an estate village set around the grandiose **Castle Leslie**.

Monaghan town

All the elements of post-Plantation urban planning are well to the fore in **MONAGHAN** town, which derived its prosperity from the linen industry and was long the base of a British garrison. To gain some understanding of the area's development, the best starting-point is the **Monaghan County Museum** (Mon–Fri 11am–5pm, Sat noon–5pm; free), just up Hill Street, which recounts local history through a varied selection of displays and interactive touch-screens, and features archeological finds, traditional crafts, railway memorabilia and an assortment of paintings, prints and photographs. The most exceptional exhibit is the **Cross of Clogher**, a glorious, finely worked silver cross dating from the early fifteenth century. The museum also hosts a changing programme of temporary exhibitions. Just downhill from here on Market Street is the late eighteenth-century **Market House**, a charming, arched limestone edifice whose exterior is embellished with exquisite carvings of oak apples and leaves.

A short distance east is **Church Square**, dominated by an impressive obelisk commemorating a garrison member who died at the Battle of Inkerman, and almost entirely surrounded by stately, early nineteenth-century buildings, including a Neoclassical courthouse, a very fetching Regency Gothic church and an appropriately sturdy bank. A hundred metres further east is the hub of Monaghan's town planning, the **Diamond**, in whose very centre stands a flamboyant nineteenth-century drinking fountain named the Rossmore monument. A seventeenth-century settlers' cross had formerly occupied the site, and was moved to Old Cross Square, at the bottom of Dublin Street.

Practicalities

Monaghan's **bus** station (Ⓣ047/82377) is on North Road, five minutes' walk north of Church Square. The **tourist office** (May–Oct Mon–Fri 9am–5pm, Sat 10am–5pm; Ⓣ047/71818, Ⓦwww.monaghantourism.com) is unhelpfully located in the leisure centre a kilometre or so up the Clones road.

Accommodation options are limited. The two classiest choices are the *Hillgrove Hotel* on Old Armagh Road (Ⓣ047/81288, Ⓦwww.hillgrovehotel.com; ❺–❻), southeast of town, with very swish doubles and suites, or the *Four Seasons Hotel & Leisure Club*, out towards Armagh in Coolshannagh (Ⓣ047/81888, Ⓦwww.4seasonshotel.ie; ❺), with equally fine rooms and its own pool and gym. Otherwise head for *Grove Lodge*, Old Armagh Rd (Ⓣ047/84677, Ⓦwww.grovelodge-bnb.com; ❷), a modern family home with pleasant en-suite rooms. For daytime **food** try the pleasant *Dinkins*, Church Square; several of the bars also serve meals, including *The Squealing Pig* on the Diamond, and *Andy's* on Market Street, which also offers more esoteric fare in its restaurant (closed Sun–Tues).

For **entertainment**, the *Westenra Hotel*, on the Diamond, has live music and DJs at weekends. *McKenna's*, Dublin Street, has rock and indie bands several nights a week and the *Shamrock Bar* on the same road has a well-regarded traditional session on Thursdays.

Around Monaghan

Monaghan's few sites of interest are scattered around the county: the town itself and south of it at **Inniskeen** while to its north and west are **Glaslough** and **Clones** respectively.

Inniskeen

Best accessed from Dundalk, a dozen kilometres east, the village of **INNISKEEN** was the birthplace of the poet and writer **Patrick Kavanagh**. His grave can be found beside St Mary's Church, while the church annexe houses the **Patrick Kavanagh Rural and Literary Resource Centre** (Tues–Fri 11am–4.30pm, plus mid-March to Sept Sat 2–6pm & June–Sept Sun 2–6pm; ⓣ042/937 8560, ⓦwww.patrickkavanaghcountry.com; €5) which has stacks of memorabilia related to the poet, as well as a specially commissioned series of twelve paintings based upon his epic and extraordinarily emotive poem *The Great Hunger*. The centre stages several weekends devoted to poetry and writing, plus an annual weekend in late November celebrating Kavanagh's life and work. If you're in need of refreshment try the aptly named *Poet's Rest* coffee shop next door. The only **accommodation** in the village is provided by *Gleneven House* (ⓣ042/937 8294, ⓦwww.gleneven.com; ❷), a hundred metres or so towards Dundalk from the Resource Centre, which has a mix of comfy en-suite and standard rooms.

Glaslough

Eleven kilometres northeast of Monaghan lies the somewhat otherworldly estate village of **GLASLOUGH**, dominated by a lengthy Famine wall which surrounds the estate of Castle Leslie. The Leslie family can reputedly trace back its origins to Attila the Hun and arrived in Ireland in 1633 in the shape of John Leslie who had been appointed Bishop of Raphoe. A colourful character, Leslie became known as the "fighting bishop", thanks to his victory as leader of an army over Cromwell at the Battle of Raphoe. When Charles II was restored to the throne, Leslie received £2000 as a reward for loyalty and used the sum to purchase Glaslough Castle and its demesne in 1665. His descendants have remained in occupation ever since and have included some equally intriguing figures. John Leslie's son Charles was charged with high treason for arguing a little too strenuously against the penal laws, but escaped and fled to France. Subsequently pardoned by George I, he returned to Glaslough where his children often entertained Jonathan Swift, who was not always complimentary about them in return:

Here I am In Castle Leslie
With Rows And Rows Of Books Upon The Shelves
Written By The Leslies
All About Themselves.

The current and very grand castle was built in the late nineteenth century and the family became connected by marriage to the Churchills – both Randolph and Winston stayed here. Later owners included Desmond Leslie who authored *Flying Saucers Have Landed*, a supposedly factual account of the first alien contact with humans.

Nowadays *Castle Leslie* (ⓣ047/88100, ⓦwww.castleleslie.com) is an utterly majestic, thoroughly relaxing place to stay, and is often patronized by the rich and famous – Paul McCartney and Heather Mills were married here. Accommodation in the castle itself is now restricted to members of its private club, but there's still the *Hunting Lodge* (❻), whose thirty sumptuously decorated rooms are comfort incarnate. Even if you're not planning to stay overnight, you can still enjoy the atmosphere here by sampling the evening menu (€52 plus wine) or indulging in one of the regular gourmet nights (€57). Otherwise you're free to wander the estate, arrange fishing in the lake (renowned for its enormous pike) or book one of the many riding packages provided by the equestrian centre.

Clones

Near the border with Fermanagh, the lively town of **CLONES** (pronounced "clo-nez") lies 20km southwest of Monaghan town, overlooking drumlin country from its hilltop perch. St Tiernach founded a monastery here in the sixth century and is supposedly buried in a reliquary stone coffin in a small graveyard off Ball Alley Lane, near which are the remains of a ninth-century **round tower** which was originally five storeys high. The monastic settlement was subsequently superseded by an Augustinian foundation and the sparse remains of the abbey are just a little way to the east, across MacCurtain Street. The town's other significant relic is a richly carved **high cross**, which stands in the Diamond, somewhat overshadowed by the sombre shape of **St Tiernach's Church** (Church of Ireland). The cross's front panels depict scriptural scenes, such as the Garden of Eden, while the reverse is devoted to scenes from Christ's life.

Just west of the town centre, above Cara Street, is the site of a **Neolithic hill fort**, which was used as the foundations for a short-lived twelfth-century Norman castle that was razed to the ground by local chieftains. Indeed the English did not regain control of Clones until 1601 and much of the contemporary town owes its layout to that period, while the presence of both Presbyterian and Methodist churches (John Wesley preached here several times in the 1770s) bears testament to the Plantation. In the nineteenth century prosperity arrived in Clones via the railways and the Ulster Canal, which connected Belfast to Lough Erne. At the bottom of Cara Street stands the **Ulster Canal Stores** (July & Aug daily 9am–5pm; Sept–June Mon–Fri 9am–5pm), which at one time served as the distribution centre for wares arriving in Clones by water. Nowadays it houses small displays on the railways,

Clones lace

The area around Clones has a strong tradition of **lace-making**, a generally home-based industry which, at its peak in the 1850s, saw more than 1500 workers supplying markets as far afield as Paris, Rome and New York. Passed on from mother to daughter, the lace-making craft was introduced to Clones by the wife of the local Church of Ireland rector, Cassandra Hands, as a means of supplying income in the desperate post-Famine times. Rather than following the time-consuming Venetian needlework style, Clones women opted for a crochet hook as a means of expediency, and began producing work embellished by the flora of their local environs, often characterized by the multi-twirled **Clones knot**. Clones lace was embroidered into blouses and dresses, but its own elaborate style was gradually replaced by simpler designs. Nevertheless, it remains an important local tradition and, in 1989, a co-operative was established to reinvigorate the craft. There are still several lace-makers in the area and some of their work is on display at the **Ulster Canal Stores** where you can enquire about the possibility of purchasing their wares.

lace-making and independence (Clones was a strong Republican base), as well as works by local artists.

Clones also houses the GAA's second largest stadium (after Croke Park), **St Tiernach's Park**, north of the town off the Roslea road, which stages the Ulster province's Gaelic-football finals in July.

Practicalities

Tourist information on the town is provided by the Ulster Canal Stores and the website ⓦwww.clones.ie. For **accommodation** head to the *Lennard Arms Hotel*, on the Diamond, which offers spacious en-suite B&B (ⓣ047/51075; ❷) and serves whopping bar **meals**. The only other option in town at the nineteenth-century *Creighton Hotel* (ⓣ047/51055, ⓔcreightonhotel@eircom.net; ❷), which has a variety of relaxing en-suite rooms, as well as a restaurant offering traditional fare.

Aside from the hotels, the only decent **place to eat** is *Cuil Darach*, Fermanagh Street (ⓣ047/52147), for substantial lunches and dinners. Packed with lively **pubs**, Fermanagh Street is the place to head for an evening's entertainment. *The Paragon* has DJs (Fri–Sun) while *Papa Joe's* offers karaoke and live music at weekends. *The Tower* is an old-fashioned long bar while *Treanors* offers the only hope of a **traditional music** session. The town's **festival** takes place over the first week in August, with plenty of entertainment on the streets and in the bars.

County Cavan

County Cavan is characterized by a serene blend of unblemished countryside and a vast complex of lakes and waterways known as **Lough Oughter**. It is very popular with anglers, attracted by the county's multitude of opportunities for **fishing**, and also offers a chance to cruise along the relatively recently developed **Shannon–Erne Waterway**, which links the waterways of the great Shannon River to Lough Erne, creating a 380-kilometre navigable stretch. Another way to enjoy the unspoilt countryside is to follow the **Kingfisher Cycle Trail** (see p.680), a 320km route which takes in many scenic spots on a circular tour through Cavan and neighbouring counties.

Cavan town itself is an agreeable enough place but has little of inherent interest, other than the nearby ecclesiastical remains at **Kilmore**, and if you want to explore the county's lakes and waterways **Belturbet** makes a much better base. The county's west provides some dramatically rugged landscapes, ideally explored via the **Cavan Way**, while, in the south, the county museum in **Ballyjamesduff** amply rewards a detour.

Cavan town and around

Nowadays a busy market town, **CAVAN** was once the seat of the O'Reilly clan who built a Franciscan abbey here in 1300, although this was burnt down by a friar in 1451. Later, the town itself was razed to the ground in 1576 by a female member of the clan and consequently rebuilt. Much of what you see today dates from the nineteenth and twentieth centuries and all that remains of the reconstructed abbey is its eighteenth-century bell tower, on Abbey Street, standing next to the grave of **Owen Roe O'Neill**. Modern Cavan does have its charms, though there's little to see here. Most of the action in terms of shops and bars takes place along Main Street.

The **bus station** (Ⓣ049/433 1353) is at the southern end of Farnham Street, and the **tourist office** (April–Sept Mon–Fri 9am–5pm, Sat 9am–1pm; Ⓣ049/437 7200, Ⓦwww.cavantourism.com) is 300m northeast along the same street in the recently constructed Johnston Library and Farnham Centre. There are a few places to stay dotted around the town, including two comfortable B&Bs on Cathedral Road, the northern continuation of Farnham Street, both offering en-suite rooms: *Glendown* (Ⓣ049/433 2257, Ⓦwww.glendownhouse.com; ❷) at no. 33, and *Oakdene* (Ⓣ049/433 1698; 2). Alternatively, bang in the centre on Main Street, the *Farnham Arms Hotel* (Ⓣ049/433 2577, Ⓦwww.farnhamarmshotel.com; ❹) provides characterful en-suite accommodation. The town's plushest option is the very swish *Cavan Crystal Hotel* (Ⓣ049/436 0600, Ⓦwww.cavancrystalhotel.com; ❺), about a kilometre southeast of town on the N3 Dublin road, which has luxurious rooms and its own pool and fitness centre.

Food options are fairly thin on the ground, but several bars on Main Street, including *An Síbín*, *The Imperial* and the *Blackhorse Inn*, serve meals or, for a bountiful range of salads and sandwiches, there's *Café Mana* on Thomas Ashe Street. *Blessings* on Main Street is a smashing old-fashioned **bar**, while the *Farnham Arms*, also on Main Street, has a renowned Wednesday-night traditional **session**. *Sports World*, 11 Town Hall St (Ⓣ049/433 1812), provides information on **fishing**, as well as rod rental and licences.

Kilmore cathedral

The **Cathedral Church of St Fethlimidh** at **KILMORE**, 5km southwest of Cavan town on the R198, stands on the site of a church built in the sixth or seventh century. Cathedral status was granted to a subsequent church in 1454, which became the See of the Bishopric of Kilmore. The current substantial edifice standing here today was completed in 1860 and constructed in a cruciform Middle Pointed style around a central tower topped by a pyramidal roof. However, its most impressive exterior feature is a wonderfully carved, four-arched Romanesque doorway, which serves as the vestry door. One of only two of its kind in the Ulster province – the other can be found on White Island (see p.682) – this doorway began life as a feature of the cathedral at Toneymore, but, when this fell into disrepair, was salvaged and moved to an abbey on Trinity Island in Lough Oughter. After the Reformation it was moved once again to the old Kilmore cathedral, now the parochial hall, before finding a last resting-place in the current building.

The cathedral is kept locked during the day, so to admire its impressive interior you'll need to attend a service or enquire locally about access. The cathedral's grounds house the grave of William Bedell, who was bishop here from 1629 to 1642 and is chiefly remembered for his translation of the Old Testament into Irish.

Ballyjamesduff

BALLYJAMESDUFF is a pleasant, small crossroads town, 15km southeast of Cavan town along back lanes or a little further via the N3. James Duff himself, the Earl of Fife, was an early Plantation landlord of the area, and one of his descendants, Sir James Duff, commanded English troops during the suppression of the 1798 Rebellion – making the more sombre Irish version of his name, "Black Séamus", rather appropriate to local ears.

The town is the location for the **Cavan County Museum** (Tues–Sat 10am–5pm; June–Oct also Sun 2–6pm; €3; Ⓦwww.cavanmuseum.ie), housed in a former convent, which has an impressive collection covering all aspects of the county's history. Many of the post-eighteenth-century exhibits in the museum were donated by Mrs Phyllis Faris from her mammoth and eclectic "Pighouse Collection" of domestic artefacts and memorabilia in Killeshandra (ignore any signs you might see around the county directing you to her own museum, as it's been closed for several years). Major items on display include the Killycluggin Stone, dating from 200 BC and decorated in classic Celtic La Tène artwork, and replicas of Celtic stone idols dating from the second century BC to the second century AD, as well as the impressive 1100-year-old Lough Errol dugout boat. There's also extensive coverage of the county's sporting prowess, including the 1947 All-Ireland Senior Gaelic football final between Cavan and Kerry which took place in New York as a special commemoration of the centenary of the worst year of the Great Famine. Also represented here is the songwriter Percy French who worked in the county for a spell as an inspector of drains – one of his more famous comic songs is *Come Back Paddy Reilly to Ballyjamesduff*.

West Cavan

To the west of Cavan town lies the assortment of loughs of varying sizes that forms the system known as **Lough Oughter**, through which the River Erne somehow contrives to manage a pathway to Upper Lough Erne (see p.684). Roads are few and landmarks limited to the occasional small hill, while the rush-fringed lakes lure many for fishing possibilities. The land gradually assumes dominance over water west of the hillside town of Belturbet. Waterside **Ballyconnell** supplies the best base for exploration, beyond which the inhospitable and bleak strip doglegs beyond between counties Fermanagh and Leitrim, becoming ever craggier as it rises through wild, boggy hills. At the county's northwestern tip, the **Cavan Way** terminates at the tiny border village of **Blacklion**.

Belturbet and around

One of the most pleasant bases for exploring the lough is **BELTURBET**, some 18km north of Cavan town, a hillside village rising steeply from the River Erne. Very popular with anglers, the village is also a base to explore the Shannon–Erne Waterway by renting a **cabin cruiser** from Emerald Star Line (€645–3150 per week depending on size and season; Ⓣ071/962 3710, Ⓦwww.emeraldstar.ie); these can be dropped off in Carrick-on-Shannon (see p.490). For **B&B**, try the busy and friendly *Church View*, 8 Church St (Ⓣ049/952 2358, Ⓦwww.churchviewguesthouse.com; ❶), just behind the library, off the main road. On the main street, *The Seven Horseshoes* is a popular if rather pricey spot for lunches and evening **meals** and also has very comfortable en-suite rooms (Ⓣ049/952 2166, Ⓦwww.sevenhorseshoes.com; ❸), or there are filling lunches at *The Harbour*, on the way to the marina. Of numerous lively **bars**, *The Widow's* has a regular Sunday-night traditional session.

▲ Drumlane Church

Apart from the delights of loughside walks and getting out on the water, the major source of interest around the lakes is **Drumlane Church**, situated just south of Miltown on the R201 from Belturbet in a beautiful setting between two lakes. St Mogue, a pupil of Wales's patron St David, founded a monastery here in the sixth century. Nearby, an eleventh-century **round tower** features now barely distinguishable carvings of birds, thought to be a cock and a hen and believed to bear some relevance to the Resurrection, while the medieval church is part of an abbey founded here by monks from Kells in County Meath (see p.173). Now ruined and roofless, the church's west doorway has carved heads of possibly ecclesiastical figures or monarchs, which probably date from the fifteenth century.

Ballyconnell

Twelve kilometres west of Belturbet is **BALLYCONNELL**, set beside the Shannon–Erne Waterway and an amenable base for enjoying the surrounding countryside, with numerous **accommodation** options. If you've got your own helicopter, you might fancy landing on the helipad at the luxurious *Slieve Russell Hotel, Golf & Country Club* (Ⓣ049/952 6444, Ⓦwww.quinnhotels.com; doubles ⑤, suites ⑨), a huge edifice about 6km towards Belturbet with its own pool, gym, tennis courts, eighteen-hole PGA championship golf course and no fewer than three restaurants. Alternatively, if means are more modest, there's the excellent *Sandville House* **hostel** (IHO; Ⓣ049/952 6297, Ⓦhomepage.eircom.net/~sandville; dorms €15, doubles ①), about 3km east of Ballyconnell, offering rooms in a nicely converted barn and space for camping. **B&Bs**

include the welcoming *Rossdean* (Ⓣ049/952 6358, Ⓔrossdeanbb@eircom.net; ❷), 500m down the Belturbet road. Ballyconnell has a few **places to eat** and all are situated on Main Street. *Pól O'D* (Ⓣ049/952 6228; Wed–Sat 6–9.30pm) is an exceptional, modern Irish restaurant– a three-course evening meal costs €35 per head without wine. Alternatively, there's excellent pub grub available at *The Angler's Rest* and several cafés in the village.

The Cavan Way and Blacklion

The county's northwestern reaches provide superb walking terrain, best accessed via the signposted 25-kilometre **Cavan Way**, which runs through jagged landscapes from Dowra in County Leitrim (see p.493) to Blacklion where it joins the **Ulster Way**. The hills above Blacklion command dramatic views across Lough Macnean to the Fermanagh lakelands in the east and the mountains of Sligo and Leitrim to the west. About halfway along the route is the Shannon Pot, the veritable source of Ireland's longest river but a mere trickle here.

The border village of **BLACKLION** derives its name from a long-defunct pub and offers both comfortable en-suite accommodation and one of the northwest's finest restaurants, in the shape of *Macnean House* (Ⓣ&Ⓕ071/985 3022; ❸; closed late Dec and Jan). The restaurant (Thurs–Sun 7–9.30pm plus July & Aug Wed, Sun also 12.30–3.30pm) is run by one of Ireland's best-known chefs, Neven Maguire, whose cooking is both classy and imaginative, uses local ingredients, and is mouthwatering throughout, especially the scrumptious desserts – expect to pay at least €45 for the set dinner, but there are cheaper à la carte options.

Travel details

Trains

Drogheda to: Belfast (6–7 Mon–Sat, 5 Sun; 1hr 40min); Dublin (29–33 Mon–Sat, 14 Sun; 30min–1hr); Dundalk (12–17 Mon–Sat, 8 Sun; 15–25min); Newry (6–7 Mon–Sat, 5 Sun; 45min).
Dundalk to: Belfast (6–7 Mon–Sat, 5 Sun; 1hr 15min); Drogheda (4–12 daily; 25min); Dublin (11–14 Mon–Sat, 6 Sun; 1hr–1hr 20min); Newry (6–7 Mon–Sat, 5 Sun; 25min).

Buses

Bus Eiveann
Ballyconnell to: Belturbet (Mon–Sat 4 daily, Sun 3; 15min); Cavan town (Mon–Sat 4 daily, Sun 3; 30min); Enniskillen (Mon–Sat 4 daily, Sun 3; 45min).
Ballyjamesduff to: Cavan town (Mon & Wed–Fri 1 daily, Tues 3; 20–40min).
Belturbet to: Ballyconnell (Mon–Sat 4 daily, Sun 3; 15min); Cavan town (Mon–Sat 4 daily, Sun 5; 15min).
Blacklion to: Enniskillen (Mon–Sat 4 daily, Sun 2; 20min); Sligo (Mon–Sat 4 daily, Sun 2; 1hr).
Carlingford to Dundalk (Mon–Sat 4 daily; 35–50min); Newry (Mon–Sat 4 daily; 25–35min).
Cavan town to: Athlone (Mon–Sat 1 daily; 1hr 55min); Ballyconnell (6–7 daily; 30min); Ballyjamesduff (Mon & Wed–Fri 1 daily, Tues 3; 20–35min); Belturbet (6–7 daily; 15min); Donegal town (4–6 daily; 2hr 20min); Dublin (17 daily; 2hr); Enniskillen (6–8 daily; 1hr 10min); Galway (Fri & Sun 1 daily; 3hr 15min); Kells (16 daily; 45min); Monaghan town (Mon–Sat 1 daily; 55min); Navan (16 daily; 1hr 5min).
Clones to: Cavan town (1–2 daily; 30min); Monaghan town (Mon–Sat 5–8 daily, Sun 1; 25min).
Donore to: Drogheda (5–6 daily; 15–30min).
Drogheda to: Belfast (9 daily; 1hr 40min–2hr); Collon for Mellifont (Mon, Wed & Fri 4 daily, Tues & Thurs 2 daily, Sat 1; 15min); Donore for Newgrange (5–6 daily; 10min); Dublin (17 daily; 1hr 5min); Dundalk (17 daily; 20–30min); Navan (Mon–Sat 8 daily, Sun 4; 30–55min).

Dundalk to: Belfast (10 daily; 1hr 15min–1hr 40min); Carlingford (Mon–Sat 5; 50min–1hr); Drogheda (16–20 daily; 20–30min); Dublin (16 daily; 1hr 30min); Inniskeen (Mon–Sat 4 daily; 20min); Louth village (Mon–Sat 5 daily; 20min); Newry (Mon–Sat 9 daily; 30–45min).
Inniskeen to: Dundalk (Mon–Sat 5 daily; 20min).
Louth village to: Dundalk (Mon–Sat 5 daily; 20min).
Monaghan town to: Cavan (Mon–Fri 2–3 daily; 1hr); Clones (Mon–Fri 2 daily, Sat 1; 30min); Derry (8 daily; 1hr 50min); Dublin (14–16 daily; 2hr–2hr 20min); Dundalk (Mon–Fri 1 daily; 1hr 10min); Omagh (16 daily; 45min).

Matthews
Ⓣ042/937 8188, Ⓦwww.matthewscoach.com.
Dundalk to: Dublin (Mon–Fri 20 daily, Sat 10, Sun 9; 1hr 30min) via Drogheda (30min).

Ulsterbus
Belturbet to: Enniskillen (Mon–Sat 3 daily; 1hr).
Cavan to: Clones (Mon–Sat 2–3 daily; 30min); Monaghan town (Mon–Sat 2–3 daily; 1hr).
Clones to: Cavan (Mon–Sat 2 daily; 30min); Enniskillen (Mon–Sat 4–6 daily, Sun 1; 1hr); Monaghan town (Mon–Sat 2 daily; 30min).
Monaghan town to: Armagh (Mon–Sat 3–5 daily, Sun 2; 30–45min); Athlone (Mon–Sat 1 daily; 2hr 15min); Belfast (Mon–Sat 2–3 daily; 1hr 45min); Cavan (Mon–Sat 1 daily; 55min); Clones (Mon–Sat 3 daily 30min); Enniskillen (Mon–Sat 2 daily; 1hr 20min).

4

The Midlands: Westmeath, Longford, Offaly and Laois

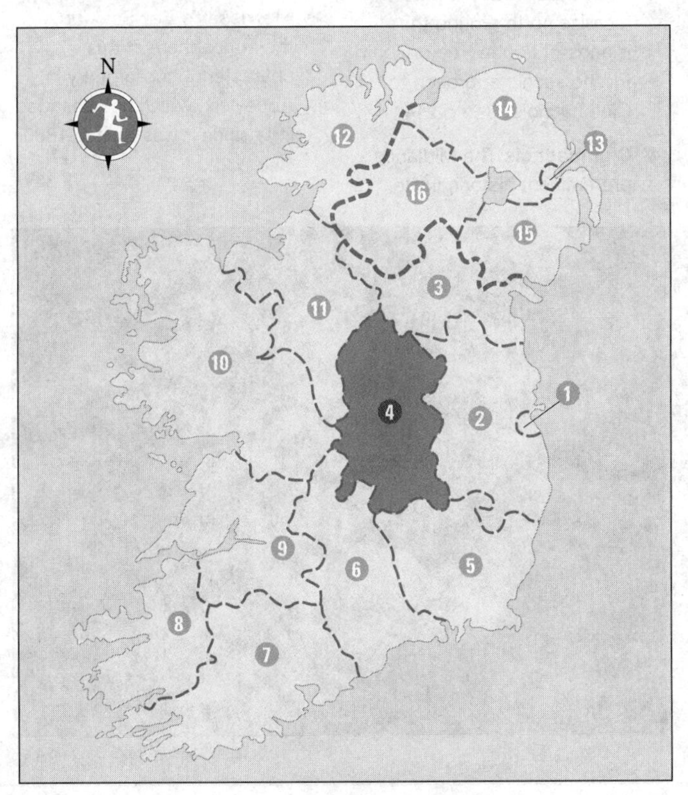

CHAPTER 4

Highlights

* **Belvedere House** A beautifully restored Georgian hunting lodge, set in attractive gardens, overlooking Lough Ennell. See p.210

* **The Fore Valley** Explore the rich ecclesiastical history of this remote, green valley or suspend your disbelief in appreciation of its Seven Wonders. See p.211

* **Boat trips from Athlone** Take a cruise north around the islands of Lough Ree or south for the scenic approach to Clonmacnois. See p.214

* **Clonmacnois** The Midlands' pre-eminent historical site, a prestigious complex of churches and ornate high-crosses overlooking the River Shannon. See p.215

* **Birr Castle** Wander around the huge and varied grounds and immerse yourself in the scientific exploits of the talented Parsons family at the Historic Science Centre. See p.219

* **Morrissey's Bar** Soak up the atmosphere at this characterful pub-grocery in Abbeyleix, which has changed little since it was built in 1880. See p.223

▲ Morrissey's Bar, Abbeyleix

4

The Midlands: Westmeath, Longford, Offaly and Laois

Obeying the siren call of the west coast, most foreign tourists, and indeed Irish holiday-makers, put their foot down to motor through **the Midlands** as quickly as possible. It's true that you're unlikely to want to make a comprehensive tour of the area, but if you fancy a stopover off the main radial routes out of Dublin, there are some compelling sights, and a surprisingly varied landscape, to discover.

County Westmeath's dairy farms are interspersed with large, glassy lakes, including Lough Ennell to the south of **Mullingar**, the county town, on whose shores **Belvedere House** is well worth a short detour off the N4. Among the county's more northerly lakes nestle the quirky gardens of **Tullynally Castle** and the pastoral charms of the **Fore Valley**, where you can poke around medieval monastic remains and be entertained by their wondrous legends. The N4 ploughs on through **County Longford**, mostly rich grasslands but blending into Ulster's drumlin country in its northern third. In the south of the county, the **Corlea Trackway Visitor Centre** gives a fascinating glimpse of a prestigious but ill-fated Iron Age road-building project.

The **River Shannon** and its seasonal floodplain delineates most of the Midlands' western border, running down through **Athlone**, a major junction town that lies on the N6, the railway and the Westmeath–Roscommon frontier, before veering southwest at Banagher: from both of these towns you can take **boat trips**, either for the day or on a live-aboard cruiser, while the major ecclesiastical site of **Clonmacnois**, just south of Athlone, enjoys a dreamy setting above the river's meanders and meadows. Elsewhere, **County Offaly** is known for its bogs, whose desolation can be definitively explored on the **Clonmacnois and West Offaly Railway**, but **Birr**, with its imposing castle and Georgian terraces, makes one of the best bases in the Midlands. Beyond the attractive bulge of **Slieve Bloom**, with its thick topping of blanket bog, **County Laois** (pronounced "leash") is mostly lush grazing and cereal land; the grounds and Neoclassical house of **Emo Court**, designed by James Gandon,

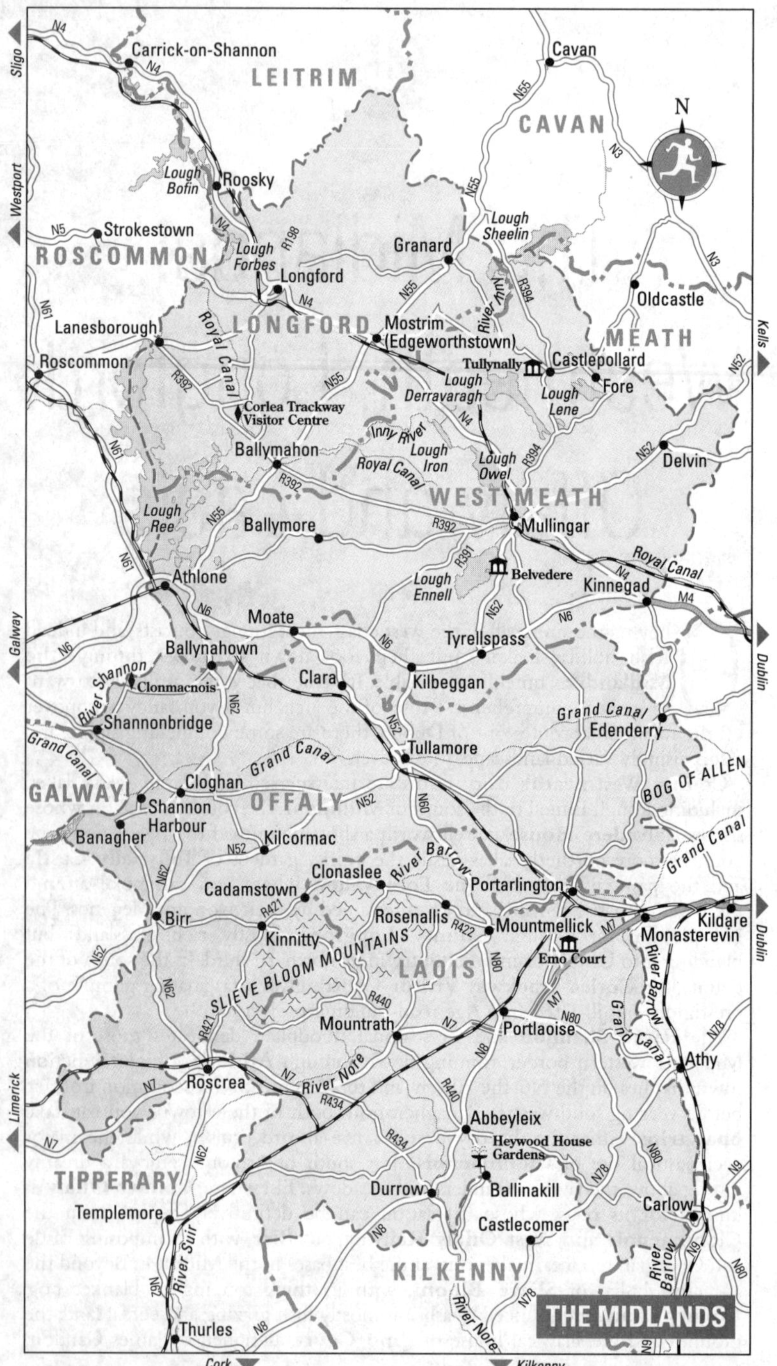
THE MIDLANDS
N
LEITRIM
CAVAN
ROSCOMMON
LONGFORD
MEATH
WESTMEATH
GALWAY
OFFALY
LAOIS
TIPPERARY
KILKENNY
BOG OF ALLEN
SLIEVE BLOOM MOUNTAINS
Sligo
Westport
Galway
Limerick
Cork
Kilkenny
Kells
Dublin
Dublin
Carrick-on-Shannon
Cavan
Lough Bofin
Roosky
Strokestown
Lough Forbes
Longford
Granard
Lough Sheelin
Oldcastle
Lanesborough
Roscommon
Mostrim (Edgeworthstown)
Tullynally
Castlepollard
Fore
Lough Derravaragh
Lough Lene
Corlea Trackway Visitor Centre
Ballymahon
Inny River
River Inny
Lough Iron
Royal Canal
Lough Owel
Delvin
Lough Ree
Ballymore
Mullingar
Belvedere
Lough Ennell
Kinnegad
Athlone
Moate
Tyrellspass
Ballynahown
Clara
Kilbeggan
River Shannon
Clonmacnois
Shannonbridge
Grand Canal
Edenderry
Tullamore
Cloghan
Shannon Harbour
Banagher
Kilcormac
River Barrow
Clonaslee
Portarlington
Cadamstown
Rosenallis
Birr
Kinnitty
Mountmellick
Emo Court
Kildare
Monasterevin
Mountrath
Portlaoise
River Nore
Athy
Roscrea
Abbeyleix
Heywood House Gardens
Ballinakill
Durrow
Templemore
Castlecomer
Carlow
River Suir
Thurles
N4
N5
N6
N7
N8
N9
N52
N55
N61
N62
N78
N80
M4
M7
N3
R198
R392
R394
R391
R421
R422
R440
R434

certainly justify a detour off the M7, while the attractive estate-town of **Abbeyleix** is your best bet for a break on the N8 Cork road.

These counties were mostly beyond the Pale, the enclave around Dublin that the Anglo-Normans retreated to in the fourteenth and fifteenth centuries, and indeed Offaly is named after the *Uí Failí* (O'Connor Faly), Irish chieftains who would attack the Pale and then retreat to their strongholds deep in the boglands. In the sixteenth century, however, this region was fairly comprehensively planted, when land was confiscated from native Irish owners and given to loyal English landlords. In 1541, Westmeath (*An Iarmhí*) was split off from County Meath, and in 1556 Offaly and Laois were created as "King's County" and "Queen's County", respectively, with the latter's main town named Maryborough (now Portlaoise) after the current monarch. Bypassed by the Industrial Revolution, many of the planned estate-towns that were attached to these landholdings remain to this day, along with the vestiges of a slow, steady rural style of living.

Of the places described here, only Athlone (on the line to Galway and Westport) and Mullingar (on the Sligo line) are served by **train**. **Buses** access all the main towns and villages, but as many of the attractions of this region are off the beaten track, you really need your own transport to get the best out of it.

Mullingar and Belvedere House

Set in lush cattle-country, **MULLINGAR**, the county town of Westmeath, holds little of interest for visitors, except as a base for visiting **Belvedere House**, a Georgian mansion in a lovely setting on Lough Ennell, or as a stop-over on a journey northwest towards Sligo. **Trains** on the main Dublin–Sligo line stop at the station on the southwest side of the centre; most **buses** call at Castle Street right in the heart of town, though some stop only at the train station. **Tourist information** is available in summer at Market House, just round the corner on Pearse Street, the westerly continuation of Austin Friars Street (May & Sept Mon–Fri 9.30am–1pm & 2–5.15pm; June–Aug Mon–Fri 9am–6pm, Sat 10.15am–1pm & 2–6pm; ⓣ044/934 8650), or year-round at the headquarters of East Coast and Midlands Tourism on the Dublin road (Mon–Fri 9.30am–1pm & 2–5.15pm; same phone number).

The pick of the **B&Bs** around Mullingar is friendly *Lough Owel Lodge* (ⓣ044/934 8714, ⓦwww.angelfire.com/tx/aginnell; April to mid-Oct; ❷), 3km north of town off the N4 and a short stroll from the eponymous lake. The en-suite bedrooms and lounges are large and attractive, with some pretty views, and the breakfast is well worth getting up for. Alternatively, try *Hilltop* (ⓣ044/934 8958, ⓦwww.hilltopcountryhouse.com; March–Oct; ❷), a modern country house with a fine garden, 2km northeast of the centre on the N52 Delvin road. Bang in the centre of town, the *Greville Arms* **hotel** is a welcoming and recently refurbished old coaching inn on Pearse Street (ⓣ044/934 8563, ⓦwww.grevillearms.com; ❹). *Gallery 29* (closed Sun & Mon) at 29 Oliver Plunkett St is a fine **café**, offering everything from breakfast, through soups, salads and sandwiches, to cakes and pastries, while *Oscar's*, a lively and unpretentious **restaurant** opposite (ⓣ044/934 4909; evenings, plus Sun lunch), is well known locally for its pasta, pizza and tasty Italian and global main courses. Pleasant **pubs** are *Canton Casey's*, with outdoor tables in front of the tourist office, and *Hughes's*, which often hosts DJs or live music, both on Pearse Street.

Belvedere House

Belvedere House stands in abundant gardens on the eastern shore of Lough Ennell, 5km south of Mullingar on the N52 (daily: March, April, Sept & Oct house 10.30am–5pm, gardens 10.30am–7pm; May–Aug house 10am–5pm, gardens 9.30am–9pm; Nov–Feb house and gardens 10.30am–4.30pm; last admission 1hr before closing; €8.75; Heritage Island; ⓣ044/934 9060 or ⓦwww.belvedere-house.ie for details of the many concerts, festivals and other events hosted at Belvedere throughout the year). The house was built in the 1740s by Richard Castle as a hunting lodge for Robert Rochfort, later the First Earl of Belvedere, the so-called "Wicked Earl", whose main pastime seems to have been making life hell for his wife and brothers. In 1743 he falsely accused his wife Mary of having an affair with his brother Arthur and imprisoned her for the next 31 years at their nearby main residence, Gaulstown. It was only when the Earl died that she was released by their son, whom she no longer recognized. Meanwhile, the Earl had successfully pressed charges of adultery against Arthur, who, unable to pay the damages of £20,000, lived out his days in debtors' prison.

The **house** itself, which commands beautiful views of the lake, has been painstakingly restored and authentically refurbished by Westmeath County Council. It holds some gorgeous fireplaces of carved Irish oak with Italian marble insets, but is most notable for the exquisite craftsmanship of its rococo ceilings, the work of a French stuccodore, Barthelemij Cramillion. Look out especially for the vivid depictions of the Four Winds, a fire-breathing dragon and a horn of plenty in the dining room, while the library, intended for night-time use, features sleeping cherubs wrapped in a blanket of clouds, a crescent moon and stars, and on the cornice a swirl of flowers with their heads closed.

As one of the county's chief amenities, the **gardens** boast all manner of attractions, even a tram that provides guided tours of the estate on certain days of the year (€2). A feud between Robert Rochfort and his other brother George was behind one of the main sights, the **Jealous Wall**. When George commissioned Richard Castle in the 1750s to build Tudenham House, a much larger mansion than Belvedere, just a kilometre away, the Earl of Belvedere spent £10,000 building this huge Gothic folly, three storeys high and nearly 60m long, just to block the view. Other sights include a Victorian walled garden, enclosing an unusual collection of Himalayan plants, a small animal sanctuary, playgrounds for kids, and a café in the old stable block by the entrance. Or you can just take a stroll around the extensive woodlands and lawns: the 45-minute Earl's Trail, for example, will take you along the lakeshore and back, past an octagonal gazebo, a folly known as the Gothic Arch and a restored ice-house.

Northern Westmeath

The far north of Westmeath shelters two compelling and whimsical attractions, the gardens of Tullynally Castle and the Seven Wonders of the Fore Valley, near **CASTLEPOLLARD**, a pretty eighteenth- and nineteenth-century village laid out around a large triangular green. With your own transport, it's easily approached from Mullingar on the R394, or from the Loughcrew Cairns near Oldcastle, just across the border in County Meath (see p.174).

Tullynally Castle

A little over a kilometre northwest of Castlepollard on the Granard road, **Tullynally Castle** has been the seat of the Anglo-Irish Pakenhams, later Earls of Longford, since the seventeenth century. Remodelled as a rambling Gothic Revival castle to the designs of Francis Johnston in the early 1800s, it remains the family home, open only to prebooked group visits (minimum 20 people) and for occasional concerts. The extensive **gardens**, however, are open to casual visitors in the summer (May & June Sat, Sun & public hols noon–6pm; July & Aug daily noon–6pm; €6; Ⓣ044/966 1159, Ⓦwww.tullynallycastle.com). Terraced lawns around the castle overlook parkland, laid out by the first Earl of Longford in 1760. From here winding paths lead through the woodland to lakes, a walled garden with a 200-year-old yew avenue and a limestone grotto, as well as the recently added Chinese garden complete with pagoda and Tibetan garden of waterfalls and streams. A **café** in the castle courtyard offers teas, coffees and home-made cakes.

The Fore Valley

To the east of Castlepollard off the R195 Oldcastle road, the **Fore Valley** is a charming, bucolic spot, sheltered between two ranges of low, green hills and dotted with some impressive Christian ruins. Around 630, St Fechin founded a monastery here, which had grown into a community of three hundred monks by the time he died in 665. Over the centuries since, various sites in the valley have become associated with Fechin's magical powers, known as the **Seven Wonders of Fore**, though in truth they're far from jaw-dropping – it's unlikely that you'll be converted to miracle-worshipping, but the wonders add some fun and interest to an exploration of the locale.

The historical and supernatural sites are all within walking distance of the village of **FORE** at the heart of the valley. The **coffee shop** here (April–Sept daily 12.30–6pm; Oct–March Sat & Sun 12.30–6pm; Ⓣ044/966 1780), as well as serving home-made soup, sandwiches, cakes and drinks, hosts a twenty-minute audiovisual on the monastery, and sells literature and provides information on the area. Ask behind the bar at the *Seven Wonders* **pub**, which opens at around 12.30pm, if you want the key for the Anchorite's Cell. **B&B** is available at *Hounslow House* (Ⓣ044/966 1144, Ⓔeithne.healy@fore-enterprises.com; April–Sept; ❷), a large, 200-year-old farmhouse set in extensive grounds with fine views of the valley, about a kilometre from the village and well signposted.

The Seven Wonders

To the west of the village, on the south side of the road, stands **St Fechin's Church**, now roofless, the oldest remaining building in the valley, dating probably from the tenth century. Over its main entrance there's a massive lintel inscribed with a small cross-in-circle: the first wonder, the **stone raised by St Fechin's prayers**. Up the slope and across from the church, you'll find the **Anchorite's Cell**, a fifteenth-century tower to which the mausoleum chapel of the Greville-Nugent family was added in the nineteenth century. Inside an inscription commemorates the last hermit of Fore, Patrick Beglin, whose body is "hidden in this hollow heap of stones" – the second wonder, the **anchorite in a stone**. Beglin had vowed to remain in the cell until he died: in 1616, he fell trying to climb out, and broke his neck – thus enacting his promise.

Back down the slope and across the road you'll see the **water that will not boil**, a holy well known to cure headaches and toothaches, where in the nineteenth century rites were performed on St Fechin's Day (January 20). In the spring stands a dead ash tree, now gaily festooned with coins, sweet wrappers, stockings and knickers – the fourth wonder, the **wood that will not burn**. Nearby, a stream that runs underground from Lough Lene to the south resurfaces at the ruined St Fechin's Mill – the **mill without a race**.

A couple of hundred metres across the marshy valley floor rise the substantial but compact remains of **Fore Priory** – the **monastery built on a bog**. It was erected in the early thirteenth century, one of very few in Ireland to follow the rule of St Benedict, the fifth-century Italian ascetic. Attached to the central cloister, of which several Gothic arches remain, you'll find the church to the north, the chapterhouse to the east, with the dormitory above, and the refectory to the south. A little away from the main buildings, up a small slope, there's a circular, thirteenth-century columbarium, where the monks kept doves, an efficient source of meat in the Middle Ages.

The seventh wonder is a little removed from the others to the south of the village – ask for directions at the coffee shop. A short woodland walk will bring you down to the attractive shore of Lough Lene, which is dotted with small, green islands. A stream flows out of the lake, apparently in the wrong direction, passing under an overgrown arched bridge, before disappearing into a sink hole (to emerge at St Fechin's Mill) – the **water that flows uphill**.

Athlone and around

Straddling the Shannon at its midpoint, **ATHLONE** (Ⓦwww.athlone.ie) is the bustling, prosperous capital of the Midlands and an important road and rail junction. It probably derives its name from the *Táin Bó Cúailnge*, in which the remains of the white bull of Connacht, the Findbennach, after its defeat by Ulster's brown bull, are scattered throughout Ireland; its loins came to rest here at *Áth Luain*, the "Ford of the Loins". A bridge was first built over this ford in 1120 by Turlough O'Connor, king of Connacht, which was replaced by a stone bridge by the Anglo-Normans in 1210, who were also responsible for the mighty castle. The latter still casts a formidable shadow over Athlone, having weathered some bloody fighting during the Cromwellian Wars and the War of the Kings of the seventeenth century. Today, the town supports an important college, the Athlone Institute of Technology, as well as various civil-service offices and high-tech firms, but its main function for tourists is as a jumping-off point for the monastic site of **Clonmacnois**. Fewer visitors know about the **Corlea Trackway Visitor Centre**, but the evocative, 2000-year-old wooden road preserved here is also well worth a visit if you have your own transport.

The imposing, grey fortifications on the west side of the main bridge now house the underwhelming **Athlone Castle Visitor Centre** (May–early Oct daily 9.30am–4.30pm; €4 for the AV; Heritage Island). In the oldest part of the castle – a substantial, ten-sided tower dating from the thirteenth century – there's a small, musty folk and historical museum, but it's currently closed – it's hoped it will reopen some time in 2008. In the adjacent building, you can watch a 45-minute audiovisual that focuses on the vicious Sieges of Athlone during the War of the Kings: in July 1690, the castle did its job, forcing William III's army to retreat after a week; they returned with some serious artillery in June of 1691, however, and after building a pontoon over the river and reducing much of the castle to rubble, they took it from the Jacobites, who lost over 1200 men. The film also covers the River Shannon and its wildlife, as well

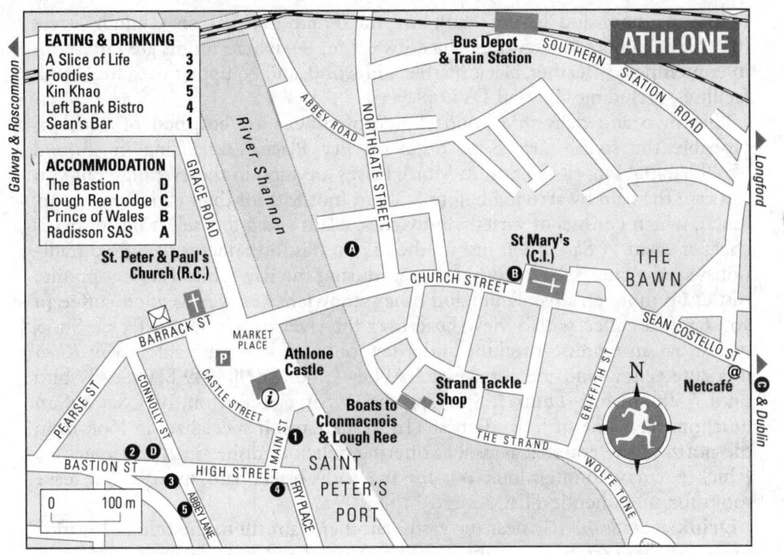

as local lad, **Count John McCormack** (1884–1945). One of the greatest bel canto singers ever – who professed himself to be "the world's worst actor" – McCormack gave up the operatic stage at a comparatively young age in 1923. He turned to concert work and recordings (tested out on the gramophone that's preserved in the museum), was made a count of the Papal Court for his charity work in 1928, and gave a tearful farewell concert at London's Royal Albert Hall in 1938.

Practicalities

The main **bus** and **train stations** lie on the north side of the centre on Southern Station Road, though private buses on their way between Galway and Dublin stop only on Dublin Road. The **tourist office** (mid-April to May & Sept Mon–Fri 10am–1pm & 2–5.30pm; June–Aug Mon–Sat 9.30am–5.45pm; ⓣ090/649 4630) is inside the castle, and **Internet** access is available at Netcafé on Sean Costello Street. You can **rent a bike** at Buckley's on Dublin Road (ⓣ090/647 8989), or a **car** from Enterprise, Dublin Road (ⓣ090/649 1030, ⓦwww.enterprise.com).

Athlone's modern, purpose-built **hostel**, *Lough Ree Lodge* (IHH; ⓣ09064/76738, ⓦwww.athlonehostel.ie; mid-May to mid-Sept), offers small dorms (from €15.50 including light breakfast), twins and doubles (❶), as well as singles and family rooms, a twenty-minute walk along the Dublin Road from the centre, opposite the college. *The Bastion*, above a clothes shop on Bastion Street (ⓣ09064/94954, ⓦwww.thebastion.net; ❷), is the pick of the town's **B&Bs**. It's an elegant, relaxing spot, hung with modern art, which serves healthy buffet breakfasts. In the centre, there are also two recently built luxury **hotels**: the environmentally conscious *Radisson SAS* on Northgate Street (ⓣ090/644 2600, ⓦwww.radissonsas.com; ❺), which enjoys a peerless setting on the east bank of the Shannon overlooking the castle and offers smart, well-designed rooms with either an urban or a soothing marine theme, a swimming pool and leisure club; and the *Prince of Wales* on Church Street (ⓣ090/647 6666, ⓦwww.theprinceofwales.ie; ⑤), where rooms are kitted out in contemporary leather, black marble and wood, and equipped with high-tech facilities, including CD and DVD players.

The town also delivers a good choice of **places to eat**, best of which is probably the stylish *Left Bank Bistro* on Fry Place, specializing in seafood (ⓣ090/649 4446; closed Sun & Mon). Prices are high in the evenings, but you can ease the pain by arriving before 7.30pm (not Sat) for their early-bird menu; lunch, which consists of varied sandwiches, salads and a few select hot dishes is cheaper again. *A Slice of Life* just up the hill on Bastion Street serves good traditional sandwiches, salads and light meals during the day, while *Foodies* opposite rustles up more creative panini and other sandwiches, as well as good coffee (if you fancy a coffee with a view, head over the river to the Strand Tackle Shop, which has an espresso machine and a few outdoor riverside tables). *Kin Khao,* in a cute yellow-and-red cottage at 1 Abbey Lane (ⓣ090/649 8805; early bird until 7.30pm Mon–Thurs & Sun, 7pm Fri & Sat; closed Mon, Tues, Sat & Sun lunchtimes), is one of Ireland's best Thai restaurants. It specializes in food from the north of the country, as well as offering delicious dishes such as *hor mok gai* (chicken curry soufflé); look out for the daily blackboard specials and leave room for an authentic Thai dessert.

Drink at *Sean's Bar*, near the castle, another claimant to the title of Ireland's oldest pub. It's certainly appealingly old-fashioned and sociable, with sawdust on the floor, live music, either acoustic or traditional, every night and a huge beer garden at the back stretching down towards the river. If, however, you're blessed with a fine evening, you might well be tempted by a sundowner on the riverside terraces of the *Radisson SAS Hotel*.

Trips to Lough Ree and Clonmacnois

On most days in the summer (roughly May–Sept), Viking Tours (ⓣ090/647 3383 or 086 262 1136) runs **boat trips** on the Shannon, which involve sailing in a replica longboat, with Viking costumes for kids to dress up in. The longboat either heads north around the islands of **Lough Ree** (90min; €10), which include Hare Island, site of a Viking encampment that has yielded considerable amounts of treasure, or south for the scenic approach to **Clonmacnois** (see opposite; about 4hr 30min round trip, including 1hr 30min at Clonmacnois; €10 one way, €20 return). Departures are from the Strand in front of the Strand Tackle Shop (ⓣ090/647 9277), where tickets can be bought. If you fancy making a whole holiday out of it, rent a self-drive **live-aboard boat** from Athlone Cruisers at the Jolly Mariner Marina on the north side of town (ⓣ090/647 2892, ⓦwww.acl.ie).

There are no buses to Clonmacnois from Athlone, but the trip is perfectly manageable in a day by **renting a bike or a car** (see p.213). The other option would be taking a **taxi** from Athlone Cabs, Dublin Road (ⓣ090/647 4400; around €60, including 1hr waiting time).

Corlea Trackway Visitor Centre

It's a little tricky to get to the fascinating **Corlea Trackway Visitor Centre** (April–Sept daily 10am–6pm; last admission 45min before closing; free), which is actually across the county border in Longford and signposted along a minor road off the R392, 20km northeast of Athlone, but its isolation in the midst of a desolate bog only adds to the appeal of the place. In 1984, Bord na Móna (the Peat Board) discovered a buried *togher*, an early Iron Age trackway, while milling turf here in Corlea raised bog. Dated to 148 BC, the trackway was made of split oak planks up to 4m in length that were meant to float on the bog surface, one of the most substantial and sophisticated of many such prehistoric roads found in Europe. However, the builders knew more about woodworking than the properties of the bog, because within ten years the heavy planks had sunk into the peat – which preserved them perfectly for the next two thousand years. The road connected dry land to the east with an island in the bog to the west, but it's clear that such a prestigious construction was intended for more than just the movement of animals by farmers: it may have been part of a ceremonial highway from the Hill of Uisneach, the ritual "centre of Ireland" that marked the division of the five ancient provinces, between Mullingar and Athlone, to the royal site of Rathcroghan in Roscommon (see p.499), via the narrow crossing of the Shannon at Lanesborough.

Excellent **guided tours** (every hour, on the hour) begin with the 18m of trackway that's been preserved under cover in the visitor centre. Another 80m has been left outside under the turf, but the guides, as well as delving into the extraordinary ecology of the bog, will take you to the wooden walkway built over it, which gives a good idea of what the trackway would have looked like, undulating over the peaty tussocks.

From Clonmacnois to Banagher along the Shannon

The stretch of the Shannon to the south of Athlone is particularly pretty, and justly popular for **cruise holidays**, with pleasant refuelling stops at the riverside villages of **Shannonbridge** and **Banagher**. Here the river descends at a shallow gradient through flat land that floods extensively in winter, which explains why there are so few bridges. In spring, however, the receding flow leaves beautiful, nutrient-rich water meadows, some of the last of their type in Europe. The **Shannon Callows**, as they are known, become the summer home of rare wild-flowers, grazing cattle, lapwings, curlews, redshanks and rare corncrakes. The region's pre-eminent attraction, the well-endowed, 1500-year-old pilgrimage site of **Clonmacnois** in the northwest corner of County Offaly, enjoys a grandstand seat above the Callows, but its tranquillity is often broken by coach tours. If you can, time your visit for late afternoon, when you might be lucky enough to catch the birds singing as the sun sets over the Shannon.

Clonmacnois

The substantial remains of **Clonmacnois**, pre-Norman Ireland's most important Christian site, enjoy an idyllic location on the grassy banks of the gently meandering Shannon, 10km south of Athlone (daily: mid-March to mid-May & mid-Sept to Oct 10am–6pm; mid-May to mid-Sept 9am–7pm; Nov to mid-March 10am–5.30pm; last admission 45min before closing; €5.30; Heritage Card; Ⓦwww.heritageireland.ie). The monastery was founded, as a satellite of St Enda's house on Inishmore (see p.430), in around 548 by **St Kieran (Ciarán)**, who with the help of Diarmuid of the Uí Néills, the first Christian High King of Ireland, erected a wooden church here. Kieran brought with him a dun cow, whose hide later became Clonmacnois' major relic – anyone who died lying on it would be spared the torments of Hell – and who was commemorated in the *Lebor na hUidre* (Book of the Dun Cow), the oldest

▲ Clonmacnois

surviving manuscript written wholly in Irish. Perfectly sited at the junction of the Slí Mhor, the main road from Dublin Bay to Galway Bay, and the major north–south artery, the Shannon, the monastery grew in influence as various provincial kings endowed it with churches and high crosses. With a large lay population, Clonmacnois resembled a small town, where craftsmen and scholars produced illuminated manuscripts, croziers and other remarkable artefacts, many of which can be seen in the National Museum in Dublin. However, between the eighth and twelfth centuries the site was plundered over forty times by Vikings, Anglo-Normans and Irish enemies, and church reforms in the thirteenth century greatly reduced its influence. In 1552, Athlone's English garrison reduced it to ruins, though, as the burial place of Kieran, it has persisted to this day as a place of pilgrimage, focused on the saint's day on September 9.

The visitor centre and high crosses

Clonmacnois' three magnificent high crosses have been moved into the excellent **visitor centre** to prevent further damage by the weather. (Outside the Office of Public Works has erected all-too-faithful replicas, complete with erosion – an attempt to re-create their appearance when first carved would have been far more constructive.) The finest is the **Cross of the Scriptures**, a pictorial sermon showing the Crucifixion, Christ in the Tomb and the Last Judgment. It was erected in the early tenth century by Abbot Colman and Flann, the High King of Ireland, who may be depicted together (with Flann holding a pole) in the bottom scene on the shaft's east face. Standing 4m high, the cross is carved from a single piece of sandstone and may originally have been coloured. The other two crosses are about a century older and much simpler, the **South Cross** featuring the Crucifixion surrounded by rich interlacing, spirals and bosses, while the **North Cross** is carved with abstract Celtic ornaments, humans and animals.

Elsewhere in the visitor centre there's a good audiovisual on Kieran's life and the history of Clonmacnois, and an interesting reconstruction of a *dairthech* (oak house), the type of small oratory that would have been built out of wood at this and other monasteries throughout Ireland before stone began to be used in the tenth century.

The site

Most of Clonmacnois' nine churches are structurally intact apart from their roofs, the largest being the **cathedral** straight in front of the visitor centre. It was built in 909 by Abbot Colman and King Flann, but its most beautiful feature now is the fifteenth-century north doorway, featuring decorative Gothic carving surmounted by SS Dominic, Patrick and Francis. The last High King of Ireland, Rory O'Connor, was buried by the altar here in 1198. Several smaller churches encircle the cathedral, notably **Temple Ciarán**, the burial place of St Kieran, dating from the early tenth century.

In the western corner of the compound rises a fine **round tower**, erected in 1124 by Abbot O'Malone and Turlough O'Connor of Connacht, High King of Ireland and father of Rory. Down towards the river, **Temple Connor**, which probably dates from the twelfth century, is still used by the Church of Ireland for Sunday services in summer. There's another round tower attached to the nave of **Temple Finghin**, which is Romanesque in style and thought to date from 1160–70.

In a peaceful, leafy glade about 500m away from the main site and signposted from the east side of the compound, the **Nun's Church** is the place to escape to if a fleet of tour coaches descends. Founded by Queen Devorguilla, who retired here as a penitent in 1170, it boasts a fine Romanesque doorway and chancel arch carved with geometrical patterns.

Practicalities

There's a small **café** in the visitor centre, and a helpful **tourist office** (mid-March to early Nov daily 10am–5.45pm; Ⓣ090/967 4134) in the car park. If you want to stay near the site, head for *Kajon House* (Ⓣ090/967 4191, Ⓦwww.kajonhouse.cjb.net; March–Oct; ❷), a friendly, comfortable **B&B**, with en-suite rooms and evening meals on offer, under 2km away on the Shannonbridge road. The *Glebe* **campsite** (Ⓣ090/643 0277, Ⓦwww.glebecaravanpark.ie) lies 5km away in Clonfanlough, signposted off the road towards Athlone.

Shannonbridge

Around 6km southwest of Clonmacnois, the village of **SHANNONBRIDGE** stands at the meeting point of counties Offaly, Galway and Roscommon and where the River Suck joins the Shannon. This strategic location is bolstered by a long, arched bridge over the Shannon and an imposing, Napoleonic-era fortification on the Roscommon bank, which has now been turned into a fine **restaurant**, the *Old Fort*, offering sophisticated fare, such as salmon stuffed with red pepper and saffron cream (Ⓣ090/967 4973; Wed–Sat evenings & Sun lunch, plus July to mid-Sept Mon, Tues & Sun evenings); it's expensive on weekend evenings after 7pm, but otherwise quite reasonably priced. The quiet, attractive stretch of river here is popular with pleasure boats, though it's overshadowed by the peat-fired colossus of West Offaly Power Station. *Rachra House*, a smart, Georgian-style modern house with en-suite rooms near the river (Ⓣ090/967 4249, Ⓦwww.rachrahouse.shannonbridge.net; May–Oct; ❷) is a good option for **B&B**, while *Killeen's*, a cosy **pub** and grocery store further down the main street, dishes up sandwiches lunchtime and evening, as well as Irish stew and other traditional hot dishes on summer lunchtimes, and hosts live music, mostly sing-along ballads, every night in summer, on weekends in winter.

If the power station happens to have aroused your curiosity about the peat industry, you can follow it up with a bog tour on the **Clonmacnois and West Offaly Railway**, 6km east of town off the R357 towards Cloghan (April, May & Sept Mon–Fri 10am–5pm; June–Aug daily 10am–5pm; €7; Ⓦwww.bnm.ie). Run by Bord na Móna, the Irish Peat Board, the 45-minute trip runs every hour on the hour, taking you on narrow gauge through the eerie landscape of Blackwater Bog, with a chance to try your hand at turf-cutting along the way.

Banagher

A little over 10km downstream from Shannonbridge, **BANAGHER** grew up around another narrow crossing of the Shannon, spanned by an arched stone bridge. Despite the establishment of a huge cement factory in more recent times, the town seems to be on the slide, with lots of unkempt disused premises in the centre. Its long main street slopes down to a huge, busy pleasure-boat marina, but the prettiest spot on the river is across on the Galway side, where in the Napoleonic era a Martello tower was erected and a Cromwellian castle was converted into a gun tower.

As well as Bus Éireann services, Banagher is on the route of Kearns Transport buses between Portumna and Dublin (see p.224). *Crank House*, an attractive Georgian building on the main street fronted by a curious pepper-pot tower, is home to the **tourist office** (Mon–Fri 10am–5pm; Ⓣ057/915 2155), which offers **Internet** access, and *Heidi's* **café**, which serves sandwiches, cakes and traditional main courses at reasonable prices and stays open in the evening on summer weekends. Your best all-round bet for hospitality in Banagher is the *Brosna Lodge* (Ⓣ057/915 1350, Ⓦwww.brosnalodge.com; ❸), a comfortable, family-run **hotel** further up the main street, which serves tasty, varied and reasonably priced **meals** in its bar and restaurant area. Comfortable, en-suite **B&B** accommodation, with fine views of the river and good rates for singles and children, can be found at *Dun Cromáin*, Crank Road (Ⓣ057/915 3966, Ⓦwww.duncromain.com; Feb–Nov; ❷), 300m off Main Street near *Crank House*. Back on Main Street, *Hough's* is a characterful, creeper-clad, old **pub**, which hosts traditional music every night in summer, at weekends in winter.

At the marina, **canoes** can be rented from Shannon Adventure Canoeing Holidays (Ⓣ057/915 1411) and **boats** for live-aboard cruises along the Shannon from Carrickcraft (Ⓣ057/915 1187, Ⓦwww.carrickcraft.com) and Silverline Cruisers (Ⓣ057/915 1112, Ⓦwww.silverlinecruisers.com). On Sundays in July, August and early September (with occasional extra sailings), Silverline's *Victoria Queen* runs ninety-minute pleasure **cruises** to Victoria Lock, a local beauty spot where the Shannon splits into two channels (€10).

Birr

At the confluence of the Camcor and Little Brosna rivers, **BIRR** (Ⓦwww.birrnet.com) is the Midlands' most attractive town, planned around the estate of Birr Castle, the home of the Parsons family, later the Earls of Rosse. Around Emmet Square – formerly Duke's Square, but the unpopular statue of the Duke of Cumberland, victor over the Jacobites at the Battle of Culloden in 1746, is long gone from the central pillar – you'll find several broad Georgian terraces, graced with fanlights and other fine architectural details. Birr is not yet on the country's main tourist trail but supports some appealing places to stay and eat, making it an excellent place from which to explore the Shannon, Clonmacnois and Slieve Bloom. The place comes to life in mid-August during its **Vintage Week and Arts Festival** (Ⓦ www.birrvintageweek.com), when shop assistants, bar staff and townspeople deck themselves out in historic regalia, and there's a varied programme of street theatre, music, and art exhibitions.

A monastery was first founded here in the sixth century, later becoming famous for the *Mac Regol Gospels* (now in the Bodleian Library, Oxford), an illuminated manuscript named after the early ninth-century abbot and bishop. Birr was settled by the Anglo-Normans, who built a castle here in 1208, later becoming the site of an O'Carroll stronghold between the fourteenth and seventeenth centuries. In the 1619 plantation of their territory, known as Ely O'Carroll, however, Sir Laurence Parsons was given Birr, which became known as Parsonstown. A descendant of his set about reconstructing the town in the 1740s in Neoclassical style, a development which continued in stages until as late as the 1830s.

Birr Castle

The forbidding, grey Gothic **castle** itself is not open to the public, but there's plenty of interest in the **Historic Science Centre** in the coach houses and the varied demesne (daily: March–Oct 9am–6pm; Nov–Feb 10am–4pm; €9; Heritage Island; Ⓦ www.birrcastle.com). In the nineteenth century, the Parsons family gained an international reputation as scientists and inventors, partly it would seem because they were educated at home. The third Earl of Rosse, William Parsons, devoted himself to astronomy, and in 1845 built the huge **Rosse Telescope**, with a 72-inch reflector, which remained the largest in the world until 1917. It was fully reconstructed in the 1990s, along with the massive, elaborate housing of walls, tracks, pulleys and counterweights needed to manouevre it, which can be seen in the garden. The fourth Earl, Laurence, and his mother, Mary, a friend of Fox Talbot's, were eminent photographers, and her darkroom, believed to be the oldest surviving example in the world, is on show. Meanwhile, Laurence's brother, Sir Charles Parsons, was carving himself a varied and colourful career, which included building a small flying machine and a helicopter in the 1890s and spending 25 years unsuccessfully trying to make artificial diamonds. He'll be best remembered, however, as the inventor of the steam turbine and for his exploits at the 1897 Spithead Naval Review, celebrating Queen Victoria's Diamond Jubilee when, frustated at the Royal Navy's foot-dragging, he gatecrashed in the *Turbinia*, the first steam-turbine ship, racing through the fleet at the unheard-of speed of 34 knots. Within a few years the technology was adopted by navies and passenger liners around the world. All of this is set in historical and global context in the Science Centre, with hoards of astrolabes, cameras and other instruments and some lively audiovisuals.

You could easily spend a couple of hours strolling around the beautiful castle **demesne**, especially if you buy the booklet on its fifty most significant trees, or in summer you could hire a horse and carriage to save the legwork. Beyond the wild-flower meadows, which are left to grow tall until July every year, lie a nineteenth-century lake, a fernery and fountain, and the oldest wrought-iron suspension bridge in Ireland, dating from 1820. The walled gardens feature the tallest box hedges in the world, which are over three hundred years old, as well as intricate parterres and paths canopied with hornbeams in the formal, seventeenth-century-style Millennium Garden.

Practicalities

O'Connell Street, which becomes Main Street, runs south from Emmet Square, where **buses** stop, to Market Square. The **tourist office** is in the civic offices on Wilmer Road, which runs very roughly parallel to and east of Main Street (mid-May to mid-Sept Mon–Sat 9.30am–1 & 2–5.30pm; ⓣ057/912 0110); it shares the complex with the public library, which provides **Internet** access.

Off the west side of Market Square, on Castle Street, is a very good value **guesthouse**, *The Maltings* (ⓣ057/912 1345, ⓔthemaltingsbirr@eircom.net; ❷). Housed in a restored 1810 warehouse that was used to store malt for Guinness and overlooks the leafy river, it offers quiet, large rooms with TVs and en-suite bathrooms. Also central is the welcoming *Townsend House*, on busy Townsend Street to the north of Emmet Square (ⓣ057/912 1276, ⓔtownshousebandb@eircom.net; ❷), which provides similar facilities and wonderful breakfasts, in an airy, high-ceilinged nineteenth-century house that's tastefully furnished with antiques. Around the corner on tree-lined Oxmantown Mall, *The Stables* (ⓣ057/912 0263, ⓦwww.thestablesbirr.com; ❸) is a fanlit nineteenth-century townhouse with comfortable, en-suite bedrooms and an open fire in its cosy lounge, as well as a home-furnishings shop and tearooms.

The town's central **hotel**, *Dooly's* in Emmet Square (ⓣ0509/20032, ⓦwww.doolyshotel.ie; ❹), is a welcoming Georgian coaching inn, with a chequered history; it was here in 1809 that the Galway Hunt partied a little too hard after a day in the field and managed to burn the hotel down, thus gaining a new name, the Galway Blazers. It's still one of the town's main social hubs, thanks partly to its fine **restaurant**, *The Emmet* – a formal, luxurious but not too pricey affair, serving dishes such as honey-roast duck stuffed with chestnuts in an apple, rhubarb and ginger sauce. For a change of continents, *Kong Lam* (ⓣ057/912 1253) on Market Square is a good Chinese option. During the day, your best bet is *Emma's*, 31 Main St, a mellow **café** – cool jazz and comfy banquettes – preparing delicious panini and cold deli plates, as well as speciality teas and coffees and a tempting array of cakes.

Craughwell's in Castle Street is a very sociable and cosy **pub**, with traditional music at weekends. *The Chestnut*, on The Green between Emmet Square and the castle, is also welcoming; stylishly outfitted with dark wood and leather seats and backed by a large beer garden, it hosts traditional sessions on Thursdays and live bands at weekends. Birr Theatre and Arts Centre on Oxmantown Mall (ⓣ057/912 2911, ⓦwww.birrtheatre.com) hosts a varied programme of drama, music and artistic events throughout the year.

Slieve Bloom

To the east of Birr, straddling the Offaly–Laois border, rises **Slieve Bloom** (ⓦwww.slievebloom.ie), the "mountain of Bladhma", named for an ancient Connacht warrior who sought refuge here. Although it extends only for about 20km across and down, the massif, from which emerge two of Ireland's principal rivers, Barrow and Nore, brings welcome relief in the vast Midland flatness. There's a large area of rugged upland blanket bog, dotted with bright purple ling heather, bog cotton and the insect-eating sundew, and home to skylark, kestrels and the rare peregrine falcon and hen harrier. The lower slopes are shaded by oak and birch in the stream valleys, as well as rather too many intrusive conifer plantations. The waymarked 77km-long **Slieve Bloom Way** describes a heavily indented circuit of most of the range, before passing underneath the highest point – Arderin (527m), which means, rather hopefully, the "height of Ireland"; shorter signposted walks are detailed on ⓦwww.slievebloom.ie. OS **map** #54 covers the whole of Slieve Bloom, while East

West Mapping produces a useful map-guide to the waymarked trail, available from local bookshops and tourist offices. For something more organized, get in touch with Gerry Hanlon (Ⓣ086 821 0056) or the Slieve Bloom Rural Development Co-operative Society at the community centre in Kinnitty (see below), who run a **walking festival** over the bank-holiday weekend in early May (coinciding with a set-dancing festival), and **guided walks** every Sunday afternoon thereafter until early November (plus occasional winter walks; €5 per person), as well as a weekend geology and natural-history festival in early September.

The best bases are on the Offaly side of the mountains, within walking distance of the Slieve Bloom Way. At the westernmost edge, the charming village of **KINNITTY** huddles around a triangular green that's traversed by a tiny stream. In the community centre here you'll find a small but helpful **tourist office** (Tues–Fri 11am–4pm; Ⓣ057/913 7299), which can advise on walks and tours. *Ardmore House* (Ⓣ057/913 7009, Ⓦwww.kinnitty.com; ❷), an attractive, nineteenth-century stone house with a fine view of the mountain, offers en-suite or standard **B&B**, home baking and turf fires and can arrange guided walking tours. There's also en-suite B&B at *The Slieve Bloom* **pub** (Ⓣ057/913 7010, Ⓦwww.kinnittynet.ie; ❷), a cosy establishment with an attractive beer garden, bar **food** and live music on Saturdays. A couple of kilometres northeast of the village on the R421, the Neogothic splendours of *Kinnitty Castle* (Ⓣ057/913 7500, Ⓦwww.kinnittycastle.com; ❽) have been tastefully renovated as a luxury hotel, complete with gym and spa, horse riding and falconry displays; attractive but cheaper rooms are also available in a guest-house on the estate (❹).

Further along the same road, 5km from Kinnitty, leafy **Cadamstown** guards an old bridge over the Silver River, which is named after the particles of silver that get washed down from the upland limestone. From the bridge, a nature trail (less than 2km there and back) runs upstream to a small waterfall and gorge, with display boards on the geology and ecology of Slieve Bloom. Refresh yourselves at the outdoor riverside tables of *Dempsey's* pub by the bridge or *My Little Tea and Craft Shop* in the front room of a nearby cottage.

Emo Court

If you're driving down the M7 towards Limerick or Cork, it's well worth planning a break at **Emo Court**, one of the very few private country houses designed by James Gandon, Ireland's greatest Neoclassical architect (early June to mid-Sept Tues–Sun 10.30am–6.30pm; tours at least hourly, last tour 5.45pm; €2.90; Heritage Card; Ⓦwww.heritageireland.ie). This lovely example of the style is surrounded by extensive **grounds** – laid out in the eighteenth century and a great spot for a picnic – which you're free to walk around at any time: lawns sweep down to an ornamental lake, there's a majestic avenue of giant sequoias, over a kilometre long, and part of the estate is now given over to thick forestry, which is crisscrossed by trails. Emo Court lies just northwest of the New Inn turn-off, between Monasterevin in County Kildare and Portlaoise, and is well signposted.

John Dawson, the first Earl of Portarlington, who had given Gandon his first job in Ireland, on Dublin's Custom House, commissioned Emo Court in 1790, though it wasn't completed until some eighty years later. Typical of Gandon is the magnificent pedimented Ionic **portico**, flanked by two delightful stone

▲ Emo Court

reliefs of cherubs; the one on the left represents music, painting, sculpture and, fittingly, architecture, while to the right is a playful agricultural scene. The tour continues into the **entrance hall**, whose ceiling is decorated with gorgeous plaster rivulets of oak leaves, in keeping with the numerous oak trees on the estate. Of the four mahogany doors here, symmetrically placed at the corners, see if you can spot which two are false. For much of the twentieth century, Emo Court housed a novitiate for the Jesuits, who couldn't resist turning the **rotunda** beyond the hall, with its double-height dome and coffered ceiling, into the sanctuary of a chapel. The **dining room** is distinguished by its handsome ceiling plasterwork of rosettes and eagles, commissioned by the second Earl of Portarlington in the 1830s from Lewis Vulliamy, a fashionable architect who also worked on London's Dorchester Hotel. The **library**, which was stripped down to become the nave of the Jesuits' chapel, has now regained its amazing rococo fireplace of Carrara marble, showing cavorting cherubs picking grapes, while the long, elegant **drawing room** beyond is broken up by grey-green Ionic columns of Connemara marble, topped with gilt capitals.

Abbeyleix

Near the southern border of Laois, the congenial market town **ABBEYLEIX** is a far preferable place for a break to the county town Portlaoise, if you're driving down the M7 and N8 towards Cashel and Cork. Of the Cistercian abbey of the name, founded in 1183, nothing remains, but the Georgian market house, terraced crescents and broad main street are still in place from the eighteenth and nineteenth centuries, when the de Vesci family, former lords of Kildare, moved their estate village onto the coach road and remodelled it.

The de Vescis' former seat, Abbeyleix House, just west of town, designed by James Wyatt in the eighteenth century, isn't open to the public, but there are a few sights in and around town where you could profitably while away an afternoon. Towards the north end of the main street, the **Sensory Garden** (June–Sept Mon–Fri 9am–4pm, Sat & Sun 2–6pm; Oct–May Mon–Fri 10am–4pm; donation requested) sits within the walls of a former Brigidine convent. Short paths lead you around pungent, lushly planted borders and rockeries, a lotus pond and a thatched gazebo. A little further out on the same road, the town's interesting and well-designed **Heritage House** (May–Sept Mon–Fri 9am–5pm, Sat & Sun 1–5pm; €3; Ⓦ www.heritagehousemuseum.com) occupies a Victorian school built by the de Vescis. Display boards relate the history of the town and county, aided by scale models of the town in the early twentieth century and of the old Cistercian abbey. A whole room is devoted to the town's famous carpet factory, which attained both apogee and nadir when its products were selected to grace the floors of the *Titanic* – its clerk, who'd been given a free ticket to promote the carpets in the US, went down with the ship, and the factory went out of business the same year, 1912.

Around 7km southeast of town (signposted from the village of Ballinakill), you can stretch your legs at **Heywood House Gardens** (Ⓦ www.heritageireland.ie; free guided tours July & Aug Sun 3pm), which were landscaped by the English architect Sir Edward Lutyens and designer Gertrude Jekyll in the early twentieth century. The house itself burnt down in 1950 and the gardens are now reached from the car park of Heywood Community School. A pergola overlooks a lily-strewn lake with a path laid out around it, and an alley of box-cut lime trees leads to a pretty walled garden enclosing an oval pond. Eight stone turtles attend the pond's oversized fountain, which is surrounded by tiers of colourful flowerbeds.

Practicalities

Abbeyleix offers little choice in the way of accommodation or food, but fortunately its one **hotel** is very good. On the N8 on the southern edge of town, *Abbeyleix Manor Hotel* (Ⓣ 057/873 0111, Ⓦ www.abbeyleixmanorhotel.com; ④) is a friendly, well-run establishment, with smart, well-equipped rooms; excellent, varied food is available in either the popular bar or the restaurant. Few people leave Abbeyleix without sampling the delights of *Morrissey's Bar*, a sociable and much-loved pub-grocery just down from the market house. Seemingly unchanged since it was built in 1880, the cavernous interior is adorned with high wooden shelves, screens and pews, as well as a cosy stove for winter evenings.

Travel details

Trains

Athlone to: Dublin Heuston (9–11 daily; 1hr 40min–2hr); Galway (5–8 daily; 1hr 10min); Westport (3 daily; 2hr).
Mullingar to: Dublin Connolly (6–9 daily; 1hr 15min); Sligo (4–6 daily; 2hr).

Buses

Bus Éireann
Abbeyleix to: Cork (6 daily; 3hr); Dublin (6 daily; 1hr 40min).
Athlone to: Birr (3–6 daily; 50min); Cork (1–2 daily; 4hr 30min); Drogheda (1–2 daily; 2hr 30min); Dublin (hourly; 2hr); Dundalk (1–2 daily; 3hr 15min); Galway (hourly; 1hr 30min); Kilkenny (1–2 daily; 2hr 50min); Limerick (2–4 daily; 2hr 10min); Mullingar (1–4 daily; 1hr); Sligo (2–6 daily; 2hr 15min–3hr); Waterford (1–2 daily; 4hr); Westport (1–3 daily; 2hr 45min).
Banagher to: Birr (1 weekly, Sat; 15min); Dublin (1 weekly, Sat; 3hr).
Birr to: Athlone (3–6 daily; 50min); Banagher (1 weekly, Sat; 15min); Cork (1–2 daily; 3hr 30min);

Dublin (1 daily; 4hr); Limerick (Mon–Fri 1 daily; 1hr 30min); Portumna (1 daily, not Sat; 20min).
Mullingar to: Athlone (1–4 daily; 1hr); Drogheda (1–2 daily; 1hr 40min); Dublin (10–13 daily; 1hr 30min); Dundalk (1–2 daily; 2hr 20min); Galway (1–2 daily; 3hr); Sligo (4 daily; 2hr 30min).

Aircoach
Ⓣ01/844 7118, Ⓦwww.aircoach.ie
Abbeyleix to: Cork (8 daily; 2hr 20min); Dublin Airport (8 daily; 1hr 40min).

Citylink
Ⓣ1890 280808, Ⓦwww.citylink.ie
Athlone to: Dublin (15 daily; 2hr); Galway (15 daily; 1hr 30min).

Kearns Transport
Ⓣ057/912 0124, Ⓦwww.kearnstransport.com
Banagher to: Dublin (1 daily; 2hr).
Birr to: Dublin (3–5 daily; 1hr 30min); Galway (via Portumna; 5–6 weekly; 2hr).

Nestor
Ⓣ091/797144, Ⓦwww.nestorlink.ie
Athlone to: Dublin (4 daily; 2hr); Dublin Airport (7 daily; 2hr 20min); Galway (7 daily; 1hr 30min).

5

Kilkenny, Carlow and Wexford

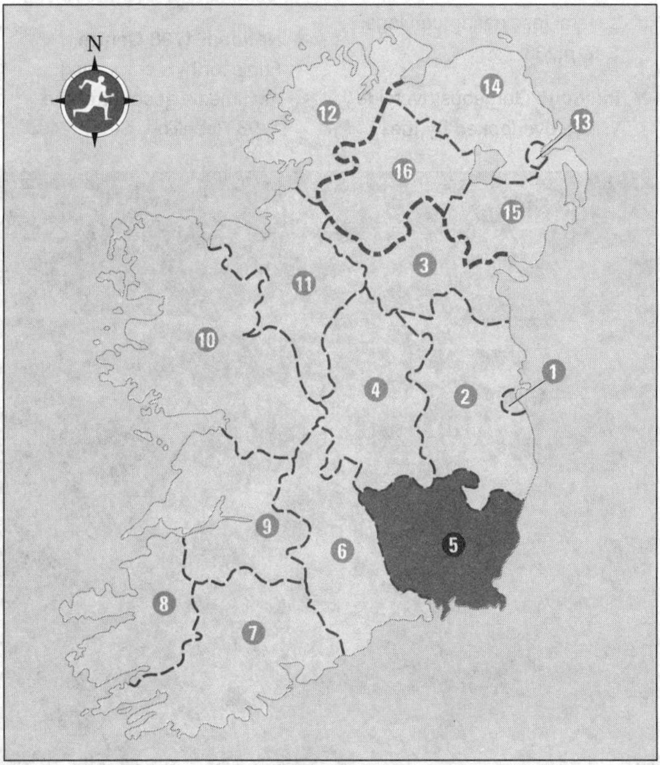

CHAPTER 5 Highlights

* **Kilkenny city** Vibrant and historic, Kilkenny retains its medieval framework, centred upon its imposing castle, and has two exciting festivals to boot. See p.229

* **Jerpoint Abbey** Atmospheric ruins of a remarkable twelfth-century foundation, featuring a wonderful colonnaded cloister and several fascinating carvings. See p.236

* **Inistioge** Gorgeous riverside village overlooked by the rejuvenated Woodstock Estate. See p.236

* **Wexford** Lively town that retains much of its medieval layout and is renowned for its prestigious Opera Festival. See p.238

* **Duncannon** A charming seaside village with a grand, sandy beach, overlooked by a looming fort. See p.246

* **National 1798 Centre** Enniscorthy's enthralling multimedia account of the 1798 Rebellion. See p.249

▲ Jerpoint Abbey

5

Kilkenny, Carlow and Wexford

The countryside of Ireland's southeastern corner is largely flat and insipid, but, thanks to its position, gets some of the best of the country's weather. County **Kilkenny**'s attractions are focused on its namesake city, an effervescent place with a flourishing arts scene and a layout reflecting its medieval origins. The county's northern reaches offer little interest bar the magnificent **Dunmore Cave**, but to the south lie the lush river valleys of the **Nore** and **Barrow** and trim waterside towns and villages. County **Carlow** has almost negligible appeal, but, if you're passing through, it does have one notable sight in the form of the gorgeous valley-set village of **St Mullins**. Conversely, County **Wexford** has much allure, especially in the genial **county town** itself and in **Enniscorthy**, a place redolent of the 1798 Rebellion. The county's eastern coastline offers numerous expansive sandy **beaches**, while its southern perimeter is characterized by inland lagoons, small fishing villages and the bleak wonders of the **Hook Head Peninsula**.

Thanks to its strategic position just across St George's Channel from south Wales, Ireland's southeast has borne the brunt of the country's colonization. The **Vikings** founded an early settlement here, which grew into Wexford town, while the **Anglo-Normans** quickly exploited the area's economic potential and greatly altered its physiognomy. They developed Kilkenny and Wexford towns and built castles across the two counties, while also transforming uncultivated areas into productive farmland. However, control was not always easily maintained. The MacMurrough-Kavanagh Irish dynasty, based in the north of County Wexford, continually frustrated English attempts to control the region and full conquest only occurred when **Cromwell** arrived in the mid-1600s. Even after this, County Wexford witnessed some of the bitterest fighting during the 1798 Rebellion, when insurgents held out longer here than anywhere else in the country, before being finally defeated near Enniscorthy.

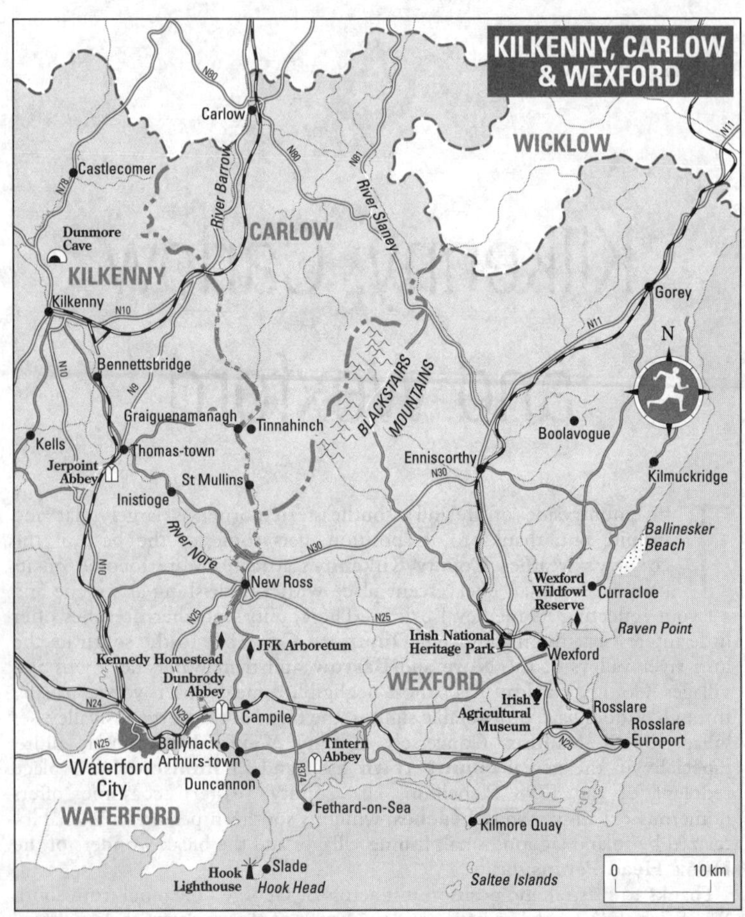

Counties Kilkenny and Carlow

Medieval **Kilkenny city** (Cill Chainnigh; Ⓦwww.kilkenny.ie) is a splendid place to pass a couple of days, thanks to its magnificent **castle** and other historical sites, and a plethora of fine pubs and restaurants. The delights of the area's countryside are best enjoyed in its southern reaches, where the lush valleys of the rivers **Nore** and **Barrow** encompass the evocative remains of monastic foundations **Kells Priory** and **Jerpoint Abbey**, and waterside towns and villages including **Thomastown**, **Graiguenamanagh**, **Inistioge** and – just over the Carlow border – **St Mullins**.

The **South Leinster Way**, a 100km waymarked trail, runs from Kildavin on the eastern border of County Carlow, via 800-metre Mount Leinster in the Blackstairs Mountains, to Carrick-on-Suir, just across Kilkenny's western border in Tipperary. The most attractive section is in southern Kilkenny, between Borris (where the path intersects the Barrow Way) and Mullinavat, especially the 16km from Graiguenamanagh to Inistioge.

Kilkenny city and around

Unquestionably Ireland's most characterful medieval city, **KILKENNY** straddles the broad River Nore, doglegging past its imposing castle. Downhill from here lies a compact grid of narrow streets, dating back to the city's origins, though little of its former gated walls remains. North of the city the major attraction is formed by the strange calcite formations in **Dunmore Cave**.

The first known settlement at Kilkenny is believed to have been a sixth-century monastic community founded by St Canice. After the arrival of the **Anglo-Normans** in 1169, Strongbow erected a motte and bailey fort, overlooking the Nore, in 1172, which was later replaced by a stronger stone structure, constructed by his son-in-law, William, the Earl Marshal. The latter set about fortifying the entire town, by means of the city walls and towers and forced the local and Catholic Irish population to construct dwellings outside its boundaries in an area still known as "Irishtown" today. Subsequently, the city's ownership passed through various hands, before James Butler, the third Earl of Ormonde, purchased the demesne in 1391.

Following the 1641 Rebellion, Kilkenny became the focus for the **Catholic Confederation**, an unlikely alliance of royalists loyal to Charles I and Irish landowners dispossessed by the Plantation. This established a parliament in Kilkenny, aimed at attaining Irish self-government and, in the process, restoring the rights of Catholics. However, its powers were short-lived, and, after Cromwell's arrival in 1650, the city's prosperity and power began to dwindle.

Nonetheless, nowadays Kilkenny still possesses an undoubted grandeur, largely untarnished by inappropriate modern building developments and, thanks to its castle and numerous other sights, as well as a lively nightlife and cultural scene, has become an integral part of the Irish tourist trail.

Arrival and information

Kilkenny's **train station** (ⓣ056/772 2024) is off Dublin Road, a ten-minute walk along John Street to the city centre. **Bus Éireann** services leave from here and also stop on Patrick Street in the centre, while **private buses** use The Parade near Kilkenny Castle. The **tourist office** is in the Shee Alms House on Rose Inn Street (May, June & Sept Mon–Fri 9.30am–6pm, Sat 10am–6pm; July & Aug Mon–Sat 9am–6pm, Sun 11am–1pm & 2–5pm; Oct Mon–Fri 9.15am–5pm, Sat 10am–6pm; Nov–April Mon–Sat 9.15am–5pm; ⓣ056/775 1500, ⓦwww.southeastireland.com) and provides free maps of the city. One-hour **walking tours** depart from here (mid-March to Oct Mon–Sat 10.30am, 12.15pm, 3pm & 4.30pm, Sun 11.15am & 12.30pm; for winter times, contact the tourist office; €6; ⓦwww.tynantours.com), and an open-top hop-on hop-off guided **bus tour** leaves from The Parade (May to Sept daily on the half-hour 10.30am–12.30pm, and on the hour 2–5pm; 45min; €10; ⓣ01/458 0054, ⓦwww.irishcitytours.com).

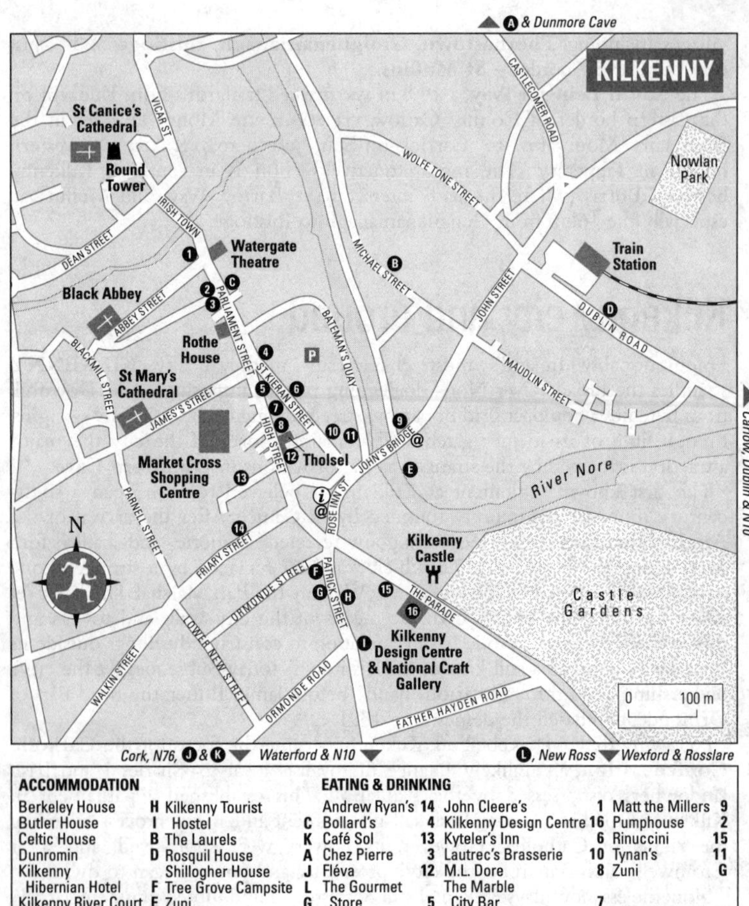

Internet access is available from E Centre, 26 Rose Inn St, and 4U Net, 79 John St.

Accommodation

Kilkenny has plenty of accommodation, but advance reservation is necessary at weekends, throughout the summer and during festivals (see p.234). For **camping**, *Tree Grove Caravan & Camping Park* (March to mid-Nov; mid-Nov to Feb available weekends, if booked in advance; ⓣ056/777 0302, ⓦwww.treegrovecamping.com) is a popular site 1.5km down the R700 New Ross road.

Berkeley House 5 Patrick St ⓣ056/776 4848, ⓦwww.berkeleyhousekilkenny.com. Centrally located Georgian townhouse, offering very pleasant accommodation in airy, tastefully decorated en-suite rooms. Private parking available. ❸

Butler House Patrick St ⓣ056/776 5707, ⓦwww.butler.ie. This expansive former dower house of Kilkenny Castle was decorously refurbished by Kilkenny Design in the 1970s. Its spacious rooms marry Georgian refinement and modern accoutrements to stunning effect, and some overlook the castle. ❺

Celtic House 18 Michael St ⓣ056/776 2249, ⓦwww.celtic-house-bandb.com. Well-maintained, modern townhouse in a quiet, fairly central location, providing en-suite, airy rooms. ❷

Dunromin Dublin Rd ⓣ056/776 1387, ⓦwww.dunrominkilkenny.com. Superbly maintained nineteenth-century dwelling on the main road near the train station, providing very comfortable en-suite rooms. April–Oct. ❷

Kilkenny Hibernian Hotel 1 Ormonde St ⓣ056/777 1888, ⓦwww.kilkennyhibernianhotel.com. Once a bank and later the HQ of a food company, this lovingly restored Victorian building features a variety of lavish accommodation, including a splendidly appointed penthouse suite. Doubles ❺, suite ❼

Kilkenny River Court John St ⓣ056/772 3388, ⓦwww.kilrivercourt.com. Plush four-star hotel, nestling beside the Nore with fine views of the castle and offering a wide range of leisure facilities, including a pool, gymnasium and treatment rooms. ❺

Kilkenny Tourist Hostel 35 Parliament St (IHH) ⓣ056/776 3541, ⓦwww.kilkennyhostel.ie. A largish and well-run hostel, featuring spacious dorms, a few private rooms, kitchen and laundry facilities. Front dorms can suffer from street noise at weekends. Dorms from €14, doubles ❶.

The Laurels College Rd ⓣ056/776 1501, ⓦwww.thelaurelskilkenny.com. A friendly and helpful purpose-built modern guesthouse, ten minutes' walk south of the centre, some of whose en-suite rooms feature king-sized beds and whirlpool baths. ❸

Rosquil House Castlecomer Rd ⓣ056/772 1419, ⓦwww.rosquilhouse.com. An elegant and welcoming upmarket guesthouse, ten minutes' walk from the centre, with spacious, stylish and well-equipped rooms, an attractive sitting room and fine breakfasts. ❸

Shillogher House 1km south of the centre on the N76 Clonmel road ⓣ056/776 3249, ⓦwww.shillogherhouse.com. Bright and colourful en-suite bedrooms and a warm welcome at this modern, purpose-built B&B set in a huge garden. ❷

Zuni 26 Patrick St ⓣ056/772 3999, ⓦwww.zuni.ie. Above the restaurant of the same name, luxurious and stylish contemporary bedrooms with a minimalist decor of dark woods and red and white furnishings; private parking available. ❹

The City

Kilkenny's medieval layout is centred on its hill and **castle**. Downhill from here the expansive **Parade**, a broad avenue that once hosted civic ceremonies and military displays, leads down to the **High Street**, the main shopping district. This wends its way to one of the city's other main landmarks, **St Canice's Cathedral**, en route passing landmarks such as the **Tholsel** and **Rothe House**, both evidence of previous periods of prosperity.

Kilkenny Castle

Kilkenny's stately **castle** (April & May daily 10.30am–5pm; June–Aug daily 9.30am–7pm; Sept daily 10am–6.30pm; Oct–March daily 10.30am–12.45pm & 2–5pm; guided tours every 30min, last tour 1hr before closing; €5.30; Heritage Card; ⓦwww.heritageireland.ie) is unquestionably the city's dominant feature. Sitting strong above the Nore, the original stone castle was built here in the early thirteenth century by William Marshall, Earl of Pembroke, replacing the previous motte and bailey fort, and purchased in 1391 by James Butler, third Earl of Ormonde. His family's wealth was founded upon huge areas of land acquired in Kilkenny and Tipperary and his descendants, surviving siege by Cromwell in 1650, subsequently built the grand entrance gateway later that century. However, James Butler, second Duke of Ormonde, one-time Viceroy of Ireland, was forced to flee to France in 1715 when he was arraigned for treason for supporting the Stuart cause. He died in Avignon in 1745, by which time the castle had fallen into disrepair, and it was only the marriage two decades later of John Butler, seventeenth Earl of Ormonde, to a local heiress that revived the family's fortunes, resulting in the creation of the parkland and modifications to the castle itself.

▲ Kilkenny Castle

Further work began around 1826, enhancing the castle's medieval exterior while adapting its interior in contemporary country-house style. The Butlers remained in residence until 1935, when another decline in the family's fortunes led to their departure and the auction of the castle's contents. The building fell into disrepair, until it was acquired by the Irish state in 1969, and was much restored over subsequent decades.

While waiting for your tour it's well worth heading down to the castle's basement, which houses a small shop and the **Butler Gallery** (Ⓦ www.butlergallery.com; free) devoted to temporary modern-art exhibitions. The **tour** itself begins with a short film on the castle's history, then leads through its expansive hall, whose chequered floor is tiled with black Kilkenny "marble" (actually a polished limestone, but prevalent enough in the hills around Kilkenny to have given it the nickname "Marble City"), via a series of extravagantly proportioned rooms, equipped with sizeable fireplaces and deeply recessed windows. En route you'll pass a portrait of the first Duke of Ormonde which, for a period in its life, hung in the gents' toilet of a restaurant in New York – a far-flung result of the 1935 auction. The castle's crowning glory is its extraordinarily long gallery, which occupies almost the entire length of the River Wing, replete with twin fireplaces and marble carvings of key moments in the history of the Butler dynasty. Its 1825 hammer-beam roof, punctuated by curving columns bearing the heads of various mythical beasts, is decorated somewhat fancifully by whimsical Pre-Raphaelite daubs.

From the castle to Irishtown

Across the Parade from the castle, converted eighteenth-century stables house the **Kilkenny Design Centre**, which retails a broad range of premium Irish crafts, and its recommended upstairs café (see p.234). Behind the shop, you'll find the attractive, airy premises of the **National Craft Gallery**, which, under the auspices of the Crafts Council of Ireland, mounts a varied programme of exhibitions by Irish and international craftspeople, ranging from stained glass to quilts (Jan–March Mon–Sat 10am–6pm; April–Dec Mon–Sat 10am–6pm, Sun 11am–6pm; free; Ⓣ056/776 1804, Ⓦwww.ccoi.ie). In the courtyard beyond the gallery, you can visit several small craft workshops; if you're interested in further similar exploration, pick up a "Craft Trail" leaflet from the gallery or the tourist office, which details half a dozen other studios around the county.

Heading down the Parade from here and across the junction to the High Street leads to the **Tholsel**, the city's erstwhile financial exchange and, subsequently, town hall, constructed in 1761. The High Street blends seamlessly into Parliament Street, both replete with shops and businesses, intriguing alleys and offshoots, as well as one of the finest remnants of the city's Tudor prosperity, **Rothe House** (April–Oct Mon–Sat 10.30am–5pm, Sun 3–5pm; Nov–March Mon–Sat 10.30am–4.30pm; €4, combined ticket with cathedral €7; Ⓦwww.rothehouse.com), a complex of three dwellings, linked by courtyards, built by a wealthy Kilkenny merchant in 1594. The building is home to the Kilkenny Archeological Society and houses a small and somewhat dull **museum** of artefacts and memorabilia. Far better are the two galleries devoted to **costumes**, featuring all manner of clothing from the last two hundred years, donated by local residents.

Just before Parliament Street becomes Irishtown, on Abbey Street stands the Holy Trinity Church, more commonly known as the **Black Abbey** thanks to the colour of the habits of its founders, the Dominicans. Dating from 1225, the abbey was suppressed during the Reformation and fell into disrepair. Now fully restored, and again a Dominican establishment, its fine carvings and glorious fifteen-panel rosary stained-glass window can be viewed after daily Masses.

St Canice's Cathedral

Kilkenny's Church of Ireland cathedral, thirteenth-century **St Canice's** (April, May & Sept Mon–Sat 10am–1pm & 2–5pm, Sun 2–5pm; June–Aug Mon–Sat 9am–6pm, Sun 2–6pm; Oct–March Mon–Sat 10am–1pm & 2–4pm, Sun 2–4pm; €4, combined ticket with Rothe House €7; Ⓦwww.stcanicescathedral.ie), looms above Irishtown. Though its spire collapsed in 1332, the rest of this grand Gothic structure remains true to its date of origin. The magnificently carved interior contains many splendid sixteenth- and seventeenth-century tombstones, often cut from black Kilkenny marble, including some remarkable effigies of the Butler family, as well as a more modern construction – a scale model showing the city's layout in 1640. In the churchyard stands a graceful, ninth-century **Round Tower**, the only vestige of St Canice's monastic settlement (same hours; €3, combined ticket with cathedral €6), whose reward for climbing its 160 steps is a superb vista of the city spread out below.

Eating, drinking and entertainment

Kilkenny has more than a smattering of decent **restaurants**, a lively **café** scene, and plenty of pubs serving excellent snacks and meals. The city has numerous attractive **bars**, many untouched by the tasteless hands of refurbishment, and there's plenty of **music** on offer too, with some splendid traditional sessions. The Watergate Theatre, Parliament Street (ⓣ056/776 1674, ⓦwww.watergatekilkenny.com), has a varied programme of drama, dance and opera, and plenty of gigs too. For information about what's on in Kilkenny, pick up one of the local newspapers, the *Kilkenny Voice* (published every Tues) or the *Kilkenny People* (Wed), or the free monthly booklet, *Whazon? Waterford and Kilkenny* (or go to ⓦwww.whazon.com/kilkenny).

A major event in the city's calendar is the ten-day **Kilkenny Arts Festival** (ⓦwww.kilkennyarts.ie), beginning in the second week of August, featuring all manner of music, as well as drama, various exhibitions and literary goings-on. In early June there's the marvellous five-day comedy festival, **The Cat Laughs** (ⓦwww.thecatlaughs.com), involving a host of comedians in a variety of venues. The four-day **Rhythm and Roots Festival** (ⓦwww.kilkennyroots.com) features more than thirty bands from around the world over the bank-holiday weekend at the start of May, with the focus on American country and roots music.

Cafés and restaurants

Café Sol William St ⓣ056/776 4987. A fine eatery whose name reflects its warm atmosphere and Spanish swing. For lunch there are sandwiches, great salads and various hot dishes, while the evening offers a wider range of meat, fish and vegetarian dishes with local ingredients well to the fore, some of which are available on the early-bird menu.

Chez Pierre 17 Parliament St. A plain French-style café serving wholesome breakfasts, lunches and delicious *tartines*, as well as simple French dinners from Thurs to Sat, with a fine range of house wines on offer.

Fléva 84 High St ⓣ056/777 0021. This bright and spacious restaurant serves a delicious and eclectic range of meals, using local ingredients like Kilkenny lamb, and tasty fish dishes like seared tuna. Enjoyment is enhanced by displays of local artwork on the walls. Closed Mon.

The Gourmet Store 56 High St. Deli supplying wonderful multilayered sandwiches to take away, as well as stocking a vast assortment of culinary delights.

Kilkenny Design Centre The Parade. The centre's self-service café offers splendid salads and sandwiches, a variety of home-made soups, and more substantial meals, all at reasonable prices.

Lautrec's Brasserie 9 St Kieran St ⓣ056/776 2720. A popular night-time bistro serving a variety of pasta dishes and pizzas, as well as specials such as grilled swordfish and Barbary duck; early-bird menu daily except Sat.

M.L. Dore 65 High St. Friendly, old-fashioned tearooms, styling itself the "nostalgia café", with a wide variety of snacks, soups, salads and meals on offer during the day and in the evening.

Rinuccini 1 The Parade ⓣ056/776 1575. Authentic, Italian-run restaurant where classily prepared, traditional dishes such as *pollo ai funghi* (chicken with mushroom cream sauce), are served with some élan; early-bird menu nightly.

Zuni 26 Patrick Street ⓣ056/772 3999. Very fine and stylish modern-Irish cooking with Mediterranean, Middle Eastern and Asian influences, served in a contemporary setting with alfresco summer courtyard dining. On the pricey side, but there's an early-bird menu every evening. Closed Mon lunchtime.

Bars and music venues

Andrew Ryan's Friary St. A popular, welcoming bar with traditional music Thurs and live bands Tues, Sat & occasional other nights.

Bollard's St Kieran St. Friendly bar with good service, fine meals, pleasant tables on the alley and traditional music Tues & Thurs.

John Cleere's Parliament St. The city's longest-running traditional-music session is here on Mon, as well as other music during the rest of the week; bigger names appear in the bar's theatre, which also hosts comedy and drama.

Kyteler's Inn St Kieran St. This medieval inn's spooky reputation is linked to erstwhile resident Alice Kyteler who was tried for witchcraft in 1324. She fled to England, leaving her maid Petronella to take the rap – and her place on the burning woodpile. The bar has plenty of nooks and crannies and offers traditional music nightly, and decent meals.

The Marble City Bar High St. Fashionable, revamped central bar serving delicious meals, including an especially good range for vegetarians, with its own daytime tearooms at the back on St Kieran St.

Matt the Millers John St. Big, bold and brash pub, dishing up a diet of live music and/or DJs every night, often with a late bar.

Pumphouse Parliament St. A big old bar that still retains a cosy feel; traditional music Mon–Wed and DJs and bands at the weekend.

Tynan's beside John's Bridge. An old-fashioned riverside bar, furnished with leather banquettes and dark wood, with a beer garden at the back.

Dunmore Cave

Northern County Kilkenny lacks instant appeal and the only significant focus of interest is **Dunmore Cave** (March to mid-June & mid-Sept to Oct daily 9.30am–5pm; mid-June to mid-Sept daily 9.30am–6.30pm; Nov–Feb Fri–Sun 10am–5pm; last admission 1hr before closing; €2.90; Heritage Card; Ⓦwww.heritageireland.ie), 10km north of the city off the N78. Buggy's Coaches (Ⓣ056/444 1264) run a twice-daily private **bus** from the Parade in Kilkenny towards Castlecomer, which will leave you with a walk of about a kilometre to the cave. Formed in a limestone outcrop of the Castlecomer plateau, Dunmore's series of chambers feature numerous beautiful calcite creations – curtains and crystals, stalactites and stalagmites; the most remarkable of the last stands some four and a half metres high. The cave is referenced in the *Annals of the Four Masters* (see box, p.512), which recounts that the Vikings massacred a thousand people here in 928, a tale partially substantiated in 1967 when excavations uncovered the skeletons of more than forty women and children, and a Viking coin.

Southern Kilkenny

Some of the county's finest spots lie towards its southern extremity, countryside defined by the lush valleys of the rivers **Barrow** and **Nore**. Near the Nore are major ecclesiastical remains at **Kells** and **Jerpoint Abbey** while, by the Barrow, both **Graiguenamanagh** and **St Mullins** are attractive places to stay. Near the beguiling village of **Inistioge**, you can explore the extensive gardens and arboretum of the Woodstock demesne.

Kells

Fourteen kilometres south of Kilkenny lies the medieval village of **KELLS**, a petite and picturesque settlement straddling a tributary of the Nore, the King's River. A short stroll from its centre stands one of the country's most atmospheric ruins, **Kells Priory** (open access), set by the river. This Augustinian foundation was established in 1193 and had a turbulent history, being sacked in both 1252 and 1327, before dissolution in the 1540s. Most of its remains date from the fourteenth and fifteenth centuries and inside the still-standing curtain wall, with its gatehouse and towers, are a church and chapel and several domestic buildings. All told, it's one of the largest and most outstanding Irish medieval sites, though the priory has no connection with the *Book of Kells* housed in Trinity College, Dublin, which is named after Kells in County Meath.

Jerpoint Abbey and Thomastown

The major tourist sight in the south of the county is **Jerpoint Abbey** (daily: March–May & mid-Sept to Oct 10am–5pm; June to mid-Sept 9.30am–6pm; Nov 10am–4pm; last tour 1hr before closing time; €2.90; Heritage Card; Ⓦwww.heritageireland.ie), which lies on the N9, 20km south of Kilkenny city. Originally founded as a Benedictine house in 1158, the abbey was colonized by Cistercians some twenty years later. The oldest remain is the twelfth-century Romanesque church, but the rest, set around a beautifully colonnaded fifteenth-century cloister, follows the characteristic Cistercian design. The abbey features a number of tomb sculptures and some intriguing carvings on the cloister arcade, including the "little man of Jerpoint" whose stomach-crossed hands and open-mouthed expression suggest either mirth or dyspepsia.

The jumping-off point for the abbey, **THOMASTOWN**, 2km to the northeast, is a pleasant riverside crossroads town on the Dublin–Waterford train line. A walled town of some note in medieval times, Thomastown now maintains scant sense of its own antiquity, other than its old **bridge** across the Nore and the ruined thirteenth-century church of **St Mary's** at the top of Market Street.

Practicalities

Accommodation is available in Thomastown at the *Tower House*, Low Street (Ⓣ056/772 4500, Ⓔtowerhousebandb@hotmail.com; ❸), actually a restored medieval tower, which provides excellent, en-suite B&B, with good rates for singles and children. Alternatively, if you've got transport, head south to Jerpoint Abbey where top-notch B&B is available at *Abbey House*, a restored, eighteenth-century mill house (Ⓣ056/772 4166, Ⓦwww.abbeyhousejerpoint.com; ❸).

Across the road from the *Tower House* in Thomastown, *Ethos* (closed Sun evening; Ⓣ056/775 4945) is a cheery, modern **café-restaurant**, serving up breakfast, sandwiches, salads and basic main courses for lunch, and more complex dishes such as baked cod with basil and parmesan crust for dinner. For a drink, head round the corner to *Carroll's* on Logan Street, a cosy, enticing **pub** that offers food and occasional live music.

Inistioge

Eight kilometres along the Nore from Thomastown is the quaint village of **INISTIOGE** (pronounced "Inisteeg"), set around a tree-lined green, an old church and a narrow-arched stone bridge over the river. Unsurprisingly, the attractive location, with its verdant hills rising above the village, has drawn film-makers and both *Circle of Friends* and *Widows' Peak* were shot here. The steep lane rising from the village green leads after a couple of kilometres to **Woodstock**, a demesne centred on a Georgian mansion designed by Francis Bindon, one of the architects of Russborough House (see p.156). When its owners left Ireland during the War of Independence, the house was taken over by the Black and Tans and, like many similarly tarnished dwellings, was burnt down after independence in 1922. However, since 1999 a project by the county council to restore the **gardens** (April–Sept 9am–8pm; Oct–March 9am–4.30pm; car €4, pedestrians free; Ⓦwww.woodstock.ie) has been ongoing and you can enjoy walks lined by firs and monkey puzzles, an arboretum, rose gardens and rockeries, and breathtaking views of the Nore valley.

The village's only **accommodation** is provided by the *Woodstock Arms* (Ⓣ056/775 8440, Ⓦwww.woodstockarms.com; ❷), a pleasant pub with tables out on the green, offering well-appointed en-suite rooms. You can admire the waterside while sampling the delights at *The Old Schoolhouse*, a crafts shop and **café** that offers soup, fresh salmon from the Nore and home-made cakes. Up in the Woodstock demesne, by the car park, is a highly recommended **restaurant**, *Bassett's* (closed Sun evening, Mon & Tues; Ⓣ056/775 8820). Either in the bright, contemporary main room or at the outdoor tables with fine views of the Nore valley, you can enjoy sophisticated dinner dishes employing home-grown vegetables, local meats and fresh seafood, such as red mullet with potato, sautéed marrow and fennel; lunch consists of simpler fare such as omelette and cannelloni.

Graiguenamanagh and St Mullins

For much of its length the Barrow forms the boundary between counties Kilkenny and Carlow. Along it, 16km east of Thomastown, sits the small market town of **GRAIGUENAMANAGH** in a perfect setting, with its smaller Carlow "twin", **Tinnahinch**, just over the bridge. Bang in the town centre stands **Duiske Abbey**, founded in 1204 by Cistercians. Much of the present building, which now functions as a parish church, dates from the nineteenth century, but parts of the original interior have been carefully maintained, including the fleur-de-lis floor tiles by the main entrance, a grand effigy of an Anglo-Norman knight, and an outstanding, embellished Romanesque doorway. The *Duiske Inn* on Main Street serves filling bar **meals**, but a more upmarket option is the *Waterside*, a nineteenth-century granite cornstore on the quay, whose restaurant serves local specialities such as smoked eel; it also offers fine en-suite rooms, all overlooking the river, which well merit a night's **stay** (Ⓣ059/972 4246, Ⓦwww.watersideguesthouse.com; ❸). Graiguenamanagh has recently taken on a literary bent, hoping to become Ireland's answer to Hay-on-Wye, with a Readers and Writers Festival on the bank-holiday weekend at the beginning of May and the Town of Books Festival in late September, which attracts dozens of small, mostly antiquarian, booksellers – for details of both go to Ⓦwww.booktownireland.com.

On the east bank of the Barrow in County Carlow lies the gorgeous village of **ST MULLINS**, its dwellings appealingly arranged at the bottom of a valley around the village green. To get there from Graiguenamanagh, either drive across the bridge and follow the signs, or walk the pretty, eight-kilometre **riverside path**, the southernmost section of the Barrow Way. Opposite the village green is a perfectly dome-shaped earthwork and just behind are the remains of a monastery founded by St Moling in 696, consisting of the remnants of a medieval church and a round tower's stump. There's no better place to enjoy this tranquil spot than *Blanchfield's* **pub** on the green, a very friendly local, while across the way and up the hill lies one of the best-set **B&Bs** in Ireland, *Mulvarra House* (Ⓣ051/424936, Ⓦwww.mulvarra.com; ❷), many of whose tastefully decorated en-suite rooms have balconies overlooking the valley. Dinner, using local, organic produce wherever possible, is available if booked in advance, as are spa treatments, and the breakfasts are superb too.

County Wexford

The relaxed town of **Wexford** (Loch Garman; Ⓦ www.wexfordtourism.com) makes an ideal base for exploring the eponymous county, and has a thriving arts scene for evening entertainment. Inland, Wexford county offers historic towns such as **Enniscorthy** and **New Ross**, while the county's coastline features numerous fine **beaches** along its eastern stretches. On its southern strip, attractions include the picturesque fishing port of **Kilmore Quay** and the windswept reach of the captivating **Hook Head Peninsula**.

Wexford town

WEXFORD is a happy-go-lucky kind of town with plenty of scope for enjoying music in its **pubs**, but it has its serious side too, not least in the shape of its internationally renowned **Opera Festival**. Though still organized around its medieval narrow lanes, there are few true remnants of the Middle Ages. The town began life as a Viking base for incursions and trading, before becoming an early Anglo-Norman conquest in 1169. Wexford later housed an English garrison whose loyalty to the Crown resulted in vicious fighting against Cromwell's army in 1649; two hundred locals were massacred in taking control. The town also played a significant role in the 1798 Rebellion, which was finally quelled at Enniscorthy (see p.249). Wexford's lengthy quays pay testimony to its re-emergence as a prosperous port in the nineteenth century, though gradual silting of the harbour's entrance and the development of Rosslare Harbour led to its demise as a competitive port.

Arrival and information

Wexford's **train station** (Ⓣ 053/912 2522), which has left-luggage facilities, and main **bus stop** are on Redmond Square at the north end of the quays. The **tourist office** (Ⓣ 053/912 3111, Ⓦ www.southeastireland.com; April–June, Sept & Oct Mon–Fri 9am–6pm, Sat 10am–6pm; July & Aug Mon–Sat 9am–7pm, Sun 11am–1pm & 2–5pm; Nov–March Mon–Sat 9.15am–1pm & 2–5pm) is around five hundred metres south of here at Crescent Quay. The Wednesday-published *Wexford Echo* and *Wexford People* provide entertainment **listings**. For **Internet access** head to Office 1 on the corner of North Main and Charlotte streets, for **bike hire**, Hayes on South Main Street (Ⓣ 053/912 2462). Hour-long **walking tours** can be arranged by appointment (Ⓣ 053/915 2900; €5), and there are summer **boat trips** from the harbour to view the **seals** at Raven Point, depending on the weather (1hr 30min; Ⓣ 086/860 3828; €10).

Accommodation

As an excellent base for touring the southeast, Wexford has a fine range of **accommodation**, though you'll need to book months in advance for rooms during the Opera Festival (see p.241). Scenic seafront **camping** is available at *Ferrybank Camping and Caravan Park* (June–Aug; Ⓣ 053/916 6926, Ⓦ www.wexfordcorp.ie), just across the bridge from the quays, past the public swimming pool.

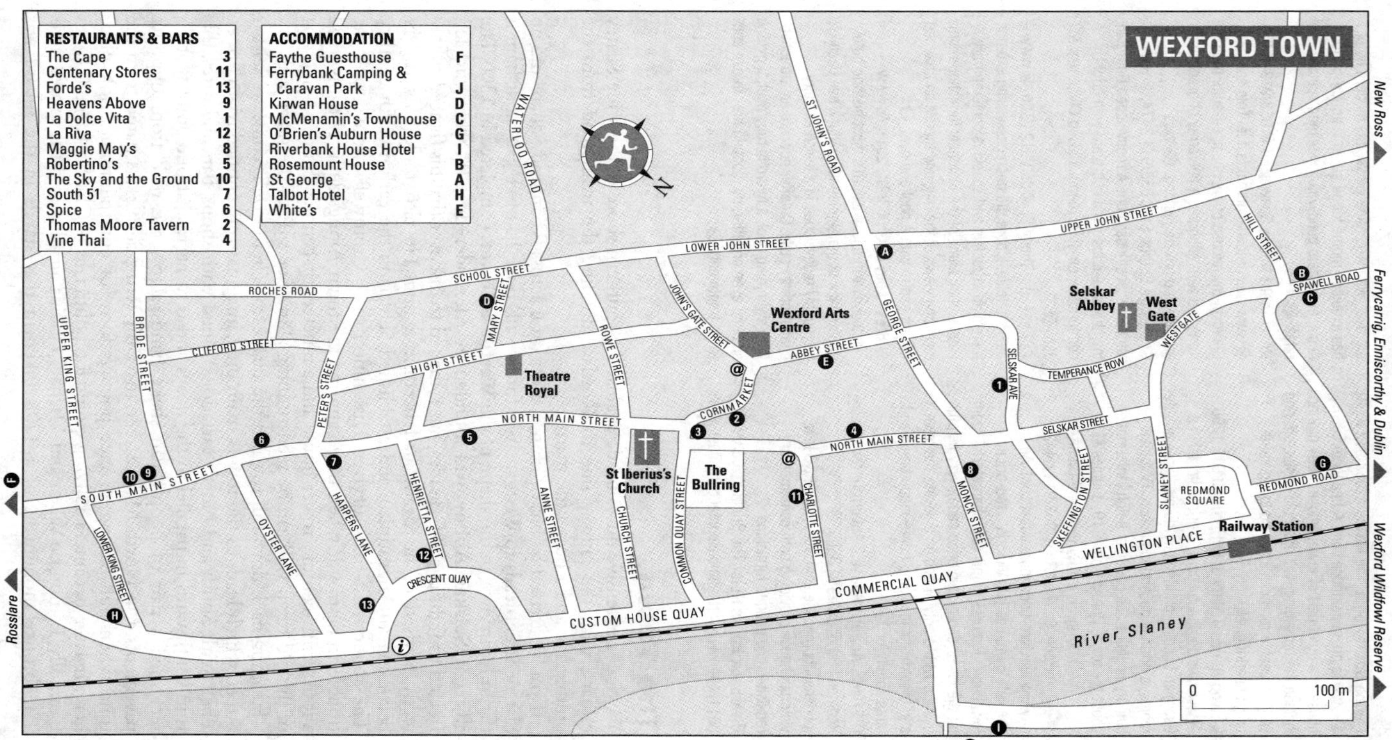

WEXFORD TOWN
New Ross
Ferrycarrig, Enniscorthy & Dublin
Wexford Wildfowl Reserve
Rosslare
F
J
RESTAURANTS & BARS
The Cape 3
Centenary Stores 11
Forde's 13
Heavens Above 9
La Dolce Vita 1
La Riva 12
Maggie May's 8
Robertino's 5
The Sky and the Ground 10
South 51 7
Spice 6
Thomas Moore Tavern 2
Vine Thai 4
ACCOMMODATION
Faythe Guesthouse F
Ferrybank Camping & Caravan Park J
Kirwan House D
McMenamin's Townhouse C
O'Brien's Auburn House G
Riverbank House Hotel I
Rosemount House B
St George A
Talbot Hotel H
White's E
N
0
100 m
WATERLOO ROAD
ST JOHN'S ROAD
UPPER JOHN STREET
LOWER JOHN STREET
SCHOOL STREET
ROCHES ROAD
HILL STREET
SPAWELL ROAD
Selskar Abbey
West Gate
WESTGATE
TEMPERANCE ROW
SELSKAR AVE
SELSKAR STREET
SKEFFINGTON STREET
SLANEY STREET
REDMOND SQUARE
REDMOND ROAD
Railway Station
WELLINGTON PLACE
COMMERCIAL QUAY
CUSTOM HOUSE QUAY
CRESCENT QUAY
River Slaney
Wexford Arts Centre
JOHN'S GATE STREET
ABBEY STREET
GEORGE STREET
CORNMARKET
NORTH MAIN STREET
MONCK STREET
CHARLOTTE STREET
The Bullring
COMMON QUAY STREET
St Iberius's Church
CHURCH STREET
ROWE STREET
Theatre Royal
MARY STREET
HIGH STREET
ANNE STREET
HENRIETTA STREET
HARPERS LANE
PETERS STREET
CLIFFORD STREET
BRIDE STREET
UPPER KING STREET
SOUTH MAIN STREET
OYSTER LANE
LOWER KING STREET

Faythe Guest House The Faythe ⓣ053/912 2249, ⓦwww.faytheguesthouse.com. A fine Victorian house in a quiet part of town, whose pretty grounds include the remaining wall of an old castle, offering very agreeable rooms, a splendid lounge and private parking. ❸

Kirwan House 3 Mary St (IHH) ⓣ053/912 1208, ⓦwww.wexfordhostel.com. Well-run hostel in a Georgian building offering airy dorms, three private rooms, a brightly decorated kitchen, TV lounge, laundry facilities and plenty of helpful information about the town. Dorms from €19, doubles ❶.

McMenamin's Townhouse 6 Glena Terrace, Spawell Rd ⓣ053/914 6442, ⓦwww.wexford-bedandbreakfast.com. An absolute gem, this late Victorian, red-brick townhouse features comfy and characterful rooms (at the lower end of this price code), very helpful owners with plenty of tips on enjoying the town, and breakfasts, including home-made bread and jams, to die for. ❸

O'Brien's Auburn House 2 Auburn Terrace, Redmond Rd ⓣ053/912 3605, ⓦwww.obriensauburnhouse.com. Very good B&B in a Victorian house providing both contemporary requisites and antique furnishing. ❷

Riverbank House Hotel The Bridge ⓣ053/912 3611, ⓦwww.riverbankhousehotel.com. Just over the river, with waterside views, this modern hotel has exquisite rooms kitted out in Victorian-period decor, and offers good-value weekend special rates. ❹

Rosemount House Spawell Rd ⓣ053/912 4609, ⓦwww.wexfordbedandbreakfast.ie. This spruce Georgian townhouse offers plush, en-suite rooms furnished with antiques, a fine array of breakfast goodies and private parking. ❸

St George George St ⓣ053/914 3474, ⓦwww.stgeorgeguesthouse.com. A redeveloped Georgian townhouse set around a courtyard with bright, comfortable, en-suite rooms. Closed Christmas & Jan. ❷

Talbot Hotel Trinity St ⓣ053/912 2566, ⓦwww.talbothotel.ie. Ignore the unprepossessing exterior, there's an attractive and spacious contemporary hotel within. Many of the tastefully furnished rooms have fine views of the bay, and there's an attached leisure centre with a pool and gym. ❺

Whites Abbey St ⓣ053/912 2311, ⓦwww.whitesofwexford.ie. Wexford's most historic hotel, dating back to the eighteenth century, has been thoroughly redeveloped in a lavish and airy contemporary style. On offer now are an attractive 20m swimming pool, a hydrotherapy pool, a gym, a spa and even cryotherapy (dubbed the "freeze and fix it" treatment). ❺

The Town

Wexford's extensive quays nestle against the southern shore of the wide Slaney estuary, with the railway line to Rosslare dividing the main road from the promenade and a busy little marina.

If you've arrived by bus or train, a short stroll across Redmond Square and up Slaney Street leads to Westgate. Wexford's walls once had five gates, but here is the only survivor in the shape of the **Westgate Tower**, completed in 1300. The adjacent **Selskar Abbey** was founded by Alexander de la Roche who left Ireland to fight in the Crusades, but returned to discover that his fiancée, incorrectly advised of his death, had become a nun. He also took holy orders, becoming an Augustinian, and established Selskar in the early twelfth century. The abbey must have survived Dissolution since Cromwell's troops took the trouble to destroy it when they captured the town. Alongside its remains stand a fourteenth-century tower house and a nineteenth-century church, while part of the old town wall can be seen running along one side of the graveyard.

Heading back downhill towards the quays from here, you'll come to Selskar Street, which leads to the town's main drag, imaginatively entitled Main Street, albeit with South and North variations. Lined with shops, bars and cafés, this runs southwards in parallel to the quays and is so narrow at one point that it's reckoned a pair of people can shake hands across the road from opposite pavements. On North Main Street, the **Bull Ring** derives its name from the time when bull-baiting, a once popular form of entertainment, took place here. It later became a rallying-point for politicians – Charles Parnell, James Connolly, Éamon de Valera and Michael Collins all addressed the crowd here. The bronze monument of a 1798 Pikeman that stands in the square was sculpted by Oliver Sheppard, also responsible for *The Death of Cúchulainn* housed in the GPO in Dublin. Beside *The Cape* bar, whose sign recalls the days when its proprietor was both landlord and undertaker, a road leads up to the Cornmarket, now an arts centre (see below), and more of the tiny lanes that characterize the town.

A little further along Main Street is Anglican **St Iberius's Church**, which dates back to the late seventeenth century but was much remodelled in 1760; it features a fine Georgian interior, possibly designed by John Roberts (see p.272). The church's unusual gallery was installed to accommodate troops stationed in the town and its broader-than-long shape was an ingenious answer to the problem of the site's proximity to the city wall. The church hosts regular classical-music concerts (Ⓣ085 713435, Ⓦwww.musicforwexford.ie).

Carrying on down South Main Street, Henrietta Street leads to **The Crescent**, a semicircular part of the quays where the original Viking shipping pool once lay. Here stands a statue of **John Barry**, the "Father of the American Navy", who originated from Tacumshane in the southeast corner of County Wexford and left to become a sailor, fetching up in Philadelphia, where he gained prosperity as master of a merchant ship. He rose to prominence as a sea captain in the American War of Independence and played a major role in the US Navy until his death in 1803. Naturally, the statue faces seawards.

Eating, drinking and entertainment

Wexford has plenty of good **cafés** and **restaurants** and numerous lively pubs, several of which serve bar meals and feature live **music**. Bigger-name acts usually play at the **Wexford Arts Centre** on Cornmarket (Ⓣ053/912 3764, Ⓦwww.wexfordartscentre.ie), which also hosts theatre, dance and comedy, as well as a lively programme of exhibitions, usually featuring Irish artists.

The biggest event in Wexford's cultural calendar is undoubtedly the renowned **Wexford Opera Festival** (Ⓣ053/912 2400 or 912 2144, Ⓦwww.wexfordopera.com), which draws not only performers and companies from around the world, but international audiences too, attracted by its distinctive programme – tickets and accommodation need to be booked months in advance. The main performances are supplemented by a variety of concerts, talks, late-night comedy and contemporary music. The festival's traditional home, the Theatre Royal, is currently undergoing a €30million rebuilding programme, but is due to reopen in time for the 2008 festival, to be held over three weeks beginning in late October. Wexford also plays host to the **Grooves Trail** (Ⓦwww.wexlive.com/grooves) in June or early July, a long weekend featuring fifty or so music gigs around the town.

Cafés and restaurants

Forde's Crescent Quay Ⓣ053/912 2816. Innovative and stylish, *Forde's* delivers the goods with some flair, offering a broad range of seasonal starters, plenty of imaginative seafood offerings, such as cod on a bed of mussels with roast red-pepper chutney, alongside succulent meat dishes and appetizing desserts. Good-value Sun lunch and early-bird menus (Mon–Sat). Mon–Sat dinner only, Sun lunch & dinner.

Heavens Above 112 South Main St Ⓣ053/912 4877. This night-time restaurant above *The Sky and the Ground* (see p.242) specializes in modern European food and some old classics such as French onion soup, employing élan in both presentation and tastebud titillation.

La Dolce Vita 6–7 Trimmer's Lane Ⓣ053/917 0806. Astonishingly good, authentic Italian food and a lengthy list of wines, served in a delightful, small, daytime café and at inexpensive prices too – come here for lunch and forget about eating later.

La Riva Crescent Quay Ⓣ053/912 4330. Characterized by excellent cooking and imaginative use of ingredients, this cosy restaurant serves delicious seafood, including catch-of-the-day risotto, as well as a variety of tasty meat dishes using local produce. Evenings only (early-bird menu Mon–Fri).

Robertino's 19 South Main St ☎053/912 3334. A local institution, this extremely popular restaurant serves a daytime menu of pizzas, burgers, salads and the like, and later transforms into the real Italian, offering a broad variety of dishes and truly attentive service.

Spice 80 South Main St ☎053/912 2011. Upmarket Indian restaurant with elegant modern decor, specializing in Keralan and other South Indian dishes – try the tasty Goan curry of king prawns and mango. Evenings only.

Vine Thai 109 North Main St ☎053/912 2388. Appealingly set in a lofty, ornately corniced first-floor room, this largely authentic spot covers all the standards, including an especially wide range of appetizers, rustled up in an open kitchen by Thai chefs.

Pubs and bars

The Cape The Bull Ring. The undertaking side of the business, as claimed by the sign, has long gone, and this popular meeting-place is very much a place to catch up with local news and watch the world pass by, while supping a good pint of Guinness.

The Centenary Stores Charlotte St. This long, congenial bar, with a pleasant outdoor area, attracts a lively and varied crowd, and hosts DJs upstairs most nights of the week plus a traditional session Sun lunchtime.

Maggie May's Monck St. Quiet in the early evening, this smart, friendly bar with a small beer garden comes to life later on, especially for the traditional-music sessions (Thurs and, in summer, Sun).

The Sky and the Ground 112 South Main St. This dark and woody bar, with a large beer garden at the back, is an atmospheric place for a pint, staging regular live music, including traditional sessions Mon & Thurs, singer-songwriters Tues.

South 51 51 South Main St. Swish, lively café-style bar, with a roof garden, a varied food menu and DJs Fri & Sat.

Thomas Moore Tavern Cornmarket. Hosting traditional-music sessions on Thurs and some other nights, this pub is cosily old-fashioned, though it was about to be refurbished at the time of writing. The bar's name recalls the poet and publisher of the hugely successful series *Irish Melodies*, whose mother, the delightfully named Anastasia Codd, was born here. There's a traditional-music session on Thurs.

Around Wexford town

To Wexford's north lies Ireland's premier wildfowl sanctuary, **Wexford Wildfowl Reserve**, while to the west is the impressive **Irish National Heritage Park**. To the south of town lies rather bland countryside, though the ornate gardens of **Johnstown Castle** and the **Irish Agricultural Museum** are well worth visiting. The small seaside resort of **Rosslare** has a splendid beach, much enjoyed by families in summer, while **Rosslare Europort** is a major point of entry into Ireland.

Wexford Wildfowl Reserve

On the north side of the Slaney estuary, the **Wexford Wildfowl Reserve** will provide fascination for twitchers and laypeople alike. It occupies a charming patch of reclaimed land, two metres below sea level, known as the North Slobs (from Irish *slab*, meaning "mud, mire or a soft-fleshed person"), a maze of channels, reed beds, grazing lands and tillage. Between early October and mid-April, this peculiarly rich habitat is home to thousands of ducks, geese and swans, while in spring and autumn large numbers of birds on migration stop to feed here. Of particular importance in the former category are the ten thousand Greenland white-fronted geese, about a third of the world's population, who winter on the reserve after nesting in Greenland, as well as the two thousand Brent geese who arrive in mid-December after breeding in Canada. Year-round inhabitants include mute swans and a healthy population of Irish hares.

To get to the reserve, head 3km up the R741 Gorey road, then turn right for 2km. As well as various hides, you'll find the well-run **visitor centre** (daily 9am–5pm; free; ⓣ053/912 3129, ⓦwww.npws.ie), which houses an observation tower and an engaging little exhibition. The centre organizes talks year round, and guided walks, workshops and other events mostly in the summer. It's not possible to walk by yourself in the protected environs of the reserve, but if you fancy stretching your legs at this stage, you could make for the nearby **Raven Nature Reserve**, an expanse of dunes and pine forest that runs down to Raven Point at the mouth of the estuary. To get there, retrace your steps to the R741, head north for 500m, then turn right; the reserve is 8km from the turn-off, via the village of Curracloe.

Irish National Heritage Park

Four kilometres west of Wexford off the N11 Dublin road at **FERRYCARRIG** is the **Irish National Heritage Park** (daily: April–Sept 9.30am–6.30pm, last admission 5pm; Oct–March 9.30am–5.30pm, last admission 3/4pm; €7.50; ⓦwww.inhp.com), devoted to full-scale reconstructions of the sites and buildings that configure Ireland's known history, right through from Mesolithic times. A roam around the park takes you past, and sometimes into, all manner of dwellings and ritual sites. The undoubted centrepiece is an impressive facsimile of a twelfth-century castle.

Irish Agricultural Museum

It's well worth taking a trip six kilometres south from Wexford town to **Johnstown Castle**. This nineteenth-century Gothic Revival mansion is not open to the public, but its extensive grounds (daily 9am–5pm; admission charges May–Sept: car €6, pedestrians/cyclists €2) feature an abundance of flora, outdoors and in hothouses, as well as ornamental lakes, rich woodland and a ruined medieval tower-house. The estate's old farm buildings are now home to the **Irish Agricultural Museum** (April–Nov Mon–Fri 9am–5pm, Sat & Sun

▲ Irish National Heritage Park

11am–5pm; Dec–March Mon–Fri 9am–12.30pm & 1.30–5pm; €6), which explores rural history via displays, artefacts, a wealth of furniture and machinery, re-created workshops and kitchens. There's also a specific display on the Famine, recounting its impact, the search for a cure for potato blight, and the massive changes in rural Ireland that ensued. The Viking Shuttlebuses to Rosslare and to Kilmore Quay from Wexford's Redmond Square each stop at the agricultural museum once a day – phone ⓣ053/914 2742 or contact the Wexford tourist office for times.

Rosslare and Rosslare Europort

Some 11km southeast of Wexford town is **ROSSLARE**, a somewhat nondescript single-street village with few attractions, though it has a massive and popular Blue Flag sandy beach and a superb **place to stay** in the form of *Kelly's Resort Hotel & Spa* (ⓣ053/913 2114, ⓦwww.kellys.ie; closed mid-Dec to mid-Feb; ❻), set right by the strand with its own thermal spa and seaweed baths, as well as a host of activities for adults and kids. It has two fine restaurants as well (both of which offer good-value lunch menus) – the rather formal *Beaches*, serving traditional classics, and the more relaxed and innovative *La Marine Bistro*.

Further southeast along the coast, **ROSSLARE EUROPORT** is a major ferry terminal (ⓣ053/57937, ⓦwww.iarnrodeireann.ie/rosslare/home), serving arrivals from Wales and France. Should you arrive by car, there's no reason to linger and, if you come on foot there are transport connections to various parts of Ireland (see p.250). The terminal hosts car-rental outlets and a bureau de change (the nearest ATM is ten minutes' walk away in the harbour village), as well as offices of the ferry companies (see also p.29), Irish Ferries (for Pembroke; ⓣ053/913 3158) and Stena Line (for Fishguard; ⓣ053/916 1560). If you're catching an early-morning ferry there's an enormous number of **B&Bs** near the harbour or a short distance away (mostly ❷), or head for *Hotel Rosslare* (ⓣ053/913 3110, ⓦwww.hotelrosslare.ie; ❹), which surveys the harbour from a cliff-top position and provides exquisitely furnished, spacious rooms, some with balconies.

The south coast and the Barrow estuary

Ireland's southeastern corner is reminiscent of the Netherlands, consisting of flat, low-lying land infiltrated by the sea, forming large lagoons. Off shore lies the bustling bird sanctuary of the **Saltee Islands**, accessible by boat from **Kilmore Quay**, while the area's sightseeing highlight is the atmospheric ruin of **Tintern Abbey**, near the neck of the blustery **Hook Head Peninsula**, which is punctuated with sandy beaches and a fascinating medieval lighthouse. Circumnavigating Hook Head brings you to the pleasant little resort of **Duncannon** and nearby **Ballyhack**, whence car ferries cross the Barrow estuary to Passage East in County Waterford. This ferry service is 20km south of the first road crossing of the Barrow, at the busy town of **New Ross**, and is certainly worth taking if you're short of time, but that way you'd miss out on several attractions on the east bank of the river, notably the glorious remains of **Dunbrody Abbey**, the **John F. Kennedy Arboretum** and the vivid **Dunbrody Emigrant Ship** at New Ross. Bus transport here is better than in many remote areas of Ireland: Bus Éireann's routes are supplemented by the sporadic services of the Rural Transport Initiative (RTI) along the Barrow estuary to Fethard-on-Sea on Hook Head (see p.251).

Across the estuary to Waterford

If you're heading for County Waterford, then the Passage East Car Ferry (Ⓣ051/382480, Ⓦwww.passageferry.com) from **Ballyhack**, a kilometre north of Arthurstown, is a boon, saving time and mileage. Ferries operate a continuous service April–Sept Mon–Sat 7am–10pm, Sun 9.30am–10pm, with a last sailing Oct–March at 8pm. The price for a car on the five-minute crossing is €8 single, €11 return; for a cycle, €2 single, €3 return; and for a pedestrian €2 (return trip included).

Kilmore Quay and the Saltee Islands

Twenty kilometres south of Wexford, the seaside village of **KILMORE QUAY** figures high in the county's supposed list of "attractions". Despite its setting and Blue Flag marina, this busy fishing port doesn't have much to recommend it, with several utilitarian fisheries and a somewhat overrated beach, but this hasn't deterred businesses from cashing in on its location. If the sun's not shining, you could occupy your time at the **Guillemot Maritime Museum** (Ⓣ053/912 1572 or 051/561144), a converted lightship that's been run aground and set in concrete by the harbour. It now houses an assortment of rather drab seafaring memorabilia, but was closed for extensive renovation at the time of writing.

However, one definite time to come here is during the village's **seafood festival** (Ⓣ053/912 9922) in mid-July, which offers much scope for tasting the delicacies on offer. Otherwise there's a fine seafood **restaurant**, *The Silver Fox* (Ⓣ053/912 9888), serving locally caught produce in smart surroundings by the harbour – it's a little pricey, but more manageable on the daily early-bird menu. Alternatively, for premium-quality bar meals there's *Kehoe's* **pub**, opposite the church, with walls bedecked in maritime mementos and a neat, little beer garden at the back. En-suite **B&Bs** in the village include the attractive *Quay House* (Ⓣ053/29988, Ⓦwww.quayhouse.net; ❸), near the church, and welcoming *Harbour Lights* (Ⓣ053/912 9881; ❷), which offers good rates for children and singles, nearer the sea.

From the harbour you can take a ninety-minute boat trip (call Ⓣ053/912 9684 or 053/912 9704; €20 per person) to the uninhabited **Saltee Islands**, some 6km off the coast, to view Ireland's largest bird sanctuary – nesting grounds for all manner of seabirds during May and June, such as puffins, kittiwakes and auks. It's also possible to get to the islands from Kilmore Quay by **kayaking**, through Sea Paddling (see p.274), or under **sail**, with Sailing Ireland (Ⓣ053/913 9163, Ⓦwww.sailingireland.ie).

Tintern Abbey

Situated 30km southwest of Wexford town off the R374 is the dramatic ruin of **Tintern Abbey** (daily: mid-June to Sept 10am–6pm; Oct 10am–5pm; last admission 45min before closing; €2.10; Heritage Card; Ⓦwww.heritageireland.ie), surrounded by 3km of woodland trails. This thirteenth-century Cistercian foundation was constructed by William Marshall, Earl of Pembroke, and was populated by monks from its better-known namesake in Monmouthshire, Wales. By the time of its dissolution in 1536, the abbey was reckoned to be the third richest Cistercian establishment in Ireland. It was then granted to one of Henry VIII's officers, Anthony Colclough, who much modified the buildings, while subsequent additions, including the battlemented walls, were made by his descendants, who lived here until the 1960s. Only part of the original cruciform church is still standing but its tower is extant and includes a small exhibition on the abbey's history.

Around Hook Head

Heading south along the R374 from the abbey brings you to **FETHARD-ON-SEA**, the eastern gateway to the **Hook Head** (Ⓦwww.thehook-wexford.com). There are few facilities on the peninsula, but this almost single-street village does have a **tourist office** (Mon–Fri 9.30am–1pm & 1.30–5pm; Ⓣ051/397502), behind the post office (which offers Internet access), a **café**, *The Village Kitchen*, and you can **stay** at the focus of local life, the *Hotel Naomh Seosamh* (Ⓣ051/397129, Ⓔabobrien@eircom.net; ❷), which has comfortable en-suite rooms and serves food all day in summer, evenings in winter. **Camping** is available at *Ocean Island Caravan and Camping Park* (Easter–Sept; Ⓣ051/397148 or 397123), on the R374 on the north side of the village.

The road from here to Hook Head passes through flat, drab farmland, but the scenery improves as the peninsula narrows. Take a detour to **SLADE**, the last place of any size before Hook Head (and that's not saying much) – a tranquil spot that time seems to have bypassed. It's set around an antiquated split harbour that's dominated by a ruined fifteenth-century castle, and, if you fancy a bracing stroll, it's less than 3km around the coast from here to Hook Head.

Hook Head itself is entirely exposed to the elements, serene in good weather – though utterly dangerous for swimming – and excitingly wild in a storm. The rocky shoreline has a wealth of fossils and it's a popular location for birdwatchers, who visit to spot migrations, as well as whale- and dolphin-watchers. The **Hook Lighthouse** (March–Oct daily 9.30am–5pm; Nov–Feb Sun 9.30am–4pm; €5.50; café open daily year-round) was built by William Marshall (see p.245) in the early thirteenth century to guide ships safely into Waterford Harbour. Apart from a short period during the 1600s, it has functioned ever since and became fully automated in 1996. Guided tours lead to the lighthouse's top, some 36 metres high, and recount its history, paying note to the monks who were the first light-keepers here.

Duncannon and around

DUNCANNON (Ⓦwww.visitduncannon.com) is a small, friendly village with an expansive Blue Flag beach protected from the elements by a rocky coastline at its southern extremity. Looming above from its lofty promontory is **Duncannon Fort** (June–Sept daily 9.30am–5.30pm; Oct–May by appointment; €5 with a guided tour, €3 without; Ⓣ051/389454), constructed in 1586, on the site of a Celtic fort and a Norman castle, as a bulwark against Spanish invasion. Much remodelled since then, the fort remained in British hands until 1919 and was burnt down by the IRA in 1922. Though Ireland was officially neutral during World War II, the fort was rebuilt on its outbreak, becoming a base for the Irish Army until 1986. As well as an art gallery and an Internet café, the complex includes a small maritime museum, a dry moat with ten-metre-high walls and, in a surviving older building, a fetid dungeon (accessible only on the guided tour) where the Croppy Boy, the subject of a well-known song of the 1798 Rebellion, was allegedly incarcerated. Over on the beach, in mid-August there's the two-day **International Sand-Sculpting Festival** (Ⓣ051/389990), in which a host of competitors produce astonishing, but sadly temporary, artworks.

For **accommodation** try the comfortable, well-kept en-suite rooms at *The Moorings* (Ⓣ & Ⓕ051/389242; March–Nov; ❷), by the fort. Nearby, overlooking the sea at the central crossroads, the *Strand Tavern* is a convivial local, serving good-value **food** all day and often has evening entertainment. On the opposite corner, *Roche's* features a cosy, old-fashioned front bar – home to traditional sessions on Fridays and bands or singer-songwriters on summer Saturdays – and larger spaces beyond, including a beer garden. Lunches here cover everything from sandwiches and salads to chowder, seafood and steaks, while *Sqigl* (evenings: summer Tues–Sat; winter Wed–Sat; ⓣ051/389188), the adjacent restaurant run by the same family and pronounced "squiggle", is a more sophisticated option, serving delicious local seafood and sublime desserts.

Just before waterside **ARTHURSTOWN**, 3km north, there's sumptuous country-house **accommodation** at *Dunbrody House* (ⓣ051/389600, ⓦwww.dunbrodyhouse.com; ❼), an 1830s mansion set in glorious parklands. The hotel houses one of Ireland's foremost cookery schools – as well as a spa offering food-based treatments – so it's unsurprising that the **restaurant** here is exceedingly good. Slightly closer to the village, with fine views of the estuary, is another late Georgian country house in expansive grounds, *Glendine House* (ⓣ051/389500, ⓦwww.glendinehouse.com; ❸), which offers luxurious, upmarket B&B, as well as dinner for guests if arranged in advance.

Dunbrody Abbey to New Ross

A few kilometres up the R733 from Arthurstown lies ruined **Dunbrody Abbey** (May to mid-Sept daily 10am–6pm; €2; ⓦwww.dunbrodyabbey.com), a Cistercian monastery founded in 1170 by Hervé de Montmorency, on the instructions of his nephew, the Anglo-Norman invader, Strongbow. Overlooking the Barrow estuary, its magnificent remains centre on a sixty-metre-long early Gothic church, whose most notable features are the elegant west doorway and east window. Following Dissolution, the abbey passed into the hands of the Etchingham family whose descendants added the tower and nearby buildings and own the land to this day. On site there's also a full-sized maze, which utilizes 1500 yew trees (€4, includes fee for pitch and putt course).

In **CAMPILE**, to the northeast, there's superb **food** to be enjoyed at the *Shelburne Restaurant* (ⓣ051/388996; Tues–Sat dinner, Sun lunch), a place with a well-merited reputation for delicious seafood and lip-smacking meat dishes. Back on the R733 look out for signs to *Kilmokea* (ⓣ051/388109, ⓦwww.kilmokea.com; Feb–Nov; ❻), a former Georgian rectory offering deluxe rooms, as well as a swimming pool, gym and spa treatments. The adjacent walled **gardens** and woodland garden beyond, which are lush with rare plants, trees and shrubs, are open to visitors (mid-March to early Nov daily 10am–6pm; €6). There's fine dining here too, as well as café lunches and cream teas served in the conservatory.

The horticultural connection continues a few kilometres north at the **John F. Kennedy Arboretum** (daily: April & Sept 10am–6.30pm; May–Aug 10am–8pm; Oct–March 10am–5pm; last admission 45min before closing; €2.90; Heritage Card; ⓦwww.heritageireland.ie), named after the former US President, who returned to visit his ancestors' homeland in 1963. The arboretum houses an astonishing assortment of more than 4500 trees and shrubs from the world's temperate regions. Its grounds sweep upwards along the slopes of Slieve Coillte, whose 270-metre summit provides panoramic views of the surrounding countryside. JFK's great-grandfather, Patrick, was born a little to the west in Dunganstown, where the **Kennedy Homestead** (May, June & Sept Mon–Fri 11.30am–4.30pm; July & Aug daily 10am–5pm; ⓦwww.kennedyhomestead.com; €5) describes his emigration to the US, fleeing the Famine in 1848, and traces the family's subsequent history.

New Ross

NEW ROSS (ⓦwww.newrosstourism.com) squats besides the River Barrow, 12km north of the arboretum, its quayside marred by poor redevelopment and heavy traffic, but there's still life in the old place, especially in the lanes behind the frontage. The river provided access to the upstream countryside of Wexford and Kilkenny, and the town's importance beyond being a local embarkation point is emphasized by the quayside presence of the **Dunbrody Emigrant Ship** (daily: April–Sept 9am–6pm; Oct–March 10am–5pm; last tour 1hr before closing; €7; Heritage Island; Ⓦwww.dunbrody.com). Though this is a reconstruction of one of the nineteenth-century vessels that conveyed numerous Irish emigrants to North America, particularly during the height of the Famine, it is actually a full-scale, fully-operable craft and occasionally takes part in tall ship races. Following a brief scene-setting video, the half-hour guided tour of the ship, complete with costumed actors role-playing passengers and crew, shows the conditions on board, stressing the variance between those who travelled steerage and first class. On board you can also access a database of virtually everyone who emigrated to North America between 1845 and 1875.

The town's **tourist office** (Ⓣ051/421857) is housed in the ship's visitor centre (same hours). Ask here about the **Ros Tapestry** (Ⓦwww.rostapestry.com), an ambitious, ten-year project to embroider the history of New Ross in fifteen colourful panels – it's nearing completion and will probably be hung in St Mary's Church on Mary Street. On the northeast side of town, 3km or so out, *MacMurrough Farm Hostel* (Ⓣ051/421383, Ⓦwww.macmurrough.com; March–Nov; dorms from €14, private rooms ❶) is a welcoming, comfortable and tranquil cottage **hostel** on a working farm, while **B&B** is available in the centre of town at homely *Riversdale House*, Lower William Street (Ⓣ051/422515, Ⓔriversdalehouse@eircom.net; ❷), which has an attractive conservatory and gardens. Several bars along The Quay serve **meals**, while the best bet for lunch is *Café Nutshell*, 8 South St (closed Sun & Mon), an excellent deli-café serving everything from juices and smoothies to meat, seafood and cheese platters and daily-special hot dishes. If you fancy lunch, afternoon tea or dinner on the water, then book a table on *The Galley*, North Quay (Ⓣ051/421723, Ⓦwww.rivercruises.ie; April–Oct), which plies between New Ross and Inistioge on the Nore, towards St Mullins on the Barrow or along the Suir to Waterford, all dependent on the tide; it may also be possible to take a **cruise** on *The Galley* without having a meal, according to demand. The **JFK Dunbrody Festival** (Ⓦwww.jfkdunbrodyfestival.org) takes place over three days towards the end of July and features a variety of musical and other events, as well as arts, craft and food fairs and a regatta.

North Wexford

The countryside of North Wexford is not especially impressive, though splendid sandy **beaches** punctuate its coastline. Energetic **Enniscorthy** is North Wexford's largest town and the centre of an area that has numerous associations with the **1798 Rebellion**, especially at nearby **Vinegar Hill** and **Boolavogue**.

North along the coast

Ten kilometres northeast of Wexford town, past Curracloe, lies the sprawling **Ballinesker Beach** whose dunes spread far into the distance. The strand deputized for Omaha Beach as the site of the D-Day landings in Stephen Spielberg's World War II epic *Saving Private Ryan*. The area's also noted for the Bronze Age gold artefacts – the Ballinesker Hoard – that were discovered here; they are now on view at Dublin's National Museum. Further up the coast near

Kilmuckridge is another broad beach popular with families, **Morriscastle**, known as "the golden mile".

Enniscorthy

Around 24km north of Wexford, the attractive old town of **ENNISCORTHY** straddles the River Slaney. Its main streets rise steeply from the river's west bank towards the Market Square where proudly stands a statue of two of the key figures in the 1798 Rebellion, Thomas Sinnott the pikeman and Father John Murphy (see p.250). From here Rafter Street leads after a ten-minute walk to the **National 1798 Centre** (Easter–Sept Mon–Fri 9.30am–5pm Sat & Sun noon–4pm; Oct–Easter Mon–Fri 9.30am–4pm; €6; ⓦwww.iol.ie/~98com), a high-tech sound-and-vision fest, capturing the excitement of events prior to the Rebellion, the Rising itself and its aftermath, all cogently set within broader intellectual and political contexts that brought about American independence and the French Revolution. There's a marvellous display on the conflict between revolution and counter-revolution set out on a giant chessboard. Another highlight is an audiovisual featuring an enthralling debate between actors playing the roles of the Dublin-born Whig politician and philosopher Edmund Burke and Thomas Paine, the English radical and American revolutionary whose *Rights of Man* (1792) was a direct riposte to Burke's more conservative *Reflections on the Revolution in France* (1790). It was on the gorse-covered **Vinegar Hill**, opposite on the Slaney's eastern bank, that the rebels of 1798 met their demise at the hands of British forces.

Occupying a much revamped thirteenth-century castle just east of the Market Square, the **Wexford County Museum** (ⓣ053/923 5926) also owns plenty of relics from the 1798 campaigns, as well as items associated with the 1916 rebellion, such as the old clock from the GPO in Dublin – it's little known that there was a coordinated rising at Easter in Enniscorthy too, and the town surrendered a day after Dublin. At the time of writing, the museum was closed for renovation by the Office of Public Works, but due to reopen in 2008.

West from here, through the Market Square and along Main Street, is **St Aidan's Cathedral**, an imposing Gothic Revival edifice, designed by the English architect Augustus Pugin, whose other works include Killarney's St Mary's Cathedral and, in collaboration with Sir Charles Barry, the interior of the Palace of Westminster. St Aidan's was built between 1843 and 1850, its tower added the following year and a spire in 1871. However, the combination of the two later features proved too heavy for the supporting pillars and the tower's lower section had to be removed. Much longer than wide and with an impressively high ceiling, the interior features high pointed arches, an oak carved pulpit, beautiful stained-glass windows depicting saints and bishops, and a small exhibition on Pugin's career.

Practicalities

Buses set down outside the Bus Stop Shop on The Shannon Quay on the eastern bank of the Slaney. The **train** station is on the same side of town, west of Templeshannon, which leads south to Enniscorthy Bridge. The **tourist office** is in the National 1798 Centre (same hours; ⓣ053/923 4699).

Enniscorthy boasts a top-notch **hotel**, *Riverside Park* on The Promenade near the 1798 Centre (ⓣ053/923 7800, ⓦwww.riversideparkhotel.com; ⑤), with modern, attractive rooms, many of which overlook the river, and its own indoor pool, gym and sauna. Out on the Gorey road, *Monart* (ⓣ053/923 8999, ⓦwww.monart.ie; ⑧) is an impressive, contemporary **spa hotel** set around a lake in extensive private woodlands, with over seventy treatments available and a fine restaurant. For **B&B** try the cosy standard and en-suite rooms at *Maura Murphy's*, 9 Main St (Ⓣ054/33522, Ⓦwww.dirl.com/wexford/enniscorthy/maura-murphy.htm; ❷), which is very centrally placed near Market Square with its own car park; or, below Vinegar Hill, *Ivella*, 9 Rectory Rd (Ⓣ053/923 3475, Ⓦwww.dirl.com/wexford/ivella.htm; ❷), an attractive old house with standard accommodation.

Good **food** in town can be found at the Tex-Mex *Alamo Restaurant* in the *Riverside Park Hotel* or at the *Galo Chargrill*, 19 Main St (Ⓣ053/923 8077; closed Mon), which specializes in traditional Portuguese cuisine. For an atmospheric pint head to *The Antique Tavern*, down Slaney Street from the Market Square, an old **bar** with a wealth of local photos and memorabilia on its walls and an upstairs balcony for absorbing views of the river and Vinegar Hill. On the quays just north of here, *The Bailey* (Ⓣ053/923 0353) does a bit of everything: converted from an old warehouse and decorated in plush, Victorian style, this new café-bar offers good food, regular live gigs and a weekend nightclub.

Enniscorthy's **Strawberry Festival** (Ⓦwww.strawberryfestival.ie) takes over a weekend at the end of June or the beginning of July and includes lots of entertainment and events as well as punnet-loads of Wexford strawberries.

Boolavogue

If you're intrigued by Wexford's role in the 1798 Rebellion, then head for the **Father Murphy Centre** (Easter–Oct Mon–Fri 10.30am–5pm, Sat & Sun noon–6pm; Ⓦwww.boolavogue.info; €6) at **BOOLAVOGUE**, 10km northeast of Enniscorthy. John Murphy was Boolavogue's parish priest for fourteen years, lodging with the Donohue family. A supporter of the United Irishmen, though compelled by his bishop to preach against them, he became a key figure in the Wexford campaign and survived all the local battles. After the Vinegar Hill defeat he fled the county, but was captured near Tullow in County Carlow and executed. The centre consists largely of a reconstruction of the Donohue farmstead, and the priest's own room features an old settle bed and a dog collar, reputed to be his, found at Vinegar Hill. There are displays on local life and the outhouses include a dairy, pigsty and trap house, plus plenty of antiquated farm machinery.

Travel details

Trains

Campile to: Rosslare Europort (Mon–Sat 1 daily; 55min); Waterford (Mon–Sat 1 daily; 25min).
Enniscorthy to: Dublin (3 daily; 2hr–2hr 15min); Rosslare Europort (3 daily; 50min); Wexford (3 daily; 30min).
Kilkenny to: Dublin (4–6 daily; 1hr 45min); Thomastown (4–6 daily; 10min); Waterford (4–6 daily; 40min).
Rosslare Europort to: Dublin (3 daily; 3hr–3hr 10min); Rosslare (3 daily; 5min); Waterford (Mon–Sat 1 daily; 1hr 20min); Wexford (3 daily; 25min).
Thomastown to: Dublin (4–6 daily; 1hr 55min); Kilkenny (4–6 daily; 10min); Waterford (4–6 daily; 30min).
Wexford to: Dublin (3 daily; 2hr 30min–2hr 45min); Enniscorthy (3 daily; 30min); Rosslare (3 daily; 20min); Rosslare Europort (3 daily; 25min).

Buses

Bus Éireann

Duncannon to: Fethard-on-Sea (1 Mon & Thurs; 25min); New Ross (Mon–Sat 1–2 daily; 45min); Waterford (Mon–Sat 1–2 daily; 1hr 20min); Wexford (1 on Mon & Thurs; 1hr 25min).

Enniscorthy to: Dublin (11–13 daily; 2hr 20min); New Ross (4 daily; 30min); Waterford (4 daily; 1hr); Wexford (8–11 daily; 25min).
Fethard-on-Sea to: Duncannon (1 Mon & Thurs; 25min); New Ross (1 Mon & Thurs; 1hr 5min); Waterford (1 on Mon & Thurs; 1hr 40min); Wexford (1 on Mon & Thurs; 1hr).
Kilkenny to: Carrick-on-Suir (6–7 daily; 50min); Cork (1–3 daily; 3hr); Dublin (6–7 daily; 2hr 15min); New Ross (1 weekly; 1hr 15min); Waterford (1–2 daily; 1hr).
Kilmore Quay to: Wexford (2 on Wed & Sat; 40–50min).
New Ross to: Dublin (4 daily; 2hr 45min); Duncannon (Mon–Sat 1–2 daily; 45min); Enniscorthy (4 daily; 30min); Fethard-on-Sea (1 on Mon & Thurs; 1hr 5min); Kilkenny (1 on Thurs; 1hr 15min); Waterford (7–11 daily; 20min); Wexford (3–7 daily; 40min).
Rosslare Europort to: Cork (3–4 daily; 4hr 15min); Dublin (11–13 daily; 2hr 25min–3hr 20min); Killarney (1–4 daily; 6hr–6hr 30min); Tralee (1–4 daily; 7hr); Waterford (3–4 daily; 1hr 25min); Wexford (11–13 daily; 30min).
Thomastown to: Dublin (5–10 daily; 2hr 5min); Inistioge (1 on Thurs; 10min); Kilkenny (1 on Thurs; 30min); New Ross (1 on Thurs; 50min); Waterford (7–10 daily; 30–40min).
Wexford to: Cork (3–6 daily; 4hr); Dublin (12–14 daily; 2hr 35min–3hr); Duncannon (1 on Mon & Thurs; 1hr 25min); Enniscorthy (9–11 daily; 25min); Fethard-on-Sea (1 on Mon & Thurs; 1hr); Killarney (1–4 daily; 5hr 30min); Kilmore Quay (2 on Wed & Sat; 35–40min); New Ross (3–7 daily; 40min); Rosslare (1 daily; 20min); Rosslare Europort (11–13 daily; 30min); Tralee (1–4 daily; 6hr 30min); Waterford (3–7 daily; 1hr).

Ardcavan
Ⓣ053/912 2561
Wexford (Crescent Quay) to: Dublin & Dublin Airport (1 daily; 2hr 30min).

J.J. Kavanagh
Ⓣ056/883 1106, Ⓦwww.jjkavanagh.ie
Kilkenny to: Clonmel (2–3 daily; 1hr); Dublin (2–5 daily; 2hr–2hr 30min).
Thomastown to: Dublin (11 daily; 2hr 30min–3hr 30min).

RTI
Ⓣ051/389418 or 087/251 9614
Fethard-on-Sea Tues, Thurs & Sat 1 daily to and from Duncannon (20min); Arthurstown (25min); Ballyhack (30min); Campile (35min); New Ross (55min); Waterford (Merchants Quay; Sat only; 1hr 20min).

Viking Shuttlebus
Ⓣ053/914 2742
Wexford (Redmond Square) to: Dublin Airport (via Enniscorthy; 4 daily; 2hr 30min); Kilmore Quay (Mon–Sat 3–4 daily; 45min); Rosslare (Mon–Sat 2–3 daily; 20min).

6

Tipperary and Waterford

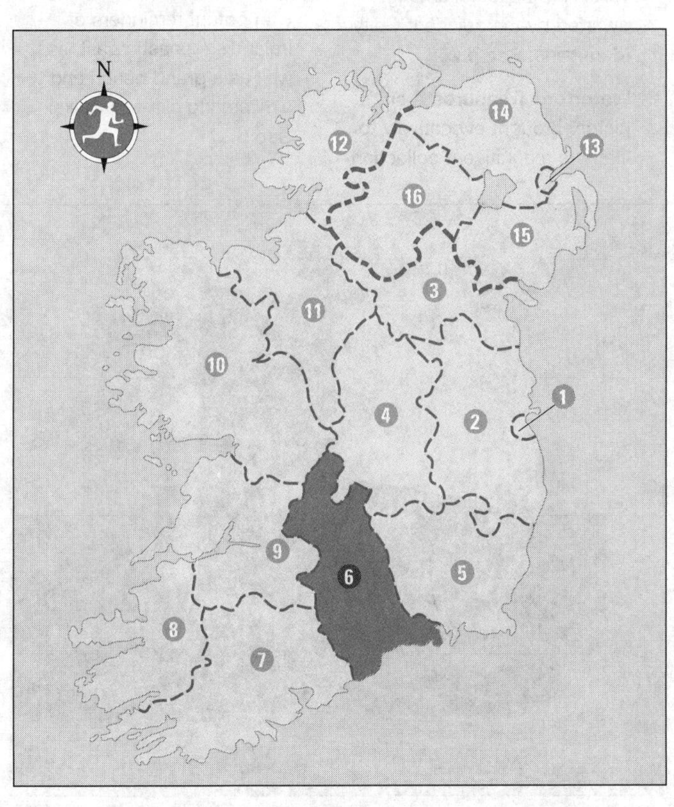

CHAPTER 6

Highlights

* **The Rock of Cashel** Stunning medieval religious site, set high above the surrounding countryside. See p.258
* **Cahir Castle** One of the country's best-preserved Anglo-Norman strongholds. See p.262
* **The Glen of Aherlow** River valley in a beautiful setting, dwarfed by the adjacent Galty Mountains. See p.265
* **Waterford Treasures** A city's history brought evocatively to life by a magnificent collection of locally found discoveries from Viking and later times. See p.271
* **Dungarvan** Clustered around its broad bay, this attractive town has plenty to enthral, including some fine traditional music. See p.275
* **Ardmore** A delightful village with potent reminders of Ireland's monastic past, as well as a grand beach and exhilarating cliff-top walks. See p.277

▲ Cahir Castle

6

Tipperary and Waterford

You're unlikely to be immediately enticed by a first sight of counties Tipperary and Waterford, much of whose countryside could well vie for the title of Ireland's dullest. However, if you're travelling west to Clare, Cork or Kerry you'll probably pass through one or other county, and there are still sufficient points of interest to merit a stop.

Most of **Tipperary**'s attractions lie in its southern reaches, notably the historic towns of **Cahir** and **Carrick-on-Suir.** The county's most outstanding site, the **Rock of Cashel**, is further north – a magnificent isolated outcrop rising from the plain and crowned by impressive Christian buildings spanning various periods. In the county's southwest lie the magical **Galty Mountains** looming over the verdant wonders of the **Glen of Aherlow**.

To Tipperary's south, **County Waterford** features a fine and varied coastline with plenty of broad bays and sheltered beaches, as well as its own array of historic and ecclesiastical sites at towns and villages such as **Ardmore**, **Lismore** and **Dungarvan**. The county's northern fringe is dominated by the lonesome and boggy **Comeragh** and **Knockmealdown** mountains while, in utter contrast, **Waterford city** is a dynamic place, renowned for its high-class crystal, and possessing a superlative museum in the form of Waterford Treasures.

County Tipperary

Tipperary (Tiobraid Árann) is the wealthiest of Ireland's inland counties, deriving its prosperity from the flat and fertile plain known as the **Golden Vale**, which provides rich pickings for dairy farmers and horse-breeders. It's also one of the largest counties, stretching over 100km from top to toe, and, uniquely, is divided into two administrative regions, North Tipperary (formerly North Riding) and South Tipperary (formerly South Riding), each with its own county town. By far the county's most breathtaking lure is the **Rock of Cashel**, soaring

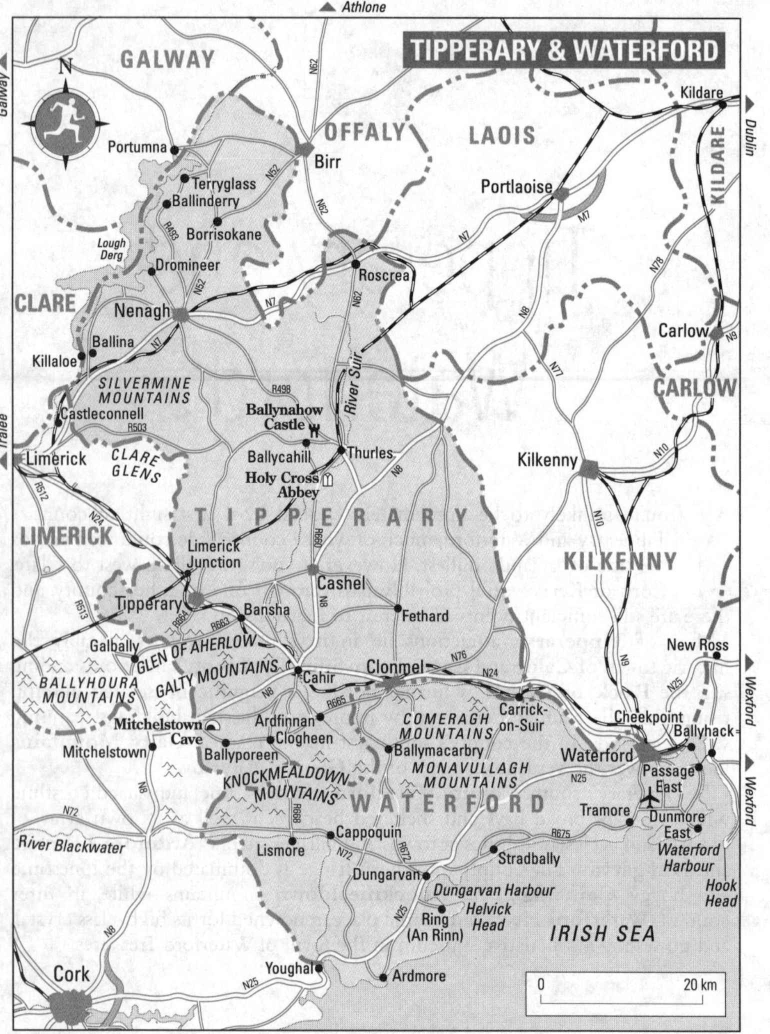

above the town's environs, and topped by the lofty walls and towers of renowned religious edifices. In the county's far northwest, the trim, historic town of **Nenagh**, administrative capital of North Tipperary, gives access to the verdant shores of **Lough Derg**, on the River Shannon. To the south of Cashel, **Cahir** holds plenty of historical interest in the shape of an imposing thirteenth-century castle and an ornamental nineteenth-century baronial villa, while to the east of here lie **Clonmel**, county town of South Tipperary, and **Carrick-on-Suir**, home to one of Ireland's most graceful mansions. In the county's far southwest, the main attractions are the fascinating calcite formations of **Mitchelstown Cave** and the idyllic **Glen of Aherlow**. Across this southern part of the county runs the **Tipperary Heritage Way** (Ⓦwww.tipperaryway.com), an easy 56-kilometre waymarked trail that runs down the Suir valley from Cashel to Cahir and Ardfinnan, finishing at the Vee (see p.279), in the Knockmealdown Mountains near the Waterford border.

Cashel and around

A small town on the main N8 Dublin–Cork road, **CASHEL** (Ⓦwww.cashel.ie) – the name derives from the Irish *caiseal,* meaning "stone fort" – is utterly overshadowed by the stunning **Rock of Cashel**, an outcrop that rears out of the surrounding fertile plain, the Golden Vale. Surmounted by important ecclesiastical remains, the Rock is a hotspot on the tourist trail, so is best visited in the early morning before the hordes arrive or in the late afternoon when the coaches have departed. The town does have some other noteworthy sights, while to its north are the **Holy Cross Abbey**, a site of major pilgrimage, and the impressively rotund **Ballynahow Castle**.

Arrival and information

Buses stop near the market house on Main Street where you'll find one of Cashel's **tourist offices** (daily 9.30am–5.30pm; mid-Oct to mid-March closed Sat & Sun; Ⓣ062/61333) – the other is in the Brú Ború Cultural Centre (see p.259). From the Main Street tourist office, **walking tours** of the town depart on summer evenings (Tues, Wed & Thurs 7pm; €7.50; Ⓣ087/285 4404). The public library on Friar Street provides **Internet** access, while McInerney's on Main Street (Ⓣ062/61225) rents out **bicycles**. Cashel's **festival** (Ⓦwww.cashelartsfest.com) offers a variety of cultural events over the month of November.

Accommodation

Despite the Rock's popularity you should have no problems finding accommodation, though prices are somewhat higher than elsewhere in Tipperary. There are plenty of B&B options in town and many more in the surrounding countryside, especially on the Dualla road.

Abbey House 1 Dominic St Ⓣ062/61104, Ⓔteachnamainstreach@eircom.net. Relaxing en-suite and standard rooms in a quiet, central location opposite St Dominic's Friary. May–Oct. ❷

Ashmore House John St Ⓣ062/61286, Ⓦwww.ashmorehouse.com. A homely, comfortably furnished Georgian townhouse with en-suite rooms and a private car park, run by friendly owners. ❷

Bailey's Main St Ⓣ062/61937, Ⓦwww.baileys-ireland.com. Stylish accommodation, featuring a twenty-metre pool and gym, in an impressive townhouse that dates back to 1709. ❺

Cashel Holiday Hostel 6 John St (IHH & IHO) Ⓣ062/62330, Ⓦwww.cashelhostel.com. Appealing, central hostel in yet another Georgian townhouse, with a well-equipped kitchen and sociable dining area, a cosy sitting room and laundry facilities. Dorms from €16, private rooms ❶

Cashel Palace Hotel Main St Ⓣ062/62707, Ⓦwww.cashel-palace.ie. Housed in the former archbishop's palace with its spacious and elegant sitting rooms, and set within extensive, peaceful gardens, this hotel offers top-notch accommodation and first-class service. ❼

Cashel Town B&B 5 John St Ⓣ062/62330, Ⓦwww.cashelbandb.com. Recently refurbished B&B, under the same management as *Cashel Holiday Hostel* next door, with a wide variety of cheery, colourful standard and en-suite bedrooms and a large sitting room. Guests have the option of cooking their own breakfast in the hostel's kitchen. Without breakfast ❶, with breakfast ❷.

O'Brien's Holiday Lodge Dundrum Road (IHH) Ⓣ062/61003, Ⓦwww.cashel-lodge.com. In a bucolic setting looking up towards the Rock, about a kilometre from the main tourist office on the northwest side of town, a well-run hostel in a renovated stone barn with an attached campsite. Dorms €17.50, private rooms ❶.

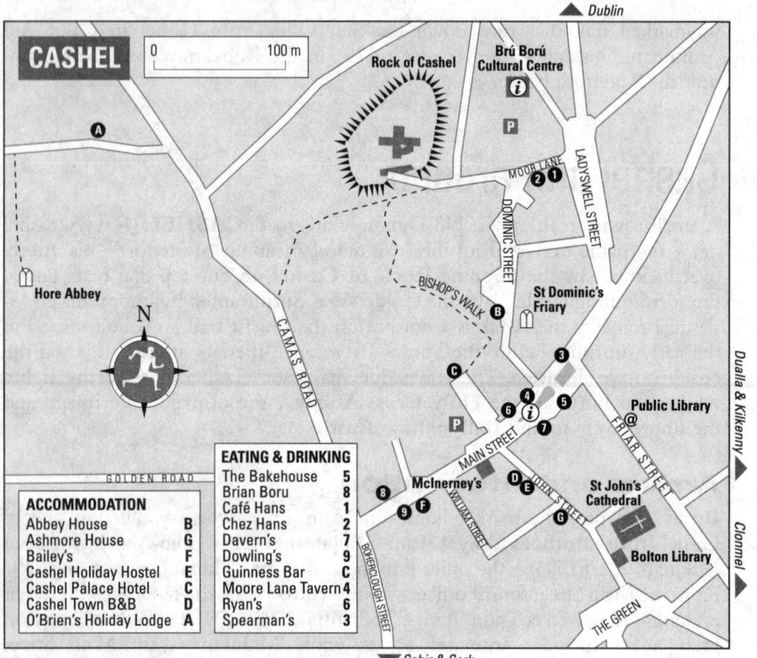

The Rock of Cashel

Viewed from afar, the **Rock of Cashel** (daily: mid-March to early June & mid-Sept to mid-Oct 9am–5.30pm; early June to mid-Sept 9am–7pm; mid-Oct to mid-March 9am–4.30pm; last admission 45min before closing; €5.30; Heritage Card; mid-March to mid-Sept free 45min guided tours every hour on the half-hour; ⓦ www.heritageireland.ie) is a captivating sight, a freak and solitary lump of limestone, reflecting the light in diverse ways throughout the day and topped by a collection of walls, towers, turrets and crenellations of *Gormenghast* proportions. It might seem heretical to suggest so, but this vista is actually the best thing about the Rock since, despite its staggering location and much-trumped billing, when you get there the site is actually far less atmospheric than other notable ecclesiastical complexes, not least Kells Priory (see p.235) and Quin Abbey (see p.387). Nonetheless, despite the swarms of coach-tour-borne tourists, there's plenty to see and much to marvel at.

The Rock is some ten minutes' walk uphill from Cashel town (or less from the signposted car park) and, once you've purchased your ticket, the first sight is the fifteenth-century **Hall of the Vicars Choral**, which once housed the choir charged with singing at the cathedral's services. Its upper floor features a minstrels' gallery as well as a fine, eighteenth-century Flemish tapestry showing Solomon receiving the Queen of Sheba, while the lower houses the original, twelfth-century **St Patrick's Cross** (the one outside – on the cross's original spot – is a replica). Badly worn, it bears a carving of Christ on one side and the saint on the other, and is unusual in not having a ring around the cross head. Next door is the **Dormitory of the Vicars Choral** where a twenty-minute video, *Strongholds of the Faith*, is shown throughout the day.

The rise of the Rock

According to legend, the Rock first rose to political prominence in the fourth or fifth century AD, when a major fortress was established by the descendants of Eógan Mór who went on to establish a dynasty of kings-cum-bishops reigning over this part of Munster. The Eóganacht were ousted from Cashel in 978 by the Dál Cais line from Killaloe in County Clare, Brian Boru becoming the overlord of Cashel, and subsequently achieving dominance over Ireland in 1002. His descendant, Murtagh, granted the Rock to the Church in 1101 and, some fifty years later, when the papacy established four archbishoprics in Ireland, one of which was at Cashel, an early medieval cathedral was built here. By then, however, the Eóganacht had regained control under Cormac Mac Cárthaigh, who built the extant **Cormac's Chapel**, finished in 1134, though the Rock subsequently changed hands once again. The adjoining **cathedral** dates from the thirteenth century and was perhaps constructed during the regime of an O'Brien archbishop. The whole site was sacked by Cromwell's forces in 1647, but was still used by the Church of Ireland until 1749 when cathedral status was granted to St John's Church on John Street.

Directly opposite is **Cormac's Chapel**, perhaps the most atmospheric of Ireland's Romanesque churches. Its appealing south facade of brown sandstone, decorated with the typical blind arcades of the period, stands in warm contrast to the grey limestone used elsewhere on the Rock and in most Irish churches. In the chancel you'll find some very rare surviving examples of medieval Irish paintwork. The most complete fragment, on the south wall, shows part of the baptism of Christ, while the ceiling features scenes relating to the Magi – though you wouldn't know it unless you were told. The elaborate chancel arch beyond, which is strangely off-centre to the nave, features vivid sculpted heads of people and animals. Although the adjacent cathedral obstructs the chapel's north door, formerly its main entrance, it's still possible to go out and have a look at a lively carving of a robust lion being hunted by a centaur, equipped with a bow and arrow and a Norman-type helmet.

Constructed on the site of the earlier establishment between 1230 and 1270, the huge Gothic **cathedral** is typically Anglo-Norman in form, with pointed arches and loftily set lancet windows. It also features some smaller quatrefoil casements, as well as a nave unusually shorter than the choir, caused by the construction of a **tower** on the west side, built for the archbishops' accommodation and refuge during the fifteenth or sixteenth century. Abutting the cathedral's north transept, the **Round Tower** is the Rock's earliest building, dating from the turn of the twelfth century. It's nearly 30 metres high but cannot be climbed, so you'll have to make do with the fine views of the lush countryside around the Rock from ground level.

Around the town

Situated on the far side of the Rock's car park is the **Brú Ború Cultural Centre** (mid-June to early Sept Tues–Sat 9am–11.30pm; early Sept to mid-June Mon–Fri 9am–1pm & 2–5pm; ⓣ062/61122, ⓦwww.comhaltas.com). The basement houses the entertaining **Sounds of History** multimedia exhibition (same hours; €5; Heritage Island) which races through the development of Irish cultural history, focusing particularly on St Patrick, Brian Boru, and traditional-music collectors such as Bunting and O'Neill. The centre's theatre hosts shows of traditional music, song and dance in summer (mid-June to early Sept Tues–Sat

9pm; €18, with dinner €48), staged by Comhaltas Ceoltóirí Éireann, the national organization for the promotion of Irish music.

Just downhill from the Rock's entrance, paths lead west and south. The former leads towards **Hore Abbey**, a thirteenth-century Cistercian monastery, probably built by those working on the Rock's cathedral. Set in open fields, the ruins themselves are impressive and afford an excellent, unobstructed view of the Rock. The southerly path is the **Bishop's Walk**, a shortcut back to the town centre via the gardens of the **Palace Hotel**, which was designed in 1730 by Sir Edward Lovett Pearce, architect of Dublin's House of Parliament, for the wealthy Archbishop Theophilus Bolton, who also provided for the restoration of Cormac's Chapel. Bolton was regarded as the leading contemporary ecclesiastical lawyer and was also an avid collector of books and manuscripts, bequeathing the fruits of his labours to the diocese. The collection forms part of the **Bolton Library** (mid-Jan to mid-Dec Mon–Fri 10am–2.30pm, though the actual hours can be irregular; ⓣ062/61944; €2) though the bulk of its rare maps, manuscripts and books, some dating back to the twelfth century, was acquired from William King, Archbishop of Dublin from 1702 to 1729. The library stands in the grounds of the elegant Palladian **St John's Cathedral**, the successor to the cathedral on the Rock, on John Street. Also in the town centre, it's worth looking in on the **Heritage Centre** attached to the tourist office (same hours; free), which is home to a scale model of Cashel as it looked in 1640 (accompanied by an audio commentary on the history of the town), as well as the original charters granted to the town in the seventeenth century by Charles II and James II.

Eating and drinking

For daytime fare there are a couple of fine **cafés** on Main Street: *The Bakehouse*, opposite the tourist office, is a bakery with an upstairs coffee shop serving breakfast, snacks and lunches; and *Spearman's* at no. 97 is an airy, attractive place providing a range of coffees, soups, sandwiches and cakes (closed Sun). Cashel's finest **restaurant** is *Chez Hans* (evenings only Tues–Sat; ⓣ062/61177), on Moor Lane on the way up to the Rock, in a building that was once a Wesleyan chapel. The food is exceptional, employing locally sourced meat and wild Irish fish, and prices are more manageable if you arrive in time for the early-bird menu (Tues–Fri until 7.15pm). The adjacent *Café Hans* (Tues–Sat noon–5.30pm; ⓣ062/63660) is a slimmed-down and more economically priced version of its sibling. In the atmospheric cellar of the *Cashel Palace Hotel*, the *Guinness Bar* serves up delicious salads and uncomplicated hot meals at reasonable prices until 8pm.

The town has an excellent choice of **pubs**, including *Ryan's*, a cosy, old-fashioned local with a beer garden, and the nearby *Moor Lane Tavern*, a long, slim bar with live music and/or DJs from Thursday to Saturday and traditional sessions on Tuesday and Sunday – both are behind the tourist office. *Davern's*, opposite the tourist office, is a pleasant spot offering good lunches and a **traditional-music** session (Mon & Wed), but the most atmospheric bar in town is *Dowling's*, further south down Main Street, a wonderful old place with lots of nooks and crannies and a tiny snug. Newest on the scene is *Brian Boru* opposite, a vast, stylish but unpretentious bar under the same ownership as Dublin's *Whelan's*, which hosts a traditional session on Monday and DJs and/or bands from Thursday to Sunday.

Holy Cross Abbey and Ballynahow Castle

Holy Cross Abbey (ⓦwww.holycrossabbey.ie), 14km north of Cashel on the R660 towards Thurles, has long been a focus of pilgrimage, since it held what was believed to be a fragment of the **True Cross**, thought to have been bestowed upon Murtagh O'Brien, King of Munster, in 1110 by Pope Paschal II. The abbey was founded by Cistercians in 1180, renovated during the fifteenth century, but then slumped into dilapidation until the twentieth. When Mass was celebrated in the roofless ruin in 1967 it was the first such occasion for more than two centuries. Shortly afterwards a full-scale restoration programme began and the abbey now operates as a parish church and a popular wedding location, especially for the photo opportunities in the cloister garth. The abbey's interior, with its groined ceiling and soaring arches, features glorious decorative stonework, not least in the chancel's fifteenth-century sedilia. On the transept's wall is an unusual fifteenth-century fresco depicting a hunting scene, a peculiar subject to find illustrated in a church. Behind the church stand the ruins of the abbot's house and the infirmary.

About 7km north of the abbey, **Ballynahow Castle** is a statuesque tower house dating from the sixteenth century. Inside, it is completely bare, though well preserved, with highlights including a tightly spiralling staircase and the corbelled roof of the second-floor room. If you are coming from Holy Cross, turn right at the green towards Thurles, then left opposite the Protestant church, and right in the village of Ballycahill and look out for the sign to the left. The castle stands in the centre of a farm, the owner of which will unlock the gate for you.

Nenagh and Lough Derg

The most attractive of the North Tipperary towns, **Nenagh** makes for a pleasing brief stop and is not far from **Lough Derg**'s eastern shoreline, studded with attractive villages.

Nenagh

NENAGH, 50km northwest of Cashel, is a busy market town and was once an Anglo-Norman power-base. Its only important remnant from those times is the robust, circular, five-storey **castle keep** on Summerhill, which was once part of a much larger pentagonal stronghold. The castle had a chequered history following its construction between 1200 and 1220 by Theobald fitzWalter, a cousin of Thomas à Becket, changing hands many times during its active life, and was much fought over during the war between James II and William of Orange.

West of the castle on Kickham Street is the town's **heritage centre** (May–Sept Mon–Fri 9.30am–5pm, Sat 10am–5pm; Oct–April Mon–Fri 9.30am–5pm; free; Ⓦwww.irishroots.net/ntipp.htm), occupying the imposing Governor's House of North Tipperary's former jail complex. Later it became a convent and then a National School – the latter is re-created in the centre, alongside an old-fashioned pub-grocery, featuring an antiquated telephone exchange. The basement houses agricultural artefacts while the top floor is devoted to temporary exhibitions.

Practicalities

Buses stop on Kickham Street, bang in the centre of town; the **train** station is southeast of the centre, off Kenyon Street. The **tourist office** (Mon–Sat 9.30am–1pm & 2–5.30pm; Ⓣ067/31610, Ⓦwww.tipperarylakeside.com) is on Pearse Street (the southerly continuation of Summerhill), where you can also rent **bikes**, from Moynan's (Ⓣ067/31293). Plush **accommodation** can be found at *Abbey Court Hotel*, Dublin Road (Ⓣ067/41111, Ⓦwww.abbeycourt.ie; ❺), which has its own pool, spa and gym, or, more modestly at *Williamsferry House*, on Fintan Lalor Street on the west side of the centre (Ⓣ067/31118, Ⓦwww.williamsferry.com; ❷), an 1830 townhouse providing very well-equipped en-suite rooms. *Country Choice*, 25 Kenyon St, is a very good deli and **café** that serves some wonderful soups, sandwiches, salads and hot lunches, while your best bet for dinner is the nearby wine bar and **restaurant**, *The Pepper Mill*, 27 Kenyon St (Ⓣ067/34598).

Lough Derg

Lough Derg's eastern shore sees far fewer visitors than its opposite bank in Clare (see p.391), mainly because the R493, accessed north of Nenagh off the N52 Borrisokane road, provides barely a glimpse of the water as it passes through sleepy villages and agreeable countryside. A certain amount of traffic is drawn to waterside **DROMINEER**, 10km northwest of Nenagh, terminus of the 64-kilometre **Lough Derg Way** walking trail from Limerick via Killaloe, and home to Shannon Sailing (Ⓣ067/24499, Ⓦwww.shannonsailing.com), who offer **sailing** tuition and boat hire. The other main attraction on this side of the lough is **TERRYGLASS**, which has a short signposted stroll leading to its quay and views of Portumna across the lake. The village is renowned for its two **pubs**, *Paddy's* and *The Derg Inn*, bang next-door to each other in the centre. Both serve excellent **food** and have a regular diet of **music** in the summer, including a fine traditional session at *The Derg* (Sun). A good **place to stay** nearby is *Lake Land Lodge* (Ⓣ067/22069, Ⓔlakelandlodge.eircom.net; ❷), and there are several other fine B&Bs in the area, including *Dancer Cottage*, Curraghmore (Ⓣ067/27414, Ⓦdancercottage.cjb.net; ❷), a modern Tudor-style house in a tranquil setting off the road from Ballinderry to Borrisokane, where dinner is available if booked in advance.

The lower Suir valley

Rising in the Devilsbit Mountains in the north of Tipperary, the **River Suir** runs down the length of the county before abruptly turning east in the face of the Knockmealdown Mountains. Along the way it nourishes countless dairy cattle and three significant towns along the southern border with Waterford. Of these, **Cahir** is by far the most compelling for visitors, with its mighty castle and the whimsical Swiss Cottage, though **Clonmel**, the capital of South Tipp, hosts some lively goings-on and **Carrick-on-Suir** is the site of a rare and well-preserved Elizabethan manor house. Feeding into the Suir to the west of Cahir, the luscious **Glen of Aherlow** is one of the county's prettiest spots and a fine base for exploring the scenic Galty Mountains. Tucked away on the south side of the range are the fantastic stalactites and stalagmites of **Mitchelstown Cave**, while the attractive villages of **Clogheen** and **Ardfinnan** lie to the east of here in the lee of the Knockmealdowns.

Cahir

The dominant feature of traffic-clogged **CAHIR**, 18km south of Cashel, is its **castle** (daily: mid-March to mid-June & mid-Sept to mid-Oct 9.30am–5.30pm; mid-June to mid-Sept 9am–7pm; mid-Oct to mid-March 9.30am–4.30pm; last admission 45min before closing; €2.90; Heritage Card; Ⓦ www.heritageireland.ie), surrounded by the waters of the River Suir at the western entrance to the town. *Cahir* itself means "fort" in Irish and the town grew up around its thirteenth-century Anglo-Norman stronghold, though much, including the restored outer walls, dates from more recent times. The castle was a power base of the influential Butlers, the Earls of Ormonde, and managed to survive a siege and bombardment by the Earl of Essex in 1599, as well as the invasions of Cromwell and William of Orange. However, after Cromwell's victory in 1650, the Butlers moved out and the castle fell slowly into disrepair, until it was given new life by the second Earl of Glengall, who impoverished himself in the process. The castle's entrance leads to the cramped middle ward, overshadowed by the thirteenth-century keep whose chambers feature various displays, including a model of the 1599 siege. To the left of here a gateway, surmounted by defensive viewpoints on each side, leads to the more expansive outer ward. In the inner ward, parts of the larger of the two towers derive from the thirteenth and fifteenth centuries, though the banqueting hall was redesigned by William Tinsley in 1840 for use as the Butlers' private chapel.

Cahir's other major attraction is the **Swiss Cottage** (mid-March to mid-April daily except Mon 10am–1pm & 2–6pm; mid-April to mid-Oct daily 10am–6pm; mid-Oct to mid-Nov daily except Mon 10am–1pm & 2–4.30pm; €2.90; last admission 45min before closing; Heritage Card), a twenty-minute riverside stroll south from the town or, if you're driving, off the Ardfinnan road. Designed by John Nash, architect of the Royal Pavilion at Brighton, this lavish, thatched cottage *orné* on the castle demesne was constructed in the early 1800s for Richard Butler, Baron Caher and later the first Earl of Glengall, though his precise reason remains unclear. A contemporary scurrilous theory held that it was to enjoy clandestine liaisons with his mistress, but there is evidence that it was used occasionally as a residence and for entertaining guests. Now thoroughly restored using appropriate timbers and period decor, entrance is via the basement kitchen. Entertaining **guided tours** starting from here visit the elegant salon, whose interior is decorated with one of the first commercially manufactured Parisian wallpapers, and music room, and ascend via a spiral staircase to the grand master bedroom with its commanding views of the countryside.

Practicalities

Cahir's **train station** is off Church Street, five minutes' walk northeast of the castle, while **buses** stop outside the **tourist office** (April–Sept Mon–Sat 9.30am–6pm; July & Aug also Sun 11am–5pm; Ⓣ 052/41453), which is right opposite the fortress. Just uphill from here is The Square, where Cahir Communications offers **Internet** access.

An enticing **place to stay**, 1km down the N8 Cork road, is *Carrigeen Castle* (Ⓣ 052/41370, Ⓦ www.tipp.ie/butlerca.htm; mid-Jan to mid-Dec; ❷), home to the modern-day descendants of the Butler family, which provides comfortable standard and en-suite rooms. Alternatively, head to The Square and all-en-suite *Tinsley House* (Ⓣ 052/41947, Ⓦ www.tinsleyhouse.com; ❷) or the *Cahir House Hotel* (Ⓣ 052/43000, Ⓦ www.cahirhousehotel.ie; ❺), a thoroughly updated Georgian townhouse, featuring comfy, colourful rooms, a gym and spa. **Campers** should head for the *Apple Camping & Caravan Park* (Ⓣ 052/41459, Ⓦ www.theapplefarm.com; May–Sept) at Moorstown, 6km east of Cahir on the main N24 road towards Clonmel.

River House, a bright, attractive **café** opposite the tourist office and the castle, dishes up soups, sandwiches, quiches and uncomplicated hot lunches, while the

Castle Arms next door serves pub grub during the day. In the evening, you can tuck into pizza and pasta at Galileo, a basic Italian restaurant in the old granary on Church Street (Ⓣ052/45689), then head for *Irwin's* on The Square, easily the liveliest **pub**, which sometimes has traditional music or a DJ.

Ardfinnan to Mitchelstown Cave

Nine kilometres south of Cahir lies the pretty riverside village of **ARDFINNAN**, and a further 5km south on the Newcastle road (signposted from the *Hill Bar* in the village centre) there's a staggeringly good **B&B**, *Kilmaneen Farmhouse* (Ⓣ052/36231, Ⓦwww.kilmaneen.com; ❷). It not only serves delicious breakfasts and dinners (guests-only; advance reservation necessary), but offers the perfect starting-point for walks in the surrounding countryside, which is traversed here by the Tipperary Heritage Way (see p.256). Nine kilometres southwest of Ardfinnan is **CLOGHEEN**, from where it's a short but steep trip up the Lismore road into the Knockmealdown Mountains, to the panoramic vantage point called The Vee (see p.279). Here there's a **campsite**, *Parson's Green* (Ⓣ052/65290, Ⓦwww.clogheen.com), and a couple of excellent **B&Bs**: *Ballyboy House* (Ⓣ052/65297, Ⓦwww.dirl.com/tipperary/cahir/ballyboyhouse.htm; ❷), a gorgeous country house, just south of the village; and *The Old Convent* on the Vee road (Ⓣ052/65565, Ⓦwww.theoldconvent.ie; ❺), an elegantly converted nunnery that styles itself a "gourmet hideaway", offering much-fêted, eight-course tasting menus in its **restaurant** (€58; Thurs–Sun evenings).

At **Ballyporeen**, 7km west, where **Ronald Reagan** came in 1984 to visit his great-grandfather's home village, follow the signs up the northern route from the central crossroads and you'll eventually arrive at **Mitchelstown Cave** (April–Sept daily 10am–6pm; winter hours variable – call Ⓣ052/67246; €4.50); alternatively, it's easily accessed via the N8 west of Cahir. The convoluted system of grottos, stretching some 3km underground, was discovered in 1833. Guided half-hour tours convey visitors through only a small section of the cavities, but these reveal some stunning calcite formations, produced by the

▲ Mitchelstown Cave

constant dripping of water on limestone over several eons. One is known as "The Pillars of Hercules", another shaped like an eagle's wing and there is also the frankly weird nine-metre high "Tower of Babel". To the northeast of here, 2km beyond the N8, is the basic, alpine-style An Óige **hostel**, *Mountain Lodge* (ⓣ052/67277; dorms €15; April–Sept), a fine starting-point for walks in the Galty Mountains.

The Glen of Aherlow

To Cahir's northwest lies the lush and resplendent **Glen of Aherlow,** spreading some 18km from **Bansha** in the east to **Galbally** in the west, just across the border in County Limerick. Lying beneath the northern facade of the Galty Mountains, the glen is a marvellous place to drive or cycle around and the scenic circular route is well worth taking. The best vantage point for spectacular views is by the entrance to the Glen of Aherlow Nature Park, 1.5km north of the junction of the R663 and R664. From here on the wooded ridge of Slievenamuck, the glen lies spread out below, light reflecting from the river, and the mountains looming beyond. A one-hour **walking** trail is laid out in the nature park, while the signposted **Ballyhoura Way** runs through the Glen to Galbally, on its eighty-kilometre journey from the train station at Limerick Junction via the Ballyhoura Mountains to St John's Bridge in north Cork.

Nearly all the Glen's amenities are near the junction, including the *Coach Road* **pub** and several **places to stay**. A former hunting lodge, *Aherlow House Hotel* (ⓣ062/56153, ⓦwww.aherlowhouse.ie; ❺) has bright spacious rooms, its own restaurant and a bar serving meals. *Ballinacourty House* (ⓣ062/56000, ⓦwww.ballinacourtyhse.com; ❷) occupies converted eighteenth-century stables and its haylofts house pleasant rooms overlooking a cobbled courtyard; there's also a reasonably inexpensive restaurant here (closed Mon–Sat lunchtime), as well as a **campsite** (ⓣ062/56559, ⓦwww.camping.ie; May–late Sept) in the grounds. There's a small **tourist information point** at the back of the *Coach Road* pub (Mon–Fri 9.30am–5pm, plus Sat 10am–4pm in summer; ⓣ062/56331, ⓦwww.aherlow.com), providing details of local walks and activities.

Clonmel

CLONMEL (ⓦwww.clonmel.ie), 16km east of Cahir, is easily Tipperary's liveliest town. Important in medieval times as a trading centre, today it supports brewing and pharmaceuticals industries. It's also known as the birthplace of **Laurence Sterne**, author of the comic masterpiece *Tristram Shandy*, in 1713. Later, it became the hub of a revolutionary communications system, founded by an immigrant from Lombardy, **Carlo Bianconi**. His horse-drawn coaches, or Bians as they became known, traversed the country from the company's headquarters on Parnell Street, and Carlo himself was twice appointed mayor of the town.

At the eastern end of central O'Connell Street stands the Neoclassical **Main Guard** (mid-March to Oct daily 9.30am–6pm; free; ⓦwww.heritageireland.ie), constructed around 1675 by the first Duke of Ormonde as the courthouse for Tipperary. From around 1715 until 1810 it was used as the market house, its arched loggia converted into shops. The building has been restored to its former glory, its sandstone arcade open to view once again. Inside are displays recounting its history and a small hall that occasionally hosts events.

Outside the library, at the top of Emmet Street (which runs off Mitchell Street, the easterly continuation of O'Connell Street), stands a statue commemorating one of Clonmel's most famous sons, the tenor Frank Patterson; more about him and the town's past can be uncovered at the **South Tipperary County Museum** in Mick Delahunty Square (Tues–Sat 10am–5pm; free; ⓣ052/34551, ⓦwww.southtippcoco.ie). It's also worth checking out the **South Tipperary Arts Centre**, east of the Main Guard on Nelson Street (ⓣ052/27877, ⓦwww.southtipparts.com), which hosts some interesting temporary exhibitions of visual arts.

Practicalities

The **train** and **bus stations** are fifteen minutes' walk north of the town centre off the road to Fethard and the N24 bypass; heading due south eventually leads down central Gladstone Street to the Main Guard. Clonmel's **tourist office** (Mon–Fri 9.30am–1pm & 2–4.30pm; ⓣ052/22960) is one block west of here, in the thirteenth-century tower house of St Mary's Church on Mary Street. **Internet** access is provided by *Circles* on Market Street, which runs east off Gladstone Street.

Hotel accommodation is available at *Fennessy's*, Gladstone Street (ⓣ052/23680, ⓦwww.fennessyshotel.com; ❷), offering revamped accommodation and old-fashioned charm, in a Georgian building above a pub; and at the luxurious, modern *Clonmel Park Hotel* off the N24 bypass at the western edge of town (ⓣ052/88700, ⓦwww.clonmelparkhotel.com; ❺), which encompasses a twenty-metre pool, leisure centre and spa. There are plenty of **B&Bs**, including the spacious *Ashbourne*, Mountain Road (ⓣ052/22307, ⓔashbourne@iol.ie; ❷), with fine rooms overlooking the river from its south bank. *Befani's*, just south of the Main Guard at 6 Sarsfield St (ⓣ052/77893, ⓦwww.befani.com; ❸), has smart, well-equipped rooms above a cheery restaurant, which serves a variety of Mediterranean **food**, including good-value tapas. For creative, mostly organic lunches and snacks head to *Angela's*, behind the Main Guard on Abbey Street (closed Sun). *Mulcahy's*, 47 Gladstone St, serves very popular bar food, while, around the corner, *Tom Skinny's* on Market Street provides good-value pizzas.

Among Clonmel's plentiful **pubs**, *Lonergan's*, O'Connell Street, has traditional music on Mondays, the aforementioned *Mulcahy's* on Wednesdays. Sports fans should head to *Gerry Chawke's*, Upper Gladstone Street, a traditional bar with a host of Gaelic-games memorabilia. Clonmel's nine-day **Junction Festival** (ⓦwww.junctionfestival.com) in early July features an innovative programme of theatre, dance, music and street entertainment, while National Hunt **horse racing** takes place at Powerstown Park on the northeast side of town a dozen times a year (ⓣ052/22611, ⓦwww.clonmelraces.ie).

Carrick-on-Suir

Close to the Waterford border lies the busy market town of **CARRICK-ON-SUIR**. Its main point of interest is multi-gabled **Ormond Castle** (guided tours mid-June to early Sept daily 10am–6pm; last admission 45min before closing; phone ⓣ056/772 4623 about winter opening; €2.90; Heritage Card; ⓦwww.heritageireland.ie), Ireland's only surviving Elizabethan manor house, which is situated at the far eastern end of Castle Street, a continuation of Main Street. Erected in the 1560s by Thomas ("Black Tom") Butler, tenth Earl of Ormonde, for an (unrealized) visit by his cousin, Elizabeth I, the house contains numerous tributes to her, most notably in the elaborate series of panels in the long gallery. Also displayed is a fine collection of royal charters, including one of 1661 granting the title Duke of Ormonde to Tom's descendant James.

In a musty converted church just off the north side of Main Street is the local **Heritage Centre** (April–Sept Mon–Thurs 10am–1pm & 2–4pm, Fri 10am–2.30pm; Oct–March Tues–Thurs 10am–1pm & 2–4pm, Fri 10am–2.30pm; €3). Exhibits include plenty of historical photographs, oddities such as the former tannery's hooter, and celebrations of local heroes: the champion cyclist Seán Kelly and the hugely influential Clancy Brothers who, in cahoots with Tommy Makem, were at the forefront of the 1960s folk revival (see p.714).

Practicalities

The **train station** is behind the town park on the northeast side of the centre, while **buses** stop outside the park, on Pill Road. The **tourist office** is in the Heritage Centre (same hours; ⓣ051/640200). The *Carraig, a* newly refurbished **hotel** on Main Street (ⓣ051/641455, ⓦwww.carraighotel.com; ❸), is the focal point of the town's hospitality, offering well-appointed rooms and fine **meals** in the bar and restaurant. For **B&B** head to *Fatima House*, John Street (ⓣ051/640298, ⓦwww.fatimahouse.com; ❷), which has pleasant en-suite rooms.

County Waterford

The attractions of **County Waterford** (Port Láirge, or the Déise) are integrally linked to the first part of its name, whether in its alluring **river valleys**, lengthy southern **shoreline**, or in **Waterford city** itself, which derived much of its prosperity from its strategic riverside setting. Nowadays a flourishing modern conurbation, with a lively nightlife and arts scene, the city houses almost half of the county's population and one of Ireland's finest museums, **Waterford Treasures**. Waterford's coastline takes in numerous **sandy beaches**, not least at **Dunmore East**, and great vantage points for panoramic views, as well as the blossoming town of **Dungarvan**, set around a gorgeous natural harbour. There are still tiny areas where old traditions survive, especially in coastal **Ring**, Ireland's smallest coastal Gaeltacht, while further west along the shoreline **Ardmore** contains enthralling relics associated with St Declan.

Though much of the county's hinterland consists of characterless farmland, there are numerous attractions towards its northern extremity. From the ancient ecclesiastical centre of **Lismore**, in the heart of the gorgeous **Blackwater** valley, the exhilarating **Knockmealdown Mountains** are readily accessible, while in the county's far northeast lies the **Comeragh** range and the pretty **Nire** valley.

Most of the county's major sights can be easily reached – public **transport** is generally pretty good here – and well-kept roads make **cycling** relatively leisurely, though there are some particularly steep inclines in the north. Note that, on the east side of the county, the most southerly road crossing of the River Barrow is up at New Ross in County Wexford – if you're driving or cycling between Waterford and Wexford, it's worth considering the **ferry** between **Passage East**, 12km east of Waterford city, and Ballyhack (see p.245).

Waterford city

In many ways **WATERFORD** (Ⓦwww.waterfordtourism.com) is Ireland's least discovered city, often bypassed by tourists heading from Rosslare for the more hyped destinations of Cork and Kerry further west. Even the hardiest defender of this dockland city's reputation would be hard-pressed to mount a campaign centred upon Waterford's immediate allures. Though neat wooded hillsides figure north of Rice Bridge, the vista mainly encompasses ugly industrial development, with cranes and a refinery dominating the skyline and unappealing quays offering barely a hint of the vibrant city lying behind.

But Waterford is one of those places where scraping the surface reveals numerous delights. Behind those ugly quays lies a complex of narrow lanes, first formed in medieval times, and many grand examples of Georgian town planning in the shape of sturdy townhouses and elegant municipal and ecclesiastical buildings. There's a lively nightlife here too, with plenty of enjoyable bars, as well as decent cafés and restaurants.

Some history

Waterford's origins are integrally linked to the River Suir. The **Vikings** built a settlement here in the early tenth century to provide shelter for their longboats and exploit trading opportunities offered by the river's confluence with the Barrow – and further upstream the Nore – providing easy access to the south-east's fertile farmland. The Viking settlement prospered and controlled much of this part of Ireland, exacting a tribute from the Celts called Airgead Sróine (Nose Money) since the punishment for welshers was to have their noses cut off.

Later, the course of both local and national history was much impacted by Strongbow's assault on the city in 1170, caused by **Dermot MacMurrough**'s attempts to gain sway over Ireland (see p.692). The success of the Anglo-Norman earl's bloody offensive not only led to his marriage to MacMurrough's daughter but brought his liege lord, **Henry II**, scurrying to Ireland the following year to assume control of the country's conquest. Henry granted a charter providing royal protection to the city and his descendant, King John, increased its size by adding new walls and towers – well-preserved examples of the latter can be seen at Castle Street and Jenkins Lane.

Though much affected by the Black Death and frequent incursions by both Irish and Anglo-Norman neighbours, Waterford continued to flourish as a **port**, reliant on trade in wool, hides and wine. Though Cromwell was repelled in 1649, a year later Ireton's troops took control and expelled many of the Catholic merchants. Protestant domination of the city's trade was reinforced by William of Orange's accession. The eighteenth century witnessed major architectural developments, mostly designed by locally born John Roberts. Shipbuilding prospered during the nineteenth century, the city becoming second only to Belfast in terms of tonnage constructed, and many Waterford-built vessels transported the city's famous **crystal**, first manufactured here in 1783. Though the plant closed in 1851, it reopened a century later and remains to this day a major local employer. Waterford suffered economically during the second half of the twentieth century, witnessing factory closures and the virtual end of shipbuilding here. However, Ireland's economic boom in the 1990s began the revival process.

Arrival and information

The **train station** (Ⓣ051/317899), which has left-luggage facilities, is just north of the river on Dock Road; Bus Éireann services use the **bus station**

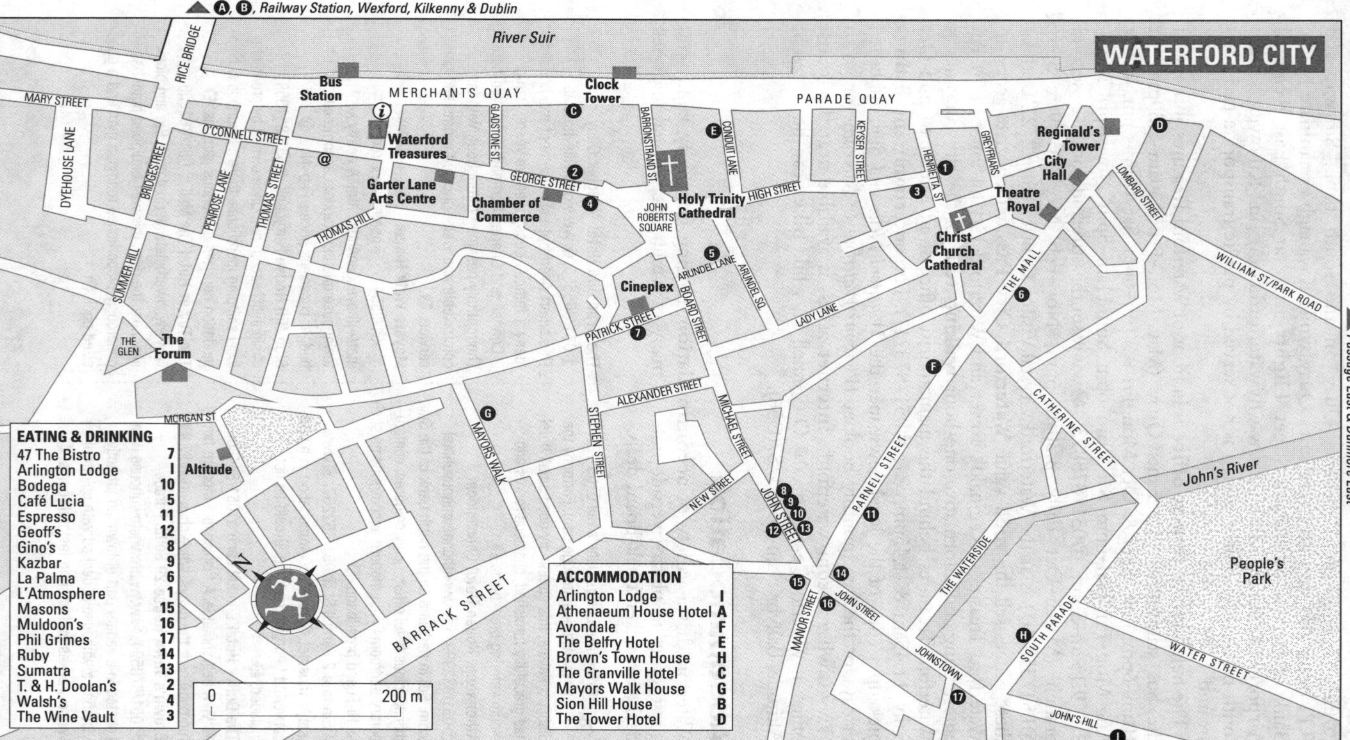
WATERFORD CITY
A, B, Railway Station, Wexford, Kilkenny & Dublin
Passage East & Dunmore East
Waterford Crystal & Cork
Waterford Airport
River Suir
RICE BRIDGE
MERCHANTS QUAY
PARADE QUAY
Bus Station
Clock Tower
Waterford Treasures
Garter Lane Arts Centre
Chamber of Commerce
Holy Trinity Cathedral
Christ Church Cathedral
Reginald's Tower
City Hall
Theatre Royal
Cineplex
The Forum
THE GLEN
Altitude
People's Park
John's River
MARY STREET
DYEHOUSE LANE
BRIDGESTREET
PENROSE LANE
THOMAS STREET
O'CONNELL STREET
SUMMER HILL
THOMAS HILL
GLADSTONE ST.
GEORGE STREET
BARRONSTRAND ST.
JOHN ROBERTS SQUARE
CONDUIT LANE
HIGH STREET
KEYSER STREET
HENRIETTA ST
GREYFRIARS
LOMBARD STREET
WILLIAM ST/PARK ROAD
THE MALL
ARUNDEL LANE
ARUNDEL SQ.
LADY LANE
BOARD STREET
PATRICK STREET
ALEXANDER STREET
MICHAEL STREET
STEPHEN STREET
MAYORS WALK
MCRGAN ST
NEW STREET
JOHN STREET
PARNELL STREET
CATHERINE STREET
THE WATERSIDE
SOUTH PARADE
WATER STREET
MANOR STREET
JOHNSTOWN
JOHN'S HILL
BARRACK STREET
N
0 200 m
EATING & DRINKING
47 The Bistro 7
Arlington Lodge I
Bodega 10
Café Lucia 5
Espresso 11
Geoff's 12
Gino's 8
Kazbar 9
La Palma 6
L'Atmosphere 1
Masons 15
Muldoon's 16
Phil Grimes 17
Ruby 14
Sumatra 13
T. & H. Doolan's 2
Walsh's 4
The Wine Vault 3
ACCOMMODATION
Arlington Lodge I
Athenaeum House Hotel A
Avondale F
The Belfry Hotel E
Brown's Town House H
The Granville Hotel C
Mayors Walk House G
Sion Hill House B
The Tower Hotel D

(Ⓣ051/879000) on Merchants Quay on the south bank. Suirway and RTI buses also stop on Merchant's Quay, while Kavanagh's terminate by the Bank of Ireland on Parnell Street. **Flights** arrive at South East Regional Airport (Ⓣ051/875589, Ⓦwww.flywaterford.com) in Killowen, 10km south of the city centre, which is not served by public transport; a taxi costs around €25.

The helpful main **tourist office** is in front of Waterford Treasures, just east of the bus station on Merchants Quay (May Mon–Fri 9.30am–5.30pm, Sat 10am–6pm; June, Sept & Oct Mon–Fri 9.30am–6pm, Sat 10am–6pm; July & Aug Mon–Fri 9am–6pm, Sat 10am–6pm, Sun 11am–5pm; Nov–April Mon–Sat 9.15am–5pm; Ⓣ051/875823, Ⓦwww.southeastireland.com); a second branch (March–Oct daily 8.30am–6pm, Nov–Feb Mon–Fri 9am–5pm; Ⓣ051/358397) is at the Waterford Crystal Visitor Centre (see p.272). Both of these offices sell the good-value **Waterford City Pass**, which gives access to Waterford Treasures, Reginald's Tower and Waterford Crystal for €11.70. An entertaining and informative one-hour **walking tour** of the city convenes at Waterford Treasures behind the main tourist office (mid-March to mid-Oct daily 11.45am & 1.45pm; €7; Ⓣ051/873711). For **entertainment listings** pick up a copy of the local newspaper, the *Waterford News and Star*, published Fridays, or the free monthly booklet *Whazon? Waterford & Kilkenny* (or go to Ⓦwww.whazon.com/waterford). **Internet** access is available near the tourist office at Waterford e-Centre, 10 O'Connell St, while **bikes** can be rented at Altitude, Ballybricken (Ⓣ051/870356).

Accommodation

Waterford has a variety of **accommodation**, ranging from cosy, family-run guesthouses to plush riverside hotels – many of which offer special midweek deals or weekend half-board deals.

Arlington Lodge John's Hill Ⓣ051/878584, Ⓦwww.arlingtonlodge.com. Formerly the Bishop's Palace, this stunningly good small hotel has gracefully furnished, spacious rooms and mouthwatering breakfasts. ❺

Athenaeum House Hotel Christendom Ⓣ051/833999, Ⓦwww.athenaeumhousehotel.com. Set in parkland on the north bank of the Suir, this spacious hotel offers richly coloured, contemporary bedrooms with modern accoutrements such as Hi-Fi and broadband. ❺

Avondale 2 Parnell St Ⓣ051/852267, Ⓦwww.staywithus.net. Spruce accommodation in a well-converted Georgian building. Breakfast not included. ❷

The Belfry Hotel Conduit Lane Ⓣ051/844800, Ⓦwww.belfryhotel.ie. A fashionable modern family-run hotel near the quays. Wheelchair-friendly. ❹

Brown's Town House 29 South Parade Ⓣ051/870594, Ⓦwww.brownstownhouse.com. Located in a sedate part of town, an attractive Victorian townhouse bedecked with colourful window boxes and offering tasteful rooms. ❹

The Granville Hotel Meagher Quay Ⓣ051/305555, Ⓦwww.granville-hotel.ie. This smart riverfront establishment has housed many a famous guest over the years; Daniel O'Connell and Charles Parnell both stayed here. Thoughtfully designed throughout, with large, comfortable and well-equipped rooms and good service. ❹

Mayors Walk House 12 Mayors Walk Ⓣ051/855427, Ⓦhomepage.eircom.net/~jfhovenden/index.htm. A neatly kept townhouse offering standard accommodation at budget-conscious prices. Feb–Nov. ❶

Sion Hill House Ferrybank Ⓣ051/851558, Ⓔsionhill@eircom.net. Once owned by prominent local shipping merchants, there's luxurious accommodation here, set in glorious gardens. ❸

The Tower Hotel The Mall Ⓣ051/862300, Ⓦwww.towerhotelwaterford.com. Big and block-like, near the river, this well-equipped hotel has generously proportioned rooms, a gym and a good-sized pool. ❺

The City

Waterford's core, and the source of much of its past wealth, is the River Suir and your first glimpse of the city will inevitably be of its quays, busy with traffic and highly industrial. The streets behind, though, bear many of the hallmarks of the Georgian era, with trim thoroughfares and stately dwellings, though, truth be told, many of the latter have seen finer days.

The city possesses an outstanding museum in the shape of **Waterford Treasures** on Merchants Quay, which houses an abundance of relics, dating right back to the Viking period. Two hundred metres east of here, opposite the clock tower, Barronstrand Street leads south to the main shopping streets, passing Holy Trinity Cathedral, and thence, via a couple of name changes, to John Street, whose bars, pubs and cafés form the nightlife focus. To the clock tower's east is the stirring and historic **Reginald's Tower**, south of which is a complex of tiny, sometimes tortuous lanes, which shelter some fine buildings including **Christ Church Cathedral**. The products of the internationally renowned glass factory, **Waterford Crystal**, a couple of kilometres from the centre, continue to embody those bygone times.

Waterford Treasures

In a stylishly renovated granary behind the tourist office on Merchants Quay lies one of Ireland's most entrancing museums, the stunning **Waterford Treasures** (April–Sept daily 9am–6pm; Oct–March Mon–Fri 10am–5pm, Sat & Sun 11am–5pm; €7; Ⓦ www.waterfordtreasures.com). Impressively designed and employing a diverse range of display techniques, the museum brings the city's history into focus, often with a telling sense of humour. The collection is organized chronologically and begins with the third-floor **Viking** galleries. These exhibit an extraordinary array of artefacts from the tenth to twelfth centuries, including a meticulously carved bird-bone flute, a gaming board and pieces, intricate jewellery and a perfectly rounded alder *hanap*, or drinking goblet. The **Anglo-Norman** era is also well represented, with a finely-worked gold stirrup-ring set with a sapphire, illuminated charters, an entire medieval

▲ Waterford Crystal

bow – the only surviving example in Ireland – and the Edward IV sword, a mighty piece of silver weaponry presented to the Mayor of Waterford in 1462.

The second-floor galleries include a superb collection of royal charters from Tudor and Stuart times before moving on to **Georgian** Waterford; here the Monstrance Throne made for a local dignitary in 1729 features dazzling silverwork, resembling a small fireplace topped by a huge crown. Displays also trace the career of the architect **John Roberts**, designer of many of the city's finest Georgian buildings. The last section on this floor vividly focuses on Waterford's strong links through emigration with Newfoundland in Canada, while the first floor hosts interesting history and art exhibitions.

The cathedrals

To the east of Waterford Treasures, Roberts was responsible for the many-windowed **Chamber of Commerce** on George Street, but his prime ecclesiastical design is **Holy Trinity Cathedral** (free) on Barronstrand Street. This dates from 1793, but was much revised in the following century, resulting in today's flamboyant building. Its heavily ornate interior features a Baroque pulpit dwarfed by a soaring baldachin, all set beneath an impressively high-vaulted ceiling.

East up the High Street will bring you to Roberts' other major creation, the Church of Ireland **Christ Church Cathedral** (April–Nov Mon–Fri 10am–6pm, Sat 10am–4pm, Sun noon–4pm; €4; Ⓦwww.christchurchwaterford.com), which took almost a quarter of a century to complete once work began in 1773. This stately, Neoclassical edifice stands on the site of a previous medieval church, utilizing the base of the previous building. It features an ornate stuccowork ceiling and a fine window, added much later, by the stained-glass artist A.E. Child, as well as the somewhat grisly tomb of James Rice, a fifteenth-century mayor of Waterford, which graphically depicts a decaying corpse fed upon by worms and a toad. Just up from here on the Mall is another Roberts design, the squat **City Hall**.

Reginald's Tower

Waterford's city walls were once punctuated by seventeen towers, of which six still survive. By far the most impressive of these is **Reginald's Tower** (Easter–May & Oct daily 10am–5pm; June–Sept daily 10am–6pm; Nov–Easter Wed–Sun 10am–5pm; €2.10; Heritage Card; Ⓦwww.heritageireland.ie), a short step up from City Hall towards the river. Dating from the late twelfth century, this bulky three-storey tower was put to many uses, including hosting the wedding of Strongbow and Dermot MacMurrough's daughter. For a time it was a mint – there's a display on the coinage produced here – later becoming an arsenal before being used as a jail from around 1819. Various displays and a short video document the tower's story and its place in Waterford's history.

Waterford Crystal

Waterford's famed crystal seems to be on sale everywhere in the city, and the **crystal factory**, a couple of kilometres down the N25 towards Cork, runs a **visitor centre** providing guided tours of the production process (March–Oct daily 8.30am–4pm, Nov–Feb Mon–Fri 9am–3.15pm; €9; Heritage Island; Ⓦwww.waterfordvisitorcentre.com). These cover the whole manufacturing shebang, from design to the intricate art of glassblowing, and display some glorious examples of the finished product – all, of course, aimed at tempting you to splash out on one of the finished works. From Monday to Saturday, city **bus** #3C from opposite the clock tower on the quays traces a circular route that includes the crystal factory.

Eating and drinking

The city has plenty of good places to **eat**, from lively cafés to upmarket restaurants, and several of the pubs serve decent bar meals – try *T. & H. Doolan's* or *Geoff's* (see below). Waterford also has many lively **bars** and several of the options on John Street and its continuation, Michael Street, including *The Wacky Apple*, feature **live music**, usually by up-and-coming local indie bands. With a few exceptions, the city is not a good place to catch traditional music, however.

Cafés and restaurants

47 The Bistro Patrick St ⓣ051/844774. This welcoming, contemporary restaurant is justly popular for its excellent, inexpensive, carefully presented offerings, which include pasta, salads, sandwiches and a few traditional dishes such as bacon and cabbage and Irish stew and dumplings.

Arlington Lodge John's Hill ⓣ051/878584. The hotel's restaurant serves a range of classic dishes in a classy setting, featuring plenty of seafood and delicious desserts.

Bodega 54 John St ⓣ051/844177. An attractive, informal setting for some inspired dishes such as fillet of hake with roast red-pepper purée; occasional live music in the evening.

Café Lucia Arundel Lane. A great daytime place for salads, panini, cakes and lunchtime specials such as Thai fishcakes. Closed Sun.

Gino's John St. Bright, neat branch of the long-running Cork institution, a no-frills restaurant dishing up pizzas, salads, wine, beer and ice cream.

La Palma 20 The Mall ⓣ051/879823. In a converted Georgian townhouse with an appealing atmosphere, an upmarket Italian restaurant offering imaginative, sometimes over-elaborate, dishes and heart-stopping desserts. Good-value set menu Mon–Thurs evenings and an early-bird menu Mon–Fri. Closed Mon–Thurs lunchtimes & Sun. Under the same management is *Espresso @ La Palma*, just down the road on Parnell St, which does pizza and pasta.

L'Atmosphere 19 Henrietta St ⓣ051/858426. Authentic, informal bistro with a growing reputation for its unfussy, classic French dishes such as cassoulet of duck confit and Toulouse sausage at reasonable prices. Range of good-value set menus including a Mon–Fri early bird. Closed Sat & Sun lunchtimes.

Sumatra 53 John St. Restful, brightly coloured and welcoming café-restaurant that dishes up very tasty sandwiches, salads, cakes and a few main dishes during the day, and hearty, global-influenced meals such as lasagne and Moroccan lamb casserole in the evening. Mon–Thurs 8.30am–7pm, Fri & Sat 8.30am–11pm, Sun 11am–9pm.

The Wine Vault High St ⓣ051/853444. Classy bistro offering an extensive menu – everything from oysters to Thai-spiced duck confit – with plenty of vegetarian options and good-value lunch and early-bird (Mon–Fri) menus. Closed Sun.

Pubs and bars

Geoff's 8–9 John St. Lots of dark and cosy corners in this characterful traditional bar which also serves excellent lunches and displays plenty of posters for local events.

Kazbar 57 John St. Louche, vaguely Egyptian decor and several tables outside for watching the world pass by at this busy café-bar, which hosts a traditional session on Thurs, live bands on Sat.

Masons Manor St. A popular and lush split-level DJ bar in a converted warehouse, whose interior features bizarre statues and rose-tinted lighting.

Muldoon's Manor St/John St. A big, bold and brassy pub with a popular club, *Oxygen*, upstairs, playing chart and R'n'B Wed–Sat.

Phil Grimes 61 Johnstown. Friendly, old-style bar with a small beer garden; traditional session Wed and singer-songwriters' open-mike night Thurs.

Ruby John St/Parnell St. Another well-populated DJ bar with a swish lounge kitted out with striking modernist paintings. Live bands Thurs–Sun.

T. & H. Doolan's 31–32 George's St. Fabulous old bar which puts on folk music and ballad singers most nights in summer and serves traditional food such as Irish stew in the evenings.

Walsh's 11 George's St. An antique bar-cum-off-licence with a grand display of whiskeys and wines in its shop window.

Entertainment and festivals

Waterford has a good selection of arts venues, and festivals occur throughout the year. **The Forum** (ⓣ051/871111, ⓦwww.forumwaterford.com) on The Glen is a lively theatre hosting a variety of gigs and comedy as well as a popular club night on Saturdays. On O'Connell Street, the **Garter Lane Arts Centre** (ⓣ051/855038, ⓦwww.garterlane.ie) exhibits artworks, shows independent films and has performances of music, comedy, dance and theatre, the latter most notably provided by the city's Red Kettle Theatre Company (ⓦwww.come.to/redkettle). A more mainstream venue for drama is the **Theatre Royal** on The Mall (ⓣ051/874402, ⓦwww.theatreroyalwaterford.com), which is also the location for the renowned late-September **Light Opera Festival** (ⓦwww.waterfordfestival.com), which features amateur operatic societies from around the world and has its own more widely arts-based Fringe Festival (ⓦwww.waterfordfringefestival.com). **Christ Church Cathedral** plays host to frequent classical-music concerts, featuring especially choirs and organ soloists (bookings through the Theatre Royal). The Cineplex **cinema** (ⓣ0818 221122) is on Patrick Street.

Other **festivals** include Spraoi (ⓦwww.spraoi.com), held over the August bank-holiday weekend, which features plenty of music and street performances and culminates in a massive parade, and the Waterford Arts Festival (ⓦwww.waterfordartsfestival.com), occupying a week in late October or early November.

Waterford's coast

Waterford's coastline lacks the wildness of the shoreline further east, but there are still glorious, enticing beaches – especially at **Dunmore East**, **Stradbally** and **Ardmore** – and plenty of balmy cliff-top walks, not least at Ardmore, which is also a major ecclesiastical site. **Dungarvan**'s highlight is its broad and splendid bay, while the county's only *Gaeltacht*, **Ring**, is renowned for its traditional music. A novel way to experience this coastline is to hook up with Sea Paddling (ⓣ051/393314, ⓦwwwseapaddling.com), who offer a variety of **sea-kayaking** courses and trips, exploring the area's sea caves, islands and coves, as well as the River Barrow and the Saltee Islands (see p.245).

Dunmore East

Appealing **DUNMORE EAST** (ⓦwww.waterford-dunmore.com), 16km southeast of Waterford, is very much a place of contrasts and something of a retreat for the city's wealthier denizens. The village is actually split in two, with the eastern part set neatly around a small sandy beach backed by sandstone cliffs, while the much busier western half is built above and around a lively fishing harbour and marina. Down by the harbour Dunmore East Adventure Centre (ⓣ051/383783, ⓦwww.dunmoreadventure.com) offers kayaking, canoeing, windsurfing and sailing as well as land-based **activities** such as climbing and orienteering. In late August, the village comes to life for the four-day **International Bluegrass Festival**.

Life in the east village is focused around the popular *Strand Inn* (ⓣ051/383174, ⓦwww.thestrandinn.com), offering plentiful outdoor tables overlooking the beach, bar meals and excellent seafood in its restaurant, as well as tasteful **accommodation** (❸). There are also excellently kept rooms opposite at the very smart, modern *Beach Guest House* (ⓣ051/383316, ⓦwww.dunmorebeachguesthouse.com; March–Oct; ❷), while uphill in the western quarter is *The Haven Hotel* (ⓣ051/383150, ⓦwww.thehavenhotel.com; ❹), set in extensive grounds. Alternatives include the very comfy rooms at *Springfield* in the east village (ⓣ051/383448, ⓦwww.springfield-dunmore.com; April–Oct; ❷). Your best bets for **eating** are the *Strand Inn* and the inexpensive daytime *Bay Café* above the harbour, which features plenty of seafood in its sandwiches, main courses and chowder, as well as tasty home-made pâté.

Tramore

Sixteen kilometres west of Dunmore East, **TRAMORE** ("big beach") certainly lives up to its name, though unfortunately the town is surrounded by ghastly housing developments and the strand itself is marred by adjacent amusement arcades, caravan parks and fast-food outlets. It's really only worth visiting if you want to indulge a special interest: **surfers** should get in touch with Surf T-bay (Ⓣ051/391297, Ⓦwww.surftbay.com), who offer courses and equipment rental; equine fanciers might be tempted by the regular **horse racing** (Ⓣ051/381425, Ⓦwww.tramore-racecourse.com); and the rejuvenated gardens at nearby **Tramore House** (May–Sept daily 10am–9pm; Oct–April Mon–Fri 10am–4pm; free) will entice anyone keen on blooms. Surfers might want to bunk down at *Beach Haven Hostel* (Ⓣ051/390208, Ⓦwww.beachhavenhouse.com; dorms €15–20, private rooms ❶), but otherwise there's no reason to stay here overnight.

Stradbally and Clonea Strand

West of Tramore the R675 to Dungarvan traverses verdant countryside, as it twists around the cliff-girt littoral known as the **Copper Coast** (Ⓦwww.copper-coast.com), after the rich deposits that were extensively mined in the nineteenth century. Because of the area's rich geological heritage, it's recently been designated a UNESCO Geopark (Ⓦwww.coppercoastgeopark.com), and there are plans to open up a full-service visitor centre. One of the best places to stop along this stretch is scenic **STRADBALLY**, with several fabulous beaches nearby, the choicest being the sheltered **Stradbally Cove**, a little way west of the village. *Park House* (Ⓣ051/293185, Ⓦwww.waterfordfarms.com/parkhouse; ❷; March–Oct) provides relaxing, standard and en-suite **B&B** and *The Cove* is a great old bar for a pint.

Seven kilometres further along the coast towards Dungarvan lies **Clonea Strand**, an expansive, Blue Flag sandy beach, full of day-trippers in summer. You can **camp** nearby at *Casey's Caravan and Camping Park* (Ⓣ058/41919; Easter to mid-Sept), or stay in some luxury at the *Clonea Strand Hotel* (Ⓣ058/45555, Ⓦwww.clonea.com; ❹) with a pool, gym, Turkish bath and seafood restaurant.

Dungarvan

Attractive, bustling **DUNGARVAN** (Ⓦwww.dungarvantourism.com) is splendidly situated on a large bay where the waters of the River Colligan broaden as they reach the sea. Unlike many of its fellow resorts, it remains largely unscathed by the blight of chain-store similitude. The main attraction here is **King John's Castle** (guided tours June–Sept daily 10am–6pm; free), squatting proudly at the eastern end of Davitt's Quay. Built in 1185 as an Anglo-Norman command base, it consists of a shell keep with a curtain wall. Inside are eighteenth-century barracks, occupied by the IRA during the Civil War and burnt down when they abandoned the site. Subsequently, these were restored to become the local Garda station and now contain displays on the castle's history. The nearby old Market House at the east end of Main Street contains an **arts centre** (Tues–Sat 11am–5pm; free; Ⓣ058/48944) which hosts art displays and has occasional events. Five minutes' walk west along Main Street will bring you to St Augustine

Street, where the **Waterford County Museum** (mid-May to mid-Sept Mon–Sat 10am–1pm & 2–5pm; mid-Sept to mid-May Mon–Fri 10am–1pm & 2–4.30pm; free; ⓦwww.dungarvanmuseum.org) houses exhibits on maritime and local history, as well as temporary exhibitions.

Practicalities

The town's **tourist office** is on Meagher Street by the bridge at the top of the bay (May–Oct Mon–Sat 9.30am–6pm; Nov–April Mon–Fri 9.30am–5pm; ⓣ058/41741, ⓦwww.dungarvantourism.com). *Lawlor's Hotel* opposite (ⓣ058/41122, ⓦwww.lawlorshotel.com; ❹) provides very comfortable **accommodation**, while *The Tannery*, near the Market House Arts Centre on Church Street (ⓣ058/45420, ⓦwww.tannery.ie; ❹), offers swish rooms in a townhouse setting. Out on the R672 Clonmel road, about 1km northwest of the centre, *Powersfield House* (ⓣ058/45594, ⓦwww.powersfield.com; ❸) has pretty rooms in a modern, Georgian-style house and offers excellent breakfasts, dinner for guests if arranged in advance, and cookery courses. Back in town, *The Moorings* rents out large, bright, en-suite rooms, some overlooking the harbour, above a pub (see below; ⓣ058/41461; ❷).

For **food**, *The Tannery* is an excellent restaurant serving modern European cuisine in a stylish setting, which runs an early-bird menu Tuesday–Friday; it's at 10 Quay St, just round the corner from the co-owned guesthouse of the same name (ⓣ058/45420; lunch Tues–Fri & Sun; dinner Tues–Sat plus Sun in July & Aug). With waterfront tables on Davitt's Quay, *Interlude* is a more informal spot that's justifiably popular for its global-influenced dishes and tapas (ⓣ058/45898; closed Sun evening & Mon). A couple of doors away is *The Moorings*, a lovely, old, nautical-themed **pub**, with harbourside tables and a large beer garden at the back; it serves good bar meals, as well as more sophisticated fare such as monkfish with crab claws in a white wine and dill sauce in its weekend restaurant. The town has plenty of other decent pubs too, including *The Local*, a cosy bar on central Grattan Square, with regular traditional music sessions (Thurs and sometimes Sat); and *Bridie Dee's*, south of the square on Mary Street, a dark and characterful bolthole which has sessions on Saturdays and Sundays in winter, every night in high summer. Dungarvan stages a major traditional-music festival, **Féile na nDeise** (ⓦwww.feilenandeise.com), in early May.

Ring (An Rinn)

Beginning 4km south of Dungarvan off the N25, and spreading east as far as **Helvick Head**, at the mouth of Dungarvan Harbour, and south almost down to Ardmore, is the *Gaeltacht* area known as **RING** (An Rinn in Irish). This is Waterford's only Irish-speaking area, home to about a thousand people, and one where the traditions of music and dance remain far stronger than anywhere else in the county.

Ring is a diffuse community of connected townlands with just a few facilities and not much to see, making the local **bars** the main attraction. The best of these is *Mooney's*, about 5km from the N25 along the main R674 road towards the headland, which offers simple lunches in summer and is a tremendous place for traditional music (Sat year-round, Fri–Sun in summer, plus impromptu sessions) – it's the home pub of the well-known band Danú. For **accommodation** your best bet is the very hospitable *Gortnadiha Lodge* (ⓣ058/46142, ⓦwww.waterfordfarms.com/gortnadiha; Feb–Nov; ❷), overlooking Dungarvan Bay about 2km along the R674, which offers excellent breakfasts and evening meals if pre-booked. Next to the Spar supermarket, about 7km along the R674, stands *An Linn Bhuidhe*, a daytime **café** serving basic lunches. The liveliest time of the year here is during the **Oyster Festival** in early August with plenty of shellfish and traditional music.

Ardmore

The seaside village of **ARDMORE**, 20km southwest of Dungarvan, is an enchanting place, rich in religious history and relics, mainly associated with St Declan who established a monastery here some thirty years before St Patrick came to Ireland. There's a kilometre-long sandy beach at the foot of the village, hemmed in by long, grassy headlands and flanked on its western side by **St Declan's Stone**. According to legend, the saint's luggage was miraculously transported by this boulder when he travelled from Wales (and thus presumably avoided excess-baggage charges). Heading up the hill towards the western headland leads past **St Declan's Well**, where the saint apparently conducted baptisms in the early fifth century, and where he later retired to a small cell for greater seclusion. From here there's a breezy five-kilometre **cliff walk**, with stunning views, around the headland, which will bring you back to the top of Main Street.

Above the town (and near the end of the cliff walk), on the site of Declan's original monastery, stands a solid-looking twelfth-century Romanesque **cathedral** and a willowy, conically capped **round tower**. The cathedral has lost its roof but its walls are impressively buttressed. Its west wall features an arcade from a previous building, embellished by remarkable carvings of Biblical scenes, while two carved ogham stones can be seen inside. In a corner of the graveyard is **St Declan's Oratory**, which possibly dates from the eighth century; the pit in the floor, once covered with a flagstone, is where he was supposedly buried.

Ardmore's **hotel** is the welcoming family-run *Round Tower*, College Road (Ⓣ024/94494, erth@tinet.ie; ④), offering restful en-suite rooms, a bar and restaurant in a former convent, as well as traditional-music sessions in the attractive garden on Sunday afternoons in summer. There are a few **B&Bs** scattered around the area, including *Cush* (Ⓣ024/94474, Ⓔmttroy@eircom.net; ②; April–Sept), a pleasant house overlooking the bay. *An Tobar* near the front has filling **bar food** and live-music sessions, sometimes traditional, on summer weekends. Nearby, the *Old Forge* is a spruce café-restaurant with pleasant outdoor tables, which operates in the daytime in winter, until 9pm in summer; on offer are tasty cakes, soups and unpretentious meals such as lasagne and salmon with lemon butter. Further up Main Street, *White Horses Restaurant* (Ⓣ024/94040; closed Mon all year and Oct–April Tues–Thurs) is a more sophisticated and expensive place with an interesting menu that stretches to dishes such as crispy duckling with caramelized orange and kumquat sauce. Ardmore Diving (Ⓣ058/46577, Ⓦwww.ardmorediving.com) offers **diving** trips and the basic range of PADI courses.

Northern Waterford

The northern stretch of the county, along the border with Tipperary, is studded with two modest but pretty mountain ranges, the **Comeraghs** and the **Knockmealdowns**, neither of which rises higher than 800 metres. **Ballymacarbry**, 25km north of Dungarvan on the R672, is the best jumping-off point for the Comeraghs, while historic **Lismore**, 25km west of Dungarvan in the beautiful Blackwater valley, provides easy access to the Knockmealdowns.

Ballymacarbry and the Comeragh Mountains

One of the best approaches to the bleak moorland of the Comeragh Mountains, with its smattering of bogs and heather, is along the Nire valley, which descends from beneath Knockaunapeebra (789m) on the Comeraghs' western fringe to waterside **BALLYMACARBRY**. The Comeragh Scenic Drive, signposted directly opposite *Melody's* pub, runs beside the river to tiny **Nire** where there's superb **accommodation** at *Hanora's Cottage* (Ⓣ052/36134, Ⓦwww.hanorascottage.com; ❼) with Jacuzzis in every room, a breakfast feast and splendid dinners in the **restaurant**. Both *Hanora's* and the attractively set and very comfortable *Cnoc-na-Rí* (Ⓣ052/36239, Ⓦhomepage.eircom.net/~cnocnaricountryhome; ❷), a little further around the Drive, are ideal bases for walking in the mountains. Alternatively, further on there's **camping** at *Powers the Pot*, Harney's Cross (Ⓣ052/23085, Ⓦwww.powersthepot.net; May–Sept), set some 365m up in the mountains with its own quaint, thatched-wine bar.

Lismore

Set amidst verdant countryside on the south side of the River Blackwater is the sleepy town of **LISMORE**, once a major religious centre. St Carthagh founded a thriving **monastery** here in 636 that became a great centre of learning and retained both religious and political importance for several centuries, despite periodic raids by the Vikings and later the Anglo-Normans. On the site of its medieval cathedral, wrecked by Edmund Fitzgibbon around 1600, stands the Church of Ireland **St Carthagh's Cathedral**, constructed some thirty years later – to get there head east up Main Street and turn left down North Mall. Much of its appearance derives from remodelling in the early 1800s, including the addition of its tower and spire, and it remains a charming building, set in a tree-lined cobblestone courtyard. Just inside the front door is a lovely stained-glass window by the Pre-Raphaelite Edward Burne-Jones, depicting two virtues: Justice and Humility. A Romanesque arch in the nave might possibly date from the original cathedral and leads to the imposing McGrath tomb which features carvings of the twelve Apostles, the Crucifixion and the martyr St Catherine. Stones set into the back wall, including a particularly stalwart bishop, date from the ninth to eleventh centuries.

Despite the cathedral's attractions it is the extravagant and graceful **Lismore Castle**, magnificently set above the River Blackwater, that overshadows the town. The Irish home of the Dukes of Devonshire was designed by Joseph Paxton (also responsible for the Crystal Palace for London's Great Exhibition of 1851) in the mid-nineteenth century, taking as his starting point the remains of a castle built by Prince John in 1185. Though the bulk of the castle cannot be visited, its extensive **gardens** (daily: April, May & Sept 1.45–4.45pm; June–Aug 11am–4.45pm; €7; Ⓦwww.lismorecastle.com) present numerous exterior views from different aspects. The gardens consist of woodlands and a host of magnolias, camellias and rhododendrons in season, as well as a yew-tree walk where Edmund Spenser is believed to have written *The Faerie Queen*. Modern sculptures dot the gardens, and the formerly derelict west wing of the castle has recently been transformed into a **gallery** that hosts some interesting exhibitions of contemporary art (Ⓣ058/54061, Ⓦwww.lismorearts.ie).

Lismore's fascinating history comes to life at the **Heritage Centre** on Main Street (May–Oct Mon–Fri 9.30am–5.30pm, Sat 10am–5.30pm, Sun noon–5.30pm; Nov–April Mon–Fri 9.30am–5.30pm; €4.50; Heritage Island; Ⓦwww.discoverlismore.com) whose galleries recount the stories of some of the town's famous figures, including the chemist Robert Boyle who was born in the castle in 1627; and there's a short and entertaining audiovisual, *The Lismore Experience*.

Practicalities

The **tourist office** is in the Heritage Centre (same hours; ⓣ058/54975) and can provide information about Immrama, a **festival** of travel writing in mid-June (or go to ⓦwww.lismoreimmrama.com). Pleasant B&B **accommodation** is available at two modern houses set in large attractive gardens: *Beechcroft*, Deerpark Road (ⓣ058/54273, ⓦwww.beechcroftbandb.ie; April–Oct; ❷), and *Pine Tree House*, Ballyanchor (ⓣ058/52382, ⓦwww.pinetreehouselismore.com; ❷), at opposite ends of the town and both well signposted from the centre. North of town is the swish and spacious *Ballyrafter House Hotel* (ⓣ058/54002, ⓦwww.waterfordhotel.com; ❺), built by the Duke of Devonshire in the early 1800s.

For **food**, your best bet is *Foley's on the Mall*, a tastefully updated pub towards the east end of Main Street, which serves a wide range of tasty, popular meals, as well as sandwiches and soups. An appealing alternative for lunch (Tues–Sat) is *Summerhouse* next door, a smart gift shop and café that also opens for tea and cakes on Sundays. For **traditional music** there's *The Classroom* bar (Thurs), also on Main Street.

The Knockmealdown Mountains

North from Lismore the R668 to Cahir undulates upwards through a lovely river valley, garnished with a mass of woody greenery, before heading into the mountains. To the east, after 10km, rises **Knockmealdown** itself (793m), whose name translates aptly as "bare brown mountain", while a little further up the road lies the spectacular viewpoint known as **The Vee** where precipitous slopes offer a chevron-shaped scene of the fields of Tipperary laid out far below, a panoply of greens, browns and yellows. Named after the road's prominent hairpin bend here, this popular beauty spot is especially famous for its magnificent display of rhododendrons, which flower in late May and early June. From here it's a downhill ride to the village of Clogheen (see p.264). The **Tipperary Heritage Way** (see p.256) north to Cashel begins here at The Vee, while the seventy-kilometre **East Munster Way** starts down at Clogheen and heads east from The Vee to Carrick-on-Suir, via Clonmel and the northern foothills of the Knockmealdowns and the Comeraghs.

Travel details

Trains

Cahir to: Carrick-on-Suir (3 Mon–Sat; 45min); Clonmel (3 Mon–Sat; 20min); Waterford (3 Mon–Sat; 1hr 10min).
Carrick-on-Suir to: Cahir (3 Mon–Sat; 45min); Clonmel (3 Mon–Sat; 25min); Waterford (3 Mon–Sat; 25min).
Clonmel to: Cahir (3 Mon–Sat; 45min); Carrick-on-Suir (3 Mon–Sat; 25min); Waterford (3 Mon–Sat; 50min).
Nenagh to: Dublin (change at Ballybrophy; 1–2 daily; 2hr 20min); Limerick (1–2 daily; 50min).
Waterford city to: Cahir (3 Mon–Sat; 1hr 10min); Carrick-on-Suir (3 Mon–Sat; 25min); Clonmel (3 Mon–Sat; 50min); Dublin (4–6 daily; 2hr 35min); Kildare (4–6 daily; 1hr 50min); Kilkenny (4–6 daily; 40min); Rosslare Europort (1 Mon–Sat; 1hr 20min).

Buses

Bus Éireann
Ardmore to: Cork (1–3 daily; 1hr 35min); Dungarvan (Mon–Sat 2–3 daily; 25–45min); Ring (2 Mon–Fri July–Aug only, 1 Fri & Sat all year; 30min); Waterford (Mon–Sat 1–2 daily; 1hr 55min); Youghal (1–3 daily; 20min).

Cahir to: Bansha (6–8 daily; 15min); Carrick-on-Suir (6–8 daily; 50min); Cashel (8–9 daily; 15min); Clonmel (6–9 daily; 20min); Cork (7 daily; 1hr 20min); Dublin (6 daily; 3hr 5min); Limerick (6–8 daily; 1hr 5min); Waterford (6–9 daily; 1hr 20min).
Carrick-on-Suir to: Ardfinnan (Mon–Sat 2 daily; 45min); Ballyporeen (Mon–Sat 2 daily; 1hr 10min); Cahir (6–8 daily; 50min); Clogheen (Mon–Sat 2 daily; 1hr); Clonmel (6–8 daily; 20min); Cork (1 daily; 2hr 15min); Dublin (5–6 daily; 3hr 10min); Kilkenny (6–8 daily; 55min); Limerick (6–8 daily; 2hr); Waterford (6–8 daily; 40min).
Cashel to: Cahir (8–9 daily; 15min); Cork (6 daily; 1hr 35min); Dublin (6 daily; 2hr 50min).
Clonmel to: Ardfinnan (2–4 daily; 20min); Ballymacarbry (1 on Tues, 2 on Fri; 20min–1hr); Ballyporeen (2–3 daily; 45min); Cahir (6–9 daily; 20min); Carrick-on-Suir (6–8 daily; 20min); Clogheen (2–4 daily; 30min); Cork (3 daily; 2hr 55min); Dublin (5–7 daily; 3hr 30min); Dungarvan (1 on Tues; 1hr 45min); Kilkenny (6–9 daily; 1hr 15min); Limerick (6–8 daily; 1hr 30min); Waterford (6–9 daily; 1hr).
Dungarvan to: Ardmore (Mon–Sat 2–3 daily; 25–45 min); Ballymacarbry (1 on Tues; 45min); Clonmel (1 on Tues; 1hr 45min); Cork (12–13 daily; 1hr 25min); Lismore (1–2 daily; 35min); Ring (2 Mon–Fri July–Aug only, 1 Fri & Sat all year; 15min); Stradbally (1 Wed & Fri; 30min); Waterford (13–14 daily; 50min); Youghal (12–13 daily; 35min).
Lismore to: Cork (1 on Fri, Sept–June 1 on Sun; 1hr 10min); Dungarvan (1–2 daily; 35min); Waterford (1 on Fri, Sept–June 1 on Sun; 1hr 20min).
Nenagh to: Dublin (14 daily; 3hr); Limerick (13 daily; 45min); Terryglass (1 Fri; 45min).
Ring to: Ardmore (2 Mon–Fri July–Aug only, 1 Fri & Sat all year; 30min); Dungarvan (2 Mon–Fri July–Aug only, 1 Fri & Sat all year; 15min); Waterford (2 Mon–Fri July–Aug only, 1 Fri & Sat all year; 1hr 35min).
Waterford city to: Ardmore (Mon–Sat 1–2 daily; 1hr 55min); Cahir (6–9 daily; 1hr 20min); Carrick-on-Suir (6–8 daily; 40min); Clonmel (6–9 daily; 1hr); Cork (12–13 daily; 2hr 15min); Dublin (5–10 daily; 3hr); Duncannon (1–2 Mon–Sat; 1hr 20min); Dungarvan (12–13 daily; 50min); Kilkenny (1–2 daily; 1hr); Killarney (10–11 daily; 4hr 10min); Limerick (6–8 daily; 2hr 30min); Lismore (1 on Fri, Sept–June 1 on Sun; 1hr 20min); New Ross (6–15 daily; 20–35min); Ring (2 Mon–Fri July–Aug only, 1 Fri & Sat all year; 1hr 35min); Rosslare Europort (3–4 daily; 1hr 25min); Stradbally (1 Wed & Thurs; 1hr 10min); Thomastown (5–12 daily; 30–40min); Tralee (10–11 daily; 4hr 45min); Tramore (21–31 daily; 25min); Wexford (3–7 daily; 1hr); Youghal (12–13 daily; 1hr 25min).

Aircoach
Ⓣ01/844 7118, Ⓦwww.aircoach.ie
Cashel to: Cork (St Patrick's Quay; 8 daily; 1hr 30min).

J.J. Kavanagh's Waterford
Ⓣ051/872149, Clonmel Ⓣ052/29292; Ⓦwww.jjkavanagh.ie
Clonmel to: Dublin (2–3 daily; 3hr); Kilkenny (2–3 daily; 50min).
Nenagh to: Dublin (4 daily; 3hr); Limerick (Arthur's Quay; 7–8 daily; 50min).
Tramore to: Dublin (10 daily; 3hr 30min–4hr 30min); Waterford (10 daily; 30min).
Waterford to: Dublin (11 daily; 3–4hr); Thomastown (11 daily; 30min).

RTI
Ⓣ051/389418 or 087/251 9614
Waterford 1 Sat to and from New Ross (25min); Campile (45min); Ballyhack (50min); Arthurstown (55min); Duncannon (1hr); Fethard-on-Sea (1hr 20min).

Suirway
Ⓣ051/382422, Ⓦwww.suirway.com
Waterford to: Dunmore East (6 Mon–Sat, plus July–Aug 6 Sun; 30min); Passage East (2–3 Mon–Sat; 30min).

Cork

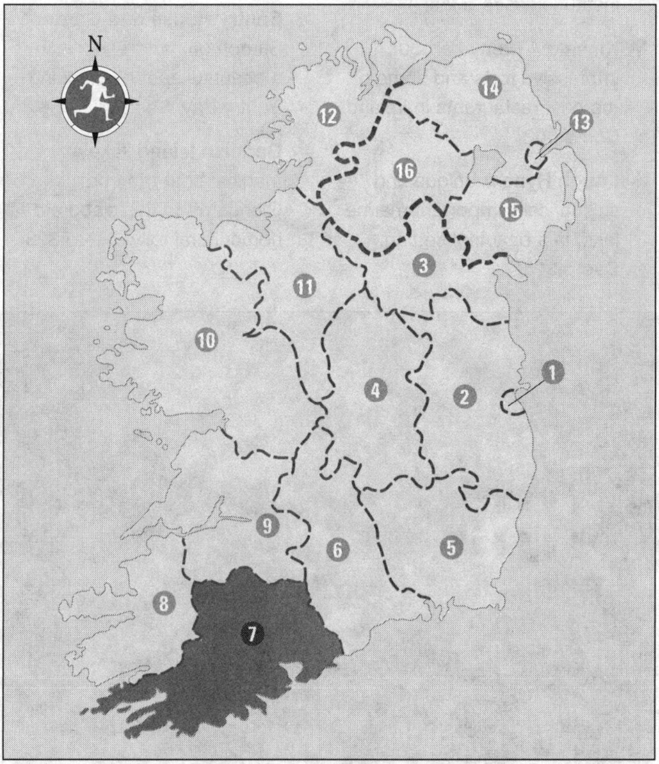

CHAPTER 7

Highlights

* **Fota House** An extravagantly decorated mansion, brought to life by imaginative displays and set in impressive grounds. See p.296
* **Ballymaloe House** For a blow-out, eat or stay at this exceptional restaurant and hotel, a uniquely Irish institution. See p.299
* **Kinsale** A pretty harbour, impressive forts and some of the best restaurants in Ireland. See p.302
* **Lough Hyne** A unique and scientifically important marine lake, in a beautiful setting. See p.313
* **Clear Island** Hop on the ferry for varied birdwatching and pleasant walking. See p.315
* **The Sheep's Head Way** The shortest and easiest walking route in southwestern Ireland, around a wild and lonely peninsula. See p.319
* **Bantry House and Gardens** Sumptuous art treasures in a beautiful spot overlooking Bantry Bay. See p.321
* **Garinish Island** Take a magical boat trip from Glengarriff to this elaborate horticultural folly. See p.323

▲ Fota House

7

Cork

Cork is far and away Ireland's largest county, but nearly all visitors simply ignore its massive hinterland of dairy farms, dotted with low mountains and evergreen plantations. The coast's the thing, and in an east–west spread of over 170km it unfurls an astonishing diversity. **Cork city**, the capital of the self-styled "rebel county", is renowned for its independent spirit, and packs a good cultural and social punch in its compact, vibrant centre, on an island in the Lee estuary. With its excellent restaurants, cafés and specialist food market, the city also sets a high culinary tone, which much of the rest of the county keeps up. Further reminders of a prosperous seafaring past can be seen hereabouts in the ports of **Cobh**, **Youghal** and especially **Kinsale**, each of which has reinvented itself in its own singular way as a low-key, pleasurable resort.

Though it meanders wildly through inlets and hidden coves, the coastline west from Cork city as far as **Skibbereen** remains largely gentle and green, with a good smattering of sandy beaches and a balminess that has attracted incomers and holiday-homers from the rest of Ireland and Europe. Facing each other across the shelter of Roaring Water Bay, the good-time ports of **Baltimore** and **Schull** are popular with a cosmopolitan, watersports crowd, but the offshore islands of **Sherkin** and **Clear** presage wild country ahead. **Mizen Head** is the first of Cork's and Kerry's five highly irregular, southwesterly fingers of folded rock, which afford spectacular views of each other and the Atlantic horizon. The next, narrow **Sheep's Head**, is perhaps the most charming, where – especially if you slow down to walking pace – you'll feel as if you're getting to know every square kilometre of gorse, granite and pasture and just about every inhabitant. Shared between Cork and Kerry, the **Beara Peninsula** is especially dramatic, epitomized by mild, verdant **Glengarriff**'s backdrop of dark, bare rock and lonely mountain passes.

Buses will get you around most of the county, and **bikes** can be rented in the main towns. Bus Éireann is augmented in the far west by a couple of private minibus services and West Cork Rural Transport (see "Travel details", p.326), but you'll need to check timetables carefully as services on the quieter routes sometimes run weekly rather than daily. The elaborate landscape of west Cork is great country for **walking** or **cycling**, both of which pursuits are served by waymarked routes on the Beara Peninsula and the Sheep's Head Peninsula.

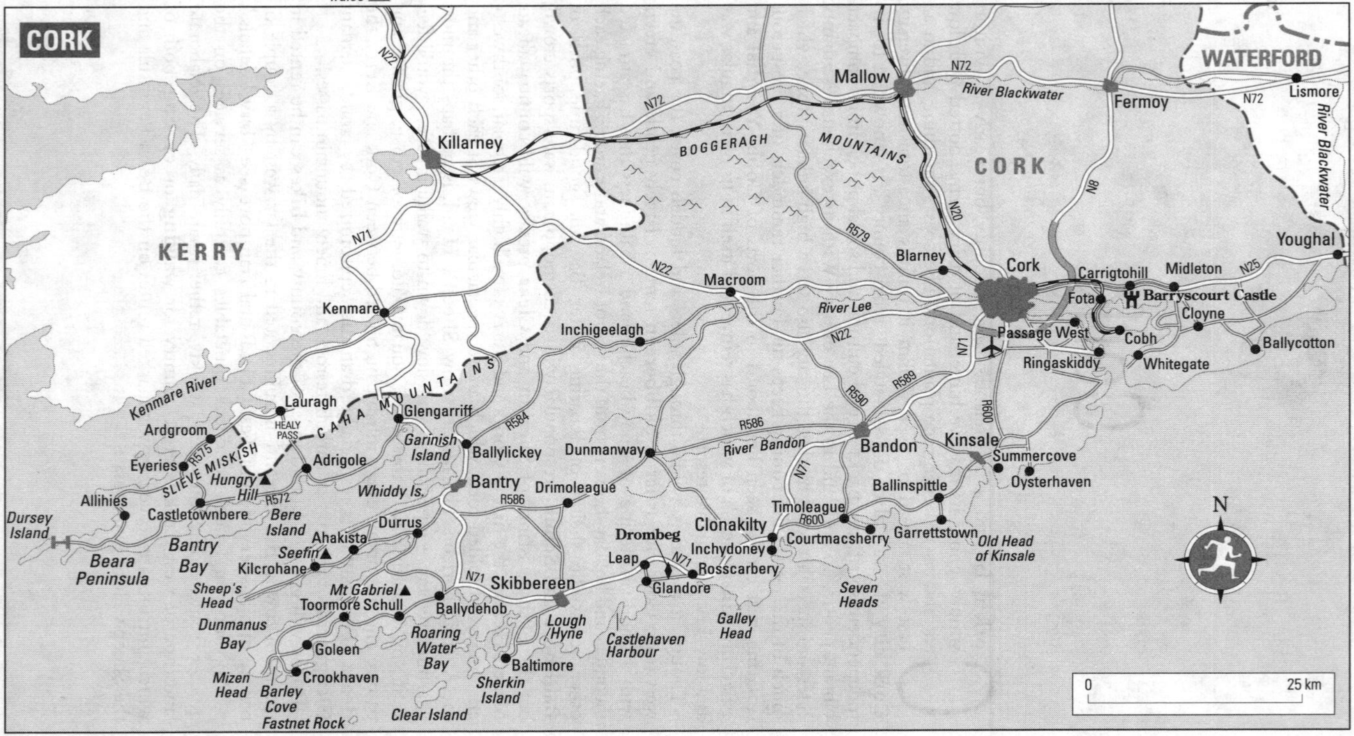

CORK

Tralee
Limerick
Dublin
Waterford
WATERFORD
KERRY
CORK
Lismore
River Blackwater
N72
Fermoy
Mallow
Killarney
N22
BOGGERAGH MOUNTAINS
N20
N8
R579
Blarney
Cork
Youghal
N25
Midleton
Carrigtohill
Fota
Barryscourt Castle
Cloyne
Ballycotton
Cobh
Whitegate
Passage West
Ringaskiddy
Macroom
River Lee
Inchigeelagh
N71
Kenmare
Kenmare River
Lauragh
HEALY PASS
CAHA MOUNTAINS
Glengarriff
Garinish Island
Ardgroom
R575
Eyeries
SLIEVE MISKISH
Hungry Hill
Adrigole
R572
Allihies
Castletownbere
Dursey Island
Beara Peninsula
Bantry Bay
Bere Island
Whiddy Is.
Bantry
Ballylickey
R584
Dunmanway
R586
Drimoleague
River Bandon
R590
R589
Bandon
R600
Kinsale
Summercove
Oysterhaven
Ballinspittle
Garrettstown
Old Head of Kinsale
Timoleague
Courtmacsherry
Seven Heads
Clonakilty
Inchydoney
Drombeg
Leap
Rosscarbery
Glandore
Galley Head
Castlehaven Harbour
Skibbereen
Lough Hyne
Baltimore
Sherkin Island
Clear Island
Ballydehob
Roaring Water Bay
Schull
Toormore
Mt Gabriel
Durrus
Ahakista
Seefin
Kilcrohane
Sheep's Head
Dunmanus Bay
Goleen
Crookhaven
Mizen Head
Barley Cove
Fastnet Rock
N
0
25 km

Cork city

The Republic's second city, **CORK** (Corcaigh, "marshy place") is strongly characterized by its geography. The centre sits tight on a kilometre-wide island, much of which was reclaimed from marshes, in the middle of the River Lee, while the enclosing hills seem to turn this traditionally self-sufficient city in on itself. Given this layout and its history, it comes as no surprise that Corkonians have a reputation in Ireland for independence of spirit, not to say chippiness. Indeed, in many ways, Cork sees itself not in second place but as a rival to Dublin. It produces its own national newspaper, *The Irish Examiner*, brews Murphy's and Beamish, its own versions of the national drink, stout, and supports a vigorous artistic, intellectual and cultural life of its own, cemented by its role as European City of Culture in 2005. Even its social divisions match Dublin's: here too the south side of the river is generally more affluent, while the north side has more public housing and a stronger working-class identification.

In colonial times, Cork also maintained its own strong links with London, through its role as a major **port**, proof of which can still be seen all around town. The main drag, curving St Patrick's Street, was originally a waterway lined with quays, while you can still spot eighteenth-century moorings on Grand Parade. Though contemporary Cork doesn't make the most of its long riverfront, much of which is now lined by major roads, the channels of the Lee, spanned by more than twenty bridges, break up the cityscape and pleasantly disorientate. The harbour area has Ireland's largest concentration of chemical factories, fortunately downstream of the centre, while the city's other main modern industry, computers, is linked to the prestigious university, to the west of the centre. All of this has spawned a widespread commuter belt, but the compact island is still the place for the many excellent restaurants, lively pubs and artistic venues, so helping to maintain the city's vibrancy.

Some history

In the seventh century, **St Finbarre** established a monastery at Cork, on the site of today's cathedral, to the southwest of the modern centre. Three centuries later, the Vikings created a separate settlement, an island in the River Lee's marshes, which was taken over in the twelfth by the Anglo-Normans. They strengthened the defences of the central part of the island with the construction of vast city walls, leaving the west and east ends to the swamp and later developing suburbs on the slopes to the north and south. The fortifications were largely destroyed, however, in the successful **Williamite siege** of 1690, and became redundant when the marshes were reclaimed soon after. The next century witnessed great wealth, through the trade in butter and pickled meat and the development of the port for provisioning westbound sailing ships. Brewing and distilling plants were established, which persist to this day, along with glass, silver and lace industries, but the Act of Union and the introduction of steamships brought stagnation in the nineteenth century. At the start of the last century, Cork took an active part in the **War of Independence** and the **Civil War**, and suffered as a consequence. In 1920, the Royal Irish Constabulary murdered the Lord Mayor, Tomás MacCurtain, and as a reprisal for an ambush, the Black and Tans burnt much of the city centre to the ground in 1921. MacCurtain's successor as mayor, Terence MacSwiney, was incarcerated and went on hunger strike, which after 74 days led to his death on October 24, 1920.

Arrival and information

Regional and national buses arrive at the **Bus Éireann station** on Parnell Place alongside Merchant's Quay (Ⓣ021/450 8188), while the **train station**, known as Cork Kent Station (Ⓣ021/450 6766), is a kilometre out of the city centre on the Lower Glanmire Road. Harrington's and O'Donoghue's **private buses** stop near the Bus Éireann station on the east side of Parnell Place, while Aircoach and Citylink buses use St Patrick's Quay on the north side of the river. **City and local buses** stop on the central St Patrick's Street.

Local buses run into the centre from the **ferry** terminal at Ringaskiddy, 13km southeast of town. Travelling by plane, you'll arrive at **Cork Airport** (Ⓣ021/431 3131, Ⓦwww.corkairport.com), which lies 7km south of the centre off the Kinsale road and has a small tourist-information kiosk. From here, you have a wide choice of bus services into the centre: Bus Éireann's coach runs to the bus station on Parnell Place in 25 minutes (frequency varies from roughly hourly on Sun to at least every half-hour Mon–Fri daytimes; €3.90 single, €6.50 return, free to Bus Éireann express-coach ticket-holders; talking timetable on Ⓣ021/422 2129, Ⓦwww.buseireann.ie); while Skylink (Ⓣ021/432 1020, Ⓦwww.skylinkcork.com; €5 single, €8 return) operates two hourly, circular routes, one via *Jury's Inn*, St Patrick's Quay, Shandon and MacCurtain Street, the other via the tourist office and the university on Western Road. If you're arriving by car, note that **parking** on the street requires a disc, which can be picked up from any newsagent. There's a useful multistorey car park on Coal Quay beside the Opera House.

The **tourist office** is on Grand Parade (Mon–Fri 9.15am–5.30pm, Sat 9.30am–5.30pm, plus Sun roughly 10am–5.30pm in July & Aug; closes 5.15pm in winter; Ⓣ021/425 5100, Ⓦwww.corkkerry.ie); you might want to ask here about a planned high-tech astronomy visitor centre at Blackrock Castle Observatory on the east side of town. From April to September, various historical **walking tours** of the city head off from the tourist office (Mon–Fri 4 daily; Ⓣ085 100 7300, Ⓦwww.walkcork.ie; €10). There's also a choice of open-top **bus tours**, both of which can be booked at the tourist office: the hop-on, hop-off Cork City Tour departs from opposite the tourist office to take in the city centre as well as passing Cork City Gaol, the public museum and the Glucksman Gallery on the west side (March–June, Sept & Oct every 45min; July & Aug every 30min; €13; Ⓣ021/430 9090); and Bus Éireann covers the city centre and runs out to Blarney, departing from the bus station on Parnell Place (May bank-holiday weekend and June–Sept 2 daily; 3hr; €11; Ⓣ021/450 8188). For those short on time, Bus Éireann and Easy Tours (Ⓣ021/454 5328, Ⓦwww.easytourscork.com) run a variety of coach tours from Cork in the summer, bookable at the tourist office.

Cork hosts plenty of lively **festivals**, of which the largest and most prestigious are the **midsummer festival**, a wide-ranging arts festival in late June (Ⓣ021/427 4077, Ⓦwww.corkfestival.com), the **film festival** in mid-October (Ⓣ021/427 1711, Ⓦwww.corkfilmfest.org), and the **jazz festival** later in the month (Ⓦwww.guinnessjazzfestival.com). There's also an international choral festival in late April or early May (Ⓦwww.corkchoral.ie), an international folk-dance festival in July (Ⓣ021/437 2035, Ⓦwww.corkfolkdancefest.com), a folk festival in late August or early September (Ⓦwww.corkfolkfestival.com), and in late September, the Beamish Experience (Ⓦwww.beamish.ie), a weekend of wall-to-wall gigs in the city's pubs and theatres, and an early-music festival, shared between the city and East Cork (Ⓣ021/463 6761, Ⓦwww.eastcorkearlymusic.ie).

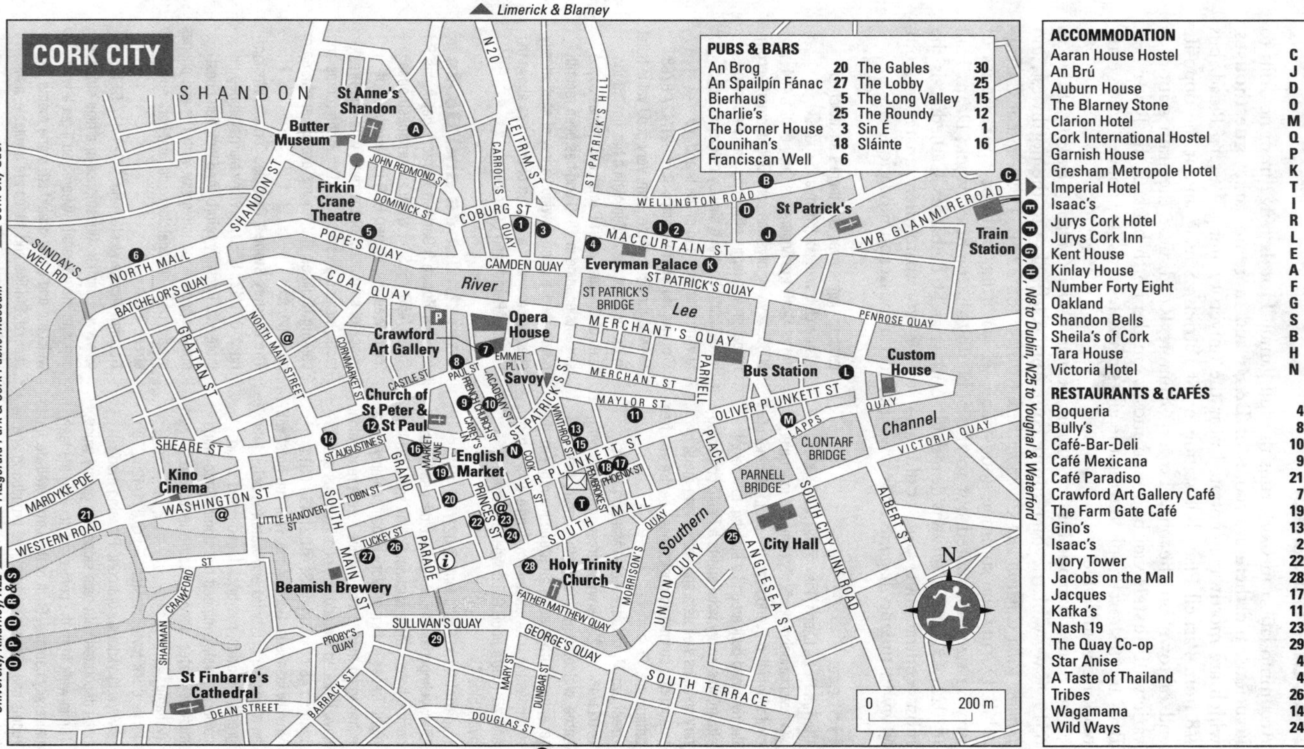
CORK CITY
Limerick & Blarney
Cork City Gaol
Fitzgerald Park & Cork Public Museum
University, Killarney, N22
O, P, Q, R & S
E, F, G, H, N8 to Dublin, N25 to Youghal & Waterford
Airport, Passage West, Ringaskiddy & Kinsale
30
SHANDON
St Anne's Shandon
Butter Museum
Firkin Crane Theatre
St Patrick's
Train Station
Everyman Palace
River Lee
Opera House
Crawford Art Gallery
Savoy
Church of St Peter & St Paul
English Market
Bus Station
Custom House
Channel
Kino Cinema
Beamish Brewery
Holy Trinity Church
City Hall
Southern
St Finbarre's Cathedral
PUBS & BARS
An Brog 20
An Spailpín Fánac 27
Bierhaus 5
Charlie's 25
The Corner House 3
Counihan's 18
Franciscan Well 6
The Gables 30
The Lobby 25
The Long Valley 15
The Roundy 12
Sin É 1
Sláinte 16
ACCOMMODATION
Aaran House Hostel C
An Brú J
Auburn House D
The Blarney Stone O
Clarion Hotel M
Cork International Hostel Q
Garnish House P
Gresham Metropole Hotel K
Imperial Hotel T
Isaac's I
Jurys Cork Hotel R
Jurys Cork Inn L
Kent House E
Kinlay House A
Number Forty Eight F
Oakland G
Shandon Bells S
Sheila's of Cork B
Tara House H
Victoria Hotel N
RESTAURANTS & CAFÉS
Boqueria 4
Bully's 8
Café-Bar-Deli 10
Café Mexicana 9
Café Paradiso 21
Crawford Art Gallery Café 7
The Farm Gate Café 19
Gino's 13
Isaac's 2
Ivory Tower 22
Jacobs on the Mall 28
Jacques 17
Kafka's 11
Nash 19 23
The Quay Co-op 29
Star Anise 4
A Taste of Thailand 4
Tribes 26
Wagamama 14
Wild Ways 24
0 200 m
N

Accommodation

Accommodation in Cork runs the full gamut. **Hotels** range from no-frills to luxurious, and there are scores of **B&Bs** and more upmarket **guesthouses**, which are mostly concentrated near the university along Western Road (bus #8 from Parnell Place bus station or St Patrick's Street), and at the opposite end of town on the busy Lower Glanmire Road, near the train station. A variety of **hostels** can be found mostly on the north bank of the River Lee. Beds are in short supply during the city's many festivals (see above), when early booking is advisable.

The nearest **campsites** are *Blarney Caravan and Camping Park* (Ⓣ021/451 6519, Ⓦwww.blarneycaravanpark.com; April–Oct), 8km to the northwest, and *Jasmine Villa Caravan and Camping Park* (Ⓣ021/488 3234), 15km east at Carrigtohill. During the summer, good-value, self-catering, **student apartments** of varying sizes are rented out to the public by the night or week; Deans Hall (Ⓣ021/431 2623, Ⓦwww.deanshall.com), near St Finbarre's Cathedral, is the most central, but you could also try Ⓦwww.parchmentsquarecork.com, Ⓦwww.studentvillage.ie or Ⓦwww.ucc.ie/campusaccommodation.

Hotels

Clarion Hotel Lapps Quay Ⓣ021/422 4900, Ⓦwww.clarionhotelcorkcity.com. Set in a quiet, central location overlooking the south channel of the river and built around a striking, full-height atrium, this luxury hotel sports a fresh, contemporary style, as well as a spa with a long menu of treatments, swimming pool, fitness centre and free broadband. 5

Gresham Metropole Hotel MacCurtain St Ⓣ021/450 8122, Ⓦwww.gresham-hotels.com. Large, welcoming, nineteenth-century hotel, recently refurbished in an attractive modern style and boasting a lavish leisure centre with a gym and 25-metre pool. Good weekend rates available. 5

Imperial Hotel South Mall Ⓣ021/427 4040, Ⓦwww.imperialhotel.ie. Cork's oldest and most central hotel, where Michael Collins spent his last night. Traces of former glory remain, notably in the extravagant marble lobby, while recent renovations have included the addition of a luxurious spa. 5

Isaac's 48 MacCurtain St Ⓣ021/450 0011, Ⓦwww.isaacs.ie. Good-value, well-run hotel with an attractive courtyard and waterfall behind its grand, Victorian, red-brick facade, and smart, colourful, well-equipped bedrooms. Good-value midweek rates; serviced apartments also available. 3

Jurys Cork Hotel Western Rd Ⓣ021/425 2700, Ⓦwww.jurysdoyle.com/cork. Pleasing modern hotel decorated with pale stone and grainy wood, 10min walk from the centre overlooking the leafy university campus. Each of the large, well-designed rooms has a music system, free broadband and a pillow-top bed, the bistro and bar feature broad terraces on the river, and there's an attached leisure club with pool, gym and spa. 6

Jurys Cork Inn Anderson's Quay Ⓣ021/494 3000, Ⓦwww.jurysinns.com. Bright, smart accommodation in a large, efficiently run, welcoming hotel. Central but in a slightly quieter location towards the east end of the island. 5

Victoria Hotel St Patrick's St Ⓣ021/427 8788, Ⓦwww.thevictoriahotel.com. Very good value hotel in the heart of the action, which has hosted the likes of Charles Stuart Parnell and James Joyce since its opening in 1810 and has been recently refurbished. It offers a wide variety of neat, mostly spacious rooms in a warren of corridors above the shops of Patrick and Cook streets. 3

Guesthouses and B&Bs

Auburn House 3 Garfield Terrace, Wellington Rd Ⓣ021/450 8555, Ⓦwww.auburnguesthouse.com. Well-maintained B&B in a central but peaceful spot north of the river, with fine breakfasts, including vegetarian, TVs in the rooms and parking facilities. Bathrooms are either shared or en suite. 2

The Blarney Stone 1 Carriglee Terrace, Western Rd Ⓣ021/427 0083, Ⓦwww.blarneystoneguesthouse.ie. Recently refurbished Victorian guesthouse opposite the university, with TVs and phones in all rooms, optional Jacuzzis, and parking off the street. 3

Garnish House Western Rd Ⓣ021/427 5111, Ⓦwww.garnish.ie. Guesthouse of a high standard opposite the university, where you'll get a warm welcome and a fine breakfast; some rooms have a Jacuzzi. Studios and suites are available, as is off-street parking. 4

Kent House 47 Lower Glanmire Rd Ⓣ021/450 4260, Ⓦhomepage.eircom.net/~kenthouse. Family-run B&B in a Victorian townhouse near the train station, offering a wide range of en-suite rooms and good single rates. ❷

Number Forty Eight 48 Lower Glanmire Rd Ⓣ021/450 5790, Ⓔjerryspillane48@hotmail.com. This brightly painted nineteenth-century townhouse offers comfortable, en-suite rooms with fine, home-baked breakfasts; good rates for singles and children. ❷

Oakland 51 Lower Glanmire Rd Ⓣ021/450 0578. B&B in a terraced eighteenth-century house near the train station, offering en-suite rooms with TVs. ❷

Shandon Bells Western Rd Ⓣ021/427 6242, Ⓦwww.shandonbells.com. Very helpful and informative B&B, offering bright, colourful, en-suite rooms with TVs and a varied breakfast menu; overlooking the southern channel of the river near the university, it's a 15min walk from the centre. ❷

Tara House 52 Lower Glanmire Rd Ⓣ021/450 0294, Ⓔtarahouse@02.ie. Family-run nineteenth-century townhouse with en-suite rooms, and TVs throughout. ❷

Hostels

Aaran House Hostel Lower Glanmire Rd (IHO) Ⓣ021/455 1566, Ⓔtracy_flynn3@hotmail.com. Comfortable townhouse by the train station with a kitchen, laundry facilities, bike rental and just 20 dorm beds. Dorms €12–16, twins ❶.

An Brú 57 MacCurtain St (IHO) Ⓣ021/455 9667, Ⓦwww.bruhostel.com. The city's most central hostel, in a former hotel above a sociable backpackers' bar. The smart, basic rooms are all en suite, and there's a kitchen, Internet access and laundry facilities. Prices include a simple breakfast. Dorms €14–22.50, doubles/twins ❶.

Cork International Hostel 1 Redclyffe, Western Rd Ⓣ021/454 3289, Ⓦwww.irelandyha.org. Well-appointed and organized 96-bed hostel that's been recently refurbished to An Óige five-star standards, with en-suite bathrooms throughout, Internet access and bureau de change. Take bus #8 from the bus station or St Patrick's Street. Dorms €15–22, twins ❶.

Kinlay House Bob and Joan's Walk, Shandon (IHH) Ⓣ021/450 8966, Ⓦwww.kinlayhousecork.ie. Large, well-run and welcoming hostel, on a quiet lane next to St Anne's Church, with laundry facilities and Internet access. Price includes a light breakfast. Dorms €13–18, twins ❶.

Sheila's of Cork 4 Belgrave Place, Wellington Rd (IHH) Ⓣ021/450 5562, Ⓦwww.sheilashostel.ie. Cork's biggest hostel, efficiently run and welcoming, with a good kitchen, laundry facilities, sauna, bike rental and Internet access; meals available. Dorms €13–19, twins ❶.

The City

The best of the city's sightseeing options are undoubtedly the **Crawford Art Gallery**, with its fine collection of eighteenth- to twentieth-century art, and the **Cork City Gaol**, which vividly evokes life in a nineteenth-century prison. In truth, however, none of Cork's sights are absolute must-sees, though it's a pleasant place to stroll around on a fine day. The city centre is essentially the eastern part of the island, with its quaysides, bridges, old warehouses and the narrow alleys of the medieval heart, plus a segment to the north of the River Lee that has MacCurtain Street as its central thoroughfare. The scale is manageable, and everything on offer can be explored on foot.

For those with a taste for it – and with shoe leather to spare – there's plenty of **Neogothic church architecture** to see, mostly along the river banks. The highlight is William Burges's **St Finbarre's Cathedral** on Proby's Quay (Mon–Sat: April–Sept 10am–5.30pm; Oct–March 10am–12.45pm & 2–5pm; €3; Ⓦwww.cathedral.cork.anglican.org), whose three soaring, French Gothic spires are visible all over the city. The well-lit interior, which is elaborately decorated with red Cork marble, stained glass and Italianate mosaics, also impresses with its lofty proportions. Leading nineteenth-century practitioners Augustus Pugin and George Pain also worked in Cork. The Church of SS Peter and Paul, just off St Patrick's Street in the centre, was designed by Pugin and sports some fine woodcarving. Pain was the architect behind Holy Trinity Church on Father Matthew Quay, with its handsome lantern spire, and St Patrick's Church out to the northeast on Lower Glanmire Road.

Blarney

Blarney, Blarney, what he says he does not mean. It is the usual Blarney.

So spoke Queen Elizabeth I, and a legend and its accompanying tourist phenomenon were born. Though supposedly loyal to the queen, the **Lord of Blarney**, Cormac MacCarthy, had been stalling her emissary, Sir George Carew, who had been sent to restore English control of Munster, sidetracking him with wine, women and words. MacCarthy, it was said, could talk "the noose off his head", and over the centuries blarney came to mean "flattering, untrustworthy or loquacious talk associated with . . . Irish people" (*The Encyclopedia of Ireland*). This story of the word's origin, however, may itself be blarney. . .

At some stage in the nineteenth century, with the beginnings of mass tourism to the southwest of Ireland, it became popular to kiss the **Blarney Stone**, part of the machicolations of **Blarney Castle**, a fine fifteenth-century tower house, set in attractive grounds, which stands in the village of the same name, 8km northwest of Cork. The stone stands over a 26-metre drop, and planting a smacker on it is meant to grant "the gift of the gab". If you're really feeling that tongue-tied, city buses run to Blarney from the bus station roughly hourly, and the castle is open year-round (May & Sept Mon–Sat 9am–6.30pm, Sun 9.30am–5.30pm; June–Aug Mon–Sat 9am–7pm, Sun 9.30am–5.30pm; Oct–April Mon–Sat 9am–6pm or sunset, Sun 9.30am–6pm or sunset; last admission 30min before closing; €8; Heritage Island; Ⓦwww.blarneycastle.ie). Legions of the verbally challenged queue up in summer, when it's best to turn up early in the morning or late in the afternoon.

The centre

Three roughly east–west arteries define Cork's commercial centre, bracketed to the west by the wide boulevard of **Grand Parade**: the crescent of **St Patrick's Street** (aka Patrick Street), bustling with major chainstores and modish boutiques; **Oliver Plunkett Street**, home to more traditional shops and pubs; and the city's grand financial and legal hub, **South Mall**. On the north side of Patrick Street, cafés and restaurants line the pedestrianized alleys of the old French quarter around **Paul Street**, though the main culinary venue is undoubtedly the covered **English Market**, a joy for the senses that's well worth wandering through. Yet stronger stimulation is provided beyond Grand Parade at the **Beamish Brewery** on South Main Street, where they've been making stout since the seventeenth century. The visit consists of an audiovisual on the brewing process (April–Oct Tues & Thurs 10.30am & noon; Nov–March Thurs 11am; €8; Ⓦwww.beamish.ie), which ends up, not surprisingly, with a sample of the black stuff.

The Crawford Art Gallery

The city's major set-piece sight is the **Crawford Art Gallery**, next to the Opera House in Emmet Place on the north side of Patrick Street (Mon–Sat 10am–5pm; free; free guided tours of the current exhibitions Sat 2.30pm; Ⓣ0121/490 7855, Ⓦwww.crawfordartgallery.ie). Its permanent collection of Irish and British art from the eighteenth century onwards, though far from compulsory viewing, is worth a couple of hours of your time, and the gallery hosts some interesting temporary exhibitions of Irish and international art in its striking modern extension and features an excellent café (see p.293). Development of the gallery is ongoing, and some works are yet to come out of storage.

The lion's share of the collection is housed on the first floor, where, at the top of the stairs, *Ulysses and a Companion Fleeing the Cave of Polyphemus* (1776), a complex allegory by Cork's greatest and most troubled painter, **James Barry**, takes pride of place. Barry depicted himself as the companion, with his friend and patron, the statesman Edmund Burke, as Ulysses, raising his index finger to counsel caution – to no avail. The outspoken nationalist Barry was the only artist ever to achieve expulsion from London's Royal Academy, and was ostracized as a result. On the landing hangs a fascinating *View of Cork*, painted in 1755 by **John Butts**. You can pick out the waterway that is now Patrick Street, the 1724 Custom House (with a Union Jack in the courtyard), which is now the gallery you're visiting, and the Dutch-style houses on the quays, evidence of Cork's role in expanding Anglo-Dutch trading influence in the North Atlantic.

Among some sentimentally cloying nineteenth- and twentieth-century works, the Gibson Galleries beyond shelter fine representative works by **Jack B. Yeats** (see p.90) and Limerick-born **Seán Keating** (1889–1977), many of whose academic realist paintings have achieved iconic status. Look out for the former's *Returning from the Bathe, Mid-day*, painted in 1948 and typical of his expressionist late work, a joyful melange of bright, summery colours and swift brush-strokes. Though obviously posed in a studio, Keating's *Men of the South* (1924) achieves the restrained grandeur of a classical frieze, depicting a grim-faced IRA column waiting to ambush British soldiers. Other highlights of the permanent collection include a piercing portrait of actor Fiona Shaw by Victoria Russell on the staircase to the first floor, and a ghostly rendition of the most famous portraits of literary icons Yeats, Beckett and Joyce by **Louis le Brocquy** on the ground floor.

West of the centre

The west end of the island narrows around a residential area, which is home to hospitals and parts of the extensive university campus. At the latter, a kilometre out of the centre off the south side of Western Road (served by city bus #8 from St Patrick's St), it's worth checking out the **Glucksman Gallery** (Tues, Wed, Fri & Sat 10am–5pm, Thurs 10am–8pm, Sun noon–5pm; free; ⓣ021/490 1844, ⓦwww.glucksman.org). This striking building of wood, glass, limestone and steel, which was shortlisted for the 2005 RIBA prize, hosts rotating exhibitions of contemporary art, as well as an attractive café. Signposted off the opposite side of Western Road, facing the leafy north channel of the River Lee, sits **Fitzgerald Park**, where you'll find the **Cork Public Museum** (Mon–Fri 11am–1pm & 2.15–5pm, Sat 11am–1pm & 2.15–4pm, plus April–Sept Sun 3–5pm; free; ⓣ021/427 0679, ⓦwww.corkcity.ie/ourservices/rac/museum), a celebration of Cork and Corkonians – including sports personalities Sonia O'Sullivan and Roy Keane, both of whom have donated shirts. The museum traces the city's history through interesting documents and memorabilia, with a particular concentration on the period from the Great Famine to The Emergency, as World War II was known in Ireland. Some beautiful examples of Cork silver- and glassware are on display, alongside archeological finds from the Neolithic era onwards and some engaging temporary exhibitions on subjects such as prehistoric gold. From here it's a fifteen-minute walk across the river and up to Cork City Gaol (see opposite), signposted over the nearby footbridge.

Shandon and the northside

To the north of the island, **Shandon**'s narrow residential streets and alleys tumble down the slope towards the River Lee. At the centre of this area stands the former **butter market**, a round, tubby building in cobbled O'Connell

Square that houses the Firkin Crane Theatre (see p.294). The fascinating story of the dairy trade and its major impact on the development of the city is told in the **Butter Museum** opposite (daily: March–June, Sept & Oct 10am–1pm & 1.30–5pm; July & Aug 10am–1pm & 1.30–6pm; Nov–Feb by arrangement; €3; Ⓣ021/430 0600, Ⓦwww.corkbutter.museum). The museum begins with dairy culture in early Ireland, as illustrated by a keg of bog butter: on remote grazing lands, milk was churned into butter on the spot and preserved in the bogs for later use; to this day, such kegs are often turned over by peat-cutters, who'll swear the butter is still edible. In the eighteenth century, thanks to its fertile hinterland and its position on the largest natural harbour in the northern hemisphere, Cork became the main provisioning port in the Atlantic for both the British Navy and trade convoys, with most Cork butter ending up in the West Indies. In the following century, the city managed to ride out the general agricultural collapse precipitated by the Napoleonic Wars and the Famine by gearing the butter trade to the English market through rigorous controls – the butter-market building you see outside was where barrels were washed and weighed at this time, to avoid underhand practices by farmers. The story is brought up to date with a film on the successful development of the Kerrygold brand by tycoon and museum sponsor, Tony (now Sir Antony) O'Reilly.

Just up the slope from here, **St Anne's Shandon** is a graceful, early eighteenth-century, Anglican church, built partly of white limestone, partly of puce sandstone – a combination that is said to have inspired the red-and-white "rebel" flag of County Cork. Its steeple, the city's most famous landmark, is flanked by four huge, notoriously unreliable clocks – earning the nickname "the four-faced liar" – and topped by a giant golden salmon as a weather vane. It's possible to climb the tower for matchless views of the city and to ring the bells (Mon–Sat: Easter–Nov 10am–5pm; Nov–Easter 10am–4pm; €6; Ⓦwww.shandonbells.org).

To the west of here, a half-hour walk from the centre along North Mall and Sunday's Well Road, is the forbidding red sandstone of **Cork City Gaol**, in the posh suburb of Sunday's Well (daily: March–Oct 9.30am–6pm; Nov–Feb 10am–5pm; last admission 1hr before closing; €7; Ⓦwww.corkcitygaol.com). Skilfully designed for its punishing purpose in 1818 by the Pain brothers, George and James, the jail operated until 1923 when Republican prisoners – among them Countess Markiewicz (see p.483) and short-story writer Frank O'Connor – were released after the Civil War. A lively and informative audio tour guides you round the well-preserved cells, where the individual stories of real-life prisoners are recounted. An audiovisual courtroom drama finishes the tour evocatively, projected onto the walls of one of the jail's imposing drum galleries.

From the late 1920s until the early 1950s, the jail was home to the studios of Radio Éireann (now RTÉ), which have now been replaced by the **Radio Museum Experience** (same times; €7, or €10.50 combination ticket with the jail). There's lots of interesting material on the pioneers of radio here, a re-creation of the old studio, a large collection of early radios, and a "juke box" of archival recordings. In high season, an attractive tearoom operates in the jail's old gatehouse.

Eating

Eating out is one of the great pleasures of Cork. The city's chefs place a high premium on sourcing the best of local, artisanal ingredients, which they creatively put to good use. And with plenty of competition and an increasingly discriminating public to keep happy, **cafés** and **restaurants** are generally good value, certainly compared with the rest of the country. The best place to get a feel for Cork's culinary enthusiasm is the **English Market**, a Victorian covered market accessed either from Princes Street or Grand Parade. As well as the city's best fishmongers, greengrocers and butchers – stocking the local delicacies of tripe and *drisheen*, a type of black pudding – there are all manner of pungent specialist stalls where you could build a great picnic: cheeses, cold meats and smoked fish, olives, salads and deli goods, bread, cakes, and even wine and chocolates.

The island

Bully's 40 Paul St ⓣ 021/427 3555. Unpretentious, comfy restaurant dishing up mostly Italian food: pizza, home-made pasta, seafood, omelettes and burgers. Reasonably priced, especially at lunchtime.

Café-Bar-Deli entrances on Academy St and French Church St. A stylish setting, with spacious red velvet seating and a marble bar, for a tried-and-trusted formula that's been very successfully road-tested in Dublin: starters, pastas, salads, pizzas and desserts, with daily specials, at moderate prices. No booking.

Café Mexicana Carey's Lane ⓣ 021/427 6433. Largely authentic, moderately priced Mexican restaurant with relaxing, warm decor and a buzzy atmosphere.

Café Paradiso 16 Lancaster Quay, Western Rd ⓣ 021/427 7939. Popular, unpretentious restaurant serving excellent and innovative Mediterranean-influenced vegetarian and vegan cuisine. Moderate lunches; expensive dinners. Closed Sun & Mon.

The Crawford Art Gallery Café Emmet Place ⓣ 021/427 4415. Classy and affordable café-restaurant in a gorgeous ground-floor room of the gallery. You can lunch on snacks such as delicious pork terrine and salad, more substantial dishes like sausage, mash and onion, or push the boat right out with three courses for €25. And after a short spin round the gallery, you might well find yourself tempted back for tea and cake. Mon–Sat 10am–4.30pm.

The Farm Gate Café Upstairs in the English Market, Princes St. Excellent daytime café-restaurant overlooking the market's bustling stalls from its skylit balconies. Great cakes and desserts and very reasonably priced lunches, which feature salads and savoury tarts, as well as many traditional dishes: Irish stew, oysters and other seafood, tripe and onions, and *drisheen*. One balcony is self-service, the other table service. Closed Sun.

Gino's Winthrop St. The epitome of cheap'n'cheerful, a bright, no-frills restaurant dishing up pizza, salads, wine and ice cream.

Ivory Tower Princes St ⓣ 021/427 4665. Small, eccentric, first-floor restaurant that draws its culinary inspirations from all over the world to produce imaginative, off-the-wall combinations, such as venison with smoked chilli and dark chocolate jus – the effects can be hit-and-miss but are never boring. €60 for a three-course set menu plus soup or sorbet. Wed–Sun evenings.

Jacobs on the Mall 30A South Mall ⓣ 021/425 1530. Top-drawer cooking, using local, seasonal produce whenever possible, that's surprisingly affordable at lunchtime. The setting's a winner too, a former Turkish bathhouse illuminated by abundant skylights, which has had a contemporary makeover in reds and blues. Closed Sun.

Jacques Phoenix St, a lane off Pembroke St by the GPO ⓣ 021/427 7387. Long-running favourite, a mellow oasis in the heart of the city, serving creative but carefully judged food – generally expensive, but great value before 7pm. Evenings only.

Kafka's 7 Maylor St. Simple, cheap daytime café close to the bus station. The menu caters roughly equally for vegetarians and meat-eaters, with great all-day breakfasts and basic, filling sandwiches, baguettes and burgers, plus coffee and cake. Closed Sun.

Nash 19 19 Princes St. Bright, efficent daytime buffet restaurant serving delicious, high-quality cuisine – including a fish, a pasta and a warm salad of the day, sandwiches, and hot and cold breakfasts – at reasonable prices. Closed Sun.

Tribes 8 Tuckey St. Relaxing meeting-place with plenty of armchairs and sofas, which caters especially for night owls with its late hours and dozens of tea and coffee varieties. The menu has recently been expanded to include hot meals such as lasagne, salads, sandwiches and desserts, as well as beer and wine. Tues–Thurs 10.30am–midnight, Fri & Sat 10.30am–4am, Sun noon–11pm.

Wagamama 4–5 South Main St. Branch of the reliable chain of Japanese noodle bars, offering tasty fried and soup noodles, rice dishes, dumplings and invigorating juices.

Wild Ways 21 Princes St. Friendly organic sandwich shop and juice bar, offering good breakfasts and coffees, and delicious wraps, focaccias, pies and soups for lunch. Closed Sun.

Off-island

Boqueria 6 Bridge St ⓣ021/455 9049. Elegant tapas bar in a skilfully converted traditional pub, with shining leather banquettes and a marble-topped bar. Delicious traditional Spanish dishes have been adapted to make the best use of local artisan produce, such as cheeses, sausages and breads, and it's great for breakfasts such as Macroom porridge, too. Closed Sun lunchtimes in summer.

Isaac's MacCurtain St ⓣ021/450 3805. Popular, informal restaurant with bare stone walls, candles and a buzzy atmosphere. The short, global menu, supplemented by daily specials, might take in Moroccan lamb-shank tagine and green Thai curry.

The Quay Co-op 24 Sullivan's Quay ⓣ021/431 7026. Self-service, mostly organic workers' co-operative café above a health-food store and bakery, serving tasty, substantial and cheap vegetarian and vegan meals (and catering for many other dietary requirements), great salads, soups, puddings, breakfasts and teas. Mon–Sat 9am–9pm.

Star Anise Bridge St ⓣ021/455 1635. Well-regarded, bright orange café-restaurant serving excellent modern food such as duck confit with rustic potatoes, green beans and balsamic cream. Very reasonable for lunch, and good-value early-bird menu Tues–Fri before 7pm. Closed Sat lunchtime, Sun & Mon.

A Taste of Thailand (BKK 93) Bridge St ⓣ021/450 5404. Stylish, moderately priced Thai restaurant, where the dishes themselves aren't all that authentic, but the flavours certainly are – try the tasty beef salad with mango and crispy noodles.

Nightlife and entertainment

The city's main performance venue is **Cork Opera House** in Emmet Place (ⓣ021/427 0022, ⓦwww.corkoperahouse.ie), which hosts high-quality drama, dance, opera, comedy and concerts of all hues; the attached **Half Moon Theatre** (ⓦwww.halfmoontheatre.ie) has a more eclectic programme of drama, comedy and music. Cork's oldest traditional theatre is the **Everyman Palace** on MacCurtain Street (ⓣ021/450 1673, ⓦwww.everymanpalace.com), which offers a varied menu of drama, dance and opera. The Firkin Crane at the Institute for Choreography and Dance, O'Connell Square, Shandon (ⓣ021/450 7487), is Cork's leading **dance** venue, while Kino, on Washington Street (ⓣ021/427 1571, ⓦwww.kinocinema.net), is an excellent **cinema**.

The city boasts dozens of great **bars**, specializing in characterful and unreconstructed old pubs. These would generally be worth seeking out for their atmosphere alone but a high proportion of them also host **music**, traditional or otherwise, as detailed below. DJ nights come and go, but the *Savoy*, a huge Art Deco theatre on Patrick Street (ⓦwww.savoycork.com), remains Cork's main **club**, featuring a wide range of DJs and live bands from Thursday to Saturday nights. The *Everyman Palace* (see above) also hosts lively club nights from Thursday to Saturday.

For **information** on the arts, nightlife and entertainment, consult the *Irish Examiner* or the free monthly leaflet, *Whazon*, which can be picked up in cafés and arts venues (or go to ⓦwww.whazon.com/cork). Plugd Records, a well-stocked music shop at 4 Washington St (ⓣ021/427 6300), is a good place to pick up info on the gig and club scenes, while The Living Tradition, 45A MacCurtain St (ⓣ021/450 2564, ⓦwww.thelivingtradition.com), which sells a wide range of Irish and world music, will have the latest on traditional sessions.

Pubs and bars

An Brog Oliver Plunkett St. Dark, grungy, sprawling and packed with students, who come for the late bar (till around 2am every night) and the music (live bands Wed, DJs Thurs–Sun).

An Spailpín Fánac 28 South Main St. Rambling, scruffy bar with live music every night, mostly traditional sessions but also bluegrass and singer-songwriters.

Bierhaus Pope's Quay. Small, lively bar with comfy leather sofas and dozens of German and other world beers on tap or in bottles, including regular guest beers; sample trays of those on draught available until 8pm. Live music Fri night.

Charlie's Union Quay. Dimly lit, grungy pub with frequent live music, mostly blues but including a popular traditional session on Sun at 3pm.
The Corner House Coburg St. Similar in feel to *Sin É* next door (see below), though more spacious, and hung with postcards from all over the world. Traditional sessions two or three nights a week, with folk, blues or bluegrass just about every other night.
Counihan's Pembroke St, by the GPO. Two styles under one large roof: welcoming, old-fashioned, tile-floored pub downstairs – where a string quartet and a group mixing Irish traditional music with Andean rhythms currently plays on Sun evenings – and a bright, trendy bar upstairs with comfy sofas.
Franciscan Well 12A North Mall. On the site of a medieval monastery, this microbrewery-bar knocks out great stout, lager, ale and wheat beer, which can be enjoyed out the back in the sunny beer-yard in summer. Trad sessions Mon nights; popular weekend beer festival every year in late Oct (Ⓦ www.franciscanwellbrewery.com).
The Gables 32 Douglas St. Very popular bar offering varied lunches and dinners (Mon–Fri), and traditional music on Wed and Sun, bluegrass on Thurs.
The Long Valley Winthrop St. Fine traditional bar, sporting a large snug at the front and decorated with plants, old views of Cork and a mishmash of old wooden furniture, some of it rescued from an old cruise-liner. Famous for its tasty doorstep sandwiches (Mon–Sat lunch).
The Roundy 1 Castle St. Attractive bar that gets its name from its position on the rounded corner of Grand Parade. Big picture-windows, leather banquettes and heated outdoor tables make the most of this location, and there's a decent range of beers; pay-in gigs upstairs feature everything from jazz to singer-songwriters.
Sin É Coburg St. Dark and cosy pub, hung with all sorts of bric-a-brac and memorabilia and offering a wide range of beers. Frequent live music, including traditional twice a week.
Sláinte Market Lane, off Patrick St near the English Market. Friendly, unpretentious bar, with a good selection of beers, a cosy snug and tables out on the alley. The varied roster of entertainment includes traditional music with The Ceili All-Stars on Wed, comedy on Sun and something called musical bingo on Mon.

Listings

Bike rental Rothar Cycles, 55 Barrack St Ⓣ 021/431 3133, Ⓦ www.rotharcycletours.com.
Bookshops Liam Ruiseal, 49 Oliver Plunkett St; Mercier Bookshop, 18 Academy St; Waterstone's, 69 Patrick St. Good Yarns in the English Market sells and buys secondhand books, while Vibes and Scribes at 3 Bridge St and 21 Lavitts Quay offers a range of new, discount and secondhand stock.
Car rental Most of the big multinationals are represented at Cork Airport, including Budget (Ⓣ 021/431 4000, Ⓦ www.budget.ie), who also have a branch in the centre on St Patrick's Quay (Ⓣ 021/450 7404). There are few local outfits, but they include Great Island Car Rentals, who are centrally placed at 47 MacCurtain St (Ⓣ 021/450 3536).
Exchange The main banks are on and around St Patrick's St, and there are bureaux de change at the GPO on Oliver Plunkett St, and at *Cork International* and *Kinlay House* hostels.
Ferry companies Swansea–Cork Ferries, Ringaskiddy Ⓣ 021/437 8036 or 1800 620397 (see "Getting there" in Basics for details); Brittany Ferries (to Roscoff), 42 Grand Parade Ⓣ 021/427 7801, Ⓦ www.brittanyferries.com.
Gaelic football and hurling Cork is one of the few counties that's strong on both Gaelic games, and won the All-Ireland Hurling Final in both 2004 and 2005. Parc Ui Chaoimh, 2km east of the centre off Centre Park Rd, is one of the country's major stadiums; for fixtures, consult the *Irish Examiner*.
Gay and lesbian information Cork Gay Project (Ⓣ 021/427 8470, Ⓦ www.gayprojectcork.com) runs *The Other Place*, a resource centre and café with Internet access at 8 South Main St. L.Inc, 11A White St (Ⓣ 021/480 8600, Ⓦ www.linc.ie), is Cork's lesbian resource centre. Cork's gay bars are *Flux*, 56 MacCurtain St; *Instinct Bar*, Sullivan's Quay; and *Loafers*, 26 Douglas St. Gay and lesbian accommodation is available at *Roman House*, 3 St John's Terrace, Upper John St (Ⓣ 021/450 3606, Ⓦ www.interglobal.ie/romanhouse), and *Emerson House*, 2 Clarence Terrace, Summer Hill North (Ⓣ 086 834 0891). For further information, go to Ⓦ www.gaycork.com.
Helplines Rape Crisis Centre, 5 Camden Place Ⓣ 1800 496496; Samaritans, Coach St Ⓣ 021/427 1323 or 1850 609090.
Hospital Cork University Hospital, Wilton Rd Ⓣ 021/454 6400.
Internet Wired to the World, 28 North Main St and 12A Washington St; Café 18, 18 Princes St.
Laundry Castle Cleaners, Shandon St Ⓣ 021/428 8893; or Western Road Launderette, 21B Western Rd Ⓣ 021/427 9937.
Left luggage Available at the Bus Éireann station (Mon–Fri 7.45am–7pm, Sat 9am–6pm, plus Sun

9am–6pm in summer; €2.70 for the first day, €2.50 for each subsequent day) and at the hostels.
Pharmacy Patrick Street Late Night Pharmacy, 9 Patrick St ⓣ021/427 2511.
Police The main police station is on Anglesea St ⓣ021/452 2000.
Taxis There are ranks on Patrick St. Cab companies include ABC (ⓣ021/496 1961), Blue Cabs (ⓣ021/439 3939) and Cork Taxi Co-op (ⓣ021/427 2222).
Travel agents USIT, 66 Oliver Plunkett St ⓣ021/427 0900.
Watersports Munster Dive and Canoe, 30 St Finbarr's Rd (ⓣ021/431 2510, ⓦwww.mdac.ie), offers diving and canoeing courses.

East Cork

East Cork (ⓦwww.eastcorktourism.com) occupies a blind spot in the eyes of many visitors, their focus set on the more spectacular coastline to the west, but several interesting places are worth considering, all of them served by public transport. A suburban train service makes possible an excellent, varied day-trip across the Lee estuary to **Fota Island**, with a sensitively restored Neoclassical hunting lodge and a wildlife park in its surrounds, and on to the attractive harbour town of **Cobh** on Great Island. Now isolated between Fota and the N25 at Carrigtohill, **Barryscourt Castle** makes for a fascinating visit, while further east lies **Midleton**, the traditional home of Jameson whiskey and a culinary hub. In an expansive setting at the mouth of the River Blackwater, the historic, easy-going resort of **Youghal**, some 40km east of Cork, marks the border with County Waterford.

Fota Island and Barryscourt Castle

As you travel from the mainland by rail or road, you're hardly aware that **Fota** is an island in Cork Harbour. Its main attraction is **Fota House** (April–Sept Mon–Sat 10am–5pm, Sun 11am–5pm; Oct–March daily 11am–4pm; €5.50; Heritage Island; ⓦwww.fotahouse.com), an elegant, mostly early-nineteenth-century hunting lodge built for the Barry family, whose main seat had by then moved from nearby Barryscourt Castle (see opposite) to Castlelyons near Fermoy. On the extravagantly decorated ground floor, good audiovisuals convey the reminiscences of gardeners and housekeepers who worked on the estate, the history and architectural quirks of the house and the conservation of the arboretum, along with a plant catalogue. The highlights of the house are the **entrance hall**, a beautifully symmetrical space divided by striking ochre columns of *scagliola* (imitation marble), and the ceiling of the **dining room**, with its gilded plasterwork birds and musical instruments and delicately painted cherubs and floral motifs. Before visiting the **servants' quarters** and their impressive octagonal game-larder, be sure to catch the audiovisual in the study, which explains such features as the gaps at the top of the windows of the butler's servery – added so that food smells would tantalize the poor servants rather than the house guests. There's a nice little café in the billiard room, where you can refresh yourself before pressing on to the estate's internationally significant **arboretum** (same times as house; free), laid out in the mid-nineteenth century. At its best in April and May, it hosts a wide range of exotic trees and shrubs, with many rare examples, including some magnificent Lebanese cedars, a Victorian fernery and a lush, almost tropical lake.

In the former estate of Fota House, **Fota Wildlife Park** (mid-March to Oct Mon–Sat 10am–6pm, Sun 11am–6pm; Nov to mid-March Mon–Sat 10am–4.30pm, Sun 11am–4.30pm; last admission 1hr before closing; €12.50, children

€8, family ticket €50; Ⓦwww.fotawildlife.ie) is renowned for its success in breeding cheetahs, which, along with monkeys, giraffes, bison and many other species, wander about in seventy acres of open countryside. There's a train tour (€2) with guided commentary to help you make the most of it.

Barryscourt Castle

The original home of the Barrys, one of the principal Anglo-Norman families in Ireland, who later built Fota House, **Barryscourt Castle** stands a few kilometres to the northeast (June–Sept daily 10am–6pm; access by guided tour, last tour 5.15pm; €2.10; Heritage Card; Ⓦwww.heritageireland.ie). It's a fine fifteenth- or sixteenth-century tower house that's been impressively restored and decked out with re-created sixteenth-century furniture. The knowledgeable guides will point out murder holes and many other doughty defensive features, a priest hole and, in the chapel, an unusual remnant of the original ceiling, made of wattle and daub covered in lime mortar. Also of special interest is the garderobe, used for bathing (an infrequent enough practice in itself in medieval times), of a rare design that incorporates a sloping floor for drainage and a limestone slab to sit on. Outside there's a re-created sixteenth-century apple and pear orchard and pungent herb garden, a surprisingly intact bawn wall, and a café (closed Mon & Thurs). Barryscourt Castle is signposted off the R624 Fota road, though if you're coming directly from Cork it's easier to get there by turning off the N25 at Carrigtohill. **Buses** towards Midleton stop at Carrigtohill, leaving just a 500-metre walk to the castle.

Cobh

On the southern coast of Great Island, with extensive views of Cork Harbour, **COBH** (pronounced "cove") makes a great escape from the city on a fine day. This historic and unpretentious resort, clinging onto a steep, south-facing slope, sports a stony beach, a promenade with a bandstand and gaily painted rows of Victorian hotels and houses. Much of the tourist traffic comes now from the dozens of huge cruise-liners that dock here every year, continuing a long tradition for this fine, natural harbour: Cobh was a port of call for the *Sirius*, the first steamship to cross the Atlantic, in 1838, and for the *Titanic* on her disastrous maiden voyage in 1912. The port was also a major supply-depot during the American and Napoleonic wars, and became Ireland's main point of emigration after the Great Famine. This long and often tragic seafaring history is vividly detailed at the **Queenstown Story** (daily: May–Oct 9.30am–6pm; Nov–April 10am–5pm; last admission 1hr before closing; €6.60; Ⓦwww.cobhheritage.com; Heritage Island), a heritage centre in the former Victorian train-station on the seafront (the town was renamed Queenstown after a visit by Queen Victoria in 1849, but its old name was restored after Independence). If your appetite for salty tales and memorabilia still hasn't been sated, get along to the **Cobh Museum** (April–Oct Mon–Sat 11am–1pm & 2–5pm, Sun 2.30–5pm; €2; Ⓦwww.cobhmuseum.com), housed in a nineteenth-century Presbyterian church on the west side of the town centre.

Glancing up from the seafront, you can't miss the French Gothic **St Colman's Cathedral**, an enormous nineteenth-century pile of Dalkey granite and Mallow limestone, with a ninety-metre spire and a forecourt that affords peerless views of the harbour. If you make the short, sharp climb up here, you'll find, beneath the impressive wooden vaulting of its beautifully proportioned nave, the typically overblown decoration of the style. The florid, gold-and-white high altar was an ill-fated gift from the priests of the diocese to one Bishop McCarthy to mark his golden jubilee – unfortunately, the first Mass to be celebrated on it was his own Requiem. The rose window over the main entrance depicts the throne of God in a rich rainbow of colours, while the tower above holds a renowned carillon of 49 bells, the largest in the country; hour-long recitals take place on most Sundays at 4.30pm from May to September.

Ireland's – and possibly the world's – first yacht club was founded in Cobh in 1720, and messing about boats is still a strong feature of life in the town. The **International Sailing Centre**, which has a town office on East Hill and its main activities base out at East Ferry Marina at the eastern end of Great Island (Ⓣ021/481 1237, Ⓦwww.sailcork.com), holds sailing courses, and rents out canoes and dinghies. There's a maritime song **festival** and a fishermen's rowing regatta in June and a people's regatta in mid-August. A Titanic Commemorative Weekend takes place in April, with lectures and guided walks, while May sees a memorial weekend for the *Lusitania* (see p.303), many of whose victims were buried in the Old Church Cemetery, 2km north of Cobh. Between June and September you can take a **harbour cruise** through Marine Transport Services at Kennedy Pier (€6.50; Ⓣ021/481 1485, Ⓦwww.mts.ie).

Practicalities

The **train station** (Ⓣ021/481 1655) is towards the western end of the seafront, while Cobh's very helpful **tourist office** (Mon–Fri 9am–5.30pm, Sat & Sun 1–5pm; Ⓣ021/481 3301, Ⓦwww.cobhharbourchamber.ie), which also offers **Internet access**, is a little to the east. The tourist office shares the old yacht club with the **Sirius Art Centre** (Ⓣ021/481 3790, Ⓦwww.iol.ie/~cobharts), home to some interesting art exhibitions, literature events and concerts. The engaging and enterprising Michael Martin runs *Titanic*-themed **walking tours** starting from the *Commodore Hotel* opposite (daily 11am, Oct–Feb pre-booking essential on Ⓣ021/481 5211 or 087 276 7218; 1hr 15min; €9.50; Ⓦwww.titanic.ie).

Between the heritage centre and the tourist office stands *Waters Edge* (Ⓣ021/481 5566, Ⓦwww.watersedgehotel.ie; ❺), a tastefully decorated **hotel**, where many of the spacious bedrooms have seafront verandas. Good, all-en-suite choices among the dozens of **B&Bs** are *Ardeen*, 3 Harbour Hill (Ⓣ021/481 1803, Ⓔardeenbandb@hotmail.com; ❷), with great views from its lofty position near the cathedral and decent child reductions; *Ard na Laoi*, a smartly kept house opposite the tourist office at 15 Westbourne Place (Ⓣ021/481 2742; ❷); and *Seafield*, in a grand period house to the west of the centre on Lower Road (Ⓣ021/481 1563, Ⓦwww.seafieldcobh.com; March–Oct; ❷).

For food, there's a pleasant self-service **café** on the old station concourse at the Queenstown Story, while *Jacobs Ladder* at the *Waters Edge Hotel*, specializing in seafood and local produce in dishes such as baked cod with a tomato salsa, is

Cork Harbour ferry

A **ferry** runs between Glenbrook near Passage West, on the mainland southeast of Cork city, and Carrigaloe, a few kilometres north of Cobh on Great Island (daily 7am–12.15am every 10min; car €6 return, €4 single; adults €1 each way; bikes carried free; Ⓣ021/481 1223). Taking just five minutes, this is especially useful for travelling between Cobh and the south side of the city, and for bypassing the city altogether if you're heading from anywhere in East Cork to Kinsale and beyond on the West Cork coast.

the best **restaurant** in town. The adjacent *Quays Bar*, a modern **pub**, also serves tasty lunch and dinner but its main draw is its very attractive harbourside patio. There are several other pleasant bars along the promenade, or try *Jack Doyle's*, a congenial, sociable spot five minutes' walk up the hill from the cathedral, which is hung with memorabilia of the eponymous local boxer and tenor, known as the "Gorgeous Gael".

Midleton

The busy market town of **MIDLETON**, burgeoning with Cork commuters, is creating a strong culinary reputation for itself. It's arrayed round a broad, lively main street, which is bypassed to the south by the N25, so makes a pleasant stopover, just 18km east of Cork. The town's main visitor activity is **The Jameson Experience** (daily: March–Oct 10am–6pm, last tour 4.30pm; Nov–Feb Mon–Sat tours at 11.30am, 1pm, 2.30pm & 4pm, Sun 12.30pm, 2.30pm & 4pm; €9.75; Heritage Island; Ⓦwww.jamesonwhiskey.com), at the **Old Distillery** off the south end of the main street. Whiskey is no longer made in this distillery, but you'll be shown around the carefully restored machinery – including the largest pot still in the world, with a capacity of 32,000 gallons – in the atmospheric old buildings, and you'll get a taste of the "water of life" (*uisce*) at the end. Midleton's friendly **tourist office** stands at the distillery entrance (summer Mon–Sat 9.30am–1pm & 2–5.15pm; Ⓣ021/461 3702). Trailways, Hikes & Walks offers local **guided walking tours** (Ⓣ087 646 4115, Ⓦwww.trailwayswalks.com), while the local holiday camp, *Trabolgan*, 15km south at Whitegate on Cork Harbour (Ⓣ021/466 1551, Ⓦwww.trabolgan.com), offers **adventure activities** ranging from abseiling to sea kayaking to day visitors, as well as **camping**.

Glenview House (Ⓣ021/463 1680, Ⓦwww.glenviewmidleton.com; ❹) is an upmarket **B&B** run by friendly and solicitous owners, 4km north of Midleton off the R626 Fermoy road. The eighteenth-century country house enjoys beautiful gardens, large, comfortably decorated bedrooms and many fine Georgian architectural features, which were rescued from Fitzwilliam Street, Dublin, when the electricity board knocked down a row of houses there in the 1960s (see p.92). If your purse strings are a bit tighter, *An Stór*, Drury's Avenue (IHH; Ⓣ021/463 3106, Ⓦwww.anstor.com), in a converted mill on Drury's Lane off the east side of Main Street, is a comfortable, welcoming **hostel**, with dorms (from €18) and twin rooms (❶), and plenty of local information at hand.

Ballymaloe

Around 10km southeast of Midleton, off the R629 Cloyne–Ballycotton road, lies *Ballymaloe House* (Ⓣ021/465 2531, Ⓦwww.ballymaloe.ie; ❼), the most famous **restaurant** in Ireland, serving exceptional modern Irish cuisine using carefully sourced local ingredients. There's much more to this grand enterprise than just a restaurant: **accommodation** in the vine-covered, originally fifteenth-century manor house and adjacent courtyard mixes country-house style with contemporary features, and there's a heated outdoor pool, five-hole golf course and tennis court in the extensive grounds. Attached to the house is a shop selling crafts and, of course, kitchenware, with an excellent daytime **café**. The nearby **cookery school** (Ⓣ021/464 6785, Ⓦwww.cookingisfun.ie) runs prestigious twelve-week certificate courses as well as a host of short courses, and you can visit the school's restored nineteenth-century **gardens**, featuring the largest formal herb garden in Ireland and a Celtic maze (May–Sept Mon–Fri 11am–5pm; €6).

▲ Ballymaloe House

One of the finest **places to eat** is *The Farm Gate*, Coolbawn, off the west side of Main Street (021/463 2771; closed Mon–Wed evenings & all Sun), a bustling café-restaurant where they prepare local ingredients carefully and simply, at reasonable prices. There's a pianist on Saturday evenings, and a deli out front that sells fresh artisanal produce. *O'Donovan's* (021/463 1255; Mon–Sat evenings), a more formal restaurant opposite the distillery on Main Street, offers excellent dishes such as local rack of lamb with mustard-herb crust and red-wine jus, a warm welcome and an early-bird menu until 7pm (not Sat). Don't be fooled by the traditional pub frontage of *Finín's* further up the high street (021/463 1878; closed Sun) – it's more restaurant than bar, decorated with colourful modern paintings, where you can choose between simple dishes such as delicious chicken-liver pâté with salad and fancier meals like steak in wine and mushroom sauce. On Saturday mornings, Midleton hosts one of the country's best **farmers' markets**, behind the courthouse off Main Street (www.midletonfarmersmarket.com), offering everything from cheese, smoked fish and meats to breads, cakes and chocolate; over a weekend in early September, there's a **food festival**.

Youghal

YOUGHAL (pronounced "yawl") enjoys a lush, picturesque setting on the west bank of the River Blackwater's estuary, the border with County Waterford. It was one of Ireland's leading ports in the medieval era, with a scattering of ancient buildings to show for it, and later became a centre for the carpet industry, but today it is popular with holidaying Irish families, who take their leisure on the long, sandy, Blue Flag beach to the southwest.

The Town

Youghal's long, gently curving high-street is lined with tall, colourfully painted nineteenth-century buildings, interspersed with a few more historic structures. Bridging the south end of the street, the most obvious of these is the Georgian **clock tower**, which stands on the site of a medieval gate. It's a huge but well-proportioned sandstone affair that once served as a prison. Further north on Main Street, you'll find the **Red House**, a typically steep-roofed Dutch-style home built around 1710, and, opposite, a restored tower house, **Tynte's Castle**, from the fifteenth century.

Turning left at the nearby seventeenth-century almshouses onto Church Street will shortly bring you up to Youghal's main historic site, the Anglican **Collegiate Church of St Mary's** (Mon–Thurs 9.30am–5pm, Fri 9.30am–4pm, guided tours at 2.30pm). On the site of the fifth-century monastic settlement of St Declan of Ardmore, it's one of the oldest functioning churches in Ireland, built in about 1220. Inside, the squat Gothic nave boasts impressive oak roof trusses, as well as an elaborate, painted sword-rest, which was used for the mayor's sword in the seventeenth century, and a beautifully carved eighteenth-century oak pulpit. Almost bursting out of the south transept, an extravagant, multicoloured monument commemorates Richard Boyle, the seventeenth-century Earl of Cork who did much to develop Youghal, along with his two wives and children, including the chemist Robert. At the top of the attractively landscaped graveyard, climb the well-preserved thirteenth-century town walls for great views of the bay.

To one side of the church you can peer through the trees at the grand outline of **Myrtle Grove** (not open to the public), the home of Sir Walter Raleigh in the late sixteenth century. Raleigh was granted Youghal as part of the Munster Plantations, but showed little interest in the place – though legend has it that he introduced the potato to Ireland here – selling his land in Cork, Waterford and Tipperary for £1000 to Richard Boyle in 1602. Another esteemed resident of the house was the great philosopher, Bishop George Berkeley, who was warden of the church's college in 1734.

Back towards the south end of town, just off Main Street by the clock tower, **Fox's Lane Museum** (summer Tues–Sat 10am–1pm & 2–6pm; rest of year open weekdays by prior appointment, call ⓣ024/91145; €4) preserves a quite different form of history: beautifully restored domestic gadgets and appliances dating from the 1850s – when the mass production of gadgetry accelerated, following the Great Exhibition of 1851 in London – to the 1950s. It's a small, personal collection, informatively labelled and with the engaging owner generally on hand to answer questions. There's also a re-created hundred-year-old kitchen, whose dresser has a built-in coop to keep the chickens safe from foxes at night.

In summer Youghal also offers an array of **water-borne activities**, mostly from the jetty behind the tourist office. Blackwater Cruises (ⓣ087 988 9076) run frequent, sedate, ninety-minute trips up the beautiful Blackwater River, lined with castles, country houses and ruined abbeys, while Kingfisher cover the same ground in a much faster and noisier airboat (ⓣ087 050 6649, ⓦwww.airboatsireland.com). Aquatrek (ⓣ024/90542, ⓦwww.aquatrek.ie) offer a wide range of sailing courses, including taster trips, as well as other marine adventures.

Practicalities

Buses stop at the north end of Main Street, while the helpful **tourist office** and the attached **heritage centre**, which recounts the port's history since the ninth century (free), are well to the south on Market Square, just behind the harbour (daily: mid-March to Oct 10am–5pm, may be extended to 9am–6pm in July & Aug; Nov to mid-March 10am–2pm; ⓣ024/20170). Interesting **walking tours** of the town depart from the tourist office (July & Aug Mon–Fri 11am; at other times, book through the tourist office; 1hr 30min; €6). The tourist office also provides details of the town's visual-arts **festival** in mid-July (or phone ⓣ087 412 6213) and historical festival in late September (ⓦwww.youghalcelebrateshistory.com), when art shows, plays and concerts accompany an international historical conference. **Internet** access is available at Cyberoom, 49 North Main St.

For **hotel** accommodation, and for food and drink (see opposite), the outstanding choice is ★ *Aherne's*, with spacious and tastefully decorated luxury bedrooms, on North Main Street (Ⓣ024/92424, Ⓦwww.ahernes.com; ❺), in the centre of town. Youghal supports dozens of centrally located **B&Bs**, including the elegant Georgian *Avonmore House*, on South Abbey (Ⓣ024/92617, Ⓦwww.avonmoreyoughal.com; ❷), and *Roseville*, an attractive detached house with a garden and good breakfasts, on New Catherine Street (Ⓣ024/92571, Ⓦwww.rosevillebb.com; closed mid-Dec to mid-Jan; ❷). Out on the Cork road near the beach, you'll find many more, such as the welcoming *Greenlawn* (Ⓣ024/93177, Ⓔtjscanlon@eircom.net; Feb–Oct; ❷), about 2km from the centre. Around 7km southwest of town on the R633 towards Ballymacoda, *Clonvilla* offers **camping**, as well as inexpensive en-suite and standard B&B (Ⓣ024/98288, Ⓔclonvilla@hotmail.com; ❶).

There are plenty of **places to eat**, too. *The Coffee Pot*, a self-service **café** on the high street, just north of the clock tower, offers a mouthwatering display of cakes and a wide if predictable range of lunches. A little further up the street at no. 56, more sophisticated daytime fare, including tasty ciabattas and bagels, are served at *The Priory*, a small deli-café in a former Benedictine priory (closed Mon). Upstairs, a sophisticated **restaurant** has recently opened, *Via* (Ⓣ024/91482; Tues–Sun evenings), offering imaginative and authentic modern Italian food. At no. 61, *Pak Fook Garden* is a popular, spick-and-span Chinese restaurant, with a takeaway branch opposite (Ⓣ024/90668). The excellent restaurant at *Aherne's* is highly regarded for its fresh seafood, or you can choose from a scaled-down menu by the open fire in its very congenial **bar**. *The Nook* (*Treacy's*), by the turn-off for St Mary's Church, is a relaxing traditional pub and café, which is very popular for its varied lunches and good coffees. Movie buffs will want to hunt down *Paddy Linehan's* opposite the tourist office: for the filming of *Moby Dick* with Gregory Peck in 1954, John Huston transformed Youghal's waterfront into New Bedford, Massachusetts, and the pub is hung with signed photos of the shoot.

In summer **traditional music** can be heard at *The Nook* on Monday and Wednesday nights, and in two staged shows: *Seisiún* (*Ceolta Sí*; Ⓣ087 793 4504, Ⓦwww.ceoltasi.com or www.comhaltas.ie), an evening of music, dance and storytelling at the *Walter Raleigh Hotel* (Mon) and the Brú na Sí Cultural Centre (Thurs), and *Dancing thru the Ages* at The Mall Arts Centre (Wed & Thurs; Ⓣ024/92571, Ⓦwww.dancingthrutheages.com), which soups it up with a bit more razzamatazz in *Riverdance* vein.

Kinsale

KINSALE (Ⓦwww.kinsale.ie), 25km south of Cork city, enjoys a glorious setting at the head of a sheltered harbour around the mouth of the Bandon River. Two imposing forts and a fine tower-house remain as evidence of its former strategic importance as a trading port, and Kinsale has built on its cosmopolitan links to become the culinary capital of the southwest. Add in plenty of opportunities for watersports on the fine local beaches and a raft of congenial pubs, and you have a very appealing, upscale resort town.

Some history

St Multose founded a monastery at Kinsale in the sixth century, and by the tenth the Vikings had established a trading post. After the Anglo-Normans walled the town in the thirteenth century, it really began to take off, flourishing on trade, fishing and shipbuilding in its excellent deep harbour, which became an important rendezvous and provisioning point for the British Navy. The **Battle of Kinsale** in 1601 was a major turning-point in Irish history, leading to the "Flight of the Earls" to the Continent six years later which saw the end of the old Gaelic aristocracy: Philip III of Spain had sent forces to Kinsale to support the Irish chieftains, but communications were poor and Chief Hugh O'Neill, more accustomed to guerrilla warfare, was defeated by Elizabeth I's army in a pitched battle.

In 1689 **James II** landed here in his attempt to claim back the throne, only to flee ignominiously from this same port a year later, after defeat at the Battle of the Boyne. His supporters fought on, however, burning the town and holing up in James Fort and Charles Fort. After a series of decisive attacks by the Duke of Marlborough, they surrendered on favourable terms and were allowed to go to Limerick for the final battle under Patrick Sarsfield (see p.375).

During World War I, in May 1915, a German submarine torpedoed the passenger liner *Lusitania* off the Old Head of Kinsale, as it was sailing from New York to England. Twelve hundred of the passengers and crew were lost, and the sinking was a major factor in the USA's eventual entry into the war.

Arrival, information and accommodation

Buses stop at the Esso garage on Pier Road, right at the heart of Kinsale, by the northwest tip of the harbour. Opposite lies the friendly, well-informed **tourist office** (March–June & Sept–Nov Mon–Sat 9.15am–1 & 2–6pm; July & Aug Mon–Sat 9.15am–7pm, Sun 10am–5pm; Dec–Feb Tues–Sat 9.15am–1 & 2–5pm; ⓣ021/477 2234), which has plenty of useful free literature on the town. From here, engaging historical **walking tours** depart twice a day in summer, once daily in winter (1hr; €7; ⓣ021/477 2873), while summer-evening ghost tours meet at the *Tap Tavern* on Guardwell (Mon–Fri; 1hr; €10; ⓣ087 855 5043). The tourist office also has the times of summertime **cruises** to the outer harbour and the Bandon River on the *Spirit of Kinsale*, or phone ⓣ021/477 8946 or 086 250 5456 (ⓦwww.kinsaleharbourcruises.com; €12.50). **Bikes** can be rented from Mylie Murphy, 8 Pearse St (ⓣ021/477 2703). Both the Outdoor Education Centre (ⓣ021/477 2896, ⓦwww.kinsaleoutdoors.com), on the harbour near the town centre, and Oysterhaven Activity Centre (ⓣ021/477 0738, ⓦwww.oysterhaven.com), 5km east of Kinsale on Oysterhaven Bay, offer **sailing**, **wind-surfing** and **canoeing**. At Blue Flag Garrettstown Beach, 12km southwest of town, H2O offers **sea-kayaking** trips and courses (ⓣ021/477 8884, ⓦwww.h2oseakayaking.com), while G Town Surf Shop offers **surfing** lessons (ⓣ021/477 8884, ⓦwww.surfgtown.com). For **horse riding**, contact Ballinadee Stables, a ten-minute drive from town off the Timoleague road (ⓣ021/477 8152).

Internet access is available at Finishing Services, 71 Main St. As well as the gourmet **festival** in October (see p.306), Kinsale hosts a varied and prestigious, week-long arts festival in July (ⓣ021/470 0877, ⓦwww.kinsaleartsweek.com) and a fringe jazz festival to coincide with the main jazz festival in Cork in late October (ⓣ021/477 4602). Pick up a copy of the free *Kinsale Newsletter* at the tourist office to check out exactly what's on around town each week.

There are dozens of **guesthouses** and **B&Bs** in Kinsale, as well as a couple of **hostels**. Booking is advisable in high summer and during the gourmet festival. **Camping** is available at *Dempsey's* hostel (see below) or *Garrettstown House Holiday Park* at Ballinspittle, 10km southwest of Kinsale (ⓣ021/477 8156, ⓦwww.garrettstownhouse.com; May to mid-Sept).

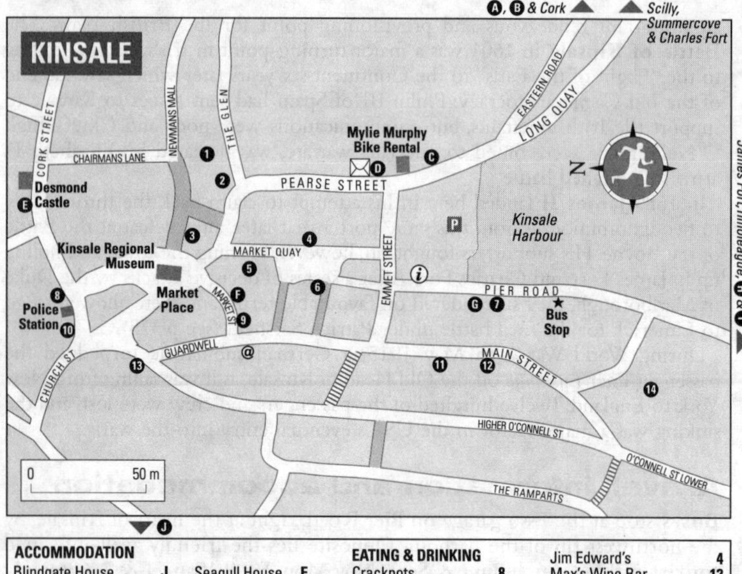

ACCOMMODATION				EATING & DRINKING			
Blindgate House	J	Seagull House	E	Crackpots	8	Jim Edward's	4
Cucina	F	Walyunga	H	Cucina	F	Max's Wine Bar	12
Dempsey's Hostel	A	Waterside	I	Dino's	7	Quay Food Company	5
Hilltop B&B	B			Fishy Fishy Café	14	Shanakee	9
Long Quay House	C			Fishy Fishy Shop	10	The Tap Tavern	13
Old Bank House	D			Gina's	6	Toddies	1
Pier House	G			The Grey Hound	3	The Vintage	11
						The White House	2

Blindgate House Blindgate ⓣ021/477 7858, ⓦwww.blindgatehouse.com. Bright, stylish and welcoming guesthouse, decorated with natural fabrics and contemporary furniture and offering great breakfasts and a quiet garden to relax in. A 5min walk west of the town centre up the hill. Closed Jan & Feb. ❺

Cucina 9 Market St ⓣ021/470 0707, ⓦwww.cucina.ie. Good-value choice in the heart of town: bright, decent-sized rooms of a plain, modern design, with TVs and white-tiled bathrooms. Above a good café (see p.306), where you can get breakfast, though it's not included in the price. ❷

Dempsey's Hostel Eastern Rd ⓣ021/477 4111 (IHH). Basic hostel with a pleasant conservatory on the main Cork road, about 1km from the centre by the Texaco garage. Private rooms, including singles, and camping available. Dorms €15, doubles ❶.

Hilltop B&B Sleaveen Heights ⓣ021/477 2612. Spacious and comfortable bungalow, with all rooms en suite with TV, plus a conservatory at the front overlooking the harbour and James Fort. Signposted off the R600 Cork road, and around a 5min walk from the centre. Closed Nov–Feb. ❷

Long Quay House Long Quay ⓣ021/477 4563, ⓦwww.longquayhousekinsale.com. All of the large, comfortable bedrooms have TVs and en-suite bathrooms, most with baths, in this ivy-clad Georgian house of fine proportions in the centre of town overlooking the harbour. Closed mid-Nov to Christmas. ❸

Old Bank House 11 Pearse St ⓣ021/477 4075, ⓦwww.oldbankhousekinsale.com. Very comfortable and luxurious Georgian-period guesthouse in a central location, with beautiful furnishings in the drawing room and lounge. Many of the well-equipped rooms overlook the harbour, and there's plenty of choice for an excellent breakfast. ❺

Pier House Pier Rd ⓣ021/477 4475, ⓦwww.pierhousekinsale.com. A charming haven in a pretty garden right in the centre of town, with a bright, contemporary-rustic look enlivened with modern art. Most of the well-equipped rooms have sleigh beds and terraces or balconies, and there's an outdoor hot-tub and sauna. ❹

Seagull House Cork Street ⓣ021/477 2240, ⓦwww.seagullhouse.com. Smart B&B next to Desmond Castle in the centre, with en-suite doubles, plus one reasonably priced single room; no child reductions. Closed Oct–Feb. ❷

Walyunga Sandycove ⓣ021/477 4126, ⓦwww.walyunga.com. Spacious and very welcoming bungalow, with landscaped gardens and outstanding sea and valley views, in a quiet location 3km from town off the R600 Timoleague road. Excellent breakfasts served on the panoramic patio in good weather. Closed Nov to mid-March. ❷

Waterside Dromderrig ⓣ021/477 4196, ⓦwww.waterside.ie. A kilometre or so from the centre on the R600 Timoleague road near the bridge over the Bandon, this large, modern house offers colourful, well-appointed rooms, all with views over the river, TVs and en-suite bathrooms, and good breakfasts from a varied menu. At the lower end of this price code; good single rates. ❸

The town centre

The **Kinsale Regional Museum** (Wed–Fri 11am–4pm, Sat noon–4pm, Sun 2.30–5pm; times may vary – check on ⓣ021/477 7930; €3; Heritage Island) is immediately recognizable in the warren of lanes behind the tourist office by its Dutch-style triple gables, which were added in 1706 to the old market house. Upstairs, the courtroom where the inquest into the loss of the *Lusitania* took place has been left partly as it was, augmented, poignantly, by an almost pristine deckchair from the wreck, as well as a medal produced in Germany to celebrate the sinking. Otherwise, the museum is a dusty collection of tools, maps and any old rope, dotted with a few curiosities such as Michael Collins' hurley and the shoes of the eight-foot three-inch Kinsale Giant, who made a fortune on the English stage in the eighteenth century as a novelty act.

Five minutes' walk up Cork Street from the museum stands a fine example of an urban tower-house, **Desmond Castle** (mid-April to Oct daily 10am–6pm, last admission 5.15pm; €2.90; Heritage Card; ⓦwww.heritageireland.ie). It was built around 1500 as a town residence and customs house by the Earl of Desmond, who had recently been given control of the wine trade from France, Spain and Portugal via Kildare to Bristol by King Henry VII. The architectural highlight is the facade, pierced by ogival windows, including unusual corner pairs on the first floor, and stamped with the Desmond coat of arms surmounted by Henry VII's royal standard. Interesting displays inside trace the building's chequered, often grim history – including stints as a jail and workhouse – as well as local connections with the global wine trade. Many of the "Wild Geese", Irishmen who fled the country in the sixteenth to eighteenth centuries, especially after the Battle of Kinsale and the Battle of the Boyne, went on to have successful second careers in viticulture, notably Richard Hennessy of Cork who settled in Cognac in the 1740s and the Lynches of Galway, producers of the famous claret, Château Lynch-Bages. These so-called "**Wine Geese**" have now formed an order of over a hundred *chevaliers* (knights), comprising wine producers of Irish descent from around the world.

The harbour

On the west side of the harbour, Kinsale spreads south for a couple of kilometres to the broad mouth of the Bandon River. On a long spit of land between the river and the outer harbour, **James Fort** is a great place to orientate yourself, with fine views that stretch from the town around to the open sea. Built in 1602–04 on the site of a walled fortification that was easily captured by the English from the Spanish forces at the Battle of Kinsale, it's a five-sided fort whose walls are now fetchingly overgrown with ferns and brambles. The new fort, however, proved equally vulnerable when, in 1649, a well-placed gun on the higher ground to the west led to its surrender to the Cromwellians, and in the 1680s, the building of Charles Fort finally rendered James Fort obsolete. On the southeast-facing side of the narrow peninsula, there's a small and pleasant sandy **beach** (signposted).

Kinsale's most compelling sight, the formidable **Charles Fort**, lies on the opposite side of the harbour, 3km southeast of town beyond the village of Summercove (mid-March to Oct daily 10am–6pm; Nov to mid-March daily 10am–5pm; last admission 45min before closing; €3.70; Heritage Card). On a fine day, the best way to get there is to **walk**, skirting round Scilly village and then following the lower, shoreline road, with refreshment available at *The Spaniard* and *The Bulman* (see opposite). It's possible also to extend the walk along the scrub-covered slopes out to the point at the end of the outer harbour (2hr return from the fort at an easy pace).

Begun in 1678, Charles Fort stands on the site of Anglo-Norman Ringcurran Castle, which had been destroyed on Cromwell's orders in 1656. Sir William Robinson, architect of the Royal Hospital, Kilmainham (see p.114), adapted the classic, star-shaped design of the great French military engineer, Vauban, but his advice to build extra fortifications at the top of the hill was not followed – though the fort was almost impregnable from the sea, the Duke of Marlborough was easily able to unseat the Jacobites by attacking on land in 1690. You can still make a complete circuit of the massive walls, but most of the buildings on the twelve-acre site were damaged during the Irish Civil War in 1922. The eerie roofless shells are substantial enough, however, to give a ready impression of what life in the fort must have been like for its garrison of four hundred, and you can flesh out the picture by sampling the fascinating displays and audio-visuals in the rebuilt Barracks Stores. The former ordnance sheds opposite now house a café (June–Sept daily; mid-March to May & Oct Sat & Sun).

Eating

Kinsale is a real honey-pot for foodies, its many cafés and restaurants making the most of local seafood and land-based ingredients, often with a French influence. In early October, there's a weekend **gourmet festival** (Ⓣ021/477 2847, Ⓦwww.kinsalerestaurants.com). The Quay Food Company on Market Quay is a fine **deli** for putting together a picnic.

Crackpots 3 Cork St Ⓣ021/477 2847. Informal, evening-only restaurant with an excellent, diverse menu that might offer swordfish with Asian slaw and mango and coriander chutney. All dishes are served on artistic crockery (also for sale), "Wine Geese" wines (see p.305) are denoted on the menu and there's a good-value early-bird menu until 7pm.

Cucina 9 Market St Ⓣ021/470 0707. Excellent daytime café-restaurant in a buzzy, contemporary setting, serving delicious sandwiches, soups and salads, plus a daily hot special, as well as varied breakfasts and very good coffees. Closed Sun. Accommodation available (see p.304).

Dino's Pier Rd. Waterfront chippy of good repute, whose menu stretches to chowder and fishcakes, with plenty of tables inside and a few outside if you want to sit down and eat.

Fishy Fishy Café Pier Rd. Highly regarded, informal restaurant (cash only, no reservations) with very attractive patio tables, serving great fish and seafood at reasonable prices. Daytime only, but in summer they stay open until 8pm Tues–Fri. Under the same ownership, the *Fishy Fishy Shop*, a fishmonger's on Guardwell, serves a simpler, more keenly priced lunch menu (closed Sun & Mon).

Gina's Market Quay. Small, bright-orange café, offering delicious wraps, panini, ciabattas and salads, as well as good coffee and cake.

Jim Edward's Market Quay. Pleasant, central pub with a posh restaurant, though you might as well stick to the excellent seafood on the bar menu: try the chowder or cod in smoked-salmon butter with (great) chips.

Max's Wine Bar Main St Ⓣ021/477 2443. Cosy, upmarket, "Irish-French" spot with a small conservatory. On the menu, meat and vegetarian dishes make an appearance alongside seafood offerings such as salmon en croute stuffed with rocket, with a lemon-butter sauce. Snack lunches and a good-value early-bird set menu (until 7.30pm) also available. Closed Tues.

Toddies The Glen ☎021/477 7769. Relaxing setting, whether in the candlelit interior hung with modern art, or at the attractive balcony tables, for top-notch cooking. A short menu, augmented by a long list of daily specials, features an excellent beef fillet *perigordine*, as well as lots of seafood – try the delicious scallop risotto. Mon–Sat evenings.

The Vintage Main St ☎021/477 2502. This formal but cosy and welcoming, oak-beamed restaurant serves up sophisticated and carefully presented, French-influenced cuisine, with a strong emphasis on seafood and locally sourced meat. Tues–Sun evenings, plus Sun lunch.

The White House The Glen. Moderately priced, first-rate bar food, with dishes such as *zarzuela*, a Spanish fish and tomato stew with saffron rice, plus a catch of the day.

Drinking and entertainment

To bolster its reputation for good living, Kinsale sports a wide array of genial **pubs**. Particularly popular is *The Grey Hound*, by the museum, a cosy, old-fashioned spot with quaint wooden partitions and seats outside on the pedestrianized alley. The rambling *Shanakee* (*An Seanachai*) on Market Street and the *White House* (see above) are regular venues for live **music**, usually traditional or ballads; or head for the *Tap Tavern* on Guardwell, a simple, sociable inn hung with bric-a-brac, for a quiet pint. Named after the plucky leader of the Spanish at the Battle of Kinsale, *The Spaniard* (☎021/477 2436) is a cosy, flagstoned pub that offers good food, either at the bar or in the restaurant, and regular traditional, folk and country music and sing-alongs; it's in the suburb of **Scilly**, just over a kilometre away around the east side of the harbour, on the way to Charles Fort. Further out towards the fort at **Summercove**, *The Bulman* (☎021/477 2131) also hosts plenty of music, ranging from bluegrass to jazz; its upstairs restaurant (Wed–Sat dinner, Sat & Sun lunch) enjoys great views of the harbour, while the attractive bar, adorned with nauticalia and warmed by open fires, dishes up soup and sandwiches.

West towards Skibbereen

Between Kinsale and Skibbereen, the main route west – the R600 and then the N71 – carves its way across the top of successive peninsulas, touching the sea only at the estuary towns of **Timoleague**, **Clonakilty** (often shortened to "Clon") and **Rosscarbery**. With names such as the **Seven Heads** (between Timoleague and Clon) these jagged-edged peninsulas are worth exploring with your own transport and no set destination in mind – crisscrossing minor roads will reveal sheltered coves, wild cliffs and balmy beaches. Clonakilty is the main base here, with the small coastal villages of **Courtmacsherry** and **Glandore**, which is handy for one of the country's finest stone circles at **Drombeg**, providing picturesque and tranquil alternatives.

Timoleague and Courtmacsherry

At **TIMOLEAGUE**, you might be tempted to break your journey westwards by the extensive remains of a **Franciscan friary**, standing on the side of the main road at the head of the muddy Argideen estuary. Built in the late thirteenth or early fourteenth century on the site of a seventh-century church, the abbey still shows the empty shells of its church, cloister, library, infirmary and dining room, though as befits the austere Franciscan order, the architectural details are plain. The village also has an excellent, relaxing **bar-restaurant**, *Dillon's*

(Ⓣ023/46390; Thurs–Sun evenings), while some of Ireland's finest smoked salmon (both wild and organically reared), as well as excellent smoked chicken and rashers, can be bought at Ummera smokehouse, a few kilometres north at Inchy Bridge (Ⓣ023/46644 for directions; Ⓦwww.ummera.com).

About 4km down the estuary on the R601, **COURTMACSHERRY** is a sheltered, tranquil, gaily painted family resort that consists mostly of holiday homes. It sparks into life with music, poetry and stories in mid-September during its **Storytelling Carnival** (Ⓣ023/46170). At the far end of the beach, Courtmacsherry Water Sports (Ⓣ023/44464, Ⓦwww.courtmacsherry watersports.com) offers **sailing** and **canoeing**, as well as land-yachting and power-boating, while **horse riding** is available via the old-fashioned, family-run *Courtmacsherry Hotel* (Ⓣ023/46198, Ⓦwww.courtmachotel.com; ❸). Cheery and cosy **guesthouse** accommodation overlooking the bay, as well as excellent breakfasts, can be had at *Travara Lodge* (Ⓣ023/46493, Ⓔtravaralodge @eircom.net; closed Nov; ❷).

Clonakilty and around

CLONAKILTY (Ⓦwww.clonakilty.ie) is an appealing if undramatic service town, which gives access to the Blue Flag beach at nearby **Inchydoney**. The town offers plenty of traditional music in the pubs, but is most famous as the home of award-winning **black puddings** and as the birthplace of Republican leader **Michael Collins**.

Information and accommodation

The helpful **tourist office** (June & Sept Mon–Sat 9.15am–6pm; July & Aug Mon–Sat 9.15am–7pm, Sun 10am–5pm; Oct–May Mon–Sat 9.15am–1pm & 2–5pm; Ⓣ023/33226) at 25 Ashe St – part of the town's long high street, which to the east becomes Wolfe Tone Street, to the west Pearse Street and then Western Road – stocks a free, weekly *What's On* guide. **Bike rental** is available at MTM Cycles, 33 Ashe St (Ⓣ023/33584), **horse riding** at Clonakilty Equestrian Centre, 500m beyond the Model Railway Village on the Inchydoney road

▲ Black pudding, Clonakilty

(Ⓣ023/33533). You can access the **Internet** at Talk and Internet Saloon, directly opposite the tourist office.

Clon can offer the full range of **accommodation**, including a **campsite**, *Desert House*, 500m from the centre near the shore (May–Sept; Ⓣ023/33331, Ⓔdeserthouse@eircom.net); head east out of town, turn right at the roundabout and follow the signs.

Bay View Old Timoleague Rd Ⓣ023/33539, Ⓦwww.bayviewclonakilty.com. Flower-bedecked, brightly decorated and welcoming en-suite B&B on the east side of town, with a pretty garden; decent single rates and reductions for children are offered. Closed Nov–Feb. ❷

Clonakilty Townhouse Wolfe Tone St Ⓣ023/35533, Ⓦwww.clonakiltytownhouse.ie. Welcoming, purpose-built guesthouse with spacious, bright, en-suite rooms, good breakfasts and Internet access, in a central location with private parking. ❸

Inchydoney Island Lodge and Spa Ⓣ023/33143, Ⓦwww.inchydoneyisland.com. Luxury retreat, beautifully sited at the mid-point of Inchydoney Beach and decorated in plush but cheery contemporary style, with extravagant touches such as espresso-makers in the rooms. Attached is a well-equipped and authentic thalassotherapy spa, offering a wide range of seawater and other treatments, as well as a large, indoor, heated seawater pool. ❽

O'Donovan's Hotel Pearse St Ⓣ023/33250, Ⓦwww.odonovanshotel.com. Parnell and Marconi stayed at this lively, traditional meeting-place on the main street, and it's still run by the O'Donovan family, retaining some of its period charm after recent refurbishment. ❹

Wytchwood Old Brewery Lane, off Emmet Square Ⓣ023/33525, Ⓦwww.wytchwood.ie. Central, comfortable and peaceful B&B in a Georgian-style house with a walled garden; en-suite throughout. Closed Oct–May. ❷

Around town

The main draw around Clonakilty is without doubt the **beach**, 4km to the south, on **Inchydoney Island**, which is now locked to the mainland by two causeway roads that enclose reclaimed pasturage. This gorgeous expanse of pristine white sand is split in two by Virgin Mary's Point, where the road ends, and flanked by headlands of rolling green fields. At the point, the West Cork Surf School offers **surfing** lessons (Ⓣ086 869 5396, Ⓦwww.westcorksurfing.com), and you don't have to be a resident of the spa hotel to avail of their thalassotherapy treatments (see above) or the varied and reasonably priced menu at their *Dunes Bar & Bistro*, which has some appealing outdoor tables.

Four kilometres east of Clonakilty, off the R600 towards Timoleague, is the eclectic but highly recommended **Michael Collins Centre** (mid-June to mid-Sept Mon–Fri 10.30am–5pm, Sat 11am–2pm; donations requested; Ⓣ023/46107, Ⓦwww.michaelcollinscentre.com). Engaging half-hour guided tours full of anecdotes, particularly about his distant relative Michael Collins, are led by Mr Crowley; features include photos, memorabilia and an audiovisual on Collins, and the Ambush Trail, a reconstruction of Collins' fatal ambush in 1921 at Beal na Bláth. On top of this there's a Michael Collins tour (by appointment, in your own car), taking in the actual Beal na Bláth and what is left of Collins' birthplace, incinerated in 1921 by the Black and Tans.

Alongside the N71 towards Bandon, also 4km east of Clon, are the lovely **Lisselan Gardens** (daily: Jan, Feb, Nov & Dec 8am–4pm; March, April & Oct 8am–5pm; May & Sept 8am–7pm; June–Aug 8am–8pm; €6; Ⓦwww.lisselan.com). A full circuit of the varied grounds here, crossing and recrossing the babbling Argideen River, takes about an hour, encompassing a fine rockery and formal gardens, lily ponds, woodland trails and a collection of fuchsias from around the world in the walled garden. The estate's nineteenth-century manor house is not open to the public, but there's an attractive tearoom in the courtyard. Lisselan takes part in the **West Cork Garden Trail**

(Ⓦ www.westcorkgardentrail.com) for two weeks in June, when other, normally private gardens open their gates to visitors.

If poor weather rules out any outdoor exploration, you could do worse than holing up in the **West Cork Regional Museum** (summer Tues, Thurs, Fri & Sat 10.30am–5pm, Sun 2–5pm, but hours sometimes irregular; €3) at the west end of Clonakilty's main street (here Western Road), which covers the area's contribution to the War of Independence and Clonakilty's once-prosperous linen industry, and displays a host of agricultural implements. Kids in particular will enjoy the **West Cork Model Railway Village** (Jan–June & Sept–Dec daily 11am–5pm, July & Aug 10am–6pm; €7, children €4.25, family ticket €22.50; Ⓦ www.modelvillage.ie), on the southeast edge of town off the Inchydoney road, which replicates the 1940s West Cork Railway and the towns it served in great detail at 1:24 scale. There's also a quirky cafeteria serving tea and cakes, housed in full-size, 1940s train carriages outside. Departing from here, a "road train" (€11, children €6.25, family ticket €33.50, all including entry to model village) makes a tour of Clonakilty several times a day, dropping down to Inchydoney beach twice daily if the narrow roads aren't too busy.

Eating and drinking

The town's main street has a good choice of **places to eat**. During the day, *Prego 2*, a small, friendly café at 6 Ashe St, rustles up excellent ciabattas, salads, soups and cakes. *An Súgán*, 41 Wolfe Tone St, specializes in seafood, in either its cosy bar or upstairs restaurant, and there's a well-run, popular Indian, the *Cobra Tandoori and Balti Restaurant* (evenings plus Fri–Sun lunchtimes; Ⓣ 023/35957), on Ashe Street. Top of the range is *Gleeson's*, a short way south of Ashe Street at 3 Connolly St (Tues–Sat evenings; Ⓣ 023/21834), an elegant spot offering sophisticated fare such as monkfish with saffron, tomato and capers and good-value set menus (Tues–Thurs all evening, Fri & Sat until 7pm).

De Barra's on Pearse Street is the pick of the **pubs**, an atmospheric old spot with live **music** most nights, including a popular traditional session on Monday night. *An Teach Beag*, a reconstructed traditional cottage behind *O'Donovan's Hotel*, has Irish music every night during July and August, and at weekends throughout the year, and there's more trad on Tuesdays in the hotel itself. *Shanley's* on Connolly Street hosts live traditional, piano and jazz, including occasional big-name Irish acts.

Rosscarbery, Drombeg and Glandore

Like Clonakilty and Timoleague, **ROSSCARBERY** (Ⓦ www.rosscarbery.ie) sits at the head of a deeply indented, southeast-facing bay. On the east side of its mouth is Owenahincha **beach**, a fine, Blue Flag stretch of sand that overlooks several rocky islets and, in the far distance, the lighthouse on Galley Head; **campers** can pitch tent here at *O'Riordan's Caravan Park* (Ⓣ 023/48216). Rosscarbery's landmark modern **hotel**, the *Celtic Ross* (Ⓣ 023/48722, Ⓦ www.celticrosshotel.com; closed mid-Jan to mid-Feb; ⑤), has large, comfortable rooms with fine views of the lagoon, a pool, sauna and gym. The area's best **B&B** is the atmospheric and welcoming *Castle Salem* (Ⓣ 023/48381, Ⓦ www.castlesalem.com; Feb–Nov; ②), a seventeenth-century farmhouse attached to a fine fifteenth-century castle, where you can enjoy home-made soda bread, scones and jams for breakfast; it's 4km away, signposted off the N71 towards Skibbereen. Hidden up a lane on the north side of the N71, Rosscarbery's attractive square shelters several **bars** and **places to eat**, notably *O'Callaghan Walshe* (Tues–Sun evenings; Ⓣ 023/48125), an informal, rustic and pricey restaurant specializing in fish. In mid-May, Rosscarbery hosts a three-day arts and literature **festival**, featuring performances, talks and workshops.

To the west of Rosscarbery lies one of the area's few compelling historical sites, the Bronze Age **Drombeg stone circle**; accessible via the R597 road towards Glandore, it's signposted after 5km. Looking out over pretty cattle pastures with the Atlantic in the distance, these seventeen well-preserved stones are associated with the winter solstice, when the sun sets on the southwest horizon at a point aligned with the lowest, axial stone (known as the "Druid's Altar") and the two tallest portal stones. Close by in the same field sits one of the best examples of a *fulacht fiadh*, a ritual cooking site (literally "deer roast"), in Ireland. It consists of a 1.5-metre-long stone-lined trough for water, into which red-hot stones from the adjacent hearth would have been rolled. Experiments have shown that this would have successfully boiled the water, and that meat wrapped in straw and plunged into the trough would have cooked in the same time it takes to do your turkey at Christmas, twenty minutes per pound, plus an extra twenty minutes for the pot.

A popular yachting haven, **GLANDORE** enjoys a particularly beautiful elevated position, overlooking the turquoise waters of a deep inlet and surrounded by lush, tree-carpeted slopes. Several **bars** set out tables and chairs to make the best of this view, including the *Glandore Inn*, recommended for its tortillas, pastas and other hearty **food**, and the very congenial *Casey's Bar* towards the east end of the village. Your best bet for accommodation is *Bay View*, a comfortable **B&B** with fine views (Ⓣ028/33115; ❷). On the R597, about a kilometre east of Glandore, you'll find the trim and peaceful *Meadow* **campsite** (Ⓣ028/33280, Ⓔmeadowcamping@eircom.net; Easter plus May to mid-Sept).

Skibbereen and around

SKIBBEREEN (often shortened to "Skibb"; Ⓦwww.skibbereen.ie), the lively administrative centre for this part of west Cork, is a good spot to take a break and recharge your batteries, with plenty of restaurants and accommodation options. To the south, it gives access to a rich coastal landscape where green pastures begin to alternate with the scrubby, rocky slopes so typical of more westerly parts. If you have your own wheels, you shouldn't miss the uniquely beautiful lagoon of **Lough Hyne**, while regular buses run down to the

Whale watching and kayaking

The seas off Skibb, rich feeding grounds for herring and sprat, are earning a reputation as one of Europe's premier **whale-watching** sites, with minke (from April), fin (from late June or early July), humpback (from September) and sometimes killer whales, as well as scores of dolphins, coming remarkably close to shore; September to November is the peak time. For further information, consult the website of the Irish Whale and Dolphin Group, Ⓦwww.iwdg.ie. Two companies run daily boat trips, costing €30–40 per person, from Reen Pier, well to the southeast of Skibb on Castlehaven Harbour: West Cork Marine Tours (Ⓣ028/36832 or 086 327 3226, Ⓦwww.whales-dolphins-ireland.com) and Whale Watch West Cork (Ⓣ028/33357 or 086 120 0027, Ⓦwww.whalewatchwestcork.com). Along the coast here between Rosscarbery and Mizen Head, there are also **sea-kayaking** trips, ranging from half a day to five-day expeditions, run by Atlantic Sea Kayaking (Ⓣ028/21058, Ⓦwww.atlanticseakayaking.com).

animated resort of **Baltimore**, which is connected by ferry to the contrasting islands of **Sherkin** and **Clear**.

The Town

Skibbereen is at its busiest on Fridays, when an afternoon country market of local produce (which is repeated on Saturday morning) coincides with the traditional weekly **cattle market**. The town's layout, bypassed by the main N71 to the north, is easy once you've got the hang of it: around a slow bend in the Ilen River, the two narrow main streets form a V shape, North Street pointing to the northeast, and Main Street (which becomes Bridge Street) pointing northwestwards. On North Street, the **West Cork Arts Centre** (Ⓣ028/22090, Ⓦwww.westcorkartscentre.com), which hosts temporary art exhibitions, drama and films, is worth a look (in the long term, the centre plans to move to a new site off Townshend Street, on the south side of town).

The first-rate **heritage centre**, in an attractively restored gasworks on Upper Bridge Street (mid-March to May & mid-Sept to Oct Tues–Sat 10am–6pm; June to mid-Sept daily 10am–6pm; last admission 45min before closing; winter opening by appointment "or just try the door"; €6; Heritage Island; Ⓣ028/40900, Ⓦwww.skibbheritage.com), is the home of two contrasting exhibitions. Introduced by actor and local resident Jeremy Irons, *The Great Famine Commemorative Exhibition* film provides a sensitive and vivid commentary on the Famine of the 1840s. The Skibbereen area was especially badly hit, with nearly a third of its population of a hundred thousand losing their lives and a further eight thousand being forced to emigrate – even though the Famine's effects on the town were widely publicized by the famous, stark drawings of James Mahony for the *Illustrated London News*. The ninety-minute **Skibbereen Trail**, marked by bronze plaques and detailed in a leaflet available from the heritage centre, takes in some of the Famine sites, including **Abbeystrewery Cemetery** on the N71 on the western edge of town, where between eight and ten thousand victims were buried in pits. The other exhibition introduces the amazing diversity of nearby **Lough Hyne** (see opposite), with an audiovisual and abundant pictures of its flora and fauna. The heritage centre also offers a genealogy service and, from June to September, runs historical **guided walks** of Skibbereen (Tues & Sat at 6.30pm; 90min; €5).

Practicalities

Buses drop off and pick up on Bridge Street, where Bus Éireann information is available from *Cahalane's* bar. The well-informed **tourist office** (June Mon–Sat 9am–6pm; July & Aug Mon–Sat 9am–7pm, Sun 10am–5pm; Sept–May Mon–Fri 9am–1pm & 2–5pm; Ⓣ028/21766) is on North Street and will provide information about the town's children's **festival** at the end of July and **food festival** in September (Ⓦwww.atasteofwestcork.com). **Bikes** can be rented from Roycroft's in Ilen Street (off Bridge St; Ⓣ028/21235), while **Internet access** is available at Skibbereen Business Services, overlooking the Super Valu car park on the south side of Main Street.

Among **B&Bs**, *Sunnyside*, at 42 Mardyke St off the south side of Bridge Street (Ⓣ028/21365, Ⓦwww.stayatsunnyside.com; closed Jan; ❷), is a comfortable and central if run-of-the-mill option, with both standard and en-suite rooms. Distinctly out of the ordinary is *Bridge House*, Bridge Street (Ⓣ028/21273; ❷), an eccentric, Victorian-styled B&B stuffed with antiques, swags and china dolls. There's a fine **hostel**, the *Russagh Mill Hostel and Adventure Centre*, in a lovingly restored mill a kilometre southeast on the R596 Castletownshend road

Irish food and drink

Like the country and culture that it springs from, Irish cuisine is imbued with a strong sense of tradition, though that's certainly not to say that changing times and tastes have passed it by. In fact, over the last two decades, something of a culinary revolution has been taking place, and modern Irish cuisine now encompasses all manner of global techniques. Most crucial, however, is what underpins it: a renewed emphasis on the finest, freshest and often locally produced ingredients that have always been at the heart of all the classic Irish dishes.

▲ Eden restaurant, Dublin

Food (*bia*)

Modern Irish cuisine's attention to ingredients has bred a new generation of high-quality, small-scale artisan **producers**, be they cheese-makers, organic farmers, fish-smokers or bakers, with the best Irish chefs seeking out this produce to re-create and adapt traditional dishes. The best places to sample the results are in big-city **restaurants** and gourmet hotspots such as Kinsale and Kenmare, but if you fancy trying your hand at preparing a few dishes yourself, head for one of the country's excellent **food markets**. Colourful, vibrant affairs worth a visit in their own right, the best are the permanent English Market in Cork city, and, on Saturdays, the Temple Bar Food Market in Dublin, the Galway city market and the Midleton market in east Cork.

Irish meat is internationally renowned, especially Aberdeen Angus **beef** and **lamb** from the west coast, the latter often appearing in a wholesome **Irish stew**, a classic broth with potatoes, onions and carrots. Interesting variants to look out for include Achill lamb from Mayo, what the French call *pré-salé*: as the animals graze on briny meadows by the sea, the meat is naturally salty and a little sweet; and delicious air-dried Connemara lamb from Oughterard, a little like Italian Parma ham. Beef, pork and lamb of course crop up in excellent sausages, which may be accompanied on your breakfast plate by **black pudding**, a sausage of pig's blood, and **white pudding**, made from pig's offal and cereals (the butchers of Clonakilty in West Cork make a speciality of these puddings). Also keep an eye out for Skeaghanore ducks from Ballydehob in west Cork, which are highly prized for their taste and texture.

Fresh **fish** and **seafood** such as prawns, lobsters and mussels, particularly from the west coast, Dublin Bay and Carlingford Lough, Dundrum Bay and Stangford Lough in the North, are also generally excellent. Among many seafood festivals around Ireland's coastline, the most famous are at Clarinbridge and nearby Galway city celebrating Galway Bay's **oysters**. These large, silky European Flat Oysters are some of the best in the world, having matured and fattened for about three years in anticipation of a season that runs from September until April. Other watery delicacies include silver or brown eels, for example from the River Bann; Ardglass

◀ English Market, Cork City

Farmhouse cheeses

Legend has it that Irish monks exported the secrets of **cheese-making** to Europe in the sixth century, while many different kinds of Irish cheese are recorded in early texts – notably the twelfth-century **Aislinge Meic Conglinne**, a brilliantly satirical tale about a king possessed by a demon of gluttony, and an underfed student monk who tries to tempt the demon out with a vision of a foodie's paradise. However, cheese-making in Ireland entirely died out in the seventeenth and eighteenth centuries, as a result partly of the plantations and partly of the rise of the international butter trade. It wasn't until the 1970s and 1980s that local cheese-making took off again, generally handmade by farmers with milk from their own cows, goats or sheep. These **farmhouse cheeses**, though often based on Continental or British recipes, have wowed the international markets and in less than quarter of a century production has rocketed to over a thousand tonnes a year, concentrated in the counties of Munster. Here are a few names to look out for on your travels:

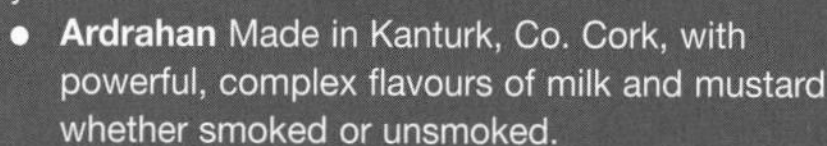

- **Ardrahan** Made in Kanturk, Co. Cork, with powerful, complex flavours of milk and mustard, whether smoked or unsmoked.

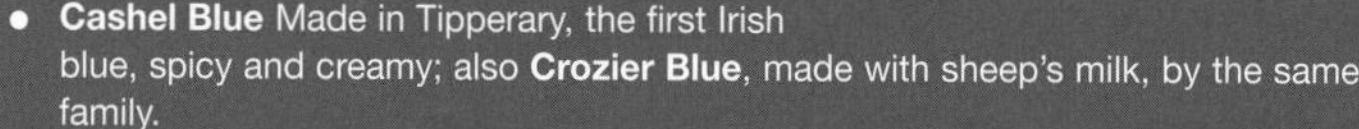

- **Cashel Blue** Made in Tipperary, the first Irish blue, spicy and creamy; also **Crozier Blue**, made with sheep's milk, by the same family.
- **Desmond** Piquant, long-matured, Swiss-style cheese from Schull in west Cork; also **Gabriel**, a hard, aromatic and full-bodied Gruyère-like cheese from the same makers.
- **Drumkeel** Mild, slightly crumbly, hexagonal, white cheese from Antrim.
- **Durrus** Semi-soft, washed-rind cheese from west Cork that scoops up frequent awards.
- **Gubbeen** Full-flavoured semi-soft from Schull, available smoked.
- **Kilshanny** Type of Gouda, sweet, hard and milky, made in Lahinch, Clare; sometimes flavoured with garlic, cumin or nettles.
- **St Killians** Soft, Camembert-style cheese with a pungent rind, from Enniscorthy, Co. Wexford; also milder **St Brendan** brie by the same cheese-maker.
- **St Tola** A fine range of goat's cheeses from Inagh, Clare.

potted herrings from Down, which are marinated in vinegar, rolled with bay leaf and breadcrumbed; and crab classically dressed with mustard and mayonnaise. Ireland is also home to dozens of excellent **smokehouses**, which smoke not only delicately flavoured, satiny salmon, but also mussels, eels, mackerel, tuna, cod and trout; one of the best, Ummera, near Timoleague in west Cork, also produces delicious smoked bacon and chicken.

Irish stew ▶

▲ The Long Hall pub, Dublin

Drink (*deoch*)

Dark, creamy **stout** has long been Ireland's most popular drink, and few visitors leave without a taster. It's always granted two minutes' settling time halfway through pouring and you should let it settle again once it's fully poured. Brewed in Dublin, Guinness is the market leader, but Beamish and Murphy's from Cork are also worth trying, as are microbrewery-produced stouts and beers.

The other indigenous tipple is **whiskey**, whose name comes from the Gaelic *uisce beatha*, the "water of life". Apart from an inexplicable change in spelling, the main differences are that whiskeys generally don't have the smoky, peaty flavour found in many Scotches, as the malt is dried in smokeless kilns rather than over peat fires; and they are triple-distilled, whereas Scotch only goes round twice, making the Irish version on the whole smoother and more refined. The main brands are Jameson's, Power's, Paddy's – all three of which are now distilled in Midleton, Co. Cork, though Paddy's is still the most popular whiskey in Munster – and Bushmills, made in Antrim and the preferred drop in the North. Whiskey, along with black coffee, sugar and cream, is one of the ingredients in **Irish coffee**, which was invented in the 1940s at the terminus of the flying-boat service in Foynes, Co. Limerick, to warm up damp and miserable transatlantic passengers.

Irish specialities

- **Bacon and cabbage** Shoulder of pork slowly boiled with cabbage.
- **Barmbrack** or **brack** (*bairín breac*, "speckled loaf") Sweet, full-flavoured, cake-like bread, made with dried fruits and spices; traditional at Halloween, when symbolic gifts (such as a ring to foretell marriage) are baked in the brack.
- **Black and Tan** Stout and ale, generally mixed in equal quantities.
- **Black velvet** Stout and champagne.
- **Boxty** Potato pancakes.
- **Carrageen** or **carrageen moss** Edible seaweed, valued for its medicinal qualities; it is often used to make a blancmange-like dessert or ice cream.
- **Champ** The Northern version of colcannon, with spring onions instead of cabbage.
- **Colcannon** Mashed potato mixed with cabbage and often leeks.
- **Crubeen** Boiled pig's trotters.
- **Drisheen** Sausage of sheep and beef blood, mixed with oatmeal and pepper, from the southwest, especially Cork.
- **Dublin coddle** Sausages and bacon boiled with potatoes and onions.
- **Dublin lawyer** Lobster cooked with whiskey and cream.
- **Dulse** Edible seaweed, rich in Vitamin A and protein.
- **Fadge** Northern Irish fried potato bread.
- **Hot port** A winter warmer, made with port, hot water, lemon and cloves.
- **Hot whiskey** or **hot toddy** As above, with whiskey instead of port.
- **Poteen** (*poitín*, "little pot") Subject of many an Irish song, a powerful, usually illicitly distilled whiskey that varies enormously in quality – some being fit only to strip paint.
- **Red lemonade** Produced since the nineteenth century and unique to Ireland, a local favourite, though it's just lemonade with red colouring.
- **Soda bread** Light, tasty bread baked with bicarbonate of soda, buttermilk and flour.
- **Tayto's** Ireland's own brand of potato crisps; the basic flavour is cheese'n'onion.

(☎028/22451, Ⓦwww.russaghmillhostel.com; IHH; closed Nov–Feb; dorms €12–14, twins ❶), which also offers walking, climbing and kayaking trips. **Camping** is possible here or at the *Hideaway Camping & Caravan Park* (☎028/22254, Ⓔskibbereencamping@eircom.net; Easter & May to mid-Sept), a little closer in on the Castletownshend road.

Your best bet for **eating** in Skibb is the relaxed and informal *Kalbo's Bistro*, 48 North St (☎028/21515; closed Sun; early-bird until 7.30pm Mon–Fri), which serves up sophisticated and not too pricey dishes such as turbot on crab risotto with lemon-butter sauce. Otherwise, try *Yassou*, a cosy café-restaurant on the corner of Bridge and Townshend streets, which does everything from authentic Greek *meze* to burgers. For a meal with a touch of adventure thrown in, make a reservation at *Island Cottage* (mid-June to mid-Sept Wed–Sat evenings; ☎028/38102, Ⓦwww.islandcottage.com; set menu €45, no credit cards), an excellent, charming restaurant on **Heir Island**; to get there you'll need to drive or cycle west along the N71 towards Ballydehob for 5km, then follow the signs down the small peninsula for about another 5km to Cunnamore, from where a small boat will ferry you across to the island in five minutes.

Among Skibb's **bars**, *Baby Hannah's* on Bridge Street is a lively spot, which hosts **traditional music** on Mondays year-round and Fridays in summer. Sessions are also held at the *Corner Bar* on the same street on Mondays and Saturdays, while at the *West Cork Hotel* on Ilen Street, the local *comhaltas* (traditional-music association) puts on a show of music, song, dance and storytelling every Wednesday from mid-July to the end of August (☎028/22739, Ⓦwww.skibbereencomhaltas.com; €10).

Lough Hyne

If you head out of Skibb on the Baltimore road and take a left turn after about 5km, you'll soon come upon **Lough Hyne**. Ireland's first marine nature reserve, this tidal lake is joined to the sea only by a narrow channel, known as the rapids, but reaches depths of 45m in places. A combination of warm waters from the Gulf Stream and diverse habitats – sea caves, whirlpools, shallow and deep areas – supports an astonishingly rich variety of saltwater species here, over a thousand in less than a square kilometre. Many are rare species that are generally only found in the deep ocean or the Mediterranean, such as the triggerfish and the red-mouthed goby. Sheltered by varied slopes of gorse, woods and bare rock, the placid waters are also popular among swimmers and kayakers. To make the most of a visit, see the exhibit at the Skibbereen heritage centre first (see opposite), where you can also pick up a brochure for the **Knockomagh Wood Nature Trail**. Beginning where the road from Skibb meets Lough Hyne, at its northwestern corner, this two-kilometre trail zigzags upwards and westwards past fine viewpoints of the lake, ancient sessile oaks and bluebell meadows, to the 197-metre summit of Knockomagh Hill, which affords a panorama of the coastline stretching from Galley Head in the east to Mount Gabriel above Schull.

Baltimore

Though isolated at the end of a stubby peninsula to the southwest of Skibbereen, **BALTIMORE** (Ⓦwww.baltimore.ie) comes as a lively surprise, bustling with fishing and pleasure boats and ferries to Sherkin and Clear islands. In fine weather, there are few pleasanter spots in Cork than the small, sun-trap square above the harbour, filled with café and bar tables. Overlooking the square stands **Dún na Séad**, a thirteenth-century tower house that was the chief residence of the infamous pirates, the O'Driscolls, but fell into ruins from the end of the seventeenth century until its painstaking recent restoration as a private home. It's worth a visit in summer (June–Sept daily 11am–6pm; €3) to see the imposing great hall on the first floor and to take in the commanding views of the harbour and Roaringwater Bay from the battlements. Basking in the shelter of large inshore islands, the port is particularly busy during the **regatta** held in early August, but the enterprising village is canny enough to lay on several other annual **festivals**. There's a fiddle fair in mid-May (ⓦ www.fiddlefair.com) and a combined food and sailing festival during the last weekend in May (ⓦ www.woodenboatfestival.com), while the annual O'Driscoll clan gathering takes place in June (ⓣ 028/20125).

Information and accommodation

As well as selling some beautiful objects made on Sherkin and Clear islands, Island Crafts, in a hut down by the quay, provides **tourist information** on Baltimore and the islands daily in summer (ⓣ 028/20347 or 20022, ⓦ www.islandscrafts.com). You can take a **diving** course or trip at Aquaventures (ⓣ 028/20511, ⓦ www.aquaventures.ie), who also offer half-day **snorkelling** trips, or Baltimore Diving Centre (ⓣ 028/20300, ⓦ www.baltimorediving.com). In summer, the ferry MV *Mystic Waters* runs guided, two-hour **boat tours** of ten of the so-called Carbery's Hundred Isles in Roaringwater Bay (Mon–Fri & Sun 2.30pm; ⓣ 087 263 8470 or 028/20218, ⓦ www.tenislandtours.com or www.islandtripper.com), while Baltimore Sea Safari offers a wide variety of trips in a smaller, speedier rib (ⓣ 028/20753, ⓦ www.baltimoreseasafari.ie). As well as operating the ferry service to Clear Island, the *Naomh Ciarán II*, *Spirit of the Isles* and *Cailín Óir* (see p.316) lay on a variety of sightseeing opportunities in summer: the first two sail out to the famous, hundred-year-old lighthouse on Fastnet Rock, via Clear, every afternoon, while the *Cailín Óir* has an imaginative menu of tours, with guided commentary, to Lough Hyne, Fastnet, around Sherkin Island and Baltimore Harbour (all weekly in the evening), as well as to Crookhaven (see p.318; bus to Barley Cove available for charter), via Clear Island, one or two days a week. Baltimore is a popular **place to stay** in July and August, over bank-holiday weekends and during its festivals (see above), when booking in advance is highly recommended.

Baltimore Bay Guesthouse ⓣ 028/20600, ⓦ www.youenjacob.com. Bright, pleasant, spacious, pine-floored rooms on the main square, most with harbour views. All have en-suite bathrooms and continental breakfast is served downstairs at *La Jolie Brise* café. ❸

Baltimore Townhouse ⓣ 028/20197, ⓦ www.baltimoretownhouse.com. Owned by *Casey's Hotel*, this gleaming new house near the village centre encompasses six stylish and well-equipped suites, each with a sitting room and small fridge. Breakfast is either continental, including freshly baked bread left hanging on your door, or full Irish, taken at *Casey's*, which is also where you check in. Good-value weekend, midweek and half-board packages. ❺

Bushe's Bar ⓣ 028/20125, ⓦ www.bushesbar.com. Basic but comfortable rooms above the pub, with TVs and en-suite bathrooms; you'll pay more for a harbour view. Breakfast is taken in bed. ❷

Casey's Hotel On the main Skibbereen road, 1km from the harbour ⓣ 028/20197, ⓦ www.caseysofbaltimore.com. Charming, family-run hotel with large, colourfully decorated and very comfortable en-suite bedrooms and good breakfasts. The restaurant (see below) and the beer garden – as well as many of the rooms – enjoy glorious views over the peaceful inlet to Ringarogy Island. All sorts of weekend, midweek and half-board packages are offered. ❺

Rolf's Left turn off the main road into the village, a 10min walk from the harbour ⓣ 028/20289, ⓦ www.rolfsholidays.eu. Civilized, tranquil spot in beautiful, subtropical gardens with fine sea views and a good restaurant (see below). The pine-furnished rooms are bright and spruce, and self-catering cottages are also available. ❸

Top of the Hill Hostel On the main road, a 5min walk from the harbour ⓣ 028/20094, ⓦ www.topofthehillhostel.ie. Bright, attractive hostel with a good-sized kitchen, lounge and patio. Dorms €15, twins and doubles ❶

Eating and drinking

Baltimore's **eateries** are diverse and generally good value, belying its scale and remoteness. The restaurant at *Rolf's* is a relaxing setting for tasty and moderately priced European dishes, using as much home-grown, organic and local produce as possible and including plenty of choice for vegetarians. *Casey's* offers various catches of the day and seafood platters at reasonable prices either in the restaurant or the bar, where simpler main courses, soup and sandwiches are also available. Back in the centre, *La Jolie Brise* does everything from breakfast to late suppers, with tables out on the square overlooking the harbour. On offer are simple main courses, such as pizza, salmon and steak, as well as cheap local oysters, mussels and prawns. The same owners run *Chez Youen* just down the street (Ⓣ028/20136; closed Sun & Mon), a homely white-tablecloth affair serving mostly French seafood dishes. *Bushe's Bar* is a friendly, popular **pub**, which serves excellent, cheap soup and seafood sandwiches during the day. The bar at *Casey's Hotel* has live music on Saturdays year-round, more frequently in high summer.

Sherkin Island

Guarding the west side of Baltimore Harbour, **Sherkin** (Inis Arcáin, "Island of the Porpoise"; Ⓦwww.sherkinisland.ie) is a tranquil, pretty island that shares the mixed scrub and pastoral landscape of the mainland hereabouts. On a half-day stroll around the boot-shaped island, you could take in the highest point, Slievemore, to the southwest on the toe of the boot, and the best beaches, Trá Bawn, Trá Eoghan Mhór and Silver Strand, to the north of Slievemore. There are **ferries** from Baltimore (5–9 daily; 10min; €10 return; Ⓣ028/20218, Ⓦwww.sherkinferry.com) and, if you fancy a spot of island-hopping, twice a week the *Cailín Óir* (see p.316) links Sherkin with Clear Island. All boats land at the easterly pier, behind which stands a plain fifteenth-century Franciscan **abbey**, with its fifteen-metre tower intact; you can still see the outline of its cloister and the walls of a curious seventeenth-century fish "palace", where pilchards were salted and barrelled for export to Spain.

If you want to stay, there's smart **B&B** at the all-en-suite *Horseshoe Cottage* (Ⓣ028/20598, Ⓦwww.gannetsway.com; ❷), a recently renovated 400-year-old house, overlooking tranquil Horseshoe Bay to the south of the pier; the owners also offer half- and full-day sailing trips and holistic massage. Set in attractive gardens to the north of the pier, *The Islander's Rest* **hotel** (Ⓣ028/20116, Ⓦwww.islandersrest.ie; ❹) offers pleasant, en-suite bedrooms with great views, as well as hearty food in the bar. *The Jolly Roger*, a cosy **pub** with a pretty terrace opposite, also offers food, as well as impromptu music sessions. You can buy supplies just up from the pier at the Abbey Store and post office.

Clear Island

Ireland's most southerly inhabited point, **Clear Island** (Oileán Chléire, also known as Cape Clear; Ⓦwww.oilean-chleire.ie) is an isolated outpost of the **Gaeltacht**, which welcomes teenagers from all over the country to two Irish colleges during the summer, and generally reaches out to visitors, with plenty of facilities and information available. The island also holds a traditional storytelling **festival**, with concerts, workshops and plenty of music (Ⓣ028/39116, Ⓦindigo.ie/~stories), on the first weekend of September.

Clear describes a very rough figure-of-eight, just six kilometres square, with **North Harbour**, where ferries dock, and cliff-girt **South Harbour**, where kayaks and snorkels can be rented, almost meeting in the middle. Its landscape of steep, rolling hills of heather and pasture is crossed by narrow, hedge-lined roads and paths, affording fine views of Roaringwater Bay and of Fastnet Rock to the west. The island is most famous as one of the best seabird-watching sites in Europe, with breeding colonies of black guillemots, choughs and rock doves and an important **bird observatory** at North Harbour (Ⓣ028/39181). Late spring and October are the best times for twitchers.

The island is reputed to have been the sixth-century birthplace of **St Ciarán of Saighir** (not to be confused with Ciarán of Clonmacnois), who is (spuriously) claimed to have brought Christianity to Ireland thirty years before St Patrick. According to legend, he ended his days in Cornwall, where he was known as St Piran and credited with the discovery of tin. His twelfth-century church, graveyard and holy well lie on the west side of North Harbour. Much more impressive is the fifteenth-century **Dún an Óir** ("Fort of Gold") to the west, a ruined O'Driscoll stronghold on an isolated and now inaccessible rocky outcrop. Up the steep bank to the east of North Harbour, visitors are welcome at **Cleire Goat Farm** (Ⓣ028/39126, Ⓦwww.emara.com), which produces ice cream, cheese and sausages. In the mornings, you can watch milking, at other times, walk down the steeply sloping pastures to see the animals – or you could sign up for a goat husbandry course. A short walk further along the same road, by the church, the tiny **heritage centre** (June–Aug Mon–Sat noon–5pm, sometimes closed for lunch; €4) hosts some detailed and interesting displays, especially on maritime history and archeology.

Practicalities

As well as summertime **ferries** from Schull (see p.318), the *Naomh Ciarán II* and *Spirit of the Isles* (both Ⓣ087 268 0760, 087 282 4008 or 028/39153, Ⓦwww.capeclearferry.com; summer 4–5 daily; winter 1–3 daily; €12 return) and the *Cailín Óir* (Ⓣ086 346 5110, Ⓦwww.islandtripper.com; summer 2–5 daily; €14 return, with guided commentary and a short tour around the intervening islands) sail from Baltimore (45min). In summer, the first two boats also do daily trips from Clear Island to Fastnet, while the *Cailín Óir* sails on from Clear to Crookhaven (see p.318) one or two days a week; Baltimore–Clear return tickets with the *Cailín Óir* are accepted on the Clear–Schull *Karycraft* ferry.

The crafts shop at North Harbour dispenses **tourist information**, and Chuck Kruger leads historical and archeological **guided walks** (Ⓣ028/39157). In the summer, the island minibus (Ⓣ028/39119 or 086 383 6759; €5 per person) runs hour-long **tours** of the island, hourly from noon. As the island can get busy in high summer, it's best to book accommodation before you come. **B&Bs** include the good-value and friendly *Cluain Mara*, attached to *Ciaran Danny Mike's* pub (Ⓣ028/39153, Ⓦwww.capeclearisland.com; self-catering cottages also available; ❷); and the welcoming *Ard na Gaoithe*, in a renovated nineteenth-century house up behind the youth hostel along a steep lane (Ⓣ028/39160, Ⓔardnagaoithe@hotmail.com; ❷); both offer particularly good rates for single rooms. The basic An Óige **hostel** occupies the old coastguard station at South Harbour (Ⓣ028/41968, Ⓦwww.anoige.fenlon.net; closed Oct–Feb; dorms €16), while **camping** is possible on a terraced site on the opposite side of the harbour (Ⓣ028/39119; June–Sept).

The island has two **pubs**, both on the road between the two harbours. *Cotter's Bar* offers tasty **food** during the day a short walk from North Harbour, while *Ciaran Danny Mike's,* overlooking South Harbour from the hill, is popular for both lunch and dinner. *Club Cléire*, the social and cultural centre beside North Harbour, hosts traditional **music** on summer weekends, and *An Siopa Beag* in the same building is the island's grocery store, with **Internet** access and a **café** serving sandwiches, salads and pizzas.

Mizen Head Peninsula

Mizen Head is a wild and beautiful peninsula, projecting southwestwards around the substantial mass of copper-rich **Mount Gabriel**. The whole of its empty northern coast consists of sheer cliffs and stupendous views. The south coast is more populous, sheltering safe harbours, the large village and resort of **Schull** and the remote, sandy beaches of **Barley Cove**, while the only tourist attraction of any note is the signal station at the very tip, the **Mizen Head Visitor Centre**.

Schull

The peninsula's main settlement, **SCHULL** (Ⓦwww.schull.ie), is a congenial harbour town that's not only popular with yachties but also has an artistic bent, with crafts shops, galleries and a weekly food and crafts market (every Sun from Easter to Christmas). It shelters in the lee of 407-metre **Mount Gabriel**, to the north, topped by an aircraft-tracking station and blessed with fine views. The walk up there (about 8km there and back) is detailed in a very useful, free, annual booklet, *Schull Visitor's Guide*, that's available around the town; since the mountain was actively mined for centuries, take care on the way that you avoid uncovered mine shafts.

Schull also boasts a **planetarium**, developed by a local German resident in the village's community college on Colla Road, which runs south off Main Street. It's generally open only in the summer (June–Sept), at Easter and over bank holidays, with a detailed programme of starshows (€5, children €3.50, family ticket €15; Ⓦwww.schullcommunitycollege.com) – call Ⓣ028/28315 or 28552 for details.

Reflecting its catholic nature, Schull's main annual events are **Calves Week** sailing regatta, in the first full week in August, and a packed **arts week** later in the month. The Schull Watersports Centre at the pier (Ⓣ028/28554) offers **kayaking**, **windsurfing** and **dinghy rental**, while **diving** is organized by Divecology (Ⓣ028/28943, Ⓦwww.divecology.com) and **horse riding** by Ballycumisk Riding School, 6km or so east of town near Rossbrin Harbour (Ⓣ028/37246 or 087 961 6969).

▲ Mizen Head

Practicalities

Internet access is available at @ Your Leisure on Main Street. *Stanley House*, about a kilometre southwest of the centre off Colla Road, provides en-suite **B&B** in a large, immaculately kept, modern house with a pleasant garden, fine views across the bay and good single rates (ⓣ028/28425, ⓦwww.stanley-house.net; March–Oct; self-catering accommodation also available; ❷). More upmarket digs, as well as Swedish-influenced cooking, can be had at *Grove House* on Colla Road itself (ⓣ028/28067, ⓦwww.grovehouseschull.com; ❸). Overlooking the harbour, this creeper-clad townhouse has been quirkily and stylishly redecorated with antiques and modern paintings. Towards the east end of Main Street stands a new **hotel**, *Harbour View* (ⓣ028/28101, ⓦwww.harbourviewhotelschull.com; ❺), which has been attractively done out with dark woods and pale stone in contemporary style; it offers good single rates, fine views of the bay, a well-equipped gym and a good-sized pool.

Schull's best **restaurant** is *The Waterside* on Main Street (ⓣ028/28203; closed Mon), a plush, upmarket spot serving up complex dishes such as Dunmanus Bay prawns with champagne-and-coriander sauce. With outside seating down at the harbour, the fish shop dishes up high-class fish and chips, as well as pizzas. Towards the east end of Main Street by the hotel, *West Cork Gourmet Store* is a popular, easy-going deli and **café**, serving high-quality soups, salads and sandwiches; in summer, it stays open Thursday–Sunday evenings to offer pizzas, pastas and salads. Several of the **pubs** also offer good food, including *Hackett's* on Main Street, a great old bar with a vaguely alternative feel, a good soundtrack and regular live music. Here you can get imaginative bar lunches of salads, sandwiches and soups and, on weekend evenings in summer, French farmhouse-style casseroles in the restaurant upstairs (ⓣ028/28625).

In summer, the *Karycraft* **ferry** (ⓣ028/28278 or 086 237 9302, ⓦwww.capeclearferries.com) runs from Schull to Clear Island (June–Aug 3 daily; early Sept 1–3 daily; phone for schedule for the rest of Sept; 45min; €13 return) and operates evening cruises, via Clear Island, around the Fastnet Rock (June & Sept 1 weekly; July & Aug 2 weekly; 2hr 30min; €14).

Goleen, Crookhaven and Mizen Head

Around 15km southwest down the peninsula from Schull lies the quiet village of **GOLEEN**. Attractively sited on the small harbour here is the charming upscale **restaurant** and **B&B**, *Heron's Cove* (ⓣ028/35225, ⓦwww.heronscove.com; ❷), which opens for dinner from April to October and for B&B year-round (with evening meals always available to guests). The tip of the peninsula, which is the southernmost point of mainland Ireland, rather surprisingly shelters a golden, sandy, Blue Flag beach in **Barley Cove**, backed by dunes and punctured by a stream. A wild spit of land pushes east of here to the village of **CROOKHAVEN**, which would feel like the end of the world were it not for the pleasure boats anchored in the long, fjord-like inlet. In the village, you'll find welcoming, en-suite **B&B** at *Galley Cove* (ⓣ028/35137, ⓦwww.galleycovehouse.com; mid-March to Oct; ❷), a modern bungalow with fine views of the sea and Fastnet lighthouse, and two cosy **pubs** with bar food and outside tables overlooking the water.

To the west of Barley Cove, the narrow road heads upwards and outwards to **Mizen Head** itself. The **visitor centre** here, which comprises a café and the famous signal station (now automatic), isn't up to much (mid-March to May & Oct daily 10.30am–5pm; June–Sept daily 10am–6pm; Nov to mid-March Sat & Sun 11am–4pm; €6; Heritage Island; ⓦwww.mizenhead.ie), but it's worth paying the entrance fee to walk out to the head, which turns out to be an island, accessed by a slender, arched bridge: with the fifty-metre Fastnet lighthouse and the tip of the Beara Peninsula to either side and the whole of Ireland behind you, you're left to plot the folds of the jagged cliffs, the movements of the clouds and the churning contours of the ocean.

Sheep's Head

The **Sheep's Head** (Ⓦwww.thesheepshead.com), a precarious sliver of land between Dunmanus and Bantry bays, is the quietest and least populous of the southwestern peninsulas. Gorse and heather sprout from its long granite spine, leaving room for narrow pockets of green pasture on its north and especially its south coast. With magnificent views of the larger peninsulas on either side, it can be best appreciated by pedalling the easy-to-follow, 90-kilometre **Sheep's Head Cycle Route**, or by walking the 88-kilometre **Sheep's Head Way**, both of which are waymarked circuits from Bantry; the latter is relatively easy walking, avoiding the round-peninsula road for most of the way, and is covered by OS Discovery Series map number 88 or the 1:50,000 map that comes with the locally available *Guide to the Sheep's Head Way*. It can be done in four days, with two nights in Kilcrohane after two long days' walking and a night in Durrus; the last day is missable, so you might want to catch a bus back to Bantry from Durrus.

At the head of Dunmanus Bay, **DURRUS** is a relatively busy junction village between the Mizen Head and Sheep's Head peninsulas, supporting several pubs and *Good Things Café*, on the Ahakista road, a bright, modern, summertime **café-restaurant** (and cookery school) that makes creative use of local land and sea ingredients (Ⓣ027/61426, Ⓦwww.thegoodthingscafe.com; mid-June to Aug Mon & Thurs–Sun lunch & dinner). A couple of kilometres southwest down the R591 towards Crookhaven, *Blairs Cove House* (Ⓣ027/61127, Ⓦwww.blairscove.ie; ❻) combines spacious luxury accommodation (March–Nov) in beautiful grounds overlooking Dunmanus Bay, with an excellent restaurant (mid-March to Oct Tues–Sat evenings), renowned for its buffet-style starters and grilled meats.

KILCROHANE, 15km southwest of Durrus, supports a combined shop and post office with a petrol pump, a couple of **bars** serving food, and a **hostel**, *Carbery View* (Ⓣ027/67035; IHO; dorms €14), where **camping** is possible. In an attractive house by the church, friendly *Bridge View House* (Ⓣ027/67086, Ⓦwww.bridgeviewhouse.com; ❷) is a highly recommended **B&B**, with excellent home-cooking. From Kilcrohane, a road loops along the north coast of the peninsula, reaching its highest point at a spectacular pass 2km north of the village; for even better views, it's possible to walk to the top of **Seefin**, Sheep's Head's highest hill (344m), in about half an hour from the pass. Further along the quieter north side, there's an outstanding **B&B** at **Glenlough**, 12km southwest of Bantry and less than a kilometre off the Sheep's Head Way: the welcoming, all-en-suite *Sea Mount Farmhouse* (Ⓣ027/61226, Ⓦwww.seamountfarm.com; March–Oct; ❷) provides magnificent views of Bantry Bay, fine home-baking, evening meals, walking tours and plenty of useful information about exploring the area.

West of Kilcrohane, the Sheep's Head is dotted with small lakes and becomes more jagged and hummocky as it narrows to a lighthouse at the tip. Where the tarmac runs out, the **Tooreen Visitor Centre** (Easter–Sept daily; Ⓣ027/67136) nourishes travellers with hearty soups, fresh salmon sandwiches, desserts and cakes, and offers walking information. From here it's a half-hour walk down to the lighthouse.

Bantry

BANTRY enjoys a glorious location, ringed first by lush, wooded slopes and then by wild, bare mountains, at the head of 35-kilometre-long **Bantry Bay**, one of the finest natural harbours in Ireland. The prime viewpoint is naturally occupied by **Bantry House**, which with its sumptuous interior and garden is one of West Cork's few unmissable historic sites. At the junction of several important roads, Bantry is also a substantial market and service town, with plenty of amenities for visitors.

Arrival, information and accommodation

Buses stop on the central Wolfe Tone Square, at the east end of which is the helpful **tourist office** (April & May Mon–Sat 9.15am–5pm; June Mon–Sat 9.15am–6pm; July daily 9.15am–6pm; Aug daily 9.15am–7pm; Sept & Oct Mon, Tues & Thurs–Sat 9.15am–5pm; sometimes closed for lunch; ⓣ027/50229). **Bike rental** is available at Nigel's, a short way out on the Glengarriff road (ⓣ027/52657), **Internet access** at Fast.net on Bridge Street, the continuation of New Street, which runs off the east end of the square.

There's a good range of **accommodation** in Bantry, with dozens of B&Bs lining the Glengarriff road on the north side of town, but it's advisable to book ahead in July and August, especially during the prestigious nine-day **West Cork Chamber Music Festival** (ⓣ027/52788, ⓦwww.westcorkmusic.ie), generally at the beginning of July, the six-day **West Cork Literary Festival** (ⓣ027/61157, ⓦwww.westcorkliteraryfestival.ie) that follows immediately after, or the five-day **traditional-music festival** in August (ⓣ027/52788, ⓦwww.westcorkmusic.ie). At Ballylickey, 6km from Bantry along the Glengarriff road, is *Eagle Point Caravan and Camping Park* (closed Oct–Easter; ⓣ027/50630, ⓦwww.eaglepointcamping.com), a large, well-organized **campsite** in a fine location, with pebbly beaches for swimming. At the time of writing, a contemporary, four-star **hotel**, *The Maritime* (ⓣ027/54700, ⓦwww.themaritime.ie), was about to open at the southwest corner of Wolfe Tone Square.

Atlanta House Main St ⓣ027/50237. Traditional, good-value, family-run guesthouse right in the heart of Bantry, with en-suite bathrooms and TVs in all the good-sized bedrooms. ❷

Bantry House ⓣ027/50047, ⓦwww.bantryhouse.com. Luxurious digs in one of the country's finest mansions, which is still the home of the White family, former Earls of Bantry. The guest lounge is the huge, chandeliered library, with its coffered ceiling and fine views of the formal garden. Closed Nov–Feb. ❻

Dunauley Seskin ⓣ027/50290, ⓦwww.dunauley.com. Signposted 2km from the centre along the steep road towards Vaughan's Pass, this welcoming and comfortable modern B&B offers fine breakfasts and magnificent views. ❷

The Mill Newtown ⓣ027/50278, ⓦwww.the-mill.net. Excellent B&B 1km along the Glengarriff road, roomy, comfortable and colourfully decorated; all the en-suite bedrooms have TVs, and there's a laundry service and great breakfasts. Closed Dec–Feb. ❷

The Town

Bantry gathers itself around the expansive, bayside **Wolfe Tone Square**, which features a statue of St Brendan the Navigator gazing west out to sea with arms outspread (see p.361) and another of Wolfe Tone pointedly holding a telescope behind his back (see below). On a rainy day, you might want to seek shelter in the **Bantry Museum**, a clutter of rat-traps, fools' gold and clippings of local sporting successes, housed in a tiny building behind the fire station near the northwest corner of the square (summer Tues–Fri 10.30am–1pm & 2–4.30pm; winter by appointment, ⓣ027/55564; €2).

On the southern approach to town, **Bantry House** is one of Ireland's most compelling country houses, both for its lavish art works and for its magnificent setting, among formal gardens overlooking the bay (March–Oct daily 10am–6pm; €10, armada exhibition and gardens only €5; the house, but not the armada exhibition and gardens, is closed to visitors in the first half of March and during the chamber- and traditional-music festivals; ⓦwww.bantryhouse.com). Built in the early eighteenth century and extended a hundred years later, it was spared destruction during the Irish Civil War, when it acted as a hospital for the wounded of both sides. Many of its beautiful furnishings were gathered by the Second Earl of Bantry on his nineteenth-century grand tour and boast name-dropping provenances, such as the gorgeous Aubusson tapestries made for Marie Antoinette on her marriage to the future Louis XVI. The highlight is the dining room, which resembles an extravagant stage-set: rich, Chartres-blue walls, a marble colonnade and vast seventeenth-century sideboards carved with cherubs and classical scenes. There's a very attractive **café**, with tables under the house's west balcony, which serves tea and simple lunches.

The display boards of the **Bantry 1796 French Armada Exhibition Centre** are housed in the East Stables. In December 1796, United Irishman **Wolfe Tone** persuaded the French to send a fleet carrying some thirteen thousand seasoned soldiers, to invade Ireland in support of a republican revolution. Contrary winds prevented them from landing in Bantry Bay – though they were "close enough to toss a biscuit on shore" according to Tone – and the fleet was forced to return to Brest. Had they landed, it's likely that they would have overwhelmed the inexperienced forces in Ireland at the time. The exhibition includes the ship's bell and a cross-section model of the scuttled frigate, *La Surveillante*, which was not rediscovered until 1981.

Eating and drinking

Bantry offers a surprisingly diverse menu of cafés and restaurants, ranging from seafood to wholefood, as detailed below, while *The Snug* on the square is your best bet for pub grub. For a drink, head for *Ma Murphy's*, a cosy bar-grocery on New Street with a cool soundtrack and a beer garden; for traditional **music**, *Crowley's* on the square, which hosts sessions at weekends and on Wednesdays in summer.

The Brick Oven Wolfe Tone Square. Accomplished all-rounder serving good, authentic pizza, plus baguettes and baps for lunch and tasty bistro dishes such as scallop, salmon and monkfish gratin in the evenings.

El Gitano New St ⓣ027/50025. Lively, mostly organic, new restaurant specializing in enticing tapas, many of which are available in two sizes. For lunch, there's also sandwiches, burgers and omelettes (plus brunch on Sun); for dinner, main courses such as seafood pasta in white wine and cream sauce. Closed Mon evenings.

O'Connor's Wolfe Tone Square ⓣ027/50221. Recently refurbished in smart, nautical style, this relaxing, high-quality restaurant specializes in local mussels, lobster, oysters, duck and lamb; good-value lunch and early-bird menus (before 7pm).

Organico Just off the square at the start of the Glengarriff road. Popular, easy-going vegetarian and organic café, above a health-food store, dishing up tasty hummus and falafel salads, sandwiches, soups and main courses such as quinoa bean stew. Internet access. Closed Sun.

Stuffed Olive New St. Excellent deli-café serving creative sandwiches, cakes, good coffees, juices and smoothies. Closed Sun.

The Beara Peninsula

The largest and most remote of Cork's peninsulas, the **Beara** (Ⓦwww.bearatourism.com) careers southwestwards for 50km between Bantry Bay and the Kenmare River. Patterns in the landscape are hard to distinguish here, and contrasts frequent. Indeed, the peninsula's most popular tourist spot, **Glengarriff**, has built an industry on the stunning contrast between its lush subtropical setting and the irregular, barren rocks of the Caha Mountains behind. The mountainous spine is often augmented by ribs, and particularly in the Slieve Miskish Mountains at the Beara's tip, the coast road is forced to climb through whatever passes can be found. Round on the north coast, half of which belongs to County Kerry (see p.350), the only settlements occupy occasional cups of green farmland beneath the stony ridges. This diverse scenery is linked together by two routes: the **Beara Way**, a 200-kilometre waymarked walk (9–11 days), following mostly tracks and minor roads from Glengarriff west (via Adrigole, Castletownbere and a ferry to Bere Island, which can easily be missed out) to Dursey Island, then along the north coast of the peninsula (via Allihies, Eyeries, Ardgroom and Lauragh) to Kenmare and back to Glengarriff; and, following roughly parallel, the 138-kilometre **Beara Way Cycle Route**. Route guides are available locally, and the Ordnance Survey 1:50,000 Discovery map 84 covers nearly the whole peninsula.

Glengarriff and around

The founders of **GLENGARRIFF** (Ⓦwww.glengarriff.ie) were perhaps having an off-day when they named it *An Gleann Garbh*, the "rugged glen" – or, to be charitable, maybe the climate has changed since then. It's true that above and behind stands the magnificent backdrop of the wild, bare Caha Mountains, but the village itself sits in a sheltered oasis of balmy greenery. This picturesque juxtaposition, warmed by the Atlantic Gulf Stream, has attracted tourists since the eighteenth century, when the *Eccles Hotel* at the east end of town was built. The landscape – and the gift shops – still pull in the coach parties, but the village's popularity also means there's a decent range of places to stay, making it a good base for exploring some of Cork's most beautiful countryside or for just hopping over to see the horticultural delights of **Garinish Island**. To the west, in the dramatic shadow of Hungry Hill, watersports and a pleasant hostel are on offer at **Adrigole**.

The microclimate is mild enough to support the **Bamboo Park** (daily 9am–7pm; €5; Ⓦwww.bamboo-park.com), a beautiful thirteen-acre private garden, planted with thirty different species of bamboo, as well as various palms, ferns and eucalyptus. The maze of paths here would be great for kids, who get in free, to have a very long game of hide-and-seek, while the seashore frontage reveals idyllic views of tufted green islets in the bay.

As well as the Beara Way and Cycle Route, there are plenty of opportunities in the immediate vicinity of Glengarriff for exploration on foot or by bike (or a combination of both). About a kilometre up the N71 Kenmare road is **Glengarriff Woods Nature Reserve**, a forest park of ancient sessile oaks, birch and holly, that shelters Mediterranean species such as strawberry trees. It's crossed by waymarked nature trails, including the short climb up to **Lady Bantry's Lookout**, which is rewarded with panoramic views of the bay. Also accessible from the N71, about 10km from Glengarriff, lies **Barley Lake**, a beautiful armchair or corrie lake.

Glengarriff practicalities

Local walking possibilities are covered in a leaflet that you can get at one of the two **tourist offices** in the main street: Fáilte Ireland's (June–Aug Mon, Tues &

Thurs–Sat 9.15am–1pm & 2–5pm; ⓣ027/63084) or the privately run office in the souvenir shop next to *Murphy's Hostel* (daily: high summer 9am–9pm; shoulder season 9am–6pm; closed roughly Oct–April; ⓣ027/63201). Note that there are no banks in Glengarriff, but the post office in the Spar supermarket can change money. Glengarriff Cabs (ⓣ027/63060 or 087 973 0741, ⓦwww.glengarrifftours.ie) run half- and full-day **tours** of the Beara and the Ring of Kerry.

Casey's (ⓣ027/63010, ⓦwww.caseyshotelglengarriff.ie; closed mid-Dec to mid-Feb; ❸) is a friendly, recently refurbished nineteenth-century **hotel** in the centre of the village, while more upmarket digs are available at the lavishly renovated *Eccles Hotel* (ⓣ027/63003, ⓦwww.eccleshotel.com; ❺) at the east end of town. Your best **B&B** option is the good-value, all-en-suite *Cottage Bar and Restaurant* (ⓣ027/63226, ⓦwww.cottagebar.com; ❷), which offers very good half-board deals and has some self-catering cottages. *Murphy's* (IHH; ⓣ027/63555, ⓔmurphyshostel@eircom.net; dorms €15, doubles ❶) is an excellent, friendly **hostel**, with double and family rooms, good showers and plenty of useful information about what to do in the area. You can **camp** in some comfort at *Dowling's* (ⓣ027/63154, ⓔnickydee@eircom.net; closed Nov–Easter), about 2km out on the R572 Castletownbere road.

Casey's Hotel does very good bar **food**, and such delights as Bantry Bay mussels in garlic butter in its smart restaurant, while the *Cottage Bar and Restaurant* is a good bet for cheap traditional food. During the day, the *Village Café* at *Murphy's Hostel* dishes up cakes, soup, sandwiches and more substantial meals, with plenty of vegatarian options, at keen prices. Glengarriff has a tight concentration of lively **pubs**, with music often on in summer at *The Hawthorn* or *Bernard Harrington's*, and on Wednesdays at the *Eccles Hotel*.

Garinish Island (Ilnacullin)

In 1910, the MP Annan Bryce bought **Garinish** (aka Ilnacullin) from the British War Office and, after shipping in all the topsoil, gradually turned the rocky inshore island into an exotic garden oasis. Having passed into public ownership in 1953, the island is now a delightful and accessible escape from the mainland, especially in summer, when colourful plants from around the world set the island alight against a backdrop of the sparse, jagged mountains just across the water. The island's centrepiece is a formal Italianate garden, surrounded by a walled garden and wilder areas, a Grecian temple with magnificent views of the Caha Mountains and a Martello tower. There's a coffee shop and a one-hour self-guided trail around the gardens, and serious horticulturalists should pick up the Heritage Service's guidebook, which includes detailed plant lists.

The ten-minute **boat trip** to the island takes you past the lush islets of Glengarriff Harbour, where you may see basking seals. It costs €12 return with Harbour Queen Ferries (ⓣ027/63116, ⓦwww.harbourqueenferry.com) from opposite the *Eccles Hotel*; €10 with the Blue Pool Ferry (ⓣ027/63333, ⓦwww.bluepoolferry.com), based next to *Murphy's* right in the centre of the village; or €7.50 with the *Lady Ellen*, from Ellen's Rock, about 2km west of the village off the Castletownbere road (ⓣ027/63110 or 087 944 3784). These prices don't include admission to the island (March & Oct Mon–Sat 10am–4.30pm, Sun 1–5pm; April Mon–Sat 10am–6.30pm, Sun 1–6.30pm; May & Sept Mon–Sat 10am–6.30pm, Sun noon–6.30pm; June Mon–Sat 10am–6.30pm, Sun 11am–6.30pm; July & Aug Mon–Sat 9.30am–6.30pm, Sun 11am–6.30pm; €3.70; Heritage Card; ⓦwww.heritageireland.ie).

Adrigole

About 25km west along the coast from Glengarriff is **ADRIGOLE**, an extended ribbon development around the junction with the scenic **Healy Pass** road that leads north to Lauragh in County Kerry (see p.350). Down by the harbour the West Cork Sailing Centre offers **sailing**, **powerboating** and **kayaking** (Ⓣ027/60132, Ⓦwww.westcorksailing.com), and a short distance west of the junction for the Healy Pass is the IHH **hostel**, *Hungry Hill Lodge* (Ⓣ027/60228, Ⓦwww.hungryhilllodge.com; dorms €17, doubles ❶), with twin, double and family rooms, meals, camping and laundry facilities available; a pub and a shop are nearby too.

Castletownbere

Over 100km west of Cork city at the end of the peninsula, the bustle of **CASTLETOWNBERE** (sometimes referred to as Castletown Berehaven or just Castletown) comes as quite a surprise. Benefiting from the country's second largest natural harbour, it's Ireland's biggest white-fish port, and especially during strong winter gales, Atlantic trawlers of many nationalities put in here. Not surprisingly, there's a good range of amenities for visitors, with the fairly compact area around the main square offering cafés, restaurants, banks and some boisterous pubs.

If you want to learn more about the Beara's (mostly) maritime history, head for the entertaining, well-designed **Call of the Sea** visitor centre on the northeast side of the centre on the Eyeries road (North Road; summer Mon–Fri 10am–5pm; last admission 4pm; call Ⓣ027/70835 about low-season opening, or just try the door; €4; Ⓦwww.callofthesea.com). It covers the themes of smuggling and copper mining, keeping watch from lighthouses and Martello towers, fishing and the naval history of Bantry Bay, through videos, hands-on activities and lively, anecdotal display-boards put together by the Beara Historical Society.

To the west of town, there's a pleasant three-kilometre walk to **Puxley Mansion**, the poignant skeleton of a Neogothic pile just off the R572 Dursey road that's slated for redevelopment into a luxury hotel. It was constructed in the nineteenth century by the Puxleys – made famous by Daphne du Maurier in her novel *Hungry Hill* – who built up a vast fortune from copper-mining in the nineteenth century but were burnt out by the IRA in 1921. Further on through the grounds, you'll come to the overgrown seafront ruins of **Dunboy Castle**, which afford dramatic views back along the Beara Peninsula. Built in the fourteenth century, the castle was besieged by the English in 1602 after the Battle of Kinsale. Facing an army of 4000, its garrison of 143 men held out for eleven days, but in the end were all slaughtered and the castle blown up. Their chieftain, **Donal Cam O'Sullivan Bere**, then embarked on his famous long **march** up to County Leitrim in the winter of 1602–03 with a thousand men, women and children. Harassed by the English and the Irish, he arrived two weeks later with just 35 followers left.

Practicalities

Buses stop on the main square, and there's a **tourist information** office just to the west along the main street (Mon–Sat 9.30am–1pm & 1.30–5pm; Ⓣ027/70054), which can give details of short, signposted loop walks on the peninsula. **Internet access** is available at Beara Computers on the square, **bike rental** from the Supervalu supermarket (Ⓣ027/70020). Guided, half- to three-day **sea-kayaking** trips can be arranged with Frank Conroy (Ⓣ027/70692, Ⓦwww.seakayakingwestcork.com), **diving trips and courses** with Beara Diving on the square (Ⓣ027/71682, Ⓦwww.bearadiving.com).

Your best **B&B** option is *Rodeen* (Ⓣ027/70158, Ⓦwww.rodeencountryhouse.com; mid-March to Oct; ❷), a family home set in beautiful subtropical gardens 2km east of town, with stylish, en-suite rooms overlooking the bay.

Hostel accommodation is on offer at both *Harbour Lodge* (☎027/71043, ⓦwww.harbourlodge.net; IHO; dorms from €15, en-suite twins ❶), a converted convent in the centre of town behind the Supervalu supermarket, and the recently built *Ocean View Lodge* on the square (call at the nearby Spar supermarket or ☎027/70057; dorms €20, doubles ❶), which has a wide variety of rooms, including singles. You can **camp** at *Berehaven Camper & Amenity Park* (☎027/70700, ⓦwww.berehavengolf.com), 5km east on the Glengarriff road at Filane.

For something to **eat** during the day, make for the inexpensive *Copper Kettle* on the square (closed Sun), which dishes up tasty baguettes, soups and salads. Your best bet for a more substantial meal is probably *The Olde Bakery* to the west of the square, an upmarket but informal spot, with dishes such as tiger prawns in Thai curry sauce and an early-bird menu until 7.30pm. Back on the square, *MacCarthy's* grocery-bar does a wide range of sandwiches and soups for lunch, and is the best place to **drink**, with regular traditional sessions. You're also likely to find **music** at *Twomey's* on Main Street, which runs set dancing on Fridays and a session on Saturdays.

On to Dursey Island and Allihies

Beyond Castletownbere, you can skirt round through a few tiny, remote but dramatically set villages to the north side of the peninsula and on towards Kerry. This end of the Beara was heavily mined for copper in the nineteenth century – walkers should watch out for unguarded shafts. Making a virtue of the solitude, around 8km west of Castletownbere, is the **Dzogchen Beara Tibetan Buddhist Retreat Centre**, where visitors are welcome to stay at the attached **hostel** or attend the daily meditation classes or longer retreats (☎027/73032, ⓦwww.dzogchenbeara.org; €15).

The Beara lays on a bit of excitement at its very end, in the form of the **cable car** across the roaring sound to **Dursey Island**. There are no facilities on the island, but you can walk its 11-kilometre stretch of the Beara Way for seemingly endless views across the Atlantic, beyond Calf, Cow and Bull islands. The small cable car, which takes about fifteen minutes, only operates three times a day (plus an extra slot June–Aug on Sun; exact times from the Castletownbere tourist office; €4 return). For a day-trip, aim to get there before 9am – note that islanders and their sheep and cattle take preference (the main livestock sales are at the end of summer). The cable-car operator and his wife run a pleasant, en-suite **B&B**, nearby on their farm overlooking Dursey Sound, *Windy Point House* (☎027/73017, ⓦwww.windypointhouse.com; meals available to guests; ❷).

Looping round an especially harsh and rocky part of the peninsula on the R575, you'll come upon the former copper-mining village of **ALLIHIES**, its brightly coloured houses dramatically huddled together against the leathery creases of Slieve Miskish's western flank and blessed with superb sunset views. The village has a sandy beach, **Ballydonegan Strand**, less than a kilometre away, as well as a dive school, Cluin (☎027/73896, ⓦwww.cluin.com), three pubs and a shop-cum-post office. On the main street in the centre, *Sea View* (☎027/73004, ⓦwww.seaviewallihies.com; ❷) offers comfortable en-suite **B&B** and good breakfasts, as well as self-catering apartments and bike rental. Also in the centre is the appealing *Allihies Hostel* (IHH; ☎027/73107, ⓦwww.allihieshostel.net; April–Oct), with dorms (from €16), twins (❶) and family rooms, and bikes to rent. **Camping** by the beach is possible at *Anthony's* small site (☎027/73002). *O'Neill's* (☎027/73008) serves **food** in both bar and restaurant, and is also your best bet for traditional music on weekends year-round.

Travel details

Trains

Cork to: Cobh (Mon–Sat at least hourly, 9 on Sun; 25min); Dublin Heuston (hourly; 2hr 50min); Fota (Mon–Sat at least hourly, 9 on Sun; 15min); Killarney (6–9 daily, sometimes with a change at Mallow; 1hr 30min); Limerick (change at Limerick Junction; 5–8 daily; 2hr); Tralee (6–9 daily, sometimes with a change at Mallow; 2hr 20min).

Buses

Bus Éireann

Bantry to: Adrigole (6–9 weekly; 1hr); Castletownbere (1–2 daily; 1hr 15min); Clonakilty (1 daily in summer; 1hr 10min); Durrus (2 on Sat; 15min); Glengarriff (2–3 daily; 25min); Kenmare, via Glengarriff (1 daily in summer; 1hr 10min); Kilcrohane (2 on Sat; 45min); Killarney, via Glengarriff (1 daily in summer; 2hr 20min); Rosscarbery (1 daily in summer; 1hr); Skibbereen (1 daily in summer; 30min).

Castletownbere to: Kenmare, via Eyeries and the north side of the Beara (summer Mon–Sat 2 daily; 1hr 20min).

Cork to: Adrigole (6–9 weekly; 3hr); Athlone (1–2 daily; 4hr 30min); Bantry (5–7 daily; 1hr 50min–2hr 20min); Birr (1–2 daily; 3hr 30min); Blarney (hourly; 20–30min); Cahir (7 daily; 1hr 20min); Carrick-on-Suir (1 daily; 2hr 15min); Carrigtohill (Mon–Fri roughly half-hourly, Sat & Sun roughly hourly; 30min); Cashel (6 daily; 1hr 35min); Castletownbere (6–9 weekly; 3hr); Clonakilty (6–9 daily; 1hr); Clonmel (3 daily; 2hr 55min); Courtmacsherry (Mon–Fri 1–2 daily; 1hr 25min); Dublin (6 daily; 4hr 30min); Ennis (hourly; 2hr 30min); Galway (hourly; 4hr 15min); Glengarriff (2–3 daily; 2hr); Goleen (1–2 daily; 3hr); Kenmare (1 daily in summer; 3hr 30min); Kilkenny (1–3 daily; 3hr); Killarney (hourly; 2hr 30min); Kinsale (3–12 daily; 40min); Limerick (hourly; 2hr); Midleton (hourly; 30min); Rosslare Europort (3–4 daily; 4hr 15min); Schull (2 daily; 2hr 30min); Shannon Airport (hourly; 2hr 30min); Skibbereen (5–10 daily; 2hr); Timoleague (Mon–Fri 1–2 daily; 1hr 15min); Tralee (hourly; 2hr 30min); Waterford (12–13 daily; 2hr 15min); Wexford (3–6 daily; 4hr); Youghal (hourly; 50min).

Skibbereen to: Baltimore (Mon–Fri 3–5 daily, plus 4 on Sat in summer; 20min); Bantry (1 daily in summer; 30min); Clonakilty (4–8 daily; 40min); Goleen (1–2 daily; 1hr); Rosscarbery (4–8 daily; 25min); Schull (2 daily; 30min).

West Cork Rural Transport

ⓣ027/52727, ⓦwww.ruraltransport.ie

Bantry to: Durrus (Mon–Fri 2–6 daily; 45min–1hr 40min); Glengarriff (1 weekly; 30min); Goleen (4 weekly; 1hr); Kilcrohane (4 weekly; 1hr); Schull (4 weekly; 35min–1hr 15min); Skibbereen (Mon–Fri 2–3 daily; 30min–1hr 30min).

Castletownbere to: Adrigole (2 weekly; 25min); Allihies (2 weekly; 30min); Dursey Sound (2 weekly; 55min).

Harrington's Buses

ⓣ027/74003

Castletownbere to: Cork (Mon–Wed & Fri–Sun 1 daily; 2hr 15min).

O'Donoghue's Buses

ⓣ027/70007

Castletownbere to: Cork (Thurs 1 daily; 2hr 45min).

Aircoach

ⓣ01/844 7118, ⓦwww.aircoach.ie

Cork to: Cashel (8 daily; 1hr 30min); Dublin (8 daily; 4hr); Kildare (8 daily; 3hr).

Citylink

ⓣ1890 280808, ⓦwww.citylink.ie

Cork to: Ennis (hourly; 2hr 35min); Galway (hourly; 3hr 50min); Limerick (hourly; 1hr 50min).

8

Kerry

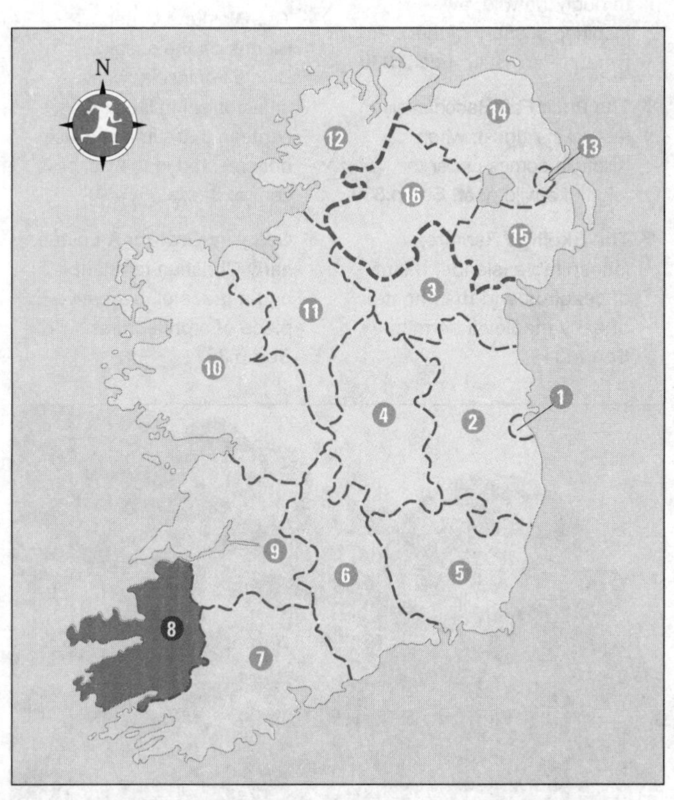

CHAPTER 8

Highlights

✱ **Killarney National Park** Beautiful – and popular – landscape of mountains and lakes, that can be explored by boat, bike and on foot. See p.334

✱ **The Kerry Way** A 213-kilometre walking route through the wild, awe-inspiring scenery of the Iveragh Peninsula. See p.339

✱ **The Puck Fair** Bacchanalian festival in August, when Killorglin comes under the reign of a wild goat. See p.339

✱ **The Skelligs** Remote, inhospitable islands, haunt of seabirds and the ghosts of early medieval hermits. See p.344

✱ **Caherdaniel** Hillside village with a great beach and plenty of outdoor activities. See p.347

✱ **Kenmare** An agreeable base with a great selection of places to eat, sleep and drink. See p.348

✱ **The Blaskets** Lonely islands off the scenic Dingle Peninsula, with an astonishing literary heritage that's imaginatively documented in the visitor centre. See p.359

✱ **Gallarus Oratory** A unique, early Christian remnant and a graceful, evocative piece of architecture. See p.361

▲Skellig Michael

8

Kerry

Kerry has been making visitors' romantic dreams of Ireland come true since the eighteenth century, when the grandeur of the lakes and mountains around **Killarney** first came to widespread attention. Encompassing the highest range in the country, **Macgillycuddy's Reeks**, the scenery here is, of course, still magnificent, and the Killarney area shelters some fine, underrated architectural sights too, while the town itself has plenty of amenities and entertainment, though little soul. Most of the one million tourists who come to Kerry every year, however, stick rigidly to Killarney and the **Ring of Kerry**, the scenic drive around the neighbouring **Iveragh Peninsula**, so it's pretty easy to avoid the crowds.

The Iveragh itself measures around sixty by thirty kilometres, with plenty of tracks across its vast, rugged hinterland and coastal branch roads such as the **Ring of Skellig** to explore by car, bike or on foot. The island of **Skellig Michael** off the end of the peninsula, one of the most remarkable hermitages in the world and now a UNESCO World Heritage Site, remains the ultimate place to get away from it all. At the southeastern corner of the peninsula, **Kenmare** contrasts well with Killarney, providing some excellent accommodation, restaurants and nightlife in a trim, picturesque setting, as well as access to further scenic delights on Kerry's part of the **Beara Peninsula**.

Kerry's other peninsula, **Dingle**, experienced its own minor visitor boom on the release of David Lean's film, *Ryan's Daughter*, in 1970, which pumped as much as £3 million into the local economy during a long and troubled location shoot here (including the near-drowning of star Robert Mitchum off Dunquin and the building of an entirely new village, Kirrary, on the remote slopes above). It's still nothing like as touristed as the Ring, and offers a jagged landscape of stark mountains and spectacular beaches, an especially rich heritage of early Christian sites, and a fine, all-round base in the main settlement, **Dingle town**.

Despite the centuries of tourist traffic, Kerry has maintained a strong sense of independence, though perhaps doesn't shout about it as much as its neighbour, Cork. It's one of the least urbanized counties in Ireland, with a sweet, country lilt to the accent. Distinctive H-shaped goalposts are everywhere, not just on village GAA fields but on most farms, evidence of the county's obsession with **Gaelic football**. The self-styled "Brazil" of the sport have won the All-Ireland County Championship far more than anyone else – 35 times and counting – and produced the finest team ever between 1975 and 1986, winning the championship eight times in those eleven years. The Dingle Peninsula, one of Ireland's strongest Gaeltacht areas, has nurtured not only great footballers, but also a fine community of musicians and the extraordinary **writers** of the wild

Blasket Islands, who put their rich oral tradition of Irish-language storytelling to paper in the early twentieth century. The county's other most obvious concentration of literary talent has been in the flatlands of **North Kerry**, as celebrated in the genial market town of **Listowel**.

Killarney and around

KILLARNEY (Ⓦ www.killarney.ie) was developed as a resort on the doorstep of Ireland's finest lakeland scenery in the eighteenth and nineteenth centuries, and remains a popular tourist town, busy, lively and easily accessible, with hundreds of places to stay in all price ranges. Backpackers are particularly well catered for, with an appealing selection of hostels and all manner of tours available for those without their own transport. The town's kiss-me-quick hedonism and souvenir shops are not to everyone's taste, but the attraction of the place is still the same as three hundred years ago: beginning in the very heart of town, **Killarney National Park** encompasses three beautiful lakes, beyond which rise the splendid **Macgillycuddy's Reeks**, Ireland's highest mountain range. The only building of architectural interest in the town is Pugin's elegant **cathedral**, but the national park shelters three diverse and very well preserved monuments, **Ross Castle**, **Muckross Friary** and **Muckross House**.

Arrival and information

Kerry's **airport** (ⓣ066/976 4644, ⓦwww.kerryairport.ie) is 15km from Killarney on the N23, a couple of kilometres northeast of the village of Farranfore, which is on the Tralee–Killarney train line. Buses between Limerick and Killarney (plus a few Tralee–Killarney services) call at the airport roughly every two hours; a taxi into town costs around €25 (call Euro Taxis on ⓣ064/37676 if you want to book one). Killarney's **train** and **bus stations** are both very central, the former off East Avenue Road (ⓣ064/71067), and the latter, which offers **left luggage**, on nearby Park Road (ⓣ064/30011).

The excellent **tourist office** on Beech Road (June & Sept daily 9am–6pm; July & Aug daily 9am–8pm; Oct–May Mon–Sat 9.15am–5pm, sometimes closing for lunch; ⓣ064/31633) shelters a bureau de change. **Bikes** can be rented from O'Sullivan's on Beech Road opposite the tourist office (ⓣ064/22389), with branches at The Outdoor Shop, 18 New St (ⓣ064/26927), and The Bike Shop, opposite the cathedral (ⓣ064/31282), as well as from several of the hostels. Budget (ⓣ064/34341, ⓦwww.budget.ie) have **car-rental outlets** both at the airport and in town, on Kenmare Place, while there's a **taxi rank** on College Street. **Internet access** can be had at Rí Rá on Plunkett Street. Killarney Riding Stables, a kilometre west of town on the Killorglin road (ⓣ064/31686, ⓦwww.killarneyridingstables.com), offer **horse riding** in the national park on day-trips, as well as on the two- or five-day Reeks Trail.

Accommodation

It's certainly worth booking **accommodation** in Killarney in advance, but there are scores of B&Bs, upmarket guesthouses and hotels in town – if none of the listings below can fit you in, the friendly tourist office should be able to help. There are several **campsites** nearby, including *Fleming's White Bridge* (ⓣ064/31590, ⓦwww.killarneycamping.com; Easter to early Oct, plus some bank holidays), a kilometre east of town, signposted off the N22 Cork road; and *Killarney Flesk* (ⓣ064/31704, ⓦwww.campingkillarney.com; Easter–Sept), a kilometre south on the N71 Kenmare road – the Kerry Way and Muckross House are easily accessed from here.

The Copper Kettle Lewis Rd ⓣ064/34164, ⓦwww.copperkettlekillarney.com. Pleasant B&B on the north side of the town centre with a variety of tasteful, en-suite rooms, all with satellite TV and video. Discounts for *Rough Guide to Ireland* readers. ❸

Fair View Michael Collins Place, off College St ⓣ064/34164, ⓦwww.fairviewkillarney.com. Attractive and welcoming central guesthouse (with parking), where the tasteful, comfortable rooms all have en-suite bathroom, satellite TV and video, and some are wheelchair-accessible; great breakfasts, too. Discounts for *Rough Guide to Ireland* readers. ❹

Fuchsia House Muckross Rd, a 10min walk from the centre ⓣ064/33743, ⓦwww.fuchsiahouse.com. Friendly, purpose-built guesthouse, set back from the main road in attractive, tree-shaded gardens, with large, homely rooms, W-iFi and a separate guest kitchen. ❸

Killarney International Hostel 5km west of town on the Killorglin road ⓣ064/31240, ⓦwww.irelandyha.org. Well-run, An Óige hostel in a renovated eighteenth-century country house with nearly 200 beds, including comfortable twin, family and en-suite rooms. Cooked meals, Internet access, bike rental, laundry facilities and bureau de change available. Courtesy bus from town in high season, or catch the Bus Éireann service towards Killorglin. Dorms from €14, twins ❶.

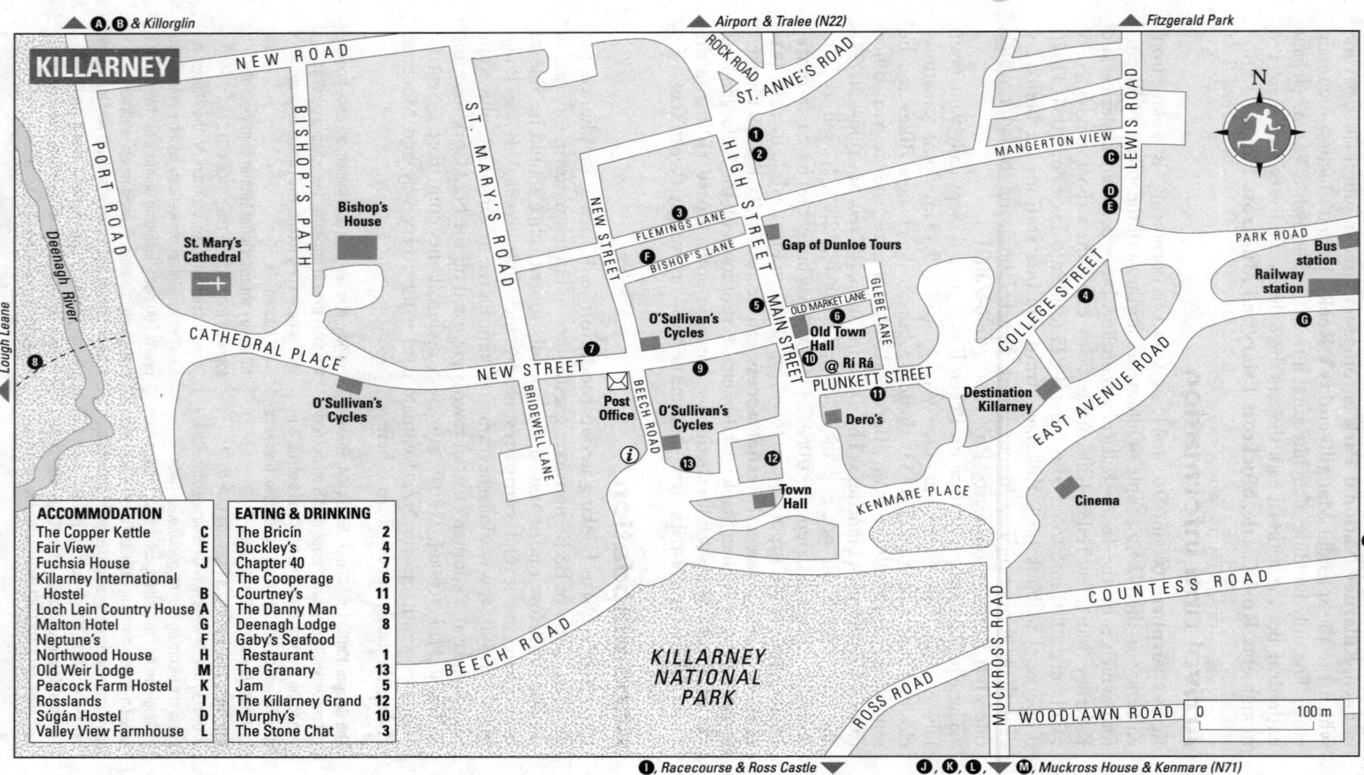
KILLARNEY
A, B & Killorglin
Airport & Tralee (N22)
Fitzgerald Park
Cork
H
I, Racecourse & Ross Castle
J, K, L, M, Muckross House & Kenmare (N71)
Lough Leane
N
NEW ROAD
ROCK ROAD
ST. ANNE'S ROAD
LEWIS ROAD
MANGERTON VIEW
PORT ROAD
BISHOP'S PATH
ST. MARY'S ROAD
NEW STREET
HIGH STREET
FLEMINGS LANE
BISHOP'S LANE
MAIN STREET
OLD MARKET LANE
GLEBE LANE
PLUNKETT STREET
COLLEGE STREET
EAST AVENUE ROAD
PARK ROAD
CATHEDRAL PLACE
BRIDEWELL LANE
BEECH ROAD
KENMARE PLACE
COUNTESS ROAD
MUCKROSS ROAD
WOODLAWN ROAD
ROSS ROAD
Deenagh River
Bishop's House
St. Mary's Cathedral
Gap of Dunloe Tours
O'Sullivan's Cycles
Old Town Hall
@ Rí Rá
Post Office
Dero's
Town Hall
Destination Killarney
Cinema
Bus station
Railway station
KILLARNEY NATIONAL PARK
0
100 m
ACCOMMODATION
The Copper Kettle C
Fair View E
Fuchsia House J
Killarney International Hostel B
Loch Lein Country House A
Malton Hotel G
Neptune's F
Northwood House H
Old Weir Lodge M
Peacock Farm Hostel K
Rosslands I
Súgán Hostel D
Valley View Farmhouse L
EATING & DRINKING
The Bricín 2
Buckley's 4
Chapter 40 7
The Cooperage 6
Courtney's 11
The Danny Man 9
Deenagh Lodge 8
Gaby's Seafood Restaurant 1
The Granary 13
Jam 5
The Killarney Grand 12
Murphy's 10
The Stone Chat 3

Loch Lein Country House Hotel Fossa, 5km west of town just off the N72 ⓣ064/31260, ⓦwww.lochlein.com. A good-value choice if you'd prefer to stay away from the town's bustle, this peaceful, welcoming and well-run small hotel has views of Lough Leane and the mountains, spacious, tastefully decorated rooms and its own restaurant. ❹

Malton Hotel East Avenue Rd ⓣ064/38000, ⓦwww.gshotels.com. Ivy-clad Victorian railway hotel, formerly the *Great Southern*, where the huge lobby sports chandeliers and marble floors, the breakfast room an ornate, gilded ceiling, and where rooms, especially in the original building, are very attractive. Extensive gardens, spa and swimming pool to relax in too. ❻

Neptune's Hostel Bishop's Lane, off New St ⓣ064/35255, ⓦwww.neptuneshostel.com (IHH & IHO). Excellent hostel, huge but welcoming, with plenty of local information on offer. Family rooms, twins and doubles, as well as Internet access, laundry facilities and cooked meals, are available. Dorms from €13, doubles ❶.

Northwood House Muckross View, off Countess Grove ⓣ064/37181, ⓦwww.northwoodhouse.com. Very helpful B&B in a recently built, palatial house on a quiet road near the centre, with fine views of the town and surrounding countryside, offering en-suite bedrooms with TVs and great breakfasts. ❷

Old Weir Lodge Muckross Rd, a 10min walk from the centre ⓣ064/35593, ⓦwww.oldweirlodge.com. Thirty-room, mock-Tudor guesthouse that feels like a hotel, with spacious, well-equipped and comfortable rooms. It retains the personal touch, with a warm welcome and plenty of local information. ❹

Peacock Farm Hostel 10km from town on the south shore of Lough Guitane, signposted off the road to Muckross ⓣ064/33557 or 086 103 9036 (IHH & IHO). Relaxing, small hostel in a traditional farmhouse with a spacious, attractive conservatory and fine lake views. Well situated for walking in the mountains. Free transport from town twice daily. April–Sept. Dorms €12, twins ❶.

Rosslands Ross Rd ⓣ064/36139, ⓦwww.rosslands.com. Pleasant B&B in a quiet, modern bungalow with a fine garden, 800m from the centre on the road to Ross Castle. En-suite rooms with satellite TV and video. Discounts for *Rough Guide to Ireland* readers. ❷

Súgán Hostel Lewis Rd ⓣ064/33104, ⓦwww.killarneysuganhostel.com (IHO). Central and cosy hostel, run by a musician, with welcoming if cramped dorms and bike rental. Staff are friendly and the hostel is a good source of local information. Dorms €15, twins ❶.

Valley View Farmhouse Lough Guitane Rd ⓣ064/31206, ⓦwww.valleyview-farmhouse.com. You'll be well looked after and enjoy tranquility and great views on this working farm, 8km southeast of town near Lough Guitane (pick-ups from town available). Most rooms en-suite; good single and children's rates. Closed Oct–April. ❷

The Town

Seat of the Bishop of Kerry, **St Mary's Cathedral** is Ireland's finest Neogothic church, built in stages between 1842 and 1912 to a design by Augustus Pugin. Set in spacious gardens by the entrance to the national park on the west side of the town centre, its exterior, with a lofty steeple over the transept, is strikingly elegant. Inside the rough grey stonework is colourfully lit by dozens of stained-glass windows, which depict in their upper range the life of Christ, in the lower the lives of the Irish saints, notably Patrick and Brendan the Navigator, patron saint of the diocese. The huge redwood tree outside the west door marks a mass children's grave from the time of the Famine: work on the church was suspended in the late 1840s, when the partly roofed building was used as a hospital and shelter.

On a rainy day, you might ask at the tourist office if the Museum of Irish Transport, a collection of bicycles, motorbikes, vintage cars, fire engines and associated memorabilia, has managed to find new premises yet. Otherwise, the main activity in the town itself revolves around seasonal **festivals** and events. In May and July Killarney's racecourse (ⓣ064/31125, ⓦwww.killarneyraces.ie), in a scenic spot on Ross Road, hosts boisterous, well-supported **racing**, while **Summerfest** (ⓦwww.killarneysummerfest.com), held over two weeks in late June or early July, features big-name concerts – the likes of Elton John, Pink and Snow Patrol – and plenty of street entertainment. The first weekend in May, when the Rally of the Lakes (ⓦwww.rallyofthelakes.com) pulls crowds of motoring fans to the area, is not a good time to experience the serenity of the mountains. Killarney is a good place to sample the Kerry fervour for **Gaelic football**: major matches are held at Fitzgerald Park on Lewis Road, which is named after Dick Fitzgerald, greatest player of the early twentieth century and author of the first training manual on the game, and enjoys a magnificent mountain backdrop from its north terraces. The local side, Dr Croke's, All-Ireland club champions in 1992, have their stadium across the road.

Eating and drinking

Eating out in Killarney is generally a pricey undertaking, though several places offer good value for it. In a tourist town that's constantly reinventing itself, it's perhaps inevitable that there are few characterful old **pubs** left. Entertainment's the name of the game, and most bars provide regular live music, of wildly varying quality.

Restaurants and cafés

The Bricín 26 High St ⓣ064/34902. Homely restaurant that serves traditional Irish food, notably filled boxties (potato pancakes), as well as more eclectic dishes such as prawns in a Calvados cream sauce. Set 3-course menus available, as well as an early-bird 2-course before 7pm. Closed Mon lunchtime & Sun.

Chapter 40 40 New St ⓣ064/71833. Welcoming restaurant in an attractive, modern setting, serving very good, global-influenced dishes such as monkfish wrapped in aubergine with couscous and raita. Mon–Sat evenings.

The Cooperage Old Market Lane, off Main St ⓣ064/37716. Funky decor complements some creative modern dishes, with game and seafood featuring heavily. There's a good-value early-bird menu before 7.30pm (not Sat) and a simpler, cheaper lunchtime menu. Evenings plus Thurs–Sat lunchtimes.

Deenagh Lodge just inside the National Park gate. In a quaint, thatched cottage hung with paintings by local artists, this inexpensive place offers tasty soups, simple sandwiches and cakes. Daytime, roughly Easter–Oct.

Gaby's Seafood Restaurant 27 High St ⓣ064/32519. Killarney's finest and most expensive seafood restaurant, formal but not at all stuffy, serving great platters of seafood and lobster from the tanks in the front window. Mon–Sat evenings only.

Jam Main St. Branch of Kenmare's modern, daytime bakery-café, serving great cakes, scones and coffee, as well as delicious sandwiches, quiches, salads and main courses. Closed Sun.

Murphy's 37 Main St. Branch of Dingle's excellent ice-cream shop (eat in or take away), which also serves great cakes and coffees.

The Stone Chat Flemings Lane, off High St. Rustic setting for a long, moderately priced menu of tasty, unpretentious dishes such as salmon with chive sauce, with a decent range of vegetarian options.

Pubs and bars

Buckley's *Arbutus Hotel*, College St. Smartly refurbished traditional bar with long, sociable bench seats, and traditional sessions Mon–Sat evenings and Sun lunchtime in summer, Fri–Mon evenings in winter.

Courtney's Plunkett St. Appealingly plain, bare-wood pub, popular among a twenty-something crowd for its traditional music on Thurs, live bands on Fri and DJ sessions on Sat.

The Danny Man New St. Huge, mock-rustic bar-restaurant, purveying traditional music and ballads in a good-time atmosphere, nightly in summer, at weekends in winter.

The Granary Beech Rd, opposite the tourist office. Stylish, modern, purpose-built bar-venue, furnished in wood, leather and bare stone, and serving an interesting selection of good food. Live bands Fri–Sun with late-night DJs Fri & Sat.

The Killarney Grand (aka *Sheehan's*) Main St. A large but often-crowded bar, popular with locals and tourists, with nightly live entertainment: ballads or traditional music between 9 and 11pm, with a cover charge for bands and a club after 11pm; on Wed evenings there's set dancing.

Killarney National Park and the Gap of Dunloe

Killarney National Park now protects the glaciated limestone valleys around the three lakes, Leane (or Lower), Muckross (or Middle) and Upper

▲ The Gap of Dunloe

(see the map on p.340). The lakeshores are covered with virgin forest that features oak and such Mediterranean plants as the arbutus, or strawberry tree – so termed because of its red, but non-edible, fruit. Among the park's notable mammals are red deer, otter, pine marten, red squirrels and Irish hare, while its 140 bird species include the peregrine falcon and the hen harrier. Running roughly parallel to the park's western border is the dramatic glacial breach known as the **Gap of Dunloe**. The **National Park Visitor Centre** (mid-March to Sept daily 9am–6pm; free) at Muckross House provides information about all aspects of the park, including a twenty-minute audiovisual on the landscape, flora and fauna, and there's an information point (July to mid-Sept daily 9.30am–6.30pm) at Torc Waterfall. The Ordnance Survey of Ireland produces a detailed, 1:25,000 **map** of the national park.

There's all manner of tours and transport available, including boats at Ross Castle (see p.336) and Muckross House (see p.337), and rented bikes (see p.331). Two-hour **guided walks** through the park set off from O'Sullivan's Bike Shop opposite St Mary's Cathedral every morning at 11am (€9; Ⓣ064/33471 or 087 639 4362, Ⓦwww.killarneyguidedwalks.com). On bank- holiday weekends, the local Chamber of Tourism and Commerce organizes guided **walking programmes**, comprising a varied selection of full-day (€10) and shorter (free) walks – go to Ⓦwww.killarney.ie or phone Ⓣ1850 566466 or 064/37928 for information and bookings. **Jaunting cars** (pony traps) tout for business at several locations, including Kenmare Place in town, Muckross House and Kate Kearney's Cottage (for the Gap of Dunloe). They generally charge around €20 per person, but it's worth haggling with the "jarveys" – as the drivers are known – depending on how many are in your group and how far you want to go. Reputable jarveys, recommended by the tourist office, include Paul and Michael Tangney, usually to be found at Kenmare Place (Ⓣ064/33358 or 087 253 2770).

Several tour operators, including Dero's, Main Street (Ⓣ064/31251, Ⓦwww.derostours.com), O'Donoghue Brothers, *Old Weir Lodge*, Muckross Road (Ⓣ064/31068, Ⓦwww.killarneydaytour.com), and Gap of Dunloe Tours, *O'Connors Pub*, 7 High St (Ⓣ064/30200, Ⓦwww.gapofdunloetours.com), offer full-day **combination tours**, which take you by bus to the starting point of Kate Kearney's Cottage, from where you walk or ride a jaunting car or pony through the Gap; then after a lunch stop at Lord Brandon's Cottage you take a boat ride through the three lakes to Ross Castle, and finally a bus brings you back into town (€27 per person, €47 with jaunting car, €62 with pony-trekking). Simpler **bike-on-boat tours** (you cycle through the Gap of Dunloe and sling your bike on a boat between Lord Brandon's Cottage and Ross Castle) can be arranged through the hostels, or Gap of Dunloe Tours, who also run a **bus to Muckross House** and back once a day.

Ross Castle and Lough Leane

The gates of Knockreer Estate, opposite the cathedral and guarded by Deenagh Lodge (now a café, see p.334), give immediate access to the national park. Paths through the grounds, which blaze in spring with rhododendrons, azaleas and magnolias, lead south after about half an hour to **Ross Castle** (mid-March to May & Sept to mid-Oct daily 9.30am–5.30pm; June–Aug daily 9am–6.30pm; mid-Oct to mid-Nov Tues–Sun 9.30am–4.30pm; tours every 40min, last admission 45min before closing; €5.30; Heritage Card; Ⓦwww.heritageireland.ie). Alternatively, a more roundabout route from the gates to the castle runs along the shore of **Lough Leane**, affording magnificent views of the lake's thirty-odd islands and the mountains to the southwest; or you can drive there via a turning off the N71 Kenmare road.

Engaging and informative 35-minute **tours** focus on the history, architecture and day-to-day life of the castle. It's an impressive example of a medieval tower house, probably built in the late fifteenth century by one of the O'Donoghue Ross chieftains, who had undisputed hold over the Killarney area at the time. They clearly had something to fear, however: the austere stronghold features murder holes and stumble steps – of irregular dimensions, designed to trip unwary attackers – while the cross-planked and spiked oak doors are further protected by raised thresholds and pointed arches. The flagstoned rooms, which include a Great Hall with its own pantry and minstrels' gallery and a tiny cubbyhole for around fifteen servants to sleep in, have been decked out with authentic fifteenth- to seventeenth-century furniture and tapestries.

From the pier at Ross Castle, **tours of the lake** are operated by large water-buses – the *Lily of Killarney* (contact O'Donoghue Brothers or Dero's Tours, as above; March–Oct) or the *Pride of the Lakes* (in town, contact Destination Killarney, Scotts Gardens, East Avenue Road Ⓣ064/32638; March–Oct) – each of which runs five one-hour trips a day, costing €8; the latter also offers a connecting shuttle bus from town (€2 return). Also at the pier, you can hire a boatman to take you out in a motorboat or rowing boat, or you can rent your own (Ⓣ087 675 7791), which will allow you to have a look at heavily wooded **Inisfallen**, the largest of Lough Leane's islets. The monastery established here by St Finian the Leper in the early seventh century became a major centre of learning, numbering among its tenth-century alumni Ireland's most famous king, Brian Boru. The *Annals of Inisfallen*, written by the monks between the eleventh and thirteenth centuries and now housed in the Bodleian Library in Oxford, are the main source for the history of Munster of the period. The original churches and dwellings are long gone, but you can see the picturesquely weathered ruins of a thirteenth-century oratory and a mostly thirteenth-century Augustinian priory.

Muckross Estate

The huge **Muckross Estate** begins about 3km south of Killarney off the N71, where a gate and a gaggle of jaunting cars signal the short walk through the woods to **Muckross Friary** (mid-June to early Sept daily 10am–5pm; last admission 45min before closing; free; Ⓦwww.heritageireland.ie). Founded in the fifteenth century, this strict Franciscan friary originally enshrined a miraculous statue of the Virgin Mary. It's in a remarkable state of preservation, with an intact two-storey cloister shaded by a gnarled yew tree at its centre.

You can continue through the estate on foot or by bike, but car drivers will have to continue down the main road for 1km to **Muckross House** (daily: mid-March to June, Sept & Oct 9am–6pm; July & Aug 9am–7pm; Nov to mid-March 9am–5.30pm, closed 1 week at Christmas; last guided tour 1hr before closing; €5.75, joint ticket including farms €9.50; Heritage Card; Ⓦwww.muckross-house.ie). The Victorian interiors of this fine, nineteenth-century Neo-Elizabethan stately home are rich, almost cloying, with fascinating display boards detailing the lives of its former inhabitants. You can watch weavers at work in both the basement and the crafts centre, where there are also displays of bookbinding and pottery. On the other side of the car park are the three traditional **working farms** where you can chat to actors playing out the roles of farmers and their wives (mid-March to April & Oct Sat, Sun & public hols 1–6pm; May daily 1–6pm; June–Sept daily 10am–6pm; last admission 1hr before closing; €5.75, joint ticket including the house €9.50; Heritage Card). In fine weather, you can sit outside at the splendid **café-restaurant** in the crafts centre, overlooking the pretty **gardens** (open all year; free), which are noted for their rhododendrons and azaleas. **Boat trips** on Muckross Lake can be organized at the nearby Dundag Boathouse (Ⓣ087 278 9335 or 087 120 0420).

Muckross Lake and the Upper Lake

Starting from the house (where you can pick up a walks leaflet), there's a delightful ten-kilometre trail around **Muckross Lake**, mostly on paved paths, but with a short section on the main Kenmare road. Passing through gnarled, mossy, ancient woods with a thick undergrowth of heather and ferns, you'll reach Brickeen Bridge where lakes Muckross and Leane meet, and shortly after the Meeting of the Waters, where the outflow from the Upper Lake runs into Muckross Lake. Just above this second meeting is a picturesque, tree-shaded pool with the arches of the ruined Old Weir Bridge as a backdrop, which must feature in a million photo albums around the world. In summer, refreshments are available at the nearby **Dinis Cottage**, an eighteenth-century hunting lodge that's recently been renovated as a tearoom. On your way back, you can take in twenty-metre **Torc Waterfall** on a short detour, or take on the steep climb up to the summit of **Torc Mountain** (535m) for magnificent views of the lakes and the Reeks.

Further down the main N71, 16km from Killarney, is **Ladies' View** (site of a café, bar and crafts shop), which apparently was chosen by the ladies-in-waiting of Queen Victoria on her visit in 1861 as the finest view in the land – with some justification. From the car park here, you look directly down on the **Upper Lake**, with its many channels running down to lakes Muckross and Leane on one side, and the Carrauntoohil massif rising on the other. Just before reaching Ladies' View on the main road, there's a signposted path, part of the Kerry Way, through Derrycunihy Woods to Lord Brandon's Cottage (see below); beyond Ladies' View, spectacular vistas continue at least as far as **Moll's Gap**, where the Avoca craft shop and its good café mark the parting of the Kenmare road and the R568 to Sneem.

The Gap of Dunloe

The **Gap of Dunloe**, a glacial defile which cuts off Tomies and Purple mountains from Macgillycuddy's Reeks, is justifiably one of the area's most popular attractions. Try, if you can, to come here late in the day, when the light is at its best and the road at its quietest.

The usual approach is from the north, where **Kate Kearney's Cottage**, a pub and restaurant 4km from Beaufort, stands at the foot of the Gap. Beyond here the road is closed to motor traffic at busy times (except for access), leaving it free for walkers, cyclists, pony trekkers and jaunting cars. It's a starkly beautiful seven-kilometre climb to the Head of the Gap, walled in by a steep patchwork of grass and bare purple rock, with tumbling waterfalls after rain, past reedy lakes and one or two sheep. Then from the Head, you can make a glorious descent into the broad **Black Valley**, hemmed in by 784-metre Broaghnabinnia at its western end and so named because all its inhabitants died during the Famine. It now supports a few sheep farms, a primary school and a basic An Óige **hostel** (closed Dec & Jan; ⓣ064/34712 or 01/830 4555; dorms €12.50–16), on the Kerry Way 3km from the Head of the Gap. About 2km further down the road, in a delightful spot at the head of the Upper Lake, is **Lord Brandon's Cottage** (open approximately April–Oct), where scones, soup and sandwiches are on offer.

The Iveragh Peninsula: the Ring of Kerry

The **Ring of Kerry** is often used as a substitute name for the **Iveragh Peninsula**, but more properly it refers to the 175-kilometre road that encircles this vast, scenic leg of land. Tourists have been coming to the peninsula in ever-increasing numbers over the past century, but most of them do the Ring by bus or car in a day from Killarney. If you stay in one of the Iveragh's few small towns or venture off the main route, you'll have to yourself this giant's landscape of mountains, lakes and long ocean views, which is at its most spectacular when illuminated by a sudden shaft of light through the clouds like a flash bulb.

Buses ply the whole Ring from June to mid-September only (1 daily), returning to Killarney from Sneem via Moll's Gap. At other times buses from Killarney only venture as far as Cahersiveen (Mon–Sat 2 daily) and Waterville (Mon–Sat 1 daily), via the north coast. On the south coast, there are buses between Sneem and Kenmare twice daily in July and August (Mon–Sat), but only once a week for the rest of the year. You can walk around the peninsula on the **Kerry Way**, as detailed in the box below, while cycling, often up steep gradients and against strong winds, is a shorter – three days at the least – but perhaps just as physically demanding option. The waymarked, 215-kilometre **Ring of Kerry Cycle Route** (map guide available from local tourist offices)

The Kerry Way and Carrauntoohil

The 213-kilometre-long **Kerry Way** is a spectacular, waymarked long-distance footpath that starts in Killarney, takes in the Muckross Estate, Torc Waterfall, the Upper Lake and the Black Valley before crossing to Glencar, then goes right around the Iveragh Peninsula anticlockwise, with short offshoots to Glenbeigh, Cahersiveen, Waterville and Caherdaniel, finally passing through Sneem and Kenmare. Mostly following a network of green roads, many of which are old "butter roads", the route provides magnificent views both of the Iveragh's mountains and of the neighbouring peninsulas, Dingle and Beara. OS 1:50,000 **map** numbers 78 and 83 are essential, and Cork Kerry Tourism produce a useful *Kerry Way Map Guide*. The whole thing can be done in nine or ten days, or, with careful study of bus timetables, you could do day-walks along the Way beyond Glenbeigh in summer, or on the section between Glenbeigh and Waterville in winter.

Accommodation in the Black Valley, Glenbeigh, Cahersiveen, Waterville, Caherdaniel and Kenmare is detailed in the text. Other accommodation – which should be enough to get you all the way round the Kerry Way – includes *The Climbers' Inn* in **Glencar**, between the Black Valley and Glenbeigh (ⓣ066/976 0101, ⓔclimbers@iol.ie; April–Oct daily, Nov–March weekends; dinner available; dorms €25 including breakfast; twins and doubles ❷); *Caitin's Hostel and Pub* in **Kells**, between Glenbeigh and Cahersiveen (ⓣ066/947 7614, ⓔpatscraftshop@eircom.net; IHO; dorms €15); *Old Convent House* (ⓣ064/45181, ⓦwww.oldconventhouse.com; April–Oct; ❷) in **Sneem**, between Caherdaniel and Kenmare; and *Greenwood Hostel* in **Templenoe** (ⓣ064/89247, ⓔgreenwoodhostel@eircom.net; IHH & IHO; dorms €15, private rooms ❶), between Sneem and Kenmare. An excellent **website**, ⓦwww.kerryway.net, provides trail descriptions, maps and full details of walker-friendly accommodation, offering services such as luggage transfer, evening meals and packed lunches, along the route.

Experienced walkers may well be tempted off the Kerry Way to tackle Ireland's highest peak, **Carrauntoohil** (1038m). Two of the finest approaches are described in *Best Irish Walks* by Josh Lynam: the Coomloughra Horseshoe, a seven-hour, occasionally vertiginous circuit, starting from the bridge at Breanlee on the Beaufort–Glencar road, which also takes in the second and third highest peaks, Beenkeragh and Caher; and a tough, nine-hour MacGillicuddy's Reeks ridge walk, beginning at *Kate Kearney's Cottage*, bagging six peaks and ending at the Breanlee bridge.

of necessity follows the main road for around a third of its journey, but includes a long, scenic loop through Ballinskelligs,Portmagee and Valentia Island and covers the north coast of the peninsula and the area around Killarney almost entirely on minor roads.

Coach tours from Killarney, which ply the Ring of Kerry in flotillas in summer, are required to travel anticlockwise: you can weigh up the disadvantages of getting stuck in a convoy – plenty of time to admire the views – against meeting the buses on the many blind corners. In the account below, we've covered the Ring anticlockwise.

West towards Cahersiveen

Nineteen kilometres from Killarney is **KILLORGLIN**, a distinctly missable town on the River Laune apart from for three mad days in the middle of August during the **Puck Fair** (ⓦwww.puckfair.ie), which draws in crowds of up to thirty thousand. First a wild goat is stalked in the mountains, then caged and crowned as king of the town, the signal for a Dionysian festival of wine and song, plus a traditional horse fair. The event has pagan roots in the Celtic harvest

KILLARNEY NATIONAL PARK & THE IVERAGH PENINSULA

Castlemaine
Castlemaine
Tralee
Cork
Lough Guitane
Kilgarvan
Castletownbere
Healy Pass & Adrigole
Bantry
Killorglin
Killarney
Fossa
Beaufort
Kate Kearney's Cottage
Ross Castle
Inisfallen
Lough Leane
Tomies Mt
Gap of Dunloe
Muckross Friary
Muckross House
Purple Mt
Muckross Lake
Torc Mountain
Upper Lake
Black Valley
Lord Brandon's Cottage
Ladies View
Mangerton Mountain
KILLARNEY NATIONAL PARK
Carrauntoohil (1038m)
MACGILLYCUDDY'S REEKS
Moll's Gap
Kerry Way
Kenmare
Templenoe
Blackwater Bridge
Tahilla
Sneem
Iveragh Peninsula
Mullaghanattin
Knockmoyle
Ballaghisheen
River Inny
Glencar
Breanlee
Caragh Lake
Glenbeigh
Seefin
Rossbeigh Strand
Dingle Bay
Ring of Kerry
Kells
Knocknadobar
Teermoyle Mt
Doulus Head
Cahersiveen
Valentia Island
Knightstown
Reenard Point
Geokaun
Chapeltown
Bray Head
Portmagee
Ring of Skellig
Mastergeehy
Puffin Island
St Finan's Bay
Ballinskelligs
Waterville
Lough Currane
Staigue Fort
Ballinskelligs Bay
Coomakista Pass
Castle Cove
Little Skellig
Skellig Michael
Bolus Head
Deenish Island
Abbey Island
Caherdaniel
Derrynane Bay
Scariff Island
Kenmare River
Ardgroom
Derreen Gardens
Lauragh
Gleninchaquin Park
CORK
Glengarriff
N22
R563
N72
N70
N71
R565
R566
R567
R568
R569
R571
R574
0 5 km

festival of Lughnasa, though these particular ceremonies are meant to commemorate the herd of goats that ran down into Killorglin, to warn the townsfolk that Cromwell's army was on its way. Your best bets for somewhere to **stay** during the festival are *Laune Valley Farm Hostel* (IHH & IHO; ⓣ066/976 1488, ⓔlaunevalleyfarm@hotmail.com), which offers dorms (from €16), private rooms (❶) and cooked meals a couple of kilometres away on the N70 Tralee road, or the well-equipped *West's* caravan park and campsite (ⓣ066/976 1240, ⓦwww.westcaravans.com; April–Sept), 1.5km out on the Killarney road. Otherwise, contact the Killorglin **tourist office**, which is based in the council offices by the central roundabout, about accommodation as early as possible (Mon–Fri 9am–5pm; ⓣ066/976 1451).

To the southwest of Killorglin, inland of the N70, **Caragh Lake** is far quieter than the lakes of Killarney and almost as scenic. Stretching for 6km in the shadow of Carrauntoohil, it's roughly circled by minor roads and flanked to the east by a forestry park, which affords fine views over the lake to the Dingle Peninsula. Several upmarket **guesthouses** cling to the northeastern corner of the lake, notably *Carrig Country House*, a pretty Victorian lodge in colourful gardens with wonderful views and a fine **restaurant** (ⓣ066/976 9100, ⓦwww.carrighouse.com; closed Dec–Feb; ❺).

GLENBEIGH, on the N70, 13km southwest of Killorglin, makes a convenient stopover on the Iveragh's north coast. The *Towers Hotel* (ⓣ066/976 8212, ⓦwww.towershotel.com; ❹), an old-fashioned staging post with a modern extension on the main junction here, will cater for most of your needs. The lively, cosy **bar** serves sandwiches, salads and plenty of seafood, and hosts traditional and other live music at weekends, while a wider choice of marine life is offered on the hotel **restaurant**'s set menu in the evenings. En-suite **B&B** in a smart dormer house with a pretty garden is available at *Glencurrah House* (ⓣ066/976 8133, ⓦwww.glencurrahhouse.com; April–Oct; ❷), while **campers** should head for *Glenross Caravan and Camping Park* (ⓣ066/976 8451, ⓦwww.killarneycamping.com; Easter & May–Sept) on the east side of the village. Just over a kilometre away to the west, there's a spectacular Blue Flag beach, **Rossbeigh Strand**, which hugs a five-kilometre-long spit of land; you can arrange **horse riding** on the beach through Burke's Activity Centre (ⓣ087 237 9110, ⓦwww.burkesactivitycentre.ie).

Cahersiveen

CAHERSIVEEN (sometimes spelt Caherciveen or Cahirsiveen, but always pronounced with the stress on the last syllable) is the main service town for the west end of the peninsula. Functional rather than attractive, its one long, narrow street – at various points named East End, Church Street, Main Street and New Street – is dotted with unkempt, disused buildings. The town's most famous son was Daniel O'Connell (see p.696), to whom the **O'Connell Memorial Church** on the main street was dedicated – a remarkable tribute for a politician. Built between 1888 and 1902, largely with money from the States and Australia, it's a huge, lumbering edifice made of concrete – now badly cracking – faced with Irish granite.

More deserving of a visit is the **heritage centre** in the fearsome, castle-like **Barracks** (June–Sept Mon–Sat 10am–5.30pm, Sun 1–5.30pm; at other times by arrangement, ⓣ066/947 2777; €4), which contains a concise history of the town, covering O'Connell and the Fenian uprising of 1867; it was the latter, when an attempt was made to cut the transatlantic cable at Valentia, that prompted the construction of these heavily fortified quarters for the Royal Irish

Constabulary. The **tourist office** in the old library on the main street (May to mid-Sept daily 9.30am–5.15pm, closing, at variable times, for lunch; ⓣ066/947 2531) can give you details of the Beentee (8km) and Laharn (12km) loop walks to the south of town and of several attractive spots on the nearby Doulus Head peninsula that are accessible on foot or by bike, including a ruined fifteenth-century tower house, a couple of well-preserved ring forts and White Strand, a fine, curving, sandy beach. **Bikes** can be rented from Casey's at the west end of the high street (ⓣ066/947 2474). From June to September, James Casey, who also arranges boat tours, leads two-hour guided historical **walks** of the town, departing from the *UN Bar* opposite the tourist office on the main street (daily at 11am; €10; ⓣ066/947 3186).

Practicalities

En-suite **B&B** is available at the smart and imposing *San Antoine* (ⓣ066/947 2521, ⓦwww.sanantoine.com; mid-March to mid-Oct; ❷) on Valentia Road at the west end of town. Contact *The Final Furlong Farmhouse and Stables* (ⓣ066/947 3300, ⓦwww.thefinalfurlong.com; April–Sept; ❷) for **horse-riding** opportunities in the local area; they also offer pleasant, seafront, en-suite, B&B accommodation on a working farm, 1.5km from the town on the road to Glenbeigh. There's a friendly **hostel** on the main street, *Sive*, 15 East End (IHH & IHO; ⓣ066/947 2717, ⓦwww.sivehostel.ie; dorms €13–16, twins ❶), a small terraced house with camping, family rooms, cooked meals and laundry facilities available. For **camping**, however, you'd be better off at the waterfront *Mannix Point Camping and Caravan Park* on the west side of town (ⓣ066/947 2806, ⓦwww.campinginkerry.com; mid-March to Sept), a well-equipped site with impromptu music sessions and a turf fire in the evening.

Good, reasonably priced bar **food** can be had at the welcoming *An Bonnán Buí (McCarthy's)* on Main Street, while *The Oratory* opposite is a civilized art gallery and café (closed Sun), serving cakes, paninis, salads and hot daily specials. As the owners come from a family of fishermen, seafood is not surprisingly the speciality at *QC's*, a stylish, nautical-themed restaurant at 3 Main St, with a cheaper menu, including tapas, available at the bar (ⓣ066/947 2244; summer closed Sun lunchtime; winter Thurs–Sun evenings only). The town has a host of characterful **bars**, notably *Mike Murt's* on East End, which has traditional music on Wednesday nights, and the aforementioned *An Bonnán Buí* (music Thurs). Cahersiveen holds a lively **music and arts festival** (ⓣ066/947 3772, ⓦwww.celticmusicfestival.com) over the bank-holiday weekend at the beginning of August, which has attracted big names such as Sinead O'Connor and the Hothouse Flowers. **Internet** access is available at an unnamed shop on Main Street, between *QC's* and the O'Connell Church.

Reenard Point and Portmagee

From **REENARD POINT**, 5km west of Cahersiveen, a **ferry** operates a continuous shuttle service across to Knightstown on Valentia Island (April–Sept Mon–Sat 8.15am–10pm, Sun 9am–10pm; cars single €5, return €8; cyclists single €2, return €3). *The Point Bar* here is very popular for its inexpensive, high-quality dishes, especially seafood.

The other jumping-off point for Valentia is **PORTMAGEE**, a harbour village situated beside the long bridge to the island. Its **Skellig Heritage Centre**, actually just across the bridge (mid-March to April, Oct & Nov Mon–Fri 10am–5pm; May, June & Sept daily 10am–6pm; July & Aug daily 10am–7pm; last admission 1hr before closing; ⓦwww.skelligexperience.com; €5; Heritage

Island), gives some fascinating background on seabirds and other marine life, lighthouses and early monastic life, with a short film about Skellig Michael. The centre also has a café with fine views of Portmagee, and runs **cruises** around, but not onto, Skellig Michael, which are useful for those who could not manage the 650 steps to the island's summit (1hr 45min; €27.50, including admission to the visitor centre; usually 3pm daily, plus others subject to demand, but Ⓣ066/947 6306 to check); in bad weather, mini-cruises around the Valentia channel may be laid on (€22, including admission to the visitor centre). Back in the centre of Portmagee, you can get tastefully decorated **accommodation** – ask for a room overlooking the harbour – and good **food**, either in the restaurant or the lively, friendly bar, at *The Moorings* (Ⓣ066/947 7108, Ⓦwww.moorings.ie; closed mid-Dec to mid-Jan; ❸); there's also traditional music on Friday and Sunday nights, plus Tuesdays in July and August. *Portmagee Hostel* (Ⓣ066/948 0018, Ⓦwww.portmageehostel.com; IHH) offers **dorms** (€14.50) and twin or double rooms (❶).

Valentia Island

Separated from the mainland by a long, narrow channel that's now bridged, **VALENTIA** barely feels like an island. For such a small, remote spot, it boasts a surprising number of claims to fame: as well as being known from the radio shipping forecasts and for Valentia slate (see below), it was from here that the first transatlantic telegraph cable was laid in 1866. To add to the island's repute, in 1992 the oldest fossilized footprints in the northern hemisphere, the so-called Tetrapod Trackway, were discovered here (see below).

Valentia's only **hostel** is the *Ring Lyne* (IHO; Ⓣ066/947 6103, Ⓔseanosullivan@hotmail.com), with dorms (€10–15), private rooms (❶), camping facilities, bar and restaurant, 4km from the bridge on the main road across the island at **Chapeltown**. Nearly all other facilities are at **Knightstown** at the northeastern tip, which provides dramatic views of the Iveragh Mountains. **B&Bs** on the waterfront here include *Spring Acre*, a spruce, en-suite bungalow with good single rates and child reductions (Ⓣ066/947 6141, Ⓔrforan@indigo.ie; March–Oct; ❷), and the *Royal* (Ⓣ066/947 6144, Ⓦwww.theroyalvalentia.com; ❶), a formerly grandiose Victorian hotel. The nearby *Fuchsia* (Ⓣ066/947 6051; Mon & Wed–Sun evenings) is a welcoming and popular **restaurant**, with courtyard tables for fine evenings, serving excellent food from around the world. The spruce *Sea Breeze* does espressos, cakes, salads, soup and sandwiches, while the *Royal Pier*, where the beer garden enjoys the finest views of the mainland, serves bar food and hosts traditional music on Wednesdays.

At the western edge of Knightstown, the **Valentia Heritage Centre** (April–Sept daily 10.30am–5pm, though hours sometimes irregular; €3; Ⓣ066/947 6411) houses a tidy display on the island's history in the old primary school. Continuing up School House Road, then forking right, will bring you after about a kilometre to **Glanleam House**, which was formerly the seat of the Knight of Kerry. Developed in the 1850s, the beautiful subtropical **gardens** here (April–Sept daily 10am–7pm; €4.50) encompass lily-of-the-valley trees, ferns and other exotic specimens from South America, Australasia and China, which thrive in this mild, sheltered location. The elegant eighteenth- and- nineteenth-century house also offers delightful **accommodation** in spacious, comfortable rooms, with especially attractive bathrooms and fine views of Valentia Harbour (Ⓣ066/947 6176, Ⓦwww.glanleam.com; mid-March to early Nov; ❺; self-catering cottages also available).

Beyond, about 5km from Knightstown near the island's northernmost tip, it's possible to see for yourself the **Tetrapod Trackway**, though you might have to show some perseverance as it's not very well signposted. From a car park by the island's coastguard station, a short path leads down to a precarious shelf of black rock by the Atlantic, on which the small foot- and tail-prints of the creature – a metre-long, lizard-like amphibian that lived some 385 million years ago – are quite clearly visible. What can feel like the end of the world on a stormy day is a suitably awesome location to come toe-to-toe with our first landborne ancestors. On the road to the Trackway, about a kilometre back, the *Lighthouse Café* (summer Tues–Sun noon–7.30pm; ⓣ066/947 6304) is a charming **café-restaurant**, serving organic, home-grown salads, local mussels and crab, with tables out on the grassy slopes to make the most of the magnificent views.

Perched high on the slopes above the Trackway is the **Valentia Slate Quarry**, which has furnished slate for the Houses of Parliament in London and the Paris Opera House; it's a noisy, open cavern, dripping with very cold water and topped by a much-revered Grotto of the Virgin, with lofty vistas over the sea. Further exciting views are provided by the spectacular **Fogher Cliffs** and **Geokaun Mountain**, the island's highest point, to the west of here, and the ruined lookout tower on **Bray Head**, at the southwestern end of the island.

The Skellig Islands

A voyage to the **Skellig Islands** (Na Scealga, "the crags"), rising sharply from the sea 10km off the tip of the Iveragh Peninsula, is one of the most exciting and inspiring trips you can make in Ireland. On top of the larger of these two inhospitable, shark's-tooth islands, **Skellig Michael** (or Great Skellig), a monastery was somehow constructed in the late seventh or early eighth century, in imitation of the desert communities of the early Church fathers. The exposed, often choppy boat-ride out, followed by Manx shearwaters, storm petrels and puffins from Puffin Island, a nature reserve at the edge of St Finan's Bay, only adds to the sense of wild isolation. **Little Skellig** is a nature reserve too, crawling with over fifty thousand gannets and now officially full (the excess

Skellig practicalities

Small **boats** run out to the Skelligs between May and September (sometimes with extra departures at the back end of April and in October) but depend on the weather being good enough for the crossing. They need to be booked the previous day at the latest – only a dozen operators are allowed to land on the island, and there's often a delay of several days before the boats will sail because of bad weather – and you're advised to phone the boatman about conditions on the morning of your trip. The trip is only for those with good mobility, as there's a vertical ladder up onto the quay, and then 650 steps to the summit; the alternative is a cruise around the islands from the Skellig Heritage Centre (see p.342). Bring walking shoes, warm waterproof clothes, water and food as there are no facilities on Skellig Michael (toilets are on the boats).

Costing €35–40 per person, the boats operate from several points around the coast. **Operators** include: Sean Feehan from Ballinskelligs (the shortest crossing to Skellig Michael at around 45min; ⓣ066/947 9182 or 086 417 6612); John O'Shea from Caherdaniel (ⓣ087 689 8431); Seán Murphy (Sea Quest; ⓣ066/947 6214 or 087 236 2344, ⓦwww.skelligsrock.com), who sails from Knightstown, via Reenard Point and Portmagee; and from Portmagee, Michael O'Sullivan (Waterville Boats; ⓣ066/947 4855), who will pick up in Waterville; the Caseys (ⓣ066/947 2437 or 087 239 5470, ⓦwww.skelligislands.com), who will pick up in Cahersiveen; and Des Lavelle (ⓣ066/947 6124). Boats depart between 10 and 11am and should allow you at least two hours on the island.

moved to the Saltees off County Wexford); landing is forbidden here, but the boatmen will come in close so you can watch the gannets diving for fish and hear their awesome din.

If you come between early spring and August, you'll have thousands of cute breeding puffins to keep you company on the 200-metre ascent from Skellig Michael's quay. The compact, remarkably well preserved **monastery** in the lee of the summit is a miracle of ingenuity and devotion. It was built entirely on artificial terraces, facing south–southeast for maximum sunlight, with sturdy outer walls to deflect the winds and to protect the vegetable patch made of bird droppings; channels crisscross the settlement to funnel rainwater into cisterns. You can walk into the dry-stone, beehive huts, chapels and refectory, which would have sheltered a total of twelve to fifteen monks at any one time and have withstood the worst the Atlantic can throw at them for 1300 years. The high cross beside the large oratory probably marks the burial of the founder, reputed to have been St Fionán, or an early saint – engaging guides, employed by the Office of Public Works, are on hand to give further background information.

At least three Viking raids in the ninth century were not enough to dislodge the monks, but during the climatic change of the twelfth century, the seas became rougher and more inhospitable. Around the same time, pressure was brought to bear on the old independent monasteries to conform, and the monks adopted the Augustinian rule and moved to Ballinskelligs on the mainland. Pilgrimages to Skellig Michael, however, continued until the eighteenth century, even after the Dissolution of the Monasteries.

The Ring of Skellig

To the south of Portmagee runs the **Ring of Skellig**, a quiet, scenic though often very steep route around the most westerly promontory of the Iveragh Peninsula, via wild and exposed **St Finan's Bay** – which is the unlikely home of the high-quality Skellig Chocolate Factory (visitors welcome to taste and buy; closed Jan; ⓣ066/947 9119, ⓦwww.skelligschocolate.com). From the highest point of the road between Portmagee and St Finan's Bay, you can climb the hill on the seaward side of the saddle in twenty minutes or so for the most magnificent views out to the Skellig Islands, across to the Dingle Peninsula and the Blaskets, and inland to the Iveragh Mountains.

On the far shore of the promontory lies **BALLINSKELLIGS** (Baile an Sceilg), behind a lovely, curving, sheltered, Blue Flag beach with great views of Waterville and the mountains, where Skelligs Surf School (ⓣ087 917 8808, ⓦwww.skelligsurf.com) offers **surfing** lessons. The monks of Skellig Michael retreated here in the twelfth century, constructing a new **abbey** which in turn was largely rebuilt in the fifteenth century. By walking south along the shoreline for five minutes, beyond a badly ruined tower-house, you can still see its delicate purple-grey sandstone church and traces of its cloister. The small but sprawling village of Ballinskelligs is part of a Gaeltacht (Irish-speaking) enclave, Uíbh Ráthach, and draws hosts of teenagers to Irish college in the summer. There's a **hostel** towards the south end (IHH; ⓣ066/947 9942, ⓦwww.skellighostel.com; dorms €14.50, private rooms ❶), while the refurbished *Ballinskelligs Inn* (ⓣ066/947 9104, ⓦwww.ballinskelligsinn.com; ❷) offers good-value, en-suite **B&B**, a **restaurant** and bar, with live music at weekends. The striking thatched roundhouse at the north end of the village is an **art gallery** and summertime café, attached to the Cill Rialaig retreat for artists, who each donate a work of art for sale here.

Waterville

On the east side of Ballinskelligs Bay, **WATERVILLE** (An Coireán; Ⓦwww.waterville-insight.com) is an incongruously genteel resort in this distant wilderness. Its exposed, pebbly beach is backed by a long, grassy promenade – now sporting a statue of Charlie Chaplin, who spent several holidays here – and large, neat houses with well-tended lawns, many of them built for workers on the transatlantic telegraph cable, which was extended from Valentia to Waterville in the 1880s. There's a small **tourist office** and bureau de change (daily: high season 9am–8pm; winter 10am–5pm; Ⓣ066/947 4212, Ⓔcraftmarket@eircom.net) in the crafts centre on the north side of town, and standard and en-suite B&B **accommodation** in part of the nineteenth-century cable station at the *Old Cable House* (Ⓣ066/947 4233, Ⓦwww.oldcablehouse.com; ❷), an attractive and congenial establishment in a pleasant garden, with dinner and **bike rental** available. On the northern edge of town overlooking Ballinskelligs, *Brookhaven* (Ⓣ066/947 4431, Ⓦwww.brookhavenhouse.com; ❹) is a well-run and helpful guesthouse with a wide variety of spacious, comfortable rooms and plenty of choices for breakfast. The welcoming, family-run *Butler Arms Hotel* (Ⓣ066/947 4144, Ⓦwww.butlerarms.com; closed mid-Oct to March; ❻) offers tastefully furnished bedrooms, many with sea views, and a pretty garden.

Waterville boasts several good **places to eat**. Opposite the crafts centre, *Paddyfrogs* (Ⓣ066/947 8766; March–Oct evenings only) is run by a Frenchman and his Irish wife, who cook up some creative continental dishes such as a seafood symphony with saffron sauce, as well as interesting options for veggies. In the centre of the village, the *Sheilin* (Ⓣ066/947 4231; evenings only) is a cosy, fairly pricey restaurant specializing in all manner of seafood, but with landborne options such as Kerry lamb and cheaper pastas also on offer. There's also plenty of seafood at reasonable prices at the nearby *Lobster Bar*, which hosts traditional music in summer. *Peter's Place*, a former hostel at the south end of town, provides good coffee and cakes, as well as **Internet** access. The adult education centre, Tech Amergin (Ⓣ066/947 8956, Ⓦwww.techamergin.com), hosts a three-day **arts festival** over the solstice in June, as well as courses in everything from archeology to the fiddle in the summer.

Several minor roads from Waterville head northeast up the **Inny Valley** towards Glencar and the heart of the Iveragh Mountains. Ten kilometres away up the valley near Mastergeehy (Maistir Gaoithe), the dorms (from €17) and private rooms (❶) of the *Brú na Dromoda* **hostel** (IHH; Ⓣ066/947 4782, Ⓦwww.dromid.ie; May–Oct) cater to walkers on the Kerry Way.

Derrynane Bay and around

Beyond Waterville, the Ring of Kerry climbs steeply to the **Coomakista Pass**, where a viewing point affords glorious views of Deenish and Scariff islands in the foreground at the mouth of the Kenmare River, and Bull, Cow and tiny Calf islands off the end of the Beara Peninsula. Hidden away beneath, at the southernmost point of the Iveragh Peninsula about 10km south of Waterville, is **Derrynane Bay** (pronounced "Derrynaan", meaning the "oak wood of St Fionán"). On the north side of the bay, **Derrynane House** (April & Oct Tues–Sun 1–5pm; May–Sept Mon–Sat 9am–6pm, Sun 11am–7pm; Nov–March Sat & Sun 1–5pm; last admission 45min before closing; €2.90; Heritage Card; Ⓦwww.heritageireland.ie) was once the home of, and is now a shrine to, Daniel O'Connell, the hugely popular, nonviolent campaigner who in 1829 achieved partial Catholic emancipation (see p.696). The plain, elegant house, which was largely rebuilt by the "Liberator" himself when he inherited it in 1825, contains all manner of memorabilia, as well as a tearoom and a lively, twenty-minute audiovisual that's well worth catching. The most striking relic is a chariot presented by Dubliners to O'Connell on his release from prison in 1844: modelled on a Roman triumphal car, with gold and purple silk, mouldings and armchairs, it carried him at the head of a crowd of 200,000 to his home in Merrion Square, Dublin.

The pretty gardens and wooded parklands around the house, accessible on signposted trails, have been declared a national historic park, and give onto wide, sandy beaches with 3km of dunes and good swimming; from the strand, you can stroll across to atmospheric Abbey Island with its graveyard and ruined abbey, founded by St Fionán in around 700. At the inlet on the western side of the island causeway, Derrynane Sea Sports (ⓣ066/947 5266) offers canoeing, sailing, wind-surfing and other **waterborne activities** in the summer. From here you can pick your way west for over a kilometre along a beautiful Mass Path – which formerly led worshippers to the secret Mass Rock at Derrynane House – to Béaltrá Pier; follow the lane uphill from the pier and turn onto the Kerry Way heading east back towards Derrynane House, for a very satisfying circular **walk** of a couple of hours or so.

CAHERDANIEL (Cathair Donál), a sprawling, attractively sited village on Derrynane Bay's steep eastern flank, is one of the nicest bases on the Ring of Kerry. There's very good **hostel** accommodation at its heart at the *Traveller's Rest* (IHO; ⓣ066/947 5175, ⓦwww.caherdanielhostel.com; dorms from €15.50, private rooms ❶), while *Kerry Way*, next to *The Blind Piper* pub, offers plain but comfortable **B&B** (ⓣ066/947 5277, ⓦwww.activity-ireland.com; ❷), as well as various **activities** including diving, hill-walking and rock-climbing. Further accommodation to the west of the village includes *Derrynane Bay House*, a kilometre or so out on the main road (ⓣ066/947 5404, ⓦwww.ringofkerry.net; closed Nov to mid-March; ❷), offering en-suite bathrooms and fine views; the *Scarriff Inn* (ⓣ066/947 5132, ⓦwww.caherdaniel.net; closed Nov to mid-March; ❸), 4km away on the N70, which has rooms with great sea views and offers good **food** in the bar or restaurant but is very popular with coach groups; and the attractive upmarket *Iskeroon* (ⓣ066/947 5119, ⓦwww.iskeroon.com; May–Sept; ❺), down the lane by the *Scarriff Inn* on a pebbly beach. *Glenbeg* (ⓣ066/947 5182, ⓔglenbeg@eircom.net; mid-April to Sept), on a sandy beach a kilometre or so east of the village, is the place to go for **camping**. Caherdaniel hosts a market for crafts and local produce in the village hall on Friday mornings in summer, and there are two vibrant **pubs** by the central crossroads, *Freddy's* and *The Blind Piper*, both with outdoor tables by a stream – at the latter you can eat well in either the bar or, in the summer, the restaurant, and you can often catch live music (Sundays are your best bet). *The Courthouse*, a **café** next to *Freddy's*, rustles up some interesting sandwiches, salads and soups at low prices.

Around 7km east of Caherdaniel on the N70, a sign points left to **Staigue Fort**, near the village of Castlecove; there's a small visitor centre (summer daily 10am–8pm; €3) near the junction, attached to a coffee shop and friendly bar with outdoor tables. After 4km up a narrow road, you'll come to a sophisticated ring fort, at least 2000 years old, with five-metre-high dry-stone walls surrounded by a bank and ditch; it's in an excellent state of preservation. Beyond Castlecove at the unexceptional village of Sneem, there's a fork in the main roads eastward: a mountain road (the R568) heads up to **Moll's Gap** (see p.338) and from there to Killarney, while the less scenic N70 continues along the seashore to Kenmare.

Kenmare and around

Sitting at the head of the Kenmare River – actually a long, narrow sea inlet – **KENMARE** (ⓦwww.neidin.net or www.kenmare.com) is an excellent base for exploring not only the Ring of Kerry, but also the **Beara Peninsula**, part of which, including the contrasting scenic beauties of **Gleninchaquin** valley and **Derreen Gardens**, lies in County Kerry. The cosmopolitan town is neat and attractive in itself, with a fine array of restaurants and accommodation and a lively, sociable nightlife.

The Town

Kenmare was established after the 1652 Act of Settlement, which followed Cromwell's brutal campaign in Ireland and forced Irish landowners to give up their estates to English settlers. Sir William Petty, who mapped and allocated these forfeited lands, managed to get hold of a quarter of Kerry for himself, and in 1670 established **Nedeen** (or An Neidín, "the little nest") here, a colony of English and Welsh Protestants to work in his lead mines, pilchard fisheries and ironworks. His descendant, the first Marquis of Lansdowne, rebuilt the town on its current X-shape in 1775, with the pretty, tree-shaded **Fair Green** (which still belongs to the Lansdownes) at its fulcrum, and rechristened it **Kenmare** – mistranslating *Neidín* as "nest of thieves", he adapted an earlier Irish name, *Ceann Mara* (head of the sea inlet), with which he was also able to honour his good friend, Lord Kenmare. The town's colourful history is carefully detailed in the **heritage centre** at the back of the tourist office (same hours – see below; free).

Kenmare's only other sight as such is a Bronze Age **stone circle**, five minutes' walk from the Green (signposted) on the riverbank. Around 17m in diameter, it's the largest of its kind in Kerry and may be orientated on the setting sun. At its centre stands a burial dolmen, three standing stones supporting a large capstone.

Practicalities

Kenmare's major streets are Henry Street and Main Street, which meet at Fair Green and are linked at their southern ends by Shelbourne Street. **Buses** stop on Main Street, while the helpful **tourist office** is on Fair Green (Easter–May, Sept & Oct Mon–Sat 9am–5pm, sometimes closing for lunch; June daily 9am–6pm; July & Aug daily 9am–7pm; ⓣ064/41233). From here, **guided walking tours** of the town or the surrounding countryside depart Monday–Saturday at 10am (€10–15; ⓣ086 325 3701). **Bikes** can be rented from Finnegan's, at the top of Henry Street (ⓣ064/41083), and **Internet access** is available at the post office opposite or at Live Wire, Rock Street (off Main Street). Seafari (ⓣ064/83171, ⓦwww.seafariireland.com) and VIP (ⓣ087 981 1155, ⓦwww.kenmareanglingandsightseeing.com) run two-hour **cruises** (€20) of Kenmare and the Iveragh and Beara peninsulas from the pier three or four times a day in high season, taking in the islands of the Kenmare River, a colony of a hundred seals and prolific birdlife. In summer Finnegan's runs scheduled minibus **tours** of the Ring of Kerry (Mon, Wed & Fri), Beara Peninsula (Tues) and Glengarriff and Garinish Island (Thurs); book at the Kenmare Lace Centre above the tourist office or phone ⓣ064/41491 or 087 248 0800 (ⓦwww.kenmarecoachandcab.com). Based at Dauros on the north shore of the Beara (with a courtesy bus to and from town), Star Sailing and Adventure Centre

(Ⓣ064/41222, Ⓦwww.staroutdoors.ie) lays on a range of activities including **sailing**, **kayaking**, **horse riding** and boat trips on the Kenmare River (€22).

Accommodation

Kenmare has an excellent choice of **accommodation**, including a couple of smart hostels and two of Ireland's finest hotels. **Camping** is available at the *Faungorth Family Activity Centre* (Ⓣ064/41770), 3km east on the Kilgarvan road.

Fáilte corner of Shelbourne and Henry streets Ⓣ064/42333, Ⓔfailtefinn@eircom.net (IHH & IHO). Spacious, well-kept hostel in the town centre, with spick-and-span rooms and a well-equipped kitchen. Closed Nov–March. Dorms from €16, twins ❶.

Foley's Henry St Ⓣ064/42162, Ⓦwww.foleyskenmare.com. Colourful, comfy en-suite rooms in a friendly and central place above a pub and restaurant – ask for a room at the back. ❸

Harbour View 6km southwest of town on the R571, near Star Sailing Ⓣ064/41755, Ⓦwww.kenmare.com/harbourview. Welcoming, traditional, en-suite B&B in a comfortable and quiet Modern house, set in a pretty garden, with fantastic views of the Kenmare River and the Iveragh mountains. ❸.

Hawthorn House Shelbourne St Ⓣ064/41035, Ⓦwww.hawthornhousekenmare.com. Highly recommended: great hospitality, stylish, well-appointed, en-suite rooms and fine breakfasts. ❷

Kenmare Lodge Hostel 27 Main St Ⓣ064/40662, Ⓔkenmarehostel@eircom.net (IHH). Smart, well-maintained rooms, some en-suite, all with towels provided, above a photographic shop; large kitchen and laundry facilities. Dorms €15, twins and doubles ❶.

Park Hotel Shelbourne St Ⓣ064/41200, Ⓦwww.parkkenmare.com. Dating from the late nineteenth century, this elegant luxury hotel stands in splendid grounds above the Kenmare River. Service is excellent, and a stunning, modern spa has been carefully blended into its leafy setting. Closed late Nov to early Feb, apart from Christmas and New Year. ❽

Rose Cottage The Square Ⓣ064/41330, Ⓦwww.kenmare.net/rose-cottage. Very comfortable and welcoming old-fashioned cottage, with pretty garden and en-suite rooms, bang in the centre of town on the Fair Green; no single rooms. ❷

Sallyport House Ⓣ064/42066, Ⓦwww.sallyporthouse.com. Spacious, upmarket guest-house on the shore of the Kenmare River on the southern edge of town. Rooms are furnished with antiques and boast large bathrooms and fine views of the gardens or the harbour. April–Oct. ❺

Sheen Falls Lodge Ⓣ064/41600, Ⓦwww.sheenfallslodge.ie. Top-notch, five-star hotel, overlooking the eponymous waterfall in a 300-acre woodland estate, 2km from town across the Kenmare River. The arm-long list of facilities includes swimming pool, spa, fitness centre, tennis and horse riding. Closed Jan. ❽

Silver Trees Killowen Rd Ⓣ064/41008, Ⓦwww.kenmare.net/silvertrees. A friendly, efficient and rather plush B&B, 5min walk from the centre, opposite the golf course on the road towards Kilgarvan, where the spacious, comfortable rooms all have their own bathroom and TV. Closed Oct–March. ❷

Virginia's Guesthouse Henry St Ⓣ064/41021, Ⓦwww.virginias-kenmare.com. Centrally located above *Mulcahy's Restaurant*, this charming, compact home-from-home has tasteful, well-equipped, en-suite rooms and excellent, varied breakfasts. ❸

Eating and drinking

Kenmare is fast acquiring a good reputation for **eating out**, with some fine **restaurants** and **cafés** (as detailed below). There's even a high-quality fish-and-chip shop, *Wharton's* on Main Street, with upstairs seating, and you can put together a fine picnic, or just buy a freshly made sandwich, at the Kenmare Food Company, a deli at 22 Henry St. Henry Street and Main Street shelter about a dozen **pubs**, so finding somewhere congenial to drink is very straightforward. *Crowley's* on Henry Street is an atmospheric, old-time bar with a snug and communal seating around the walls, and traditional music on Tuesday, while *The Wander Inn* opposite hosts a session on Thursday. *McCarthy's* over on Main Street is a lively, sociable spot that pulls in the thirty-somethings on weekends with live bands and singers, and hosts an early-evening traditional session Tuesday to Thursday.

Bácús Main St ⓣ064/48300. Excellent, welcoming bistro, hung with black-and-white Robert Doisneau photos of Paris, serving delicious, mostly classic, dishes such as roast poussin with stuffing and root vegetables, at very fair prices, using local, seasonal produce where possible; leave room for desserts such as fuchsia and honey jelly with Irish Mist mousse.

Jam Henry St. Very successful update of a traditional, self-service bakery-café. Good cakes and scones, and excellent coffee, as well as delicious sandwiches, quiches and lasagne. Closed Sun.

Lime Tree Shelbourne St ⓣ064/41225. Reliable, fairly pricey restaurant and art gallery in a sensitively converted schoolhouse, serving continental dishes such as beef fillet with aubergine purée and wild mushroom and pepper cream.

Mulcahy's 16 Henry St ⓣ064/42383. Crisp, modern decor and pricey but excellent, creative cuisine with global influences. Summer Mon & Wed–Sun evenings, winter Mon & Thurs–Sun evenings.

Packies Henry St ⓣ064/41508. Homely, upmarket restaurant with a good reputation, under the same management as *The Purple Heather*, cooking up plenty of seafood as well as dishes such as rack of lamb with mint and redcurrant jus. Mon–Sat evenings.

Prego Henry St ⓣ064/42350. Inexpensive, candlelit Italian café-restaurant, serving tasty risottos, pizzas, pastas and salads, as well as varied breakfasts, and sandwiches and simple main courses for lunch.

The Purple Heather Henry St ⓣ064/41016. A relaxing, daytime bistro-bar, serving light meals such as home-made chicken-liver paté with Cumberland sauce. Mon–Sat till 6pm.

South of Kenmare: the Beara Peninsula

To the south of Kenmare lies the **Beara Peninsula**, most of which is in County Cork (see p.322). At first the countryside here is green and thickly wooded, but head west on the R571 towards the end of the peninsula, or uphill on the scenic N71 towards Glengarriff, and the terrain soon becomes more windswept and lonely.

Around 13km from Kenmare along the R571, it's well worth turning onto the dramatic minor road up **Gleninchaquin**, a narrow coombe valley which bowls out at its head around the eponymous lake. After 3km, you'll come upon **Uragh Stone Circle** in a truly magical setting: hemmed in by glaciated hills, on a slender rise between lakes Inchaquin and Uragh, with views down the valley and across to Macgillycuddy's Reeks. To the south runs **Uragh Wood**, one of Ireland's few remaining stands of sessile oak, where numerous birds of prey, red squirrels and stoats reside.

Five kilometres further up the road, you'll reach **Gleninchaquin Park** (daily dawn–dusk; €4.50; ⓦwww.gleninchaquin.com), where easy-to-follow walks have been laid out around the head of the beautiful valley. It's not the wild, man-against-nature experience of the Beara Way, but it seems to be a neat solution to the problems between walkers and farmers that have been occurring in some parts of the country – and it's hard to get lost. The main, two-hour, circular trail takes you up via a corrie lake to the top of the waterfall, which affords the most spectacular views of the valley. If you fancy an easier outing, there's a river and water garden walk (30min), with rock pools for bathing, a farm walk (1hr) and a heritage trail (90min), or you can opt for longer trails (4hr or 7hr) taking in further lakes above the waterfall; however long your exertions, you can refresh yourself with tea, coffee and home-made cakes at the farmhouse. Back on the R571, almost opposite the turn-off for Gleninchaquin, *The Peacock* (ⓣ064/84287, ⓦwww.bearacamping.com) provides **camping** and **dorm** accommodation (€9–15) in two-person huts or four-person cabins, as well as a café-restaurant.

On the northwest side of **Lauragh**, 25km southwest of Kenmare, the extensive, subtropical **Derreen Gardens** (April–Sept daily 10am–6pm; €6) run down to the sea. Still owned by the descendants of Sir William Petty, they're planted with mature exotic species such as giant Australian ferns, Chilean myrtles, acacias, bamboo, rhododendrons and mighty eucalyptus trees. There are plenty of marked trails to keep you going for anything from thirty minutes to two hours, including paths along Kilmakilloge Harbour where a belvedere affords fine views across to the Iveragh Peninsula. South of Lauragh towards Adrigole, the R574 climbs to the county border at the narrow and dramatic **Healy Pass**, which affords magnificent views, passing after 1km a small **campsite**, *Creveen Lodge* (Ⓣ064/83131, Ⓦwww.creveenlodge.com; mid-April to Oct). Around 3km from Lauragh at Glanmore Lake, near the Beara Way and accessible by a minor road that runs west of and roughly parallel to the R574, there's a simple An Óige **hostel** in an old schoolhouse (closed Oct–May; Ⓣ064/83181, Ⓦwww.irelandyha.org; dorms €11–15).

The Dingle Peninsula

One wonders, in this place, why anyone is left in Dublin, or London, or Paris, when it would be better one would think, to live in a tent, or a hut, with this magnificent sea and sky, and to breathe this wonderful air, which is like wine in one's teeth.

J.M. Synge, *In West Kerry*

The last of southwestern Ireland's five great peninsulas, **Dingle** (Ⓦwww.dingle-peninsula.ie) is perhaps the most distinctive of them all. Arrowing westwards for over 50km, its heavily glaciated topography is especially irregular, with an L-shaped ridge of mountains that peaks at its north end at **Mount Brandon**, the highest summit in Ireland outside of Macgillycuddy's Reeks. Five-hundred-metre **Mount Eagle** at the very tip of the peninsula sets up a truly spectacular drive, cycle or walk around **Slea Head.** On the coasts, the long, exposed sandbars at **Castlegregory** and **Inch** draw surfers and windsurfers, while the deeply recessed, sandy beaches at **Ventry** and **Smerwick Harbour** encourage gentle swimming.

Dingle has an unusually rich heritage, including over five hundred Celtic *clocháns* (corbelled, dry-stone beehive huts), among which the most compelling is **Dún Beag**, dramatically perched along the Slea Head Drive. A satisfying day-trip beyond Dún Beag and Slea Head loops round to the early Christian **Gallarus Oratory**, whose stunningly simple dry-stone construction is perfectly preserved after 1300 years. The peninsula is also one of the strongest **Irish-speaking** districts in the country, known as **Corca Dhuibhne** (meaning "the

The Dingle Way

Probably the best way to soak up the Dingle Peninsula's dramatic, shifting landscapes is to walk all or part of the waymarked, 180-kilometre **Dingle Way**, which begins in Tralee, heads west to Camp, then loops round the rest of the peninsula, via long, sandy beaches, the steep north face of Mount Brandon and most of Dingle's major sites and villages. The whole thing can be done in seven or eight days, catching a bus out towards Camp on the first day to avoid repeating the stretch between there and Tralee. An excellent **website**, Ⓦwww.dingleway.net, provides trail descriptions, maps and full details of walker-friendly accommodation, offering services such as luggage transfer, evening meals and packed lunches, along the route. OS 1:50,000 **map** no. 70 covers most of the route, with the eastern end of the peninsula on no. 71, and Cork Kerry Tourism produces a useful 1:50,000 map-guide.

▲ Gallarus Oratory

followers of Davinia", a Celtic goddess); **courses** in Irish language and culture can be arranged at Feileastram Teo, An Portán, Dunquin (see p.360), and through the museum in Ballyferriter (see p.360). As the main settlement at the heart of this thriving Gaeltacht (which officially begins just west of Anascaul and Castlegregory), **Dingle town** (An Daingean) feels like a capital. It supports some top-notch restaurants and places to stay, complemented by a vibrant traditional-music scene, and is perfectly located for varied day-trips. One of the best of these is the boat trip to the abandoned **Blasket Islands** just off Slea Head, which were responsible for an astonishing body of Irish-language writing in the early twentieth century.

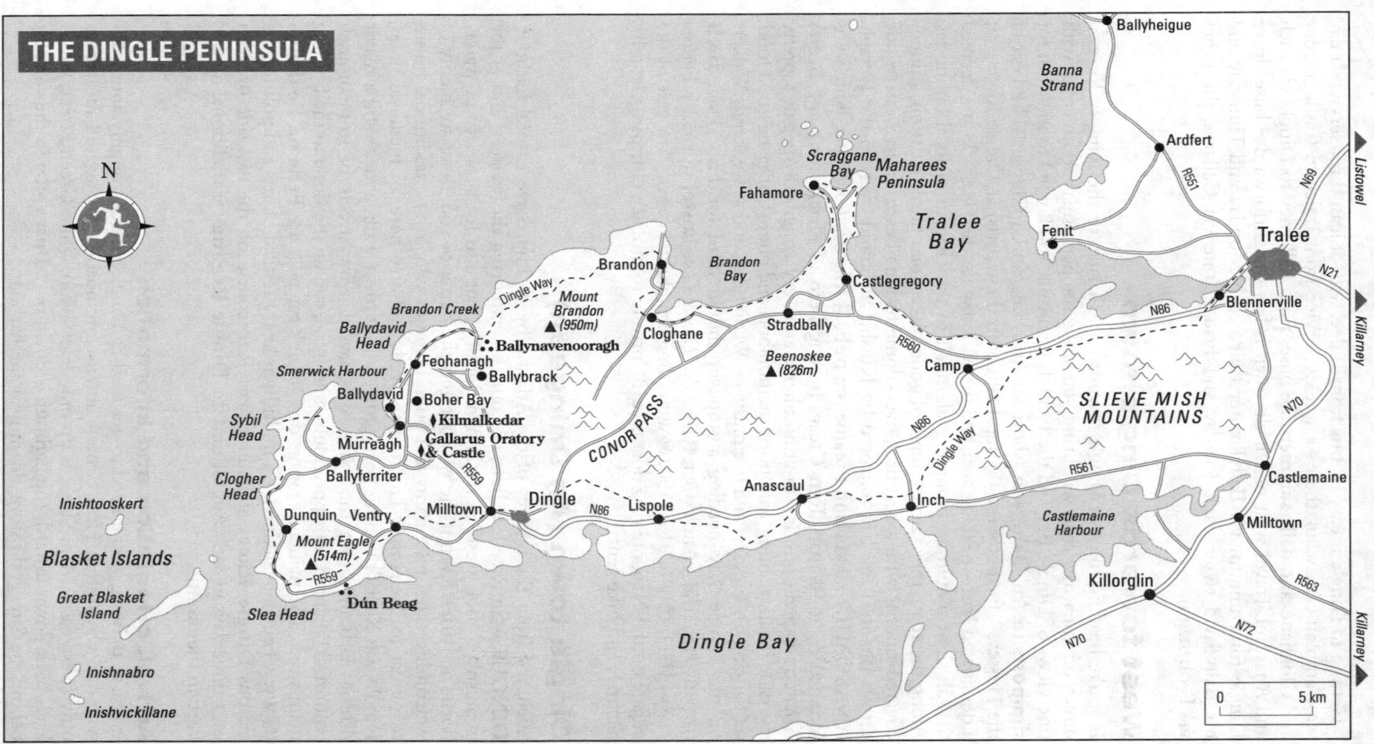
THE DINGLE PENINSULA
N
Ballyheigue
Banna Strand
Ardfert
R551
N69
Listowel
Scraggane Bay
Maharees Peninsula
Fahamore
Tralee Bay
Fenit
Tralee
N21
Killarney
Blennerville
Brandon
Brandon Bay
Castlegregory
Dingle Way
Mount Brandon (950m)
Brandon Creek
Cloghane
Stradbally
N86
Ballydavid Head
Ballynavenooragh
R560
Beenoskee (826m)
Camp
Feohanagh
Smerwick Harbour
Ballybrack
Ballydavid
Boher Bay
SLIEVE MISH MOUNTAINS
Kilmalkedar
Sybil Head
Murreagh
Gallarus Oratory & Castle
CONOR PASS
N70
Clogher Head
Ballyferriter
R559
R561
Castlemaine
Anascaul
Inch
Inishtooskert
Dunquin
Ventry
Milltown
Dingle
Lispole
Castlemaine Harbour
Milltown
Mount Eagle (514m)
Blasket Islands
Killorglin
Great Blasket Island
Dún Beag
R563
Slea Head
Dingle Bay
N72
Inishnabro
Inishvickillane
0
5 km

Getting to Dingle is easy by **bus** from Tralee, with at least three services a day via Camp and Anascaul; there's a weekly service from Tralee to Castlegregory and Cloghane, and daily summertime buses from Killarney to Dingle via Inch and Anascaul. Travel west of Dingle town is less straightforward – buses leave Dingle for Dunquin via Ballyferriter twice each Monday and Thursday and for Ballydavid twice each Tuesday and Friday (one via Gallarus, the other via Feohanagh).

West towards Dingle town

If you're heading towards Dingle town from Killarney or the Ring of Kerry, a direct, often narrow road will bring you along the peninsula's south coast, with fine views of Dingle Bay and the Iveragh Peninsula. You'll need to look out for **signposts** to **An Daingean** (short for An Daingean Uí Chuise, "The Fort of the Husseys", formerly the big local family in these parts) as Dingle town is in a designated Irish-speaking area, and the Ministry for the Gaeltacht has decreed that all signs should be monolingual, much to the chagrin of local businesses. Along the coast, there are a couple of good places for a break. At **Inch**, a dune-covered sandbar with a beautiful, five-kilometre-long beach on its western side thrusts out into the bay, mirrored by Rossbeigh Strand over on the Iveragh. **ANASCAUL**'s main claim to fame is a **pub**, *The South Pole Inn*, which was founded by local man, Tom Crean, unsung hero of Shackleton's and Scott's Antarctic expeditions. It's an atmospheric and very congenial spot in a pretty riverside location, hung with polar memorabilia and photos, offering good food, set dancing on Tuesdays and live music on Wednesdays and at weekends. Walkers on the Dingle Way needing a stopover should head for *Four Winds* **B&B** (ⓣ066/915 7168; March–Oct; ❷), or the *Dingle Gate* **hostel** (formerly *Fuchsia Lodge;* IHH; ⓣ066/915 7150, ⓦwww.dinglegatehostel.com), 2km east of the village on the N86, offering dorms (€13), private rooms (❶), **camping**, laundry facilities and bike rental.

Dingle town (An Daingean)

Sheltered from the ravages of the Atlantic by its impressive natural harbour, **DINGLE** is an excellent base, not only for exploring the western end of the peninsula ("back west" as it's known locally), but also for a variety of water-borne activities. Even if the weather gets the better of you, there are plenty of welcoming cafés, restaurants and pubs, many of which host traditional music, to retreat to. Tourism is far from the only industry here: in medieval times, Dingle was Kerry's leading port, protected by town walls, and it's still a major fishing harbour. From the extensive quays, narrow streets of stone houses, colourfully painted and appealingly substantial, run up the slope to the bustling main street. The principal events on Dingle's calendar are **Feile na Bealtaine** (ⓦwww.Feilenabealtaine.ie), a multidisciplinary festival of arts and politics, the riotous **Dingle Races** at Ballintaggart Racecourse on the east side of town over three days in early August, and the **Dingle Regatta** for traditional *currachs* later in the month.

Arrival, orientation and information

If you're **driving**, you'll need to get used to Dingle's fierce, roughly anticlockwise one-way system. Holy Ground and its continuation, Dykegate Lane, are up only (west–east), Main Street is up only (east–west), while Green Street, which leads back down towards the harbour, is down only. **Buses** stop in the car park behind the Supervalu store, down near the harbour.

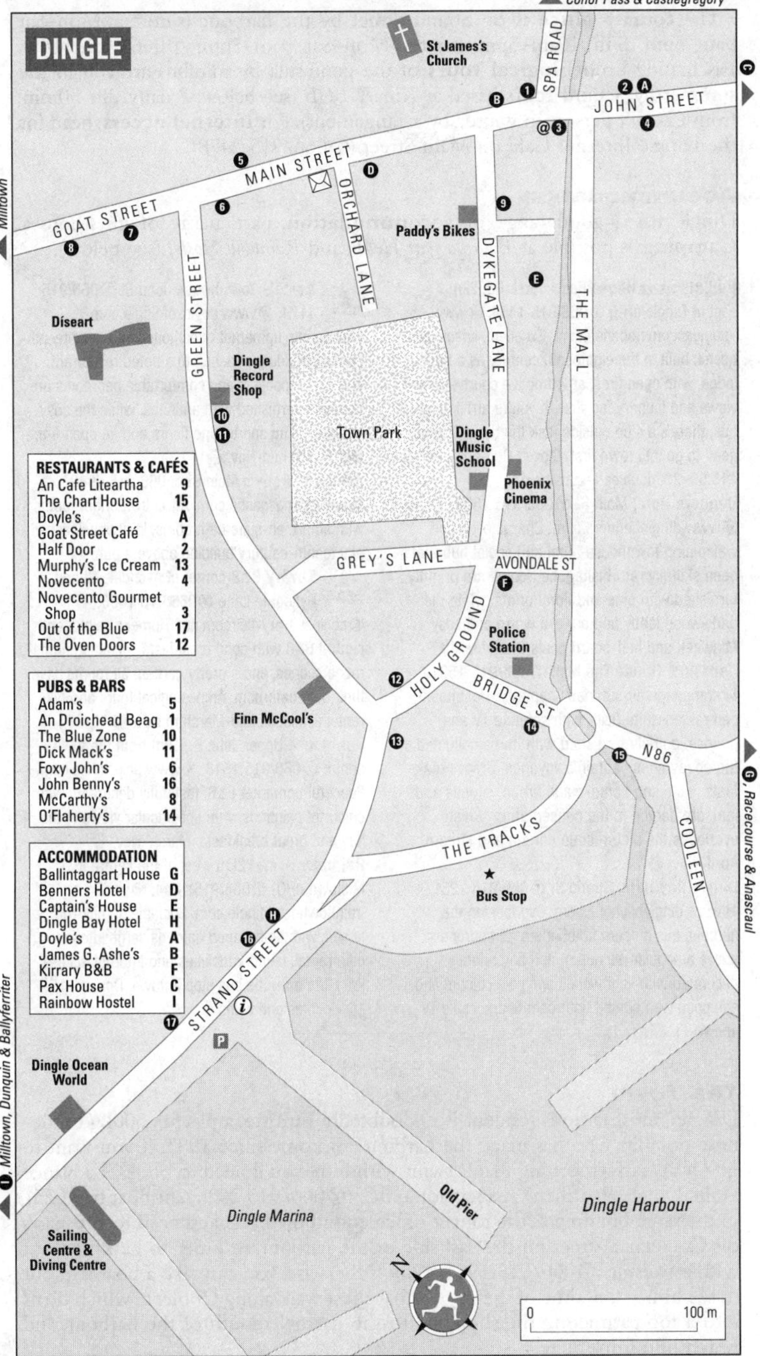
DINGLE
St James's Church
Conor Pass & Castlegregory
SPA ROAD
JOHN STREET
MAIN STREET
GOAT STREET
Milltown
ORCHARD LANE
Paddy's Bikes
DYKEGATE LANE
THE MALL
GREEN STREET
Díseart
Dingle Record Shop
Town Park
Dingle Music School
Phoenix Cinema
GREY'S LANE
AVONDALE ST
HOLY GROUND
Police Station
BRIDGE ST
Finn McCool's
N86
G, Racecourse & Anascaul
COOLEEN
THE TRACKS
Bus Stop
STRAND STREET
Dingle Ocean World
I, Milltown, Dunquin & Ballyferriter
Old Pier
Dingle Marina
Dingle Harbour
Sailing Centre & Diving Centre
N
0
100 m
RESTAURANTS & CAFÉS
An Cafe Liteartha 9
The Chart House 15
Doyle's A
Goat Street Café 7
Half Door 2
Murphy's Ice Cream 13
Novecento 4
Novecento Gourmet Shop 3
Out of the Blue 17
The Oven Doors 12
PUBS & BARS
Adam's 5
An Droichead Beag 1
The Blue Zone 10
Dick Mack's 11
Foxy John's 6
John Benny's 16
McCarthy's 8
O'Flaherty's 14
ACCOMMODATION
Ballintaggart House G
Benners Hotel D
Captain's House E
Dingle Bay Hotel H
Doyle's A
James G. Ashe's B
Kirrary B&B F
Pax House C
Rainbow Hostel I

8 KERRY

The **tourist office** is on Strand Street by the harbour (summer Mon–Sat 9am–6pm, Sun 10am–5pm; winter Mon–Sat 9am–5pm; ⓣ066/915 1188). Fascinating **archeological tours** of the peninsula by minibus are run in the summer by Sciúird Tours based at *Kirrary B&B* (see below; 2 daily, 2hr 30min; from €20 per person; in winter, by arrangement). For **Internet access**, head for the Dingle Internet Café on Main Street (ⓣ066/915 2478).

Accommodation

Dingle has a good range of **accommodation**, particularly of guesthouses. **Camping** is possible at *Ballintaggart House* and *Rainbow Hostel* (see below).

Ballintaggart House Racecourse Rd, 2km east of Dingle (IHH) ⓣ066/915 1454, ⓦwww.dingleaccommodation.com. Excellent, spacious hostel, built in the eighteenth century as a hunting lodge, with open fires, an attractive courtyard, fine views and laundry facilities. If you're arriving by bus, there's a stop outside (ask the driver), so no need to go into town first. Closed Oct–April. Dorms €13.50–20, doubles and twins ❶.

Benners Hotel Main St ⓣ066/915 1638, ⓦwww.dinglebenners.com. Characterful and welcoming townhouse hotel and social hub that's been skilfully refurbished: bedrooms are brightly furnished with pine and floral prints, while the dark-wood lobby and bar are warm and cosy. Midweek and half-board deals available. ❻

Captain's House The Mall ⓣ066/915 1531, ⓦhomepage.eircom.net/~captigh/. Hospitable, central, en-suite B&B, with satellite TV and phones, quirkily furnished with items collected on the eponymous captain's voyages. Great breakfasts, including home-made bread, scones and jam, are served in the conservatory, which overlooks the picturesque garden and stream. April–Nov. ❸

Dingle Bay Hotel Strand St ⓣ066/915 1231, ⓦwww.dinglebayhotel.com. Overlooking the harbour, this modern hotel offers 25 bedrooms above a popular restaurant and bar, brightly decorated with light woods and pale colours and equipped with heated bathroom floors, cable TV and Wi-Fi. ❺

Doyle's Townhouse John St ⓣ066/915 1174, ⓦwww.doylesofdingle.com. Welcoming, upmarket guesthouse in an eighteenth-century building attached to a noted restaurant. The eight spacious and comfortable bedrooms are tastefully furnished with antiques, while the cosy drawing room sports pine floors and an open fire. Mid-Feb to mid-Nov. ❺

James G. Ashe's Main St ⓣ066/915 0989, ⓦwww.jamesgashe.com. Attractive, bright rooms with smart, en-suite bathrooms, in a whitewashed nineteenth-century building above a pub. ❷

Kirrary B&B corner of Avondale St and Dykegate Lane ⓣ066/915 1606, ⓔcollinskirrary@eircom.net. Homely, helpful and central B&B with good breakfasts, including home-made scones, and a pretty garden; all rooms have their own bathroom. Archeological tours and bike rental available. Mid-March to Nov. ❷

Pax House Upper John St, 1km from the town centre ⓣ066/915 1518, ⓦwww.pax-house.com. Peaceful upmarket B&B, tastefully decorated with colourful paintings, with spectacular views of the bay and great breakfasts. March–Nov. ❸

Rainbow Hostel 2km west of the centre in Milltown (IHO) ⓣ066/915 1044, ⓦwww.rainbowhosteldingle.com. Sociable, family-run hostel, with landscaped gardens, large kitchen, bike rental, laundry facilities and Internet access. Free lifts from the bus stop in town. Dorms €15–16, doubles and twins ❶.

The Town

Dingle's most famous resident is undoubtedly **Fungie**, a playful, 300kg bottle-nose dolphin who has made the harbour his home since 1983. If you want to go for an early-morning (8am) swim with him, you'll need to book in advance at the Dingle Boatmen's Association office (ⓣ066/915 2626; 2hr boat trip €25), in the same building as the tourist office, round the back, and head to Brosnan's on Cooleen, a street on the east side of the harbour, in order to be kitted out with a wetsuit (ⓣ066/915 1967; €25). Otherwise, you can take a boat trip out to see him at any time of the day (€16), or just walk along Cooleen, which turns into a footpath along the shoreline to the narrow mouth of the harbour, and watch him from there.

Dingle offers several other opportunities for enjoying the water, including trips to **Great Blasket** (see p.359). **Surfboards** and wetsuits can be rented from Finn McCool's in Green Street, and surfing lessons, with free shuttle transport from town, are provided by West Coast Surf School (ⓣ086 836 0271). Dingle Sailing Centre at the marina (ⓣ086 847 8745, ⓦwww.saildingle.com) offers **sailing** courses and rents out dinghies and **kayaks**, while **diving** trips, mostly to the Blasket Islands, and PADI courses can be arranged at the nearby Dingle Marina Diving Centre (ⓣ066/915 2789, ⓦwww.divingdingle.ie). Back on land, you can go **riding** at Coláiste Íde Stables, 3km southwest from Dingle at Burnham (ⓣ066/915 9100), and rent **bikes** from Foxy John's on Main Street, Paddy's on Dykegate Lane and *Kirrary B&B*.

If nautical pursuits have whetted your curiosity, head for **Dingle Oceanworld** (Mara Beo) on the waterfront (May, June & Sept daily 10am–6pm; July & Aug Mon–Fri 9am–8.30pm, Sat & Sun 9.30am–8.30pm; Oct–April daily 9am–4.30/5pm; €11, child €6.50, family €30; ⓦwww.dingle-oceanworld.ie). As well as a centre for marine conservation, Oceanworld is a richly detailed aquarium, where you can stick your hands in the touch pool, observe sharks, stingrays, piranhas and eels at close quarters and walk underneath a variety of fish from around the Irish coast in the tunnel tank.

Back in the centre of town at Díseart Institute of Education and Celtic Culture, a former convent of the enclosed order of Presentation Sisters on Green Street, you can admire twelve **stained-glass windows** by Harry Clarke, one of the foremost artists in the medium in the last century (Mon–Sat 9am–5pm, sometimes closed for lunch in winter; €2, or €3.50 with guided tour); commissioned in 1922, they depict scenes from the life of Christ in opulent detail. Díseart also shelters an exhibition on the making of *Ryan's Daughter* on the peninsula in the 1960s (see p.329) and hosts an interesting variety of **courses** and talks on Irish and Celtic culture (ⓣ066/915 2476, ⓦwww.diseart.ie).

Eating and drinking

Although it doesn't promote itself as a foodie town, Dingle has several first-rate **restaurants**. Seafood, naturally, features strongly on their menus, and also in the town's **bar food**, while a couple of homely **cafés** are great for whiling away rainy afternoons. Pubs that are known best for their live music are detailed overleaf, while good options for a sociable **drink** include *Foxy John's* combined hardware shop and bar on Main Street, and *Dick Mack's* on Green Street, a crusty, beery, former cobblers' shop, with stars on the pavement outside to commemorate such diverse former customers as Robert Mitchum and Julia Roberts.

Adam's Main St. Cheap and tasty home-made lunches – including lemon and walnut chicken salad and Irish stew – at this likeable pub.

An Cafe Liteartha Dykegate Lane. Bookshop-café that offers a wide range of mostly Irish-interest books (including local guidebooks) out the front, and cheap, unpretentious food at the back: soup, scones, cakes and sandwiches, and good tea and coffee.

The Chart House by the roundabout at the bottom of The Mall ⓣ066/915 2255. Relaxing restaurant in a stone cottage with posh-rustic decor, preparing creative cuisine, such as John Dory with apple and fennel salad and an orange and basil sauce. Evenings only.

Doyle's Seafood Restaurant John St ⓣ066/915 1174. Upmarket but cosy and informal bar-restaurant which enjoys a widespread reputation for its seafood, including lobster from its own tank and adventurous dishes such as scallops and monkfish teriyaki. Land delicacies, plus one or two dishes for veggies, also available, as well as a good-value early-bird menu until 7pm. Mon–Sat evenings.

Goat Street Café Goat St. Civilized and sociable café, rustling up imaginative, tasty salads, Thai curries and other hot dishes, soups and desserts, at reasonable prices. Closed Sun.

Half Door John St ⓣ066/915 1600. Relaxing, white-tablecloth restaurant with excellent cooking – mostly seafood – a good wine list, delicious desserts such as apple and pear crumble, and friendly, efficient service. It's pricey, but there are various set menus on offer, which are especially good value at lunchtime and early evening.

John Benny's Strand St. Cosy, refurbished pub popular with locals and tourists for its bar food: bacon and cabbage, seafood, salads and sandwiches, with vegetarian options.

Murphy's Ice Cream Strand St. Delicious home-made ice cream to eat in or take away, as well as other great desserts, and excellent coffee.

Novecento John St ⓣ066/915 2584. Deliciously authentic Italian restaurant with wonderful service. Choose from a wide range of *antipasti*, reasonably priced home-made pastas, such as tasty macaroni with Italian sausage and tomato cream sauce, and a variety of daily seafood specials. Good-value three-course menu before 7pm. Evenings only, closed Wed. *Novecento Gourmet Shop*, nearby on Main St, dishes out great pizzas, either whole or by the slice, to take away (evenings, plus Mon–Fri lunchtimes).

Out of the Blue Opposite the tourist office on Strand St ⓣ066/915 0811. Simple seafood restaurant, dishing up whatever fish and shellfish are fresh from the pier opposite, in excellent dishes such as langoustine green curry. Pricey for dinner, simpler, cheaper menu for lunch. Closed Wed lunchtime & when there's no fresh fish.

The Oven Doors (Dingle Tea Rooms) Holyground. Long-established daytime café at the bottom of Green St, serving good, cheap pizzas, sandwiches, baked potatoes, tea, coffee and great cakes, in a bright, cheerful setting.

Live music and entertainment

Dingle is a hotbed of **traditional music**, with some locally based, nationally known performers turning up in the town's **pubs**. Cosy *An Droichead Beag*, at the bottom of Main Street, has great sessions just about every night, as does *O'Flaherty's*, a spartan but sociable pub, hung with interesting memorabilia, on Bridge Street down by the roundabout. *John Benny's*, nearby on Strand Street, puts on traditional music every night in summer, and keep an eye out for occasional sessions in the back room of *McCarthy's (Mac Carthaigh)* on Goat Street. In summer, there's a well-received series of folk and traditional **concerts** (3 weekly; ⓣ087 284 9656, ⓦwww.whatsondingle.com), with some contemporary music thrown in, at the pretty St James's Church in Main Street; tickets can be bought at the tourist office or the Dingle Record Shop, Green Street, a good source of information about sessions and of traditional CDs, especially by local musicians, at keen prices. You can even learn to **play** the *bodhrán* or tin whistle at the Dingle Music School on Dykegate Lane (ⓣ086 319 0438, ⓦwww.dinglemusicschool.com). For something completely different, *The Blue Zone*, a late-night wine bar above the Dingle Record Shop on Green Street, offers **jazz** and pizzas, and there's a good **cinema**, The Phoenix, on Dykegate Lane (ⓣ066/915 1222), and an acclaimed **theatre** company, Beehive, based at the Studio on Cooleen (ⓣ066/915 2924, ⓦwww.beehivetheatre.com).

Ventry to Slea Head

The next bay west of Dingle is just as impressive, sheltering a crescent of fine, sandy beach and low dunes in the lee of 514-metre Mount Eagle. The strand here was the suitably epic location for the legendary single combat between Fionn Mac Cumhaill and Daire Donn, the King of the World, to save Ireland from invasion by Daire's armies. In the village of **VENTRY** (Ceann Trá), which straggles around the bay, Penny's Pottery near the post office has a sporadically open summertime **café**, while *Páidí Ó Sé's* **pub**, further round the semicircle by the church, serves lunch and dinner; owned by a famous former Kerry Gaelic footballer and manager, it's hung with sporting memorabilia. On the west side of the bay, it's well worth calling in to the small but fascinating **Celtic**

and Prehistoric Museum (March to mid-Nov daily 10am–5.30pm; in the off-season call ⓣ066/915 9191; €4; ⓦwww.celticmuseum.com). Here you can gawp at a fossilized nest of dinosaur eggs, a baby dinosaur skeleton and the complete skull and tusks of a woolly mammoth, of the type that would have been roaming Ireland over twenty thousand years ago. From the Stone Age come jewellery, statuettes and tools – when the engaging owner is around, he'll show you how they were used. There are also some lovely Bronze Age spiral ornaments and Celtic amulets, money and burial offerings.

Beyond Ventry, it's a fine drive or cycle to **Slea Head** (Ceann Sléibhe), as the road narrows and the slopes of Mount Eagle steepen towards the end of the peninsula. This landscape is dotted with several Iron Age dry-stone forts, known as the **Fahan Group**, of which the most arresting is the first, around a kilometre beyond the museum. In a spectacular setting overlooking the Iveragh Peninsula, **Dún Beag** (entry €3, including a ten-minute audiovisual upstairs in the *Stonehouse* restaurant) has partly fallen into the Atlantic, and the location still feels precarious, at the base of Mount Eagle with the sea boiling around the black rocks below. Plenty of interest remains, however, including four lines of defensive banks and five corresponding ditches, traversed by a sixteen-metre souterrain, or underground escape route, which you can see beneath the flagstones of the entrance path. Within the three-metre-high walls stands a slightly disorientating beehive hut, or *clochán*, circular from the outside, rectangular within. Opposite the fort and built in a loosely similar, *clochán* style, *The Stonehouse* **café-restaurant** (closed Tues; ⓣ066/915 9970) offers reasonably priced lunchtime dishes such as crab salad with basil pesto and a more sophisticated menu in the evenings (booking essential).

The Blasket Islands and Dunquin

Just off Slea Head lie the **Blaskets** (Na Blascaodaí), island mountains with steep, gashed sides, like the Skellig Islands on the other side of Dingle Bay. Despite their inhospitableness, the largest island, **Great Blasket** (An Blascaod Mór), was inhabited by up to two hundred people for at least three centuries until 1953, when, with no school, shop, priest or doctor, it was finally abandoned. Because of their isolation, however, the islanders maintained a rich oral tradition in the Irish language, which in the early twentieth century, encouraged by visiting scholars, evolved into a remarkable body of written **literature**. Works such as *An tOileánach* (*The Islandman*) by Tomás Ó Criomhthain, *Fiche Blian ag Fás* (*Twenty Years A-Growing*) by Muiris Ó Súilleabháin and *Peig* by Peig Sayers (an oral account written down by her son) give a vivid insight into the hardships of island life.

The island's story is told with great imagination at the Great Blasket heritage centre, **Ionad an Bhlascaoid Mhóir**, on the mainland opposite, at the north end of Dunquin (Easter to June, Sept & Oct daily 10am–6pm; July & Aug daily 10am–7pm; last admission 45min before closing; open on request in winter, ⓣ066/915 6444; €3.70; Heritage Card; ⓦwww.heritageireland.ie). Though the building doesn't look like much as you approach, inside is a beautiful museum space. There are excerpts from the island writers, and a moving section on Great Blasket's abandonment in 1953 and the migration of many islanders to Springfield, Massachusetts – where they still receive the *Kerryman* newspaper from Tralee every week. There's a good bookshop run by *An Café Liteartha* (see p.357), and the **café** is a good spot for lunch, with fine views of the islands.

In the summer, **boats** to Great Blasket leave the pier on the south side of Dunquin in good weather every half-hour or so (15–30min; €30 return;

Ⓣ066/915 6422, Ⓦwww.blasketisland.com, or Ⓣ066/915 4864, Ⓦwww.blasketislands.ie). In the afternoon, there are also guided cruises around the Blasket Islands from Dunquin (locally termed "Eco Tours"; 2hr 30min; €40; same contact details), taking in the spectacular Cathedral Rocks on Inishnabro, puffins (in spring and early summer, depending on the weather) and grey seals on Inishvickillane, and possibly basking sharks, whales and dolphins. These boats also pick up on Great Blasket, so if you caught an earlier boat across from Dunquin, it would be possible to combine a walk on the island with a guided cruise. In addition, ferries run from Dingle town to Great Blasket every two hours (35min; €35 return; Ⓣ066/915 1344, Ⓦwww.blasketisland.com); guided cruises around the islands from Dingle may be added in the future. All boats can be booked at the Dingle Boatmen's Association office (Ⓣ066/915 2626), in the same building as the tourist office in Dingle town.

Once **on Great Blasket**, you can wander the white-sand beach, Trá Bán, at its eastern end and the grassy footpaths that cross its six-kilometre length, passing the ghosts of the old village. Accompanied by seals, puffins, storm petrels and shearwaters, you can contemplate the 3000km that separates you, here on Europe's most westerly islands, from North America where most of the islanders ended up, and the treacherous 2km of Blasket Sound which made living on the island untenable. Wild camping is possible on the island, but the hostel and café are indefinitely closed.

There are several comfortable **places to stay** back in **DUNQUIN** (Dún Chaoin), including a modern An Óige hostel, with dorms (from €12.50), twins (❶) and family rooms (Ⓣ066/915 6121; Feb–Nov). *An Portán* provides en-suite **B&B** in decent-sized, bright rooms and a reasonably priced **restaurant**, as well as Irish-language courses for adults (Ⓣ066/915 6212, Ⓦwww.anportan.com; ❷). Across from here *Kruger's* **pub** offers lunchtime soup and sandwiches and traditional music on Saturdays year-round (plus an early-evening session on Sun in summer). Around 3km north around Clogher Head from Dunquin, *Tig Áine* (Ⓣ066/915 6214) is a laid-back summertime **café** and crafts gallery with fine views of Sybil Head, serving cakes, sandwiches, tasty soups and imaginative salads; writing courses are held here (Ⓦwww.dinglewritingcourses.ie) and an evening-time restaurant is planned. Just beyond is the pottery and shop of one of Ireland's leading potters, Louis Mulcahy (Ⓣ066/915 6229, Ⓦwww.louismulcahy.com), where, between Easter and September, you can have a go yourself in the workshop.

Ballyferriter

Two kilometres further on from Louis Mulcahy's pottery, **BALLYFERRITER** (Baile an Fheirtearaigh) is a byword for remoteness in Ireland, but actually ticks a surprising number of boxes when it comes to amenities. There's a lovely beach, **Wine Strand**, just to the north on sheltered **Smerwick Harbour**, and some pleasant walking to the northwest where the peaks of **Sybil Head** and the **Three Sisters** rise like a row of waves to meet the sea. The old village school has been converted into the **Músaem Chorca Dhuibhne** (Museum of the Dingle Peninsula; April, May, Sept & Oct daily 10am–5pm; June–Aug daily 10am–5.30pm; in winter by appointment; Ⓣ066/915 6100, Ⓦwww.corca-dhuibhne.com; €2.50), which houses a small but tidy display on the archeology and history of the peninsula since Mesolithic times, its geology and its more recent role as a location for movies such as *Ryan's Daughter*. There's a café at the museum, which as part of the peninsula's development co-operative also organizes courses in Irish language and culture (Ⓦwww.cfcd.ie).

Just down the road from the museum, *Óstán Ceann Sibéal* (ⓣ066/915 6433, ⓦwww.ceannsibealhotel.com; ❹) is a stylish, contemporary **hotel**, hung with paintings by local artists, serving bar food as well as dishes such as confit of lamb shank in its **restaurant**. *Tigh an tSaorsaigh* (*Sears*) is a genial old, flagstoned pub with a piano, traditional sessions at weekends in summer and pleasant, en-suite **B&B** upstairs (ⓣ066/915 6344, ⓦwww.searspub.com; ❷). The village's other characterful bar, *Tigh Uí Chatháin* (*Kane's*), boasts fine views from its rear terrace, is very popular for lunch and dinner, and hosts a traditional-music club, Siar Ó Thuaidh, with three or four gigs a month (ⓣ066/915 6359, ⓦwww.dinglearts.com). For **hostel** accommodation, as well as camping, head to *The Black Cat*, the grocery shop at the south end of the village (IHO; ⓣ & ⓕ066/915 6286; dorms €14). In late February, the village hosts a five-day **traditional-music festival**, Scoil Cheoil an Earraigh (ⓣ066/915 5399, ⓦwww.scoilcheoil.com), featuring concerts, dancing, lectures and other events.

Gallarus to Ballynavenooragh

Five kilometres east of Ballyferriter, off the R559 towards **Murreagh** (An Mhuiríoch), the beautiful **Gallarus Oratory** is Dingle's most compelling historic monument. A 1300-year-old church built entirely of dry gritstone in the shape of an upturned boat, it sits proudly in its field at the very western edge of Europe like a Platonic ideal of architectural purity, still quite intact and unadorned. Its stones, carefully selected and smoothed off inside and out, and gracefully corbelled to form the roof, are now weathered to soft tones of green, brown, purple and orange. It's lit by a single window opposite the doorway, while the only features inside are two large, pierced stones above the lintel which probably served for the attachment of a door. Access to the oratory, which is in state care, is absolutely free, so there's no need at all to pay €3 at the privately run visitor centre, which comprises a gift shop, café and fifteen-minute audiovisual, sitting between the most obvious car park and the church; instead, continue a short way along the hedgerowed lane to a tiny car park which gives direct access to the oratory.

Mount Brandon and St Brendan

Dingle's highest peak, **Mount Brandon** (Cnoc Bréanainn; 950m), is firmly associated in mythology with sixth-century **St Brendan the Navigator**, Kerry's patron saint. Variously, according to the legends, he ousted Crom Dubh, the pagan harvest god, from the mountain and prayed here before beginning a seven-year journey across the Atlantic to discover North America. However, scholars now regard the story of the voyage as a too-literal interpretation of the *Navigatio Sancti Brendani*, Ireland's finest contribution to medieval literature, which was in fact a sophisticated allegory of the monastic life.

An eighteen-kilometre waymarked pilgrim path, **Cosán na Naomh** (The Saint's Road), has been laid out from Ventry Strand to the mountain, with an associated map-guide available locally or from the Heritage Council (ⓣ056/777 0777, ⓦwww.heritagecouncil.ie). It runs mostly on minor roads and lanes past Ballyferriter, Gallarus and Kilmalkedar to the western foot of the mountain. The official waymarked trail stops at a grotto at Ballybrack (An Baile Breac) because of insurance problems, but experienced walkers can happily continue due northeastwards to the summit, ascending through 750m in 3.5km, for some stupendous views on a clear day. It's also possible to ascend the mountain's easterly flank, marked by yellow painted arrows, from Faha, 2km northwest of Cloghane.

Adjacent to the oratory is the *Teach an Aragail* **campsite** (ⓣ066/915 5143; April–late Sept), whose owner, TP, also offers Irish cultural activities, including language-learning, music, dancing, archeological tours and walking (ⓣ086 819 1942, ⓦwww.gaeilgebeo.com or ⓦwww.dingleactivities.com). Nearby stands **Gallarus Castle**, an austere but well-preserved fifteenth-century tower house guarding Smerwick Harbour (June–Sept daily 10am–6pm, last admission 5.15pm; free; ⓦwww.heritageireland.ie). You can either look around by yourself or take a guided tour of its four extant storeys, which were inhabited by the Fitzgeralds, the lords of West Kerry, until the end of the seventeenth century. The castle, which has limited parking space, is about 300m down a narrow lane to the right off the R559, just beyond the campsite; there's also a direct path from the private car park at the oratory.

At the crossroads at Murreagh, the R559 turns right, passing after 2km **Kilmalkedar**, an attractive, mid-twelfth-century church in the Irish Romanesque style. In the surrounding graveyard, you'll find an ogham stone, an early sundial and a high cross. The left turn at Murreagh will bring you to the pier at **BALLYDAVID** (Baile na nGall), where *Tigh TP's* **pub** occupies a glorious location on Smerwick Harbour. Cosy for a drink in winter, it offers bar and restaurant food and outdoor bayside tables in summer, as well as budget **accommodation** in en-suite four-bed rooms with TVs and access to a kitchen (ⓣ066/915 5444; ❶; see above for details of TP's cultural activities).

The road straight ahead from the Murreagh crossroads leads after a couple of kilometres to *Tigh an Phóist*, a **hostel** at Boherboy (Bothar Buí) offering dorms (from €14), private rooms (❶) and bike rental (IHH; closed Nov to mid-March; ⓣ066/915 5109, ⓦwww.tighanphoist.com). Further north around the bay at Glaise Bheag on the way to Feohanagh (An Fheothanach), *Gorman's Clifftop House & Restaurant* (ⓣ066/915 5162, ⓦwww.gormans-clifftophouse.com; ❹) offers upmarket **B&B**, fine **dining** and great views from its cliff-top perch. Around 4km northeast of Feohanagh, just off the signposted "Slea Head Drive" (also the Dingle Way here), you'll come to dramatic **Brandon Creek** (Cuas an Bhodaigh). This abrupt, cliff-girt slash in Dingle's north coast is supposedly where St Brendan set sail for America and is still used as a harbour by small fishing boats. One kilometre south of here, it's worth making a short, signposted detour east off the "Slea Head Drive" to visit the impressive ring fort of **Ballynavenooragh** (Cathair na bhFionnúrach), about which a detailed leaflet is available from the Ballyferriter museum. Slightly elevated on the flank of Mount Brandon, the ring fort commands fine views of the massive landscape to the west, including Smerwick Harbour, the Three Sisters and Sybil Head, and Tiaracht beyond, one of the Blaskets. Probably built between the eighth and tenth centuries AD and occupied until the thirteenth, the fort comprises a circular, dry-stone wall, 3m thick and extant up to 2m in height, surrounding a two-roomed house; underneath, you can make out the entrance to a souterrain, a subterranean passage used for refuge and storage.

The Conor Pass and the north coast of the peninsula

To the northeast of Dingle town rises a great L-shaped ridge of mountains, running south from the highest, Mount Brandon, and across to Beenoskee (826m). The steep and narrow **Conor Pass** road, which cuts across the ridge to the peninsula's north coast, ascends to over 500 metres giving spectacular views of stark uplands, corrie lakes and the huge sweep of **Brandon Bay** below. The best base for walking here is **CLOGHANE** (An Clochán), a tiny village flanked by lovely beaches on the eastern flank of Mount Brandon: signposted archeological and walking trails, including the Dingle Way, criss-cross the area, and the *Cloghane and Brandon Walking Guide* is available from the small, summer-only tourist office in the village (ⓣ066/713 8277). There's good **food** and en-suite **rooms** at *O'Connor's* characterful pub (ⓣ066/713 8113, ⓦwww.cloghane.com; closed Nov–Feb; ❷), while *Mount Brandon House* **hostel** (IHO; ⓣ066/713 8299, ⓦwww.mountbrandonhostel.com) has small dorms (from €18), private rooms (❶) and **camping**. Cloghane comes to life at the end of July for the four-day **Feile Lughnasa** (ⓣ066/713 8137, ⓦwww.irishcelticfest.com), celebrating the Celtic harvest festival with guided walks, poetry, dancing and music.

Separating Brandon Bay from Tralee Bay, the **Maharees Peninsula** is an exposed, beach-girt spit of land to the north of the village of **CASTLEGREGORY**. What's reckoned to be some of the best **wind-surfing** in the world is possible here – it's good in all wind directions, with a variety of west-, north- and east-facing spots suitable for all levels of ability; there's a good break for **surfers**, too. Based about halfway along the peninsula, Jamie Knox is the best contact for information, as well as for wind-surfing, surfing and **kite-surfing** tuition and rental, and other watersports such as canoeing (ⓣ066/713 9411, ⓦwww.jamieknox.com); en-suite **B&B** is also available here (❷), as well as packages combining accommodation and tuition. **Diving** trips and courses are run by Waterworld, a PADI Gold Palm IDC Centre, from their base, Harbour House, at Scraggane Bay at the end of the Maharees (ⓣ066/713 9292, ⓦwww.waterworld.ie); they too offer en-suite **accommodation** (❸), as well as an indoor swimming pool, gym, sauna and a scenic **restaurant** specializing in seafood. If all that sounds too energetic, just flop out on the nearest beach to Castlegregory, east-facing, Blue Flag **Sandy Bay**.

Back on Strand Street in town, the **Castlegregory Visitor Information Centre** (Mon–Fri 9.30am–5pm, sometimes closing for lunch; ⓣ066/713 9422, ⓔcastleinfo@eircom.net) offers **Internet** access, and *Fitzgerald's Euro-Hostel* (ⓣ066/713 9133) has **dorms** (€15) and private rooms (❶) above a shop and bar. Out on the Tralee road is the well-signposted, beachfront *Anchor* **campsite** (ⓣ066/713 9157, ⓦwww.caravanparksireland.net; Easter–Sept). Surfies refuel on sandwiches, Irish stew and cakes at *Phil's* **café** during the day, and on steaks, seafood and pizza at the *Village Bistro* (ⓣ066/713 9878) in the evening, both on Strand Street near the Spar supermarket. On the west side of town, *Ned Natterjack's* **pub**, named after the toads that make their home in Castlegregory's dunes, has bar food all day, a beer garden and regular live music.

North Kerry

North Kerry, flat, rich farming land that runs as far as the Shannon estuary, feels quite different from the rest of the county – and they've even been known to play hurling rather than Gaelic football up here. Instead of the remote, spectacularly set coastal villages of the peninsulas, you'll find – or avoid – the traditional, kiss-me-quick resorts of Ballyheigue and Ballybunion, while the county town of **Tralee** seems quite anodyne if you've just come up from Dingle, for example. It is worth making time, however, for **Listowel**, a characterful small town that's a hotbed of literary activity. North again from here, the useful **Shannon ferry** (see p.395) cuts down travelling time to County Clare from **Tarbert**, which has a good hostel, *The Ferry House* (IHH; ⓣ068/36555, ⓦwww.ferryhostel.com), with dorms (from €12), private rooms (❶) and meals available, if you need a stopover.

Tralee and Ardfert

Although **TRALEE** (ⓦwww.tralee.ie) has a long history as a market town, originally built around an Anglo-Norman castle and priory, its attractions today are modern and rather functional. Chief among them is the **Kerry County Museum** in the Ashe Memorial Hall, Denny Street (Jan–March Tues–Fri 10am–4.30pm; April, May & Sept–Dec; Tues–Sat 9.30am–5.30pm; June–Aug daily 9.30am–5.30pm; €8; Heritage Island; ⓦwww.kerrymuseum.ie), which incorporates a comprehensive but rather dry run-through of the history of Ireland and Kerry since the Stone Age, as well as the Medieval Experience, a series of re-created scenes of mid-fifteenth-century Tralee complete with artificial smells. The narrow-gauge, three-kilometre **Tralee to Blennerville Steam Railway** (ⓣ066/712 1064), from Ballyard Station on the southwest side of town, was having engine problems at the time of research but should be at full steam again by the time you read this. The railway leads southwest to the largest working windmill in Ireland and Britain, the **Blennerville Windmill** (April, May, Sept & Oct daily 9.30am–5pm; June–Aug daily 10am–6pm; €5), which has its own visitor and crafts centre.

Probably the most interesting visit you can make in the Tralee area is to the ruined **cathedral** at **ARDFERT**, 9km to the northwest, on the site of a monastery that was supposedly established by St Brendan the Navigator in the sixth century at his birthplace (mid-April to Sept daily 9.30am–6pm; last admission 45min before closing; €2.10; Heritage Card; ⓦwww.heritageireland.ie). The slender tenth-to-thirteenth-century cathedral is the largest pre-Gothic church in Ireland and features fine lancet windows behind the altar. Look out especially for some beautiful Romanesque sandstone carving, in geometric and floral designs, on the west doorway and around the window of the small, nearby church. The **bus** schedules between Tralee and Ardfert only allow a day-trip to the cathedral in July and August (when extra services to the beach resorts beyond are laid on).

Tralee practicalities

The adjacent **train** (ⓣ066/712 3522) and **bus** (ⓣ066/712 3566) stations are just a few minutes' walk northeast of the centre of town. The friendly and helpful **tourist office** (Jan & Feb Mon–Fri 9.15am–1pm & 2–5pm; March, Nov & Dec Mon–Sat 9.15am–1pm & 2–5pm; April & Oct Mon–Sat 9.15am–5pm; May, June & Sept Mon–Sat 9am–6pm; July & Aug Mon–Sat 9am–7pm, Sun 10am–6pm; ⓣ066/712 1288) is in the Ashe Memorial Hall underneath the Kerry County Museum. You can **rent bikes** from Tralee Gas Supplies in Strand Street (ⓣ066/712 2018) and access the **Internet** at Antech, 40 Bridge St, next to *Sean Óg's* pub.

Tralee's smartest **hotel** is the welcoming *Manor West*, with elegant, contemporary bedrooms, a leisure club and spa; it's attached to the large shopping centre of the same name, on the Killarney road on the east side of town (ⓣ066/719 4500, ⓦwww.manorwesthotel.ie; ❺). The town also has dozens of **B&Bs**, including *Leeside*, a hospitable, en-suite place with fine breakfasts and good single rates on Edward Street, Oakpark (ⓣ066/712 6475, ⓦwww.dowlingsleeside-bnb.com; March–Sept; ❷), about a kilometre northeast of the centre beyond the train station;

and *Brook Manor Lodge* (Ⓣ066/712 0406, Ⓦwww.brookmanorlodge.com; ❸), a comfortable, well-equipped upmarket guesthouse with excellent breakfasts, in a peaceful, scenic setting 3km northwest of the centre on the Fenit road. *Finnegan's* (Ⓣ066/712 7610, Ⓦwww.finneganshostel.com; IHH & IHO) is a well-appointed, central **hostel** in a characterful Georgian townhouse on Denny Street, where four- to eight-bed dorms (from €17) and en-suite doubles and twins (❶) come with a light continental breakfast. There's also a well-equipped **campsite** at *Woodlands Park*, Dan Spring Road (Ⓣ066/712 1235, Ⓦwww.kingdomcamping.com; mid-March to Sept), ten minutes' walk south of the centre of town.

Tralee is home to one of Kerry's finest **restaurants**, *Restaurant David Norris*, Ivy Terrace (Ⓣ066/718 5654; Tues–Sat evenings; early-bird available Tues–Fri), a relaxing, civilized spot for well-judged, meticulously prepared dishes such as lemon and thyme-scented chicken with pancetta and pea, onion and chive cream. Otherwise your best bet is *Val's*, an attractive modern pub on Bridge Street offering good-value light meals for lunch, tapas, and varied dinner menus in either the bar or the upstairs bistro (Ⓣ066/712 1559; winter Wed–Sat only). Nearly a dozen of Tralee's lively **pubs** boast regular traditional music, notably *Seán Og's* on Bridge Street (most nights), *Betty's Bar*, Strand Street (Fri, plus Sun in summer) and *Baily's Corner*, Ashe Street (Tues, plus Mon & Fri in summer).

Next to the tourist office is the **National Folk Theatre of Ireland**, Siamsa Tíre (Ⓣ066/712 3055, Ⓦwww.siamsatire.com), which usually has excellent shows in the summer and a varied programme of drama, music, dance and literary events during the rest of the year. Towards the end of August, the five-day **Rose of Tralee International Festival**, which is followed immediately by the boisterous **Tralee Races** (also held in late May; Ⓦwww.traleehorseracing.com), takes over the town. It's a slightly questionable but generally good-natured beauty and talent contest, accompanied by much merry-making, which is open to women of Irish birth or ancestry. Contact the festival office in the Ashe Memorial Hall, Denny Street (Ⓣ066/712 1322, Ⓦwww.roseoftralee.ie), for more information. There's also a family **arts festival** at Easter, **Samhlaíocht**, including puppet shows, exhibitions, music and street entertainment (Ⓣ066/712 9934, Ⓦwww.samhlaiocht.com), followed immediately by a **short-film festival** (Ⓦwww.kerryfilmfestival.com).

Listowel

Up the N69, 27km northeast of Tralee, **LISTOWEL** (Ⓦwww.listowel.ie) is a congenial market town in a leafy setting on the north bank of the River Feale. It's best known for its literary associations, boasting an annual five-day festival of literary workshops and events, called, with due poetic licence, **Writers' Week** and taking place over the bank-holiday weekend at the beginning of June (Ⓣ068/21074, Ⓦwww.writersweek.ie). Listowel's most celebrated literary figure is probably the late **John B. Keane**, author of plays such as *Sive*, a powerful romantic tragedy, and *The Field*, a dramatization of a shocking murder that took place in this region in the 1950s.

In the imposing town square stands **Seanchaí**, the **Kerry Literary and Cultural Centre** (June–Sept daily 9.30am–5pm, last admission 4pm; Oct–May Mon–Fri 10am–4.30pm, last admission 3pm; €5; Heritage Island; Ⓣ068/22212, Ⓦwww.kerrywritersmuseum.com). The centre includes rooms devoted to local writers such as Keane, Brian MacMahon and Brendan Kennelly, which have been imaginatively designed, with recorded extracts, to reflect the personality of each. There are some interesting audiovisuals, including Kerryman Eamon Kelly, Ireland's most famous story-teller (or *seanchaí*, pronounced "shanakee").

From Seanchaí's reception informative and entertaining tours depart for formidable **Listowel Castle** next door (June–early Sept daily 9.30am–4.45pm; hours may be extended in future, depending on demand; free; Ⓦwww.heritageireland.ie). When the castle was built in the early or mid-fifteenth century for the Fitzmaurices, the Lords of Kerry, the adjacent River Feale would have been navigable and was probably forded at this point, but from the eighteenth century onwards, in more peaceful times, the building fell into disrepair and was quarried for stone. Nevertheless, two of the four original towers remain, rising to a height of 15m, and have recently been restored by the Office of Public Works.

On the north side of town off John B. Keane Drive, you can take a highly unusual train ride on the **Lartigue Monorail** (May–Sept daily 2–5pm; €6; Ⓣ068/24393 or 22212). First opened in 1888, this low-cost railway system covered the 15km between Listowel and Ballybunion on the coast. The steam locomotive and a 500-metre section of the track have recently been restored for short jaunts, and a museum and café, as well as longer opening hours, are planned.

Practicalities

Listowel's lively all-round venue, **St John's Theatre and Arts Centre** (Ⓣ068/22566, Ⓦwww.stjohnstheatrelistowel.com), is based in the former church in the middle of the square. It hosts drama, dance, all kinds of music and art exhibitions, as well as the **tourist office** (June & Sept Mon–Sat 9.30am–1pm & 2–5.15pm; July & Aug daily 9.30am–1pm & 2–5.15pm; Ⓣ068/22590). You can access the **Internet** round the corner at Antech, 18 Church St.

Listowel's **accommodation** ranges from the recently refurbished traditional charms of the *Listowel Arms* on the square (Ⓣ068/21500, Ⓦwww.listowelarms.com; ❹), to B&Bs such as *Allo's* (❸), which has three lovely rooms furnished with antiques, including one with a four-poster and a huge bathroom, above a bistro (see below); and the simpler *Ashford Lodge*, a bungalow on Tarbert Road with standard and en-suite rooms and decent rates for singles and children (Ⓣ068/21280, Ⓔashfordlodge@eircom.net; ❷).

There's a good, cheap **café** at the literary centre (Mon–Fri), and decent **bar food** is available at *The Mermaids* on William Street, just north of the square. For a blow-out dinner – or a better-value lunch – head for *Allo's* characterful bar and **bistro**, 41 Church St (Ⓣ068/22880; Tues–Sat), where you can feast on dishes such as crab, mascarpone and wild garlic risotto.

In July and August, Listowel flaunts its theatrical and musical credentials, with outdoor **performances** of music, drama and storytelling at Seanchái (Fri 1.30pm; free); lively nights at the excellent *John B. Keane* **pub** on William Street (Tues comedy, Wed folk music, Thurs extracts from Keane's plays; free); and an evening show of traditional music, dance and storytelling at the *Listowel Arms* (€10; Ⓦwww.comhaltas.ie). Towards the end of September, the town comes raucously to life again for the week-long **Listowel Races** (Ⓣ068/23037, Ⓦwww.listowelraces.ie), and in November there's a five-day **food festival** (Ⓣ068/23034, Ⓦwww.listowelfoodfair.com).

Travel details

Trains

Killarney to: Cork (6–9 daily, sometimes with a change at Mallow; 1hr 30min); Dublin (8 daily, most with a change at Mallow; 3hr 30min); Tralee (7–9 daily; 40min).

Tralee to: Cork (6–9 daily, sometimes with a change at Mallow; 2hr 20min); Dublin (8 daily, most with a change at Mallow; 4hr 5min); Killarney (7–9 daily; 40min).

Buses

Dingle to: Ballydavid (Tues & Fri 2 daily; 20–40min); Dunquin (via Ballyferriter, Mon & Thurs 2 daily; 45min).

Kenmare to: Bantry, via Glengarriff (daily in summer; 1hr 10min); Castletownbere (summer Mon–Sat 2 daily; 1hr 20min); Lauragh (summer Mon–Sat 2 daily, winter 1 on Fri; 40min); Sneem (summer Mon–Sat 2 daily, winter 1 on Fri; 35min).

Killarney to: Bantry, via Glengarriff (daily in summer; 2hr 20min); Caherdaniel (summer 1 daily; 2hr); Cahersiveen (summer 1–3 daily, winter Mon–Sat 2 daily; 1hr 30min); Cork (hourly; 2hr); Dingle, changing at Tralee (3–6 daily; 1hr 35min–2hr 30min); Dingle, via Inch and Anascaul (summer 2 daily; 1hr 20min); Dublin (5–6 daily; 6hr); Kerry Airport (Farranfore; 6–9 daily; 20min); Glenbeigh (summer 1–3 daily, winter Mon–Sat 2 daily; 50min); Kenmare (summer 3–5 daily, winter Mon–Fri 2 daily; 45min); Killorglin (4–7 daily; 30min); Limerick (6–7 daily; 2hr); Listowel (5–7 daily; 1hr 30min); Ring of Kerry (summer 1 daily; 4hr 45min); Shannon Airport (6–7 daily; 2hr 45min); Tralee (11–16 daily; 40min–1hr); Waterford (10–11 daily; 4hr 10min); Waterville (summer 1–2 daily, winter Mon–Sat 1 daily; 1hr 45min); Wexford (1–4 daily; 5hr 30min).

Tralee to: Ardfert (winter Mon–Fri 2 daily, summer 2–3 daily; 15min); Castlegregory (2 on Fri; 40min); Cloghane (2 on Fri; 1hr 10min); Cork (hourly; 2hr 15min–2hr 45min); Dingle (3–6 daily; 1hr 20min); Dublin (8–10 daily, change at Limerick; 6hr); Limerick (8–11 daily; 2hr 5min); Listowel (8–10 daily; 40min).

Travel details

9

Limerick and Clare

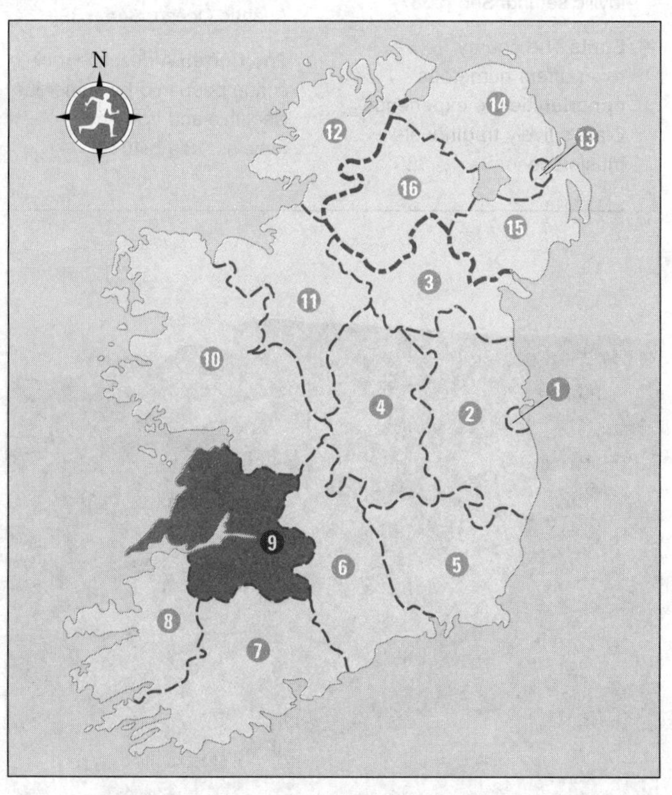

CHAPTER 9 Highlights

* **Hunt Museum** Limerick's finest attraction, a diverse, personal collection of beautiful art and antiquities. See p.378
* **Lough Gur** Atmospheric rural lake surrounded by fine Neolithic remains. See p.382
* **Quin Abbey** Evocative monastic remains in an utterly idyllic setting. See p.387
* **Ennis** The county town offers numerous opportunities to experience Clare's lively traditional-music scene. See p.388
* **Scattery Island** Deserted for more than thirty years, this tranquil island in the middle of the Shannon estuary was once a major ecclesiastical settlement. See p.395
* **The Cliffs of Moher** Massive sea-battered cliffs, providing exhilarating views of the Atlantic Ocean. See p.399
* **The Burren** A desolate rock-scape peppered by numerous Neolithic and Iron Age remains. See p.401

▲ The Cliffs of Moher

9

Limerick and Clare

Limerick is the least attractive county on Ireland's west coast, featuring ugly industrial development along the Shannon and a rich but bland agricultural hinterland and, consequently, is often passed through rapidly by tourists. **Limerick city**, however, does have some lures, notably a vibrant cultural life and the superb **Hunt Museum**, housing the Republic's richest art and antiquities collection outside Dublin. Away from here, the planned and deliberately pretty village of **Adare** has a lingering appeal, while the dramatic area around **Lough Gur** is riddled with major prehistoric remains.

In utter contrast, the neighbouring county of **Clare**, across the broad **River Shannon**, has a wealth of scenic attractions. Its coastline all the way from **Kilkee** to **Fanore** is dotted with golden beaches, sometimes of breathtaking quality. Near the village of **Doolin**, famed for its year-long, tourist-driven diet of traditional music, stand the awesome **Cliffs of Moher**, while the county's northern interior is characterized by the craggy, barren landscape of **The Burren**, home to numerous prehistoric sites. The county town, **Ennis**, is a true hotbed of traditional music, with fabulous sessions year-round, and the county's eastern border is defined by the waters of the impressive **Lough Derg**.

Limerick and Ennis are interconnected by rail and bus, and in high season you can reach most outlying attractions by bus.

County Limerick

County Limerick (Luimneach) divides itself largely between dairy farming on the fertile Munster plain and manufacturing along the River Shannon, though neither is likely to tempt you to stay here long. **Limerick city**, however, is worth a stopover to see the sights and sample its cultural scene and nightlife, while the beautiful Neolithic sites of **Lough Gur** and the quaint, historic village of **Adare** are the main reason to get out into the county. You'll need your own transport for the latter, but the city is well served by **trains** – from Ennis and points east and south via Limerick Junction – and by **buses** from just about anywhere.

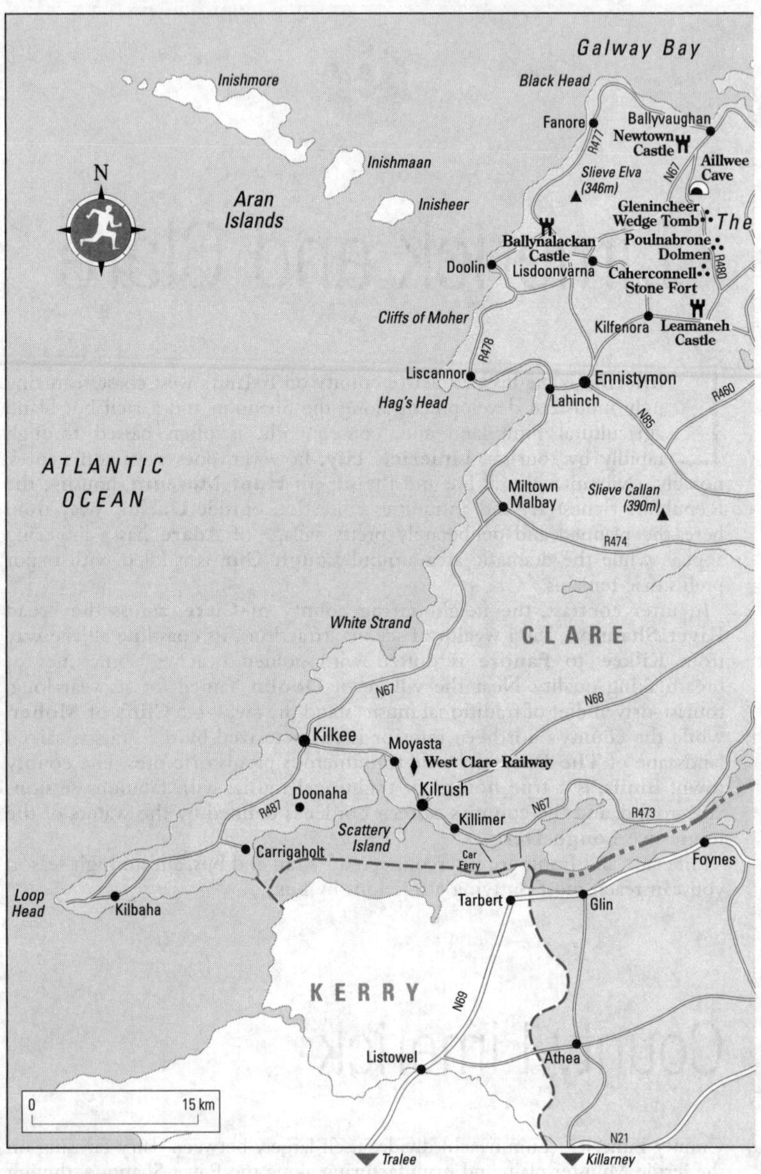

Limerick city

All manner of routes – by road, rail and even air, to nearby Shannon Airport – lead to **LIMERICK** (Ⓦ www.visitlimerick.com), the Republic's third city, yet few visitors bother to stop. The instantly appealing landscapes of Clare and Kerry are just a short hop further on, and it has to be said that Limerick has an

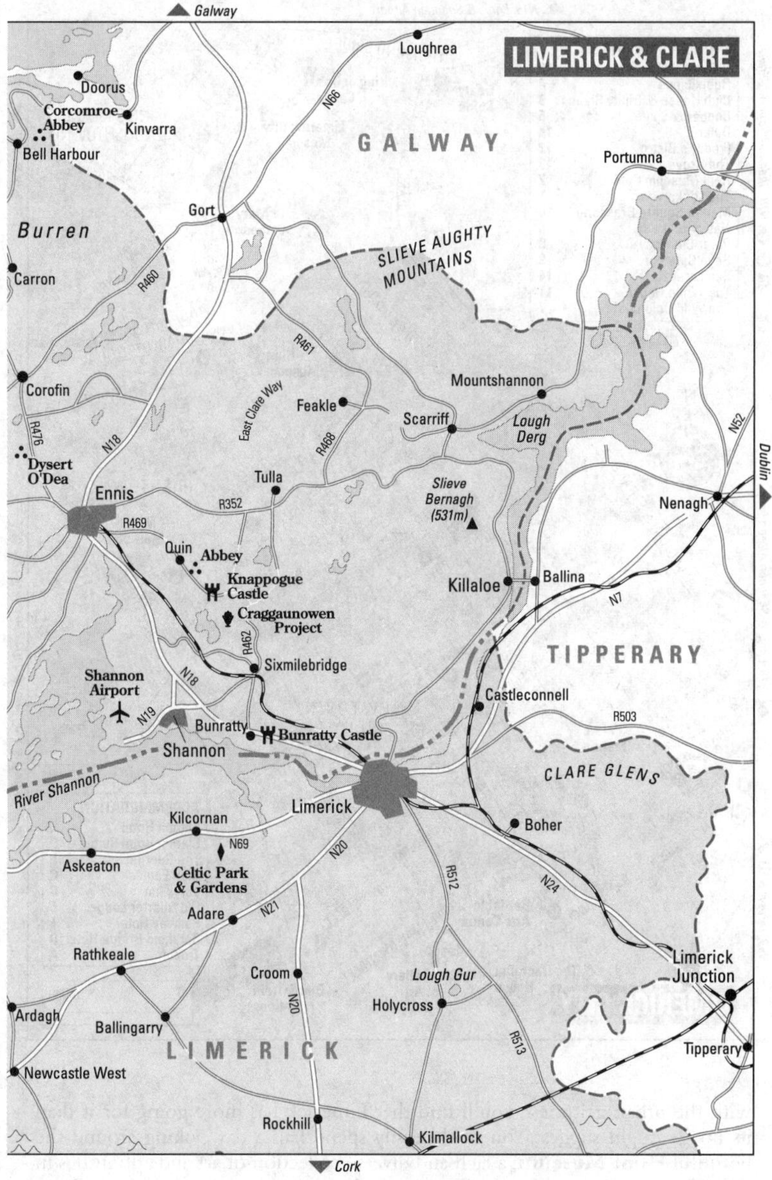

image problem – and an excessively visceral nickname, "Stab City", to go with it – that it just can't seem to shake off. Unfortunately, stories of gangland violence in the city keep cropping up in the Irish news media with depressing regularity, and while this shouldn't impinge on the casual visitor, there is sometimes an unmistakable air of intimidation in certain areas, which you might not be expecting on the west coast of Ireland. However, if you can live

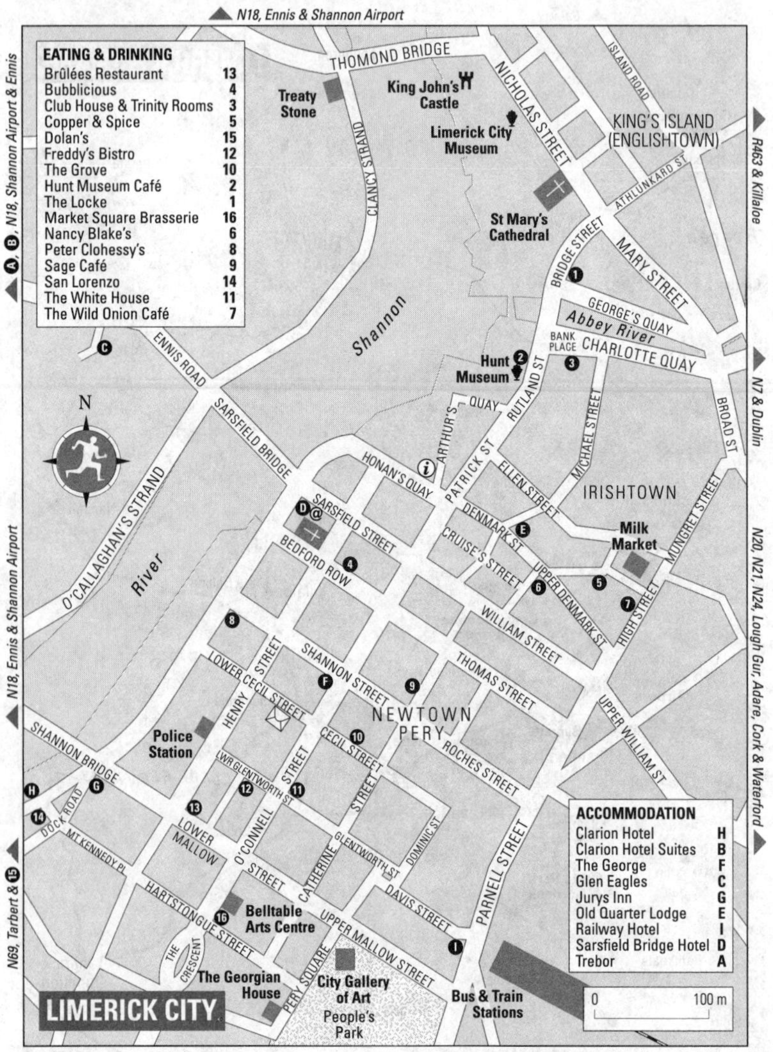

with the urban grittiness, you'll find that Limerick has more going for it than its image might suggest. You could easily spend half a day poking around the beautiful **Hunt Museum**, a rich and diverse collection of art and antiquities in the Georgian Custom House. The Anglo-Norman **castle** and **cathedral** are also both impressive, and it's well worth checking out the year-round roster of vibrant **festivals**. As well as substantial renovation of the Shannon quays, regeneration efforts have included the extensive campus at Plassey, 3km southeast, which is also the site of the National Technological Park – the three colleges here, the university, Institute of Technology and College of Education, certainly help to enliven the city's cultural life and **nightlife**.

Limerick festivals

The city lays on a compelling menu of **festivals** throughout the year. Undoubted highlights include **ev+a** (Exhibition of Visual-plus Art; ⓣ061/310633, ⓦwww.eva.ie), Ireland's pre-eminent annual exhibition of contemporary art. From the end of March to late June, works by Irish and foreign artists, as selected by a leading international curator, are installed at the Belltable, the City Gallery of Art and around the cityscape. In late June and early July, **Blas**, a highly regarded, two-week, summer school of traditional music and dance, takes place at the Irish World World Academy of Music and Dance, Limerick University (ⓦwww.ul.ie/~iwmc/blas), with plenty of associated concerts and sessions around the city. In mid-July, the **Shannon International Music Festival** is a five-day showcase for the Irish Chamber Orchestra and prestigious guest artists (ⓣ061/202620, ⓦwww.irishchamberorchestra.com). From late July to mid-August, **Summer Music on the Shannon** (ⓣ065/708 7566, ⓦwww.summermusicontheshannon.com) is Ireland's largest summer music-school and festival, with performers from over twenty countries presenting concerts and operas. An international poetry festival, **Cuisle**, encompassing readings, open-mike sessions and workshops, takes place in October (ⓣ061/407421, ⓦwww.limerickcity.ie).

Some history

The Vikings sailed up the Shannon in about 922 and established a settlement here on a river island, formed by a narrow branch off the main flow that is today called the Abbey River. This port at the lowest fording point of the river was coveted by the Anglo-Normans, who in 1197, decisively seized, and set about fortifying, the town. This involved building high city walls around what became **Englishtown**, to keep out the local Irish, who retreated to a ghetto to the southeast across the Abbey River – **Irishtown**.

In the late seventeenth century, the final bloody scenes of the War of the Kings were played out here. After their defeat at the Boyne in 1690, the Jacobite forces in Limerick castle, under the Earl of Tyrconnell and local hero **Patrick Sarsfield**, refused to surrender. Though beset by a vastly superior force, Sarsfield managed to raise the siege by creeping out at night with five hundred men and destroying the Williamite supply train. When William's army came back in 1691, however, the medieval walls of the castle were unable to withstand the artillery bombardment. Tyrconnell having died of a stroke, Sarsfield surrendered on October 3, 1691, on supposedly honourable terms, according to the **Treaty of Limerick**. The Jacobites – some twelve thousand in all, later known as the "**Wild Geese**" – were permitted to go to France, in whose cause Sarsfield fought and later died. The treaty also promised Catholics the comparative religious toleration they had enjoyed under Charles II, but the English went back on the deal, and between 1692 and 1704 the Irish Parliament passed the harshly anti-Catholic penal laws.

The eighteenth century proved to be far more prosperous for Limerick, which in the 1750s received a grant of £17,000 from the Irish Parliament towards a major redevelopment. Completed in 1840 and named after the local MP, **Newtown Pery** comprised a grid of broad Georgian terraced streets, built well to the south of the cramped, fetid medieval city. In the early twentieth century, however, Limerick suffered greatly during the nationalist struggles, which, in 1919, gave rise to a radical movement that's unique in Irish history. In protest against British military action during the War of Independence, the local Trades Council called a general strike and proclaimed the **Limerick Soviet**. With help from the IRA, they took over the city, controlling food distribution, setting up a citizens' police force and even printing their own money. It lasted only a few

▲ Georgian doorway, John's Square

weeks, however, collapsing under pressure from the Catholic bishop. In 1921, both Limerick's mayor, George Clancy, and the former mayor, Mícheál O'Callaghan, were murdered by the Royal Irish Constabulary. One of the effects of the Troubles was that the rich were persuaded to move out of the city: many of their Georgian houses in Newtown Pery became tenements and remain dilapidated to this day, while recent investment has concentrated on developing an industrial base around the city and on renovating the quaysides.

Arrival and information

The adjacent **train** (ⓣ061/315555) and **bus** (ⓣ061/313333) stations are on Parnell Street on the south side of the centre. Limerick is also the nearest city to **Shannon International Airport** – see p.386 for transport details and other information.

The **tourist office** (June Mon–Sat 9.30am–5.30pm; July & Aug Mon–Sat 9am–6pm, Sun 9.30am–1pm & 2–5.30pm; Sept–May Mon–Sat 9.30am–1pm & 2–5.30pm; ⓣ061/317522) is on Arthur's Quay, near the top of O'Connell Street, and dispenses a useful guide-map of the city and county. From here depart two **walking tours** of the city that last about two hours each: a Historical Walking Tour (daily 11am; €10), and an *Angela's Ashes* Walking Tour (daily 2.30pm; €10), which seeks out the grinding slums of Frank McCourt's childhood in the 1930s and 1940s, as described in his bestselling memoir.

Accommodation

Limerick offers plenty of generally good-value, central **accommodation**. There are no hostels, but during the summer the university's Mary Immaculate College opens up its **student accommodation** to visitors at Courtbrack, out on the N69 Tarbert road, about fifteen minutes' walk southwest of the city centre (ⓣ061/302500, ⓦwww.courtbrackaccom.com; IHH; mid-June to early Sept; dorms €23.50, singles €30, twins ❶, light breakfast included). If you're staying in the centre and have a car, you'll need to secure it either in the hotel car park or in one of the many multi-storeys overnight.

Clarion Hotel Steamboat Quay ⓣ061/444100, ⓦwww.clarionhotellimerick.com. A striking addition to the Limerick cityscape, this oval hotel, the tallest in Ireland, juts out over the river, with spectacular views. Stylish, contemporary rooms, a health and leisure club with swimming pool overlooking the river, and good food, either European in the restaurant or Thai and Malaysian in the bar. ❹

Clarion Hotel Suites Ennis Rd ⓣ061/582900, ⓦwww.clarionsuiteslimerick.com. Spacious and very good value suites, a 10min walk from the centre. The public rooms, including a European and Asian restaurant, occupy a sympathetically modernized Georgian mansion, while the suites, in the adjacent contemporary block, have either 1 or 2 bedrooms, a sitting room with dining area and a small kitchen area. There's a gym on site and guests have access to the *Clarion Hotel*'s leisure centre (see above). ❸

The George O'Connell St ⓣ061/460400, ⓦwww.thegeorgeboutiquehotel.com. Boutique hotel on the upper floors above the main street, offering well-equipped rooms done out in dark wood and green in contemporary style. Nice touches include cafetières and iPod stations in the rooms; free parking available. ❹

Glen Eagles 12 Vereker Gardens ⓣ061/455521, ⓔgleneaglesbandb@eircom.net. The closest B&B to the city centre on a peaceful cul-de-sac off the N18 Ennis road. All rooms are en suite with TVs, and there are decent rates for singles. Closed mid-Dec to mid-Jan. ❷

Jurys Inn Lower Mallow St ⓣ061/207000, ⓦwww.jurysinns.com. Well-run, no-frills hotel with over 150 smart and comfortable rooms. Very handy for the centre, but right on one of Limerick's busiest junctions, so unless you're eager for a view of the river, ask for a room at the back. ❸

Old Quarter Lodge Denmark St ⓣ061/315320, ⓦwww.oldquarter.ie. Right in the heart of the city centre, above a sometimes-noisy café-bar, this guesthouse has recently been refurbished in crisp, modern style, with en-suite bathrooms, satellite TV and wireless Internet, as well as an attractive, first-floor breakfast conservatory. ❸

Railway Hotel Parnell St ⓣ061/413653, ⓦwww.railwayhotel.ie. Brightly painted, traditional hotel opposite the train station, offering comfortable, standard and en-suite accommodation and a welcoming, family-run atmosphere. ❷

Sarsfield Bridge Hotel Sarsfield Bridge ⓣ061/317179, ⓦwww.tsbh.ie. Bright, comfortable, en-suite rooms in a modern, landmark hotel, looking out on the busy bridge and, in the distance, King John's Castle; secure car parking. ❹

Trebor Ennis Rd ⓣ061/454632, ⓦwww.treborhouse.com. Clean and comfortable rooms, which have been tastefully decorated and equipped with en-suite bathrooms, in a welcoming townhouse, a short walk from the city centre. May–Sept. ❷

The City

The traditional distinctions between **Englishtown** – focused on the castle and now signposted as **King's Island** – **Irishtown** and **Newtown Pery** no longer matter very much, as there's little of the medieval city left in the first two areas, while Newtown Pery's grid of dilapidated Georgian terraces is scattered with modern developments. All the sights can be easily covered on foot, and the shops, restaurants and pubs congregate around the main artery of **O'Connell Street**.

The Hunt Museum

The beautiful and fascinating displays in the **Hunt Museum**, dating from the Stone Age to modern times, are the best place to start a tour of the city (Mon–Sat 10am–5pm, Sun 2–5pm; €7.50; Heritage Island; ⓣ061/312833, ⓦwww.huntmuseum.com). Over the course of the twentieth century, John and Gertrude Hunt gathered together this diverse collection of art and antiquities, especially known for its religious works, and bequeathed it to the people of Ireland. You'll get the best idea of the spirit of the place in the Epilogue Room, which juxtaposes pieces of wildly different origins, such as an eighteenth-century Chinese porcelain cockerel and an English stone rabbit from the fifteenth century. In the 1990s, a fitting venue was found for the bequest in the old **Custom House** on Rutland Street, built in the 1760s in elegant Palladian style and best appreciated from the river side.

Besides the permanent collection, the museum mounts a major summer show and other temporary exhibitions throughout the year. There are guided tours every day (phone for details) and a fine café (see p.381). Don't forget to poke around in the drawers in the galleries, where you're as likely to find a Gauguin watercolour as some bronze axe-heads – with over two thousand works in the collection, this is the museum's way of having as many as possible accessible to the public.

Particular pieces to look out for include the beautiful, early ninth-century *Antrim Cross*, one of the finest examples of early Christian metalwork from Ireland. Made of bronze decorated with enamel in geometric and animal designs, it was discovered by chance in the River Bann in the nineteenth century. Keep an eye out also for the *Beverley Crozier*, a piece of walrus ivory intricately carved with miracles of healing, dating from the eleventh century; a vivacious, rearing bronze horse by Leonardo da Vinci; and a ten-drachma coin, minted in Syracuse in the fourth or fifth century BC, which is reputed to be one of the thirty pieces of silver received by Judas for betraying Christ – it was highly revered from the thirteenth century on as a relic of the Crucifixion, despite its portrayal of the pagan Greek demigods, Arethusa and Nike. Other highlights include works by fine Irish artists such as William Orpen, Jack B. Yeats and Roderic O'Connor, and a whole room devoted to depictions of the Crucifixion – which the museum's map-guide aptly misspells as "Crucifixation".

St Mary's Cathedral

Just across the river from the Hunt Museum, the Church of Ireland **St Mary's Cathedral** (summer Mon–Sat 9am–4.30pm, except during services; winter Mon–Fri 9am–4.30pm, Sat 9am–1pm, except during services; suggested donation €2; ⓦwww.cathedral.limerick.anglican.org) boasts a fine, almost homely interior of rough stone walls, ample, brightly coloured stained glass and beautiful barrel-vaulted ceilings. It was founded on the site of the Viking *thingmote* or meeting place in 1168 – from which time dates the Romanesque west doorway, carved with monstrous heads, stylized flowers and chevrons – but has gained so many accretions over the centuries that it's now as broad as it is long, with an intriguingly confused layout.

The cathedral's highlight is its set of dark-oak **misericords** in the Jebb Chapel, the only example left in Ireland. Dating from the late fifteenth century, they're ornately carved with symbols of good and evil, including a delicate, sinuous swan, cockatrices, griffins and all sorts of other mythical monsters. Look out also for the limestone **reredos** behind the main altar, which was carved in Celtic Revival style by Michael Pearse, father of the Irish patriot, Pádraig, and the nearby tomb of the cathedral's founder, King Donal Mór O'Brien of Munster, decorated with three heraldic lions and a Celtic cross.

King John's Castle and around

Continuing up Nicholas Street from the Anglican cathedral, you'll reach **King John's Castle** (daily: April–Oct 9.30am–5.30pm; Nov–March 10.30am–4.30pm; last admission 1hr before closing; €9; Heritage Island; Ⓦwww.shannonheritage.com), one of the country's most imposing Anglo-Norman castles, especially when viewed from the banks of the Shannon. A five-sided fortification inaugurated by the king himself in 1210, it had no keep and, originally at least, no tower at its southeast corner facing Englishtown; at the beginning of the troubled seventeenth century, however, a rectangular artillery bastion was added here. You enter through an incongruous modern interpretive centre, overlooking a small piazza on the eastern side – the site developers' original plan had been to faithfully rebuild the east curtain wall, but during the work, pre-Norman houses were unearthed here, which are now preserved underneath the raised entrance building.

The **interpretive centre** focuses on the horrific sieges the castle suffered in the seventeenth century. In 1642, it was successfully beset by the Royalist Confederation of Kilkenny, who in turn were winkled out by Cromwell's son-in-law, Henry Ireton, in 1651. An emotive audiovisual show relates the final terrible siege in 1691 by the Williamite forces, returning after being repelled the previous year by the Jacobite defenders. From here you can explore the extant walls and round towers, which offer some fine views of the

▲ King John's Castle

city and the Shannon. It may well strike you, however, that the most constructive use of the castle was in the 1930s, when after the departure of the British Army, neat, terraced council houses with back gardens onto the river were built within the walls.

On the south side of the small castle piazza stands **Limerick City Museum** (Tues–Sat 10am–1pm & 2.15–5pm; free; Ⓦwww.limerickcity.ie/museum), which is stuffed with grandfather clocks, medals and an old-fashioned diving suit, as well as examples of Limerick silver and lace, prehistoric finds and relics of the Limerick Soviet (see p.375) – currency notes and *The Bottom Dog*, a Labour news-sheet of the time. If you want to see the infamous **treaty stone** on which the surrender terms of the 1691 siege were signed, cross Thomond Bridge to the west bank, where the stone was put on a pedestal, over 2m high and facing the castle, in 1865.

The Georgian House and Limerick City Gallery of Art

No. 2 Pery Square, on the south side of the centre, one of a terrace that's regarded as the best example of late Georgian architecture in the city, has been renovated and opened to the public as the **Georgian House** (Mon–Fri 10am–4pm; €6; Ⓦwww.georgianlimerick.com). Built in 1838 by James Pain, the elegant facade, with fluted columns and an ornate fanlight around the door, looks onto what is now the People's Park. In the interior, which is quite plainly decorated and has been furnished with rather lacklustre exhibits and labels, you're left to admire the grand, airy proportions of the 23-room mansion – the visit is not a patch on the similar Georgian houses open to the public in Dublin.

By the entrance to the People's Park stands **Limerick City Gallery of Art** (Mon–Wed & Fri 10am–6pm, Thurs 10am–7pm, Sat 10am–5pm, Sun 2–5pm; free; Ⓣ061/310633, Ⓦwww.limerickcity.ie/lcga). Displayed on a rotating basis, the permanent collection of eighteenth- to twentieth-first-century paintings and drawings by artists such as Sean Keating, Paul Henry and Jack B. Yeats will appeal to aficionados of Irish art, but the gallery is more likely to be of interest for its exciting programme of **contemporary exhibitions** by Irish and international artists. Further similar exhibitions are mounted each month by the Belltable arts centre, around the corner on O'Connell Street (see below).

Eating, drinking and entertainment

There's no shortage of decent **places to eat out** in Limerick – notably upmarket restaurants and a diverse roster of daytime cafés – and on Saturday mornings, you could put together a nifty picnic at the **Milk Market**, a farmers' market of stalls selling olives, cheese, pies, salamis, breads, pastries and chocolate. A few, mostly traditional, **pubs** stand out from the crowd, while *The Trinity Rooms* at The Granary (the same complex as the *Club House*, see below; Ⓦwww.trinityrooms.ie) is the best **club**. Top dog for **live music** is *Dolan's* on Dock Road (Ⓣ061/314483, Ⓦwww.dolanspub.com), which features traditional music in the bar every night and everything from jazz to singer-songwriters, from indie to tribute bands, in its two gig venues, *The Warehouse* and *Upstairs*. Limerick's only **gay bar** and nightclub, *Bubblicious*, Bedford Row (Ⓦwww.bubbliciousbar.com), serves up cabaret on Friday nights, and DJs until late from Thursday to Sunday.

The **Belltable**, 69 O'Connell St (Ⓣ061/319709, Ⓦwww.belltable.ie), is the city's main **arts centre**, hosting a stimulating mix of drama, poetry, cabaret, dance, opera, music and film. For details of all arts and nightlife events, pick up a copy of the *Limerick Events Guide* (*LEG*), a free, monthly **listings magazine** available in bars and the tourist office.

Cafés and restaurants

Brûlées Restaurant 21 Henry St ⓣ061/319931. A trim, white-tablecloth affair in a Georgian townhouse on a prominent corner. Delights such as duck-leg confit with rosemary and ginger-scented lentils are expensive, but there are good-value early-bird (before 6.30pm) and lunch menus. Dinner Tues–Sat, lunch Thurs & Fri.

Copper & Spice 2 Cornmarket Row ⓣ061/313620. Welcoming, popular restaurant with warm, modern decor and a pan-Asian menu: a lot of dishes are classic Thai, but the majority are authentic Indian, including a delicious vegetarian *thali* and other veggie choices. Tues–Sat dinner, Sun lunch & dinner.

Freddy's Bistro Theatre Lane, an alley between Lower Glentworth St and Mallow St ⓣ061/418749. Pricey bistro – though there's an early-bird until 7pm – with a cosy, rustic feel and a strong French influence, whose speciality is fillet steak with brandy, bacon and mushrooms. Tues–Sat evenings.

The Grove Cecil St. Cheap and cheerful café serving tasty vegetarian wholefood: pizza, nut burgers, lasagne, pies, a wide variety of salads, juices and scones, either to eat in or take away. Closed Sat & Sun.

Hunt Museum Café (Ducartes) Rutland St. In a bright, airy, popular, self-service café overlooking the river, lunch might range from bacon and cabbage to baked salmon with fennel. A creative range of salads, open sandwiches, soup and cakes are also on offer, all at very reasonable prices. Opening hours same as museum; on Sun, drinks and cakes only.

Market Square Brasserie 74 O'Connell St ⓣ061/316311. Popular, sophisticated spot offering dishes like grilled polenta and vegetable terrine with *peperonata* alongside soup, fish and surf'n'turf daily specials. It's housed in a small cellar with bare brick walls that manages to be both formal and cosy.

Sage Café Catherine St. Seductive, airy, daytime café decorated in off-white colours and light woods, rustling up excellent, global-influenced hot dishes, creative salads, delicious sandwiches on home-made brown bread, soup and cake. Closed Sun.

San Lorenzo Steamboat Quay, Dock Rd ⓣ061/311500. Attractive and authentic Italian restaurant – jointly run by a Sicilian and a Sardinian – overlooking the river. Tasty, moderately priced pasta and pizza, as well as a long menu of meat and fish dishes – and an early-bird before 7pm. Evenings only.

The Wild Onion Café High St. Genuine American café-diner, with a down-home Southern welcome guaranteed – and authentically inexpensive. Excellent all-day breakfasts – try the French toast with sausage meat and hash browns – hot and cold sandwiches, omelettes, plus fine coffee, cookies and desserts. Tues–Fri 8am–4pm, Sat 9am–3pm.

Pubs and bars

The Club House The Granary, Bank Place. Upbeat, contemporary bar in a reconstructed 250-year-old granary, with great leather sofas, a spacious courtyard outside and a wide range of food, including pizzas.

The Locke 3 George's Quay. Large, congenial pub, offering good meals from the bar or in the upstairs bistro, as well as music ranging from traditional to jazz on Tues, Thurs and Sun. Great on a sunny day, when you can sit at the tables out front overlooking the Abbey River.

Nancy Blake's Upper Denmark St. Welcoming, old-fashioned pub with bare wooden floors covered in sawdust, home to traditional music Mon and Wed evenings, and Sat afternoon. Through the back is a large, covered and heated courtyard and a modern bar that hosts a DJ on Fri.

Peter Clohessy's Howley's Quay. Attractive complex of bars in a recent riverside development, owned by legendary Munster and Ireland rugby prop, "The Claw". There are plenty of big screens for watching sport, of course, outdoor tables on the river, and live bands on Wed; the aptly named *Sin Bin* club downstairs plays chart music Wed–Sat.

The White House (James Gleeson's) 52 O'Connell St. Established in 1812, this is Limerick's finest old pub, characterful and cosily furnished in dark wood. Traditional music on Sun, acoustic singers with open mike on Tues, and a well-attended poetry session – open mike, plus a guest published poet – on Wed (ⓦwhitehousepoets.blogspot.com).

Listings

Bicycle rental Emerald Cycles, 21 Upper Roches St ⓣ061/417000.

Bookshops Dineen's, 95 Henry St ⓣ061/413326; O'Mahony's, 120 O'Connell St ⓣ061/418155.

Car rental Irish Car Rentals, Dock Rd ⓣ061/226300, ⓦwww.irishcarrentals.ie; O'Mara Freeway, Ennis Rd ⓣ061/451611.

Hospital Limerick Regional Hospital, about 2km south of the centre in Dooradoyle ⓣ061/301111.

Internet access Bethel Business Centre, Sarsfield St, near the bridge.

Laundrette Speediwash, 11 St Gerrard's St, off O'Connell Ave (the continuation south of O'Connell St) ⓣ061/319380.

Left luggage At the bus station, Parnell St.
Pharmacy O'Sullivan's, Sarsfield St ☎061/413808, is open late 7 days a week.
Police Divisional HQ, Henry St ☎061/212400.
Taxis Castletroy ☎061/332266; Tower Cabs ☎061/444444.
Tours If you're short of time, you might want to consider taking a coach tour with Barratt Tours (☎061/384700, ⓦwww.4tours.biz), who run to the Cliffs of Moher every day except Fri, as well as to further-flung destinations; or with Railtours (☎01/856 0045, ⓦwww.railtoursireland.com), who take in the Cliffs of Moher and Bunratty Castle every day except Sun.
Travel agent USIT, O'Connell St ☎061/415064.

Lough Gur

Twenty kilometres south of Limerick city on the R512 towards Kilmallock, a cluster of grassy limestone hills spring unexpectedly from the plain, sheltering in their midst **Lough Gur**, the site of dozens of largely prehistoric monuments. Their importance lies in the fact that many of them are not ceremonial sites but stone dwelling places, dating from around 3000 BC onwards, which have furnished archeologists with most of their knowledge of the way of life in Neolithic Ireland. That's not to say that this curious landscape did not have a ritual aspect, as it was also revered as the territory of the sun goddess, Áine, and accrued a powerful mythical reputation, for example as the location of some of Fionn Mac Cumhaill's adventures in the *Ulster Cycle*.

Before it was partly drained in the nineteenth century, the lake (now C-shaped) formed an approximate square, with a nine-kilometre shoreline around a large triangular island, **Knockadoon**.The drainage, which left a marsh on the eastern side of the island and lowered the lake's level by 3m, revealed hoards of prehistoric items. These included myriad bones of ritually slaughtered oxen, gold and bronze spearheads, a bronze shield, swords and dozens of stone and bronze axes, all of which appear to have been thrown in as offerings to the gods of the lake but which are now scattered around the museums of the world. The tranquillity of the lake, broken only by the sounds of geese and a wealth of other birdlife, allows you easily to set your imagination to work on how life would have been here five thousand years ago.

You'll need your own **transport** to get to Lough Gur, as the only buses from Limerick are in the late afternoon. We've described the sites below in the order you'll come to them, though you may want to get the background at the visitor centre first before your explorations.

The stone circle and gallery grave

The first site you'll come to, on the R512 to the west of the lake, is the largest and finest **stone circle** in Ireland. Now set in a grassy glade surrounded by majestic trees, it consists of 113 large stones propped upright in sockets, around an artificial floor of gravelly earth 70cm above the original ground level; all of this is surrounded by a huge bank of earth, turf and small stones. Built around 2100 BC, the circle is associated with **Crom Dubh**, the harvest god, with its only entrance, to the northeast, precisely aligned to receive the sunrise on the quarter-day of August 1, the harvest festival of Lughnasa. On the opposite side to the entrance, large quantities of organic debris were found behind two especially tall stones, which point to sunset at Samain, the November 1 quarter-day; it may be that ritual bulls were eaten here to celebrate the traditional start of winter (when it made sense to cull the herd before the fodder shortage).

About a kilometre south of the stone circle at Holycross, the access road to Lough Gur heads west off the R512 around the south shore. Just over a kilometre in, on the south side of the road, you'll see the so-called Giant's Grave, a wedge-shaped **gallery grave** dating from about 2600 BC, where the remains of eight adults and four children were discovered. It's yet another ancient Irish site where Diarmuid and Gráinne are meant to have lain together on their flight from Fionn Mac Cumhaill, though it has added significance as Gráinne is the alter ego of Áine, the sun goddess. Until about a century ago, couples would mimic their divine coupling by making love in such graves.

The visitor centre and Knockadoon

Nearly 2km on from the gallery grave, at the northeast corner of the lake, lies the **visitor centre** (May to mid-Sept daily 10am–6pm; €5; ⓦwww.shannonheritage.com). Housed in replica Neolithic huts, it gives a fair idea of what life was like for the early inhabitants through artefacts, display boards and an audiovisual.

Causeways lead across from near the visitor centre and from near the Giant's Grave to the island of **Knockadoon**, which is fun to explore though parts are covered in dense woodland. Visible from the visitor centre at the northeast corner of the island is **Bourchier's Castle**, a privately owned, fifteenth-century tower house, while the overgrown remains of the thirteenth-century **Black Castle** face the Giant's Grave from the southern shore. Working west from here, you'll see traces of huts and ring forts on the grassy slopes, and around on the northwest-facing shore of the island, a limestone seat on a small, grassy mound known as the **Housekeeper's Chair**. This was held to be the birth-chair of Áine, from which she turned green corn to gold, for Crom Dubh to carry off at harvest time. A little further on, near the northernmost point of the island, is a **cave** that was held to be the entrance to Tír na nÓg, the land of eternal youth.

Adare and around

Around 15km southwest of Limerick on the N21 towards Tralee and Killarney, **ADARE** draws in coach parties from far and wide, with a reputation for prettiness that's perhaps a little overblown – it is quaint, but don't expect it to take your breath away. As the Heritage Centre reveals, it was made picturesque by design: the earls of Dunraven, landlords of Adare Manor, beautified their estate village with ornamental thatched cottages in the early nineteenth century, according to the current fashion for pastoral romanticism, and with Arts and Crafts–style houses in the early twentieth century. The attraction of Adare, which gathers itself around a broad main street and a prim town park on the south bank of the River Maigue, is enhanced by some impressive remnants, mostly ecclesiastical, of its medieval heyday.

The best place to start is the **Heritage Centre** (winter Mon–Sat 9.30am–1pm & 2–4.30pm, Sun 10am–1pm & 2–4/4.30pm; summer daily 9am–5/6pm; €5; Heritage Island; ⓣ061/396666, ⓦwww.adareheritagecentre.ie), centrally located opposite the park on Main Street, which furnishes plenty of interesting detail on the town and its early thirteenth-century **Desmond Castle**. The castle, on the north side of the Maigue River bridge, is coming towards the end of a lengthy restoration, but can be visited on 50-minute guided tours from the Centre (June–Sept & sometimes Oct daily, phone for times; €6, or €10 combined ticket with Heritage Centre).

The limerick

Limericks became common in Britain in the nineteenth century, popularized by Edward Lear, but their origin is shrouded in the mists of time. One possible theory is that the form derives from the satirical rhymes of the **Maigue Poets** (named after the river that runs through Adare), who were translated from Irish into English in the mid-nineteenth century.

The Catholic parish church next door to the Heritage Centre, a trim, multi-aisled affair with an imposing, oak-beamed roof, was part of the **Trinitarian Abbey** until the mid-nineteenth century. Founded around 1230 with an attached hospital, it was the only house of the Order of the Holy Trinity in Ireland. Down an alley to one side is a circular stone tower with a conical roof, where the monks kept pigeons – not as a hobby, but for the refectory table. Five minutes' walk away, on the south side of the Maigue bridge, stands the **Augustinian Friary**, which is now an Anglican parish church and school (access not permitted roughly Mon–Fri 9am–3pm during school term). Founded in 1315, it has an attractive, fifteenth-century cloister, which was carefully restored by the Dunravens in the nineteenth century then spoiled by the insertion of their brutal family mausoleum. Arriving late on the scene, in 1464, the **Franciscans** built their **friary** – which was also known as the "Poor Abbey" because of their strict emphasis on poverty, or the "Grey Abbey" because they made their habits of undyed wool – on the north side of the river beyond the castle. It's now part of a golf course, but it's worth asking at the clubhouse for permission to view the cloister and other well-preserved ruins.

Practicalities

The Heritage Centre houses a very helpful **tourist office** (Feb to mid-May & mid-Sept to Dec Mon–Sat 9am–1pm & 2–5pm; mid-May to mid-Sept daily 9am–6pm; ⓣ061/396255), a library where you can access the **Internet** and a popular café, serving tasty sandwiches, soup and simple hot dishes. The Dunravens' many-turreted pile, built in 1832 in Gothic style and set in huge grounds on the east side of the main street, has now been converted into the luxurious *Adare Manor* **hotel** (ⓣ061/396566, ⓦwww.adaremanor.com; ❽), which boasts its own golf course, swimming pool and spa. A pool and spa are also part of the deal at the comfortable and very welcoming *Woodlands House Hotel* (ⓣ061/605100, ⓦwww.woodlands-hotel.ie; ❹, with good-value midweek breaks also available), 2km from the centre in a secluded setting off the Limerick road. There are dozens of **B&Bs** in and around Adare, including neat and homely *Berkeley Lodge*, Station Road (ⓣ061/396857, ⓦwww.adare.org; ❷), and *Clonunion House*, 1km out of town off the Limerick road (ⓣ061/396657, ⓦwww.adarevillage.com; April–Oct; ❷), a two-hundred-year-old farmhouse with large, antique-furnished rooms, set in spacious gardens. There's a **campsite**, *Adare Camping and Caravan Park* (ⓣ061/395376, ⓦwww.adarecamping.com; mid-March to Sept), 4km south of Adare off the R519 Ballingarry road.

Several of Main Street's thatched cottages have been turned into gift and craft shops or **restaurants**, including the excellent *Wild Geese* (ⓣ061/396451; Tues–Sun evenings), purveying well-judged French-influenced cuisine such as fillet of beef topped with a herb crust. Cheaper but more predictable meals are on offer at *The Arches Restaurant*, just along from the Heritage Centre. In summer, **traditional music** is played on Saturday and Sunday at nearby *Lena's*

pub, and around the corner on the Rathkeale road (N21) at *Bill Chawke's* on Thursday and at *Seán Collins'* on Sunday, while on Tuesday evenings in July and August the Heritage Centre hosts a show of music, dance and storytelling, mounted by Comhaltas, the national cultural organization (Ⓦwww.comhaltas.ie), as part of their Seisiún programme (€10).

BALLINGARRY, 5km southwest down the R519, is home to a first-class **hostel**, *Trainor's* (Ⓣ069/68164, Ⓔtrainorhostel@eircom.net; IHH; mid-March to Sept; dorms from €15, twins ❶), and *Echo Lodge*, a luxurious country-house **hotel** in a converted nineteenth-century convent, containing one of Ireland's foremost **restaurants**, *The Mustard Seed* (Ⓣ069/68508, Ⓦwww.mustardseed.ie; closed first 2 weeks of Feb; ❺).

The Celtic Park and Gardens

The Celtic Park and Gardens (mid-March to mid-Oct 9.30am–6pm; at other times by appointment, Ⓣ061/394243; €6) are well worth a short detour if you have your own transport, situated 8km northwest of Adare or 3km off the N69, to the south of Kilcornan. On the site of a Celtic lakeside settlement, all manner of Irish historic monuments have been lovingly re-created, including a stone circle, an ogham stone and a holy well. A local church of the Knights Templars has been rebuilt, complete with thatched roof, while each feature's explanatory note is full of interesting detail – you'll learn, for example, that the same cooking method as a *fulacht fiadh*, a stone-lined trench filled with water and hot stones for boiling meat, is still used in parts of New Guinea. All of this is set in lush woodlands and meadows where over 150 species of wild flowers and plants are found between spring and August. At the end of the walk before returning to the tearoom, you'll come upon an original, unexcavated circular fort, surrounded by a deep ditch, and a pleasant formal garden, sporting an ornamental lily pond and hundreds of roses.

County Clare

Renowned worldwide for its vibrant musical traditions, **County Clare** draws a multitude of aficionados to its numerous **pub sessions** as well as major **festivals** such as the Willie Clancy Summer School. Its county town, **Ennis**, is an animated place with many excellent music pubs and some atmospheric religious remains, further examples of which are dotted around the countryside, such as at **Quin Abbey**, **Dysert O'Dea** and the settlement on **Scattery Island**. The castles and tower houses of Clare's erstwhile dynasties, the O'Briens and MacNamaras too inform the landscape, notably at **Bunratty, Knappogue** and **Leamaneh**.

Elsewhere the county's attractions are largely set beside the water, mostly along its Atlantic shoreline and most dramatically at the vertiginous **Cliffs of Moher**. Here too you'll find attractive seaside towns, often equipped with tremendous sandy beaches, such as **Kilkee** and **Lahinch** and the village of **Fanore.** At Clare's eastern extremity lies the expansive **Lough Derg**, whose waters are best explored by renting your own boat or taking a cruise. In utter contrast, in North Clare the heights of **The Burren**, a mass of jumbled, broken limestone, provide desolate though dramatic landscapes and numerous **Stone** and **Iron Age** antiquities. Its best bases for exploration are the attractive villages of **Ballyvaughan** and **Lisdoonvarna**, the latter renowned for its annual matchmaking festival.

Shannon International Airport, in Clare's southeast, lies within easy reach of Ennis, which itself is the county's **transport** hub. Clare is reasonably well covered by buses in summertime, though the county's north is best accessed from Galway.

Southeast Clare

Heading north from Limerick to Galway along the busy N18 it's easy to miss some of the attractions of the county's nether region. Consisting largely of flat farmland, its lanes, ideal for cycling, lead to several sites of historic interest. The most southerly is the impressive **Bunratty Castle**, while a short hop further north encompasses the imaginative **Craggaunowen Project** with its re-creations of dwellings from bygone times, another stately Anglo-Norman stronghold, **Knappogue Castle**, and the idyllically set monastic site of **Quin Abbey**.

Bunratty Castle

Some twelve kilometres west of Limerick, bypassed by the main N18 Ennis road, lies the village of Bunratty whose **castle** and **folk park** (daily 9am–5.30pm; June–Aug open till 6pm; last admission to castle 4pm and to folk park 1hr 15min before closing; €14; ⓦwww.shannonheritage.com; Heritage Island) form one of Ireland's most popular attractions. A castle was first built here in 1277 during the Anglo-Normans' brief occupation of southeast Clare, though the present version dates back to the mid-fifteenth-century and was constructed for the MacNamaras, a branch of the O'Brien clan. Majestically restored in the 1950s, its keep contains an impressive array of artwork and furniture, mostly dating from the fifteenth and sixteenth centuries. In the evenings "medieval" banquets are staged here (daily subject to demand 5.30pm & 8.45pm; €57.50), their entertainment consisting of a somewhat twee form of

Shannon International Airport

Shannon International Airport (ⓣ061/712000, ⓦwww.shannonairport.com) serves direct flights from North America, the UK and several other European countries, as well as Irish internal services. The airport has good bus links with Limerick, 20km to the southeast (where you can access the rail network), and Ennis, 20km north, as well as to Cork, Dublin, Galway and Killarney (for timetables call Bus Éireann ⓣ061/313333 or 065/682 4177, ⓦwww.buseireann.ie). A taxi to either Limerick or Ennis will cost around €32 – there's a 24-hour taxi desk (ⓣ061/471538) in the arrivals hall.

The airport's **tourist office** (daily 6.30am–6pm; ⓣ061/471664) is in the arrivals hall, where there's also a bank (Mon 10am–5pm, Tues, Thurs & Fri 10am–4pm, Wed 10.30am–4pm), a bureau de change (daily 6am–10pm), ATMs, several **car-rental** outlets and the airport's information desk (daily 6am–midnight). Accommodation can be booked through the tourist office (€4). Alternatively, there's the modern *Park Inn* (ⓣ061/471122, ⓦwww.rezidorparkinn.com; ④ plus breakfast) within walking distance of the terminal and numerous B&Bs in and around Shannon town itself, a sprawling and unappealing place – it's better to head to Ennis (see p.388), a far livelier and more attractive stop.

traditional dance, music and song. The expansive castle grounds host the folk park, a re-creation of a nineteenth-century village, replete with post office, shops, a church and a pub, all populated by actors in contemporary dress.

In the village centre, the Georgian *Bunratty Castle Hotel* (ⓣ061/478700, ⓦwww.bunrattycastlehotel.com; ⑤) has excellent **accommodation** in period-furnished rooms, as well as fine meals and its own spa. The village is awash with B&Bs, especially on Low Road, including *Bunratty Woods Country House* (ⓣ061/369689, ⓦwww.bunrattywoods.com; ③; mid-March to mid-Nov), a beautifully furnished guesthouse; other comfortable options include *Innisfree* (ⓣ061/369773, ⓔinnisfree@unison.ie; ②) and *Bunratty Villa* (ⓣ061/369241, ⓦwww.bunrattyvilla.com; ②; late March to Nov). *Durty Nelly's* **pub**, across from the *Bunratty Castle Hotel* at the beginning of Low Road, features traditional-music sessions (Tues & Thurs), though these are often geared to meet more popular tastes.

The Craggaunowen Project

Around 7km northeast of Bunratty, just past Sixmilebridge, a turning leads east off the R462 to the **Craggaunowen Project** (mid-April to mid-Oct daily 10am–6pm; last admission 5pm; €8.50; ⓦwww.shannonheritage.com), which features reconstructions of dwellings, hunting sites and other aspects of life during prehistoric and early Christian times.

The hour-long self-guided tour begins with a sixteenth-century tower house whose displays of medieval art and artefacts include some notable European wood-carvings, before moving on to re-creations of a *crannóg*, ring fort and souterrain, as well as **The Togher**, a real Iron Age wooden roadway, which was moved here from County Longford (see p.214). Proof that replicas can sometimes match the real McCoy comes in the form of **The Brendan**, a *curragh* whose hull consists of leather hides stretched over an ash frame, in which Tim Severin and his four-man crew crossed the Atlantic in 1976. A ninth-century manuscript describes how St Brendan the Navigator became the first European to reach the Americas in the sixth century in such a boat – and, though impossible to prove that Brendan did so, Severin certainly demonstrated that the technology described was sufficient for the task.

Knappogue Castle and Quin Abbey

Heading back to the R462 and a few kilometres to the north is **Knappogue Castle** (May–Sept daily 9.30am–5pm; €7; ⓦwww.shannonheritage.com), an imposing fortified structure constructed in 1467 by Seán MacNamara. His descendants lived here until the nineteenth century, apart from a brief hiatus when it was occupied by Cromwell's troops, but debts forced its sale and it passed through several owners before being purchased by a former US Navy bureaucrat, who began restoration work in the late 1960s. The interior now features elegant oak furnishings, though the undoubted centrepiece is the hall used for "medieval" banquets (May–Oct daily 6.30pm, according to demand; €54.50). The castle's grounds include an impressive walled garden (same hours as castle; free), dating from 1817, whose centrepiece is a bust of Bacchus.

From Knappogue the road heads north to **Quin** where the ruined **friary** (June–Sept Wed–Mon 10am–5pm; free) occupies a glorious pastoral setting. Unusually, the original building incorporated parts of a castle, built by Thomas de Clare in the late thirteenth century, which was subsequently attacked by the Irish, leaving it "a hideous, blackened cave" according to one contemporary observer. In the 1430s the MacNamaras brought Franciscans to Quin to found the friary and used the ruins of the old castle as a base, constructing a remarkable edifice in the process, including a striking colonnaded cloister and a tall, trim tower. The friary was dissolved in 1541, but the friars returned after the death of Elizabeth I, only to be expelled again a few years later.

Ennis

With a population of around twenty five thousand, **ENNIS** is by far and away Clare's largest town. It began its life in the thirteenth century as a small settlement grouped around a long-disappeared O'Brien castle. Nowadays, it's a buzzing town, set on both sides of the River Fergus, and still largely based around its medieval street pattern and the central, often traffic-clogged artery, O'Connell Street. Though there's little to see here apart from the ruins of a medieval **friary**, to the north of O'Connell Street, the town is thoroughly enjoyable in its own right, with plenty of decent restaurants and, above all, a thriving **traditional-music** session scene.

Arrival and information

Both the **bus station** (Ⓣ065/682 4177) and the **train station** (Ⓣ065/684 0444) are fifteen minutes' walk from the town centre on Station Road. For details of getting into town from **Shannon Airport**, see the box on p.386.

The **tourist office** (July & Aug daily 9.30am–5.30pm, Sat & Sun closed 1–2pm; Sept–June Mon–Sat 9.30am–1pm & 2–5.30pm, Jan & Feb closed Sat;

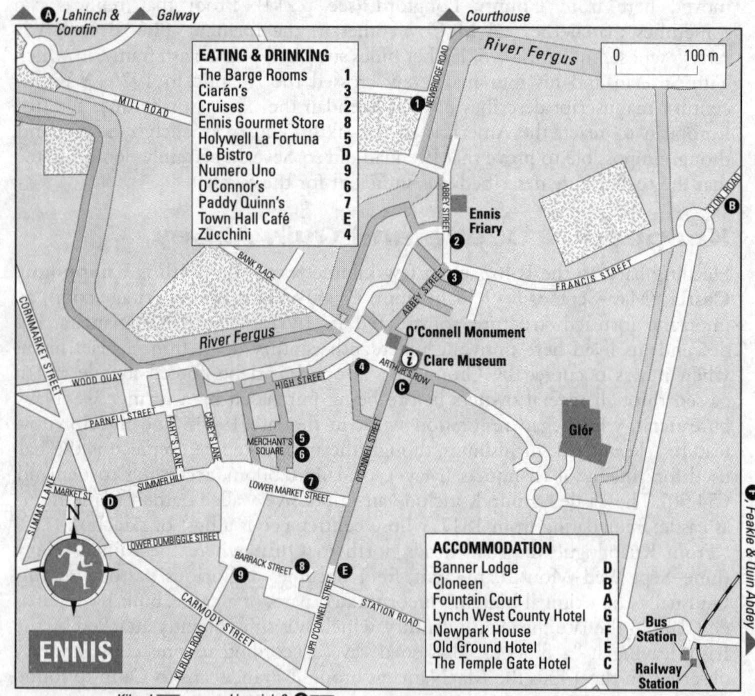

Ⓣ065/682 8366, Ⓦwww.shannonregiontourism.ie) is down Arthur's Row, an alley towards the northern end of O'Connell Street. **Walking tours** of the town (May–Oct Wed–Mon 11am & 7pm; 1hr 30min; Ⓣ087/648 3714, Ⓦwww.enniswalkingtours.com; €8) begin from outside the tourist office. If you want to take a **coach tour** of Clare's major sites, contact Barratt Tours (Ⓣ061/348700, Ⓦwww.4tours.biz), which operates summer trips (daily except Fri; €27) to the Cliffs of Moher and the Burren. **Internet** access is available at the excellent *Coffee and Bytes*, Lower Market Street.

Accommodation

Ennis has a reasonably broad range of **accommodation**, though can get very busy during July and August and at festival times (see p.390), when it's worth booking ahead.

Banner Lodge Market St Ⓣ065/682 4224, Ⓦwww.bannerlodge.com. This town-centre guesthouse has eight very restful and sizeable en-suite rooms, all maintained to a high standard. ❷

Cloneen Clon Rd Ⓣ065/682 9681. Near the roundabout at the end of Francis Street, *Cloneen* provides both standard and en-suite accommodation, and bike-storage space for cyclists. Mid-April to mid-Oct. ❷

Fountain Court Lahinch Rd Ⓣ065/682 9845, Ⓦwww.fountain-court.com. Three kilometres down the N85 Lahinch road, this guesthouse provides a relaxing rural setting, its own peaceful gardens, and very comfortable rooms, featuring king-sized beds. Mid-March to Nov. ❸

Lynch West County Hotel Clare Rd Ⓣ065/682 3000, Ⓦwww.lynchhotels.com. A big modern hotel, 1km south of town with its own leisure centre, complete with three swimming pools, gym, spa and solarium. The hotel runs its own programme of entertainment for children, based around its play centre. ❸

Newpark House Tulla Rd Ⓣ065/682 1233, Ⓦwww.newparkhouse.com. A couple of kilometres east of Ennis off the R352 Scarriff road in a woodland setting, this splendid house dates from 1650 and provides stylish period rooms, some including canopy beds. Mid-March to mid-Nov. ❸

Old Ground Hotel O'Connell St Ⓣ065/682 8127, Ⓦwww.flynnhotels.com. Probably the town's best-known hotel, the ivy-clad *Old Ground* dates from the eighteenth century and has its own relaxing gardens. Rooms are spacious, elegantly designed and furnished, and include a number of suites. There's a library too, plus a fine restaurant, popular bar (with its own menu) and the stylish *Town Hall Café* (see p.390). Doubles ❺, suites ❻

The Temple Gate Hotel The Square Ⓣ065/682 3300, Ⓦwww.templegatehotel.com. A blend of the old and new, this hotel's swish design incorporates a nineteenth-century former convent. Rooms are modishly decorated, especially the classy suites, which feature king-sized beds and tapestry wall coverings. Doubles ❺, suites ❼

The Town

Ennis's only real edifice of note is its Franciscan **friary** (April, May & mid-Sept to Oct Tues–Sun 10am–5pm; June to mid-Sept daily 10am–6pm; €1.60; Heritage Card). It's best to take the optional guided tour, which explains the friary's importance from its inception in the late thirteenth century by the O'Briens, then rulers of much of north Munster, who had rooms here and were buried here. At one time the friary was regarded as one of Ireland's major educational institutions. While other such establishments did not survive the Reformation, this one did, thanks to Murchadh O'Brien's acknowledgement of the rule of the Tudors – he become the first Earl of Thomond in the process, though the friars were finally expelled in the 1570s. Subsequently, the buildings were used as assizes and a jail, as well as providing rooms for visiting dignitaries. In the late seventeenth century the friary became a parish church of the Church of Ireland and was renovated at various times, before finally being abandoned in 1871. What's left remains impressive, especially the fifteenth-century tower and the perfectly formed arches of the cloister garth. In a niche on one of the tower's piers is a carved **relief** of St Francis, complete with a habit whose girdle bears the three characteristic knots of the Franciscans, representing chastity, poverty and obedience, while his body and limbs bear several stigmata; the south transept includes a carving of Christ, hands tied and accompanied by tokens of the Crucifixion. In the chancel is the **Creagh Tomb** which dates from 1843 and incorporates sculptured panels from an earlier fifteenth-century tomb, decorated with astonishingly detailed scenes of Christ's suffering.

Away from the friary are several monuments devoted to Ennis's later political significance. O'Connell Square is dominated by a tall obelisk celebrating **Daniel O'Connell**, elected as Clare's MP in 1828. As a Catholic he could not take his seat, but his large majority was a factor in Westminster's subsequent implementation of the Catholic Emancipation Act and he was able to attend the Commons when re-elected in 1830. The former Taoiseach **Éamon de Valera**, who represented East Clare (including Ennis) at the Dáil for more than thirty years, is commemorated by a monument outside the Courthouse on Gort Road.

For a fuller picture of Clare's history it's best to visit the **museum**, which shares the same building as the tourist office on Arthur's Row (June–Sept Mon–Sat 9.30–5pm, Sun 9.30am–1pm; Oct–May Tues–Sat 9.30am–1pm & 2–5pm; free; ⓦwww.clarelibrary.ie) and covers everything from local archeological finds to the West Clare Railway (see p.396), taking in a re-creation of a Viking longboat, sport, music and dance on the way.

Eating

The range of Ennis's culinary delights has developed in leaps and bounds over recent years and there's now more than a few places guaranteed to titillate your tastebuds.

Ennis Gourmet Store 1 Barrack St. The place to pick up premium ingredients for a snack or picnic also serves terrific lunchtime sandwiches and salads and, unquestionably, the town's finest coffee. Closed Sun.

Holywell La Fortuna 8 Merchants Square ⓣ065/684 2420. Branch of the excellent Clare/Galway chain serving gargantuan pizzas and reasonably priced pasta dishes.

Le Bistro *Temple Gate Hotel*, The Square ⓣ065 682 3300. Award-winning modern European food, served in splendid surroundings – the enormous Sun lunches are especially popular.

Numero Uno 3 Old Barrack St ⓣ065/684 1740. Excellent pizzas at this tiny but very popular restaurant. Open until 1am Fri & Sat.

O'Connor's 10 Merchants Square. A stylish café-bistro offering a range of meals, including an especially good goat's-cheese salad.

Town Hall Café *The Old Ground Hotel*, O'Connell St ⓣ065/682 8127. Occupying, as the name suggests, Ennis's former municipal centre, this splendidly spacious room is the venue for everything from coffee to filling lunches, tea and scones, and an imaginative evening menu, including treats such as steak cooked in a mustard and whiskey sauce.

Zucchini 7 High St ⓣ065/686 6566. Very fine food indeed, especially its imaginative range of seafood and vegetarian dishes, served in an atmospheric and cosy setting. Expect to pay around €45 plus wine, though there's an early-bird special at €24.50 (5–7pm).

Nightlife and entertainment

As Christy Moore advised in his famed song *Lisdoonvarna*, "If it's music you want – go to Clare" and Ennis offers a host of places to enjoy the experience. A purpose-built concert hall on Friar's Walk, **Glór** (ⓣ065/684 3103, ⓦwww.glor.ie), often features traditional-music concerts as well as other events, and Ennis is home to two major festivals: the **Fleadh Nua** (ⓦwww.fleadhnua.com), over the last week of May, and the **Ennis Traditional Music Festival** (ⓦwww.ennistradfestival.com), which runs for four days in mid-November. The best source for information about the local traditional-music scene, and a good place to pick up CDs by Clare musicians, is Custy's Music Shop on Cook's Lane, off O'Connell Street (Ⓦwww.custysmusic.com).

At other times, for **traditional-music sessions**, head for **bars** such as *Cruises*, Abbey Street (Wed–Sat), a stone-floored place with a roaring fire in winter; lively *Ciarán's* on Francis Street (summer Wed–Sun; less frequently off-season); or cosy *Paddy Quinn's*, Lower Market Street (Sat all year). For more eclectic fare cross the river to *The Barge Rooms*, 1 Newbridge Place, which stages musical entertainment in its bar as well as hosting a late-night club.

East Clare

Less visited than other parts of the county, East Clare still has plenty of attractions, most focused upon small towns and villages, such as **Killaloe** and **Mountshannon**, sitting by the edge of **Lough Derg**. The lake itself constitutes the county's eastern boundary and is very popular with the more upmarket set, with its picturesque villages reminiscent of the English Cotswolds; offering numerous angling opportunities, it attracts a boating crowd. Away from the Lough the countryside has a vastly different character from the remainder of Clare – it's a mass of hills and a warren of tiny lanes, with interest focused upon two of the county's greatest traditional-music centres, **Feakle** and **Tulla**.

Tulla and Feakle

The crossroads village of **TULLA**, some twenty kilometres east of Ennis, is renowned for its **traditional music**, mostly through the efforts of the Tulla Céilí Band, though you're more likely to catch the band at a festival somewhere else than in their homeplace. However, you'll probably find a session at either *Torpey's* or *McCarthur's* at weekends and there's very welcoming **B&B** at *Clondanagh Cottage* (Ⓣ065/683 5429, Ⓦwww.clondonaghcottage.com; ❷) in a rural setting a couple of kilometres or so northeast of the village. For stylish **food** in pleasant surroundings, head to *Flappers* (Ⓣ065/683 5711; closed Sun).

A better bet for music is tiny **FEAKLE**, 13km further east, with sessions at *Pepper's* (Wed) – where you can also get bar **meals** (from breakfasts to dinners) – and *Shortt's* (Thurs), as well as a seven-day **International Traditional Music Festival** (Ⓦwww.feaklefestival.ie) in early August, featuring major singers and musicians. Village **accommodation** consists of a well-equipped hostel in the centre, *Loughnane's* (IHO; Ⓣ61/924200, Ⓦwww.eastclarehostels.com; dorms €20, private rooms ❶; May–Dec), and farmhouse B&B at *Laccaroe House* (Ⓣ061/924150, Ⓦwww.laccaroehouse.com; ❷; March–Nov), past *Pepper's* bar towards Scarriff.

Mountshannon

Lough Derg's western shore is sparsely populated, with just a few small villages on the road to Portumna (see p.425) in County Galway. The pretty loughside village of **MOUNTSHANNON**, 14km east of Feakle, is the best place to head for, its long, straight main street revealing the village's origins as a planned eighteenth-century settlement.

Mountshannon is popular with anglers and there are several places offering **accommodation**. In the village centre is the hospitable, family-run

Mountshannon Hotel (ⓣ061/927162, ⓦwww.mountshannon-hotel.ie; ❸), while B&B options to the north include *Oak House* (ⓣ061/927185, ⓔhowemaureen@eircom.net; ❷; April–Oct), with its own private beach, and *Derg Lodge* (ⓣ061/9271980; ❶), an agreeable modern bungalow. *Lakeside Holiday Park* (ⓣ061/927225, ⓦwww.lakesideireland.com; May–Sept), just off the Portumna road, offers **camping** as well as renting kayaks and boats for exploring the lough. In the village, you'll find the *Cois na hAbhna* **bar**, which has occasional traditional sessions in summer and serves wholesome meals. The village's **Iniscealtra Festival** (ⓦwww.iniscealtra-artsfestival.org), covering contemporary visual arts as well as traditional dance and music, happens over ten days from late May.

Killaloe

Hillside **KILLALOE** commands a strategic position above the point where the Shannon leaves Lough Derg. It was here that Brian Ború, the eleventh-century High King of Tara and founder of the O'Brien clan, built his palace, Kincora, a massive fort that was the centre of power in Ireland until Brian's death at the Battle of Clontarf in 1014 (see p.692). This stood on the summit of the hill in the spot now occupied by the Catholic church, though no trace of the building remains. However, about a kilometre or so to the north of the town, off the Scarriff road, is the Bronze Age ring fort **Béal Ború**, perhaps occupied by Brian before Kincora's construction. For more about him visit the **Brian Ború Heritage Centre** (May–Sept 10am–6pm; €3.20; ⓦwww.shannonheritage.com; Heritage Island) on the old stone bridge which leads to Killaloe's "twin-town", Ballina in Tipperary.

Killaloe later became a religious centre, based around thirteenth-century **St Flannan's Cathedral**, just down Royal Parade from the bridge. This features an impressive Romanesque doorway, taken from an earlier church that occupied the site, as well as a low, square bell-tower. Just beside the doorway is the massive **Thorgrim Stone**, unusually bearing both runic and ogham inscription. Who or what "Thorgrim" was is unknown – the stone gained its name because the word appears twice in the carvings.

Practicalities

The very helpful **tourist office** is in the Brian Ború Heritage Centre on the bridge (May–Sept daily 10am–5.30pm; ⓣ061/376866). Lough **cruises** on *The Spirit of Killaloe* (May to mid-Sept daily; call ⓣ086/814 0559 for times; €10; ⓦwww.killaloe.ie/thespiritofkillaloe) leave from across the bridge in Ballina, while **boats** can be rented from Whelan's Foodstore, Main Street (ⓣ061/376159). **B&Bs** include the attractive townhouse, *Kincora House*, Church Street (ⓣ061/376149, ⓦwww.kincorahouse.com; ❷; May–Sept), and the welcoming *Derg House*, Royal Parade (ⓣ061/375599, ⓔ_ictekirl@eircom.net; ❷). The *Lakeside Hotel* (ⓣ061/376122, ⓦwww.lakeside-killaloe.com; ❹), in Ballina, has an unbeatable waterside location.

Cherry Tree (ⓣ061/375688; open Tues–Sat evenings and Sun lunchtime) is a decidedly upmarket **restaurant** near the *Lakeside Hotel*, offering stunning locally sourced food in a loughside setting (with a three-course dinner at around €50 and Sun lunch for €29 plus wine). Other food options include *Crotty's Courtyard Bar*, Bridge Street, serving meals which can be enjoyed alfresco, and *Gooser's*, a lively bar/restaurant just down the Limerick road in Ballina. Traditional-music sessions are currently thin on the ground, but both *The Anchor Inn*, Bridge Street, and *Molly's* in Ballina are worth a try. The local festival is **Féile Brian Ború** (first weekend in July; ⓦ www.feilebrianboru.killaloe.ie) with plenty of music in the pubs, street entertainment and a mass Shannon swim.

North of Ennis

Three kilometres north of Ennis, the R476 road heads through flat agricultural land towards the busy village of **Corofin**. On the way a worthy excursion can be made west to **Dysert O'Dea**, a major religious foundation.

Dysert O'Dea

Well signposted off the R476, the **O'Dea Castle** (May–Sept daily 10am–6pm; €4) was the stronghold of the O'Dea branch of the O'Brien clan until 1691.

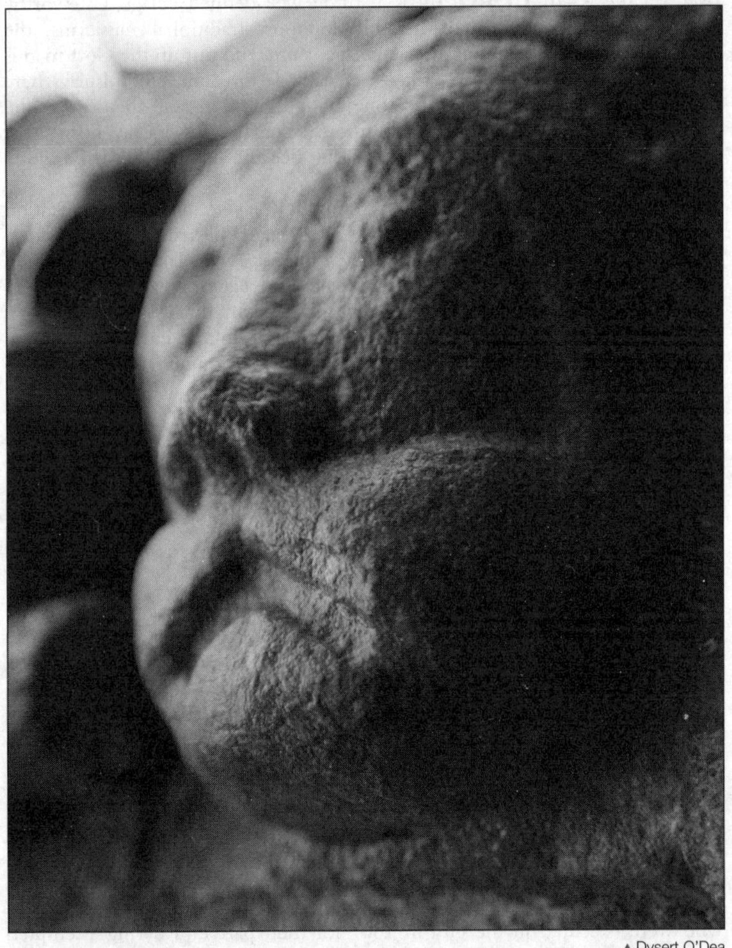

▲ Dysert O'Dea

Nowadays it houses an archeological centre and is the best starting-point for a history trail leading across fields to **Dysert O'Dea**. St Tola founded a monastery here in the eighth century and there are several later religious remains, including a twelfth-century Romanesque church, extensively rebuilt in the seventeenth. This features a finely carved doorway and gargoyle-like carvings of human faces and animal heads. Nearby stands a round tower, badly damaged by Cromwell's guns, and the twelfth-century **White Cross of Tola**, which bears elaborate patterning and several impressive carvings, including a Crucifixion scene set above a powerful-looking bishop. Dysert O'Dea witnessed a major battle in 1318 when Sir Richard de Clare's army was defeated by the O'Briens, quelling attempts to enforce Anglo-Norman sovereignty over Clare – it would be another two centuries before they were successful.

Corofin

Back on the R476, **COROFIN** is a sturdy, well-defined village, noteworthy as the birthplace of one of Ireland's foremost traditional musicians, the accordionist Sharon Shannon. In the village centre and just up the Gort road is the **Clare Heritage Centre** (May–Oct daily 10am–6pm; €4). Displays here provide a fascinating glimpse of bygone living conditions and focus upon the Famine years and emigration. A side-room celebrates the locally born artist Sir Frederick Burton (1816–1900), who later became the director of London's National Gallery.

B&Bs include comfortable en-suite rooms at *Corofin Country House*, Station Road (Ⓣ065/683 7791; ❷; March–Nov), and similarly pleasant accommodation at *Lakefield Lodge*, Ennis Road (Ⓣ065/683 7675, Ⓦwww.lakefieldlodgebandb.com; ❷; March–Oct). The family-run *Corofin Village Hostel* on Main Street (IHH & IHO; Ⓣ065/6837683, Ⓦwww.corofincamping.com; dorms €16, doubles ❶; April–Sept) offers comfortable budget accommodation and **camping**. Several pubs serve **meals**: the *Corofin Arms* has an impressive dinner menu, including rack of Clare lamb, and is a popular spot for Sunday lunch too, while *Bofey Quinn's* provides filling fodder, such as a tasty fish-and-potato pie. You can catch a pub **session** at the *Corofin Arms* (Tues & Fri–Sun), *Campbell's* (Tues), *Bofey Quinn's* (Wed) or *Inchiquin Inn* (Fri).

Southwest Clare

It's a relatively long haul from Ennis to Clare's southwest, but well worth the effort for the attractions offered by two popular holiday spots and the chance to explore the glorious scenery of the **Loop Head peninsula**. Of the resorts, **Kilkee** is the livelier, with a sweeping beach and access to Loop Head; **Kilrush** is more stolid, but still attractive in its own way and is a base for watersports, dolphin watching and the ferry to **Scattery Island**, a major monastic site.

Kilrush

Forty-odd kilometres from Ennis, **KILRUSH** is a graceful planned town whose broad main drag, Frances Street, leads down to a bustling marina where you can catch a ferry to Scattery Island (see opposite). At the town's core stands the **Maid of Éireann** statue, honouring the Manchester Martyrs, three Fenians who were executed in the city in 1867 for their part in a daring attempted rescue of some of their comrades arrested during a failed uprising.

Killimer car ferry

A few kilometres east of Killimer on the N67 Ennis–Kilrush road is the Shannon **car ferry** which crosses to Tarbert in Kerry (April hourly Mon–Sat 7am–9pm, Sun 9am–9pm; May–Sept Mon–Sat hourly 7am–10am & 6–9pm, half-hourly 10.30am–5.30pm, Sun hourly 9–10am & 6–9pm, half-hourly 10.30am–5.30pm; Oct–March hourly Mon–Sat 7am–7pm, Sun 9am–7pm; the operating hours from Tarbert are 30min later than Killimer; one-way: car €15, pedestrians/cyclists €4; return: €25/€6; ⓣ065/905 3124, ⓦwww.shannonferries.com). This saves a trip of more than 130 kilometres via Limerick if you're planning to visit Kerry or, alternatively, en route from Kerry to Clare.

In the early nineteenth century, wealthy landlord John Ormsby Vandeleur built Kilrush House, which stood in an estate eight hundred metres or so east of town by the Killimer road (N67). The building was demolished in 1973, but the restored **Vandeleur Walled Garden** (daily: April–Sept 10am–6pm; Oct–March 10am–4pm; €5; ⓦwww.vandeleurwalledgarden.ie) is an attractive, sheltered spot, featuring an abundance of subtropical plants. Vandeleur himself, however, is not remembered with any affection, having evicted many of his tenants during the worst years of the Great Famine.

The Shannon estuary is home to the country's only resident group of **bottle-nosed dolphins**, whose calving season takes place between May and August, and so far more than a hundred individuals have been identified. To enjoy a sight of them you can take a two-hour trip on the MV *Dolphin Discovery* from the marina on Merchants Quay (July & Aug 11am, 2pm & 4.30pm; April–June, Sept & Oct call for times; €20; ⓣ065/905 1327, ⓦwww.discoverdolphins.ie).

Practicalities

The **tourist office** is on Frances Street (June–September Mon–Sat 10am–1pm & 2–6pm, Sun 10am–2pm; ⓣ065/905 1577, ⓦwww.kilrush.ie). **Internet** access is provided by Internet Bureau, also on Frances Street.

The town has a few **B&Bs**, of which the most central is *Crotty's* pub (ⓣ065/905 2470, ⓦwelcome.to/crottys; ❷) on Market Square, which has charmingly furnished standard rooms, while out of town, and opposite the Vandeleur Walled Garden, is *Bruach na Coille* (ⓣ065/905 2250, ⓦwww.clarkekilrush.com; ❷), a Georgian-style house in splendid grounds with comfy rooms and a generous breakfast menu. *Katie O'Connor's* **hostel** (IHO; ⓣ065/905 1133, ⓦwww.westclare.com; dorms €16, doubles ❶; mid-March to Sept) is a well-run place on Frances Street.

Near the marina *The Harbour Restaurant* (ⓣ065/905 2836) offers a variety of **meals** such as pasta, cajun chicken and wraps. Good-value bar food is available at *Crotty's*, which also hosts a traditional-music session (Tues) and is the focus for the mid-August traditional-music festival **Éigse Mrs Crotty** (ⓦwww.eigsemrscrotty.com), celebrating the late owner of the pub, an accomplished concertina-player. Other sessions occur at *The Way Inn*, Vandeleur Street (nightly in summer).

Scattery Island

In high season some three or four daily ferries run from Kilrush's marina to **Scattery Island**, two and a half kilometres offshore (Scattery Island Ferries; ⓣ065/905 1327, ⓦwww.discoverdolphins.ie; €12). A monastery was established here by St Senan in the sixth century, and the island retained ecclesiastical importance until its exposed position attracted Viking raiders in 870, who

The West Clare Railway

A few kilometres north of Kilrush at Moyasta is the only extant section of the renowned **West Clare Railway**, which opened in August 1892 and linked Ennis – via a roundabout route through Corofin – to southwest Clare until its closure in 1961. Much of the track was then sold to a Kenyan railway company, but the Moyasta station house and a two-kilometre stretch of the line have been restored and it's possible to take an enjoyable trip back and forth (April–Sept Mon–Sat 10am–6pm, Sun noon–6pm; €6; Ⓦwww.westclarerailway.ie).

The railway's fame owes much to the composer and singer Percy French who, along with his troupe of music-hall entertainers was due to play an engagement in Kilkee. Unfortunately, the train broke down in Miltown Malbay and, by means of a much-delayed replacement, French arrived late, discovering that most of his audience had already left. He sued the railroad for damages, winning the princely sum of £10 and wrote the song *Are Ye Right There Michael* as an account of his experiences, the Michael in question being Michael Talty, who was the guard on the train when the incident occurred.

occupied it until defeated by Brian Ború in the late tenth century. Medieval church building is evident in the form of several ruins, and there is a 35-metre-high **round tower** in reasonably well-preserved condition, which is most impressive when the sun seems to reflect off its yellowy, lichen-covered stone. This tower's door is at ground level whereas most others had an entrance above head-height, accessed by a ladder which could be withdrawn for defensive purposes. Derelict since the last inhabitants left almost thirty years ago, like many an abandoned Irish island, Scattery has a timeless air. A trip to its southern point, where a lighthouse and gun battery remain from the time of the Napoleonic wars, is well worth making, to experience a sense of peaceful isolation and enjoy the spectacular views from the elevated battery.

Kilkee

Thirteen kilometres northwest of Kilrush, **KILKEE** is a jaunty holiday resort, long popular with Limerick city folk, whose main attraction is a gorgeous, sandy, crescent-shaped **beach** that offers breathtaking cliff-top walks at both its ends. If the sun's obscured, there are plenty of other activities in Kilkee, including **scuba diving** at the Ocean Life Dive Centre at the East End Pier (Ⓣ065/905 6707, Ⓦwww.oceanlife.ie), and nearby Kilkee Waterworld (late April to May Sat & Sun 11am–5pm, June–Aug daily 11am–6pm; €6; Ⓣ065/905 6855, Ⓦwww.kilkeewaterworld.com), an indoor complex featuring an exciting sixty-metre water slide and other delights.

Kilkee's **tourist office**, on The Square (June to early Sept daily 9.30am–1pm & 2–5.30pm; Ⓣ065/905 6112, Ⓦwww.kilkee.ie), can help find rooms, and you might need its assistance during July and August. **B&B** choices include the seafront *Strand Guest House*, Strand Line (Ⓣ065/905 6177, Ⓦwww.clareguesthouse.com; ❸), and the *Thomond Guesthouse*, Grattan Street (Ⓣ065/905 6742, Ⓦwww.kilkeethalasso.com; ❷), which also provides thalasso therapy in the form of seaweed baths and other related relaxations (not included in the accommodation price). Alternatively, there's the *Marine Hotel* at the southern end of O'Curry Street (Ⓣ065/905 6722, Ⓦwww.marinhotelkilkee.ie; ❹), a modern establishment within a stone's throw of the seafront.

The best **eating** places include *Murphy Blacks* on The Square (Ⓣ065/905 6854) for excellent seafood and classic Irish specials and *The Strand Restaurant*,

Strand Line (Ⓣ065/905 6177), overlooking the beach, for more seafood delights. *Myles Creek* on O'Curry Street provides filling bar meals. Kilkee has plenty of **pubs** – *O'Mara's*, O'Curry Street, is a decent old-fashioned bar and sometimes has live music.

Loop Head

A tapering, elongated stretch of land, the **Loop Head peninsula** reaches southwest from Kilkee for some 25km. Though mostly low-lying, there are some staggering cliff-top walks; alternatively, it's possible to encompass virtually the whole peninsula by taking a very scenic signposted drive, either from Kilkee or from a couple of kilometres west of Moyasta. The latter route rounds Poulnasherry Bay before heading along the northern shore of the Shannon estuary, where there's a well-equipped **campsite** in a picturesque setting at **Doonaha** – *Green Acres* (Ⓣ065/905 7011; April–Sept).

Further on, the charming village of **CARRIGAHOLT** houses the ruins of a fifteenth-century castle commanding its harbour. *The Long Dock* nearby is a notable **traditional-music** pub (summer sessions Wed & Fri–Sun) and has filling bar **meals**. Alternatively, there's top-notch seafood at *Fennells* (Ⓣ065/905 8107; closed Mon & Tues) almost opposite. From the harbour Dolphinwatch runs summer trips to see and hear (through a hydrophone) the Shannon **dolphins** (see p.395; €22; 2hr; Ⓣ065/905 8156, Ⓦwww.dolphinwatch.ie; advance booking essential).

At scenic **KILBAHA**, approaching the peninsula's tip, *The Lighthouse Inn* serves both a decent pint and filling bar meals. To the north are the so-called **Bridges of Ross** at Ross Bay – natural arches formed by the ocean's erosion of the cliffs – though in fact there's now only one of the two. Five kilometres further west from Kilbaha, Loop Head itself has tremendous views of the Kerry Mountains to the south and as far north as the Twelve Bens of Connemara.

West Clare

More than any other area of Clare, the county's west is associated with **traditional music**. There's many a vibrant session in village pubs all along the coast and the town of **Miltown Malbay** hosts one of Ireland's major music festivals. There are plenty of sandy **beaches** too, notably at the attractive small resort of **Lahinch**. The famous towering **Cliffs of Moher** are further north near **Liscannor**, and close to the traditional-music magnet of seaside **Doolin** and, inland, the charmingly old-fashioned, small town of **Ennistymon**.

Miltown Malbay

Though set back some distance from the sea, **MILTOWN MALBAY**, 30km northeast of Kilkee, originated as a Victorian holiday resort. The town hosts the week-long **Willie Clancy Summer School** (Ⓦwww.setdancingnews.net/wcss/wcsst.htm), beginning on the first Saturday in July and named after the *uilleann* piper, singer and raconteur who died in 1973. More than a thousand people from all over the world turn up for the school's classes, and seats in the town's pubs for the sessions and at the concerts are at a premium.

Accommodation needs to be reserved well in advance, too, during the festival. B&Bs – all a little way out of town – include *An Gleann* (Ⓣ065/708 4281, Ⓔangleann@oceanfree.net; ❷) on the Ennis road, and *Berry Lodge*

(Ⓣ065/708 7022, Ⓦwww.berrylodge.com; ❷) south of the town in Annagh; owned by chef Rita Meade, cookery courses are offered here, and there is a fine **restaurant** (July & Aug; advance booking essential). Several bars in town also serve meals, but, for a treat, a better option is *The Black Oak* (May–Nov; closed Mon; Ⓣ065/708 4403), north of town in Rineen, which provides good-value and excellently presented dinners (around €30 plus wine) in a sea-view location. Of the attractive old **bars** along Miltown's main street, the best bets for **sessions** outside "Willie Week" are *Lynch's* (Wed, Fri & Sat) and *Hillery's* (Mon, Wed & Fri–Sun).

Lahinch

The little seaside resort of **LAHINCH**, 12km north of Miltown Malbay, is renowned for its glorious sandy strand. Right by the beach is **Seaworld**, with a 25-metre swimming pool, plus an aquarium with rock and touch pools, sea horses and lobsters (July–Sept; pool: daily 10am–8.30pm; aquarium: daily 10am–6pm; call for hours during other months; pool €8, aquarium €8, combined ticket €13; Ⓣ065/708 1900, Ⓦwww.iol.ie/~seaworld).

There's plenty of **accommodation** here, including the impressive family-run *Atlantic Hotel*, Main Street (Ⓣ065/708 1049, Ⓦwww.atlantichotel.ie; ❹), and a fine selection of B&Bs offering en-suite rooms – two just down the Ennistymon road are *Mulcarr House* (Ⓣ065/708 1123, Ⓦwww.esatclear.ie/~mulcarrhouse; ❷; mid-March to Oct) and *Tudor Lodge* (Ⓣ065/708 1270; ❷; April–Oct). Alternatively, there's *Lahinch Hostel* (IHH; Ⓣ065/708 1040, Ⓦwww.visitlahinch.com; dorms €17, doubles ❶) by the church at the bottom of Main Street, which rents bikes and has laundry facilities.

When hungry, head for *The Shamrock Inn*, Main Street, which serves very good bar **meals**. Nearby alternatives include *Danny Mac's*, a popular café-bar selling filling pancakes and providing **Internet** access, and *The Cornerstone*, which offers good seafood dishes. For a more upmarket marine dinner/Sunday lunch option, there's *Barrtrá* (Ⓣ065/708 1280; July & Aug daily, March–June & Sept closed Mon, Oct–Dec Fri–Sun only; closed all Jan & Feb; expect to pay around €40 plus wine), just over 5km south of Lahinch on the N67, which proffers not only excellent seafood, but has vegetarian options too. Several bars have **traditional music** in summer, including *The Cornerstone* (Thurs) and *The Nineteenth* (Sat), while *The Shamrock Inn* has a variety of other music at weekends.

Ennistymon

The relaxed town of **ENNISTYMON**, 4km east of Lahinch, promotes itself as "the town of old shop fronts", to which its long main street bears ample testimony. The town straddles the River Cullenagh and the **Cascades Walk**, signposted on Main Street, leads a little way along the bank past the falls whose waters tumble over rocks by an old arched bridge. Ennistymon's most famous son was the poet **Brian Merriman**, born here in 1747, who wrote the epic and particularly bawdy 1200-line poem, *The Midnight Court*.

Just down the Lahinch road, the Georgian-style *Falls Hotel* (Ⓣ065/707 1004, Ⓦwww.fallshotel.ie; ❺), set in woodlands by the water, provides very spruce and spacious **accommodation**. Excellent B&B is provided at *Byrne's* on Main Street (Ⓣ065/707 1080; ❷), with some rooms overlooking the river; there is also a **restaurant** providing fresh seafood. Another food option on the same street is *An Teach Bia*, which serves everything from full Irish breakfasts to fresh mussels. Main Street's old **bars** are especially good for traditional music so, for a session, head to *Daly's* (Thurs & Sun) or *Cooley's House* (Wed & Fri). There aren't many **ATMs** in West Clare, but you'll find one here on Parliament Street.

Liscannor and the Cliffs of Moher

The petite fishing village of **LISCANNOR**, with its trim cottages and tiny harbour, is a grand base for visiting the Cliffs of Moher. A couple of kilometres towards the cliffs, **The Rock Shop** shows an interesting film recounting the story of Liscannor flag, the local flagstone that peppers the area and used to be used in house building, as well as retailing handicrafts and numerous locally-found crystals and fossils. Liscannor's shoreline is dominated by *Logue's Liscannor* **hotel** (ⓣ065/708 6000, ⓦwww.loguesliscannorhotel.com; ❸), with very stylishly furnished rooms overlooking the bay, while opposite is the new and more petite *Cliffs of Moher Hotel* (ⓣ065/708 6670, ⓦwww.cliffsofmoherhotel.ie; ❺) which provides classy accommodation and service. For **B&B** try *Sea Haven* (ⓣ065/708 1385, ⓦwww.seahaven-liscannor.com; ❷), offering comfortable en-suite rooms with sea views. Both the hotels have decent restaurants and *Vaughan's* **pub** serves astonishingly good seafood all day, while the bar at the *Cliffs of Moher Hotel* commemorates locally born John P. Holland, a nineteenth-century pioneer in the development of the submarine.

Some 5km north of Liscannor are the **Cliffs of Moher**, stretching downwards to the Atlantic for almost 200m. The cliffs take their name from an old promontory fort, Mothar, and extend some 8km from Hag's Head, west of Liscannor, to a little beyond O'Brien's Tower, which was constructed by a local altruist in 1835 at their highest point. Access to the cliffs remains unrestricted, but, if you're travelling by car you'll be compelled to pay Clare County Council's extortionate parking charge of €8 for the privilege. Said sum "entitles" visitors (though exactly the same facilities are available if you arrive on bike or foot) to free entry to the controversial new €31.5million **visitor centre** (Jan & Feb 9.30am–5pm, March–April 9am–6pm, May & Sept 8.30am–7pm, June–Aug 8.30am–8.30pm, Oct 8.30am–6pm, Nov & Dec 9am–5pm) and to the infrequent "cliff edge" guided tours – enquire at the main desk for details.

Tucked away within the hillside, there's no doubting that the centre is an impressive architectural feat – and its first-floor **restaurant** does offer panoramic seascapes and a reasonable choice of meals – but to reach it you'll pass a somewhat tacky range of souvenir shops and find more of the same kind of "Oirish" gifts on sale within. The centre also houses the **Atlantic Edge** exhibition (same hours; €4; Heritage Island) whose interactive touch-screens, computer games and 3-D film (all to the accompaniment of ethereal "Celtic hush"–style music), do in part provide lucid explanations of the cliffs' evolution and wildlife, but overall form a ludicrous electronic counterpoint to the actual glories outside.

All told, the best bet is to head straight past the centre and to the newly erected steps which curve upwards towards the cliff-top. Then you can opt for turning south towards Hag's Head or in the opposite direction to O'Brien's Tower where the latter's viewing platform offers the best sight of the wave-battered cliffs below, enhanced by the resonant roar of the Atlantic waves pummelling the rocks at shore level. The optimum time to visit is around sunset when the heights and sea are spot-lit by the rays of the evening sun. Alternatively, you can gain a different perspective of their prodigious stature from one of the regular **boat-trips**. Cruises to view the cliffs operate from the pier at Doolin (see below; April–Oct 4 sailings daily; €25; ⓣ065/707 5949, ⓦwww.mohercruises.com).

Doolin

In the 1960s the then tiny village of **DOOLIN**, 7km north of the Cliffs of Moher, developed a reputation for its **traditional music**, largely thanks to the reputation of a bachelor farmer **Micho Russell**, a singer, flute and whistle player. Appreciation for his very natural and rhythmic playing resulted in TV and radio appearances and an international touring career. Attracted by his music, a trickle of enthusiasts began to visit Doolin's pubs to hear the playing of Micho and his two brothers Packie and Gussie, all sadly departed. Today, Doolin is awash with tourists virtually throughout the year, cramming into its **pubs** (*O'Connor's* in Fisher Street on the way to the harbour, *Fitzpatrick's Bar* in the *Hotel Doolin* – see below – and *McGann's* and *McDermott's* at the northern end) enticed by the village's renown. Unfortunately, most of the music churned out nightly is not the "pure drop", but either neatly adjusted to suit popular tastes or simply amplified garbage, and in truth there are many other and better places to hear Clare's often fabulous traditional music.

The village itself is not especially attractive either, sprawling across mainly flat land towards the sea and cluttered by an incoherently planned jumble of modern houses. Yet, for all its faults, you will occasionally strike lucky with a session and there's no doubting that the place does possess a certain charm.

There is a new attraction in the shape of **Doolin Cave** (mid-Feb to mid-March & Nov Fri–Sun noon–5pm; mid-March to June daily 11am–5pm; July–Sept daily 10am–6pm; Oct daily noon–5pm; €15, tickets purchased from the *Bruach na hAille* restaurant – see below; Ⓦwww.doolincave.ie), unquestionable highlight of the underground tour is a seven-metre silver-gleaming stalactite hanging from the ceiling of the dome-like central cavern.

Three local companies offer **boat-trips** from Doolin pier to the Aran Islands (see p.405 & p.432) and one of these, Moher Cruises, also provides trips to view the Cliffs of Moher.

Accommodation

Considering its size, Doolin probably offers more **accommodation** per square metre than anywhere else in Ireland and has several hostels to boot; plus you can **camp** by the sea at *Nagel's* (Ⓣ065/707 4558; April–Sept), near the pier.

Aille River Hostel Ⓣ065/707 4260, Ⓦwww.esatclear.ie/~ailleriver. Centrally situated cottage-style hostel offering a variety of small dorms and camping facilities. Dorms €15, doubles ❶.

Aran View House Ⓣ065/707 4061, Ⓦwww.aranview.com. Set above the village on the coast road, this is a fine country-house hotel offering tremendous views from its very attractive rooms and tasty seafood in its restaurant.

Cullinan's Guesthouse Ⓣ065/707 4183, Ⓦwww.cullinansdoolin.com. Excellent B&B run by welcoming hosts, adjacent to the T-junction in the village centre. It features very comfortable and well-appointed en-suite rooms, and has a splendid restaurant specializing in seafood. ❸

Doonmacfelim House Ⓣ065/707 4503, Ⓦwww.doonmacfelim.com. Also in the village centre, this is a beautifully kept farmhouse with its own tennis court. ❷

Hotel Doolin Ⓣ065/707 4111, Ⓦwww.hoteldoolin.ie. Opposite *Cullinan's*, this new establishment certainly offers Doolin's plushest accommodation and includes a restaurant, pizzeria, café and *Fitzpatrick's Bar*. ❺

Rainbow Hostel Ⓣ065/707 4415, Ⓔrainbowhostel@eircom.net. Unquestionably the cosiest Doolin hostel, by *McDermott's* pub in the north of the village. It's well-equipped and family-run with bike rental available. Dorms €15, doubles ❶.

Eating

Most **restaurants** are at Doolin's northern end and tend to open only in the evenings. They include: the swish *Bruach na hAille* (Ⓣ065/707 4120), by

McGann's, with fine seafood and vegetarian options; just around the corner, the *Lazy Lobster* (☎065/707 4390; closed Mon), offering a delicious seafood menu; and *Roadford House* (☎065/707 5050), which serves fish, shellfish and meat dishes. All three pubs and several accommodation providers (see above) also serve meals at reasonable prices.

The Burren

The Burren's name derives from the Irish word *boireann*, meaning "stony place", a particularly apt description for this massive, desolate plateau that occupies most of the county's northwest. Its northern and western reaches almost clutch the sea while, to the south and east, the rocks gently slope towards lush green fields. Formed mainly of fissured limestone pavement, pitted by occasional valleys hidden beneath ominous-looking cliffs, The Burren is a thoroughly unworldly place with barely a sign of life. The starkness of the landscape, crisp white in sunlight, deep grey-brown in rainfall, has a primeval allure and remains utterly fascinating. Few now live within its bounds, but many endured this harsh environment in the distant past, leaving many relics of their inhabitation. Ancient burial practices are reflected in the abundance of **Stone Age** monuments, while later inhabitants built ring forts, circular stone dwellings, during the **Iron Age**, many of which remain in a fine state of preservation. Most of the subsequent medieval **Christian remains** are scattered around the area's more fertile fringes.

The area's coastal outskirts include attractive resorts such as lively **Ballyvaughan** and tiny **Fanore**, while inland are the spa town of **Lisdoonvarna**, famous for its matchmaking festival, and the renowned traditional-music village **Kilfenora**; all make fine bases for investigating The Burren. If you lack your own **transport**, bikes can be rented in Doolin and Ballyvaughan, or you could take a coach trip from Ennis. However, a grasp of the landscape's subtleties can

▲ The Burren

only really be achieved by **walking**. Tim Robinson's exceptionally detailed **maps**, covering different parts of the area are widely available in the county; a compass is an advisable accessory as there's a dearth of obvious landmarks. Alternatively, an excellent way to explore the area is via a trip organized by Burren Hill Walks, Corkscrew Hill, Ballyvaughan (Ⓣ065/707 7168, Ⓦhomepage.eircom.net/~burrenhillwalks), which runs a mixture of themed walks and treks.

Lisdoonvarna

LISDOONVARNA, 8km east of Doolin, is an attractive small town that developed in the nineteenth century around its old spa – its sulphated waters can usually be sampled at the **Spa Wells Health Centre**'s pumphouse (closed at the time of writing). Reinvigoration aside, Lisdoonvarna's calendar is focused upon its **matchmaking festival** (Ⓦwww.matchmakerireland.com), an annual September rally for the lovelorn, which runs for almost a month. The festival dates back to the times when dealers at street fairs acted as matchmakers, arranging marriages for bachelor farmers, too land-tied to seek their own nuptial bliss. Today, the event features all manner of entertainment in the bars and hotels geared towards bringing couples together. Drawing an international attendance, it's a hugely popular affair and accommodation can be hard to find for miles around while it's on.

Awash with **hotels** (though most close once the matchmaking festival is over or even earlier), two of the town's smaller establishments are the most appealing. Both offer very amenable rooms: welcoming *Rathbaun Hotel* (Ⓣ065/707 4009, Ⓦwww.rathbaunhotel.com; ❷; April to mid-Oct), and attractive *Sheedy's Country House Hotel* (Ⓣ065/707 4026, Ⓦwww.sheedys.com; ❹; mid-March to Sept), the oldest building in the village, but with a stylishly refurbished interior. For **B&B** there's the very comfortable *Marchmont* (Ⓣ065/707 4050; ❷; March–Nov), a modern townhouse, or pleasant *Blackbridge House* (Ⓣ065/707 5934, Ⓦwww.blackbridgehouse.com; ❷; March to mid-Oct). Lastly, just down the road to Doolin is the new and excellently equipped An Óige–affiliated *Sleepzone* **hostel** (Ⓣ091/566999, Ⓦwww.sleepzone.ie/sleepzonebur.html; dorms €18, doubles ❶), set in the landscaped grounds of a former hotel

Most of the town's pubs and hotels serve **food**. *The Roadside Tavern* is particularly fine, especially for Sunday lunch and offers the best summertime **traditional music** (Thurs–Sat) alongside the *Royal Spa Hotel* which has nightly sessions in summer and also serves excellent pizzas.

Kilfenora

Nine kilometres southeast of Lisdoonvarna, the village of **KILFENORA** is one of Clare's most celebrated **traditional-music** centres. Its fame is intrinsically linked to the Kilfenora Céilí Band, Ireland's oldest and most illustrious, and on summer Wednesday nights the KCB plays in *Linnane's* pub. *Vaughan's* pub has set dancing in its barn (Thurs & Sun) as well as a session in the pub itself (Tues), while *Nagle's* has a session on Sundays.

Here too is the **Burren Centre** (daily: mid-March to May, Sept & Oct 10am–5pm; June–Aug 9.30am–6pm; €6; Ⓦwww.theburrencentre.ie; Heritage Island), which provides an entertaining account of the area's history, including imaginatively constructed, sometimes interactive displays and models explaining its geology and antiquities. Hard by the Centre stands the ruined twelfth-century **Kilfenora Cathedral**, the site of the county's largest concentration of high crosses. The twelfth-century Doorty Cross in the chancel is especially impressive; its faces depict various ecclesiasts and a scene from the Crucifixion.

The village has a central **B&B**, *Murphy's* (ⓣ065/708 8040, ⓔlika@eircom.net; ❶), offering en-suite accommodation, as well as two more down the Lisdoonvarna road. The very well equipped *Kilfenora Hostel* (IHO; ⓣ065/708 8908, ⓦwww.kilfenorahostel.com) is situated next door to *Vaughan's* pub and has spacious dorms (€20) and private rooms (❶).

Around the coast to Ballyvaughan

One of the most dramatic routes around The Burren is the R477, which traces the shoreline from a few kilometres northwest of Lisdoonvarna to the striking village of **Ballyvaughan**. Inland, and inaccessible by car, is a crisscross pattern of the old "green roads", offering splendid upland walking and majestic panoramic views.

From Lisdoonvarna to Ballyvaughan

Just 3km northwest of Lisdoonvarna, near the junction with the R479 Doolin road, you'll spot **Ballynalackan Castle**, a fifteenth-century tower house, perched high above the road. If you fancy splashing out on a **meal**, it's well worth taking the signposted lane up to *Ballinalacken Country House* (ⓣ065/707 4025, ⓦwww.ballinalackencastle.com; mid-April to Oct), a converted Victorian mansion serving sumptuous dinners (closed Tues), often using local produce such as scallops and lamb. Accommodation is also available (❺) and some of the bedrooms enjoy fantastic views of the Aran Islands and the Cliffs of Moher.

The coast road north of Ballynalackan is dramatic but desolate, sometimes shrouded in the mornings by the haze of a sea-fret. The only sizeable place on the way to Ballyvaughan is the straggling street-village of **FANORE** which has a sweeping Blue Flag beach, the excellent *Holywell La Trattoria* (ⓣ065/707 6971; June–Sept evenings plus Sat & Sun lunchtimes) and *O'Donoghue's* pub, which has ballad singers on summer Saturday nights. **B&Bs** in the village include *Annaly House* (ⓣ065/707 6154, ⓦhomepage.eircom.net/~annalyhsfanore; ❶; April–Oct), set on a working farm, and *Seacoast Lodge* (ⓣ065/707 6250 ⓔseacoastbb@eircom.net; ❷; mid-March to Oct), near the beach, both offering very relaxing en-suite rooms. The Burren Riding Centre (ⓣ065/707 6140, ⓔburrenriding.ennis@eircom.net) operates **horse riding**, including trails along the "green roads", trekking in The Burren and beach hacks. If you fancy learning to **surf**, then the Aloha Surf School (ⓣ087 213 3996, ⓦwww.surfschool.tv) provides all necessary equipment.

Five kilometres further on, the road rounds Black Head where you can climb up to **Caheerdooneerish** ring fort and gaze across Galway Bay before heading onwards to Ballyvaughan.

Ballyvaughan

Built in 1829 to assist the fishing industry, **BALLYVAUGHAN**'s harbour saw the village develop as a major trading centre and, not long afterwards, steamers began to ply between here and Galway, bringing visitors and establishing the tourist trade. It's an eye-catching village, especially when the sun gleams on its predominantly white and cream houses, and an ideal base for exploring The Burren. **Accommodation** includes eighteenth-century *Hyland's Burren Hotel* (ⓣ065/707 7037, ⓦwww.hylandsburren.com; ❹; closed Jan), with pleasant modern facilities, as well as high-quality B&B at *Ballyvaughan Lodge* (ⓣ065/707 7292,

Ⓦwww.ballyvaughanlodge.com;❷).Tranquil *Dolmen Lodge*, Tonarussa (Ⓣ065/707 7202, Ⓔolmenlodge@eircom.net; ❷; April to mid-Oct), a farmhouse 800m east of the village, has a more rural setting; or there's the luxurious, eighteenth-century *Gregans Castle Hotel* (Ⓣ065/707 7005, Ⓦwww.gregans.ie; doubles ❺, suites ❼; April to late Oct), 5km south of Ballyvaughan on the N67, which offers stylish rooms and suites in a very scenic location. Just down the N67, J. Connole (Ⓣ065/707 7061) rents **bikes** and operates a service **laundry**. The adjacent Brendan's Boats provides **Internet access**.

Ballyvaughan has plenty of **eating** places. Out on the Galway road, the seaside *Whitethorn Restaurant & Crafts* (Ⓣ065/707 7044; mid-March to Oct daily 9.30am–6pm, Fri & Sat until 9.30pm) supplies a delicious range of modern Irish cuisine, and back in the village, *Hyland's Burren Hotel* provides wholesome bar meals. For summertime **traditional music**, head to *Hyland's Burren Hotel* (Mon) or *O'Brien's* (Fri–Sun).

Burren sites

Roads south from Ballyvaughan lead to a wealth of ancient and some medieval sites. A kilometre or so down the R480 and off to the west is **Newtown Castle** (June–Sept daily; free; call Ⓣ065/707 7200 for times), a restored sixteenth-century tower house with walls almost four metres thick, murder holes and gun loops, now part of the grounds of the Burren College of Art. The ground-floor circular chamber was once a larder and a spiral stair leads upwards to the main hall on the third floor, where windows offer magnificent views in every direction. Back on the R480 and a little further south, **Aillwee Cave** (6 tours daily 10am–5.30pm; July & Aug until 6.30pm; closed Dec afternoons; €12; Ⓦwww.aillweecave.ie; Heritage Island) is reckoned to be two million years old. Guided tours visit caverns and bridged chasms, allowing you to marvel at weird rock formations, numerous stalagmites and stalactites, and the hibernation chambers of a long-extinct species of brown bear.

About 3km south of the cave, and just off the eastern side of the R480, is the **Gleninsheen Wedge Tomb**, the best preserved of its kind in the area. In 1930 a remarkable finely worked gold collar was discovered here by a boy hunting rabbits and is now held by Dublin's National Museum. Just a kilometre south from here is the **Poulnabrone dolmen**, the best known of The Burren's seventy or so megalithic tombs. When excavated in 1986 the remains of some thirty people were uncovered along with several tools, utensils and items of jewellery, providing evidence that the tomb dated from around 2500 BC.

A kilometre further south is **Caherconnell Stone Fort**, the most substantial of The Burren's many ancient remains. Such circular homesteads, with their dry-stone walling, were built from around the fifth century onwards; this one is some 40m in diameter with nearly four-metre-thick walls. The **visitor centre** here (daily: March–June & Sept–Oct 10am–5pm; July & Aug 10am–6pm; €5; Ⓦwww.burrenforts.ie) provides a "virtual tour" of the fort with displays recounting how the daily life of its residents might have been spent, as well as describing the building's design and other Burren monuments.

Continuing onwards, by the junction with the R476 is another O'Brien fortress, **Leamaneh Castle** (open access), which, though long abandoned, is still in reasonable shape. Its tower dates from around 1480 and the adjoining four-storey house with its segmented windows was added in 1640 by Conor O'Brien.

From here it's worth backtracking past Caherconnell and taking a detour along the first road east to **CARRON**, birthplace of Michael Cusack, a co-founder of the Gaelic Athletic Association (see p.117), commemorated by a monument next to the old school and by a recently built **visitor centre** (April–Oct daily 10am–5.30pm; €5; ⓦwww.michaelcusack.ie) which incorporates the Cusack family cottage and provides information on not only his life and times, but the history of the GAA and the local Burren environment. The hamlet also contains *Cassidy's* pub, housed in a former barracks, with excellent bar **meals** (April–Oct) and traditional-music sessions on Fridays plus a folk singer or session on Saturdays, and a pleasant **hostel**, *Clare's Rock* (ⓣ065/708 9129; dorms €14, ❶; late-April to Sept).

Corcomroe Abbey and New Quay

Heading north from Carron, the barren Burren gradually descends, becoming increasingly lush as it approaches the coast. Just before Bell Harbour, a turning leads to the well-preserved remains of twelfth-century **Corcomroe Abbey**, a Cistercian foundation set in a valley. Inside the church is an altar-tomb bearing an effigy of a king, believed to be an O'Brien, who died in 1267. Other buildings include an infirmary-cum-guesthouse and a gatehouse, plus part of a cloister. Some 4km north of Bell Harbour, off the N67 Galway road, is tiny **New Quay**, a fishing village renowned for *Linnane's Lobster Bar*, which serves delicious seafood.

Travel details

Ferries to the Aran Islands

Aran Islands Fast Ferries
ⓣ065/707 4550 or 086 881 9052, ⓦwww.aranislandsfastferries.com.
Doolin to: Inisheer (April–early Sept every 90min in peak season; 25min) and Inishmore (April to early Sept 2–4 daily; 1hr); calls at Inishmaan if there's enough demand.

Doolin Ferries
ⓣ065/707 4455, ⓦwww.doolinferries.com
Doolin to: Inisheer (April, May, Sept & Oct 3 daily, June–Aug 4 daily; 30min); Inishmore (April–Oct 2 daily; 1hr 15min).

Moher Cruises
ⓣ065/707 5949, ⓦwww.mohercruises.com
Doolin to: Inisheer (April–Oct 1–2 daily; 30min).

Trains

Ennis to: Limerick (8–9 daily; 40min).
Limerick to: Cork (7–9 daily, with a change at Limerick Junction; 2hr); Dublin Heuston (11–14 daily, often with a change at Limerick Junction; 2hr 20min–2hr 40min); Ennis (8 daily; 40min); Waterford (Mon–Sat 3 daily, with a change at Limerick Junction; 2hr 40min).

Buses

Bus Éireann
Services are listed below and, in addition to these, the #50 operates from late June to the end of August from Galway to Tralee (via Ballyvaughan, Lisdoonvarna, Doolin, the Cliffs of Moher, Lahinch, Miltown Malbay, Kilkee and Kilrush) at 8.40am daily – during the same period a 2pm service goes as far as Lahinch and a 6pm one terminates in Doolin. The return service during the same period and via the same route leaves Tralee at 3.30pm daily and there's also one from Doolin to Galway (Mon–Sat 8.40am). These services are not included in the following listings.
Ballyvaughan to: Cliffs of Moher (1 daily; 55min); Doolin (Mon–Sat 2 daily, Sun 1; 40min); Galway (Mon–Sat 2 daily, Sun 1; 1hr 10min); Kinvara (Mon–Sat 2 daily, Sun 1; 30min); Lisdoonvarna (Mon, Wed, Fri & Sat 2 daily, Tues, Thurs & Sun 1 daily; 25min).
Bunratty to: Ennis (14 daily; 35min); Limerick (Mon–Sat 22–24 daily, Sun 11; 25min).
Corofin to: Ennis (1 daily; 15–25min); Ennistymon (1 daily; 25min); Kilfenora (1 daily; 15min); Lahinch (1 daily; 35min).
Doolin to: Ballyvaughan (2 daily; 40min); Cliffs of Moher (3 daily; 15–30min); Ennis (2 daily; 1hr 30min); Ennistymon (2 daily; 45min); Galway (2 daily; 1hr 35min–2hr 10min); Lahinch (2 daily;

1hr 10min); Lisdoonvarna (3–4 daily; 15min).
Ennis to: Bunratty (14 daily; 35min); Cliffs of Moher (2–3 daily; 50min); Cork (12 daily; 3hr 5min); Corofin (1 daily; 20min); Doolin (3 daily; 1hr 15min); Ennistymon (Mon–Sat 3–4 daily, Sun 2; 35min); Feakle (Thurs 1; 55min); Galway (14–15 daily; 1hr 20min); Kilkee (Mon–Sat 4 daily, Sun 2; 1hr 10min); Kilfenora (Tues–Thurs & Sat 1 daily; 40min); Kilrush (Mon–Sat 4 daily, 2 Sun; 55min); Lahinch (Mon–Sat 3–4 daily, Sun 2; 40min); Limerick (12–14 daily; 50min); Liscannor (2–3 daily; 45min); Lisdoonvarna (2–3 daily; 1hr 10min); Shannon Airport (10–14 daily; 50min–1hr); Tulla (Thurs 1; 35min).
Ennistymon to: Doolin (2 daily; 40–50min); Ennis (2 daily; 35min); Lahinch (2 daily; 5–10min).
Feakle to: Ennis (1 Thurs; 50min); Gort (Fri 1; 35min); Tulla (1 Thurs; 20min).
Kilfenora to: Corofin (Tues–Sun 1 daily; 15min); Ennis (Tues–Sun 1 daily; 40min); Ennistymon (Tues–Sun 1 daily; 10min); Lahinch (Tues–Sun 1 daily; 20min).
Kilkee to: Ennis (Mon–Sat 2 daily, Sun 1; 1hr 10min); Kilrush (Mon–Sat 2 daily, Sun 1; 15min).
Killaloe to: Limerick (Mon–Sat 2–3 daily; 55min); Nenagh (Mon–Fri 2 daily; 35min).
Kilrush to: Ennis (Mon–Sat 3 daily, Sun 2; 55min); Kilkee (Mon–Sat 3–4 daily, Sun 2; 15min).
Lahinch to: Cliffs of Moher (2 daily; 10min); Doolin (2 daily; 45min); Ennis (1 daily; 45min–1hr); Ennistymon (2 daily; 5–10min); Liscannor (2 daily; 5min); Lisdoonvarna (2 daily; 30min); Miltown Malbay (Mon–Sat 1 daily; 20min).
Limerick to: Adare (hourly; 20min); Athlone (2–4 daily; 2hr 10min); Birr (Mon–Fri 1 daily; 1hr 30min); Bunratty (10–17 daily; 20min); Cliffs of Moher (1–3 daily; 1hr 50min); Cork (hourly; 1hr 50min); Doolin (1–2 daily; 2hr 15min); Dublin (hourly; 3hr 40min); Ennis (hourly; 50min); Galway (hourly; 2hr 30min); Killaloe (4–5 Mon–Sat; 50min); Killarney (every 2hr; 2hr); Lisdoonvarna (1–2 daily; 2hr); Listowel (8–9 daily; 1hr 30min); Mount-shannon (1 Sat; 1hr 25min); Nenagh (13 daily; 45min); Shannon Airport (Mon–Sat frequent service, Sun at least hourly; 30–55min); Tralee (8–9 daily; 2hr); Tulla (1 Wed; 55min); Waterford (6–8 daily; 2hr 30min).
Lisdoonvarna to: Ballyvaughan (Mon–Sat 2 daily, Sun 1; 25–45min); Cliffs of Moher (3 daily; 15–25min); Doolin (3 daily; 15min); Ennis (2 daily; 1hr 10min); Lahinch (2 daily; 35min); Galway (2 daily; 1hr 20min).
Miltown Malbay to: Ennis (Mon–Fri 2 daily, Sat & Sun 1 daily; 40min–1hr 20min); Ennistymon (Mon–Sat 1 daily; 30min); Lahinch (1 daily; 20min).
Mountshannon to: Limerick (Sat 1; 1hr 20min).
Shannon Airport to: Cork (13 daily; 2hr 35min); Ennis (Mon–Sat 13–15, Sun 10; 35–50min); Galway (12 daily; 1hr 50min–2hr10min); Limerick (Mon–Sat 24–28 daily, Sun 11; 50min).
Tulla to: Ennis (Thurs 1; 35min); Feakle (Thurs 1; 20min); Limerick (Wed 1; 50min).

10

Galway and Mayo

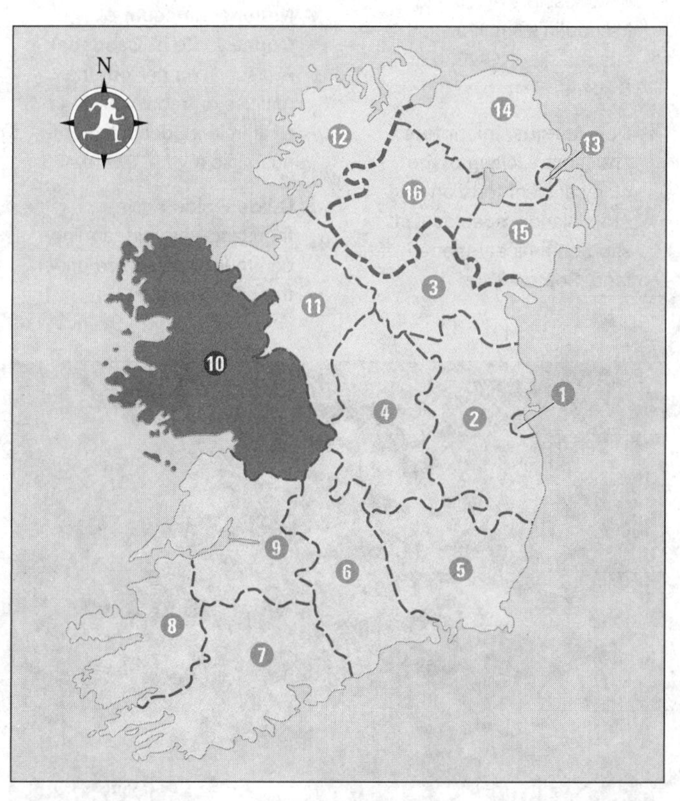

CHAPTER 10 Highlights

* **Galway festivals and pubs** It's hard not to have a good time in the vibrant, youthful capital of the west. See box on p.412 & p.420

* **Islands** Choose between the wild beauty of the Arans, the grandiose scenery of accessible Achill and Inishbofin's small-scale charms. See p.429, p.464 & p.449

* **Dun Aengus, Inishmore** The most exciting of the many ancient forts on the Aran Islands, spectacularly sited on a ninety-metre cliff face. See p.435

* **Walking in Connemara** The best way to appreciate the dramatic mountains, bogs and lakes. See box on p.441

* **Croagh Patrick** A tough climb, enriched by historical and religious associations, and outstanding views. See p.458

* **National Museum of Country Life at Castlebar** A fascinating peek at the realities of traditional life in rural Ireland, debunking the nostalgic myths. See p.463

* **Céide Fields** A five-thousand-year-old farming community preserved under the bog. See p.467

▲ Galway nightlife

10

Galway and Mayo

Sweeping strokes of geology have carved up the landscape of Galway and Mayo, forming a many-pronged block between Galway and Donegal bays that's almost cut off from the mainland by a string of lakes. In the south, the forty-kilometre stretch of Lough Corrib neatly bisects **County Galway**, the second largest county in Ireland after Cork. On one side, the largely flat, gentle grasslands of **east Galway** stretch across to the Shannon, sheltering a fascinating diversity of historic castles, cathedrals, monasteries and country estates. Between Corrib and the sea, however, stands the violent jumble of **Connemara**, a much-romanticized land, but with plenty to get sentimental about. Interest here is provided in abundance by the ever-changing scenery of beaches, bogs, lakes and wild mountains, though if you're looking for specific tourist attractions, there's a diverting cluster around the lakeside village of **Oughterard**. **Clifden**, however, is the main base, boasting a fine range of facilities at the heart of the mountains.

On the narrow neck of land between these eastern and western halves sits **Galway city**, an animated historic town with an enjoyable social, musical and artistic life. The city gives a whiff of the Gaelic culture that's far more noticeable out on the **Arans**, starkly beautiful islands that used to form a barrier across the entrance to Galway Bay. As well as sheltering some breathtaking prehistoric and early Christian sites, the islands are part of the country's largest Irish-speaking area, which also comprises the eastern section of Connemara.

Though ranking just behind Galway in terms of size, **County Mayo** has only half its population and is far less developed for tourism. An exception is the eighteenth-century planned town of **Westport**, a comfortable, elegant base from which to tackle the pilgrims' path to the top of **Croagh Patrick**, and to visit the diverse inhabited **islands** at the mouth of Clew Bay. In the north of the county, the intriguing Neolithic agricultural remains at **Céide Fields** provide a compelling focus, surrounded by kilometre after unexplored kilometre of desolate bogland and rugged seascapes.

Galway city

Known for its festivals, music and bars, **GALWAY** (Gaillimh; Ⓦwww.galway.net) is a vibrant, fun-loving city and, though it has few sights to visit, many people end up staying here longer than intended. In the last thirty years, Galway has rediscovered the prosperity that came from trading in the fifteenth to seventeenth centuries and is now the fastest growing city in western Europe. Conveniently,

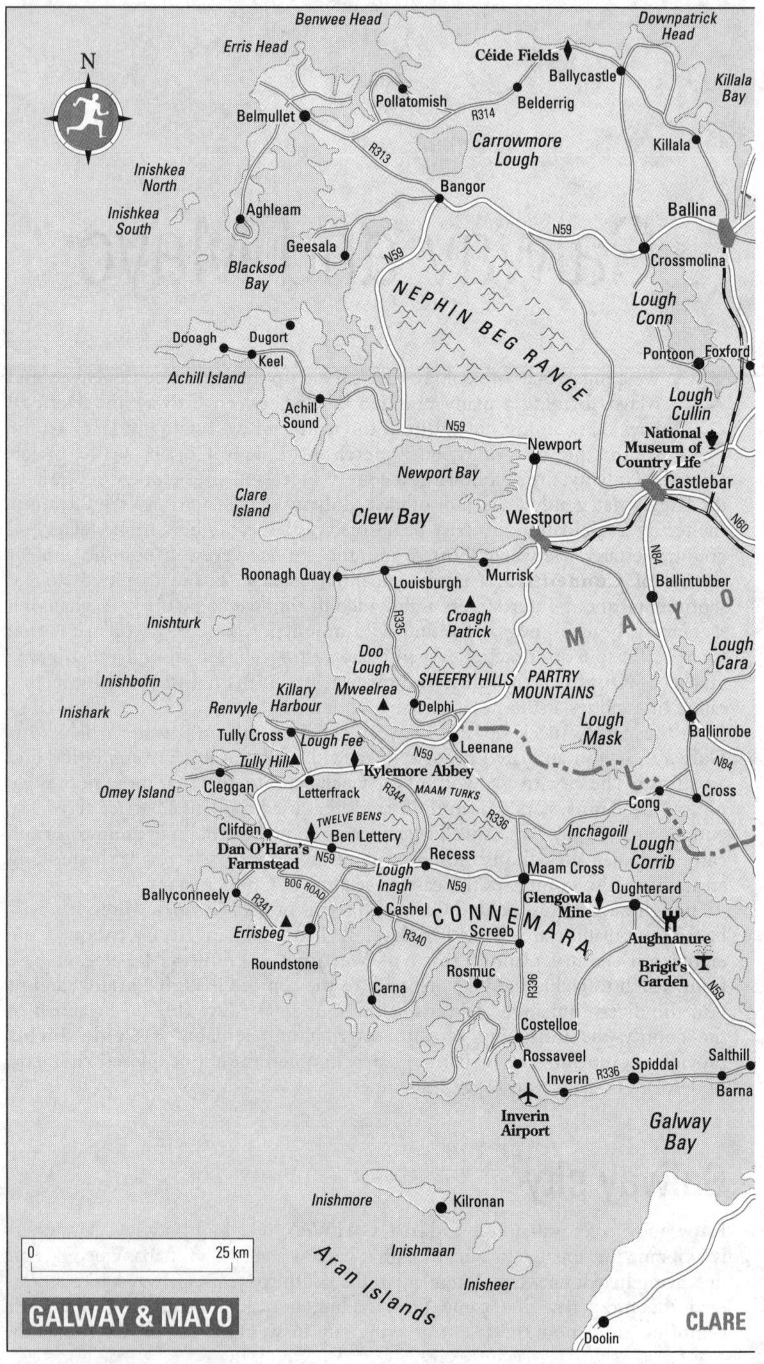
N
Benwee Head
Erris Head
Downpatrick Head
Céide Fields
Ballycastle
Killala Bay
Pollatomish
Belderrig
Belmullet
R314
Carrowmore Lough
Killala
R313
Inishkea North
Inishkea South
Aghleam
Bangor
Ballina
Geesala
N59
Crossmolina
Blacksod Bay
NEPHIN BEG RANGE
Lough Conn
Dooagh
Dugort
Keel
Achill Island
Pontoon
Foxford
Achill Sound
Lough Cullin
N59
National Museum of Country Life
Newport
Newport Bay
Castlebar
Clare Island
Clew Bay
Westport
N60
N84
Roonagh Quay
Louisburgh
Murrisk
Ballintubber
R335
Croagh Patrick
MAYO
Inishturk
Lough Cara
Doo Lough
SHEEFRY HILLS
PARTRY MOUNTAINS
Inishbofin
Killary Harbour
Mweelrea
Inishark
Renvyle
Delphi
Lough Mask
Ballinrobe
Tully Cross
Lough Fee
Leenane
Tully Hill
N59
Kylemore Abbey
N84
Omey Island
Cleggan
Letterfrack
R344
MAAM TURKS
Cross
Cong
TWELVE BENS
R336
Inchagoill
Clifden
Ben Lettery
Lough Corrib
Dan O'Hara's Farmstead
N59
Recess
Lough Inagh
Maam Cross
BOG ROAD
N59
Oughterard
Ballyconneely
Glengowla Mine
R341
Cashel
CONNEMARA
Errisbeg
Screeb
Aughnanure
R340
Roundstone
Brigit's Garden
Rosmuc
R336
N59
Carna
Costelloe
Rossaveel
Salthill
Spiddal
Inverin
R336
Barna
Inverin Airport
Galway Bay
Inishmore
Kilronan
0
25 km
Inishmaan
Aran Islands
Inisheer
GALWAY & MAYO
CLARE
Doolin

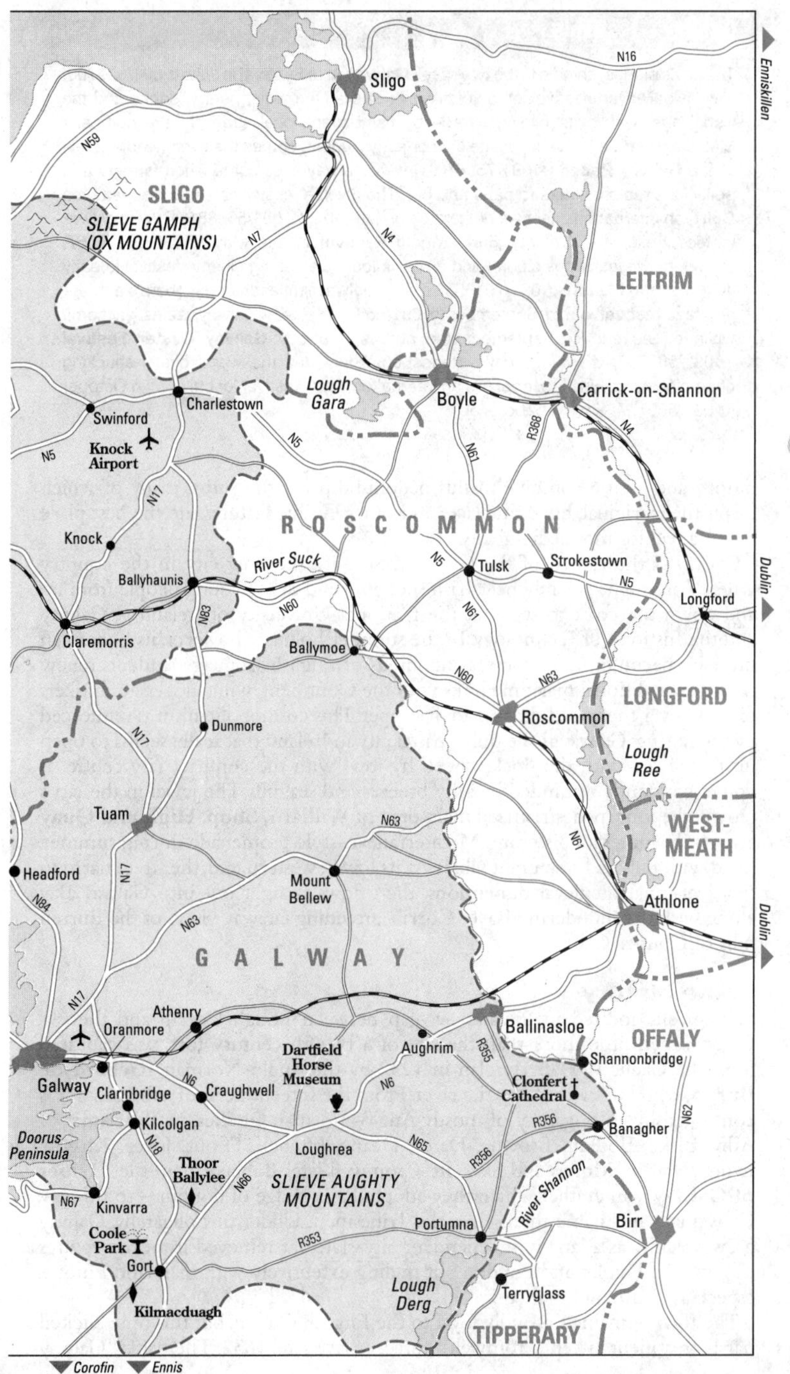

Sligo
N16
Enniskillen
N59
SLIGO
SLIEVE GAMPH
(OX MOUNTAINS)
N7
N4
LEITRIM
Lough
Gara
Charlestown
Boyle
Carrick-on-Shannon
Swinford
R368
N4
Knock
Airport
N5
N5
N61
N17
ROSCOMMON
Knock
River Suck
N5
Tulsk
Strokestown
Dublin
Ballyhaunis
N5
Longford
N83
N60
N61
Claremorris
Ballymoe
N60
N63
LONGFORD
Roscommon
Dunmore
N17
Lough
Ree
Tuam
N63
WEST-
MEATH
N61
Headford
N17
Mount
Bellew
N84
Athlone
Dublin
N63
GALWAY
N17
Athenry
Oranmore
Ballinasloe
OFFALY
Dartfield
Horse
Museum
Aughrim
R355
Shannonbridge
Galway
N6
Clarinbridge
Craughwell
N6
Clonfert
Cathedral
Kilcolgan
R356
Banagher
N62
Doorus
Peninsula
N18
Loughrea
N65
R356
Thoor
Ballylee
N66
SLIEVE AUGHTY
MOUNTAINS
River Shannon
N67
Kinvarra
Portumna
Birr
Coole
Park
R353
Gort
Lough
Derg
Terryglass
Kilmacduagh
TIPPERARY
Corofin
Ennis

Galway's festivals

The city's biggest shindig is the two-week **Galway Arts Festival** in July (Ⓣ091/509700, Ⓦwww.galwayartsfestival.ie), a volatile mix of drama, music, poetry, dance and the visual arts, with a headlining parade by flamboyant local street-theatre company Macnas. Hard on its heels, in late July or early August, comes the even headier brew of the **Galway Races** (Ⓣ091/753870, Ⓦwww.galwayraces.com), when farmers and politicians rub shoulders to party and bet. The diverse festival calendar also features **Cúirt**, an international festival of literature in late April (Ⓣ091/565886, Ⓦwww.galwayartscentre.ie), the **Galway Early Music Festival** in late May (Ⓣ090/662 5057, Ⓦwww.galwayearlymusic.com) and a prestigious, week-long cinema festival in early July, the **Film Fleadh** (Ⓣ091/751655, Ⓦwww.galwayfilmfleadh.com). There's a three-day **jazz festival** in mid-September (Ⓣ091/569777, Ⓦwww.galwayjazzfestival.com), while at the end of September, the riotous, four-day **Galway Oyster Festival** (Ⓣ091/587992, Ⓦwww.galwayoysterfest.com) includes the world oyster-shucking championships. Finally, **Baboró** is an international arts festival for children in October (Ⓣ091/569777, Ⓦwww.baboro.ie).

history and leisure combine in this hedonistic place: the **pubs**, many of which retain their original, huge fireplaces and other Gothic features, are the best place to get a feel for the medieval city.

Galway is the capital of the Gaelic West – it's the only city in the country where you might possibly hear Irish spoken – and draws young people from up and down the coast to study at the National University of Ireland at Galway and the Institute of Technology. In the summer holidays, however, its bohemian diversity becomes more overt, as hundreds of English-language students renew the city's traditional maritime links with the Continent, while dozens of buskers from all over the world sing for their supper. This cosmopolitanism is reinforced by the setting: Galway is the only coastal city in Ireland that really seems to open up to the sea, with the docks cheek by jowl with the compact city centre, as you're constantly reminded by salty breezes and seagulls. The jewel in the city's crown, the long, pedestrianized main drag of **William, Shop, High and Quay streets**, becomes a boisterous, Mediterranean-style promenade during summer, lined with pub and restaurant tables. At its lower, western end, the street narrows to its original medieval dimensions, then flows straight out into Galway Bay along with the thundering River Corrib, providing faraway views of the Burren hills of County Clare.

Some history

Strategically located in the narrow gap between Lough Corrib and the sea, Galway, then little more than the site of a twelfth-century fort, was captured from the Gaelic O'Flaherty clan in 1232 by the Anglo-Norman **Richard de Burgo**, who built a castle by the river. From the fifteenth century, the town was controlled by an oligarchy of mostly Anglo-Norman families, by the names of Athy, Blake, Bodkin, Browne, Darcy, Deane, Ffrench, Ffront, Joyce, Kirwan, Lynch, Martin, Morris and Skerrett. Cromwell later dubbed them the "**Tribes of Galway**", an epithet which they adopted as a badge of honour – to this day, Galwegians nickname themselves the Tribesmen. Under this oligarchy, Galway grew wealthy as a largely independent city-state, far removed from the centres of power in Dublin and London but trading extensively with mainland Europe, especially Spain and France.

The town remained proudly loyal to the English Crown, but this only elicited harsh treatment when Cromwell's forces arrived in 1652. Thereafter, Galway

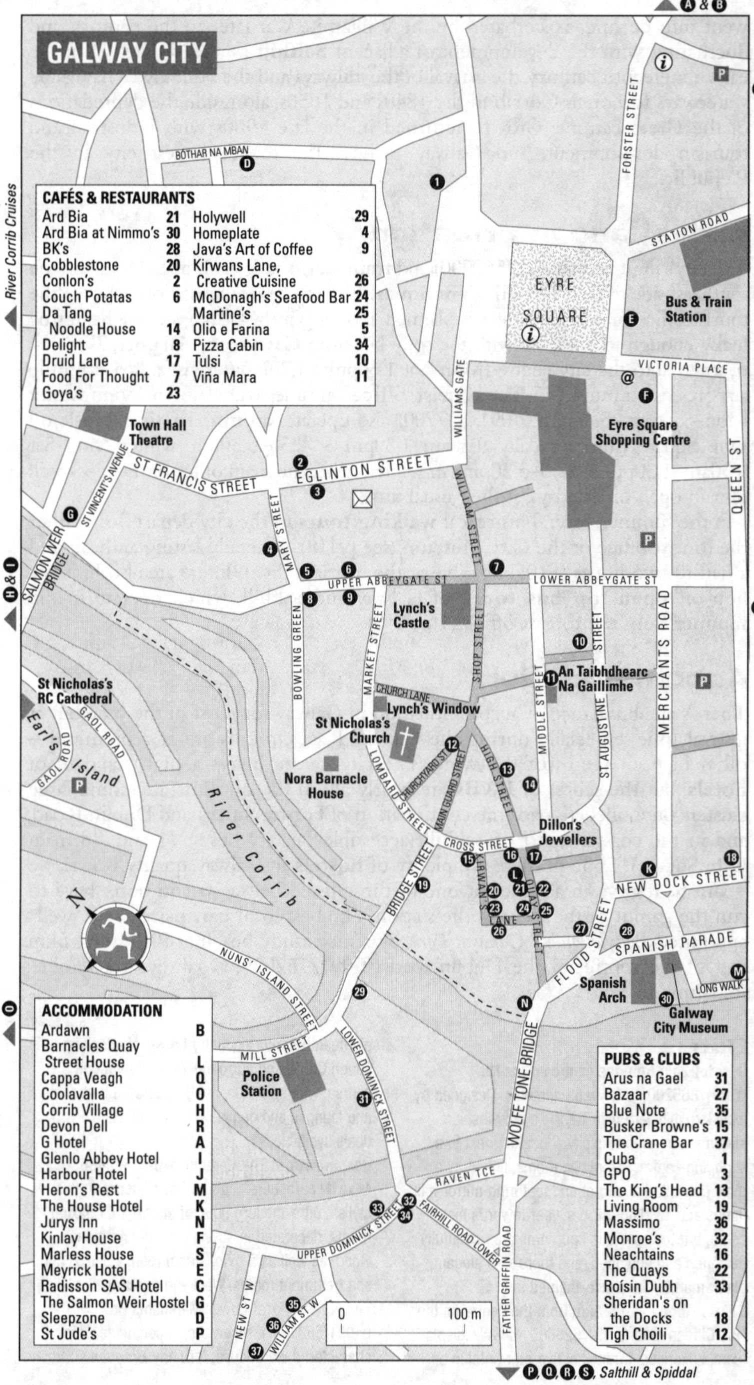

10

GALWAY AND MAYO

went into decline, exacerbated by the Williamite War later in the century, and fluctuating with the development of adjacent **Salthill** as a seaside resort in the early nineteenth century, the arrival of the railways and the building of navigable waterways to Lough Corrib in the 1840s and 1850s, alongside the depredations of the Great Famine. Growth returned in the late 1960s with industrial and tourism development, and Galway is now the fourth largest city in the Republic.

Arrival and information

The city's joint **bus** (Ⓣ091/562000) and **train stations** (Ⓣ091/561444) are on the southeast side of the landmark **Eyre Square**, though a new bus station opposite the tourist office on Forster Street is planned. Coming in by plane, you might just be lucky enough to coincide with the daily bus from **Carnmore Airport**, 7km east of town, into the city centre (Mon–Sat 1.30pm; €4.70); otherwise a taxi from the airport costs around €15. The **tourist office** (summer daily 9am–5.45pm; winter Mon–Sat 9am–5.45pm; Ⓣ091/537700) also operates an **information kiosk** on Eyre Square (summer daily 9.30am–1.30pm & 2.30–5.30pm; winter Mon–Sat 9.30am–1.30pm & 2.30–5.30pm); in winter, either the main office or the kiosk will remain open on Sundays, at their usual times.

In the summer, several historical **walking tours** of the city depart from either the tourist office or the City Museum (see p.418), generally lasting an hour and a half to two hours (€10; bookable at the tourist office). There are also hop-on, hop-off **open-top bus tours** of Galway and Salthill, which operate in the summer from the tourist office (1hr; €10).

Accommodation

There's an abundance of accommodation in Galway for most of the year, but at festival time, especially during the Galway Races, rooms are at a premium – often in both senses of the word. The city centre boasts a high standard of **hotels**, but the scores of **B&Bs** are nearly all on the outskirts, including large clusters on College Road (the continuation of Forster Street) and Dublin Road, and in the coastal resort of Salthill (accessible on city buses #1 and #8 from Eyre Square). Though there are plenty of **hostels** in Galway, quality is variable – aim to reserve in advance at one of those listed below so you don't have to run the gamut of the touts at the station. The best local **campsite** is the well-appointed *Ballyloughane Caravan Park*, by a nice sandy beach at Renmore, 5km east of the centre off the Dublin road (Ⓣ091/752029, Ⓔgalwaycamp@iol.ie; mid-June to Aug).

Hotels

G Hotel 2km from the centre on the N6 Ⓣ091/865200, Ⓦwww.theghotel.ie. Designed by local lad, milliner Philip Treacy, a bold fashion statement in an inauspicious location next to a shopping centre. The public rooms, linked by a pink, catwalk-like carpet and featuring mirror-ball lamps and swirling mirrors, veer towards high camp, but the spacious bedrooms are beautifully designed and equipped, and there's an elegant, black-marble, Japanese-themed spa. ❼

Glenlo Abbey Hotel 5km from the centre on the N59 Clifden road Ⓣ091/526666, Ⓦwww.glenlo.com. Luxurious, traditional five-star hotel in an eighteenth-century country house, overlooking Lough Corrib and surrounded by its own golf course, with spacious, richly decorated bedrooms and lounges and genial, helpful staff. Half-board deals available. ❽

Harbour Hotel The Harbour Ⓣ091/569466, Ⓦwww.harbour.ie. Right on the waterfront, this stylish, ultra-modern hotel offers bright, relaxing rooms, decorated in strong colours and blonde wood, as well as a gym, steam room, Jacuzzi and spa treatment rooms. Weekend deals available. ❻

The House Hotel Lower Merchants Rd Ⓣ091/568166, Ⓦwww.thehousehotel.ie. This characterful warehouse, formerly *Brennan's Yard*

Hotel, has been transformed into a luxurious but cosy boutique hotel, featuring stylish, well-equipped rooms with sound-proofed windows and colourful, contemporary public rooms; in-room spa treatments available. 6

Jurys Inn Quay St ⓣ091/566444, ⓦwww.jurysinns.com. This large, well-run, chain hotel offers spacious, comfortable rooms with all the facilities you might need and is handily placed at the bottom of Quay Street overlooking the river. 4

The Meyrick Eyre Square ⓣ091/564041, ⓦwww.monogramhotels.ie. This imposing Victorian railway hotel, formerly the *Great Southern*, has been renovated and brought into the same stable as the *G Hotel*, retaining its large, graceful bedrooms, but now offering an outdoor hot tub, gym and spa treatments. Weekend deals available. 6

Radisson SAS Hotel Lough Atalia Rd ⓣ091/538300, ⓦwww.radissonhotelgalway.com. Bright, modern, Scandinavian-run luxury hotel overlooking Galway Bay from a fine position on the northeast side of the train station. A long list of leisure facilities includes an extensive spa, swimming pool, gym and, of course, sauna. 7

B&Bs

Ardawn 31 College Rd ⓣ091/568833, ⓦwww.galway.net/pages/ardawn-house. A welcoming, upmarket B&B ten minutes' walk from the centre in a red-brick, modern house. Very comfortable and smart rooms and lavish breakfasts. At the lower end of this price code. 4

Cappa Veagh 76 Dalysfort Rd, Salthill ⓣ091/526518, ⓦwww.cappaveagh.com. Welcoming, comfortable and clean modern house, close to the seafront and a city bus stop (#1), with en-suite rooms with TVs, and very helpful and knowledgeable hosts. March–Oct. 2

Coolavalla 22 Newcastle Rd ⓣ091/522415, ⓔcoolavalla@eircom.net. Large, trim family house by the hospital and university, ten minutes' walk west of the centre, with one en-suite and two standard rooms, and good single rates. Closed Nov–March. 1

Corrib Village Newcastle ⓣ091/527112, ⓦwww.corribvillage.com. This huge complex on the campus of Galway University offers a wide variety of standard and en-suite B&B accommodation or apartment rentals in the summer (June–Aug) on the banks of the River Corrib 3km north of the centre. The village includes a café, supermarket, kids' club, tennis courts, laundry facilities and a complimentary shuttle bus to Eyre Square, and guests have access to the university's wide-ranging sports facilities. 2

Devon Dell 47 Devon Park, Lower Salthill ⓣ091/528306, ⓦwww.devondell.com. Welcoming, helpful and well-run en-suite B&B near the seafront with delicious breakfasts that include pancakes, croissants and smoothies. Closed Dec–Feb. 2

Heron's Rest 16A Long Walk ⓣ086 337 9343, ⓦwww.theheronsrest.com. Hospitable B&B in a peerless location, steps from the city centre but overlooking the quiet river and Galway Bay. Attractive rooms and excellent breakfasts featuring home-baked bread and muffins. May–Sept. 3

Marless House Threadneedle Rd, Salthill ⓣ091/523931, ⓦwww.marlesshouse.com. Comfortable, mock-Georgian modern home, 3km from the centre by the beach, with spacious, en-suite rooms. Closed mid-Nov to mid-Jan. 2

St Jude's 110 Lower Salthill ⓣ091/521619, ⓦwww.st-judes.com. Grand, manorial family home with elegant, en-suite bedrooms and good breakfasts, a 10min walk from the centre. Dinner, half-board rates and good single rates available. Closed mid-Dec to mid-Jan. 2

Hostels

Barnacles Quay Street House 10 Quay St (IHH) ⓣ091/568644, ⓦwww.barnacles.ie. A large, welcoming and efficiently run hostel in the heart of Galway's nightlife. All rooms are en suite, with twins and doubles available, there are laundry and kitchen facilities, and light breakfast is included. Dorms from €12, doubles 1.

Kinlay House Merchants Rd, Eyre Square (IHH & IHO) ⓣ091/565244, ⓦwww.kinlaygalway.ie. Huge, modern hostel that's friendly and well run, with laundry and bureau de change facilities and two kitchens. Many dorms are en suite, and double and twin rooms are available. Prices include a simple continental breakfast. Dorms from €14, doubles 1.

The Salmon Weir Hostel St Vincent's Ave, Woodquay (IHO) ⓣ091/561133, ⓦwww.salmonweirhostel.com. Small and simple, this comfortable hostel has two kitchens and Internet access and a friendly atmosphere; breakfast included in the price. Dorms from €12, doubles 1.

Sleepzone Bóthar na mBan, Woodquay ⓣ091/566999, ⓦwww.sleepzone.ie. Modern, well-maintained hostel affiliated to An Óige, five minutes' walk north of Eyre Square. All rooms are en suite, with singles, twins and doubles available, as well as Internet access, laundry facilities and a bureau de change. Prices include a light breakfast. Dorms from €13, doubles 1.

The City

The natural place to begin an exploration of the city is **Eyre Square**. This former common land, jousting ground and market square outside the city walls has recently been renovated, with plenty of greenery and pedestrianized areas. Surviving the facelift are a splendid **fountain**, erected in 1984 to mark the city's quincentenary, which evokes in rusted metal and rushing water a hooker, the traditional sailing boat of Galway Bay; and the **Browne doorway** marooned at the top of the square, the finely carved entrance and surrounding windows of a mercantile townhouse, bearing the 1627 coats of arms of the Brown and Lynch families, that's rather forlornly set in a concrete wall. In the Eyre Square Shopping Centre, on the southwest side, stands an extensive, heavily restored section of the medieval **city wall** with a couple of towers, now built into the back wall of Dunnes Stores.

The old centre

Strolling down William Street and Shop Street from Eyre Square, you'll come upon **Lynch's Castle**, home of the city's leading family of the fifteenth to seventeenth centuries, who provided no fewer than 84 mayors of Galway – it's now a branch of the Allied Irish Bank. Dating from the fourteenth and fifteenth centuries, it's probably the finest medieval townhouse in the country, with several elaborately sculptured slabs on the facade: among various Lynch coats of arms, you can make out the insignia of King Henry VII, featuring a dragon and greyhound, and above the doorway, an image of an ape holding a child – legend has it that the monkey saved one of the Lynch children from a fire. In the bank vestibule are display boards on the history of the house and the family and an impressive fireplace, which was probably carved to commemorate the intermarrying of the notable Blake and Ffrench families in 1627.

The most famous story of the Lynches is embodied in the ornately carved **Lynch's Window**, around the corner on Market Street behind St Nicholas's Church. In the 1490s young Walter Lynch Fitzstephens, jealous of the attentions a Spanish guest was giving his girlfriend, Ann Blake, stabbed the man and threw him into the sea. When the boy was duly sentenced to death, however, the town was up in arms pleading for mercy for the popular youth, and the usual executioner refused to do his duty. It was left to the boy's father, James, the mayor, to hang him from this jail window, which is now carved with a skull and crossbones. Galwegians claim this to be the origin of the term "lynching".

Founded in around 1320, the adjacent **Collegiate Church of St Nicholas** is the largest functioning medieval church in Ireland, but only by virtue of several slate-grey extensions over the centuries which have given it a particularly disharmonious external appearance. Dedicated to the fourth-century St Nicholas of Myra, patron saint of sailors and also revered as Santa Claus, the interior, however, is worth a quick look. There's a simply but beautifully carved font dating from around 1600 to the right of the entrance, while a banner in the north aisle shows the arms of the fourteen Tribes of Galway, many of whom endowed the church. Most of the interest lies in the south transept, built by the Lynches and containing many of their ornate tombs – including Mayor James Lynch Fitzstephens – and a curiously personal thirteenth- or fourteenth-century tomb of a Crusader, Adam Bure, promising that "whoever will pray for his soul will have twenty days' indulgence".

On Bowling Green, the lane running off the north side of the church, sits the **Nora Barnacle House**, the family home of James Joyce's wife and muse (mid-May to mid-Sept Mon–Sat 10am–1pm & 2–5pm; €2.50; ⓦwww.norabarnacle.com). As much for its memorabilia of Joyce, enthusiastically

▲ Lynch's Castle

explained by the curator, the tiny, one-up, one-down house is worth visiting for its insight into urban living conditions in the late nineteenth and early twentieth century. The Barnacles and most of their eight kids slept in the upstairs room, while the downstairs room was kitchen, dining and living room, and often bedroom, with perhaps a few chickens in the minuscule backyard.

Back on the main drag, at the corner of Cross and Quay streets, a small, informal museum at the back of Dillon's Jewellers traces the engaging cultural history of the **Claddagh ring**. Designed by a late seventeenth-century Galwegian who had been captured by pirates and enslaved to a Moorish goldsmith, this style of ring has been worn by the likes of Queen Victoria and

John Wayne. It features a pair of hands, symbolizing friendship, a heart, for love, and a mitred crown, traditionally for loyalty, and is often given as a love token. The museum also displays old photos of **The Claddagh** (An Cladach, "a flat, stony shore"), a former fishing village on the south bank of the river. When the Anglo-Normans took over and walled the town, the native population moved across the Corrib and remained there, Irish-speaking and with a certain measure of independence, until the 1930s when their thatched cottages were knocked down to make way for modern housing.

The river

Down by the river, near the sixteenth-century **Spanish Arch**, stands the swanky, new, glass-fronted **Galway City Museum** (June–Sept daily 10am–5pm; Oct–May Tues–Sat 10am–5pm; free; Ⓣ091/532460, Ⓦwww.galwaycitymuseum.ie). It currently exhibits relatively few artefacts (though more are planned as the museum finds its feet), but traces the city's history in vivid fashion, dealing with The Claddagh (see above) on the second floor, the medieval town on the first, and bringing matters up to date on the ground floor. The highlights are a nine-metre hooker, a traditional sailing boat suspended in all its glory in the atrium that was specially commissioned for the museum; and a statue of Galway-born Pádraic Ó Conaire (1882–1928; see p.726), the first modernist fiction writer in Irish. The museum also hosts some interesting temporary exhibitions, as well as a regular series of poetry readings at Friday lunchtimes. From the museum, you can take a short, pleasant stroll either down to the river mouth for views across the bay to the Burren hills, or upstream along a quiet path that passes weirs, fishermen and a few patches of lawn.

From the quays further upstream, beyond Salmon Weir Bridge and behind the Town Hall Theatre, two companies run ninety-minute, summertime **cruises** up the river for 8km, passing suburbs, leafy countryside and a couple of ruined castles, before entering Lough Corrib; tickets for both are available from the tourist office. The *Corrib Princess* (May, June & Sept 2 daily; July & Aug 3 daily; €14; Ⓣ091/592447, Ⓦwww.corribprincess.ie) is a large cruiser with a sundeck and covered saloon, while Celtic Boat Safari operates a smaller, open boat (Mon–Fri 3 daily; €10; Ⓣ087 981 1579).

Salthill

About a kilometre southwest of Wolfe Tone Bridge begins the resort suburb of **Salthill**, Galway's summer playground. It's a Sunday-afternoon tradition to walk the long promenade – lined with high-rise apartment blocks, hotels and amusement arcades, as well as safe beaches with fine views across the bay to the Burren – and kick the wall at the end by the diving platform for good luck, before turning back. On the front, the National Aquarium of Ireland, **Galway Atlantaquaria** (Mon–Fri 9am–5pm, Sat & Sun 10am–5pm; Nov–Feb closed some Mon and Tues for tank maintenance; €9, children €5.50; Ⓣ091/585100, Ⓦwww.nationalaquarium.ie), is a big draw for kids, entertainingly showcasing Ireland's sea, river and canal life. Beyond Salthill and just 5km west of the centre, **Silver Strand** is the nicest beach in the vicinity of the city, a small, sandy affair with a Blue Flag and a gentle shelf, beneath a grassy headland. It's accessible on buses towards Spiddal.

Eating

It's claimed that Galway pays too much attention to drinking and not enough to eating, but it actually holds a wide variety of good-quality **restaurants**, ranging from traditional seafood joints to characterful upmarket bistros, alongside authentic Chinese and Indian offerings. Among the **pubs**, *Busker Browne's*, *The King's Head* and especially *Sheridan's on the Docks* serve great food, but if you're sick of hanging out in bars, there are plenty of very appealing **cafés**, a few of which – notably *Ard Bia* – stay open in the evenings. Sheridan's Cheesemongers, an all-round deli opposite St Nicholas's Church on Churchyard Street, and the Saturday market (see "Listings", p.422) are great places to pick up a picnic.

Cafés

Ard Bia 2 Quay St ☎091/539897. Lively, first-floor social and culinary hub, especially popular for weekend brunch, with plain, bright decor and windows perched above the action on the main street. During the day, it's a global café, serving salads, sandwiches, burgers and soup, as well as cakes and a wide choice of juices and teas; in the evening it reopens as a restaurant with dishes such as saddle of Wicklow venison. Closed Sun & Mon evenings.

Cobblestone Kirwan's Lane. Traditional-style café decorated with old prints and subdued colours, with tables out on the quiet lane. Dishes include soups, salads and delicious wraps such as smoked salmon and cream cheese, with plenty of vegetarian options, as well as delicious cakes.

Delight 29 Upper Abbeygate St. Great coffee, juices and breakfasts, as well as some novel sandwiches, bagels and salads, to eat in on the few bar stools or take away. Closed Sat & Sun.

Food For Thought Lower Abbeygate St. Cheap wholefood and vegetarian snacks, sandwiches, salads, hot dishes, cakes and good coffee, to take away or eat in.

Goya's Kirwan's Lane. Elegant, modern café with tables out on the alley, serving excellent home-baked cakes and coffee, as well as soups, quiches, sandwiches and pies. Closed Sun.

Java's Art of Coffee 17 Upper Abbeygate St. Arty hangout that's open till 3 or 4 every morning, offering great coffee and cool sounds, as well as tapas, sandwiches, salads, a tempting variety of meat and cheese plates, cakes and breakfasts.

Olio e Farina Upper Abbeygate St. Mouthwatering Italian deli with a small café area at the back, offering fresh pasta dishes, gourmet ciabattas, salads and plates of cured meats from their own farm in Tuscany. Closed Sun.

Restaurants

Ard Bia at Nimmo's Long Walk, Spanish Arch ☎091/561114. Offshoot of the Quay Street café in a characterful medieval stone building overlooking the river, offering delicious, good-value cooking with strong Greek, Middle Eastern and North African influences in the evening, and for lunch (Thurs–Sun only), classy sandwiches, salads, and cheese and meat platters.

BK's Spanish Parade ☎091/568450. Despite the address, this easy-going wine bar and bistro couldn't be more French. Dine on classic dishes such as duck *magret* in prune and fig sauce, or simpler, cheaper fare such as plates of cheese and charcuterie – sometimes to the accompaniment of a piano or live jazz. Cheap three-course set menu. Poetry readings some Thurs evenings.

Conlon's Eglinton St. Popular, cheap seafood restaurant, specializing in Galway Bay oysters, seafood salads, and fish and chips in plain but comfortable surroundings. The day's catch is chalked up on a blackboard. Closed Sun lunchtime.

Couch Potatas Upper Abbeygate St. The national vegetable baked in dozens of creative ways, with the added pleasure of puzzling over the meaning of names like "Paris by Night". Cheap and plenty for veggies, of course, plus starters and salads.

Da Tang Noodle House Middle St ☎091/561443. Hung with art exhibitions, this cosy spot provides excellent, authentic, mostly northern Chinese noodles – either in soup, sauce or pan-fried – as well as salads, sizzling dishes and hotpots. Closed Sun lunch.

Druid Lane 9 Quay St ☎091/563015. Relaxed, informal restaurant, with helpful staff and excellent, global-influenced food, such as duck breast with cranberry and port jus; or you can perch at the bar for a glass of wine and snacks. Early-bird menu until 7pm. Closed Mon–Thurs lunchtimes.

Holywell Bridge Mills, O'Brien Bridge. In an atmospheric converted mill, with a gorgeous sun-trap riverside terrace, this branch of the County Clare franchise dishes a short but winning menu of very tasty, classic pastas and pizzas at low prices.

Homeplate Mary St. Cosy, basic and cheap restaurant serving everything from herbal teas and cakes, through salads and ciabattas to main courses such as chicken curry. Mon–Thurs noon–8pm, Fri & Sat noon–9pm, Sun noon–7pm.

Kirwans Lane, Creative Cuisine Kirwans Lane, off Upper Cross St ☎091/568266. Popular, welcoming, upmarket restaurant with quiet outdoor tables, offering a range of international cuisine, such as turbot fillet with prawn bisque. Closed Sun lunch.

McDonagh's Seafood Bar 22 Quay St. A Galway seafood institution, attached to a fishmonger's. Simple, traditional fish dishes in the friendly restaurant (Mon–Sat evenings), or high-quality fish and chips and chowder from the takeaway section (closed Sun lunch), which has a few simple tables inside and out on the street.

Martine's Quay St ⓣ091/565662. Friendly, reasonably priced, wood-panelled bistro, with a lovely, dark bar and tables outside. Sandwiches, salads and pastas for lunch (Fri & Sat only), and a fairly conservative evening menu, featuring rack of lamb and lasagne, alongside a more interesting list of daily specials.

Pizza Cabin Upper Dominick St ⓣ091/582887. Delicious, cheap pizzas to take away or eat in, either on the narrow counters here or in *Monroe's* pub next door.

Tulsi Buttermilk Walk, Middle St ⓣ091/564831. Galway's best Indian restaurant rustles up very good vegetarian and meaty food and even tries its hand at Indo Galwegian fusion dishes such as tandoori mackerel. Good-value buffet lunch on Sun.

Viña Mara 19 Middle St ⓣ091/561610. Aptly decorated in warm, sunny hues, this restaurant and wine bar offers carefully prepared, mostly Mediterranean dishes, such as braised confit of belly pork, sometimes with a modern twist, and attentive service. Simpler lunch and early-bird (Mon–Fri until 7.30pm) menus. Closed Sat lunchtime & Sun.

Drinking, nightlife and entertainment

A slow crawl through the **pubs** of Shop, High and Quay streets is a must, soaking up the cosy atmosphere of their historic interiors in winter, and the buzzy streetlife at their outdoor tables in summer. You're bound to find a traditional session here, though the best two places for **live music** are probably *The Crane* and *Roísin Dubh*, which share with a casino and a lap-dancing club the seedier, more alternative area on the right bank of the river around Dominick Street.

Together with DJ bars, there are plenty of **clubs** in Galway, among which *Cuba* and *GPO* stand out. **Listings** publications in Galway come and go frequently, the latest incarnation being *Xposed, a* free, fortnightly leaflet and map; more steadfast is the free newspaper, the *Galway Advertiser* (based at the top of Eyre Square), which comes out every Thursday and goes like hot cakes.

Built in the 1820s, the **Town Hall Theatre**, Courthouse Square, Woodquay (ⓣ091/569777, ⓦwww.townhalltheatregalway.com), is the city's main performance venue, putting on drama, dance, music and opera by visiting companies throughout the year. Look out especially for performances by local theatre company, **Druid** (ⓦwww.druidtheatre.com), whose highly acclaimed recent productions have included the complete cycle of six plays by John Millington Synge. Founded in 1928, **An Taibhdhearc na Gaillimhe** in Middle Street (ⓣ091/563600, ⓦwww.antaibhdhearc.com) is the national Irish-language theatre, and hosts a well-regarded show of traditional and folk dance and music in the summer, Music at the Crossroads (ⓦwww.music-crossroads.com).

Pubs and clubs

Arus na Gael 45 Dominick St. Cavernous Irish-speaking pub and club, with traditional music on Sat, and DJs on Fri.

Bazaar Quay Lane. Incongruous Moroccan-themed bar in a venerable, heavy-stoned building, with plenty of scatter cushions and low lighting, as well as tables outside on the piazza; DJs most Sats, live traditional music early evening Sat & Sun.

Blue Note William St West. Despite its name and the huge mural outside, this is not a jazz club. DJs play funk, soul and other laid-back sounds into the farthest snugs of this dimly lit, slightly scruffy but fun bar.

Busker Browne's Cross St. This welcoming, popular bar in a former Dominican convent offers original medieval fireplaces, a lofty, Gothic hall on the third floor, and floor upon floor of alcoves and armchairs in a complementary modern design for comfy eating and drinking. Seafood chowder, salads and full meals are served daily till late, and there's DJs at weekends, jazz at Sun lunchtimes.

The Crane Bar Sea Rd. Invariably busy bar owned by two musicians, with excellent traditional and country sessions, plus singer-songwriters, every night.

Cuba Eyre Square ⓣ091/565991, ⓦwww.cuba.ie. Three floors of pulse-raising beats at this club with an unobtrusive Cuban theme, which hosts DJs and live bands throughout the week, as well as a comedy club on Sun.

GPO Eglinton St ⓣ091/565376 ⓦwww.gpo.ie. Lively club popular with students offering a wildly varied programme, ranging from hip-hop to indie, which occasionally includes top live acts and international DJs.

The King's Head High St. Busy three-storey pub in an impressive medieval building with flagstone floors, bare stone walls and a seventeenth-century bridal fireplace, that's a great spot for lunch, or pizzas in the evenings. Cromwell's military governor, Colonel Peter Stubbers, who was widely rumoured to have been Charles I's executioner, requisitioned this building, hence the name. Live music nightly – anything from rock to big bands, though not traditional – followed Thurs–Sat by DJs until 2am.

Living Room Bridge St. Trendy, popular makeover of the old *Lisheen Bar*, though not strictly bang up to date: the place now has a strong Seventies retro feel, heavy on browns, reds and pale wood, with plenty of padded bench seats. DJs and a late bar Thurs–Sun nights, and decent food during the day.

Massimo William St West. Stylish, modern bar done out with comfy booths and couches, soft lighting and lots of bare wood, hosting up-tempo DJs at weekends.

Monroe's Upper Dominick St. Huge, sociable and unpretentious pub with traditional or acoustic music nightly, sometimes with set dancing or a sing-along, and pizzas available from *Pizza Cabin* next door.

Neachtains 17 Cross St. Galway's finest traditional pub, in what was once the town house of Humanity Dick (see p.445). In winter, the homely warren of small rooms, bars, bench seats and snugs draws a diverse crowd, who tend to migrate to the plentiful tables on the busy corner of Cross and Quay streets in summer. Live music, usually Thurs–Sun, might feature traditional, bluegrass and jazz.

The Quays Quay St. Regular two-storied facade conceals an eccentric, warren-like, medieval superpub, decorated with mullioned and stained-glass windows, carved beams and Gothic wooden arches. Early-evening traditional sessions Fri & Sun, plus a balconied venue with a large stage for regular live bands and DJs.

Roísin Dubh 9 Upper Dominick St ⓣ091/586540, ⓦwww.roisindubh.net. This pub is Galway's best live venue, hosting gigs of every style from rock and reggae to folk and funk, with a late bar every night and a pleasant terrace overlooking the river. Comedy club Wed night.

Sheridan's on the Docks Queen St. An offshoot of the excellent deli on Churchyard St, this spruce but cosy gastro-pub serves soups, salads, sandwiches, oysters and delicious plates of cheese, meat and smoked fish. There's also a huge selection of wines and beers, including the local, microbrewed Galway Hooker, a pale ale from County Roscommon. Closed Mon–Wed lunchtimes & Sun (though this may change if they're granted the necessary licence).

Tigh Choili Mainguard St. Welcoming, central and sociable traditional pub with daily sessions around 6pm and 9.30pm, plus 2pm on Sun.

Listings

Airport ⓣ091/755569, ⓦwww.galwayairport.com.

Bike rental Europa Bicycles, Earls Island, opposite St Nicholas's Catholic Church (ⓣ091/563355); Mountain Trail Bike Shop, The Cornstore, Middle St (ⓣ091/569888, ⓦwww.bikehireireland.com).

Bookshops Charlie Byrne's, The Cornstore, Middle St, stocks a good range of new, secondhand and discounted books; Eason's, 33 Shop St, is a large general bookshop and sells a few foreign newspapers.

Car rental Budget has offices both at Carnmore Airport (ⓣ091/564570) and on Eyre Square (ⓣ091/566376), ⓦwww.budgetcarrental.ie; or try local company, Windsor, based at Monivea Rd, Ballybrit ⓣ091/770707, ⓦwww.windsor-galway.ie.

Gay information ⓦwww.queergalway.com. Bars at *Strano's*, William St West (ⓦwww.stranos.ie), and *The Stage Door*, Wood Quay (ⓦwww.thestagedoor.ie). Information line for gay men ⓣ091/566134 Tues & Thurs 8–10pm, for lesbians ⓣ091/564611 Wed 8–10pm.

Helplines Samaritans, 14 Nun's Island Rd ⓣ091/561222; Rape Crisis Centre, 7 Claddagh Quay ⓣ1850 355355.

Horse riding Rusheen Riding Centre, at the west end of Salthill ⓣ091/521285, ⓦwww.galwayhorseriding.com.

Hospital University College Hospital, Newcastle Rd ⓣ091/524222.

rnet Port, Victoria Place, Eyre Square.
dry At the hostels, or Launderland, near the office on Bóthar na mBan.
Left luggage At the train station (Mon–Fri 8am–6.15pm, Sat 10am–6.15pm; €2.50) or the hostels.
Market The huge Saturday market around St Nicholas's Church hosts craftspeople and some great foodstalls, where you could make up a picnic of cheese, home-made bread, smoked salmon, hummus and olives.
Massage Excellent Thai-yoga massages and other treatments are provided by Denise Delaney (Ⓣ085 132 5700) at The Acupuncture Clinic, 2 Churchyard St, and Devonpark Holistic Health Clinic, 108 Lower Salthill, while Sinead Murphy (Ⓣ087 624 5685) offers deep-tissue, reflexology and other massages at Devonpark.
Parking Pay and display on the street, or use a car park – useful locations include next to the tourist office off Forster St and the multistoreys on Dock Rd and Merchants Rd.
Police Mill St Ⓣ091/538000.
Taxis Claddagh Cabs, William St West Ⓣ091/588434; Galway Taxis, 7 Mainguard St Ⓣ091/561111. There are taxi ranks at Eyre Square.
Tours For walking and bus tours of the city, see p.414. If you're short on time, you might want to sign up for a half- or full-day bus tour of Connemara or the Burren and Cliffs of Moher at the tourist office (€20–25). Operators include Bus Éireann (Ⓣ091/562000, Ⓦwww.buseireann.ie), Galway Tour Company (Ⓣ091/566566, Ⓦwww.galwaytourcompany.com), Healy (Ⓣ091/770066, Ⓦwww.healytours.ie), Lally (Ⓣ091/562905, Ⓦwww.lallytours.com) and O'Neachtain (Ⓣ091/553188, Ⓦwww.ontours.biz).
Travel agent USIT, 16 Mary St Ⓣ091/565177, Ⓦwww.usit.ie.
Watersports Windsurfing rental and tuition, plus canoe rental, at Rusheen Bay, at the west end of Salthill Ⓣ087 260 5702, Ⓦwww.rusheenbay.com. Sea-kayaking trips and courses through Ireland West Sea Kayaking (Ⓣ086 173 3610, Ⓦwww.irelandwestseakayaking.com) or Kayakmór (Ⓣ087 756 5578, Ⓦwww.kayakmor.com).

East Galway

East Galway (Ⓦwww.galwayeast.com) is a vast tract of fertile, flat land bordered by the Shannon and its tributary the River Suck, the southern half of which shelters some compelling places to visit. **Kinvarra** is a justly popular honeypot on the shores of Galway Bay, while several historic attractions ring the inland town of **Gort**, notably **Coole Park**, Lady Gregory's idyllic woodland estate, and W.B. Yeats's tower house, **Thoor Ballylee**. Out on a limb on the shores of Lough Derg, **Portumna** is an easy-going boating resort, with a notable castle and forest park, which gives access to **Clonfert Cathedral**, one of the country's finest Romanesque churches. Back towards Galway city, Arts and Crafts fans shouldn't miss the richly ornamented St Brendan's Cathedral in **Loughrea**, while the west's first designated "heritage town", **Athenry**, is a fascinating, congenial place to visit and stay. All of these spots have decent **bus** links with Galway city, and Athenry is the last calling point for Dublin–Galway **trains**.

Galway Bay

East of Galway city, the N18 runs south around the eastern shores of Galway Bay, which are lined with native European Flat Oyster beds. There are some renowned **oyster pubs** here, including *Paddy Burke's Oyster Tavern* at Clarinbridge (Ⓣ091/796226) and Kilcolgan's *Moran's Oyster Cottage*, a bar-restaurant prettily set by the bay (Ⓣ091/796113), while the fifty-year-old **Clarinbridge Oyster Festival** (Ⓣ091/796766, Ⓦwww.clarenbridge.com) over three days in early September kicks off the season, which lasts until April. Beyond Kilcolgan, the N18 heads inland towards Gort, Ennis and Limerick, while the N67 towards the Burren hugs the coast via the quaint village of Kinvarra.

Kinvarra and around

Tucked away at the head of its own inlet in the southeastern corner of the bay, **KINVARRA** (ⓦwww.kinvara.com) is a popular getaway for Galwegians, with several attractive, lively pubs – and **buses** from the city between one and five times a day, many of which continue to Doolin and the Cliffs of Moher. The pretty, harbourside village also boasts a notable historic site, **Dunguaire Castle** (mid-April to early Oct Mon, Tues & Fri–Sun 9.30am–4.30pm, Wed & Thurs 9.30am–5pm; €5.50), an intact, four-storey tower house, built in 1520. The name comes from Guaire, the seventh-century king of Connacht who was so renowned for his generosity that his right arm was said to have grown longer than his left, and *dún* (fort), which may refer to the ancient earthwork on the headland to the east. You can poke around the many rooms, with their intricate vaults and corbels, and get out onto the roof for gorgeous views of Kinvarra Harbour and the Burren beyond. The castle also hosts medieval banquets, with a literary pageant, a harpist and singers, and decent food (mid-April to early Oct Mon, Tues & Fri–Sun twice nightly, subject to demand; €51; ⓣ1800 269811), and, more mundanely, a bureau de change (there's no bank in Kinvarra, though there is an ATM at the Londis supermarket).

On the west side of Kinvarra Bay, the tranquil **Doorus Peninsula**, which was an island until the eighteenth century, shelters on its north shore **Traught beach**, a broad, stony Blue Flag strand, and provides ample opportunity for scenic walks or cycle rides – *Kinvarra: A Ramblers' Map and Guide* can be picked up from Murphy Store, a crafts and coffee shop in a restored grain store on the Quay, and **bikes** can be rented from the hostel (see below).

Practicalities

The village **hotel** is the *Merriman* on the main street, named after the satirical, eighteenth-century, Irish-language poet (see p.717)from nearby Ennistymon in Clare ⓣ091/638222, ⓦwww.merrimanhotel.com; closed early Jan–early March; ❹). Boasting one of Ireland's largest thatched roofs, it is tastefully decorated inside, with well-appointed bedrooms, an excellent restaurant and *M'Asal Beag Dubh*, a good pub with decent bar food. Among **B&Bs** in the village, *Cois Cuain* (ⓣ091/637119; April to mid-Oct; ❷), a cottage on the Quay with a fine garden, is your best bet. Out near the northeastern corner of the Doorus Peninsula, *Breacan Cottage* (ⓣ091/638266, ⓦwww.breacan.com; ❷) is a very welcoming, tastefully designed modern house on the seafront, with excellent breakfasts and views across Galway Bay. You can also stay on the peninsula at the nearby An Óige **hostel**, *Doorus House* (ⓣ091/637512, ⓦwww.kinvara.com/doorushouse; €12–16), a nineteenth-century mansion which has family rooms, a small shop, laundry facilities, bike hire and Internet access and offers courses in Irish dancing and traditional music. From Galway or Kinvarra, there are one to five Doolin-bound buses a day to Doorus Cross, leaving you with a three-kilometre walk to the hostel, and one daily (Mon–Fri; #423) to *Fahy's Travellers' Inn* pub and shop at Nogra, which will leave a 1.5-kilometre walk.

Besides the *Merriman*, good **eating** options in Kinvarra include *Keogh's Bar and Restaurant* on the main street (ⓣ091/637145), highly recommended for its varied, reasonably priced snacks and full meals, including local smoked salmon and oysters in season; *The Pier Head Bar and Restaurant* (ⓣ091/638188), which has a pricier menu, also featuring plenty of seafood, with the bonus of fine views of the harbour and bay; and the quaint and much-photographed *Café on the Quay (Pizza Café*; closed Mon & Tues in winter), offering breakfast, sandwiches and salads during the day, and pizza and more substantial dishes in the evening, as well as **Internet** access. Among the village **bars**, *The Ould Plaid*

Shawl on the main street, nineteenth-century birthplace of poet and patriot Francis Fahy and named after his most famous song, is good for a quiet pint, while several places have live music: *Keogh's*, hosts two to four nights a week of traditional, blues or country; flower-bedecked *Connolly's,* at the corner of the Quay and the main street, offers attractive outdoor tables and Wednesday and Saturday sessions (plus some Sun afternoons); and *Greene's* opposite is a lively, old-fashioned spot which often has great, impromptu traditional sessions.

For a bit of pampering, the Seaweed Treatment Company just off the south side of the main street offers wraps of local seaweed and foot massages, as well as smart self-catering accommodation (Ⓣ091/444123 or 637760, Ⓦwww.seaweedtreatment.com). Kinvarra lays on a music **festival**, the *Fleadh na gCuach* (the Cuckoo Fleadh), usually over the bank-holiday weekend at the start of May, and the *Cruinniú na mBáid* (the Meeting of the Boats), usually on the second weekend in August (depending on the tides). The latter features the racing of Galway Bay's traditional, wooden, red-sailed boats, known as **hookers**, which can often be seen docked in the harbour. For those heading on to Clare, *Café Beo* on the main street contains a small information point about the Burren (Ⓦwww.burrenbeo.com).

Gort and around

About 12km southeast of Kinvarra and 19km south of Kilcolgan, **GORT** (Ⓦwww.gortonline.com) is a traffic-laden town of multicoloured houses on the busy N18 Galway–Limerick road, with some relief provided by the large, triangular market square in the centre. Kinvarra and Galway city would be more congenial bases for exploring the surrounding historic sites but the town does have a handful of noteworthy amenities. On the north side of the square, *The Gallery* is a hip, friendly **café** hung with modern art, which stays open in the evening, serving delicious soups, pizzas, salads, quiches and sandwich platters and great tea and coffee. The owners lay on live music, anything from folk to classical, on Sunday evenings, as well as other nights of spoken word or open-mike, and run a basic **hostel** upstairs (Ⓣ091/630630, Ⓦwww.myspace.com/gallerycafegort; dorms €15). A little way out on the Ennis road, the *Lady Gregory* **hotel** (Ⓣ091/632333, Ⓦwww.ladygregoryhotel.ie; ⑤) offers well-appointed rooms, a decent-sized swimming pool, spa and fitness club. At the southeast corner of the market square, *O'Donnell's* is a characterful warren of an old **pub**, which hosts traditional music twice a week.

Coole Park

Coole Park, around 3km north of Gort on the N18, is the former estate of **Lady Augusta Gregory** (1852–1932), dramatist, folklorist and co-founder of the Abbey Theatre in Dublin, the world's first national theatre. At the beginning of the last century, Coole was the centre of the Irish Literary Revival, visited by Synge, Shaw, O'Casey and most of all Yeats, who spent over twenty summers there. After Lady Gregory's death, however, the estate passed into the hands of the Department of Agriculture and Lands, who left the house to fall into disrepair and demolished it in 1941. The demesne is now a beautiful woodland park, home to pine martens, red deer and red squirrels and laid out with two signposted nature trails, which will bring you down to a seasonal lake and its many swans. In the walled garden stands the **autograph tree**, a beautiful, swooping copper beech on which all the great writers and painters who stayed here carved graffiti.

The **visitor centre** (April, May & Sept daily 10am–5pm; June–Aug daily 10am–6pm; €2.90; Heritage Card; Ⓦwww.coolepark.ie) features a highly engaging exhibition based on the memoirs of Lady Gregory's granddaughter, who was born and brought up at Coole, including computer re-creations of the house, and film footage and sound recordings of Yeats. The nearby **café**, which dishes up everything from breakfast to hot lunches such as lasagne, is attractively sited under the arches of the old stable block.

Thoor Ballylee

Five kilometres north of Coole Park on the N18, a signpost points eastward to W.B. Yeats's former home, **Thoor Ballylee**, 3km away along the back roads (June–Sept Mon–Sat 9.30am–5pm; €6). Set by a beautiful, shady stream, this thirteenth- or fourteenth-century tower house, with adjoining nineteenth-century thatched cottage, was bought by Yeats for £35 in 1916 and restored as a summer residence for his family. The narrow tower, with one large room on each floor, has been renovated again, and simply furnished as it would have been in 1926 when Yeats last came here. In addition, rare editions of Yeats's work are on show, while taped commentaries in each room feature apposite recitals, including extracts from *The Tower*, a collection published in 1928 that contains a number of poems written at and about Thoor Ballylee. The souvenir shop has a local **tourist-information** point (Ⓣ091/631436).

Kilmacduagh

Around 6km southwest of Gort, a little way off the R460 to Corofin, the extensive monastic ruins of **Kilmacduagh** stand in an unspoilt setting with magnificent views of the Burren's limestone terraces to the west. The monastery was founded by St Colman Mac Duagh, a member of one of the local royal families, around 632, but the buildings you can see today date mostly from around five hundred years later. They're impressive by virtue of their scale and quantity – a cathedral, four churches, the "Glebe House" (possibly the abbot's house) and a 35-metre-high, leaning round-tower – rather than any architectural finery, but look out for the grim-faced bishop carved over the cathedral's south doorway.

Portumna and around

PORTUMNA, 47km east of Gort through the pine-clad Slieve Aughty mountains, is a compact market town surrounded by forests and open land that run down to the meeting of the River Shannon with Lough Derg. In summer, lough-cruiser tourism generates a welcoming, low-key holiday atmosphere, with plenty of late-night live music in the pubs.

On the southwest side of the town centre stands the early seventeenth-century fortified mansion **Portumna Castle** (early April–Oct 10am–6pm, last admission 45min before closing; hours around Easter may vary, phone Ⓣ090/974 1658; €2.10; Heritage Card), which was gutted by fire in 1826 and is currently being renovated. Work is under way to open up the first floor, for a better appreciation of the Jacobean internal architecture and views of the lake, but currently you're confined to the ground floor, which is arrayed with interesting display boards on the de Burgo family who lived here, the house and its conservation. Look out for the gun holes in the impressively thick walls, reflecting how unsettled life was in seventeenth-century Ireland. In front of the house, the elegant Renaissance garden, one of the first in Ireland, has been re-created (at its best in July when the seventeenth-century breeds of roses come out), as has the walled kitchen garden to one side.

Beyond the castle gatehouse, about 400m down the road towards the lake, lie the extensive remains of **Portumna Friary** in a leafy setting. Originally

▲ Portumna Castle

a Cistercian chapel, it was rebuilt by the Dominicans in the early fifteenth century, with ornate, traceried windows in the east wall and south transept of the church, and a small, pretty cloister, now heavily restored. Part of Portumna Castle's former estate – still home to a sizeable herd of fallow deer – constitutes the **Portumna Forest Park** (access from the marina beyond the friary, from the castle or off the Gort road to the west of town), where you can stroll along marked trails through the woodland to the lake shore.

Practicalities

The helpful **tourist office** (June–Aug Mon–Fri 9.30am–1pm & 1.45–5pm; ⓣ090/974 1910, ⓔinfo@southeastgalway.com) is on Abbey Street, which runs parallel to and south of Main Street (where Bus Éireann and Kearns Transport buses stop). **Internet access** is available at the Integrated Rural Development office next door. If you're so tempted by the water that you want to live on it for a week or two, contact Emerald Star, who rent out **self-drive cruisers** from the marina at the east end of town (ⓣ090/974 1120, ⓦwww.emeraldstar.ie).

There's plenty of **accommodation** in Portumna, including several B&Bs on quiet Dominick Street, the continuation of Abbey Street: try *Auvergne Lodge* (ⓣ090/974 1138, ⓔauvergnelodge@eircom.net; ❷), a friendly, modern family home with en-suite bedrooms on Dominick Street; or pricier *Shannon Villa*, about a kilometre east of the town centre on Bridge Road (ⓣ090/974 1269, ⓔshannonvilla@ireland.com; March–Oct; ❷), where you can get dinner and relax in the peaceful conservatory. If you fancy something a bit swankier, book into the *Shannon Oaks Hotel and Country Club* (ⓣ090/974 1777, ⓦwww.shannonoaks.ie; ❺; good weekend deals and self-catering also available), which boasts a long list of facilities including a popular restaurant and bar, a swimming pool and gym, in spacious grounds at the west end of Main Street.

The Beehive (closed Sun lunch & Mon), a basic **café-restaurant** on St Patrick's Street, just off the south side of Main Street, serves salads, sandwiches, traditional main courses and cakes, plus tasty, popular pizzas in the evenings.

Opposite is *Dyson's* (☎090/974 2333; Wed–Sun evenings; early-bird until 6.30pm), a smart, pricey restaurant that rustles up such delights as rack of lamb with a cassoulet of cabbage, leeks and bacon. Portumna boasts more than twenty **pubs**, with live music, including traditional, just about everywhere on weekend nights in the summer. Regular traditional sessions are held at *Stronges* on Main Street (Wed), and there could be an impromptu session at *Horan's* (*The Corner House*), at the corner of Main and St Patrick's streets, on any night.

Clonfert Cathedral

It's a pleasant drive or cycle ride along flat country roads to beautiful, tree-girt **Clonfert Cathedral**, which is noted especially for its exuberant Romanesque doorway, 25km northeast of Portumna. The church was founded in the sixth century by St Brendan (see p.361), who was later buried here, and the present building has been in continuous service from around the tenth century, though it's now only infrequently used by the Church of Ireland. Regarded as the high point of Irish Romanesque, the rounded, golden-brown, sandstone doorway, topped by a triangular gable, may have been added for a synod held at Clonfert by St Laurence O'Toole, Archbishop of Dublin, in 1179. It's carved with a remarkable diversity of inventive motifs, some of which have been traced to Scandinavia and western France, including human and animal heads, interlace and other geometrical devices. The innermost order, inserted immediately around the door in around 1500, features a small angel and two conspicuous figures, one of whom is probably St Brendan. The church interior is fairly plain, but look out for a vivacious carving of a mermaid on the chancel arch. Dating from around 1600, the adjacent bishop's palace later became home to the English fascist, Oswald Mosley, but has rapidly rotted since it was accidentally burned down in 1954.

Loughrea and around

LOUGHREA, 32km northwest of Portumna, is a small market town on the lake of the same name. It's unlikely that you'll want to stay here, but it's well worth detouring off the N6 bypass to visit the late nineteenth-century **St Brendan's Cathedral**, a shining product of the Arts and Crafts movement – which in its Irish manifestation is often referred to as the Celtic Revival. The church is on Barrack Street, which runs parallel to and south of Main Street, and a detailed, well-written, thirty-minute audio-tour is available from the adjacent presbytery (€2.50). The interior is decorated with rich marble, playfully carved Irish-oak pews and Mediterranean-style column capitals in the nave telling the story of St Brendan (see p.361). Its most notable feature, however, is its stained glass, which was mostly produced by **An Túr Gloine** (The Shining Tower), a co-operative Arts and Crafts studio based in Dublin from 1903 to 1944. Look out especially for the 1930s works by the Dublin-born artist **Michael Healy**, who was heavily influenced by the Renaissance art he'd studied in Florence. His *St Joseph* in the right-hand aisle is sombrely emotive, but in *The Queen of Heaven*, further down the same aisle, he deals only in brilliant colours and composition, to convey Mary's regal splendour. Healy's masterpieces are *The Ascension* and *The Last Judgement* in the west transept, sparkling tapestries of colour inlaid with the dramatic heads of his characters, notably the terrified sinners in the right-hand work surrounded by hellish red and purple.

The adjoining **Clonfert Museum** (open on request, preferably Mon–Fri mornings; ☎091/841212; donation requested) houses some beautiful tapestries designed by Jack B. Yeats and made by the **Dun Emer Guild**, the weaving and printing arm of the Irish Arts and Crafts movement, founded in 1902 and named after the needleworking wife of the mythical hero, Cúchulainn. There's also a primitive, polychrome carving of the Virgin and Child dating from the late twelfth or early thirteenth century, the oldest surviving wooden statue in Ireland. Among the town's **places to eat**, *Catherine's Kitchen*, a bakery next door to the cathedral, is a good daytime option, offering fresh sandwiches and simple meals.

Six kilometres east of Loughrea off the N6, those of a horsey persuasion might be tempted by the **Dartfield Horse Museum** (daily 9.30am–6pm, last admission 5pm; ⓣ091/843968, ⓦwww.dartfieldhorsemuseum.com; €8; Heritage Island), to watch equine audiovisual displays, try out a riding machine and go into the stables to admire the beasts. Pony and carriage rides are also on offer if pre-booked, as well as more serious lessons and treks, including multi-day jaunts across Connemara (ⓦwww.aillecross.com).

Athenry

ATHENRY's name in Irish, Baile Átha an Rí, "town of the ford of the king", reveals its ancient significance as a crossing point of the River Clarin, 20km east of Galway city on what was the main route to Dublin. By some murky logic of local politics, the N6 now dips south to take in Loughrea, leaving Athenry and its many well-preserved historic sites in peace, including nearly all of its fourteenth-century town **walls**, plus the North Gate, five towers, and the **castle**. Dating back to the thirteenth century, this forbidding, almost windowless three-storey tower stands at the northeast corner of the walls, guarding the ford (April & Oct daily 10am–5pm; May–Sept daily 10am–6pm; last admission 45min before closing; €2.90; Heritage Card; ⓦwww.heritageireland.ie).

Opposite the castle, but also accessible from the market square, is the lively and enterprising **heritage centre** (April–Sept daily 11am–5pm; €3, or €5 including archery in the grounds and a guided walking tour of the town; discount with Heritage Card; ⓣ091/844661, ⓦwww.athenryheritagecentre.com). Occupying a nineteenth-century church built within the ruins of a medieval predecessor, it recounts the town's history using well-presented touch-screen audiovisuals. There are stocks, a re-created dungeon, a wooden maze and lots of objects for kids to handle, and everyone, big or small, gets to wear a medieval costume. The centre hosts frequent special events and activities, including a festival of medieval crafts and re-enactments one Sunday in late August. Out in the market square stands the only **market cross** in situ in the country, though it's badly damaged; dating from the fifteenth century, it's carved with scenes of the Crucifixion and the Virgin and Child. East from here, just across the river, the extensive remains of the thirteenth-to-fifteenth-century Dominican **Priory of SS Peter and Paul** include a fine collection

The Fields of Athenry

Athenry is probably most famous for the song **The Fields of Athenry**, penned by singer-songwriter Pete St John in 1979, as an adaptation of a poignant 1880s ballad about the abominations of the Famine. It's an emotive, catchy number, popular in pubs and at soccer and rugby matches, and you may well find yourself joining in at least the chorus:

Low lie the fields of Athenry, Where once we watched the small, free birds fly,
Our love was on the wing, We had dreams and songs to sing,
It's so lonely round the fields of Athenry.

of carved grave slabs from medieval times on (the interior is accessible on guided tours from the heritage centre).

Athenry's outstanding **B&B** choice is *Caheroyan House* (Ⓣ091/844858, Ⓦwww.caheroyanhouseathenry.com; ❸; self-catering also available), five minutes' walk northeast from the North Gate on the Monivea road. This tastefully refurbished eighteenth-century manor house in a pretty garden offers spacious en-suite bedrooms, walks in its forty hectares of organic farmland and woodland, and tennis courts. Around 7km southeast of Athenry, east of the village of Craughwell, *St Clerans* (Ⓣ091/846555, Ⓦwww.stclerans.com; ❽) is a luxurious and relaxing **hotel** with a fine European and Oriental restaurant, in an elegant, eighteenth-century manor house that used to belong to film director John Huston. North Gate Street is flanked by a couple of good, inexpensive **places to eat**. In a whitewashed traditional cottage that's signposted down a small alley, the Indian-run *Curry Cottage* (Ⓣ091/875685; Tues–Sun evenings) rustles up all your subcontinental favourites, including a wide selection of vegetable dishes, while the popular *Castlegate Hotel* offers tasty soup and sandwiches in the bar and more substantial dishes in the attached *Pepper Mill* restaurant.

The Aran Islands

Once part of a land barrier across the south side of Galway Bay, the **Aran Islands** (Oileáin Árann) – **Inishmore**, **Inishmaan** and **Inisheer** – have proved alluring to travellers for centuries. Until recently, their isolation allowed the continuation of an ancient Gaelic culture, traces of which remain, along with Irish, still the main language of the islands. Fishing and farming are to this day the main activities on Inishmaan, while tourism is the major earner on Inishmore and Inisheer, attracting around a quarter of a million visitors a year.

As well as the islands' heritage, their dramatic landscapes, continuing the limestone pavement of the Burren in County Clare into the sea, are a major draw. This bleak geology manages to sustain over four hundred varieties of wild flower, including the rare Alpine Spring gentian, as well as a healthy population of butterflies and endangered bird species such as the chough and the Little Tern. And strewn across the islands is one of the richest concentrations of pre-Christian and early Christian archeological sites in Europe, encapsulated by **Dun Aengus**, a spectacular prehistoric ring fort on the edge of Inishmore's sea cliffs.

The Ordnance Survey cover the Arans on a single, 1:25,000 **map**, while *The Aran Islands: A World of Stone* is an excellent introductory **book**, published by O'Brien Press. Tim Robinson has produced a comprehensive map and guidebook of the islands, which is great on archeology and the derivation of Irish place names, while his books, *The Aran Islands: Pilgrimage* and *Labyrinth*, provide even more detailed and fascinating analysis. Meanwhile, Breandán and Ruairí Ó hEithir's *An Aran Reader* is an absorbing anthology of writing about the Arans, from the chronicler Giraldus Cambrensis to Seamus Heaney.

Some history

Few areas of Ireland are as rich in ancient remains as the Aran Islands, notably the massive **stone forts** that so enhance the grandeur of the landscape. The dating of these forts, however, is tricky, especially as their functions and significance seem to have varied over the centuries, but it's clear that all seven forts

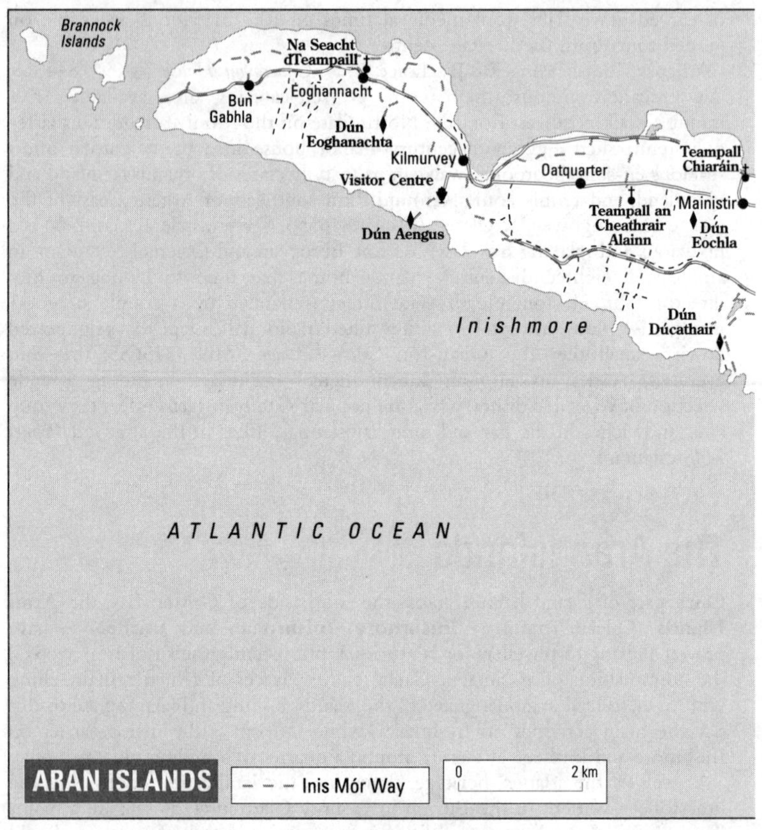

on the Arans were in use around 800 AD, while some are as old as 1100 BC, during the Bronze Age. Meanwhile, from the fifth or sixth century onwards, the islands were a centre of **monastic learning**, their wildness and remoteness drawing students from far and wide. St Enda's monastery on Inishmore was one of the most influential of the age, training monks who went on to found important houses of their own, such as Brendan of Clonfert, Ciarán of Clonmacnois and Colmcille of Iona.

The monasteries of the Arans had gone into decline by the early thirteenth century, at which time Galway city began to take off as a trading port under the Anglo-Normans. For controlling piracy – and their own piratical instincts – in Galway Bay, the Gaelic lords of Aran, the **O'Briens** of County Clare, received an annual payment from the city. In the sixteenth century, however, the O'Briens fell into dispute with the O'Flahertys of west Galway over the islands – to their mutual detriment. The argument was eventually resolved by Queen Elizabeth I, who, seeing the Arans as strategically important against the Spanish and French, annexed the islands to the Crown. In 1588, the Arans were sold to the Lynch family of Galway, who were required to keep a garrison of soldiers there. The family, however, remained loyal to the king during the English Civil War of the 1640s, and the victorious Cromwell declared Sir Robert Lynch a traitor and his lands forfeit.

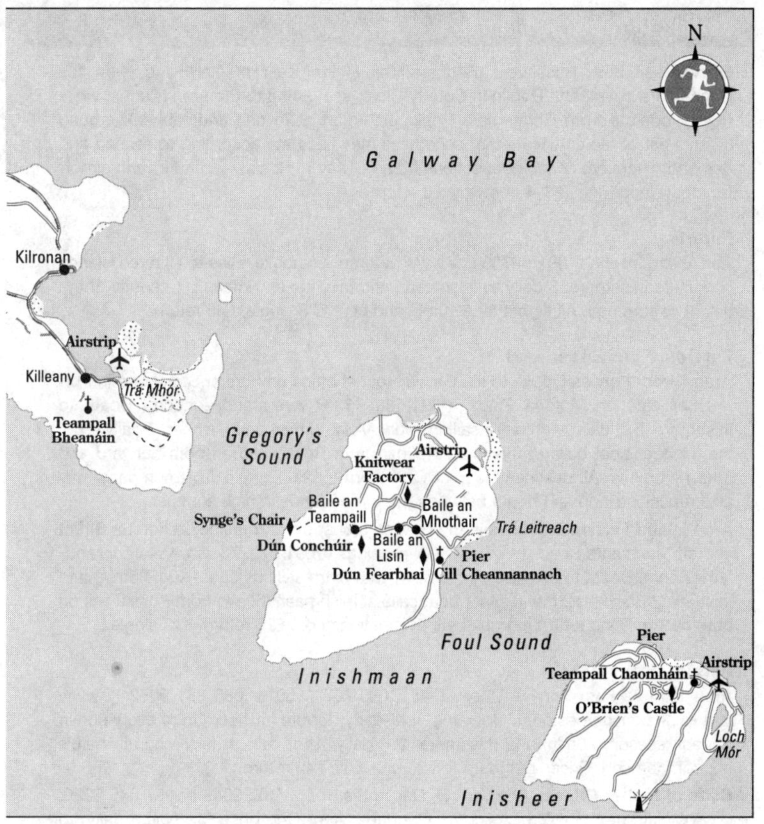

Thereafter, the islands passed through a succession of landowners, whose main interest was the income from ever-increasing rents. The islands escaped the worst effects of the Famine of the 1840s, as the availability of food from the sea and the shore helped to compensate for the failure of the potato crop. Indeed, the populations of Inishmaan and Inisheer increased during the decade, perhaps because they provided refuge for mainlanders. It wasn't until 1922 that the absentee landlords sold their interests and the islands' farmers finally came to own their land.

Inishmore

One of the great attractions of **Inishmore** (Inis Mór, "Big Island", but often referred to simply as Árainn) is its topography, stark, simple and easily appreciated. Sheer cliffs run the fourteen-kilometre length of its south coast, lashed at their base by the relentless Atlantic, while their tops offer an ethereal panorama, the echoing wall of the Cliffs of Moher to the southeast, and to the north across Galway Bay, the Connemara Mountains, tinged with green, purple and gold. The land declines northwards in a geometric pattern of grey stone, the parallel grooves of its limestone pavement overlaid by ten thousand kilometres of

Getting to the Aran Islands

Ferries sail from Rossaveel (Rós an Mhíl; 40km west of Galway city on the Connemara coast) and Doolin in County Clare (see p.400) to the Aran Islands, while **flights** operate from Connemara Regional Airport at Inverin (Indreabhán), around 30km west of the city. Note that schedules may fluctuate according to season and demand. There are coach connections from Galway to Rossaveel and Inverin airport for most departures (€3–4 one way, €6 return).

Flights

Aer Árann Inverin ⓣ091/593034, ⓦwww.aerarannislands.ie. Flies to all three islands (2 daily to Inishmore, 3 daily to Inishmaan and Inisheer in winter, up to hourly at the height of summer). All flights take 10min and cost €23 single, €45 return.

Ferries from Rossaveel

Aran Direct Ferries Opposite the Galway tourist office on Forster Street and in Port Internet café on Victoria Place ⓣ091/566535, ⓦwww.arandirect.com. Boats to Inishmore (2–3 daily, with extra sailings June–Aug; 35min) and Inisheer (2 daily; 1hr); the Inisheer boat calls at Inishmaan (50min from Rossaveel) on both outward and return journeys. All destinations cost €25 return, €12.50 single. This company may also run island-hopping boats between the three islands in high summer.

Aran Island Ferries Branches in the Galway tourist office, outside on Forster Street and on Merchants Road ⓣ091/568903, evenings ⓣ091/572273, ⓦwww.aranisland-ferries.com. Boats to Inishmore (2–3 daily, with extra sailings June–Aug; 35min) and Inisheer (2 daily; 1hr); the Inisheer boat calls at Inishmaan (50min from Rossaveel) on both outward and return journeys. All destinations cost €25 return, €13 single.

Ferries from Doolin

Aran Islands Fast Ferries Doolin Pier ⓣ065/707 4550 or 086 881 9052, ⓦwww.aranislandsfastferries.com. Operates April–early Sept to Inisheer (up to every 90min in peak season; 25min) and Inishmore (2–4 daily; 1hr); calls at Inishmaan if there's enough demand. Prices range up to €25 one way, €40 return.

Cliffs of Moher Cruises (the *Jack B*) Doolin Pier ⓣ065/707 5949 or 087 245 3239, ⓦwww.cliffs-of-moher-cruises.com. Operates April–Oct once or twice daily to Inisheer (30min). €15 one way, €30 return.

Doolin Ferries Doolin Pier ⓣ065/707 4455, 707 4466 or 707 4189, ⓦwww.doolinferries.com. Operates April to Sept or Oct to Inisheer (at least 3 daily; 25min) and to Inishmore (2 daily; duration depends on number of stops on the way), sometimes calling at Inishmaan. Prices range up to €20 one way, €40 return.

dry-stone walls, which parcel up man-made fields, painstakingly nurtured out of sand, seaweed and what handfuls of soil there are. There's more greenery and a smattering of villages towards the sheltered north coast, which is lined with rock pools and several sandy beaches.

This landscape is strewn with a wealth of spectacular dry-stone **ring forts**, notably **Dun Aengus**, and fascinating **early churches**. Consequently, and with frequent bus and boat links to Galway city, Inishmore receives crowds of day-trippers in the summer and is the most tourist-oriented of the Arans, now even boasting a branch of *Supermac's*, Ireland's very own burger chain. However, you really need two full days to visit the historic sites, which will also allow you time to soak up the scenery, enjoy the relative quiet of the evenings here and even have a swim at beautiful **Kilmurvey beach**.

The island's main **festival** is Féile Patrún Inis Mór, over a weekend in late June or early July, featuring *currach* racing and other traditional sports, accompanied by plenty of music and open-air set dancing. In late February or early March, themed events and parties celebrate cult classic *Father Ted*, the TV comedy whose setting, Craggy Island, was inspired by the Arans (Ⓦwww.friendsofted.org for information and tickets).

Information and getting around

Ferries dock at **KILRONAN** (Cill Rónáin), the main village. At the helpful **tourist office** (April, May, Sept & Oct daily 10am–6pm; June–Aug daily 10am–6.45pm; Nov–March Mon–Fri 11am–5pm, Sat & Sun 10am–5pm, sometimes with an hour's lunch break; Ⓣ099/61263, Ⓔaran@failteireland.ie) opposite the pier, it's worth asking if the Aran Heritage Centre on the north side of the village has reopened. Kilronan has a surprisingly large and well-stocked Spar **supermarket**, with an **ATM**, not far from the village **post office** and the Bank of Ireland, which opens on Wednesdays year-round, plus Thursdays in July and August. You can **change money** at the tourist office, which also offers a **left-luggage** service (€1 per day).

The most scenic way to get around is on the waymarked **Inis Mór Way**, which covers the whole of the island on its fifty-kilometre route, though it can easily be broken up into shorter chunks and satisfying circular walks; a leaflet is available at the tourist office. Or you can rent a **bike** from Aran Bicycle Hire or Burkes, which are both by the pier in Kilronan; it's easier on the legs and lungs if you go out on the coast road and come back by the hillier middle road, with the prevailing west wind at your back. **Pony buggies** offer tours of the island (€40–60 for a group of up to four adults, with a choice of 3 set routes), as do the **minibuses** that line up at the pier waiting for the boats to come in. The latter follow an established route around the island that takes two and a half to three hours, including an hour and a half at Dun Aengus and fifteen minutes at the Seven Churches, and charge €10 per person; you could also negotiate with them for a taxi service. Lastly, there's a public **bus**, which runs across to Bun

The Aran Islands and the Gaelic Revival

In the late nineteenth century, the Arans became a living museum for anthropologists, antiquarians and linguists, seeking out the unbroken heritage of Gaelic language, beliefs and customs here, which in turn provided fuel for the **Gaelic Revival** and the Nationalist movement. Written and spoken Irish was a particular focus of interest, as even by this time the islands were one of the few areas of the country where the native language was in daily use. Patrick Pearse came specifically to learn Irish on Inishmaan, which was also visited by writers Yeats, Lady Gregory and, most notably, J.M. Synge – George Russell later joked that Synge's knack was to discover that if you translated Irish literally into English, you achieved poetry.

The Arans themselves have nurtured several excellent writers. **Liam O'Flaherty** (1896–1984) of Inishmore wrote many highly regarded short stories and novels, notably *The Informer* (1925), a salty tale of an ex-IRA man who betrays an associate to the police and is hunted down by his former colleagues. Meanwhile poet **Máirtín Ó'Direáin** (1910–88), also from Inishmore, explored themes of alienation and the anonymity of city life in the Irish language.

In 1934, the documentary-maker **Robert Flaherty** released his classic *Man of Aran*, in which he sought to record the islands' vanishing way of life, though some of it had already disappeared – he wasn't averse to re-creating scenes that were no longer witnessed. A few of the traditions captured in the film still exist – you'll still see people collecting seaweed for fertilizer, building dry-stone walls and fishing from **currachs** (traditional pointed skiffs), though these are no longer covered with animal skins.

Gabhla and back via the middle road three or four times a day (Mon–Sat; €3), departing from Kilronan's supermarket.

Accommodation

Out of a dozen or so **B&Bs** in **Kilronan**, *Seacrest* (Ⓣ099/61292; ❷) is a good bet in the centre, with smart en-suite rooms, a spacious living room and hearty breakfasts. The friendly and richly decorated *Pier House* (*Teach na Ceibe*; Ⓣ099/61417, Ⓦwww.pierhousearan.com; closed Nov to mid-March; ❸) occupies a peerless spot by the jetty with panoramic views. On the southwest side of Kilronan now stands a smart, modern **hotel**, *Óstan Árann* (Ⓣ099/61104, Ⓦwww.aranislandshotel.com; ❺), tastefully fitted with pine floors and bare stone walls, and with fine views of the bay and Internet access. Two kilometres southeast of Kilronan in the village of **Killeany** (Cill Éinne), *Tigh Fitz* (Ⓣ099/61213, Ⓦwww.tighfitz.com; closed most of Dec; ❸) is a congenial pub offering cosy and well-equipped en-suite rooms. On a rise at the east end of Killeany is *Ard Einne* (Ⓣ099/61126, Ⓦwww.ardeinne.com; closed Nov–Jan; dinner available; ❸, midweek deals available), a welcoming and well-run spot, with fine views from all its rooms, which are en suite and cheerfully done out in pine and floral prints.

Above the beach in **Oatquarter** (Fearann an Choirce), towards the west end of the island, Conneely's *Beach View House* (Ⓣ099/61141, Ⓔbeachviewhouse@eircom.net; mid-April to Sept; ❷) has en-suite and standard rooms, and is good value at the lower end of the price code. In **Kilmurvey** (Cill Mhuirbhigh) near the Dun Aengus visitor centre stands *Kilmurvey House* (Ⓣ099/61218, Ⓦwww.accommodationaranislands.com; April–Oct; dinner available if booked in advance; ❸), an impressive and welcoming nineteenth-century country house with a ruined church in its extensive garden. Film buffs will relish staying at the thatched and whitewashed *Man of Aran Cottages*, in a colourful garden on the west side of Kilmurvey beach (Ⓣ099/61301, Ⓦwww.manofarancottage.com; March–Oct; ❷), which Robert Flaherty built in the local style as a set for his film, *Man of Aran*; there are six attractive, en-suite bedrooms with fine views of Connemara, and guests can enjoy delicious, mostly organic dinners, using herbs and vegetables from the garden.

Among Inishmore's **hostels**, the IHO-affiliated *Kilronan Hostel* in downtown Kilronan (Ⓣ099/61255, Ⓦwww.kilronanhostel.com; from €13.50) includes breakfast in the price and has family rooms available – though they probably won't get many takers as it's above *Tigh Jo Mac's*, a popular pub. A quieter alternative, located just above Killeany and signposted from the main road, is the well-equipped, spacious *Killeany Lodge Pilgrim Hostel* (Ⓣ099/61393, Ⓔphostel@hotmail.com; April–Oct; IHO; dorms €15, twins ❶), with a pretty garden, great views and cooked meals available. To the west, on the main road to Kilmurvey, is the *Mainistir House Hostel* at **Mainistir** (Ⓣ099/61169, Ⓦwww.mainistirhousearan.com; IHO; dorms €17, twins ❶; breakfast included), a basic but comfortable hostel, which offers Internet access and very good, mostly vegetarian buffets in the evenings.

A basic **campsite** (Ⓣ099/61185), with toilets and washbasins but no showers or cooking facilities, lies a twenty-minute walk from Kilronan along the coast road towards Teampall Chiaráin, but you'd be better off camping in the garden of the *Killeany Lodge Pilgrim Hostel* (see above), where you can share the hostel's facilities.

Around the island

Heading west from Kilronan, minibuses and bicycles can make the main road across the island to Kilmurvey – the **middle road** – a little hectic in high season, but you can still escape what crowds there are by taking the less hilly **coast road** along the north shore (turn right at *Joe Watty's* pub), or by walking along the southerly, partly paved **rock road**, which cuts across the highest part of the island.

West to Kilmurvey

About 1.5km northwest of Kilronan on the coast road, **Teampall Chiaráin** is believed to have been founded in the sixth century by St Ciarán, a disciple of Enda's, who went on to establish one of the great monasteries in Ireland, at Clonmacnois. The plain, rectangular west doorway is eighth or ninth century, but the church was enlarged around it in the twelfth century, including the arched Romanesque east window. At the east end, look out for an ancient slab inscribed with a cross and a circle, and pierced with a hole through which people pass handkerchiefs for luck.

Three kilometres from Kilronan off the middle road, near the island's highest point, stands **Dún Eochla** (Fort of the Yew Wood). Heavily reconstructed in the nineteenth century, it's an oval hill fort consisting of two massive, roughly concentric walls, with great views across Galway Bay. A couple of kilometres further along the middle road, it's well worth breaking your journey at the fifteenth-century **Teampall an Cheathrair Alainn** (the Church of the Four Beauties), named after four saints who are said to have lived and been buried here. This picturesque ruined chapel is reached along a rough, signposted path through grassy fields and over stone walls; water from the well on its south side, hung with crosses and other votive offerings, is believed to cure eye complaints.

The middle and coast roads meet at the beautiful horseshoe of **Kilmurvey beach**, a gently sloping, Blue Flag stretch of fine sand, with magnificent views across to Connemara.

Dun Aengus (Dún Aonghasa)

Signposted to the south of Kilmurvey, **Dun Aengus** is by far the Aran Islands' most compelling prehistoric site, a semicircular fort of three concentric enclosures, hard up against the edge of sheer, ninety-metre sea cliffs. From here, you can see Kerry Head, northwest of Tralee, on a clear day and occasionally Mount Brandon on the Dingle Peninsula – and if you're truly blessed the island of Hy Brasil to the west (see p.436). The fort is named after Aengus of the **Fir Bolg**, a legendary ancient race, who were said to have been of Greek origin and to have ruled Ireland for 37 years, before being conquered by the equally mythical Tuatha Dé Danann.

The inner citadel comprises a wall, six metres high and four metres wide, of massive blocks of limestone that were quarried on site and put together without mortar. In the site's heyday, the inhabitants would have lived here and in the middle enclosure, while the outermost enclosure would have been for livestock. Some time after 500 BC, however, Dun Aengus contracted and a still-imposing *chevaux-de-frise* was constructed between the middle and outer walls, a ten-metre-wide field planted with razor-sharp standing stones up to 1.8 metres high, designed to slow down attackers.

Daytime access to the site is via a **visitor centre** (daily: March–Oct 10am–6pm; Nov–Feb 10am–4pm; €2.10; Heritage Card; Ⓦwww.heritageireland.ie), with an attached café, from where it's an uphill walk of nearly a kilometre to the fort. Built on the site of an early medieval monastery, the visitor centre compellingly puts Dun Aengus into its historical context, based on the results of major excavations carried out here between 1992 and 1995. After hours, you can get up to the fort through the side gate next to the visitor centre.

Hy Brasil

From Dun Aengus, you might be lucky enough to see the famous mirage known as **Hy Brasil** (after which the South American country was named), which appears in the sea to the west as a mountainous island. Local folklore represents this mythical land variously as the island of the blessed, the Garden of Eden, Tír na nÓg (the land of eternal youth), the Isle of Truth, of Joy, of Fair Women and of Apples. In the early twentieth century, islanders believed it appeared once every seven years, but up until the mid-nineteenth century it was actually shown on some sea charts of the Atlantic. On the unforgiving, sea-battered Arans, it's easy to understand how this fantasy of a prosperous paradise grew up.

There's evidence of human activity at Dun Aengus from 1500 BC to 1000 AD, with the first enclosure dated to around 1100 BC and the most dynamic period of activity around 800 BC. Prompted by the site's extremely exposed location and lack of water, various theories have been put forward over the years about it being a storm temple or some kind of ceremonial theatre, but archeologists have now returned to the obvious explanation: that it was indeed an inhabited fortress, probably the capital of the Arans, built partly to demonstrate the islands' power when viewed from the sea and located on a site that may have had ritual significance.

West of Kilmurvey

Just under 2km northwest of Kilmurvey, signposts point south along a dwindling trail for the twenty-minute walk up to the impressive **Dún Eoghanachta**. Probably built between 650 and 800 AD, it's the smallest of the Aran forts, a perfect circle of rectilinear, almost brick-like, light-grey, limestone blocks. Lying within reach of some relatively good farming land, it would have been a defended homestead and still shelters the remains of three *clocháns*.

A little further along the road, on the north side of the straggling village of Eoghannacht, stands an interesting monastic complex called **Na Seacht dTeampaill** or the **Seven Churches**, though it actually consists of the substantial ruins of two churches and five domestic buildings. It was founded by St Brecan, who arrived on the island in the fifth or early sixth century, succeeded Enda as the abbot of the main monastery at Killeany, and was famous for his piety and severity. Occupying good land with a permanent supply of fresh water and some of the deepest soil on the island, the site is still used as a graveyard. The older of the churches, Teampall Bhreacáin, dates from the eighth century but was gradually enlarged with some fine arches. Teampall A'Phoill (Church of the Hollow), which goes back only as far as the fifteenth century, was used as a parish church until relatively recently. Near the northeastern corner of the site, you can see the incised base of a high cross, which originally consisted of a single, four-metre-high limestone slab.

South and east of Kilronan

Dún Dúcathair (Black Fort) enjoys a spectacular location on a promontory to the south of Kilronan. Guarded by cliffs on three sides, and a *chevaux-de-frise* on the fourth, the fort consists of a single massive wall, 60m long, that slices across the neck of the headland. Once through the narrow entrance at the eastern end – the main gate here collapsed into the sea in the early nineteenth century – you'll find the remains of four oval *clocháns*. The fort lies on a branch of the Inis Mór Way about 3km from Kilronan – head south along the main road for a kilometre after which a turning is signposted off to the right along an increasingly rocky path.

In a magnificent hilltop location that's especially lovely at sunset, eleventh-century **Teampall Bheanáin** stands just south of and above the village of Killeany. Built of huge stone slabs, it's notable for its north–south alignment, its unusually steep gables and for its size, just 5m long – some claim it to be the smallest church in Europe. It was probably part of St Enda's early monastic site, formed around 490 (*Cill Einne* means "Church of Enda"), which was torn down by Cromwell's soldiers to strengthen Arkin Castle in the village in 1652. Beyond Killeany and the airstrip, Trá Mhór is a huge stretch of sandy **beach** that's good for swimming.

Eating and drinking

No one comes to Inishmore just for the food, though the **restaurants** offer plenty of local lobster if you have the cash. With fine views from its terrace tables, the *Pier House* in Kilronan (see p.434) is a great spot for lunch on a sunny day, serving tasty panini, salads, chowder and more substantial seafood dishes; dinner, which may include Aran lobster, oysters and wild salmon sushi, is much more sophisticated and pricey. Cheaper fare, notably fish and chips, chowder and other marine delicacies, can be had at *An tSean Ceibh* (*The Ould Pier*), a no-frills restaurant with a few outdoor tables. *Lios Aengus*, a **café** and book exchange by the Spar supermarket, serves up fine breakfasts and lunches of sandwiches, salads and baked potatoes, as well as cakes and great coffee. In the evening, you could reserve a place for yourself at *Mainistir House Hostel*'s buffet (see p.434).

The pick of Inishmore's **pubs** are *Tigh Jo Mac's* in the centre of Kilronan, a convivial spot with impromptu traditional music and a terrace with good views over the harbour; and *Joe Watty's*, which has a tree-shaded beer garden on the northern edge of Kilronan and all sorts of live music most nights in summer; it's also very popular for its baguettes and hot meals. In summer, *Tigh Fitz's* at Killeany offers daytime bar food and live music at weekends.

Inishmaan

Approaching from the west or east, **Inishmaan** (Inis Meáin, "Middle Island") looks like a rising wave about to break over Galway Bay to the north. From the grey, fissured limestone pavement at its northern end, tiny, green pastures separated by a maze of dry-stone walls rise to the main east–west ridge – along which lies a ribbon of villages – while the "back of the island" beyond slopes off more gradually to the south. This is the most unspoilt of the Arans, and the most thoroughly Irish-speaking (though English is understood), where people are still mostly engaged in farming and fishing. Wild salmon are caught from black, pointed *currachs* – now with outboard motors – and on Sundays, older women wear traditional multicoloured shawls to go with their thick woollen skirts. The island's historic sites are on a smaller scale than Inishmore's – though the imposing ring fort of **Dún Conchúir** is worth singling out – and there are far fewer amenities, but for some people this tranquil, low-key place will be the perfect getaway.

Inishmaan's most famous visitor was **J.M. Synge**, who, on the advice of W.B. Yeats, spent long periods of time here between 1898 and 1902, living on mackerel and eggs. He found artistic liberation here, as well as plenty of plot ideas in the stories told him by the islanders, writing his first play, *When the Moon has Set* in 1901. His book *The Aran Islands* is a moving account of the way of life he encountered.

Around the island

The island's sights are linked by the **Inis Meáin Way**, an eight-kilometre walking route, which runs across the centre of the island and back and is marked with yellow arrows on limestone plaques. Immediately southwest of the pier on the east side of the island, you'll see **Cill Cheanannach**, a tiny, roofless church with steeply pitched gables, built some time before 1200. Just to the north in the graveyard lies a curious, roughly triangular slab of limestone: the end-stone of a tomb-shrine, it's pierced with a hole through which pilgrims could touch the bones of the saint inside (possibly the shadowy Cheanainn). **Dún Fearbhaí** perches on the slope above Cill Cheanannach, a small, rectilinear ring fort, probably dating from the ninth century AD or later, that's now atmospherically overgrown. North of the pier runs **Trá Leitreach**, a safe, sheltered **beach**.

From the pier, the island – and the main road – rises in rough steps through the adjoining hamlets of Baile an Mhothair and Baile an Lisín to Baile an Teampaill at its midpoint. It's well worth calling in to the village church here to see the gorgeous **stained-glass windows** executed by Harry Clarke in 1939. Made up of glass pieces of varying thicknesses, the richly coloured images swim before your eyes – look out especially for Cavan (Caomhán), the patron saint of Inisheer, with a man rowing a *currach* behind his feet.

A little further along on the right stands **Teach Synge** (June–Sept afternoons, variable hours, usually daily though sometimes closed Sun; ⓣ099/73036; €3), where Synge stayed on Inishmaan, as well as Lady Gregory, W.B. Yeats and Patrick Pearse before him. It's a charming 300-year-old cottage, thatched and whitewashed, with typically small windows (rents on the islands were often calculated on the basis of the size and number of windows). A dresser, a butter churn and most of the other furniture from Synge's time are still inside, and there are some fascinating photos taken by the playwright himself, on the first camera to be brought to the island.

Signposted up a lane from Teach Synge, near Inishmaan's highest point, **Dún Conchúir** is one of the Arans' most imposing forts, with fine views of Connemara and down Ireland's west coast. Its ramparted, dry-stone walls are 5m thick and 6m high, with a walled gateway defending the main entrance at the northeastern corner. According to legend, Conchúir was the younger brother of Aengus, who is commemorated with his own fort on Inishmore, backing up the theory that there was a prehistoric confederation of the islands, with its capital at Dun Aengus. The last inhabitant of the fort was a nineteenth-century Connemara man called Malley, who had accidentally killed his father and hid out here for several months, before escaping to America – a tale used as inspiration by Synge for the plot of *Playboy of the Western World*.

About twenty minutes' walk west of Baile an Teampaill is the playwright's favourite contemplative spot, **Synge's Chair**, a semicircle of stones he gathered himself, on the site of an old look-out post facing Gregory's Sound. From here, it's possible to hike down the west coast, along towering, rectangular cliffs, to the blowholes at the southwest corner, before cutting up the middle of the island to the village after about two and a half hours.

Practicalities

Bikes can be rented just up from the pier, on the main road towards Baile an Mhothair, while information is available from the **Inishmaan Island Co-operative** (ⓣ099/73010, ⓔccimeain@indigo.ie), near the **post office** in the centre of the island; the Bank of Ireland operates on the second Tuesday of every month.

The small, modern island **hotel**, *Óstan Inis Meáin* (Ⓣ099/73020, Ⓦwww.inismeainhotel.com; ❸), has comfortable, en-suite rooms and a bar, towards the north end of the island near the airstrip. The family that runs the knitwear factory (see below) have recently built an excellent **restaurant** and set of **suites** nearby, in a smart, contemporary style that skilfully blends in with the island landscape (Ⓣ086 826 6026, Ⓦwww.inismeain.com; March–Oct; restaurant weekends only; ❻). Each suite has a huge picture window to make the most of the views of Galway Bay and a large living area, where substantial breakfasts, delivered on a tray, are taken. With very welcoming and knowledgeable owners, *An Dún*, just below Dún Conchúir (Ⓣ099/73047, Ⓦwww.inismeainaccommodation.com; ❷), offers attractive, well-designed, en-suite, **B&B** rooms with great views, and delicious food in their daytime **café** and evening **restaurant**, including local wild salmon, seafood and vegetables; in the off season, they provide pick-ups from the pier and aromatherapy packages on certain weekends. Or there's the cheaper and very hospitable *Ard Alainn* (Ⓣ099/73027 or 087 285 6778, Ⓔardalainn_inismeain@eircom.net; ❷; self-catering also available; phone for pick-up from the pier), with standard and en-suite rooms and good rates for singles, in a lofty position between Dún Conchúir and Synge's Chair offering a fine panorama of Galway Bay that stretches from the Burren right round to Inishmore. The best place to **camp** is in the sand dunes by the beach, Trá Leitreach. The island's quaint, thatched **pub**, *Teach Ósta*, in Baile an Mhothair, hosts impromptu sessions of traditional music.

On the north side of Baile an Mhothair, the Inis Meáin Knitting Company (Ⓣ099/73009, Ⓦwww.inismeain.com) produces beautiful **knitwear** and linen based on traditional Aran patterns, usually for exclusive export markets, but available here from the factory at discounted prices. Also based on Inishmaan is the Aran Islands Dive Centre, which organizes **scuba diving** off the Arans in summer (Ⓣ099/73134, 091/505943 or 087 919 2212, Ⓔatlanticdiving@eircom.net).

Inisheer

Lying just 10km off the Clare coast, **Inisheer** (Inis Oírr, "East Island"; Ⓦwww.inisoirr-island.com) is the smallest and least dramatic Aran. Its historic sites aren't quite as appealing as Inishmaan's, and it's much more of a lively pleasure ground, attracting crowds of teenagers to Irish college and day-trippers from Doolin in summer. There's a lovely, partly sheltered, sandy **beach** east of the **pier** on the north coast, along which nearly all of the habitation on this three-kilometre-wide island spreads.

Above and behind the beach, **O'Brien's Castle** (Caisleán Uí Bhriain) is attractively sited above low, ivy-covered cliffs, a short, green valley and a network of dry-stone walls. It's well worth walking up to the castle for views of the harbour and the north half of the island, if nothing else. Covered in brown lichen, it's extant up to two storeys, with some crenellations and one roofed room remaining. This fourteenth- or fifteenth-century tower house was built by the O'Brien clan of County Clare, who ruled the Arans at the time, within an early medieval ring fort, **Dún Formna**, which is not as impressive as similar forts on the other islands.

Climb the sand dune, topped with modern gravestones and wild flowers, on the southeast side of the beach and you're in for a surprise: sunk into the dune's summit lies **Teampall Chaomháin**, a roofless church dedicated to St Cavan (still a common boy's name on the island), who is thought to have been the brother of St Kevin of Glendalough. Retaining walls now help to protect the ruin from the shifting sand, but it still has to be shovelled out every year on June 14, the saint's feast day. The primitive, lintelled doorway of the original, tenth-century oratory here was retained as the main west entrance of this larger, late-medieval church, while an ornately carved slab just to the northeast marks Cavan's grave. Southeast again from here is **Loch Mór**, a pretty lake inhabited by wildfowl.

The ten-kilometre, waymarked **Inis Oírr Way** traces a circular route round the northern half of the island, taking in these sites, and you could easily branch off between Teampall Chaomháin and Loch Mór to add on a walk down the road to the **lighthouse** at the southeastern tip of the island, which affords fantastic views of the Cliffs of Moher.

Practicalities

The **Inisheer Island Co-operative** beyond the east end of the beach (T099/75008, E ccteo@eircom.net) can provide information, as well as **Internet** access (Tues, Thurs & Sat afternoons only). There's no bank on the island, but the hotel can change money, and the Bank of Ireland visits every second Tuesday in summer and on the fourth Tuesday of the month in winter. The multipurpose **arts centre**, *Áras Éanna* (T099/75150, W www.araseanna.ie), a fifteen-minute walk south from the west end of the village, has a gallery showing temporary exhibitions by artists in residence, runs crafts courses and demonstrations of traditional basket-making in the summer and hosts music, films and plays in its small theatre. **Bikes** can be rented from the helpful office in front of the pier, while forty-minute **tours** of the island are provided by pony buggies (€10 per person).

There's usually enough **accommodation** on Inisheer to meet demand, but it might well be worth booking ahead at the height of the season, especially for the bank-holiday weekend at the start of August. The island **hotel**, the *Óstán Inis Oírr* near the pier (T099/75020, W www.ostaninisoirr.com; Easter–Sept; 3), has cosy, en-suite rooms. Hard by the pier is the *Brú Radharc na Mara* **hostel** (T099/75024, E radharcnamara@hotmail.com; IHH & IHO; mid-March to Oct), which offers dorms (€15), twin (1) and family rooms, as well as smarter, en-suite accommodation in the attached **B&B** (2). Among the island's other B&Bs, *Radharc an Chláir* by the castle (T099/75019, E bridpoil@eircom.net; 2) has a good reputation for its fine views and great meals, with good rates for singles and children. The only place to **camp** is on the official site by the beach, which has toilets and hot showers.

At the west end of the village, *Fisherman's Cottage*, an attractive, welcoming **café-restaurant** done out in marine colours (T099/75073, W www.southaran.com), serves tasty dinners and simpler lunches, using mostly organic ingredients. They also offer cookery and yoga courses, as well as kayaks to rent, and are planning to build a guesthouse. In summer there's music most nights of the week at the hotel bar (which stays open year-round and does popular pub grub), *Tigh Ruairí*, an easy-going **pub** next door, or *Tigh Ned's*, a cosy spot by the hostel with a lovely garden overlooking the harbour.

Connemara

Comprising all of Galway to the west of the city, **Connemara** (W www.connemara-tourism.org) is a ravishingly diverse tract of land. Cut off from the

Walking in Connemara

Connemara offers a fantastic variety of **walking**, including mountains over 700 metres – though remember the nearest rescue team is in Galway. A good **map** and guidebook for serious walkers is *The Mountains of Connemara*, with a 1:50,000 scale map derived from aerial photography and fieldwork by Tim Robinson, and an excellent guide to eighteen walks of varying length and difficulty by Joss Lynam. It's available by post from the publishers – Folding Landscapes of Roundstone, Connemara, Co. Galway – or from bookshops and tourist offices. The Ordnance Survey has recently resurveyed the area, producing their own maps at 1:50,000.

A good introduction to the Maam Turks, with fantastic views of the Twelve Bens across Lough Inagh, would be the ascent of **Cnoc na hUilleann** and **Binn Bhriocáin** from the Inagh Valley back road north of Recess, on a three- to four-hour circuit described in *Mountains of Connemara* (part of it on the Western Way). Also described are the classic Twelve Bens walk, the seven-hour **Gleann Chóchan Horseshoe**, starting from the *Ben Lettery* youth hostel and bagging six of the peaks; and the tough, high-level **Maam Turks Walk**, which traverses the range from north of Maam Cross to Leenane – it can be done in one very long day, but most people will want to do it in two, staying down in the Inagh valley, either at the very welcoming and friendly, en-suite *Lough Inagh Ranch* (ⓣ095/34716, ⓔjuliastaunton@hotmail.com; ❷) or at *Lough Inagh Lodge* (ⓣ095/34706, ⓦwww.loughinaghlodgehotel.ie; closed mid-Dec to early March; ❻), a characterful country house, built as a fishing lodge in the nineteenth century.

Mountains of Connemara also covers the waymarked **Western Way**, which runs for 50km from Oughterard to Leenane. This varied, low-level trail starts as a pleasant, sometimes boggy walk beside Lough Corrib, before crossing over from the village of Maam into the dramatic Inagh valley, which runs between the Bens and the Turks. The walk can be done in two long days, with an overnight near Maam, where **B&B** is available at *Leckavrea View House* (ⓣ & ⓕ094/954 8040; March–Nov; ❷), or in the Inagh valley (see above). There's also a new waymarked route, the **Slí Chonamara**, which runs mostly on roads for 250km with quite a few spur trails through the Gaeltacht (details from local tourist offices); the main path follows the coast round from Galway through Spiddal and Rosmuc to Recess, with plenty of accommodation options along the way.

Worthy **short walks** include the ascent of Errisbeg and other routes near Roundstone as described on p.445, the sky road from Clifden on p.448, the trails at Connemara National Park on p.450 and the climb up Tully Hill on p.451.

Walking tours are organized from Clifden by Connemara Safari on the sky road (ⓣ095/21071 or 1850 777200, ⓦwww.walkingconnemara.com), which runs five- and seven-day walking and island-hopping trips.

rest of the county by the sweep of Lough Corrib, the lie of the land at first looks simple, with two statuesque mountain ranges, the **Maam Turks** (Mám Tuirc, the "boar pass") and the **Twelve Bens** (or sometimes Twelve Pins; Na Beanna Beola, the "Peaks of Beola", a mythical giant), bordered by the deep fjord of Killary Harbour to the north. The coast, however, is full of jinks and tricks, a maze of little islands, winding roads, bogs and hills, where it can be hard to tell small loughs from sea inlets. All around the littoral are quiet, white-sand **beaches** that are great for swimming.

Connemara's harsh land, however, has always been thinly populated and isolated, though this has ensured the persistence of rural traditions and of the **Irish language**. It contains the country's largest Gaeltacht, stretching as far west as Roundstone, and Raidió na Gaeltachta and TG4, the Irish-speaking radio and TV stations, are broadcast from here. Four-week **Irish-language courses** for adults, supplemented by cultural activities and singing and dancing classes, are held each summer by NUI Galway at Árus Mháirtín Uí Chadhain (Ⓣ091/595101, Ⓦwww.nuig.ie) in An Cheathrú Rua (Carraroe).

The major route through the area is the N59 from Galway, which cuts across to Clifden before skirting the Twelve Bens on its way to Westport, but there are plenty of scenic side-roads through the mountains and around the frilly coastline. It's hard to miss out **Clifden** on your travels, the likeable and lively main town, poised dramatically between steep hills and the harbour. Other likely bases are the pretty fishing village of **Roundstone** and **Oughterard**, an angler's delight, not far out of Galway city on the lush banks of Lough Corrib. Oughterard has a good selection of visitor attractions, but the only really compelling historic sight in west Connemara is **Kylemore Abbey and Gardens**. Just off shore near here, you can sample easy-going island life on **Inishbofin**.

Bus Éireann services from Galway run along the coast via Spiddal to Carraroe, and around the N59 via Oughterard, Clifden and Letterfrack to Leenane (with a summer extension on to Westport), branching off to Roundstone, Cleggan, the Renvyle Peninsula, between Leenane and Maam Cross, and between Cong and Clifden, via Leenane, in summer. As we were going to press, a long-running private bus company in Connemara, Micheal Nee Coaches, was bought by major operator, Citylink (Ⓣ1890 280808, Ⓦwww.citylink.ie). Their main route from Galway via the N59 to Clifden, Letterfrack and Cleggan for the ferry to Inishbofin will continue, but it's unclear what will happen to the summertime services between Clifden and Cashel via Ballynahinch, and between Clifden and Kylemore Abbey via Letterfrack. Companies offering coach tours of Connemara are detailed on p.422.

Oughterard and around

Around 28km from Galway on the N59, **OUGHTERARD** (Ⓦwww.oughterardtourism.com) is a busy little town, with plenty of varied attractions in the surrounding area to keep you occupied. Its main asset, however, is not immediately obvious from the long main street: behind the trees to the north of town lies the great expanse of **Lough Corrib**, a paradise for angling or for just messing about in boats, studded with hundreds of tree-clad islets (365 of them, one for each day of the year, if you believe the locals).

The easiest way to get out onto the lake is to take a passenger cruise on the *Corrib Queen*, from the pier 2km north of the main street, to lovely **Inchagoill** island (late April to Sept 3 daily; 30min each way, plus 30min on the island; trips also possible from March and into Oct if there's enough demand; book at the tourist office or call Corrib Cruises on Ⓣ087 283 0799, Ⓦwww.corribcruises.com; €18). Little is known of this uninhabited island's history beyond the meaning of its name, "Isle of the Foreigners". It was the site of an early monastery, featuring the Romanesque Saints' Church, which was restored by Sir Benjamin Guinness in the nineteenth century and is most notable for its attractively carved west doorway. It's also possible to hop onto the same company's *Isle of Inishfree* at Inchagoill to go across to **Cong** (see p.454) in County Mayo (€20 Oughterard–Cong one way, €28 return), either as a quick route north or, if you catch the first boat from Oughterard, a full-day round trip, allowing half an hour to have a brief look around Cong.

To the east of Oughterard stands a particularly impressive and well-preserved early sixteenth-century tower house, **Aughnanure Castle** (April–Oct daily 9.30am–6pm, last admission 5.15pm; €2.90; Heritage Card;

Ⓦwww.heritageireland.ie), which rises to six storeys and still retains its outer defensive walls; it occupies what is virtually a rocky island near the banks of Lough Corrib, about 1.5km off the N59 (signposted 3km from the centre of Oughterard). The strongest bastion of the O'Flahertys, who were masters of Connemara from the thirteenth to the sixteenth century, Aughnanure boasts a frightening array of defensive features, including arrow slits aimed at the main staircase, secret prison chambers and a trap door in the hall above a subterranean river, through which were thrown guests who had outstayed their welcome.

Four kilometres southeast of the turn-off for the castle, signs point the short distance off the N59 to the delightful **Brigit's Garden**, named after the saint (see p.158) whose feast day, February 1, and symbol, the snowdrop, mark the start of spring (currently early April to Sept Mon–Sat 9.30am–5.30pm, Sun 12.30–5.30pm, but may in future years open in Feb and close in Oct; quiet time for meditation or reflection Wed 6–8pm & Sun 10am–noon; €7, children €4, family ticket €20; Ⓣ091/550905, Ⓦwww.brigitsgarden.ie). This beautifully designed four-hectare garden includes an area devoted to the four Celtic seasons, featuring sculptures, standing stones, symbolic plantings and a thatched roundhouse. Beyond this, you'll find a stand of ancient woodland, wild-flower meadows, a ring fort, a small lake and the largest sundial in Ireland, with nature discovery trails laid on for adults and kids (who also get to cavort in the willow play area). There's an excellent **café**, as well as an interesting programme of talks, events and festivals for visitors of all ages; the garden opens Sunday morning year-round for guided meditation (donation requested).

For a fascinating change from all the glorious scenery hereabouts, head underground into the recently restored **Glengowla Mine** (March–Nov daily 10am–6pm; for visits at other times, call Ⓣ091/552360; €8), 3km west of Oughterard on the N59. This silver and lead mine was worked between 1850 and 1865 and reluctantly yielded from the area's tough marble around three hundred tonnes of the ore galena. Entertaining guided tours bring to life the hardships of drilling by hand and blasting the rock, often in deep pools of water and always by candlelight.

Practicalities

Oughterard's very helpful **tourist office** is on Main Street (May–Aug Mon–Sat 9.30am–5.30pm, Sun 9.30am–1.30pm; Sept–April Mon–Fri 9.30am–5.30pm; Ⓣ091/552808, Ⓦwww.connemarabegins.com) and has leaflets on walks in the area, including the Western Way (see box, p.441), as well as **Internet** access. You can also ask here about the rowing regatta in July and the horse show at the end of August, which are both combined with live music and other entertainments.

To make the most of Oughterard's setting, the best **places to stay** are the high-standard B&Bs and guesthouses near the lake. A short stroll from the tourist office, on the north side of town off Camp Street, *Camillaun* (Ⓣ091/552678, Ⓦwww.camillaun.com; March–Nov; ❷) is a tastefully decorated, welcoming modern B&B with open fires, set in pretty gardens on the banks of the Owenriff River (where you can rent rowing and motor boats). A little out of town, northwest on the Glann road, lies *Waterfall Lodge* (Ⓣ091/552168, Ⓦwww.waterfalllodge.net; ❷), a handsome Victorian house in wooded gardens by a stream, offering fine breakfasts. Six kilometres out on the same road, *Currarevagh House* (Ⓣ091/552312, Ⓦwww.currarevagh.com; April–late Oct; ❺, half-board deals available) is a charming, traditional country house built in the 1840s on the lake shore, which serves excellent, unpretentious meals based on local produce. It has its own boats and ghillies, plenty of walks on the wooded forty-hectare estate and immaculate gardens with fine views of the lake and a tennis court. Oughterard also has a high-quality **hostel**, *Canrawer House* (Ⓣ091/552388, Ⓦwww.oughterardhostel.com; IHH; Feb–Aug; dorms €17 including light breakfast, twins ❶), where rooms have en-suite bathrooms, and **camping** and boat rental is available; it's in a large, modern house with an extensive lawn, which is signposted off the west end of the main street, less than a kilometre from the tourist office.

The town is not so well off for **places to eat**, as many visitors seem to dine at their hotel or B&B. Indeed, the best restaurant is probably at *Currarevagh* (see above), where non-guests can dine if they book in advance. Great places to shop for a picnic are *The Yew Tree*, by the central junction on Main Street, an artisan bakery that also sells hummus, cheeses and good coffees; and McGeough's butcher's on Camp Street, who smoke and air-dry Connemara lamb (a little like Italian Parma ham) and sell cheeses. *Breathnach's Bar* by the central junction is a welcoming **pub**, offering sandwiches, salads, chowder and seafood tagliatelle, among more traditional hot dishes, as well as music at weekends.

West around the coast

The R336 coast road arrows west out of Galway through a gently sloping landscape of shrubs, ferns and boulders, offering fine views of the slate-grey Burren across the water but marred by a monotonous ribbon development of white bungalows. Relief comes after 18km with the lofty trees and church of **SPIDDAL** (An Spidéal, "the hospital"), the effective capital of the Gaeltacht, which is known for its traditional-music sessions. The main daytime draw here is the **Spiddal Craft Village** (Ceardlann an Spidéil; Ⓣ091/553376, Ⓦwww.spiddalcraftvillage.com), a group of studios – with an on-site bistro-café – making and selling fine pottery, weaving, jewellery, woodwork, leather goods, sculpture and musical instruments. For **accommodation**, *An Crúiscín Lán* (Ⓣ091/553148, Ⓦwww.cruiscinlanhotel.com; ❹) is a good upmarket option, with large, bright rooms – some with sea-view balconies – and a smart, evening **restaurant**. For **B&B** your best bet is *Cala 'n Uisce* (Ⓣ091/553324, Ⓦwww.geocities.com/spiddalgalway; May–Sept; ❷), a large, welcoming country home with en-suite bedrooms, set in attractive gardens on the west side of town. **Campers** should head for the well-equipped *Páirc Saoire an Spidéil* (Ⓣ091/553372, Ⓔpaircsaoire@eircom.net), 1.5km inland from the centre of the village. To catch some **music**, try centrally located *Tigh Hughes*, *An Calad Mór* or *An Crúiscín Lán*, which also boasts a beer garden and bar food.

West of Spiddal the road passes **Inverin** (Indreabhán), site of the airport for the Aran Islands, and **Rossaveel (**Rós an Mhíl), the main ferry port for the islands. Here, as the Maam Turks and the Twelve Bens hove into sight for the first time, the land becomes abruptly harsher and rockier, splintering into dozens of tiny, disorientating islands. North of Rossaveel, you can head straight up the R336 to Maam Cross to join the N59 into Clifden, or you can continue winding round the coast on the R340, which would eventually bring you out near Cashel and Roundstone.

Near **Rosmuc**, at the end of a small peninsula off the R340, stands **Teach an Phiarsaigh** (Easter Sat, Sun & Mon 10am–5pm; June to mid-Sept daily 10am–6pm; late Sept Sat & Sun 10am–6pm; last admission 45min before closing; €1.60; Heritage Card; Ⓦwww.heritageireland.ie), a thatched and whitewashed traditional cottage, which was the summer residence of the revolutionary and writer, Patrick Pearse (see p.107). Here Pearse ran summer schools for his pupils from St Enda's in Rathfarnham, Dublin, and wrote his famous eulogy for the nationalist Jeremiah O'Donovan Rossa on his death in 1915. Inside are mementos and an exhibition on Pearse, but the cottage is more noteworthy for its atmosphere and setting, with dramatic views of the sea and mountains.

Roundstone and around

On the R341 coast road, which eventually loops round into Clifden, **ROUNDSTONE** (Cloch na Rón, "seal rock") is a picturesque fishing village set in some of Connemara's finest scenery. Nestling into an east-facing slope to shelter from the ocean, the stone harbour looks out on the many islands of Bertraghboy Bay and across to the peaks of the Twelve Bens and the Maam Turks, while behind looms a lone mountain, three-hundred-metre Errisbeg. Three kilometres southwest of the village, the beautiful, sandy beaches of **Gurteen Bay** and **Dog's Bay** are separated by a narrow, dune-covered isthmus.

The village is well known for its **crafts shops**, including a famous *bodhrán* workshop in a former Franciscan monastery at the south end of the village (Ⓣ095/35808, Ⓦwww.bodhran.com). Here you can watch the drums being made, test them out in a sound room or have one painted in the Celtic motif of your choice while you wait. The old monastery also shelters a silver-jewellery workshop and pottery.

From the centre of the village, you can take on a very satisfying short **walk** to the summit of **Errisbeg**, which offers majestic views in all directions. Take the paved lane beside *O'Dowd's* bar and follow the rough track that it turns into; you'll have to pick your way over often boggy ground and boulders towards the top which, despite appearances from below, turns out to be a ridge of three summits – with a little trial and error, you'll find the one with the scenery you like best. On three sides runs a hopelessly indented coastline of white-sand beaches, where peninsulas are barely distinguishable from islands; to the north, set against one of the finest prospects of the Bens and the Turks, lies huge, sparse **Roundstone Bog**, one of the finest blanket bogs in the country, covered with a glittering crazy-paving of tiny lakes and crossed by a single narrow road.

There are some beautiful woodland **walks** along lake shore and river bank in the estate of Ballynahinch Castle (see below), which are described in a leaflet available from the hotel reception. Starting from a double gate about 1km south of the castle (as detailed in the leaflet), on the north side of Cloonbeg Bridge just off the R341, it's also possible to walk along the path of the old railway line from Galway, through conifer plantations and across the bog, all the way to Clifden if you like.

Practicalities

Good options for **B&B** include *St Josephs* (Ⓣ095/35865, Ⓦwww.connemara.net/stjosephsb&b; ❷), a cosy, welcoming and good-value en-suite place with great breakfasts in the heart of the village. Six kilometres northeast on the R341 towards the N59 is the upmarket *Angler's Return* (Ⓣ095/31091, Ⓦwww.anglersreturn.com; mid-March to Nov; ❸), a tranquil and stylish 1820s sporting lodge set in pretty gardens. There are several **campsites** to the west of Roundstone, including the *Gurteen Bay Caravan Site* beside the beach of the same name (Ⓣ095/35882; March–Sept). A couple of exceptional **hotels** enliven the harsh landscape to the northeast of Roundstone. Set on its own fishing river and lake towards the N59, eighteenth-century **Ballynahinch Castle** was once the home of Richard Martin – aka Humanity Dick – the animal-rights campaigner and co-founder of the RSPCA in 1824, and later of cricketing maharaja,

Ranjitsinhji. It's now a grand, romantic luxury hotel in a glorious estate setting, with an excellent restaurant and a cosy fisherman's bar where good food is also available (Ⓣ095/31006, Ⓦwww.ballynahinch-castle.com; closed Feb; half-board deals off-season; ❼). Near the village of **Cashel** (An Caiseal), about a fifteen-minute drive round the bay from Roundstone, *Cashel House Hotel* (Ⓣ095/31001, Ⓦwww.cashel-house-hotel.com; closed early Jan to early Feb; ❼), is an elegant country house set in varied and beautiful **gardens** that are open to non-residents (early Feb to Nov daily 10am–5pm; €5 donation to charity requested).

The best place to **eat and drink** in Roundstone is lively, sociable *O'Dowd's*, which serves excellent bar food; attached to the pub is a fine restaurant and the *Roundstone Café*, offering good coffee, sandwiches, pizzas, seafood chowder and **Internet** access. Ferron's Supermarket contains a post office and **ATM**. The village hosts a small arts **festival** in late June or early July (Ⓦwww.roundstoneartsweek.com), a hooker regatta in late July and Summerfest in mid-August (Ⓦwww.roundstonesummerfest.com).

Clifden and around

CLIFDEN, the English-speaking capital of Connemara, is a popular, animated service town for both tourists and locals, enhanced by a spectacular setting: it perches on a steep, verdant hillside, where the lofty, grey spires of the Catholic and Anglican churches compete for attention, while on its western side the land plunges abruptly down to the deeply indented harbour. Several stately townhouses sprinkle the three major streets – **Main Street**, the continuation of the Galway road culminating in Market Square, with **Bridge Street** and **Market Street** branching off it at either end and meeting to form a rough triangle. By basing yourself in one of the town's fine accommodation options, you'll be able to explore the varied attractions of coast and mountain hereabouts – especially if you have your own car or are prepared to hire a bike – and return to sample the often lively nightlife.

There's not much to do on a rainy day in the town itself, although you may find some diversion at the **Station House Museum** near the tourist office (May–Oct Mon–Sat 10am–5pm, Sun noon–6pm; €2), which has displays on local history and on the history, breeding and racing of Connemara ponies. These rugged, passive workhorses have their day in mid-August, when they're judged at the **Connemara Pony Show** (Ⓦwww.cpbs.ie). The other highlight of Clifden's calendar is the prestigious and lively **arts festival** (Ⓦwww.clifdenartsweek.ie) at the end of September.

Information and accommodation

For information on the town and the whole of Connemara, head for the **tourist office**, part of the development around the old station on the Galway road (mid-March to May & Sept to mid-Oct Mon–Sat 10am–5.20pm; June, July & Aug daily 10am–5.50pm; Ⓣ095/21163). You can access the **Internet** upstairs at *Two Dog Café* (see below), and **rent a bike** at John Mannion's, Bridge Street (Ⓣ095/21160). **Horse and pony trekking**, often on one of the area's fine beaches, is available at several riding schools nearby, including Errislannan Manor (Ⓣ095/21134; closed Sun), about 8km away, signposted 3km south of town off the Ballyconneely road, and Cleggan Beach Equestrian Centre (Ⓣ095/44746, Ⓦwww.clegganridingcentre.com), 10km to the northwest.

Clifden boasts a high standard of **accommodation** in all price ranges, including some excellent, mid-range guesthouses. **Camping** is available at

Shanaheever Campsite (Ⓣ095/22150, Ⓦwww.clifdencamping.com; mid-April to Sept), 2km out of town off the Westport road.

Ardagh 2km south of town on the Ballyconneely road Ⓣ095/21384, Ⓦwww.ardaghhotel.com. Relaxing and comfortable, family-run hotel with fine views of the bay, pleasant staff and an excellent restaurant. Early April–Oct. Weekend packages available. ❺

Atlantic Hotel Market St Ⓣ095/30590, Ⓦwww.hotelclifden.com. Recently refurbished by the owners of the *Old Monastery Hostel* in Letterfrack (see p.451), offering large, bright, simple rooms and healthy breakfasts of porridge, home-made bread and scones. The ground-floor bar-café (which hosts live country and blues), and sun terrace overlook the harbour; art exhibitions and inexpensive, mostly vegetarian, buffet dinners planned. ❷

Ben Lettery Hostel 13km east of Clifden on the N59 (An Óige) Ⓣ095/51136, Ⓦwww.anoige.ie. Right at the foot of Ben Lettery, one of the Twelve Bens, with fine views, this is a cosy and welcoming, forty-bed hostel, with family rooms available. It's geared towards walking in the mountains, with drying rooms and laundry facilities. March–Nov. Dorms from €12.

Ben View House Bridge St Ⓣ095/21256, Ⓦwww.benviewhouse.com. Very central, flower-bedecked nineteenth-century house, offering friendly and comfortable B&B and plenty of local information. ❷

Brookside Hostel Fairgreen (IHH & IHO) Ⓣ095/21812, Ⓦwww.brookside-hostel.com. Overlooking the showground at the bottom of Market St, a basic but pleasant hostel with a laundry, where you can get information about local walking and cycling. Feb–Oct. Dorms from €13.50, doubles ❶.

Buttermilk Lodge 400m out on the Westport road Ⓣ095/21951, Ⓦwww.buttermilklodge.com. Friendly and very well appointed modern guest-house, with spacious, en-suite bedrooms set in a large garden. Closed early Jan–Feb. ❷

Clifden Town Hostel Market St (IHH) Ⓣ095/21076 or 21936, Ⓦwww.clifdentownhostel.com. Excellent, attractive hostel, with family rooms, two well-equipped kitchens and a comfy sitting room. Dorms from €15, twins and doubles ❶.

Dan O'Hara's Farmhouse Lettershea, around 7km east of Clifden off the N59 Ⓣ095/21246 or 21808, Ⓦwww.connemaraheritage.com. B&B upstairs from the heritage centre (see below) in bright and airy en-suite rooms; entry is included in the price. ❷

Dolphin Beach House 5km west on Lower Sky Rd Ⓣ095/21204, Ⓦwww.dolphinbeachhouse.com. Renovated, welcoming 200-year-old farmhouse by the seashore with its own sandy cove and spectacular views, where you can sleep in elegantly simple bedrooms, lounge in spacious, open-fired sitting rooms and dine on local meat, seafood and organic vegetables. ❺

The Quay House down on the harbour Ⓣ095/21369, Ⓣwww.thequayhouse.com. Set in the characterful, early nineteenth-century harbourmaster's house, which later became a convent, this is an outstanding guesthouse with a sociable, house-party atmosphere. Excellent breakfasts are served in the large conservatory; rooms are elegantly decorated with antiques and paintings, most overlook the water, and some have working fireplaces, four-posters or fitted kitchens. Mid-March to Oct. ❺

Sea Mist House just down from Market Square towards the harbour Ⓣ095/21441, Ⓦwww.seamisthouse.com. Tranquil, relaxing and central stone cottage in a lush garden with stylish en-suite rooms, excellent breakfasts and plenty of local knowledge. ❸

Winnowing Hill 1km out on the Ballyconneely road Ⓣ095/21281, Ⓦwww.winnowinghill.com. Peaceful, modern B&B with comfortable, en-suite rooms and an attractive conservatory, set on a hill with fine views of the town and the Twelve Bens. Mid-March to early Nov. ❷

Eating, drinking and entertainment

Clifden boasts a healthy choice of modern and traditional **cafés**, and although the **restaurant** scene hasn't quite taken off in the same way as some of the tourist honeypots in Cork and Kerry, there are a couple of good choices, as detailed below.

Among the **pubs**, *Mannion's* on Market Street is the best spot for **food**, with daily specials and seafood platters, all in hearty portions. There's a more varied menu at *Conneely's* opposite, a contemporary-style bar and night club on the other side of Market Street, but what really makes it stand out are the gorgeous views of the harbour from its rear balcony. *Conneely's* hosts live **music** or DJs (summer Thurs–Mon, winter Sat), as do several other watering holes in Clifden: *Mannion's* or *Lowry's* on the same street are the likeliest places for traditional music, which may also make an appearance at *E.J. King's* on Market Square, along with country and western and ballads. Loud and lively *Mullarkey's* at the back of *Foyles Hotel* on Market Square is the best spot for modern folk, blues, bluegrass and singer-songwriters, with regular open-mike nights. From June to August, Tuesday and Thursday evenings see a performance of traditional music, song and dance at the Town Hall, just west of Market Square.

Cullen's Café-Bistro Market St. Basic, economical and easy-going place serving unpretentious dishes such as poached Connemara salmon and rhubarb crumble.

G's Market Square ⓣ095/22323. Welcoming and attractive restaurant with a few harbour-view tables and a Malaysian chef, who turns his hand successfully to modern Irish dishes (scallops with scallion mash) as well as fusion (crispy Peking duck breast with poached pears and red cabbage). Evenings (in winter, Thurs–Sun only).

Mitchell's Market St ⓣ095/21867. Probably Clifden's best restaurant, providing well-judged and beautifully presented cuisine, heavily weighted towards fresh fish and seafood. Cheaper, simpler dishes available at lunchtime. Closed early Nov to mid-March.

Steam in the old station complex on the Galway road. Global-influenced menu of delicious salads, wraps and ciabattas, as well as cakes and coffees, with a few quiet outdoor tables for a sunny day. Mon–Sat daytimes.

Two Dog Café Church Hill, just off Market Square. Excellent and imaginative sandwiches, salads and soups, finished off with delicious desserts such as lemon drizzle cake and great coffee. Tues–Sat daytimes.

Walsh's Bakery Market St. Traditional daytime café serving good cakes and a varied menu of sandwiches and unpretentious meals; in summer it stays open till 9pm on weekdays.

Around Clifden

Outside town, the main set-piece tourist attraction, at Lettershea, 7km east on the N59, is **Dan O'Hara's Farmstead and the Connemara Heritage and History Centre** (April–Oct daily 10am–6pm; €7.50; Heritage Island; ⓦwww.connemaraheritage.com), which sounds rather kitsch but is actually very engaging. Fascinating display boards by local archeologist Michael Gibbons and a twenty-minute video introduce you to the history of Clifden and Connemara, and to Dan O'Hara himself. A tenant farmer whose house was famous for its céilís (it was known as the local "ballroom of romance"), O'Hara was evicted in 1845 and eventually found his way to New York, where, having little English, he sold matches and inspired the famous eponymous song. Outside in the grounds, you can view reconstructions of an oratory, a dolmen tomb, a wooden ring fort and a *crannóg*, a thatched dwelling set in a small lake. If there are enough people around, you can take a guided tour in a tractor-borne bus up to Dan O'Hara's refurbished cottage for great views south over the bogs and lakes to Roundstone and Errisbeg and for demonstrations that might include sheep-shearing, thatching and turf-cutting. There's also a daytime café at the centre and B&B is available (see p.447).

An alternative diversion is to walk or cycle the spectacular **sky road** on the west side of the town, which loops scenically round the narrow peninsula on the north side of Clifden Bay (13km in total). It ends up by the long, thin inlet of Streamstown Bay, passing a quarry for the streaky, green Connemara marble, before hitting the Westport road just north of Clifden.

To the south of Clifden, the R341 begins its scenic loop round, via the village of Ballyconneely, towards Roundstone (see p.445), with the highly irregular sea shore and a dozen or so fine beaches to its right. You can complete an excellent, scenic bicycle tour from Clifden by turning left, 4km north of Roundstone, onto the **bog road**, which undulates westward across the stark peatland back to town. About 5km south of Clifden on the R341, on the right-hand side, you'll pass a three-metre limestone sculpture of an aeroplane wing commemorating the first transatlantic flight, by **Alcock and Brown** in June 1919. The intrepid aviators circled Clifden twice in celebration, but then nosedived into the bog here, wrecking their plans to continue their triumphal flight to London. On the opposite side of the Ballyconneely road is the site of a telegraph station, where **Marconi** sent the first commercial wireless transmission across the Atlantic in 1907; the station was burnt out by Republicans during the Civil War in 1922 and abandoned, with around a thousand local people losing their livelihoods.

Inishbofin

INISHBOFIN (Ⓦwww.inishbofin.com) continues the diversity of the Connemara landscape into the sea, though in a gentler, miniature format. Just 5km wide, the island encompasses cliffs and the rocky outcrops known as **The Stags** on its western side, tranquil, reedy **Lough Boffin**, the haunt of swans, at its centre, and several sandy beaches, but rises only to 90m at its highest point, **Cnoc Mór**, which is carpeted by a springy layer of grass. This all makes for gentle, low-key exploration, complemented by a choice of good accommodation and plenty of traditional music, featuring the island's own renowned céilí band.

The first historical reference to Inishbofin comes from the seventh century: after the Irish and Roman Churches fell out at the Synod of Whitby in 664, St Colman left Lindisfarne and journeyed here via Iona. Though the monastery he established was destroyed in 1334, you can still see the atmospheric shell of a fourteenth-century **chapel** on the site, to the east of the pier, beyond a small, lily-strewn lake. In the island cemetery surrounding the chapel, two stone crosses and a couple of holy wells are said to date from Colman's foundation. The island's other historic site is visible on the right as you enter the excellent natural harbour, a forbidding, mottled-black **castle**, built in the sixteenth century and strengthened by Cromwell, which is accessible at low tide.

You can walk right around the island in a day, quite easily taking in the sites mentioned above, as well as the small but interesting **heritage museum** and gift shop a short way east of the pier (June–Aug daily noon–1.30pm & 3–5pm, Sept Sat & Sun noon–1.30pm & 3–5pm; hours extended if the island's busy with visitors; donation requested; Ⓣ095/45950), the sandy **beach** in the southeast corner, which provides the best swimming, the broad horseshoe of **Rusheen Bay** a little way up the east coast, and **Trá Ghael**, a beautiful beach beneath Cnoc Mór in the west, where the currents are too dangerous for swimming.

Getting to Inishbofin

The **ferry**, MV *Island Discovery* (Ⓣ095/45819 or 44878, Ⓦwww.inishbofinislanddiscovery.com; €20 return), crosses to Inishbofin from **Cleggan**, 11km away and 10km northwest of Clifden, three times a day (30min) from June to August, and two or three times a day for the rest of the year. In winter, Bus Éireann offers one **bus** from Galway, one from Clifden, to Cleggan on Saturdays; see p.442 concerning Citylink buses. If you have time to spare in Cleggan, you can get tasty seafood meals at *Oliver's*, a popular, well-run **bar** and **restaurant**, which also offers **B&B** (Ⓣ095/44640, Ⓦwww.oliversbar.com; ❷) and traditional music on Saturday nights. Plans for an **airstrip** on Inishbofin, handling flights from the Galway mainland, were nearing completion at the time of writing.

Practicalities

You can get **tourist information** at the friendly heritage museum or the island community centre above the pier (Mon–Fri irregular hours; ⓣ095/45861 or 45895), and access the **Internet** at the latter. **Maps** of the island are available on the boat or at the heritage museum. At the pier, you can arrange a **boat trip** with Aidan Day (ⓣ095/45974), or rent a **bike** (if there's no sign of Paddy Joe King and his bikes, head to his house 700m east of the pier near the hostel; ⓣ095/45833). **Scuba diving** can be arranged through Islands West (ⓣ087 222 7098, ⓦwww.islandswest.ie). The island shop (and post office) near the pier is expensive, so it's best to bring as much stuff over with you as you can. A lively, three-day **arts festival** takes place over a weekend in May or sometimes early September.

The pick of the accommodation on Inishbofin is the recently rebuilt *Day's Inishbofin House* just east of the pier (ⓣ095/45809, ⓦwww.inishbofinhouse.com; closed mid-Dec to mid-Feb; ❺; at busy times, half-board only), a chic, modern **hotel** with a marine spa offering hydrotherapy baths and seaweed-based treatments, where most bedrooms have balconies overlooking the harbour. Its more traditional, long-standing competitor, the *Doonmore Hotel* (ⓣ095/45804, ⓦwww.doonmorehotel.com; ❹; Easter–Sept), 2km west of the pier, has fine sea views, plain, comfortable rooms, a restaurant open to non-residents (booking essential) and a bar with decent food. Meanwhile, the new kid on the block is the welcoming *Dolphin Hotel*, 700m east of the pier (ⓣ095/45991, ⓦwww.dolphinhotel.ie; in winter, weekends only; ❸), offering large, bright, well-equipped en-suite rooms, some with outdoor terraces. The island's best **B&B** is *Elliott's* (ⓣ095/45853, ⓔjoanne@inishbofin.com; March–Oct; ❷), who rent out an elegant, secluded room with its own entrance and a panoramic conservatory, 500m east of the pier. The excellent *Inishbofin Island* **hostel**, 700m east of the pier (IHH & IHO; ⓣ095/45855, ⓦwww.inishbofin-hostel.ie; Easter–Sept; dorms €15, twins ❶), is welcoming and well maintained, and offers family rooms, laundry facilities and space for **camping**.

The daytime **café** at *The Galley* in Rusheen Bay serves delicious smoked fish in various combinations, as well as soups and desserts. The *Dolphin Hotel* offers dishes such as roast chicken with spinach and Gruyère mousse and plenty of fish and scallops (depending on what's fresh) in its **restaurant**, as well as bar food. Otherwise your best bet is the bar food or the sophisticated evening restaurant specializing in seafood at *Day's Inishbofin House*. Nearby *Day's* **pub** is a congenial place and in summer hosts regular traditional-music sessions. The Inishbofin Ceili Band are a fixture at the *Doonmore Hotel* on Saturday nights, and tour the other hotels on other nights.

Letterfrack and Connemara National Park

The tiny, nineteenth-century Quaker village of **LETTERFRACK**, around 15km northeast of Clifden, is the main access point for the **Connemara National Park**, which covers a thin slice of the northwest sector of the Twelve Bens, stretching east as far as Benbrack, Bencullagh, Muckanaght and Benbaun. The park's **visitor centre** on the west side of the village (early March–May, Sept & Oct daily 10am–5.30pm; June–Aug daily 9.30am–6.30pm; hours may be variable, so worth checking on ⓣ095/41054; free; ⓦwww.heritageireland.ie) gives access to an excellent, newly constructed walkway to the top of **Diamond Hill** (about 2hr 30min return), which affords fantastic views of Kylemore Abbey and the mountains, bays and islands all around. There are also three shorter **nature trails** across the lower slopes, through some natural woodland and over bogland, with free guided walks on Monday, Wednesday and Friday mornings in June, Monday, Wednesday, Friday, Saturday and Sunday mornings in July and August. The centre contains a fascinating exhibition on the wildlife and geology of Connemara and a café, and in July and August hosts worthwhile, free nature and heritage talks on Wednesday evenings and plenty of activities for kids.

On the south side of the village's central junction (where the supermarket contains an ATM), the *Old Monastery* **hostel** (IHH & IHO; ⓣ095/41132 or 087 234 9543, ⓦwww.oldmonasteryhostel.com; dorms €15, twins and doubles ❶) is a characterful warren with plenty of sitting areas inside and out. **Bike hire**, **Internet** access and **camping** are on offer, as are big breakfasts of porridge and home-baked bread and scones (included in the price), and vegetarian, mostly organic, buffet dinners. The owner also runs Western Explorer, offering **boat trips** most days in summer (according to demand; about €50 per person for a full day), which take in seal colonies, swimming and deserted islands, with the opportunity to spot plenty of birds and possibly whales and dolphins. At the other end of the scale is *Rosleague Manor* (ⓣ095/41101, ⓦwww.rosleague.com; mid-March to mid-Nov; half-board, low-season and online deals available; ❻), an elegant, early nineteenth-century **hotel** 1.5km west of the village, with a relaxed, country-house atmosphere, great **restaurant** and charming sitting rooms. The extensive grounds stretching down to the sea contain a tennis court, and there are fine walks through gardens, woodlands and along the Rosleague Peninsula (gardens – €2.50 charity donation requested – afternoon tea and dinner available to non-residents).

At the east end of the village is an excellent **restaurant**, *Pangur Bán* (ⓣ095/41243; evenings & Sun lunch), which serves up delicious fare, such as rabbit and Toulouse sausage casserole with butter beans, at quite reasonable prices in a relaxing ambience. *The Bard's Den* by the central junction lays on a wide variety of cheaper fare including pizzas, hosts sessions on Sundays, discos on winter Saturdays and offers en-suite **B&B** rooms (ⓣ095/41042, ⓦwww.bardsden.com; ❶).

The Renvyle Peninsula

North of Letterfrack, it's well worth exploring the minor roads that crisscross the **Renvyle Peninsula**, eventually looping around by the gentle waters of Lough Fee to meet the N59 near Killary Harbour. On the south side of the peninsula, 3km from Letterfrack overlooking Ballynakill Harbour, you'll come to the **Ocean and Country Visitor Centre** (mid-March to early Nov daily 10am–6pm; ⓣ095/43473 or 086 199 1988; €6.50, €20 with a cruise), which features exhibits of sea life and local maritime history, lots of children's activities, an attractive café and hour-long wildlife cruises in a glass-bottomed boat three or four times a day to view deserted islands and, hopefully, seals and dolphins. From the museum quay, a walk up **Tully Hill** is highly recommended (about 3hr return), whose 355-metre summit affords a matchless panorama, with the towering mountains of Connemara arrayed to the east for your viewing pleasure.

The peninsula's main settlements are the adjacent hamlets of **Tully Cross** and **Tully**, 4km due north of Letterfrack. By the crossroads, *Paddy Coyne's* is a popular, cosy **pub**, which has frequent live **music**, including traditional on Wednesdays, while in summer Tully's Teach Ceoil ("music cottage") plays host to a show of Irish music, song, dance and storytelling (Tues 9pm; €10; ⓣ095/41047 or 43446, ⓦwww.comhaltas.ie) and various other gigs, including a fiddler and singer-songwriters on Sunday. Two kilometres west of Tully Cross towards the end of the peninsula is *Renvyle Beach* (Ⓣ095/43462, Ⓦwww.renvylebeachcaravanpark.com; mid-March to Sept), a good **campsite**, with direct access to a fine beach, and a further kilometre on, in a dreamy position seemingly on the edge of the world, *Renvyle House* (Ⓣ095/43511, Ⓦwww.renvyle.com; closed early Jan to early Feb; midweek deals available; ⑥). This former home of the surgeon, writer and wit Oliver St John Gogarty (see p.120) is now a relaxing luxury **hotel**, offering facilities such as golf, tennis, boating and a heated outdoor swimming pool.

By heading east from Tully Cross, you'll reach **Lettergesh Beach** after 5km, a concave stretch of fine sand with views of the offshore islands and a popular **campsite** nearby, *Connemara* (Ⓣ095/43406; May–Sept). There's another great beach just over 2km further on at **Glassillaun**, a wild, north-facing crescent with the bulk of Mweelrea Mountain over in Mayo looming to the northeast. Based here is Scuba Dive West (Ⓣ095/43922, Ⓦwww.scubadivewest.com), offering courses and **diving** off the coast and nearby islands.

Kylemore Abbey and Garden

Five kilometres east of Letterfrack on the N59, in a gorgeous setting behind a glassy lake against the rugged, green backdrop of Dúchruach hill, sits grey, castellated **Kylemore Abbey** (abbey daily: mid-March to Oct 9am–5.30pm, Nov to mid-March 10am–4.30pm; gardens mid-March to Oct 10am–5pm; €12; Heritage Island; Ⓦwww.kylemoreabbey.com). Though it's now a small girls' boarding school, run by a semi-enclosed order of Benedictine nuns, you can visit the library, dining room, morning room and main hall (it's planned to open up more rooms), and learn about the place's history from the interesting display

▲ Kylemore Abbey

boards and audiovisual presentation. Also on the lake shore is a beautiful Neogothic **church**, which incorporates elements copied from the great English cathedrals of the late twelfth and early thirteenth centuries. The abbey boasts an extensive **crafts shop** and **restaurant**, and **fishing** on the lake and Kylemore River can be arranged at the nearby hut (Ⓣ095/41178).

From the abbey a shuttle bus runs about every ten minutes to the restored **walled garden**. Laid out in the 1860s with no fewer than 21 glasshouses, the huge garden deteriorated after the estate was sold in 1903, but an ambitious project has returned it more or less to its former state, using only original Victorian plant specimens. Walking through the walls into the beautifully tended ornamental flower garden is a rather surreal experience, like entering a Victorian English municipal park in the wilds of Connemara. Beyond the flower garden lie stream and fern walks and vast beds of herbs and vegetables, with everything from dill to parsnips (all labelled), divided by a long, pretty herbaceous border. Two of the glasshouses have been reinstated, while the head gardener's house and his workers' far more basic bothy have been refurbished, but the most poignant remnants are the very fine, original cabbage trees.

Killary Harbour and Leenane

Killary Harbour is one of Ireland's very few fjords, a truly dramatic oddity with Connacht's highest mountain, Mweelrea (817m), plunging sheer into the dark water on its north bank. This glacial gouge runs for 16km between the uplands of Galway and Mayo, and with a typical depth of 15 metres is perfect for salmon and mussel farms. The only waterside settlement, **LEENANE** (Leenáun), enjoys a snug, scenic location near the head of the fjord. The **Sheep and Wool Centre** in the village (generally April–Oct daily 10am–6pm, last admission 5.15pm, but may open outside these months; €4, €2 children, €8 family ticket; Ⓣ095/42323, Ⓦwww.sheepandwoolcentre.com) may not sound too promising, but makes for a fascinating little visit, especially if you have kids. Accompanied by an enthusiastic guide, you'll get to see demonstrations of spinning and weaving, motley breeds of sheep and a sheepdog at work; children can card wool and feed the animals, and the centre also has a good, inexpensive café-restaurant. The **Killary Adventure Centre**, about 5km west of Leenane on the N59 (Ⓣ095/43411, Ⓦwww.killary.com), offers all manner of activities and courses, either by the day or residential, from rock-climbing to sailing, kayaking and wind-surfing. For a gentler way onto the water, take a ninety-minute **cruise** on the fjord with Killary Cruises, based at Nancy's Point, 2km west of Leenane (April–Sept 4 daily, plus evening barbecue cruises in July & Aug; Oct 2 daily; €20; Ⓣ091/566736, Ⓦwww.killarycruises.com).

Of the village's **accommodation**, the outstanding B&B choice is the fjord-side *Convent* (Ⓣ095/42240; April–Nov; ❷), which retains some fine stained glass from its previous incarnation as a nunnery, while the *Leenane Hotel* (Ⓣ095/42249, Ⓦwww.leenanehotel.com; closed mid-Nov to March; ❹), a recently refurbished traditional coaching inn, boasts an even better setting, with a delightful garden and fountain right on the water's edge. Built from environmentally sustainable materials, *K2*, the hostel at the Killary Adventure Centre, offers spacious rooms with a view, while the upstairs lounge, bar and restaurant area enjoys an astonishing panorama. Back in the village, the *Blackberry Café* (Ⓣ095/42240) is a very attractive and welcoming **restaurant**, offering well-prepared and reasonably priced dishes, such as wild salmon with dill sauce.

County Mayo

Far from pulling up at the county border, the wonderful mountain scenery found in Connemara marches on into the south of **County Mayo** (Maigh Eo; Ⓦwww.visitmayo.com), in the substantial shape of Mweelrea, the Sheefry Hills and the Partry Mountains. These ranges culminate in the conical peak of Ireland's holy mountain, **Croagh Patrick**, beyond which change is announced by the trough of **Clew Bay**, the extension of a geological fault that runs all the way to the Scottish Highlands. Unless you're beetling direct to Westport on the N59, two possible routes out of Connemara into south Mayo present themselves. You can detour east to the abbey town of **Cong**, right on the county border, sharing many similarities with Oughterard, to which it is linked by boat trips across Lough Corrib. Or you can forge through the heart of the mountains from Leenane to **Louisburgh**, which gives access to the charming islands of **Inishturk** and **Clare** at the mouth of Clew Bay. Either way, you're almost certain to end up in **Westport**, a refined, lively, Georgian base, terminus of the railway line from Dublin and hub for local buses.

The county's other main tourist centre is **Achill** at the northwest corner of Clew Bay, Ireland's largest island and a popular resort. Beyond this, there's mile after mile of wild, dramatic landscape, but only a few specific attractions: the stunning discovery of a Neolithic farm system at **Céide Fields** justifies a journey to the north coast if you have the time, while a short way east of Westport is the impressive **National Museum of Country Life** at Castlebar. Further inland, **Knock Airport** (Ⓣ094/936 8100, Ⓦwww.knockairport.com), built to bring in pilgrims to the nearby Marian shrine, is a useful, often cheap way into the county, with car rental offered by, among others, Avis (Ⓣ09493/67707, Ⓦwww.avis.ie) and Casey's (Ⓣ094/936 7456, Ⓦwww.caseycar.com); the airport is served by a Bus Éireann shuttle to Charlestown, 5km away at the junction of the N17 and N5, with connections in all directions, including buses to Westport, Galway and Sligo.

Cong

Right on the border between the green plains of south Mayo and Galway's Connemara Mountains (with a summertime bus service via Leenane to Clifden) sits the pretty village of **CONG**, on the neck of land separating loughs Corrib and Mask. Its main claim to fame these days is that the movie *The Quiet Man*, an iconic if sentimental, emigrants' portrayal of Ireland that starred John Wayne and Maureen O'Hara (who was herself born in Dublin), was filmed here in 1951. If you're happy to get into the kitschness of it all, head for the **Quiet Man Museum** (Easter to mid-Oct daily 10.30am–4.30pm, closed half-hour for lunch; €5) just around the corner from the tourist office, a painstaking replica of the cottage built for the making of the film; the only "real" thing in it is a horse's harness used in the film. From roughly Easter to September, the museum runs guided tours of locations around the village used in the film (daily at noon & 2pm; 35min; €15, including entry to the museum).

The village does boast a site of genuine historical interest, **Cong Abbey**, originally founded in the seventh century and rebuilt in the twelfth and thirteenth centuries by Turlough, Rory and Cathal O'Connor, kings of Connacht and the last high kings of Ireland. The ruined Augustinian abbey's fine sculpture-work suggests links with western France, particularly the very fine geometrical and foliate carvings on the doorways to the chapterhouse from the cloister. The elaborate **Cross of Cong**, which was created for

Turlough O'Connor in 1123 (now in Dublin's National Museum, see p.89), reflects the place's former wealth, which at one time housed a population of three thousand – the logistics of feeding such a crowd are hinted at in the fishing house over the River Cong, from where a line ran to a bell in the refectory to let cook know when fish had been caught. From the bridge over the river by the abbey, you can stroll through the woods to Lough Corrib, passing through *Ashford Castle Hotel*'s grounds, though in summer be aware that it charges €5 for the privilege.

Practicalities

The **tourist office** opposite the abbey (March–early Dec daily 10am–5.45pm, closing 1–2pm for lunch on some days; June to mid-Sept daily 9.30am–6.45pm; Ⓣ094/954 6542) has a **bureau de change** and plenty of detailed literature about the area's sights. By Water (Ⓣ087 225 5569, Ⓦwww.bywater.ie) runs **kayaking** trips on the Cong River, loughs Corrib and Mask. The *Isle of Inishfree* **cruises** from *Ashford Castle* or Lisloughry pier (near the hostel) across Lough Corrib to **Inchagoill** Island (see p.442; 2 daily; €18; Ⓣ094/954 6029 or 087 679 6470, Ⓦwww.corribcruises.com), with the possibility in summer of sailing on to Oughterard, on the Connemara shore, on the *Corrib Queen* (€20 one way, €25 return from Cong); from June to September, the *Isle of Inishfree* also offers hour-long evening cruises with live traditional music and a bar (daily 6pm; €18).

The well-run, comfortable *Cong* **hostel**, 2km from the centre of the village off the Headford road in Lisloughry (Án Oige, IHH & IHO; Ⓣ094/954 6089, Ⓦwww.quietman-cong.com; dorms €18, en-suite twins and doubles ❶), screens *The Quiet Man* every night, rents out rowing and motor **boats**, and has a **campsite**, a playground and a bureau de change; bike rental may also be available in the future. Also on site is *Michaeleen's Manor* (❷), a smart, en-suite, *Quiet Man*-themed **B&B** – named after the film's drunken matchmaker – with a tennis court, sauna and hot tub, as well as a DVD player in every room to watch the film. At the opposite end of the price scale is lavish *Ashford Castle*, built by Sir Arthur Guinness in the nineteenth century, whose grounds are far larger than the adjoining village of Cong. Standing at the point where the Cong River runs into Lough Corrib, it's now a luxury **hotel** with fine views, a health spa and a raft of outdoor activities, including horse riding and falconry (Ⓣ094/954 6003, Ⓦwww.ashford.ie; ❽).

Danagher's on Abbey Street offers reasonably priced bar **meals**, salads and sandwiches, while *The Hungry Monk* (March–Oct), a smart little café with **Internet** access near the tourist office, rustles up delicious salads and sandwiches, as well as great coffee. In the grounds of *Ashford Castle Hotel*, *Cullen's at the Cottage* (Ⓣ094/954 5332; March–May closed Tues & Wed; June–Sept daily) is an informal, seasonal bistro in a traditional thatched cottage with outdoor seating, serving everything from soups, salads and sandwiches to fresh lobster from the tank.

Delphi and Louisburgh

The obvious road north from Connemara into Mayo is the N59 from Leenane to Westport, but the seemingly impenetrable mountains on the north side of Killary Harbour conceal a far more scenic route. Winding between the Mweelrea massif and the Sheefry Hills, the R335 brings you first to the noted fishing lake at **Delphi**, so named by the second Marquis of Sligo in the early nineteenth century: after swimming the Hellespont with Byron, the Marquis arrived at Delphi in the mountains of central Greece, where he was overcome with homesickness as it reminded him so much of his fishery back here in Mayo. After his return in the 1830s, the Marquis built, in a glorious setting by the lake facing the lower slopes of Mweelrea, *Delphi Lodge*, which is now a traditional luxury **hotel** (ⓣ095/42222, ⓦwww.delphilodge.ie; closed Christmas and New Year; ⑥; half-board packages and self-catering cottages also available). Decorated in opulent but relaxing fashion, the lodge is notably sociable, featuring excellent, imaginative dinners taken around one huge table, with the angler who has caught the biggest fish that day at the head.

The Delphi valley now also shelters an **adventure centre**, about 1km south of the lodge (ⓣ095/42208, ⓦwww.delphiadventure.com), running activities and courses in surfing, canoeing, mountaineering and more for both adults and kids. The centre is attached to the *Delphi Mountain Resort and Spa* (ⓣ095/42987, ⓦwww.delphiescape.com), a luxury **spa** that's currently closed for major refurbishment but due to reopen some time in 2008.

Beyond Delphi, the road skirts the black water of **Doo Lough**, past an interesting memorial. In March 1849, hundreds of men, women and children marched the 16km from the small crossroads town of Louisburgh through this bleak, exposed valley to Delphi Lodge, where the Famine Commissioners were staying. When they arrived, the commissioners were eating a hearty lunch and would not be disturbed, then refused any help, leaving the starving people to struggle back through the snow to Louisburgh, a journey on which many of them died. Every year in May, there is a Famine Walk to commemorate the event (and modern-day famines; ⓣ098/68218), which also forms part of the exhibition at the **Granuaile Centre** in the library at **LOUISBURGH** (June–Sept Mon–Fri 10am–5pm; rest of the year Mon–Fri 10am–2pm by appointment; ⓣ098/66341; €4). The centre's main subject, however, is seafaring in Ireland in the sixteenth century, in particular **Grace O'Malley** (Gráinne Ní Mháille, often corrupted to Granuaile; c. 1530–1603), the formidable sea captain and pirate queen of Clare Island, who ruled the sea from Galway Bay to Donegal Bay. About 4km west of Louisburgh at Carrownisky Strand, **surfing** instruction and equipment hire is available through Surf Mayo (ⓣ087 621 2508, ⓦwww.surfmayo.com). Over the bank-holiday weekend at the start of May, Louisburgh hosts a lively **festival** of traditional music, Féile Chois Cuain (ⓦwww.feilechoiscuain), featuring concerts, classes and plenty of impromptu sessions. If you're ready for something to eat in Louisburgh, head for *Louisburgh 74* just off the main square on Chapel Street (closed Mon), a spruce **café** and crafts shop that serves cakes, tasty and substantial sandwiches, salads and a wide variety of hot dishes; in the summer, it stays open till 8pm. The sparsely inhabited coastline southwest of Louisburgh is lined with sandy beaches, notably **White Strand**, a long, west-facing stretch around the mouth of a stream about 15km away, and **Silver Strand** a couple of kilometres on at the end of the road, a great desert of a beach at the mouth of Killary Harbour, flanked by rocks and low dunes in the shadow of bulky Mweelrea.

Clare Island

A minor road heads due west from Louisburgh to **Roonagh Quay** at the southwestern corner of Clew Bay, where **boats** (May–Sept at least 7 boats a day; in winter at least 2 boats a day: contact O'Malley's ⓣ098/25045, ⓦwww.omalleyferries.com; or O'Grady's ⓣ098/25212 or 28288, ⓦwww.clareislandferry.com; €10 single, €15 return) depart for the fifteen-minute voyage to **Clare Island** (ⓦwww.clareisland.info). There are currently no buses to Roonagh Quay, but it's always worth ringing the boat operators to see if you can arrange a lift from Westport.

Measuring 8km by 5km, Clare Island manages to cram in two hills, Knockmore (462m) and its little brother Knocknaveen (223m) to the east, behind which the mighty sea cliffs along the northwest shore are home to important breeding colonies of seabirds, notably fulmars. Other rare birds found on the island include peregrines, choughs and barnacle geese, while notable plants include petalwort, a species of liverwort. A leaflet available on the boats details five **walks** on the island, including a complete circuit which takes about six hours. If you're not up to that, you can rent **bikes** or a minibus **taxi** from the pier (ⓣ098/25640 or 086 161 0557).

The harbour, which shelters a Blue Flag **beach** with fine views of the mainland mountains, is guarded by a well-preserved, sixteenth-century **tower house**, which was the main stronghold of Grace O'Malley (see opposite). In the middle of the island's south shore near the post office and shop, she – or more likely a relative of hers – is buried in an ornate Gothic tomb in the mid-thirteenth-century Cistercian **abbey**. More notable from an artistic point of view are the **frescoes** in the chancel, among the finest extant medieval paintings in Ireland, which depict cattle raids, people hunting and fishing, musicians, dragons and griffins. Towards the lighthouse at the northern tip is the Ballytoughey Loom and Craft Shop (ⓣ098/25800, ⓦwww.clareisland.info/loom), where you can watch **weaving** and spinning, buy wool, linen and silk, or even enrol on a summertime course. Nearby is a **yoga retreat centre** (ⓣ098/25412, ⓦwww.yogaretreats.ie), which also offers courses in vegetarian cookery, meditation and eco-building; B&B (❷; minimum stay 2 nights) and self-catering accommodation are sometimes available outside of the summer season when no course is running. **Scuba diving** can be arranged through Islands West (ⓣ087 222 7098, ⓦwww.islandswest.ie).

Internet access is available at the library in the community centre on the west side of the harbour (ⓣ098/29838). The main **festivities** on the island are a *currach* and yawl regatta in July and singles weekends for the over-thirties in June and September. **B&Bs** offering both en-suite and standard accommodation include the friendly *Seabreeze* (ⓣ098/26746, ⓕ25649; ❷), above the harbour behind the community centre, where evening meals are available if requested in advance; and the O'Malleys' *Cois Abhainn* (ⓣ & ⓕ098/26216 or ⓣ086 081 9896; Feb–Nov; ❷), 3km from the harbour at the island's southwest tip – the owner will pick you up and make evening meals. You can **camp** in the field behind the beach, with toilets, showers and a laundry available in the community centre.

Inishturk

To the south of Clare Island lies the even smaller and less developed island of **Inishturk** (ⓦhomepage.eircom.net/~inishturkisland), a tranquil, hospitable, two-hundred-metre-high lump of rock and grass that survives on farming and lobster fishing. O'Grady's **boats** (see above) run over from Roonagh Quay (10 weekly, though may be affected by the weather in winter; 50min; €10 single, €20 return) and from Clare Island (3 weekly; 50min; €10), while Jack Heanue's mail boat crosses from Cleggan (see p.449) twice a week (1hr; ⓣ098/45541 or 086 202 9670; €25 return). From the tiny harbour, the island's paved road branches north and south: to the north, there's a particularly fine **walk**, veering west off the road around a small lake, before climbing to a ruined watchtower in around 45 minutes. The south road rises to the **community centre** after about fifteen minutes, opposite which a narrow gate points down through the fields to the island's finest sandy **beach**, a gorgeous, sheltered strand with clear, blue water and great views of the mainland.

B&Bs include Delia Concannon's by the pier (Ⓣ098/45610; ❷), which offers brightly coloured rooms, lunch and dinner, and a pretty garden with outdoor tables; and *Tránaun House* (Ⓣ098/45641, Ⓔtranaunhouse@gmail.com; mid-March to Dec; ❷; good rates for singles and children), a ten-minute walk up the south road at the **post office**, with en-suite rooms, seafood dinners and pick-ups from the harbour. The community centre doubles up as the island **pub** in the evenings with regular music sessions and céilís.

Croagh Patrick

Rising to 764m to the east of Louisburgh, the cone of **Croagh** (pronounced "croak") **Patrick** dominates Clew Bay and the Westport area. It was the pagan home of the mother goddess, now converted into the holiest mountain in Christian Ireland, and on a fine day offers an awesome panorama, stretching from the Twelve Bens in the south to Slieve League in the north.

The starting point for the ascent of Croagh Patrick is the excellent **visitor centre** on the R335 on the north side of the peak (March–Oct daily 11am–4.30pm or longer hours – phone Ⓣ098/64114 to check; free; Ⓦwww.croagh-patrick.com). Here you'll find lockers, showers, advice about the climb and the weather, an excellent **café** and a DVD on the **history** of the mountain (on request). During his long missionary tour of the island, **St Patrick** is supposed to have passed the forty days of Lent in 441 alone on the mountain, finding time to hurl all of Ireland's snakes to their deaths over the precipice of Lugnanarrib just to the south of the summit. This association with the saint has made Croagh Patrick the focus of major **pilgrimages**, which take place three times a year, on March 17 (St Patrick's Day), August 15 (Assumption Day) and – the main event – on the last Sunday in July, Reek Day (which coincides with the pagan harvest festival of Lughnasa). On this day, tens of thousands of pilgrims still make the climb to attend Mass on the summit, some of them fasting and walking barefoot.

The **climb** itself, taking on average 3hr 30min return, is easy to follow though very steep in places – you'll need good walking shoes and preferably a stick, available from the visitor centre. At the summit you'll find a small **chapel** that took twelve men six months to construct in 1905, though archeologists have discovered evidence of much earlier building work up here, a massive rampart dating from pagan times.

In a small park opposite the visitor centre stands the national **monument** to *an nGórta Mór* (the Great Famine), commissioned in 1997 for the 150th anniversary. The bronze sculpture of a coffin ship, with skeletons floating around its masts and prow, looks more eerie and shocking now that it's been weathered green by the rain. On the shoreline behind the sculpture, well-preserved **Murrisk Abbey**, which features some unusual battlements on the south wall of the church, was established by the O'Malley family in 1457. An Augustinian foundation dedicated to St Patrick, in former times it housed famous relics such as the Shrine of St Patrick's Tooth and his Black Bell, both now in Dublin's National Museum. From the abbey there are fine views of the islands of **Clew Bay**, which are actually half-submerged drumlins (see p.746); there are said to be enough of them for a year and a day – 366 – of which only seven are now inhabited.

If you're relying on public transport for a day-trip to Croagh Patrick, Thursday (the main shopping day in Westport) is the best day to attempt the climb, with

▲ National Famine Monument

three or four **buses** in each direction between the town and Louisburgh; Tuesdays and Saturdays are also possible, but you won't be able to dawdle on the mountain if you're going to make the bus back. For **B&B** in the area, try *Béal-an-t-Sáile* (Ⓣ098/64012, Ⓦwww.bealantsaile.com; ❷), overlooking the sea less than a kilometre east of the visitor centre, with great breakfasts. *The Tavern*, on the main road near the visitor centre, does very good **food** and has pleasant outdoor tables.

Westport

Set on the picturesque shores of Clew Bay, **WESTPORT** (Ⓦwww.westporttourism.com) is an agreeable, easy-going town that matches its location with some fine architecture. Its main visitor attraction is **Westport House**, a graceful, Georgian mansion now surrounded by a country park of rides and amusements, which separates the town centre from Westport Harbour. The centre itself was laid out in classical style in 1780 for the Browne family of Westport House by James Wyatt, who built a striking, octagonal square and canalized the Carrowbeg River, flanking it with the tree-lined Mall. More recently, the town has developed an artsy, cosmopolitan feel, attracting many visitors and residents from other parts of Ireland and Europe. During the summer, the place is abuzz, especially for the prestigious, ten-day **Arts Festival** in September (Ⓣ098/29551, Ⓦwww.westportartsfestival.com).

Arrival, orientation and information

The centre of Westport consists of two parallel main thoroughfares, **James Street**, with the Octagon at its southwestern end, and below that **Bridge Street**, with a clock tower at its southwestern end. At their northeastern ends, the two streets end at **The Mall** and the Carrowbeg River. From the clocktower, High Street runs south, while Mill Street, where **buses** stop, runs east; the **train station** is less than a kilometre out in the same direction. From the Octagon, Quay Hill and Quay Road head west for about 2km to **Westport**

Harbour, where you'll find the entrance to Westport House, along with several restaurants and pubs.

The **tourist office** on James Street (March–June, Sept & Oct Mon–Fri 9am–5.45pm, Sat 10am–5.45pm; July & Aug Mon–Sat 9am–6pm, Sun 10am–6pm; Nov–Feb Mon–Fri 9am–5.45pm, Sat 10am–1pm; Ⓣ098/25711) houses a good **heritage centre** downstairs (€3) tracing the development of the town. It also dispenses maps of the town and useful leaflets on nearby walks (*Westport Walks*, covering 6 circular routes of 1–3hr) and on the Clew Bay Trail, linking 21 archeological sites between here and Clare Island (Ⓦwww.clewbaytrail.com).

From the tourist office, Bus Éireann runs full-day **bus** tours from late June to early September, taking in Leenane, Kylemore Abbey and Cong on Tuesdays, Achill Island on Thursdays (€22; Ⓣ096/71800, Ⓦwww.buseireann.ie). You can access the **Internet** at Gavin's video shop on Bridge Street, and rent a **bike** from Sean Sammon's fuel yard on James Street (Ⓣ098/25471). **Horse riding** can be arranged, for example, at the Drummindoo Equitation Centre (Ⓣ098/25616), 1km from the centre of town on the Castlebar road, **sailing** via Glenan's, Collanmore Island (Ⓣ098/26046). Clew Bay Sea Safaris (Ⓣ087 126 6516), Clew Bay Ecotours (Ⓣ087 966 9332, Ⓦwww.clewbayecotours.com) and the *Lady Slievemore* (Ⓣ098/26852 or 085 131 1453, Ⓦwww.achilladventures.com) offer **boat tours** of Clew Bay in summer, while Croagh Patrick Walking Holidays (Ⓣ098/26090, Ⓦwww.walkingguideireland.com) run **guided walks** in the area, lasting from a day to a week. Horizon Activity Centre on North Mall (Ⓣ098/50290, Ⓦwww.horizonireland.com) lays on half- and full-day activity programmes, including **kayaking** and **surfing**, for kids and adults.

Accommodation

As evidence of its success as a tourist destination, Westport boasts several new and renovated **hotels**, as well as an abundance of **B&Bs** and a couple of good hostels. **Campers** should head for the *Parklands Caravan and Camping Park* (Ⓣ098/27766, Ⓦwww.westporthouse.ie; mid-May to early Sept) on the Westport House estate.

Abbeywood Hostel Newport Rd Ⓣ098/25496, Ⓦwww.abbeywoodhouse.com. With stained glass, parquet floors and a comfy sitting room in the old oratory, this former monastery is very central but quiet, set back from the road in its own garden. Rooms are large, bright and airy, and the engaging owner bakes bread every evening for the next day's continental breakfast (included in the price); Internet access and laundry facilities available. Open May–Sept daily, rest of the year at weekends. Dorms from €18, twins and doubles ❶.

Altamont House B&B Ballinrobe Rd Ⓣ098/25226. Hospitable and well-run, this flower-strewn place with both standard and en-suite rooms is located between the centre and the train station. Mid-March to Nov. ❷.

Carrabaun House B&B 1km out on the Leenane road Ⓣ098/26196, Ⓦwww.anu.ie/carrabaunhouse. Highly recommended B&B in a spacious, en-suite, period-style modern house with fine views and good breakfasts. ❷

Castlecourt Hotel Castlebar St, just east of the Mall Ⓣ098/55088, Ⓦwww.castlecourthotel.ie. Together with the adjacent co-owned *Westport Plaza*, this hotel offers a spa, swimming pool, gym, a wide choice of restaurants, a kids' club in school holidays, and all manner of theme breaks, half-board offers and other packages. This is the livelier and more family-oriented of the two hotels, where the decor is fairly traditional but fresh and colourful, and enlivened in the public areas by vibrant landscape paintings. ❺

Cedar Lodge B&B Kings Hill Ⓣ098/25417, Ⓦwww.cedarlodgewestport.com. Welcoming, quiet, en-suite bungalow set in colourful, landscaped gardens, five minutes' walk from the centre, off the N59 Newport road. Mid-March to Oct. ❷

Newport House 12km north of town in Newport Ⓣ098/41222, Ⓦwww.newporthouse.ie. The area's finest traditional country-house hotel, a creeper-clad Georgian affair in pretty grounds overlooking its private fishery on the Newport

River. Sitting rooms are airy and elegant, the bedrooms simpler but spacious and very comfortable, and there's an excellent restaurant, serving local produce in a mostly classic French style. Mid-March to early Oct. ❻

Old Mill Hostel Barrack Yard, James St (IHH & IHO) ⓣ098/27045, ⓦwww.oldmillhostel.com. Through an archway next to the tourist office, this former mill and brewery is now a comfortable and characterful hostel, with a light breakfast included in the price and laundry facilities. Closed Christmas & New Year. Dorms from €17.50, doubles ❶.

Westport Plaza Hotel Castlebar St, just east of the Mall ⓣ098/51166, ⓦwww.westportplazahotel.ie. Welcoming, chic and contemporary hotel, offering spacious and well-equipped rooms with king-sized beds, Italian marble bathrooms and Jacuzzi baths. For facilities, see *Castlecourt Hotel* above. ❺

Wyatt Hotel The Octagon ⓣ098/25027, ⓦwww.wyatthotel.com. Congenial and stylish small hotel, done out in bare wood and bold colours, in an unbeatable central location; ask about its various special deals. ❹

The Town

Not one for the historical purists, **Westport House** has wholeheartedly embraced the concept of a former stately home as a modern pleasure-ground (11.30am–5.30pm: house & gardens April–Sept daily, March & Oct Sat & Sun; attractions Easter week daily, May Sun, June Thurs–Sun, July & Aug daily; house and gardens €11.50, children €6.50; house, gardens and all attractions €20, children €14, family €68; ⓦwww.westporthouse.ie). On the estate, which is entered from Westport Harbour, are a host of attractions and rides, such as a miniature railway, an animal and bird park, a log flume ride, pitch and putt, archery, kayaking, rowing boats and swan pedaloes.

Nevertheless, the gardens are still well worth a stroll, and the creeper-clad Georgian **house** overlooking the lake is beautiful. It was built in 1730 by Richard Castle, with alterations later in the century by James Wyatt, and is still home to the Browne family, descendants of the pirate queen, Grace O'Malley. Highlights include the hall, with its fine barrel ceiling and ornate marble mantelpiece designed by Castle, the cantilevered marble staircase, executed by Italian craftsmen brought over specially for the purpose, and a delicate portrait by Sir Joshua Reynolds of Denis Browne, a member of Grattan's Parliament, in the Long Gallery. The large dining room is one of the finest examples of Wyatt's work, sporting boldly carved mahogany doors and relief medallions in Wedgwood style on playful classical themes. The rooms upstairs are as usual less compelling – though look out for the playwright J.M. Synge's violin in one of the corridors. Downstairs in the dungeons, which house various children's amusements, you can see the remains of one of Grace O'Malley's many fortresses around Clew Bay.

Near the gates to Westport House, where Quay Road meets the Quay, the **Custom House Studios** (ⓣ098/28735) host interesting monthly exhibitions of contemporary art. Ten minutes' walk west around the harbour, the **Clew Bay Heritage Centre** (April, May & Oct Mon–Fri 10am–2pm; June & Sept Mon–Fri 10am–5pm; July & Aug Mon–Fri 10am–5pm, Sun 3–5pm; €3; Heritage Island; ⓣ098/26852, ⓦwww.museumsofmayo.com) traces the history of Westport and the Clew Bay area through photographs, documents and other interesting artefacts; it also offers a genealogical service and runs guided **walking tours** of the town (July & Aug Tues & Thurs 8pm; €6), starting from the clock tower at the top of Bridge Street.

Eating, drinking and entertainment

Westport has a decent, though not exceptional, range of **places to eat**, spread between the centre and the harbour, as detailed below. Overall, *The Lemon Peel* is your best bet, while among several reasonably priced Italian restaurants on and around Bridge Street, *Il Vulcano* stands out.

▲ Matt Molloy's

The town's most famous **pub** is *Matt Molloy's*, owned by the flautist of The Chieftains, a rambling, characterful old place on Bridge Street that fills up for its frequent **traditional-music** sessions. *McGing's* on High Street is a cosy, congenial, traditional bar that boasts the best pint of Guinness in Mayo and is enlivened on Sundays and Mondays by a guitarist. Over on James Street, the simple, wooden decor of *Walsh's* (*Blouser's*) is popular with a 30-something crowd, who come for the weekend DJ nights and the live music and salsa nights during the week. The town also has a number of quiet, old-fashioned grocery bars, such as *Moran's* on Bridge Street.

Antica Roma Bridge St. Cheap, basic pizzeria and fish'n'chip shop, to eat in or take away.

Il Vulcano High St ☎098/24888. Bustling, authentic Italian restaurant with an open kitchen, just up from the clock tower, which provides pasta, risotto, pizza, and some very good meat and seafood main courses.

The Lemon Peel The Quay ☎098/28795. Imaginative, global-influenced cuisine in an attractive restaurant above *The Asgard* pub, with seafood a particular strength; good-value early-bird menu until 7pm. Evenings: summer Tues–Sun, winter Tues–Sat.

McCormack's Bridge St. Brightly painted, inviting café and art gallery above a butcher's, which serves coffee, salads, home-made soup and fine sandwiches. Closed Wed.

Nicola's Food Emporium Lime Court. Small deli-café, just off James St opposite the tourist office, featuring paninis, salads, hot dishes and delicious juices and smoothies.

Orient Aroma Bridge St. Decent Chinese restaurant and takeaway offering some unusual dishes and early-bird set menus until 6.30pm.

Quay Cottage The Quay ☎098/26412. This restaurant in a pretty, atmospheric stone cottage by the gates to Westport House has a good, long-standing reputation locally, especially for its seafood dishes. Evenings, daily in summer, Tues–Sat in winter.

Sol Rio Bridge St ☎098/28944. Colourful and informal upstairs restaurant, with a Portuguese influence, that efficiently covers all the bases: salads, pasta, pizza and more expensive fish and meat dishes, augmented by sandwiches at lunchtime. Closed Tues.

Castlebar and around

CASTLEBAR, the county town of Mayo, has a lot less going for it than Westport, just 18km away to the west, but has recently been given a shot in the arm with the opening of the **National Museum of Country Life** at nearby **Turlough**. The **tourist office** (June–Aug Tues–Sat 10am–5pm, with a break for lunch; hours variable, so best to phone to check – ⓣ094/902 1207) is in the Linen Hall Arts Centre on central Linenhall Street. It's unlikely that you'll want to stay here, with congenial Westport so close, but there is a good spot for **lunch** around the corner from the tourist office on New Antrim Street, *Café Rua* (closed Sun), which serves fine sandwiches and imaginative, tasty home-cooking.

The National Museum of Country Life

The **National Museum of Country Life** (Tues–Sat 10am–5pm, Sun 2–5pm; free; ⓦwww.museum.ie) trumpets its theme early on, with a board near the entrance juxtaposing images of romanticism against reality, of a heavily tinted poster for John Wayne in *The Quiet Man* against a roughly contemporary photo of Inisheer men wading in freezing-cold seas to gather seaweed. The aim is to dig beneath the dewy-eyed nostalgia that besets popular images of rural Ireland, to reveal the harsh realities of country life from 1850 to 1950, and the museum achieves this with admirable balance and imagination. Even the scenic approach, 8km east of Castlebar off the N5, fits into the picture, the sleek, modern lines of the new building reflected in the beautiful lake of Turlough Park, with a lofty round-tower in the background for good measure. From Monday to Saturday, it's quite possible to get there by **bus** from Westport (though it's worth double-checking with Bus Éireann or the tourist office): catch the 12.35pm to Castlebar, where you'll wait about half an hour and change onto the 1.40pm service (towards Ballina) to Turlough; returning, the 5.09pm bus from Turlough runs all the way through to Westport. Taxis are available in Castlebar on, for example, ⓣ094/903 4700.

The exhibition works its way downstairs from the entrance, where there's a short introductory audiovisual presentation. **Level -1** includes a brief but very worthwhile history of the period from an ordinary person's point of view and gives examples of the ingenious uses to which twisted straw rope was put: baskets, hens' nests, mattresses, stools and horse collars. The meat of the exhibition is on **Level -2**, which comprehensively chronicles the unremitting work of farming and fishing, of housewives, craftsmen and tradesmen. Nice touches here are a recording of a poignant letter home from an emigrant to America, and footage of men making a coracle on the River Boyne – exactly like weaving a huge basket. Probably the most interesting section deals with the seasons and festivals: churning butter on May Day to ward off evil, leaving food and drink out for dead relatives on Halloween, and grainy footage of **Wren Boys**, who would knock on doors on St Stephen's Day (Dec 26) with the corpse of a wren, asking for money to bury it while singing songs and telling jokes – the money, of course, would be spent on a party. **Level -3** presents personal reminiscences of the changes in rural life, revealing how horses weren't actually very good at ploughing. As a contrast to the main part of the museum, it's also possible to look inside the adjacent "Big House" of the landowners, **Turlough Park House**. The library and drawing room of this nineteenth-century Gothic Revival pile, designed by Thomas Newenham Deane, architect of the National Museum in Dublin, have been accurately refurbished.

As well as a good **café** and shop, there are **guided tours** of the museum every day (€2), and an exciting range of workshops, demonstrations and performances, especially on Wednesday and Sundays (Ⓣ094/903 1751 for details).

Achill Island

The grandeur of **ACHILL**'s scenery, encompassing towering sea-cliffs and bulky, bare mountains that rise over 650m, can seem grey and forbidding in poor weather, but on a sunny day is quite magnificent. It's the largest of the Irish islands and, now connected to the mainland by a road bridge, one of the most developed, with plenty of hotels, B&Bs and hostels, and a ribbon of white-painted holiday homes on the south coast. Drawn by sweeping sandy beaches (five of which have earned a Blue Flag) and fairground rides, Irish fun-seekers descend in droves on August weekends, when the place can get a bit rowdy. Germans are also attracted to Achill, by associations with novelist and Nobel Laureate Heinrich Böll, who lived at Dugort in the 1950s. The island was until recently entirely Irish-speaking and its eastern half is still a designated Gaeltacht area, hosting teenagers at Irish college in their summer holidays.

One of the best times to come is during **Scoil Acla** (Ⓣ098/43107, Ⓦwww.scoilacla.com), a lively week of cultural programmes and workshops, with plenty of traditional music, usually at the end of July; at this time, and continuing until early September, a **yawl festival** is held, featuring races, mostly at weekends, of the area's traditional, wooden sailing boats. There's also a walking festival in mid-March, the Heinrich Böll literary festival in early May and a

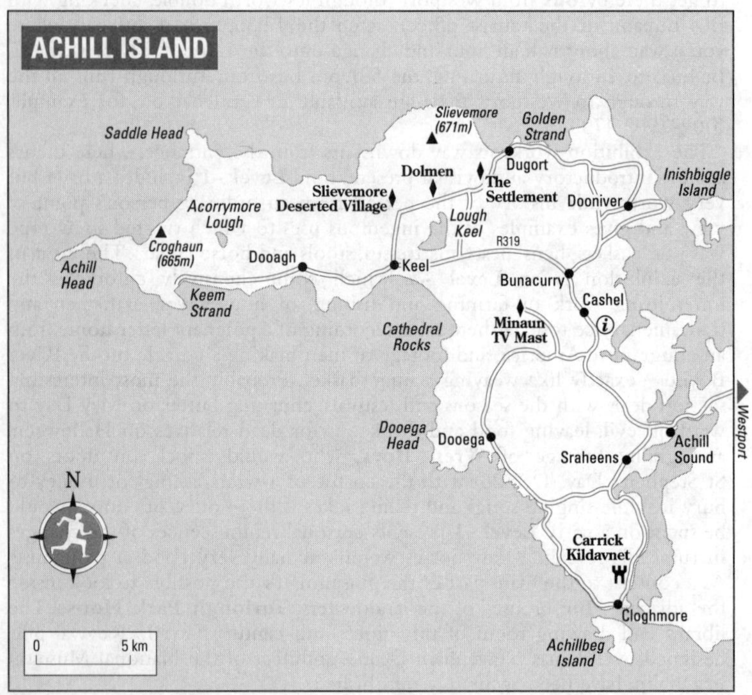

seafood festival in mid-July. Note that the island's only **ATM** is at Achill Sound, though travelling **banks** pitch camp in the centre of Keel on Monday, Tuesday and Wednesday mornings, and at *Gray's* guesthouse in Dugort and the garage in Cashel on Tuesday lunchtimes.

Achill Sound

The road bridge crosses the narrow, winding strait to the island at **ACHILL SOUND** (Gob an Choire), which is not the best base for exploration but has some useful facilities, including good accommodation. On the island side of the bridge, there's an **ATM** at the side of *Sweeney's* restaurant and supermarket (which offers **Internet** access), and a summertime Fáilte Ireland **tourist office** next to *McLoughlin's* pub (July & Aug Mon–Fri 10am–5pm; ⓣ098/45384). On the left immediately before crossing the bridge stands a comfortable, very welcoming **hotel** and local social hub, *Óstán Oileán Acla* (ⓣ098/45138, ⓦwww.achillislandhotel.com; ❹), which has fine views of the island, a good restaurant and bar, and regular live music and discos. On the opposite side of the road before the bridge is the *Railway* **hostel** (IHO; ⓣ098/45187; dorms €12, doubles ❶), a cosy spot in the old station with big log fires, where some of the rooms are en suite and **camping** is possible.

The south end of the island

The "Atlantic Drive" around the south end of the island from Achill Sound brings you after 6km to the ruined eighteenth-century **church** and holy well of Damhnait (Davnet or Dympna), a seventh-century saint who sought refuge and built a church (*cill*) here. Just beyond, its pink stone set attractively on the shoreline, rises the redoubtable outline of **Carrick Kildavnet**, an almost perfectly preserved, fifteenth-century, O'Malley tower house. Fantastic views of the Atlantic open up as you round the nearby headland, continuing as far as the village and Blue Flag beach of **Dooega**. Above the settlement looms **Minaun**, Achill's third highest mountain; a left turn will bring you up to the TV mast near its summit for one of the island's most spectacular panoramas.

The Atlantic Drive rejoins the main road across the island just before **CASHEL** (Caiseal), home to the multi-tasking Lavelle's petrol station and pub. Here you'll find the very helpful **Achill Tourism Office** (Mon–Fri 9am–5pm, plus Sat 11am–5pm in summer; ⓣ098/47353 or 47392, ⓦwww.achilltourism .com), which publishes a weekly entertainment guide in summer and sells detailed maps of the island and a guide to fourteen circular walks. The garage also offers **car rental** (ⓣ098/47242) and holds an interesting Friday-morning **market**, selling crafts, cheese and home-made cakes and bread. Behind the garage, Achill Computer Solutions offers **Internet** access.

Keel

The lively village of **KEEL**, a few kilometres west of Cashel, boasts a lovely three-kilometre Blue Flag sandy **beach**, backed by a large lake, as well as a branch office of **Achill Tourism** at the entrance to *Keel Sandybanks* campsite (May & Sept daily 11am–5pm; June–Aug daily 11am–7pm).

Good **B&Bs** include the small, very friendly, all en-suite *Fuchsia Lodge*, with bright, pine-furnished rooms and a guest kitchen, at the west end of the village (ⓣ098/43350, ⓔfuchsialodge@eircom.net; ❷). Back in the centre of the village, but giving directly onto the west end of the beach, *Bervie* (ⓣ098/43114, ⓦwww.bervieachill.com; April–Oct; dinner available for residents; ❸; minimum 2-night stay in peak season) is a civilized retreat in the former coastguard station, with fetching, summery ground-floor rooms around a pretty garden. Swiss-run *Ferndale* (ⓣ098/43908, ⓦwww.ferndale-achill.com; ❹), 200m up the lane by the *Annexe* pub, has just three rooms, but they're lavishly furnished, with four-poster beds and, in the Heidi Suite, a whirlpool bath. At the west end of the village, *Richview* **hostel** (ⓣ098/43462 or 086 231 5546; dorms €12, doubles ❶) is run by a friendly musician and set in an attractive old house with great views. There's a swanky caravan park and **campsite**, *Keel Sandybanks* (ⓣ098/43211, ⓦwww.achillcamping.com; late May to early Sept), on the beach.

Superior options for **eating** are the *Beehive*, a smart, daytime café-restaurant and crafts shop with outdoor tables, serving everything from cakes to wild Achill salmon; *Ferndale* (see above), which offers an ambitious range of world cuisine, an impressive wine list and a huge picture-window overlooking the bay; and *Calvey's* (ⓣ098/43158; April–Sept), a smart restaurant with comfy banquettes and great views, conveniently next to its own butcher's shop for dishes such as fresh Achill mountain lamb.

For a **drink** head to *The Minaun View* or *The Annexe*, which are both likely to have live music in summer. The combined post office and supermarket has **bike rental**. **Wind-surfing** courses and board rental are available from Windwise by the lake at the east end of town (ⓣ098/43958, ⓦwww.windwise.ie), and **scuba diving** can be arranged through Joseph Carey (ⓣ087 234 9884, ⓦwww.achilldivecentre.com), **surfing** through Shane Cannon (ⓣ086 228 8566, ⓦwww.achill-surf.com). Meanwhile, *McDowell's Hotel* (see opposite) offers all manner of watery pursuits, including **sailing** and **kayaking**, through its outlets on the beach and the lake. Calvey's (ⓣ087 988 1093, ⓦwww.calveys.com), just north of the village on the lower slopes of Slievemore, offers **horse-riding** treks and tuition, and you can access the **Internet** at Keel's Achill IT Centre (ⓣ098/43292).

Dooagh and beyond

West along the road from Keel is the small village of **DOOAGH**, overlooking its own sandy beach. At its base here, the enterprising **Achill Field School** (ⓣ098/43564, ⓦwww.achill-fieldschool.com) lays on a raft of interesting activities, including weekly lectures from June to August and a fortnightly film club; cultural and historical exhibitions are also planned. The field school also runs one- to eight-week archeology courses, featuring the dig at the Deserted Village (see below) and summer open days at the Deserted Village. On the west side of Dooagh, *Croaghan* offers comfy, en-suite **beds** and good breakfasts (ⓣ098/43301, ⓔteachcruachan@eircom.net; ❷), as well as **guided tours** of the island. *Gielty's*, a large, modern **pub**, café and bistro at the west end of the village, has plenty of outdoor tables and live music, including regular traditional sessions.

Beyond Dooagh, the main road rises and descends very steeply to Blue Flag **Keem Bay**, a gorgeous strip of white sand hemmed in by steep, green slopes – on a sunny day, you'll feel as if you're looking down on a Mediterranean cove, with basking sharks often visible in the limpid waters. A turning off the up-slope towards Keem Bay will bring you to **Acorrymore Lough**, a black corrie lake, now reservoir, cradled by grassy scree slopes. From here you can set out on the steep ascent of **Croghaun**, the island's second highest mountain (665m), which boasts spectacularly high cliffs on its seaward side. An easier walk, with only slightly less dramatic views, begins at the Keem Bay car park, heading up to the cliff tops and west along the humped back of **Achill Head** to the end.

The north end

Heading north from Keel, a side road runs along the west side of the lake, then skirts east around **Slievemore**, Achill's highest mountain at 671m, before looping around the north end of the island. About 2km from Keel, you'll see over to the left the **Deserted Village**, a strange unnamed linear settlement of almost a hundred stone dwellings. Its most recent period of habitation came to an end in the early twentieth century, when locals used it as a *booley*: during the summer, they would occupy the cottages while grazing their cattle on the mountainside, but would return to their homes in Dooagh for the winter months. This is one of the last places in Europe to have practised *booley*-ing, or transhumance, but the village's abandonment is still a mystery, though it's being excavated by the Achill Field School (see opposite) every summer. Around 2km further east on Slievemore's southern flank, a signposted, ten-minute walk up from the road will bring you to a keyhole-shaped **dolmen** which enjoys fine views of Keel Bay. It is possible to **stay** near the southeastern corner of the mountain at *McDowell's Hotel and Activity Centre* (Ⓣ098/43148, Ⓦwww.achill-leisure.ie; ❸), a spacious, welcoming place, which offers a huge range of **outdoor activities** for adults and children, as well as renting out all sorts of adventure-sports equipment to non-guests.

A kilometre or so to the north is the site of **the Settlement**, the first Protestant mission in Ireland to minister in the Irish language. It was founded in 1834 by a Church of Ireland vicar, Edward Nangle, and at first proved successful, with stone cottages, schools, a small hospital and a printing press churning out regular publications. During the 1840s Famine, the Settlement came under fire for encouraging converts, known as "soupers" or "jumpers", with offers of soup and grain. The Catholic Church, who had previously been indifferent to the islanders' education, fought back by opening a National School in 1852, and the Settlement, further rocked by emigration and financial difficulties, eventually closed in 1886. Approached by an avenue of trees on the east side of the road, the mission's **church** of 1855 is still standing, containing a prominent memorial to Nangle. *Gray's* (Ⓣ098/43244; ❸) occupies several houses of the former Settlement, a relaxing, comfortable **guesthouse** with a garden and croquet lawn, where dinner is available.

Less than a kilometre beyond lies **Dugort Beach**, a gently curving, Blue Flag stretch of sand in the shadow of Slievemore, overlooked to the east by the small village of Dugort. **Boat trips** around the coast on the *Lady Slievemore* depart from here and several other points on the island (Ⓣ085 131 1453). Around 3km east, Blue Flag **Golden Strand** is flanked by *Lavelle's* **campsite** (Ⓣ098/47232; Easter–Oct). Ten minute's walk beyond is the *Valley House* **hostel** (Ⓣ098/47204, Ⓦwww.valley-house.com; IHO; dorms from €13, doubles ❶), a fine, mid-nineteenth-century house, formerly the Earl of Cavan's hunting lodge, with a sociable courtyard bar and camping.

Céide Fields and Ballycastle

Isolated on Mayo's dramatic, cliff-girt north coast, the prehistoric site of **Céide** (pronounced "cage-a") **Fields** is difficult to get to, but repays the effort. Here, archeologists have discovered a unique, 5000-year-old agricultural landscape, miraculously preserved under a thick layer of peat and undisturbed by later farming. A highly organized system of dry-stone field walls, dotted with individual houses and gardens in what were apparently peaceful times, covers an area of thirteen square kilometres, the largest Stone Age monument in the world. What's remarkable about the site is its very ordinariness, its similarity to much of the Irish countryside today, as Seamus Heaney noted in *Belderg*:

A landscape fossilized, its stone wall patternings
Repeated before our eyes in the stone walls of Mayo.

Rough contemporaries of the tomb-builders of Newgrange, these farmers cleared the area's forest to make fields for their cattle, sheep, wheat and barley, and built wooden houses, of which trenches and postholes are now the only traces. However, after only five hundred years, the climate deteriorated, causing the bog to gradually rise up over their farms.

The site is commemorated by an impressive, well-designed **visitor centre** (late Feb to mid-Oct daily 10am–6pm; €3.70; Heritage Card; ⓦwww.heritageireland.ie), which features exhibitions and audiovisuals on the history and geology of the area and the formation of the bog, as well as a viewing platform and a fine café. Regular forty-minute guided tours (last tour 5pm) take visitors outside to see excavated walls, animal and house enclosures and to learn about the ecology of the bog that swallowed them up. From the adjacent clifftop viewpoint, you can see Donegal's Slieve League on a clear day, and in the near distance the sea stack of Downpatrick Head, neatly layered and tufted with grass: according to legend, this is the severed head of the last snake that St Patrick chased from Ireland.

The nearest town to Céide Fields is **BALLYCASTLE** (ⓦwww.ballycastle.ie), 8km to the east, which comes as a pleasant surprise among the barren, grossly proportioned mountains of North Mayo: set in the broad Ballinglen valley, it's surrounded by green fields, trees and cattle, with a fine sandy beach at the river mouth. **Tourist information** is available at the Ballycastle Resource Centre (Mon–Fri 10am–5/6pm, closing for lunch; ⓣ096/43407). Changing exhibitions of works by internationally known artists attached to the local **Ballinglen Arts Foundation** are held at the gallery opposite *Polke's* **pub**. A traditional, welcoming grocery-bar, *Polke's* itself is hung with paintings by Ballinglen artists who have searched for the muse there. For accommodation, head for the welcoming *Keadyville* **B&B** (ⓣ096/43288 or 086 088 9010; ❶), where there are great breakfasts and sea views, or the elegantly refurbished former coastguard station and convent, the *Stella Maris* **hotel**, which offers beautiful views of the bay, meticulous luxury and an excellent, creative **restaurant** (ⓣ096/43322, ⓦwww.stellamarisireland.com; April–Sept; ❻). You can also eat very well at *Mary's* homely **café** and bakery on the main street (closed Sun in winter; ⓣ096/43361).

There's no public transport to Céide Fields but Ballycastle is linked by **bus** to Ballina, 28km to the southeast, which in turn has regular services to and from Westport and Castlebar. Further exploration of the coast could be based on the **North Mayo Sculpture Trail**, marked by brown *Tír Sáile* (Land of the Salty Wind) signposts, a striking and ever-growing series of modern outdoor sculptures, celebrating the wild beauty and cultural heritage of the area; for further information, phone ⓣ098/45107 or go to ⓦwww.mayoireland.ie/tirsaile.htm.

Travel details

Trains

Dublin Heuston to: Athenry (5–7 daily; 2hr 30min); Ballina (3–4 daily, most via a connection at Manulla Junction; 4hr); Castlebar (3 daily; 3hr 15min); Galway (5–7 daily; 2hr 30min–3hr); Westport (3 daily; 3hr 30min–3hr 50min).
Galway to: Athenry (5–8 daily; 15min); Athlone (5–8 daily; 1hr); Dublin (5–7 daily; 2hr 30min–3hr); Kildare (2–5 daily; 2hr 15min).
Westport to: Athlone (3–4 daily; 2hr); Castlebar (3–4 daily; 15min); Dublin (3–4 daily; 3hr 30min–3hr 50min).

Buses

Bus Éireann

Ballina to: Ballycastle (Mon–Fri 2–3 daily; 30min–1hr); Castlebar (3–8 daily; 1hr).
Dublin to: Castlebar (2–5 daily; 4hr 45min); Galway (hourly; 3hr 40min); Portumna (Mon–Fri & Sun 1 daily; 3hr); Westport (2–5 daily; 5hr).
Galway to: Achill (2 weekly, on Fri & Sun; 3hr); Athenry (Mon–Sat 4 daily; 35min); Athlone (hourly; 1hr 30min); Castlebar (4–7 daily; 1hr 45min); Clarenbridge (hourly; 20min); Clifden (1–6 daily; 1hr 45min–2hr 15min); Cliffs of Moher (summer 2–3 daily, winter 1 daily; 2hr); Cong (2–5 daily; 1hr); Cork (hourly; 4hr 15min); Doolin (summer 2–4 daily, winter 1–2 daily; 1hr 30min); Dublin (hourly; 3hr 45min); Ennis (hourly; 1hr 15min); Gort (hourly; 45min); Kilcolgan (hourly; 30min); Killarney (every 2hr; 4hr); Kinvarra (1–5 daily; 30min–1hr); Kylemore (winter 2 weekly, summer Mon–Sat 2 daily; 1hr 30min–2hr); Leenane (winter 2 weekly, summer Mon–Sat 2 daily; 1hr 30min–2hr); Letterfrack (winter 2 weekly, summer Mon–Sat 2 daily; 2hr); Letterkenny (3–5 daily; 4hr); Limerick (hourly; 2hr); Loughrea (hourly; 35min); Oranmore (at least hourly; 10min); Oughterard (5–7 daily; 40min); Portumna (5 weekly; 2hr); Rosmuc (Mon & Fri 1 daily; 1hr 15min); Roundstone (winter 4 weekly, summer 1–2 daily; 1hr 30min); Shannon Airport (4 daily; 2hr); Sligo (5–6 daily; 2hr 15min); Spiddal (3–8 daily; 40min); Westport (4–5 daily; 2hr).
Westport to: Achill (1–3 daily; 1hr 10min–1hr 50min); Athlone (1–3 daily; 3hr); Ballina (2–7 daily; 1hr); Castlebar (6–12 daily; 20min); Clifden (summer Mon–Sat 1 daily; 1hr 30min); Cong (2 weekly; 1hr); Kylemore (summer Mon–Sat 1 daily; 1hr); Leenane (summer Mon–Sat 1 daily; 45min); Letterfrack (summer Mon–Sat 1 daily; 1hr 15min); Louisburgh (Mon–Sat 2–4 daily; 35min); Sligo (2–4 daily; 2hr 40min).

Private buses

Bus Nestor (Ⓣ091/797144, Ⓦwww.nestorlink.ie) and **Citylink** (Ⓣ091/564163 or 1890 280808, Ⓦwww.citylink.ie) each run several coaches a day between Galway City (from the coach park beside the tourist office) and Dublin airport and city centre, via Athlone. Citylink also runs several coaches a day to Shannon Airport, to Limerick and Cork, and to Clifden, Letterfrack and Cleggan (see also p.442).
Feda O'Donnell Coaches (Ⓣ091/761656, Ⓦwww.fedaodonnell.com) operates daily services between Galway City, Knock, Sligo, Bundoran, Donegal, Letterkenny and Gweedore.
Kearns Transport (Ⓣ057/912 0124, Ⓦwww.kearnstransport.com) runs daily services between Portumna and Dublin, via Banagher and Birr, and at weekends between Portumna and Galway city via Loughrea.

11

Sligo, Leitrim and Roscommon

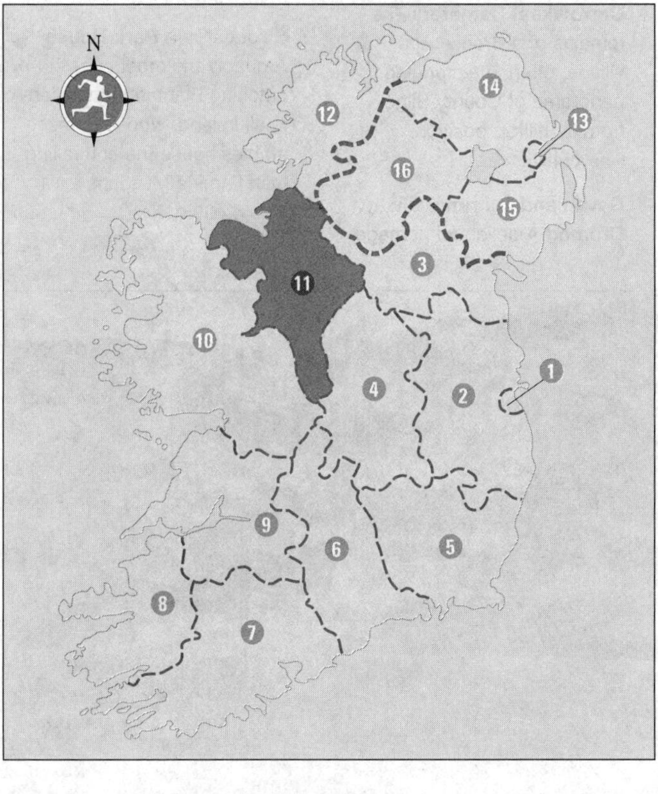

CHAPTER 11

Highlights

* **Lough Gill** Utterly tranquil and unspoilt and the inspiration, alongside its island, Innisfree, for much of the poetry of Yeats. See p.481

* **Lissadell House** A fine Neoclassical mansion replete with memories of the Gore-Booth sisters and the poet Yeats. See p.483

* **Carrowkeel Cemetery** The remains of a Bronze Age village, offering a stunning panorama of County Sligo from its hilltop position. See p.487

* **Cavan and Leitrim Railway, Dromod** A delightful homage to the railways of the past – a fully operating steam railway, staffed by some of the most knowledgeable and go-ahead enthusiasts around. See box on p.492

* **Arigna Mining Experience** Devoted to the vicissitudes of life for the miners who once literally scraped a living in the mountains here – completely gripping. See p.497

* **Strokestown Park House** Arguably the most eye-catching Plantation mansion in all Ireland, whose former stables house the enthralling Irish Famine Museum. See p.499

▲ Lough Gill

Sligo, Leitrim and Roscommon

Counties Sligo, Leitrim and Roscommon are renowned for the rhythmic sway and gentle flamboyance of their traditional music, characterized by flutes and fiddles and often known as the North Connacht style of playing. Topographically, however, they have less in common, with **Sligo** possessing the most allure: though it might feel less wild and remote than nearby Mayo and Donegal, the county still features atmospheric Megalithic monuments, mountains that, in the form of Benbulben and Knocknarea, dominate the skyline, and some of Ireland's best surfing beaches. It also shares two gorgeous loughs – Gill and Glencar – with sparsely populated **Leitrim**, one of Ireland's hidden gems – a sweet melange of secluded lakes and drumlins, offering fine hiking territory and, thanks to its proximity to the Shannon, numerous boating and fishing opportunities. Southernmost **Roscommon** largely consists of unexciting farmland, especially the less appealing nether region to the west of Lough Ree, though further north, near the vibrant town of Boyle, it becomes more enthralling, blending attractive lakes with the dramatic reaches of the Arigna Mountains, Ireland's former coal-mining base.

The three counties are reasonably well served by **public transport**, not least in the form of the mainline railway which links the towns of Sligo, Boyle and Carrick-on-Shannon, though bus services in more remote areas are infrequent.

County Sligo

The county's hub, lively **Sligo town**, is one of Ireland's foremost traditional music centres, offering many an enjoyable session, and has the best facilities for visitors keen to explore the local countryside. Easy trips from here could include the bracing seaside resorts of **Strandhill** and **Rosses Point**, as well as Megalithic sites **Carrowmore Cemetery** and **Medb's Cairn**, set atop

SLIGO, LEITRIM & ROSCOMMON
0
15 km
N
Bundoran
DONEGAL
Lower Lough
Omagh
A32
Mullaghmore
Mullaghmore Head
N15
Inishmurray
Cliffony
Creevykeel Court Tomb
R281
Lough Melvin
Streedagh Point
Grange
Benbulben (528m)
FERMANAGH
Glenade Lough
DARTRY MOUNTAINS
Lissadell House
Carney
Enniskillen
Drumcliffe
Glencar Lough
R280
R282
R283
R281
Sligo Bay
Raghly
Rosses Point
Manorhamilton
A4
Blacklion
Coney Island
N16
Aughris Head
Easkey
Killaspugbrone Church
Sligo
R286
N16
Killala Bay
Aughris
Split Rock
Strandhill
Parke's Castle
Lough Gill
Innisfree
Leitrim Way
Upper Lough Erne
Medb's Cairn
Skreen
R287
R287
Carrowmore Megalithic Cemetery
Dromahair
R297
Enniscrone
N59
N59
LEITRIM
Ballysadare
Dowra
R280
Coolaney
Collooney
CAVAN
Ballinaglera
R284
SLIEVE GAMPH (OX MOUNTAINS)
N4
Drumfin
Lough Allen
Ballina
SLIGO
Riverstown
Heapstown Cairn
ARIGNA MOUNTAINS
N17
R293
R207
Ballymote
Castlebaldwin
Slieve Anierin (586m)
Aghacashel
Templehouse Lake
Lough Arrow
Arigna
BRICKLIEVE MOUNTAINS
Lough Talt
R294
Carrowkeel Cemetery
Keadue
R208
Ballinamore
Tubbercurry
Drumshanbo
Lough Conn
N26
R294
Lough Scur
CURLEW MOUNTAINS
R294
Lough Key
R209
R209
R280
Fenagh
R204
Keshcarrigan
N17
Foxford
Gurteen
LOUGH KEY FOREST PARK
Carrick-on-Shannon
R293
Boyle
N5
N4
R202
Charlestown
Lough Gara
Swinford
Mohill
R201
MAYO
N61
N4
R202
Lough Rinn

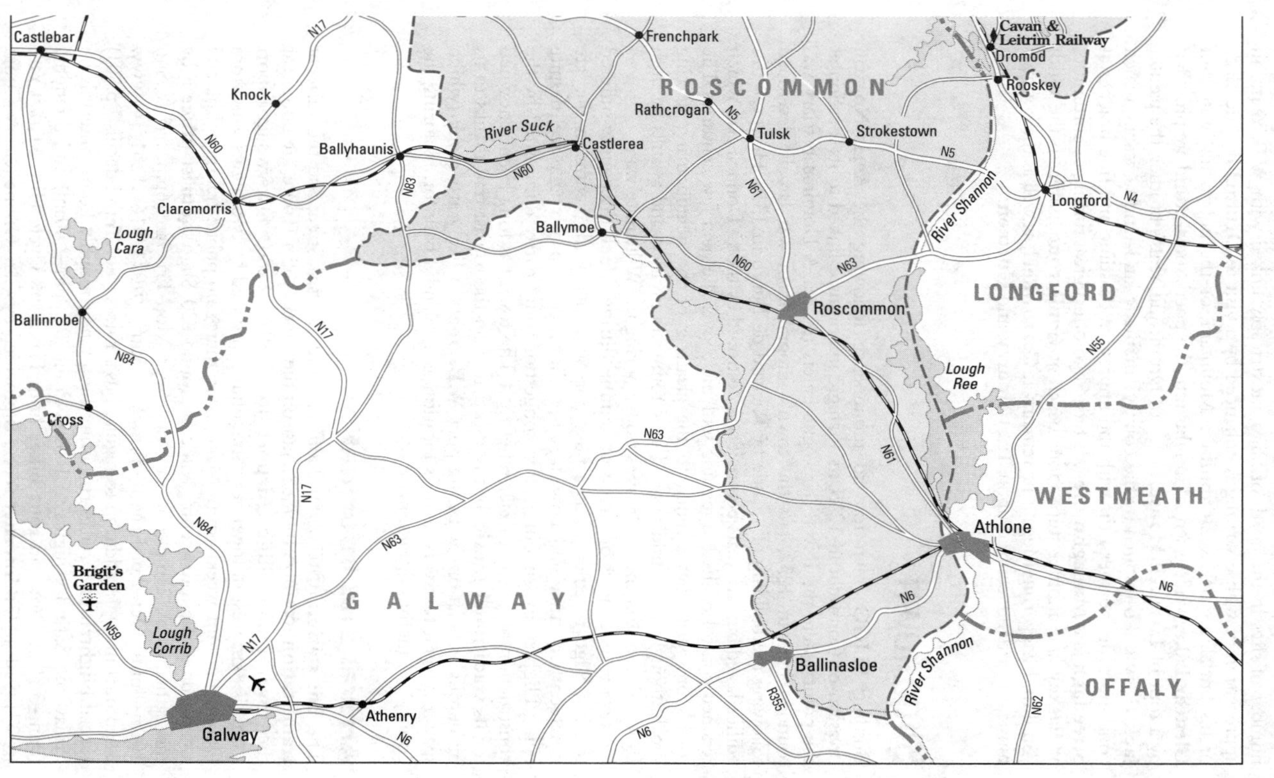

Castlebar
Knock
Claremorris
Lough Cara
Ballinrobe
Cross
Brigit's Garden
Lough Corrib
Galway
Athenry
N60
N17
N84
N59
N6
Ballyhaunis
N83
River Suck
Castlerea
Ballymoe
Frenchpark
ROSCOMMON
Rathcrogan
N5
Tulsk
Strokestown
N61
N60
Roscommon
N63
GALWAY
Ballinasloe
R355
Cavan & Leitrim Railway
Dromod
Rooskey
Longford
N4
River Shannon
LONGFORD
N55
Lough Ree
WESTMEATH
Athlone
OFFALY
N62

Knocknarea Mountain, though you'll need your own transport to reach them. Majestic **Lough Gill**, and its celebrated island **Innisfree** is, along with a number of sites in the north of Sligo, inextricably linked with **W.B. Yeats**, an appreciation of whose writing is enhanced by a visit to **Drumcliffe**, the place of his burial, set below **Benbulben** Mountain, or the entrancing waters of **Glencar Lake**, while essential insights into the poet's social world are provided by a tour of **Lissadell House**, north of Drumcliffe. Yeats's brother, the painter **Jack B.**, was also inspired by the county's dramatic land- and seascapes, which continue to its northern tip with the impressive coastline and fine beaches at **Streedagh** and **Mullaghmore**. Western Sligo offers great surfing opportunities at **Easkey** and another stupendous beach at **Enniscrone**, while to the south you'll find staggering Megalithic remains at **Carrowkeel**, as well as the county's musical heartland, centred upon **Tubbercurry** and **Gurteen**.

Sligo town

Bustling **SLIGO** town rose to prominence following the Anglo-Norman invasion of Connacht in 1235, its strategic importance linked to its location at the point where the River Garavogue enters the sea. A Dominican friary was founded here in 1252, but the town's integral form was largely developed following the building of a castle by Richard de Burgo in 1310. However, this edifice lasted but five years before it was destroyed by the O'Donnell clan which retained control of the burgeoning settlement over the next few centuries. The town's prosperity owed much to the gleaning of the neighbouring herring shoals, though it was undermined by Cromwell's invasion and assaults by both James II's and William of Orange's troops during the Williamite war.

After the exigencies of the Great Famine, during which the county suffered terribly, Sligo re-emerged as a busy port and mercantile centre in the late nineteenth century and nowadays is a thoroughly absorbing place, despite being blighted by ongoing traffic congestion, only partly diminished by the construction of a recent inner relief road. The town has long been renowned for its **traditional music**, but is also firmly on the tourist trail thanks to its numerous associations with the poet **W.B. Yeats**, a lively arts scene (which spawns several **festivals**) and its location as a splendid base for exploring the county's numerous attractions.

Arrival and information

The **bus station** (Ⓣ071/916 0066) on Lord Edward Street and the adjacent **train station** (Ⓣ071/916 9888), just off the Inner Relief Route, are both near the town centre. **Sligo Airport** (Ⓣ071/916 8280, Ⓦwww.sligoairport.com) is 8km west of town near Strandhill and served by two flights daily from Dublin and four weekly from Manchester; there's no public-transport link and a taxi ride to the town centre will cost around €20. Sligo's **tourist office** is by the cathedral on Temple Street (May–Sept Mon–Fri 9am–6pm, Sat & Sun 10am–4pm; Oct–April Mon–Fri 9am–5pm; Ⓣ071/916 1201, Ⓦwww.sligotourism.ie). In addition to regular bus services (see "Travel details", p.501) special **Nightrider** services run from the town at roughly hourly intervals on Friday and Saturday nights to Rosses Point (9.30pm–2.40am) and Strandhill (9pm–3.50am). You can **rent bikes** from Flanagan's Cycle Hire, Market Yard (Ⓣ071/914 4477). **Internet** access is provided by Café Online, Cabry Court, Stephen Street, and Cygo Internet Café, behind 19 O'Connell St.

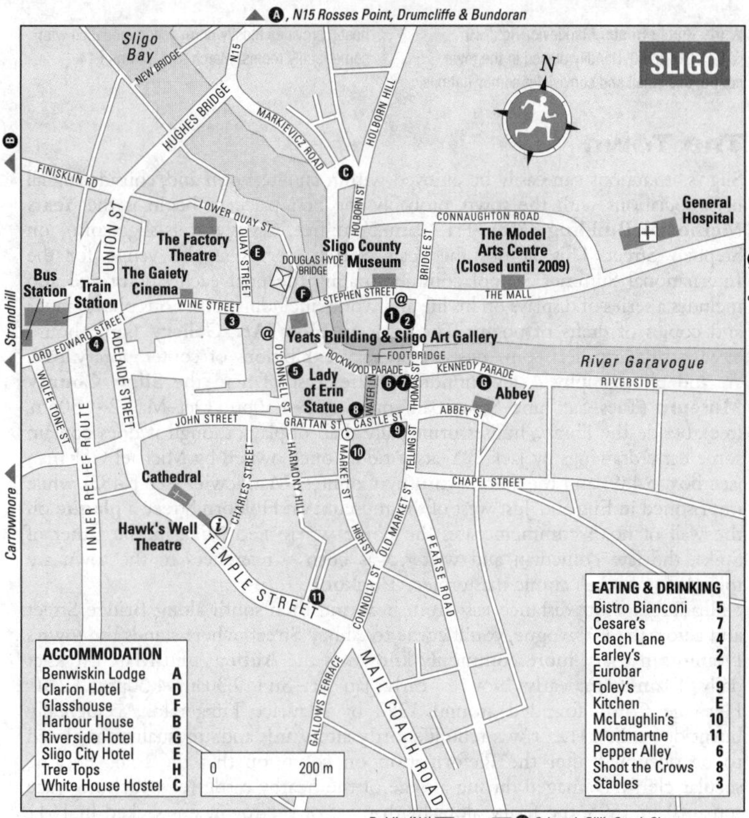

Accommodation

There are numerous **hotel** options dotted around, plus plenty of **B&B**s along the main roads leading out of the town. For **camping** your best bets are in Strandhill and Rosses Point (see p.480 & p.482).

Benwiskin Lodge Shannon Eighter ⓣ071/914 1088, ⓦwww.benwiskin.com. A delightful country house offering charming en-suite accommodation, just 50m off the N15 Donegal road, 2km north of town. ②

Clarion Hotel Clarion Rd, Ballinode ⓣ071/911 9000, ⓦwww.clarionhotelsligo.com. Very swish and modern establishment, offering remarkably good room-rate deals, 1km out of town off the N16 Enniskillen road. ③

The Glasshouse Swan Point ⓣ071/919 4300, ⓦwww.theglasshouse.ie. This literally dazzling (when the sun shines) place by Hyde Bridge offers a dramatic glassy counterpoint to the adjacent waters of the Garavogue. Its chic rooms offer floor-to-ceiling windows and a high degree of comfort. ⑤

Harbour House Finisklin Rd (IHH & IHO) ⓣ071/917 1547, ⓦwww.harbourhousehostel.com. Set in the old harbourmaster's house, and offering very pleasant en-suite rooms and dorms, its only disadvantage is the kilometre-long walk from town. Dorms €18, doubles ①.

Sligo City Hotel Quay St ⓣ071/914 4000, ⓦwww.sligocityhotel.com. Plush new hotel providing elegant accommodation and extremely efficient service. ⑤

Tree Tops Cleveragh Rd ⓣ071/916 0160, ⓦwww.sligobandb.com. A comfortable and well-appointed guesthouse with a pleasant garden, just off Pearse Road. ②

White House Hostel Markievicz Rd (IHH) ☎071/914 5160. Handily placed in the town centre, this small and convivial if somewhat basic hostel provides mostly dorm accommodation with some family rooms; March–Oct. Dorms €14.

The Town

Sligo's attractions can easily be enjoyed within an afternoon and, considering all his associations with the town, probably the best place to begin is the **Yeats Memorial Building** (Mon–Fri 10am–5pm; free; Ⓦwww.yeats-sligo.com), on Stephen Street. This houses the Yeats Society, serves as the venue for the International Summer School commemorating the poet each August and also includes a series of displays on his life and works, including numerous photographs and copies of drafts of poems. The adjacent **Sligo Art Gallery** (same hours; Ⓦwww.sligoartgallery.com) hosts temporary exhibitions of contemporary Irish art and photography. A few hundred metres east of here, the **Sligo County Museum** (Tues–Sat: June–Sept 10am–noon & 2–4.50pm; Oct–May 2–4.50pm; free), beside the library, houses principally drab displays, though it does contain some early drawings by Jack B. Yeats, a fiddle once owned by Michael Coleman (see box, p.489) and the apron worn by Countess Markiewicz (see p.483) while imprisoned in England. Just west of the museum on Holborn Street, a **plaque** on the wall of no. 5 commemorates the house where Leo Milligan, the father of Spike, the late comedian and writer, was born – references to the town are included in Spike's comic masterpiece **Puckoon**.

Heading a short distance east from here and then south along Bridge Street and across the Garavogue, you'll come to Abbey Street, where stands the town's Dominican friary, more commonly known as the **Abbey** (mid-March to Oct daily 10am–6pm; early Nov to early Jan Fri–Sun 9.30am–4.30pm; €2.10; Heritage Card), founded around 1252 by Maurice Fitzgerald. Accidentally burnt down in 1412, it was rebuilt shortly afterwards and, unusually, continued to be occupied after the Reformation on condition that the friars became secular clergy. Damaged during a siege of the nearby castle (of which no trace remains) in 1595, the friary, along with most of the town, was sacked in 1641 by Sir Frederick Hamilton and his Puritan army, and its friars massacred. However, the friary's remains are in remarkably good condition and include a delicately decorated high altar, gracefully carved tombs and sculptures, and well-preserved cloisters. West of the friary, at the bottom of Market Street, the **Lady of Erin** statue commemorates the 1798 uprisings.

Eating

You won't be spoilt for choice in terms of the range of **restaurants** in Sligo and most won't threaten your bank balance; many of the pubs also serve bar lunches at reasonable prices.

Bistro Bianconi 44 O'Connell St ☎071/914 1744. Convivial Italian restaurant serving excellent pasta and pizza. Closed Sun.

Cesare's Rockwood Parade ☎071/914 1386. Though it deals in Italian standards, this cosy riverside restaurant also includes some very successful exotic blends, such as Thai tagliatelli.

Coach Lane Above *Donaghy's Bar*, 1–2 Lord Edward St ☎071/916 2417. A diverse mix of meat, seafood and vegetarian dishes from around the world, with a pleasant terrace for alfresco summer dining.

Eurobar Stephen St Car Park. Probably Sligo's best coffee, served in a stylish modern setting.

The Kitchen *The Glasshouse Hotel*, Swan Point ☎071/919 4300. Superb main courses firmly focused upon modern Irish cuisine and a range of staggering desserts. Expect to pay around €50 plus wine.

Montmartre 1 Market Yard. The town's most upmarket restaurant, French-run and offering a deliciously varied menu including rabbit in mustard crust and fresh Lissadell lobster. Expect to pay around €40 plus wine, though there's an early-bird special for approx. €16 Tues–Fri. Closed Mon.

Pepper Alley Rockwood Parade. A spacious riverside café, serving a grand mix of breakfasts, lunches and snacks.

Pubs

Sligo has a plethora of splendid old-fashioned **pubs**, many offering lively **traditional-music** sessions.

Earley's Bridge St. This cosy old bar features a great Thurs-night session and other music on Fri and Sat.

Foley's Castle St. Traditional bar with a superb range of whiskeys, and sessions year-round on Thurs & Sat, plus Wed from June to Sept.

McLaughlin's Market St. Another very convivial pub, staging a fine session on Tues.

Shoot the Crows Castle St. Lively, slightly dishevelled bar across from the *Lady of Erin* statue with sessions on Tues and Thurs.

Stables Wine St. Friendly bar with a great session on Friday nights.

Entertainment, festivals and sport

On Temple Street the Hawk's Well **theatre** (Ⓦwww.hawkswell.com) presents a range of dramatic productions and a variety of musical events and is one of the main venues for the Yeats International Summer School (first two weeks in August; Ⓦwww.yeats-sligo.com). The Factory Theatre, Lower Quay Street (Ⓦwww.blueraincoat.com), is host to the innovative Blue Raincoat Theatre Company and also hosts other cultural events. The Gaiety (Ⓣ071/917 4002, Ⓦwww.gaietysligo.com), a twelve-screen **cinema**, can be found on Wine Street. The town's major **music festival** is Sligo Live (Ⓦwww.sligolive.ie), held over the October public-holiday weekend and featuring a host of traditional-music sessions, as well as a variety of major acts. For info on other events check one of the two weekly newspapers, *The Sligo Champion* or *Sligo Weekender*, or the fortnightly freesheet *The Scene* (Ⓦwww.scene.ie).

The town's **association football** club, Sligo Rovers, plays at The Showgrounds, Knappagh Road (Ⓣ071/917 1212, Ⓦwww.sligorovers.com for details of games). If you fancy a flutter, head for the **Sligo Races** (Ⓣ071/918 3342, Ⓦwww.countysligoraces.com) on Cleveragh Road, where there are eight meetings between May and early October.

Around Sligo town

West of Sligo town lies the famous surfing beach at **Strandhill**, a grand base for exhilarating coastal walks, while inland is one of Europe's most significant collections of passage graves at **Carrowmore Megalithic Cemetery**. Both the resort and the graveyard are overlooked by the numinous Knocknarea Mountain, on whose summit sits the mystical **Medb's Cairn**.

Strandhill and around

Seaside **STRANDHILL**, 8km west of Sligo town, remains remarkably unexploited despite its gorgeous position, the village and its beach set against the backdrop of the looming Knocknarea Mountain. On the way into the village look out for **Dolly's Cottage** (June Sat & Sun 2–6pm; July & Aug daily 2–6pm; free), a tiny thatched dwelling named after its last occupant, Dolly

▲ Celtic Seaweed Baths

Higgins, who died in 1970. Maintained as it was, with a turf fire and a tiny pouch bed, the cottage now sells various handicrafts, as well as home-made jams and preserves.

Strandhill's **beach** is its most renowned feature, a wild stretch pounded by huge Atlantic breakers. Though it's absolutely unsafe for swimming, it's massively popular with **surfers** and regularly witnesses the Sligo Open Championship over the first weekend in August. Right by the beach the Perfect Day Surf School (Ⓦwww.perfectdaysurfing.com) offers a range of classes. Adjacent on the front you can luxuriate in the curative and pleasantly soporific waters of the **Celtic Seaweed Baths** (Mon–Fri 10am–9pm, Sat & Sun 10am–8.30pm; Ⓦwww.celticseaweedbaths.com; €20 single, two adults sharing €30), which also offers aromatherapy, reflexology and massage treatments (€30–60).

The beach offers bracing walks, especially a few kilometres north past tiny Sligo Airport to **Killaspugbrone Church**, whose ruins largely date from the twelfth and thirteenth centuries, though its tower is a later addition. Visiting the church some centuries earlier St Patrick somehow contrived to stumble and dislodge a tooth in the process, which he promptly donated to the sacristan, Bishop Bronus. This relic was kept and passed down and, in the fourteenth century, an exquisite casket, the Fiacal Pádraig, was created to house it – the tooth subsequently disappeared, but its container is on view at Dublin's National Museum.

The village has few **accommodation** options. Nearest the beach on Shore Road is *Knocknarea House* (Ⓣ071/916 8313, Ⓦwww.strandhillaccommodation.com; ❷; March–Oct), a modern family home with congenial en-suite rooms and an attached, well-equipped hostel, *Strandhill Lodge* (dorms €16, doubles ❶). Heading uphill will bring you to the very amenable *Ocean View Hotel* (Ⓣ071/916 8115, Ⓔoceanviewhotel@eircom.net; ❹; mid-March to Oct), some of whose pleasant en-suite rooms overlook the village. Alternatively, **camping** is available at *Strandhill Caravan and Camping Park* (Ⓣ071/916 8111; April to mid-Sept). Back at the bottom of Shore Road, *The Strand* **bar** offers a turf fire, cosy snugs and wholesome pub meals.

Carrowmore Cemetery and Medb's Cairn

Four kilometres southwest of Sligo town, **Carrowmore Megalithic Cemetery** (Easter–Oct daily 10am–6pm; last admission 5pm; €2.10; Heritage Card) presents a remarkable array of some thirty Megalithic **passage tombs**, easily the biggest prehistoric graveyard in Europe. This oval-shaped cluster of monuments spreads out within a 1km-by-600m field and ranges from the most basic, a small circle of stones surrounding a central roofed chamber, through to the largest, known as Listoghill, covered by an impressive rounded cairn. Excavations have uncovered cremated human remains as well as jewellery carved from bones and antlers; it's suggested that some of the tombs were created as far back as 4800 BC, though they continued to be used for burial over the next three millennia.

Carrowmore is made all the more atmospheric for being set below one of Ireland's most significant burial places, the massive **Medb's Cairn**, standing on the summit of Knocknarea Mountain – 55m wide and 10m high, and surrounded by a three-metre-high earthen bank. Whether Medb, the legendary queen of Connacht and one of the protagonists of the **Táin Bó Cúailnge**, is actually buried here is unknown, since the site has not been excavated, but it's well worth making the trek, not only for views of the cairn itself, but for spectacular outlooks north to Donegal and west to Mayo. To get there from Carrowmore head west for 1km, take a right turn at the junction with the R292, then left at the first crossroads – after another kilometre a lane leads right towards the car park at the base of the mountain, from which it's a steep four-kilometre hike to the summit. On your way up to the top pick up a stone and leave it on the cairn, making a wish as you do so and, as local legend has it, the force of Queen Medb may be with you.

Lough Gill

To the east of Sligo town lies one of Ireland's most entrancing lakes, **Lough Gill**, set beneath wooded slopes which provide the backdrop to almost all its 40km shoreline. The best route around the lough, and one easily navigable in less than a day's cycling, is to follow the shore clockwise starting off by following the R286 from Sligo town, and taking in the plantation **Parke's Castle** on the way, from which you can take a water tour and catch a sight of idyllic **Innisfree**.

Parke's Castle

A few kilometres further on, towards the lake's eastern extremity, the R286 hugs the shoreline as it enters County Leitrim on its way to **Parke's Castle** (mid-March to Oct daily 10am–6pm; €2.90; Heritage Card). This picturesque plantation castle was erected by Captain Robert Parke in the 1620s and elegantly restored in the late twentieth century by the Office of Public Works. A moated tower-house once stood here, home of the Irish chieftain Brian O'Rourke, who in 1588 was charged with high treason after sheltering Francesco de Cuellar, one of the few survivors of the Armada ships wrecked off the Sligo coast (see p.485). O'Rourke was hanged at Tyburn in 1591 and his lands confiscated, later being distributed to the Leitrim planters, whose number included Parke. Inside are reconstructed some of the features of the inner courtyard, such as a blacksmith's forge, a well and a water gate. You can wander around the battlements, admire expansive views of the lough and also take in an exhibition on the remodelling of the castle with displays on other notable vernacular buildings.

Innisfree

From the pier beside Parke's Castle the **Wild Rose of Innisfree waterbus** operates a tour of Lough Gill (Easter–Oct daily 11am & hourly from 12.30–4.30pm; ⓣ071/916 4266, ⓦwww.roseofinnisfree.com; €10), taking in views of Yeats's beloved isle of **Innisfree**, and featuring recitals of the poet's works by the skipper, almost certainly including the poet's **Lake Isle of Innisfree**:

I will arise and go now, and go to Innisfree,
And a small cabin build there, of clay and wattles made:
Nine bean-rows will I have there, a hive for the honey-bee,
And live alone in the bee-loud glade.

Alternatively, head a few kilometres southwards through Dromahair and pick up the R287. About 4km along this a signposted lane leads down to the water where there's a fabulous view of the lough and Innisfree in all its serene beauty.

North Sligo

The majority of North Sligo's attractions are easily accessible from the county town. Much of the landscape is irrevocably associated with W.B. Yeats, particularly **Benbulben** Mountain, under whose green-tinged slopes and surmounting tableland the poet is buried at **Drumcliffe**. To the mountain's south lie the magical waters of **Glencar Lake** with its exhilarating waterfall, while to its west is **Lissadell House**, home to Yeats's friends, Eva Gore-Booth and Constance Markiewicz, tours of which provide valuable insights into the poet's social milieu. The coastline from **Raghly** northwards is less stimulating, though does include the gorgeous **Streedagh Strand** and another fine beach at **Mullaghmore**, a quaint harbour village not far from one of Ireland's major funerary monuments, **Creevykeel Court Tomb**.

Rosses Point

Eight kilometres northwest of Sligo town, off the N15, **ROSSES POINT** is a picturesque seaside resort which has not moved with the times and is all the better for its lapse. There's a grand **beach**, ideal for swimming, and splendid views across the bay, both of which provided inspiration for Jack B. Yeats, the poet's artist brother. From here there are fine, often blustery walks around the headland and, in the village itself, top-notch **accommodation** available at the grandiose *Yeats Country Hotel & Leisure Club* (ⓣ071/917 7211, ⓦwww.yeatscountryhotel.com; ❻), a very child-friendly place which has elegantly furnished rooms, plenty of which offer sea views, and its own swimming pool and gym. Alternatively, for B&B, there's the congenial *Oyster View* (ⓣ071/917 7201; ❷; March–Sept), also with sea views. You can **camp** at *Greenlands Caravan* *and Camping Park* (ⓣ071/917 7113; Easter to mid-Sept). For **food** try *The Waterfront* (ⓣ071/917 7122), which serves delicious marine delicacies and has its own bakery, coffee shop and art gallery, or *Austie's*, a very cosy, traditional **bar**.

Drumcliffe and Glencar Lake

Eight kilometres due north of Sligo along the N15, the tiny seaside village of **DRUMCLIFFE** is the site of a **monastery** established in 574 by St Colmcille, though only a round tower and an eleventh-century high cross, set on opposite sides of the main road, remain today. The graveyard of the adjacent and somewhat stark nineteenth-century church is where the poet **W.B. Yeats** is buried and, as a consequence, is very much on the tourist trail. Yeats died in 1939 in Roquebrune, France, but before doing so requested that his body be interred locally for "a year or so" before being returned to Sligo. His wishes were granted in 1948 when his remains were transferred from France to Drumcliffe, where his great-grandfather had been rector, and buried, as one of his last poems stated, "Under bare Ben Bulben's head". His headstone, which also marks the resting place of his wife George, bears the last three lines of that poem, **Under Ben Bulben**:

Cast a cold Eye
On Life, on Death.
Horseman, pass by!

Next to Drumcliffe church is a good **café** and craft shop situated in the former visitor centre. Alternatively, *The Yeats Tavern*, a hundred metres further along the main road, offers substantial **bar** meals.

Heading east from Drumcliffe along minor roads you'll come to **Glencar Lake** after some 8km, gorgeously set amid tree-lined slopes. Near the eastern extremity of its northern shore a signposted footpath leads up to an impressive fifteen-metre-high **waterfall**, cascading down into a deep pool from the rocky mountainside above, which provided the inspiration for part of Yeats's poem *The Stolen Child*:

Where the wandering water gushes
From the hills above Glen-car,
In pools above the rushes that
Scarce could bathe a star.

Lissadell House

Just north of Drumcliffe a signpost points west to Carney and **Lissadell House** (April–Sept 10.30am–6pm; tours on the hour 11am–5pm; house €6, gardens €5, coach house €5, combined ticket €12; ⓦwww.lissadellhouse.com), a grey-walled Neoclassical mansion built by Sir Robert Gore-Booth in 1830. The house's notability partly rests on its associations with Yeats who became friends with Robert's granddaughters, **Eva** and **Constance**, in the 1890s. Nowadays owned by two Kildare barristers, the house is gradually undergoing restoration and its hugely informative and entertaining tour is well worth taking. The tour begins in the ground-floor billiards room, featuring numerous Gore-Booth family photos and the hunting equipment of the Arctic explorer, Henry Gore-Booth, and then ventures upstairs via an imperial staircase of Kilkenny marble to the pokey little guestroom where Yeats used to stay; on its walls hang some of his brother Jack's early cartoons and pictures of boatmen.

▲ Lissadell House

Returning downstairs, the next stop is the gallery-cum-music-room, designed like a Greek temple and featuring ten-bulb gasoliers – Lissadell was the first house in Ireland to be gas-lit – before passing through a pre-prandial anteroom; note where Constance has engraved her name on a window, and her charcoal pictures, which were produced during a stint in Paris. The dining room itself, equipped with an Egyptian-style plaster ceiling, has entrancing full-scale mural portraits by Constance's husband, Count Casimir Markiewicz, featuring her brother Jocelyn and family retainers. Constance herself played a major role in the 1916 Easter Rising, though by 1918 had not only been elected as Britain's first woman MP, but also subsequently became Minister of Labour in the Dáil's first post-Independence cabinet.

Downstairs, the servants' hall features numerous drawings by Eva Gore-Booth, Yeats's confidante as he struggled to come to terms with his unrequited love for Maud Gonne, as well as an elaborate butler's indicator-box whose lights provided details about where his services were currently required.

To the house's northwest stands the recently restored **Coach House** (same hours), home to both a tearoom and an exhibition devoted to the Countess Markiewicz which includes a wealth of memorabilia, photographs and paintings, the last including a somewhat chilling death-bed portrait by her husband Casimir. Elsewhere in the estate the walled **kitchen garden** and seaside **alpine garden** (both same hours) have undergone massive reinvigoration and feature a wealth of rare plants, including a variety of Lissadell's own daffodil strains, as well as extremely enjoyable walks.

Raghly Point to Streedagh Strand

Tiny **RAGHLY** lies just a few kilometres west of Lissadell House. Its harbour serves as the starting point for a two-kilometre stroll along the coast that loops back down a lane, offering tremendous views out to sea and inland to the mountains. Just before the village's restored castle – painted a rather brash yellow – which is not open to the public, you can **stay** very comfortably indeed at a charming mid-Victorian mansion, *Ardtarmon House* (ⓣ071/916 3156, ⓦwww.ardtarmon.com; ❸), set in expansive grounds beside the bay.

From Raghly an intricate network of lanes runs further up the coast and it's best to follow signposts towards Grange up to **Streedagh Strand**, some 7km north. The beach is a tremendous expanse of sand, absolutely ideal for horseback hacking (try Island View stables on ⓣ071/916 6156), and there is a two-kilometre walk north to Streedagh Point. Just offshore from here stands **Carraig na Spáinneach** (Spaniards' Rock), where Armada ships were wrecked in 1588. Many of the boats' survivors managed to swim ashore, only to be slaughtered by the English and locals when they dragged their exhausted bodies from the water – stones on the beach are said to indicate various mass graves. One notable survivor, though, was Captain Francesco de Cuellar whose diary, describing his experiences, is held by Madrid's Academia del Historia.

Cliffony and Mullaghmore Head

Twenty-two kilometres north of Sligo town, **CLIFFONY**'s erstwhile post office houses one of the northwest's finest **restaurants**, *The Old Post House* (ⓣ071/917 7688; closed Mon & Tues), which offers inventive takes on modern Irish fish and meat cuisine (expect to pay around €45 plus wine for three courses). Just north of the village lies the more historically noteworthy **Creevykeel Court Tomb** (open access), probably the best example of its kind in Ireland. A cairn-covered, trapeze-shaped barrow constructed between 3500 and 3000 BC, though now lacking many of its stones, this features two central burial chambers, faced by an oval-shaped court in which rituals were conducted. Excavations in 1935 uncovered cremated remains, alongside Neolithic pottery, arrowheads, axes and artefacts, all now held by Dublin's National Museum.

Just before Creevykeel a lane leads northwards for 4km to **MULLAGHMORE**, an enticing village set around a secluded, walled harbour with a glorious expanse of sandy beach just to its south, offering fabulous views north to the mountains of Donegal and back towards Benbulben. The village has two splendidly equipped **hotels** – the *Pier Head Hotel* (ⓣ071/916 6171, ⓦwww.pierheadhotel.ie; ❻) and the *Beach Hotel and Leisure Club* (ⓣ071/916 6103, ⓦwww.beachhotelmullaghmore.com; ❹), which both offer grand rooms with views of the harbour or Atlantic, various leisure facilities and weekend activity breaks. Alternatively, the nearby B&B *Seacrest* (ⓣ071/916 6468, ⓦwww.seacrestguesthouse.com; ❷) is beautifully appointed and has a wonderful location overlooking the beach. You can sample fine seafood in the hotels' **restaurants**, but it's hard to surpass the marine treats on offer at *Eithna's Seafood Restaurant* (daily 6.30–9.30pm; ⓣ071/916 6407; Sept–May call for opening times), where the house speciality of lobster features among other locally caught delights (expect to pay around €50 plus wine for a three-course meal).

West Sligo

Sligo's western shoreline, stretching from near Sligo town almost as far as Mayo's Ballina, is probably the least visited in the county. Yet set against the looming southern backdrop of the Ox Mountains, it offers plenty of diversions including bracing seascapes at **Aughris**, Ireland's surfing capital **Easkey** and a dazzling beach at **Enniscrone**. A little way inland, the memorable funerary sepulchres at **Skreen** are well worth a detour en route.

Skreen and Aughris

Twenty-five kilometres west of Sligo town along the N59, the tiny village of **SKREEN** is worth visiting for the astonishing collection of 23 **box tombs** situated in the graveyard adjacent to its Church of Ireland and created by a local family of stonemasons, the Diamonds, between 1774 and 1886. Named after one Andrew Black, who had the tomb erected in memory of his father in 1825, the most remarkable of these is known as the Black Monument, which carries an ornate carving of a ploughman, atypically dressed Fred Astaire–style in top hat and tails. Other tombs feature the more sinister piratical decoration of a skull and crossed bones.

Back on the N59 and just west of the village a signpost points towards the secluded seaside hamlet of **AUGHRIS**. From the pier here you can follow a bracing five-kilometre cliff walk, which takes in splendid views and sights of numerous seabirds and, from June to August, basking dolphins. Next to the pier is the wonderful *Beach Bar*, a thatched pub which began life in the eighteenth century as a shebeen known as *Maggie Maye's*. The bar not only serves a variety of sumptuous seafood dishes, and offers occasional traditional-music sessions in summer, but also provides extremely amenable en-suite **B&B** in an adjacent bungalow (Ⓣ071/916 6703, Ⓦwww.thebeachbarsligo.com; ❷).

Easkey to Enniscrone

The somewhat decaying small village of **EASKEY**, 15km west of Aughris, began life as a monastic community, much later becoming the base for the MacDonnells, originally gallowglasses who served the ruling O'Dowd clan and built seaside **Roslee Castle** (now ruined) in the fifteenth century. Thanks to the constancy of its waves, Easkey is a popular **surfing** centre and houses the headquarters of the Irish Surfing Association. The Tourist Information Office stands on Main Street (Mon–Fri 10.30am–2.30pm; Ⓣ096/49020) and provides details on local surfing and other attractions. There's little **accommodation** available, and your best bet is *The Fisherman's Weir* pub, also on Main Street (Ⓣ096/49525, Ⓦwww.fishermansweir.net; ❶), which provides very reasonably priced en-suite rooms and serves light **meals** all day.

Just a couple of kilometres southeast of Easkey, by the R297, stands the bizarre **Split Rock**, a three-metre-high glacial oddity which is reckoned to have arrived here when Fionn Mac Cumhaill attempted to throw a boulder from the Ox Mountains into the sea, losing a bet in the process. In a fit of rage he chased after the rock and sundered it with one blow of his sword.

Some 14km southwest along the coast from Easkey, **ENNISCRONE** is blessed with a gorgeous, five-kilometre arc of golden **strand**. Its other main draw is **Kilcullen's Bath House** (May–Oct daily 10am–9pm; Nov–April Mon–Fri noon–8pm, Sat & Sun 10am–8pm; bath and steam €20 or €35 for a twin room; Ⓦwww.kilcullenseaweedbaths.com), where you can wallow in a bath full of seaweed – the iodine-rich water is not only sheer relaxation but is also reckoned to offer relief for rheumatism and arthritis – before enjoying a hot steaming in a cedarwood cabinet. The centre of town life is the welcoming *Castle Arms Hotel* on Main Street (Ⓣ096/36156, Ⓦwww.castlearmshotel.com; ❷), which offers good-value en-suite **accommodation**, and has a lively bar, excellent carvery and a programme of summer entertainment. Alternatively, there's very comfortable en-suite B&B at *Enniscrone Lodge*, Pier Road (Ⓣ096/36181, Ⓦhomepage.tinet.ie/~ennislodge; ❷), which serves grand breakfasts, or you can **camp** at the *Atlantic Caravan Park* (Ⓣ096/36132; March–Sept) by the golf course.

South Sligo

South Sligo's attractions are spread over a wide area, ranging from the glorious **Lough Arrow** in the east, via Megalithic sites, such as **Heapstown Cairn** and the atmospheric **Carrowkeel Cemetery**, set in the Bricklieve Mountains, to the equally gorgeous **Lough Talt** in the west. Above all, however, the area is renowned for its **traditional music**, especially within the triangle formed by the towns of **Ballymote**, **Gurteen** and **Tubbercurry**.

Riverstown and Lough Arrow

The tranquil village of **RIVERSTOWN**, some 20km southeast of Sligo, is home to the **Sligo Folk Park** (May–Sept Mon–Sat 10am–5.30pm, Sun 12.30–6pm; Oct–April Mon–Fri 10am–5pm; €6; Ⓦwww.sligofolkpark.com), a well-designed collection of buildings that includes a museum devoted to rural history and farm implements, re-created craft workshops with occasional craft demonstrations, a nature trail along the banks of the Unshin, plus a crafts shop and café. Over the August bank-holiday weekend the village is taken over by the **James Morrison Traditional Music Festival** (Ⓦwww.morrison.ie), celebrating the music of the famous fiddler, born in nearby Drumfin in 1893. Just outside the village on the road to Drumfin you can **stay** at elegant *Coopershill* (Ⓣ071/916 5108, Ⓦwww.coopershill.com; ❻; April–Oct), a striking Georgian mansion set in expansive grounds, which has been the residence of the same family since its construction in 1774. Its exquisite rooms feature four-poster beds, while the house itself is furnished with a dazzling array of antiques.

Five kilometres south of the village, by the road to Ballindoon, stands the impressive **Heapstown Cairn**, which, at 60m in diameter, is Ireland's largest Megalithic passage tomb outside the Boyne Valley. Indeed, it may have once been the country's biggest, but many stones have been removed for use as building material. According to legend the cairn was constructed by the Fomorians following a battle with the Tuatha De Danann and is also the supposed burial place of Aillil, brother of King Niall of Tara.

From the cairn it's a short jaunt to the eastern shore of **Lough Arrow**, whose limpid waters are peppered with tiny islands. If you can't resist the undeniable temptation to explore the lough, a fly-fisherman's paradise, then several locals rent out **boats** (including Finian Dodd Ⓣ071/916 5065 and John Hargadon Ⓣ071/966 6666). Alternatively, you can rent one from the *Rock View Hotel* (Ⓣ071/966 6073, Ⓔrockhotel@eircom.net), about halfway along the eastern shore, which also offers reasonably comfortable accommodation (❷). Right next door is the *Lough Arrow Touring Park* (Ⓣ071/966 6018; April–Oct) where **tents** can be pitched.

Castlebaldwin and Carrowkeel Cemetery

At **CASTLEBALDWIN**, 6km south of Riverstown on the N4, the very upmarket *Cromleach Lodge* (Ⓣ071/916 5155, Ⓦwww.cromleach.com; ❼; Feb–Oct) provides elegant, well-equipped accommodation, and a modern Irish restaurant of equal stature (expect to pay at least €65 plus wine for three courses). From here, minor roads of diminishing width and reliability lead towards the Bronze Age **Carrowkeel Cemetery** (open access). The last kilometre or so has to be negotiated on foot, but your efforts will be rewarded with a spellbinding panoramic view of the surrounding countryside. Here on the uplands of the Bricklieve Mountains is a remarkable collection of fourteen cairns, plus an assortment of other stonework. Excavation in 1911 produced a wealth of jewellery and relics, and several of the cairns, consisting of roofed, cruciform **passage graves**, can be entered. The most striking is cairn K, which, in complete contrast to County Meath's Newgrange (see p.178), is illuminated by the sun's rays during the summer solstice (June 21).

Ballymote and around

The largest place in southern Sligo is **BALLYMOTE**, 20km from the county town, which is celebrated in the title of one of Ireland's best-known jigs, *Famous Ballymote*. Richard de Burgo built a **castle** here in 1300 which, switching ownership numerous times during its history, proved to be a veritable straw in the wind of Irish politics. In 1317 it fell to the O'Connors and remained in Irish hands until captured by Bingham, the governor of Connacht, in 1584. It was soon afterwards reclaimed by the McDonaghs who then sold it to Red Hugh O'Donnell (see p.535) – he marched from here to catastrophic defeat at Kinsale in 1601. Later taken by Cromwell's army, it fell yet again to the O'Connors in 1690, before they in turn surrendered the castle to Williamite troops who determined to put an end to the whole farrago by tearing down much of the building and filling in the moat. The ruins lie just west of the town centre, and the stripped interior can be visited by acquiring a key from the Enterprise Centre (Mon–Fri 8.30am–4pm) on Grattan Street. Towards the end of the fourteenth century, the **Book of Ballymote** was assembled here, significant not just for the vast deal of information on Irish lore and history it contains, but also because it unlocks the secrets of the carved ogham letters that appear on numerous Neolithic standing stones. The book is held by the Royal Irish Academy in Dublin.

Five kilometres northwest of town at Portinch, the **Irish Raptor Research Centre** (April to early Nov daily 10.30am–12.30pm & 2.30–4.30pm; €8; Ⓦwww.eaglesflying.com) is a sanctuary for numerous birds of prey and owls. It's well worth catching a demonstration of free-flying here (11am & 3pm daily; 1hr) to watch falcons and eagles swoop and soar; there is also a pet zoo for children, but don't tell them they're looking at the eagles' dinner.

Practicalities

The **railway station** is opposite the castle ruins, off the Tubbercurry road. For **information** about the town and local **events** visit Ⓦwww.ballymote.ie. The area's most elegant **accommodation** is offered by *Temple House* (Ⓣ071/918 3329, Ⓦwww.templehouse.ie; ❺; April–Nov), in a lakeside setting, just after the Irish Raptor and Research Centre 5km northwest of town and well signposted from the Collooney road. Dating originally from the late seventeenth century, this majestic country house now offers six of its hundred rooms as guest accommodation, and residents can also sample a fine modern European three-course dinner here for around €40 (plus wine). Back in town, reasonably priced en-suite **accommodation** is available at the *Coach House Hotel*, Grattan Street (Ⓣ071/918 3111, Ⓔcoachhousehotel@eircom.net; ❸), where you can see a facsimile of pages from *The Book of Ballymote* and also obtain very reasonably priced **lunches** and dinners. Alternatively, you might head for agreeable, modern *Millhouse* (Ⓣ071/918 3449, Ⓔmillhousebb@eircom.net; ❷), at the south end of town, which serves delicious breakfasts. *Stonepark* and the adjacent *The Corran* on Teeling Street are, respectively, a restaurant and café serving decent **meals** and *Hayden's*, just up Lord Edward Street, is a great old-style **bar**. For the best chance of a music session, head to another equally welcoming hostelry, *Doddy's*, just to the south on O'Connell Street. Ballymote holds the Paddy Killoran Tradititional Music **festival** annually on the third weekend in August (Ⓦcomhaltas.ie/events/detail/paddy_killoran_traditional_festival) in honour of the late and much-acclaimed fiddler.

Gurteen

South of Ballymote the R293 runs parallel to the Dublin railway line before drifting away through fertile farmland and reaching the crossroads village of **GURTEEN** after 11km. Gurteen sits at the heart of South Sligo's **traditional-music** scene, and its greatest son was the fiddler Michael Coleman (see box below). Right by the crossroads stands the **Coleman Irish Music Centre** (Mon–Sat 10am–5pm; Ⓦwww.colemanirishmusic.com), which stages traditional music and dance shows (July & Aug Wed, Thurs & Sat 9pm; €10), and has a shop retailing a very good range of books and CDs, including several collections of recordings from its own archives. Gurteen hosts the **Coleman Traditional Festival** over the last weekend in August, while regular sessions are held in *Teach Murray* (Mon) and the *Roisín Dubh* (Tues & Sat) **pubs**. The best place to **eat** in the village is the *Crossbar*, Main Street, serving a range of bar meals in the evenings, while there's a centrally placed **B&B** on Main Street in the shape of *Church View* (Ⓣ071/918 2935, Ⓦwww.thechurchview.com; ❷), offering attractive en-suite rooms.

Tubbercurry and around

Some 30km southwest of Sligo, **TUBBERCURRY** is a rather docile small town but traditional music thrives here, focused on the week-long **South Sligo Summer School** (Ⓦwww.sssschool.org) held in mid-July. In addition to various classes, there are plenty of pub sessions and an end-of-school concert. Tubbercurry's origins date back to the late fourteenth century when the O'Connors built a fortress here, but it remained a sleepy little settlement until becoming a stop on one of Bianconi's coaching routes (see p.265) in 1853. The burgeoning town was all but destroyed by fire during a zealous Black and Tan reprisal in 1920, and little remains from before that time.

Michael Coleman

Arguably the greatest of Irish fiddlers, **Michael Coleman** was born in 1891 in Killavil, just north of Gurteen, and grew up in a household noted for its strong musical tradition. Taking up the fiddle in early childhood, he developed rapidly under the tuition of his elder brother James and acquired a phenomenally extensive repertoire. Coleman moved to New York in 1914, where he found a living playing first on the vaudeville circuit and later in the city's Irish dancehalls and bars. With a ready-made Irish market for the nascent US recording industry, Coleman made his first 78s in 1921 and over the next fifteen years released numerous others on a variety of labels, while frequently broadcasting on the radio. He made his last recording in 1936.

The impact of these recordings, the embodiment of the fluid **Sligo-style** of music – characterized by its sweet tone and sometimes flamboyant ornamentation – was enormous not just in the US but also back home, and the approach taken by Coleman and his fellow Sligo émigrés, Paddy Killoran and James Morrison (see p.713), came to dominate Ireland's traditional music. Coleman died in 1945, but you'll still encounter many a traditional session throughout Ireland where the sequence of tunes exactly replicates one of his 78rpm recordings.

Tubbercurry isn't exactly awash with facilities, though *Killoran's* coffee shop on Main Street supplies filling **breakfasts and lunches**, while the smartly refurbished *Murphy's Hotel* opposite (Ⓣ071/918 5598, Ⓦwww.murphyshotel.ie; ❸) provides admirably accoutred en-suite **rooms** as well as a range of **meals** in both its restaurant and bar. Alternatively, you might head to *Cawley's* on Emmet Street (Ⓣ071/918 5025, Ⓔawleysguesthouse@eircom.net; ❷), a comfortable **guesthouse** with a restaurant open to non-residents serving a mix of French-inspired and traditional Irish cuisine. Another accommodation option is *Cruckawn House* (Ⓣ071/918 5188, Ⓔcruckawn@esatclear.ie; ❷), offering welcoming en-suite B&B in a modern house a few hundred metres down the Ballymote road.

Some 15km to Tubbercurry's west, along a lonely road that passes through flat land before rising into the Ox Mountains, lies the gorgeous **Lough Talt**. Trout-rich, the lake attracts plenty of anglers as well as walkers keen to enjoy the 6.5km path circumnavigating its waters.

County Leitrim

Ireland's least populated county by some stretch, **Leitrim** crams a dizzying diversity into its ever-attractive countryside, though lacks any really notable sights. Bordering no fewer than six other counties, Leitrim extends some 80km from its southeastern border with Longford to a narrow strip of Atlantic shoreline in the northwest, with the expansive **Lough Allen** at its core. Two of its most attractive assets lie to the west, spanning the border with Sligo – **loughs Gill and Glencar**. In the south the River Shannon is the principal feature, not least in the county town, **Carrick-on-Shannon**, while rolling countryside to the river's east, especially between **Keshcarrigan** and **Ballinamore**, is sprinkled with tiny lakes and drumlins.

Carrick-on-Shannon

Other than messing about on the water, **CARRICK-ON-SHANNON**, Leitrim's county town, does not offer a vast amount to see or do, but with plenty of facilities it's a pleasant enough focus for investigating the area. The town owes much of its prosperity to its proximity to the water, and in summer its busy marina is jam-packed with barges and cruisers. Carrick originally grew up around a strategic crossing point on the River Shannon, the importance of which was recognized by the English who began building a planned settlement that was incorporated as a borough in 1613. Nothing remains from those times and the modern town only really began to develop in the nineteenth century, particularly after the 1840s when the Shannon navigation scheme reached the town. Its stone bridge and quays date from this period.

Arrival and information

Buses (☎071/916 0066) arrive either beside or opposite *Coffey's Pastry Case*, by the Shannon bridge, depending on which direction you've come from. The **train station** (☎071/962 0036) is a short distance down the Elphin road on the southern side of the river.

The amenable **tourist office** (May–Sept Mon, Thurs & Fri 10am–1pm & 2–5pm, Tues & Wed 10am–1pm & 2–4pm, Sat 10am–1pm & 2–4.45pm; ☎071/962 0170, Ⓦwww.leitrimtourism.com) is in the Old Barrel Store, under the bridge. Carrick has an active festival calendar, with a lively **regatta** (Ⓦwww.carrickrowingclub.com) at the beginning of August providing the high point of the boating season, while there is a week-long festival devoted to **coarse fishing** in mid-September (☎071/962 0313). The town's Water Music **festival** (Ⓦwww.carrickwatermusic.com) is held over the second weekend in August and features all manner of musical concerts and events, in genres ranging from traditional to classical.

Accommodation

Carrick has a fairly limited range of **accommodation**, though there are plenty of B&Bs in its environs, especially east of town on the Dublin road.

Aisling Town House St Mary's Close, Main St ☎071/962 0131. Set just back from the main drag, this B&B has very cosy en-suite rooms. April–Oct. ❷

The Bush Hotel Main St ☎071/967 1000, Ⓦwww.bushhotel.com. Recently expanded, this hotel remains traditional in style. Though rooms range in size, they are all more than a notch above average. ❺

Hollywell Liberty Hill ☎071/962 1124, Ⓔhollywell@esatbiz.com. A grandiose, ivy-clad period house in a riverside setting just a short walk from the centre of town near the station, with beautifully furnished and very spacious rooms, two of which overlook the Shannon. ❹

The Landmark Hotel Dublin Rd ☎071/962 2222, Ⓦwww.thelandmarkhotel.com. A modern hotel with sprucely furnished rooms overlooking the Shannon, offering a wide range of facilities, including an indoor pool. ❺

Scregg House Off the Elphin road, just over the Roscommon border ☎071/962 0210. Great breakfasts and well-kept en-suite rooms in a splendid farmhouse, some 5km from town and very handy for the sessions at *Anderson's* (see p.492). June to mid-Sept. ❷

The Town

Just above the river, off the top of Bridge Street, stands the town's only real building of note, the former courthouse, built in 1821 and known as **The Dock** (☎071/965 0828, Ⓦwww.dock.ie). It houses the Leitrim Design House (Ⓦwww.leitrimdesignhouse.ie), showcasing works by local artists and craft workers, as well as hosting regular exhibitions, and also includes a one-hundred-seater performance space staging regular theatre, comedy and music events.

Most people come to Carrick for its water-based activities. Moon River runs **trips** along the river (call ☎071/962 1777 for times, Ⓦwww.moon-river.net; €12) from the bridge, while several companies offer **Shannon cruisers** for weekly rental (two- to twelve-berth), including Emerald Star (☎071/962 7633, Ⓦwww.emeraldstar.ie) and Carrick Craft (UK ☎01/278 1666, Ⓦwww.cruise-ireland.com) – expect to pay around €700–3200, depending on the size of the boat and season. More information on the Shannon–Erne waterway can be obtained from the Inland Waterways Association of Ireland (Ⓦwww.iwai.ie), which also retails guides and navigation charts.

Eating, drinking and entertainment

Several of Carrick's **pubs** serve estimable food, including *The Oarsman* on Bridge Street, which also offers imaginative modern Irish cuisine in its restaurant (☎071/962 1733) for half the price you'd pay in Dublin (around €40 for three courses plus wine). Just to the west by the rowing club on Quay Road, *Victoria Hall* (☎071/962 0320) offers a great mélange of Thai and modern Irish food – a three-course meal here will set you back around €45, but there's also an early-bird option (5–7.30pm, €30) and a daytime "bento box" special at €15.50. Elsewhere, *The Landmark Hotel* offers plenty of variety in its cafés and restaurants and *Coffey's Pastry Case*, by the bridge, is a great place for coffee and light bites. Over the bridge and south of town off the Boyle road, Carrick Cineplex (☎071/967 2000, Ⓦwww.carrickcineplex.ie) is a multiscreen **cinema** which also hosts an **internet café**. For **traditional music**, head to *An Poitín Still* on Main Street (Fri), *Cryan's* (Sat & Sun) or, 5km south of town on the R368 Elphin road, *Anderson's Thatch Pub*, a cosy bar with superb sessions nightly from June to August, and on Wednesday and Saturday the rest of the year.

Around Carrick

After Carrick the Shannon meanders northwards before entering the vast **Lough Allen** just by pleasant **Drumshanbo**, a place with a rich musical tradition. It's a fine base for investigating the local countryside, which with rivers, streams and, to the east, a collection of tiny lakes provides plenty of opportunities for watersports enthusiasts.

Drumshanbo and Lough Allen

Some 12km north of Carrick, **DRUMSHANBO** is a lively village at the tip of **Lough Allen**'s southern shore. Right in its centre, the **Sliabh an Iarainn Visitor Centre** (May to mid-Sept Mon–Fri 9am–5pm; €3) is a good source of detailed background information on local customs and history, including the iron-and-coal mining industries centred on Arigna in County Roscommon (see p.497), as well as a reconstruction of a typical sweathouse. Drumshanbo has a strong musical tradition and, in the third week of July, holds the seven-day Joe Mooney Summer School (Ⓦwww.joemooneysummerschool.com), offering **traditional-music** classes and concerts. At the beginning of June it also hosts the **An Tostal Festival** (Ⓦwww.antostalfestival.ie), with a variety of music and street entertainment, while a more recent arrival on the scene is the three-day **Sliabh an Iarainn Music and Arts Festival** (Ⓦwww.saifestival.com), Leitrim's answer to Glastonbury, held over the August public-holiday weekend.

The Cavan and Leitrim Railway

Seventeen kilometres southeast of Carrick, and next to the existing Dublin–Carrick mainline railway station in the small village of **DROMOD**, is the starting point for what's left of the **Cavan and Leitrim Railway** (Mon & Sat 10am–5.30pm, Sun 1–5.30pm; train rides €7; Ⓦwww.irish-railway.com). Staffed by informative and dedicated enthusiasts, this is a fully operational narrow-gauge steam railway, along which trains run some 500m or so up the restored track to Clooncolry.

The most upmarket **place to stay** is the *Ramada Hotel* (T 071/964 0100, W www.loughallenhotel.com), set in a stunning location beside Lough Allen, which has elegantly furnished bedrooms (5) and spectacular suites (7), all overlooking the water, as well as its own spa, fitness centre and pool. If means are more modest, head to *Fraoch Ban* (T 071/964 1260, E fraochban@eircom.net; 2; April–Oct), a comfortable modern bungalow also surveying the lake, a kilometre up the Dowra road.

Astonishingly good-value bar **meals** are served all day at *Henry's Haven*, Convent Avenue, or head to *The Galley*, High Street, a café serving a delicious range of light bites and more substantial lunches. Traditional-music **sessions** are currently thin on the ground in Drumshanbo, though well worth trying is *Olivia D's* (last Fri of each month), a friendly, old-style bar, and, if you've transport, *The Mountain Tavern* (Wed 9pm & Sun 6pm) in Aghacashel, some 6km to the northeast, which also serves very wholesome **lunches** and dinners (Wed–Sun). **Bikes** can be rented from Moran's on Convent Avenue (T 071/964 1974).

From Drumshanbo roads lead north along both eastern and western shores of **Lough Allen**. The western route crosses into County Roscommon and skirts the Arigna Mountains (see p.497), while its alternative to the east heads up through bleak flatlands below Slieve Anierin. The waymarked 48-kilometre **Leitrim Way** (map available from local tourist offices) follows Lough Allen's shoreline before taking in higher ground on its way to the remote village of **Dowra**, the starting point for the **Cavan Way** (see p.202). At **Ballinaglera**, 13km north of Drumshanbo, the **Lough Allen Adventure Centre** (W www.loughallenadventure.com) offers a variety of waterborne activities, such as windsurfing and kayaking, as well as hill-walking.

East of Drumshanbo

Taking the R208 east from Drumshanbo and then heading along the R210 and joining the R209 leads to a jumble of little lakes surrounded by low hills. **KESHCARRIGAN**, about 8km east of Drumshanbo on the Shannon–Erne Waterway, is worth a stop (even though the village has been partly blighted by inappropriate modern housing developments) for its amiable **bar**, the *Canal Stop*, right beside the canal. Six kilometres east, **FENAGH** was once an important ecclesiastical centre, founded by St Caillin in the sixth century. The area's history is recounted in the recently opened **Heritage Centre** (May–Sept Wed–Fri 10am–5.30pm, Sat & Sun noon–5.30pm; Oct–April Wed–Sun noon–5.30pm; W www.fenagh.com), which also includes a café and an indoor soft play area. Just down the Mohill road are the remains of St Caillin's **monastery** (open access; free), and a short distance further southwards there's splendid **accommodation** at *The Old Rectory* (T 071/964 4089, W www.theoldrectoryireland.com; 2), a very child-friendly Georgian house on a working farm offering well-kept en-suite rooms, brilliant breakfasts and views of Fenagh Lough from the grounds.

BALLINAMORE, 5km northeast of Fenagh, is a focus for **cruising** on the Shannon–Erne Waterway, with barges available from Riversdale Barge Holidays (T 071/964 4122, W www.riversdalebargeholidays.com; €560–1370 per week). There's little to see in the town itself, but it still offers a pleasant overnight stop. Central **accommodation** options include very agreeable en-suite rooms at *Hamill's B&B* (T 071/964 4211, W www.hamillsbedandbreakfast.com; 2), just off the High Street, or further up the main drag, the spacious rooms offered by the *Commercial and Tourist Hotel*

(Ⓣ071/964 4675, Ⓔcommercialhotel@gmail.com; ❸). *Smyth's*, a popular **bar** on the High Street, provides hearty pub grub.

County Roscommon

County Roscommon is renowned as one of Ireland's dullest counties, thanks to its largely uninspiring scenery. In its far north, however, the **Arigna Mountains** provide a wild and vivid contrast to the flat landscape that defines most of the county, and can be explored from the lively, historic town of **Boyle** towards Roscommon's northern extremity. Further south, sites around **Tulsk** are intrinsically associated with major events in Celtic mythology, and the planned town of **Strokestown** features a memorable Georgian mansion with a hugely impressive museum devoted to the Great Famine. Southern Roscommon, however, including its eponymous county town, provides little to warrant investigation.

Boyle and around

Rising gently above its own namesake river, engaging **BOYLE** is an easygoing town, pleasant to stroll around, with plenty of congenial bars, a couple of sites of noteworthy historical interest and a lively arts festival. It also makes an excellent base for exploring not only Roscommon's northern attractions, such as **Lough Key Forest Park**, but neighbouring Leitrim and South Sligo too.

Boyle's origins lie in the establishment of a Cistercian monastery in 1161, but as it was situated on an important trading route, the abbey became embroiled in numerous inter-clan and Irish–English skirmishes and was sacked on a number of occasions. It lingered on for several decades after the Dissolution – its last abbot was executed in 1584 for refusing to disavow his allegiance to Rome – and from 1599 until the end of the eighteenth century it was used as a barracks by the English and known as Boyle Castle. In 1603 the building passed into the hands of Sir John King and remained in the family's possession until 1892. It was Staffordshire-born King who transformed Boyle, constructing a grand mansion to the west of the abbey and an avenue (now the town's Main Street) leading up to it. At the same time he began to amass thousands of acres of land, which would eventually become the largest estate in County Roscommon, **Rockingham**.

Arrival, information and accommodation

Boyle's **train station** (Ⓣ071/966 2027) is two hundred metres south of the centre on Elphin Street, while **buses** set down on Carrick Road. The **tourist office** (June to mid-Sept daily 10am–1pm & 2–5.30pm; Ⓣ071/966 2145, Ⓦwww.visitroscommon.ie) is just by the entrance to King House and stocks information on the area. There are several summer **festivals**, of which the biggest is the week-long Boyle Arts Festival (Ⓦwww.boylearts.com) at the end of July – its broad-ranging programme includes plenty of drama, comedy, poetry readings, concerts, exhibitions and lectures.

Boyle has just a few **places to stay**. In the abbey's shadow is the delightful Victorian *Abbey House* (ⓣ071/966 2385, ⓔabbeyhouse@eircom.net; ❷; March–Oct), with spacious and well-furnished en-suite rooms, while opposite the abbey on the main road is the hospitable *Cesh Corran* (ⓣ071/966 2255, ⓦwww.marycooney.com; ❷), with well-appointed rooms and great breakfasts. Right in the town centre on Bridge Street, the 250-year-old *Royal Hotel* (ⓣ071/966 2016; ❸) has modernized, comfortable en-suite rooms, some of which overlook the river. Alternatively, there's the recently opened *Lough Key House* (ⓣ071/966 2161, ⓦwww.loughkeyhouse.com; ❸), an exquisite Georgian house set in beautiful grounds adjacent to the main entrance to Lough Key Forest Park, offering sumptuous breakfasts and tastefully decorated en-suite bedrooms. The nearest **campsite** is in Lough Key Forest Park (see p.496).

The Town

It's easy to find your way around Boyle and the town's two major attractions are well signposted from the centre. The first of these is **Boyle Abbey** (Easter–Oct daily 10am–6pm; €2.10; Heritage Card), consecrated in 1218, whose alluring remains lie down by the river on the eastern side of town. Despite various onslaughts during the course of its history, it remains perhaps the finest surviving Cistercian church in Ireland and its sixty-year building process bears traces of both the Romanesque and then newly arrived Gothic styles of architecture. Trim and tightly organized, the abbey's ruins are entered via its gatehouse, which contains a small exhibition on the foundation's history and a model of how it once might have looked. Inside the nave the transition from Romanesque to Gothic is neatly contrasted by windows and arches, circular facing pointed. Some of the capitals bear intriguing secular decorations – one features little figures standing between trees and clutching the branches somewhat stiffly – while high on the western wall is a carving of a Sheila-na-Gig (see p.748).

The original seat of the King family (see opposite) was destroyed by fire, but its replacement, **King House** (April–Sept daily 10am–6pm; €7; ⓦwww.kinghouse.ie; Heritage Island), is well worth visiting. This impressive stone mansion was built around 1730 and sold to the War Office when the Kings moved to Rockingham, becoming the barracks for the Connaught Rangers from 1788 until 1922. The Irish Army then occupied the building till the 1940s, after which it passed into private hands, becoming at one time a store for feed and fuel, before falling into dereliction. Now thoroughly restored, its ground floor houses Boyle's **Civic Art Gallery**, largely displaying works by local painters, while upper storeys employ interactive high-tech gadgetry to retell the story of the house and the family who built it, with plenty of child-oriented exhibits. The story of Henry's son Edward, who built Rockingham, is wittily recounted in one exhibit, "How to become an earl in six easy stages", describing how he rose to become Earl of Kingston in 1768. One section of the house is devoted to the Connaught Rangers and recalls their role in various military campaigns.

Eating, drinking and entertainment

Daytime **eating** options include the restaurant run by King House (see opposite) for wholesome snacks and lunches, and the snug *Stone House Café*, by the river, which offers equally filling home-cooking. The *Royal Hotel* has a very popular coffee shop, as well as reasonably priced meals in its bar and restaurant. Several of the pubs serve bar meals, including *The Moving Stairs* and *Tapster's* on The Crescent.

The best places for **traditional music** are *Kate Lavin's* (Thurs), Patrick Street, a dark and cosy old-style bar, and *Wynne's*, Main Street (Fri), which is more modern but equally welcoming. The *Moylurg Inn* on The Crescent has a variety of music, including ballad-singing, at weekends. Kings House runs a programme of **classical-music** events in summer.

Lough Key Forest Park

Just off the N4, 3km east of Boyle, lies **Lough Key Forest Park** (March–June, Sept & Oct daily 10am–6pm; July & Aug Mon–Thurs 10am–6pm, Fri–Sun 10am–9pm; Nov–Feb Fri–Sun noon–4pm; car €4, though free if spending €20 or more on activities; Ⓦwww.loughkey.ie; Heritage Island), an area once the focal point of the Kings' Rockingham estate. However, the demesne was abandoned by the family in 1957 after their mansion, designed by the English architect John Nash, was destroyed by fire – all that now remains of the grandiose 365-windowed creation are two still-accessible subterranean servants' tunnels through which the Kings' menials scurried to fulfil their duties.

Though almost all of the park's woodland and trails remain unsullied, a recent massive commercial re-vamp has restricted access to certain areas, focal to which is the newly constructed **Visitor Centre** at the end of a driveway 2km from the park's Gothic gateway on the N4. It's here that you can buy tickets to the newly installed **Lough Key Experience** (last admission 90min before closing; €7.50) and pick up the headset that provides a guided commentary to a walking trail around a segment of the park. Apart from recounting the park's history and describing its wildlife and flora, this takes you through the aforementioned tunnels as well as to the top of the five-storey Moylurg viewing tower which commands splendid vistas of the lake and its numerous islands, including **Trinity Island**, which was once the site of a Cistercian foundation and a medieval castle. It holds a special place in Irish mythology as the last resting place of Una Bhán MacDermott, who died of grief after being forbidden to marry her lover Thomas Costello – the song **Una Bhán**, recounting the tale, is one of the great songs of the **sean-nós** tradition (see p.715). The trail concludes with the 300-metre-long **Tree Canopy Walk** whose timber-and-steel construction rises steadily to a nine-metre-high view of the park from the treetops.

Elsewhere, near the visitor centre there's also the outdoor children's **Adventure Play Kingdom** (last admission 1hr before closing; €5) and **Boda Borg** (last admission 2hr before closing; minimum of three participants; €16), a Swedish-designed two-storey puzzle-house which relies upon teamwork to solve various instruction-less problems.

If you don't wish to embark on any of these constructed activities, you can still enjoy the circular five-kilometre walk around the waters of the lough, which encompasses various Megalithic and medieval ruins. There are numerous other signposted trails around the estate, too, and you can also take a **boat trip** out on the lake or hire a rowing boat during the summer months (Ⓣ071/966 7037, Ⓦwww.loughkeyboats.com). There's a somewhat pricey **restaurant** too and you can also **camp** at the *Lough Key Caravan and Camping Park* (Ⓣ071/966 2212; early April to mid-Sept).

The Arigna Mountains

The far north of County Roscommon stretches up to Lough Allen where gentle farmland ascends to the moors and lakes of the **Arigna Mountains**. Albeit small-scale, this was once one of the few areas of Ireland to play a role in the Industrial Revolution, based first on **iron** extraction for a fifty-year period after 1788 – the local ironworks forged pikes in preparation for the 1798 Rebellion – and, subsequently, **coal**, which was worked here until 1990. The **Arigna Miners Way** (Ⓦwww.arignaminerswayandhistoricaltrail.com) is a waymarked 120-kilometre walking trail through the area, linking up with both the Leitrim Way and a historical trail taking in Boyle and parts of Sligo. Nearby, the appealing village of **Keadue** is worth a visit for its musical heritage.

Keadue

KEADUE, 12km northeast of Boyle, is an attractive village of traditional cottages, stone walls and well-kept gardens. It is associated with the blind harper Turlough O'Carolan (see p.711), whose grave lies by the ruins of Killronan Abbey, just out on the Sligo road. The musician is commemorated at the **O'Carolan Heritage Park**, a well-kept public park in the heart of the village with, as its centrepiece, a bronze replica of one of his harps. Keadue also hosts two musical events in July/August: first a traditional-music summer school, which is followed by a major harp and traditional-music **festival** (Ⓦwww.ocarolanharpfestival.ie). You can stay very comfortably at the *O'Carolan B&B* (Ⓣ071/967 4257; ❷; May–Sept), a pleasant bungalow by the church, while both *McCabe's* and the *Harp and Shamrock* **pubs** are friendly places for a pint.

Arigna Mining Experience

From the dusty village of **Arigna** itself, a little further north, a winding lane leads a couple of kilometres upwards, past a smokeless fuel plant, to the **Arigna Mining Experience** (Jan to mid-March Mon–Fri 10am–5pm; mid-March to Dec daily 10am–5pm; €8; Ⓦwww.arignaminingexperience.ie; Heritage Island). Perched high on a hilltop and commanding stunning views of Lough Allen and the surrounding countryside, this brilliantly designed and utterly enthralling museum is based around one of the last working pits in the area. The history of local coal mining is well documented in the reception area, but, once equipped with hard hat, it's the forty-minute **tours** of the mine that are most informative and thought provoking. Led by ex-miners, these are rich in anecdote and thoroughly explore both the industry's nature itself and the atrocious and exploitative working conditions the miners endured. The tour is packed with atmosphere: the tunnels are dark and foreboding, and the sound of dripping water and footsteps amplified by the acoustics. Especially astonishing was the ability of the miners to squeeze themselves into the tightest of seams in the quest for coal.

Frenchpark to Strokestown

South of Boyle lies rolling agricultural land, punctuated by several notable historical attractions, all situated close to the main N5. These include a museum at **Frenchpark**, devoted to Ireland's first president and Irish-language campaigner Douglas Hyde, numerous ancient remains around **Tulsk** and the impressive planned settlement of **Strokestown**. The area is easily accessible on a day-trip from Boyle or, if you want to spend more time here, Strokestown provides the best base.

Frenchpark

Fourteen kilometres southwest of Boyle lies the village of **FRENCHPARK**, where the former Church of Ireland parish church is home to the **Douglas Hyde Interpretive Centre** (May–Sept Tues–Fri 2–5pm, Sat & Sun 2–6pm; free). The centre recounts the life of Douglas Hyde (1860–1949), one of the key figures in the Irish cultural revival, with numerous informative displays and an entertaining film.

Born in Castlerea, 13km south of Frenchpark, to Anglo-Irish Ascendancy stock, Hyde learnt Irish at an early age and developed a lifelong interest in the nation's rich vernacular tradition and folklore. After attending Trinity College he became professor of Modern Irish Language and Literature at the National University of Ireland and produced numerous articles, essays and reviews in Irish, as well as collaborating on a number of Irish-language plays with Lady Gregory. Hyde also travelled the country widely, gathering material, much of which was transcribed into collections such as the highly influential *Love Songs of Connaught*. In 1893, he was one of the founders of the **Gaelic League**, which aimed to enhance Irish culture via the revival of musical and linguistic traditions, though Hyde later became concerned by the League's increasing links with the Independence movement and resigned as its president in 1915. Elected to the Irish Senate in 1925, he retired from public life in 1932 until he was appointed the country's first president in 1938. After his death Hyde was interred in the graveyard of his father's former parish – his grave is the last of eight family members in the corner behind the statue erected in his honour.

Tulsk and around

Located around the village of **TULSK**, 15km southeast of Frenchpark, is a rich array of earthworks, ring forts, standing stones and caves betokening one of Ireland's major mythological areas. According to *The Annals of the Four Masters* (see p.512) it was here that Medb, the warrior queen and earth goddess who features heavily in the *Táin Bó Cúailnge* (see p.193), sited her palace Cruachan, the location of the epic's opening and gory conclusion. Away from the world of legend, Tulsk was certainly the seat of the Kings of Connacht, and the ruins of their medieval castle are visible in the village.

Before visiting the monuments, it's wise to head for the informative **Cruachan Aí visitor centre** (pronounced "crew-han ee") just west of the crossroads in Tulsk (June–Oct Mon–Fri 9am–6pm, Sat 10am–6pm, Sun 1–6pm; Nov–May Mon–Sat 9am–5pm; €5; Ⓦ www.cruachanai.com; Heritage Island), which also has a decent café. The sites were identified in 1837 by John O'Donovan who, working with the Ordnance Survey of Ireland, fixed their locations and allocated the names still in use today, such as Rathcroghan in place of Cruachan. With entertaining high-tech wizardry, including an inspired multimedia presentation on the **Táin**, the centre attempts to explain the purpose of the various rocky lumps and earthy bumps – though little is actually known, not least because the majority have yet to be fully excavated.

A map of the sites is contained in the centre's leaflet and it's essential to ask the staff about which are currently accessible. The majority are situated just east of the N5, about 5km northwest of Tulsk near the **RATHCROGHAN** crossroads. Medb's palace, an elevated ring barrow with views of the surrounding monuments, is appropriately set in a cattle field; nearby are **Oweynagat**, a souterrain that supposedly provided the entrance to the Otherworld, and **Relig na Rí**, the legendary burial place of the Kings of Tara.

Strokestown

Just 11km east of Tulsk is one of Ireland's most striking planned towns, **STROKESTOWN**, the story of which in many ways retells the country's troubled history in microcosm. The land on which the town lies and the surrounding area, known as Corca Achlann, belonged for more than a thousand years to the MacBranan clan, underlords of the powerful O'Connor kings who ruled Connacht, until dispossessed by Cromwell in the 1650s. Subsequently, part of their territory was granted by Charles II to Nicholas Mahon, whose kin later amassed more than 30,000 acres for their huge estate, second only in size to Rockingham (see p.494) in Roscommon, becoming one of the great landed families of Ireland in the process. In the early nineteenth century, his descendant Lieutenant General Thomas Mahon, Second Lord Hartland, requiring a grandiose symbol reflecting the extent of his property, determined to have constructed a central avenue wider than Vienna's Ringstrasse. This tree-lined mall leads a couple of hundred metres both east and west from the town centre. At its western end sits an octagonal church, deconstructed but still with its spire, now housing the **County Roscommon Heritage and Genealogy Centre** (ⓣ071/963 3380, ⓦwww.roscommonroots.com) which conducts research for anyone seeking to trace their Roscommon roots; the eastern end of the mall terminates in a three-arched gateway, marking the entrance to the Mahon's massive estate.

Strokestown Park House

The magnificent Georgian **Strokestown Park House** (mid-March to Oct daily 11am–5.30pm; house, famine museum & gardens €5 each, combined ticket €8 for any two & €12 for all three; house tours daily at 11.30am, 2pm & 4pm, plus Sat & Sun 5pm; ⓦwww.strokestownpark.ie; Heritage Island) was the seat of the Mahon family from its completion in 1696 for almost three hundred years. This huge mansion originally consisted of a two-storey central block and basement until the 1740s when Thomas Mahon, MP for Roscommon, hired the architect Richard Castle to construct a third storey and two extra wings. Mahon's son, Maurice (who became the First Lord Hartland in 1800), made subsequent additions including the library and many decorative features, such as cornices and chimneypieces, while the Second Lord Hartland added the porch and its huge pilasters. The house remained in Mahon ownership until 1979 when it was sold, along with its contents, to a local garage owner who undertook restoration work and opened it to the public in 1987.

Few Irish "big houses" retain their original-owners' property (in this case ranging from furniture to children's toys) and this is a vital factor in making the **guided tours** so entertaining. The main hall features early eighteenth-century wood panelling while the spacious dining room, decorated in rich rose-pink damask wallpaper, is equipped with furniture from the early 1800s and a mammoth turf-bucket. The library was originally a ballroom – hence the bowed space at one end, which housed musicians – and has glorious Chippendale bookcases, while the smoking room was converted into a laboratory and

▲ Strokestown Park House

photographic darkroom by Henry Pakenham-Mahon in the 1890s. The house's north wing includes a superb kitchen, replete with spits and ovens, and, looking upwards, you'll see a balustraded gallery, the only surviving example in Ireland of a kind favoured by Castle, from which the housekeeper could keep an eagle eye on business down below and, according to Strokestown legend, drop menus for the week's meals down to the cook.

The Irish Famine Museum

Among the property passed on by the Mahons were numerous documents and letters relating to the family's role in relation to the Great Famine of 1845–51. The house's former stables, marvellously vaulted buildings in their own right, house an often chilling and ever stimulating **museum** detailing the Famine's effects upon the Mahons' tenants and its wider impact across Ireland. The intricate but ever informative displays and films focus on the concatenation of factors in Ireland – the growth of the rural population, the conacre system of agricultural tenancy, the reliance on the potato crop and the spread of the potato blight – that combined with Britain's economic policy of non-interference to have such a devastating effect on human life. Exhibits also highlight the role in local events of Major Denis Mahon, who had inherited the Strokestown estate after the death of the third and last Lord Hartland in 1845. An innate malevolence seems to have coursed through Denis's veins since he not only evicted the majority of his tenants, but contracted dangerously unseaworthy vessels (the infamous coffin ships) to transport some of them in atrocious conditions to North America. Displays document contemporary newspaper reports condemning his actions and, in 1847, his assassination by vengeful ex-tenants.

Practicalities

Accommodation includes the *Percy French Hotel* on Bridge Street (Ⓣ071/963 3300; ❷), very much the town's centre of life, which has pleasant en-suite rooms, a decent **restaurant** and a bar that also serves meals, and *Mrs Martin's* welcoming guesthouse on Church Street (Ⓣ071/963 3247; ❶). Opposite the hotel is a grand old-style **pub**, *Hanly's*, which sometimes hosts **traditional-music** sessions. Strokestown holds a major poetry **festival** over the May public-holiday weekend (Ⓦwww.strokestownpoetry.org) and a traditional-music festival, Féile Frank McGann (Ⓦwww.feilefrankmcgann.com), in early October.

Travel details

Trains

All services operate 4–5 times daily.

Boyle to: Ballymote (15min); Carrick-on-Shannon (15min); Dublin (2hr 30min); Mullingar (1hr 25min); Sligo (40min).

Carrick-on-Shannon to: Boyle (15min); Dromod (15min); Dublin (2hr 15min); Mullingar (1hr 10min); Sligo (55min).

Sligo to: Ballymote (20min); Boyle (40min); Carrick-on-Shannon (55min); Dublin (3hr 10min); Mullingar (1hr 55min).

Buses

Bus Éireann

Ballinamore to: Drumshanbo (Fri & Sat 1 daily; 25min); Fenagh (Thurs 1; 10min); Sligo (Fri & Sat 1 daily; 1hr 35min–2hr 5min).

Ballymote to: Boyle (Mon–Wed & Sat 1 daily; 30min); Gurteen (1 Sat; 20min); Sligo (Mon–Wed 1 daily, Sat 2; 40min); Tubbercurry (Wed 2; 30min).

Boyle to: Carrick-on-Shannon (4–5 daily; 15min); Dublin (4–5 daily; 3hr); Gurteen (Thurs 2; 25min); Riverstown (Thurs & Fri 1 daily; 35min); Sligo (4–5 daily; 40min); Strokestown (Mon–Sat 1 daily; 40min).

Carrick-on-Shannon to: Boyle (5–6 daily; 15min); Dromod (5–6 daily; 20min); Drumshanbo (Sat 1; 25min); Dublin (5–6 daily; 2hr 30min–3hr); Sligo (5–6 daily; 1hr).

Dowra to: Drumshanbo (Sat 1; 25 min); Sligo (Sat 1; 1hr 15min).

Drumcliffe to: Ballyshannon (Mon–Sat 8–9 daily, Sun 3; 35–50min); Sligo (Mon–Sat 8–9 daily, Sun 4; 15min).

Drumshanbo to: Ballinamore (Fri & Sat 1 daily; 25min); Carrick-on-Shannon (Sat 1; 25min); Dowra (Sat 1; 25min); Keadue (Fri 1; 20min); Sligo (Fri 1, Sat 2; 1hr 10min–1hr 40min).

Easkey to: Enniscrone (Mon–Sat 3–5 daily, Sun 1; 35–50min); Sligo (Mon–Sat 3–5 daily, Sun 1; 50min).

Enniscrone to: Easkey (Mon–Sat 3–5 daily, Sun 1; 35–50min); Sligo (Mon–Sat 3–5 daily, Sun 1; 1hr 15min).

Frenchpark to: Strokestown (6 daily; 25min); Tulsk (4–5 daily; 10min).

Gurteen to: Ballymote (Sat 1; 20min); Boyle (Thurs 2; 25min); Sligo (Sat 2; 55min–1hr 5min); Tubbercurry (Sat 1; 25min).

Keadue to: Drumshanbo (Fri 1; 20min); Sligo (Fri 1; 50min).

Riverstown to: Boyle (Thurs & Fri 1 daily; 35min); Sligo (Thurs & Fri 1 daily; 40min).

Rosses Point to: Sligo (Mon–Fri 7, Sat 5; 20min).

Sligo to: Ballymote (Mon–Wed 1 daily, Sat 2; 35–45min); Ballyshannon (Mon–Sat 9 daily, Sun 3; 40min–1hr); Boyle (5–6 daily; 40min); Bundoran (Mon–Sat 9–10 daily, Sun 3; 35–55min); Carrick-on-Shannon (5–6 daily; 1hr); Derry (Mon–Sat 7 daily, Sun 3; 2hr 30min); Donegal (Mon–Sat 7 daily, Sun 3; 1hr 5min); Drumcliffe (Mon–Sat 9–10 daily, Sun 3; 15min); Dublin (5–6 daily; 3hr 15min–3hr 50min); Easkey (Mon–Sat 3–5 daily, Sun 1; 55min); Enniscrone (Mon–Sat 3–5 daily, Sun 1; 1hr 15min); Enniskillen (Mon–Sat 4 daily, Sun 2; 1hr 25min); Galway (Mon–Sat 5–7 daily, Sun 4; 2hr 30min); Gurteen (Sat 2; 50min–1hr 5min); Keadue (Fri 1; 50min); Lissadell (2 Mon–Fri during school terms, 2 Sat all year; 20min); Riverstown (Thurs & Fri 1 daily; 40min); Rosses Point (Mon–Fri 7, Sat 5; 20min); Skreen (Mon–Sat 2–3 daily; 30min); Strandhill (Mon–Fri 7, Sat 5; 20min); Strokestown (Mon–Sat 1 daily; 1hr); Tubbercurry (Mon–Sat 5–7 daily, Sun 4; 35min); Westport (1–2 daily; 1hr 50min).

Strandhill to: Sligo (Mon–Fri 7, Sat 5; 20min).

Strokestown to: Boyle (1 daily; 40min); Dublin (6 daily; 2hr 25min); Frenchpark (6–7 daily; 25min); Sligo (Mon–Sat 1 daily; 1hr); Tulsk (5 daily; 15min).

Tubbercurry to: Ballymote (Wed 2; 30min); Galway (Mon–Sat 5–7 daily, Sun 4; 1hr 55min); Gurteen (Sat 1; 25min); Sligo (5–6 daily; 35min); Westport (1 daily; 1hr 20min).
Tulsk to: Frenchpark (4–5 daily; 10min); Strokestown (4–5 daily; 15min).

Feda O'Donnell
Ⓦ www.fedaodonnell.com

Sligo to: Donegal (Sat–Thurs 2 daily, Fri 4; 50min); Galway (Mon–Thurs & Sat 2 daily, Fri & Sun 3 daily; 2hr 10min).

Ulsterbus
Ballinamore to: Enniskillen (1 Mon–Sat; 50min).

12

Donegal

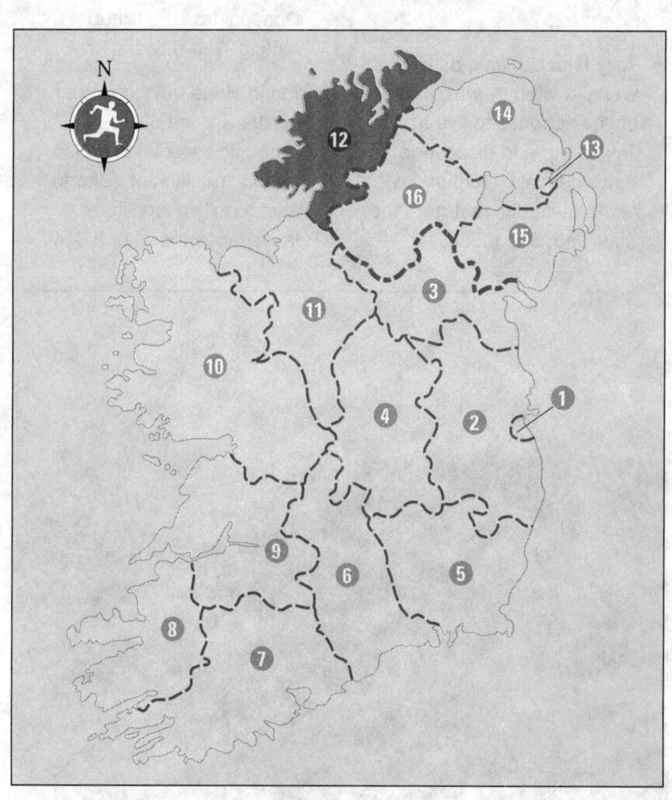

CHAPTER 12

Highlights

* **Slieve League** No visit to Donegal would be complete without a walk along the top of this mountain's awesome sea-cliffs. See p.516

* **Húdaí Beag's pub** Unquestionably, one of the best traditional-music sessions in Ireland takes place here on Monday nights. See p.525

* **Tory Island** Bleak, barren, wet and windy – why would anyone choose to live here? Take a trip and discover a thriving local culture and a world quite different from the mainland. See p.526

* **Glebe House** Home of the late artist Derek Hill, Glebe House contains some of the most remarkable modern art in Ireland. See p.530

* **The Grianán Ailigh** This restored, circular stone fort commands unbeatable panoramic views of Donegal from its hilltop setting. See p.541

* **Malin Head** Ireland's most northerly point offers dramatic seascapes and, thanks to a lack of visitors, wonderfully unspoilt landscapes too. See p.544

▲ The Grianán Ailigh

12

Donegal

Second in size only to County Cork, **County Donegal** has unquestionably the richest scenery in the whole of Ireland, featuring a spectacular three-hundred-kilometre coastline – an intoxicating run of headlands, promontories and peninsulas rising to the highest sea-cliffs in Europe at **Slieve League**. Inland is a terrain of glens, rivers and bogland hills, of which the best-known destinations are the Glencolmcille Peninsula and around Ardara and Glenties in the southern part of the county. The **Glencolmcille** area attracts more visitors than any other, yet the landscape of **northern Donegal** is, if anything, even more satisfying, especially the Rosguill and Inishowen peninsulas (though certain parts have been blighted by ugly, modern housing developments) and the interior region around Errigal Mountain, Lough Beagh and Lough Gartan. Other noteworthy areas are the **Rosses** and **Gweedore**, which are reminiscent of the more barren stretches of Connemara and make up the strongest Irish-speaking districts in the county.

Donegal's original name was *Tír Chonaill*, which translates as "the land of Conal"; Chonaill was one of the twelve sons of Niall of the Nine Hostages, reputed to have ruled Ireland in the fifth century. After the Flight of the Earls in 1607 (see p.693), the English changed the name to that of their main garrison *Dún na nGall* ("fort of the foreigners"), which has a certain irony, because Donegal always eluded the grip of English power thanks to its wild and infertile terrain. Donegal is the most northerly part of Ireland, which confuses some into believing that it is part of Northern Ireland. It never actually has been, since in 1922, at the time of Partition, the Unionists believed that Donegal's Catholic population would threaten the stability of the new statelet by voting the county and the whole of the North back into the Republic.

The county has an extensive network of public and private **bus services** with Letterkenny and Donegal town as its major transport hubs. However, there are limited services to some areas, especially outside high season, but you'll need your own transport to reach some outlying attractions, such as Glenveagh and parts of the Rosguill, Fanad and Inishowen peninsulas.

South Donegal

Entered via the N15 from Sligo (which now largely bypasses the most scenic spots), South Donegal might lack the wildness characteristic of much of

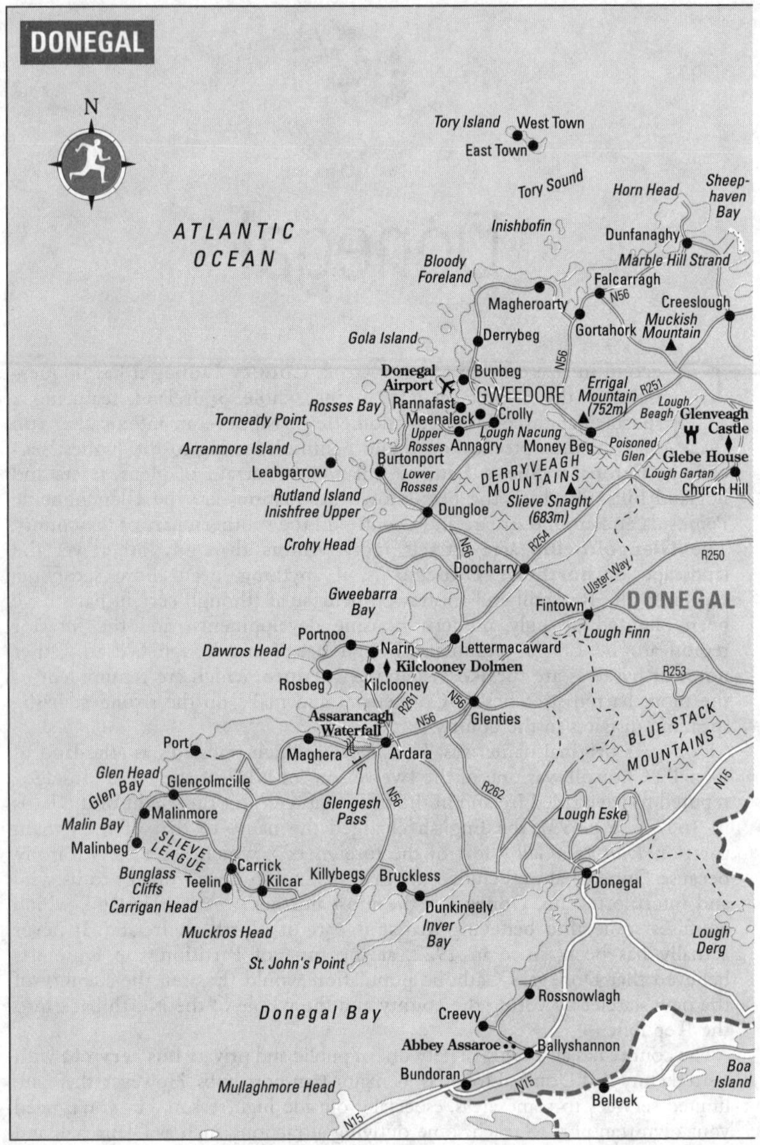

Donegal's coastline, but the area still has some marvellous beaches, especially at **Bundoran** and **Rossnowlagh**, both popular surfing spots, while **Ballyshannon** is an attractive hillside town situated at the mouth of the River Erne. Further north, **Donegal town** has a pleasant bayside setting and remains of a notable castle, while to its north and southeast respectively lie graceful **Lough Eske** and **Lough Derg**, a major site for Catholic pilgrimage.

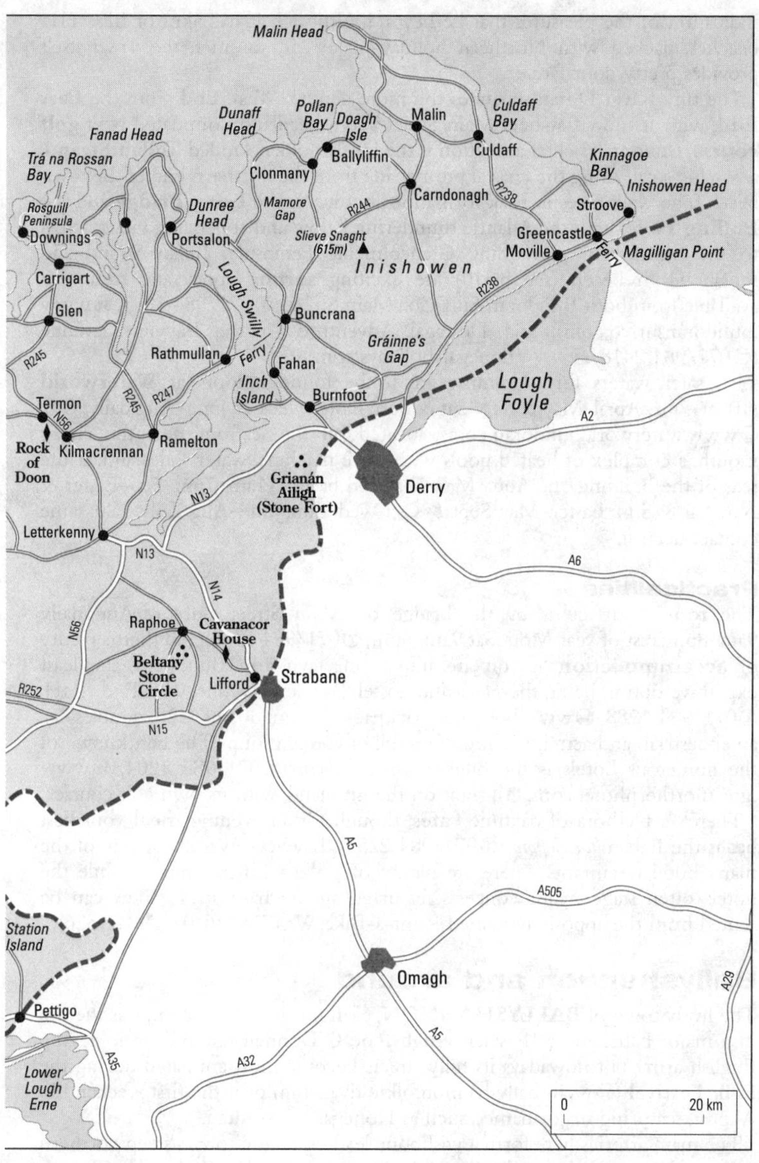

Bundoran

Once described by an Irish newspaper as like "the back streets of Las Vegas only with cheaper hookers", **BUNDORAN** isn't quite that bad, but it's hard to avoid disappointment if the town is your first sight of Donegal. Lying at the county's southern extreme, this popular, though tacky, seaside resort offers no indication of the pleasures that lie beyond. Although it has 5km of Blue Flag beaches, packed with Northern holiday-makers in summer, the town itself provides pretty dour fare.

The tiny River Doran separates the more genteel **West End** from the **East End**, with its down-at-heel Main Street and a headland dominated by a **golf course**. Bundoran's chief attraction is the lovely golden-sanded **Tullan Strand**, a bracing stroll along the coastal promenade from the northern end of the town beach. The walk takes in rock formations known as the **Fairy Bridge** and the **Puffing Hole**, with the Atlantic thundering below and appetizing views across to the much more rewarding Glencolmcille Peninsula. Tullan Strand and Rossnowlagh beach (see p.510) are exciting **surfing** spots, and tuition is available from both Bundoran Surf Co., Main Street (Ⓣ071/984 1968, Ⓦwww.bundoransurfco.com), and Donegal Adventure Centre, Bayview Avenue (Ⓣ071/984 2418, Ⓦwww.donegal-holidays.com).

Far safer waters for swimming are to be found indoors at **Waterworld** (10am–7pm: April, May & Sept Sat & Sun; Easter week & June–Aug daily; €10; Ⓦwww.waterworldbundoran.com), located on the seafront near the river's mouth, a complex of heated pools with wave machine, water slides and, at the rear of the building, the Aqua Mara seaweed baths (11am–7pm: Feb–Easter & Nov Sat & Sun; Easter–May, Sept & Oct Wed–Sun; June–Aug daily; €20; same contact details).

Practicalities

The **tourist office** is by the bridge on Main Street (July & Aug daily 9am–8pm; rest of year Mon–Sat 9am–6pm; Ⓣ071/984 1350) and there's plenty of **accommodation** if you are intent on staying in Bundoran, the least expensive option being the *Homefield* hostel, Bayview Avenue, West End (IHH; Ⓣ071/984 1288, Ⓦwww.homefieldbackpackers.com; dorms €20, doubles ❶), an equestrian and activity centre often full of young groups. The best known of the numerous hotels is the huge *Great Northern* (Ⓣ071/984 1204, Ⓦwww.greatnorthernhotel.com; ❺), right on the headland, with its own golf course.

There's a plethora of daytime **cafés**, though for an evening **meal** your best bet is the Italian *La Sabbia* (Ⓣ071/984 2253), Bayview Avenue, or one of the many hotel restaurants. There are plenty of **pubs** with live music, while the hotels often stage major concerts featuring ageing Irish stars. **Bikes** can be rented from the appositely named Rent-a-Bike, West End (Ⓣ071/984 1526).

Ballyshannon and around

The lively town of **BALLYSHANNON**, 6km north of Bundoran, was the site of a major battle in 1591 when Hugh Roe O'Donnell saw off the besieging English army, but nowadays its hilly streets become most animated during the **Folk Festival** (Ⓦwww.ballyshannonfolkfestival.com) over the first weekend in August, featuring major names, such as Donegal's own Altan.

The main arteries here form a wishbone leading up the town's steep northern slope, and signposted near the top of the left-hand branch is **St Anne's Church** and graveyard, built on the site of the ancient palace of Mullaghanshee. A simple marble slab, inscribed with the word "poet", lies left of the church, marking the burial place of locally born **William Allingham** (1824–89). His first volume, *Poems* (1850), includes his most well known work, *The Fairies* ("Up the airy mountain/Down the rushy glen/We daren't go a-hunting/For fear of little men…"). Such verse attracted him to the Pre-Raphaelites – another work, *Day and Night Songs*, was illustrated by Rosetti and Millais – before Allingham

Rory Gallagher

A more recently renowned scion of Ballyshannon than Allingham was the blues-rock guitarist **Rory Gallagher**, who was born in 1948 in the East Port area (head south across the river and roundabout and take the first left). After learning his trade in show bands, he formed the power trio Taste in the 1960s before embarking on a successful solo career. Known as much for his broad-checked shirts as the vivacity of his playing and live performances, Gallagher died prematurely in 1995 after years of alcohol abuse. Opposite the library in East Port, there's a commemorative plaque, quoting lyrics from one of his best-known and most appropriate songs, *Going to My Home Town*; a weekend of music in early June (ⓦwww.goingtomyhometown.com) celebrates his life. Someone who might have come across Gallagher's records is the rock-loving ex-British prime minister **Tony Blair**, whose late mother also hailed from Ballyshannon.

moved on to the more serious poetic subject of his homeland. His posthumously published *Diary* recounts his friendships with literary contemporaries, most notably Tennyson.

Practicalities

Ballyshannon's **tourist office** (Mon–Fri 9.15am–1pm & 2–5pm; ⓣ071/982 2888) is just north of the bridge and has plenty of information on the town and surrounding area. **Internet access** is available at the Tirhugh Resource Centre, The Mall (ⓣ071/985 2476).

The town has a fair number of **B&Bs**. Across the river and over the roundabout there's the very well furnished and friendly *Elmbrook*, East Port (ⓣ071/985 2615, ⓔelmbrookbandb@eircom.net; ❷; March–Oct), or head to popular *Mullac Na Si*, Bishop Street (ⓣ071/985 2702, ⓦwww.mullacnasi.com; ❷; April–Oct). More luxurious accommodation is provided by *Dorrian's Imperial Hotel* on Main Street (ⓣ071/985 1147, ⓦwww.dorriansimperialhotel.com; ❺), a refurbished eighteenth-century building whose facilities include a pool and gym. Waterside **camping** is available at the *Lakeside Caravan and Camping Park* (ⓣ071/985 2822; Easter–Sept) off the R230 Belleek road.

Eating places, however, are sparse. During the day try *Shannon's* on Bishop Street for excellent-value breakfasts and lunches, but the best evening option is *Sweeny's White Horse*, a pub 200m down Bundoran Road, serving a surprisingly imaginative menu. Alternatively, *Soprano's*, opposite the tourist office, offers a variety of Italian standards and bar snacks.

Ballyshannon's most atmospheric **pub** is *The Thatch*, Bishop Street, with cottage-kitchen interior and **traditional music** in summer on the first and third Saturdays of each month. Other kinds of music can be found at *Finn McCool's* on Main Street and *Dicey Reilly's* on Castle Street, or *Josie's Bar*, East Port. The **Abbey Centre** at the top of Market Street (ⓣ071/985 2928, ⓦwww.abbeycentre.net) hosts a range of musical and theatrical events and has a two-screen **cinema**. At **Ballintra**, 7km along the Donegal road, there's **horse racing** in the open fields on the first Monday in August.

Abbey Assaroe

Instead of taking the main road from Ballyshannon to Donegal town, the left turn at the top of Main Street heads along the more pleasant Rossnowlagh road, where, after about 800m, a signposted left turn leads to the sparse remains of **Abbey Assaroe**, founded by the Cistercians in 1184. Past the abbey and round to the left, you'll come to a restored **mill** beside a bubbling stream. This makes a pretty picture of millrace and rotating cogwheels, and there's a small **interpretive centre** (Easter week & June–Sept daily 11am–7pm; rest of year Sun 2.30pm–7pm; free), explaining the restoration project and the role of the Cistercians in medieval Ireland, as well as an adjacent café.

The log gate by the old bridge takes you onto the stream's bank and leads to two artificial **caves**. One is a small grotto known as Catsby's; the other – nearly 30m deep – is said to have once reached all the way under the abbey and run for 3km towards Rossnowlagh. The grotto was once a site for secret Masses, held here to evade the enforcement of the penal laws in the eighteenth century. A couple of hundred metres upstream are *Eas Aedha Ruadh*, the **falls** of the chieftain Red Hugh O'Donnell, who reputedly drowned here.

Creevy and Rossnowlagh

Back on the Rossnowlagh road, 3km on, a turning leads to the tiny seaside hamlet of **CREEVY**. It's a tranquil though lonely spot, and a memorial on the pier sadly records the death of three local fishermen in 1988, testament to the occasional ferocity of the waters in the bay. Should you fancy **staying**, there's the very pleasant *Creevy Pier Hotel* (ⓣ071/985 8355; ❸), where you can watch the waves from the bar and sample fresh seafood in its restaurant.

ROSSNOWLAGH lies about 5km further north, with good cliffs for walks overlooking a magnificent expanse of beach that is raked by Atlantic surf but is also sometimes blighted by boy racers. Rossnowlagh has a private **surfing** club beside the swish and elegant *Sandhouse Hotel* (ⓣ071/985 1777, ⓦwww.sandhouse.ie; ❹), but one of the many surfing buffs should be able to help you out with equipment, or at least suggest where to acquire some. The village is also the site of the only **Orange Order parade** (see box, p.659) in the Republic, which takes place on the weekend before July 12. On the cliff-top, there's the excellent *Ard na Mara* **B&B** (ⓣ071/985 1141, ⓦardnamara-ire.com; ❷) and the splendidly situated *Smugglers Creek* **inn**, offering superb seafood and live **music** at weekends. A kilometre or so north of Rossnowlagh towards Ballintra lies **Glasbolie Fort**, a huge earthen rampart 6m high and nearly 300m round, said to have been the burial place of a sixth-century High King of Ireland.

Donegal town and the loughs

DONEGAL town is not the most exciting of places, but it's a pleasant enough spot to pass a few hours. It's not even the county town (which is Lifford – see p.540) but, thanks to the bypass, traffic no longer crams its triangular and central **Diamond**, the old market place.

Many tourists head for Donegal town in the mistaken belief that they'll find themselves in the midst of the county's famously wild terrain, and then discover its rather more sedate setting. However, southeast of the town, the landscape is replete with little lakes well stocked for fishing; the largest of these, and a place of pilgrimage, is **Lough Derg**. Less than 8km upriver from Donegal town is another spot of gentle natural beauty, **Lough Eske**, from where you can walk into the wilds of the **Blue Stack Mountains**, which rise to the north.

Arrival and information

Buses stop outside the *Abbey Hotel* on The Diamond, with timetables available from the **tourist office** in its new waterside building in The Quay car park (Sept–May Mon–Fri 9.30am–5.30pm; June–Aug Mon–Fri 9am–6pm, Sat 10am–6pm; also July & Aug Sun 11am–3pm; ⓣ074/972 1148). **Internet access**

is available at the Cyber Café, above *The Blueberry Tearooms*, Bridge Street. **Bikes** can be rented from The Bike Shop, Waterloo Place (Ⓣ074/972 2515).

Accommodation

Donegal town has plenty of **accommodation**, including a staggering number of **B&Bs**, in all price ranges, so you should have no difficulty finding somewhere to stay.

The Abbey Hotel The Diamond Ⓣ074/972 1014, Ⓦwww.abbeyhoteldonegal.com. A very comfortable central option, offering use of the adjacent *Central*'s leisure facilities. ❺

Atlantic Guest House Main St Ⓣ074/972 1187, Ⓦwww.atlanticguesthouse.ie. Good-quality en-suite rooms bang in the town centre, though some can suffer from street noise. ❶

The Central Hotel The Diamond Ⓣ074/972 1027, Ⓦwww.centralhoteldonegal.com. Refurbished hotel with bright and airy rooms (some overlooking the bay) and its own leisure centre. ❹

Donegal Town Independent Hostel Ⓣ074/972 2805, Ⓔlincunn@eircom.net. One of the county's best hostels, situated 800m down the Killybegs road, welcoming and efficiently run; IHH; dorms €16, doubles ❶.

Ernan's House Hotel Off the Sligo road Ⓣ074/972 1065, Ⓦwww.sainternans.com. An absolute gem of a small country-house hotel, built by Wellington's nephew in 1826 and situated on its own private island. Rooms are spacious and stylish and its two suites utterly gorgeous. Open mid-April to Oct. Doubles ❻ & ❼, suites ❽.

The Water's Edge Glebe Ⓣ074/972 1523, Ⓦwww.littleireland.ie/thewatersedge. Very well kept house on the shores of the bay, a few hundred kilometres up the Sligo road, offering comfortable en-suite rooms. ❷

The Town

Donegal's original "fort of the foreigners" was thought to have been built on the banks of the River Eske by invading Vikings. Later, the first Red Hugh O'Donnell, king of Tir Chonaill, had a Norman-style tower house, known as **O'Donnell's Castle**, constructed on its site in the fifteenth century. When the English defeated the second Red Hugh in 1603, Sir Basil Brooke was given command of the town and it was he who rebuilt and extended the old castle, retaining the lower parts of the original tower, which had been razed to the ground by Red Hugh to prevent its capture. This well-restored example of Jacobean architecture sits on Tirconnell Street by The Diamond (mid-March to Oct daily 10am–6pm; Nov to mid-March Fri–Sun 9.30–4.30; €3.70; Heritage Card). It's a fine marriage of strong defence and domestic grace, featuring mullioned windows, arches, ten gables and no fewer than fourteen fireplaces, over the grandest of which are carved the escutcheons of Brooke and his wife's family, the Leicesters. Brooke topped the tower with a Barbizon turret and added the mansion on the left, with the kitchens and bakery on the ground floor and living quarters on the floor above. Brooke was highly prolific in Donegal and was responsible for the overall design of the town.

Down at the quay a **Waterbus** (Ⓣ074/972 3666 for times; €15) offers a seventy-minute trip around Donegal Bay. The County Donegal Railway, which formerly ran from Derry to Ballyshannon, closed in 1959, and its history is told at the **Donegal Railway Heritage Centre** at the Old Station House on Tirconnell Street (Mon–Fri 10am–5pm; also July & Aug Sat & Sun 2–5pm; €3.50; Ⓦwww.countydonegalrailway.com). Here you'll find a model of the old railway and lovingly restored railcars and carriages from the steam age.

Just outside town down the Sligo road lies the **Donegal Craft Village** (Mon–Sat 9.30am–5.30pm), whose seven workshops are well worth visiting to view and perhaps buy a range of glassware, handwoven products, jewellery, sculptures and other artworks.

The Annals of the Four Masters

In Donegal town's Diamond stands an obelisk commemorating the compilers of the famed **Annals of the Four Masters**. The Annals were begun in the town's **Franciscan friary**, whose ruined remains stand on the left bank of the River Eske, and were a systematic attempt to collect all known Irish documents into a history of the land beginning in 2958 BC, including mythical invasions by Firbolgs and Milesians, and ending in 1616 AD. The friary itself was built in 1474 by the first Red Hugh and his wife Nuala O'Brien of Munster. It was occupied by the English in 1601 and seriously damaged by the besieging O'Donnell army, being finally abandoned after the Flight of the Earls (see p.693). The *Annals* were completed by friars who had moved to a site by the River Drowse, near Kinlough, Country Leitrim. Manuscript copies of the *Annals* are occasionally on display at Trinity College library in Dublin.

Eating

Eating places are plentiful in Donegal town, though for something special it's best to head out to *Harvey's Point* (see opposite).

Aroma Donegal Craft Village. Exceptionally good coffee shop and home bakery serving a range of salads and savouries, including some superb Mexican specials.

The Blueberry Tearooms Castle St. A friendly place serving excellent soups, sandwiches and lunches.

The Central Hotel The Diamond. The carvery here is very popular with locals and good value, though the new *It's Thai!* restaurant is also earning plaudits for the authenticity of its cuisine.

Dom's Quay St. Popular bar and restaurant serving an extensive menu of traditional and contemporary cuisine.

The Harbour Quay St. A local institution, offering a wholesome range of pizzas, meat and fish dishes.

The Krusty Kitchen Main St car park. Welcoming café dishing up breakfasts, snacks and filling lunches.

La Bella Donna Bridge St ☎074/972 5789. Reasonably priced restaurant providing a range of well-prepared Italian standards.

Entertainment and bars

Donegal holds a summer **festival** in late June with plenty of music and street entertainment. Many of the town's **pubs** offer entertainment year-round, and Thursday's *Donegal Democrat* newspaper provides local **listings**.

Opposite the castle, the *Scotsman's Bar* has traditional music on Fridays. At the top of Main Street *The Schooner*, just past the cathedral, has a nautical interior, an original nineteenth-century bar and music at weekends. For a quiet pint, try *Tírconaill*, an old-time bar on The Diamond. The most popular **club** nights are in the *Abbey Hotel* (Sun 10.30pm–2am; sometimes also Fri in summer).

Lough Eske and the Blue Stacks

The soft beauty of **Lough Eske** is easily accessible from Donegal town. To get there take the minor road that runs north of the river, signposted "Lough Eske Drive", 500m out on the Killybegs road. This leads to a forgotten forested estate, once belonging to the Brooke family but now owned by the Forestry Commission. The lough is no longer a particularly great fishing spot, though it is known as a place to catch char, a tasty 20cm-long species of the salmon family, which lurk in the depths at the centre of the lake, moving out to the shallower edges around late October, where they can easily be fished using worms. The sandy banks of the River Eske are also known for freshwater oysters – some of which are reputed to contain pearls – but they're a protected species so it's illegal to take them. The ruins of an **O'Donnell tower**, once a prison, stand on one of the small islands on the lake.

At the southern end of the lough is *Harvey's Point Country Hotel* (074/972 2208, www.harveyspoint.com; 7), which offers superb **accommodation** and one of the best **restaurants** in the county (expect to pay around €35 for lunch and €55 for dinner; Nov–March closed Sun eve and all day Mon & Tues), serving tantalizing French-inspired cuisine.

Carrying on along the western shore of Lough Eske, you'll reach the point where the river flows in at the lough's northern tip. A dirt road here runs off to the left into the **Blue Stack Mountains**. At the top of the pathway that leads on from the track there are superb views over the lough and, nearby, the tumbling **Doonan waterfall**. From here you can join the waymarked **Bluestack Way**, which passes Lough Belshade, guarded in legend by a huge black cat. If you're intending to tramp around the mountain range, it's best to keep to the skirts of the hills as there are many marshy patches on lower ground – and be prepared for misty pockets during bad weather.

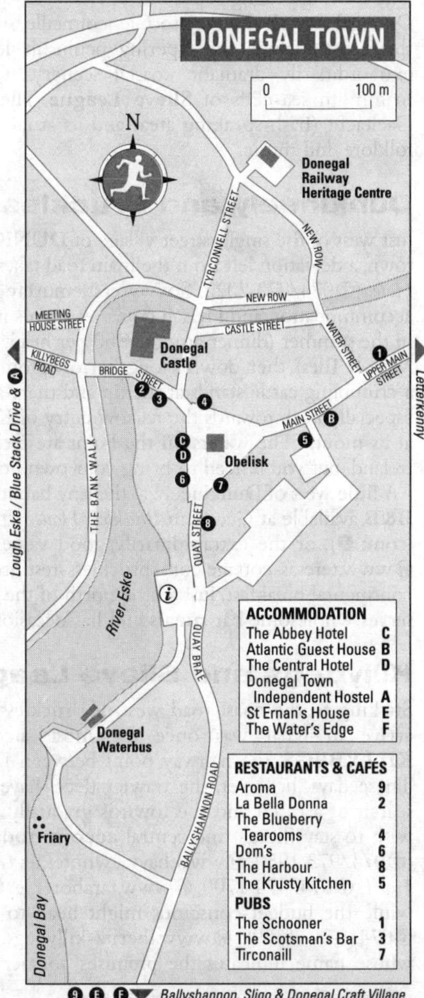

Lough Derg and Station Island

In the middle of **Lough Derg**, 25km east of Donegal town, is a rocky islet known as **Station Island** or, more popularly, St Patrick's Purgatory, a retreat for Catholics needing rigour and solitude to recharge their faith. A national shrine of pilgrimage since the fifth century, it was described by Girardus Cambrensis in *Topography of Ireland* (1186) as "an island, one part of which is frequented by good spirits, the other by evil spirits". Contemporary scholars have argued that, as St Patrick never referred to Lough Derg in his writings, he probably never visited the island, but nevertheless it still thrives today as a strong centre for **pilgrimage**.

Participants in the three-day retreats (June to mid-Aug; €45) abjure sleep and food (apart from black tea and toast) and walk barefoot over rocks, praying at Stations of the Cross around the island. One-day retreats (May, Aug & Sept; €27) are less austere. *Station Island*, a collection by Seamus Heaney, contains a number of poems dealing with the mystique surrounding this ritual, while the late Pete McCarthy graphically recounted his experience of a retreat in *McCarthy's Bar* (see p.739). If you want to participate, contact ⓣ071/986 1518, ⓦwww.loughderg.org. The island is approached via the R233 from **Pettigo**, nine kilometres south. A bus from Ballyshannon or Enniskillen will drop you in Pettigo village, though some continue to Lough Derg in the summer. Pettigo also has a remarkable number of pubs for such a small village, suggesting an importance placed on spiritual nourishment of a rather different kind. Should you require alimentary sustenance, *Miler's Restaurant* in the *Pettigo Inn* serves reasonably priced **meals**.

Southwest Donegal

The most appealing route out of Donegal town heads west along the shore of Donegal Bay all the way to Glencolmcille, some 50km away. Highlights along this coast include the tapering peninsula leading to **St John's Point** and extraordinarily dramatic coastal scenery, which reaches an apogee in the mammoth sea-cliffs of **Slieve League**. The **Glencolmcille Peninsula** is a Gaeltacht (Irish-speaking area) and its attractive villages are rich in traditional folklore and music.

Dunkineely and Bruckless

Just west of the single-street village of **DUNKINEELY**, 17km west of Donegal town, a deviation left from the main road takes you first past *Castle Murray House Hotel* (ⓣ074/973 7022, ⓦwww.castlemurray.com; ❹), noted for its comfortable accommodation and French gourmet **meals** including delicious seafood specials in the summer (dinner around €50 per head, Sun lunch €30; Oct–April closed Mon & Tues), then down a long, narrow promontory to **St John's Point**, where a crumbling castle stands at the tip and there are great **views** over Donegal Bay, especially back towards the narrow entry of Killybegs Bay, with **Rotten Island** at its mouth. The waters off the Point are reckoned to offer the best **diving** in Ireland, but you'll need to bring your own boat and equipment.

A little west of Dunkineely, at the tiny hamlet of **BRUCKLESS**, there's stylish **B&B** available at Georgian *Bruckless House* (ⓣ074/973 7071, ⓦwww.bruckless.com; ❸), or the extraordinarily good value *Bruckless Rest* (ⓣ074/973 7517, ⓦwww.teresas-cottage.com/bruckless-rest.htm; ❶), whose low prices include a continental breakfast. Just a little north of the village is the *Ring Fort Inn*, which serves wholesome bar **meals** and has occasional live music.

Killybegs and Slieve League

Sticking to the coast road west of Bruckless, you'll round Killybegs Bay and arrive in what was once the most successful fishing port in Ireland: **KILLYBEGS**, the halfway point between Donegal town and Glencolmcille. These days, however, the trawler fleets have moved to more distant parts in search of a catch and the town is gradually sinking into decline. Should you wish to stay there's fine central **accommodation** at both the *Bay View Hotel* (ⓣ074/973 1950, ⓦwww.bayviewhotel.ie; ❺) and the more recently built *Tara Hotel* (ⓣ074/974 1700, ⓦwww.tarahotel.ie; ❹), both overlooking the harbour, while the budget-conscious might head to the adjacent *Ritz* **hostel** (IHO; ⓣ074/973 1309, ⓦwww.theritz-killybegs.com; dorms €20, doubles ❶) whose name indicates the premises' former existence as a cinema. The best

▲ Cliffs of Teelin

places to eat include the two hotels and, nearby, the locals' daytime favourite, *Melly's Café*.

Five kilometres westwards, the route to Kilcar passes *Kitty Kelly's* **restaurant** (evenings only; ⓣ074/973 1925), which offers particularly good locally caught seafood. A few kilometres further on the road divides: for the scenic way, take the lefthand fork, a narrow switchback ride along the coastline with stupendous views over the ocean, especially from **Muckross Head**, and the looming presence of the hills and mountains to your right.

The roads meet again at **KILCAR**, a pleasant village and a centre for the Donegal **tweed industry**: there are a couple of small factories open to visitors. The village has a **sea-angling festival** at the beginning of August, followed shortly afterwards by a raucous **street festival**. **Boats** can be rented from Jim Byrne (ⓣ074/973 8224), while Paddy Clarke (ⓣ074/973 8211) offers guided archeological tours and hill-walking. *John Joe's* **bar** hosts regular Friday-night sessions. *Teach Barnaí* (ⓣ074/973 8160), across the road, is a great **restaurant**, serving superb French-inspired evening meals and extremely popular Sunday lunches.

Should you wish to stay, Kilcar has welcoming seaside **B&B** at *Ocean Spray* (ⓣ074/973 8438; ❷) back on the road towards Muckross Head. Alternatively, 3km west on the coast road towards Carrick is *Derrylahan* (IHH & IHO; ⓣ074/973 8079, ⓦhomepage.eircom.net/~derrylahan; dorms €16, doubles ❶), set on a working farm and one of the friendliest and busiest **hostels** in the country.

Derrylahan is an ideal base for exploring the beautiful countryside around **CARRICK**, especially Teelin Bay and the awesome Slieve League cliffs to the west. In the pretty village of Carrick itself the *Sliab Liag* **pub** has live music and DJs at the weekend and, if you want to stay, there's **B&B** at *Cairnsmore* (ⓣ074/973 9137; ❷; March–Oct), a wonderfully situated bungalow with very comfortable en-suite rooms, 500m towards Glencolmcille.

The southern road from Carrick to **TEELIN** follows the west bank of the River Owenee, whose rapids and pools are good for **fishing** – licences are

Climbing Slieve League

There are two routes up to the ridge of **Slieve League**. The less-used back one, known as Old Man's Track, follows the signpost pointing to the mountain just before Teelin and looks up continually to the ridge, while the frontal approach follows the signs out of Teelin to **BUNGLASS**, swinging you spectacularly round sharp bends and up incredibly steep inclines to one of the most thrilling cliff scenes in the world, the **Amharc Mór**. These are allegedly the highest marine cliffs in Europe, and standing here that seems all too possible. The sea moves so far below that the waves appear silent, and the 600m face glows with mineral deposits in tones of amber, white and red. They say that on a clear day it is possible to see one-third of the whole of Ireland from the summit. **Sightseeing tours** of the cliffs from the waters below are organized from Teelin, weather permitting (see below).

If you want to make a full day of it, you can climb up to the cliffs from the Bunglass car park and follow the path along the top of the ridge, which eventually meets Old Man's Track. From here One Man's Pass, a narrow path with steep slopes on each side, leads up to the summit of Slieve League. Bear in mind that the route can often be muddy and very windy – it is certainly not advisable in misty weather or if you suffer from vertigo. From the top of Slieve League, you can either retrace your steps back to Teelin or continue west over the crest of the mountain and down the heather-tufted western slope towards the verdant headland village of **MALINBEG**, where there's a sublime, crescent-shaped golden strand enclosed by a tight rocky inlet. Malinbeg itself is a village of white bungalows, with the land around ordered into long narrow strips. The *Malinbeg hostel* (IHH & IHO; ⓣ074/973 0006, ⓦwww.malinbeghostel.com; dorms €16, doubles ❶) is comfortable and well-equipped and offers exhilarating views from most of its rooms. On the cliff edge a ruined Martello tower faces **Rathlin O'Beirne Island**, 5km offshore, a place with many folklore associations. There are occasional boats across (enquire in Teelin – see below), but nothing to see aside from some early Christian stone relics and a ruined coastguard station.

Beyond Malinbeg, it's relatively easy to extend your walk through **MALINMORE**, where the large *Glen Hotel* (ⓣ074/973 0003, ⓦwww.glenhotel.com; ❸) has great views from its en-suite rooms and serves food, and on to Glencolmcille. The whole distance from Teelin to Malinmore can be comfortably completed in six hours.

available from Teelin Sea Angling Club (ⓣ074/973 9079). Sea-angling and sightseeing **boat trips** to the Slieve League cliffs are provided by Paddy Byrne (ⓣ074/973 9365). The village is Irish-speaking and rich in folklore, which has been recorded over the last half-century by the late Seán Ó'hEochaidh, Donegal's great folklorist. Teelin has a long musical tradition and you're more than likely to catch a Saturday session in *The Rusty Bar*, the only **pub**, whose cosy lounge is often the venue for dynamic music and traditional song.

Glencolmcille and around

As the road from Carrick approaches **GLENCOLMCILLE**, it traverses desolate moorland that's dominated by oily-black turf banks amidst patches of heather and grass. After this, the rich beauty of the Glen, as it's known, comes as a welcome surprise. Settlement in the area dates back to the Stone Age, as testified by the enormous number of **megalithic remains** scattered around the countryside, especially court cairns and standing stones. There's evidence, too, of the Celtic era, in the form of earthworks and stone works. According to tradition, **St Columba** founded a monastery here in the sixth century and some of the **standing stones**, known as the Turas Cholmcille, were adapted for Christian usage by the inscription of a cross. Every Columba's Day (June 9) at midnight, the locals commence a barefoot circuit of the fifteen Turas, including Columba's Chapel, chair, bed, wishing stone and Holy Well, finishing up with Mass at 3am in the village church. (Columba and Columbcille/Colmcille are the same person – the latter is the name by which he was known after his conversion, and means "the dove of the church".)

Widespread emigration post-Famine and in the early twentieth century left the Glencolmcille area a typical example of rural decay. In 1951, however, a new and energetic curate, Father James McDyer, instigated efforts to revitalize the community, while retaining and strengthening its culture. Electricity arrived and road improvements reduced its isolation and allowed new collective enterprises in knitting and agriculture to thrive, and encouraged the development of local tourism.

One of McDyer's major initiatives stands in **Doonalt** down by the beach – the **Folk Village Museum and Heritage Centre** (Easter–Aug Mon–Sat 10am–6pm, Sun noon–6pm; Sept Mon–Fri 11am–5pm, Sun noon–6pm; €3.50; Ⓦwww.glenfolkvillage.com), a cluster of replica thatched cottages, each equipped with the furniture and artefacts of the era it represents. A reception building introduces you to the area's history and cultural heritage, including a reputed visit by Charles Stuart (Bonnie Prince Charlie). The **National School** replica has a display of informative photographs and research projects, and a section on the American painter Rockwell Kent, who painted marvellous treatments of the area's landscapes. At **Sheebeen** house, you can try seaweed wine and other locally made concoctions, such as honey, fuchsia and elderberry (most much better than they sound); there's also a teahouse and crafts shop. On the way down the main street to the Folk Village sits the **Ulster Cultural Centre** which hosts the many **courses** run by Oideas Gael (Ⓦwww.oideas-gael.com), including Irish language, painting, music and dance, archeology and hill-walking.

From behind the hostel (see below), **cliff walks** steer off around the south side of the bay above a series of jagged drops. Rising from the opposite side of the valley mouth, the promontory of **Glen Head** is surmounted by a Martello tower. On the way out you pass the ruins of **St Colmcille's Church**, with its "resting slab" where St Columba would have lain down exhausted from prayer. North across this headland you can climb and then descend to the forgotten little cove of **Port** a few kilometres away, a village deserted since the 1940s. Absolutely nothing happens here – although Dylan Thomas once stayed in the next valley at **Glenlough**, renting a cottage for several weeks in a doomed attempt to "dry out" in an area replete with poteen stills.

Practicalities

En-suite **B&B** accommodation is available at *Corner House* (Ⓣ074/973 0021; June–Aug; ❶) in Cashel or at *Brackendale* (Ⓣ074/973 0038; March–Oct; ❷). You can catch the sunset at the beautifully positioned *Dooey* **hostel** (IHO; Ⓣ074/973 0130, Ⓦwww.dooeyhostel.com; dorms €14, doubles ❶), set high above the fine shingle strand at the mouth of the valley; it also offers **camping**. To get there on foot, keep on the village road as far as the Folk Village, and then take a path up to the left; in wet weather the longer route by road may be easier (fork left 800m before the Folk Village). The teahouse at the Folk Village does moderately priced **food**, though the most popular place for everything from breakfast to evening meals is *An Cistín*, part of the Ulster Cultural Centre.

Glen's **bars** tend to come alive at weekends, especially if the superb local fiddler James Byrne is present, and during the **fiddle festival** at the beginning of August. Glencolmcille's **community festival** takes place during the second week of August.

The Glengesh Pass and Maghera

Heading northeast from Glencolmcille, the minor road to Ardara runs through the heart of the peninsula, travelling via the dramatic **Glengesh Pass** before spiralling down into wild but fertile valley land. Just before reaching Ardara, a road to the left runs along the southern edge of **Loughros Beg Bay** for 9km to **MAGHERA**, passing the transfixing **Assarancagh Waterfall**, from where you can embark on a hardy ten-kilometre waymarked walk uphill to the Glengesh Pass.

Maghera itself is an enchantingly remote place, dwarfed by the backdrop of hills and glens and fronted by an expansive and deserted strand that extends westwards to a rocky promontory riddled with **caves**. One of the largest is said to have concealed a hundred people fleeing Cromwell's troops; their light was spotted from across the strand and all were massacred except a lucky individual who hid on a high shelf. Most of the caves are accessible only at low tide and a torch is essential. Beware the **tides**, however, as even experienced divers have been swept away by the powerful currents. Behind the village, a tiny road, unsuitable for large vehicles, runs up to the **Granny Pass**, an alternative and very scenic route to Glencolmcille.

Central Donegal

The area around the bustling town of **Ardara** contains some of the most contrasting landscapes in Donegal. Rugged mountains lie to the southwest, traversed by the steeply sinuous **Glengesh Pass** and fringed by the unspoiled expanse of **Maghera** strand. Inland to the northeast sits the stately village of **Glenties**, while to the north the coastline forms peninsulas punctuated by the **Gweebarra** River, which, in turn, leads inland to the tranquil villages of Doocharry and Fintown, virtually surrounded by mountain scenery of an almost lunar quality.

Ardara

Sixteen kilometres north of Killybegs on the N56 lies lively **ARDARA**. Traditionally a weaving and knitwear centre, this is an excellent place to buy **Aran sweaters**, sometimes at half the price of elsewhere in Ireland. Molloy's, a kilometre south of town, is the biggest outlet, but Kennedy's, uphill from The Diamond, is handier (its owner is also a mine of local tourist information); both stores are well stocked with hand-loomed knitwear and tweeds.

The Catholic **church** west of Ardara's Diamond has a striking stained-glass window, *Christ among the Doctors*, by the Modernist-inspired **Evie Hone**, one of the most influential Irish artists of the twentieth century. The authors of the Gospels are depicted symbolically with the infant Christ at the centre and David and Moses above and below.

Accommodation options include the renovated and very grand *Nesbitt Arms Hotel* (ⓣ074/954 1103, ⓦwww.nesbittarms.com; ❹), while a kilometre east of town is the stylish, seventeenth-century *Woodhill House* (ⓣ074/954 1112, ⓦwww.woodhillhouse.com; ❹), set in its own extensive grounds. Comfortable central **B&B** is provided by *Brae House*, Front Street (ⓣ074/954 1296, ⓔbraehouse@eircom.net; ❷). **Bike rental** is available from Don Byrne, just west of the Catholic church (ⓣ074/954 1658).

Good **places to eat** include *Woodhill House*, whose restaurant offers classic Irish cuisine and is well worth the asking price of €40 or so per head for dinner and €30 for Sunday lunch, while the *West End Café* on Main Street offers not only Donegal's best fish and chips, but a range of exceptionally good snacks and meals at very affordable prices. Ardara's L-shaped main street is crammed with **pubs** of which the best is *Nancy's*, a more than two-hundred-year-old warren of small, cosy rooms on Front Street, run by the same family throughout its history, and which serves grand bar meals. Equally friendly is the atmospheric *Corner House* bar on The Diamond, which sometimes has traditional-music at weekends. The town's **Cup of Tae** traditional music festival (ⓦwww.cupoftaefestival.com) takes place over the first weekend in May.

Glenties

Set at the foot of two glens 10km east of Ardara, **GLENTIES** is a tidy village of Plantation grandeur. It also sports one of the largest **clubs** in the northwest, the *Limelight*, at the northern end of Main Street, and a host of bars. Another more spiritual attraction is a beautiful modern **church** at the Ardara end of town, designed by the Derry architect Liam McCormack; the vast sloping roof reaches down to 2m from the ground, and rainwater drips off the thousand or so tiles into picturesque pools of water. Opposite the church, **St Conall's Museum and Heritage Centre** (June–Sept Mon–Sat 10am–1pm & 2–4.30pm; €2.50) is one of the best small-town museums in the country and displays much material of local interest, focusing on wildlife, Donegal's railways, antiquities, and the effects of the Great Famine. There's a special display on local music, featuring the travelling Doherty family (see box, p.521) and an old 1885 Edison phonograph. Upstairs is devoted to the playwright **Brian Friel**, whose mother hailed from here – his *Dancing at Lughnasa* bears a dedication to "The Glenties Ladies" and was partly filmed in the neighbourhood – and the town's most famous son, **Patrick MacGill** (see box below).

Practicalities

Accommodation includes the comfortable *Highlands Hotel* on Main Street (ⓣ074/955 1111, ⓦwww.thehighlandshotel.com; ❸), with a plaque commemorating the room where actress Meryl Streep stayed for the local premiere of *Dancing at Lughnasa*. Among several **B&B** choices are *Marguerite's*, a cosy townhouse at the north end of the same street (ⓣ074/955 1699, ⓦmargueritesbandb.com; ❷). Just outside the village, heading towards Ardara, are two very pleasant alternatives: spacious *Lisdanar* (ⓣ074/955 1800, ⓦwww.lisdanar.com; April–Oct ❷), and, a little further on, welcoming *Ardlann*

Patrick MacGill

Born in Glenties in 1890, young **Patrick MacGill** was sold by his parents at a hiring fair for servants. He escaped and fled to Scotland, working as a farm labourer and a navvy, while also writing poems and attempting to sell them. Eventually, he attracted patronage and ended up working on the *Daily Express*, was wounded in France fighting for the British in World War II, then returned to Ireland before marrying the American author Margaret Gibbons and emigrating to the US where he died in 1963. His best-known work is the semi-autobiographical *Children of the Dead End*, which brilliantly recounts the wayward lives of migrant navvies, while *The Rat Pit* parallels this in its tale of young Irish women forced into prostitution. A **summer school** is held in his honour in mid-July, drawing hundreds of people to its exhibitions, seminars and literary debates (ⓦwww.patrickmacgill.com).

(Ⓣ074/955 1271, Ⓔardlann@eircom.net; ❷). **Eating** choices are limited, but the excellent *Highlands Hotel* offers a wide range of food – the gargantuan lunches are exceptional value. Alternatively, try one of the several cafés on Main Street.

All of the **pubs** are on Main Street and most get crowded at weekends, with several offering pre-*Limelight* music for clubbers. A quieter alternative is down-to-earth *Ó Faolain's*, an old-fashioned bar frequented by characterful locals. For **traditional music**, the *Highlands Hotel* has a Sunday-night session and also hosts the **fiddlers' weekend** at the beginning of October; otherwise head for the *Glen Inn*, a bar-cum-grocery 5km out on the Ballybofey road, beautifully situated by the river at the foot of the Blue Stack Mountains. There are sessions here most Friday and Saturday nights, often featuring one of the Campbell brothers, well-known fiddlers in these parts and beyond.

The Dawros Head Peninsula

To the immediate north of Ardara, the **Dawros Head Peninsula** is much tamer than Glencolmcille, with many tiny lakes dotting a quilt of low hills. The terrain of purple heather, fields, streams and short glens makes a varied package for the enthusiastic walker. The first turning off the R261 Narin road leads to **ROSBEG**, an isolated village, straggling beside a series of rock-strewn coves, but you can **camp** among the dunes at **Tramore Beach** (Ⓣ074/955 1491; Easter–Sept). It's even lonelier out at **Dawros Head** itself, but at least there's the welcoming *Dawros Bay House*, a bar serving great seafood.

If you've headed directly from Ardara towards Narin and Portnoo, in **KILCLOONEY**, just before the pastel-shaded church on the right, is the **Kilclooney dolmen**, probably the best-preserved portal stones in the country. The capstone is over 4m long and the structure is reckoned to date from around 3500 BC.

Continuing onwards towards Narin, the most worthwhile sight on the peninsula is **Doon Fort**, which occupies an entire oval-shaped islet in the middle of **Lough Doon**. To get there turn left at the "Rosbeg/Tramore Beach" signpost a kilometre or so before Narin, then head right up the lane just after a school. A few hundred metres later you'll see a sign for **boat rental** leading down to a farmhouse, where you can rent a rowing boat inexpensively to take you across to the island. The idyllic setting, rarely disturbed by visitors, makes the hassle worth it: although its walls are crumbling, the fort has been untouched for over two thousand years. The walls stand 5m high and 4m thick; their inner passages were used in the 1950s for storing poteen.

In **NARIN** the spearheaded, four-kilometre-long **strand** is a wonderful beach, safe for bathing. At low tide you can walk out to **Iniskeel Island**, where St Conal founded a monastery in the sixth century. This has long since disappeared, but there are the ruins of two twelfth-century churches with some cross-inscribed slabs. *Roaninish* (Ⓣ074/954 5207, Ⓔeileentomburke@eircom.net; mid-June to mid-Sept; ❷) offers very comfortable **B&B**, while the *Lake House* **hotel** in Clooney (Ⓣ074/954 5123, Ⓦwww.lakehousehotel.ie; ❸), 1.5km east of Narin, dates from 1847 and provides high-quality accommodation and a fine **restaurant**.

Doocharry and Fintown

East of Narin the N56 hugs the shoreline, twisting and turning until it crosses the Gweebarra and enters Lettermacaward. From here a minor road follows the river 8km inland to **DOOCHARRY**, a tiny place with just a pub and a

John Doherty

The greatest Donegal traditional fiddler, **John Doherty** (c.1895–1980), is buried in Fintown cemetery. Born in Ardara into a family of travellers and musicians descended in part from the MacSweeney clan, erstwhile underlords of parts of Donegal, Doherty spent most of his life on the roads between Ballybofey and Glencolmcille, earning his keep by working as a tinsmith and playing the fiddle at house dances. By his 20s his dynamic yet intricate style of playing guaranteed his living, but for the first fifty or so years of his life his reputation remained firmly within the environs of his travelling beat. In the 1950s he began to be sought out by music collectors and folklorists and subsequently he made commercial recordings (several excellent CDs of his work are available). Many of the tunes played in Donegal today owe their origins to the repertoire of John Doherty and his brothers Mickey and Simon, and despite almost thirty years passing since his death he remains a major influence on the region's driving style of fiddle playing.

grocery, which acts as the gateway to some of the most dramatic scenery in the county. From Doocharry, you can head further upstream northeast along a narrow and tortuous lane past **Slieve Snaght**, through the **Glendowan**

▲ John Doherty

Mountains and skirting the southern edge of the **Glenveagh National Park** to **Lough Gartan** (see p.530). The desolate though beautiful countryside bears little sign of human impact and you'll be lucky to see any life beyond the odd sheep or fluttering bird.

A more major road heads 9km southeast from Doocharry through rugged, rock-strewn moorland to **FINTOWN**, a simple roadside village set at the foot of towering mountains in the Finn Valley where the river broadens to form an elongated strip of lake. You can take a waterside trip along a small section of the old narrow-gauge **railway** (late June to mid-Sept Mon–Sat 11am–4pm, Sun 1–5pm; €6; ⓦwww.antraen.com).

The Rosses

The **Rosses**, a vast expanse of rock-strewn land and stony soil, is a strong Gaeltacht area. Dotted with over 120 tiny lakes, the crumpled terrain stretches from **Dungloe** in the south to **Crolly** in the north, but the forbidding nature of much of the landscape meant most settlements could only survive near the sea, so following the shoreline route around the Rosses is far more rewarding than the more direct road north.

Dungloe

An Clochán Liath is the name you'll see on signposts approaching **DUNGLOE**, referring to the grey-coloured stepping-stones that were once used to cross the river here. The modern Anglicized version comes from Dún gCloiche, the name of a stone fort situated on a rock a few kilometres offshore. When the fair that was held at the fort moved in the eighteenth century to the village of An Clochán Liath, which had grown up around the stepping stones, the fort's name stuck, though Irish-speakers still refer to the town by its original name.

For most of the year, there's little to detain you in Dungloe. At the end of July, however, the **Mary From Dungloe festival** (ⓦwww.maryfromdungloe.com), centred around a rather wholesome beauty pageant, provides a good pretext for general festivities, plenty of music and street entertainment. There's no antiquity behind the festival's origins or name – it dates from 1968 and the title comes from an Irish hit single by the Emmet Spiceland band.

Dungloe is also synonymous with the rejuvenating work of **Paddy "the Cope" Gallagher** (1871–1966), who envisaged the salvation of these then poor communities through cooperative ventures, in particular by reducing their dependency on moneylenders. Oddly enough, the enterprise's practical origins lay in Paddy's discovery that the price of manure was reduced when purchased by societies. As a result, he founded the Templecrone Co-operative Agricultural Society (the "Cope") in 1906, and its central branch still stands proudly on Dungloe's main street with others elsewhere in the Rosses.

The very helpful **tourist office** (June Mon–Fri 10am–1pm & 2–5.30pm; July–Sept Mon–Fri 10am–1pm & 2–5.30pm, Sat 10.30am–1pm & 2–4pm; ⓣ074/952 1297) is in the town's library, in the old church just off the top of Main Street. The library also offers **Internet** facilities. Upmarket **accommodation** is provided by *Óstán na Rosann*, Mill Road (ⓣ074/952 2444, ⓦwww.ostannarosann.com; ❹), which has its own leisure centre and pool, or you can stay very comfortably near the centre of town at *The Rockeries* (ⓣ074/952 2082, ⓦwww.rockeries.com; ❶), a short distance up the Crolly road.

Eating options on Main Street include *Doherty's Restaurant*, a good low-priced chipper and grill, or for evening meals there's modern Irish cuisine at *Ostán na Rossan*. *Patrick Johnny Sally's* **bar** near the top of the hill is a genuine old-timers' pub with a fabulous view of the ocean. Further down Main Street, *Beedy's Bar* has traditional sessions on Tuesdays, and there's assorted entertainment in the *Bayview Lounge* at weekends.

Burtonport

Seven kilometres northeast of Dungloe, **BURTONPORT** is the embarkation point for **Arranmore Island** and, if you can find a boatman at the harbour to take you out, for other smaller islands. In the late eighteenth century, the village's founder, William Burton, attempted to establish **Rutland Island**, just offshore, as a major trading centre and, consequently, this area became the first English-speaking district in the whole of Donegal. During the 1798 rebellion James **Napper Tandy** landed on the island with French troops, but became somewhat inebriated on hearing of Wolfe Tone's capture and was carried back on board (see p.696). Apart from busy activity at the harbour, Burtonport has little to say for itself. For **eating**, *The Lobster Pot* specializes in delicious seafood and the *Skipper's Tavern* offers occasional traditional **music**.

Arranmore

There are now two year-round **ferries** to Arranmore, both charging €15 return, for the short trip from Burtonport to **Arranmore Island**, which pass through the straits between the nearest cluster of islands, and then across to the main village on Arranmore, **LEABGARROW**. If you want to get there quickly, there's a fast ferry which takes just five minutes (daily 5–8 sailings; ⓣ087/317 1810, ⓦwww.arranmorecharters.com). For a more leisurely journey taking around half an hour there's a **car ferry** (daily 3–8 sailings; ⓣ074/952 0532, ⓦwww.littleireland.ie/arranmoreferry). **Accommodation** on the island is limited, but there's *Claire's B&B* (ⓣ074/952 0042; ❷) and *Bonner's* (ⓣ074/952 0532, ⓦwww.littleireland.ie/arranmoreferry/bonnersbb.htm; ❷), both in Leabgarrow and providing en-suite rooms. The island's permanent population of around eight hundred people is almost entirely concentrated along the eastern and southern coastlines. The high centre-ground of bogland and lakes reaches a greater altitude than anywhere else in the Rosses and it's well worth hiking a few hundred metres upland for great views back across the water to Burtonport.

A circuit of the whole island, with cliff-top view of the Atlantic, takes around six hours and the terrain isn't especially taxing though it can be blustery. A great tragedy occurred off the very southeastern tip during the stormy night of November 9, 1935, when a sailing ship carrying returning islanders ran aground on the rocks. Nineteen people died, including seven from the same family – the eighth member was the only survivor. Many ships have foundered in the choppy seas hereabouts, but, in 1983, the lone American yachtsman Wayne Dickenson landed on the island's west coast after 142 days at sea in the smallest boat ever to cross the Atlantic. In the cliffs below St Crone's Church on the southern shore is **Uaimh an Áir** (the "cave of slaughter"), where seventy hiding islanders were massacred in the seventeenth century by a certain Captain Conyngham, in an action that lay somewhat outside his remit from Charles I to rid the Rosses of "rogues and rapparees". Two islanders later took revenge by killing the captain in Dunfanaghy. Uninhabited **Green Island**, at the southwestern tip, is now a **bird sanctuary** and rare species have been spotted hereabouts, including the snowy owl in 1993. The most dramatic of the several **beaches** is at the northwestern end of the island, on the way to the lighthouse and approached by a set of steps down the side of a perpetually crumbling cliff.

Facilities on Arranmore are limited, but there are seven **pubs**, including *Pally's* which has regular entertainment. You can eat at *Bonner's Ferryboat* **restaurant** or, more expensively, the *Glen Hotel*, while *Phil Bán's* bar serves snacks all day.

Around the Rosses to Crolly

The road through the Rosses to Gweedore cuts across a wild and crazed terrain of granite boulders and stunted vegetation. About 8km northeast of Burtonport is the small **Carrickfinn Peninsula**, which boasts a fine strand and **Donegal Airport** (2 daily flights to Dublin and 3 weekly to Prestwick by Aer Árann; ⓣ074/954 8284, ⓦwww.donegalairport.ie). A short distance east from here is **ANNAGRY**, where *Dannie Minnie's* **restaurant** (ⓣ074/954 8201, ⓦwww.dannieminnies.com) has superb seafood specialities – expect to pay around €45 for dinner plus wine – and very svelte accommodation (❸). Annagry's **festival** at the beginning of June is one of the biggest in the Rosses.

A short detour north of Annagry leads to **RANNAFAST**, a village with an astonishing Irish literary heritage. The oral tradition has always been strong in the Rosses, but its writers only came to prominence once the school system was improved early in the twentieth century. Foremost were three brothers from Rannafast's **Clann Mhic Grianna** (*clann* being Irish for "family"): Séamus Ó'Grianna, the author of 27 books under the pseudonym Máire, and a popular choice for School Leaving Certificate examinations; Seosamh Mac Grianna, whose most famous works are *An Druma Mór* and his autobiography, *Mo Bhealach Féin*; and Séan Bán Mac Grianna, the youngest of the lot and the poet of the family. The village also hosts a large **Irish-language college**. All its pubs were closed to prevent students from undermining their studies and it remains dry to this day.

In the townland of **MEENALECK**, just before Crolly, a sign points to *Leo's Tavern*. The proprietors, Leo and Baba Brennan, were both well known on the dance-band circuit in the 1950s and 1960s, but other family members have achieved greater fame. Three of their children (Máire, Pól and Ciarán) were members of the group **Clannad** and another is the celebrated singer/musician **Enya** – the pub's walls are decorated with a variety of awards and mementos. The *Tavern*, which was recently rebuilt from scratch and serves excellent **food**, is hugely popular with tourists, and features a range of music including a Thursday-night traditional session and sometimes singalongs, often featuring Leo himself on piano accordion. You're more likely to meet the locals at *Tessie's* across the road, one of the friendliest bars in the county. Just up the road from here you can **camp** at *Sleepy Hollows* (ⓣ074/954 8272, ⓦhomepage.eircom.net/~sleepyhollows; Easter–Sept), which also offers budget-priced and comfortable **B&B** (❶).

CROLLY marks the end of the Rosses and the beginning of neighbouring Gweedore. Just after the bridge, a narrow road leads up into the **Derryveagh Mountains** (see p.527). This passes lovely **Lough Keel** before reaching its highest point by an abandoned school and swinging sharply right to return to Dungloe. If you head straight on instead, you'll arrive at the most wonderfully situated and very congenial **hostel**, *Screag an Iolair* (IHO; ⓣ074/954 8593, ⓔisai@eircom.net; April to early Sept; dorms €18, doubles ❶), with cosy rooms, traditional music, lots of advice on walking and a splendid place to spend a few days. Nestling in beautiful semi-wild gardens on the side of **Cnoc na Farragh Mountain**, the hostel (whose name means "eagle's nest") provides magnificent views of mountains, lakes, distant Arranmore and, when on offer, spectacular sunsets.

Gweedore and Tory Island

Like its southern neighbour, the Rosses, the interior of the **Gweedore** district is largely desolate and forbidding country, and settlements again cling to the shoreline. To the southwest lie the villages of **Bunbeg** and **Derrybeg**, their cottages sprinkled across a blanket of gorse and mountain grasses. The ruggedness intensifies as it continues up the coast and round the Bloody Foreland to Gortahork in the Cloghaneely district, yet surprisingly, there has been significant house-building here and the area is quite densely populated. Some distance offshore lies Ireland's most literally isolated community, Irish-speaking **Tory Island**, a place rich in folkloric and musical traditions.

Gweedore

BUNBEG has a gorgeous little harbour, packed with smallish trawlers, 1.5km from the village along an enchanting rollicking road. There's a regular year-round **ferry** service to Tory Island (see box, p.527), and it's possible also to take a boat trip from the pier to uninhabited **Gola Island** in summer (ⓣ087/660 7003; €10).

For **accommodation**, there are several hotels on or near the road from Bunbeg to Derrybeg. With its own leisure centre *Óstán Gweedore* (ⓣ074/953 1177, ⓦwww.ostangweedore.com; ❺) is the plushest, but *Óstán Radharc na Mara* (ⓣ074/953 1159, ⓦwww.visitgweedore.com; ❹) doesn't lag far behind; both have excellent **restaurants**. At Bunbeg harbour, there's very fine **B&B** at *Bunbeg House* (ⓣ074/953 1305, ⓦwww.bunbeghouse.com; March–Oct ❷), with pleasant waterside views from its rooms. The best **bar** is *Teach Húdaí Beag*, by the harbour crossroads, which hosts a famous Monday-night traditional session, sometimes involving as many as twenty musicians, as well as a smaller Friday-night one too, and also has comfortable en-suite rooms (ⓣ074/953 1016; ❶). *Seán Óg's* pub has a Wednesday-night session and other music throughout the week.

At **GLASSAGH**, about 7km north of Derrybeg, the road climbs abruptly to Knockfola, loosely translated as the **Bloody Foreland**, a grim, stony, almost barren zone, crisscrossed by stone walls, and so-called because of the red hue acquired by its heather from the light of the setting sun. If you fancy lingering a while, the best **place to stay** is *Teac Jack* (ⓣ074/953 1173, ⓦwww.teacjack.com; ❷), which has a fine restaurant and a bar often hosting traditional music, as well as set-dancing on Tuesday and Sunday nights. From Knockfola, the road turns eastwards hugging the side of the mountain, with the bogland and its hard-worked turf banks stretching below towards the Atlantic. You should be able to spot the distinctive shape of **Tory Island** far out to sea and, at **MAGHEROARTY**, 8km east of Derrybeg, a road runs down to the pier, where you can pick up a ferry to the island (see p.527) and possibly arrange a trip to largely deserted **INISHBOFIN**, just offshore.

There's little to do on the island except relax and wander or perhaps muse on the strange fate of **Arthur Kingsley Porter**. A Harvard professor and owner of Glenveagh Castle (see p.529), Kingsley Porter was living in a small house on the island when he failed to return from a walk in July 1933. Though he probably drowned, rumours concerning his whereabouts flourished, some even suggesting that he had been sighted at continental art galleries. Whatever the case, his inquest was the first in Ireland to take place without a body, and a verdict of misadventure was recorded.

Tory Island

With its ruggedly indented shores pounded by the ocean, **TORY ISLAND**, though only 12km north of the mainland, is notoriously inaccessible. Yet despite the island's barren landscape and the ferocity of the elements, the Tory islanders are thriving, a situation no one could have predicted after the events of 1974 threatened to curtail thousands of years of settlement. During that winter the harshest of **storms** battered Tory for over eight weeks, severing all communications and preventing helicopters from landing. When it finally abated, two dozen families applied for mainland housing, ten eventually moving to Falcarragh. It later transpired that Donegal County Council had drawn up a full-scale evacuation plan.

As in Glencolmcille (see p.516), the arrival of a new priest, **Father Diarmuid Ó Péicín**, stimulated a transformation. Visiting on a day-trip in 1980, he ended up staying for four years as the island's pastor. Conditions were poor and the islanders dispirited. Essential amenities such as a water supply, proper sanitation and reliable electricity were lacking. There was no ferry service and, even if there had been, the harbour was unfit to receive it. Rallying the islanders, the pastor began to lobby every possible target, securing support from such disparate characters as the US senator Tip O'Neill (who had Donegal ancestry) and Ian Paisley. The campaign attracted media attention and conditions gradually began to improve thanks to the eventual support of the embarrassed state and the financial assistance of an American philanthropist. Nowadays, around 150 people live permanently on the island and 25 children attend the local junior school, a happy sign of the island's revival (older children spend term times in Falcarragh).

Tory's inaccessibility has long reinforced its remoteness, ensuring the retention of a powerful culture that has almost vanished from the mainland, referred to by islanders as "the country". Only 4km long and less than 1.5km wide, its vulnerability to the elements means little can grow here, and what does has to be protected from the salty winds behind stone walls. The Irish-speaking islanders have a deep respect for the island and its landscape, both as inspiration for their musicians, storytellers and artists and as a powerful source of legend.

According to local mythology, Tory was the stronghold of the **Fomorians**, who raided the mainland from their island base and whose most notable figure was the cyclops **Balor of the Evil Eye**, the Celtic god of darkness. Intriguingly, the local legend places his eye at the back of his head. There's also said to be a crater in the very heart of the island that none of the locals will approach after dark, for fear of incurring the god's wrath. In the sixth century, **St Colmcille** landed on Tory with the help of a member of the Duggan family. In return, the saint made him king of the island; the line has been unbroken ever since and you're more than likely to meet the present king, **Patsy Dan Rodgers**, who regularly greets arrivals at the harbour. Some monastic relics from St Columba's time remain on Tory, the most unusual of which – now the island's emblem – is the **Tau Cross**. Its T-shape is of Egyptian origin, and is one of only two such monuments in the whole of Ireland. It has now been relocated and set in concrete on Camusmore Pier in West Town, one of the island's two villages. There are other mutilated stone crosses and some carved stones lying around,

Ferries to Tory Island

There are now two **ferry services** to Tory Island, both charging around €20 for a return trip. The first is operated by Turasmara Teo (Ⓣ074/953 1320, Ⓦwww.toryislandferry.com). It has a daily sailing between April and October, which leaves Bunbeg at 9am and heads back from Tory soon after dropping off at around 10.30am depending on the tides (Nov–March sailings Mon–Fri only). There are additional sailings from **Magheroarty** (April–Oct daily 11.30am & 5pm plus July & Aug 1.30pm). *Óstán Thoraigh* (see below) also operates a daily service from Easter to October, leaving Magheroarty at 11am, 1pm, 4.30pm and 7pm. Departure times for both services may be affected by the tides and the weather, so always call ahead to check. Whatever the weather, be prepared for sudden changes and for a forced overnight stay on the island.

several by the remains of the **round tower** in West Town, which is thought to date from the tenth century and is uniquely constructed from round beach stones. A local superstition focuses on the **wishing stone** in the centre of the island, three circuits of which will supposedly lead to your desires being granted. According to legend, it was used to defeat invaders by wrecking their ships: the British gunboat *Wasp*, sent to collect taxes in 1884, was caught in a sudden storm that killed all but six of its crew.

Tory islanders are famed for their **painting**, a development that originated in a chance encounter between the English painter Derek Hill and one of the island's fishermen, **James Dixon**, in 1968, both now deceased. Dixon had never lifted a brush before the day he told Hill that he could do a better job of painting the Tory scenery, but he went on to become the most renowned of the island's school of **primitive painters** – Glebe House has a remarkable painting by him (see p.530). You can view the islanders' work and, more than likely, meet the artists, at the **James Dixon Gallery**, the originator's former home, a little way to the east of the harbour.

You'll find most of the amenities in **WEST TOWN**. *Óstán Thoraigh* provides comfortable **accommodation** (Ⓣ074/913 5920, Ⓦwww.toryhotel.com; ❸), has one of the only two bars on the island, a fine **restaurant** serving seafood, and organizes a range of summer events, including traditional music and song, painting and birdwatching weekends, as well as running the Dive Tory centre for aquatic fans. For **B&B**, there's nearby *Teach Bhillie* (Ⓣ074/916 5145, Ⓦwww.toraigh.net; ❷), which offers decent en-suite rooms and a small self-catering kitchen. The **Social Club** in West Town is one of the hubs of island life, with a bar and regular traditional music and dancing.

The Derryveagh Mountains and Glenveagh

Inland from Gweedore lies some of the most dramatic scenery in Donegal, an area dominated by mountains such as **Errigal** and **Slieve Snaght** and loughs of startling beauty. This is popular hill-walking country, especially along the Poisoned Glen, part of the much-visited **Glenveagh National Park**. Further on, towards Letterkenny, the countryside becomes gentler and increasingly verdant, especially in the environs of **Lough Gartan**, an area rich in associations with St Columba.

The loughs and Mount Errigal

Heading east on the N56 from Gweedore, the imposing and starkly beautiful mass of **Mount Errigal** becomes increasingly prominent. From a distance the mountain appears to be snow-covered, but skirting the northern shore of **Lough Nacung**, it becomes apparent that the white colouration has geological, rather than meteorological, causes. You can **stay** very comfortably near the lough at *An Chúirt* hotel (Ⓣ074/953 2900, Ⓦwww.anchuirt-hotel.ie; ❹) or, if you want to press on, the minor R251 road leads to **MONEY BEG**, where the brand new *Errigal* An Óige **hostel** (Ⓣ074/953 1180, Ⓦwww.errigalhostel.com; dorms €21, doubles ❶) sits at the foot of the mountain. It's a stunning purpose-built place, entirely in keeping with the area, and features private en-suite doubles, plus four-bed rooms and innovative split-level six-bed dorms plus an Internet room, self-catering kitchen and a reasonably priced diner.

Quite often the area around Errigal is shrouded in mist, but on a clear day the beauty of the mountain is unsurpassable, its silvery slopes resembling the Japanese artist Hokkusai's images of Mount Fuji. The hour-long hike up to the top is a must, and there's a waymarked trail from the road, 2km past the Poisoned Glen turn-off, up the southeast ridge. The climb to the summit is well worth it for the stupendous **views**: virtually all of Donegal, and most of Ulster, is visible and you could easily spend several hours just sitting and absorbing the contrasts provided by coastline, loughs and mountains.

Back down in Money Beg, a lane runs south to the narrow strip of land, which divides Lough Nacung from Dunlewey Lough. On the way there's the **Dunlewey Lakeside Centre** (mid-March to early Nov Mon–Sat 10.30am–6pm, Sun 11am–6pm; Ⓦwww.dunleweycentre.com; tour of farm and outbuildings €6, boat trip €6, combined ticket €10), an impressive visitor centre by the shore. There's an excellent **restaurant** here and a

▲ Mount Errigal

book-cum-crafts shop, with maps of the area on sale. It's very child-friendly outside with a small farmyard "zoo", adventure playground and pony rides on offer. For adults the highlight is the re-creation of the home of the notable local weaver, Manus Ferry; the **boat trip** around Dunlewey Lough is also a lovely excursion. The centre hosts a superb series of traditional-music concerts (July & Aug Tues), as well as a Sunday-afternoon session at 2.30pm, and is also the focus for one of Ireland's major **traditional-music** events, the Frankie Kennedy Winter School (commemorating the late Altan flute player; Ⓦwww.frankiekennedy.com) over the New Year, which has plenty of instrumental classes and nightly concerts by some of the country's best-known musicians. A new 500-seater theatre-cum-concert-hall will open here in 2008.

Glenveagh National Park

According to legend, the **Poisoned Glen**, east of Dunlewey Lough, is where the cyclops Balor of the Evil Eye (see p.526) was slain by Lugh, poisoning the ground on which his single orb fell. There are many other explanations for the origins of its name, from the darkly conspiratorial (the glen's waters were polluted to kill English soldiers) to the purely botanical (poisonous Irish spurge used to grow here).

To reach the glen, head a little way further east of Money Beg on the R251 and take the signposted lane leading downhill to the right. Just below the ruined church at the eastern end of Lough Nacung turn off to the left and follow the track over the old bridge. The path dwindles away and you should follow the left bank of the river deep into the gorge until it turns sharply left. Walk through the water here, usually just a trickle in summer, to the opposite bank and climb up towards a granite crest. From here walk beside the small stream through a gully and finally you'll emerge on a ridge. It's not an easy tramp, for a lot of the ground is marshy, but the views are fantastic, with the River Glenveagh flowing into Lough Beagh down below. You're now in the **Glenveagh National Park** and may well see deer hereabouts. If you don't want to retrace your tracks and are prepared for a longer hike, you have a number of options. However, it's vital to follow all the basic rules of hill-walking and essential to keep to the designated roads and paths during the winter deer-culling season (Sept–Feb), or you run the risk of being shot. Experienced hill-walkers will probably be tempted by the sight of **Slieve Snaght**, the highest point in the park, off to the southwest. Alternatively, if you head downhill to the southeast, the Glendowan road at the bottom leads eastwards to **Lough Gartan** (see p.530) and westwards to **Doocharry** (see p.520). If you take this road east towards Gartan for a short distance, an old disused vehicle track to the left will lead you down the barrel of the glen alongside the river to Lough Glenveagh.

A less arduous approach to Glenveagh is to follow the R251 alongside the mountains until it curves to meet Lough Beagh's northern tip. A little further on is the official National Park **visitor centre** (Feb–Nov daily 10am–6.30pm; free). The centre has detailed and interactive displays on the area's ecology and geology, as well as information on the eagles which have been introduced in the park in the hope of establishing a viable breeding stock, and there's also a reasonably priced restaurant. Minibuses (€2 return) ply between here and **Glenveagh Castle** (same hours; tours €2.60; Heritage Card), built on a small promontory for wealthy landowner George Adair between 1870 and 1873. Adair was the creator of the estate that now forms much of the park, but while you might admire the end product it's impossible to condone the means by which it was achieved. Though some land was obtained through purchase, during what is now known as the **Derryveagh Evictions**, Adair evicted 244 tenants during the bitterly cold April of 1861, forcing many into the workhouse and others to emigrate to Australia. The rhododendron-filled gardens surrounding the castle were very much the work of Adair's wife, Cornelia, who also introduced herds of red deer to the estate. The steep ascent to the viewpoint behind the gardens is more than worthwhile for the wonderful views down to the castle and along the lough deep into the glen. Guided tours of the castle focus on the collection of furniture and artwork collected by the millionaire Irish-American, Henry McIlhenny, the last owner of Glenveagh, who bequeathed the castle and its contents to the nation. An earlier proprietor was Arthur Kingsley Porter who disappeared in mysterious circumstances on Inishbofin Island (see p.525).

Lough Gartan and around

The environs of **Lough Gartan** are one of the supreme beauties of Ireland. **St Colmcille** was born into a royal family here in 521; his father was from the house of Niall of the Nine Hostages and his mother belonged to the House of Leinster. If you walk over from Glenveagh you'll pass his **birthplace** – take the first road right at the first house you see at the end of the mountain track, and you'll come to a colossal **cross** marking the spot; the site is also signposted from the road running along the lough's southern shore. Close by is a slab known as the **Flagstone of Loneliness**, on which Colmcille used to sleep, thereby endowing the stone with the miraculous power to cure the sorrows of those who also lie upon it, though nowadays it's bestrewn with coins. During times of mass emigration, people used to come here on the eve of departure in the hope of ridding themselves of homesickness. Archeologically, it's actually part of a Bronze Age gallery tomb and has over fifty cup marks cut into its surface.

Going back to the track leading downhill will bring you to the lakeside road, where a left turn leads to the remains of a church known as the **Little Oratory of St Colmcille**. It's an enchanting ruin, no larger than a modern living room, with a floor of old stone slabs with grass growing up through the cracks. A holy well is here too and nearby the Natal Stone, where the baby Colmcille first opened his eyes; to this day pregnant women visit the slab to pray for a safe delivery.

Glebe House and around

Glebe House (daily: June to mid-Oct 11am–6.30pm; June & Sept to mid-Oct closed Fri; tours €2.90; Heritage Card) is a gorgeous Regency building set in beautiful gardens on the northwest shore of Lough Gartan. Richly decorated both inside and out, it owes its fame to the time of its tenure by the English artist Derek Hill (1916–2000), though it's now run as a **gallery** by the Heritage Service. The converted stables are used for visiting exhibitions, while the rooms of the house itself display a rich collection of paintings, sketches and numerous other items once owned by Hill, including works by Kokoschka, Yeats, Renoir and Picasso. The study is decked out in original William Morris wallpaper and there are Chinese tapestries in the morning room. The kitchen has various paintings by the Tory Island group of primitive painters (see p.527), most remarkably James Dixon's impression of Tory from the sea. It's well worth buying the guidebook and taking the tour.

Moving on round the northeast of the lake, in the direction of Church Hill, a right turn immediately after crossing the bridge will take you down to the modern **Colmcille Heritage Centre** (Easter week & May–Sept Mon–Sat 10.30am–6.30pm, Sun 1–6.30pm; €2.50), on the opposite shore from Glebe. The exhibition space is devoted to St Colmcille's life and the spread of the Celtic Church throughout Europe. If you have no interest in ecclesiastical history, there are other intriguing items, including very beautiful stained-glass windows of biblical scenes by Ciarán O'Conner and Ditty Kummer, and a step-by-step illustration of vellum illumination and calligraphy.

The road to the heritage centre continues a little further on to the **Gartan Outdoor Adventure Centre** (ⓣ074/913 7032, ⓦwww.gartan.com), which runs a range of outdoor activities, including courses in mountain skills. Continuing east from here towards Letterkenny, you ascend from the northern shore to the village of **Church Hill**, with superb cross-country views as far north as the peninsulas.

Doon and Kilmacrennan

Lying a few kilometres northeast of Lough Gartan, **the Rock of Doon** and **Doon Well** are signposted off the R255 shortly after the village of **Termon** on the way to Kilmacrennan. Following the directions leads to a rural cul-de-sac right next to the well. A path from here ascends to a large bushy outcrop that is the Rock of Doon. From 1200 to 1603 this was the spot where the O'Donnell kings were crowned, standing above a huge gathering of their followers. The inauguration stone on the summit is said to bear the imprint of the first Tír Chonaill king, a mark into which every successor had to place his foot as his final confirmation. Doon, an ancient pagan healing **well**, is still a place of pilgrimage, marked out by a bush weighed down with personal effects left behind by the sick, hoping for a cure. You're meant to take off your shoes as you approach and be well intentioned before taking the water.

KILMACRENNAN is a sweet-looking village on the road southeast to Letterkenny. Four hundred metres down the Ramelton road from here is yet another site with Colmcille connections, **Cill Mhic n-Eanain**, where Columba was fostered and educated by Cruithnechan in around 528. A monastery stood here from the sixth century to 1129, and it was also the site of the O'Donnells' religious inauguration following the rites at Doon. The ruins on the left are of a sixteenth-century Franciscan **friary**, while the Church of Ireland building to the right dates from 1622 and fell into disuse around 1845. Back in the village, both the *Angler's Haven* and the *Village Tavern* **pubs** have reasonably priced food.

The north Donegal coast

Running from the Cloghaneely district, which adjoins Gweedore, the **north Donegal coast** holds some of the most spectacular scenery in the whole country, where the battle between the elements is often startlingly apparent. Overshadowed at first by the bleak beauty of **Muckish Mountain** to the south, the main road from **Gortahork** to Milford passes through verdant countryside as it meanders around the deep bays and inlets and alongside the glorious and often deserted beaches which punctuate the shoreline. On the way, the Plantation town of **Dunfanaghy** provides a good base for exploring one of the coastline's two breathtaking peninsulas: **Horn Head**, with its rugged, sea-battered cliffs; and, further to the east, **Rosguill**, almost circumscribed by the marvellous Atlantic Drive.

Gortahork to Falcarragh

The first place you'll encounter in **Cloghaneely**, east of the Bloody Foreland, is **GORTAHORK**, an Irish-speaking village with a strong cultural history, home to the country's greatest contemporary Gaelic poet, **Cathal Ó Searcaigh**. There's little to see in the village, but it makes a grand base for exploring the surrounding countryside. *Teac Maggie Dan's* (ⓦwww.maggiedans.ie; daily 6pm–midnight) is an all-purpose **café/bar** with its own **theatre** named after the poet. The village's **hotel**, *Óstan Loch Altan* (ⓣ074/913 5267, ⓦwww.littleireland.ie/lochaltan; ❸) is modern, though somewhat functional, but offers a good range of meals in its bar and restaurant. For **music**, head to *Teac Billie*, an old- man's drinking place with Tuesday-night sessions.

Three kilometres east of Gortahork, **FALCARRAGH** is livelier and better supplied with shops. A short distance east of the central crossroads is **An tSean Bhearic** (Mon–Fri 10am–5pm, Sat & Sun noon–5pm; free; ⓦwww.little ireland.ie/falcarraghvisitorcentre), housed in the old police barracks. This has a craft shop and café, as well as displays on the town and its policing history, and regularly hosts temporary exhibitions and cultural events. Falcarragh **beach** is reached by heading north at the village crossroads and turning right about 1.5km further on, then continuing east for 3km. This is one of the more beautiful strands on this northwest coast, but a strong undercurrent makes it **unsafe for swimming**.

The road south from Falcarragh to Glenveagh passes through **Muckish Gap**. The slate-grey mass of **Muckish Mountain** dominates the view, its sides pitted with old workings where quartzite sand was extracted for the manufacture of optical glass. It's a relatively easy climb from the roadside shrine at the Gap up a grassy ridge to the **summit** and, on a clear day, the entire coastline from the Bloody Foreland to Malin Head is splendidly visible from here.

Dunfanaghy and around

The small Plantation town of **DUNFANAGHY**, 10km east of Falcarragh, is the gateway to the **Horn Head Peninsula**. On its western outskirts is the **Workhouse** (Easter–Sept Mon–Sat 10am–5pm, Sun noon–5pm; €4.50), sympathetically restored as a local history and community centre. Built in 1845 on the eve of the Great Famine, at first it had only five inmates, but by 1847, as the Famine intensified, over six hundred people were crowded inside. The Famine story is recounted upstairs through the tale of one local inmate, Hannah Herrity, who lived until 1926 – though the narrative method (a distinctly dull and disappointing series of tableaux) undermines the power of her story. The centre also displays work by local artists and has a coffee shop. Dunfanaghy's **hotel** is *Arnold's* (ⓣ074/913 6208, ⓦwww.arnoldshotel.com; late March to Oct; ❺), which also has riding stables, organizes a variety of activity breaks (including writing, photography, painting and golf) and serves excellent-value **food** in both its bar and restaurant.

There are plenty of **B&Bs**, including *Rosman House* (ⓣ074/913 6273, ⓦwww.rosmanhouse.ie; ❷) and *The Whins* (ⓣ074/913 6481, ⓦwww.thewhins .com; ❷), both of which are a cut above the average. As a less expensive, though comfortable, alternative, the excellent *Corcreggan Mill* **hostel** (IHH; ⓣ074/913 6409, ⓦwww.corcreggan.com; dorms €12, double ❶), 2km west towards Falcarragh, has private rooms in a converted railway carriage and **camping**.

As for **places to eat**, apart from *Arnold's*, there's *Danny Collins* pub, which serves bar meals; in the square, *Muck and Muffins* is a popular **café** which also exhibits and sells the owners' pottery; while the diner at the back of Ramsay's stores, off the square, is very reasonably priced. *McColgan's* **bar** is bright and breezy and has a regular Monday-night traditional session.

Horn Head

Horn Head is magnificent, an almost two-hundred-metre rock face scored by ledges on which perch countless guillemots and gulls. Puffins are also returning in significant numbers. The best view of the cliffs, sea-stacks and caves is from the water, but the cliff road is vertiginous enough in places to give you a good look down the sheer sides.

To get there take the slip road at the western end of Dunfanaghy village; it descends to skirt the side of a beautiful inlet before rising steeply to go round the east side of the head. A spectacular vista of headlands opens up to the east – Rosguill, Fanad and Inishowen – but none can match the drama of Horn Head's **cliffs**, their tops clad in a thin cover of purplish heather. Alternatively, you can walk from Horn Head Bridge, 800m from Dunfanaghy on the Horn Head road, and head west across the dunes to **Tramore Beach**. Then follow the sheep track north, passing two small blowholes called the **Two Pistols** and then a much larger one, **McSwyney's Gun**, so called because of the power of the sonic boom produced by the explosion of compressed air from the cavern. Erosion has occurred over the years, however, and you'll be lucky to hear anything these days. Continuing onwards, you'll come to **Pollaguill Bay** and beach. The next wondrous site is the more than twenty-metre high **Marble Arch**, cut by the sea through the base of Trawbreaga Head. Horn Head itself soon becomes visible as you ascend the next headland.

The **walk** as far as here takes around three hours from Dunfanaghy and you can either complete the whole circuit of the peninsula or head back by road.

Marble Hill and Ards Forest Park

East of Dunfanaghy, the road follows the edge of **Sheephaven Bay**, and, shortly after passing through Portnablagh, a signposted turn-off leads to **Marble Hill Strand**, a vast sweep of sand and the location for the *Shandon Hotel* (Ⓣ074/913 6137, Ⓦwww.shandonhotel.com; mid-March to Oct; ❻), equipped with grand rooms, a spa, heated pool and tennis courts. Overlooking the strand, Marble Hill House was once owned by **Hugh Law**, TD for Donegal in the first Irish Parliament of 1922, who entertained all manner of celebrities here, including W.B. and Jack Yeats. Nearby, **Ards Forest Park** (daily: April–Sept 10am–9pm; Oct–March 10am–4.30pm; free) occupies the former demesne of the Capuchin friary of Ard Mhuire; a 1.5km-long avenue alongside Lough Lilly takes you into its centre, where there are fine walks through the woodland as well as along the shore of Sheephaven Bay.

Creeslough and around

The sleepy village of **CREESLOUGH** occupies a slope commanding gorgeous views across the head of Sheephaven Bay. Partway down its main street is a **church** designed by Liam McCormack, its whitewashed whorl and back-sloping table roof reflecting the thickly set Muckish Mountain nearby. **Lackagh Bridge**, about 6km east of Creeslough, offers a tremendous viewpoint of Sheephaven Bay, the curving silted shoreline lying downstream and a ginger-brown picture of rushes and heather reaching deep into the hills. Immediately after the bridge there's a turn-off running for 3km to **GLEN**, well worth taking for the opportunity to drop in at the *Olde Glen* **bar**, a low-ceilinged, atmospheric place, which serves incredibly good evening meals in its restaurant (closed Mon). A minor road south from Glen leads up through gorgeously lonely landscapes and a tremendous viewpoint overlooking Lough Salt before descending to Termon (see p.531).

The Rosguill Peninsula

The route onto the extremely beautiful and very manageable **Rosguill Peninsula** starts by the side of the church in **Carrigart**, 13km northeast of Creeslough, and passes rabbit-infested dunes at the back of a tremendous and usually deserted **beach**. At the top of the strand is **DOWNINGS**, a sprightly holiday centre patronized mainly by Northern Irish tourists, with caravan sites hogging the rear end of the beach and holiday chalets creeping up the hillside behind the village. The one **pub** you should head for is *Downings Bar*, uphill at the far end of the village, a welcoming place with an open fire, lots of *craic* and music at weekends. The most luxurious **place to stay** is the *Rosapenna Hotel* (Ⓣ074/915 5301, Ⓦwww.rosapenna.ie; mid-March to Oct; ❻), next to its own eighteen-hole golf course. Alternatively, there's en-suite **B&B** at *Dun Roamin* (Ⓣ074/9155716, Ⓦwww.littlebandb.com; April–Sept; ❷), up the right-hand fork as you enter Downings and overlooking Sheephaven Bay. You can **camp** at *Casey's Caravan Park* (Ⓣ074/915 5301; April–Sept).

Downings' main street runs on round the west side of the headland to become the panoramic **Atlantic Drive**, which runs around the headland and also makes for a stupendous thirteen-kilometre walk. The range of views encompasses the essence of Donegal – rugged landscapes in constant tussle with the Atlantic Ocean – though, sadly, this is becoming increasingly blighted by large numbers of new-build houses and caravan sites. About halfway along, a turning leads to **Melmore Head**, where you'll find, perfectly placed at **Trá na Rosann** beach, an Alpine-style An Óige **hostel** (Ⓣ074/915 5374; late May to Sept; dorms €15). A quicker way to get here is to take the right-hand fork on the way into Downings from Carrigart.

The Fanad Peninsula

The least tempting of Donegal's peninsulas is **Fanad**, circumnavigated by the well-signposted **Fanad Drive**. However, the western shoreline has little to offer scenically, and the whole peninsula is best approached along the eastern coast road from Letterkenny through the pleasant towns of **Ramelton** and **Rathmullan**, the latter with some very swish accommodation, before heading on to **Fanad Head** itself.

Ramelton and Rathmullan

RAMELTON, 13km northeast of Letterkenny, is a quaint and sedate little town sitting attractively on the eastern bank of the broad black flow of the salmon-rich River Leannan, currently undergoing a degree of rejuvenation. Those with forebears from the county should visit **Donegal Ancestry** (June–Sept Mon–Thurs 9am–5pm, Fri 9am–4pm; also July to mid-Sept Sat 9am–5pm; Ⓦwww.donegalancestry.com), occupying the old Steamboat Store built in 1853 on The Quay. The building houses a genealogical research centre (fees dependent on the amount of work undertaken) and the **Ramelton Story** (€4.50), which recounts through interesting displays and audiovisual material the story of the town from its role as the seat of the O'Donnells in the twelfth century through to the Plantation and Georgian periods.

Should you decide to stay, there's fine **B&B** at *Ardeen* (Ⓣ074/915 1243, Ⓦwww.ardeenhouse.com; April–Oct; ❷), overlooking Lough Swilly, or right in the centre at *Crammond House*, an eighteenth-century townhouse in Market Square (Ⓣ074/915 1055, Ⓦwww.ramelton.net/Accommodation/Crammond-House.htm; April–Oct; ❷). The best **food** can be found at *Mirabeau* (Ⓣ074/915 1138), a popular restaurant serving steaks and seafood at reasonable prices – expect to pay around €35. For weekend **entertainment**, try the *Bridge Bar*, naturally, by the bridge, or the thatched *Conway's* on Castle Street.

The next stop north, **RATHMULLAN** is a pretty place, with its long row of multicoloured houses facing Lough Swilly. In 1587 the rebellious **Red Hugh O'Donnell** was lured onto a British merchant ship here on the pretext of a merry drink, and ended up in Dublin jail for six years; and in 1607 Rathmullan was a departure point for the **Flight of the Earls**, the event that marked the end of the Gaelic nation. **Rathmullan Heritage Centre** (Easter–Sept Mon–Sat 10am–1pm & 2–5pm, Sun noon–5pm; €5) recounts this event and the impact of the flight, as well as mounting an exhibition of works by local artists between July and September. In October 1798 the French frigate *Hoche*, with Wolfe Tone on board, was intercepted in the lough nearby and Tone was captured and taken to Dublin for trial.

Accommodation options are not for the budget-conscious, but well worth a splurge: Georgian *Rathmullan House* (Ⓣ074/915 8188, Ⓦwww.rathmullanhouse.com; ❽) has elegantly furnished rooms, some with sea views, a very fine restaurant (plus great bar meals too) and a heated swimming pool; a short distance up the road to Portsalon the *Fort Royal Hotel* (Ⓣ074/915 8100, Ⓦwww.fortroyalhotel.com; April–Oct; ❺) dates from 1820, is set in expansive grounds, and has stylish and restful rooms and another modish restaurant. Gourmets and wine buffs are also catered for by *An Bonnan Buí* (Ⓣ074/915 8453; closed Mon & Tues) on Pier Road – a three-course meal will cost around €45 plus wine. Alternatively, there's the newly built lough-side *Water's Edge* (Ⓣ074/915 8182, Ⓦwww.theblaneygroup.com; ❹), offering high-quality modern Irish cooking and very amenable accommodation.

You can savour the Lough Swilly view over a pint in the friendly *Beachcomber* **bar** or take one of the **lough cruises** or **angling trips** operated by Rathmullan Charters (Ⓣ074/915 8129, Ⓦwww.rathmullancharters.com).

Portsalon and Fanad Head

North of Rathmullan the R247 climbs to give great views across to **Dunree Head** and the **Urris** range of mountains on the Inishowen Peninsula to the east. Taking the first right turn will lead you along a minor road hugging the coastline, passing *Knockalla Caravan and Camping Park* (Ⓣ074/915 9108; mid-March to mid-Sept) as it twists and turns up to the cliff-top approach to **Saldanha Head**. Here you'll witness the most spectacular views on the entire peninsula, looking across to Inishowen and down onto the five-kilometre stretch of golden sand at Ballymastocker Bay. Sadly, the attraction of the once tiny village of **PORTSALON** has been irrevocably destroyed by new housing, though it's still worth popping into *The Stores* pub which sits by the harbour, and was rebuilt around a tiny public bar with 1950s-style decor, wooden counter and shelves for sweets and bottled drinks; you can enjoy filling **meals** at *Sarah's Restaurant*, set above the bar. The Portsalon **golf course** (Ⓣ074/915 9459) has one of the most picturesque settings in the country.

Most of the eight-kilometre route north from Portsalon to **Fanad Head** is through humpy and barren land, with clusters of granite pushing through marshy ground. Before reaching the Head, there is one curiosity worth taking in, just a couple of kilometres north of Portsalon: the rock formation known as the **Seven Arches**, created by the constant erosive battering of the waters. To get there, follow the signpost on the right of the road, then take the path down to the new house, and finally cross the fields to the rocky strand. Alternatively, there's private access to the arches from nearby **Ballydaheen Gardens**, a gorgeous five-acre spread of flora, herbs and vegetables (mid-May to Aug Mon–Sat 10am–5pm; €5). From here the main road leads straight on to **Fanad Head**, where it reaches a dramatically placed cliff-edge **lighthouse** and its namesake **pub**, the *Lighthouse Tavern*.

Letterkenny

Whatever your means of transport, if you're travelling through northern Donegal, you're almost certain to pass through the county's boom town, **LETTERKENNY**, the largest place in Donegal; there's enough here to merit a stop, including a lively arts scene and thriving nightlife.

Arrival and information

The **bus station** is at the bottom of Port Road; both Bus Éireann and Lough Swilly operate services from here. North West Busways depart from *Charlie's Café* on Pearse Road. The **tourist office** (June–Aug Mon–Fri 9.15am–5pm, Sat 10am–2pm, Sun noon–3pm; Sept–May Mon–Fri 9.15am–5pm; ⓣ074/912 1160, ⓦwww.irelandnorthwest.ie) is on Neil T. Blaney Road, 800m out of town towards Derry. **Internet** access is available at Cyberworld, below the *4 Lanterns* café on Main Street.

Accommodation

Letterkenny's boom has been matched by a staggering increase in the numbers of **hotels** and **B&Bs**, although there are still relatively few in the town centre. Apart from the listings below, other accommodation can be found along or near the R245 Ramelton road.

Castle Grove Country House Ballymaleel ⓣ074/915 1118, ⓦwww.castlegrove.com. Three kilometres out on the Ramelton road, this elegant seventeenth-century house, overlooking Lough Swilly, offers splendidly furnished rooms and an excellent restaurant. ❺

Glencairn House Ramelton Rd ⓣ074/912 4393, ⓦwww.glencairnhousebb.com. A spacious B&B in a bungalow 2km from town, with pleasant gardens offering great views of the surrounding countryside. ❷

Gleneany Guesthouse Port Rd ⓣ074/912 6088, ⓦwww.gleneany.com. Pleasant, well-kept rooms characterize this comfortable, family-run guesthouse with its own popular restaurant. ❹

Letterkenny Court Hotel 29–45 Main St ⓣ074/912 2977, ⓦwww.letterkennycourthotel.com. This stylish town-centre hotel offers luxurious accommodation in its apartment-style suites and en-suite bedrooms. Doubles ❹, suites ❻.

Oaklands 8 Oaklands Park, Gortlee Rd ⓣ074/912 5529, ⓦwww.letterkennybandb.com. A comfortable, modern B&B in a quiet setting fifteen-minutes' walk northeast of the centre. ❷

Radisson SAS The Loop Road ⓣ074/919 4444, ⓦwww.radissonsas.com. A plush modern hotel, offering stylish, comfortable accommodation, including some family rooms, as well as bargain midweek breaks. ❹

Ramada Encore Lower Main St ⓣ074/912 3100, ⓦwww.encoreletterkenny.com. The latest addition to the town's accommodation scene, this new-build hotel has comfortable if somewhat functional rooms, but offers remarkably good deals for advance bookings, though breakfast is extra. ❹

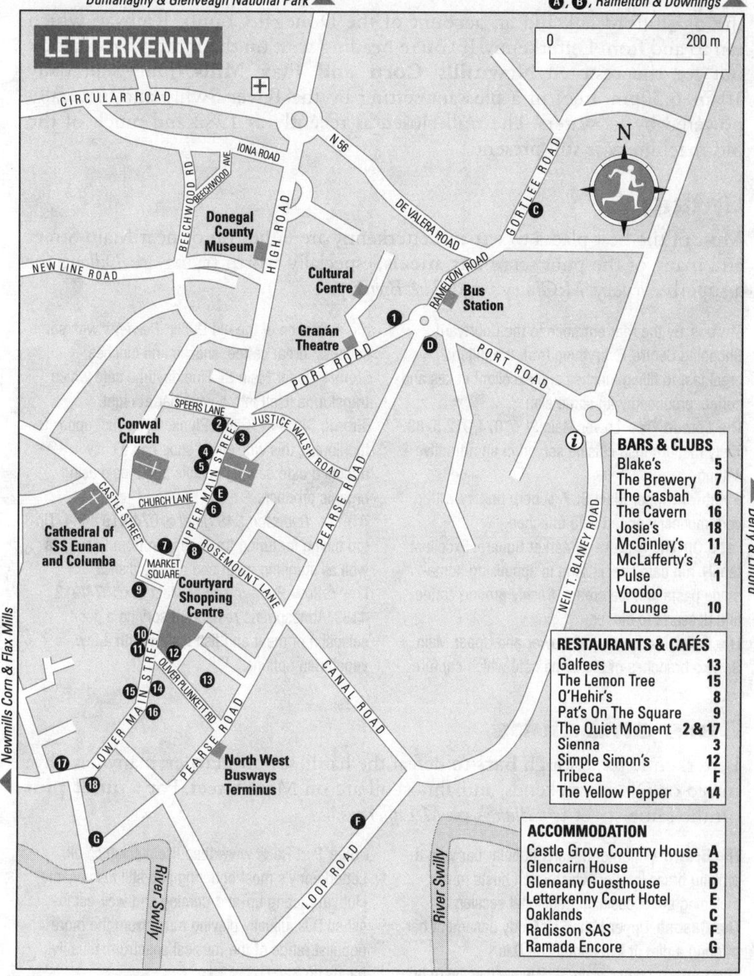

The Town

Letterkenny has undergone massive redevelopment in recent years with new shopping centres and a growing industrial sprawl beyond its boundaries. Although the town sits at the mouth of Lough Swilly, there's no water in sight, and the most notable visual element is the huge nineteenth-century **Cathedral of Saints Eunan and Columba** at the top of Church Street, with its intricate stone-roped ceiling, flying buttresses and Gaelicized Stations of the Cross. The only other place of interest in town is the **Donegal County Museum** (Mon–Fri 10am–12.30pm & 1–4.30pm, Sat 1–4.30pm; free), housed in part of the old Letterkenny workhouse on High Road. Temporary exhibitions occupy the downstairs area while upstairs is a typical display of artefacts from megalithic to more recent times, including the keys and lock of the old Lifford jail, and an account of the Donegal County Railway, which ran to and from Letterkenny. If you're heading west on the Fintown road, look out for the restored **Newmills Corn and Flax Mills** (June–Sept daily 10am–6.30pm; free) in a pleasant setting by the River Swilly and, naturally, powered by its waters. The mill closed as recently as 1982 and much of the old machinery is still present.

Eating

Most of the best places to **eat** in Letterkenny are either on or near Main Street and many of the pubs serve **bar meals**; especially worth trying are *Dillon's* for a superb carvery, *McGinley's* and *The Brewery*.

Galfees By the rear entrance to the Courtyard Shopping Centre. Everything from the full Irish breakfast to filling lunches and excellent cakes and coffee, produced with some élan.

The Lemon Tree Lower Main St ⓣ074/912 5788. Tasty modern Irish cuisine served in an attractive setting.

O'Hehir's Upper Main St. A superb bakery with a very modestly priced café attached.

Pat's On The Square 9 Market Square. Excellent family-run café specializing in appetizing home-made pasta and ice cream, freshly ground coffee and desserts to die for.

The Quiet Moment Both Lower and Upper Main St. Two branches of the same café which capture the ambience of the old Dublin *Bewley's* with some success; great coffee, snacks and lunches.

Sienna Upper Main St. Fine daytime café which transforms itself into a wine bar at night.

Simple Simon's Oliver Plunkett Rd. Just opposite the library, this wholefood shop has a cosy attached café serving snacks and meals using organic produce.

Tribeca *Radisson SAS Hotel* ⓣ074/919 4444. Tip-top dining featuring fresh salmon from Fanad, as well as stunning meat and poultry dishes.

The Yellow Pepper Lower Main St ⓣ074/912 4133. Atmospheric restaurant serving a good selection of meat and fish dishes with a few vegetarian options.

Bars and clubs

Letterkenny has enough **bars** to defeat the hardiest pub-crawler; many have live music or DJs at weekends, and almost all are on Main Street. For a **quiet pint** on the same street try *Blake's* or *McLafferty's*.

The Brewery Market Square. Popular bar with a striking brass interior, which often hosts music, including the occasional traditional session.

The Casbah Upper Main St. Moody basement bar offering a diet of live bands and DJs.

The Cavern Lower Main St ⓦwww.thecavern.ie. Bold and brash bar with regular live music and big screen sports on offer.

Josie's Lower Main St. A busy place offering floor-thumping rhythms at weekends.

McGinley's Lower Main St. A comfortable, woody, split-level bar popular with late-20 and 30-somethings.

Pulse Port Rd ⓦwww.thepulseniteclub.co.uk. Letterkenny's most enduring and still fashionable club, attracting up-and-coming and well-established DJs, usually playing tunes from the more populist range of the musical spectrum, plus live bands on Sat.

Voodoo Lounge Lower Main St ⓦwww.voodoolk.com. State-of-the-art multi-roomed new club-cum-live-venue with top-name DJs at weekends and live bands every night.

Theatre, arts and festivals

The local **theatre**, An Grianán (ⓦwww.angrianan.com), on Port Road, offers an impressive drama programme and has a reputation as one of Ireland's best **music** venues (from traditional to classical). Just behind it is the newly constructed regional **Cultural Centre** (ⓦwww.donegalculture.com), which mounts a variety of exhibitions and a regular programme of concerts, covering jazz to traditional music. On Pearse Road is the multi-screen Century **cinema** (Ⓦ www.centurycinemasletterkenny.com). Letterkenny also hosts the two-week **Earagail Arts Festival** in mid-July (Ⓦ www.earagailartsfestival.ie).

South of Letterkenny

The gently rolling countryside **south of Letterkenny** is probably the least visited of any populated area in the county, but includes a major Stone Age site near **Raphoe** and a couple of enticing lures at **Lifford**.

Raphoe and the Beltany stone circle

Thirteen kilometres southeast of Letterkenny, **RAPHOE** is set trimly around one of the largest diamonds in the county. Its erstwhile ecclesiastical importance is still indicated today by its inclusion in the Church of Ireland bishopric of Derry and Raphoe, though it was once a see in its own right. The town's **cathedral**, dedicated to St Eunan, was founded in the ninth century, but the present plain Gothic-cathedral version dates merely from 1702. Transfixed in the inner wall is a stone block with some peculiar, indecipherable carvings, and there's a very impressive and resonant, wooden baptismal chapel.

The major reason for visiting here, however, lies 3km to the south – the **Beltany stone circle**. To get there, follow the signs from the south of The Diamond in Raphoe and you'll arrive at the entrance to a farm. The circle is 400m up the bridle path to the right, over a stile and across a field full of sheep. This is one of the best-preserved circles in the country, consisting of approximately sixty stones, varying in height between 30cm and over a metre. It's easy

▲ The Beltany stone circle

to comprehend one of the reasons for its construction, as there's a marvellous panoramic view of the local valleys and the distant mountains.

Lifford

Six kilometres southeast of Raphoe, **LIFFORD** has a couple of sights for which it's worth dallying. This was formerly Donegal's legal centre and the County Council is still based here. The graceful **Old Courthouse**, dating from 1746, houses a **visitor centre** (Mon–Fri 10am–5pm, Sun 12.30–5pm; €6; Ⓦ www.liffordoldcourthouse.com), which tells the story of the O'Donnell clan and notable events in Donegal's history, as well as using tableaux of models and new technology to re-enact old trials, including that of Napper Tandy (see p.523). In the basement cells there's a pretty gruesome re-creation of the prison conditions and you can have your mugshot taken behind the bars for an additional €3. A few kilometres northwest of Lifford, off the N14, is **Cavanacor House** (Easter–Oct Tues–Sat noon–6pm; free; Ⓦ www.cavanacorgallery.ie), a fine seventeenth-century mansion where **James II** dined in 1689, and which was also the ancestral home of **James Knox Polk**, US president from 1845 to 1849. The real treat is its **art gallery**, displaying a changing array of work by contemporary Irish painters and sculptors.

The Inishowen Peninsula

The **Inishowen Peninsula** in the northeast of County Donegal is perhaps the great overlooked treasure of the Irish landscape (and certainly has the longest signposted scenic drive – the "Inishowen 100"), offering a diverse and visually exciting terrain, where the views usually encompass the waters of the loughs or the Atlantic waves. Virtually every aspect of the landscape is superb – the beaches (especially Kinnego Bay, Culdaff, Tullagh and Pollan), the towering headland bluffs (Malin, Inishowen, Dunaff and Dunree) and the central mountain range, with towering **Slieve Snaght** at the middle of it all.

The peninsula derives its name from **Eoghán**, who was made First Lord of the island by his father Niall, High King of Ireland. Phases of the peninsula's history before and after Eoghán have left a legacy of fine antiquities, from the **Grianán Ailigh** fort to a host of beautiful early **Christian crosses** (Cloncha, Mura, Carrowmore and Cooley).

Public **transport** services on the peninsula have diminished in recent years and, though you can reach places such as **Buncrana**, **Carndonagh** and **Moville** pretty easily, you'll need your own transport to explore **Malin Head**.

Burt Church and the Grianán Ailigh

The approach to the most stimulating of all Inishowen's sights, the ancient fort known as the Grianán Ailigh, passes the Liam McCormack–designed **Burt Church**, near Bridgend on the N13 Letterkenny–Derry road, the most beautiful twentieth-century church in all Ireland – like other McCormack designs in Donegal, its structure is evocative of the mystical landmark nearby. The seating is set concentrically, under a whitewashed ceiling that sweeps up into a vortex to allow sunlight to beam down directly upon the altar; the allusions in every detail to Neolithic sepulchral architecture (especially

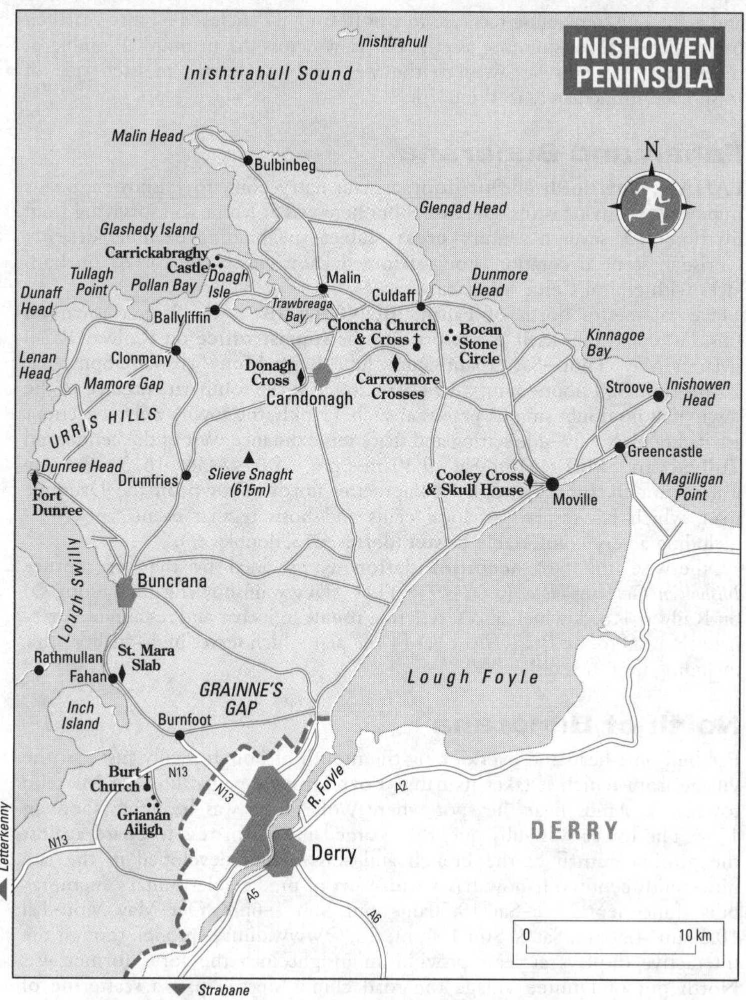

Newgrange – see p.178) are fascinating and very atmospheric. In a survey of architects the church was voted Ireland's building of the twentieth century.

The origins of the **Grianán Ailigh**, 3km up the hill from the church, date from 1700 BC, and it's thought to be linked to the Tuátha Dé Danann, pre-Celtic invaders. It was sufficiently significant to be included by Ptolemy, the Alexandrian geographer, in his second-century AD map of the world, and was the base of various northern Irish chieftains. Here, in 450, St Patrick is said to have baptized Eoghán, the founder of the O'Neill clan that ruled the kingdom of Ailigh for more than five hundred years. In the twelfth century, the fort was sacked by Murtagh O'Brian, King of Thomond, in retribution for a raid on Clare, and a large amount of its stone was carried away. Today's impressive building was largely reconstructed in the 1870s by Walter Bernard from Derry and is the only remaining terraced fort in Ireland. It's enclosed by three earthen banks, but its most stunning asset is the view across the primordial jumble of mountains and hills far away to the west and the loughs to each side of Inishowen immediately to the north.

Fahan and Buncrana

FAHAN, 6km north of **Burnfoot**, a main entry-point to Inishowen, boasts impressive monastic ruins. The first abbot here was St Mura, and surviving from his time is a seventh-century **cross slab**, a spellbinding example of early Christian stone decoration. Long-stemmed Latin crosses are carved on both faces with typical Celtic interlacing.

Five kilometres north of Fahan, **BUNCRANA** is the largest town on Inishowen and bills itself as a resort, and the **tourist office** on Railway Road (March–May Thurs–Sat 10am–5pm; June–Sept Mon–Fri 9am–5pm, Sat 10am–2pm, Sun noon–3pm; ⓣ074/936 2600), at the southern entrance to the town, will no doubt sing its praises as such. Frankly, the town's only attractions are its Lough Swilly–side setting and that's some distance west of the centre, and **Tullyarvan Mill** (Mon–Sat 9.30am–6pm; ⓣ074/936 1613, ⓦwww.tullyarvanmill.com), a couple of kilometres north of town off the Drumree road, which has displays of local crafts and hosts regular events as well as including a very comfortable **hostel** (dorms €15, doubles ❶).

Otherwise, the best **accommodation** is provided by the very spruce *Inishowen Gateway Hotel* (ⓣ074/936 1144, ⓦwww.inishowengateway.com; ❹) on Railway Road, which also serves fine **meals** in its bar and restaurant. Alternatively, head to the *Beach House* bar by the pier which serves high-quality grub, including fresh fish dishes.

North of Buncrana

Perched on a headland overlooking the mouth of Lough Swilly, just past the village from which it takes its name, **Fort Dunree** began life as a Martello tower and stands near the spot where Wolfe Tone was brought ashore in 1798. The tower was subsequently enlarged into a fortress to guard against the possible return of the French and was further developed in the late nineteenth century. It now has a **museum** of predictable military memorabilia (June–Sept Mon–Sat 10.30am–6pm, Sun 1–6pm; Oct–May Mon–Fri 10.30am–4.30pm, Sat & Sun 1–6pm; €5; ⓦwww.dunree.pro.ie), though the interactive displays at least provide an insight into the fort's former use. North out of Dunree village the road climbs steeply past a scattering of weather-beaten thatched cottages before crossing a small bridge close to the **Mamore Gap**, which seems like a chunk bitten out of the Urris Hills. From the top of the Gap the road spirals steeply downwards, each bend providing an ever wider and more spectacular view of the flat foreground to **Dunaff Head**. The 1.5-kilometre-long **Tullagh Strand** to the east of Dunaff Head is a safe bathing beach, with *Bayside Caravan Park*, which has space for **camping** just behind it (ⓣ074/937 6729; March–Oct). *The Rusty Nail* **pub**, by the roadside, has music at weekends and offers good-value bar food and Sunday lunch, and there's fine **accommodation** at *Four Arches* (ⓣ074/937 6561, ⓦwww.fourarches.btinternet.co.uk; ❷), a modern bungalow in a splendid setting near the Mamore Gap.

The route from here works its way inland between the mountains to **CLONMANY**, a neat village of predominantly cream-coloured terraced houses, quiet for most of the year but almost hyperactive during its week-long

festival at the beginning of August (Ⓦwww.clonmany.com) – *The Square Bar* has a **traditional-music** session on Sundays. A couple of kilometres onwards is the more upmarket **BALLYLIFFIN**, where the Glashedy **golf** course (Ⓣ074/937 6119) is reckoned to be one of the toughest in Ireland.

North of Ballyliffin is the entrancing **Pollan Strand**, at whose furthest tip stands the ruin of **Carrickabraghy Castle**, a sixteenth-century O'Doherty fortification. Much weathered by spray and sea salt, the castle's stones are streaked with colours ranging from the darkest hues to golden yellows. The strand itself has wonderfully wild breakers, which unfortunately make swimming dangerous. The castle sits on the western side of **DOAGH ISLE**, now linked to the mainland through centuries of silt accumulation, on whose eastern edge lies **Trawbreaga Bay**, an exquisite piece of coastline. The mouth of the bay is bewitching: strolling onto the beach here you'll discover rocks fashioned into extraordinary shapes and colours by the sea.

Carndonagh

Coming into **CARNDONAGH** from Ballyliffin, look out for the church on the corner against whose wall is the elegantly shaped and decorated seventh-century **Donagh Cross**, with two diminutive pillar stones on each side. The latter show figures with rather large heads, while the cross depicts evil little characters jumping out of its Celtic interlacing – all of which harks back to the druidic religion.

Carndonagh's buildings are stacked up the hillside, and most of the activity occurs around its central Diamond where you'll find the **Inishowen Tourist Office** (Mon–Fri 9.30am–5.30pm; June–Aug also Sat same times; Ⓣ074/937 4933, Ⓦwww.visitinishowen.com), whose friendly staff can supply you with information on the whole peninsula.

For **accommodation**, try *Ashdale Farmhouse* (Ⓣ074/937 4017, Ⓦwww.ashdalehouse.net; ❷), 500m north on the Malin road, or *An Caisléan* (Ⓣ074/937 4537, Ⓔancaislean@vodafone.ie; ❷), 1.5km south in Millbrae – both offer well-appointed en-suite rooms. **Food** options are limited. The best daytime option is *The Quiet Lady* pub, just down the Malin road, which serves astonishingly good-value lunches, while *The Arch Inn* on the Diamond offers coffee, soup and sandwiches. In the evening just about the only choice is *Simpson's*, a couple of hundred yards down the road to Culdaff. The *Persian Bar* on The Diamond has a traditional **session** on Wednesdays while both *The Arch Inn* and adjacent *Tully's* have singers or bands at weekends.

Culdaff

CULDAFF, 10km northeast of Carndonagh, is a cosy village whose nearby **beach** forms a stunning natural crescent. There's a major **sea-angling festival** here at the end of July and, in mid-October, a cultural weekend commemorates the eighteenth-century actor, **Charles Macklin** (Ⓦwww.charlesmacklin.com). However, for the rest of the year, it's *McGrory's* **bar** that's the centre of attention. It may be hard to credit, considering its isolated location, but the *Back Room* here is one of the best venues in Ireland for **live music**, and there are also traditional sessions in the bar on Tuesdays and Fridays. Equally excellent are its bar meals, featuring delights such as Donegal rock oysters, and its more upmarket **restaurant**. You can also **stay** very comfortably here (Ⓣ074/937 9104, Ⓦwww.mcgrorys.ie; ❹), as well as at *Village House*, Main Street (Ⓣ074/937 9972, Ⓔvillagehouseculdaff@eircom.net; ❷).

Malin and Malin Head

Five kilometres north of Carndonagh is the planter settlement of **MALIN**, tucked picturesquely into the side of Trawbreaga Bay, with a charming grassy Diamond at its centre. The village has a couple of **pubs**, and the recently modernized *Malin* **hotel** (Ⓣ074/937 0606, Ⓦwww.malinhotel.ie; ❹), which hosts a variety of entertainment and features a very good **restaurant**. A little way north of Malin, a signpost points to **Five Fingers Strand**, across the bay from Doagh Isle – it's worth the diversion to experience the ferocity of the breakers on the beach and the long walks on its sands, though the strand has undergone recent severe coastal erosion.

Sixteen kilometres north of Malin village, **Malin Head**, the northernmost extremity of Ireland, might not be as stupendous as other Donegal headlands but is nevertheless excellent for blustery, winding coastal walks – and for ornithologists: choughs, with their glossy black plumage, red legs and bill, inhabit the cliffs, and the rasping cry of the rare corncrake can be heard in the fields. The tip of the headland is marked by **Bamba's Crown**, a ruined Napoleonic signal tower, and the western path from here heads out to **Hell's Hole**, a 75-metre chasm in the cliffs, which roars with the onrushing tide.

There are two excellent **hostels** on the headland and both **rent out bikes**. The *Malin Head Hostel* (IHH; Ⓣ074/937 0309, Ⓦwww.malinheadhostel; dorms €13, ❶), on the way into Bulbinbeg, is well equipped and has private rooms, and the owner, who also offers reflexology and aromatherapy sessions, is a mine of information on the area. Alternatively, *Sandrock Holiday Hostel* (IHH; Ⓣ074/937 0289, Ⓦwww.sandrockhostel.com; dorms €12) at Port Ronan Pier – fork left at the *Crossroads Inn*, just north of the *Malin Head Hostel* – has wonderful sea views. Just about the only place to eat is the **restaurant** at *Seaview Tavern* (with a tiny public-bar-cum-hardware-shop); take the right fork heading north at the *Crossroads Inn* and then the first turning on the right. *Farren's* **bar** in Bulbinbeg is a cosy place to sit and chat to the locals.

Eastern Inishowen

Set on a gentle Foyle-side hillock, **MOVILLE**, 15km southeast of Culdaff, is an agreeable resort and was once a port of call for transatlantic liners, though there's little activity in today's compact harbour. The village rarely stirs itself to offer anything more than the odd tingle of excitement. For **B&B** try welcoming *Dunroman* (Ⓣ074/938 2234; ❷), offering en-suite rooms, just north of the town, or *Admiralty House* (Ⓣ074/938 2529, Ⓔsuzannemcfeely@eircom.net; May–Sept; ❷), overlooking the bay a little further north. *Barron's* café, Lower Main Street, offers economical daytime **meals**, while *Rosatos*, Malin Road, is the best place for an evening meal. There's set-dancing at *Rawdon's Bar*, Malin Road, on Tuesdays, while the *Hair of the Dog* **pub** by the pier has live music at weekends.

The most notable historical remains in the district are the **Cooley Cross** and **Skull House**, approached by taking the left turn just before the petrol station on the way into Moville. Follow the turn-off up the steep hill for just over a kilometre, always bearing right, and you'll discover an ancient Celtic wheel-cross guarding the entrance to a walled graveyard. There are very few examples of this kind of cross with the pierced ringhole in its head – the hole was once a pagan device used to clinch serious treaties, the hands of the opposing parties being joined in amity through it. The Skull House in the graveyard is in the form of the beehive huts of early monks and it was once possibly an oratory before becoming an ossuary. Any bones that were stored here have long since vanished.

The harbour village of **GREENCASTLE**, 4km north of Moville, has a pleasant view across to Magilligan Strand on the opposite side of Lough Foyle and there's a regular **ferry** service from here to Magilligan Point (April–Sept Mon–Sat 7.20am–9.50pm, Sun 9am–9.50pm; Oct–March service ends two hours earlier; ⓣ074/938 1901, ⓦwww.loughfoyleferry.com; pedestrians €4.50 single, €7 return, cars €15 single, €22.50 return). By the harbour, in the old coastguard station, is the **Maritime Museum and Planetarium** (Easter–Sept Mon–Sat 10am–6pm, Sun noon–6pm; Oct–Easter Mon–Fri 10am–5pm; museum €5, museum, planetarium and laser shows €10; ⓦwww.inishowenmaritime.com), which recalls maritime travel from bygone times through a range of Irish boats from to two to twenty metres in length. Among the maritime memorabilia, pride of place goes to a nineteenth-century rocket cart used to fire flares to aid survivors of wrecked ships. The state-of-the-art planetarium takes you on exhilarating trips through the universe, while regular laser light shows feature a traditional-music soundtrack; there are also custom shows (min. ten people) where you can choose your own musical backing.

By the road to Stroove (see below) are ruins of a fourteenth-century Anglo-Norman **castle**, built on a rocky knoll to guard the narrowest part of the lough. It was briefly captured in 1316 by Edward Bruce of Scotland who crowned himself King of Ireland, but was retaken shortly after. Later the castle fell into the hands of the O'Dohertys, but it was badly damaged by an attack by their rival Calvagh O'Donnell. Though there were subsequent attempts at renovation, by 1700 the castle was a complete ruin and has remained so ever since. Greencastle is a great place for seafood and the place to aim for is *Kealy's* **restaurant** (ⓣ074/938 1010; closed Mon), reckoned to be one of the best in Donegal (around €35 per head plus wine).

At **STROOVE** (pronounced "shroove"), the scenery becomes more exciting, with lovely clambering walks along its coastline to the lighthouse. There you'll have to return to the road to reach the small beach, from where doughtier walkers can resume the clamber as far as the cliffs of the awesome **Inishowen Head**. An easier way to the head is simply to follow the road until it turns left, at which point you carry on straight on up the hill; a car can make it the first few kilometres, though after that you risk getting stuck in a rut. From the head, it's a beautiful but tiring walk to isolated **Kinnagoe Bay**, one of the most secluded sandy beaches around, tucked between the rocky walls of headland against which the waves throw a delicate lacy spray. The alternative route here entails going back to the main road and following it to the right turn by the thatched cottage in Stroove – this will take you along the narrowest of roads over the headland and through two beautiful glens. A plaque by the roadside at Kinnagoe Bay records the sinking of *La Trinidad Valencera* from the Spanish Armada and other ships around the coast. Forty of its crew died in the water, and most of the remaining three hundred survivors were killed outside Derry by an English army. Salvaged treasures from *La Trinidad Valencera* are on view in Derry's Tower Museum (see p.608). Back in Stroove, the *Drunken Duck Seafood Bar* (ⓣ074/938 1362) is well worth a visit for its good **food** and fantastic views.

Travel details

Donegal has a plethora of **bus** services, divided here between public and private companies. Apart from express services, few companies operate on Sundays and many services are much reduced in winter.

Public bus companies

Bus Éireann

Ⓣ074/912 1309, Ⓦwww.buseireann.ie.

Note that services from Donegal town to Killybegs, Kilcar, Carrick and Glencolmcille are much reduced outside high season (late June to late Aug).

Ardara to: Donegal town (Mon–Thurs & Sat 2–3 daily, Fri 4, Sun 1; 35min–1hr 15min); Dungloe (Mon–Sat 1 daily; 40min); Glenties (Mon–Fri 4–6 daily, Sat 2; 10–20min); Killybegs (Mon–Thurs & Sat 1–2 daily, Fri 3; 20min).

Ballyshannon to: Belleek (4–6 daily; 20min); Bundoran (Mon–Sat 9–10 daily, Sun 5; 10min); Donegal town (Mon–Sat 12–14 daily, Sun 9; 20min); Lough Derg (June to mid-Aug Mon–Sat 1 daily; 40min); Sligo (Mon–Sat 8–9 daily, Sun 5; 45min–1hr).

Bundoran to: Ballyshannon (Mon–Sat 9–10 daily, 3 Sun; 10min); Sligo (Mon–Sat 8–9 daily, Sun 5; 35–50min).

Carrick to: Donegal town (2–3 daily; 1hr–1hr 15min); Glencolmcille (2–3 daily; 15min); Kilcar (2–3 daily; 10min); Killybegs (2–3 daily; 30min).

Donegal town to: Ardara (Mon–Sat 3 daily; 25min–1hr 10min); Ballyshannon (9–11 daily; 20–30min); Bundoran (5–6 daily; 30min); Carrick (2–3 daily; 1hr–1hr 15min); Derry (Mon–Sat 7 daily, Sun 3; 1hr 25min); Dublin (6 daily; 3hr 10min–3hr 45min); Dungloe (Mon–Sat 2 daily; 1hr–1hr 30min); Enniskillen (5 daily; 1hr 10min); Galway (3–4 daily; 3hr 45min); Glencolmcille (2–3 daily; 1hr 15min–1hr 30min); Glenties (Mon–Sat 3 daily; 35min–1hr 20min); Kilcar (2–3 daily (50min–1hr 5min); Killybegs (Mon–Sat 6–8 daily, Sun 2; 30–45min); Letterkenny (Mon–Sat 7 daily, Sun 3; 50min); Sligo (Mon–Sat 5 daily, Sun 3; 1hr 5min).

Dungloe to: Ardara (2 daily; 40min); Donegal town (2 daily; 1hr 15min–1hr 30min); Glenties (2 daily; 30min).

Glencolmcille to: Carrick (2–3 daily; 15min); Donegal town (2–3 daily; 1hr 15min–1hr 30min); Kilcar (2–3 daily; 25min); Killybegs (2–3 daily; 45min).

Glenties to: Ardara (2–3 daily; 10–20min); Donegal town (2–3 daily; 45min–1hr 30min); Dungloe (Mon–Sat 1 daily; 30min).

Kilcar to: Carrick (2–3 daily; 10min); Donegal town (2–3 daily; 50min–1hr 5min); Glencolmcille (2–3 daily; 25min); Killybegs (2–3 daily; 20min).

Killybegs to: Ardara (Mon–Thurs 3 daily, Fri 5, Sat 1; 20min); Carrick (2–3 daily; 30min); Donegal town (Mon–Sat 5–6 daily, Sun 1; 30–45min); Glencolmcille (2–3 daily; 45min); Glenties (Mon–Fri 1 daily; 50min); Kilcar (2–3 daily; 20min).

Letterkenny to: Derry (Mon–Sat 8 daily, Sun 3; 35min); Donegal town (Mon–Sat 7 daily, Sun 5; 50min); Dublin (9–10 daily; 4hr); Dublin Airport (9 daily; 3hr 35min); Lifford (Mon–Sat 16–17 daily; Sun 10; 25–45min); Monaghan (9–10 daily; 1hr 45min); Omagh (9–10 daily; 1hr); Raphoe (Mon–Sat 7 daily; 30min); Sligo (5 daily; 2hr).

Lifford to: Letterkenny (Mon–Sat 14–15 daily, Sun 11; 25–45min); Raphoe (Mon–Sat 5 daily; 15min).

Lough Derg to: Ballyshannon (June to mid-Aug Mon–Sat 1 daily; 40min).

Pettigo to: Enniskillen (Mon–Sat 1 daily; 40min).

Raphoe to: Letterkenny (Mon–Sat 5 daily; 30min); Lifford (Mon–Sat 5 daily; 15min).

Ulsterbus

Ⓣ028/9066 6630, Ⓦwww.translink.co.uk.

Ballyshannon to: Belleek (Mon–Sat 1–2 daily; 10–15min); Bundoran (Mon–Sat 1 daily; 10min); Pettigo (Mon–Sat 1–2 daily; 30–45min).

Bundoran to: Ballyshannon (Mon–Sat 1–2 daily; Belleek (Mon–Sat 1–2 daily; 20–25min); 10min); Pettigo (Mon–Sat 1–2 daily; 40–55min).

Pettigo to: Ballyshannon (Mon–Sat 1 daily; 30min); Belleek (Mon–Sat 1 daily; 20min); Bundoran (Mon–Sat 1 daily; 40min); Enniskillen (Mon–Sat 5–6 daily; 50min–1hr 5min).

Private bus companies

Patrick Gallagher (Churchill)

Ⓣ074/913 7037, Ⓦwww.patrickgallagher.net.

Downings to: Letterkenny via Ramelton (Mon–Fri 1 daily; 1hr).

Letterkenny to: Downings via Ramelton (Mon–Fri 1 daily; 1hr).

Patrick Gallagher (Gweedore)

Ⓣ074/953 1107, Ⓦwww.gallagherscoaches.com.

Crolly to: Belfast (1 daily; 3hr 50min) via Derry (2hr 20min) and Letterkenny (1hr 50min).

Lough Swilly

Derry ⓣ028/7126 2017; Letterkenny ⓣ074/912 2863.

A service operates from **Letterkenny** (Mon–Fri 4.15pm) to Dungloe (1hr 55min) and Burtonport (2hr 5min) via Kilmacrennan, Creeslough, Dunfanaghy, Falcarragh, Gortahork, Bunbeg and Crolly. There's also a bus from **Falcarragh** (Mon–Fri noon) to Dungloe (1hr 10min) via Gortahork, Bunbeg, Crolly, Annagry, Kincasslagh and Burtonport. The return service from **Dungloe** (Mon–Fri 9am) to Letterkenny consists of two buses, one taking the coastal route via Burtonport, Kincasslagh and Annagry and the other the more direct route via Crolly; they hook up at Falcarragh ready for a 10.35am departure to Letterkenny. A further service leaves Dungloe for Falcarragh (1hr 30min) Mon–Thurs at 4.05pm, taking in all the intervening places mentioned above en route.

Buncrana to: Ballyliffin (Mon–Fri 2 daily, Sat 1; 30min); Carndonagh (Mon–Fri 2 daily, Sat 1; 45min); Clonmany (Mon–Fri 2 daily, Sat 1; 25min); Derry (Mon–Sat 9–10 daily, Sun 3; 35min).

Carndonagh to: Ballyliffin (Mon–Fri 2 daily, Sat 1; 15min); Buncrana (Mon–Fri 2 daily, Sat 1; 45min); Clonmany (Mon–Fri 2 daily, Sat 1); Derry (Mon–Sat 2–3 daily; 50min).

Greencastle to: Derry (Mon–Fri 2 daily, Sat 3; 1hr); Moville (Mon–Fri 2 daily, Sat 3; 10min).

Kilmacrennan to: Letterkenny (Mon–Fri 4 daily, Sat 2; 20min).

Letterkenny to: Creeslough (Mon–Sat 2 daily; 35min); Derry (Mon–Fri 9 daily, Sat 5; 30–40min); Kilmacrennan (Mon–Sat 2 daily; 20min); Ramelton (Mon–Fri 3 daily, Sat 2; 20min); Rathmullan (Mon–Fri 1 daily, Sat 2; 30min).

Moville to: Derry (Mon–Fri 2 daily, Sat 3; 50min); Greencastle (Mon–Fri 2 daily, Sat 3; 10min).

Ramelton to: Letterkenny (Mon–Fri 2 daily, Sat 3; 20min).

Rathmullan to: Letterkenny (Mon–Fri 1 daily; 35min).

John McGinley

ⓣ074/913 5201, ⓦwww.johnmcginley.com.

Crolly to: Dublin (3–4 daily; 5hr 25min) via Bunbeg, Dunfanaghy and Letterkenny.

Moville to: Dublin (Mon–Sat 2 daily, Sun 1; 5hr 15min) via Carndonagh, Buncrana and Derry.

North West Busways

ⓣ074/938 2619, ⓦwww.foylecoaches.com.

Buncrana to: Carndonagh (Mon–Sat 2–4 daily; 35min); Letterkenny (Mon–Sat 2–4 daily; 45min); Moville (Mon–Sat 2–3 daily; 1hr).

Carndonagh to: Buncrana (Mon–Sat 2–3 daily; 35min); Culdaff (Mon–Sat 2 daily; 15min); Derry (Mon–Sat 3–4 daily; 45min); Malin (Mon–Sat 1 daily; 10min); Moville (Mon–Sat 2–3 daily; 20–30min).

Culdaff to: Buncrana (Mon–Fri 2 daily, Sat 1; 40–55min); Carndonagh (Mon–Fri 2 daily, Sat 1; 10–15min); Derry (Mon–Sat 2 daily; 1hr–1hr 15min); Letterkenny (Mon–Sat 1–2 daily; 1hr 40min); Malin (Mon–Sat 2 daily; 10min).

Greencastle to: Derry (Mon–Sat 3 daily; 1hr 10min); Moville (Mon–Sat 3 daily; 25min).

Letterkenny to: Buncrana (Mon–Sat 2–4 daily; 45min); Carndonagh (Mon–Sat 2–4 daily; 1hr 20min); Culdaff (Mon–Sat 1 daily; 1hr 40min); Malin (Mon–Sat 1 daily; 1hr 30min); Moville (Mon–Sat 3–4 daily; 55min–1hr 45min).

Malin to: Carndonagh (Mon–Sat 2 daily; 10min); Culdaff (Mon–Sat 1 daily; 10min); Derry (Mon–Sat 2 daily; 1hr 10min).

Moville to: Ballyliffin (Mon–Fri 3 daily, Sat 2; 25–45 min); Buncrana (Mon–Fri 3 daily, Sat 2; 50min–1hr 15min); Carndonagh (Mon–Fri 3 daily, Sat 2; 20–35min); Clonmany (Mon–Fri 3 daily, Sat 2; 30–50min); Culdaff (Mon–Fri 2 daily, Sat 1; 10–20min); Derry (Mon–Sat 4 daily; 45min); Greencastle (Mon–Sat 4 daily; 10–20min); Letterkenny (Mon–Fri 3 daily, Sat 2; 1hr 35min–2hr); Malin (1–2 daily; 25min); Stroove (Mon–Sat 3 daily; 15–25min).

Feda Ó Donnell

ⓣ074/954 8114, ⓦwww.fedaodonnell.com.

Crolly to: Galway (Mon–Thurs & Sat 2 daily, Fri & Sun 3 daily; 5hr 50min) via Dunfanaghy, Letterkenny (1hr 30min), Donegal town (2hr 20min) and Sligo (3hr 30min).

Belfast

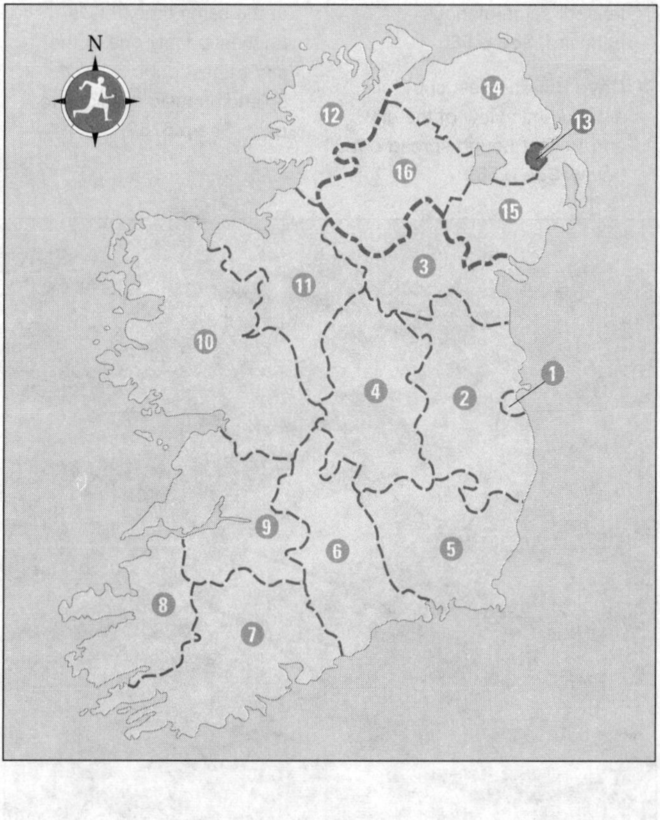

CHAPTER 13

Highlights

* **The Laganside** Nowhere has the city seen more recent change than in its harbour and docklands, revitalized by developments such as the Odyssey Arena and the Waterfront Hall. See p.562

* **Stormont** The seat of government in Northern Ireland, set in glorious parkland. See p.568

* **Cave Hill** The best spot for a panoramic view of the city and Belfast Lough spread out below. See p.569

* **West Belfast** An essential part of any visit to the city: the murals, Peace Line, cemeteries and fortified bars put everyday life into stark political context. See p.569

* **The John Hewitt** Both modern and traditional at the same time, this is unquestionably one of the city's finest pubs, with splendid music sessions to boot. See p.575

▲ The Laganside

13

Belfast

The North's largest city by some distance, **BELFAST** has a pace and bustle you'll find almost nowhere else in the six counties that make up Northern Ireland. For many, however, Belfast will always be remembered as the focus of the **Troubles** that dominated Northern Ireland's politics for almost three decades from the late 1960s and scarred so many personal lives. Indeed, as the North still continues to come to terms with the aftermath of the peace process, instigated by the 1998 Good Friday Agreement, the city remains in some ways on a knife's edge, always expecting some new predicament to emerge.

In appearance Belfast closely resembles Liverpool, Glasgow or any other industrial port across the water, and, similarly, its largely defunct **docklands** – in which, famously, the *Titanic* was built – are undergoing massive redevelopment. Though the city centre is still characterized by numerous elegant **Victorian** buildings, there's been an enormous transformation here, too, not least in the greater prosperity of the shopping streets leading northwards from the hub of Belfast life, **Donegall Square**. Yet economic improvement is not reflected in every aspect of Belfast life. Some areas of the city display obvious economic decline, most notably North Belfast and the once-thriving so-called **Golden Mile** (now little more than a silver two hundred yards at each end). On weeknights the city centre can resemble a ghost town, though there's no doubt that Belfast continues to thrive culturally. Theatre and the visual arts are flourishing, and there are plenty of places to catch the city's booming traditional- music scene.

Belfast is a place for getting out and about, and has plenty of attractions to experience. A couple of days are enough to get a feel for the city, although it is a good base from which to visit virtually anywhere else in the North. In the city centre, concentrate on the glories resulting from the Industrial Revolution – grandiose **architecture** and magnificent Victorian **pubs** – and the rejuvenated area from Ann Street to Donegall Street now known as the **Cathedral quarter**. To the south lies **Queen's University** and the extensive collections of the **Ulster Museum**, set in the grounds of the **Botanic Gardens**. A climb up **Cave Hill**, a couple of miles to the north, rewards you with marvellous views of the city spread out around the curve of its natural harbour, **Belfast Lough**. The city's once-formidable security presence and fortifications are now virtually invisible, but the iron blockade known as the **Peace Line** still bisects the Catholic and Protestant communities of **West Belfast**, a grim physical reminder of the city's and country's sectarian divisions – and there are certain **flashpoints** such as the Short Strand in East Belfast and North Belfast's Ardoyne area that it is still inadvisable to visit.

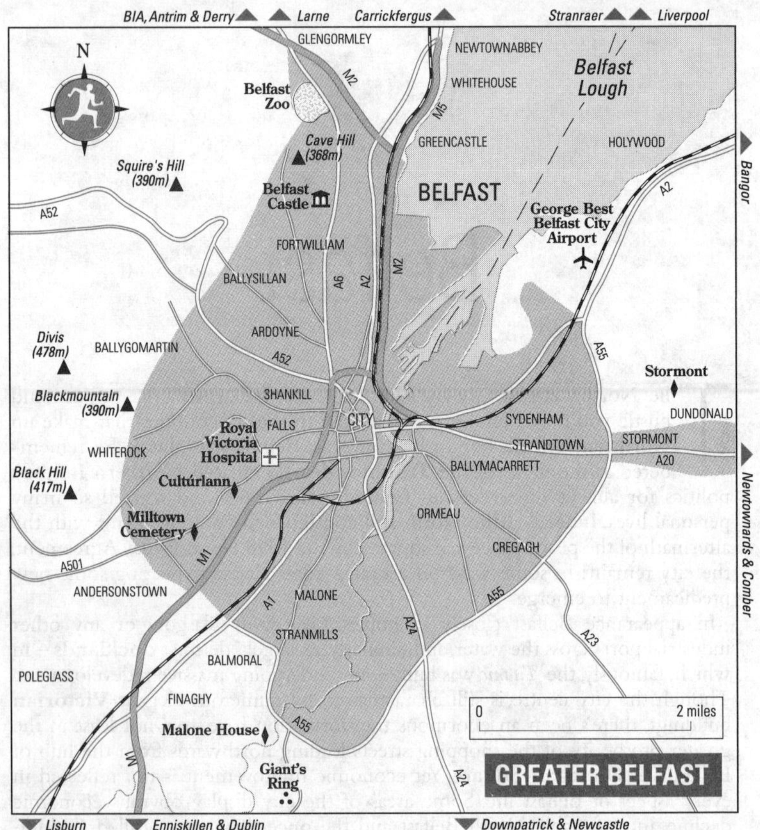

Some history

Belfast began life as a cluster of forts built to guard a ford across the **River Farset**, which nowadays runs underground beneath the High Street. An **Anglo-Norman castle** was built here in 1177, but its influence was limited, and within a hundred years or so control over the Lagan Valley had reverted firmly to the Irish, under the O'Neills of Clandeboye. In 1604, **Sir Arthur Chichester**, whose son was to be the First Earl of Donegall, was "planted" in the area by James I, and shortly afterwards the tiny settlement was granted a charter creating a corporate borough. It was not until the end of the seventeenth century though that Belfast began to grow significantly, when French Huguenots fleeing persecution brought skills which rapidly improved the fortunes of the local **linen industry** – which, in turn, attracted new workers and wealth. Through the eighteenth century the cloth trade and **shipbuilding** expanded tremendously, and the population increased tenfold in a hundred years. With economic prosperity, Belfast became a city noted for its **liberalism**: in 1791, three Presbyterian Ulstermen formed the **Society of United Irishmen**, a gathering embracing Catholics and Protestants on the basis of common Irish nationality, from which sprang the **1798 Rebellion**.

However, the rebellion in the North was quickly and ruthlessly stamped out by the English, and within two generations most Protestants had abandoned the

Nationalist cause. Presbyterian ministers began openly to attack the Catholic Church, resulting in a **sectarian divide** that as time drew on became wider and increasingly violent. At the same time, the nineteenth century saw vigorous commercial and industrial expansion, and by the time Queen Victoria granted Belfast **city** status in 1888, its population had risen to 208,000, soon exceeding that of Dublin.

With **Partition** came the creation of Northern Ireland with Belfast as its capital and Stormont as its seat of government. Inevitably this boosted the city's status, but also ensured that it would ultimately become the focus for much of the Troubles. Though its fortunes now reflected the status of the British economy, Belfast mainly fared well, despite major German bombing raids during World War II. However, the economic status of the Catholic population was deliberately maintained at a low level by the Stormont government, largely consisting of Protestant landowners and businessmen, which saw no reason to challenge existing sectarian employment, housing and policing policies – all fuel to the fire which was to follow.

For 25 years from 1969, Belfast witnessed the worst of the **Troubles** (see box on p.569) and, by the time the IRA declared a **ceasefire** in 1994, much of the city resembled a battle site. Then followed a sea change in the city's fortunes as Britain and the EU funded a **revitalization** programme costing billions of pounds. Major shopping centres were built, swish hotels, bars and restaurants seemed to spring up almost overnight, and buildings such as the Waterfront Hall and Odyssey complex have fundamentally altered the city's skyline. Young Belfast partied like never before – and to some extent still does – while the atmosphere of the whole city centre has changed irrevocably.

Nevertheless, Belfast continues to hit the headlines in a variety of ways, not all positive. In December 2004, the Northern Bank in Donegall Square suffered the biggest bank robbery in Irish history, to the tune of £26 million, allegedly committed by the IRA. And further news coverage has derived from feuding both within or between rival Loyalist paramilitary groups, their attacks on Belfast's ethnic minorities, and incidents such as the murder of Robert McCartney, a Catholic, outside a pub in the Markets area, purportedly committed by members of the IRA. Belfast remains a city divided, reflecting the political gulf between the DUP and Sinn Féin. Furthermore, all evidence suggests that sectarian attitudes are hardening, especially among young people.

Arrival, information and transport

Belfast's two airports are well connected to the city centre by public transport, though only taxis serve the ferry terminals. The city has an efficient bus network, which provides comprehensive coverage of all the outlying attractions, while a wealth of local information is available at the city's very helpful Welcome Centre.

Arrival

Belfast is served by two **airports**. Most flights arrive at **Belfast International Airport** (Ⓣ028/9448 4848, Ⓦwww.belfastairport.com), nineteen miles west of the city in Aldergrove; from here, there are airport buses to Europa Buscentre operating 24 hours (Mon–Fri every 10min–1hr, Sat every 20min–1hr, Sun every 30min–1hr; £6 single, £9 return). A taxi to the centre costs around £25.

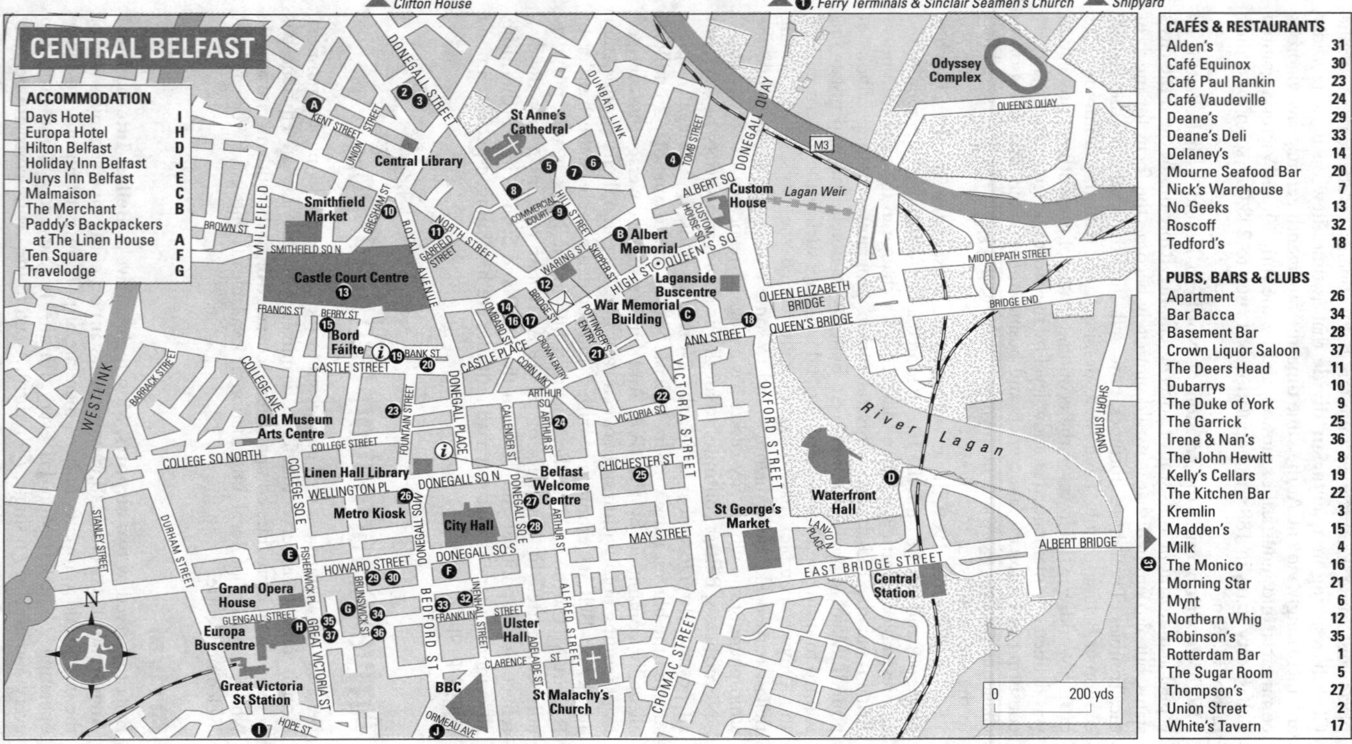
CENTRAL BELFAST
Clifton House
1, Ferry Terminals & Sinclair Seamen's Church
Shipyard
ACCOMMODATION
Days Hotel I
Europa Hotel H
Hilton Belfast D
Holiday Inn Belfast J
Jurys Inn Belfast E
Malmaison C
The Merchant B
Paddy's Backpackers at The Linen House A
Ten Square F
Travelodge G
CAFÉS & RESTAURANTS
Alden's 31
Café Equinox 30
Café Paul Rankin 23
Café Vaudeville 24
Deane's 29
Deane's Deli 33
Delaney's 14
Mourne Seafood Bar 20
Nick's Warehouse 7
No Geeks 13
Roscoff 32
Tedford's 18
PUBS, BARS & CLUBS
Apartment 26
Bar Bacca 34
Basement Bar 28
Crown Liquor Saloon 37
The Deers Head 11
Dubarrys 10
The Duke of York 9
The Garrick 25
Irene & Nan's 36
The John Hewitt 8
Kelly's Cellars 19
The Kitchen Bar 22
Kremlin 3
Madden's 15
Milk 4
The Monico 16
Morning Star 21
Mynt 6
Northern Whig 12
Robinson's 35
Rotterdam Bar 1
The Sugar Room 5
Thompson's 27
Union Street 2
White's Tavern 17
Odyssey Complex
St Anne's Cathedral
Central Library
Smithfield Market
Castle Court Centre
Bord Fáilte
Custom House
Lagan Weir
Albert Memorial
Laganside Buscentre
War Memorial Building
Old Museum Arts Centre
Linen Hall Library
Metro Kiosk
City Hall
Belfast Welcome Centre
St George's Market
Waterfront Hall
Central Station
Grand Opera House
Europa Buscentre
Great Victoria St Station
BBC
Ulster Hall
St Malachy's Church
River Lagan
DONEGALL STREET
KENT STREET
UNION STREET
DUNBAR LINK
TOMB STREET
DONEGALL QUAY
QUEEN'S QUAY
M3
MILLFIELD
BROWN ST
SMITHFIELD SQ N
GRESHAM ST
ROYAL AVENUE
NORTH STREET
GARFIELD STREET
COMMERCIAL COURT
HILL STREET
WARING ST
SKIPPER ST
HIGH ST
QUEEN'S SQ
ALBERT SQ
CUSTOM HOUSE SQ
MIDDLEPATH STREET
QUEEN ELIZABETH BRIDGE
BRIDGE END
QUEEN'S BRIDGE
ANN STREET
FRANCIS ST
BERRY ST
BANK ST
CASTLE STREET
CASTLE PLACE
LOMBARD ST
BRIDGE ST
POTTINGER'S ENTRY
CROWN ENTRY
CORN MKT
ARTHUR SQ
ARTHUR ST
VICTORIA SQ
VICTORIA STREET
OXFORD STREET
SHORT STRAND
WESTLINK
BARRACK STREET
COLLEGE AVE
FOUNTAIN STREET
DONEGALL PLACE
CALLENDER ST
COLLEGE STREET
COLLEGE SQ NORTH
COLLEGE SQ E
WELLINGTON PL
DONEGALL SQ N
DONEGALL SQ W
DONEGALL SQ E
DONEGALL SQ S
CHICHESTER ST
MAY STREET
LANYON PLACE
ALBERT BRIDGE
EAST BRIDGE STREET
STANLEY STREET
DURHAM STREET
FISHERWICK PL
HOWARD STREET
BRUNSWICK ST
BEDFORD ST
FRANKLIN STREET
LINENHALL STREET
ALFRED STREET
GLENGALL STREET
GREAT VICTORIA ST
CLARENCE ST
ADELAIDE ST
CROMAC STREET
HOPE ST
ORMEAU AVE
N
0
200 yds

The airport's arrivals hall has an ATM, a bureau de change, car rental outlets and a tourist information desk (Mon–Sat 7.30am–7pm, Sun 8am–5pm). Many domestic flights from Britain use the smaller George Best **Belfast City Airport** (Ⓣ028/9093 9093, Ⓦwww.belfastcityairport.com), named after the city's greatest footballer (see p.567) and three miles northeast of the centre, from which bus Metro #600 runs to the Europa Buscentre (Mon–Sat every 20–30min 6am–10pm, Sun every 40min 7.30am–9.25pm; £1.30 single, £2.20 return). Alternatively, you can take the free shuttle bus to Sydenham train station and hop on a train to Belfast Central or Great Victoria Street stations (Mon–Fri every 20–30min 6.20am–11.20pm, Sat every 30min 6.20am-10.50pm, Sun hourly 9.20am–10.20pm; £1.30). A taxi from City Airport to the centre costs around £6. The terminal's ground floor houses ATMs, a bureau de change, car rental outlets and a tourist information desk (Mon–Sat 8am–7pm, Sun 10am–5pm).

Ferries from Britain arrive at various dockside terminuses. Stena high-speed ferries from Stranraer dock at the terminal on **Corry Road** some twenty minutes' walk from the central Donegall Square – a taxi from here will cost around £6. Norfolkline ferries from Liverpool dock further north on **West Bank Road**; expect to pay a taxi fare from here of at least £7. P&O ferries from Cairnryan, Fleetwood and Troon dock at the town of **Larne**, twenty miles north (see p.586), which is connected by Ulsterbus to the Europa Buscentre and by train to Great Victoria Street and Central stations.

The majority of **trains** call at **Great Victoria Street Station** in the centre, with the exception of trains from Dublin and some from Larne, which terminate at **Central Station** near the Waterfront Hall on East Bridge Street, a little way east of the centre. Various Metro buses stop outside the Central Station en route to Donegall Square – travel is free to holders of railway tickets. From Central Station you can also hop on a connecting train for the ten-minute journey to Great Victoria Street Station, which stops en route at Botanic and City Hospital stations – both of which are useful if you're staying in the university quarter.

Express **buses** arrive at one of Belfast's two stations. The **Europa Buscentre**, accessed via the Great Northern shopping mall on Great Victoria Street, handles services to the Republic and airports as well as all parts of Northern Ireland except North Down and the Ards Peninsula which utilize the **Laganside Buscentre** in Queen's Square near the Albert Clock, though on Sundays even these use the Europa.

Aircoach services from Dublin Airport arrive outside *Jurys Inn*, Great Victoria Street.

Information

The **Belfast Welcome Centre** at 47 Donegall Place, just north of Donegall Square (Mon–Sat 9am–5.30pm extended June–Sept to 7pm, Sun 11am–4pm; Ⓣ028/9024 6609, Ⓦwww.gotobelfast.com), stocks a vast range of information on the city and the rest of the North, provides an accommodation booking service (£2) and sells tickets for events. It also has an Internet café and the only left-luggage facilities in the city (£3 per item for up to 4 hours, £4.50 per item for longer; all items must be collected at least 15min before closing). **Bord Fáilte**, which supplies tourist information for the Republic, is located at 53 Castle St (Mon–Fri 9am–5pm, Sat 9am–12.30pm; Ⓣ028/9032 7888). The **West Belfast Tourist Information Point** (Mon–Fri 9.30am–5.30pm; Ⓣ028/9096 4188) is in the Cultúrlann McAdam Ó Fiaich centre, 216 Falls Rd, and provides details of local attractions and events.

Guided tours

One of the best ways of seeing the city's attractions or getting to grips with its political history is to take a tour. Locally operated tours are not only hugely informative, but invariably rich in colourful anecdotes.

City Sightseeing runs a hop-on and hop-off **open-top bus tour** of the Belfast sights (March–Oct Mon–Fri every 30min–1hr 10am–4.30pm, Sat & Sun every 20–30min 10am–4.30pm; Nov–Feb Mon–Fri 10am–4pm every 45min–1hr, Sat & Sun 10am–4pm every 30–45min; ⓣ028/9028 6888, ⓦwww.city-sightseeing.com; £11), running from Castle Place and taking in the Laganside, West Belfast and the university quarter. There are eighteen stops around the city and the full tour lasts ninety minutes.

West Belfast is one of the features of several guided **taxi tours**, including Belfast Black Taxi Tours (ⓣ077 6293 6704), Black Cab Tours NI (ⓣ077 9860 2401, ⓦwww.blackcabtoursni.com), Black Taxi Tours (ⓣ0800 052 3914, ⓦwww.belfasttours.com), Harpers Taxi Tours (ⓣ028/9074 2711, ⓦwww.harperstaxitours.co.nr), Original Black Taxi Tours (ⓣ077 5156 5359) and West Belfast Taxi Tours (ⓣ028/9031 5777, ⓦwww.taxitrax.com) each of which provides around a ninety-minute tour of the Falls and Shankill roads (including the murals and the Peace Line), plus Milltown Cemetery, the docks and the university. Tours operate daily year-round, must be pre-booked and cost from £8 per person, usually with a minimum rate of £25 per taxi-load.

There are a variety of **walking tours** available. "Historic Belfast" (Wed, Fri & Sat 2pm; also Sun 2pm; 1hr 30min; £6) covers the major central sites while "The Blackstaff Way" (Sat 11am; 1hr 30min; £6) explores the heart of the old city. Both tours depart from the Belfast Welcome Centre. In addition, there's the "Historical Pub Tour" (May–Oct Thurs 7pm & Sat 4pm; 2hr; ⓣ028/9268 3665, ⓦwww.belfastpubtours.com; £6), which begins upstairs in the *Crown Liquor Saloon*, Great Victoria Street, and features six pubs, while the "Literary Tour" (Mon 7pm; 1hr; £5) departs from the Linen Hall Library on Fountain Street and takes in various sites associated with Belfast writers before culminating at the *Kitchen Bar* for a complimentary pint. Tickets for all of these may be purchased at the Belfast Welcome Centre, which also publishes a range of leaflets describing other walks in the city. Additionally, there are extensive three-hour political walking tours of West Belfast (Mon–Sat 11am, Sun 2pm; £8; ⓣ028/9020 0770, ⓦwww.coiste.ie) which depart from the Divis Tower at the city end of the Falls Road; advance booking is essential. Lastly, Belfast Safaris (ⓣ028/9031 0610, ⓦwww.belfastsafaris.com) offers a variety of "neighbourhood tours", including areas such as the Shankill and East Belfast, plus maritime, the "1700s and the United Irishmen" and nature trails (£6 per tour; call for times and details).

For a guide to entertainment in the city, consult the monthly **listings** freesheet *The Big List* (ⓦwww.thebiglist.co.uk) or the bimonthly *Belfast in Your Pocket* (ⓦwww.inyourpocket.com), both available at the Welcome Centre and from pubs, clubs and record shops. The *Belfast Telegraph* evening newspaper (ⓦwww.belfasttelegraph.co.uk) has daily listings, while the monthly freebie *Art* (ⓦwww.artslistings.com) and the free monthly *Whatabout?* listings guide are also good sources of information and available from the Welcome Centre. Finally, in an attempt to enliven the city centre in the evenings, the city council's quarterly free magazine *More Time* provides all kinds of details about shopping, eating out, nightlife and events; again this is available from the Welcome Centre.

City transport

Although you can easily walk around the city centre, distances to some of the outlying attractions are considerable, and a number of places to stay are also a little way out. The excellent **Metro** service provides frequent buses to almost every conceivable destination within the city, while the blue-and-white long-distance services of **Ulsterbus** – which principally covers the rest of the North beyond Belfast's boundaries – connect to some of the sights on the city's fringes, such as the Giant's Ring.

Almost all Metro buses set off from Donegall Square or the streets immediately around it. You can pick up a network **map** from the Welcome Centre or the Metro kiosk in Donegall Square West (Mon–Fri 8am–6pm, Sat 8.30am–5.30pm; bus information on ⓣ028/9066 6630, ⓦwww.translink.co.uk). In general buses operate from around 6am until 11pm Monday to Saturday and between 9am and 11pm on Sunday. Saturday-night **Metro Nightlink** services run from Donegall Square West along nine routes, though you're unlikely to need to use them unless you're staying outside the city (1am & 2am; £3.50).

Metro **fares** are determined by a zonal system. The city centre is covered by the Inner Zone and fares for journeys within it cost £1; most other journeys cost £1.30 or £1.60. If you're planning on making several journeys in one day it's well worth buying one of the **day-tickets** from the bus driver. These cover unlimited travel anywhere on the Metro network (£3.50, £2.50 if purchased after 10am). Alternatively, there are multi-journey **Smartlink Cards**, available in either five- or ten-journey options, and costing from £4 to £12.50 depending on the number of journeys and zones covered, plus a £1.50 one-off charge for the card itself. Cards can be purchased from the Metro kiosk, the two central bus stations and any Smartlink agent (including many newsagents).

Taxis and car parking

London-style metered black **taxis**, based at the main rank in Donegall Square East and other points throughout the city, charge a minimum £2.70, which rapidly starts to increase if you're going any distance. Alternatively, you can phone a **minicab** (try City Cabs ⓣ028/9024 2000, fonaCAB ⓣ028/9033 3333, Rent-a-cab ⓣ028/9024 2222 or Value Cabs ⓣ028/9080 9080); these too are metered, charge similar rates to the black cabs and are a good idea late at night as passing taxis are hard to grab.

There are plenty of **car parks** and pay-and-display parking operates in many of the streets. Following several arson attacks, if you're driving a car with **Republic of Ireland plates** you'd be strongly advised to seek secure, off-street parking at night.

Accommodation

Belfast now has a staggering range of **accommodation**, especially at the top end of the market. However, there's still a relative dearth of budget places and it's worth booking ahead in the summer season and during festival time. Much of the city's accommodation is concentrated around **Great Victoria Street** and south of the centre in the **university quarter**, particularly on and around Botanic Avenue and in the network of streets running between the Malone and Lisburn roads. Many hotels and guesthouses are geared towards business travellers and so frequently offer significant reductions for weekend breaks.

City centre

Days Hotel 40 Hope St ⓣ028/9024 2494, ⓦwww.dayshotelbelfast.co.uk. A Gargantuan seven-storey modern establishment, in an unappealing location near Sandy Row, but offering splendid rooms and a fine buffet breakfast (not included in the room rate). ❹

Europa Hotel Great Victoria St ⓣ028/9027 1066, ⓦwww.hastingshotels.com. Bombed on numerous occasions in the past, this massive city-centre hotel near the Opera House offers a variety of rooms and lavish executive suites. The bar, with its huge windows overlooking the city's main drag, is a poseur's paradise. ❼

Hilton Belfast 4 Lanyon Place ⓣ028/9027 7000, ⓦwww.hilton.co.uk/belfast. Huge and extravagant dockland addition to the Belfast skyline with staggering views across the city and a range of lavish rooms and suites. ❼

Holiday Inn Belfast 22–26 Ormeau Ave ⓣ028/9032 8511, ⓦwww.belfast.holiday-inn.com. Another huge modern edifice, offering excellently equipped bedrooms and a health and leisure centre. ❻

Jurys Inn Belfast Fisherwick Place, Great Victoria St ⓣ028/9053 3500, ⓦwww.jurysinn.com. A mammoth, 190-bed branch of the Dublin chain, with rooms that can fit up to three adults or two adults and two children – handily, prices are per room no matter how many stay. ❹

Malmaison 34–38 Victoria St ⓣ028/9022 0200, ⓦwww.malmaison-belfast.com. Installed in an elegantly converted warehouse, *Malmaison* features sumptuous suites named after the Samson and Goliath cranes, chic doubles and an attractive bar and restaurant. Doubles ❻, suites ❾.

The Merchant 35–39 Waring St ⓣ028/9023 4888, ⓦwww.themerchanthotel.com. Once the HQ of the Ulster Bank, this substantial Victorian edifice has been converted into a wonderful hotel, complete with many of the original Italianate fittings and its own art gallery. Rooms are spacious and luxuriously furnished and its suites are impeccably elegant. Doubles ❽, suites ❾.

Ten Square 10 Donegall Square South ⓣ028/9024 1001, ⓦwww.tensquare.co.uk. A gem of a hotel in a much-refurbished, former linen house bang opposite City Hall, featuring just 23 individually designed rooms and suites, with an utterly opulent feel that draws its influences from colonial Shanghai. Doubles ❼, suites ❾.

Travelodge 15 Brunswick St ⓣ028/9033 3555, ⓦwww.travelodge.co.uk. Modern, budget-conscious en-suite accommodation, featuring king-sized beds, right in the city centre. ❸

University area and around

Avenue House 23 Eglantine Ave ⓣ028/9066 5904, ⓦwww.avenueguesthouse.com. Pleasant Victorian townhouse providing well-equipped en-suite accommodation, including one family room and two others which sleep three people. ❷

Camera House 44 Wellington Park ⓣ028/9066 0026, ⓔcamera-gh@hotmail.com. Very luxurious, elegantly decorated townhouse offering en-suite and standard accommodation. ❸

Dukes Hotel 65–67 University St ⓣ028/9023 6666, ⓦwww.welcome-group.co.uk. Smart, modern redevelopment of a fine Victorian building, featuring 12 elegant bedrooms, a small gym and sauna, and a fashionable bar. ❹

Express by Holiday Inn 106 University St ⓣ028/9031 1909, ⓦwww.exhi-belfast.com. The smaller sister to the Ormeau Ave branch (see above) might lack its sibling's amenities, but its cheery, well-equipped rooms still provide very restful accommodation and at a grand price. ❸

Kate's B&B 127 University St ⓣ028/9028 2091, ⓔkatesbb127@hotmail.com. A popular budget choice offering standard rooms in a well-converted townhouse. ❷

Madison's 59–63 Botanic Ave ⓣ028/9030 9800, ⓦwww.madisonshotel.com. A plush, economically priced hotel with spacious rooms and a bar/nightclub popular with 30-somethings. ❸

Malone Lodge Hotel 60 Eglantine Ave ⓣ028/9038 8000, ⓦwww.malonelodgehotel.com. Welcoming and well-equipped hotel near Queen's, with off-street parking, pleasantly decorated rooms and a notable restaurant. ❺

Marine Guest House 30 Eglantine Ave ⓣ028/9066 2828, ⓔmarine30@utvinternet.com. A large Victorian guesthouse in a quiet setting offering attractive, spacious en-suite rooms. ❷

The Old Rectory 148 Malone Rd ⓣ028/9066 7882, ⓦwww.anoldrectory.co.uk. This beautifully converted former clergyman's house, about a mile south of the university, offers both standard and en-suite rooms, and high-quality breakfasts. ❸

Roseleigh House 19 Rosetta Park ⓣ028/9064 4414, ⓦwww.roseleighhouse.co.uk. Deluxe accommodation, including a family room, in a quiet area at the bottom of the Ormeau Rd, about three miles from the city centre. ❸

Tara Lodge 36 Cromwell Rd ⓣ028/9059 0900, ⓦwww.taralodge.com. This guesthouse off Botanic Ave has swish decor and excellent facilities. ❹

Hostels

The Ark 18 University St ⓣ028/9032 9626, ⓦwww.arkhostel.com. Clean, cosy, well-equipped hostel in a welcoming terraced house, with 34 beds, laundry and cooking facilities; there is a 2am curfew. Dorms £10.90, doubles ❶.

Arnie's Backpackers 63 Fitzwilliam St ⓣ028/9024 2867. Convivial IHH- & IHO-affiliated hostel with 22 beds in five dorm rooms, plus laundry and cooking facilities, and a pair of friendly Jack Russells. Dorms £11.

Belfast International Hostel 22–32 Donegall Rd ⓣ028/9032 4733. Large HINI hostel near the Protestant enclave of Sandy Row: plenty of twins and a couple of double en-suite rooms, but mainly four- and six-bed dorms. The hostel has its own café, self-catering kitchen and laundry, and organizes regular tours of Belfast and to the Giant's Causeway. Dorms £9.50–14, doubles ❶.

Paddy's Backpackers at The Linen House 18–20 Kent St ⓣ028/9058 6400, ⓦwww.belfasthostel.com. This 130-bed IHH hostel, near the northern end of Royal Ave, has a mix of doubles and twins, as well as small four- to eight-bed dorms and a much larger 18-bedder. There are also a large kitchen and laundry facilities. Dorms £6.50–10, doubles ❶.

The City

The core of Belfast is the stately, though often traffic-clogged, **Donegall Square**: in its centre stands the City Hall, and buses and taxis depart for every part of the city from the sides of the square. The main shopping area lies a stone's throw north and the prime areas for entertainment and accommodation are immediately south. Most of the grand old Victorian buildings that characterize the city are to the north and east, towards the river.

Further out, **North Belfast** boasts Cave Hill, with its castle and zoo, and **South Belfast** is home to the **Golden Mile**, leading down to the university, Botanic Gardens and Ulster Museum. The River Lagan flows towards Belfast Lough along the eastern side of the city centre and offers riverside walks, and is also the focus for the most radical development in the last few years, the **Laganside**. In **East Belfast**, across the river beyond the great cranes of the Harland & Wolff shipyard, lies suburbia and very little of interest apart from **Stormont**, the former Northern Irish parliament and home to the modern Assembly. Working-class **West Belfast**, by contrast, seems almost a separate city, divided from the rest by the speeding traffic of the Westlink motorway, pierced by the Catholic Falls Road and Protestant Shankill Road, and providing many insights into Belfast's turbulent political history.

The city centre

Belfast's **city centre** is fairly compact and easy to wander around. The heart of the old city can be found in the narrow, atmospheric lanes of the former commercial district, the **Entries**, about five minutes' walk northeast of Donegall Square. On a grander scale, many of Belfast's most handsome buildings, evidence of the city's transformation during the Industrial Revolution, are concentrated further north and east, between **St Anne's Cathedral** and the River Lagan. Right by the river you'll find the huge Laganside development, focused on the **Waterfront Hall** and the **Odyssey Complex** across the water.

Donegall Square and around

City Hall dominates Donegall Square and the entire centre of Belfast. Completed in 1906, it's a smug-looking building of bright white Portland stone, quadrangular and squat, and with its turrets, saucer domes, scrolls and pinnacle pots is representative of all the styles absorbed by the British Empire. In front of the building stands an imposing statue of Queen Victoria, the apotheosis of imperialism, her maternal gaze unerringly cast across the rooftops towards the Protestant Shankill area. At her feet, sculpted in bronze, stand proud figures showing the city fathers' world-view: a young scholar, his mother with spinning spool and his father with mallet and boat, the three of them representing "learning, linen and liners", the alliterative bedrock of Belfast's heritage.

The City Hall offers the only opportunity to be shown around one of Belfast's many Neoclassical buildings; guided **tours** last 45 minutes (at the time of writing City Hall was closed for refurbishment; call ⓣ028/9027 0456 to check progress and opening times) and access is through a security entrance at the rear, opposite Linenhall Street. Inside, the **main dome**, with its (inaccessible) whispering gallery, arches 50m above you. Modelled on St Paul's Cathedral in London, the dome is adorned around its rim with zodiac signs, both painted and in stained-glass windows. The marbled **entrance hall** itself is palatial, with staircase pillars, colonnades and bronze and marble statues. Two of the statues portray Frederick Robert Chichester, Earl of Belfast (1827–53): the first, upright and stern, stands on the principal landing, while the other, showing Frederick embraced by his mother on his deathbed, has been hauled out of the rain into the Octagon entrance porch. Also on the principal landing is a **mural**, executed in 1951 by John Luke, celebrating Belfast's now mostly defunct traditional industries – rope-making, shipbuilding, weaving and spinning. Oddly though, the central position in the picture is occupied by the town crier, a cryptic reference perhaps to Belfast having the oldest continuously published newspaper in the world – *The Newsletter*, founded in 1737. The tour also takes in the **robing room**, where the trick is to ask to try on one of the civic cloaks for a snapshot. The building's highlight is the oak-decorated **council chamber**, with its hand-carved wainscoting and councillors' pews as well as a visitors' gallery. Council meetings are often stormy, but, in their absence, it's a very urbane scene with a backdrop of portraits of British royalty and aristocracy.

At the northwest corner of Donegall Square stands Belfast's oldest library, the **Linen Hall Library** (Mon–Fri 9.30am–5.30pm, Sat 9.30am–1pm; ⓦwww.linenhall.com), established in 1788. The library has latterly been substantially revamped and is now entered via 52 Fountain St, just around the corner from the square. It has a huge array of Irish literature, language and reference books as well its Political Collection: a unique accumulation of over 100,000 publications reflecting every aspect of Northern Irish political life since 1966. This encompasses numerous election posters, and documents ranging from party political ephemera to doctoral theses sent in from all over the world; also here are prison letters smuggled out of Long Kesh which, in its more widely used name of the Maze, was the scene of the 1981 hunger strike (see p.705). The Linen Hall is an independent institution and visitors are free to examine its collection: there's a computerized catalogue on the first floor, use of which is free, though a donation is welcome. The library also boasts excellent facilities for tracing family trees, a café, and stocks all the daily newspapers.

Between the back of the City Hall and the BBC, on Alfred Street, look out for the turrets of the strange and wonderful Catholic **St Malachy's Church** (1844), the finest Victorian building in Belfast. The interior's fan-vaulted ceiling is modelled on that of Henry VII's chapel in London's Westminster Abbey, while other elaborate features include the canopied pulpit and carved marble altar, both dating from a 1926 restoration.

The Entries and around

The predominantly pedestrianized streets north from Donegall Square lead you into downtown Belfast. The main shopping street, **Donegall Place**, continues into Royal Avenue and houses familiar chain-store names. Castle Place, off Donegall Place, was once the hub of Victorian Belfast, and the grand old department stores here, in creams, pinks and browns, have been transformed into a plethora of voguish shops, though happily only the ground-floor frontages have been converted, leaving the lofty grandeur of the storeys above undisturbed.

East along Castle Lane or Castle Place leads to Ann Street and the High Street, interlinked by the narrow alleyways known as the **Entries**. You'll stumble across some great old saloon **bars** down here, like *The Morning Star* in Pottinger's Entry, with its large frosted windows and Parisian-café-like counter, and *White's Tavern* in Winecellar Entry, which dates from the seventeenth century. Crown Entry was where the Society of United Irishmen (see p.695) was born, led by the Protestant triumvirate of Wolfe Tone, Henry Joy McCracken and Samuel Nielson. Nielson also printed his own newspaper in this area, the *Northern Star*; heavily influenced by the French revolutionary ideals of liberty, equality and fraternity, the newspaper's inflammatory material led to him being hounded out of town.

From the High Street, a similar set of Entries used to run through to Waring Street to the north, but was destroyed by bombing in World War II. Still, this end of the High Street, with the River Farset running underground, is the oldest part of the city, its atmosphere in places redolent of the eighteenth century.

On Waring Street itself stands the **War Memorial Building**, containing a small exhibition commemorating the role of Northern Ireland in World War II (Mon–Fri 9am–4.30pm; free). At the rear is the **Royal Ulster Rifles Museum** (Mon–Fri 10am–12.30pm & 2–4pm, Fri closes 3pm; £1; Ⓦwww.geocities.com/rurmuseum), which features the usual array of insignia, uniforms and weaponry, as well as Billy, a rather despondent-looking regimental dog, stuffed in 1901. **Number 2 Waring Street** was originally built as a market house in 1769, but is more renowned as the venue for the **1792 Belfast Harp Festival:** by the end of the eighteenth century, the old Gaelic harping tradition had reached almost terminal decline and the convention was a deliberate attempt by its organizers, the United Irish Society, to record some of the harpers' airs for posterity. The transcriber, Edmund Bunting, was stimulated to tour Ireland collecting further airs, 77 of which were published in his illustrious collection of 1809.

St Anne's Cathedral and around

The area north of Waring Street has seen much redevelopment in recent years, with plenty of new restaurants and bars opening up – some of which offer a wide range of entertainment, such as the excellent *John Hewitt* (see p.575) – leading to its acquisition of the term **Cathedral quarter** to suggest a Parisian ambience, though one as far removed from the Left Bank as it's possible to imagine.

A couple of hundred yards north of Waring Street on Donegall Street you'll find the most monolithic of all the city's grand buildings, the Protestant **St Anne's Cathedral** (Mon–Sat 10am–4pm, Sun open roughly noon–3pm – between services; free; Ⓦwww.belfastcathedral.org), a neo-Romanesque basilica started in 1899, but not fully completed until 1981. Entrance is via the huge west door, immediately to the right of which is the baptistery, with an intricately designed representation of the Creation on its ceiling consisting of 150,000 tiny pieces of glass. Most significant, however, is the cathedral's only tomb, marked by a simple slab on the floor of the south aisle, which contains the body of **Lord Edward Henry Carson** (1854–1935). His is a name that Northern Ireland has never forgotten: the bodily symbol of Partition, he's seen either as the province's saviour or as the villain who sabotaged Ireland's independence as a 32-county state. A Dubliner of Scots-Presbyterian background, Carson took the decision in 1910 to accept the leadership of the opposition to Home Rule, which in effect inextricably allied him to the Ulster Unionist resistance movement. Yet, though this association is about the only thing for which he is remembered, his personality and integrity went far deeper than this. He abhorred religious intolerance, and behind the exterior of a zealous crusader was a man who sincerely believed that Ireland couldn't prosper without Britain and only wished that a federalist answer could have involved a united Ireland. Nonetheless, this was the same man who, as a brilliant orator at the bar, and in the role he loved the most, brought about the humiliating destruction of Oscar Wilde at the writer's trial in 1895.

As it continues north, Donegall Street becomes Clifton Street, which takes its name from **Clifton House** (built 1771–74), just around the corner at 2 North Queen St. Better known as the "Poor House", or the "Charitable Institute for the Aged and Infirm", it's a handsome Georgian construction with an octagonal-based stone spire at its rear and symmetrically projecting wings. Though simple, this is one of the more effective buildings that Belfast has to offer, yet was designed by an amateur architect and local paper merchant, Robert Joy, uncle of the hapless Henry Joy McCracken. The Institute was built at a time of much poverty and unrest, brought about by the Donegalls' eviction of tenants when their leases started running out – the very same Donegalls whose name is tagged to so many of Belfast's streets. The house is not regularly open to the public, but does offer tours on request (Ⓣ028/9089 7354, Ⓦwww.cliftonbelfast.org.uk).

A little further along is the **Clifton Street Graveyard**, which contains the graves of Robert Joy and Mary Anne McCracken, Henry Joy's sister, along with several United Irishmen, including Dr William Drennan, reputed to have been the originator of the phrase "Emerald Isle".

The Laganside

At the eastern, docks end of the High Street stands the **Prince Albert Memorial Clock Tower**, built in 1867–69 and tilting slightly off the perpendicular as a result of its construction upon gradually sinking wooden piles. It's a strange memorial, especially as Prince Albert never had anything to do with Belfast, but it's a handy landmark.

North of the Albert Memorial, along Dunbar Link, you'll come across a series of grand edifices inspired by the same civic vanity as that behind the design of the City Hall. The restored **Custom House** on Donegall Quay is a Corinthian-style, E-shaped edifice designed between 1854 and 1857 by Charles Lanyon, who was responsible for several of the city's finest buildings. Unfortunately, it's not open to the public, leaving you unable to verify rumours of fantastic art masterpieces stored in its basements – though it is known that Anthony Trollope, the nineteenth-century novelist (and inventor of the pillar box), once worked here as a surveyor's clerk.

Just beyond the Custom House on Donegall Quay is the ambitious **Laganside** development project, the first component of which to be completed was the **Lagan Weir**, designed to protect the city against flooding. Millions of pounds have been pumped into dredging the river to maintain water levels and revive the much depleted fish population – successfully it seems: there was salmon fishing on the weir's inauguration day. However, little can be done to restore the river's erstwhile crucial role in the successful development of the city as a centre for industries as diverse as linen, tobacco, rope-making and shipbuilding – a glance across the river to the Harland & Wolff shipyard confirms that the last-named still survives.

In summer, **boat trips** on the Lagan (March–Dec Tues–Thurs 12.30pm & 2pm, April–Sept also 3.30pm; £7; Ⓣ028/9033 0844, Ⓦwww.laganboatcompany.com) leave from opposite the Laganside Buscentre just south of the

Lookout – the company also operates a **Titanic** tour of the harbour and shipyards (Fri–Mon same times and price). If the sea air's twitching your nostrils, head a few hundred yards further north towards the ferry terminals, where you'll find the restored **Harbour Office** and nearby **Sinclair Seamen's Church** (Sun services 11.30am & 7pm; visits Wed 2–5pm) on Corporation Square. The latter is yet another Lanyon design, but it's the contents that are most intriguing. Sailors must have felt truly at home among the cornucopia of maritime equipment – an old-fashioned wooden wheel, the bell from HMS *Hood*, assorted navigation lights and a ship's prow for a pulpit.

The most obvious changes to the city's skyline can be seen from almost any river viewpoint: further south along Oxford Street sits the glittering two-thousand-seater **Waterfront Hall** concert venue, a housing development and a *Hilton* hotel.

The Odyssey and the SS Nomadic

Across the river on Queen's Quay, the massive **Odyssey** leisure complex features a ten-thousand-seater indoor arena, cinemas and a complex of bars, restaurants and shops. Also here is the **Whowhatwherewhenwhy** scientific discovery centre, known as **W5** (Mon–Sat 10am–6pm, Sun noon–6pm, Sept–June closes Mon–Thurs 5pm, last admission one hour before closing; adults £6.50, children £4.50; Ⓦwww.w5online.co.uk; Heritage Island) with over a hundred and fifty interactive exhibits, aimed primarily at children. Best of these is the See/Do section in which you can create your own animated cartoon and have a go at composing on a laser harp. From mid-July to August, W5 also runs a series of special workshops for children – the subjects change annually. There is also an **IMAX cinema** here (see p.578). To get to Odyssey, cross the river via Queen's Bridge (opposite Ann Street) and immediately take the first street left, or catch Metro bus #600 from the Europa Buscentre or a train from Great Victoria Street Station.

During 2006 and 2007, the **SS Nomadic** (Ⓦwww.nomadicpreservation society.co.uk) was moored at Queen's Quay and open to the public for visits. The steamship was built by Harland & Wolff for the White Star Line and, after its launch in 1911, acted as a tender, conveying passengers from Cherbourg harbour to the awaiting *Titanic*. The last time it fulfilled this task was on April 10, 1912, the beginning of the *Titanic*'s infamous and inaugural voyage. Subsequently, the *Nomadic* was requisitioned by the French government during World War I, an act repeated by the British during World War II, then operated as a tender for the Cunard Line, again from Cherbourg until 1968. Following that, the ship served time as a floating restaurant in Paris before being declared unsafe in 2002. A public appeal successfully raised enough funds to return the ship to Belfast in 2006. At the time of writing the *Nomadic* was undergoing vital repairs in dry dock but was expected to reopen to the public some time in 2008.

The Golden Mile

The strip of Belfast running south along Great Victoria Street to Shaftesbury Square and thence to the university area and beyond is ascribed the name of the "Golden Mile", though in its present state it is in truth mostly a pretty depressing stretch of empty businesses and building sites.

It begins at the grandiose, turn-of-the-century **Grand Opera House**, which sits just a short distance west of Donegall Square at the northern end of Great Victoria Street – backstage tours of the theatre are available (Wed–Sat 11am;

£5; Ⓦwww.goh.co.uk). At the northern head of the street, almost opposite the *Europa Hotel*, stands one of the greatest of Victorian gin palaces, the **Crown Liquor Saloon** (Ⓦwww.crownbar.com). The saloon has a glittering tiled exterior – amber, carmine, rouge, yellow, green, blue and smoke-grey – resembling a spa baths more than a serious drinking institution. The rich, High Victorian stuccowork continues inside, too: the scrolled ceiling (recently cleansed of all its nicotine stains), patterned floor and the golden-yellow and rosy-red hues led John Betjeman to describe it as his "many coloured cavern". Once armed with drinks (and if it's not too crowded, or lunchtime when they're reserved for diners only), grab one of the snugs, much resembling an old railway-carriage compartment and press the push-button to receive service. If the snugs are all busy, it's still a great experience to sit or stand at the bar, with its carved-timber dividing screens, painted mirrors and frieze-decorated oak panelling. The pub featured in the 1946 British movie, *Odd Man Out*, starring James Mason as a wanted IRA gunman, and the film was used as a model for the *Crown*'s restoration after it had suffered from the repeated bombing of the *Europa Hotel* in the 1970s.

Before heading into the university quarter, sidestep off Great Victoria Street into **Sandy Row**, which runs parallel to the west. A strong working-class Protestant quarter (with the tribal pavement painting to prove it), it's one of the most glaring examples of Belfast's divided world, wildly different from the city centre's increasingly cosmopolitan sophistication, yet only yards away. In Blythe Street and Donegall Road, off to the west, are some of the murals that characterize these sectarian areas (see box, p.570). Sandy Row used to be the main road south and, although hard to credit today, it was once a picturesque stretch of whitewashed cottages.

South Belfast

Towards the Golden Mile's southern extremity lies the **university area**, the focal point for South Belfast's attractions (Ⓦwww.visitsouthbelfast.com). You're likely to spend much of your time in the area, since it boasts plenty of eating places, pubs and a range of accommodation. Near Queen's University are the lush **Botanic Gardens**, within which sits the vast **Ulster Museum**, displaying everything from dinosaur bones to contemporary art but closed for refurbishment at the time of writing. Heading south from here along Stranmillis Road it's a relatively short step east to the **Lagan Towpath**, running several miles southwest to Lisburn (see p.627), while a detour along the way leads to the Neolithic earthwork known as the **Giant's Ring.**

The university quarter

Just south of Shaftesbury Square stand three churches – Moravian, Crescent and Methodist – whose distinctive steeples frame the entrance to the **university quarter**. From here, leading up to the university buildings, the roads are lined with early Victorian terraces that represent the final flowering of Georgian architecture in Belfast. The **Upper Crescent** is a magnificent curved Neoclassical terrace, built in about 1845 but sadly neglected since; it is now used mainly for office space. The **Lower Crescent**, perversely, is straight.

Queen's University is the architectural centrepiece of the area, flanked by the most satisfying example of a Georgian terrace in Belfast, **University Square**, where the red brickwork mostly remains intact, with the exception of a few bay windows added in the Victorian era. The university building itself was constructed in 1849 as a mock-Tudor remodelling of Magdalen College, Oxford, to a design by Lanyon, and houses a visitor centre (Mon–Fri 10am–4pm, May–Sept also Sat

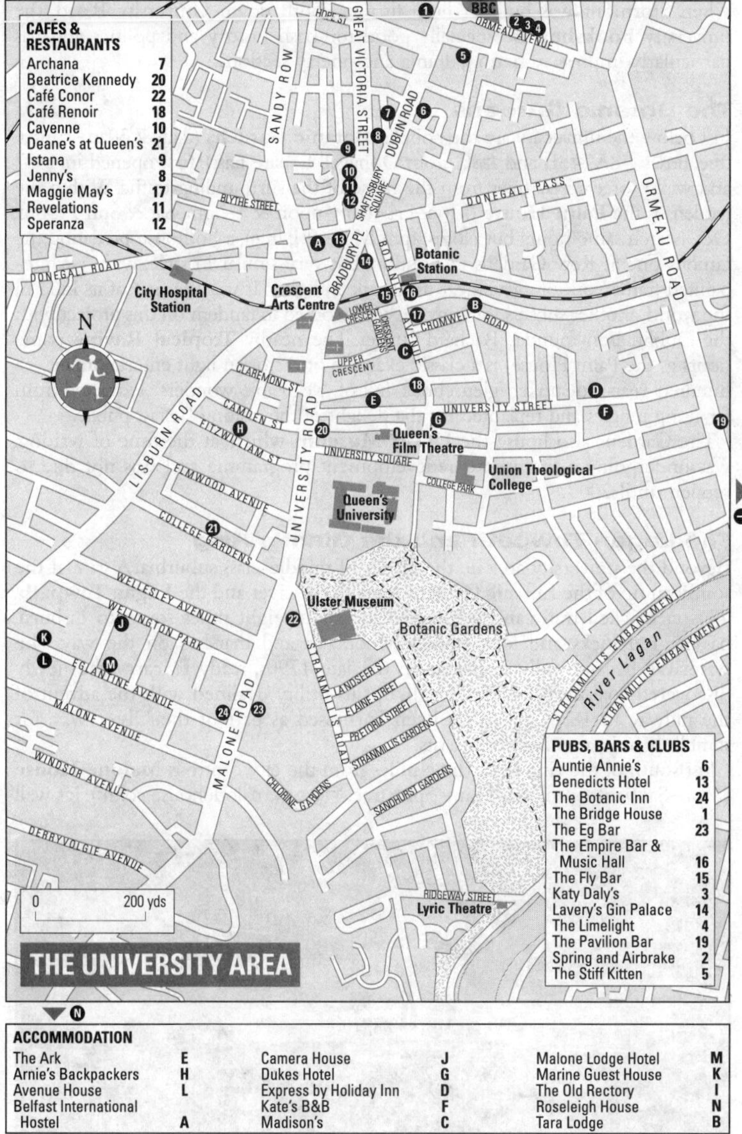

same times; Ⓦ www.qub.ac.uk/vcentre) which provides information about the university, hosts a series of art exhibitions as well as a permanent display of Seamus Heaney memorabilia (see p.618), and runs guided tours (Sat noon; £5; 1hr). Across the road from here is the Students' Union, a white 1960s design. The Italianate **Union Theological College**, nearby on College Park, also by Lanyon, was temporarily the site of the Northern Ireland Parliament until 1932 when Stormont was built. A little further south down University Road, the university **bookshop** is especially good for Irish history and politics and has particularly impressive fiction, drama and poetry sections.

The Botanic Gardens

Just below the university are the popular **Botanic Gardens** (daily 7.30am–sunset; free; buses #8A, #8B and #8C from Donegall Square East), first opened in 1827 and well protected by trees from the noise of the surrounding traffic. Within the gardens is the **Palm House** (Mon–Fri 10am–noon & 1–5pm, Sat & Sun 2–5pm; Oct–March same hours but closes 4pm Mon–Fri; free), a hothouse predating the famous one at Kew Gardens in London, but very similar in style, with a white-painted framework of curvilinear ironwork and glass. It was the first of its kind in the world, another success for Lanyon, who worked in tandem on this project with the Dublin iron-founder Richard Turner. The nearby **Tropical Ravine** (same hours as the Palm House) is a classic example of Victorian light entertainment – a hundred-year-old sunken glen chock-full of "vegetable wonders" extracted from far-flung jungles and replanted for the delight of the visiting Belfast public.

The Gardens also house the **Ulster Museum** which, at the time of writing, was undergoing a mammoth redevelopment programme and was not due to reopen until 2009.

The Lagan Towpath and the Giant's Ring

Beyond the university area lie the glades of middle-class suburbia. A gate at the southern tip of the Botanic Gardens leads to the river and the **Lagan Towpath**. This tarmacked trail can be tramped for about eight miles south to Lisburn, passing old locks and lock houses, woodland and marshes on the way. The waterway became fully navigable in the late 1790s, ready to carry the newly discovered coal from Lough Neagh, but its utility declined with the advent of the railway in 1839. Today, it's been harnessed as part of the Ulster Way, for rambling and canoeing enthusiasts.

Just south of the ring road, three miles from the city centre is **Malone House** (Mon–Sat 9am–5pm, Sun 11am–5pm; free; Ⓦwww.malonehouse.co.uk). It's well

▲ The Botanic Gardens

George Best

Maradona good, Pele better, George Best (popular Belfast sporting adage)

Born in East Belfast in 1946, **George Best** became (and remains to this day) Northern Ireland's most celebrated footballer. Rejected by local clubs, he was signed by Manchester United, then as now England's glamour team. He made his debut aged 17, playing a major role in the side's winning of the Football League Championship in the 1964–65 season. United repeated the feat in 1966–67, by which time George's reputation as a dazzling, jinking, goal-scoring winger, capable of bemusing opposing defenders, had brought him stardom. His good looks, long hair, gift of the gab and love of the high life also led to his acquisition of the sobriquet "the fifth Beatle". Further fame was assured when he played a major role in United's defeat of Benfica in the 1967 European Cup Final, scoring one of the goals in that 4–1 victory and running the Portuguese team's defence so ragged before a vast televised audience that his award of **European Footballer of the Year** was a foregone conclusion.

The latter half of the 1960s saw Best's celebrity lifestyle (by then he owned nightclubs and boutiques and had dated at least one Miss World) becoming increasingly prey to gambling, alcohol and an inveterate passion for sex – as he famously declared in a drunken appearance on BBC TV's *Wogan Show* in 1990. He walked out of United in 1974, and after that his footballing career declined rapidly, taking in spells in the US and Australia. He never played in the top flight of English football again.

Alcohol addiction led to a stint in prison in 1984, after Best was found guilty of drunk driving and assaulting a police officer. By 2002 his health was in such poor state that he underwent a liver transplant, but continued to drink after its success and eventually succumbed to multiple organ failure in November 2005.

Some 100,000 mourners lined the streets of Belfast as Best's coffin travelled to his **funeral** service at Stormont. Belfast City Airport was subsequently renamed in his honour and, in 2006, the Ulster Bank issued one million £5 notes bearing his picture – the entire issue was rapidly snapped up for keepsakes, with some notes selling for several times their value on eBay.

The great sadness of George's football career was that, despite 37 caps for Northern Ireland, he never appeared in a major international competition (such as the World Cup or European Nations Cup), but he certainly inspired a host of Northern Irish and other young footballers and, indeed, numerous jokes, not least his own oft-quoted remark: "I spent a lot of my money on booze, birds and fast cars. The rest I just squandered."

worth climbing up the adjacent hill for the views of the surrounding area and to see the house itself, an almost pristine, white, bow-fronted late-Georgian mansion, built for William Wallace Legge, a prominent local merchant. It was rebuilt by Belfast Council following a devastating fire in 1976 and is now mainly used as a conference centre, though you can visit the Higgin Gallery (Mon–Sat 11am–5pm, Sun noon–5pm; free), which hosts regular art exhibitions.

Alternatively, if you leave the towpath at Shaw's Bridge (the ring-road crossing), it's a mile-long signposted walk along country lanes to the **Giant's Ring** (free access dawn to dusk), a colossal, two-hundred-yard-wide earthwork thought to be a burial ground or meeting place. You wouldn't be far wrong in thinking that its inwardly sloping wall would make an excellent speed-track circuit, for in the eighteenth century it was used for horse racing: six circuits made a two-mile race, with the punters jostling for position on the top of the rampart. Most captivating of all is the huge dolmen at the central hub of this cartwheel structure. As a single megalithic remain, it is immediately more impressive than even the great structures of the Irish High Kings at Tara, though here there's little information concerning its origins and usage. The setting chosen for the site, high above the surrounding lowlands (probably once marshy lake), is impressive – there's a powerful feeling that the great dramas and decision-making of the ancient northeast must have been played out here. To save you walking the whole way back, you can catch Ulsterbus #13D or #313 back to the city from Shaw's Bridge; it runs every hour or so to the centre.

East Belfast

East Belfast's skyline is dominated by the Samson and Goliath cranes which tower above the **Harland & Wolff shipyard**. The shipyard is the city's proudest international asset – the ill-fated *Titanic* was built here – and is said to possess the largest dry dock in the world: over 600m long and 100m wide. Unfortunately, the area is very security-conscious and access is impossible without making a formal application.

East Belfast is trying hard to draw interest to its few attractions: there are notable **murals** at **Freedom Corner** near the beginning of the Newtownards Road, and the area does have some well-known scions. The theologian and author of the Narnia chronicles, **C.S. Lewis**, was born in Dundela Villas, and there's a plaque commemorating him at Dundela Flats, which stand on the site where the house once stood, off Dundela. Another plaque on Burren Way in the Cregagh estate commemorates the childhood home of the late footballer **George Best** (see p.567). And **Van Morrison** fans might get a thrill from seeking out his birthplace, a private house (with no public access) at 125 Hyndford St, off Beersbridge Road, and the many streets that feature in his songs (Cyprus Avenue, Castlereagh Road and others).

Four miles east of the centre, off the Newtownards Road, is **Stormont** (buses #20A and #23 from Donegall Square West), the home of the Northern Ireland Parliament until the introduction of direct rule in 1972, and now housing the Assembly created by the 1998 Good Friday Agreement. You can't visit the house itself, unless invited by an Assembly member, but it's an impressive sight, a great, White Neoclassical mansion crowning a rise in the middle of a park (with adjacent cricket field) at the end of a magnificent long, straight drive. You can wander freely in the grounds, a popular place for a walk. Also here, though obviously not open to the public, is **Stormont Castle**, the office of the British Secretary of State for Northern Ireland.

North Belfast

North Belfast's attractions amount to no more than a castle and the city's zoo, both out on the Antrim Road and conveniently alongside one another on the slopes of Cave Hill, served by bus #1 from Donegall Square West.

Built in 1870 to the designs of Lanyon, the sandstone **Belfast Castle** and its wooded estate are open to the public (Mon–Sat 9am–10pm, Sun 9am–6pm; free; Ⓦwww.belfastcastle.co.uk). The exterior is in Scottish Baronial style, inspired in part by the reconstruction of Balmoral Castle in Aberdeenshire in 1853, with a six-storey tower, a series of crow-stepped gables and conically peak-capped turrets. The most striking feature of all, however, is the serpentine Italianate stairway that leads down from the principal reception room to the garden terrace below. Restored and refurbished in 1990, the interior is sadly virtually empty of Victorian period accoutrements, but upstairs the revamped **visitor centre** traces the locality's history from prehistoric cave-dwellers to the castle's construction.

The Troubles in West Belfast

The Troubles in West Belfast have their origins in the nineteenth century, when the city's population expanded dramatically as people flocked from the countryside to work in the booming new flax and linen industries. Many of these migrants were crammed into jerry-built housing in the grids of streets which still today define this part of the city. Conditions were deplorable and did nothing to ease tensions between Catholic and Protestant residents. There were numerous sectarian riots – the worst was in 1886, during the reading of the Home Rule Bill, when 32 people died and over 370 were injured – leading to the almost inevitable definition of two separate neighbourhoods, as Protestant and Catholic families alike began to migrate to more secure surroundings.

In 1968 and 1969, this division was pushed to its limit when, across the city, sectarian mobs and gunmen evicted over eight thousand families from their homes, mainly in Catholic West Belfast. The Royal Ulster Constabulary, or RUC, called for government assistance, and British troops arrived on the streets on August 15, 1969. A month later the makeshift barrier dividing the Catholic **Falls** from the Protestant **Shankill** had become a full-scale reinforced "peace line". British intervention may have averted a civil war, but it failed to prevent an escalation in sectarian conflict. Indeed, the army soon came to be viewed as an occupying force and a legitimate target for a reviving IRA. In return, Loyalist paramilitaries sought to avenge Republican violence, often through indiscriminate acts of aggression, such as the atrocities carried out by the **Shankill Butchers** in the 1970s, so called because they use butchers' knives to first maim then murder their Catholic victims, selected at random.

Over the next 25 years, West Belfast remained the major battleground of the Troubles. The busy **Westlink motorway** separates West Belfast from the rest of the city, and at the height of the conflict the various overhead bridges and roundabouts were used by the police and army as virtual border crossings to control access to and from the area.

Adjoining the castle is the well-landscaped parkland of **Belfast Zoo** (daily: April–Sept 10am–5pm; Oct–March 10am–2.30pm; adults £7.80, children £4.10, Oct–March adults £6.30, children £3.20; Ⓦ www.belfastzoo.co.uk), which stretches up towards Cave Hill. A fifteen-year renovation programme and an investment of £10 million has left the zoo looking much less like an animal prison than it once did. Within, you'll find primates and big cats, elephants, penguins and sea lions, and a free flight aviary, where rare species have room to breed.

Castle and zoo aside, though, it's **Cave Hill** itself that should be your target in the area. Several paths lead up from the castle estate to the hill's summit – a rocky outcrop known as "Napoleon's Nose" – which affords an unsurpassable overview of the whole city and lough. From here you can't help but appreciate the accuracy of the poet Craig Raine's aerial description of the city in his *Flying to Belfast* as "a radio set with its back ripped off". Cave Hill was once awash with Iron Age forts, for there was flint (for weapon making) in the chalk under the basalt hill-coverings. In 1795, Wolfe Tone, Henry Joy McCracken and other leaders of the United Irishmen stood on the top of Cave Hill and pledged "never to desist in our efforts until we have subverted the authority of England over our country and asserted our Independence".

West Belfast

Though the nexus of the Troubles for 25 years, today **West Belfast** (Ⓦ www.visitwestbelfast.com) is as safe as anywhere else in the city to visit. However,

Belfast murals

As much a marker of an area's allegiances as painted kerbstones or fluttering flags and bunting, the politically inspired **murals** of Northern Ireland are among the most startling sights not just in Belfast, but of the whole country. This ephemeral art form, which recycles the images and slogans of the Troubles, characterizes the violent struggles of the last few decades. Though many have been in place now for a decade, some of the slogans and murals mentioned here may have vanished by the time of your visit: new murals are painted over old ones or the houses they adorn are demolished. A detailed archive of Northern Ireland's murals is maintained by the University of Ulster at Ⓦcain.ulst.ac.uk/mccormick and another large collection of photographs can be found at Ⓦwww.belfastmurals.net.

Loyalist murals

For most of the twentieth century, mural painting in Northern Ireland was a predominantly **Loyalist** activity. The first mural appeared in East Belfast in 1908 and, like many of its successors, celebrated **King Billy**'s victory at the **Battle of the Boyne**. Loyalist murals have tended to use imagery symbolic of power, such as the clenched scarlet fist, known as the **Red Hand of Ulster**, or flags, shields and other heraldic icons. However, the Loyalist response to the Troubles translated into what is now the most common form of painting, the militaristic mural. If King Billy appears at all, it is often with a guard of balaclava-clad, weapon-toting **paramilitaries**, accompanied by a threatening slogan. Inspired by the desire for "no surrender" and preservation of the status quo, Loyalist mural-painting is certainly less dynamic and diverse than its Republican counterpart. A typical example, on Hopewell Crescent in the Lower Shankill, shows two masked gunmen crouching beside a clenched red fist which is surrounded by the Union Flag and the flags of Ulster, the UFF and UDA – part of the slogan reads "Lower Shankill UFF. Simply the best."

Recently, Loyalist murals have sought to undermine Sinn Féin's role in the peace process by attacking the IRA – a striking five-panelled example on the Shankill Road recalls a number of IRA bombings of Loyalist targets and carries the slogan, "30 Years of Indiscriminate Slaughter by So-Called Non-Sectarian Irish Freedom Fighters".

The greatest concentration of Loyalist murals is to be found on and around the Shankill Road, especially the Shankill Estate, to the north, and Dover Place, off Dover Street, to the south. Other areas are Sandy Row and Donegall Pass in South Belfast, and Newtownards Road, Martin Street and Severn Street in East Belfast.

Republican murals

Republican murals were at first limited to simple sloganeering or demarcation of territory, the best-known example being the long-standing "You are now entering Free Derry" in that city's Bogside district (see p.610). As with much else in Republican politics, however, the 1981 **hunger strikes** had a significant influence. Murals in support of the ten hunger strikers abounded and the (usually smiling) face of **Bobby Sands** – the IRA commander in the Maze prison who led the strike – remains an enduring image. Murals soon became a fundamental part of the Republican propaganda campaign and an expression of the community's current cultural and political concerns, though militaristic images have never really dominated Republican murals as much as they have done Loyalist ones. Prominent themes have been **resistance** to British rule, the call for the **withdrawal of troops** and questioning the **validity of the police**.

More recently, however, Republican muralists have turned increasingly to **Irish legends** and history as their sources of inspiration and the only militaristic murals tend to be found in flashpoints such as the Ardoyne. Equally, artists have paid tribute to other international **liberation movements**, as in a striking series of murals on Divis Street just before the beginning of the Falls Road. Further Republican murals can be found nearby on Beechmount Avenue, on Lenadoon Avenue in Andersonstown, and on New Lodge Road in North Belfast.

there's little of architectural note among the mainly residential streets and most of the "sights" are associated with the area's troubled past. Much of the old terraced housing has been replaced in recent years by rows of modern estates, but it's impossible to miss examples of the partisan **mural paintings** that decorate walls and gable ends in both Catholic and Protestant areas (see box opposite). Tourist information about the area is available from the West Belfast Tourist Information Point (see p.555).

The Falls

From the city centre, Divis Street, a westward continuation of Castle Street, leads to the **Falls Road**, which heads on for a further two miles west past Milltown Cemetery (see below) and into Andersonstown. The first part of the Falls Road is known as the **Lower Falls** where most of the land to the left (south) consists of modern red-brick terraced housing estates. The right-hand side of the road is more of a hotchpotch and features some of the local landmarks: the bright blue swimming baths and the DSS (the Department of Social Security, known as "the Brew" – a corruption of "bureau"), cooped up in an awning of chicken-wire. Down Conway Street (by the DSS), stands the old **Conway Mill** (Mon–Fri 9am–5pm; Ⓦwww.conwaymill.org), revitalized by a concerted community effort spearheaded by local activist Father Des Wilson. Inside you can investigate the wares of the numerous small businesses and local artists who operate from here, as well as an art gallery and a small exhibition depicting the mill's history. All the way along the Falls Road you'll spot, blocking the ends of the streets to the right, walls of iron sheeting. These comprise the "**Peace Line**", and directly behind them is the Protestant working-class district of Shankill.

Further west lie the red-brick and more recent buildings of the **Royal Victoria Hospital**, at the junction with Grosvenor Road. During the Troubles, the Royal, as it's known locally, received international acclaim for its ability to cope with the consequences of the violence. Just beyond it, in a disused Presbyterian church at 216 Falls Rd, is the **Cultúrlann MacAdam Ó Fiaich** (Mon–Wed & Sun 9am–9pm, Thurs–Sat 9am–10pm; Ⓦwww.culturlann.com), a cultural centre for Irish-speakers, housing an extensive bookshop (also selling traditional-music CDs), an excellent café and a thriving theatre, often the host to musical events. Although you are unlikely to hear it being spoken on the streets or in most pubs, the Irish language is flourishing in Catholic areas of Belfast and throughout the North; the first Irish-speaking primary school is over twenty years old, and the first secondary school was opened in 1991.

Milltown Cemetery

Follow the Falls Road west for another mile and you'll come to **Milltown Cemetery**, the main Republican burial ground in Belfast, situated opposite a fortified police station. Enter through the stone arch and you're immediately surrounded by a numbing array of Celtic and Roman crosses. If you're in search of the Republican plots, continue directly on from the entrance for about 100m, then veer right, heading towards a corrugated warehouse shed just outside the perimeter of the cemetery. Along the way are two plots, marked off by a low, green border fence. The nearer one holds a large memorial tablet listing the Republican casualties in the various uprisings from 1798 to the present day, behind which lies an empty plot still awaiting the body of Volunteer Tom Williams, hanged in Belfast Jail in 1942 and and still buried within its precincts. The far plot contains a modern granite-block sculpture, and also the graves of Bobby Sands (see p.705), Mairéad Farrell and Seán Savage, who were killed in 1988 by a British SAS unit in Gibraltar, and others. Once you start to look, it's not difficult to spot the graves of many other victims of the Troubles, a devastatingly long list of (usually young) men and women.

The M1 motorway runs along the bottom of the burial park. It was onto this stretch of road in 1988 that Michael Stone was pursued after he'd opened fire and hurled grenades at mourners attending the funeral of Seán Savage.

Shankill

The Protestant population of West Belfast lives in the area abutting the Falls to the north, between the **Shankill Road** and the Crumlin Road. As with the Falls, there's little here of special interest, apart from an array of Loyalist murals (some even including Web addresses). Along the **Crumlin Road**, in particular, are a number of evocative sites symbolizing the worst years of the Troubles. From the Westway you'll pass between the courthouse and the notorious **Crumlin Road Gaol**, the two connected by an underground tunnel; former inmates include Éamon de Valera (see p.701), Gerry Adams (see p.706) and Ian Paisley (see p.589), and it closed in 1996. One million pounds is being spent to redevelop the gaol and there are plans to open it to visitors as well as continue its occasional staging of cultural events (see Ⓦ www.dsdni.gov.uk/nbcau-index.htm). Despite many other obvious signs of redevelopment and renovation – the most apparent being the recently constructed leisure centre – the area is in decline, its population shrinking in inverse proportion to the Catholic population on the other side of the Peace Line.

Eating

Eating out in Belfast is very much a movable feast with new places popping up and others vanishing or relocating. There are plenty of options for food during the day in the centre and at the southern end of the Golden Mile, ranging from new **cafés** (many of which in the city centre stay open until 8.30pm on Thurs nights) to **traditional pubs** (which generally only serve lunch but in some cases continue providing food until 9pm – see p.574).

Most of the city's well-established **restaurants** are around Donegall Square or in the university area. Bear in mind that they are often fully booked on Friday and Saturday evenings, so you need to reserve a table unless you are prepared to eat early. There is a fair choice of cuisine, from modern Irish and European, with French and Italian especially popular, to a smattering of Indian and Chinese restaurants. Standards are generally high and often exceptionally good value for money. The choice is limited for **vegetarians**, and there's a complete dearth of wholefood restaurants, but many places now include veggie options on their menus.

Cafés

Café Conor 11A Stranmillis Rd. Opposite the Ulster Museum in the artist Willie Conor's former studio, this café has an interesting, affordable Mediterranean-style menu, and is good for brunch. Daily 9am–11pm.

Café Equinox 32 Howard St. One of the recent bloom of café-society hangouts, at the back of the Equinox interiors shop. As you'd expect, it looks good, with food to match.

Café Paul Rankin 27–29 Fountain St. Modernist interiors, gourmet coffees and, best of all, choice Mediterranean breads.

Café Renoir 93–95 Botanic Ave. Very popular branch of the local chain, offering everything from coffee and snacks to bistro-style meals and a pizzeria.

Café Vaudeville 25–39 Arthur St. Laughably pretentious on some levels, this "Art Nouveau" café-bar, somehow transplanted from Montmartre to Belfast, does serve some of the city's finest coffee and its meals successfully blend Parisian élan with down-to-earth Antrim cooking.

Deane's Deli 44 Bedford St. Offshoot of the restaurant (see below), serving splendid sandwiches and more substantial meals. Open till 10pm Wed–Sat.

Delaney's 19 Lombard St. Economical, wholesome food from a self-service café handily placed in the main shopping area.

Jenny's 81 Dublin Rd. Plain but cosy café, offering sandwiches, curries and bakes.

Maggie May's 45 Botanic Ave. Huge, economically priced portions of wholesome Irish cooking with lots of veggie choices. Be prepared to queue and bring your own wine.

Revelations 27 Shaftesbury Square. Internet café with a range of coffees and sandwiches on offer. Mon–Fri 8am–10pm, Sat 10am–6pm, Sun 11am–7pm.

Restaurants

Alden's 229 Upper Newtownards Rd ⓣ028/9065 0079. This East Belfast outpost, a mile or so out towards Stormont, is well worth the trek for its top-quality fish and seafood menus; prices for a two-course meal start from around £20 plus wine. Closed Sat lunch and Sun all day.

Archana 53 Dublin Rd ⓣ028/9032 3713. Possibly Belfast's finest Indian restaurant, serving spicy, good-value curries and balti dishes and plenty of vegetarian options.

Beatrice Kennedy 44 University Rd ⓣ028/9020 2290. Serves a cosmopolitan menu, largely focused on seafood and poultry, at around £25 per head with an early-bird two-course special for £12.95 (5–7pm). Closed Mon.

Cayenne 7 Ascot House, Shaftesbury Square ⓣ028/9033 1532. Founder of the acclaimed *Roscoff* (see below), Paul Rankin's club-meets-bistro offers everything from oysters to the best of modern Irish cuisine, heightened by adroit use of spices; expect to pay around £25 plus wine.

Deane's 34–40 Howard St ⓣ028/9033 1134. The North's only Michelin-starred restaurant is an elegant venue for stunning modern Irish cuisine with a strong French influence, but expect to pay at least £30 plus wine for two courses. There's also a brasserie here with a more affordable menu. Closed Sun. Owner Michael Deane has also recently opened *Deane's at Queen's*, 36–40 College Gardens (ⓣ028/9038 2111), which offers a more limited range of meals (some may baulk at paying £11 for fish and chips); again it's closed on Sun.

Istana 127 Great Victoria St ⓣ028/9032 2311. Very amenable restaurant serving a delicious range of good-value Malaysian specialities.

Mourne Seafood Bar 34–36 Bank St ⓣ028/9024 8544. Cracking new place for all piscivores, serving everything from shellfish and oysters to exotic dishes incorporating hake or monkfish. Reasonably priced too, and there's even an on-site fishmonger's if you fancy cooking your own. Closed Sun & Mon evenings.

Nick's Warehouse 35 Hill St ⓣ028/9043 9690. Chic, pricey and cosmopolitan restaurant upstairs and an atmospheric wine bar and less expensive menu downstairs. Closed Sun.

▲ Crown Liquor Saloon

Roscoff 7 Linenhall St ⓣ028/9031 1150. The flagship of Paul Rankin's culinary operations serves a wonderful range of French-inspired food and has the ambience to match; from around £30 plus wine for a two-course meal. Closed Sun.

Speranza 16–19 Shaftesbury Square ⓣ028/9023 0213. Massive, reasonably priced pizza and pasta specialist in plush modern surroundings.

Tedford's 5 Donegall Quay ⓣ028/9043 4000. Another great place for fresh seafood, including lobster and king scallops, as well as an enticing range of meat dishes; expect to pay around £30 plus wine for two courses though there's also a theatre menu (£18.95), in keeping with its handiness for the Waterfront Hall. Closed Mon & Tues lunch and Sun all day.

Drinking, nightlife and entertainment

Belfast has numerous excellent **pubs** concentrated in the city centre and the **club** and **music** scenes continue to thrive on Fridays and Saturdays, although Sundays can be quiet, with many bars closing early or remaining shut all day. To tap into the city's pulse, your best bet is to wander around the Entries or up and around Donegall Street, while there's plenty of action at each end of the Golden Mile. For the latest **information** on what's going on, the monthly listings freesheet *The Big List* is essential, though the *Belfast Telegraph* also features extensive, if somewhat disorganized, listings.

Pubs and bars

As always in Ireland, the **pubs** are the heart of the city. The liveliest in the evenings are on Great Victoria Street, on and near Donegall Street, and around the university, and if you start drinking at the famed *Crown Liquor Saloon* (see p.564 and below) you can manage a substantial pub crawl without moving more than a few hundred yards. If you're short of time, you could always join the **Historical Pub Tour**, covering six of Belfast's best-known bars (see box on p.556). For pub reviews, check ⓦwww.belfastbar.co.uk.

In addition to the handful of places mentioned here, there are dozens of pubs around the city which double up as venues for live music of one sort or another; we've listed these separately below.

The Bridge House 35–37 Bedford St. A Wetherspoon's mega-pub offering probably Belfast's cheapest pint of stout and a range of cheap meals.

Crown Liquor Saloon 46 Great Victoria St, opposite the *Europa Hotel*. The most famous and spectacular pub in Belfast, with a clientele that thinks itself intellectual (there's no music). Good repertoire of Ulster food – champ, colcannon and the like – and also Strangford oysters in season, which usually go by early afternoon.

The Deers Head 1 Lower Garfield St. Fine, traditional pub, offering very filling bar meals.

The Monico 17 Lombard St. Tiled floors, wood panelling and snugs galore characterize this traditional pub.

Morning Star 17 Pottinger's Entry. This fine old-fashioned bar, busy in the day, quiet at night, is one of Belfast's best preserved and provides a wonderfully good value buffet lunch.

Live music

The best Belfast entertainment is **music** in the pubs, and most tastes can be satisfied by the diversity on offer. The number of visiting international performers has increased dramatically since the opening of the Waterfront Hall and Odyssey Arena, and the local scene is thriving too – there are always good up-and-coming bands playing in the city, just waiting to get noticed. While traditional music usually comes free with your pint, rock venues may

Gay and lesbian Belfast

The main resource of Belfast's **gay scene** is Queerspace, part of Cara-Friend, Cathedral Buildings, Donegall Street (Ⓦwww.queerspace.org.uk), a collective that aims to serve the needs and raise the profile of the gay, lesbian, bisexual and transgender community of Belfast and Northern Ireland; it holds weekly drop-in sessions on Saturday afternoons (3–6pm). Alternatively, there's Ⓦwww.gaybelfast.net which provides plenty of information on entertainment and nightlife. **Helplines** include Cara-Friend (Ⓣ028/9032 2023; Mon–Wed 7.30–10pm) and Lesbian Line (Ⓣ028/9023 6668; Thurs 7.30–10pm). Belfast's **Gay Pride** (Ⓦwww.belfastpride.com) week begins on the last Saturday in July.

The number of gay bars and venues has increased substantially over the last few years (though the majority are geared towards men) and include:

Dubarrys 10–14 Gresham St Ⓣ028/9032 3590, Ⓦwww.dubarrysbar.co.uk. Plush new three-storey bar-cum-venue in one of the city's most run-down areas, certainly more laid-back than its competitors and featuring a lesbian night on the first Friday of each month in its top-floor *Seduction Lounge*.

Forbidden Fruit at *The Potthouse*, 1 Hill St (see below). Long-standing Monday-night gay-men's mega-bash, featuring two rooms full of commercial and house sounds and compere Titty von Tramp.

Kremlin 96 Donegall St Ⓣ028/9031 6060, Ⓦwww.kremlin-belfast.com. Ireland's biggest gay venue, featuring three bars and various themed nights of music, fun and games, including the hugely popular "Revolution" on Saturdays.

Mynt 2–16 Dunbar St Ⓣ028/9023 4520, Ⓦwww.myntbelfast.com. Lounge bar for all of the week whose downstairs (Wed–Sun) and upstairs (Fri & Sat) areas provide all manner of fun. The former concentrates on participatory entertainment such as quizzes and karaoke, while the latter is firmly aimed at all dance maniacs.

Union Street 14 Union St Ⓣ028/9031 6060, Ⓦwww.unionstreetpub.com. This daytime gastropub also hosts a variety of themed nights for gay men, ranging from karaoke to bingo, via deck-thumping DJs.

charge between £4 and £15 depending on the act's reputation. Pre-booked tickets for the biggest names will usually cost much more – between £15 and £50.

Traditional music

The Duke of York 11 Commercial Court, off Donegall St. Convivial bar with a traditional session on Thurs often featuring the fine fiddler Dónal O'Connor.

The Garrick 29 Chichester St. Fine old bar serving excellent lunches throughout the week plus Irish stew and a pint for a fiver on Sun at 5pm; traditional sessions Wed (9pm) and Fri (5pm).

The John Hewitt 53 Donegall St. Light and airy pub run by the Belfast Unemployed Resource Centre, with newspapers, paintings by local artists on sale, plus excellent traditional sessions (Tues 9.30pm, Fri & Sat 6pm) as well as traditional jazz on Fri (8.30pm) and singer-songwriters on Mon (9pm). Also serves healthy, reasonably priced meals.

Kelly's Cellars 30 Bank St. Belfast's oldest surviving continually run pub and, according to legend, a frequent meeting place for the United Irishmen behind the doomed 1798 rebellion – Henry Joy McCracken hid under the bar counter from British soldiers. Good lunches, including thumping portions of home-made Irish stew and steak pie, and traditional music several nights a week.

Madden's Berry St. Wonderful, unpretentious, atmospheric pub, with lots of locals drinking in two large rooms, one upstairs, one downstairs. Serves cheap stew and soup and there are excellent traditional sessions (Mon, Fri & Sat 9.30pm).

White's Tavern Winecellar Entry, High St. Atmospheric old Entries bar, with stone floors and an open fire, serving excellent lunches and hosting traditional sessions downstairs (Fri–Sun) and DJs upstairs (Fri & Sat).

Rock, indie, blues and beyond

Auntie Annie's Dublin Rd ⓣ028/9050 1660, ⓦwww.the-limelight.co.uk. Large drinking emporium with music on two floors most nights (singer-songwriters downstairs; rock, indie and DJs upstairs).

The Botanic Inn 23 Malone Rd ⓣ028/9050 9740, ⓦwww.thebotanicinn.com. Perhaps inevitably known as the "Bot", this place caters almost entirely to students and has plenty of atmosphere. Features events nightly, including folk music (Wed), live singers or bands (Thurs) and DJs at the weekend.

The Empire Bar & Music Hall 42 Botanic Ave ⓣ028/9030 8112, ⓦwww.thebelfastempire.com. Cellar bar in a former church just up from the station, with a boisterous beer-hall atmosphere. Good-value food and bands most nights of the week with DJs and bigger-name bands upstairs.

Katy Daly's/The Limelight/Spring and Airbrake 15–19 Ormeau Ave ⓣ028/9032 5968, ⓦwww.the-limelight.co.uk. These three places under the same management are, respectively, a cavernous and popular bar club with a broad-ranging music programme; one of the North's leading live-music venues; and a smaller bar-cum-club offering an eclectic mix of singers and bands, plus DJs.

The Kitchen Bar 36–40 Victoria Square. Sadly, the atmospheric old bar was demolished to facilitate the area's redevelopment, but this much grander and airier version has been constructed nearby. Still under the same welcoming management, the bar features superb-value lunches, jazz on Thurs (5–7pm) and acoustic music on Fri (8.30pm).

Lavery's Gin Palace Ssee opposite.

The Odyssey Arena 2 Queen's Quay ⓣ028/9073 9074, ⓦwww.odysseyarena.com. The place where the biggest rock and pop singers and bands perform.

The Pavilion Bar 296 Ormeau Rd ⓣ028/9028, 3283, ⓦwww.laverysbelfast.com/thepavilion/index.asp. Possibly "the" place to catch up-and-coming young indie bands.

Robinson's 38 Great Victoria St. Theme bar spread over four floors and overshadowed by the *Crown* next door, *Robinson's* is packed at lunchtimes with local workers taking advantage of the cheap menus. Live folk and traditional music nightly in the *Fibber McGee's* section, and DJs upstairs in *Roxy* (Fri & Sat 9pm–1am).

Rotterdam Bar 54 Pilot St ⓣ028/9074 6021, ⓦwww.rotterdambar.com. A dockland institution, with bands most nights, leaning towards singer-songwriters, blues, rock and new country. Somewhat off the beaten track, a mile or so northeast of the centre, it's best to take a taxi to get here.

Clubs and DJ bars

Belfast's **club scene** isn't what it was ten years ago, but there are still plenty of dance dens, as well as pre-club **DJ bars** around. Check *The Big List* for who's on when; you'll find most venues run different clubs on different nights. Venues are scattered fairly evenly around the city centre; students – not surprisingly – tend to dominate those closest to the university area. Admission may be free early in the week (and at some places all week) and as low as £2 or £3 up to Thursday nights, while weekend prices are usually around £5 to £10. Many places stay open until 1am Monday to Thursday and till 2am on Fridays and Saturdays.

Apartment 2 Donegall Square ⓣ028/9050 9777, ⓦwww.apartmentbelfast.com. Describing itself as "urban living made easy", this swish bar gives denizens the chance to look down on the square and is the place for bright young Belfast to be seen, even when eating breakfast; DJs most nights. Mon–Sat 8am–1am, Sun noon–midnight.

Bar Bacca 43 Franklin St ⓣ028/9023 0200, ⓦwww.barbacca.com. Exceedingly hip establishment, right down to the Oriental furnishings and a giant Buddha above the door, popular with the cocktail crowd who soak up Thurs acoustic nights and Fri/Sat club nights with DJs spinning everything from Augustus Pablo to Funkadelic. Mon–Fri noon–1am, Sat 4pm–1am.

Basement Bar 16 Donegall Square East ⓣ028/9033 1925, ⓦwww.basementbistrobar.co.uk. Popular underground bistro-bar dishing up good-value meals (Mon–Sat noon–9pm) with live jazz-funk on Fri and guest DJs on Sat. Closed Sun.

Benedicts Hotel 7–21 Bradbury Place ⓣ028/9059 1999, ⓦwww.benedictshotel.co.uk. Gothic-themed bar (architecturally, not musically) offering live music (Mon–Wed) and DJs (Thurs–Sun); strict dress code – no sportswear – and over-21s only.

The Eg Bar 32 Malone Rd ⓣ028/9038 1994, ⓦwww.egbar.co.uk. Located across the road from the "Bot" (see above), this is another student-packed place. Very crowded, with DJs most of the week.

The Fly Bar 5–6 Lower Crescent Ⓣ028/9050 9750, Ⓦwww.theflybar.com. Vibrant three-storey venue, though when it's empty it really does feel empty. DJs from the more populist end of the market (Wed–Sat).
Irene & Nan's 12 Brunswick St. Busy designer pub with DJs at the weekend.
Lavery's Gin Palace 14 Bradbury Place Ⓣ028/9087 1106, Ⓦwww.laverysbelfast.com. Snazzy outside but a regular pub within. The *Back Bar* has music of the live or DJ variety every night, including a reggae, ska and dub club on Mon and the definitely "Eclectic Electric" (Sat). The *Bunker Bar* features live bands most nights of the week.
Milk 10–14 Tomb St Ⓣ028/9027 8876, Ⓦwww.clubmilk.com. Ever-popular and ever-packed docklands club offering dance music to suit all tastes Thurs–Sun.
Northern Whig 2–10 Bridge St. Massive but comfy bar in the premises of the old newspaper, featuring DJs Fri & Sat.
The Stiff Kitten 1 Bankmore Square Ⓣ028/9023 8700, Ⓦwww.thestiffkitten.com. The city's new kid on the block, a tasty bar serving great-value meals during the daytime and a diverse range of spun music in the evenings.
The Sugar Room Above *The Potthouse*, 1 Hill St Ⓣ028/9024 4044, Ⓦwww.potthouse.co.uk. Major club in a renovated seventeenth-century pottery, dishing up a raucous diet of R&B, funk and house for over-21s. Fri & Sat.
Thompson's 3 Patterson's Place, Arthur St Ⓣ028/9032 3762, Ⓦwww.clubthompsons.com. Once a garage owned by aviation freak Harry Ferguson, this place now hosts a variety of club nights featuring commercial house, funk and R&B.

Classical music and opera

Almost all classical-music concerts take place in the Ulster or Waterfront halls, while opera fans are catered for by the Grand Opera House. Tickets for the Ulster Orchestra's performances at the Waterfront, Ulster and Whitla halls are available from Elmwood Hall, Queen's University Belfast, 89 University Rd (Ⓣ028/9066 8798, Ⓦwww.ulster-orchestra.org.uk).

Grand Opera House Great Victoria St Ⓣ028/9024 1919, Ⓦwww.goh.co.uk. Belfast's most prestigious venue, featuring regular operatic performances as well as many of London's West End productions.
Ulster Hall Bedford St Ⓣ028/9032 3900, Ⓦwww.ulsterhall.co.uk. Most of the city's classical-music performances are given by the Ulster Orchestra; the hall is also used for big rock and pop concerts. At the time of writing the hall was closed for major refurbishment.
Waterfront Hall Lanyon Place, Laganside Ⓣ028/9033 4400, Ⓦwww.waterfront.co.uk. Hosts classical music and ballet, mainstream jazz and occasional big names from the moribund world of middle-of-the-road pop and rock.
Whitla Hall Queen's University Ⓣ028/9027 3075. Stages some professional and amateur classical concerts.

Theatre, cinema and art

Most of Belfast's theatres and cinemas are concentrated in the south of the city. Although the choice for both is relatively limited, there is still enough to please most tastes.

Theatres and arts centres

Crescent Arts Centre 2–4 University Rd Ⓣ028/9024 2338, Ⓦwww.crescentarts.org. A focus for much of Belfast's left-field arts and performance activities and home to the Fenderesky Gallery (Tues–Sat 11.30am–5pm), displaying often splendid works by local artists.
Lyric Theatre 55 Ridgeway St, off Stranmillis Rd Ⓣ028/9038 1081, Ⓦwww.lyrictheatre.co.uk. Stages more serious contemporary drama, and gave actor Liam Neeson an early platform.
Old Museum Arts Centre 7 College Square North Ⓣ028/9023 5053, Ⓦwww.oldmuseumartscentre.org. The place to go for experimental or fringe productions; also hosts regular art exhibitions.

Cinemas

Mainstream **cinemas** showing general releases include the multi-screen Movie House on Dublin Road (Ⓣ028/9024 5700, Ⓦwww.moviehouse.co.uk) and Storm Cinemas in the Odyssey Complex (Ⓣ028/9073 9134, Ⓦwww.stormcinemas.co.uk). Alternatively, Queen's Film Theatre, 20 University Square (Ⓣ028/9097 1097, Ⓦwww.queensfilmtheatre.com), has two screens screening art-house movies and late-night shows at exceptionally good prices. Additionally, the Odyssey Complex includes the Sheridan IMAX cinema (Ⓣ028/9046 7000, Ⓦwww.belfastimax.com), with a screen ten times larger than normal.

Spectator sports

Though watching, discussing and betting on **sport** is as much of a pastime in Belfast as anywhere else, you'll find very few locals expressing particularly passionate opinions about the city's teams and players, with the notable exception of boxing. Indeed, when people watch sport here, it's usually the televised variety, and attendances for most events are relatively small, an indifference that applies equally to the North's national teams. Nevertheless, if you're interested in attending a match of whatever kind, there are plenty of opportunities, and the *Belfast Telegraph* usually has the details.

The Northern Ireland **football** (soccer) team has enjoyed little success on the international stage over the last twenty years, but lit a blaze of glory in the summer of 2005 when it defeated England 1–0 in Belfast, reignited by a 3–2 victory over Spain the following year. Internationals are played at **Windsor Park** (the home ground of the Linfield club) near the Lisburn Road (buses #9A and #9B to Lower Windsor Avenue). The biggest club sides in Belfast – paradoxically enough – are Glasgow's Celtic and Rangers, generally supported respectively by Catholics and Protestants, as well as Liverpool and Manchester United.

Since football is the Belfast sport, success at either **hurling** or **Gaelic football** has been lacking, and County Antrim (which in this case includes Belfast for sporting purposes) has never won either All-Ireland Senior Final. You can see both sports most weekends at Roger Casement Park, on Andersonstown Road (buses #10A, #10B, #10C and #10D), where the Ulster Hurling Final is held in July.

The provincial **rugby-union** team, Ulster, plays its games at the Ravenhill Grounds, Ravenhill Park (bus #79), and features in both the Celtic League and the Heineken Cup. Perhaps the most popularly attended matches are the **ice-hockey** games at the Odyssey Arena (see p.563), featuring the Belfast Giants.

Listings

Airlines Aer Árann Ⓣ0870 876 7676, Ⓦwww.aerarann.com; Aer Lingus Ⓣ0870 876 5000, Ⓦwww.aerlingus.com; bmi Ⓣ0870 670 0555, Ⓦwww.flybmi.com; bmibaby Ⓣ0870 224 0224, Ⓦwww.bmibaby.com; City Jet Ⓣ0870 142 4343, Ⓦwww.airfrance.co.uk; Continental Ⓣ0845 607 6760, Ⓦwww.continental.com; easyJet Ⓣ0871 244 2366, Ⓦwww.easyjet.com; flyBe Ⓣ0871 522 6100, Ⓦwww.flybe.com; Fly Whoosh Ⓣ0871 282 6767, Ⓦwww.flywhoosh.com; jet2.com Ⓣ0871 226 1737, Ⓦwww.jet2.com; Manx2 Ⓣ0871 200 0440, Ⓦwww.manx2.com; Ryanair Ⓣ0871 246 0000, Ⓦwww.ryanair.com; Zoom Airlines Ⓣ0870 240 0055, Ⓦwww.flyzoom.com.

Bike rental McConvey Cycles, 183 Ormeau Rd Ⓣ028/9033 0322, Ⓦwww.rentabikebelfast.com.

Books Bookfinders at 47 University Rd has second-hand books and, alternatively, there's Harry Hall's at 39 Gresham St. There's also the University Bookshop, 91 University Rd (see p.566); Waterstone's on Fountain St; and branches of Eason's on Botanic Ave and Donegall Place. No Alibis, 83 Botanic Ave, specializes in crime books.
Car rental Alamo at Belfast International Airport (BIA) and George Best Belfast City Airport (GBBCA) ⓣ0870/191 6921; Argus at Belfast International Airport (BIA) and George Best Belfast City Airport (GBBCA) ⓣ00353 1/499 9600; Avis at 69–71 Great Victoria St ⓣ028/9024 0404, BIA ⓣ0870 608 6317 and GBBCA ⓣ0870 608 6317; Budget at 96–102 Great Victoria St ⓣ028/9023 0700, BIA ⓣ028/9442 3332 and GBBCA ⓣ028/0945 1111; Enterprise at 1 Boucher Crescent ⓣ028/9066 6767; Hertz at BIA ⓣ028/9442 2533 and GBBCA ⓣ028/9073 2451.
Ferries Norfolkline, West Bank Rd ⓣ0870 600 4321, ⓦwww.norfolkline.com; P&O Irish Sea, Larne Harbour ⓣ0870 242 4777, ⓦwww.poirishsea.com; Stena Line, Corry Rd ⓣ0870 570 7070, ⓦwww.stenaline.co.uk.
Festivals The Belfast Festival at Queen's University (ⓦwww.belfastfestival.com), which lasts for two to three weeks from late Oct to Nov, claims to be Britain's second-biggest arts festival after Edinburgh. Others are the week-long Titanic Made in Belfast Festival in mid-March with plenty of shipping-related events and exhibitions; the Belfast Film Festival in mid-April (ⓦwww.belfastfilmfestival.org); the Cathedral Quarter Arts Festival for ten days in early May (ⓦwww.cqaf.com); Orange Parades on July 12 (and marching season from Easter onwards); and the Open House folk and traditional-music festival (ⓦwww.openhousefestival.com), running for five days or so in late Sept. In addition, early Aug sees the West Belfast Féile An Phobail (ⓦwww.feilebelfast.com), a week-long music and dance festival.
Hospitals Belfast City Hospital, Lisburn Rd ⓣ028/9032 9241; Royal Victoria Hospital, Grosvenor Rd ⓣ028/9024 0503.
Internet access Belfast Welcome Centre, 47 Donegall Place; Friends Café, 109–113 Royal Ave; No Geeks, Castle Court Centre; *Revelations*, 27 Shaftesbury Square.
Laundry Globe, 37–39 Botanic Ave ⓣ028/9024 3956.
Left luggage Belfast Welcome Centre, 47 Donegall Place.
Lost property Musgrave Police Station, Ann St ⓣ028/9065 0222.
Markets The huge St George's Market in May St (Fri 6am–2pm & Sat 9am–3.30pm) is the liveliest; the Fri food and variety market is by far the more popular, with about two hundred traders taking part, while Sat focuses on organic produce and gardens. The Smithfield Retail Market, at the back of the Castle Court development on West St/Winetavern St, is also pretty good; it operates from about thirty shop units and sells new and second-hand goods and clothes.
Pharmacies Boots, 35–47 Donegall Place; Bradbury Pharmacy, 24–31 Shaftesbury Square.
Police In an emergency, call ⓣ999 or 112. The main city-centre police station is in North Queen St.
Post offices 12–16 Bridge St and Shaftesbury Square (Mon–Sat 9am–5.30pm).

Travel details

Trains

Belfast (Central) to: Antrim (Mon–Sat 9–10 daily, Sun 6; 25min); Ballymena (Mon–Sat 9–10 daily, Sun 6; 35min); Bangor (Mon–Sat every 15–30min, Sat every 30 min, Sun hourly; 20–30min); Carrickfergus (Mon–Sat every 30min, Sun 9; 25min); Cultra for the Ulster Folk and Transport Museum (Mon–Sat every 20–30min, Sat every 30 min, Sun hourly; 15min); Derry (Mon–Sat 9 daily, Sun 4; 2hr 10min); Drogheda (Mon–Sat 7 daily, Sun 5; 1hr 35min); Dublin (Mon–Sat 8 daily, Sun 5; 1hr 50min–2hr 15min); Dundalk (Mon–Sat 7 daily, Sun 5; 1hr 10min); Larne harbour (Mon–Sat 15–16 daily, Sun 9; 55min); Larne town (Mon–Fri 23 daily, Sat 18, Sun 9; 50min); Lisburn (Mon–Sat every 15–30min, Sat every 30 min, Sun hourly; 15–30min); Newry (Mon–Sat 7 daily, Sun 5; 55min).
Belfast (Great Victoria St) to: Antrim (Mon–Sat 9–10 daily, Sun 6; 35min); Ballymena (Mon–Sat 9–10 daily, Sun 6; 45min); Bangor (Mon–Sat every 15–30min, Sun hourly; 25–40min); Cultra for the Ulster Folk and Transport Museum (Mon–Sat every 20–30min, Sat every 30 min, Sun hourly; 20min); Derry (Mon–Sat 9 daily, Sun 4; 2hr 20min); Lisburn (Mon–Sat every 15–30min, Sat every 30 min, Sun hourly; 10–25min).

Belfast (Yorkgate) to: Larne harbour (Mon–Fri 14 daily, Sat 17, Sun 9; 50min); Larne town (Mon–Fri 20 daily, Sat 18, Sun 9; 45min).

Buses

Only details of direct services from Belfast are listed. Call **Ulsterbus** on ⓣ028/9066 6630 for information on bus connections to places not included here.

The **Antrim Coaster** service runs from Belfast/Larne to Coleraine via the Glens of Antrim, Ballycastle and the Giant's Causeway; see p.620 for full details.

Note that services on the Belfast–Dublin Airport–Dublin route depart from Glengall St, adjacent to the Europa bus station, between 1am and 5am, and that all Laganside services operate from Europa on Sun.

Belfast (Europa) to: Annalong (Mon–Sat 3 daily, Sun 1; 1hr 35min); Antrim (Mon–Fri 21 daily, Sat 18, Sun 2–3; 35–40min); Armagh (Mon–Fri 14 daily, Sat 5, Sun 3; 1hr 5min–1hr 30min); Athlone (Mon–Sat 1 daily; 4hr 50min); Ballymena (Mon–Fri 25 daily, Sat 13, Sun 2–3; 1hr); Cavan (Sat–Thurs 2 daily, Fri 3; 2hr 40min–3hr 45min); Derry (Mon–Fri 33 daily, Sat 20, Sun 11; 1hr 40min); Downpatrick (Mon–Fri 15 daily, Sat 11; 1hr–1hr 10min); Drogheda (9 daily; 1hr 40min); Dublin (20 daily; 2hr 40min–2hr 55min); Dublin Airport (20 daily; 2hr 10min–2hr 35min); Dundalk (9 daily; 1hr 10min–1hr 20min); Dungiven (Mon–Fri 33 daily, Sat 20, Sun 11; 1hr 5min); Enniskillen (Mon–Fri 16 daily, Sat 9, Sun 2; 1hr 50min–2hr 15min); Galway (Fri & Sun 1 daily; 6hr 45min); Hillsborough (Mon–Fri 24 daily, Sat 15, Sun 8; 25min); Kilkeel (Mon–Sat 3 daily, Sun 1; 1hr 50min); Larne (Mon–Fri 13 daily, Sat 6, Sun 3; 55min); Limavady (Mon–Sat 2 daily, Sun 1; 1hr 35min); Magherafelt (Mon–Sat 4 daily, Sun 2; 1hr 10min–1hr 20min); Monaghan (Sat–Thurs 2 daily, Fri 3; 1hr 35min–2hr); Moneymore (Mon–Sat 4 daily, Sun 2; 1hr 25min–1hr 35min); Newcastle (Mon–Fri 5 daily, Sat 4, Sun 1; 1hr 10min); Newry (Mon–Fri 29 daily, Sat 15, Sun 8; 1hr 10min); Omagh (Mon–Fri 17 daily, Sat 10, Sun 6; 1hr 30min–1hr 45min).

Belfast (Laganside) to: Bangor (Mon–Sat 24 daily, Sun 8; 45min); Cultra for the Ulster Folk and Transport Museum (Mon–Sat 24 daily, Sun 8; 30min); Newtownards (Mon–Fri 44 daily, Sat 25, Sun 14; 35min); Portaferry (Mon–Fri 6 daily, Sat 8, Sun 2; 1hr 15min–1hr 45min).

14

Antrim and Derry

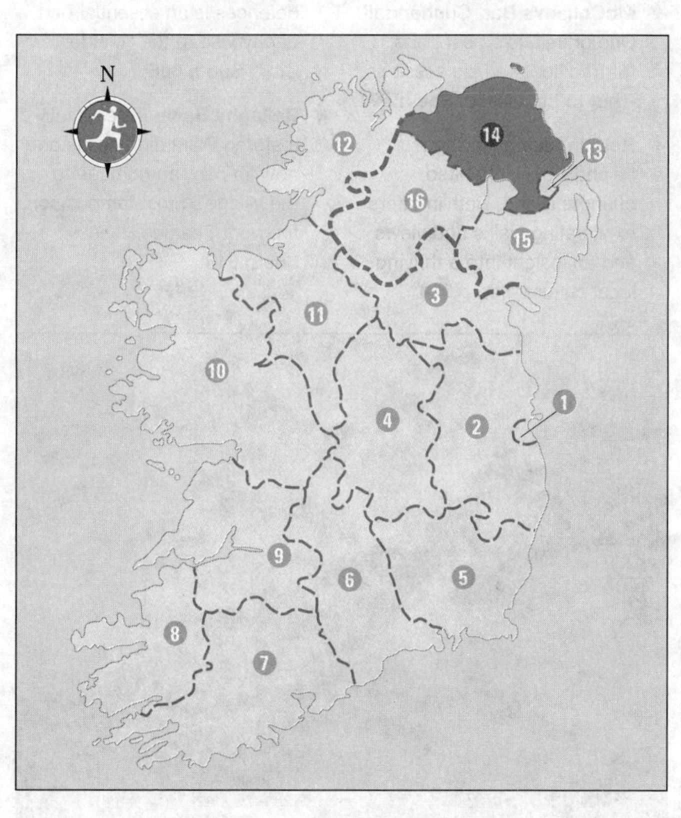

CHAPTER 14

Highlights

* **The Antrim Coast Road** The route from Larne to Portrush, skirting the Glens of Antrim, is one of Ireland's most scenic, with magical seascapes, staggering cliff-top walks and some of the North's prettiest villages. See p.588

* **McCollam's Bar, Cushendall** One of Ireland's best pubs for traditional-music sessions – not to be missed. See p.591

* **Rathlin Island** Northern Ireland's only inhabited offshore island, Rathlin offers exhilarating walks and views and an insight into a thriving local culture. See p.594

* **The Giant's Causeway** Get there early to beat the crowds and marvel at one of the strangest geological formations in Europe. See p.596

* **The Walls of Derry** A circuit of these seventeenth-century defences is an essential part of any visit to the "Maiden City". See p.606

* **Bellaghy Bawn** A beautifully restored Plantation castle and now, in part, an homage to the village's most famous son, the poet Seamus Heaney. See p.618

▲ The Antrim Coast Road

Antrim and Derry

Much of the coastline of **County Antrim** is as spectacular as anything you'll find across the whole of Ireland and, consequently, unlike other parts of the North, it has always attracted an abundance of tourists. North from the ferry port of **Larne**, the A2 coast road takes in attractive villages and small towns, such as **Carnlough**, **Cushendall** and the port of **Ballycastle**, all set against or within the verdant Antrim **Glens**. A short boat trip from Ballycastle lies rugged **Rathlin Island**, while further along the coast to the west, blustery cliff-top walks lead to the strange basalt formations of the **Giant's Causeway**. With an attractive backdrop, **Portrush** and, just over the border in Derry, **Portstewart** are popular seaside holiday resorts. In contrast, inland Antrim is a pretty dull mix of bland farmland and dour Loyalist towns, though **Ballymena** does offer the notable ecology-focused ECOS Centre.

County Derry's coastline is also blessed with wonderful strands, overlooked by **Mount Binevenagh** and the eccentric **Mussenden Temple**. **Derry city** itself is a lively place, set on the banks of the **Foyle**, with its hilltop core still enclosed by one of the best-preserved city walls in Europe. The county's hinterland is more dramatic than Antrim's, especially where it skirts the Sperrin Mountains around historic **Dungiven**. The flatter territory towards Lough Neagh features some noteworthy Plantation settlements at **Magherafelt** and **Moneymore**.

The two counties have a more than decent transport infrastructure, including an extensive bus network and the rickety but generally efficient rail line from Belfast to Derry. The latter city is also a hub for buses to Donegal.

County Antrim

County Antrim's major attractions are the nine **Glens of Antrim** in its northeast corner, fertile green fingers probing inland from high cliffs, and, in its northwestern corner, the weird geometry of the **Giant's Causeway**. Much of the predominantly Protestant population here has it roots in Scotland and, on fine days, their homeland in the shape of the Mull of Kintyre and the islands of Islay and Jura are clearly visible across the water. As you follow the coast road (A2) further west, you'll come to one of the North's great seaside resorts, **Portrush**, a popular holiday spot with sandy beaches and waves perfect for surfing.

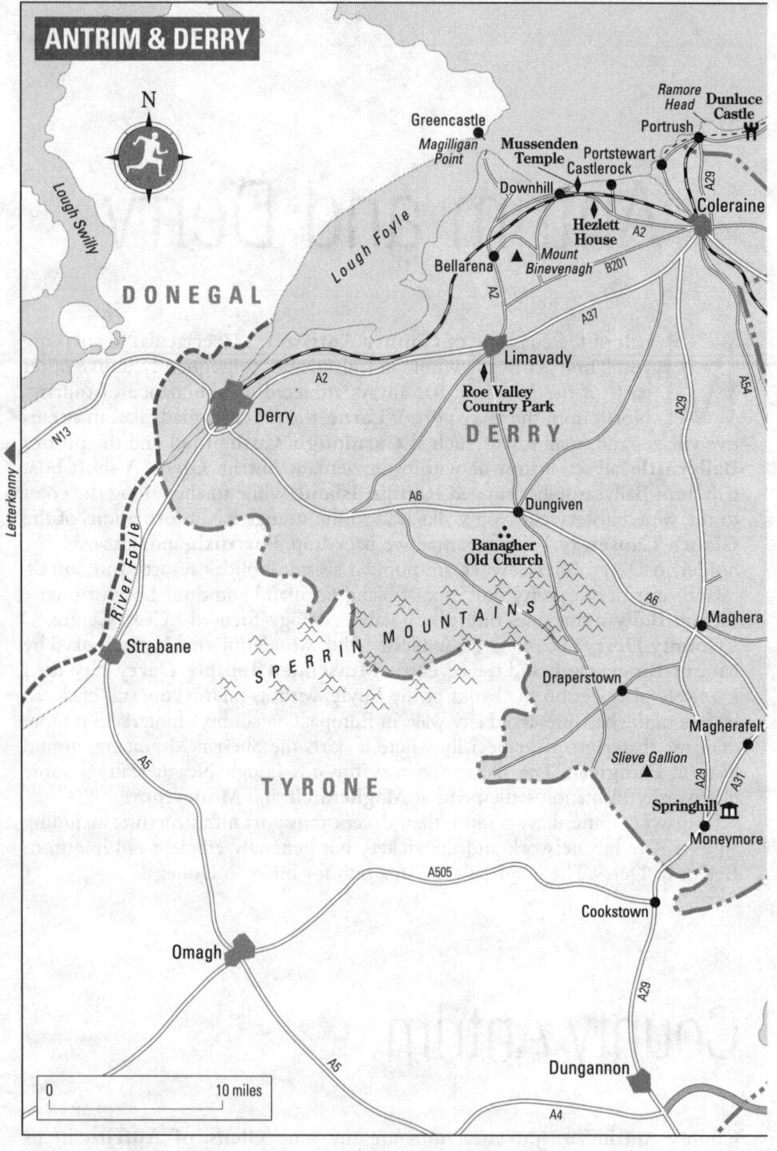

If you're not driving, **transport** around the coastline can be a problem. **Buses** are infrequent, although there are summer specials to the various sights, or you can take the **train**, though it cuts a less-interesting inland route through bland farming country on its way via Coleraine to Portrush.

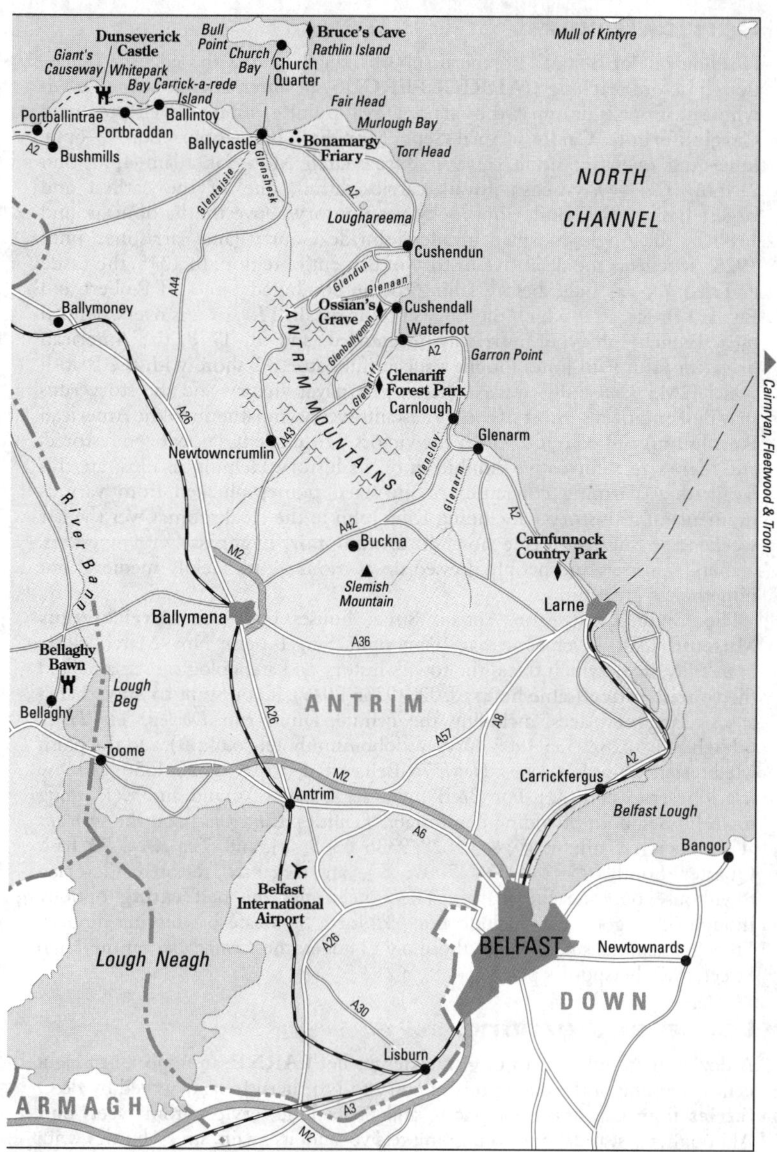

North from Belfast

The coastal strip from Belfast to Larne is largely uninspiring farmland, although there are a few spots to detain you as you head towards the more enticing Antrim Glens further north.

Carrickfergus

Heading out of Belfast's northern suburbs, the A2 skirts the edge of Belfast Lough before reaching **CARRICKFERGUS**, an unremarkable seaside town whose seafront is dominated by its only real point of interest, well-preserved **Carrickfergus Castle** (April–Sept Mon–Sat 10am–6pm, Sun 2–6pm; June–Aug opens at noon on Sun; Oct–March Mon–Sat 10am–4pm, Sun 2–4pm; £3; Ⓦwww.ehsni.gov.uk/carrick.shtml), one of the earliest and largest Irish castles. Built on a rocky promontory above the harbour around 1180 by the Anglo-Norman invader John de Courcy (and garrisoned until 1928), it reflects the defensive history of this entire region. In 1315, the castle endured a year's siege before falling to the combined forces of Robert and Edward Bruce, after which the English retook it. In 1760, it was overwhelmed by a French force but hurriedly recaptured, and, in 1778, the American privateer John Paul Jones fought a successful battle off-shore with the British vessel HMS *Drake*; this was America's first naval victory, and the story runs that Belfast citizens (most of the Protestants were sympathetic to the American Revolution) rushed out to cheer the victors. The castle has now been restored, and there's an informative exhibition on its history. Helping to illustrate this is a rather alarming collection of life-sized figures plucked from various moments of its history – including King John in the cloakroom. Over the last weekend in July the castle hosts an **annual fair**, Lughnasa, with wrestlers, archers, minstrels and people dressed up as monks – it's tackily medieval but nonetheless great fun.

The **Civic Centre** on Antrim Street houses both the **Carrickfergus Museum** (April–Oct Mon–Sat 10am–6pm, Sun 1–6pm; Nov–March closes 5pm daily; free), which traces the town's history and archeological remains, and the **tourist office** (same hours; Ⓣ028/9335 8049). If you want **to stay**, there's a scattering of places, including the central, family-run *Dobbins Inn Hotel*, 6 High St (Ⓣ028/9335 1905, Ⓦwww.dobbinsinnhotel.co.uk; ❸), and the plush Mediterranean-style *Clarion Hotel*, 75 Belfast Rd (Ⓣ028/9336 4556, Ⓦwww.clarioncarrick.com; ❹). For B&B there are a pair of grand and welcoming town houses, both providing comfortable facilities: *Langsgarden*, on the seafront at 70 Scotch Gardens (Ⓣ & Ⓕ028/9336 6369; ❷), and *The Keep*, 93 Irish Quarter South (Ⓣ028/9336 7007; ❷), an elegantly restored Victorian townhouse opposite the marina. The hotels offer the best **eating** options, though other good bets include *Ecu*, 63 North St, a café-bar serving modern French/Italian cuisine, and, for those on a budget, the *Central Bar* on the High Street, a Wetherspoon's pub.

Larne and around

A dozen or so miles north of Carrickfergus lies **LARNE**, an important freight centre and one of the main ports of entry to Northern Ireland, served by P&O **ferries** from Cairnryan and Troon and Stena Line services from Fleetwood. Although its seaside position is impressive and its main street bustles with shoppers, it is a grim and ugly place, paint-splattered with Loyalist slogans, symbols and insignia. The town's **history** is inextricably linked to its convenience as a landing stage, perhaps most notably one night in April 1914 when the Ulster Volunteers, opposed to the Irish Home Rule Bill, unloaded some 140 tons of German arms – an astonishing 35,000 rifles and five million rounds – on the quayside here and rapidly distributed them to supporters throughout Ulster by a motorcade of several hundred vehicles. They made such a racket that local residents believed an invading army had arrived.

Three-quarters of a mile north of Larne on the Antrim coast road stands a large **monument** to the engineer of this road, William Bald, and his stalwart workers, who blasted their way through, over and round the cliffs and rocky shoreline to create this route in the 1830s. The impressive scale of this achievement becomes apparent the moment you leave Larne's dull suburbs and the view expands to take in the open sea and, beyond it, the low outline of the Scottish coast. About three miles north of Larne, **Carnfunnock Country Park** (daily 9am–dusk; free, though various charges apply for parking and activities) is a good place to stop for a walk, with a walled garden, a time garden – with a collection of sundials ranging from the simple to the arcane – a maze in the shape of Northern Ireland, and a nine-hole golf course. There are free Sunday-afternoon concerts by flute, pipe and accordion bands in summer. You can also **camp** here (Easter–Oct; ⓣ028/2827 0541).

Ferry information for P&O services from Larne can be obtained on ⓣ0870/242 4777 or for Stena Line on ⓣ0870/520 4204, local **bus** information on ⓣ028/2827 2345. If you need to stay in Larne, the **tourist office** in Narrow Gauge Road (Mon–Fri 9am–5pm; May–Sept also Sat 9am–5pm; ⓣ028/2826 0088) will book B&B **accommodation** for you, and there is plenty to choose from if you're catching an early ferry or arrive late at night. Near the ferry terminal is the comfortable *Manor Guest House*, 23 Olderfleet Rd (ⓣ028/2827 3305, ⓦwww.themanorguesthouse.com; ❷), or the equally good *Seaview Guest House*, 154–156 Curran Rd (ⓣ028/2827 2438, ⓦwww.seaviewlarne.co.uk; ❷), near the harbour. There's a **campsite** at *Curran Court Caravan Park*, 131 Curran Rd (Easter–Oct; ⓣ28/2827 3797), but you're better off at Carnfunnock Country Park (see above).

Inland Antrim

Inland Antrim consists mainly of rolling farmland, broken only by the looming bulk of **Slemish Mountain**. Though there's little to whet the appetite, the larger population centres, such as **Ballymena**, **Antrim** and Lisburn (see p.627) possess a few items of cultural interest.

Antrim town

ANTRIM is a largely undistinguished place, with a centre that demonstrates the decay that typically follows the construction of out-of-town shopping developments. The town does however possess a **tourist office**, at 16 High St (May, June & Sept Mon–Wed 9am–5pm, Thurs & Fri 9am–5.30pm, Sat 10am–1pm; July & Aug Mon–Fri 9am–5.30pm, Sat 10am–3pm; Oct–April Mon–Fri 9am–5pm; ⓣ028/9442 8331). If you've time to kill, there are a couple of diversions: a tenth-century **round tower** in Steeple Park, a mile north of town, marking the site of an important monastery that flourished between the sixth and twelfth centuries; and a pretty, if unremarkable, eighteenth-century cottage, **Pogue's Entry**, on Church Street (call ⓣ028/9448 1338 for opening times; free), the preserved childhood home of Alexander Irvine, author of *My Lady of the Chimney Corner*, which recalled his boyhood years before the Famine. Popping through the Castle Gate on Dublin Road, you'll find yourself in the pleasant gardens of the old **Antrim Castle**. The building itself was totally destroyed by fire in 1922, but the carriage house and stables now contain the **Clotworthy Art Centre** (Mon–Fri 9.30am–9.30pm, Sat 10am–5pm; July & Aug also Sun 2–5pm; ⓣ028/9448 1338; free), which is worth a look for its galleries of work by local artists and occasional international exhibitions; the centre also stages a programme of evening events.

Ballymena and around

BALLYMENA is a predominantly Protestant town and most of its original Plantation settlers came from Scotland's southwest; the Ballymena accent still retains traces of Scottish lowlands speech. Originally a linen town, the alleged tightfistedness of its residents earned it the sobriquet of the "Aberdeen of Ireland", though significant redevelopment has left little surviving from the pre-Victorian era. The town's biggest attraction is the **ECOS Environmental Centre**, Kernohans Lane, Broughshane Road (Mon–Fri 9am–5pm; also July & Aug Sat 10.30am–5pm, Sun noon–5pm; free; Ⓦwww.ecoscentre.com), a mile northeast from the centre, which features high-tech interactive galleries focusing on biodiversity, energy sustainability and alternative energy sources, as well as walking and cycling trails around its 150 acres of parkland. There is also a local **museum** (Mon–Fri 10am–5pm, Sat 10am–1pm; Oct–April closed Mon–Fri 1–2pm; free), offering plenty of information on the area's history and housing a variety of temporary exhibitions, located just behind the **tourist office**, which is at 76 Church St (Mon–Fri 9am–5pm, Sat 10am–4pm; Ⓣ028/2563 8494). At the time of writing both the museum and the tourist office were due to form part of a new development called The Braid, also featuring an arts centre, on Bridge Street, in 2008; as a result opening hours and contact numbers may change.

For miles around Ballymena the landscape is dominated by one of County Antrim's most mystical reference points, 488-metre-high **Slemish Mountain**, which is best approached from the village of **Buckna**, eight miles or so east. This extinct volcano is said to be the place where St Patrick herded swine as a slave-boy after being captured and brought to Ireland, and is consequently a place of pilgrimage on March 17 – though others claim his writings indicate that the place of his captivity was Killala, County Mayo. Whatever the truth, the mountain is a steep climb of about 240m from the car park to the summit, but the **views** are well worth the effort; to the north, you can see the ruins of **Skerry Church**, the ancient burial place of the O'Neills of Clandeboye (see p.552).

The Glens of Antrim and Rathlin Island

Northwest of Larne lie the nine **Glens of Antrim**, a curious landscape in which neat seaside villages contrast vividly with the rough moorland above. Despite their proximity to the Scottish coast, the Glens were extremely isolated until the completion of the coast road in the 1830s. Their largest town is **Ballycastle**, which is also the departure point for the ferry to rugged **Rathlin**, Northern Ireland's last inhabited offshore island, in one of whose caves Robert the Bruce of Scotland acquired a legendary lesson in patience from a spider spinning and re-spinning its web. The best base for exploration of the area, though, is **Cushendall**, a charming village 26 miles along the coast from Larne.

Glenarm

The southernmost of the Glens, **Glenarm**, is headed by a village of the same name, which grew up around a hunting lodge built by Randal MacDonnell

Ian Paisley

Born in Armagh in 1926 to a Baptist-preacher father and equally devout mother, Ballymena has long been the base of the Right Hon Reverend **Dr Ian Paisley** MP, ex-MEP, MLA, Moderator of the Free Presbyterian Church of Ulster, and leader of the now dominant force in Unionist politics, the **Democratic Unionist Party** (DUP) (Ⓦwww.ianpaisley.org). Often referred to as "Dr No", thanks to his expressed opposition to anything threatening to undermine Unionism, Partition or the Protestant faith, and possessed of one of the loudest voices, both literally and figuratively, in Northern politics, Paisley is an undeniably charismatic figure whose hefty frame, despite recent ill health, remains imposing.

Paisley sprang to prominence in the 1960s as a hard-line opponent of Republicanism and the Civil Rights Movement (see p.704), his standpoint succinctly summed up by his **no surrender** catchphrase. In 1966 he established the Ulster Protestant Volunteers, which began a bombing campaign (though Paisley has never been officially connected with it), aimed at destabilizing the government of prime minister Terence O'Neill. Three years later he was jailed for organizing an illegal counter-demonstration against a civil-rights march in Armagh. The increasing strength of his power base became clear, however, during opposition to the Sunningdale Agreement (see p.705), which was brought down by the Ulster Workers' Strike, in which both he and his supporters played a key role.

In 1971 Paisley founded the DUP as a more working-class, uncompromising alternative to the Ulster Unionists and, in 1979, was elected as one of three Northern Ireland representatives to the European Parliament, marking his arrival on the assembly's first day by attempting to shout down the then president of the European Council, former Irish prime minister Jack Lynch. During an address to the parliament by the late Pope John Paul in 1988, Paisley was ejected by fellow MEPs after interrupting the pontiff's speech by yelling repeatedly "I denounce you, Antichrist!"

One of Paisley's most notorious campaigns was the homophobic "Save Ulster from Sodomy", recently revived in opposition to the civil marriage of gay couples, but he engendered rather more publicity through his opposition to the 1985 Anglo-Irish Agreement – "Ulster Says No" – which saw him once again ejected from the Strasbourg assembly, this time for heckling Margaret Thatcher. Around this time he is alleged to have established a paramilitary unit, the Third Force, which is believed to have imported arms from South Africa, though the organization itself quickly disappeared and its weaponry is believed to have been passed on to other Loyalist paramilitary groups. Indeed, Paisley's links with Loyalist paramilitaries have always been obfuscated, not least during the controversial Drumcree Church Orange parades, which Paisley attended and addressed. And though he has never been a member of the Orange Order, he fully backs its right to march.

Paisley's loyalty to the British Crown was sorely tested during the affirmation of the 1998 Good Friday Agreement, during which he referred to Queen Elizabeth II as Tony Blair's "parrot". His position appeared to be strengthened in 2004, when the Assembly elections resulted in the DUP becoming the dominant force in political Unionism, a situation enhanced by its virtual annihilation of the Ulster Unionists in the 2005 General Election. However, Paisley's refusal to share power in the Assembly with the majority Republican party, Sinn Féin, despite the IRA's historic decision to abandon its armed campaign, led to the suspension of the Assembly until November 2006. It was not until January 2007, following further DUP successes in Assembly elections of that month, that he took up his position as First Minister, with Sinn Féin's Martin McGuinness as his deputy.

In September 2007 Paisley suddenly announced that he was stepping down in January the following year from his position as Moderator of the Free Presbyterian Church of Ulster, amid rumours of increasing disquiet amongst both that church's and DUP members about his power-sharing with Republicans.

after Dunluce Castle, further up the coast, was abandoned (see p.599). Glenarm became the major seat of the Earls of Antrim, something that might lead you to expect that **Glenarm Castle**, on the site of the lodge, would be worth seeing, but major rebuilding in the eighteenth and nineteenth centuries has left it an architectural mishmash of conflicting styles. From May to September the castle (Ⓣ028 2884 1203, Ⓦwww.glenarmcastle.com) has a few open days, focusing upon garden events and classical music. **GLENARM** village itself, though, is a delight and gives a taste of what's to follow along the coast, with a narrow main street of colour-washed buildings broadening out as it approaches an imposing gateway, the old estate entrance, which now provides access to the glen itself and a pleasant walk beside the river. Back in the village, you'll find a few cosy **bars**, the *River Café*, serving coffee and snacks, and a salmon-processing plant on the outskirts with a shop where you can inspect the wares. There's a smattering of comfortable and affordable **places to stay**, including *Riverside House*, 13 Toberwine St (Ⓣ028/2884 1474, Ⓔfaith.p.a@btopenworld.com; ❷), which offers en-suite accommodation.

Carnlough, Waterfoot and Glenariff

Rounding the next bay from Glenarm, you'll arrive at **CARNLOUGH**, standing at the head of **Glencloy**. Until the 1960s, Carnlough's way of life was linked to its limestone quarries, and the village's most striking feature today remains its sturdy limestone buildings, dating mainly from the mid-nineteenth century. Right in the village centre, running over the main road, there's a solid **stone bridge** that once carried a railway bringing material down to the **harbour**, which itself has an impressive breakwater, clock tower and limestone courthouse. On the seafront, the solid *Londonderry Arms Hotel* (Ⓣ028/2888 5255, Ⓦwww.glensofantrim.com; ❺), originally a coaching inn and once briefly owned by Winston Churchill, is a comfortable **place to stay**; you can also sample local Glenarm smoked salmon in the restaurant here, or just go for a drink and admire the bizarre collection of mementos of the 1960s champion steeplechaser Arkle. For cheaper B&B, there are rooms above the *Bridge Inn* in Bridge Street (Ⓣ028/2888 5669, Ⓦwww.mcauleyscarnlough.com; ❶).

From Carnlough the road skirts round a gaunt shoulder of land and on to **WATERFOOT**, a short strip of houses with a couple of bars that comes to life in the evenings. There are plenty of **B&Bs** around, including *Dieskirt Farm*, 104 Glen Rd (April–Dec; Ⓣ028/2177 1308, Ⓦwww.dieskirtfarm.co.uk; ❷), a very welcoming farmhouse whose recently refurbished en-suite rooms offer tremendous views of the surrounding countryside.

It's **Glenariff**, though, that is the real attraction here, a wide, lush and flat-bottomed valley that is abruptly cut off by the sea. A few miles up the glen from Waterfoot is the **Glenariff Forest Park** (daily 9am–dusk; car £4, pedestrians £1.50), which has a **campsite** (Ⓣ028/2955 6000; contact the head forester in advance) and a number of waymarked trails. Opt for the Waterfall Trail to see a spectacular series of **cascades**, skirted by a timber walkway.

Cushendall and around

CUSHENDALL, which lies at the head of three of the nine Glens, is a delightfully understated village, its charming colour-washed buildings grouped together on a spectacular shore. The red-sandstone **tower** at the central crossroads was built in 1817 by one Francis Turnley, an official of the East India Company, as "a place of confinement for idlers and rioters", and, though there's little else to see here, the village makes a fine base for exploring the local countryside and catching a traditional-music session. The village comes alive during the weekend of the **Heart of the Glens** festival in the middle of August, one of the area's oldest events, replete with traditional music, sporting events and much merriment, culminating in a huge street céilí on the Sunday.

Cushendall's **tourist office** (Mon–Fri 10am–1pm & 2–5.30pm, also July & Aug Sat 9am–6pm; ⓣ028/2177 1180) is on Mill Street, west of the central crossroads. The village is well provided with **accommodation**, with the most comfortable option *The Glens Hotel* (ⓣ028/2177 1223, ⓦwww.theglenshotel.com; ❸), right in the centre, which has a regular programme of live entertainment. The most central B&B option is *Riverside* on Mill Street (ⓣ028/2177 1655; ❶), though this has only standard, but otherwise well-equipped, rooms. Two options slightly outside town are *The Meadows*, heading about half a mile towards Waterfoot at 81 Coast Rd (ⓣ028/2177 2020; ❷), which is friendly and spacious and offers disabled access, and the welcoming *Cullentra House*, 16 Cloghs Rd (ⓣ028/2177 1762, ⓦwww.cullentrahouseireland.com; ❷), a mile northwest of the village off the Cushendun road, with wonderful views. **Camping** is available at *Cushendall Caravan Park*, 62 Coast Rd (April–Sept ⓣ028/2177 1699), next to Cushendall Boat Club, three-quarters of a mile towards Waterfoot.

For **traditional music** head to *McCollam's*, a cottage-style pub on Mill Street known to all as *Johnny Joe's*, which hosts sessions on Friday throughout the year plus Tuesdays, Saturdays and Sundays in high season. Another great session takes place every Wednesday and Saturday at *The Skerry Inn* in **Newtowncrumlin**, eight miles southwest off the Ballymena road.

Eating options include *Harry's* (ⓣ028/2177 2022), at 10 Mill St, which offers exceptional, good-value meals in its downstairs bar, including huge roast dinners and fresh fish, and more refined modern Irish fare upstairs. Across the road, the first-floor rooms above *McCollam's* now house *Upstairs at Joe's* (ⓣ028/2177 2630), a top-notch restaurant serving a wide range of meat and seafood dishes.

Layd Old Church and Ossian's Grave

For the best walk from Cushendall, head east along Shore Road to the beach and then north and uphill to a cliff-top path. Offering splendid views of Scotland across the water, this leads after about half a mile to the enchanting ruins of the early fourteenth-century **Layd Old Church** (free access), which began life as a Franciscan foundation before serving as a parish church until around 1790. The church was the chief burial place of the MacDonnells: wandering around the graveyard you'll find a cross indicating the grave of Dr James McDonnell, who not only pioneered the use of chloroform in surgery, but was one of the organizers of the 1792 Belfast Harp Festival (see p.561).

Another interesting trip from Cushendall is to **Ossian's Grave**, signposted a couple of miles along the main road to Cushendun. There's a double fake involved here. Ossian, the legendary son of Fionn Mac Cumhaill, was the supposed author of the popular Ossianic cycle of poems, though these were in fact largely fabricated by James Macpherson in the 1760s. The poems inspired the early Romantic movement, particularly in Germany, where Goethe quoted Ossian at length in *The Sorrows of Young Werther*. However, the tomb has nothing to do with either the legendary or poetic incarnation as it's really a Neolithic court grave. All the same, standing in a sloping field above the valley, with views to Glendun, Glenaan and, in the distance, Scotland, it oozes atmosphere. The stone cairn here commemorates a more substantial literary figure, **John Hewitt**, known as the Poet of the Glens. Beyond the grave runs **Glenaan**, one of the smallest of the Glens, which soon peters out to little more than a dip of red reeds and black seams of peat between two hills of heather and cotton grass.

Cushendun to Fair Head

The once-fashionable resort of **CUSHENDUN** is an architectural oddity almost entirely designed by Clough Williams-Ellis, the innovative architect of Portmeirion in Wales, and constructed between 1912 and 1925. Built to a commission from Ronald McNeill, the first (and last) Lord Cushendun, and his Cornish wife, Maud, Cushendun's houses are of rugged, rough-cast whitewash with slate roofs – a Cornish style that clearly weathers the Atlantic storms as efficiently here as in Cornwall. All of Cushendun is National Trust property, and it shows. It's a tiny and well-tended place where tourists – and everyone else – seem peculiarly out of place. The high spot of the village calendar is unquestionably its **festival week** towards the end of July, which features plenty of music, competitions and sporting events. Otherwise it's a place for summer strolls and watching the fishing boats.

The village is blessed with an excellent **bar-restaurant**, *Mary McBride's*, whose home-made chowder and more substantial fish lunches and dinners are well worth sampling, if a touch pricey at around £20 for two courses (excluding drinks). **B&Bs** include the award-winning *Sleepy Hollow*, 107 Knocknacarry Rd (Ⓣ&Ⓕ028/2176 1513; ❶), *Drumkeerin*, out towards Torr Head at 201A Torr Rd (Ⓣ028/2176 1554, Ⓦwww.drumkeeringuesthouse.com; ❷), and *Villa Farmhouse*, 185 Torr Rd (Ⓣ028/2176 1252, Ⓔmaggiescally@amserve.net; ❷). The council caravan park on Glendun Road (April–Sept; Ⓣ028/2176 1254) has space for **camping**.

The main road from Cushendun northwest to Ballycastle runs inland, traversing some impressively rough moorland, and passes **Loughareema**, the "vanishing lake", so termed because of its tendency to drain away completely in hot weather. A mile further on, **camping** is available at *Watertop Open Farm* (April–Oct; Ⓣ28/2076 2576, Ⓦwww.watertopfarm.co.uk), a working farm (July & Aug 11am–5.30pm; £2) that can also arrange **pony trekking** and fishing. However, if you take the main road, you'll be missing some of the best of the northern coastline. The narrow, winding **coastal road**, edged with fuchsia and honeysuckle, switches back violently above the sea to **Torr Head**, the closest point on the Irish mainland to the Mull of Kintyre in Scotland.

Murlough Bay and Fair Head

Murlough Bay is the most spectacular of all the bays along the northern coast. From the rugged cliff-tops, the hillside curves down to the sea in a series of wild flower meadows that soften an otherwise harsh landscape. As much as anywhere else on the Irish coastline, this is a place for just spending time and drinking it all in.

The last headland before Ballycastle is **Fair Head**, whose massive two-hundred-metre cliffs offer a truly spectacular view across the North Channel to Scotland – the Mull of Kintyre and further to Islay and the Paps of Jura – a proximity that sheds light on the confusion of land ownership between Ireland and Scotland. Nearby Rathlin Island (see p.594) was hotly contested up until the seventeenth century, while the MacDonnells owned land both here and on Kintyre (which was considered dangerous enough to English interests to be settled, or "planted", with people from elsewhere in Scotland, as occurred in Ireland). **Lough na Cranagh**, one of three lakes in the hinterland behind the cliffs, houses a *crannóg*, encircled by a parapet wall. A walk from the Fair Head car park to Murlough Bay takes about 45 minutes, but muddy paths and changeable weather make walking boots and a waterproof essential.

Ballycastle

The lively market town and port of **BALLYCASTLE** sits at the mouth of the two northernmost Antrim Glens, **Glenshesk** and **Glentaisie**, and makes a pleasant base for exploring the Causeway Coast or the Glens themselves. The best time to visit Ballycastle is at the time of the **Ould Lammas Fair**, Ireland's oldest fair, dating from 1606. Held on the last Monday and Tuesday in August, it features sheep and pony sales. Stallholders do a roaring trade in **dulse**, an edible seaweed, and **yellowman**, a tooth-breaking yellow toffee that's so hard it needs a hammer to break it up. These delicacies feature in a sentimental song that originates locally:

Did you treat your Mary Ann
To dulse and yellowman
At the Ould Lammas Fair in Ballycastle–O?

The Town

Ballycastle has a solid, prosperous feel about it that derived originally from the efforts of an enlightened mid-eighteenth-century landowner, Colonel Hugh Boyd, who developed the town as an industrial centre, providing coal and iron ore mines, a tannery, a brewery and soap, bleach, salt and glass works, all now defunct. It was from its **coal mines** particularly that the town garnered most of its wealth; lignite was mined at Ballintoy on the coast a few miles further west, an enterprise which came to an abrupt end when the entire deposit caught fire and burned for several years. More recently, the **harbour** area was redeveloped to cater for the now-defunct ferry to Campbeltown on the Mull of Kintyre, and remains the springboard for trips to Rathlin Island.

At the seafront there's a memorial to **Guglielmo Marconi**, the inventor of the wireless, who in 1898 made his first successful radio transmission between Ballycastle and Rathlin. From here, Quay Road leads gradually uphill past houses and shops to **The Diamond**, the town's focus. From here, head up the steeper Castle Street to find the town's tiny **museum** (July & Aug Mon–Sat noon–6pm; free), which occupies the old eighteenth-century courthouse. Temporary exhibitions are hosted upstairs, while the former cells downstairs hold a collection of artefacts produced by the pre–World War I Irish Home Industries Shop. Pride of place goes to the Glentaisie banner for the first *Feis na nGleann* ("festival of the Glens") in 1904.

Just out of town, on the Cushendall road, are the ruins of **Bonamargy Friary** (free access), founded by the dominant MacQuillan family around 1500. One family member, Julia, insisted on being buried in the main walkway, so that she might be humbled by others' stepping feet even in death. A number of the rival MacDonnell family are also buried here, including the hero of Dunluce Castle, Sorley Boy MacDonnell, and his son Randal, first Earl of Antrim (see p.599). An indication of the erstwhile strength of the Irish language in these parts is that the tomb of the second earl, who died in 1682, is inscribed in Irish as well as the usual English and Latin; the Irish translation reads, "Every seventh year a calamity befalls the Irish", and, "Now that the Marquis has departed, it will occur every year". The **River Margy**, on which the Friary stands, is associated with one of the great tragic stories of Irish legend, that of the Children of Lir, whose jealous stepmother turned them into swans and forced them to spend three hundred years on the Sea of Moyle (the narrow channel between Ireland

and the Scottish coast). Also on the stretch of shore near Ballycastle is **Carraig Uisneach**, the rock on which the mythical Deirdre of the Sorrows, her lover Naoise and his brothers, the sons of Uisneach, are said by some to have come ashore after their long exile in Scotland.

Practicalities

The helpful **tourist office** in Sheskburn House on Mary Street (July & Aug Mon–Fri 9.30am–7pm; Sept–June Mon–Fri 9.30am–5pm; ⓣ28/2076 2024) can assist with **accommodation**. For more generous budgets, the *Marine Hotel*, at the bottom of Quay Road (ⓣ028/2076 2222, ⓦwww.marinehotel.net; ❹), is very hospitable. Otherwise opt for the stunning seascape views from comfortable *Kenmara House*, 45 North St (ⓣ028/2076 2600; ❷), uphill from the front, the very place where Marconi conducted his tests. Almost next door to the *Marine* is the small *Ballycastle Backpackers Hostel* (ⓣ028/2076 3612, ⓦwww.ballycastlebackpackers.net; dorms £10, doubles ❶), which offers a mix of twin and family rooms and six-bed dorms. The nearest campsite is at *Watertop Open Farm* (see p.592).

For **food**, *Wysner's* restaurant, 16 Ann St (closed Sun), has an adventurous and inexpensive menu, often including salmon from Carrick-a-rede (see opposite), and is next door to the famous butcher of the same name. The *Anzac Bar*, 5 Market St, also has a deserved reputation for its splendid meals while there's an innovative menu at *The Cellar* (ⓣ028/2076 3037) on The Diamond. You'll find Ballycastle's **pubs** surprisingly lively: *O'Connor's* has **traditional music** on Thursdays; the *House of McDonnell* (also known as *Tom's*), on the main street, is young and buzzy, with traditional music on Fridays; and the *Central Bar* opposite has sessions on Wednesdays. Down on the seafront, the friendly *Bakewell's* is a great place to end the evening.

Rathlin Island

Rathlin Island lies five miles north of Ballycastle and just twelve miles west of the Mull of Kintyre in Scotland. Shaped like a truncated figure seven, Rathlin is an impressive, craggy place, with a coastline consisting almost entirely of cliffs, and a lighthouse at each tip. As the island's width is never more than a mile, the sea dominates the landscape and its salty winds discourage the growth of vegetation – wind turbines harness this energy source for electricity generation. The presence of dry-stone walls and numerous ruined cottages indicates a time when the population was far larger than the hundred or so current inhabitants concentrated in **Church Quarter**.

Halfway towards the western lighthouse is the site of a **Stone Age** axe-making site, and, to its north, earthworks known as **Doonmore**. In the early Christian period, the island was a haven for monks, who left evidence of their presence in the form of a sweathouse (a kind of primitive sauna) at **Knockans**, back towards Church Bay. In 795 AD Rathlin was the first place in Ireland to be raided by the **Vikings**. Later raids saw two bloody massacres, first by the English and then by the Scots. In 1575, the mainland MacDonnells sent their women, children and old people to Rathlin for safety from the English, but that didn't stop the invading fleet, under the Earl of Essex (whose soldiers included Sir Francis Drake), from slaughtering the entire population. In 1642, a later generation of MacDonnells was then butchered by their Scottish enemies, the Campbells, causing Rathlin to be deserted for many years afterwards. You can discover more about the island's history and culture in the Boathouse, down by Church Quarter's harbour, which has been converted to house a **visitor centre** (May–Aug daily 10.30am–4pm; ⓣ028/2076 2024; free).

The island's cliffs are superb for **birdwatching**, particularly **Bull Point**, on the western tip, part of a large RSPB nature reserve. The **viewpoint** at the western lighthouse (April–Aug; contact warden in advance on ⓣ028/2076 3948) provides wonderful views of Northern Ireland's largest colony of seabirds – a minibus plies between here and Church Bay in summer. The foot of the cliff is punctured by **caves**, many of them accessible by boat only in the calmest of weather (enquire at the Boathouse about trips). A number are filled with detritus from wrecked ships, brought to the surface by storms. **Bruce's Cave**, on the northeast point of the island, below the lighthouse, is a cavern in the black basalt where, in 1306, so the story goes, the despondent Robert the Bruce retreated after being defeated by the English at Perth. Seeing a spider determinedly trying to spin a web gave him the resolve to "try, try and try again", so he returned to Scotland and defeated the English at Bannockburn.

Practicalities

Caledonian MacBrayne **ferries** (ⓣ028/2076 9299, ⓦwww.calmac.co.uk) make the 45-minute trip from Ballycastle harbour to Rathlin four times daily between April and September; a return ticket costs £10. Outside these months services are reduced to twice daily but in winter the wreck-filled waters in the "race" (as the stretch of water is known locally) can become too treacherous for the boat to make the return trip, or even to sail at all, so it's worth booking ahead to make sure you find a bed on the island, as **accommodation** is very limited.

There's **B&B** by the harbour at the *Manor House* (ⓣ028/2076 3964, ⓦwww.rathlinmanorhouse.co.uk; ❷), a restored late-Georgian home with its own excellent tearoom. Overlooking Mill Bay ten minutes' walk to the south is the tiny *Soerneog View Hostel* (ⓣ028/2076 3954, ⓦwww.n-irelandholidays.co.uk/rathlin; dorms £10), which also rents out **bikes**. **Campers** can pitch their tents for free on the east side of Church Bay.

In Church Quarter *Bruce's Kitchen* serves bar **meals** and you can get snacks at *McCuaig's* pub, and lunches and teas at the *Manor House*. Rathlin's two major events are the week-long **festival** in mid-July, with everything from céilís to model-yacht racing, and the **regatta** on the last weekend in August.

The north Antrim coast

The north coast of County Antrim, west of Ballycastle, is dominated, from a tourist perspective, by Northern Ireland's most famous tourist attraction, the bizarre formation of basalt columns at **the Giant's Causeway**. On the way, near the town of **Ballintoy**, there are several pleasant diversions, not least the precarious rope bridge to **Carrick-a-rede Island**. West of the Causeway, you can sample some whiskey at **Bushmills** and visit the imposing and well-preserved remains of **Dunluce Castle**, the stronghold of the local MacDonnell clan. The coastline west of Dunluce is another major holiday spot, with the resort of **Portrush** filled with tourists in July and August and students the rest of the year.

Carrick-a-rede and Ballintoy to Dunseverick Castle

As you draw level with **Carrick-a-rede Island**, not far outside Ballintoy on the coast road west from Ballycastle, you'll see the island's **rope bridge** (daily, weather permitting: March to late May & early Sept to Oct 10am–6pm; late

May to Aug 10am–7pm; £3 rising to £3.30 in July & Aug). Strung almost 25m above the sea, the rope-connected planks lead to a commercial salmon fishery on the southeast side of Carrick-a-rede (the name means "rock in the road": the island stands in the path of migrating salmon) – but its main function seems to be to scare tourists, something it does very successfully. Walking its eighteen-metre length, as the bridge leaps and bucks under you, is enough to induce giggles and screams from the hardiest of people.

BALLINTOY itself has a dramatic harbour, much loved by artists, with a dark, rock-strewn strand contrasting oddly with the neat pale-stone breakwater. It's lively with boats in the summer, but bleak and exposed in winter. At the top of the harbour road stands a little white **church**, which replaced an earlier one in which local Protestants took refuge from Catholics in 1641 before being rescued by the Earl of Antrim. If you're tempted to **stay** in the village, try the comfortable *Fullerton Arms*, 22 Main St (ⓣ028/2076 9613, ⓦwww.fullertonarms.co.uk; ❸), or, for sea views, *Portcampley House*, 8 Harbour Rd (ⓣ028/2076 8200, ⓦwww.portcampley.co.uk; ❷). **Hostel** accommodation is available at the well-equipped *Sheep Island View Hostel*, 42A Main St (IHH & IHO; ⓣ028/2076 9391, ⓦwww.sheepislandview.com; dorms £12, doubles ❶), which also has space for **camping**.

Continuing west along the coast, **Whitepark Bay** is a delightful, mile-long sweep of white sand with an HINI **hostel** (ⓣ028/2073 1745; dorms £14, twins ❶; April–Oct), which organizes all manner of events and activities. The coastal path from Ballintoy leads west past here to **PORTBRADDAN**, a tiny hamlet of multicoloured houses, where St Gobban's, a slate-roofed little church, just four metres by two, is supposedly the **smallest church in Ireland**. Needless to say, there are other contenders: the ruins of an even smaller one, St Lasseragh's, stand on the cliff above.

From Portbraddan the coast path leads round a headland, through a spectacular hole in the rock and then, by degrees, up to the cliffs of **Benbane Head**. The road and path almost converge at the ruins of a sixteenth-century gatehouse, all that's left of **Dunseverick Castle**. This was once the capital of the old kingdom of Dalriada, which spread over north Antrim and Scotland, and the terminus of one of the five great roads that led from Tara, the ancient capital of Ireland. Its location, naturally enough, made it one of the main departure points for the great Irish colonization of Scotland that took place from the fifth century onwards, and later the castle was stormed by the **Danes** in the ninth and tenth centuries.

The Giant's Causeway

Ever since 1693, when the Royal Society first publicized it as one of the great wonders of the natural world, the **Giant's Causeway** has been a major tourist attraction. The highly romanticized pictures of the polygonal basalt rock formations by the Dubliner Susanna Drury, which circulated throughout Europe in the eighteenth century, did much to popularize the Causeway; two of them are on show in the Ulster Museum in Belfast (see p.566). Not everyone was impressed, though. A disappointed William Thackeray commented, "I've travelled a hundred and fifty miles to see *that*?", and especially disliked the tourist promotion of the Causeway, claiming in 1842 that "The traveller no sooner issues from the inn by a back door which he is informed will lead him straight to the causeway, than the guides pounce upon him." Although the tourist hype is probably now less overtly mercenary, the Causeway still attracts hundreds of thousands of visitors annually, filling the visitor centre and the

▲ The Giant's Causeway coast

minibus that scurries back and forth. But even in high season it's easy to escape the crowds by taking to the cliffs.

For sheer otherworldliness, the Causeway can't be beaten. Made up of an estimated 37,000 black **basalt columns**, each a polygon – hexagons are by far the most common, with pentagons second, though sometimes the columns have as many as ten sides – it's the result of a massive subterranean explosion, some sixty million years ago, that stretched from the Causeway to Rathlin and beyond to Islay, Staffa (where it was responsible for the formation of Fingal's Cave) and Mull in Scotland. A huge mass of molten basalt was spewed out onto the surface, which, on cooling, solidified into what are, essentially, crystals. Though the process was simple, it's difficult, when confronted with the impressive regular geometry of the columns, to believe that their production was entirely natural.

Fionn Mac Cumhaill: the Causeway legends

According to mythology, the Giant of the Causeway was Ulster warrior **Fionn Mac Cumhaill** (also known as Finn McCool), and two legends of Fionn's exploits provide an entertaining alternative to geologists' explanations of the Causeway's origins. In one, Fionn became besotted with a woman giant who resided on the Scottish island of Staffa (where the Causeway's fault-line resurfaces) and constructed a highway across the sea by which he could travel to woo his inamorata. An alternative version of the story suggests that Fionn built the Causeway in order to head over to Scotland to give another giant a good kicking, but, when confronted by his enemy's superior size, fled back to Ireland and hid in an extra-large cot which he'd persuaded his wife to construct. When the pursuing Scots giant arrived, he took just a glance at the sheer size of Fionn's supposed "baby" and fled back to Scotland.

Visiting the Causeway

Public transport to and from the Causeway is well organized with regular bus services (see "Travel details", p.620), and there's also a restored **narrow-gauge railway** that runs here from Bushmills (see opposite; June, Sept & Oct Sat & Sun; July & Aug daily; 7 trains daily on the hour from 11am–5pm, returning 30min later from the Causeway; 20min; ⓣ028/2073 2844, ⓦwww.freewebs.com/giantscausewayrailway; single £4.50, return £6). If you want to **stay** close to the Causeway, try the refurbished nineteenth-century *Causeway Hotel* (ⓣ028/2073 1210, ⓦwww.giants-causeway-hotel.com; ❸) near the visitor centre, or *Carnside Farmhouse*, 23 Causeway Rd (March–Oct ⓣ028/2073 1337, ⓦwww.carnsideguesthouse.co.uk; ❷), which has superb views.

The Causeway's **visitor centre** (daily: March–June, Sept & Oct 10am–5pm; July & Aug 10am–6pm; Nov–Feb 10am–4.30pm; free; ⓦwww.giantscausewaycentre.com) was severely damaged by fire in 2000 and continues to be housed in temporary accommodation on the cliff-top awaiting a permanent replacement. As well as providing tourist information, the centre offers the usual range of "Celtic" gifts and a **café**, while regular announcements are made for the frankly ignorable twelve-minute Causeway audiovisual presentation in the adjacent theatre (£1) and the unnecessary guided tours (£2.50). Avoidance of the council's extortionate car-park charge (£5) is virtually impossible unless you're prepared to park some distance away and walk.

From the visitor centre, it's wise to resist the temptation to follow the crowds on the ten-minute walk along the lane straight down to the Causeway, and to dodge the minibus that runs every ten minutes (June & Sept 10am–6pm; July & Aug 10am–7pm; Oct–May 10am–4.30pm; £1 single, £2 return), the only form of transport allowed here except bicycles; instead take a far more scenic route – a round trip of roughly two miles. Follow the cinder path up behind the visitor centre and round the edge of several promontories, from which you can gasp at the Causeway from above and watch the eider and gannets wheeling across from Ailsa Craig, thirty miles away in Scotland. A flight of 162 steps takes you down to sea level and a junction in the path. Following the path west will bring you to the Giant's Causeway but if you continue round the bay to the north you'll reach a series of rock formations, the first of which is the twelve-metre basalt columns known as the **Organ Pipes**. Many of the other formations have names invented for them by the guides who so plagued Thackeray and his contemporaries – the Harp, for example – but at least one, **Chimney Point**, further north, has an appearance so bizarre that in September 1588 it persuaded the crew of the *Girona*, a ship of the Spanish Armada, to think it was

Dunluce Castle (see opposite), where they thought they might get help from the MacDonnells. Instead, their vessel was wrecked on the rocky shore at **Port-na-Spánaigh**, just before Chimney Point. Its treasure was recovered by divers in 1968, and some of the items are on show in the Ulster Museum in Belfast (see p.566) when it reopens, and, the Tower Museum in Derry (see p.608). Sadly, extensive cliff erosion prevents any further exploration and prohibitive costs are likely to deter future reparation.

Bushmills and Dunluce Castle

The next stop on the main road beyond the Causeway is **BUSHMILLS**, whose foremost attraction is the **Old Bushmills Distillery** on the outskirts of town. Whiskey has been distilled here legally since 1608, making it the oldest licit distillery in the world, and it's well worth taking the **tour** (April–Oct Mon–Sat 9.30am–5.30pm, Sun noon–5 pm, last tour 4pm; Nov–March open daily, but call for tour times; £5; ⓣ028/2073 1521, ⓦwww.bushmills.com). Bushmills whiskey is distilled three times, once more than Scotch, but perhaps the biggest surprise is just how little subtlety is involved in the industrial manufacture of alcohol, despite all the lore that surrounds it. The distillery is a massive factory where an extraordinary range of (mostly unpleasant) smells assail your nostrils, making it difficult to imagine that the end product really does delight the taste buds. At the end of the tour you'll be offered a tot of the hard stuff: your best bet is the unblended malt, representative of what goes on in Bushmills itself, as the grain whiskey that goes into the blend is almost all distilled in Cork; alternatively ask for a tot of Coleraine whiskey, only a tiny amount of which is still produced. They also serve hot toddies, which may be more in order in winter. To find the distillery, follow the signs from the cenotaph in the centre of town – it's barely a quarter of a mile.

Accommodation in the town includes the fabulous *Bushmills Inn*, 9 Dunluce Rd (ⓣ028/2073 3000, ⓦwww.bushmillsinn.com; ❽), a former coaching inn with a cottage-style interior, spacious and exquisitely furnished rooms, and a superb **restaurant** featuring a range of fine traditional dishes – particularly fish – given an inspired contemporary zest. The HINI **hostel**, 49 Main St (ⓣ028/2073 1222; dorms £15, twins ❶), is equipped with small, en-suite rooms, and for **B&B** there's *Ballyness* (ⓣ028/2073 1438; ❷), half a mile south of the village down the B66. There's also space for a few tents at the adjacent *Ballyness Caravan Park* (mid-March to Oct; ⓣ028/2073 2392).

A detour westwards along the minor coast-road from Bushmills will take you past the narrow-gauge railway station for trips to the Giant's Causeway (see opposite) to the decorous little seaside village of **PORTBALLINTRAE**, about a mile away. Here, you'll find **accommodation** at the very comfortable *Bayview Hotel*, 2 Bayhead Rd (ⓣ028/2073 4100, ⓦwww.bayviewhotelni.com; ❼), and seaside B&B at nearby *Manor House*, 51 Beach Rd (ⓣ028/2073 2002; ❷).

The main road rejoins the coast a couple of miles west of Bushmills. Here you'll see the most impressive ruin on this entire coastline, the sixteenth-century **Dunluce Castle** (daily: April–Sept 10am–5.30pm; Oct–March 10am–4.30pm; £2; ⓦwww.ehsni.gov.uk/dunluce.shtml). Perched on a fine headland, high above a cave, it looks as if it only needs a roof to be perfectly habitable once again. Its history is inextricably linked to that of its original owner, **Sorley Boy MacDonnell**, whose clan, the so-called "Lords of the Isles", ruled northeastern Ulster from this base. English incursions into the area culminated in 1584 with Sir John Perrott laying siege to Dunluce, forcing Sorley Boy ("Yellow Charles" in Irish) to leave the castle. But as soon as Perrott departed, leaving a garrison in charge, Sorley Boy hauled his men up the cliff in baskets and recaptured the castle, later repairing the damage with the proceeds of the salvaged wreckage of the *Girona* and arming the fort with three of its cannons. Having made his point, Sorley Boy agreed a peace with the English, and his son, **Randal**, was created Viscount Dunluce and Earl of Antrim by James I. In 1639, Dunluce Castle paid the penalty for its precarious, if impregnable, position when the kitchen fell off the cliff during a storm, complete with cooks and dinner. Shortly afterwards, the MacDonnells moved to more comfortable lodgings at Glenarm, and Dunluce was left empty.

The castle remains an extraordinary place. The MacDonnells' Scottish connections – Randal continued to own land in Kintyre – are evident in the **gatehouse**'s turrets and crow-step gables, and in the tapering chimneys of the seventeenth-century **Great Hall**. There's a strange touch of luxury in the **loggia**, though it oddly faces away from the sun. A spectacular scramble (particularly in wild weather) takes you down to the **cave** below the castle that pierces right through the promontory, with an opening directly under the gatehouse.

Portrush

The town of **PORTRUSH**, on the Ramore Peninsula, has everything you'd expect from a seaside resort, from sandy **beaches** backed by dunes, which run both east and west, to summer drama in the town hall and plenty of amusements for children. Many students from the University of Ulster at Coleraine live here and make it a considerably livelier place than you might expect, even out of season; the huge popularity of the local dance scene draws clubbers from all over the North and the town can have a distinctly raucous feel at weekends. The long, sandy beach towards Dunluce ends at the **White Rocks**, where the weather has carved the soft limestone cliffs into strange shapes, most famously the so-called "Cathedral Cave", nearly 60m from end to end.

Portrush's wide range of activities and entertainments for children and wet afternoons include the all-weather **Waterworld**, by the harbour (Easter week, July & Aug Mon–Sat 10am–8pm, Sun noon–8pm; May & Sept Sat & public hols 10am–6pm, Sun noon–6pm; June Mon–Sat 10am–7pm, Sun noon–7pm; £4.50), with water flumes, slides, sauna, Jacuzzis, aquarium and restaurant, and **Barry's Fairground**, just behind the seafront. The **Dunluce Centre**, 10 Sandhill Drive, a little south of the town centre (April Sat & Sun noon–6pm; May, June, Sept & Oct Mon–Fri noon–5pm, Sat & Sun noon–6pm; July & Aug daily 10.30am–6.30pm; £3.50–4.50 per attraction, £8.50 combined ticket; Ⓦ www.dunlucecentre.co.uk), houses the tourist office (see opposite), a viewing tower and a variety of interactive and cinematic experiences, including a simulated ghost train, a high-tech treasure hunt and an interactive adventure playground. The former bathhouse for the well-heeled patrons of the *Northern Counties Hotel* on the seafront is now **The Coastal Zone** (10am–5pm: June & Sept Sat & Sun; which July & Aug daily; free; Ⓦ www.ehsni.gov.uk/portrush .shtml), which features interactive exhibits exploring local marine life (including a fascinating rock pool), and coastal change in the area.

There is rewarding **surfing** off West Strand and White Rocks; you can rent boards and gear, and take lessons, at Troggs Surf Shop, 88 Main St (Ⓣ 028/7083 3361), who'll also advise on the condition of the waves. Safety considerations are seemingly jettisoned, however, during the annual **raft race** at the end of May, when participants race each other across the harbour on home-made rafts. The main sporting attraction here, though, is the **Royal Portrush Golf Club** (Ⓣ 028/7082 2311), whose vistas offer a welcome distraction from your handicap. The Royal Portrush is the North's premier club, and boasts one nine-hole and two eighteen-hole courses. Demand is high in the summer, especially in good weather, and it's wise to book ahead.

Practicalities

The **train station** is a short hop south of the town centre on Eglinton Street; **buses** stop at various points around the town. The friendly and efficient **tourist office** (March & Oct Sat & Sun noon–5pm; April–June & Sept Mon–Fri 9am–5pm, Sat & Sun noon–5pm; mid-June to Aug daily 9am–7pm; ⓣ028/7082 3333) is in the Dunluce Centre (see opposite).

Note that **accommodation** fills up quickly in high season, especially in July for the major golf championships, and also in mid-May during the North West 200 motorbike road races. Top of the range is the central and recently refurbished *Ramada Portrush* at 73 Main St (ⓣ028/7082 6100, ⓦwww.ramadaportrush.com; ❺). There are dozens of **B&Bs**, too, most of them very friendly and welcoming: try *Glenkeen Guest House*, 59 Coleraine Rd (ⓣ028/7082 2279, ⓔglenkeen@btinternet.com; ❷), which provides splendid breakfasts, or *Belvedere House*, 15 Lansdowne Crescent (ⓣ028/7082 2771, ⓦwww.belvederetownhouse.co.uk; ❷), offering well-furnished en-suite rooms in a pleasant location overlooking the sea. **Campsites** abound in the area, though most of them are actually fairly unattractive caravan parks that also take a few tents; closest to town is the municipal *Carrick Dhu Caravan Park*, 12 Ballyreagh Rd (April–Oct; ⓣ028/7082 3712), a mile west on the A2, or there's the *Ballymacrea Caravan and Camping Park*, 220 Ballybogey Rd (March–Oct; ⓣ028/7082 4507), a mile and a half down the B62 Ballymoney road.

For **food** try *55° North* (ⓣ028/7082 2811) at the seaside end of Causeway Street, which offers a mix of modern Irish and Italian food and has a downstairs coffee shop. Alternatively, down at the harbour (and all run by the same management), there's *Coast* (ⓣ028/7082 3311; closed Mon & Tues in winter), an upmarket Italian **restaurant**, while above it the *Ramore Wine Bar* (ⓣ028/7082 6969) serves good-value meat and seafood dishes with a few veggie options. On the second floor there's the *Ramore* restaurant itself (ⓣ028/7082 6969; closed lunchtimes and Mon & Tues all day), which specializes in pan–East Asian cuisine.

The town has a few convivial **pubs** – the nicest bar in town is the *Harbour Inn* – and there's a regular traditional session at the *Springhill Bar* on Causeway Street (Thurs). **Nightlife** is quite a serious business here, mostly centred on one of the North's biggest clubs, Saturday-night's *Lush*, in *Kelly's Hotel* on Bushmills Road (ⓣ028/7082 6600), which attracts major DJs and, consequently, clubbers from far and wide. Alternatively, there's *Club Soi* in the *Traks Complex*, Station Square (ⓣ028/7082 2112, ⓦwww.traks-complex.com), with well-known DJs on both Friday and Saturday nights.

County Derry

County Derry stretches all the way from **Lough Neagh** in its southeast corner, skirting the northern fringes of the Sperrin Mountains to the west on its way towards Donegal. In its far northwest, modern **Derry city** sprawls around the old steep, walled town and spills over the banks of the River Foyle. A border town, with a substantial Catholic majority, it was traditionally the starting point for emigrants from Donegal and around on their journey to the Americas. The county's coastline, from **Magilligan Point** to **Downhill**, **Castlerock** and, across the River Bann, **Portstewart** features some fabulous beaches. Inland offers fewer attractions, though there are important religious remains at **Dungiven** and examples of settler endeavour in orderly plantation towns such as **Magherafelt** and **Moneymore**.

Overall, the county is well served by **public transport**. Buses cover just about everywhere while the rail service provides rapid access to the county's coastline and to some towns inland. If you're heading on to Donegal, you can take one of the many buses from Derry city.

Derry city

DERRY, which lies at the foot of Lough Foyle, is a crossroads city in more ways than one: roads from all cardinal points arrive here, but it was also a major point of emigration from the eighteenth century onwards, an exodus that reached tumultuous proportions during the Great Famine. Derry is the fourth largest city in Ireland and the second biggest in the North, but it has a markedly different atmosphere from Belfast, being two-thirds **Catholic**. While roads into the city are signposted in Irish welcoming visitors to Derry, the city still appears as "**Londonderry**" on many road maps and signs, a preference adhered to by the British government, Unionists and television news bulletins. Indeed, it has also acquired the nickname "**Stroke City**" – a reference to the tactful placating of both Nationalist and Unionist traditions by entitling it "Londonderry/ Derry". Whatever the case, locals of both persuasions now generally refer to their city as "Derry".

Approached from the east in winter twilight or under a strong summer sun, the city presents a beguiling picture, with the vista of the **River Foyle** and the rise of the city's two hillsides, terraced with pastel-shaded houses and topped by the hueless stone spires of the ever-present religious denominations. With its rich history, Derry has several worthwhile attractions, mostly enclosed within the seventeenth-century **walls**, themselves the most significant reminder of the city's past.

Outside Ireland, the name of Derry recalls the Troubles and savage events like the **Bloody Sunday** massacre. Unlike Belfast, the cutting edge of violence receded considerably here even before the ceasefires, and the city is still imbued with a real sense of optimism, despite losing trade to nearby Letterkenny whenever the euro falls against the pound. However, be aware that Derry is gaining a reputation for on-street violence of the after-closing-time variety and, in particular, has seen some nasty homophobic attacks in the town centre and along the riverside.

Some history

Though **St Columba** established a monastery here in 546 AD, the development of Derry (originally called Doire Calgaigh, "oakwood of Calgach", after a legendary warrior) only really began in medieval times, when in the fourteenth century it was granted to the Anglo-Norman de Burgos. By 1500, the power of the O'Dohertys had spread from Inishowen and they constructed

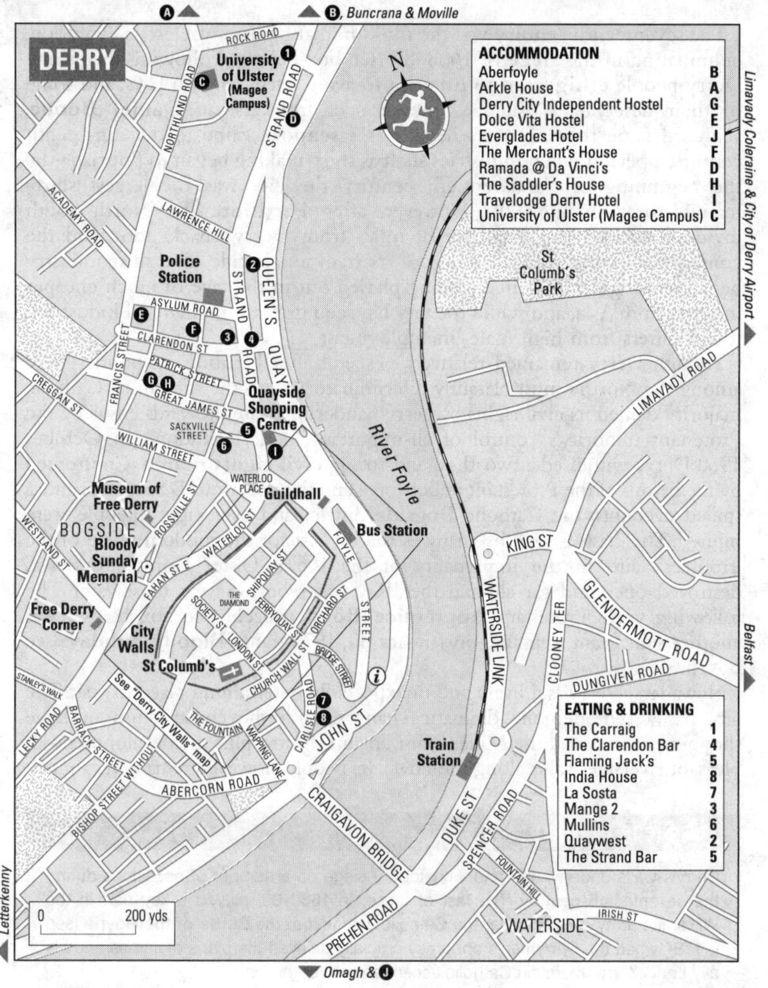

a tower house, which was later absorbed into the seventeenth-century walls (see p.608).

Towards the end of the sixteenth century the uprising of Hugh O'Neill, Earl of Tyrone, provoked an English invasion. Doire's strategic position on the River Foyle was quickly appreciated though it took some years for it finally to be captured. In 1600, the English commander **Sir Henry Docwra** began fortifying the remains of the medieval town as a base for incursions against the Irish, but in 1608 Sir Cahir O'Doherty rebelled against Docwra's successor, Pawlett, and burnt Doire, by now **anglicized** as Derry, to the ground. This destruction made the city ripe for the **plantation** of English and Scottish settlers, and the financial assistance of the wealthy businessmen of the City of London was obtained to achieve this. A new walled city was constructed and renamed **Londonderry** in 1613 in honour of its backers, the Twelve Companies of the Corporation of London.

The seventeenth century was the most dramatic phase of Derry's evolution, culminating in the **siege** of 1688–89 (see box below). Following this, many Derry people **emigrated** to America to avoid harsh English laws, and some of their descendants, such as the pioneer frontiersman **Daniel Boone**, achieved fame there. Derry's heyday as a **seaport** came in the nineteenth century, a period when industries such as shirt-making began to flourish – by the beginning of the twentieth century the city was the largest shirt-manufacturer in the UK. However, after **Partition**, the North–South dividing line lay just a couple of miles from Derry's back door, and the consequent tariffs reduced much of its traditional trade. The shirt industry began its long decline, finally being phased out in the face of much cheaper imports from Asia, and while the city has seen growth in chemical industries, it still suffers from high male unemployment.

Though Derry remained relatively peaceful after Partition, its politics were among the North's most blatantly discriminatory, with the substantial Catholic majority denied its civil rights by gerrymandering geared towards ensuring the Protestant minority's control of all-important local institutions. In October 1968 Derry witnessed a two-thousand-strong **civil rights march**. Confronted by the batons of the Protestant police force and the notorious B Specials, rioting spilled over into the Catholic **Bogside** district and over eighty people were injured. The clash is seen by many as the catalyst for the modern phase of the Troubles: faith in the impartiality of the Royal Ulster Constabulary was destroyed once and for all, and the IRA was reborn a year or so later. The following year's Protestant **Apprentice Boys' march** (see box below) was another significant step and, on January 30, 1972, came **Bloody Sunday** (see box, p.611).

Nowadays, Derry is a lively and unexpectedly entertaining place to visit. The city has also undergone dramatic changes, with the construction of huge shopping centres and the Millennium Forum theatre, plus the developments of pleasant riverside walks along the Foyle. Its people, however, remain very much

The Siege of Derry

Derry's walls underwent – and withstood – siege on a number of occasions during the seventeenth century. The last of these, in **1688–89**, played a key part in the Williamite army's victory over the Catholic James II at the **Battle of the Boyne** (see p.179), when the Derrymen's obduracy crucially delayed the plans of James and his ally Louis XIV to maintain Catholic ascendancy over the kingdom.

The suffering and heroism of the fifteen-week **siege**, the longest in British history, still have the immediacy of recent history in the minds of Derry Protestants. James's accession in 1685 had seen the introduction of a policy of replacing Protestants with Catholics in leading positions in the Irish administration and army. In December 1688, a new garrison attempted to enter the city, but was prevented when a group of young **apprentices** seized the keys and locked the city's gates. Eventually, after negotiation, an all-Protestant garrison under Governor Robert Lundy was admitted. Over the following few months the city's resident population of two thousand swelled to thirty thousand as people from the surrounding area took refuge from Jacobite forces advancing into Ulster. Fearing that resistance against the Jacobite army was futile, Lundy departed; his effigy is still burnt each December by Protestants. Around seven thousand Protestants died during the siege that followed, the survivors being reduced to eating dogs, cats and rats. Today, the siege is commemorated with a skeleton on the city coat of arms, and the lyrical tag "maiden city", a somewhat sexist reference to the city's unbreached walls.

physically divided, with Catholics living to the west of the Foyle and Protestants mainly residing to the river's east.

Arrival and information

The tiny **City of Derry Airport** (ⓣ028/7181 0784, ⓦwww.cityofderryairport.com) is seven miles northeast of town on the A2 road. It's connected by Ulsterbus services #143A and #234 to the train station and Foyle Street bus station; a taxi from the airport to the city centre costs around £10. The Airporter coach service (Mon–Fri 4am–7.30pm, Sat 6am–4pm, Sun 8am–4pm; Mon–Fri 13 daily, Sat & Sun 6 daily; single £15, return £25; couples £25 single & £40 return; ⓣ028/7126 9996, ⓦwww.airporter.co.uk) runs services to and from Belfast International (1hr 30min) and Belfast City (2hr) airports from outside the Quayside Shopping Centre, Strand Road.

Derry's **train station** (ⓣ028/7134 2228) is situated in the Waterside district across the River Foyle and a 15min walk to the town centre. The central **bus station** is on Foyle Street and is served by Ulsterbus (ⓣ028/7126 2261) for all the main Northern Ireland destinations and Bus Éireann (information from Ulsterbus), which operates buses to Dublin, Donegal town, Galway and Sligo. In addition, Lough Swilly (ⓣ028/7126 2017) and North West Busways (ⓣ074/938 2619) run services across the border into Donegal; the former operates from the bus station and the latter from Patrick Street. Local city buses leave from stops along Foyle Street. **Black taxis** operate from Foyle Street and William Street, or call Delta Cabs (ⓣ028/7127 9999) or the Derry Taxi Association (ⓣ028/7126 0247).

The **tourist office**, 44 Foyle St (March–June & Oct Mon–Fri 9am–5pm, Sat 10am–5pm; July–Sept Mon–Fri 9am–7pm, Sat 10am–6pm, Sun 10am–5pm; Nov to mid-March Mon–Fri 9am–5pm; ⓣ028/7126 7284, ⓦwww.derryvisitor.com), books accommodation, has a **bureau de change**, provides a mass of information about both the North and the Republic, and offers bicycle lockers. Grab a free, pocket *Visitor Guide* for up-to-date information about the city's attractions and facilities. The Nationalist *Derry Journal* newspaper (Tues & Fri; ⓦwww.derryjournal.com) is good for entertainment listings. **Walking tours** of the historic centre leave from the tourist office (July & Aug Mon–Fri 11.15am & 3.15pm; Sept–June Mon–Fri 2.30pm; ⓣ028/7137 7577; £6, includes entry to St Columb's Cathedral). Alternatively, the Free Derry walking tour (10am & 2pm daily; £4; ⓣ028/7126 2812, ⓦwww.freederry.net; advance booking essential) takes in the Bogside, politics and murals, and leaves from Pilot's Row Community Centre, Rossville Street. Should you wish to follow your own route you can hire a wireless **digital tour guide** from the tourist office (£4, credit card only), a location-aware device whose headset supplies you with appropriate details as you wander within the walled city.

Additionally, you can also take an hour-long open-top guided **bus** tour of the city (April–Oct daily & hourly 10am–4pm; £8; ⓣ077 4024 9998), which departs from near the tourist office and also picks up by the Guildhall, or take a **cruise** up the River Foyle from Queen's Quay (May–Sept daily 2pm; Oct–April Sat & Sun 2pm; 1hr 15min; £8; ⓣ028/7136 2857, ⓦwww.foylecruiseline.com).

Accommodation

Although Derry has plenty of upper-end **accommodation**, finding a more economically priced room in the centre can be difficult, especially in high season and at weekends. It's worth **booking in advance** or calling in at the tourist office when you arrive.

Hotels and B&Bs

Aberfoyle 33 Aberfoyle Terrace, Strand Rd ⓣ028/7128 3333, ⓔaberfoyle33@btinternet.com. Pleasant Victorian house offering en-suite B&B just a little way north of the Queen's Quay roundabout along Strand Road. ❷

Arkle House 2 Coshquin Rd ⓣ028/7127 1156, ⓦwww.derryhotel.co.uk. Refurbished, late nineteenth-century "gentleman's residence" with many original fittings, about a mile and a half from the city centre. ❷

The City Hotel 14–18 Queens Quay ⓣ028/7136 5800, ⓦwww.cityhotelderry.com. Huge monument to elegant minimalism with spacious rooms offering views of the Foyle and all the leisure facilities imaginable. ❺

Everglades Hotel 41–53 Prehen Rd ⓣ028/7132 1066, ⓦwww.hastingshotels.com. Top-of-the-range, high-quality accommodation providing elegantly furnished rooms, set on the southern banks of the Foyle a couple of miles southwest of the centre. ❺

Ramada @ Da Vinci's 15 Culmore Rd ⓣ028/7127 9111, ⓦwww.davincishotel.com. Impressively modish, modern hotel offering a range of stylish, well-furnished and very comfortable rooms. ❹

The Saddler's House 36 Great James St ⓣ028/7126 9691, ⓦwww.thesaddlershouse.com. Stylish, period-furnished Victorian townhouse B&B very near the city centre, off Strand Road. Its friendly, knowledgeable owners also run the equally grand, Georgian *The Merchant's House* (❷) at 16 Queen St, nearby. ❷

Tower Hotel 7–17 Butcher St ⓣ028/7137 1000, ⓦwww.towerhotelgroup.com. A modern 90-room establishment providing bright and airy rooms, all equipped with cable TV, just inside the city walls, with a flash bistro and excellent café-bar. ❺

Travelodge Derry Hotel 22 Strand Rd ⓣ028/7127 1271, ⓦwww.travelodge.co.uk. Modern if somewhat functional rooms in a prime city-centre location. ❸

Hostels and self-catering

Cathedral Cottages 14 & 16 London St ⓣ028/7126 9691, ⓦwww.thesaddlershouse.com. These two eighteenth-century houses in the centre of the old city are run by the owners of *The Saddler's House* B&B and make an ideal place for a self-catering, week-long stay, though you can stay for shorter periods (minimum two nights). No. 16 sleeps 4 and no. 14 5–6. Costs are £350 and £450 per week respectively; per night ❸–❹.

Derry City Independent Hostel 44 Great James St ⓣ028/7128 0542, ⓦwww.derry-hostel.co.uk. Welcoming IHH hostel offering a mix of private rooms and small dorms; prices include breakfast and free Internet access. Dorms £11, doubles ❶.

Dolce Vita Hostel 4 Asylum Rd ⓣ028/7128 7989, ⓔderryhostel@hotmail.com. Smaller sister of the *Derry City* hostel, geared more towards couples than individual travellers. Dorms £11, doubles ❶.

University of Ulster (Magee Campus) Northland Rd ⓣ028/7137 5255, ⓦwww.accommodation.ulster.ac.uk/casuallet.html. Accommodation in en-suite study bedrooms available from mid-June to early Sept. ❶

The City

Derry's centre, focused on its **medieval walls**, is remarkably compact, and it's easy to combine all the main attractions in one circuit. A tour of the walls also includes views of the Catholic **Bogside** area, whose political murals symbolize key moments in Derry's history during the Troubles.

The walls

Derry's **city walls** are one of the best-preserved defences in Europe. A mile in length and never higher than a two-storey house, they are reinforced by bulwarks and bastions and a parapeted earth rampart as wide as any thoroughfare. Within their circuit, the original medieval street-pattern has remained, with four **gateways** surviving from the original construction, albeit in slightly revised form.

The Guildhall and around

The best approach to the walls is from the Guildhall Square, once the old quay, east of Shipquay Gate. The Neogothic ecclesiastical appearance of the **Guildhall** (Mon–Fri 9am–5pm; free) belies its true function as the headquarters of the City Council. Inside, the city's history is depicted in a series of stained-glass

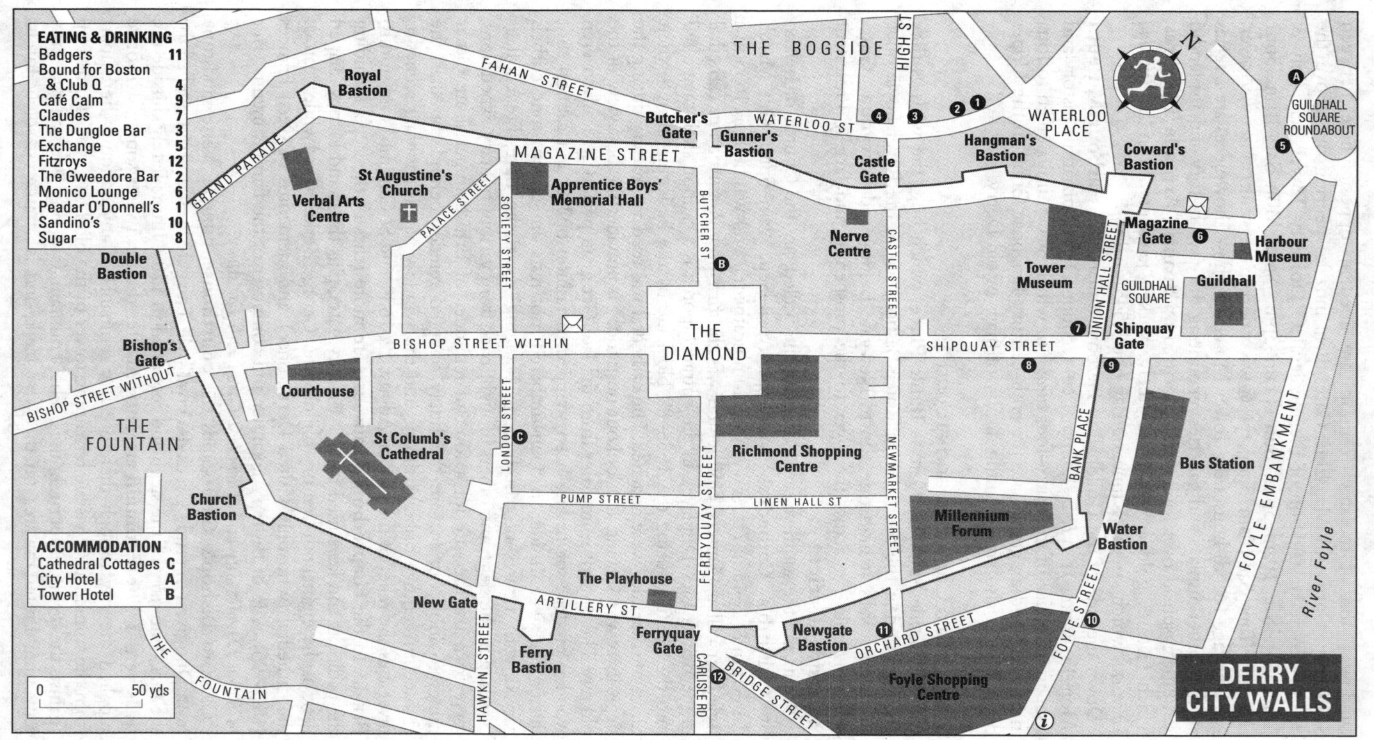
DERRY CITY WALLS
EATING & DRINKING
Badgers 11
Bound for Boston & Club Q 4
Café Calm 9
Claudes 7
The Dungloe Bar 3
Exchange 5
Fitzroys 12
The Gweedore Bar 2
Monico Lounge 6
Peadar O'Donnell's 1
Sandino's 10
Sugar 8
ACCOMMODATION
Cathedral Cottages C
City Hotel A
Tower Hotel B
0 50 yds
THE BOGSIDE
THE FOUNTAIN
THE DIAMOND
Royal Bastion
Double Bastion
Bishop's Gate
Church Bastion
New Gate
Ferry Bastion
Ferryquay Gate
Newgate Bastion
Water Bastion
Shipquay Gate
Magazine Gate
Coward's Bastion
Hangman's Bastion
Castle Gate
Gunner's Bastion
Butcher's Gate
Verbal Arts Centre
St Augustine's Church
Apprentice Boys' Memorial Hall
Nerve Centre
Tower Museum
Harbour Museum
Guildhall
GUILDHALL SQUARE
GUILDHALL SQUARE ROUNDABOUT
Courthouse
St Columb's Cathedral
Richmond Shopping Centre
Millennium Forum
The Playhouse
Foyle Shopping Centre
Bus Station
FAHAN STREET
GRAND PARADE
MAGAZINE STREET
WATERLOO ST
WATERLOO PLACE
HIGH ST
PALACE STREET
SOCIETY STREET
BUTCHER ST
CASTLE STREET
UNION HALL STREET
BISHOP STREET WITHIN
BISHOP STREET WITHOUT
SHIPQUAY STREET
LONDON STREET
PUMP STREET
FERRYQUAY STREET
LINEN HALL ST
NEWMARKET STREET
BANK PLACE
ARTILLERY ST
HAWKIN STREET
THE FOUNTAIN
CARLISLE RD
BRIDGE STREET
ORCHARD STREET
FOYLE STREET
FOYLE EMBANKMENT
River Foyle

windows. Most of the city's cannons are lined up opposite here, between **Shipquay Gate** and Magazine Gate, their muzzles peering out above the ramparts. A reconstruction of the medieval **O'Doherty Tower** here (July & Aug Mon–Sat 10am–5pm, Sun 11am–3pm; Sept Mon–Sat 10am–5pm; Oct–June Tues–Sat 10am–5pm; £4; Ⓦwww.derrycity.gov.uk/museums/tower.asp; Heritage Island) houses the Tower Museum, whose showpieces are a series of stimulating displays and galleries recounting the city's history and a splendid exhibition, spread over four storeys, focused on **Spanish Armada Treasures**, which features gold artefacts and finely worked jewellery from *La Trinidad Valencera*, which sank in Kinnegoe Bay (see p.545) in 1588.

Down the side of the Guildhall in Harbour Square, the **Harbour Museum** (Mon–Fri 10am–1pm & 2–4.30pm; free) recounts Derry's maritime history and contains a replica of the thirty-foot *currach* in which St Columba sailed to Iona in 563 AD, and an actual late fifteenth-century longboat found in the Upper Bann. There's also an intriguing display of maps of old Derry.

St Columb's Cathedral and around

Left and inside Shipquay Gate is **Bank Place**, which hugs the walls as they dogleg round at the southeastern Water Bastion, where the River Foyle once lapped the walls at high tide. On to Newgate Bastion and **Ferryquay Gate**, you can look east across the river to the prosperous and largely Protestant **Waterside district**.

Occupying the southwestern corner of the walled city, the Church of Ireland **St Columb's Cathedral** (Mon–Sat: April–Sept 9am–5pm; Oct–March 9am–1pm & 2–4pm; £2; Ⓦwww.stcolumbscathedral.org) was built in 1633 in a style later called Planters' Gothic and was the first post-Reformation cathedral in the British Isles. Displayed in the entrance porch is a cannon shell catapulted into the church during the 1688–89 blockade by the besieging army – their terms of surrender were attached. The cathedral was used as a battery during the siege, its **tower** serving as a lookout post; today it provides the best view of the old city. The present spire dates from the late Georgian period, its lead-covered wooden predecessor having been stripped to fashion bullets and cannon shot during the siege. Inside, an open-timbered roof rests on sixteen stone corbels carved with figures of past bishops. Hanging above the nave, French flags captured in the siege, and others brought back from various military expeditions, serve to make the interior a forceful reminder of British imperialism. Other things to look out for are the finely sculpted reredos behind the altar, the eighteenth-century bishop's throne and the window panels showing scenes as diverse as the relief of the city on August 12, 1689, and St Columba's mission to Britain. In the **chapterhouse museum** are more relics of the siege, including the padlocks and keys used to lock the city gates, plus the grand kidney-shaped desk of the eighteenth-century philosopher George Berkeley, erstwhile dean of the cathedral (who only visited Derry once), and mementos of Cecil Frances (1818–95), wife of Bishop Alexander and composer of the famous hymns *Once in Royal David's City* and *There is a Green Hill Far Away*.

Close to **Bishop's Gate** stands the **courthouse**, built of white sandstone from Dungiven in crude Greek-Revival style. The gate itself was remodelled for the first centenary of the siege and reopened in 1789. Immediately outside the walls here is **The Fountain** area, named after the freshwater source that once supplied the city, though there are few remnants of any antiquity here apart from the immediately visible remaining tower of the old Derry jail, jammed up against the grim modern houses. The Fountain is a tiny enclave, the only remaining Protestant area on the west bank, and is of interest solely for its

Union Jack kerb paintings and huge **murals**, which read as direct responses to the more famous Catholic "Free Derry" mural in the next valley. Until recently, the Fountain area had the oldest mural in the North. Painted in the early part of the twentieth century by Bobby Jackson, it showed the Siege of Derry and the Battle of the Boyne, and was repainted every year. In the 1970s, when the area was redeveloped, the wall was painstakingly dismantled, moved, reassembled and repainted, but it finally disintegrated in 1994. A replica was painted the following year on a special Bobby Jackson memorial wall.

The Double Bastion and Royal Bastion

Continuing north from Bishop's Gate, you reach the **Double Bastion**, where the "Roaring Meg" cannon sits. During the siege, it was said that "the noise of the discharge was more terrifying than were the contents of the charge dangerous to the enemy". Just by here is the **Verbal Arts Centre** (Ⓦwww.verbalartscentre.co.uk), a unique project aimed at sustaining and promoting forms of communication and entertainment once central to Irish culture: legend, folklore, *sean-nós* – an unaccompanied narrative form of singing (see p.715) – and story-telling performed by a *seanachie* (story-teller). The centre, incorporating designs by Louis le Brocquy, commissions works from writers,

▲ Roaring Meg

and hosts poetry readings and story-telling events, and has a pleasant **café** (Mon–Thurs 10.30am–3.30pm, Fri 10.30am–2.30pm).

The nearby **Royal Bastion** was constructed between 1826 and 1828 and used to be topped by a three-metre-high statue of Reverend George Walker, the defender of Derry "against an arbitrary and bigoted monarch" (to quote the still-legible inscription). The statue was blown up in 1973 and the surrounding area remains a significant flashpoint every August 12 when the Apprentice Boys march in their predecessors', and Walker's, memory (see box, p.604). The view from here across the Bogside district (see below) is expansive.

A little further downhill, on the south side of Magazine Street, is the main focus of Derry's dynamic cultural world, **The Nerve Centre** (ⓣ028/7126 0562, ⓦwww.nerve-centre.org.uk), which contains all manner of sound, film and video studios and editing suites, alongside an art-house cinema, music venue and coffee bar.

The Bogside

In the valley below the northern city walls is the Catholic **Bogside** district, where, at the start of the Troubles, ferocious rioting took place following the Apprentice Boys' march, with the army and police responding to bricks and petrol bombs with tear gas, rubber bullets and careering Saracen armoured cars. The area at the foot of the escarpment used to be full of streets of compact terraced housing but was redeveloped in the 1960s in the form of a dual carriageway, an estate of tenement flats and empty concrete precincts. But clinging to the opposite hillside is a classic urban landscape, with turn-of-the-century terraces of stucco facades, blue tile roofs and red chimney-stacks.

Most eye-catching in this panorama is a gable-end **mural** showing the former Independent Republican MP and one of the organizers of the People's Democracy movement Bernadette Devlin, megaphone in hand, in front of the old "You are now entering Free Derry" mural. Other murals visible nearby include a massive hunger-strike mural featuring one of the blanket-clad participants, Raymond McCartney, while another, the "Death of Innocence" mural commemorates a 14-year-old girl, Annette McGavigan, who died in 1971, caught in crossfire between the British Army and IRA. There are also striking murals featuring a gas-mask-clad petrol bomber and a British soldier smashing down a door with a sledgehammer during Operation Motorman (see box opposite). These and the nearby 1968 civil-rights-march mural were painted by the Bogside artists Kevin Hasson, Tom Kelly and William Kelly, who have published an illustrated book on their work, available from Bookworm (see opposite). Another mural, on Westland Street, depicts those killed on Bloody Sunday.

Just off Rossville Street at 55 Glenfada Park is **The Museum of Free Derry** (Mon–Fri 9.30am–4.30pm, also March–Sept Sat 1–4pm & June–Sept Sun 1–4pm; £3; ⓦwww.museumoffreederry.org). This explores the city's troubled history, focusing especially on the decade following the origin of the civil rights movement; it features a wealth of intriguing displays, photographs and posters related to that period.

Eating

Although **eating out** in Derry has improved dramatically in recent years, you still won't be faced with a bewildering selection, though prices remain incredibly reasonable compared with other parts of Ireland. Several pubs dish up very

Bloody Sunday

For the first two years of the Troubles, the area of the Catholic Bogside area beyond the original "Free Derry" mural was a notorious no-go area, the undisputed preserve of the IRA, its boundary marked by a gravestone-like monument declaring, "You are now entering free Derry". This autonomy lasted until 1972, when the British army launched **Operation Motorman**; the IRA men who had been in the area were tipped off, though, and got across the border before the invasion took place.

To the right of the "Bernadette Devlin" mural in the Bogside stands a **memorial pillar** to the thirteen Catholic civilians killed by British paratroopers (a fourteenth died later of his wounds) on **"Bloody Sunday"**, January 30, 1972, in the aftermath of a civil- rights demonstration. The soldiers immediately claimed they had been fired upon, an assertion later disproved, though some witnesses came forward to report seeing IRA men there with their guns. The bitter memory of the subsequent Widgery Commission's failure to declare anyone responsible for the deaths festered in Catholic Derry, and pressure was maintained on successive governments to reopen investigations. In 1999, after years of mounting demands for a full investigation, the British government established the Saville Inquiry, which conducted its proceedings in Derry's Guildhall until moving to Westminster in 2002 to continue its investigation. At the time of writing it was still to report its conclusions.

decent **bar meals**, two of the best being *Badgers*, Orchard Street, and the *Monico Lounge*, opposite the main post office. All the large hotels also have their own restaurants.

Café Calm 4 Shipquay Place. Pleasant café serving splendid coffee and a wide range of snacks and bites.

The Exchange Exchange House, Queen's Quay ⓣ028/7127 3990. This wine bar is currently the spot to be seen and offers a cosmopolitan menu too.

Fitzroys 2–4 Bridge St ⓣ028/7126 6211. A chic city-centre brasserie just outside Ferryquay Gate, open for lunch and evening meals.

Flaming Jacks 31–35 Strand Rd ⓣ028/7126 6400. Absolutely brilliant bistro-style place serving an eclectic range of dishes inspired by all four corners of the planet at very economical prices; booking ahead is essential.

India House 51 Carlisle Rd ⓣ028/7126 0532. The city's best Indian restaurant, offering a reasonably priced menu.

La Sosta 45A Carlisle Rd ⓣ028/7137 4817. Authentic Italian food in a pleasant, family-run establishment.

Mange 2 2 Clarendon St ⓣ028/7136 1222. Arguably the city's most innovative restaurant, and certainly one of its most popular, serving tasty, French-influenced cuisine such as mussels in garlic, delicious paté and excellent pasta.

Quaywest 28 Boating Club Lane ⓣ028/7137 0977. Pleasant wine bar/restaurant with perhaps the North's most cosmopolitan menu – everything from Mexican chicken to Spanish seafood, via notable Southeast Asian influences.

Pubs, nightlife and entertainment

What Derry lacks in restaurants, it makes up for, inevitably, in **pubs**. Congenial and conversational places include *The Clarendon Bar*, 44 Strand Rd, *Badgers*, 18 Orchard St (for an older clientele), and *Mullins* on Sackville Street.

The best place for **traditional music** is *Peadar O'Donnell's* on Waterloo Street, a retro pub with sessions most nights of the year. The attached *Gweedore Bar* has a mixed bag of rock music and DJs, while just up the hill *The Dungloe Bar* has entertainment every night except Mondays and *Bound for Boston* also offers live music, tending to focus on rock or ballads; the latter also includes *Club Q* for weekend dance fanatics. *Sandino's* on Water Street features occasional concerts, as well as DJs and/or live music on Thursdays and Fridays, plus a regular traditional-music session on Sunday afternoons followed by jazz that same evening. For more **nightlife**, make for Shipquay Street, where *Sugar* at *Downey's* has DJs most nights. Also worth checking out for DJs are the *Strand Bar* and the *Carraig*, both on Strand Road, though most stick solidly to the chart-hits formula.

The huge Millennium Forum **theatre** on Newmarket Street (Ⓣ028/7126 4455, Ⓦwww.millenniumforum.co.uk) offers a broad, if somewhat middle-of-the-road, programme, including well-known ballets and opera. More innovative theatre and dance can often be found at The Playhouse on Artillery Street (Ⓣ028/7126 8027, Ⓦwww.derryplayhouse.co.uk), while, across the river, The Waterside Theatre (Ⓣ028/7131 4000, Ⓦwww.waterside theatre.com) dishes up a mixed bag of a programme, ranging from classic drama to local versions of TV game shows. **Film** buffs are catered for by the Strand Multiplex cinema in the Quayside Centre (Ⓣ028/7137 3900, Ⓦwww.strandmultiplex.com), as well as by The Nerve Centre (see p.610), which stages regular screenings of left-field films.

Festivals

Several **arts festivals** take place at regular times throughout the year. A week-long drama festival is held at the Waterside Theatre in early March (Ⓦwww.watersidetheatre.com), while early May sees the Jazz and Big Band Festival (Ⓦwww.cityofderryjazzfestival.com); the Celtronic Dance Music Festival takes place at various venues across the city in late June (Ⓦwww.celtronic2007.com); the Big Tickle Comedy Festival occupies eleven days in early September (Ⓦwww.thebigtickle.com); and the Foyle Film Festival takes place in November (Ⓦwww.foylefimfestival.org). Additionally, there's the mammoth **Halloween Carnival**, five days of mayhem culminating in a massive costume parade and spectacular fireworks display on October 31 (Ⓦwww.derrycity.gov.uk/halloween).

Listings

Airlines British Airways Ⓣ0870 850 9850, Ⓦwww.britishairways.com; Ryanair Ⓣ0906 270 5656, Ⓦwww.ryanair.com.

Bike rental Bee's Cycles, 4 Waterloo St (Ⓣ028/7137 2155).

Bookshops Bookworm, 18–20 Bishop St (Ⓣ028/7128 2727), has good coverage of contemporary and historical Irish works. Books in Irish can be found at An Gaeláras, 34 Great James St (Ⓣ028/7126 4132, Ⓦwww.gaelaras.ie).

Car rental Desmond Motors, Strand Rd (Ⓣ028/7136 7137); Driver Hire, 74 Duke St (Ⓣ028/7131 2777). Additionally, the following agencies are based at the City of Derry Airport: Avis (Ⓣ028/7181 1708, Ⓦwww.avis.co.uk); Europcar (Ⓣ028/7181 2773, Ⓦwww.europcar.co.uk); Ford (Ⓣ028/7136 7137); Hertz (Ⓣ028/7181 1994, Ⓦwww.hertz.co.uk); Kings (Ⓣ028/9335 2557, Ⓦwww.kingscarhire.com).

Hospital Accident and emergency department, Altnagelvin Hospital, Glenshane Rd (Ⓣ028/7134 5171); call this number also for dental emergencies after working hours or at weekends.

Internet access Claudes, Shipquay St.

Laundry and dry cleaning Smooth Operators, Sackville St (Ⓣ028/7136 0529).

Market Bottom of William St – stalls most days, but busiest on Saturday.

Police The main police station is on Strand Rd (Ⓣ028/7136 7337).

Post office Custom House St (Mon 8.30am–5.30pm, Tues–Fri 9am–5.30pm, Sat 9am–12.30pm; Ⓣ0845 722 3344) and 3 Bishop St (Mon–Fri 9am–5.30pm, Sat 9am–12.30pm).

Records and CDs Sounds Around, 24 Waterloo St (Ⓣ028/7128 8890), has one of the best selections of music in Ireland, including plenty of rare traditional albums.

Northern County Derry

East of Derry city the A2 traverses drab agricultural land before reaching the small manufacturing town of **Limavady**, which retains a few remnants of Georgian times. From here, the road first heads north and then twists east, taking in marvellous beaches all the way from **Magilligan Point** to **Portstewart**, near which it crosses the River Bann. On the way there are stunning views from the land around **Mount Binevenagh** and impressive seascapes visible from the clifftop **Mussenden Temple**.

Limavady and around

LIMAVADY was once a major settlement, its old site lying two miles further south down the valley of the River Roe. The town was re-founded as Newtown Limavady in the early seventeenth century by Thomas Phillips, speaker of the Irish House of Commons, and, in recent years, has undergone major economic expansion. Although its population has consequently increased, there's still relatively little to do or see here, though the town does possess a couple of interesting features of its illustrious past: the six-arch **bridge** spanning the river was built in 1700, and Main Street, which runs down from it, is still recognizably Georgian. Limavady hosts an excellent jazz and blues **festival** in the second week of June (Ⓦ www.limavadyjazzandblues.com), as well as the Roe Valley Folk Festival in late October (Ⓦ www.roevalleyfolkfestival.com).

Tourist information is available from the council offices at 7 Connell St (Mon–Fri 9am–5pm, extended July & Aug to 5.45pm; also May–Sept Sat 9.30am–5.30pm; Ⓣ 028/7772 2010). There are some lively **bars** in the centre of town, including the atmospheric *Owen's* on Main Street. **Accommodation** in the area is limited, though just a mile south of the town is the luxurious *Radisson SAS Roe Park Resort* (Ⓣ 028/7772 2222, Ⓦ www.radissonroepark.com; ❻) which has its own golf course, leisure centre and spa facilities; alternatively, there are several B&Bs some 3–5 miles out of town along the Magilligan road.

The **Roe Valley Country Park**, a couple of miles south of Limavady, preserves Northern Ireland's first hydroelectric power station, opened in 1896, with much of the original equipment intact and viewable, as well as a visitor centre (daily: April–Sept 9am–6pm; Oct–March 9am–5pm; free) and the **Green Lane Museum** (May–Sept daily 1–5pm; May, June & Sept closed Wed; free). This focuses on the area's history, including its erstwhile importance in linen production, and features craft displays on Saturdays (2–4pm).

Danny Boy

The lyrics for the quintessential "Oirish" ballad **Danny Boy** were actually composed by an English lawyer, Fred E. Weatherley, in 1912 and, a year later, fitted to *The Londonderry Air*, a tune collected by Jane Ross, a resident of 51 Main Street, Limavady, from a travelling fiddler in 1851. The song achieved renown in Ireland when recorded in the 1930s by Margaret Burke-Sheridan and has since seen many other tear-jerking renditions (Sinéad O'Connor recorded an idiosyncratically spine-tingling version); it still remains endearingly popular with dewy-eyed expats and Irish-Americans. Limavady holds the annual Danny Boy **festival** over the first weekend in May (Ⓦ www.dannyboyfestival.com), featuring a fiddle competition and plenty of other traditional music.

The Derry coast

North of Limavady, the A2 coast road and railway skirts around **Mount Binevenagh**. The land around the mountain is now a conservation park, dedicated to the preservation of birds of prey, in particular falcons and kestrels. The easiest way of reaching the fabulous viewpoints commanded by the mountain is to take the B201 shortly after leaving Limavady and then turn left a couple of miles further on.

In **BELLARENA**, three miles north of Limavady, stands **Bellarena House**, a plantation mansion, dating back in parts to the seventeenth century. This was once the home of Sir John Heygate, a minor novelist now long out of print, who achieved some notoriety when he travelled with his more famous Fascist-sympathizing colleague Henry Williamson (author of *Tarka the Otter*) to pay homage to Adolf Hitler in the 1930s. Unfortunately, the house is no longer open to the public, but it is visible from the common ground banks of the River Roe.

A couple of miles after Bellarena train station, a turning leads to **Magilligan Point**, running across the dunes past an open prison (once an army base and later an internment camp) before reaching the tip of the peninsula. Here, at the narrow entrance to Lough Foyle, stands a **Martello tower** (free access), with walls more than three metres thick. There's the *Point Bar*, too (open summer only), to provide succour, and a regular daily **ferry** service to **Greencastle** across the water in County Donegal (pedestrians £3 single, £4.50 return; cars £10 single, £15 return; see p.545 for details). One of Ireland's most famous harpers, Dennis Hempson, was from the Magilligan townland and attended the great Belfast Harp Festival of 1792 (see p.561), where he performed the *Londonderry Air*. Hempson was one of the last harpers to play the then brass-strung instrument with long fingernails. The Ordnance Survey project to **map** the whole of Ireland began at Magilligan Strand in 1824 when Lt Col Thomas Colby established a baseline here for a network of imaginary triangles covering the whole country, from which measurements could be calculated using trigonometry.

East of the Point the A2 passes **camping** opportunities at the *Benone Tourist Complex* (April–Sept; ⓣ028/7775 0555) and the adjacent *Golden Sands Caravan Park* (April–Sept; ⓣ028/7775 0324), before hugging the cliffs as it enters **DOWNHILL** hamlet, where you'll find the excellent and spacious *Downhill* **hostel** (IHH; March to Dec; ⓣ028/7084 9077, ⓦwww.downhillhostel.com; dorms £12.50, doubles ❶), also a working pottery, on the edge of the hugely long **beach**. Overlooked by Mussenden Temple on the cliff-edge above, the beach is accessible by car, though with no shops or pubs in Downhill, stock up on provisions in advance if you intend to stay.

Just uphill from here a pair of huge, ornate gates alongside the A2 mark the main entrance to the ruins of **Downhill Palace** (daily dawn–dusk; free), built in the 1780s by **Frederick Augustus Hervey**, Anglican Bishop of Derry and fourth Earl of Bristol. Hervey was an enthusiastic grand traveller (all the many Hotel Bristols throughout Europe are named after him), and was also an art collector and great sportsman, once organizing a pre-prandial race between Anglican and Presbyterian clergy along the local strand. His palace, accessed through pleasant gardens, was last occupied by US troops, billeted here during World War II, and was dismantled on their departure.

Across fields at the back of the palace is the diminutive **Mussenden Temple** (call ⓣ028/2073 1582 for opening times; £2.20), which clings precariously to the eroding cliff-edge and offers stunning sea views. Its classic domed rotunda was apparently modelled on the Temple of Vesta in Rome and was built by Hervey in honour of his cousin Mrs Frideswide Mussenden, who died aged 22 before it was completed, after which it was used as a summer library. Later, with characteristic generosity and a fairly startling lack of prejudice, Hervey allowed a weekly Mass to be celebrated in the temple, as there was no local Catholic church. The inscription on the temple frieze translates rather smugly as: "It is agreeable to watch, from land, someone else involved in a great struggle while winds whip up the waves out at sea."

A short distance further on, at the Castlerock crossroads, is **Hezlett House** (call ⓣ028/2073 1582 for opening times; £3; ⓦwww.ntni.org.uk), built in 1690 and restored after a fire in 1986. The house is a fine example of cruck-truss construction, an early method of prefabricated building using wooden frames filled with clay and rubble that was common in England but is enough of a rarity here to warrant preservation by the National Trust. The last owner of the house is buried in the graveyard at Downhill (see opposite), where his gravestone quaintly bears both his own version of the spelling of his name and that of his father, a Mr Hazlett.

The small resort of **CASTLEROCK**, a mile north, has a long strand reaching eastwards to the Barmouth, where the River Bann's estuary draws flocks of migratory birds and birdwatchers. Unless you're a surfer, there's not much else to tempt you, apart from the renovated but still cosy *Bertha's Bar* (known locally as *Love's*) at the beginning of the promenade.

Portstewart

Derry's largest coastal resort, **PORTSTEWART**, like its near neighbour Portrush (see p.600), is full of Victorian boarding houses. Of the two, Portstewart is decidedly more sedate and has always had more airs and graces: the train station is said to have been built a mile out of town to stop hoi polloi from coming. In terms of sheer location, though, Portstewart wins hands down. Just west of the town is **Portstewart Strand**, a long sand beach firm enough to drive on (cars March–June & Sept £4.50, July & Aug £5) – which the locals delight in doing – with some of the best **surfing** in the country. It's a grand place, too, if you hit fine weather and feel like getting out your bucket and spade. The best way to take the sea air is the bracing **cliffside walk**, which runs between the beach and the town, passing battlements and an imposing Gothic mansion, now a Dominican college.

The **tourist desk** in the library on The Crescent (July & Aug Mon–Sat 10am–1pm & 2–4.30pm; ⓣ028/7083 2286) can help with **accommodation** bookings if you have any problems. **B&Bs** are mostly along the promenade or nearby and include the large and comfortable, three-star *Anchor Bar*, 87–89 The Promenade (ⓣ028/7083 2003, ⓦwww.theanchorbar.co.uk; ③), but if you want to be near the strand, there's *Cul-Erg House*, 9 Hillside (ⓣ028/7083 6610, ⓦwww.culerg.co.uk; ③), a large and modern B&B with very airy en-suite rooms. There's also the well-run *Rick's Causeway Coast* **hostel** at 4 Victoria Terrace (IHH; ⓣ028/7083 3789, ⓔrick@causewaycoasthostel.fsnet.co.uk; dorms £10, doubles ①), and the municipal *Juniper Hill Caravan Park* at 70 Ballyreagh Rd (April–Oct; ⓣ028/7083 2023), a mile down the A2 towards Portrush, which offers **camping**. *Morelli's*, 53–58 The Promenade, is justly famous for its ice cream, and also serves snacks and light meals. The busy local haunt *Shenanigans*, 78 The Promenade (ⓣ028/7083 6000), is a mid-priced **restaurant** on the main drag serving a range of modern Irish dishes; the *Anchor Bar* also provides filling bar food. The **Flowerfield Arts Centre**, 103 Coleraine Rd (Mon–Fri 9am–5pm, Sat 10am–4pm; ⓦwww.flowerfield.org), runs a variety of courses and stages exhibitions and occasional concerts covering a variety of genres. For advice on local **surfing** and equipment visit Ocean Warriors, 80 The Promenade (ⓣ028/7083 6500).

Southern County Derry

The Derry–Antrim A6 road follows a river valley through fertile farming land before reaching **Dungiven**, then ascends to the Glenshane Pass on the north-eastern fringe of the **Sperrin Mountains**. Southeast from here are a number of entirely **planned towns**, such as **Magherafelt** and **Moneymore**. The huge expanse of Ireland's biggest lake, **Lough Neagh**, laps against the county's south-eastern corner and here too is one of the must-see sights of the entire North, **Bellaghy Bawn** castle.

Dungiven

DUNGIVEN, some twenty miles southeast of Derry, is a fairly unremarkable town, though it does harbour one or two ruins of interest. Originally a stronghold of the O'Cahan clan, Dungiven was given to the Skinners' Company of London to settle in the seventeenth century. The remains of the O'Cahan fortifications are incorporated into the newly restored **castle**, whose battlemented outline gives Dungiven a particularly historic aspect when approached from the south. The castle dates back to 1839 and is set in 22 acres of parkland with views across to the Sperrins. During World War II, it was used as a dance hall by American troops, and in 1971 it was the scene of an attempt to set up an independent Northern Ireland parliament. Following restoration work, it now houses en-suite hostel-style **accommodation**, including double and family rooms (Ⓣ028/7774 2428, Ⓦwww.dungivencastle.com; call for prices).

Dungiven Priory (free access), signposted down a footpath half a mile out of the town towards Antrim, gives a taste of the pioneering life of the early plantation settlers, and of the continuity of tradition. No more than a ruin, the Augustinian priory stands on an imposing site on a bluff above the river. Founded in 1100 by the O'Cahans, it belongs to the first wave of European monastic orders that arrived in Ireland to supplant the Celtic Church. The priory contains what is rated the finest **medieval tomb** in Northern Ireland, that of Cooey na Gall O'Cahan, who died in 1385: beneath the effigy are six bare-legged warriors in kilts, presumably denoting Scotsmen, who represent the O'Cahan chieftain's foreign mercenaries, from whom he derived his nickname "na Gall", or "the foreigner". At some point, the O'Cahans added a defensive tower to the west end of the church, and later – when Dungiven was granted to the Skinners' Company, in the person of Sir Edward Doddington – this was enlarged to become a two-and-a-half-storey defensive manor house. There's an evocative artist's impression on the site of what that building looked like. Although the church hasn't been used since 1711, Dungiven Priory remains a religious site of sorts. A tree knotted with pilgrim's offerings – handkerchiefs, torn-off bits of summer dresses, socks – stands over a deeply hollowed **stone**, originally used by the monks for milling grain and now, owing to a local legend, an object of pilgrimage for people seeking cures for physical illness.

The ruined **Banagher Old Church**, a couple of miles southwest of Dungiven, was founded in the twelfth century by St Muiredach O'Heney, who is buried in the well-preserved mortuary house built on a sand hill in the churchyard. Banagher sand is said to bring good fortune to the founder's line and perhaps did so to a famous modern bearer of the saint's name, **Seamus Heaney** (see box, p.618), who is known to have visited for the explicit purpose of acquiring some. The ruins themselves are sedately impressive, as are the walks around the nearby **Banagher Glen Nature Reserve** (open access; free).

The plantation towns

Southeast of Dungiven and over the Glenshane Pass on the way to the northern tip of Lough Neagh, it is worth making a detour to see some interesting examples of town planning – the **plantation towns** of the London companies, most of them characteristically focused around a central Diamond.

One such town is **MAGHERAFELT**, granted to the Salters' Company by James I, which has a wide, sloping main street and makes a reasonable base for exploring the lough and the Bellaghy area. The amenable **tourist office** (Mon–Wed & Fri 9.30am–5.30pm, Thurs 9.30am–8pm, Sat 9.30am–5pm; ⓣ028/7963 1510) is in The Bridewell, 2 Churchwell Lane. There's **accommodation** at the ivy-clad *Laurel Villa Townhouse*, 60 Church St (ⓣ028/7930 1459, ⓦwww.laurel-villa.com; ❸), a Victorian townhouse with elegantly furnished en-suite rooms which also organizes poetry readings and other literary events. The best **eating** option is *Gardiners*, 7 Garden St (ⓣ028/7930 0033; closed Mon all day and lunchtimes except Sun), which serves an imaginative menu of Irish classics with a European twist. One of the best **pubs** is *Mary's*, an exceptionally pleasant old-time pub on the Market Square.

Originally a real gem, **MONEYMORE**, about five miles further south, had until recently degenerated into a run-down, traffic-choked disgrace but is thankfully undergoing renovation to reinvigorate some of its once-graceful pedimented buildings. Originally constructed by the Drapers in the early seventeenth century (and restored by them in 1817), these structures face each other across a wide main street topped by an Orange Hall; there are plenty of red, white and blue kerbstones here indicating the continuing strength of local Loyalism. Moneymore was the first town in the North to have piped water – amazingly enough, as early as 1615.

A mile outside town off the B18, **Springhill** (mid-March to early April, mid-April to June & Sept Sat & Sun 1–6pm; Easter week daily 2–6pm; July & Aug daily 1–6pm; £4.80; ⓦwww.ntni.org.uk) is a grand plantation manor-house built between 1680 and 1700 by William "Good-Will" Conygham in order to fulfil a marriage contract with the father of his bride-to-be, Anne Upton. Elegant both without and within, its sober whitewashed architecture houses fine rooms, equipped with original period furniture and paintings belonging to William and his descendants, who occupied the house until 1959. Upstairs, the Blue Room is said to be haunted by the ghost of Olivia Lenox-Conyngham, whose husband George was found shot here in 1816. Outside, the stables house a **costume collection**, which adopts a specific theme each year, drawing upon three thousand items collected from the mid-seventeenth century to the 1970s. There are also delightful gardens, a tower dating from the 1730s, which was probably originally part of a windmill, and a pleasant walk through beech and yew trees.

Lough Neagh and Bellaghy

East of Magherafelt and Moneymore are the fish-filled waters of the biggest lake in Ireland, **Lough Neagh**. Tributaries flow from every point of the compass: the Lower Bann, which drains the lake and runs north to **Lough Beg** (finally reaching the sea north of Coleraine), contains some huge **trout**, including the dollaghan, unique to these waters. Similar to salmon – which are also common – dollaghan grow by three pounds every year and can be caught by spinning, worming and fly-fishing: the Ballinderry Black and the Bann Olive are famous flies derived from this region. The best fishing is from mid-July to October but you will need a Fisheries Conservation Board Rod **licence**, available from the Antrim tourist office (see p.587). Information on day-tickets for fishing and specialist boat-trips, respectively issued and run by the Lough Neagh Angling Association, can also be obtained from the tourist office.

Like many of the plantation settlements in the area, **BELLAGHY**, just west of Lough Beg, has a history that reflects the divisions between communities. Indeed, no fewer than two of the ten 1981 hunger strikers (see p.705) – cousins Francis Hughes and Thomas McElwee – came from the village, and Orange parades have been a regular flashpoint. Bellaghy is neatly laid out around a T-junction, and wandering south past the whitewashed terraces on Castle Street leads to one of the best surviving examples of a plantation castle, **Bellaghy Bawn** (Easter–Aug daily 10am–6pm; Sept–Easter Mon–Sat 9am–5pm; £2; Ⓦwww.ehsni.gov.uk/bellaghy.shtml), built in 1618 by the Vintners' Company. Most of its fortifications were lost in 1641, but it still retains a striking circular flanker tower which has been well restored. Inside you'll find fascinating interpretive displays explaining the 7000-year-old history of the settlements in this area, the construction of the village – today's houses still occupy the same original allocated plots of land – and the diverse ecology of the Lough Beg wetland area. The real treasure here, however, is the dedication of much of the Bawn's space to one of the world's greatest living poets, **Seamus Heaney**, who

Seamus Heaney

There was a sunlit absence.
The helmeted pump in the yard
heated its iron,
water honeyed

in the slung bucket
and the sun stood
like a griddle cooling
against the wall
of each long afternoon.

(From *Mossbawn: 1. Sunlight*)

It's impossible to conceive of a contemporary poet, Irish or otherwise, whose works are more evocative of time and place than **Seamus Heaney**. He was born, the eldest of nine children, on the family farm of Mossbawn (itself the title of two poems in his fourth collection, *North*), in the townland of Tamniarn, near Bellaghy, on April 13, 1939. Heaney's family background, his Catholic upbringing and his study of Irish at school imbued him with a strong sense of being Irish in a state that considered itself British, a paradox that would form a major motif in his work during the 1970s. While at Queen's University, Belfast, he was further influenced by the literature he discovered in Belfast's Linen Hall library, especially the works of John Hewitt, the Antrim-born "Poet of the Glens", and the English "naturalist" poet Ted Hughes, in whose work he found an "association of sounds in print that connected with the world below". The rural Monaghan setting of Patrick Kavanagh's poetry further echoed his own experience and vision.

Heaney's first poem, *Tractors*, was published in the *Belfast Evening Telegraph* in 1962. His first significant collection, *Death of a Naturalist*, followed in 1966 and was immediately recognized for its earthiness and command of diverse metrical forms. In the 1960s, while lecturing at Queen's, Heaney's career expanded into journalism and television and he became increasingly involved in the **civil-rights** was born and raised nearby (see box below). Heaney himself is the star of a unique and atmospheric film showing in the Bawn, *A Sense of Place*, in which he reflects on the influence of his upbringing, local character and landmarks on his poetry. His father, for instance, rented grazing rights on the strand at Lough Beg; in his poem *Ancestral Photograph*, Heaney recalls helping to herd the cattle that grazed there down Castle Street on their way to market. Prints of other poems are displayed on the walls of various rooms, and the Bawn's library contains the ultimate collection of his works, including first drafts and extremely limited editions.

You can see the shimmering Lough Beg from the windows of the flanker tower, and a stroll down to the lake is well worthwhile. In summer, its waters recede and **Church Island** becomes accessible from the shore. Besides a walled graveyard, you'll find the ruins of a medieval church here, said to have been founded centuries before by the ubiquitous St Patrick, with a tower and spire added in 1788 by the eccentric Frederick Augustus Hervey (see p.614) to improve his view from Ballyscullion House on the mainland nearby. He commissioned Charles Lanyon to build a huge replacement for the original house which stood here, with, apparently, 365 windows, but died abroad before ever moving in, and the building subsequently fell into ruin.

movement. His response to the Troubles saw him seeking for "images and symbols adequate to our predicament" and he began to see poetry as a mode of resistance. Eventually, though, the violence so disturbed him that he moved with his family to County Wicklow, prompting Ian Paisley's *Protestant Telegraph* to bid farewell to "the well-known papist propagandist" on his departure to his "spiritual home in the popish republic". While his 1970s collections *North* and *Field Work* had mixed receptions – some saw the strong influence of Robert Lowell on the former – Heaney found himself turning increasingly to his Irish heritage as a source of inspiration, particularly the long medieval poem *Buile Suibhne (The Madness of Sweeney)*, and published his own *Sweeney Astray* collection in 1983. The following year's *Station Island* drew on his experiences as a participant in St Patrick's Purgatory (see p.513).

The hunger strikes of the early 1980s brought a new urgency to Northern politics and a revival of Heaney's polemicism. Prompted by the staging in Derry in 1980 of Brian Friel's play *Translations*, which showed English surveyors travelling through eighteenth-century Ireland anglicizing all the place names, Heaney cofounded the **Field Day Theatre Company** with Friel, his old friend and fellow academic Séamus Deane, the actor Stephen Rea and others. While the group's theatrical activities were themselves controversial, it was their publications that engendered the most antipathy. Their pamphlets were criticized as attempts to over-intellectualize the Troubles and the 1991 *Field Day Anthology of Irish Writing* was decried for its under-representation of work by women writers, though a subsequent volume entirely devoted to them has since been published.

Heaney's reputation, however, has remained largely unsullied, maintained not merely by the sheer literary strength of his work and its ready accessibility, but by his undoubted charisma and a lack of pomposity. In 1995, his body of work was more widely recognized by the award of the **Nobel Prize for Literature**. Heaney's recent works include: a translation of the Anglo-Saxon epic poem *Beowulf*, his dramatic retelling of this tale of monster- and dragon-slaying managing to breathe new life into a work that was long considered too dense and metaphorical for a modern readership; and his latest collection, *District and Circle*, which won the prestigious T.S. Eliot Prize for Poetry in 2006.

Travel details

Trains

Antrim to: Ballymena (Mon–Fri 14 daily, Sat 9, Sun 5; 15min); Belfast (Mon–Fri 14 daily, Sat 9, Sun 5; 35min); Derry (Mon–Sat 9 daily, Sun 5; 1hr 45min).
Ballymena to: Antrim (Mon–Fri 14 daily, Sat 9, Sun 5; 15min); Belfast (Mon–Fri 14 daily, Sat 9, Sun 5; 50min); Derry (Mon–Sat 9 daily, Sun 5; 1hr 30min).
Carrickfergus to: Belfast (Mon–Fri 38 daily, Sat 30, Sun 10; 30min); Larne (Mon–Fri 23 daily, Sat 18, Sun 10; 30min).
Castlerock to: Derry (Mon–Sat 9 daily, Sun 4; 40min).
Derry to: Antrim (Mon–Sat 9 daily, Sun 4; 1hr 45min); Ballymena (Mon–Sat 9 daily, Sun 4; 1hr 30min); Belfast (Mon–Sat 9 daily, Sun 4; 2hr 20min); Castlerock (Mon–Sat 9 daily, Sun 4; 40min).
Larne to: Belfast (Mon–Fri 24 daily, Sat 18, Sun 10; 1hr); Carrickfergus (Mon–Fri 24 daily, Sat 18, Sun 10; 30min).
Portrush to: Coleraine (Mon–Sat 19–20 daily, Sun 9; 15min) for connections to Belfast (Mon–Sat 9–11 daily, Sun 4; 1hr 30min).

Buses

All services are operated by Translink unless stated otherwise.
The **Antrim Coaster** (Goldline Express Service #252) operates from Belfast all the way around the Antrim coast to Portrush (via Larne, the Glens, Ballycastle and the Giant's Causeway) and Portstewart before terminating at Coleraine. The service operates all year from Mon to Sat, leaving Belfast Europa Buscentre at 9am and reaching Colerane at 1pm. A second bus departs from Larne at 3pm, arriving in Coleraine at 5.55pm. The respective returns leave Coleraine at 9.50am (to Larne only) and 3.40pm (all the way to Belfast). From July to late Sept the timetable is extended to include Sun, operating at the same times from both directions.
The **Bushmills Open Topper** (☎028/7032 5400) runs from Coleraine through Portrush and Bushmills to the Giant's Causeway, weather permitting, four times daily during July and late Sept; an all-day hop-on, hop-off fare is £4.80.
The **Causeway Rambler** runs from Bushmills to Carrick-a-rede seven times daily, via the Giant's Causeway, Dunseverick Castle and Ballintoy from early June to mid-Sept; an all-day ticket is £4.10. The three services above are not included in the following listings.
Antrim to: Ballymena (Mon–Fri 20 daily, Sat 14, Sun 6; 20–30min); Belfast (Mon–Fri 18 daily, Sat 11, Sun 3; 40min).
Ballycastle to: Ballintoy (Mon–Fri 7–9 daily; 15min); Ballymena (Mon–Fri 6–7 daily, Sat 4; 55min–1hr 20min); Bushmills (Mon–Fri 7–8 daily, Sat 1; 35min); Giant's Causeway (Mon–Fri 7–8 daily; 30min).
Ballymena to: Antrim (Mon–Fri 18 daily, Sat 13, Sun 3; 20–30min); Ballycastle (Mon–Sat 5–6 daily; 55min–1hr 20min); Belfast (Mon–Sat 17–18 daily, Sun 3; 1hr–1hr 20min); Carnlough (Mon–Sat 4–5 daily; 50min); Cushendall (Mon–Sat 3–4 daily; 45min); Cushendun (Mon–Sat 4–5 daily; 45min–1hr); Glenarm (Mon–Sat 4–5 daily; 55min).
Bellaghy to: Magherafelt (Mon–Fri 8 daily, Sat 5; 15min).
Carricbfergus to: Belfast (Mon–Sat 30 daily, Sun 8; 40min).
Carnlkough to: Ballymena (Mon–Sat 4 daily; 15min); Glenarm (Mon–Sat 9–10 daily; 5–15min).
Castlerock to: Limavady (Mon–Sat 6–9 daily; 45min).
Cushendall to: Ballymena (Mon–Fri 5 daily, Sat 3; 50min–1hr); Cushendun (Mon–Sat 3–4 daily; 10min); Glenariff (Mon–Fri 5 daily, Sat 3; 10min); Waterfoot (Mon–Fri 5 daily, Sat 3; 5min).
Cushendun to: Ballymena (3–5 Mon–Sat; 55min); Cushendall (Mon–Fri 5–6 daily, Sat 3; 10min).
Derry to: Belfast (Mon–Fri 32 daily, Sat 19, Sun 10; 1hr 40min); Buncrana (*Lough Swilly*: Mon–Sat 9–10 daily, Sun 3; 35min); Carndonagh (*Lough Swilly*: Mon–Sat 2 daily; 50min; & *North West Busways*: Mon–Sat 3–4 daily; 45min); Culdaff (*North West Busways*: Mon–Sat 1 daily; 1hr 5min); Derry Airport (Mon–Fri 7 daily, Sat 3, Sun 1; 20min); Donegal town (*Bus Éireann*: Mon–Sat 6 daily, Sun 3; 1hr 25min); Dublin (*Bus Éireann*: 9 daily; 4hr); Dungiven (Mon–Fri 32, Sat 19, Sun 10; 30min); Galway (*Bus Éireann*: Mon–Sat 4 daily, Sun 3; 5hr 10min–5hr 30min); Greencastle (*Lough Swilly*: Mon–Fri 2 daily, Sat 3; 1hr; *North* West Busways: Mon–Sat 2 daily; 1hr–1hr 40min); Letterkenny (*Bus Éireann*: Mon–Sat 6 daily, Sun 3; 35min; *Lough Swilly*: Mon–Fri 9 daily, Sat 5; 30–45min); Limavady (Mon–Fri 13 daily, Sat 8, Sun 4; 45min); Malin town (*North West Busways*: Mon–Sat 1 daily; 55min); Monaghan (*Bus Éireann*: 9 daily; 1hr 50min); Moville (*Lough Swilly*; Mon–Fri 2 daily, Sat 3; 50min; *North West Busways*: Mon–Sat 4 daily; 40min); Omagh

(Mon–Fri 11 daily, Sat 8, Sun 4; 1hr 5min); Raphoe (*Bus Éireann*: Mon–Sat 4 daily; 45min); Sligo (*Bus Éireann*: Mon–Sat 5 daily, Sun 3; 2hr 30min).
Dungiven to: Belfast (Mon–Fri 32 daily, Sat 19, Sun 10; 1hr 10min); Derry (Mon–Fri 34 daily, Sat 20, Sun 11; 30min); Limavady (Mon–Fri 9 daily, Sat 5, Sun 3; 25min).
Glenarm to: Ballymena (Mon–Sat 4 daily; 25min); Carnlough (Mon–Sat 11–13 daily; 5–15min).
Larne to: Belfast (Mon–Fri 18 daily, Sat 8; 55min–1hr 35min); Carnlough (Mon–Sat 6 daily; 35min); Glenarm (Mon–Sat 6 daily; 30min).
Limavady to: Belfast (Mon–Sat 2 daily, Sun 1; 1hr 35min); Castlerock (Mon–Sat 6–8 daily; 45min); Derry (Mon–Fri 14 daily, Sat 8, Sun 4; daily; 40–55min).
Magherafelt to: Belfast (Mon–Sat 4 daily; 1hr 10min); Bellaghy (Mon–Fri 7 daily, Sat 5; 15min); Moneymore (Mon–Sat 4 daily; 15min).
Moneymore to: Belfast (Mon–Sat 4 daily; 1hr 30min); Magherafelt (Mon–Sat 4–5 daily; 15min).
Portrush to: Portstewart (Mon–Sat 26–30 daily, Sun 10; 15min).
Portstewart to: Portrush (Mon–Sat 26–29 daily, Sun 7; 15min).

15

Down and Armagh

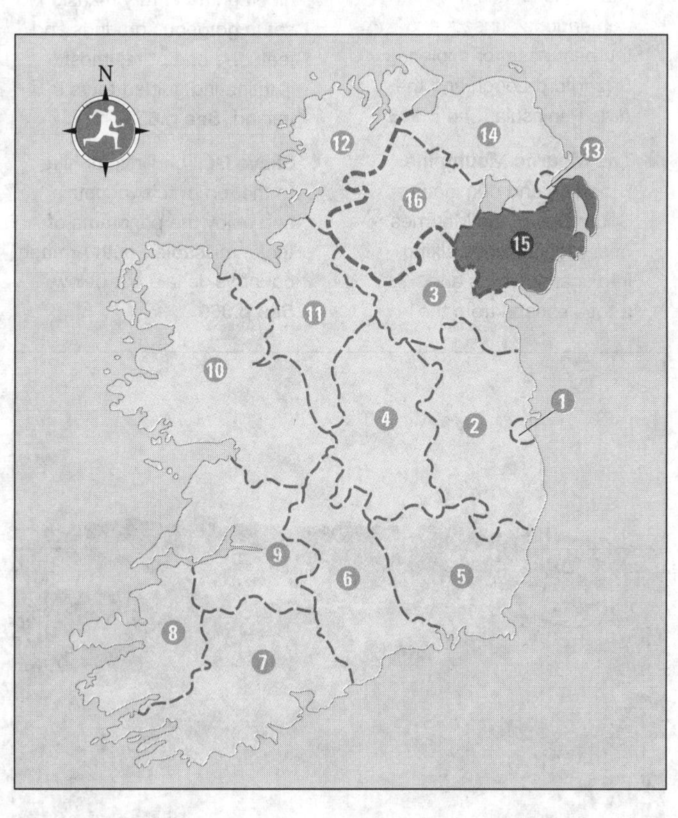

CHAPTER 15 **Highlights**

* **The Ulster Folk and Transport Museum** Possibly the best museum in Northern Ireland – it consummately encapsulates much of the North's cultural and industrial history. See p.630

* **Portaferry** A superb waterside location, tremendous sunsets and the best base for exploring Strangford Lough and the Ards Peninsula. See p.635

* **The Mourne Mountains** Brooding and dominating South Down, the Mournes offer magnificent walking, intoxicating views and a total escape from the contemporary world. See box on p.646

* **Armagh city** Probably the most graceful city in the North, with two cathedrals and a captivating Mall. See p.652

* **The Argory** A magnificent nineteenth-century mansion, set in gorgeous grounds and featuring one of the most illuminating guided tours in Ireland. See p.658

* **Slieve Gullion** Drive or hike to the top of this mountain and enjoy the panorama of the unmissable South Armagh countryside laid out below. See p.660

▲ Portaferry

15

Down and Armagh

Counties **Down** and **Armagh** occupy the southeastern corner of Northern Ireland, between Belfast and the border and contain some of the region's most attractive countryside, especially around the coast. You're also never far away from places associated with **St Patrick**, who sailed into Strangford Lough to make his final Irish landfall in County Down, founded his first bishopric at Armagh and is buried at either Downpatrick or Armagh, depending on whose claim you prefer.

Heading south from Belfast, the glowering **Mourne Mountains** increasingly dominate the panorama, and it's in this direction that most of the attractions lie. If you simply take the main roads in and out of Belfast – the A1 for Newry and the border, or the M1 motorway west – you'll come across very little to stop for: it's in the rural areas, the mountains and coast, that the charm of this region lies. One of the best options is to head east from Belfast around the Down shore – past the **Ulster Folk and Transport Museum**, one of the best in the North, and the blowsy suburban resort of **Bangor** into the **Ards Peninsula** or along the banks of **Strangford Lough**. There are plenty of little beaches, early Christian sites, defensive tower-houses and fine mansions to visit on the way towards **Newcastle**, the best base for excursions on foot into the Mourne Mountains. Beyond the Mournes a fine coast road curves around to **Carlingford Lough** and the border.

Inland there's less of interest, certainly in County Down. **Armagh city**, though, is well worth some of your time for its ancient associations, cathedrals and fine Georgian streets. South Armagh has some startlingly attractive country, especially around the peak of **Slieve Gullion**.

Getting around by public transport is relatively easy, though you'll need to out a bike or walk to enjoy the best of Stranford Lough's Western shore.

County Down

The coast and the **Mourne Mountains** in the south are the major attractions of County Down. The big towns in the north, **Newtownards** and **Bangor**, are much less appealing, but beyond them the A2 road clings to the coast for much of the way down the **Ards Peninsula** and, via the Strangford ferry, all the way to **Newry**. Other routes follow the shores of **Strangford Lough** towards

Downpatrick and its associations with the arrival of St Patrick. There are numerous small resorts around the coast, including big and blousy **Newcastle**, a good base for exploring the mountains. Inland, **Hillsborough**, much resembling an English Cotswolds-style village, is closely linked to the political development of the North, while **Lisburn**, a bustling manufacturing town (actually just over the border in County Antrim) has long been associated with the linen industry.

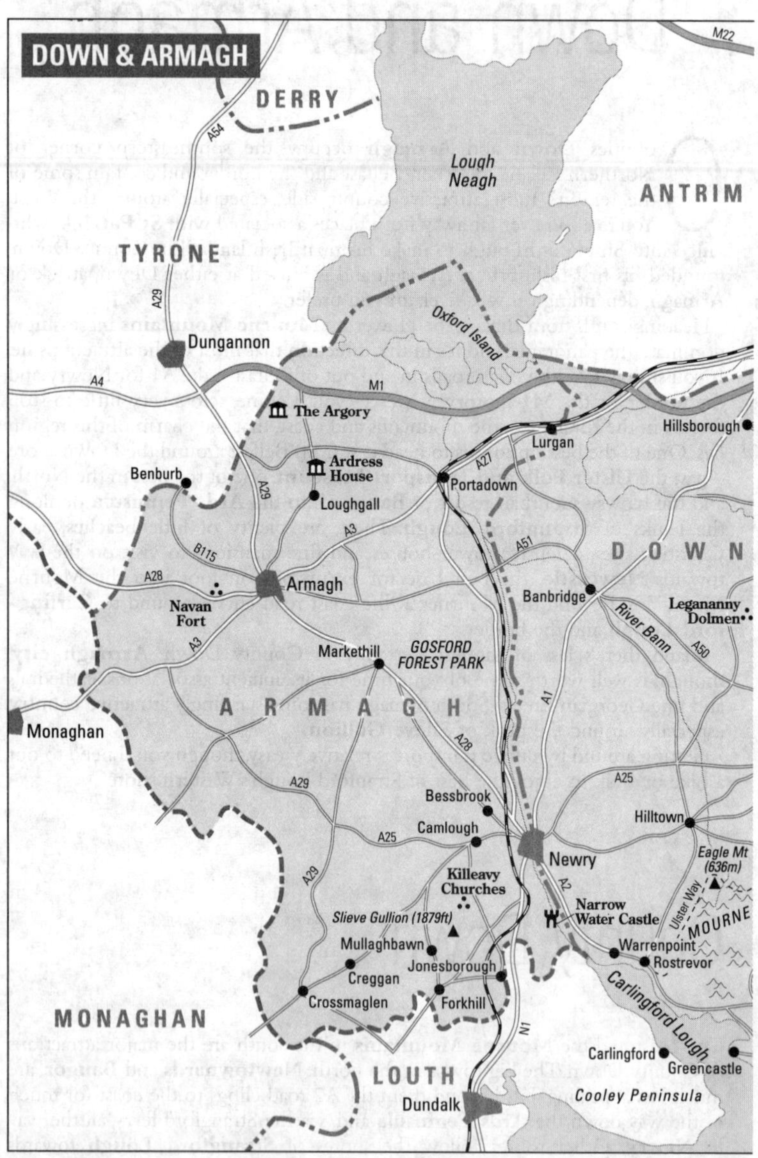

Lisburn and around

LISBURN, eight miles southwest of Belfast, basks in its acquisition, in 2002, of city status – though you'd never guess it merited such from the relatively small size of the place, its busy shopping-streets indicating ongoing commercial success perhaps unknown since its days as an important linen town. Lisburn's

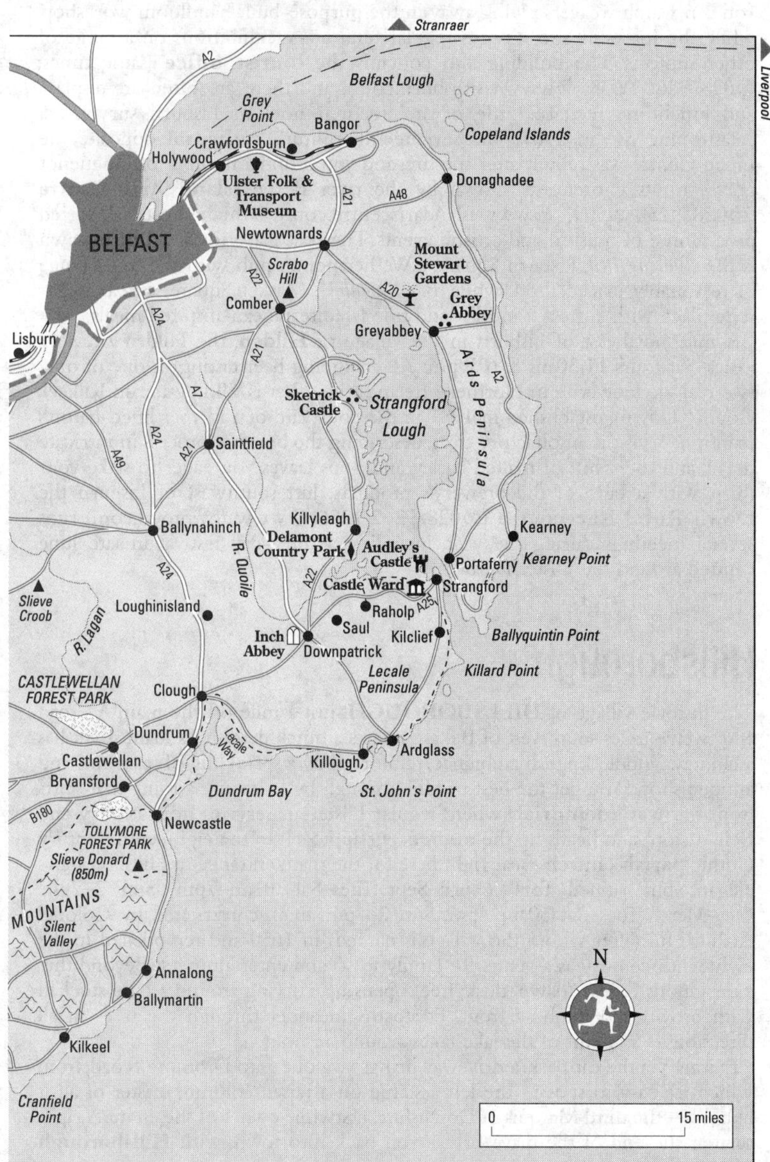

origins as a linen centre began with the establishment of the first bleach greens, the starting point for the linen manufacturing process, on the River Lagan in 1626 at **Lambeg**, a mile downstream from the town; but the industry received a boost with the arrival of French and Dutch Huguenots in 1685.

Lisburn's main attraction is the **Irish Linen Centre and Museum** (Mon–Sat 9.30am–5pm; free), in the eighteenth-century assembly rooms in the Market Square. A permanent exhibition recounts the industry's history, and you can watch weavers plying away in the purpose-built handloom workshop, while the museum also mounts regular temporary exhibitions on a range of other subjects. The building also contains the **tourist office** (same times; Ⓣ028/9266 0038, Ⓦwww.visitlisburn.com), and there are often art displays and lunchtime recitals. Little of architectural note in Lisburn survived a catastrophic fire in 1707. The seventeenth-century **cathedral** opposite the Linen Centre was rebuilt after the fire, and you'll find a number of Huguenot graves in its churchyard. Down by the river is the **Island Arts Centre** (Ⓣ028/9250 9509, Ⓦwww.islandartscentre.com), which hosts a varied programme of musical and artistic events. The best place for a **drink** in town is the *Tuesday Bell*, Lisburn Square, a Wetherspoon's pub with the usual range of reasonably priced food, while *Bar Burgundy*, Market Square, is a bodega-style place with a great wine-list and fine Mediterranean-inspired meals.

A mile northeast of Lisburn in the village of **Hilden**, the Hilden Brewery (Tues–Sat tours 11.30am & 6.30pm; £4, including beer tasting) is one of only two real-ale breweries in Northern Ireland (the other is Whitewater in Kilkeel, County Down), established in 1981 in the courtyard of a former linen-baron's mansion. A visit is an olfactory treat, describing the brewing process in intricate detail, and the whiff of malted barley and hops leaves you eager to slake your thirst with a taste of the brewery's products. Just southwest of Lisburn the **Down Royal Racecourse** (Ⓣ028/9262 1256, Ⓦwww.downroyal.com) runs several meetings during the year, including a three-day festival in late June centred around the Ulster Derby.

Hillsborough

The historic village of **HILLSBOROUGH**, just a mile off the main A1 road and twelve miles southwest of Belfast, merits a quick detour. Its main street has a chintzy, Middle English ambience, reinforced by a sprinkling of tearooms and antique shops. You get the best of Hillsborough by following a route that starts from the **war memorial** (where regular Ulsterbus services from Newry and Belfast stop) and heads up the magnificent approach to the eighteenth-century Gothic **parish church**. Bear right here for the main entrance to Hillsborough's elegant but ruined **fort** (April–Sept Tues–Sat 10am–7pm, Sun 2–7pm; Oct–March Tues–Sat 10am–4pm, Sun 2–4pm; free), constructed by Colonel Arthur Hill (after whom the village is named) in 1650 and remodelled in the eighteenth century as a venue for family feasts and entertainment. Beyond this, a deciduous **forest** (dawn–dusk; free) opens up, curving around a **lake** stocked with brown and rainbow trout. Footpaths meander through the trees in all directions – a circuit of the lake takes around an hour.

Exiting via the car park, a driveway brings you out onto Dromore Road, from which it's easy to spot to the left a statue on a raised column, master of all it beholds – the third Marquis of Downshire, erstwhile owner of the estate. A right turn at the end of the drive brings you back into town, with **Hillsborough**

Castle on your left (hourly tours: May & June Sat 10.30am–4pm; castle £5, gardens £2.50; call ⓣ028/9268 2244 to confirm detail, ⓦwww.nio.gov.uk). The mansion itself dates from 1797, and from 1925 to 1973 was the residence of the governor of Northern Ireland. Since then it's been used mainly to house visiting diplomats, although it hit the headlines when the Anglo-Irish Agreement was signed here in 1985. More recently, Tony Blair stayed here during the April 1997 peace-settlement talks, and the castle is now the official residence of the British secretary of state for Northern Ireland. Tours take you through the State Drawing and Dining Rooms, replete with Georgian furniture and silver from HMS *Nelson*; while the gardens, which you're free to roam through, are particularly lovely in May and June, when the many roses and Europe's largest rhododendron bush are in bloom.

Practicalities

Hillsborough's **tourist office** (Mon–Sat 9am–5.30pm; July & Aug also Sun 2–6pm; ⓣ028/9268 9717) is housed in the elegant Georgian courthouse on The Square at the top of Main Street. There's a mildly interesting exhibition on the court system here and **walking tours** of Hillsborough (June–Aug Sat 2pm; £2.50) leave from outside. The village has several excellent options for **food**, including *The Plough Inn*, opposite the courthouse, and, just down the hill, the seventeenth-century *Hillside Inn*, both of which serve bar meals and more substantial fare in their restaurants; the latter also has jazz on Sunday evenings. If you want to **stay** in the area, try *Fortwilliam*, 210 Ballynahinch Rd (ⓣ028/9268 2255, ⓦwww.fortwilliamcountryhouse.com; ❸), a pleasant country house a couple of miles southeast of the village.

East of Belfast

Heading east into County Down from Belfast, you've a choice of two routes: the A20, which heads due east past Stormont (see p.568) to **Newtownards**, at the head of Strangford Lough; or the A2, which heads northeast past the excellent **Ulster Folk and Transport Museum** to **Bangor**.

Newtownards and around

Following the A20, the single interesting sight as you near Newtownards is **Scrabo Tower** (April–Sept Mon–Thurs & Sat 10.30am–6pm; free), whose looming presence dominates the surrounding area. The tower protrudes from the top of a rocky, gorse-strewn hump of a hill (a long-extinct volcano), but getting to it after you've spotted it is quite a circuit – follow the signs to **Scrabo Country Park** and you'll arrive in the car park just below. The hill itself is pitted with quarries used to extract Scrabo stone, employed for all manner of local buildings, including Grey Abbey (see p.635). Up close the tower looks like a monstrous rocket in its launcher, hewn out of rough black volcanic rock. It was built in 1857 as a memorial to the third Marquess of Londonderry, General Charles William Stewart-Vane, in recognition of his efforts for his tenants during the Great Famine. The spot was originally a Bronze Age burial cairn, probably the resting place of one of the grand chieftains of the area, and there's evidence of a huge hill fort here, too. It's well worth ascending the 122 steps to the tower's top for the wonderful **views** across Strangford Lough and the healthy, blustery weather that often curls around the side of the hill.

The woodland immediately behind is a country park open to the public (free access); in contrast to the tamed, prosperous countryside round about, Scrabo is the only piece of ground for miles around to feel at all wild.

Scrabo Tower looks down on **NEWTOWNARDS**, a place strong on manufacture but unexciting for the traveller. Despite its name, it's an old town, founded in 1244, though there's little evidence of this beyond the ruined Dominican priory just off Castle Street. The Scrabo-stone **Market House** (1765), now the town hall and arts centre, lords it over a large square filled on Saturdays by market activity. The **tourist office** is near the bus station at 31 Regent St (Mon–Fri 9.15am–5pm, Sat 9.30am–5pm; ⓣ028/9182 6846, ⓦwww.www.ards-council.gov.uk). The town is the main base for the **Festival of the Peninsula** in mid-September (ⓦwww.festivalofthepeninsula.info) and a major international **Guitar Festival** (ⓦwww.ardsguitar.com) in mid-October. **Bikes** can be rented from Mike the Bike, 53 Francis St (ⓣ028/9181 1311; £12 per day).

Two miles north on the A21 Bangor road, you'll find the **Somme Heritage Centre** (April–June & Sept Mon–Thurs 10am–4pm, Sat noon–4pm; July & Aug Mon–Fri 10am–5pm, Sat & Sun noon–5pm; Oct–March Mon–Thurs 10am–4pm & first Sat of each month noon–4pm; tours £3.75; ⓦwww.irishsoldier.org; Heritage Island), with re-created frontline trenches staffed by guides in battledress who provide a sobering and moving account of the role of the Irish and Ulster divisions in the futile World War I battle that took place in July 1916 – 5500 men of the 36th (Ulster) Division alone were reported dead, wounded or missing in only the first two days. Across the main road is **Ark Open Farm** (March–Sept Mon–Sat 10am–6pm, Sun 2–6pm; rest of year closes 4pm; £3.90; ⓦwww.thearkopenfarm.co.uk), Ireland's first public rare-breeds farm, where you can compare Irish Moiled and Kerry cattle alongside llamas, reindeer, and an assortment of goats and sheep.

The Ulster Folk and Transport Museum

The A2 towards Bangor is both more scenic and more interesting than the A20, and still within easy reach of a day-trip from Belfast. There's a lovely fifteen-mile walk from **HOLYWOOD** (pronounced "Hollywood") to Helen's Bay, along a mildly indented estuary coast with some beautiful silvery-sand beaches, especially the small crescent-shaped ones at Helen's Bay itself. The **train** line runs between the path and the road, with a couple of stations where you can pick up services on towards Bangor.

At Cultra station you can alight for one of the most fascinating museums in the North, the **Ulster Folk and Transport Museum** (March–June Mon–Fri 10am–5pm, Sat 10am–6pm, Sun 11am–6pm; July–Sept Mon–Sat 10am–6pm, Sun 11am–6pm; Oct–Feb Mon–Fri 10am–4pm, Sat 10am–5pm, Sun 11am–5pm; museums £5.50 each, combined ticket £7; ⓦwww.uftm.org.uk; Heritage Island) – also served by Ulsterbus #B2 from Belfast's Laganside Buscentre. The main site is an open-air **museum village** where about thirty typical buildings from all over the North, some dating from the eighteenth century, have been taken from their original sites and rebuilt complete with authentic furnishings, including an entire street from Dromore and Belfast terraces. Conceptually, you can walk from one part of Northern Ireland to another, amid appropriate scenes. Traditional **farms** have also been created and assorted livestock roam between the buildings. The starting point is a gallery on Ulster's social history and an introduction to the buildings themselves. From here you walk around the grounds, visiting the various buildings, including a small village street with church and rectory, two schools, various typical farm dwellings, a forge and other buildings used in light manufacture. Each of these is "inhabited" by a member of staff, garbed in period costume and informative about the building and its origins. Such historical realism is impressive, though sometimes a little disquieting: the Kilmore Church graveyard contains real tombstones donated by family members.

On the far side of the main road, across a bridge, are the **transport galleries**, where the exhibits include every conceivable form of transport, from horse-drawn carts to lifeboats and a vertical take-off plane, but especially veteran cars, motorcycles and trams. You'll also meet **Old Maeve**, the largest locomotive ever built in Ireland, and a DeLorean sports car from the infamously defunct factory, while the **Titanic** exhibit documents the origins and fate of the Belfast-constructed liner. "The Flight Experience" examines the history of aviation through films, models and interactive displays. Outside the galleries there's a miniature railway that runs on summer Saturdays, and back in the main section there's a decent **restaurant**, located in the Education Centre. The museum also regularly stages temporary exhibitions and occasional cultural events.

Crawfordsburn

The short stretch of coast east from Helen's Bay is part of the **Crawfordsburn Country Park** (April–Sept 9am–8pm; Oct–March 9am–4.45pm; free), an estate handed down from the Scottish Presbyterian Crawford family, then acquired by Lord Dufferin (whose mother Helen gave her name to the bay) and which is now in public hands. Its glens and dells are replete with beeches, cypresses, exotic conifers, cedars, the usual burst of rhododendrons and also a Californian giant redwood, but the park's best features are the wild-flower meadow and the woodland planted with native species.

One of the most scenic of the waymarked trails is the path to **Grey Point Fort** (April–Sept Mon & Wed–Sun 2–5pm; Oct–March Sun 2–5pm; free), which leads through the best of the woodland, under a fine nineteenth-century railway viaduct and up to a waterfall at the head of the glen and thence to the bay. Positioned to command the mouth of Belfast Lough, along with its sister fort at Kilroot on the other side, Grey Point has an impressive battery of gun emplacements, ready to challenge the shipping that entered the lough during the two world wars. In the event, the two six-inch breech-loading guns were never fired except in practice (local residents had to be warned to open their windows and doors to prevent blast damage), apart from one occasion in World War II, when a merchant ship failed to respond to the signal "heave to or be sunk" and received a warning shot across its bows. The guns were sold for scrap in 1957 when the Coast Artillery was disbanded. After the fort was opened to the public in 1987, an identical six-inch gun was relocated here from the prison on Spike Island in Cork harbour. There's also a selection of photos showing the original guns and their positions; but it's really as a viewpoint that the fort is worth a visit for nowadays.

The park's **visitor centre** (daily 10am–5pm; free; Ⓦ www.ehsni.gov.uk) has a café and an incredible amount of information on local ecology and wildlife. **Helen's Tower**, which can be seen from a considerable distance from various vantage points, was built by Lord Dufferin in the nineteenth century to honour his mother, and as a famine relief project.

CRAWFORDSBURN village is on one of Ireland's most ancient highways, a track that ran from Holywood to Bangor Abbey (now the B20), and has a nice but (like many things in this part of the world) twee, early seventeenth-century **pub**, *The Old Inn*, 15 Main St (Ⓣ 028/9185 3255, Ⓦ www.theoldinn.com; ⑤), a partly thatched coaching-inn offering elegant en-suite accommodation and an excellent, popular **restaurant**, serving imaginative takes on standard meat and fish dishes (set dinner £30 plus wine), a four-course Sunday lunch worth starving yourself for (£19), as well as cheaper options in its bar.

Bangor

BANGOR probably takes its name from its curving bay set between a pair of symmetrical headlands, and its sheltered position made it ideal for exploitation as a holiday resort. The town has been hugely popular with Belfast people since the railway came in the 1860s, but today it's as much a suburb of Belfast as a holiday spot. It still possesses a tawdry charm, stuck in a 1960s time warp with all the appropriate bucket-and-spade paraphernalia – giant swan boats to paddle around a mini-lake in the fun park, a miniature railway and amusement arcades. There's also a 500-berth **marina**, which makes Bangor a good place for stocking up on provisions or exploring the coast, while for the land-based the town is well equipped as a stop-off point for dinner and a stroll along the promenade.

Bangor's period of greatest historical significance was almost entirely associated with its **abbey**, which was founded by St Comgall in 586 AD, and from which missionaries set forth to convert pagan Europe. Though the abbey remained powerful for eight hundred years, there's not a trace of the building left. The only vestige of its fame is the *Antiphonarium Benchorense*, one of the oldest-known ecclesiastical manuscripts, consisting of collects, anthems and some religious poems; the original now lies in the Ambrosian Library in Milan, but you can view a facsimile of it in the **North Down Heritage Centre** (July & Aug Tues–Sat 10.30am–5.30pm, Sun 2–5.30pm; rest of year closes 4.30pm; free; Ⓦwww.north-down.gov.uk/heritage), tucked away at the back of the town hall. Other displays trace the rise of the Ward family (see p.641), who were largely responsible for the town's development and built Bangor Castle (now the town hall), and an account of the life and work of songwriter and performer Percy French. There's also a fascinating collection of Eastern **objets d'art** collected by a local-born diplomat, Sir John Jordan, and a collection of archeological discoveries, featuring the Ballycroghan swords, a wonderful pair of bronze weapons dating from 500 AD, and the engraved, bronze ninth-century Bangor hand-bell.

Practicalities

The **tourist office** is opposite the marina in the Tower House on Quay Street (July & Aug Mon, Tues, Thurs & Fri 9am–6pm, Wed 10am–6pm, Sat 10am–5pm, Sun 1–5pm; Sept–June closes one hour earlier and all day Sun; Ⓣ028/9127 0069, Ⓦwww.northdowntourism.com).

As you'd expect, there are dozens of **places to stay** here. The two most luxurious **hotels** are on Quay Street – the *Marine Court* (Ⓣ028/9145 1100, Ⓦwww.marinecourthotel.net; ④) and the *Royal* (Ⓣ028/9127 1866, Ⓦwww.royalhotelbangor.com; ③) – but you'll find plenty of less-expensive **B&Bs** on Princetown and Seacliff roads.

Most of Bangor's **restaurants** are dotted along the seafront or up nearby side-streets. Well worth trying are *Jeffers by the Marina* on Gray's Hill (Ⓣ028/9185 9555; daily 10am–10pm except closes Mon 4.30pm & Sun 8pm) which serves everything from hearty breakfasts to afternoon tea and tasty evening meals. The same chef also operates *The Boat House* near the tourist office at 1A Seacliff Rd (Ⓣ028/9146 9253; closed Mon & Sun), providing exquisite seafood dishes. *Coyle's*, 44 High St, is a popular spot for pub meals and *Rioja*, 119 High St (Ⓣ028/9147 0774; closed Mon & Sun all day and Sat lunchtime), offers an attractive selection of Iberian dishes.

Festive Ireland

As might be expected from a country where the *craic*'s the thing, Ireland's not short of a festival or two – in fact, it's positively awash with them throughout late spring and summer, from local weekend events to grander affairs starring big-name performers and drawing international audiences. Visiting the major ones will usually require some degree of advance planning, whether it's booking tickets or finding somewhere to stay during these busy periods, but a sense of spontaneity is often key to the fun. Nowhere is this more evident than at the fairs and traditional music festivals, which are as much an excuse for serious partying as anything else, with celebrations spreading outwards from the main event into the surrounding streets and pubs – and with all comers welcome.

St Patrick's Day

Ireland's patron saint may have led an ascetic life, but his self-denial is certainly not reflected in the wave of partying in his honour that sweeps across Ireland (and many other countries with expat communities) on March 17. At the very least, most towns and quite a few villages will hold a commemorative parade, with virtually all the pubs hosting various kinds of music. In places associated with the saint, such as Armagh or Downpatrick, or in the cities, you'll find that the day itself may just be the culmination of a longer celebration. Indeed in Dublin, where Ireland's most renowned **St Patrick's Day** festivities take place, there is a week's worth of events, including the céilí mór, a day of traditional dancing, running up to a mammoth parade and a closing fireworks spectacular.

▲ St Patrick's Day

The arts

The most prestigious arts event is the **Galway Arts Festival**, held in mid-July. An enormous, fourteen-day event that seems to take over the whole city, the programme is characterized by sheer diversity, with a host of theatrical and dance events, plenty of visual-arts displays, gigs, traditional-music sessions and comedy. A major highlight is the Sunday-afternoon parade, which often incorporates a major performance production – in 2007, giant insects and prehistoric monsters roamed the city's streets – while other past events have included life-sized puppets appearing unexpectedly in city locations. Meanwhile, Clonmel's July **Junction Festival** is justly regarded as one of the most innovative events, thanks to another wide-ranging agenda of theatrical and musical performances, the latter often involving international artists making their Ireland debut.

▲ Galway Arts Festival

Musical events

The bulk of the many music festivals staged throughout the year revolve around traditional music, often commemorating local musical scions and drawing a horde of Irish and international artists. Many take place in the counties along the western seaboard, one of the biggest being the **Willie Clancy Summer School**, named after the much-loved *uilleann* piper, singer and raconteur and held in Miltown Malbay in early July, when the crowds pack the town as they check out the often memorable sessions. In late August there's also the **Fleadh Cheoil na hÉireann**, usually held in a different town each year, an occasion that sees musicians competing for all manner of All-Ireland instrumental and singing titles, with a multitude more flocking to take part in pub sessions. Even outdoors, impromptu sessions will be breaking out wherever and whenever artists fancy playing, so you're just as likely to hear great music on a street corner as in a jam-packed pub.

By contrast, rock festivals tend to come and go, though Dublin's **Heineken Green Energy festival**, held in May in the grounds of Dublin Castle,

Cork Jazz Festival ▶

▲ Puck Fair

▼ Oyster Festival

is more enduring than most, featuring premier bands and singers. As for jazz, look no further than the prestigious **Cork Jazz Festival** in October, which features the best of the small, but growing Irish scene, as well as international stars such as Gary Burton and Miroslav Vitous. Opera aficionados are well served by the highly esteemed **Wexford Opera Festival** in October, which sees companies from around the world performing lesser-known works alongside a host of big-name concerts and recitals.

Local events

Some local festivals have become major national events over the years, not least the **Puck Fair** at Killorglin in Kerry each August, during which a goat is crowned king of the town, and Galway's September **Oyster Festival**, where an erstwhile oyster-opening competition has developed into a major crowd-puller with thousands turning up for the associated *craic*. **Halloween**, meanwhile, goes down a storm throughout much of Ireland but is most enthusiastically celebrated in Derry, where costumed parades and festivities culminate in a carnival pageant and a huge fireworks display.

Alternatively, you could head along to the Ballycastle's **Ould Lammas Fair** in August, watch the traditional livestock sales, and enjoy delights like the edible seaweed, dulse, and the rock-hard local toffee, yellowman. Elsewhere there's many a local *féis*, as they're often termed, where crisp-eating contests, over-50s hurling matches and tugs-of-war between local Gardaí and publicans are the order of the day. Whatever the case, the fun will be riotous.

"Lovely girls"

Ireland is one of the last bastions of the **beauty contest**, with events held in every Irish county during the summer, when local contestants vie to be sent forward to major competitions (British TV's *Father Ted series* wickedly satirized such shenanigans in an episode that saw the eponymous priest hosting a shambolic "Lovely Girls" competition). The most famous of these is Kerry's **Rose of Tralee**, a highly slick affair each August that draws competitors from across the globe and is surrounded by all manner of other entertainment, while its major competitor is Donegal's lower-key **Mary from Dungloe**, held in July. Less a beauty contest than a kind of nuptial quest, September's **Matchmaking Festival** in Clare sees a multinational cast of participants flocking to Lisdoonvarna with aspirations of finding the perfect partner.

Most of the **pubs** opt for DJs or rock bands in the evening, but you'll find regular **traditional music** at Friday-night sessions at *Fealty's* (also known as the *Ormeau Bar*) on the High Street. A few doors down, *Café Ceol* is a lively and popular place with a varied music programme. Bangor Boats (ⓣ07050/608036) runs regular **deep-sea fishing trips** from the harbour (July & Aug 9.30am & 7pm; £12), and short **boat trips** (July & Aug 2–6pm; £5) around the bay from the Pickie Fun Park.

Donaghadee and the Copeland Islands

East of Bangor's sprawling suburbs, **DONAGHADEE** is the first place of any size. It's a small market town whose origins lie in its proximity to the Scottish coast – on a clear day, it's easy to see Galloway across the water if you climb up the little hill to remains of **The Moat**, a folly-like edifice constructed in 1818 to house explosives used in the construction of the town's harbour. From the seventeenth century until the middle of the nineteenth, ferries ran between here and Portpatrick in Galloway, the shortest sea-crossing available. Various notables arrived in Ireland by this route, including, in 1818, **John Keats** on his walking tour of the British Isles. He was reputedly so depressed by the poverty he saw on his way to Belfast, and the mockery attracted by his fancy London clothes, that he soon returned to Scotland. *Grace Neill's Inn*, on the High Street, dates back to 1611 and claims to have put up Peter the Great of Russia during his European tour.

Donaghadee's decline began when the ferry service was transferred to Larne in 1849. Nowadays, apart from watching the dulse-gatherers at low tide or fishing activity at the harbour, there's little going on here, and the town's only other claim to fame is that its lighthouse received a lick of paint from Brendan Behan when he was employed after the war by the Commission for Irish Lights. More enticing is the possibility of visiting the three **Copeland Islands**, a mile or so offshore and uninhabited since the 1940s. The middle one, Cross Island, is now a bird sanctuary run by the RSPB, which arranges cruises to it (ⓣ028/9049 1547); Nelson's Boats in Donaghadee run regular trips to the other two (June–Sept; call ⓣ028/9188 3403 for times and prices, ⓦwww.nelsonsboats.co.uk).

The **bistro** in *Grace Neill's* is a popular upmarket option for meals, or there's *Pier 36*, The Parade, a **pub** by the pier serving generous helpings of seafood.

Strangford Lough

Ancient annals record that **Strangford Lough** was formed around 1650 BC by the sea sweeping in over the lands of Brena. This created a beautiful, calm inlet, the archipelago-like pieces of land along its inner arm fringed with brown and yellow bladderwrack and tangleweed, and tenanted by a rich gathering of bird life during the warmer months and vast flocks of geese and waders in the winter. It's an attractive haven for small boats and yachts, and several picturesque halts for the land-bound make the road along the lough's western shore the most interesting route leading south from Belfast.

The eastern shore

The eastern edge of Strangford Lough is not as indented as its opposite shore but betters it in having a major road (the continuation of the A20) that runs close to the water virtually all the way down. Also the scenery is delightful, and there are two places to stop off en route to Portaferry – the **Mount Stewart** gardens and **Grey Abbey**.

Mount Stewart

Five miles southeast of Newtownards, served by Ulsterbus #9 and #10 from Belfast's Laganside Buscentre, is the former family home of the Londonderry family, the National Trust–owned **Mount Stewart House and Gardens** (opening times differ, see below; £6.50 for house, gardens and temple, £5 for gardens only; ⓦwww.ntni.org.uk; Heritage Island).

The 98 acres of **gardens** (lakeside gardens daily: April 10am–6pm, May–Sept 10am–8pm, Nov–March 10am–4pm; formal gardens mid- to late March Sat & Sun 10am–4pm, April & Oct 10am–6pm daily, May–Sept 10am–8pm daily) were laid out by Lady Londonderry, wife of the seventh marquess, in the 1920s – and a thorough job she made of it: among others, there are Spanish and Italian gardens, a Space Garden and the Shamrock Garden (with a topiary harp and an appropriately leaved Red Hand of Ulster). The trees and shrubs here are no more than seventy to eighty years old, but they've grown at such a remarkable rate that they look twice that. The principal reason for this is the unusually warm and humid microclimate: the gardens catch the east-coast sun, causing a heavy overnight dew, and the Gulf Stream washes the shores only a stone's throw away. Despite the northerly latitude, conditions here rival those of Cornwall and Devon.

Although the gardens are the highlight, the **house** is also worth viewing (mid-March to April & Oct Sat, Sun & public hols noon–6pm; May Wed–Mon 1–6pm; June daily 1–6pm; July & Aug daily noon–6pm; Sept Wed–Mon noon–6pm). The family was a leading member of the Protestant Ascendancy and its members included Lord Castlereagh, who was Foreign Secretary under Pitt the Younger and is best remembered for guiding the Act of Union into operation. Among the splendid (and occasionally eccentric) furniture inside is a set of 22 Empire chairs used by the delegates to the Congress of Vienna in 1815, who included the Duke of Wellington and Talleyrand; the chairs were a gift to

▲ Mount Stewart House and Gardens

Castlereagh's brother Lord Stewart, another high-ranking diplomat of the time. The Continental connection is flaunted further in bedrooms named after various historically important cities: Rome, St Petersburg, Madrid, Moscow and Sebastopol (from the time of the Crimean War). The house contains a number of paintings, particularly portraits of Castlereagh's political contemporaries, but the most notable and largest is **Hambletonian** (1799) by George Stubbs, showing the celebrated thoroughbred being rubbed down after a victory at Newmarket.

A little to the east of the estate's main entrance, the octagonal **Temple of the Winds** (April–Oct Sun 2–5pm) is a remodelling by James "Athenian" Stuart (1713–88), one of the pioneers of Neoclassical architecture, of Athens' Tower of Andronicus Cyrrhestes. The temple is set on a promontory overlooking Strangford Lough, making it a great place for birdwatching.

Grey Abbey

A couple of miles south on the shore road, **Grey Abbey** (April–Sept Tues–Sat 9am–6pm, Sun 1–6pm; Oct–March Sat 10am–1pm & 2–4pm; free) lies half a mile to the east of the village which later developed around it. The abbey was founded in 1193 by Affreca, daughter of Godred, King of Man, and wife of John de Courcy, as a thanksgiving for having made a safe sea-crossing during a storm. Typical of the **Cistercian** order, of which Mellifont was the mother house in Ireland, the abbey sits in once-remote parkland beside a rivulet,which would have been a source of fresh water and fish – self-reliance was crucial to Cistercianism. Even today, that setting is barely disturbed, and reason in itself to visit, with a substantial set of ruins to complete the picture. The abbey was burnt in 1572 by Brian O'Neill to prevent the English turning it into a fort and was subsequently granted to the Montgomery family in 1607 – slabs in the walls of the church designate the tombs of various family members.

Following the standard design of Cistercian abbeys, it has a church at one end and the living and working quarters of the monks ranged around a **cloister**, a plain structure without distracting embellishments. Grey Abbey is unusual for Ireland, though, in showing early Gothic features at a time when late Romanesque work was still common here. Among the best-preserved remains are the **west door**, much of whose carved decoration can still be made out, and the fine lancet windows in the east end. Another unusual feature is that the church is a simple hall, with no aisles. Outside the church there's a re-created "physic garden" and the notes on display help you to imagine the elongated cloister when it was overshadowed on three sides by the chapter house, dormitories and refectory, which are now no more than stumps. The gatehouse also now houses a small **museum** recounting the abbey's history and the role of the Cistercian order in Ireland.

GREYABBEY village is renowned for its numerous **antiques** shops. The *Wildfowler Inn* on Main Street is a deservedly popular choice for its bar meals and **restaurant**. Nearby **B&Bs** offering pleasant en-suite accommodation are *Quarry House*, 14 Ballywater Rd (Ⓣ028/4278 8552, Ⓔtandybriggs @yahoo.com; ❷), and *Ballynester House*, 1A Cardy Rd (Ⓣ028/4278 8386, Ⓦwww.ballynesterhouse.com).

Portaferry and around

PORTAFERRY, at the mouth of the lough, is the home of the **Exploris** aquarium (April–Aug Mon–Fri 10am–6pm, Sat 11am–6pm, Sun noon–6pm; Sept–March Mon–Fri 10am–5pm, Sat 11am–5pm, Sun 1–5pm; £6.90; Ⓦwww .exploris.org.uk; Heritage Island), which has a touch-tank for the brave to stroke a stingray, and an open-sea tank where you can view the odd roaming shark and basking seals. However, the town's main attraction is the marvellous **sunset** looking across the "Narrows" to Strangford, a view enhanced by a ten-minute climb to the stump of the old windmill just behind the town.

Ferries leave every half-hour for the five-minute ride across the lips of the lough to Strangford (Mon–Fri 7.45am–10.45pm, Sat 8.15am–11.15pm, Sun 9.45am–10.45pm; ⓣ028/4488 1637; £1.10 single, £1.80 return; car £5.30 single, £8.50 return). The **tourist office** is in The Stables, Castle Street (Easter–Sept Mon–Sat 10am–5pm, Sun 2–6pm; ⓣ028/4272 9882), next to the ruined tower house. Should you be looking for somewhere to **stay**, you will find the *Portaferry Hotel*, 10 The Strand (ⓣ028/4272 8231, ⓦwww.portaferryhotel.com; ❹), is relatively luxurious and has a popular **restaurant** specializing in fish meals; or try the brilliantly designed *The Narrows*, 8 Shore Rd (ⓣ028/4272 8148, ⓦwww.narrows.co.uk; ❹), where every room has a stupendous view across the lough. There's great food here too and all manner of special craft and activity weekends on offer. For good-value **B&B** try *Adair's*, 22 The Square (ⓣ028/4272 8412; ❶), or the *Fiddlers Green* pub, 10–14 Church St (ⓣ028/4272 8383, ⓦwww.fiddlersgreenportaferry.com; ❷). Bear in mind that accommodation may be hard to find during the Castle Ward opera season in June (see p.641). Portaferry also has a budget self-catering option in *Barholm*, 11 The Strand (ⓣ028/4272 9598, ⓦwww.barholmportaferry.co.uk; singles £15, doubles ❶), handily placed next to the ferry.

Food options are limited, but apart from the hotels the *Quarter Deck* restaurant at the *Fiddlers Green* pub provides a range of enjoyable fare, and Jumbo's, Castle Yard, is fine for coffee and brunch. The **pubs** are good at just about any time of year, with singalong folk sessions and traditional music at the *Fiddlers Green* most nights.

The coast road south of Portaferry leads to **Ballyquintin Point** and, on the way, passes the entrance lane to **St Cowey's Wells**, where the faithful optimist is spoilt for choice: there's a drinking well, a wishing well and a well for bathing sore eyes. Look out for the rock nearby – the indentations are supposed to mark the places where the saint's hands and feet rested as he prayed. Northeast from here **KEARNEY** is a charming seaside village, consisting almost entirely of whitewashed cottages and now mostly owned by the National Trust. You can walk from here to **Kearney Point**, an often blustery ten-minute stroll with panoramic views across the Irish Sea. Cherry Tree Riding Centre, 5 Newcastle Rd (ⓣ028/4272 9639), offers rides along the beach. The road north of Kearney leads up to Cloghy Bay and another tower-house, **Kirkistown Castle** (July & Aug Tues, Fri & Sat 10am–1pm, Wed & Thurs 2–6pm; free), built in 1622 by Roland Savage and remodelled in Neogothic style in the nineteenth century.

The western shore

Leaving Scrabo Tower just east of Belfast on the A22, you'll pass through **COMBER** – famous for its potatoes – before reaching a turning east to **Castle Espie Wildfowl and Wetland Centre** (March–June & Sept–Oct Mon–Fri 10.30am–5pm, Sat & Sun 11am–5.30pm; July & Aug Mon–Fri 10.30am–5.30pm, Sat & Sun 11am–5.30pm; Nov–Feb Mon–Fri 11am–4pm, Sat & Sun 11am–4.30pm; £5.50; ⓦwww.wwt.org.uk), where admission earnings are ploughed back into conserving the wetlands area for the seven thousand birds that visit it as well as the resident population of waterfowl. The centre also has a coffee shop and art gallery and hosts numerous events throughout the year, related both to ornithology and arts and crafts, as well as plenty of activities for children.

From Castle Espie, you can wind along the very edge of the lough on a series of minor roads. Travelling this scenic route is enjoyable in itself, but there are a couple of spots worth making for. First of them is **Mahee Island**, named for St Mochaoi, supposedly the first abbot of the island, and reached via a twisting lane and several causeways. Heading past the crumbling remains of Mahee Castle at the entrance to the island, and over the final causeway, you come to the Celtic **Nendrum Monastic Site**, a few hundred yards further on. It's a marvellously isolated spot, surrounded on three sides by water. Annals and excavations indicate that a sizeable community lived here from the seventh century onwards, but the remaining ruins probably date from the twelfth century at the very earliest. It was clearly a substantial establishment, with church, round tower, school and living quarters all housed in a cashel of three concentric wards. Today, the inner wall shelters the ruined church, and a reconstructed sundial uses some of the original remnants. There's an illuminating reconstruction map at the site and a helpful **visitor centre** (April–Sept Tues–Sat 9am–6pm, Sun 2–6pm; Oct–March Sat 10am–4pm; free).

Back on the road along the lough, follow the signs to Ardmillan, Killinchy and then Whiterock to reach Sketrick Island (which itself is not signposted). As with Mahee Island, there's a **castle** to guard the entrance, which collapsed in a storm in 1896 and now provides no more than a shattered reminder of its purpose. *Daft Eddie's Pub and Restaurant*, behind the castle, offers bar snacks as well as a more elaborate restaurant menu. The tiny coves and inlets at the feet of little drumlins continue as far as Killyleagh, almost any of them worth exploring.

Killyleagh

Approaching **KILLYLEAGH**, what looks like a huge Gothic fantasy comes into view, a sight wholly out of character with the area: the **oldest inhabited castle** in Ireland, it was erected by John de Courcy in the late twelfth century, but was rebuilt by the Hamilton family in 1648 and again in 1850 to give it the Bavarian **Schloss** appearance it has today. It's still a private house, and when viewed close up it's much more gaunt, with a squat mixture of crenellations, turrets and cones. The stone outside the castle gates commemorates the town's most famous son, Hans Sloane (1660–1753), physician to King George II and founder of both the British Museum and Kew Gardens – London's Sloane Square is named after him. A little way back down the hill, the *Dufferin Arms* coaching inn (ⓣ028/4482 1134, ⓦwww.dufferincoachinginn.co.uk; ❸) offers extremely comfortable **B&B** and organizes a wide range of activity breaks.

The Lecale region

Jutting into the southern reach of Strangford Lough, the **Lecale Peninsula** is above all **St Patrick** country. Ireland's patron saint was a Roman Briton, first carried off as a youth from somewhere near Carlisle in northern England by Irish raiders. He spent six years in slavery in Ireland before escaping home again and, at the age of 30, decided to return to Ireland as a bishop, to spread Christianity. Christianity had already reached Ireland a while earlier, probably through traders and other slaves, and, indeed, St Patrick was not in fact the first bishop of Ireland, but he remains easily the most famous. He arrived in Ireland this second time, according to his biographer Muirchú (also his erstwhile captor, converted), on the shores of the Lecale region, and his first Irish sermon was preached at **Saul** in 432. Today the region commemorates the association with sites at Struell Wells and Saul, as well as at **Downpatrick**.

The **Lecale Way** is an almost forty-mile waymarked walking tour of the peninsula starting in Raholp and running to Strangford and thence around the coast to Clough and onwards to Newcastle (maps available from the Downpatrick tourist office). If you've had enough of St Patrick and his seeming connection with nearly every landmark, alternative ways of exploring the peninsula are the **nature rambles** and **horse rides** available at the Quoile Countryside Centre just outside Downpatrick.

Downpatrick

DOWNPATRICK, 23 miles south of Belfast, is a pleasant enough place of little more than ten thousand people, and its compact size and the proximity of some rich and well-preserved historical sites make for an easy and worthwhile day's visit.

The **Hill of Down**, at the north of the town, was once a rise of great strategic worth, fought over long before the arrival of St Patrick made it famous. A **Celtic fort** of mammoth proportions was built here and was called first Arús Cealtchair, then later Dún Cealtchair. Celtchar was one of the Red Branch Knights, a friend of the then King of Ulster, Conor MacNessa, and, according to the *Book of the Dun Cow*, "an angry terrific hideous man with a long nose, huge ears, apple eyes, and coarse dark-grey hair". The Dún part of the fort's name went on to become the name of the county, as well as the town.

By the time the Norman knight **John de Courcy** made his mark here in the late twelfth century, a settlement was well established. Pushing north out of Leinster, and defeating Rory MacDonlevy, King of Ulster, de Courcy dispossessed the Augustinian canons who occupied the Hill of Down to establish his own **Benedictine abbey**. He flaunted as much pomp as he could to mark the occasion, and one of his festive tricks was to import what were supposedly the disinterred bodies of St Brigid and St Columba to join St Patrick, who was (allegedly) buried here. One of the earliest accounts of Patrick's life asserts that he's buried in a church near the sea; and since a later account admits that "where his bones are, no man knows", Downpatrick's claim seems as good as any.

The Town

The lavish **St Patrick Centre** (April, May & Sept Mon–Sat 9.30am–5.30pm, Sun 1–5.30pm; June–Aug Mon–Sat 9.30am–6pm, Sun 10am–6pm; Oct–March Mon–Sat 10am–5pm; March 17 9.30am–7pm; last admission 90min before closing; £4.90; Ⓦ www.saintpatrickcentre.com), just off the main drag Market Street, aims to recount the life of the saint and his influence in extensive detail. Its hagiographic, multimedia approach is pretty arid, however, and by the time you've been round its maze of interactive displays and sat through the five-screen 180-degree virtual helicopter ride through Christian history, you might even wish you'd never heard of him.

Signposts next to the centre point the way uphill to the elegant, spacious Mall, at the end of which stands **Down Cathedral** (Mon–Sat 9.30am–4.30pm, Sun 2–4.30pm; free; Ⓦ www.downcathedral.org). The site of the three graves of Columba, Patrick and Brigid is meant to be just to the left of the tower entrance and is marked today by a rough granite boulder, put there around 1900 to cover a huge hole created by earlier pilgrims searching for the saints' bones. The cathedral built by de Courcy was destroyed in 1316 during Edward Bruce's invasion, and a new abbey erected in the early sixteenth century was even more short-lived. Today's cathedral dates basically from the early 1800s, though it incorporates many aspects of earlier incarnations. Its unique feature is the private box-pews, characteristic of the Regency period and the only ones remaining in use in Ireland.

Leaving the cathedral and retracing your steps a little down English Street, which is crowded with Georgian buildings, you come to the eighteenth-century jail, home to the **Down County Museum** (Mon–Fri 10am–5pm, Sat

On the trail of St Patrick

About four miles west of Inch Abbey (take the B2 to Annacloy and then the first turning on the left), **Loughinisland** is probably the most worthwhile of all the sites in the area associated with St Patrick, and indeed one of the most idyllic spots in County Down. It comprises a reed-fringed lake contained by ten or so little drumlin hills, one of which forms an island in the lake. Here, across a short causeway, are the ruins of three small churches, set next door to each other. The smallest one, **MacCartan's Chapel** (1636), has an entrance door no taller than four or five feet. The larger northern church was used by both Catholics and Protestants until they quarrelled on a wet Sunday around 1720 over which camp should remain outside during the service. The Protestants left and built their church at Seaforde instead.

The next St Patrick landmark is at **SAUL**, a couple of miles northeast of Downpatrick off the Strangford road. St Patrick is said to have landed nearby, sailing up the tiny River Slaney, and it was here that he first preached, immediately converting Dichu, the lord of this territory. Dichu gave Patrick a barn as his first base and the saint frequently returned here to rest from his travelling missions – legend has it that he died here in 461. Today a **memorial chapel** and round tower in the Celtic Revival style, built of pristine silver-grey granite in 1932 to commemorate the 1500th anniversary of the saint's arrival, is open to visitors (9am–5pm daily). Two cross-carved stones from between the eighth and twelfth centuries still stand in the graveyard, though there's not a trace of the medieval monastery built here by St Malachy in the twelfth century.

A short distance further south, between Saul and Raholp, **St Patrick's Shrine** sits atop Slieve Patrick, a tract of hillside much like a slalom ski-slope, with the Stations of the Cross marking a pathway up. This huge Mourne-granite statue, clad at the base with bronze panels depicting Patrick's life, was erected in the same year as Saul church. The summit is no more than a twenty-minute climb and offers a commanding view of the county, a vista of the endless little bumps of this drumlin-filled territory.

At **RAHOLP** is the ruined church of **St Tassach**, named after the bishop from whom the dying Patrick received the sacrament. Patrick gave Raholp to Tassach as a reward for crafting a case for Christ's crozier, the Bachall Isú, one of Ireland's chief relics until its destruction in 1538. The ruins here were mainly restored in 1915 from the rubble that lay around, but their material is thought to date from the eleventh century. If you're eager for the complete St Patrick experience, it's a mile from the car park of the *Slaney Inn* (which serves superb bar meals) in Raholp to the spot on the lough shore where he is believed to have first landed: head towards Strangford, then left down Myra Road; cross the main Strangford road and turn left at the first fork; at the bottom of the hill, take the track on the right to the shore.

The easiest way to find the last St Patrick site, **Struell Wells**, is to return to Downpatrick. Take the Ardglass road southeast, turn left just past the hospital, then right down a narrow track into a secluded rock-faced valley and you'll come to the wells. The waters here, believed to be the wells referred to in early accounts of Patrick's mission, have been attributed with healing powers for centuries. In 1744 Walter Harris described the scene: "Vast throngs of rich and poor resort on Midsummer Eve and the Friday before Lammas, some in the hopes of obtaining health, and others to perform penance." The site contains a couple of wells, one for drinking and another known as the eye well whose waters are supposed to have curative powers, and men's and women's bathhouses. Mass is still said here on midsummer night, and people bring containers to carry the water home with them.

& Sun 1–5pm; free; ⓦwww.downcountymuseum.com). The three-storey Georgian **Governor's House** in the centre of the walled courtyard houses a somewhat lacklustre local-history gallery, though there are often more interesting temporary exhibitions elsewhere on the site; at the time of writing the house was being refurbished to provide extended galleries. The cell block at the back of the enclosure once held the United Irishman Thomas Russell, who had already survived the 1798 Rebellion but was found guilty of complicity in Robert Emmet's uprising and was duly hanged in 1803 from a sill outside the main gate of the jail.

Turn downhill between the jail and the barricaded courthouse and, inauspiciously tucked behind a secondary school, you'll find the **Mound of Down**, a smaller prominence than the Hill of Down and half-submerged in undergrowth. It's in fact 60ft high and inside its outer ditch is a horseshoe-shaped central mound of rich grass. Once a rath, or round hill fort, it was considerably altered and enlarged to create a Norman motte-and-bailey fortification, with a **bretasche** (a wooden archery tower) at the centre. Its view of the Hill of Down clearly displays the attractions the hill had for its earliest settlers; it's believed by some to be the site of the palace of the kings of Ulster.

At the rear of the market car park on Market Street, is the enthusiast-run **Downpatrick and County Down Railway** (ⓦwww.downrail.co.uk), which operates short steam-train trips up along a restored section of the Belfast–Newcastle main line to Inch Abbey (public holidays, mid-June to mid-Sept Sat & Sun 2–5pm; £4.70 return). The station has a small photographic exhibition (same times; free) on railways in County Down, as well as several steam and diesel locomotives on show. A little further along Market Street is **Downpatrick Racecourse** (ⓦwww.downpatrickracecourse.co.uk), the second oldest in Ireland and home to the Ulster Grand National in late February and several other meetings between March and December.

Practicalities

The **bus station** (ⓣ028/4461 2384) is on Market Street, a hundred yards south of the St Patrick Centre, where you'll find the **tourist office** (July–Sept Mon–Fri 9am–6pm, Sat 10am–6pm, Sun 2–6pm; Oct–June Mon–Fri 9am–5pm, Sat 9.30am–5pm; ⓣ028/4461 2233). The best and most central of the town's **B&Bs** are *Denvir's*, 16 English St (ⓣ028/4461 2012, ⓦwww.denvirshotel.com; ❸), which offers en-suite accommodation in one of Ireland's oldest coaching inns, and *Hillside*, 62 Scotch St (ⓣ028/4461 3134; ❶), in a listed Georgian townhouse. Out of town, try *The Mill at Ballydugan*, Drumcullen Road (ⓣ028/4661 3654, ⓦwww.ballyduganmill.com; ❹), a converted flour mill dating from 1792 featuring elegant rustic-style rooms and with its own café and restaurant, or the splendid *Pheasant's Hill Farm*, 37 Killyleagh Rd (ⓣ028/4461 7246, ⓦwww.pheasantshill.com; ❸), offering one of the best breakfasts in the North and a pleasant rural setting. If you're **camping**, your best bet is to go to *Castle Ward Park* (see p.642), six miles northeast on the A25 towards Strangford.

Downpatrick boasts a number of fine **cafés**, including the one in the Down Arts Centre (see below), for soups, salads and imaginative sandwiches, and *Harry Afrika's*, in the shopping centre on Market Street, for its phenomenal breakfasts. *Denvir's* (see above) serves superb lunches and evening meals, while *Justine's*, 19 English St (ⓣ028/4461 7886; lunch daily, dinner Thurs–Sun), offers a menu providing innovative variations on the standard steak and seafood.

The best **traditional-music** session is on Friday nights at *Speedy Mullan's* on Church Street, while *Hogan's* on Market Street has live bands and DJs at weekends. There may be occasional performances in the excellent **Down Arts**

Centre, 2–6 Irish St (Mon–Fri 10am–4.30pm, Sat 9am–4pm; Ⓦwww.downartscentre.com), which has an art gallery and performance space. Parallel to the Castle Ward opera season in mid-June the town mounts its own **Opera Fringe** festival with all manner of activities, including recitals and exhibitions (Ⓦwww.operafringe.com).

Around Downpatrick

A mile northwest of Downpatrick, on the other side of the Quoile Marsh, lie the remains of the Cistercian **Inch Abbey** (free access). The exquisite setting is visible from the town, but the river's intervention means that the only access is a mile out along the Belfast road, taking the left turn down Inch Abbey Road just before the defunct *Abbey Lodge Hotel*, followed by another signposted left turn shortly afterwards – alternatively you can take a train ride from Downpatrick (see above). The site was once an island, and an earlier nearby foundation was destroyed by John de Courcy in 1177 because it was fortified against him. In atonement he built a replacement here and, in 1180, invited Cistercian monks from Furness Abbey in Lancashire over to populate the building, with the intention of establishing a strong centre of English influence. Little of it is now left standing – it was burnt in 1404 and monastic life was completely over by the mid-sixteenth century. Still, its setting, among small glacial drumlins and woodland, is picturesque, and strolling up the valley sides is a pleasant way to pass half-an-hour or so.

About two miles northeast of Downpatrick, off the A25 Strangford road, the **Quoile Countryside Centre** (April–Aug daily 11am–5pm; Sept–March Sat & Sun 1–5pm; free; Ⓦwww.ehsni.gov.uk) focuses attention on the natural habitats created by the building of a tidal barrier to prevent local flooding. It organizes **nature rambles**, seal watches in Strangford Lough, dawn-chorus walks on Quoile River and even butterfly trips. Tullymurray Equestrian Centre on Ballydugan Road organizes **trail rides** to forest parks and Castle Ward – or along the coast, with beach rides to Newcastle and Tyrella (details from Ⓣ028/4481 1880).

Strangford and Castle Ward

If you're following the A2 round the coast of the Ards Peninsula, your arrival on Lecale will be at tiny **STRANGFORD** village, directly opposite Portaferry and linked by a regular ferry service (see p.636). The earlier name of this inlet was Lough Cuan (*cuan* being Irish for "harbour" or "haven"), but it was renamed Strangfiord by the Vikings over a thousand years ago because of the strong eight-knot current in the narrows. Its small harbour makes a pleasant setting for watching the to and fro of the ferry boats, and the *Lobster Pot* **inn**, on the front, has a welcome garden and middle-of-the-range prices for fine evening meals. **Places to stay** include the elegantly furnished *The Cuan* (Ⓣ028/4488 1222, Ⓦwww.thecuan.com; ❹), which has a deserved reputation for its splendid restaurant and equally friendly bar, and very upmarket B&B at *Strangford Cottage*, 41 Castle St (April–Sept; Ⓣ028/4488 1208, Ⓔstrangfordcottage@gmail.com; ❺).

Immediately around Strangford are a few houses and castles worth visiting, the first of them on the road back towards Downpatrick. **Castle Ward** (house: 1–6pm St Patrick's Day, Easter week, June Fri–Wed, July & Aug daily, Sept Sat & Sun; grounds: April–Sept 10am–8pm, Oct–March 10am–4pm; house and grounds £6.50, grounds only £4.50; Ⓦwww.ntni.org.uk; Heritage Island) is Ireland's Glyndebourne: for three weeks every June, **opera** enlivens the

▲ Castle Ward

house and grounds, and *bon viveurs* flock here with picnic hampers, starched napkins and candlesticks (tickets £40.50–55; ⓣ028/9263 9545, ⓦwww.castlewardopera.com). The house, which was the eighteenth-century residence of Bernard and Anne Ward, later Lord and Lady Bangor, is now owned by the National Trust. It's a positively schizophrenic building, thanks to the opposed tastes of its creators (they later split up): Bernard's half is in the Classical Palladian style, Anne's Neogothic, a split carried through into the design and decor of the rooms inside. Outside there are pleasant **gardens** (daily 10am–dusk) and preserved farm buildings. There's also a sixteenth-century tower house (Old Castle Ward) inside the grounds; the fifteenth-century **Audley's Castle** just outside on the lough shore, with a superb view across the lough (though there's a better example of a tower house just south of Strangford at Kilclief; see below); and the **Strangford Lough Wildlife Centre** (same hours as Castle Ward house; no extra charge), housed in a restored barn. If you want to stay, you can **camp** in the castle estate (ⓣ028/4488 1680).

From Strangford to Ardglass

A signposted turning one mile south of Strangford directs you to the **Cloghy Rocks** observation point. The rocks themselves are 20yd or so out in the lough and for most of the day look decidedly inconsequential, but at low tide you can spot basking **seals**. They're well camouflaged against the seaweed, so a pair of binoculars would be handy.

Further south, **Kilclief Castle** (July & Aug Tues–Fri 10am–6pm, Sat & Sun 2–6pm; free) is one of Ireland's earliest tower-houses, a well-preserved fifteenth-century example that was originally the home of John Cely, Bishop of Down – until he was defrocked and thrown out of the Church for living with someone else's wife.

The next stop is **St Patrick's Well**, set on a wonderful rocky shore between Ballyhornan and Chapeltown. You can get to within a few hundred yards of the well by road, but the best approach is to start from Ballyhornan – where you'll see a narrow strip of water separating the village from Guns Island, accessible at low tide and still used for grazing – and follow the foreshore path for about a mile. The well is easily spotted: it looks rather like a sheep dip with concrete walls, but with a crucifix at its head. Its holy water has turned into something closer to stagnant consommé than an ever-youthful source of new life.

Half a mile or so before you reach Ardglass, the ruin of fifteenth-century **Ardtole Church** is well signposted just a few hundred yards east of the road. It's set on the spur of a hill, which gives it a fine perspective out to sea and back across the undulating flat of Lecale. Once dedicated to St Nicholas, patron saint of sailors, the church was used by English fishermen until a quarrel broke out with the Irish around 1650. The story goes that the fishermen tied a sleeping Irish chief to the ground by his long hair so that he couldn't get up when he awoke. Tradition has it that Swift derived the similar episode in *Gulliver's Travels* from this tale, and certainly the Ardtole region runs amok with tiny drumlins – very much like the description of the Lilliputian mountains.

Ardglass and Killough

ARDGLASS is set on the side of a lovely natural inlet. Its domestic buildings, rising steeply from the harbour, are interspersed with seven fortified mansions, towers and turrets, dating from a vigorous English revival in the sixteenth century, when a trading company first arrived to found a colony here. The best preserved of the fortifications, though it's no longer open for visits on safety grounds, is **Jordan's Castle**, next door to the *Anchor* pub on the Low Road, the most elegant and highly developed of all the Down tower-houses. The tall, crenellated building with white-plaster trimming up on the hill was once **King's Castle**; its nineteenth-century renovation is obvious, as is modern work to turn it into a nursery. The lone ornamental-looking turret on the hilltop is **Isabella's Tower**, a nineteenth-century folly created by Aubrey de Vere Beauclerc as a gazebo for his disabled daughter. Overlooking the sea is one of the North's most attractively set **golf courses** (Ⓦwww.ardglassgolfclub.com).

In the nineteenth century, Ardglass was the most thriving **fishing** port in the North; and even today, aside from the prawns, herrings and whitefish brought in by the fishing fleet, there's very good rod-fishing to be had off the end of the pier for codling, pollack and coalfish. The supermarket on the quay is wonderfully stocked with a vast range of **seafood** (scallops, monkfish, oysters, salmon and more), enough in itself to entice a quick shopping visit. It's also sometimes possible to buy direct from fishing boats or from the cannery on the quay. The old **inn**, the very convivial *Commercial*, on the main street, has a well that is still in use; it's covered over with glass on the lounge floor. You can eat well at the popular *Aldo's* Italian **restaurant**, 7 Castle Place (Ⓣ028/4484 1315; Oct–April closed Mon–Wed), which serves evening meals and Sunday lunch, or head for delicious seafood at *Curran's Bar* in Chapeltown, a couple of miles towards Killough and a very cosy pub with snugs and open fires. There's very comfortable **B&B** at *Burford Lodge*, 30 Quay St (Ⓣ028/4484 1141; ❷), a Georgian house on the seafront, and the cosy *Margaret's Cottage* (Ⓣ028/4484 1080, Ⓦwww.margaretscottage.co.uk; ❷), next door to *Aldo's*.

KILLOUGH, a few miles west of Ardglass, is a tranquil village stretching around a harbour that is much larger than its neighbour's but is now silted up. Killough's main street is a fine French-style avenue of sycamores with a string of picturesque cottage terraces at its southern end, making an unlikely major thoroughfare. The Wards, of Castle Ward, built the harbour in the eighteenth century, and there's still a road running inland, virtually in a straight line, from

Killough to their castle. Untouched by tourism, there is no accommodation in the village and only bar meals in a couple of pubs.

From the southern end of Killough you can head out to **St John's Point** – much favoured by birdwatchers – on which lie the ruins of one of the North's best examples of a **pre-Romanesque church**; it's an enjoyable two-and-a-half-mile walk. The tiny west door of the tenth-century church has the distinctive sloping sides, narrowing as the doorway rises, that were a common feature of these early churches. Also still apparent are the **antae**, enclosures created by the extension of the west and east walls to give extra support to the roof. Excavations in 1977 showed up graves that extended under these walls, indicating that an even earlier church existed in the early Christian period, probably made of wood.

Dundrum

Although it's not officially in the Lecale region, whose inland ending is at Clough, **DUNDRUM**, just a few miles down the Newcastle road, has some quite spectacular ruins of a large Norman **castle** (April–Sept Tues–Sat 9am–6pm, Sun 1–6pm; Oct–March Sat 10am–4pm, Sun 2–4pm; free). The town lies beside a hammer-headed tidal bay, with the ruins sitting dramatically above, a steep fifteen-minute walk uphill from the village. The castle has a central circular donjon (with a fine spiral stairway in its walls), a fortified gateway and drum towers, all set upon a motte and bailey. In its time it was described as the most impenetrable fortress in the land, yet it was captured on several occasions and partly dismantled by Cromwell's soldiers in 1652. Some say it was a de Courcy fortress, designed for the Knights Templar, but the circular keep, a rarity in Ireland, is unlike the other fortresses de Courcy built to defend the stretch of coast from Carlingford right up to Carrickfergus. De Courcy's successor, de Lacy, is a more likely candidate – his Welsh connections tie in with the castle's similarity to the one at Pembroke in west Wales.

Newcastle, the mountains and the coast

Newcastle, with its lovely stretch of sandy beach, is the biggest seaside resort in County Down – packed with trippers from Belfast on bank holidays and summer weekends – and, with Slieve Donard rising behind the town, it's by far the best base if you want to do any serious walking or climbing in the **Mourne Mountains**. On busy days the main drag, with raucous rock bands performing outside the pubs, can feel like nothing more than a soulless strip of amusement arcades, fast-food outlets and tacky souvenir stores, but the town's more sedate qualities can be appreciated when the trippers have gone.

The Mournes are a relatively youthful set of granite mountains, which explains why their comparatively unweathered peaks and flanks are so rugged, forming steep sides, moraines and occasional sheer cliffs. Closer up, these give sharp, jagged outlines; but from a distance they appear much gentler, like a sleeping herd of buffalo. The wilder topography lies mostly in the east, below Newcastle, although the fine cliff of **Eagle Mountain** (636m), to the southwest, is wonderful if you can afford the time and effort to get there, and the tamer land above Rostrevor has views down into **Carlingford Lough** that rival any in Ireland.

In summer at least (winters can be surprisingly harsh), there are plenty of straightforward hikes in the Mournes that require no special equipment, with obvious tracks to many of the more scenic parts. For further information, and maps, go to the Newcastle tourist office or the Mourne Countryside Centre (see box, pp.646–647). There are also, of course, more serious climbs: **climbing courses** in the Mournes are run by the Tollymore Mountain Centre in Bryansford (Ⓦwww.tollymoremc.com), but they must be booked well in advance.

Newcastle

NEWCASTLE isn't exactly exciting, but it's well equipped for a range of outdoor activities, including **walking** in the Mourne Mountains southwest of town, **pony trekking** and **fishing** on the river. Golfing enthusiasts may be tempted by Newcastle's Royal County Down **golf course** (Ⓦwww.royalcountydown.org), which has a reputation as one of the most challenging links worldwide. During July and August there are all kinds of activities available with children in mind, including the **Tropicana Complex**'s heated outdoor swimming and play pools by The Promenade.

The town has a few literary connections: **Séamus Heaney** was a waiter in the 1950s at the long-gone *Savoy Café*; Brook Cottage (now a hotel), on Bryansford Road, was home to the dramatist and dialect-poet Richard Valentine Williams, better known as Richard Rowley; and a fountain on The Promenade commemorates the popular Irish songwriter Percy French, composer of *The Mountains of Mourne* and numerous comic songs. Behind the Newcastle Centre, a plaque celebrates one of the first powered flights in Ireland, undertaken in 1910 by **Harry Ferguson** to win a £100 prize – he was later to become famous through the success of the Massey Ferguson tractor.

Practicalities

The **bus station** (Ⓣ028/4372 2296) is on Railway Street at the eastern end of Main Street, which, a couple of hundred yards west, becomes The Promenade. Here you'll find the very helpful **tourist office** at 10–14 Central Promenade (Mon–Sat 10am–5m, Sun 2–6pm; Ⓣ028/4372 2222). There's a wide choice of **places to stay**. The best of the more upmarket **hotels** is the *Slieve Donard*, Downs Road (Ⓣ028/4372 1066, Ⓦwww.hastingshotels .com; ❼), with its own spa, though it's closely followed by the *Burrendale Hotel & Country Club*, 51 Castlewellan Rd (Ⓣ028/4372 2599, Ⓦwww.burrendale.com; ❺). Cheaper central **B&Bs** with sea views include *Beach House*, 22 Downs Rd (Ⓣ028/4372 2345, Ⓔmyrtle.macauley@tesco.net; ❸), in a refurbished Victorian dwelling, or the congenial *Dacara*, 47 South Promenade (Ⓣ028/4372 6745, Ⓔdacara@thechefshop.net; ❷). Newcastle's HINI **hostel** is in a townhouse on the seafront at 30 Downs Rd, near the bus station (Ⓣ028/4372 2133; dorms £13). There are also several **caravan and camping sites** around Newcastle, though the best are located in the forest parks (see box on pp.646–647).

For seafood treats head to the *Sea Salt Bistro*, 51 Central Promenade (Ⓣ028/4372 5027), which operates as a café in the mornings, then serves appetizing lunches and very substantial dinners (Thurs–Sat only) at reasonable prices, though you'll need to bring your own wine. Other **meal** options include the *Burrendale Hotel & Country Club*, whose *Vine Restaurant* is extremely popular while the *Slieve Donard Hotel*, Downs Road, serves good-value food in both its *Oak Restaurant* and *Percy French* bar. Otherwise there are plenty of **cafés**, the best of which is *Café Crème*, 139–141 Main St, and plenty of fast-food joints.

The Legananny dolmen

The **Legananny dolmen** is worth a considerable detour, which it will be wherever you are, due to its remoteness; it's signposted at the village of Leitrim, three miles north of Castlewellan. Approaching the site you'll find yourself on

Walks in the Mournes

While there's little to see in Newcastle itself, the **Mourne Mountains** offer some beautiful walks close to the town, and, for more serious walking, plenty of good hiking routes throughout the range. Before you set off it's worth visiting the Mourne Countryside Centre, 87 Central Promenade, in Newcastle (Mon–Fri 9am–5pm; July & Aug also Sat & Sun 9am–4pm; ⓣ028/4372 6493), for information on walks, access and the local ecology.

The climb up **Slieve Donard**, just south of Newcastle, is the obvious first choice. Although at 850m it's the highest peak in Northern Ireland, the ascent is a relatively easy one on a well-marked trail that starts three miles out of town on the Annalong road at Bloody Bridge (see below) and ends at the massive hermit cell on the summit; from here the views across the whole mountain landscape are quite spectacular.

For gentler local walking, there are several pleasant parks created from the estates of old houses in the vicinity. The nearest is **Donard Park** (free access) on the slopes of Slieve Donard. There's a good meander along the River Glen from Newcastle town centre to the park, and if you keep following this path uphill you'll emerge on the other side and eventually come to the Saddle, a col between the two mountains of Slieve Donard and Slieve Commedagh. If you want to carry on further into the mountains from here, a good route is via **Trassey Burn** towards the **Hare's Gap**, where minerals have seeped through the rock to form precious and semiprecious stones – topaz, beryl, smoky quartz and emerald – in the cavities of the **Diamond rocks** (hidden behind an obvious boulder stone on the mountainside). Around this point in spring, you might hear the song of the ring ouzel, a bird that migrates from Africa to breed in these upland areas.

Two miles inland from Newcastle, along the Bryansford road, **Tollymore Forest Park** (daily 10am–dusk; ⓦwww.forestserviceni.gov.uk; cars £4, pedestrians £2) is considerably bigger and better equipped than Donard, and has a **campsite**. The park creeps up the northern side of the Mournes, and its picturesque trails wind through woodland and beside the river. You enter the park by one of two ornate Gothic folly gates – there are more follies in Bryansford nearby – and there's an **information kiosk** in the car park.

narrow humped lanes, gradually ascending the southern edge of the Slieve Croob range, and feeling increasingly distant from modern realities. You may also experience a sense of *déjà vu* when you arrive at the site, for the dolmen is a popular choice of guidebook and tourist-board photographers. There's no doubting the impressiveness of the structure, looking for all the world like a giant stone tripod. Not too far away on the Castlewellan road to the east is a welcome oasis, the *Slieve Croob Inn* (ⓣ028/4377 1412, ⓦwww.slievecroobinn.com; ❸), a wonderfully situated **hotel** whose bistro-style **restaurant** serves mouthwatering meals, including delicious oven-baked fresh salmon, and a range of very tempting desserts.

Annalong and Silent Valley

The A2 south along the coast from Newcastle is a beautiful road, trailing the shore around the edge of the mountains. It takes you past the chasm known as **Maggie's Leap**, after a local woman who jumped to avoid the attentions of an unwanted suitor, and over the **Bloody Bridge**, reputedly so called because of a nearby massacre during the 1641 Rebellion. Further along the way, the fishing harbour towns of **Annalong** and **Kilkeel** are alternative bases for **walking** or exploring the mountains.

The small fishing harbour of **ANNALONG** is a pleasantly relaxed seaside town during the summer, with a stony beach and Slieve Binnion providing a

Castlewellan Forest Park (same hours and prices) is also inland about five miles further north, outside the elegant market town of Castlewellan. The estate lies in the foothills of the Mournes, and a two-and-a-half mile trail from the entrance leads to the highest point in the forest, **Slievenaslat**, providing panoramic views over the mountain range. A wonderful **arboretum**, dating originally from 1740 but much expanded since, is the forest park's outstanding feature: the sheltered south-facing slopes of its hills, between the Mournes and the Slieve Croob range, allow exotic species to flourish. There's trout **fishing** in its main lake and coarse fishing in the smaller lakes (enquire at the Newcastle tourist office for details of this and other local fisheries). There's a pleasant campsite in the park here, too (call the forest officer on Ⓣ028/4377 8664), as well as the Bluelough Mountain & Watersports Centre (Ⓦwww.mountainandwater.com) which runs various activities breaks. The park also hosts the Celtic Fusion festival (Ⓦwww.celticfusion.co.uk) in mid-July, which includes concerts by major folk and traditional musicians. Nearby **riding schools** offering trekking through the forest parks include Mount Pleasant Riding and Trekking Centre, 15 Bannanstown Rd, Castlewellan (Ⓣ028/4377 8651, Ⓦwww.mountpleasantcentre.com), and Mourne Trail Riding Centre, 96 Castlewellan Rd, a couple of miles out of Newcastle on the A50 (Ⓣ028/4372 4351, Ⓦwww.mournetrailridingcentre.com).

If you're planning on more serious hiking in the Mournes, heights worth chasing include **Slieve Binnian**, beyond the Hare's Gap, reached through the Brandy Pad passes by the Blue Lough and Lough Binnian; **Slieve Commedagh**, with its Inca-like pillars of granite; and **Slieve Bearnagh**, up to the right of the Hare's Gap. Also, try and cross the ridge from **Slieve Meelmore** to **Slieve Muck**, the "pig mountain", descending to the shores of Lough Shannagh, where there's a beach at either end – useful for a dip, though the water's freezing. In the panorama beyond the Hare's Gap, the places not to miss are the eastern slopes of the **Cove Mountain** and **Slieve Lamagan**. If you're sticking to the roads, all you can really do is circle the outside of the range, though there is one road through the middle, from Hilltown to Kilkeel.

grandiloquent backdrop. In the harbour, pleasure craft are tied up alongside the fishing boats and small trawlers; the whiff of their herring catches sometimes permeates the whole town. Just off the main road in Marine Park stands an early nineteenth-century **cornmill**, still in working order and open for visits (call Ⓣ028/4175 2256 for opening times; £1.90).

B&Bs here include a former farmhouse, *The Sycamores*, 52 Majors Hill (March–Nov; Ⓣ028/4376 8279, Ⓔbbsycamores@yahoo.co.uk; ❷), and luxurious country-house accommodation at *Glassdrumman Lodge*, 85 Mill Rd (Ⓣ028/4376 8451, Ⓦwww.glassdrummanlodge.com; ❻), which has its own stylish restaurant. There's little in the way of other **places to eat**, but right on the harbour, the refurbished *Harbour Inn* serves hearty lunches and evening meals except on Mondays and Friday and Saturday evenings. Otherwise, the *Halfway House*, north of town on the A2, offers bar meals and Sunday lunches.

Inland a mile or so from Annalong, signposts point to the aptly named **Silent Valley** (daily: April–Sept 10am–6.30pm; Oct–March 10am–4pm; pedestrians £1.50, car £4.50), where you'll find Belfast and County Down's **reservoir**, a huge thirty-year engineering project that was completed in 1933. There's a car park by the lower reservoir, bounded by the Mourne Wall, a sturdy 22-mile-long granite boundary to the catchment area that links the summits of fifteen mountains along its route. The views out to Slieve Binnian and Ben Crom, behind it to the west, are worth the effort of the three-mile circular **Viewpoint Walk** (starts at the car park). Less energetic, but still superb, is the half-mile Sally Lough stroll (or you can take the shuttle bus; May, June & Sept Sat & Sun, July & Aug daily; £1.50 return) up to the dam at Ben Crom; again the views are spectacular.

Kilkeel

Continuing south, **KILKEEL** is a much grander version of Annalong, remarkable mainly for the even heftier stench of fish from the canneries on the harbour; the town is home to nearly a hundred trawlers. The biggest excitements here are the fish auctions that take place on the quayside when the fishing boats come home, and the annual summer **harbour festival**.

The ruined **Old Church**, built in the fourteenth century, stands in the centre of Kilkeel in a ring fort. Kilkeel is a prosperous, predominantly Protestant place, but behind the village on the banks of its river memories of less happy days remain – small grave markers identify where the inmates of Kilkeel workhouse are buried. One of those buried here is the infamous **William Hare**, who murdered sixteen people in the space of a year in Edinburgh. Hare owned a lodging house, and when an old lodger died owing rent, he and his accomplice William Burke decided to sell the body to a medical school. The £7.10 they were paid spurred them on to greater efforts; however, their enthusiasm eventually raised the neighbours' suspicions and their profitable venture came to an end. Hare turned king's evidence and got his freedom, while Burke was hanged. Deciding to lie low, Hare came to Kilkeel and soon landed in the workhouse; his identity was only revealed to the locals when a Dr Reid, a former medical student from Edinburgh, recognized him. A local man with a somewhat loftier reputation was Giant Murphy, reputedly 8ft 10in tall, and who toured the world with a travelling circus.

Practicalities

There's a small **tourist office** in Kilkeel at 28 Newcastle St (Mon–Fri 9am–1pm & 2–5.30pm; also March–Oct Sat same hours; ⓣ028/4176 2525), which can find **places to stay** in town. The most comfortable option is the recently refurbished *Kilmorey Arms Hotel*, 41 Greencastle St (ⓣ028/4176 2220, ⓦwww.kilmoreyarmshotel.co.uk; ❸), whose **restaurant** is also the town's most attractive eating option. The best sites for **camping** are along Cranfield Point, a flat piece of grassy land jutting out at the entrance to Carlingford Lough with a superb and long Blue Flag beach: try *Sandilands Caravan Park* on Cranfield Road (mid-March to Oct; ⓣ028/4176 3634) or *Chestnutt Caravan Park*, next to the beach on Grange Road (mid-March to Oct; ⓣ028/4176 2653). Five miles north of Kilkee, up the B27 Hilltown road, Gamekeeper's Lodge Equestrian Centre (ⓣ028/4176 4771) offers **horse riding** and beach and Mourne treks.

Rostrevor

Four or five miles west of Kilkeel along the A2 a signpost points to the **Kilfeaghan dolmen**, a mile inland then a short walk through a couple of fields and kissing gates. Its capstone is enormous and could only have arrived here during the retreat of the glacial drift.

Further up the lough, the village of **ROSTREVOR** lies at the point where the bay waters dramatically begin to narrow towards Newry – and where the population and political climate turn more in favour of the Nationalist communities of County Armagh and those across the ever-nearing border. Rostrevor is a charming and sleepy village of Victorian terraces and friendly pubs, meandering up the lower slopes of **Slieve Martin**. There are a few small **B&Bs**, including *An Tobar*, 2 Cherry Hill (Ⓣ28/4173 8712, Ⓦwww.kilbroney.net; ❷), and *Glenbeigh*, 18 Victoria Square (Ⓣ028/4173 8025, Ⓔglenbeigh@hotmail.com; ❷). **Camping** is available at *Kilbroney Caravan Park*, Shore Road (Easter–Oct; Ⓣ028/4173 8134), where you can hike up the hill to the thirty-ton **Cloughmore** ("big stone") for views across the lough to the Cooley Mountains over the border; geologists reckon the stone is a remnant of the Ice Age, but locals prefer a more spectacular story involving Fionn Mac Cumhaill. Opposite the church, *The Kilbroney Inn* is deservedly acclaimed for its wonderful **food**, including specialities such as roast monkfish. Alternatively, *Celtic Fjord*, 8 Main St (Ⓣ028/4173 8005; closed Mon & Tues), serves an imaginative blend of modern and classic Irish cuisine. The **Fiddler's Green Festival** (Ⓦwww.fiddlersgreenfestival.co.uk) in the last week of July is a big, enjoyable event, attracting folk and traditional musicians from across Europe.

Warrenpoint

WARRENPOINT is as picturesque as Rostrevor, with a colourful esplanade of seafront housing and a spacious central square. It's a much more traditional seaside resort than its neighbour and has been attracting visitors since the early nineteenth century, when an enterprising local man advertised warm baths for the "gentry, nobility and public".

Less than a mile northwest of Warrenpoint along the Newry Road is the **Narrow Water Castle** (guided tours: July & Aug Tues, Fri & Sat 10am–1pm, Wed & Thurs 2–6pm; free). The original was built in 1212 by Hugh de Lacy to guard against access to Newry via the river, but this was burnt down during the 1641 Rebellion and the ruins here are of a building erected some twenty years later; there are very slight remains of the earlier castle nearby.

Warrenpoint's **tourist office** (Mon–Fri 9am–1pm & 2–5pm; Ⓣ028/4175 2256) is in the town hall on Church Street. You shouldn't have any trouble finding **accommodation** here, except perhaps during the four-day **Blues on the Bay** music **festival** in late May (Ⓦwww.bluesonthebay.com) or when the **Maiden of the Mournes festival** (Ⓦwww.maidenofthemournes.com) takes place over the second week of August, a local version of the Rose of Tralee (see p.365). Lough-shore **B&Bs** include the tiny *Lough View*, 10 Osborne Promenade (Ⓣ028/4177 3067; ❷), and the more lavish *Whistledown & Finns*, 6 Seaview (Ⓣ028/4175 4174, Ⓦwww.whistledown.co.uk; ❸).

While wholesome **food** is available at several **pubs**, including *Bennett's* on Church Street and *The Duke* on Duke Street, for something a little special head to *Copper Restaurant* (Ⓣ028/4175 3047; closed Mon all day and Sat lunchtime) which serves a very broad range of modern Irish cuisine – its set menu is reasonably priced at £23.50, though there's a special "tasting menu" on Saturdays (booking essential) whose seven courses will satisfy many an epicure for the sum of £50.

Newry

Although **NEWRY**, astride the border of Down and Armagh, is this region's most important commercial centre, bustling with urban vibrancy and its city status acquired in 2002, it's worth little more than a short visit. Traditionally, it was the place for people from the Republic to come and shop, and the town still thrives economically, its already traffic-clogged streets suffering gridlock on **market days** (Thurs & Sat). Given its key position, you're highly likely to pass through here, and, while it does make a possible base for exploring Slieve Gullion and the south Armagh district, you're unlikely to be tempted to stay.

Newry was founded by Cistercian monks in 1144, but for most of its history has been a **garrison**, guarding the borders of Ulster at the narrow point between hills on either side known as the Gap of the North. There's no trace at all of the bitterly contested early fortresses; what you see dates mostly from the eighteenth and nineteenth centuries, when a canal to Lough Neagh (cut in 1742, the first in the British Isles) brought the produce of the inland towns to the markets here.

One of the most interesting buildings in town is the **Catholic Cathedral** (daily 8.30am–5pm) on Hill Street. Constructed in 1829, it was the first such building to be opened following Catholic Emancipation. Despite an unpromising granite exterior, the rich mosaic pattern along its interior walls gives a Byzantine feel, and there's also a striking vaulted ceiling of decorative sweeping plaster arcs and vivid stained-glass windows. Nearby, there's a strange bronze totem-pole by sculptor Paddy McElroy, which depicts, in tortured relief, scenes from Newry's past. Not far away, the **Town Hall** is remarkable mainly because it's built on a bridge over the River Clanrye – it's half in Down, half in Armagh and was deliberately positioned here to avoid inter-county rivalry. Just opposite, the **Séan Hollywood Arts Centre** (Mon–Fri 9am–5pm & 6.30–9.30pm, Sat 9am–1pm; ⓣ028/3031 3180), on Bank Parade, hosts exhibitions of local artists' work, plays and all types of music in the auditorium, as well as housing the **Newry and Mourne Museum** (Mon–Fri 10.30am–1pm & 2–4.30pm; free; ⓦwww.bagenalscastle.com). The museum contains Nelson's table from HMS *Victory*, as well as plenty of information on local history and a re-created eighteenth-century panelled room, featuring period furniture and locally carved panelling salvaged from a house on North Street.

Another recent archeological find is **Bagenal's Castle**, the remains of which were discovered within the former McCann's Bakery on Abbey Way. This one-time Cistercian abbey was confiscated during the Reformation of 1548, and the premises were leased to a certain Nicholas Bagenal, who had apparently earlier fled his native Staffordshire to escape indictment for murder. After acting as a secret agent infiltrating the O'Neill clan, he was granted a pardon and subsequently became marshal of the English army in Ireland and established a garrison in Newry. While Bagenal was largely successful in defending the area against the O'Neills, his daughter Mary eloped and married Hugh O'Neill, a story that became the subject of Brian Friel's play **Making History**. At the time of writing, plans were afoot to move both the museum and tourist office to the restored building.

Practicalities

Newry's **bus station** (ⓣ028/3026 3531) is on The Mall alongside the canal, while the **train station** (ⓣ028/3026 9271) is a mile west of town on Millvale Road and connected to the centre by local bus #341.

The **tourist office** is in the city hall (all year Mon–Fri 9am–1pm & 2–5pm; also April–Sept Sat 10am–1pm & 2–4pm and July–Sept Tues–Fri open until 7pm; ⓣ028/3026 8877, ⓦwww.seenewryandmourne.com). The most luxurious **accommodation** is provided by the canalside *Canal Court Hotel*, Merchants Quay (ⓣ028/3025 1234, ⓦwww.canalcourthotel.com; ④), which is equipped with a gym and sauna. There are also a fair number of **B&Bs** scattered around town. Newry isn't exactly the North's gourmet capital, but you can certainly find appetizing menus at *Soho Place* (☎028/3083 3333; closed Mon eve), by the canal at 15 The Mall, or in the *Old Mill Restaurant* in the *Canal Court Hotel*. Alternatively, *The Bank Bar* opposite city hall on Trevor Hill serves reasonably priced meals in its bistro.

The Cove on Hilltown Road has a renowned Tuesday-night **traditional-music** session and there's another at the *Railway Bar*, Monaghan Steet (Thurs). **Internet** access is provided by *Coffee-Net* in the bus station on The Mall.

County Armagh

Below **Lough Neagh**, the north of County Armagh is dominated by the developed industrial strip running under the name of **Craigavon** and containing the towns of **Lurgan** and **Portadown,** and there is little in this urban hinterland to attract you. Away from the towns, however, there are a number of points of interest, and two stately homes, **Ardress** and the **Argory**, are features of some excellent cycling country north of **Loughgall**. The villages of **South Armagh** – a predominantly Catholic area – were the heartland of violent Republicanism, so much so, in fact, that it was often referred to as "Bandit Country" or "The Killing Fields", even by locals. Yet the county does warrant exploration, for it has some luscious landscapes and a history as rich as any county in Ireland: **Armagh city** has strong associations

▲ Armagh city

with St Patrick and early Christianity, while the sedately rural areas harbour some sites redolent of the island's legendary past, notably **Navan Fort** and **Slieve Gullion**.

Armagh city and around

ARMAGH is one of the most attractive places in the North, and the rich history of the city and its surroundings has plenty to keep you occupied for a day or two. The city offers **cathedrals** and **museums** set in handsome Georgian streets, and two miles west is the ancient site of once-grand **Navan Fort**. Armagh has been the site of the **Catholic** primacy of All Ireland since St Patrick established his church here, and has rather ambitiously adopted the title of the "Irish Rome" for itself – like Rome, it's positioned among seven small hills. Paradoxically, the city is also the seat of the **Protestant** Church of Ireland's archbishop of Armagh.

Armagh has a number of events during the year, and, as you'd expect, the local **St Patrick's Day Parade** (March 17) is one of the largest in the country. The County **fleadh** (traditional music and dancing festival, usually with plenty of sessions around town) takes place in June. November sees one of Ireland's major **uilleann** piping events (see p.712), the five-day **William Kennedy Piping**

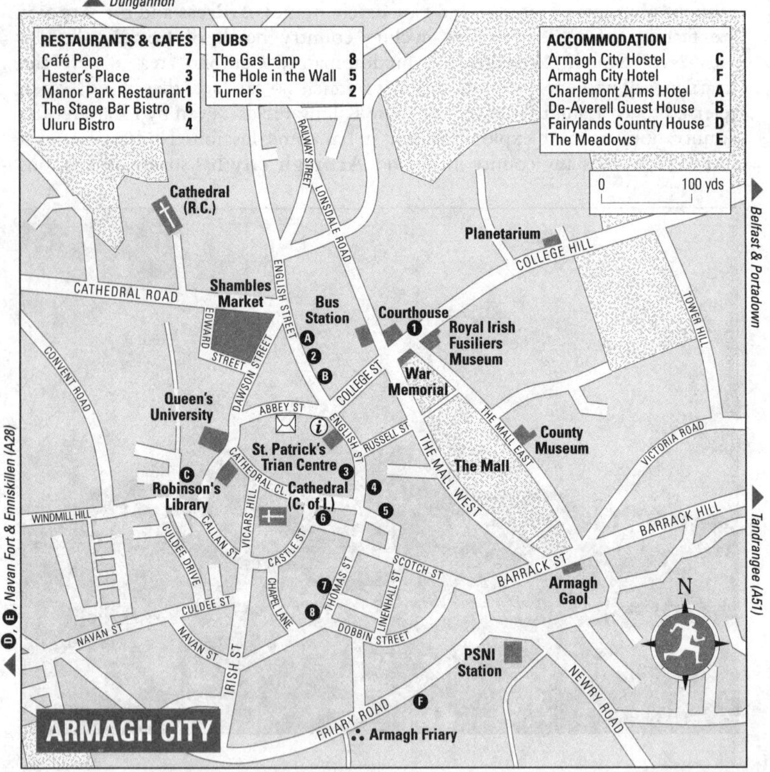

Festival (Ⓦwww.armaghpipers.com), and, at the end of the month, the **Bard of Armagh** humorous-poetry competition (Ⓦwww.bardofarmagh.com).

Arrival and information

The **Ulsterbus** station (Ⓣ028/3752 2266) is on Lonsdale Road, just north of the centre, and the **tourist office** is in the Old Bank Building, in front of the St Patrick's Trian Centre at 40 English St (all year Mon–Sat 9am–5pm, Sun noon–5pm; Sept–May Sun 2–5pm; Ⓣ028/3752 1800, Ⓦwww.visitarmagh.com); **walking tours** of the city operate from here during the summer (June–Sept Sat 11am & Sun 2pm; 90min; £5; Ⓦwww.armaghguidedtours.com).

Accommodation

For a city with so many attractions Armagh is certainly deficient in terms of **accommodation** within easy reach of the centre, and prices tend to be above average for Northern Ireland, though there is one budget option. The nearest **camping** is at *Gosford Forest Park*, seven miles southwest along the A28 near Markethill (Ⓣ028/3755 1277), with fine facilities set in wooded grounds around a castle.

Armagh City Hostel 39 Abbey St Ⓣ028/3751 1800. Modern, excellently equipped HINI hostel superbly situated near the Church of Ireland Cathedral. Dorms £15, twins ❶.

Armagh City Hotel Friary Road Ⓣ028/3751 8888, Ⓦwww.armaghcityhotel.com. Behind the facade of its soulless exterior this modern hotel does offer very plush accommodation indeed, but, as its main business is conferences and weddings, you'll need to book well in advance. ❺

Charlemont Arms Hotel 57–65 English St Ⓣ028/3752 2028, Ⓦwww.charlemontarms.hotel. Long-established, family-run establishment offering a congenial welcome and very comfortable en-suite rooms. ❸

De-Averell Guest House 47 English St Ⓣ028/3751 1213, Ⓦwww.deaverellhouse.com. Finely converted townhouse, providing restful en-suite rooms, whose owner is a mine of information on the area and a top-class chef; plus there's a cosy bar for residents and free Internet access. ❸

Fairylands Country House 25 Navan Fort Rd Ⓣ028/3751 0315, Ⓦwww.fairylands.net. Congenial place offering en-suite rooms in a quiet rural setting a mile from the centre. ❷

The Meadows 18 Monaghan Rd Ⓣ028/3752 5257. Excellent family-run B&B, a mile from the centre, providing en-suite accommodation and very tasty breakfasts. ❷

The City

The best way to get your bearings is to walk up the steps of **St Patrick's Roman Catholic Cathedral** (daily: April–Oct 10am–5pm; Nov–March 10am–4pm; free; Ⓦwww.armagharchdiocese.org), built on a hillside just northwest of the Shambles Market. The view of the town from here is impressive, and you should be able to identify most of the key sites spread out below. The cathedral's foundation stone was laid in 1840, but completion was delayed by the Famine and a subsequent lack of funding. Whilst the pope and local nobility chipped in, money was also raised by public collections and raffles – one prize of a grandfather clock has still not been claimed. On the outside, the cathedral first appears little different from many of its nineteenth-century Gothic-Revival contemporaries, but it is impressively large and airy. Inside, as befits the seat of the cardinal archbishop, every inch of wall glistens with **mosaics**, in colours ranging from marine- and sky-blue to terracotta pinks and oranges. Other striking pieces include the white-granite "pincer-claw" **tabernacle holder**, reflected in a highly polished marble floor, and a **statue** of the Crucifixion, which suggests (deliberately or otherwise) the old city's division into **Trians**.

St Patrick's Church of Ireland Cathedral

Heading south along Dawson Street, you'll soon reach Cathedral Close and **St Patrick's Church of Ireland Cathedral** (daily: April–Oct 10am–5pm; Nov–March 10am–4pm; free tours June–Aug Mon–Sat 11.30am & 2.30pm; free; Ⓦwww.stpatricks-cathedral.org). This lays claim to the summit of the principal hillock, Drum Saileach, where St Patrick founded his first church in 445 AD. It commands a distinctive Armagh view across to the other hills and down over the clutter of gable walls and pitched roofing on its own slopes. A series of churches occupied the site after 445 and, although the core of the present one is medieval, a nineteenth-century restoration has coated the thirteenth-century outer walls in a sandstone plaster of which Thackeray remarked, "It is as neat and trim as a lady's dressing room." Many of the ancient decorations were removed, leaving the spartan interior you see today. Just as you enter from the highly distinctive timber porch, you'll see a few remnants of an eleventh-century **Celtic cross** and a startling **statue** of Thomas Molyneux. Inside, high up, you should be able to sight the medieval carved heads of men, women and monsters. One other unusual feature is the tilt of the chancel, a medieval building-practice meant to represent the slumping head of the dying Christ. The **chapterhouse** has a small collection of stone statues (mostly gathered from elsewhere), the most noticeable of which are the Stone Age **Tandragee Idol** and a Sheila-na-Gig (see p.748) with an ass's ears. Outside the north transept a plaque on the west wall commemorates the burial of **Brian Ború**.

Armagh is known for its **choral music**, and the cathedral hosts the annual week-long Charles Wood Summer School in mid-August (Ⓦwww.charleswoodss.org), featuring a daily series of recitals.

The public library

Just down the hill from the cathedral, the **public library** (known locally as Robinson's (Mon–Fri 10am–1pm & 2–4pm; free, donations welcomed; Ⓦwww.armaghrobinsonlibrary.org) has, among many rare tomes, a first edition of **Gulliver's Travels** annotated by Swift himself, and an early edition of Raleigh's **History of the World** (1614), as well as a collection of engravings, including some by Hogarth. The library was founded in 1771 by Archbishop Richard Robinson, who was described as converting Armagh "from mud to stone" and who is responsible for almost all the older buildings in the city – the nearby infirmary was one of his, too, though it's now occupied by the university.

St Patrick's Trian Centre

Cathedral Close leads downhill to the main shopping area and walking a little way north up English Street, you'll come to **St Patrick's Trian Centre**, an ambitious complex containing the tourist office and three separate **exhibitions** (Mon–Sat 10am–5pm, Sun 2–5pm; joint ticket £4.75; Ⓦwww.visitarmagh.com; Heritage Island). The first of these, peopled with figures representing the land of Lilliput and Jonathan Swift's connection with Armagh, occupies the former Presbyterian Meeting House, which was partly constructed from the ruined abbey of St Peter and St Paul – Swift is reputed to have commented that the masons were "chipping the popery out of the stones". The second installation, "The Armagh Story", is a multimedia account of the town's growth and the nature of belief; while the third, "Patrick's Testament", is an interactive account of the saint's association with Armagh.

The Mall

Russell Street leads down to **The Mall**, an elegant tree-lined promenade fringed to the east by two terraces of handsome Georgian houses designed by the Armagh-born architect Francis Johnston, who worked primarily for Archbishop Robinson. Johnston was responsible for many of Dublin's best Georgian buildings, and you'll encounter more examples of his work around town, including the classical **courthouse** at The Mall's northern end; the former **gaol** occupies the southern end. In its late eighteenth-century heyday The Mall was a racecourse; nowadays there's nothing more athletic than the occasional jogger and Saturday cricket matches.

The County Museum

A former schoolhouse on the east side of The Mall houses the **County Museum** (Mon–Fri 10am–5pm, Sat 10am–1pm & 2–5pm; free; Ⓦwww.armaghcountymuseum.org.uk), an old-fashioned museum with all the usual local miscellany on display, including an alarmingly vivid collection of stuffed wildlife, plus a little **art gallery** tucked away on the upper floor. Here there are twenty or so mystical pastels, oils and cartoon sketches by the Irish turn-of-the-century poet **George Russell**, a much-neglected companion to Yeats, who acquired the alias Æ as a result of a Dublin newspaper misprinting a letter that he had signed "Aeons". The prolific local artist J.B. Vallely is also represented with a superb oil showing five musicians enjoying a session; the theme of traditional music figures in more than three thousand of Vallely's canvases and, with his wife Eithne, he currently runs the town's Armagh Pipers' Club (their children are all well-known traditional musicians). Elsewhere, a display devoted to railway history recounts the story of Ireland's worst railway disaster, when two passenger trains collided outside Armagh in 1889, killing 89 people, many of whom are buried in nearby St Mark's churchyard.

The Royal Irish Fusiliers Museum

Further north along The Mall is the **Royal Irish Fusiliers Museum** (Mon–Fri 10am–12.30pm & 1.30–4pm; free), built from the leftovers of the court-house. It's pretty much as you'd expect: tons of weaponry, uniforms, medallions and silverware from the regiment formed in 1793 in response to the Napoleonic crisis and subsequently known as the Faughs from their battle-cry **Faugh a Ballagh!** ("Clear the way!"). The Fusiliers subsequently fought in the Crimean and Boer wars (where they relieved the Siege of Ladysmith) and in both world wars before amalgamating with the Inniskilling Fusiliers (see p.678) and Ulster Rifles in 1968.

Armagh Planetarium

A couple of hundred metres up College Hill from the northern end of The Mall is the recently and completely refurbished **Armagh Planetarium** (call Ⓣ028/3752 3689 for show and opening times; adults £6 per show, children 6–15 £5; Ⓦwww.armaghplanet.com; Heritage Island). It lays claim to "the world's most advanced digital production projection system, Digistar 3" with full animation of the planetarium's dome (and reclining seats to enjoy the full effects), as well as an extraordinarily good sound setup. Various shows (30–40min each) are on offer including the child-oriented "Secret of the Cardboard Rocket" which explores the solar system; "Pole Position", touring the constellations; and the historically focused "Dawn of the Space Age". Inside there's also an exhibition hall (£2) featuring a range of high-tech interactive displays of the

Road bowls

The sport of **road bowls** is popular in Holland and Germany and was once played throughout Ireland, but is now limited mainly to Cork and Armagh, where it's also known as "road bullets".

The principle of the game is simple: a pair of rival contestants each propels a 28oz (800g) solid-iron ball along a course of country roads (usually about two-and-a-half miles long), the winner being the player who reaches the finishing line with the **fewest number of throws**. In practice, it's a complicated business. The Armagh roads twist and turn, up and down, and bowlers are assisted by a team of camp followers, including managers and road guides who advise on the most advantageous spots to aim for and the force of the throw. Traditionally a male sport, it's become increasingly popular with women, who've held their own championship since 1981.

Roads around Armagh where you're likely to catch sight of the game – usually on Sunday afternoons – include Cathedral Road, Napper Road, Blackwater Town, Rock, Tassa, Keady, Newtownhamilton and Madden roads. The most reliable information on forthcoming games is probably to be had in local pubs. The **Ulster Finals** are held in the city over two weekends in late June, with the **All-Ireland Road Bowls Final** in early August.

cosmos, as well as images of deep space and an assortment of meteorite chunks from the Moon and Mars. Outside there's the landscaped Astropark (free), a series of trails depicting the extent of the solar system in comparison to the known universe – a stroll up the Hill of Infinity leads to its very edge and also offers a glorious view of the city.

Armagh Friary

The ruins of **Armagh Friary**, founded by the Franciscans in 1263, lie within easy walking distance south of the city centre, just off Friary Road by the entrance to the grounds of the Archbishop's Palace (now the District Council offices). The ruins are those of the church alone, and the site is an unfortunate example of how atmosphere can be destroyed when a major road runs alongside. The focus now is the **Palace Stables Heritage Centre** (April, May & Sept Sat & Sun noon–5pm; June–Aug Mon–Sat 10am–5pm, Sun noon–4pm; £4.75; Ⓦwww.visitarmagh.com; Heritage Island) where tableaux of life-sized figures depict July 23, 1776, the day on which Archbishop Robinson entertained the notable English agriculturalist and writer Arthur Young – his **Tour of Ireland** was published in 1780 – and you're guided around the exhibits by living history interpreters garbed in contemporary costumes. From here you move into the main part of the palace, which dates from around 1770, though the final storey was added in 1825, and was inhabited by subsequent archbishops until 1975, when the private Primate's Chapel next door was deconsecrated. In the grounds there's a well-preserved **ice house**, a curious **tunnel** by which servants accessed the basement kitchens, a stimulating **sensory garden** and, somewhat incongruously, the municipal dog-pound.

Eating

Several of Armagh's pubs serve **bar food** at lunchtime, but eating in the evening can be more problematic, especially on Monday evenings.

Café Papa 15 Thomas St. Excellent little establishment dishing up the city's best coffee and sandwiches; closed Sun.

De-Averell Guest House 47 English St ⓣ028/3751 1213. Innovative basement restaurant whose owner-chef regularly produces imaginative and often zesty dishes; closed Mon.

Hester's Place 12 Upper English St. Very reasonably priced daytime café serving soups, sandwiches and filling lunches.

Manor Park Restaurant 2 College Hill ⓣ028/3751 5353. Upmarket and very tasty Irish cuisine with high prices to match, unless you head here for lunch or opt for the early-bird special (£16); closed Mon.

The Stage Bar Bistro The Market Place Theatre and Arts Centre, Market Square ⓣ028/3752 1828. A café during the day and a bistro at night, the latter with a predilection for big meat dishes, though the "catch of the day" is often very tempting; closed Mon eve.

Turner's 57 English St. Good-value lunches and somewhat pricier evening meals served downstairs in this popular bar specializing in traditional Irish cooking; closed Mon.

Uluru Bistro 16–18 Market St ⓣ028/3751 8051. The North's only Australian restaurant and a must for anyone keen to explore the delights of marinated kangaroo medallions or various cuts of crocodile and ostrich – the less adventurous will stick with the steaks and seafood; closed Mon all day and Sun lunch.

Drinking and entertainment

The most atmospheric **pub** for a pint is the *Hole in the Wall Bar* in McCrum's Court. English Street is a good area to pub-crawl in search of **music**; weekends are best but many places have sing-songs on Tuesdays and Thursdays, though **Turner's** has a Saturday-night traditional session. *The Gas Lamp* is a popular retro-style pub on Thomas Street and the bar at the **Market Place Theatre** has live music on Saturday nights. The *Armagh City Hotel* has both live music and DJs at weekends.

The **Market Place Theatre and Arts Centre** (ⓣ028/3752 1820, ⓦwww.marketplacearmagh.com) features a four-hundred-seat auditorium, a smaller studio theatre, gallery, a bar, coffee house and bistro, and has an imaginative programme of theatrical and musical events. Also on the Market Place is the **Armagh City Film House** (ⓣ028/3751 1033, ⓦwww.armaghfilmhouse.com), a four-screen cinema with a regular late show on Friday and Saturday nights. There's a small Saturday **market** in Market Place Square, and the bigger **Shambles Market**, just off Cathedral Road, is open Tuesdays and Fridays from 9am to 5pm.

Navan Fort

For nearly seven hundred years **Navan Fort** (open access; free) was the great seat of northern power, rivalling Tara in the south. It was here that the kings of Ulster ruled and Queen Macha built her palace on the earthwork's summit. It's a site of deeply mystical significance, but one also of enormous archeological interest. The court of the **Knights of the Red Branch**, Ireland's most prestigious order of chivalry, was based here too. The knights, like those of the Round Table, are historical figures entirely subsumed into legend, their greatest champion being the legendary defender of Ulster, **Cúchulainn**. The stories of these warriors' deeds are recited and sung in what's now known as the **Ulster Cycle**. Their dynasty was finally vanquished in 332 AD, when three brothers (the Collas), in a conquest known as the Black Pig's Dyke, destroyed Navan Fort, razing it to the ground and leaving only the earthen mounds visible today. The defeated Red Branch Knights were driven eastwards into Down and Antrim, and were little heard of again.

The fort lies two miles west of Armagh on the A28 (bus #73) and stands adjacent to the multimillion-pound **Navan Centre** (April, May & Sept Sat & Sun noon–5pm; June–Aug Mon–Sat 10am–5pm, Sun noon–5pm; £4.75; ⓦwww.visitarmagh.com; Heritage Island), which reopened a couple of years back after several years of inactivity and features multimedia displays on archeology and the legends of the Ulster cycle – frankly, unless you're keen on Celtic legends or fond of "ethereal" music in the style of Clannad, you'd be well advised to give it a miss.

Skirting this building, you'll discover that the site area is defined by a massive bank with a defensive **ditch**. When you reach the fort, you'll find an **earthen mound**, which gives a commanding view but no hint of its past. Excavation of the mound took place over a ten-year period (1961–71) and revealed a peculiar structure, apparently unique in the Celtic world. Archeologists reckon that around 100 BC the buildings that had existed since the Neolithic period were cleared, and a huge structure 108ft in diameter was constructed. An outer wall of timber surrounded five concentric rings of large posts, 275 in all, with a massive post at the very centre. This was then filled with limestone boulders and **set on fire**, creating a mountain of ash that was then covered with sods of clay to make a high mound. It is anybody's guess what the purpose of the structure was – possibly a temple, or maybe a monumental funeral pyre.

Nearby you can visit for free other ancient archeological structures: a second fort, the earliest known artificial lake in Ireland and a large natural lake that has yielded various archeological finds.

Loughgall and around

LOUGHGALL, a tranquil and pretty estate village about five miles west of Portadown (and the same distance north of Armagh along the B27), lies in the middle of apple-orchard country, beautiful in the spring, and is worth visiting mainly for its historical connections. Like many of its neighbours in Armagh's rural north, Loughgall is strongly **Protestant**. It was three miles northeast of the village at Diamond Hill that the Battle of the Diamond took place in 1795, which led to the foundation of the first Protestant **Orange Order** (see box opposite) in **Dan Winter's** (Mon–Sat 10.30am–5.30pm, Sun 2–5.30pm; voluntary donation; Ⓦwww.orangenet.org/winter), in a nearby farmyard just down Derryloughan Road, which displays maps and relics from the battle alongside seventeenth-century furniture; the cottage roof still contains original lead-shot.

Back in Loughgall, off Main Street, you'll find the **Loughgall Country Park** (daily 9am–dusk; car £2; Ⓦwww.loughgallcountrypark.com), which offers waymarked trails, an 18-hole golf course and children's play areas. Main Street also features a couple of fine antique shops, while, two miles east on Ballyhagan Road (off the B77 to Portadown), is *The Famous Grouse*, a lively **bar** with the best **restaurant** for miles around plus regular live music.

Five miles or so north of Loughgall are two National Trust stately homes a few miles apart that are worth visiting if you're spending more than a day in the area. **Ardress House** (mid-March to late Sept Sat, Sun & public hols 2–6pm; £4; Ⓦwww.ntni.org.uk) is a seventeenth-century manor house with ornate plasterwork by Michael Stapleton, a good collection of paintings, a sizeable working farmyard and wooded grounds. More enticing, however, is **The Argory** (1–6pm: mid-March to May & Sept Sat, Sun, Easter week & public hols; June–Aug daily; £4.50; Ⓦwww.ntni.org.uk), a fine Neoclassical building dating back to 1824 and set in 350 acres by the River Blackwater. The splendid **grounds** (daily: May–Sept 10am–7pm; Oct–April 10am–4pm; car £3) include very pleasant gardens, but it's the house that's the real attraction. Built of Caledon stone, its entrance hall features a fine, cantilevered staircase, and the rooms contain Victorian and Edwardian furniture among many other period items, including a fabulous cabinet barrel organ. The house is still lit by an original 1906 acetylene gas plant in the stable yard, and

The Orange Order and the marching tradition

Ireland's oldest political grouping, **The Grand Orange Lodge of Ireland**, was founded in September 1795 following the so-called **Battle of the Diamond**, which took place in or near Dan Winter's farm near **Loughgall**. The skirmish involved the Peep O'Day boys (Protestants) and the Defenders (Catholics) and was the culmination of a long-running dispute about control of the local linen trade. The Defenders attacked an inn, unaware that inside the Peep O'Day boys were armed and waiting. A dozen Defenders were killed, and in the glow of victory their opponents formed the Orange Order.

The first Orange Lodge march in celebration of the 1690 **Battle of the Boyne** (see p.179) took place in 1796, and they've been happening ever since. The Boyne is the Loyalist totem, even though the actual battle at Aughter that ended Jacobite rule did not take place until the following year. **William of Orange** is their icon, despite the fact that his campaign was supported by the pope and most of the Catholic rulers of Europe, and that William himself had a noted reputation for religious tolerance. For Protestant Ulster, the Boyne came to represent a victory that enshrined Protestant supremacy and liberties, and the Orange Order became the bedrock of Protestant hegemony. Between 1921 and 1969, for example, 51 of the 54 ministers appointed to the Stormont government were members of the Orange Order; at its peak, so were two-thirds of the Protestant male population of the North.

The **Loyalist** "marching season" begins in March and culminates in celebration of the **Battle of the Boyne** on July 12, followed by the **Apprentice Boys'** traditional march around the walls of Derry on August 12. Most Loyalist marches are uncontentious – small church parades, or commemorations of the Somme – but it can't be denied that some of them are something other than a vibrant expression of cultural identity. Marching can be a means by which one community asserts its dominance over the other – Loyalists selecting routes that deliberately pass through Nationalist areas, for instance, or their "Kick the Pope" fife-and-drum bands deliberately playing sectarian tunes and making provocative gestures such as the raising of five fingers on Belfast's **Lower Ormeau Road** (where five Catholics were shot dead in 1992). Though Loyalist marches have tended to be the flashpoints for major disturbances in recent years, not least in the late 1990s at **Drumcree** near Portadown, it shouldn't be forgotten that the marching tradition is common to both communities. Around three thousand marches take place throughout Northern Ireland each year and, although the vast majority are Loyalist parades, a significant number are **Nationalist**. The latter include the St Patrick's Day (March 17) marches of the Ancient Order of Hibernians and the Irish National Foresters, and commemorative parades and wreath-laying ceremonies by Sinn Féin and other Republican bodies on Easter Monday and various anniversaries.

during the summer it stages musical events and organized garden walks. Tours provide entertaining anecdotes about the house's erstwhile owners, the McGeough-Bonds.

South Armagh

Overshadowed by Slieve Gullion, the **South Armagh** (ⓦwww.south-armagh.com) countryside is among the most attractive in the North. Proximity to the border and a predominantly Catholic population resulted in this once being a nucleus of resistance to British rule, and some evidence of military occupation remains. There's much evidence of prehistoric settlement here, important ecclesiastical remains and plenty of traditional music.

The Ring of Gullion

Most of South Armagh's attractions are concentrated in and around the area known as the **Ring of Gullion**, a naturally formed ring-dyke of low-lying hills that encircles (and predates) the mountain at its core. People have lived here for more than six thousand years, and there's a rich heritage of remains and monuments. On the ring's western fringe is the **Dorsey Enclosure**, two huge earthen banks and ditch ramparts dating from the Iron Age, running for a mile either side of the old route to Navan Fort. Elsewhere are numerous dolmens and cairns, Christian relics and monuments from the Plantation era.

Slieve Gullion, which dominates the southeastern corner of County Armagh, is one of the most mysteriously beautiful mountains in the country. A store of romantic legends is attached to it, especially concerning **Cúchulainn**, who took his name here after slaying the hound (Cú) of the blacksmith Culainn. Due south at Glendhu is where Cúchulainn single-handedly halted the army of Queen Medb of Connaught, who was intent on capturing the great bull of Cooley. **Fionn Mac Cumhaill**, who founded the **Fianna**, a mythical national militia whose adventures are told in the *Fenian Cycle*, also appears in stories here.

A scenic way to approach the mountain is from the north, passing the turning to **BESSBROOK**, a nineteenth-century model village developed by a Quaker linen entrepreneur; the Cadbury family's Bourneville estate in Birmingham, England, followed a very similar layout. After **CAMLOUGH** turn off the main road to go down by the eastern slopes of Camlough Mountain and you'll see the beautiful **lake**, set like a jewel within its green banks. A little further on, between Camlough Mountain and Slieve Gullion, are the ruined **Killeavy churches**. Two churches of different periods share the same gable wall: the west church is pre-Romanesque and one of the most important survivors of its kind in the country; the other, larger church dates from the thirteenth century. A granite slab marks the **grave of St Monenna**, the founder of a fifth-century nunnery sited here – there's a holy well dedicated to her a little further up the slopes of Slieve Gullion, which pilgrims visit on her feast day (the Sunday nearest to July 6).

The official, tarmacked entrance up into Slieve Gullion is on the mountain's forested southern face, after you've passed through the village of **KILLEAVY**. You'll find a small **forest park** (10am–dusk daily; free), fronted by the **Courtyard Centre**, where there's a small exhibition on the area, craft workshops and a café. From the centre it's an eight-mile winding drive up to the summit (or you can follow a walking trail), where there's a couple of megalithic **cairns**. Fionn Mac Cumhaill was legendarily bewitched here by Miluchra, and local superstition holds that bathing in the small summit **lake** will turn your hair white; another tale states that under certain conditions a visitor to the site will be given the power to foresee everything that will happen that day. Various vertiginous viewpoints offer spectacular **views** over the Ring of Gullion and the surrounding countryside.

Forkhill and Mullaghbawn

You might expect **FORKHILL** to lie in an elevated position, but this tiny village set in the southwestern foothills of Slieve Gullion derives its name from the Irish **foirceal** ("trough"). It's a simple, quiet and remote-looking place, though dominated by the massive army encampment stacked on the crown of an overlooking hill. The village is strong on traditional culture: *O'Neill's Welcome Inn* has **sessions** most Tuesday nights (and other music at the weekends); there's weekend music, too, at *The Forge*.

Neighbouring **MULLAGHBAWN**, to the north, has *O'Hanlons' Bridge House*, which holds regular sessions (Fri–Sun) and there's trad too at *The Real McCoy* on Tuesdays, plus the innovative **Tí Chulainn centre** (Ⓦwww.tichulainn.ie), which runs a variety of courses and activities dedicated to the promotion of the area's culture and literary heritage.

There are a couple of **B&Bs** in Forkhill: *Lakeview Cottage*, 34 Church Rd (Ⓣ028/3088 8382, Ⓔlakeviewb.bforkhill@talk21.com; ❷), with fine views of the mountain, and *Greenvale*, 141 Longfield Rd (Ⓣ028/3088 8314, Ⓔgreenvaleequestriancentre@yahoo.com; ❷), which also offers **pony trekking**. In Mullaghbawn, there's *Adrigole House*, 4 Bun Sleibhe (Ⓣ028/3088 8689; ❷), very close to the Tí Chulainn centre.

Jonesborough

JONESBOROUGH, east of Slieve Gullion, is the venue each Sunday for a vast open-air **market** (11am–5pm), drawing traders and customers from both sides of the border. The range of goods on offer is equally enormous and it's well worth experiencing. The excellent *Flurrybridge Inn* serves lunches Thursday to Sunday and holds occasional sessions.

Two miles south of Jonesborough is the **Pillar Stone of Kilnasaggart**, a beautifully inscribed monument dating from 700 AD, which lies on the ancient road from Tara to Dunseverick. Some thirteen crosses marked within circles are engraved on its faces and the defaced markings on its edges are possibly **ogham** writing. It's surrounded by several other tiny stones with similar cross markings, all held within a pentagonal enclosure three fields away from the roadside, behind a farmhouse. Excavations here during the 1960s uncovered graves positioned radially around the pillar stone which itself is directed to face the rising sun.

Crossmaglen and around

In the far southwestern corner of Armagh just inside the border, **CROSSMAGLEN** has reputedly the largest market square in Ireland, the scene of a fortnightly Friday **market**. During the Troubles the town's reputation for armed struggle against the British was fearsome, and, in truth, it has been a cauldron of activity ever since Partition. Indeed, had the 1924 Boundary Commission's proposals been fully implemented, the town and surrounding countryside would have been transferred to Dublin rule rather than staying inside the North. All this said, on arrival you'll find the pubs much friendlier than you might have expected.

Practicalities

The extremely helpful **tourist office** (Mon–Fri 9am–5pm, extended to 6pm and weekends in summer; Ⓣ028/3086 8900, Ⓦwww.south-armagh.com) is in Ó Fiaich House on The Square. The recently opened *Cross Square Hotel* on The Square (Ⓣ028/3086 0505, Ⓦwww.crosssquarehotel.com; ❸) provides very amenable **accommodation** and there's also pleasant **B&B** at *Murtagh's Bar*, 13 North St (Ⓣ028/3086 1378, Ⓔaidanmurtagh@hotmail.com; ❷). **Eating** options are limited, but include the restaurant at the *Cross Square Hotel* or *Ma Kearney's* bar on Newry Street. *Keenan's* bar on The Square hosts a notable **traditional-music** session on Tuesdays. Crossmaglen is at the forefront of the local revival of interest in Gaelic games, and the town's **Gaelic football** team have been recent All-Ireland club champions as well as providing the backbone of the 2002 Senior Championship-winning county team.

A couple of miles east of Crossmaglen on the B30 Newry road, **CREGGAN** has a **Poets' Graveyard**, so named because three eighteenth-century Gaelic poets are buried there: Art Mac Cooey, Patrick Mac Aliondain and Séamus Mór Mac Murphy (who was also an outlaw of some notoriety). The inscription on Mac Cooey's stone is taken from his most famous poem, *Úr-Chill an Chreagáin* – "That with the fragrant Gaels of Creggan I will be put in clay under the sod". A small **visitors' centre** here (open by arrangement; free; call ⓣ00353/42 932 1402 unless within the Republic) features displays on Creggan and the poets.

East of Creggan, a turning off the main road leads to **GLASSDRUMMOND** and *Hearty's Folk Cottage* (aka *The Red Fella's Bar*), a cosy, old-fashioned place which has regular Sunday-evening traditional-music sessions.

Travel details

Trains

Bangor to: Belfast (Mon–Sat every 15–30min, Sun hourly; 30min).

Lisburn to: Belfast (Mon–Fri every 20–30min, Sat every 30min, Sun hourly; 10–20min).

Newry to: Belfast (Mon–Sat 8–9 daily, Sun 5; 50min–1hr); Drogheda (Mon–Sat 7, Sun 5; 40min); Dublin (Mon–Sat 7, Sun 5; 1hr 20min); Dundalk (Mon–Sat 7, Sun 5; 20min).

Buses

All services are operated by Translink unless stated otherwise.

The **Mourne Rambler** (ⓣ028/9066 6630) is a circular service running in July and August from Newcastle to the Silent Valley and back. Buses depart Newcastle six times daily between 9.30am and 4.30pm; an all-day ticket costs £4.50.

Annalong to: Kilkeel (Mon–Fri 15 daily, Sat 11, Sun 6; 15min); Newcastle Mon–Fri 15 daily, Sat 11, Sun 6; 20min).

Ardglass to: Ballyhornan (Mon–Sat 4–5 daily, Sun 2; 10min); Downpatrick (Mon–Fri 14 daily, Sat 7, Sun 2; 20–25min); Killough (Mon–Fri 12 daily, Sat 7, Sun 2; 5min).

Armagh to: Belfast (Mon–Fri 12 daily, Sat 7, Sun 8; 1hr–1hr 20min); Benburb (Mon–Fri 2 daily; 25min); Cavan (Mon–Fri 2 daily; 1hr 45min); Loughgall (Mon–Fri 8 daily; 15min); Markethill (Mon–Fri 17 daily, Sat 6, Sun 3; 20min); Monaghan (Mon–Fri 9 daily, Sat 5, Sun 3; 30–45min); Navan Fort (Mon–Fri 12 daily; 10min); Newry (Mon–Fri 12 daily, Sat 6, Sun 3; 35–45min).

Ballyhornan to: Ardglass (Mon–Sat 4–5 daily, Sun 2; 10min); Downpatrick (Mon–Sat 4–6 daily, Sun 2; 30min).

Bangor to: Belfast (Mon–Sat 25–29 daily, Sun 9; 45min); Donaghadee (Mon–Sat 15–18 daily, Sun 4; 25min); Newtownards (Mon–Sat 26–30 daily, Sun 7; 20min).

Castlewellan to: Downpatrick (Mon–Sat 6 daily, Sun 2; 30min); Newcastle (Mon–Sat 10–11 daily, Sun 8; 10min).

Comber to: Killyleagh (Mon–Fri 10 daily, Sat 5, Sun 2; 15min); Newtownards (Mon–Fri 21 daily, Sat 11, Sun 6; 20min).

Crossmaglen to: Mullaghbawn (Mon–Fri 7 daily, Sat 4; 25min); Newry (Mon–Fri 9 daily, Sun 4; 55min).

Donaghadee to: Bangor (Mon–Fri 22 daily, Sat 14, Sun 4; 25min).

Downpatrick to: Ardglass (Mon–Fri 15 daily, Sat 7, Sun 2; 15–25min); Ballyhornan (Mon–Fri 7 daily, Sat 4, Sun 2; 20–30min); Belfast (Mon–Sat 24–35 daily, Sun 7; 1hr); Castlewellan (Mon–Sat 6 daily, Sun 2; 30min); Killough (Mon–Fri 13 daily, Sat 7, Sun 2; 15min); Killyleagh (Mon–Fri 10 daily, Sat 6; 20min); Newcastle (Mon–Fri 21 daily, Sat 13, Sun 5; 25–35min); Newry (Mon–Sat 6 daily, Sun 2; 1hr 15min); Raholp (Mon–Sat 6–8 daily; 15min); Strangford (Mon–Fri 11 daily, Sat 6; 30min).

Forkhill to: Newry (Mon–Sat 4–5 daily; 35min).

Greyabbey to: Belfast (Mon–Sat 9 daily, Sun 4; 50min–1hr); Newtownards (Mon–Fri 17 daily, Sat 10, Sun 6; 15–25min); Portaferry (Mon–Fri 18 daily, Sat 11, Sun 6; 25–45min).

Hillsborough to: Belfast (Mon–Fri 25 daily, Sat 13, Sun 8; 25min); Lisburn (6–13 daily; 20min); Newcastle (Mon–Sat 3–4 daily; 1hr 5min).

Jonesborough to: Newry (Mon–Sat 2–3 daily (40min).

Kilkeel to: Annalong (Mon–Fri 15 daily, Sat 11, Sun 6; 15min); Newcastle (Mon–Fri 15 daily, Sat 11, Sun 6; 35min); Newry (Mon–Sat 10–11 daily, Sun 4; 50min); Rostrevor (Mon–Sat 10–11 daily, Sun 4;

25min); Warrenpoint (Mon–Sat 10–11 daily, Sun 4; 35min).
Killough to: Ardglass (Mon–Fri 13 daily, Sat 7, Sun 2; 5min); Downpatrick (Mon–Fri 12 daily, Sat 7, Sun 2; 15min).
Killyleagh to: Comber (Mon–Fri 11 daily, Sat 6, Sun 2; 15min); Downpatrick (Mon–Fri 10 daily, Sat 6; 15min).
Lisburn to: Belfast (Mon–Fri every 10–15min, Sat every 20min, Sun every 30min; 30–40min); Hilden (Mon–Sat 12–13 daily); Hillsborough (6–13 daily; 20min); Newcastle (Mon–Sat 3 daily; 1hr 20min).
Loughgall to Armagh (Mon–Fri 5 daily; 15min).
Loughinisland to: Newcastle (Mon–Sat 3 daily; 20min).
Mullaghbawn to: Crossmaglen (Mon–Fri 8 daily, Sat 4; 25min); Newry (Mon–Fri 7 daily; Sun 4; 30min).
Navan Fort to: Armagh (Mon–Fri 12 daily; 10min).
Newcastle to: Annalong (Mon–Fri 14 daily, Sat 11, Sun 6; 20min); Belfast (Mon–Fri 18 daily, Sat 13, Sun 9; 1hr 20min–1hr 45min); Bryansford (Mon–Fri 7 daily, Sat 2; 10min); Castlewellan (Mon–Fri 13 daily, Sat 10, Sun 3; 10min); Downpatrick (Mon–Fri 18 daily, Sat 13, Sun 4; 25–35min); Hillsborough (Mon–Sat 3–4 daily; 1hr 5min); Kilkeel (Mon–Fri 14 daily, Sat 11, Sun 6; 35min); Lisburn (Mon–Sat 3–4 daily; 1hr 20min); Loughinisland (Mon–Fri 3–4 daily; 20min); Newry (Mon–Sat 6 daily, Sun 2; 55min).
Newry to: Armagh (Mon–Fri 11 daily, Sat 8, Sun 3; 35–45min); Belfast (Mon–Fri 29 daily, Sat 13, Sun 7; 1hr 10min); Carlingford *Bus Éireann*: Mon–Sat 2 daily; 20min); Crossmaglen (Mon–Fri 10 daily, Sat 4; 55min); Downpatrick (Mon–Sat 6 daily, Sun 2; 1hr 15min); Dublin (14 daily; 2hr); Dundalk *Bus Éireann*: Mon–Sat 7 daily; 30–40min); Forkhill (Mon–Fri 7, Sat 4; 35min); Jonesborough (Mon–Fri 2–3, Sat 1; 40min); Kilkeel (Mon–Sat 11 daily, Sun 4; 50min); Mullaghbawn (Mon–Fri 8 daily, Sat 4; 30min); Newcastle (Mon–Sat 6 daily, Sun 2; 55min); Rostrevor (Mon–Sat 17–19 daily, Sun 7; 25min); Warrenpoint (Mon–Sat 19–22 daily, Sun 11; 15min).
Newtownards to: Bangor (Mon–Sat 26–32 daily, Sun 7; 20min); Belfast (Mon–Sat every 10–20min, Sun every 30min–1hr; 15min); Comber (Mon–Fri 18 daily, Sat 12, Sun 6; 20min); Greyabbey (Mon–Fri 16 daily, Sat 11, Sun 6; 15–25min); Portaferry (Mon–Fri 17 daily, Sat 12, Sun 6; 50min–1hr 15min).
Portaferry to: Belfast (Mon–Fri 6 daily, Sat 10, Sun 4; 1hr 25min–1hr 45min); Greyabbey (Mon–Fri 18 daily, Sat 10, Sun 7; 25–45min); Newtownards (Mon–Fri 17 daily, Sat 12, Sun 6; 50min–1hr 15min).
Raholp to: Downpatrick (Mon–Sat 6–8 daily; 15min); Strangford (Mon–Sat 5–6 daily; 15min).
Rostrevor to: Kilkeel (Mon–Sat 11 daily, Sun 4; 25min); Newry (Mon–Sat 16–20 daily, Sun 8; 25min); Warrenpoint (Mon–Sat 16–20 daily, Sun 8; 10min).
Strangford to: Downpatrick (Mon–Fri 9 daily, Sat 6; 30min); Raholp (Mon–Sat 6 daily; 15min).
Warrenpoint to Kilkeel (Mon–Sat 11 daily, Sun 4; 35min); Newry (Mon–Sat 18–23 daily, Sun 11; 15min); Rostrevor (Mon–Sat 17–19 daily, Sun 7; 10min).

16

Tyrone and Fermanagh

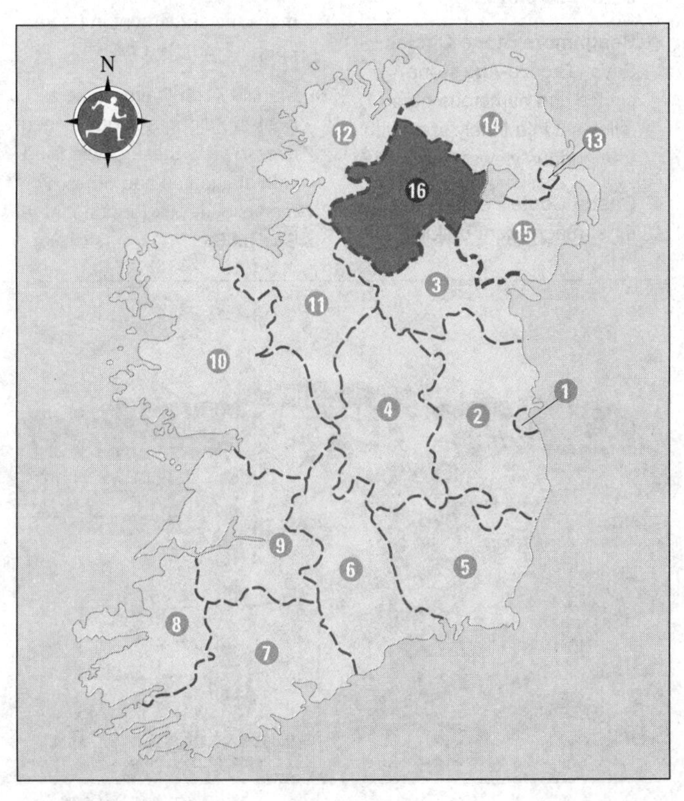

CHAPTER 16 **Highlights**

* **Lough Neagh** Ireland's largest lake – and indeed the biggest in the British Isles – is best viewed from the churchyard at Ardboe. See p.669

* **The Sperrin Mountains** Ruggedly picturesque, the Sperrins offer a splendid variety of hikes and trails. See p.671

* **Beaghmore Stone Circles** Seven Bronze-Age stone circles and numerous other relics set in a lonely spot with tremendous views. See p.672

* **Castle Coole** Perhaps the most magnificent building of its kind in Northern Ireland, this gorgeous eighteenth-century mansion is richly decorated inside and set in wonderful grounds. See p.680

* **Devenish Island** Getting out on the water is an essential part of any trip to Fermanagh, and there's no better place to do it than at this former monastic settlement in Lower Lough Erne. See p.681

* **Marble Arch Caves** Take a boat trip along a subterranean river to view these caves filled with stalactites and other marvellous rock formations. See p.686

▲ Castle Coole

16

Tyrone and Fermanagh

Much of inland Northern Ireland is formed by neighbouring **Tyrone** and **Fermanagh**, predominantly rural counties whose few sizeable towns, with the exception of **Omagh**, lie at the eastern and western fringes of the region. The chief scenic attractions of Tyrone are to be found in the wild and desolate **Sperrin Mountains** in the north, and the undulating **Clogher Valley** in the south. Other features include a scattering of archeological sites and several notable heritage centres, including the stimulating **Ulster American Folk Park**, close to Omagh.

In contrast to Tyrone, Fermanagh attracts plenty of visitors – chiefly for its watersports, boating and fishing. At its core is **Lough Erne**, a huge lake complex dotted with islands and surrounded by richly beautiful countryside. Fermanagh's main town, **Enniskillen**, evokes a strong sense of history, while the remnants of the medieval past – along with those of the seventeenth and eighteenth centuries – are found all over the region, on islands and mainland alike. As in Tyrone, sights of interest are dispersed, and buses can be very infrequent away from the main routes. The key to enjoying Fermanagh, though, is to get out onto the water – and this is easy enough from Enniskillen or from a number of the villages that rest on the lakes' shores.

County Tyrone

Stretching from the shores of the vast **Lough Neagh** in the east to the border of the Republic and Donegal in the west, County Tyrone lies bang in the middle of Northern Ireland. Its northeastern limits are high in the desolate and beautiful **Sperrin Mountains**, while in its south the **Clogher Valley** reaches towards the lakes of County Fermanagh. This is first and foremost farming country, with little evidence of industrialization apart from starchily neat

planters' villages that grew up with the linen industry and a smattering of heavier industries in the towns near Lough Neagh.

The Sperrin range offers major scenic attractions: it's rich in wildlife and is an excellent target for determined, lonesome walking. The best place to base yourself is **Gortin**, a village on the **Ulster Way** footpath and the most easily accessible overnight stop in the area. Tyrone also has no shortage of archeological remains, the most remarkable being the **Beaghmore Stone Circles**, in the southeast of the Sperrins. The towns, though, are not much of a draw. **Omagh** is the largest, agreeable enough though lacking in sights, but provides a good alternative to Gortin as a base to explore the Sperrins. Otherwise the main point of interest in the county is the **Ulster American Folk Park** near Omagh which explores the connections between the Ulster province and the US.

The region's **Ulsterbus** services are reliable along main routes but infrequent elsewhere. However, so scattered are Tyrone's attractions that you're likely to see little of the most interesting parts without a car or a bike. The one exception, of course, is in the Sperrins, where **hiking** is the best way to get around, although sporadic buses also serve the area.

Eastern Tyrone

The only places in the east of County Tyrone that could be described as anything more than villages are the rather drab towns of **Cookstown** and **Dungannon**. The dominant feature is the western shore of **Lough Neagh**, and there are a number of relics of both the region's historical heritage, such as the high crosses at **Ardboe** and **Donaghmore**, and its more recent industrial past at the **Wellbrook Beetling Mill**, close to Cookstown. The village of **Benburb**, to the south, is one of the most attractively situated in the North.

Around Lough Neagh

According to legend, **Lough Neagh** (pronounced "nay") owes its origins to the mythical giant Fionn Mac Cumhaill, who was so unimpressed by east Tyrone's low-lying terrain that he took a massive lump of land from Ulster and hurled it across the Irish Sea. It landed midway and became the Isle of Man, and the hole it left behind became the lough. Its shores, which form the county's eastern boundary, provide excellent **fishing** and plenty of bird life, though both the surrounding land and lake itself are almost featureless. Small settlements house eel fishermen, whose catches go to the Toome Eel Fishery at **Toome** at the northern tip of the lake, the largest of its kind in Europe.

Slight relief is to be found at lakeside **ARDBOE**, halfway along the lough's western shore, where there's a tenth-century **high cross**. The elements have eroded the various biblical scenes carved onto the sandstone almost beyond recognition, but its exceptional size – almost six metres high – is impressive. The cross stands in the grounds of an early monastery associated with **St Colman**, but the ruined church nearby dates from the seventeenth century and is of little interest. On a humid day in early summer, you'll also not fail to be impressed by the swarms of black Lough Neagh mayflies.

A planters' town, **COOKSTOWN**, ten miles west of Lough Neagh, boasts the longest main street in Ireland – over a mile and a quarter – which is the site of an extensive Saturday **market**. The **tourist office** is at The Burnavon, Burns Road (June–Sept Mon–Sat 9am–5pm, also July & Aug Sun 2–4pm; Oct–May Mon–Fri 9am–5pm, Sat 10am–4pm; ⓣ028/8676 9949, ⓦwww.cookstown.gov.uk), and has plenty of information about sights and events across the county. Four miles west off the A505 is the **Wellbrook Beetling Mill**, an eighteenth-century water-powered linen mill (mid-March to June & Sept Sat, Sun & public hols 2–6pm; July & Aug daily 2–6pm; £3.50; ⓦwww.ntni.org.uk). "Beetling" was the final stage of production whereby linen was given a sheen and smoothness by hammering with heavy wooden "beetles". Though it ceased operation in 1961, the mill is extremely well preserved, and all the engines still work and can be viewed in action.

DUNGANNON, about ten miles south of Cookstown, is another dreary town with no trace of its illustrious past as the hilltop seat of the O'Neills, from which they ruled Ulster for over five centuries. Just outside town, on the A45 Coalisland road, is the **Tyrone Crystal Factory** (Mon–Sat 9am–5pm, Sun 1–5pm; £5; ⓦwww.tyronecrystal.com), where you can see demonstrations of glass-blowing and hand-cutting.

At **DONAGHMORE**, three miles northwest of Dungannon, there's another **high cross** dating from the tenth century in front of the parish church, though whoever reassembled it in the nineteenth century clearly botched the job as there's an obvious join halfway down the shaft. A couple of miles southwest from here in **CASTLECAULFIELD** lie the ruins of a fortified **mansion** built by Sir Toby Caulfield in 1619, while the village **church** has a plaque commemorating the poet Charles Wolfe (1791–1823), author of *The Burial of St John Moore* and curate of Donaghmore for a few years.

Benburb

Between Dungannon and Armagh, to the south, the picturesque village of **BENBURB** merits a detour. The tiny cottages on Main Street were once apple-peeling sheds, and the parish **church**, dating from 1618, is one of the oldest still in regular use in Ireland. The church stands next to the gates of a **Servite priory** – the monastic order of Servants of the Virgin, which, though founded in Florence in 1233, did not establish itself in Ireland until 1948. The priory grounds offer a pleasant stroll, but far better are the walks along the Blackwater River in **Benburb Valley Park** (daily 9am–dusk; free), accessed from Main Street, where, perched on a rock thirty metres or so above the water, are the substantial remains of a **castle** built by Viscount Powerscourt in 1615, which offer commanding views of the Blackwater valley.

The Clogher Valley

In the far south of County Tyrone the Blackwater River runs through the **Clogher Valley**, a twenty-mile stretch running from the market town of Aughnacloy through the villages of **Ballygawley**, **Augher** and **Clogher** to **Fivemiletown**. There's little here of special interest, but the pleasantly rolling countryside is sufficient in itself to justify a diversion.

At one time a railway connected the valley's villages, and at **AUGHER** you can sample home baking in the old station, which now houses *Rosamund's Coffee Shop*. The village makes much of its connection with the writer **William Carleton** (1794–1869), whose most notable novel was *Black Prophet*, a sombre tale of the Famine years. A summer school (Ⓣ028/8776 7259) celebrates his life and work annually over five days in early August.

A couple of miles northwest of Augher lies **Knockmany Forest**, where a cairn on the top of a steep wooded hill protects a Bronze Age passage tomb, said to be the resting place of Ainé, the mother-goddess with whom Fionn Mac Cumhaill was infatuated. The stones in the tomb are inscribed with complex swirling patterns, but you can merely peer at them from a distance through a locked grille.

Three miles further west, **CLOGHER**'s main street climbs gently upwards to its eighteenth-century Church of Ireland **cathedral**. The village lays claim to the oldest bishopric in Ireland – its first bishop was St MacCartan, a disciple of St Patrick. There is also evidence of the place's earlier significance – in the park behind the cathedral is an Iron Age **hill fort**, thought to be the seat of the old kings of Oriel. Inside the cathedral is the "golden stone", a slab cross dating from the ninth century, and a gallery of portraits of former bishops bearing expressions of appropriate solemnity. The best **food** (including sumptuous breakfasts) and **accommodation** in the area is provided by *Corick House*, 20 Corick Rd (Ⓣ028/8554 8216, Ⓦwww.corickcountryhouse.com; ④), a late seventeenth-century house with a fine restaurant serving modern Irish fare.

The **Clogher Valley Scenic Drive** is ideally accessed from **FIVEMILETOWN**, seven miles west of Clogher, though the lack of signposts at certain crucial junctions means it's best tackled with an Ordnance Survey map. The complete circuit runs for about 25 miles in a loop either side of the A4, but the southerly section is easily the more enjoyable and takes you into the most isolated part of the county outside the Sperrins. Head south from the crossroads in Fivemiletown and once you've picked up the first sign you'll find yourself on narrow woodland lanes gradually ascending towards **Slieve Beagh**. It's more than likely that sheep will be your only company unless you encounter the odd hiker on the Ulster Way (see box, p.685), which you'll traverse as the route enters moorland. The whole valley can be surveyed from the car-park viewpoint before you descend into **Fardross Forest**. The only other site of note is a few miles on. Look out to your left for a bizarre, three-tiered hilltop tower known as **Brackenridge's Folly**, named after one George Brackenridge, who had the tower constructed as his mausoleum – thus compelling the squirearchy who had looked down on him during his lifetime to look up to him once he was dead.

The Sperrins

The impressive, undulating **Sperrin Mountains** form the northeastern limits of County Tyrone. Wild, empty and beautiful, they reach 2240ft at their highest point, yet the smooth and gradually curving slopes give them a deceptively low appearance. The covering of bog and heather adds to this effect, suggesting nothing more than high, open moorland. For all this, views from the summits are panoramic, and the evenness of texture can make these mountains sumptuous when bathed in evening light. Once in the mountains, it's impossible not to catch sight of the **wildlife**. Sparrowhawks and kestrels hover above, and you might see buzzards or the far more rare hen harrier, attracted by a rich range of prey in a landscape mostly undisturbed by development – the mountains teem with assorted rodents, including even the rare Irish hare. Over the years there's been many a tale about the discovery of "gold in them there hills" and you might encounter the occasional panner testing the story's veracity.

Walking the Sperrins

The forty-mile-wide range of the Sperrin Mountains offers good long-distance **walking**, without necessarily involving steep inclines. You can ramble wherever you like, but remember that – despite appearances – these are high mountains, and changeable weather makes them potentially dangerous. A map and compass are essential for serious walking.

For those not equipped for the high ground, the **Glenelly and Owenkillen** river valleys run through the heart of this fine countryside from Plumbridge and Gortin, respectively, and are particularly enjoyable for cyclists who should pick up a copy of the Sperrins cycling guide from tourist offices (also downloadable from Ⓦwww.sperrintourism.com). The **Central Sperrins Way** (map available from most tourist offices) is a 25-mile waymarked trail, which begins and ends at Barnes Gap, halfway between Plumbridge and Cranagh. The two-day walk takes in a variety of countryside with spectacular views of the mountains, moorland and Glenelly Valley. The exposed moorland can often be very wet and boggy underfoot, and, as there is no accommodation en route, taking a tent is essential.

The **Sperrins Walking Festival** (Ⓣ028/8634 7700, Ⓦwww.sperrintourism.com) is held over the first weekend in August and involves various guided daily walks, graded according to difficulty.

Much depopulated over the years, the local sheep-farming community is now sparsely scattered across the region; there are few facilities such as shops or pubs and little accommodation (except in Gortin – see below), so **planning ahead** is essential if you're intending to walk in the mountains. The Central Sperrins are tricky to reach without your own transport, otherwise you'll be dependent on the Monday-to-Saturday **Sperrin Rambler bus** (see "Travel details", p.687).

Gortin and around

If you're tackling the Sperrins to the north of Omagh (see p.673), there are really only two villages that can offer you any amenities at all – Gortin and its near-neighbour Plumbridge. And even these are comatose for much of the year.

GORTIN, ten miles north of Omagh, is a long one-street village with a surprising number of **pubs**, one of which, the *Foot Hills* bar, offers lunches and evening **meals**. Alternatively, there's an innovative menu at *The Pedlar's Restaurant*. **Accommodation** is available at the *Gortin Accommodation Suite and Activity Centre*, 62 Main St (Ⓣ028/8164 8346, Ⓦwww.gortin.net), which offers dorms (£10), family rooms (❷) and self-catering cottages (sleep 4–8; £300–400 per week). Three miles south of the village is the **Gortin Glen Forest Park** (daily 10am–dusk; pedestrians £1, cars £3), which offers a five-mile forest drive and various trails leading to viewpoints of the area, en route to which you may encounter members of the park's herd of Sitka deer. Gortin Glen is accessible on any bus between Omagh and Gortin (see p.687).

PLUMBRIDGE, three and a half miles north of Gortin, sits clustered prettily on the banks of the Glenelly River. Apocryphally, it gets its name from the building of the village bridge: the engineer in charge didn't have a plumb line and so, from his scaffolding, spat in the water, using his spit to take the perpendicular. There's little here beyond a few bars and a couple of shops, and the liveliest times are during the annual Glenelly **sheepdog trials** in August. However, you might meet the odd optimistic gold-panner, convinced that the river's waters hold the key to his fortune.

Three and a half miles east of Gortin on the B46 Creggan road is tiny **ROUSKEY**, with the ruins of a **sweat lodge**, an early form of sauna (after the steam treatment, the luckless invalid was plunged into the icy stream nearby). Widespread use of these died out after the Famine, possibly because the failure to combat typhoid dealt a severe blow to people's confidence in traditional medicinal treatments, though some were still functioning up to the 1920s. Also in the village is Teach Ceoil (Ⓣ028/8164 8882), a restored stone barn worth investigating for its evenings of **traditional music** and dancing held on the last Friday of each month.

The Beaghmore Stone Circles and An Creagán

Tyrone is peppered with **archeological remains**: there are more than a thousand standing stones in the Sperrins alone, and the county as a whole boasts numerous chambered graves. The most impressive relics are the Bronze-Age **Beaghmore Stone Circles**, in the southeast of the Sperrins. From Gortin, take the B46 east onto the A505, from where they're well signposted up a track three and a half miles north off the road. Although most of the stones on this lonely site are not more than a metre high, the complexity of the ritual they suggest is impressive: there are seven stone circles, ten stone rows and a dozen round cairns (burial mounds, some containing cremated human remains). All of the circles

▲ Beaghmore Stone Circles

stand in pairs, except for one, which is filled with over eight hundred upright stones, known as the Dragon's Teeth. The alignments correlate to movements of the sun, moon and stars; two of the rows point to sunrise at the summer.

Just off the A505, roughly halfway between Omagh and Cookstown, is the **An Creagán Visitor Centre** (daily: April–Sept 11am–6.30pm; Oct–March 11am–4.30pm; Ⓦwww.an-creagan.com; £2), modelled on the many cairns that surround it. The centre is circular and built from local stone on the land of one of the district's last native Irish-speakers, who died in the 1950s. It's actually more of a cultural centre than a museum, with locals coming along to the occasional **traditional-music** concerts, dancing, storytelling and singing events and there's also a bar and restaurant – the latter is particularly popular for Sunday lunch. But An Creagán also explores the rare, raised bog terrain all around, with interpretive displays and signposted **rambling and cycling routes** over the countryside (bike rental is also offered). The farmers driven to these bogs in the eighteenth century made huge efforts to reclaim the soil: there are limekilns from which they treated the reclaimed land, and you can still see their **potato ridges** – these grassed-over Copney spade ridges point back to the devastating Famine of 1845–51 and illustrate the farmers' desperate attempts to survive. You can organize self-catering **accommodation** here (Ⓣ028/8076 1112; £150–330 per week) in the traditional *clochán* settlement, with open turf fires supplemented, fortunately, by central heating.

Omagh and around

The name of Tyrone's largest town, **OMAGH**, is synonymous with the worst single atrocity in the history of the Troubles when, on the afternoon of Saturday, August 15, 1998, a five-hundred-pound **car bomb**, planted by the dissident Republican group the Real IRA, exploded on Market Street. Twenty-nine people died and more than two hundred were injured. Much of the eastern part of Omagh's main street was devastated by the bombing and has since undergone major reconstruction. The area uphill to the west, originally thought to be the bombers' target on the basis of their misleading warning, remained unscathed and contains two adjacent buildings that would grace any town – the fine classical **courthouse** and the irregular twin spires of the Catholic **Sacred Heart Church**. Though there's little to see in the town itself, it's a useful place to base yourself for exploring the area.

Practicalities

The **bus station** (ⓣ028/8224 2711) is just across the river from the town centre in Mountjoy Road. The **tourist office** is based in the ground floor of the riverside Strule Arts Centre on Townhall Square, just west of the bus station (Mon–Sat 10am–6pm; ⓣ028/8224 7841, ⓦwww.flavouroftyrone.com), though you'll need your own transport to see most of the region it promotes.

Accommodation

If you're hiking the Sperrins, a better bet might be to base yourself in Gortin (see p.672), but a classy option closer to town is the elegant *Erganagh House* (ⓣ028/8225 2852, ⓔerganaghhouse@tiscali.net; ④), which provides spacious en-suite rooms in a renovated eighteenth-century rectory, four miles up the Gortin road. Within Omagh itself, *Silverbirch Hotel*, 5 Gortin Rd (ⓣ028/8224 2520, ⓦwww.silverbirchhotel.com; ④), offers luxurious en-suite accommodation, while the nearest **B&B** to the town centre is *Ardmore*, a comfortable townhouse at 12 Tamlaght Rd (ⓣ028/8224 3381, ⓔrismccann@hotmail.com; ①), up the left fork in front of the Sacred Heart and along the second turning on your right. The welcoming *Omagh Independent* **hostel** is two and a half miles north of town, at 9A Waterworks Rd (IHH; ⓣ028/8224 1973, ⓦwww.omaghhostel.co.uk; dorms £10, doubles ①), signposted off the B48 and A505, but also offers a free pick-up service from the bus station.

Eating, drinking and entertainment

Omagh is a good place to stop for **food**, particularly during the daytime. The recently opened *Thyme*, 29 High St, is a popular spot for lunch and snacks, and there's also *The Riverfront Café*, 38 Market St, for excellent coffee. Plenty of pubs serve food, though the best is undoubtedly *The Coach Inn*, 1 Railway Terrace, offering tasty lunchtime specials and an extensive evening menu. *Bogan's* on Market Street serves a filling Irish stew and *Grant's*, 29 George St (ⓣ028/8225 0900), offers a bistro menu or snacks in the wine bar.

The town's spanking-new Strule Arts Centre (ⓣ028/8224 7831, ⓦwww.struleartscentre.co.uk) is on Townhall Square, signposted to the right off the High Street, and stages a lively programme of **music**, **drama** and other events. The Dún Úladh Cultural Heritage Centre, just outside town on the B4 Carrickmore road (ⓣ08224 2777), promotes Irish **traditional music** and culture and has a traditional session on Saturday nights. **Bars** offering traditional-music sessions include *Sally O'Brien's* (Thurs) and *McCann's* (Sun), both on John Street, while *Bogan's*, Market Street, is a pleasant place for a pint. **Clubbers** head for *Utopia*, 55–57 Market St, at weekends for the latest dance hits and occasional guest DJs.

The Ulster American Folk Park

The most successful of Northern Ireland's American-heritage projects is the **Ulster American Folk Park** (April–Sept Mon–Sat 10.30am–6pm, Sun &

public hols 11am–6.30pm; Oct–March Mon–Fri 10.30am–5pm; last admission 1hr 30min before closing; £5; Ⓦwww.folkpark.com), three miles north of Omagh in Camphill, a short hop on one of the regular Strabane-bound buses (see "Travel details", p.687). The first significant **emigration** from Ireland to North America was that of Ulster folk in the early eighteenth century, many of whom were of Scottish Protestant origin. Of all the immigrant communities in the United States, it was the Irish who most quickly – and profoundly – made their mark: the three first-generation **US presidents** of Irish origin were all of Ulster stock, and nine overall could trace their roots to here. Throughout the eighteenth and nineteenth centuries thousands of people left to establish new lives in North America, a steady flow of emigrants that became a torrent during the Famine years.

You can find detailed information on the causes and patterns of migration in the folk park's indoor **gallery**, which surprisingly pays little attention to the Native Americans dispossessed by the Ulster settlers, but the real attractions lie outside in the park itself, where **original buildings** have been transplanted or replicas constructed to provide a sense of Ulster life in the past. The disparity in living conditions in nineteenth-century Ireland is illustrated by the juxtaposition of a typical pre-Famine **single-room cabin** from the Sperrins, with the **Mellon Homestead**, a significantly more substantial dwelling from which the local Mellon family migrated in 1818. A re-created Ulster street, including the impressively authentic Reilly's Spirit Grocers, whose shelves are packed with appropriate period stock, leads to the *Union*, a full-sized **brig**, reconstructed to demonstrate the gruelling conditions endured during the voyage across the Atlantic. An American street leads to edifices constructed by the **Pennsylvanian settlers**, including a multipurpose log barn and massive six-roomed log farmhouse. There are plenty of other buildings, and you'll meet costumed guides and craftworkers ready to explain their activities and answer questions, augmenting the folk park's attention to authenticity. One event of note here is the annual **Bluegrass Festival** over the first weekend in September.

The complex also houses the **Centre for Migration Studies** (Mon–Fri 10.30am–4.45pm), a major reference and research library that contains an enormous variety of material, such as emigrants' letters, passenger lists and contemporary newspaper articles.

There's a **café** on the site, but for more substantial fare head up the road to the *Mellon Country Inn* (Ⓣ028/8166 1224, Ⓦwww.melloncountryhotel.com; ❸), which has a restaurant that gives a modern twist to traditional Irish dishes; it also offers stylish **accommodation**.

County Fermanagh

Fermanagh is justly famous for the intense beauty of its **lakes**. Much of the landscape is dominated by their waters, which, along with numerous rivers, constitute more than a third of the county's area. Though there are several attractive smaller loughs, it's the two interconnected parts of **Lough Erne** that draw the most visitors – Lower Lough Erne in the northwest and Upper

Lough Erne in the southeast. Surrounding hills are wooded with oak, ash and beech, producing a scene of fresh green in spring and rich and rusty colours in autumn. The water's rippling surface reflects whatever light there is, mirroring the palest of skies through to the ruddiest of magenta sunsets. It's a breathtaking landscape, where land and water complement each other in a resonant, stately harmony.

In winter **Lower Lough Erne** has the character of an inland sea, dangerous waves making even the locals wary of sailing. Fabulous vistas reach across to the shores of richly wooded, mostly uninhabited islands, on which are scattered early Christian ruins and evidence of earlier pagan cultures. The **Upper Lough** is quieter and less spectacular. The waterway here is a delightful muddle of little inlets and islands, where waters are shallower and shorelines reedy. Fields have shocks of bristly marsh-grasses; definitions between land and water are blurred. There are plenty of opportunities for **watersports**, while the less energetic can get out onto the lough by renting a boat or taking one of the lough cruises. **Walkers** will find the countryside to be mostly gentle hills and woods, which rise to small mountains in the south and west of the county, made accessible by the Ulster Way. For **cyclists**, there are well-surfaced, empty roads though routes around the Upper Lough are harder to negotiate, with little lanes often leading only to the empty, reed-filled shore – often an atmospheric spot for a picnic.

The county town of **Enniskillen** sits at the point where the Upper and Lower loughs meet. Long a strategic bridging-point, it has more amenities than the rest of Fermanagh put together and, consequently, is a good base for exploring the region. With your own transport you can easily access Fermanagh's impressive series of **planters' castles**, while two of the county's stately houses, **Florence Court** and **Castle Coole**, are open to the public.

Enniskillen and around

A pleasant, conservative little town, **ENNISKILLEN** sits on an island like an ornamental buckle, the two narrow ribbons of water that pass each side connecting the Lower and Upper lough complexes. The strategic strength of this position has long been recognized – indeed, the town takes its name from Innis Ceithleann, "the island of Kathleen", wife of Balor (see p.526), who sought refuge here after a defeat in battle. Later the island became a Maguire stronghold before William Cole, a planter from Cornwall, was appointed governor in 1607. The town played a major role in the 1641 Rebellion and the later Williamite Wars, the latter leading to the formation of its two famous regiments, the **Inniskilling Dragoons** and the **Royal Inniskilling Fusiliers**, which played a significant role in the victory at the Battle of the Boyne.

With its **castle** and proximity to the elegant **Castle Coole**, plus a town centre relatively unspoilt by shopping developments, Enniskillen is worthy of a day's visit in its own right. It's also ideally situated as a base for exploring Lough Erne and touring the attractive local countryside. However, the name Enniskillen is still often associated with one of the most devastating atrocities of the Troubles. On Remembrance Day 1987, an IRA **bomb** killed eleven and injured 61 people as they gathered to commemorate the dead of the two world wars. The resulting widespread outrage was instrumental in directing parts of the Republican movement towards seeking a political solution to the Troubles.

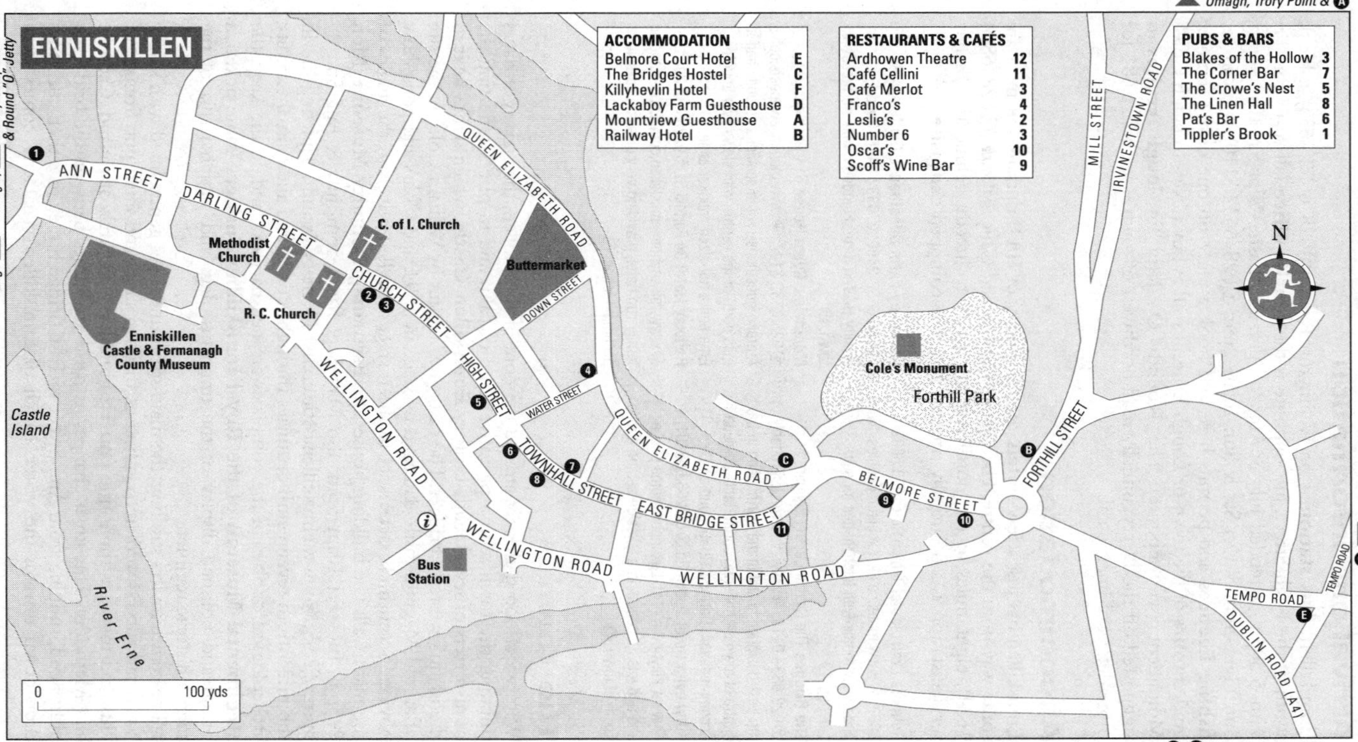
ENNISKILLEN
ACCOMMODATION
Belmore Court Hotel E
The Bridges Hostel C
Killyhevlin Hotel F
Lackaboy Farm Guesthouse D
Mountview Guesthouse A
Railway Hotel B
RESTAURANTS & CAFÉS
Ardhowen Theatre 12
Café Cellini 11
Café Merlot 3
Franco's 4
Leslie's 2
Number 6 3
Oscar's 10
Scoff's Wine Bar 9
PUBS & BARS
Blakes of the Hollow 3
The Corner Bar 7
The Crowe's Nest 5
The Linen Hall 8
Pat's Bar 6
Tippler's Brook 1
Omagh, Trory Point & A
F, 12 & Castle Coole
D
Donegal, Blaney Campsite & Round "O" Jetty
Sligo
ANN STREET
DARLING STREET
CHURCH STREET
QUEEN ELIZABETH ROAD
DOWN STREET
HIGH STREET
WATER STREET
TOWNHALL STREET
EAST BRIDGE STREET
BELMORE STREET
WELLINGTON ROAD
FORTHILL STREET
MILL STREET
IRVINESTOWN ROAD
TEMPO ROAD
DUBLIN ROAD (A4)
C. of I. Church
Methodist Church
R. C. Church
Buttermarket
Enniskillen Castle & Fermanagh County Museum
Cole's Monument
Forthill Park
Bus Station
Castle Island
River Erne
N
0
100 yds

Arrival and information

Enniskillen's **bus station** is on Wellington Road (Ⓣ028/6632 2633), a block south of the High Street. Just opposite is the **tourist office** (all year Mon–Fri 9am–5.30pm, extended July & Aug to 7pm; also Easter–Sept Sat 10am–6pm, Sun 11am–5pm & Oct Sat & Sun 10am–2pm; Ⓣ028/6632 3110). You can get **fishing licences** and permits here, and book a place on one of the summer guided **tours** of the town or Lough Erne, as well as buy tickets to climb Cole's Monument (see opposite). The Round "O" Jetty for **lough cruises** is signposted off the Derrygonnelly road northwest of town – see box, p.681 for more details of boat rental.

Accommodation

Enniskillen has just a few **hotels** though plenty of **B&B** options, but most are some way from the centre. The *Blaney Caravan and Camping Park* (Ⓣ028/6864 1634), eight miles to the northwest off the A46 directly behind the Blaney service station, is a beautifully situated and well-equipped **campsite**.

Belmore Court Motel Tempo Rd Ⓣ028/6632 6633, Ⓦwww.motel.co.uk. Excellent doubles, twins and family rooms with kitchenettes for self-catering. ❷

The Bridges The Clinton Centre, Belmore St Ⓣ028/6634 0110, Ⓦwww.hini.org.uk. Probably the best-designed hostel in the North, bang in the centre of town and offering comfortable en-suite accommodation. Dorms £12.50, doubles ❶.

Killyhevlin Hotel Dublin Rd Ⓣ028/6632 3481, Ⓦwww.killyhevlin.com. Luxurious rooms plus a spa and leisure centre, in a lakeside setting a mile south of town. ❻

Lackaboy Farm Guesthouse Old Tempo Rd Ⓣ028/6632 2488, Ⓕ6332 0440. Good-quality B&B in a rural setting a mile northeast of town. ❷

Mountview Guest House 61 Irvinestown Rd Ⓣ028/6632 3147, Ⓦwww.mountviewguests.com. A grand guesthouse set in spacious grounds half a mile north of the centre, with views over Lough Erne and a full-sized snooker table. ❷

Railway Hotel 34 Forthill St Ⓣ028/6632 2084, Ⓦwww.railwayhotelenniskillen.com. Long-standing family-run hotel, providing very pleasant en-suite accommodation. ❸

The Town

Waterways loop their way around the core of Enniskillen, their glassy surfaces imbuing the town with a pervasive sense of calm and in places reflecting the mini-turrets of seventeenth-century **Enniskillen Castle**, which stands next to the island's westerly bridges. The castle was rebuilt by William Cole on the site of an old Maguire castle damaged by siege in 1594, and Cole's additions show obvious Scottish characteristics in the turrets corbelled out from the angles of the main wall. The building houses the **Fermanagh County Museum** (Mon 2–5pm, Tues–Fri 10am–5pm; also May–Sept Sat 2–5pm, July & Aug Sun 2–5pm; £2.95; Ⓦwww.enniskillencastle.co.uk; Heritage Island), depicting life in the fifteenth to seventeenth centuries through models and audiovisual exhibits, archeological displays in the complex's arcaded barracks, and, in the keep, the **Regimental Museum of the Royal Inniskilling Fusiliers** (same ticket), a proud and polished display of the uniforms, flags and paraphernalia of the town's historic regiment.

The centre invites strolling: the main street undulates gently, lined with sturdy Victorian and Edwardian townhouses, thriving shops and smart pub fronts, and, clustered together, three fine **church** buildings – Church of Ireland, Catholic and Methodist. This street changes its name five times between the bridges at either end, running from Ann Street to East Bridge Street; to either side, lanes drop down towards the water. Much of Enniskillen's character comes from wealth derived from the care of a colonial presence. Evidence of British influence is widespread: on Windmill Hill to the west, the stately **Portora Royal School** overlooks the town, carrying a discreet reminder of the continued elitism in the social order. The school was founded by Charles I in 1626, though the present building dates from 1777; old boys include **Oscar Wilde** – the pride of the school, until his trial for homosexuality – and **Samuel Beckett**. Over on a hill to the east, **Cole's Monument**, a statue commemorating one of Wellington's generals keeps an eye on the town from Forthill Park; if you catch the park-keeper you can ascend to the viewing gallery (April–Sept daily 1.30–3pm; £1; tickets from the tourist office or museum). Immediately below is the war memorial, scene of the 1987 bombing.

On Down Street, just off the High Street, the **Buttermarket** (Mon–Sat 10am–5.30pm; Ⓦwww.fermanaghcraft.com) is a craft and design centre with a range of artisans working on site all year round. These wonderfully renovated dairy-market buildings date from 1835. For something less sedate, Thursday's general street **market** on Forthill Street is worth a trip.

Eating and drinking

Enniskillen has plenty of reasonably priced **places to eat**, with restaurants, cafés and no shortage of cheerful pubs and bars – especially, *Pat's* and *The Linen Hall*, both on Townhall Street – serving decent food. For an atmospheric **pint**, look no further than the Victorian *Blakes of the Hollow*, on Church Street, or the amicable *Tippler's Brook*, just west of the centre on The Brook. It's a lively town at night, with bar extensions until 1am commonplace in summer. **Traditional music** options are limited, but *The Corner Bar*, Townhall Street, has a regular Thursday-night session, while *The Crowe's Nest*, High Street, hosts rock and indie bands at the weekend.

Restaurants and cafés

Ardhowen Theatre Dublin Rd. A mile south of town, this theatre restaurant is worth visiting for its waterside setting (you can also enjoy the view from an excellent bar) for a bite after a traipse around Castle Coole (see p.680). Open Mon–Sat lunchtime only.

Café Cellini at the bottom of East Bridge St. A great little haunt for coffee and snacks and for looking out across the water.

Café Merlot 6 Church St. Part of *Blakes of the Hollow*, this café offers a range of inspired light meals with an Irish–Asian twist.

Franco's Queen Elizabeth Rd t0Ⓣ028/6632 4424. Mouthwatering pizza, pasta and seafood served in a cosy yet sophisticated setting.

Leslie's 10 Church St. A fine café serving home-bakes and salads or, for takeaway, great filling sandwiches or baguettes.

Number 6 Church St Ⓣ028/6632 0918. Inventive modern Irish cuisine, with some vegetarian options. Open Fri & Sat eve only.

Oscar's 29 Belmore St Ⓣ028/6632 7037. Offers a wide range of enticing East Asian and European dishes, with an unusually adventurous children's menu. Closed lunchtime & all day Sun.

Scoff's Wine Bar 17 Belmore St Ⓣ028/6634 2622. Next to *Oscar's*, serving a variety of fish and meat dishes. Closed Mon–Sat lunchtimes.

Entertainment

The hub of Enniskillen's **arts scene** is the Ardhowen Theatre (see "Restaurants and cafés", above; Ⓣ028/6632 5440, Ⓦwww.ardhowentheatre.com), which has a year-round programme of top-quality drama, film and ballet, and hosts a great range of music events – traditional Irish, jazz, opera, country, classical – as well as productions by local community groups, a **theatre festival** in March and a **jazz and blues festival** over the first weekend in June. Check with the

The Kingfisher Cycling Trail

Enniskillen is a good starting point for the 192-mile **Kingfisher Cycling Trail**, which skirts Lower Lough Erne before running through the Leitrim lakelands to Carrick-on-Shannon (see p.490), then east to Belturbet in County Cavan (see p.200), and back, via Clones in County Monaghan (see p.197), around the Upper Lough to Enniskillen. The route passes through a wonderful variety of countryside, and though some of the hills are pretty steep, they are rarely too arduous to deter cyclists. You can either bring your own bike and plan your own accommodation or take advantage of various **tour packages** available (visit Ⓦwww.cycletoursireland.com for details). Tours include two- or three-day short breaks and longer six- to eight-day casual, active or challenging rides. Accommodation is usually in B&Bs (though you can choose to stay in hotels or hostels), 18-speed bikes and essential equipment are provided, and your luggage is transported to and from each night's stop.

tourist office for dates of the Fermanagh *feis* in March – lots of traditional music, dancing, drama and crafts – and the county Fleadh, the competitive traditional-music festival, in June. The Enniskillen Omniplex on Factory Road, a mile north of town (Ⓣ08717/200400, Ⓦwww.omniplex.ie/cinema/enniskillen.htm.), is a multiscreen **cinema** showing the usual range of general-release films.

Castle Coole

Evidence of how the richest of the Enniskillen colonists lived is found about a mile southeast of the town centre at **Castle Coole** (house open St Patrick's Day and Easter week daily 1–6pm; April, May & Sept Sat & Sun 1–6pm; June Fri–Wed 1–6pm; July & Aug daily noon–6pm; guided tours hourly, last tour starts 1hr before closing; grounds open daily: April–Sept 10am–8pm; Oct–March 10am–4pm; house £5, grounds £2 per car unless visiting house; Ⓦwww.ntni.org.uk; Heritage Island), designed by James Wyatt and completed in 1798 as the lakeside home of the Earls of Belmore. The house can be approached either from the Dublin road (signposted just opposite the Ardhowen Theatre) or across the golf course from the Castlecoole road.

A perfect Palladian-fronted building of silver Portland stone, the mansion is part of a huge seven-hundred-acre estate, whose beautiful landscaped grounds feature an impressive avenue of stately oak trees and a wealth of woodland walks. Inside, the house features scagliola columns, exquisite plasterwork, a cantilevered staircase, a state bedroom decorated for George IV (who didn't actually come – the room was never subsequently used), Hogarth prints and an elegant library boasting Regency furnishings and fireplaces. The informative guided tour is well worth taking.

Lough Erne

Lough Erne has a profoundly important place in the history of Fermanagh. The earliest people to settle in the region lived on and around the two lakes; many of the islands here are in fact *crannógs*. The lough's myriad connecting waterways were impenetrable to outsiders, protecting the settlers from invaders and creating an enduring cultural isolation. Evidence from stone carvings suggests that Christianity was accepted far more slowly here than elsewhere: several pagan idols have been found on Christian sites, and the early Christian remains to be found on the islands show the strong influence of pagan culture. Here, Christian carving has something of the stark symmetry, as well as a certain vacancy of facial expression, found in pagan statues. Particularly suggestive of earlier cults is the persistence of the human-head motif in stone carving – in pagan times a symbol of divinity and the most important of religious symbols.

Devenish Island and **White Island**, the most popular of the Erne's ancient sites, are on the Lower Lough, as is **Boa Island** in its far north, which is linked to the mainland by a bridge at each end. The **Upper Lough** is less rewarding, but has interesting spots that repay a leisurely dawdle. Aside from **cruising** the waterways (see box below) and visiting the islands, there are a number of minor attractions around the loughs that are worth dropping into during your stay. Perhaps the most impressive are the early seventeenth-century planters' **castles** scattered around the shoreline.

Devenish Island

Heading around the eastern shores of Lower Lough Erne, if you don't have transport of your own, note that the easiest place to visit from Enniskillen is **Devenish Island**. **Ferries** run to the island from Trory Point, three miles north of Enniskillen off the A32 Irvinestown road (April–Sept daily 10am, 1pm, 3pm & 5pm; ⓣ028/6862 1588; £3), though it's advisable to check times with the tourist office before setting out, as poor weather can sometimes delay or cancel departures. To get to Trory Point from Enniskillen, take the Omagh bus and ask to be set down at the Kesh turn-off.

A monastic settlement was founded on Devenish by St Molaise in the sixth century and became so important during the early Christian period that it had 1500 novices attached. Though plundered by Vikings in the ninth century and again in the twelfth, it continued to be an important religious centre up until the beginning of the seventeenth century. It's a delightful setting, not far from the lough shore, and the ruins are considerable, spanning the entire medieval

Lough Erne cruises and rentals

The MV *Kestrel*, run by Erne Tours (May, Sept & Oct Tues, Sat & Sun 2.15pm; June daily 2.15pm; July & Aug daily 10.30am, 12.15pm, 2.15pm & 4.15pm; £9; ⓣ028/6632 2882), sails from the **Round "O" Jetty** northwest of Enniskillen (see p.678) around the Lower Lough, calling at Devenish Island. There are also additional evening dinner cruises to the *Killyhevlin Hotel* on the Upper Lough shore (May–Sept Sat 6 pm; £25).

The *Inishcruiser* sails around the Upper Lough from the **Share Holiday Village** (see p.684) at Smith's Strand (Easter–Sept Sun & public holidays 2.30pm; 1hr 30min; ⓣ028/6722 2122; £7).

Renting your own boat is another possibility, and there are a number of operators. Most offer open rowing boats, with or without outboard motor, though some have larger six-metre boats available. Prices range accordingly from £20 to £120 for a full day, depending on the operator and boat size. The tourist office in Enniskillen has lists of rental companies and, if you fancy something grander, of cruisers available for rent (weekly prices in high season range from around £600 for smaller boats to £2500 for 8-berth specials). Unless you're going out on a small lake you should always let the boat owner know where you're going and ask to borrow navigation charts – Lough Erne can be dangerous, especially outside the summer months.

period. Most impressive are the sturdy **oratory** and perfect **round tower**, both from the twelfth century; **St Molaise's church**, a century older; and the ruined **Augustinian priory**, a fifteenth-century reconstruction of an earlier abbey. The priory has a fine Gothic sacristy door decorated with birds and vines. To the south is one of Ireland's finest **high crosses**, with highly complex, delicate carving. Other treasures found here – such as an early eleventh-century book shrine, the Soiscel Molaise – are now kept in the National Museum in Dublin, while the island's own small **museum** (joint ticket and same hours as ferry, or 75p if you've arrived in your own boat) includes other less notable relics and detailed information about Devenish itself.

Castle Archdale and White Island

To immerse yourself thoroughly in the beauty of the lough scenery it's well worth making a trip to **Castle Archdale Country Park** (daily 9am–dusk; free) near Lisnarick, about ten miles north of Enniskillen, off the B82 Kesh road. If you're relying on public transport, the Pettigo **bus** will drop you a mile away at the park entrance; otherwise take one of the buses from Enniskillen to Kesh as far as Lisnarick and walk or hitch. The park is perfectly placed for getting out on the lough and has its own **campsite** (April–Oct; ☎028/6862 1333), which has a small supermarket and a fast-food outlet in high season. The **ferry** to White Island (see below) leaves from the nearby marina and you can also **rent boats** (half-day £45, full day £60; ☎028/6862 1156) and **bikes** (£12 per day; same contact details) here in July and August, as well as hiring **fishing rods** (£6 per half-day including bait). And, should you fancy exploring the area on **horseback**, try Drumhoney Riding Stables (☎028/6862 1892), which is also not far from the marina.

Mounted on the wall of a **ruined abbey**, the seven early Christian carvings of **White Island** look eerily pagan. Discovered early in the nineteenth century, they are thought to be **caryatids** – columns in human form – from a monastic church of the ninth to eleventh centuries. The most disconcerting statue is the lewd female figure known as a **Sheila-na-Gig**, with bulging

▲ White Island

cheeks, a big grin, open legs and arms pointing to her genitals. This could be a female fertility figure, a warning to monks of the sins of the flesh or an expression of the demoniacal power of women, designed to ward off evil. (In the epic *Táin Bó Cúailnge*, Cúchulainn was stopped by an army of 150 women led by their female chieftain Scannlach. Their only weapon was their display of nakedness, from which the boy Cúchulainn had to avert his face.) Less equivocal figures continue left to right: a seated Christ figure holding the Gospels on his knees; a hooded figure with bell and crozier, possibly St Anthony; David carrying a shepherd's staff, his hand towards his mouth showing his role as author and singer; Christ the Warrior holding two griffins by the scruff of their necks; and another Christ figure with a fringe of curly hair wearing a brooch on his left shoulder and carrying a sword and shield – here he is the King of Glory at his Second Coming. There is an unfinished seventh stone and, on the far right, a carved head with a downturned mouth, which is probably of later origin than the other statues. The **church** of White Island also contains eleventh-century gravestones; the large earthworks round the outside date from an earlier monastery.

A **ferry** from Castle Archdale Country Park marina runs to White Island on the hour (April–June & Sept Sat & Sun 10am–1pm & 2–6pm; July & Aug daily 10am–1pm & 2–6pm; ⓣ028/6862 1156; £3).

From Boa Island to Belleek

One of the most evocative of the carvings of Lough Erne is the double-faced Janus figure of **Boa Island**, six miles west of Kesh at the northern end of the Lower Lough – barely an island at all these days, as it's connected to the mainland by bridges. The landmark to look out for is **Caldragh cemetery**, signposted off the A47 about a mile west of Lusty Beg Island. Follow the signs down a lane and the graveyard is through a gate to your left.

Boa Island takes its name, not from a connection with snakes, but from Badhbh, a Celtic war-goddess. This ancient Christian burial-ground of broken moss-covered tombstones, encircled and shaded by low hazel trees, has an almost druidic setting. Here you'll find the **Janus figure**, an idol of yellow stone with very bold, symmetrical features. It has the phallus on one side, and a belt and crossed limbs on the other. The figure was probably an invocation of fertility and a depiction of a god-hero, the belt being a reference to the bearing of weapons. Alongside it stands the smaller "**Lusty Man**", so called since it was moved here from nearby Lustymore Island. This idol has only one eye fully carved, maybe to indicate blindness – Cúchulainn had a number of encounters with war-goddesses, divine hags described as blind in the left eye.

Quiet **Lusty Beg Island** just off Boa Island is a popular weekend retreat for Enniskillen people: you'll find luxury **log cabins** with saunas (ⓣ028/6863 3300, ⓦwww.lustybegisland.com; sleep 4–6; £370–600 a week), **B&B** in *The Courtyard* guesthouse (same phone & website; ④), **canoeing**, gentle walks and a good **restaurant**. A free car ferry will take you across; dial ⓣ0 from the telephone on the pier. A couple of miles further west there is splendid accommodation available at *Dreenan Cottage* (ⓣ028/6863 1951; ②), a restful and tastefully designed bungalow set right by the water, with en-suite rooms. The owners are a mine of information on the area and have fishing boats for rental.

Continuing along the northern shore, the **forest of Castle Caldwell**, on the A47 near the western extremity of Lower Lough Erne, is formed by two narrow promontories, which make it a natural breeding site for waterfowl and a habitat of rarities such as the hen harrier, peregrine falcon and pine marten. However, its seventeenth-century **castle** has long been dilapidated, and the surrounding estate is now a commercial, state-owned forest of spruce, pine and larch. At the castle's entrance, look out for the giant stone fiddle in front of the gate lodge, the sobering memorial to Denis McCabe, a local musician who in 1770 tumbled from the Caldwells' barge while inebriated and drowned. Its inscription "DDD" supposedly stands for "Denis died drunk!"

Five miles further west, lively **BELLEEK**'s main attraction is the famous **Belleek Pottery** (tours every 30min: Mon–Thurs 9.30am–12.15pm & 1.45–4.15pm, Fri 9.30am–12.15pm & 2.15–3.30pm; £4; Ⓦwww.belleek.ie; Heritage Island), which offers interesting tours of the works and a chance to buy its rather fussy products. On Main Street you'll find **Fermanagh Crystal** (Mon–Sat 10am–5pm; free), where you can watch the creation of glassware and even, funds permitting, commission your own piece. Belleek's streets host a massive **market** on Tuesdays. Belleek has grand **accommodation** at the riverside *Hotel Carlton* (Ⓣ028/6665 8282, Ⓦwww.hotelcarlton.co.uk; ❹), at the bottom of Main Street, and **B&B** further up the road in *The Fiddlestone* pub (Ⓣ028/6865 8008; ❶) where there's often the possibility of a traditional-music session. Also on Main Street, *The Thatch* **café** serves good-value snacks and coffee, and *The Black Cat Cove* provides excellent **bar** meals in an atmospheric setting. **Bikes** can be rented from Belleek Bicycle Hire, based in *The Thatch* (Ⓣ028/6865 8181; £10 per day).

Monea Castle to Lough Navar Forest

In a beautiful setting at the end of a beech-lined lane, **Monea Castle** (free access), seven miles northwest of Enniskillen off the B81, is a particularly fine ruin of a planters' castle. Built around 1618, it bears the signs of Scottish influence in its design, with similar features to the reworked Maguire Castle in Enniskillen. It was destroyed by fire in the Great Rebellion of 1641 and by Jacobite armies in 1689, and was eventually abandoned in 1750 after another fire. Five miles further north, beyond Derrygonnelly, the fortified house and *bawn* of restored **Tully Castle** (Easter–Sept daily 10am–6pm; free), itself burned by the Maguires in 1641, sits down by the lough shore. Further to the west, there are tremendous views of the lough and surrounds from **Lough Navar Forest** (daily 10am–dusk; car £3).

Upper Lough Erne and Lisnaskea

Upper Lough Erne possesses neither the historic sites nor the scenic splendour of the Lower Lough, though it does have the best preserved of the planters' castles nearby. Should you be tempted to venture further into the lough's maze of reeds and water, there are **cruises** (see box on p.681) from the **Share Holiday Village** (Easter–Oct; Ⓣ028/6722 2122, Ⓦwww.sharevillage.org) at Smith's Strand, signposted off the Lisnaskea–Derrylin road, which offers water-based activity holidays with facilities for disabled travellers, self-catering chalets (sleep 4–12; £480–590 per week) and a **campsite**.

The National Trust's **Crom Estate** (mid-March to Sept Mon–Sat 10am–6pm, Sun noon–6pm; July & Aug till 8pm; car or boat £4.75; Ⓦwww.ntni.org.uk), three miles west of Newtownbutler on the eastern shore of the lough, has the largest surviving area of **oak woodland** in Northern Ireland, home to rare species such as the purple hairstreak and wood white butterflies. There's a café and interpretive centre here, and you can rent **rowing boats** too. Unfortunately, the modern Crom Castle is privately occupied and not open to the public, though you can visit the ruins of the **old castle**. The estate has renovated courtyard **cottages** (Ⓣ0870/458 4442, Ⓦwww.nationaltrustcottages.co.uk; £243–655 per week for 2–6 people).

Almost five miles north of Newtownbutler, **Castle Balfour** (free access) at **LISNASKEA** was built for Sir James Balfour, a Scottish planter, in the early seventeenth century and shows strong Scottish characteristics in its turrets and parapets, high-pitched gables and tall chimneys. The town has several lively **bars** along Main Street, including the wonderfully named *Shoe the Donkey*, while the best place to **eat** is unquestionably the *Donn Carragh Hotel*, which specializes in seafood and provides well-equipped en-suite rooms, and is the only local **accommodation** (ⓣ028/6772 1206, ⓦwww.donncarraghhotel.com; ❷). There's a **campsite** two miles north of Lisnaskea at Mullynascarthy (April–Oct; ⓣ028/6772 1040).

Western Fermanagh

The stretch of countryside on the western edge of the county offers some good **walking** opportunities, particularly in the hills to the south. The **Ulster Way**, which runs northwest from the Upper Lough and east towards Tyrone, makes the riches of the terrain easily accessible.

This region also has two attractions that are well worth seeking out. The magnificent eighteenth-century **Florence Court** is the most assured achievement of the

The Ulster Way

From Marble Arch Caves the **Ulster Way** heads past Lower and Upper Lough Macnean before taking you through the bog and granite heights of the Cuilcagh Mountains to **Ballintempo Forest**, where there are fabulous views over the loughs. The Way then continues north, through the **Lough Navar Forest**, a well-groomed conifer plantation with tarmacked roads and shorter trails. Although a great deal of fir-plantation walking is dark and frustrating, this forest does, at points, provide some of the most spectacular views in Fermanagh, looking over Lower Lough Erne and the mountains of Tyrone, Donegal, Leitrim and Sligo. The Lough Navar Forest also sustains a small herd of red deer, as well as wild goat, fox, badger, hare and red squirrel.

Before setting out, it's well worth obtaining a copy of **The Ulster Way: Southwest Section** from the tourist office in Enniskillen (see p.678). This describes in detail the five connected trails constituting the Way's route through the county.

Accommodation along the Way is limited. There are several B&Bs near **Belcoo**, two and a half miles west from the trail's ascent to the Ballintempo Forest, including the very comfortable *Customs House Country Inn* in the centre of the village at 25–27 Main St (ⓣ028/6638 6285, ⓦwww.customshouseinn.com; ❸), which has a very popular restaurant, or, a few minutes' walk away, there's *Bella Vista*, Cottage Drive (ⓣ028/6638 6469, ⓔbellavistabelcoo@aol.com; ❷). Belcoo also has camping available at *Rushin House Caravan Park* (March–Oct; ⓣ028/6638 6519), a mile up the road to Garrison. There's also *Meadow View*, Sandhill (ⓣ028/6864 1233; ❷), half a mile north of **Derrygonnelly** on the B81. A bit further away from the route of the Way, west near the border at **Garrison** (take the minor road from Derrygonnelly), the *Lough Melvin Holiday Centre* (ⓣ028/6865 8142, ⓦwww.melvinholidaycentre.com; ❶) offers archery, caving, canoeing, wind-surfing and hill-walking courses and has a restaurant, hostel-style accommodation and camping, although you should ring ahead to check on space if you want to stop here. Finding **places to eat** can be tricky: the *Customs House Country Inn* in Belcoo serves food all day (or there are alternatives in Blacklion, just across the bridge; see p.202), but you'll only come across fast food and basic bars in Derrygonnelly (though there is often great **traditional music** at weekends).

colonists, built 150 years after the initial defensive planters' castles. If you have your own transport, a visit to the house can be combined with an hour or so at the **Marble Arch Caves**, the finest cave-system in Northern Ireland. Walkers can reach both along the Ulster Way, accessible from the A4 near Belcoo; the path runs four miles south past Lower Lough Macnean to the Marble Arch Caves and then a further five miles east to Florence Court.

Florence Court

The magnificent three-storey mansion of the National Trust–owned **Florence Court**, about eight miles southwest of Enniskillen (house open St Patrick's Day and Easter week daily 1–6pm; April, May & Sept Sat & Sun 1–6pm; June Wed–Mon 1–6pm; July & Aug daily noon–6pm; £5; grounds and forest park open all year 10am–dusk; £3.50 per car; Ⓦwww.ntni.org.uk), was commissioned by John Cole, one of the Earls of Enniskillen, and named after his wife. The house, completed around 1775, is notable for its restored rococo plasterwork and rare Irish furnishings; the dining room is especially lavish, its ceiling hosting a cloud of puffing cherubs with Jupiter disguised as an eagle in the centre, all flying out of a duck-egg-blue sky. Unfortunately, the top floor of the house was completely destroyed by a fire in 1955 and has never been renovated internally.

To get to the house from Enniskillen, follow the A4 Sligo road for three miles, branching off on the A32 Swanlinbar road and taking the signposted right turn four miles further on. The only public transport from Enniskillen is the infrequent #192 Swanlinbar service; ask to be dropped off at Creamery Cross whence it's a two mile walk to the house.

You can **stay** in the pretty *Rose Cottage* in the Florence Court walled garden (Ⓦwww.nationaltrustcottages.co.uk; sleeps 5; £269–£7230 per week), which is well equipped and has two double bedrooms. There's also award-winning accommodation nearby at *Arch House*, 59 Marble Arch Rd (Ⓣ028/6634 8452, Ⓦwww.archhouse.com; ❸), which offers splendid en-suite rooms and a **restaurant** providing hearty daytime meals.

The Marble Arch Caves and around

Fermanagh's caves are renowned, and while some are for experts only, the most spectacular system of all, the **Marble Arch Caves**, five miles west of Florence Court, is accessible to anyone. A tour of the system lasts around an hour and a quarter, beginning with a boat journey along a **subterranean river**, then on through brilliantly lit chambers, calcite-walled and dripping with stalactites and fragile mineral veils. **Tours** of the caves (daily: late March to June & Sept 10am–4.30pm; July & Aug 10am–5pm; £8; Ⓣ028/6634 8855, Ⓦwww.marblearchcaves.net; Heritage Island) are sometimes booked out by parties, so it makes sense to call ahead to check that your journey won't be wasted; in a steady Irish downpour the caves can be flooded, so check weather reports as well. You'll need to wear sturdy walking shoes and bring warm clothing as the temperature can drop significantly.

From whichever direction you approach the caves, you'll travel along the **Marlbank Scenic Loop**, with tremendous views of Lower Lough Macnean, and on either side you'll see limestone-flagged fields, much like those of The Burren in County Clare. It was fifty thousand years of gentle water seepage through the limestone that deposited the calcite for the amazing stalactite growths in the caves below.

Almost opposite the caves' entrance is the **Legnabrocky Trail**, which runs through rugged limestone scenery and peatland to the shale-covered slopes of

Cuilcagh Mountain. This forms part of an environmental conservation area and offers a strenuous six- or seven-hour walk to the mountain's summit and back (be prepared to turn back if the weather turns sour). A part of the Marble Arch Caves centre is now devoted to an exhibition describing the restoration of the mountain park's damaged peatland and bogland habitats.

Travel details

Buses

All **Ulsterbus** unless stated otherwise.

The **Sperrin Rambler** runs twice daily from Omagh throughout the year (Mon–Sat 10.05am & 1.45pm) via Gortin and Plumbridge through the Sperrins to Cranagh and on to Draperstown and Magherafelt in Co. Derry (the return service operates Mon–Sat 10.10am & 1.45pm from Magherafelt).

An Creagán Centre to: Omagh (Mon–Fri 3 daily; 40min).

Clogher to: Omagh (Mon–Fri 2 daily; 45min).

Enniskillen to: Ballyshannon (*Bus Éireann*; 5–7 daily; 45min); Belcoo (Mon–Fri 7–8 daily, Sat 3, Sun 1; 25min); Belfast (Mon–Fri 17 daily, Sat 8, Sun 4; 2hr 15min); Belleek (*Bus Éireann*; 5–7 daily; 35min); Belturbet (Mon–Sat daily 3–4; 50min–1hr); Blacklion (*Bus Éireann*; Mon–Sat 4 daily, Sun 2; 25min); Cavan (*Bus Éireann*; 4–5 daily; 1hr 10min); Clones (Mon–Sat 3 daily, Sun 1; 55min); Derrygonnelly (Mon–Fri 6 daily, Sat 3; 25min); Donegal town (*Bus Éireann*; 7 daily; 1hr 10min); Dublin (*Bus Éireann*; 4–6 daily; 2hr 35min–3hr); Florence Court (Mon–Sat 2–4 daily; 15min); Lisnarick (Mon–Sat 4–5 daily; 20–35min); Lisnaskea (Mon–Fri 4–6 daily, Sat 3, Sun 1; 30min); Monaghan (Mon–Sat 2 daily; 1hr 20min); Omagh (Mon–Fri 7 daily, Sat 3, Sun 1; 1hr); Pettigo (Mon–Sat 4 daily; 40min–1hr); Sligo (*Bus Éireann*; Mon–Sat 4 daily, Sun 2; 1hr 25min).

Gortin to: Omagh (Mon–Fri 9 daily, Sat 2; 30min).

Omagh to: An Creagán Centre (Mon–Fri 3 daily; 40min); Belfast (Mon–Fri 16 daily, Sat 11, Sun 5; 1hr 50min); Clogher (Mon–Fri 2 daily; 35–45min); Derry (Mon–Fri 13 daily, Sat 10, Sun 5; 1hr 10min); Dublin (*Bus Éireann*; 9–10 daily; 3hr); Enniskillen (Mon–Fri 7 daily, Sat 3, Sun 1; 1hr); Gortin (Mon–Fri 9 daily, Sat 2; 30min); Letterkenny (*Bus Éireann*; 8–9 daily; 1hr 5min); Monaghan (*Bus Éireann*; 9–10 daily; 45min); Ulster American Folk Park (Mon–Fri 5 daily, Sat 3, Sun 1; 15min).

Ulster American Folk Park to: Omagh (Mon–Fri 6 daily, Sat 1; 15min).

Contexts

Contexts

History

Ireland's history is as rich and colourful as that of any European nation and comprehending its troubled past is vital to an understanding of its current situation. Though the following pages can merely summarize key events, our book list (see pp.735–737) provides sources of further enlightenment.

Prehistory

Originally connected to mainland Europe, and at times completely glaciated, Ireland's geographical form has over the last two million years been as a result of global climate change. The end of the last major **Ice Age** saw sea levels rise and the gradual separation of both Britain and Ireland from the European landmass, leaving just a few connections between the two regions. The first plant-life is reckoned to have appeared around 12,000 BC, and the first mammals, such as reindeer, arrived a millennium or so later. A subsequent period of glaciation resulted in their extinction in Ireland, though warming again occurred around 9000 BC, at which point the country began its long process of forestation and various animals crossed the last remaining land-bridges.

The **first human settlements** are thought to date from around 8000–7000 BC, from evidence of archeological findings. These Mesolithic hunter-gatherers, who made various implements and artefacts from flint, lived largely around coastal areas, such as Belfast Lough and the Shannon estuary. Developments elsewhere were slow to reach Ireland and it was not until the **Neolithic** period, around 3500 BC, that people skilled in farming settled here – equipped with stone axes (numerous examples of which have been found across the country), they were capable of clearing forests for their crops and animals. These people subscribed to ritual and magic, notably in their burial ceremonies, and left numerous megalithic monuments across Ireland, including graves and stone circles (see p.11) similar to those found throughout the coastal areas of Western Europe, indicating their place in a much broader culture. Archeological discoveries reveal the increasing subtlety of the products of this culture, first in the form of pottery and later, after the arrival of the technique of casting bronze around 2000 BC, jewellery.

The Iron Age

Ireland is usually considered a Celtic country, one colonized by the Indo-European people who spread rapidly across continental Europe from the East from around 1000 BC onwards. However, while they certainly reached the French coast recent evidence suggests that far from being Celtic themselves, the peoples of Britain and Ireland gradually became Celticized through contact with traders. As a result iron reached Ireland around 700 BC and, over the course of the next few centuries, Ireland's inhabitants adopted the Celtic ritual-based culture and language, though this would diversify significantly over the next millennium.

Other innovations followed, including the development of stone-built ring forts, a response to the need for protection brought about by Celtic ideas regarding land ownership and fealty, which increasingly produced intertribal warfare. A hierarchical system was gradually established, with individual **kingdoms** forming parts of larger fiefdoms based on the five provinces of Connacht, Leinster, Meath, Munster and Ulster. These fiefdoms in turn supposedly paid homage to a High King (*Ard Rí*) based at Tara, though in fact no such regal figure really gained sway over the whole of Ireland until Brian Boru (see below). However, like its Norse contemporary, this was also a myth-making culture, based on the cult of the hero. One of these, Cúchulainn, features in the Irish epic nonpareil, the *Táin Bó Cúailnge*, a bloodthirsty tale of war and revenge whose characters are ever prey to the whims of their gods.

Early Christianity

If the myths are to be believed, then Ireland embraced **Christianity** with remarkable rapidity thanks to the efforts of its patron saint, **St Patrick** (who also eradicated the snakes that had never inhabited the island). Truth be told, the process was far more gradual and never entirely included the abandonment of Celtic pagan beliefs, as proven by the presence of Sheila-na-Gigs (see p.748) in medieval church-building. Missionaries began to arrive from the fourth century AD onwards, though the establishment of monastic settlements did not really begin for another two hundred years. By the eighth and ninth centuries monasteries such as Clonmacnois in County Offaly and Lismore in County Waterford had risen to become major seats of learning in an increasingly church-focused Europe. Extant evidence of such prowess exists in the form of **illuminated manuscripts**, such as the *Book of Durrow* and the renowned *Book of Kells*, on show in the Library of Trinity College, Dublin. At this time, using well-established trading routes, the Irish also began to send forth their own missionaries, including **St Columban**, who founded various monasteries in mainland Europe before his death in 615.

The Vikings and the Normans

The **Vikings** reached Ireland towards the end of the eighth century and conducted sporadic raids on coastal areas, usually on monasteries – the defensive round-tower dates from this period – before embarking on a more coordinated assault in 914. The upshot was the formation of fortified settlements at places such as Dublin, Cork and Waterford, though one hundred years later the Norsemen were vanquished at the Battle of Clontarf by the *Ard Rí*, Brian Boru.

Though one branch of the Norsemen, in the shape of the **Normans**, finally conquered England in 1066, it was more than a century before a successful Anglo-Norman incursion was made into Ireland, when Irish infighting resulted in Dermot MacMurrough, the dethroned king of Leinster, seeking the support of Henry II to regain his throne. The English king agreed to allow one of his knights, Richard FitzGilbert de Clare ("Strongbow"), to take a contingent of troops across the Irish Sea, but soon became concerned by the extent of Strongbow's success and arrived shortly afterwards to claim sovereignty over Ireland and establish a court in Dublin.

However, Norman rule over Ireland was largely restricted to the former Viking townships and attempts to introduce feudalism foundered against the resistance of the Irish chieftains. In reality, the process of assimilation, which saw many of the victors becoming "more Irish than the Irish", resulted in the conquest becoming limited to a small area surrounding Dublin. This became known as the "English Pale" (from the word for an enclosure), and those who lived beyond its bounds were demeaningly described as "beyond the pale", a term which subsequently became synonymous with barbarism.

Attempts to coerce the Irish into submission by force were abandoned and those Norman settlers who had established themselves gradually became integrated into a society, now usually described as Gaelic, founded on the domains of Irish chieftains. The upshot was a flowering of Gaelic culture, with its emphasis on the place of the bard (a combination of court musician and poet) in storytelling and music-making. However, this did not prevent certain Anglo-Norman dynasties from broadening their own power bases, not least the de Burgo family in Ulster and Connacht, and the Fitzgeralds of Kildare.

Tudor and Stuart incursions

The succeeding centuries saw various English interlopers attempting to establish themselves in Ireland, but it was not until **Henry VIII** broke with Rome that a concerted effort to demolish the hegemony of the Irish overlords began, linked to the dissolution of the powerful Irish monasteries with their wealth up for the grabs of any supporter of the Tudor regime. An abortive insurrection in 1534 offered Henry the excuse to send troops to Ireland, quash the revolt and establish himself as both sovereign ruler and ecclesiastical head of his domain.

His daughter **Elizabeth I** continued the process, but adopted much more stringent and far-reaching tactics, geared towards undermining Gaelic authority and its allegiance to Catholicism while simultaneously reinforcing Ireland's position as an English colony. Taking up her elder sister Mary's policy of **plantation**, during whose reign parts of Laois and Offaly had been sequestered from their Irish owners, Elizabeth unsuccessfully attempted to "plant" colonists from Scotland in the area around Belfast Lough during the 1570s.

The threat of further infiltration provoked Irish offensive reaction, of which the most crucial was the revolt led by **Hugh O'Neill** of Ulster. This Irish chieftain had been deliberately targeted by the Tudors as a potential convert to the Protestant plantation process, but, realizing he had been duped, he took up arms against the Crown. At first successful, his armies were crucially defeated at Kinsale in 1601 and, finally forced into submission by a siege at Mellifont in County Louth in 1603, he signed a treaty granting all his land and that of his underlords to the English, which was leased back to them under an oath of fealty. This opened the door for a flood of "planters", mainly ex-soldiers from England and the Scottish Lowlands who were encouraged to establish themselves in the newly gained territories. Though the Irish chiefs were still ostensibly in control of their land, their power was utterly diminished and a significant number decided to leave their country en masse in 1607, embarking from Rathmullen, County Donegal, in what was later described as the **Flight of the Earls**. The power of the old Gaelic kingships was at an end, and the plantation broadened its scale as **James I** urged more Lowland Scots to cross over to Ulster and take over the Earls' impounded lands. This established a significant division between the Protestant planters and the evicted Catholic Irish, the ramifications of which endure to this day.

The 1641 Rebellion and Oliver Cromwell

Concerns about the apparently pro-Catholic religious policies of James I's successor, **Charles I**, resulted in a Scottish rebellion in 1640. Having failed to persuade Parliament to vote for taxes to raise new troops to quell the Scots, he negotiated a deal with Irish Catholics whereby Irish troops would be provided to suppress the rising in return for concessions regarding land ownership and religious tolerance. Alarmed that the king might be about to impose Catholicism on his entire domain, a Scottish–Parliamentarian alliance proposed invading Ireland to subdue the population. A small group of Irish landowners planned their own rebellion in turn, conspiring to take Dublin Castle, Derry and other northern towns on October 23, 1641. The assault on Dublin was foiled by an informer, but Phelim O'Neill's Ulster campaign was initially successful, despite the loss of more than four thousand Protestants in the fighting and a further eight thousand who died in the harsh winter conditions after being expelled from their homes. Charles himself sent an army to put down the rising (and the Scots sent their own to protect Ulster Protestants), but the outbreak of the English Civil War delayed the resolution of the Irish question.

An Irish alliance called the **Catholic Confederation** was created to coordinate attacks on English and Scottish troops in Ireland, though **Oliver Cromwell**'s victory in the Civil War saw the overthrow of the monarchy and a determination to conquer all of Ireland. Cromwell arrived in Dublin with a large contingent of his New Model Army in August 1649 and embarked on a merciless and bitterly fought crusade to establish his authority. His prime targets were those towns occupied by Royalist garrisons, first taking Drogheda, where he massacred the troops and numerous citizens, before sweeping down through the southeast of Ireland and on to Cork and Kinsale. By 1652 all of Ireland was under Cromwell's control, his bloodthirsty troops slaughtering a quarter of the Catholic population in the process and dispatching many others into slavery in the Caribbean. The subsequent **Act of Settlement** saw widespread sequestration of Catholic-held land and all the evictees were instructed to move west of the Shannon River by the beginning of May 1654 or face death – in Cromwell's cold terms, "to Hell or to Connacht". Many more died on the journey to places such as Connemara and the boglands of Mayo, while Cromwell's troops were rewarded with their confiscated land. Unsurprisingly, Cromwell's name remains reviled across much of Ireland.

The Williamite War and the penal laws

Though the monarchy was restored in 1660, Charles II remained in thrall to his Protestant Parliament and it was not until he was succeeded by his brother, the

Catholic **James II** in 1685, that Irish hopes were revitalized. However, anti-Catholic concerns, particularly about James's close relationship with Louis XIV of France, resulted in the English Parliament's offer of the throne to the Dutch **Prince William of Orange**. James took flight to Ireland and enlisted an army to try and overthrow what had become known as the "Glorious Revolution". Though initially successful, the city of **Derry** presented a major stumbling block (see p.604), allowing William's forces the time to arrive in Ireland. James was finally defeated at Limerick, though the most celebrated encounter in William's campaign took place earlier, on July 12, 1690, when he was victor at the **Battle of the Boyne**, an event commemorated as the highpoint of the Loyalist marching season.

Subsequently, under William, the English Parliament consolidated the legal process (begun under Charles II) of furthering control over Ireland by diminishing the rights of the native Catholic population in terms of land ownership, marriage, religion and enfranchisement. A series of Acts passed between 1695 and 1728, which later became known as the **penal laws**, effectively aimed at safeguarding the Protestant planters while suppressing Irish Catholic identity and culture and dragging the population into penury. Catholics were barred from purchasing land and on a landowner's death his property was split equally between all of his sons, thus incrementally diminishing familial wealth by each generation (an essential factor in the Great Famine of the nineteenth century – see p.697), though any son who converted to Protestantism became entitled to his brothers' inheritance. Catholic priests were banned from practising unless they paid two £50 bonds for registration, and even then were not allowed to say Mass; alternatively, conversion to the Church of Ireland attracted a £20 stipend, levied on their former congregations. Targeting cultural transmission, Catholics were barred from teaching, though some operated surreptitious "hedge schools" in the countryside, using the Irish language as a medium. Despite these exigencies, native Irish culture somehow managed to survive.

Revolution and rebellion

Towards the end of the eighteenth century revolution was in the air throughout much of bourgeois Europe. Its initial catalyst was the **American War of Independence**, which saw British troops diverted from Ireland to be sent across the Atlantic. The series of laws establishing the primacy of the Anglican Church had not only affected Irish Catholics, but Presbyterian Ulster planters, too, and many had emigrated to the Americas (see p.674), bringing about some sympathy among Ireland's burgeoning Protestant mercantile class for Washington's campaign demand of "no taxation without representation". Though not directly taxed by the English Parliament, Ireland was the subject of numerous trade levies and the American war led **Henry Grattan**, leader of the Patriot Party, not only to make increasing demands for proper representation at Westminster and some form of constitutional independence, but to recruit troops to replace the departing English militia in order to defend Ireland against the threat of a French invasion.

More crucially, segments of the Irish middle-class saw the **French Revolution** of 1789, with its underlying concepts of liberty, equality and fraternity, reinforced by the publication of Thomas Paine's *Rights of Man* (1792), and the consequent possibility of an invasion from France, as the potential means of securing independence. Formed by Belfast Protestants in 1791, the **Society of United**

Irishmen promulgated Nationalist views regarding democratic reform and Catholic emancipation never likely to be taken up by the Grattan Parliament. After the English declaration of war against France in 1793, the Society was forced underground, and adopted agitational policies geared towards severing the link with Britain, linking up with militant Catholic agrarian groups in the process. France became seen as a means of breaking the connection with England and one of the Society's leaders, Theobald **Wolfe Tone**, a Protestant barrister from Dublin, was dispatched there to secure French support for an insurrection. Recognizing the possibility of gaining victory over England via the back door, a French army set sail to invade Ireland, but was prevented from landing in Bantry Bay in 1796 by bad weather and indecisiveness (see p.321).

Plans revised, the **Rebellion** finally took place in 1798 (see p.249), but was brutally resisted by English troops, who had been tipped off by informers and were supported, especially in the North, by Protestant yeomanry (many of whom belonged to the Orange Society, established in 1795 to resist Catholic Emancipation, which was later to become the Orange Order – see box, p.659). The French, under General Humbert, finally landed at Killala, County Mayo, in late August, by which time much of the uprising had been quelled. Drawing local support they proceeded to march towards Dublin, until defeated at the Battle of Ballinamuck in County Longford. Subsequently, a larger Gallic force, with Tone on board, attempted to land in County Donegal, but was intercepted by the British navy. Tone was taken to Dublin and sentenced to death, but slit his own throat before the execution.

As a result the British government enacted the 1801 **Act of Union**, dissolving the Dublin parliament and ensuring total legislative control over Ireland, which now became part of the United Kingdom. However, this decree did not deter one further Irish revolutionary, **Robert Emmet**, whose wholly ill-planned attempted coup failed ignominiously in 1803.

Catholic Emancipation

The cause of Catholic enfranchisement became the major focus for agitation. At its forefront was the lawyer **Daniel O'Connell**, who founded the Catholic Association in 1823 to build on successful British popular campaigns to expand the franchise beyond its previously limited bounds, and was returned to the British Parliament as the Member for Clare in 1828. Though legislation prevented him from taking up his seat, his victory played no small part in the subsequent passage of the Catholic Emancipation Act, which, though it only enfranchised a tiny number of middle-class voters, had enormous repercussions in making Catholics eligible for a number of public offices from which they had been previously excluded.

O'Connell was elected as Dublin's first Catholic Lord Mayor in 1841 and subsequently embarked on a campaign to repeal the Union with Britain. Adopting populist techniques acquired from the Chartists, he called a series of "**monster meetings**" throughout all of Ireland except Ulster, attended on each occasion by as many as 100,000 people. Alarmed, the British government declared his October 1843 assembly at Clontarf illegal and jailed O'Connell for sedition. More radical supporters of independence, the Young Ireland Movement, grouped around *The Nation* newspaper, attempted their own uprising in 1848, but such was its lack of support that it became known as "The Battle of Widow McCormack's Cabbage Patch".

▲ Statue of Daniel O'Connell, Dublin

The Great Famine and the diaspora

The **Great Famine** of 1845 to 1851, during which Ireland's population declined by 1.5 million – almost twenty percent – was one of the most devastating tragedies in human history. In the early 1840s a potato blight spread across Western Europe, and, while resolved reasonably well elsewhere, struck at the core of an Irish peasantry excessively dependent on the yields of their potato crops. Britain conducted a laissez-faire economic policy when starvation began to strike and continued to export from Ireland other agricultural products, which might have alleviated the situation, throughout the Famine years. By the worst year of the Famine, **Black '47**, hundreds of thousands of people faced starvation, a situation exacerbated by mass evictions in many parts of the country when landlords removed tenants unable to pay their dues. Workhouses became crammed to overcapacity and, while some people were fed by soup kitchens or received support from individual landlords, the majority faced either death or emigration.

Though Dublin, Belfast and much of the Ulster province remained relatively unscathed, at least a million people died during the Great Hunger and hundreds of thousands migrated to Britain or risked their lives by taking passage on one of the infamous "coffin ships" to North America and Australasia, many of which, often crammed beyond capacity, were not fit to sail and floundered en route.

Even when the blight was finally quelled, a pattern had been set, with **emigration** becoming regarded as the only means of escaping incipient poverty. Sixty years after the Famine, Ireland's population had sunk to just over half its 1841 level of 8.2 million, and further waves of emigration occurred during the twentieth century. This diaspora established massive Irish communities in other countries, not least in the USA, where Irish-Americans played a major role in supporting moves towards independence and remain to this day a powerful lobbying group. An early sign of such backing was the aid provided to the Nationalist organization the **Irish Republican Brotherhood** (sometimes termed Fenians) whose abortive uprising of 1867 incurred a massive backlash, though it failed to destroy the organization.

Nationalist action had been fuelled by British policy during the Famine years. Agrarian groups focused particularly on **absentee English landlords** and those who continued to evict tenants unable to pay their rent – one of the most notorious wide-scale evictions took place at Derryveagh in Donegal (see p.530).

The Home Rule Movement

Over the remaining decades of the nineteenth century the struggles over land and tenants' rights retained pivotal importance and were given added impetus with Michael Davitt's formation of the **Land League** in 1879. Its aims, however, became increasingly linked to a concerted campaign to secure independence via parliamentary democracy. The movement's guiding light was **Charles Stewart Parnell** (1846–91), who stood successfully for the **Home Rule Party** in the County Meath election of 1875 and became the party's leader two years afterwards. Parnell gained huge popularity in Ireland not only for his support of the ideal of an Irish Parliament, but also for his use of obstructive tactics in the House of Commons and his full-blooded backing for agrarian action against recalcitrant landlords and their employees, using the tactic of social excommunication. One of the first victims, in 1880, of this device was a Mayo estate factor, Captain Charles Boycott – the action introduced his eponym into the English language.

William Gladstone's government put Parnell, Davitt and other leaders of the Land League on trial for seditious conspiracy in 1881 and, though the jury failed to agree a verdict, Davitt was shortly afterwards re-arrested for breaching his "ticket of leave". A new Land Act, based on the principles of fair rent, fixed tenure and freedom of sale became law later that year, but was rejected by the Land League which embarked on a new campaign of violence against landowners and thus was declared illegal. On the very day of Davitt's release from prison the following year, the British viceroy Lord Frederick Cavendish and his Under Secretary T.H. Burke were assassinated in Phoenix Park by a Fenian group calling itself "The Invincibles". Parnell denounced the murder in the Commons, but attitudes hardened against the Irish.

Though Gladstone had been persuaded by Parnell's arguments, his first Home Rule Bill failed in 1886 (a fate shared by its successor in 1893), while Parnell's political career was terminated when his long-term affair with Kitty O'Shea saw him named as co-respondent in a divorce trial launched by her husband.

Towards identity

From the late nineteenth century onwards Nationalist ideas became increasingly intertwined with the concept of cultural revival, with two new organizations formed that had a profound effect on opinion. Founded in 1884, the fundamental aim of the **Gaelic Athletic Association** was to preserve and nurture Irish pastimes such as Gaelic football and hurling. Avowedly Nationalist, its members were banned from playing foreign games and Crown forces were excluded from membership. The **Gaelic League** was formed nine years later. While its initial aim was the preservation and maintenance of the Irish language and native culture, it too became increasingly nationalistic, viewing its goals as central to the "de-Anglicization" of Ireland. At the same time, a group of writers, centred on W.B. Yeats and Lady Gregory, set about establishing a **cultural revival**, based on the creation of distinctly Irish works written in English.

Almost simultaneously, and in response to Parnell's failure to achieve Home Rule via parliamentary means, a current of opinion developed, promulgated by a Dublin printer, **Arthur Griffith**, in his newspaper *The United Irishman* (established 1898). Initially, this espoused self-determination, involving the withdrawal of Irish MPs from Westminster and the establishment of an independent Irish parliament in Dublin as the only means to achieve economic and political freedom. Supporters of this view coalesced to form the political party **Sinn Féin** in 1905, an organization increasingly influenced by the views expounded by **James Connolly**'s Irish Socialist Republican Party, which sought to establish a workers' republic in Ireland. A significant further factor was the rise of the trade-union movement in Ireland, especially the role of the militant workers' leader **James Larkin**, who established the Irish Transport and General Workers' Union in 1909. Its philosophy was encapsulated in Larkin's slogan, "The land of Ireland for the people of Ireland".

Resistance and revolt

The General Election of 1910 resulted in the slimmest of majorities for Asquith's Liberal Party, leaving it utterly reliant on the Irish Nationalist Party to enact legislation. Seizing the moment, the Nationalists pressed for a new Home Rule Bill, which the Commons passed in 1912. This aroused a bitterly intransigent response from Northern Protestants who united under the direction of **Sir Edward Carson**, a Dublin barrister, Tory MP and leader of the Irish Unionists. In September 1911 he and James Craig initiated a campaign to resist Home Rule and any threat of the imposition of Catholicism on Protestant Ulster. More than 200,000 signed up to a covenant pledging to defeat Home

▲ Éamon de Valera

Rule by "all means necessary". In readiness for such action, Protestants formed their own militia, the **Ulster Volunteers**, which was armed by munitions from Germany – indeed Carson went so far as to lunch with the Kaiser in 1913 to discuss German aid for the resistance strategy.

Unsurprisingly, Nationalists and the British responded vigorously. The former founded its own armed force, the **Irish Volunteers**, the second Nationalist militia to form after James Connolly's Irish Citizen Army. The British responded by banning the use of armed weapons in Ireland and went so far as to plan a raid on the Ulster Volunteers, though this was abandoned when troops stationed in Ulster refused to take action against the militia. Lloyd George devised a compromise whereby the province of Ulster would be excluded from the introduction of Home Rule for six years, but the whole issue was deferred when war broke out between Britain and Germany late in the summer of 1914.

While Carson and the Irish Nationalist leader **John Redmond** pledged the support of both the Ulster and Irish Volunteers in guarding Ireland from German invasion (and, indeed, more than 230,000 Irishmen enlisted in the British Army), others saw the war as a fruitful opportunity ripe for the picking. In particular, leaders of the Irish Republican Brotherhood (IRB) made preparations for a rising, using the strength of the Irish Volunteers, to be enacted if the Germans entered Ireland or if the British tried to implement conscription. When army and police embarked on a series of raids against Irish Nationalist and revolutionary newspapers in late 1914, plans were made for a rising in September 1915, but were deferred when the Volunteers' leaders declared themselves unready. The IRB sent an envoy to Germany, the former British diplomat **Sir Roger Casement**, who successfully secured German support for the rising.

When it finally occurred on Monday, April 24, 1916, the **Easter Rising** (as it became known – see p.107) was a drastically limited affair. The British had already captured the German ship bringing arms and arrested Casement when he landed from a German submarine in Cork four days earlier. Tipped off by informers, the British had also made plans to arrest all the leaders of the various organizations involved on that Easter Monday (though such action was then largely deferred until the rebels' surrender), and the leader of the Irish Volunteers, Eoin MacNeill, ordered his men not to take part in the rebellion. In the regions, action was limited to the north of County Dublin, Enniscorthy in Wexford and parts of County Galway, while the focus for the rebels' action became the Dublin General Post Office with simultaneous assaults on key targets across the city. Pearse delivered the **Proclamation of the Irish Republic** from the steps of the GPO, but the rebels were powerless to resist the heavy British bombardment that ensued. After five days of fighting the leaders surrendered, though it was two more days before combat ended. Over the course of the week, more than 1350 people were killed or wounded and numerous buildings in central Dublin destroyed.

Dubliners were initially aghast at their city's devastation, and public anger turned to outcry when all of the rising's leaders and numerous other insurgents, with the exception of **Éamon de Valera** who had US citizenship, were executed by the British after a secret court martial. Connolly himself was so ill from infected wounds that he wouldn't have survived long enough for the planned execution and was shot while tied to a chair. As a result of the resulting public revulsion, all other death sentences were commuted with the exception of Casement, who was hanged in London in August.

The War for Independence

Far from losing support, as the British had hoped, the rebels' ideals were embraced by the next wave of leaders. Key figures were **Michael Collins**, working within the Irish Volunteers, and de Valera, who was elected MP for East Clare in 1916. The Volunteers grew in strength and Sinn Féin achieved a crushing success in the 1918 General Election, though none of its elected members took their seats, instead convening as the Dáil Éireann ("Ireland's parliament") and issuing a declaration of independence. With de Valera as its leader and Collins as Minister of Finance, the Dáil reorganized the Volunteers and Citizen Army under the new name of the **Irish Republican Army (IRA)**. The British poured troops into Ireland and war effectively began in

September 1919, when a soldier was killed in Fermoy, County Cork, and the British subsequently sacked the town.

In consequence, a campaign of guerrilla warfare broke out across most of Ireland which the Royal Irish Constabulary proved powerless to restrain. Irish sentiment was much heightened by the arrival of the **Black and Tans**, British soldiers re-recruited after World War I (and so called because of the colour of their uniforms), whose reprisals were merciless. However, even they were unable to prevent the situation of virtual stalemate, which dragged on until a truce was called in July 1921.

Meanwhile, in 1920 Westminster passed the **Government of Ireland Act**, establishing separate new parliaments for the six counties of "Northern Ireland" and the residual 26 of "Southern Ireland". Elections the following year resulted in a simple reinforcement of the Nationalist majority in the latter, which promptly reconstituted itself as Dáil Éireann, led by de Valera, and demanded independence as a 32-county state. Since Ulster's Protestants clearly held sway in the North and the armed independent struggle had reached deadlock, de Valera sent a delegation to London to negotiate an agreement with Lloyd George (thus absolving himself of any role in the process). In the face of the British prime minister's intransigence regarding the Unionist stand-off, the representatives, who included Michael Collins, agreed to the partition of Ireland as defined by the 1920 legislation, with the South gaining independence as the Irish Free State but retaining allegiance to the Crown through membership of the Commonwealth.

The Irish Civil War

A provisional government was established in the South shortly after the signing of the **Anglo-Irish Treaty** in December 1921, which granted independence at the cost of partition. However, while Collins had signed the treaty on the basis that it was a major leap towards independence and a halfway step towards gaining control of all 32 counties, de Valera rejected the proposals as a diminution of Republicanism and refused to truck with their enactment. By July 1922, pro- and anti-Treaty forces had become embroiled in a bitter **civil war** which would have a lasting impact on Ireland's politics and economy. Though most of the population of the 26 counties supported the "Free Staters", opinion was seriously divided owing to the scale of the fighting and the reprisals taken by the provisional government, not least the execution of the prominent Republican Erkine Childers (who had run guns into the country in 1914 and been arrested for possessing a revolver given him by Collins), and the counter-reprisals that ensued. Eventually, the much weaker Republican forces were restricted to control of parts of the southwest and west and were forced to surrender in May 1923. Collins himself died in an ambush in Cork.

The Free State

Since one of the main candidates, Arthur Griffith, had also died (of a brain haemorrhage) during the civil war, leadership of the new government passed on to **William T. Cosgrave**, whose regime set about establishing a new infrastructure for the country's development, including the formation of a civil service and police force. Republicans boycotted the Dáil until 1926 when de Valera formed a new political party, **Fianna Fáil**, drawing members largely from the anti-Treaty element within Sinn Féin. Cosgrave remained in power until 1932, overseeing the initiation of the Shannon hydroelectric scheme and the foundation of the Electricity Supply Board, but his Cumann na nGaedheal party lost the election that year to Fianna Fáil ushering in de Valera's subsequent sixteen-year reign as Taoiseach. Cumann na nGaedheal itself merged with the National Centre Party and the right-wing Army Comrades Association (known as the "Blueshirts") the following year to form **Fine Gael**.

Throughout this period, the economic situation remained austere, exacerbated first by the Depression after 1929 and then by high British trade-levies on imports from Ireland, a result of de Valera's refusal to repay land annuities to Britain, which forced the government into frugality and self-sufficiency. These stern policies were reflected in Ireland's social and cultural life, and ties with the Catholic Church were reinforced at the time. However, de Valera's government also saw the establishment of state boards for road, rail and air transport (Aer Lingus) and peat production.

De Valera's determination to sever links with Britain resulted in a new **constitution** in 1938 whose central premise was the renunciation of Crown sovereignty and a new system of government for the state henceforth known as **Éire**. The model adopted was bicameral with the Dáil retained, but a new upper chamber, the Seanad (or Senate), added, and the role of president (Uachtarán) created – the first holder of the office was the Protestant Douglas Hyde (see p.498).

Northern Ireland's first decades

Following the enactment of the Anglo-Irish Treaty, Northern Ireland's newfound status as a largely self-governing entity had begun in June 1921 with the establishment of its parliament under James Craig, whose **Ulster Unionist Party (UUP)** would run the statelet until 1972. Rather than including all nine counties of the Ulster province, leaders of the majority Protestant community had negotiated a settlement for their separation from the Free State on the basis of just six, thus ensuring the retention of a secure mandate which might have been threatened by the inclusion of the largely Catholic counties of Donegal and Cavan. Though a significant and gradually increasing Catholic minority remained, it was largely concentrated on agricultural areas west of the River Bann, plus the city of Derry, while the economically thriving linen and shipbuilding industries east of the river remained almost entirely in Protestant hands.

Britain needed Belfast's industrial strength as much as the UUP wanted Britain's economic and financial support and Unionists quickly set about reinforcing their domination. As well as establishing a largely Protestant police force, the **Royal Ulster Constabulary (RUC)**, and a military adjunct, the B Specials, the new parliament (originally based in Belfast, but moved to Stormont in 1932) strengthened its position by favouring the Protestant population with economic support, housing allocations and gerrymandering (for decades, Derry's electoral boundaries were changed to ensure a Protestant council despite the city's two-thirds Catholic majority, for example).

World War II

As part of the United Kingdom, Northern Ireland was heavily involved in the war effort, particularly Belfast, whose shipyards proved a major target for German bombing raids. In contrast, Éire adopted a position of neutrality throughout and negotiated its security with Germany, though it did make certain concessions to the UK regarding flights over its airspace. It also remained utterly dependent on imports from the UK and suffered drastically when British ships carrying goods such as coal and cattle feed were attacked by U-boats.

The post-war Republic

De Valera lost the 1948 election to a wide-ranging coalition of opposition parties, led by John A. Costello's Fine Gael, which set about the removal of any surviving legislative links with Britain by establishing Éire as the **Republic of Ireland** in 1949. However, the new Republic's economic position remained dire and the early 1950s were characterized by new waves of emigration, largely from rural areas either to Dublin or abroad. De Valera was returned as Taoiseach twice during the decade (in 1951 and 1957) but it was not until his long-serving deputy Seán Lemass took office in 1959 that the policies needed to boost Ireland's stagnant economy began to be enacted. Lemass directed Ireland away from protectionism and firmly towards free trade, drawing foreign investment in the process, and sowed the seeds for membership of the **European Economic Community** in January 1973 – though by this time Jack Lynch's government was fully embroiled in developments in the North (see below).

While the Republic, not least its farmers, initially prospered from EEC membership, the country suffered badly during the recession of the early 1980s, leading to a new wave of emigration. Its remaining population seemed to become increasingly conservative, rejecting referenda to allow abortion and divorce in 1983 and 1986 respectively.

The Troubles

By the 1980s Northern Ireland had been racked by violence for almost twenty years. Though its population had benefited hugely from the social policies begun by the post–World War II Labour government, not least in terms of health and social care, the Catholic population continued to suffer levels of social deprivation far worse than anywhere else in the UK. In 1967 the **Civil Rights Movement**, a nonsectarian coalition demanding equal rights, was formed, promoting its campaign via protest marches. One of these, through Derry in 1968, saw demonstrators attacked by a police baton charge and television pictures of the West Belfast MP Gerry Fitt with blood streaming down his face from a wound – transmitted around the world, these provoked international condemnation of the RUC's tactics. Severe rioting the following year following the Apprentice Boys' August parade led to the barricading of the Bogside area of Derry and Irish Taoiseach Jack Lynch's movement of Irish troops to the border to await developments.

British troops arrived shortly afterwards, ostensibly to keep the peace in Derry and Belfast, where Protestant assaults on West Belfast's Catholics had taken place. Though initially welcomed by Catholics, the army soon shifted its approach in line with the laissez-faire and often repressive tactics of the RUC. After years in the wilderness, and bolstered by new recruits, the IRA took up the gauntlet as defenders of the Catholic turf, though its own internal disputes led to the formation of the **Provisional IRA**, which broke away from the Dublin-led Official IRA and began a campaign of militant aggression against the army, RUC and Loyalists. As a result, the British introduced **internment without trial**, indiscriminately rounding up any Catholic thought to be linked to the violence. On January 30, 1972, British paratroopers shot and killed thirteen unarmed civil-rights demonstrators in Derry in an incident known ever afterwards as **Bloody Sunday**. Three days later the British Embassy was burnt down and shortly afterwards Westminster's direct rule was reinstated over Northern Ireland. On **Bloody Friday**, July 21, 1972, the IRA exploded twenty car bombs in Belfast's city centre, killing nine people and injuring 130.

The 1970s were marked by increasing violence and diplomatic attempts to produce a political solution. A first attempt at power-sharing, established by the 1973 **Sunningdale conference**, proved impossible to implement in the face of a massive campaign of disruption led by the **Reverend Ian Paisley** (see box, p.589) and the strike called by the Ulster Workers Council in May 1974, which paralyzed much of Northern Ireland. During the strike the UDA set off three car bombs in central Dublin, killing 33 people. The power-sharing executive was disbanded and direct rule reinstated once again, which continued until 1999.

Meanwhile, the IRA had transferred its bombing campaign to mainland Britain in an attempt to force the reunification of Ireland, and in 1974 set off massive **explosions** in pubs in Birmingham, Woolwich and Guildford, killing 28 people. It declared a ceasefire later that year – subsequently discovered to be a consequence of clandestine negotiations with the British Government – but the failure to secure a lasting agreement led to the resumption of the campaign the following year. In retaliation, Harold Wilson introduced the **Prevention of Terrorism Act**, allowing extended detention without charge. In two major trials, those found guilty of the Guildford and Birmingham bombings were sentenced to life imprisonment, but increasing concerns about the reliability of the forensic evidence and their confessions led to the release of the Guildford Four in 1989 and the Birmingham Six in 1991.

In the late 1970s IRA inmates at Long Kesh prison (also known as The Maze) began a series of protests against the abolition of the Special Category Status they had been granted, which gave them the right to be treated as political prisoners. This began as a "**blanket protest**" in which prisoners refused to wear prison clothes, instead opting to remain naked under a blanket draped over their shoulders, and later moved on to the infamous "**dirty protest**" where the inmates smeared their cell walls with excrement rather than emptying their chamber pots. Despite a 1978 European Court of Human Rights verdict finding the British Government guilty of "inhuman and degrading treatment", the British position remained intransigent, both under the outgoing Labour Government and even more so when a new regime under Conservative leader **Margaret Thatcher** was elected in 1979. The H-blocks of The Maze had become a hotbed for Republican education and action and, in the early 1980s, a new tactic was employed – the **hunger strike**. The first of these ended ignominiously in 1980, but the second, led by **Bobby Sands**, commander of the Provisional IRA within the prison, who was elected MP for Fermanagh and

South Tyrone in the course of the fast, had more effect. The hunger strike resulted in ten deaths, including Sands' own, but Thatcher remained obdurate despite worldwide condemnation of Britain's position.

However, her government did attempt another power-sharing initiative with the formation of the **Northern Ireland Assembly** in 1982, but this was shunned by both Nationalists and Republicans. Conversely, the **Anglo-Irish Agreement** of 1986, which strengthened the relationship between Britain and the Republic, was rejected by Unionists because of the increased consultative role given to Dublin in terms of Northern affairs.

The IRA notoriously bombed the Brighton hotel hosting the Tory party conference in 1984, almost killing Thatcher in the process. Parallel political developments saw a sea change in the form of the Republicans' tactical decision to employ the democratic process to assist their aims, encapsulated in Belfast Republican Danny Morrison's famous declaration to the Sinn Féin party's annual conference – "... will anyone here object if, with the ballot box in one hand and the Armalite in the other, we take power in Ireland?" Under the Sinn Féin banner, **Gerry Adams** became MP for West Belfast in June 1983 and was elected party president later that year, both positions he still held at the time of writing. In 1997 his colleague **Martin McGuinness** would also be elected to Westminster, and Sinn Féin would rise to become a significant force in the Republic's politics.

The rise and fall of the Celtic Tiger

The 1990s witnessed a remarkable resurgence in the Republic's economy, leading to the country's acquisition of the soubriquet **Celtic Tiger**. Ireland's emergence resulted from a combination of huge European Union subsidies (especially to farmers) and massive tax concessions to multinational companies, encouraging them to site operations in Dublin and elsewhere. For the first time in decades, Irish people actually returned home from abroad to seek work, reinvigorating an economy already bolstered by an increase in the number of graduates emerging from the country's universities. The most visible changes were apparent in the Dublin skyline, where new edifices seemed to emerge almost daily, and in the wave of "mansion" building reflecting the increasing affluence of Ireland's nouveau riche. Additionally, sparked partly by the redevelopment of Dublin's Temple Bar, the vigorous local music scene (epitomized by the worldwide success of the band U2) and the liberal tax concessions given to artists, writers and musicians, Ireland became for the first time a hip place to visit.

However, as it later emerged, the economy's growth was largely that of a boomtown built on silt, with vast wealth created for a relatively small number of investors in high-tech industries, but little legislation to tackle the social deprivation facing those way down the pecking order.

The election of **Mary Robinson** as Ireland's first woman president in 1991 heralded a more liberal outlook, but the decade remained coloured by the sweaty flesh of scandal. Taoiseach **Charles Haughey** was the first to go in 1992, his administration smeared by long-lasting and later substantiated allegations of corruption, and brought down by the revelation that journalists' private telephone calls had been tapped by the Republic's police. In 1994 his successor,

Albert Reynolds, was also forced to resign after revelations that his government had covered up allegations of paedophilia made against a Catholic priest.

Following a brief interlude of a Fine Gael coalition under **John Bruton**, the Republic has ever since been run by a series of Fianna Fáil–headed alliances with the tiny Progressive Democrat party. The Taoiseach since June 1997 has been **Bertie Ahern**, whose ministries have been dogged by further revelations of financial corruption involving key members of his party, resulting in the establishment of the **Flood Commission**'s long-standing investigations into innumerable transactions, as well as major enquiries into the operation of Ireland's police force, centred on various nefarious goings-on in County Donegal.

Ahern's government somehow stumbled on and, in 2007, secured a third consecutive general-election victory, though its hold on government was only maintained via an alliance with the Green Party. Many felt that Fianna Fáil had succeeded only by default, thanks to the hapless ineptitude of its erstwhile rival Fine Gael's election campaign. Despite electoral success, Ahern and Fianna Fáil remain deeply unpopular, and viewed as an administration which lacks any understanding of or commitment to Ireland's cultural heritage (especially through its determination to obliterate the Hill of Tara via a motorway development – see p.170), fails to counter the activities of criminal gangs in Dublin and Limerick, and still seems utterly in thrall to the agricultural and road haulage lobbies. In 2007 it proved incapable of preventing the airline Aer Lingus from uprooting its base from Shannon to Belfast, while its policies on health care, social welfare and the assimilation of migrant workers and refugees remain shambolic at best. Ahern also found himself caught up in the Mahon Tribunal's investigations into political corruption – a matter unresolved at the time of writing.

Towards the Good Friday Agreement and the Assembly

The IRA kept up its bombing campaign during the 1990s, beginning with a brazen mortar attack in February 1991 on a Cabinet meeting chaired by the new British leader, John Major. By now, however, the number of victims of Loyalist random attacks on Catholics had far outstripped those resulting from IRA activities. Undeterred, Major concluded an agreement with Albert Reynolds in December 1993, the **Downing Street Declaration**, largely shaped by the diplomacy of the SDLP's leader, **John Hume**, which sought to bring peace to Northern Ireland by democratic means.

The IRA launched another audacious mortar attack, this time on Heathrow Airport, in March 1994, but after focused lobbying by Dublin and US vice-president Al Gore, announced a ceasefire at the end of August, followed two months later by a similar Loyalist move. The following year witnessed intense negotiations involving the London and Dublin governments and the Republicans, which floundered in the face of the IRA's refusal to decommission its weaponry. Its bombing of Canary Wharf in London's financial centre in February 1996 re-emphasized its determination to continue the armed struggle, but lobbying for all-party talks on a resolution of the settlement intensified further. The key players were John Hume, who repeatedly met Gerry Adams with the intention of restoring the IRA's ceasefire, and the US president

Bill Clinton, whose involvement and support for change went way beyond any intention to ramify his Irish-American electoral support.

The most significant broker, however, became British prime minister **Tony Blair**, the Labour leader elected with a vast majority in 1997, alongside his Northern Ireland Secretary, **Mo Mowlam**. They targeted a solution by diplomatic discussions with Ahern's government and the securement of the commitment of the **David Trimble**-led Ulster Unionists and Gerry Adams to all-party talks on Northern Ireland's future. The IRA's resumption of a ceasefire in July 1997 eased the process, but continuing violence throughout the following months, including the assassination of the LVF leader, Billy Wright, inside The Maze, provided further stumbling blocks.

Blair's commitment to a democratic solution culminated on April 9, 1998. After anxious negotiations late into the night an accord was somehow agreed, and the **Good Friday Agreement** was signed the following morning. The Agreement committed its signatories "to partnership, equality and mutual respect as the basis of relationships within Northern Ireland" and reaffirmed the participants' dedication "to exclusively democratic and peaceful means of resolving differences on political issues".

More vitally, the agreement laid down the principle that any subsequent changes in the government of Northern Ireland – whether it remained part of the UK or opted to amalgamate with the Republic – relied entirely on the consent of the majority of both the Catholic and Protestant communities. An **Assembly** would be elected, based on proportional representation, with an executive of ministers drawn equally from both camps operating departments previously run by the British. Political prisoners would be rapidly released and an independent commission appointed to determine the future of Northern Ireland's policing.

The agreement was ratified by the North's population in May and elections in June 1998 saw the UUP's David Trimble returned as First Minister and the SDLP's **Séamus Mallon** as his deputy.

Impasse – and resolution

Almost as soon as the agreement was signed, however, the new administration, opposed by Ian Paisley's DUP and numerous other Loyalists, became embroiled in debate regarding the right of the Orange Order to march from a Presbyterian church in Drumcree, prior to celebrations of the Battle of the Boyne (see p.179), through Catholic areas of Portadown. Drumcree became a significant annual flashpoint over the next few years and the marching issue remains a significant element in the sectarian divide to this day, as riots following Orange Order parades in Belfast in 2005 clearly revealed.

It was not just Loyalist unrest that threatened to derail the peace process, though. A breakaway Republican grouping, the soi-disant **Real IRA**, soon perpetrated the most murderous act of the whole history of the Troubles. As part of a campaign of town-centre assaults, it exploded a car bomb in the centre of **Omagh**, County Tyrone, on Saturday August 15, 1998, killing 29 people and injuring hundreds more. In the face of uniform condemnation, the group declared a ceasefire two weeks later.

David Trimble and John Hume were jointly awarded the **1998 Nobel Peace Prize**, and politicians prepared for the opening of the Assembly in 1999, while paramilitaries maintained their ceasefires (with the exception of the small breakaway Continuity IRA, which had never declared one). However, while general optimism remained in place, the ramifications of the implementation of parts of the Good Friday Agreement soon became apparent, as the UUP became concerned at the reduction of army numbers and many of their security installations, including some notable Belfast landmarks, were demolished or removed. Their worries were exacerbated by the report of the **Patten Commission** into the future of the **Royal Ulster Constabulary**, which proposed the force's abolition and replacement by a new body – with a new name – whose members were to be recruited equally from Catholic and Loyalist communities. The loss of the words "Royal" and "Ulster" from the new organization's title were impossible for Unionists to accept, and the new secretary of state, **Peter Mandelson** (who had replaced Mo Mowlam), bowed to pressure by rejecting many of the Commission's findings, despite strong Nationalist and Republican protest. The new **Police Service of Northern Ireland** (**PSNI**), however, came into existence in November 2001, but has not recruited equally from the two communities. Indeed, Sinn Féin has refused to nominate members to its overseeing Police Board, though its position may be mellowing.

However, the two key issues, interrelated in the eyes of many Unionists, were the release of political prisoners and the **decommissioning of weaponry**. While the release of prisoners passed relatively smoothly, the operation of the Assembly was thoroughly bedevilled by the decommissioning issue from the day it opened for business on December 1, 1999, and over the next six years its powers were regularly suspended by a succession of different British Northern Ireland Secretaries – at the time of writing its reopening remains deferred. One key event happened on May 6, 2000, which even the most hardened participants in Northern Ireland's political rollercoaster ride would have found hard to predict. It came in the form of an unexpected **statement from the IRA's leadership** which, while not renouncing its avowed aim of securing a united Ireland, declared its continued commitment to the peace process. While this itself was of extreme significance, another part of the statement immediately changed the whole context of political debate in Northern Ireland by declaring that "the IRA leadership will initiate a process that will completely and verifiably put IRA arms beyond use". This would involve a number of its arms dumps being sealed and inspected by agreed third parties.

Neither the UUP nor the DUP, which despite its complete abhorrence of the Good Friday Agreement had taken its seats in the Assembly, would accept that the IRA really meant business, despite the reports of the arms inspectorate led by the Canadian General John de Chastelain. In response, Sinn Féin's leadership of Gerry Adams and Martin McGuinness argued that, as a political party, it had met all the conditions of the Good Friday Agreement and had no powers over decommissioning. Many now worried for the future of devolution, fearing that this apparent dead-end in the political process would see many IRA members defecting to the reactivated Real IRA (which indeed subsequently began a bombing campaign in London), based on the belief that the Adams–McGuinness strategy for political progress had been a mistake. If Gerry Adams could not persuade the IRA to decommission, they reasoned, then nobody could.

As the impasse continued, with no obvious external target, Loyalist paramilitaries became involved in a massive feud, largely concerned with control of criminal activities, particularly the drugs market. There were occasional violent incidents too, at flashpoints such as the interface areas of Belfast's Ardoyne and Short Strand districts, but the IRA's ceasefire remained firmly in position. However, in December 2004, Belfast's Northern Bank was the subject of the then biggest armed robbery in UK history when a gang got away with £26.5 million. Fingers were immediately pointed towards the IRA, but so far nobody has been charged with the burglary. In January 2005 a Catholic from the Short Strand, **Robert McCartney**, was murdered outside a bar in Belfast's Markets area, allegedly by IRA members, resulting in a huge cover-up and a well-publicized campaign by his bereaved sisters and partner to seek as yet unresolved justice. Later that year a senior Sinn Féin apparatchik who had originally been arrested as part of an alleged spy ring at Stormont admitted that he had long been paid to spy on the party itself by British Intelligence.

However, local and national **elections** in May 2005 witnessed a sea change in public opinion. The SDLP suffered badly at the hands of Sinn Féin, while the UUP was virtually wiped off the political map by the DUP, leading to Trimble's resignation as minister. The centre ground had now completely disappeared, leaving hardline Republicans and Loyalists as the arbiters of the peace process's continuation. In September 2005 the IRA announced that it was putting all of its weaponry beyond use, thus effectively declaring the end of its armed struggle for unification and against British rule (the UVF would follow suit in 2007).

Assembly elections in early 2007 ratified the DUP's and Sinn Féin's positions as the North's two leading parties. Subsequently, following the ending of a suspension which had begun in late 2005, Ian Paisley and Martin McGuinness took up their positions as, respectively, leader and deputy leader of the Assembly.

Traditional music

Ireland and music are as inseparable as fish and chips. Though the country has developed a thriving rock-music scene over the last forty years and artists such as U2, Sinéad O'Connor and Van Morrison have achieved massive international success, it's Ireland's traditional music that in many ways continues to hold centre stage.

While the musical traditions of other Western European countries were dissipated by the process of industrialization and political change, Ireland's indigenous music remained at the centre of its people's social life until well into the twentieth century, when its survival became threatened by emigration and governmental controls aimed at curbing dance forms regarded as immoral. It needed two major shots in the arm in the 1960s – the **folk song boom**, which originated in the USA, and the pioneering work of **Seán Ó Riada** in establishing ensemble playing as the new norm – to reinvigorate its existence.

Ireland's greatest musical ambassadors, **The Chieftains**, emerged from Ó Riada's initiative in the 1960s, and the following decade saw the formation of the country's two most influential groups, **Planxty** and **The Bothy Band**. Their performances and recordings effectively laid out the ground for others to tread, not least **De Dannan**, the Donegal-based **Altan**, and, in more recent times, **Lúnasa**, **Danú** and the US-based **Solas**.

However, the country's musical traditions remain essentially based on the age-old practice of passing down tunes and songs by oral transmission, from generation to generation and from friend to friend. Its core has become the **pub session**, where the richness of the musical tradition can be experienced at first hand, and the *craic* (or crack) – that idiosyncratically Irish, heady combination of drink-fuelled chat, banter and fun – simply takes over.

The tunes

Almost all of Ireland's traditional music tunes are based on imported **dance** forms. The only exceptions to this rule are slow airs which largely owe their origins to the song tradition (see p.715), a few special pieces belonging to the *uilleann* piping tradition (such as *The Fox Chase*, in which the instrument mimics the sound of fox, hunters and hounds), and a body of more than two hundred tunes composed by the blind itinerant harper **Turlough O'Carolan** (1680–1738), which carry some influence by Italian classical composers of that era.

There are several thousand reels, jigs (in various formats), hornpipes, barndances, strathspeys, waltzes and numerous other dance tunes, though many are only rarely played. At most sessions it is reels and jigs that predominate. Particular tune forms are favoured in different parts of the country – the polka for example is especially popular in Cork and Kerry. The authors of the vast majority of tunes are unknown, though some do bear their composer's name, such as *Martin Wynne's No. 1*, and many more are added to the canon each year in the form of new compositions. Apart from such eponymous works, tune titles should not be taken as anything more than a labelling device (and some have particularly arcane titles – witness *Wallop the Spot* or *The Cat That Kittled in Jamie's Wig*).

This depth of the tradition owes much to fears at certain times in Ireland's history that it was on the wane, spurring collectors to amass as much information

Instruments and players

We've included mention of some of the best instrumentalists on the Irish music scene in this roundup of traditional instruments. If you get the chance to see any of them at the festivals, don't miss it.

Uilleann pipes

The English folk singer Martin Carthy once aptly described seeing the renowned **Séamus Ennis** playing the *uilleann* pipes as like "watching a man wrestling an octopus". The world's most complex set of bagpipes (variously pronounced "illun" or "illyun") is an extraordinarily temperamental creature and notoriously hard to master. The instrument has several components, consisting of a nine-holed chanter capable of producing a double-octave range, powered by air squeezed from a bag positioned under the left arm, itself driven by bellows pressed against the player's torso by his or her right elbow. The pipes also come equipped with three drones and a set of three regulators that can be flipped on and off to provide chordal accompaniment. No other instrument in the Irish canon is as capable of replicating the vocal ornamentations of *sean-nós* singers via the playing of slow airs.

Since the late nineteenth century two distinct styles of playing have evolved: one more gentle and ornamentally delicate, exemplified by Séamus Ennis and **Leo Rowsome**; and the other (often termed "open" or "legato") much more intricate, crisp, showy and rhythmically driven, and associated with members of the Traveller community who earned a living playing at country fairs – key protagonists of this style were the late brothers **Johnny and Felix Doran**, and, more recently, **Davy Spillane**.

Pipers have long held a special place in Ireland's musical heritage and among today's virtuosos are **Liam O'Flynn**, famed for his solo recordings, work with the classical composer Shaun Davey and poet Seamus Heaney, and membership of Planxty. **Paddy Keenan**, memorably once described as "the Jimi Hendrix of the *uilleann* pipes", rose to fame via The Bothy Band and continues to produce performances of astonishing majesty. Other pipers of note include **Neillidh Mulligan**, perhaps the best exponent of slow airs, **Ronan Browne** of the band Cran, the Belfast-born **John McSherry** and the phenomenally talented young Dubliner **Seán McKeon**.

Flutes and whistles

The flute preferred by Irish musicians is the simple wooden version with fingers used to cover the holes rather than keys as in its classical cousin, though some players do employ semi-keyed instruments. The long-standing hotbed of Irish flute music is North Connacht, famed for its seeming production-line of players incorporating a mellifluous, sometimes flamboyant style in their music. The most well known of these is **Matt Molloy** of The Bothy Band and The Chieftains, but **Séamus Tansey** has also been hugely influential. Belfast too has produced some fine flute players, often influenced by the North Connacht style or that of neighbouring Fermanagh (from which **Cathal McConnell** is a major figure), including **Desi Wilkinson** and **Harry Bradley**, while Dublin's **Paul McGrattan** has drawn much from the Donegal fiddle tradition.

The essential learning instrument of Irish music is the tin whistle and one still carried around by many players of other instruments keen to learn new tunes quickly — if you're tempted to buy one, make sure it's a D-whistle, as many tunes are played in this key. In the hands of a skilled operator – such as **Mary Bergin**, **Gavin Whelan** or **Bríd O'Donohue** – the whistle utterly surmounts its apparent technical limitations.

Fiddles

The fiddle is Ireland's most popular traditional instrument and perhaps the best exemplar of regional musical styles (although these have been undermined as players learn their tunes and adaptations from the radio, CDs and MP3s rather than their neighbours). Donegal is famed for its captivating rhythmic style, often referred to as "driving" and best heard in the recordings of **John Doherty** (see p.521) and **Tommy**

Peoples. The Sligo style, encapsulated in the recordings of **Michael Coleman** (see p.489) and **James Morrison**, is generally regarded as more ornamented and flashy, but continues to be a major influence. The eastern parts of Galway and Clare are noted for their more lonesome style, produced by a tendency to play in flattened key signatures and exemplified by the playing of **Martin Hayes**, who uses his native tradition as an extraordinary springboard for musical exploration. To the south, in Kerry and Cork, the polka remains the most popular dance tune and much of the most atmospheric playing dates back to the fiddle-master **Pádraig O'Keeffe**, though his enduring influence can be heard in the playing of **Matt Cranitch** and **Séamus Creagh**.

Melodeons, accordions and concertinas

Squeeze-boxes come in a variety of shapes and sizes in traditional music. The simplest is the one-row button accordion, usually known as a melodeon in Ireland. Now rarely seen, one of its true masters is the Connemara box-player **Johnny Connolly**, generally regarded as the acme of accompanists for dancing. The far more popular two-row button accordion comes in a range of tunings, usually either B/C (favoured by the highly influential **Joe Burke**), which produces a more rolling and frilly style of play, or the C sharp/D variety (whose well-known exponents include **Dermot Byrne** and **Séamus Begley**). Also well worth seeking out are **Jackie Daly** and **Máirtín O'Connor**, both of whom play boxes in a variety of tunings, while the music of Clare's **Sharon Shannon** continues to attract a global audience. The piano accordion is less well favoured, though there are some cracking musicians using it, including **Alan Kelly**, **Mirella Murray** and **Martin Tourish**.

The smaller concertina was once thought of as primarily a women's instrument and was especially popular in County Clare (for too many reasons to list here). Again, it's ideal for accompanying dancers. Probably the best-known exponents are **Mary Mac Namara**, **Noel Hill**, **Chris Droney** and **Micheál Ó Raghallaigh**.

The bouzouki and other stringed instruments

The Greek *bouzouki* was first introduced to Ireland by **Johnny Moynihan** of the band Sweeney's Men in the late 1960s and made popular by **Dónal Lunny** of Planxty and The Bothy Band and **Alec Finn** of De Dannan. Along with the guitar, it's the most common form of stringed accompaniment found at sessions, though, thanks to its open tuning and flat back, it's nowadays more akin to the mandolin than its Greek forebear. As a relatively quiet instrument, the mandolin itself, as played by **Paul Kelly**, is rarely seen at sessions, though you may see a larger version known as the mandola, whose well-known protagonists include **Andy Irvine**. Lastly, there's the banjo, an instrument reviled by many for its "plunker-plunker" sound, but which does have some exceptional exponents, including **Gerry O'Connor** and **Darren Maloney**.

The bodhrán

This goatskin frame drum (pronounced "bore-run" or "bough-ron"), resembling a tambourine without jingles and played with the hand or a wooden beater, divides opinion among Irish sessioneers more than any other instrument. Some musicians appreciate the driving rhythm provided by a good percussionist (the most currently acclaimed player is **John Joe Kelly** of Flook), but others regard it as the devil's detritus and sounding, in one fiddler's memorable words, "like a sack of spuds tipped down the stairs". Originally associated with the "wren boys" who went out revelling ("hunting the wren") and playing music on St Stephen's Day (Dec 26), it was adopted for ensemble playing by **Seán Ó Riada** in the 1960s. Many music or souvenir shops sells the drum and, if you're tempted to buy one, do listen to recordings of the best players (**Johnny McDonagh** and **Colm Murphy** with De Dannan or **Donnchadh Gough** with Danú) before even considering whether your own formative skills might be welcome at a session.

as possible from musicians. The most notable collector was **Captain Francis O'Neill**, erstwhile Chicago police chief, who in the early twentieth century gathered tunes together in publications such as *The Dance Music of Ireland*. Later collectors of note include **Séamus Ennis**, who assiduously accumulated material for Radio Éireann and the BBC, and **Breandán Breathnach**, who published several volumes of material under the title *Ceol Rince na hÉireann* ("Dance Music of Ireland"). Today Dublin's Irish Traditional Music Archive continues the process of storing and cataloguing newly found material.

While these tunes were originally played at house or "crossroads" dances (held in a suitable open space – frequently a road junction), and often at weddings or wakes, they form merely a staging post for skilled traditional musicians, who embellish their renditions with all manner of musical ornamentation, though rarely straying from the essential rhythms of the dance. Nowadays, most dance tunes are played as part of a set, usually consisting of two or three of the same form, each played through a couple of times (or sometimes more) before segueing into the next one.

Sessions

The pub session as we know it today is in fact another import, having emerged in pubs in London and elsewhere where there were plenty of Irish émigrés in the years following World War II. During the folk and ballad boom of the 1960s, led by **The Clancy Brothers and Tommy Makem** and their more raucous contemporaries **The Dubliners**, Ireland's pub landlords began to welcome traditional musicians and the practice continues to this day. The session has become the focal point for the tradition and usually consists of a regular gathering of local musicians on a particular evening, one of whom is usually paid to ensure that it takes place.

The majority of sessions (except some in extremely popular tourist areas) are relatively informal affairs where the musicians play the tunes of their choice, breaking off whenever they feel like doing so for a chat or an outdoor fag-break. Sessions can be found throughout the year in cities such as Belfast, Cork, Dublin and Galway, but in smaller towns and rural areas the months between June and September are usually the best time. Most begin at around 9.30pm, though on the west coast in high summer you'll find plenty not starting until 10.30pm and sometimes later. The lure for the pub's punters is the chance to hear top-class musicianship for the price of a pint or two, as well as participating in the associated *craic*.

Bear in mind that the musicians' seats are sacrosanct, so don't plonk yourself down next to a fiddler to enjoy the music from a closer aspect – the vacant seat you've just occupied was reserved for a musician who might or might not appear later.

You'll only rarely come across dancing at a session (and you'll probably be in Kerry or Clare if you do), thus the best bet, if you want to twirl the light fantastic, is to look out for a céilí dance. Plenty of these take place during local festivals, but there are also a number of renowned venues along the west coast that feature regular nights of set-dancing to the accompaniment of a céilí band. These bands normally feature just the usual main traditional instruments, though some also include oddities such as the saxophone and accompaniment via piano and/or snare drum.

The song tradition

Sadly, unaccompanied songs also play little part in today's sessions, despite Ireland's remarkable vocal tradition. Essentially, this falls into two categories: songs in the Irish language and songs in English. Many Irish-language songs are of great antiquity and together they form part of what has become known as **sean-nós**, which literally means "old style". The tradition is strongest in the Irish-speaking areas of the west coast, particularly in West Kerry, Connemara and Donegal, and incorporates an unaccompanied singing style of great emotional intensity when applied to the "big songs" of the tradition – tales of love, loss and longing – or sprightly frivolity when handling more light-hearted matters. Singers essentially construct a soundscape in which their use of vocal ornamentation and changes in tempo and tone lead the listener through the lyrics' twists and turns. Though knowledge of the Irish language is essential to a full understanding of their abilities, even without this it's still possible to appreciate singing that can be very beautiful. Some of the best contemporary members of the tradition, not least **Iarla Ó Lionáird** (from West Cork), well known through his work with the Afro Celts fusion band, and **Lasairfhíona Ní Chonaola** (from the Aran Islands), have produced albums of extraordinary splendour.

Simultaneously, Ireland possesses a vast wealth of traditional songs in English, including many derived from the broadsheet ballad-sellers of the nineteenth and earlier twentieth centuries and others shared with the heritage of England and Scotland, and there are traditional singing clubs in several of Ireland's towns and cities. The country's foremost interpreter of these and many other contemporary songs is unquestionably **Christy Moore**.

▲ Christy Moore

Literature

For an island of less than six million people, Ireland has an astonishingly rich literary tradition, the oldest in Europe outside of Italy and Greece. While most of this literature up to the seventeenth century was written in Gaelic (usually called Irish in Ireland today), and to a lesser extent Latin, English would become pre-eminent from the eighteenth century onwards and is today the first language not just of most Irish writing but also of the vast majority of Irish people. Ireland's literary tradition has developed over two thousand years from the first markings on rocks around the time of Christ, to the acclaimed poetry, prose and theatre of writers such as W.B. Yeats, James Joyce and Samuel Beckett, producing startling works of originality and influence.

Beginnings

The oldest writing in Ireland was ogham script, a system of parallel notches that survives on standing stones from the fourth century AD, but was likely in existence for several hundred years previous. However, it was the arrival of Christianity in the fifth century that would have the most significant early influence on the emergence of literature in Ireland. With the growth of the monasteries between the seventh and tenth centuries, a rich culture of Latin manuscripts developed, the finest surviving example of which is the *Book of Kells* in Trinity College, Dublin (see p.86).

During the same period, a thriving literary culture in the vernacular of Irish life, Gaelic, began to emerge and develop, too. While the oldest surviving manuscripts in this language date from around the twelfth century, much of the material was copied and recopied for many hundreds of years before that. The oldest datable work of Gaelic literature is **Amra Choluim Chille** (Elegy of St Columba), a poem attributed to the poet Dallán Forgaill and written soon after the death in 597 of one of Ireland's most famous early saints, Colmcille, regarded as the patron saint of Irish poets. The Gaelic manuscripts also incorporated ancient, often fantastic and supernatural tales which had been preserved in a primarily oral culture. One such classic Irish story is the **Táin Bó Cúailnge** (The Cattle Raid of Cooley), which features the legendary figures of Cúchulainn, the larger-than-life Ulster warrior, and Queen Medb of Connaught.

While the manuscript tradition preserved tales concerning Cúchulainn, found in a larger narrative called the Ulster Cycle, a further popular hero in Gaelic oral culture was **Fionn Mac Cumhaill**, the leader of a band of warriors defending Ireland called the Fianna. The stories of Fionn and his men are commonly referred to as the *Fiannaíocht* tales and include the classic *Tõraíocht Dhiarmada agus Gráinne* (The Pursuit of Diarmuid and Gráinne), in which Fionn's intended, Gráinne, seduces one of his handsome warriors, Diarmuid, and elopes across Ireland, chased by Fionn and his men. Another famous early Gaelic tale is **Buile Shuibhne** (The Frenzy of Sweeney), the story of Suibhne Geilt, a king who, after being cursed by a local cleric, is transformed into a bird, banished and condemned to wander through Ireland's most desolate landscapes enduring great hardship and loneliness. These Gaelic legends have provided recurring inspiration for Irish writers, including W.B. Yeats, Synge, Joyce, Beckett, Flann O'Brien and Seamus Heaney.

The arrival of the Anglo-Normans in Ireland in the twelfth century brought another influence to bear on the Gaelic language and literature, and some of the finest poets of the Middle Ages would descend from Anglo-Norman stock, including in the fourteenth century Gearóid Iarla Fitzgerald, the Third Earl of Desmond. The thirteenth-century version of what is today known as Middle Irish was preserved as a literary language through the **bardic schools** that emerged in this period and continued in Ireland down to the mid-seventeenth century. These provided structured training for the *filí*, or poets, who were both feared and highly respected in a very hierarchical society. One significant aspect of poetry in this period was its close association with music, an association that would continue throughout the history of Irish literature. Surviving records suggest that bardic poetry was always performed with the accompaniment of the harp, the instrument that remains the national emblem of Ireland today. The esteem in which these poets were held is evident from the fact that many examples of this richly ornate and highly sophisticated bardic poetry survive, despite the tumultuous events that would lead to the decline of Gaelic Ireland.

With the undermining of the Gaelic order following the Battle of Kinsale in 1601, the structures that had supported indigenous poetic and musical production went into decline. Furthermore, as the power of musicians and poets had been feared by the British establishment throughout the sixteenth century, efforts were made to persecute them and generally limit their influence. Formerly exalted *filí* were now often reduced to **sráid-éigse** or "street poetry". The result was to bring the formerly independent professions of musician and poet together in the one performer whose compositions, particularly by the eighteenth century, gradually became more and more associated with the folk tradition of song. Indeed, for much of the succeeding two centuries the passing on of Irish poetry through song ensured its survival such that some songs from the eighteenth century, including *Dónal Óg* and *Úna Bhán*, continue to be sung today in the *sean-nós* or old-style tradition.

The eighteenth century would also witness, inspired by the Jacobite insurrections in Scotland of 1715 and 1745, the emergence of an indigenous, politically engaged poetry, as poets such as Piaras Mac Gearailt, Seán Ó Tuama, Seán Clárach Mac Domhnaill and Eoghan Rua Ó Súilleabháin produced work confident of the return of the Catholic Stuart kings to power and the revival of the Gaelic aristocracy. One of the most popular genres to evolve in this period was the **aisling**, its finest exponent **Aogán Ó Rathaille** in works such as *Mac an Cheannaí* (The Merchant's Son) and *Gile na Gile* (Brightness Most Bright). These "vision poems" feature the poet, on falling asleep, imagining he is visited by a beautiful woman who reveals herself as Ireland and laments her oppression. Such was the popularity of the *aisling* that one of the finest Gaelic poems of the eighteenth century is actually a parody of the genre, **Brian Merriman**'s *Cúirt An Mheán Oíche* (The Midnight Court). Here the poet encounters no beautiful maiden but rather an old hag, who summons him to a court where he witnesses an attack by Queen Aoibheal on the young men of Ireland for their refusal to marry and lack of virility. A ribald and satiric piece, regarded as the greatest comic poem in the language, it was banned in English when translated by Frank O'Connor in 1945, though the Irish-language version remained on the shelves.

Another highly accomplished Gaelic work of the eighteenth century is the *Caoineadh Airt Uí Laoghaire* (Lament for Art Ó Laoghaire), a long, traditional *caoineadh* or lament composed *ex tempore* by **Eibhlín Dhubh Ní Chonaill**, the aunt of Daniel O'Connell. It is a haunting piece lamenting the killing of Eibhlín's husband by the local sheriff, Abraham Morris, for refusing to sell his horse to him for £5, at a time when no Catholic was allowed under the hated penal laws to own a horse worth more than that figure.

The emergence of Irish literature in English

While Irish-language literature took a downturn from the seventeenth century onwards, Irish literature in English began to come to the fore, most importantly in the angry little shape of the poet, essayist and satirist **Jonathan Swift** (see p.103). Other notable writers in English from the eighteenth century include **Laurence Sterne**, the Tipperary-born clergyman and author of the innovative and highly influential satire on the biographical novel, *The Life and Opinions of Tristram Shandy, Gentleman*; the Longford doctor, **Oliver Goldsmith**, best known for his elegy *The Deserted Village*, novel *The Vicar of Wakefield* and play *She Stoops to Conquer*; and **Richard Brinsley Sheridan**, author of *The Rivals* and *The School for Scandal*, one of the first in a long tradition of leading Irish playwrights in the English language.

Despite the decline of Gaelic language and culture, the late eighteenth and early nineteenth centuries were nonetheless important for the rejuvenation of Irish nationalism, Irish music and the emergence of a distinctive Irish poetry in English. The efforts of primarily Anglo-Irish antiquarians, concerned to promote the distinctiveness of the adopted country of their ancestors, would help to preserve some of the native literature and music. In 1789, the first translations of Gaelic poetry and songs, *Reliques of Irish Poetry*, were published by **Charlotte Brooke**, a pioneering mediator between the Anglo-Irish Ascendancy and the local tradition. Her work would inspire subsequent antiquarians such as **Sir Samuel Ferguson**, the most important collector and translator of Gaelic poetry and mythology in the nineteenth century and a crucial influence on the writers who emerged in the Literary Revival at the end of the century, including W.B. Yeats.

Thomas Moore and the Young Ireland Poets

In the early nineteenth century, "the darling of the London drawing rooms" was **Thomas Moore**, born of a Catholic family in Dublin, whose romantic and nostalgic nationalist compositions – such as the still-popular songs *The Minstrel Boy* and *The Last Rose of Summer* – were included in *Irish Melodies*, published in ten volumes between 1808 and 1834. These poems were set to traditional Irish tunes from Edward Bunting's *General Collection of Ancient Music of Ireland* (1796), a compilation of the airs of some of the few remaining Irish harpists who performed at the Belfast Harpers' Festival of July 1792. Moore's *Melodies* has been called "the secular hymn-book of Irish nationalism" in the nineteenth century and he was regarded by many during his lifetime as Ireland's national poet. He represents the beginnings of the articulation of Irish identity and culture, on a national scale, in the English language.

While Moore had found in Irish music a means of access to what he believed to be the national spirit, the **Young Ireland Poets** associated with the nationalist newspaper, *The Nation* (which began publication in 1842), would find similar sustenance in the ballad. Among the most influential contributors to *The Nation* were **Thomas Davis** and **James Clarence Mangan**, both of whom would be alluded to in the work of W.B. Yeats and Joyce. While Davis's *A Nation Once Again* is still sung and was given serious consideration as the national anthem of Ireland, his emphasis on the importance of literature for national identity would have a vital influence on the Literary Revival. Mangan's free translation of the Gaelic song *Róisín Dubh* (Dark Rosaleen) has been described as the "most widely known nationalist poem" of the nineteenth century, but his overall ambivalence towards the nationalist project would find resonance in the work of Joyce, who wrote an essay on the poet.

Irish playwrights of the nineteenth century

Born in Dublin of Huguenot stock, **Dion Boucicault** found inspiration in Irish history and legend for plays such as *The Colleen Bawn* (1860), *The Shaughran* (1875) and *Robert Emmet* (1884). His work was renowned for its humour and enjoyed considerable popular success in Ireland, Britain and the US during his life, but subsequent Irish writers and commentators would accuse him of perpetuating the figure of the drunken and pugnacious "stage Irishman", a popular stereotype that had gained currency in the early eighteenth century in the work of Irish playwright George Farquhar.

Better known to her readers by her pseudonym **Speranza**, Jane Francesca Wilde was an Anglo-Irish author and literary hostess who contributed nationalist poems and anti-British writings to *The Nation*. While her work was of limited artistic value, her son **Oscar Wilde** would become one of the most famous (and eventually infamous) dramatists of the British stage in the late nineteenth century. Oscar did not share his mother's engagement with Irish politics and left the country for England shortly after graduating from Trinity College, where he was an outstanding student of classics, in 1874. He was awarded a scholarship to Magdalen College, Oxford, where he joined the Aesthetic Movement, a society dedicated to making an art out of life. Although Wilde published prose – his novel *The Picture of Dorian Gray* provoked a storm of protests in Victorian society because of its implied homoerotic theme – and poetry, his dazzling plays, including *Lady Windermere's Fan* and *The Importance of Being Earnest*, enjoyed the most success during his lifetime and continue to be performed today. Wilde managed to satirize the pretensions of the English upper and middle classes with humour and insight in a way that only someone coming from outside this society could. He was respected on both sides of the Atlantic for his work and enthralling lectures, and admired in polite society for his ability as a raconteur. However, a homosexual relationship with Lord Alfred Douglas, son of the Marquis of Queensbury, would eventually lead to his demise following a conviction and imprisonment for gross indecency. He was sentenced to two years' hard labour, an experience, given chilling insight by one of his finest works *The Ballad of Reading Gaol*, that would break him both physically and psychologically. Wilde died in Paris on November 30, 1900, a broken man who could never ignite his fires of creativity after prison. He left not just great

▲ Oscar Wilde

literature but also some of the most memorable aphorisms in the English language, some of which too sadly described his own fate: "The secret of life is to appreciate the pleasure of being terribly, terribly deceived."

The other major playwright to emerge in England in the late nineteenth century was also Irish, the Dublin-born, life-long socialist, **George Bernard Shaw** (see p.96), whose career and influence extended well into the twentieth century. Shaw's work for the theatre was ground-breaking in bringing his own economic, moral and political concerns to the fore, but like Wilde he was also a legendary wit, combining acerbic humour with potent insights into human nature: "Gambling promises the poor what property performs for the rich – something for nothing." Nothing short of prolific, Shaw wrote over sixty plays, including *Arms and the Man*, *John Bull's Other Island* and *Pygmalion*, as well as five less successful novels and an impressive array of literary criticism and political commentary, before his death at the age of 94 in November 1950.

The emergence of the Irish novel

A relatively new form that was to play an increasingly central part in cultural life in the nineteenth century, the novel in Ireland generally traces its beginnings to *Castle Rackrent* (1800), written by **Maria Edgeworth**. Although from an Anglo-Irish Ascendancy family, who gave their name to Edgeworthstown in Co. Longford, Edgeworth reveals the inequitable and sometimes abusive treatment estate tenants endured at the hands of their landlords. *Castle Rackrent* began one of the most popular genres in Irish literature, the "Big House" novel, concerning the experiences of the landholding class on an Anglo-Irish estate.

Though dominated by writers from the Ascendancy class in Ireland, the nineteenth century was also important for the emergence of female writers such as Edgeworth. Others include **Lady Morgan** (Sidney Owenson), whose *The Wild Irish Girl* (1806) is regarded as an important early feminist text, and the co-authors Edith Somerville and her cousin Violet Martin, known for works such as *The Irish R.M* written under their pseudonyms **Somerville and Ross**.

Other important writers of fiction to emerge in the nineteenth century include **William Carleton**, whose *Traits and Stories of the Irish Peasantry* would be a very influential text for writers such as Yeats; the brothers **John and Michael Banim**, whose major work is the 24 volumes of *The Tales of the O'Hara Family*; and Limerick-born novelist **Gerald Griffin**, whose *The Collegians* was based on events surrounding a trial in which Daniel O'Connell acted as attorney for the defence. The most popular novel in Ireland of the nineteenth century, however, was *Knocknagown; or The Homes of Tipperary* (1879), a convoluted and sentimental account of Tipperary rural life and critique of landlordism, written by the patriot and Young Irelander, **Charles Kickham**.

The Gothic genre was given much of its shape by Irish writers in this period, including **Charles Robert Maturin**, particularly in his dark tale of a man who sells his soul to the devil, *Melmoth the Wanderer* (1820); and **Joseph Sheridan Le Fanu**, the leading ghost-story writer of the nineteenth century, best known for his novel *Uncle Silas* (1864) and collection of short stories *In a Glass Darkly* (1872). But they pale in comparison to **Bram Stoker**, whose *Dracula* (1897) is still one of the most popular and adapted works of fiction today. Born in Dublin and educated at Trinity College, Stoker spent most of his life in London as manager to the famous Shakespearean actor, Henry Irving. However, in its pseudo-folkloric style and its preoccupations – the nature of the soul set against the temptations of the flesh, the noble serfs against the aristocratic fiend – his most famous novel remains curiously Irish.

The Literary Revival

While Oscar Wilde and George Bernard Shaw were dominating the stage in Britain at the end of the nineteenth century, Irish cultural nationalism was on the rise back home. This period is collectively referred to as the **Irish Literary Revival**, though there were at least two revivals apparent: the Anglo-Irish, concerned with the promotion of Hiberno-English, the English language as sculpted by the particularities of Irish accent and the structures of Gaelic; and the Gaelic Revival, focused on the Irish language, which by now had been devastated by famine, emigration, poverty, lack of support and, indeed, outright discouragement in education. During the Literary Revival, literature in both languages would become a central focus for the revitalization of Irish culture, though attempts were also made through organizations such as Conradh na Gaeilge (the Gaelic League), founded in 1893, to preserve and encourage indigenous musical practices. The League's first president **Douglas Hyde**, who later became Ireland's first president, would do much to popularize the Gaelic poetic tradition through his translations in *Abhráin Grádh Chúige Connacht* (The Love Songs of Connacht; 1893) and *Abhráin Diadha Chúige Connacht* (The Religious Songs of Connacht; 1905). These collections were an important inspiration for both Irish- and English-language writers, contributing to the idealization of the rural peasantry of the west, particularly in Yeats's work, as the well-spring from which, it was thought, a new, invigorated Irish literature and identity would emerge.

W.B. Yeats

Though **William Butler Yeats** was born in Dublin in 1865 into an aristocratic Protestant family, it was Sligo in the west of Ireland, where he spent a considerable part of his formative years, that would fire his creative imagination. The most important writer of the Revival period, Yeats was in many ways the father of modern Irish literature. One of his major roles was in bringing material in Irish – including elements from the *Táin* and *Fiannaíocht* tales – into mainstream English-language literature through collections such as *The Wanderings of Oisin* (1889). But, more importantly, as a dramatist, essayist and, above all, poet, Yeats brought Irish culture onto a world stage, winning the Nobel Prize for Literature in 1923 and producing some of the finest poetry in any language of that era. While influenced by and commenting on the turbulent years in Ireland of the early twentieth century, his work resonated internationally in a time of calamity and change during and after World War I, with the lines of *The Second Coming*, published in 1921 as the Irish war of independence was coming to an end, still among the most quoted in modern literature:

Things fall apart; the centre cannot hold;
Mere anarchy is loosed upon the world,
The blood-dimmed tide is loosed, and everywhere
The ceremony of innocence is drowned;
The best lack all conviction, while the worst
Are full of passionate intensity.

From his Late Romantic beginnings, Yeats's work developed through the trauma of lost love – Maude Gonne, a recurring presence throughout his work – and the disappointment of the Ireland he saw emerging, more mercantile than artistic, to produce a harder, more realist and direct poetry. Among the best examples of this work are *September 1913*, *Easter 1916* – his elegy for the executed leaders of the Republican Rising of that year – and *The Fisherman*. But it was in Yeats's last decade that the challenges of aging and declining health inspired some of the finest moments in modern poetry, including *Among School Children* and *Sailing to Byzantium*. Yeats died in January 1939 in France, with his body returning to Ireland after the war in 1948 to be reburied in Drumcliffe churchyard in County Sligo.

The Abbey and Synge

One of the major ambitions of Yeats, Lady Gregory and other leaders of the Literary Revival was the development of an Irish national theatre, realized with the opening of the **Abbey Theatre** in 1904. The Abbey would define a distinct form of Irish theatre, combining a concern with the English language as spoken in Ireland with an attempt to revive belief in the value of Irish culture. In its early years, its greatest playwright was **John Millington Synge**, whose work would provide some of the most memorable characters and narratives of this period, particularly in his masterpiece *The Playboy of the Western World*, first performed in 1907. This dark and yet at times very humorous play, featuring Christy Mahon who achieves fame in a rural Mayo community by claiming that he killed his father, was more than the nationalist audience of its day could accept and resulted in a riot during its first performance. Synge was not afraid to reveal the full gamut of the rural peasant's language, inflected with the Irish language, in both its vulgarity and wit, and an audience that had been conditioned to view the peasant as the very paragon of pure Irishness could not tolerate such a blasphemy. Synge died all too young at the age of 37 in 1909, but helped to inspire later dramatists to create realistic depictions of Irish life.

Joyce

James Joyce was born in Dublin in 1882 into a middle-class Catholic family, which by his early teens had declined into considerable poverty, due largely to his father's carelessness with money. Joyce's challenging experiences, however, provided considerable material for characters and narratives, giving rise to one of the most innovative and imaginative voices in English literature. Although Joyce began writing when the Literary Revival was at its height, he would become one of its strongest critics: as Stephen Dedalus, the protagonist of his semi-autobiographical *A Portrait of the Artist as a Young Man* (1916), remarks to his nationalist school-friend Davin, "You talk to me of nationality, language, religion. I shall try to fly by those nets." For Joyce, each of these elements placed constraints on the writer that could only limit his creativity and expression, something he could not countenance. In the end, he found Ireland too oppressive socially and culturally for his art and headed for the continent, rarely returning to the country of his birth after 1904, and visiting for the last time in 1912. However, while much of his writing was done in Trieste, Paris and Zürich – the city in which he died in 1941 – Ireland, and particularly Dublin, remained the central locale of his work. Indeed, arguably no other writer in twentieth-century literature mapped a city so effectively, epitomized in his finest work, *Ulysses* (1922), which recounts the happenings of a single day in the life of Dublin. Joyce's partner, and eventual wife, during his years on the continent was Nora Barnacle, and the day on which they first met in Dublin, June 16, 1904, has become immortalized as "Bloomsday" (see also p.110), the day on which all the events of the novel, concerning the life and ruminations of a Jewish advertising canvasser, Leopold Bloom, take place.

Irish literature after the Revival

The generation of writers that emerged after the establishment of the Irish Free State in 1923 would be characterized by a wish to debunk myths promulgated during the Literary Revival, including the idealization of the peasant. This concern was accompanied by a profound suspicion, and often outright rejection, of the increasingly Catholic-controlled orthodoxy that characterized the new state, as reflected in the strict Censorship of Publications Act (1929), which was responsible for the banning of many works by Irish and international authors. Figures such as Austin Clarke, Patrick Kavanagh, Frank O'Connor, Seán Ó Faoláin, Flann O'Brien and Sean O'Casey would all write work critical of Ireland as it developed in this period. Meanwhile O'Casey, Samuel Beckett and others found the climate so constraining that they decided to live outside Ireland, though their work would continue to be influenced by Irish themes.

Irish fiction after Joyce

The short story, a form pioneered in Ireland by George Moore in *The Untilled Field* (1903) and developed by Joyce in *Dubliners* (1914), has been an important genre for Irish writers ever since. **Liam O'Flaherty**, born in 1896 on the Irish-speaking Aran Islands off Galway, wrote several acclaimed novels, including *The Informer* (1925), yet it is his short stories, in both English and his native Irish, including "Going into Exile", "The Shilling" and his Irish-language collection, *Dúil* (1953), that constitute his best work. Two other notable exponents of the short-story form were **Seán Ó Faoláin** and **Frank O'Connor**. Among Ó Faoláin's finest collections are *Midsummer Night Madness and Other Stories* (1932) and *The Man Who Invented Sin* (1948), while his story "Lovers of the Lake" remains a classic in modern Irish writing. Ó Faoláin was also an editor of the seminal literary journal *The Bell*, and an outspoken critic of the anti-intellectualism that characterized Irish society during his life, under the considerable influence of the Catholic Church. While O'Connor also worked as a translator, essayist and biographer, it is for his short stories that he is best remembered, including "The First Confession" and "The Luceys" and the collection *Guests of the Nation* (1931).

One of the most experimental writers of the twentieth century was **Flann O'Brien**, born Brian Ó Núalláin in 1911. While O'Brien's finest work is arguably found in the novel *At Swim-Two-Birds* (1939), his wonderfully surreal and funny *The Third Policeman* (1967) recently enjoyed renewed popularity after its brief appearance in the TV serial *Lost*. O'Brien's first language growing up in Tyrone and later Dublin was Irish and he also wrote some of the most satirically humorous work in this language, including *An Béal Bocht* (The Poor Mouth; 1941), published under the pseudonym Myles na gCopaleen. A parody of the celebrated Blasket Island autobiographies of writers such as Tomás Ó Criomhthain and Peig Sayers, *An Béal Bocht* is an unrestrained attack on the pretensions of the Irish-Ireland movement.

Irish poetry after Yeats

The generation of poets that followed Yeats could not escape the long shadow cast by the Nobel Laureate, but were also concerned to critique the legacies of the Literary Revival. While **Austin Clarke** charted the urban experience, Patrick Kavanagh's work provided one of the first authentic catalogues of rural life in twentieth-century poetry. Clarke began writing verse in the 1910s much influenced by early Yeats and concerned with similar goals of bringing Gaelic literature into the English language; for example in his free translations of stories about Fionn Mac Cumhaill in *The Vengeance of Fionn*. As his work matured, he became one of the most consistent and acerbic commentators on Irish life and particularly the suffocating influence of the Church, apparent in one of his finest poems *Martha Blake at 51*, and his short lyric *Penal Law*:

Burn Ovid with the rest. Lovers will find
A hedge-school for themselves and learn by heart
All that the clergy banish from the mind,
When hands are joined and head bows in the dark.

Clarke's legacy has been particularly influential in the work of **Thomas Kinsella**, who continues Clarke's mapping of the urban geography of Dublin. Kinsella has also turned to Gaelic literature and Irish mythology for themes and motifs in his work and, influenced by Jungian psychology, as part of his exploration of his own unconscious, in collections such as *Notes from the Land of the Dead* (1973) and *Fifteen Dead* (1979). Kinsella has also been one of the most important translators of Gaelic literature into English, in works such as *The Táin*, *An Duanaire 1600–1900: Poems of the Dispossessed* and *The New Oxford Book of Irish Verse*.

The poetry of **Patrick Kavanagh**, who was born in 1904 and raised on a small farm near Inniskeen, County Monaghan, revealed the challenges of rural life in a manner that included an implicit, and sometimes explicit, critique of the Revival's pretensions. Though his work also includes striking lyrics recognizing the power and beauty of the natural world, for Kavanagh rural life was often characterized by deprivation, both physical and psychological, as demonstrated in *The Great Hunger* and the pounding rhythms of *Stony Grey Soil*:

O stony grey soil of Monaghan
The laugh from my love you thieved;
You took the gay child of my passion
And gave me your clod-conceived.

Kavanagh, who died in 1967, has been arguably the most influential Irish poet after Yeats for contemporary poets such as Seamus Heaney and **John Montague**. Raised in Tyrone, Montague inherited Kavanagh's rural concerns, but added to it a political consciousness focused on the Troubles in Northern Ireland, apparent in the volume *The Rough Field* (1972).

As Montague's work, and that of other Northern poets suggests, the setting-up of Northern Ireland in 1920 created distinct historical and political processes within that region. Issues such as culture, language, history and identity became all the more important to writers attempting to articulate distinctive voices in a contested space, coming to a head with the outbreak of the Troubles in the late 1960s. However, these themes were already apparent in the work of the major writers from Northern Ireland in the early and mid-twentieth century: **John Hewitt** and **Louis MacNeice**. In the work of MacNeice, who is often associated with the British poetry movement of the 1930s that included Cecil Day Lewis, Stephen Spender and W. H. Auden, one finds an ambiguous relationship with the country of his birth, though his focus on the west of Ireland in particular, in poems such as *Galway* and *Western Landscape*, anticipates the concern with this part of the island in the work of the next generation of Protestant poets, Michael Longley and Derek Mahon. Meanwhile Hewitt promoted his belief in cultural regionalism, in writing from and for the community in the North from which he emerged:

I write for my own kind
I do not pitch my voice
that every phrase be heard
by those that have no choice:
their quality of mind
must be withdrawn and still,
as moth that answers moth
across a roaring hill.

Irish-language literature in the twentieth century

The challenge for Irish-language poets in the early twentieth century lay in finding appropriate forms for their work, and whether to turn to the Gaelic models of the seventeenth and eighteenth centuries or the living language of the surviving Irish-speaking regions of the country. This debate would somewhat hinder creativity during the Gaelic Revival with little poetry of merit being produced in this period.

Nonetheless, the Gaelic Revival was important for the emergence of prose writers in Irish, most notably Galway-born **Pádraic Ó Conaire**, the author of over four hundred short stories, several plays, numerous essays and the groundbreaking novel *Deoraíocht* (Exile; 1910), still one of the most remarkable Irish works of fiction and regarded as the first modern novel in the Irish language. Set in London at the turn of the twentieth century, the narrative concerns an Irish emigrant, who after losing an arm and a leg and being seriously disfigured in an accident shortly after arriving from Galway, ends up working in a travelling circus as a sideshow freak.

Autobiography emerged as an important form in Irish-language literature in the early twentieth century. This was most apparent in the work of writers from the now-uninhabited **Blasket Islands** (see p.359) off the coast of Kerry, including Peig Sayers, Muiris Ó Súilleabháin and Tomás Ó Criomhthain, whose *An tOileánach* (The Islandman; 1929) is probably the most accomplished of all these texts.

The dwindling audience for Irish-language literature would be a matter of concern for writers throughout the twentieth century. As **Máirtín Ó Cadhain**, author of the century's most innovative novel in Irish, *Cré na Cille* (Graveyard Clay; 1948), remarked, "[i]t is hard for a man to give of his best in a language which seems likely to die before himself, if he lives a few years more". Despite the decline in the number of native speakers, however, writers like Eoghan Ó Tuairisc, Bréandán Ó hEithir, Pádraig Standún, Mícheál Ó Siadhail and Pádraig Ó Cíobháin have all produced substantial fiction in Irish, while Pádraic Breathnach, Alan Titley and Micheál Ó Conghaile continue to produce critically acclaimed collections of short stories.

In poetry, the major Irish-language writers to have emerged in the mid-twentieth century were **Máirtín Ó Direáin**, **Máire Mhac an tSaoi** and **Seán Ó Ríordáin**. For Ó Direáin, from his first self-published collection, *Coinnle Geala* (1942), the speech of the Aran Islands where he grew up was an important source, but he would turn, particularly from the collection *Ó Mórna agus Dánta Eile*, to forms apparent in the work of earlier Gaelic poets. Mhac an tSaoi would bring a thorough knowledge of the Gaelic literary tradition to her work, reflected in her use of both bardic and *amhrán*, or Gaelic song, metres in poems such as *Caoineadh* and *Ceathrúintí Mháire Ní Ógáin*. For collections such as *Brosna* (1964), Ó Ríordáin is regarded as the great modernist of Gaelic poetry, whose conscious rearranging of language would produce an original and, for many, controversial poetics in Irish.

Other accomplished Irish-language poets over the past thirty years have included Michael Hartnett – who was also a major poet in English – Michael Davitt, Gabriel Rosenstock, Liam Ó Muirthile, Nuala Ní Dhomhnaill, Cathal Ó Searcaigh, Gréagóir Ó Dúill, Micheal O'Siadhail, Áine Ní Ghlinn, Biddy Jenkinson, Colm Breathnach and Louis de Paor. Many of these writers have at some point been associated with **Innti**, an Irish-language poetry movement (and literary journal) that emerged in Cork in the early 1970s, which has been one of the most important initiatives in building a new audience for poetry generally in Ireland, often through public readings.

Irish theatre after Synge

Whereas Synge had focused on rural Ireland, the Abbey's next great dramatist, **Sean O'Casey**, would bring the lives and challenges of the urban poor onto the stage, in some of the theatre's most famous and controversial productions, including *The Shadow of a Gunman* (1923) and *Juno and the Paycock* (1924). As with Synge's *Playboy of the Western World*, O'Casey's next, and arguably finest play, *The Plough and the Stars*, resulted in a riot in the theatre when first staged in 1926. Depicting the events of the 1916 Rising from the perspective of ordinary tenement-dwellers in Dublin, O'Casey cast a critical eye over events considered sacred in Irish nationalist history, regarding the leaders as more concerned with their own egos than with the welfare of the populace. O'Casey, however, felt suffocated as many Irish writers before and after by the oppressive forces of religion and orthodoxy in Ireland. After his subsequent play, the experimental *The Silver Tassie* dealing with World War I, was rejected by the Abbey, he left Ireland in 1928 for the remainder of his life, settling in Devon, England, until his death in 1964.

Among those who assisted James Joyce in his work during his years in Paris was a young writer who had similarly left Ireland in his early twenties, and would himself go on to achieve worldwide fame as a modernist writer: **Samuel Beckett**. If Joyce wished to be remembered for the humour of his work, few writers have cast as pessimistic an eye on the world as Beckett. While creating some of the century's most memorable dramatic works – including *Waiting for Godot* (1952), *Endgame* (1958) and *Krapp's Last Tape* (1959) – Beckett developed a minimalist and sometimes severe theatre of the absurd, if one relieved by occasional moments of insight and humour. He brought to his writing the attention to detail and exactness characteristic of one writing in an acquired tongue (many of his greatest works were written in French) and was awarded the Nobel Prize for Literature in 1968.

Brendan Behan is today unfortunately remembered almost as much for his effusive personality and drunken interviews as for his important literary work, which included the autobiographical *Borstal Boy* (1958) and the plays *The Quare Fellow* (1954) and *The Hostage* (1958; originally produced in Irish as *An Giall*), a piece that in many respects anticipated the narrative of Neil Jordan's Oscar-winning 1992 film, *The Crying Game*. Behan's weakness for alcohol was a major factor in both his small, if accomplished, output as a writer and his early death at the age of only 41.

Among the recurring themes of Irish theatre since the middle of the twentieth century has been the legacy of colonialism, including the Troubles in Northern Ireland and the failures of the independent state to the south. While recent playwrights are increasingly concerned with placing contemporary Ireland on the stage, few have returned more effectively to the past in their excavation of Irish identity than **Brian Friel**, whose *Translations* (1980) and *Dancing at Lughnasa* (1992) remain modern classics of the Irish stage. Friel's work has often reflected his nationalist background, but one of the most important studies of Unionist identity is found in the Donegal-born **Frank McGuinness**'s *Observe the Sons of Ulster Marching Towards the Somme* (1985). Similar critical acclaim has attended **Thomas Kilroy** (*The Death and Resurrection of Mr Roche*, 1968; *The O'Neill*, 1969; *Sex and Shakespeare*, 1976) and **Tom Murphy** (*Famine*, 1968; *Conversations on a Homecoming*, 1985; *Bailegangaire*, 2001), while **Hugh Leonard** and **John B. Keane** have written some of the most popular dramatic works since the 1960s, several of which have been adapted for film including Leonard's *Da* (originally produced in 1977) and Keane's *The Field* (1965).

A significant development over the past thirty years has been the emergence of new theatre companies to challenge the dominance of the Abbey, including **Field Day**, founded in 1980 in Derry by Seamus Heaney, Brian Friel and Thomas Kilroy, among others. Galway's **Druid Theatre** has produced some of the most important contemporary works on the Irish stage, including the plays of **Martin McDonagh**, born in London of Irish descent. McDonagh, who won an Academy Award for best short film in 2006 and has cited Quentin Tarantino as an influence, has garnered widespread critical acclaim for his provocative and violent work, notably *The Beauty Queen of Leenane* (1996). A feature of younger playwrights such as **Conor McPherson**, **Enda Walsh** and **Mark O'Rowe** has been a willingness to bring the vernacular and popular culture onto the stage. Each of these writers has moved between theatre and film, with Walsh's *Disco Pigs* (1996) being adapted for the screen by Kirsten Sheridan in 2001, O'Rowe providing the script for one of the most successful independent Irish films in recent years, *Intermission* (2003), and McPherson going on to direct his own films, including *Saltwater* (2000) and *The Actors* (2003) starring Michael Caine. One of the most significant new voices to have emerged from the North is **Gary Mitchell**, whose plays such as *As the Beast Sleeps* (1998), *The Force of Change* (2000) and *State of Failure* (2006) draw strikingly on his own Belfast working-class Loyalist experience. However, following first threats then full-scale intimidation by the paramilitaries (angered by TV adaptations of his work), Mitchell and his family were forced to flee Belfast and continue to live in hiding. Other playwrights of note to emerge in recent years include Paul Mercier, Marina Carr, Christian O'Reilly and Sebastian Barry, who has also achieved recognition for his fiction, including *A Long Long Way*, which was shortlisted for the 2005 Man Booker Prize.

Contemporary Irish poetry

Undoubtedly the leading light of the contemporary poetry scene is Nobel Prize–winner **Seamus Heaney** (see p.618), who has built on the legacy of Patrick Kavanagh to produce lyrical verse relating the experiences of rural life. Heaney has unearthed empowering metaphors in the Irish, and Danish, landscape, particularly bogs, for the Troubles, finding parallels for contemporary violence in ancient ritualistic killings, in poems such as *Bogland*, *Punishment* and *Tollund Man*:

Out here in Jutland
In the old man-killing parishes
I will feel lost,
Unhappy and at home.

Michael Longley, born in Belfast in 1939, the same year as Heaney, has written some of the most evocative poems of the Troubles, including *Wounds* and *Ceasefire*, which draws on Book XXIV of the *Iliad* and was printed on the front page of the *Irish Times* on the eve of the IRA ceasefire on August 31, 1994. Indeed, Northern Ireland has been a particularly fertile ground for poetry since the 1960s. Other poets of note from the region include **Padraic Fiacc**, **Derek Mahon**, **Paul Muldoon**, the Armagh-born but American-based poet whose collection *Moy Sand and Gravel* won the 2003 Pulitzer Prize for poetry, and **Ciaran Carson**, one of the most distinctive and innovative voices to emerge since the 1970s and also a fiction writer of considerable talent, in novels such as *The Star Factory*, *Fishing for Amber* and *Shamrock Tea*.

Significant women's voices in Irish poetry have emerged, including **Eavan Boland**, **Eiléan Ní Chuilleanáin**, **Medbh McGuckian**, **Paula Meehan**, **Rita Ann Higgins, Mary O'Malley** and **Sinead Morrisey**, each of whom has brought the female experience to the fore, while critiquing previous representations of women in a primarily male-dominated canon. Another important development in recent years has been the growing number of literary festivals – including the Cúirt Festival in Galway, Listowel Writers' Week and the Dublin Writers' Festival – and the increasing engagement of contemporary poets in the performance of their work. Audiences have had many more opportunities to encounter new writers, and poets such as **Paul Durcan**, **Brendan Kennelly** and **Gearóid Mac Lochlainn** have established considerable reputations through performing.

Contemporary Irish prose

Irish prose in the past thirty years has been characterized by an increased focus on the urban experience and by a willingness to explore different possibilities of place and identity. Much as in poetry, the North of Ireland has produced some of the most popular and interesting work, often inspired by the traumatic events of the Troubles and the subsequent peace process. **Bernard MacLaverty** is one of the most admired fiction writers to emerge from the North since World War II, a position reaffirmed with the publication of his latest collection of short stories, *Matters Of Life & Death*, in 2006. **Eoin McNamee**'s *Resurrection Man* (1994), a disturbing fictionalized account of the notorious loyalist paramilitaries, the Shankill Butchers, was adapted into a film of the same name, while **Glenn Patterson** has turned to moments before the Troubles in Belfast to explore other possibilities that might have emerged, in *Burning Your Own* (1988) and *The International* (1999). One of the most innovative voices to emerge from the North has been **Robert McLiam Wilson**, notably in his 1996 novel *Eureka Street*, focusing on the relationship between a Catholic and a Protestant before and after the IRA ceasefire in 1994. Derry-born **Sean O'Reilly** has been compared to Isobel Allende, producing experimental and magical realist prose in works such as the short-story collection *Curfew and Other Stories* (2000) and novel *Watermark* (2005).

The death in 2006 of **John McGahern** robbed contemporary readers of one of the finest Irish writers since Joyce. McGahern had an almost uncanny insight into human nature and rural Irish society – he was born and lived for most of his life in County Leitrim – and rarely has a writer managed to realize as effectively the details of his life experience in literature. From his first novel *The Barracks* (1963) to his final autobiographical work *Memoir* (2005), McGahern's work evinced a deceptively accessible plain technique, which disguised a unique stylistic meticulousness and inner order.

While Wicklow-born **Claire Keegan**'s work – including her acclaimed 2007 short-story collection *Walk the Blue Fields* – has been indebted in style and theme to McGahern, **Colm Tóibín** has also sometimes been regarded as the heir to the Leitrim writer in his focus on aspects of the rural Irish experience. Tóibín's childhood town of Enniscorthy provides the setting for some of his most accomplished work including *The Heather Blazing* (1992) and *The Blackwater Lightship* (1999), a novel that explores the theme of homosexuality in contemporary Ireland. Fellow Wexford-born novelist **John Banville** has expressed a wish to develop a style with "the kind of denseness and thickness that poetry has", and this is evident in the elegance and supreme craftsmanship of his writing. Banville, like many of his contemporaries, has moved outside the Irish context, with subjects ranging from eminent European scientists (*Dr Copernicus*, *Kepler* and *The Newton Letter: An Interlude*), to reflections on a European city (*Prague Pictures: Portrait of a City*). He remains the most critically acclaimed of modern Irish authors, winning the Man Booker Prize in 2005 for his novel, *The Sea*.

Colum McCann has also moved outside his Irish roots for inspiration and subject matter, in novels such as *The Dancer* (2003), concerning the Russian ballet legend Rudolf Nureyev, and *Zoli* (2007), focused on the gypsies of Eastern Europe. One of the most important influences on McCann's work was the novelist and short-story writer **Desmond Hogan**, who along with Neil Jordan founded the influential **Irish Writer's Cooperative** in 1971. Hogan focuses repeatedly on the marginalized, isolated and unconventional, in settings that include rural County Galway where he grew up (*The Ikon Maker*), 1950s Dublin (*The Leaves on Grey*), and continental Europe and the United States in the wanderings of the central protagonist Des in *A Farewell to Prague*. While **Neil Jordan** is better known today for his Oscar-winning film work, he continues to produce some of the most well-crafted and, indeed, powerfully visual work in Irish literature, including his 2004 gothic tale *Shade*, entirely narrated by a murder victim.

Other members of the Writer's Cooperative include **Ronan Sheehan**, author of *The Tennis Players* and *Foley's Asia*, and **Dermot Bolger**. A poet and dramatist as well as novelist, Bolger has charted Dublin life, especially the Northside, since his first novel *Night Shift* (1985), including reimagining in the context of contemporary working-class Dublin *Caoineadh Airt Uí Laoghaire* (see p.717) as the play *The Lament for Arthur Cleary* (1989). Bolger also founded Raven Arts Press in 1979, one of several Irish publishers, including Dolmen, Gallery, Brandon, Salmon and Arlen House, that have emerged since the 1960s to provide a vital outlet for the work of Irish writers.

Clones-born **Patrick McCabe** has written some of the most innovative, provocative and sometimes deeply unsettling fiction of the past twenty years including *The Butcher Boy*, *Breakfast on Pluto* and his most recent work

Winterwood. Meanwhile, few have managed as successfully to chart the urban experience in contemporary Ireland as **Roddy Doyle**, notably in the Barrytown trilogy (*The Commitments*, *The Snapper* and *The Van*) and the 1993 Booker Prize-winning *Paddy Clarke Ha Ha Ha*, an absorbing portrayal of a child's experience growing up in Dublin in the 1960s. His 2007 collection of short stories, *The Deportees*, is just one of a growing number of texts to treat of Ireland's increasingly multicultural society.

Edna O'Brien has remained in the vanguard of Irish novelists since her pioneering work charting the female experience in 1960s Ireland, including the Country Girls trilogy: *The Country Girls, Girl with Green Eyes* and *Girls in Their Married Bliss*. O'Brien, whose twentieth work of fiction *The Light of Evening* was published in 2006, has been an inspiration to subsequent women writers like **Emma Donoghue**, a pioneering force herself in Irish lesbian fiction with works such as *Stirfry*, *Hood* and *Slammerkin*. Meanwhile, the award of the 2007 Man Booker Prize to **Anne Enright** for her fourth novel *The Gathering*, a powerful study of the trauma of suicide for those family members left behind, confirmed her position as one of the leading novelists of her generation. Described by John Banville as "one of the subtlest and most penetrating of the latest generation of Irish writers", **Mary Morrissey** has followed Banville in focusing on non-Irish themes, in particular in *The Pretender* (2000), the story of a Polish factory worker who claims to be the daughter of the last tsar of Russia. **Eilis Ní Dhuibne**, who writes in both Irish and English, has also attracted increasing attention for her work internationally, including her 1999 novel *The Dancers Dancing*. One of the most innovative voices to emerge from Northern Ireland in the 1990s was **Antonia Logue**, notably in *Shadow Box*, while **Anne Haverty's** *The Free and Easy* (2006) marked a movement among contemporary novelists to finally explore twenty-first-century Ireland in their work, rather than setting, as was frequently the case, their narratives in the past.

In similar vein, Cork-born poet, short-story writer and novelist **William Wall** wrote in 2005 one of the most pointed critiques of the Celtic Tiger, *This is the Country*, featuring a man trying to leave a life of drug abuse behind in an increasingly corrupt and uncaring Ireland. **Mike McCormack** also cast a critical eye on the new Ireland, though in a futuristic context, in *Notes from a Coma* (2005), an account of a penal experiment in which five volunteers, including the former Romanian orphan J.J. O'Malley, are kept in a coma for three months aboard a prison ship in Killary Harbour. The academic **Seamus Deane** emerged as one of the most accomplished contemporary writers with the 1996 publication of his semi-autobiographical *Reading in the Dark*. While Deane focused on his formative experiences in the North, one of the most popular recent works of autobiography was **Frank McCourt**'s Pulitzer Prize-winning *Angela's Ashes* (1996), an evocative, and at times deeply moving, account of growing up in poverty in 1930s Limerick. Dublin-born **Keith Ridgway** has also attracted increasing notice since his debut novel *The Long Falling* in 1998. While **Joseph O'Connor** began his career as a journalist and writer of popular nonfiction – including the satirical and insightful *The Secret World of the Irish Male* (1994) – he has turned in recent years to fiction, often informed by a meticulous study of history. His 2002 bestselling novel *Star of the Sea* explored the experiences of travellers on a famine ship sailing to the United States in 1847.

Seán Crosson

Books

Most of the books listed below should be available around the English-speaking world, though you may need to visit one of Ireland's many good bookshops to track down one or two.

Prose fiction

John Banville *The Sea*. One of Ireland's most innovative stylists, the former literary editor of the *Irish Times* won the 2005 Booker Prize for this tale of a widower returning to the seaside village where he spent a formative childhood summer.

Sebastian Barry *A Long Long Way*. Though better known as a playwright, Barry was nominated for the 2005 Booker Prize for this moving story, based on his grandfather's experiences, of a young Dubliner fighting for the British army in World War I, who questions his loyalties after the 1916 Easter Rising.

Dermot Bolger *The Valparaiso Voyage*. A tale of a violent homecoming, dealing with themes of political corruption and alienation in contemporary Ireland. *The Family on Paradise Pier* is a vivid account of an eccentric Protestant Big House family as their world collapses after 1915.

Ciaran Carson *Fishing for Amber*. A "long story" by one of Ireland's most original writers that pulls together Irish fairy tales, Ovid's *Metamorphoses* and the history of the Dutch Golden Age into the form of a magic alphabet. *Shamrock Tea* is a wildly imaginative fantasy based on a herbal remedy that can cleanse the windows of perception infiltrating a Belfast reservoir.

John Connolly *The Unquiet*. The latest blend of horror and suspense from Ireland's leading crime writer.

J.P. Donleavy *The Ginger Man*. Riotous and roguish, this is a semi-autobiographical tale of a Trinity College student, full of energy and humour, which unsurprisingly fell foul of the Irish censor in the 1950s.

Roddy Doyle *Barrytown Trilogy* (*The Commitments*, *The Snapper* and *The Van*). The former Dublin teacher made his name with these humorous tales of the ups and downs of working-class Dublin life, and later won the 1993 Booker Prize for *Paddy Clarke Ha Ha Ha*, which shifted the focus, still laced with comedy, to family breakdown. His latest work, *The Deportees and Other Stories*, which began life in *Metro Éireann*, a newspaper set up by two Nigerian journalists living in Dublin, deals with the multicultural "New Ireland".

Anne Enright *The Pleasure of Eliza Lynch*. Historical novel, based on the true story of the nineteenth-century Irish courtesan, who became the richest woman in the world, and her adventures in Paraguay. Enright's latest, *The Gathering*, a bleak, compelling tale of family dysfunction, won the 2007 Man Booker Prize.

Myles na gCopaleen *The Best of Myles*. Funny, quirky collection of *Irish Times* columns, under Flann O'Brien's other pseudonym.

Oliver Goldsmith *The Vicar of Wakefield*. Goldsmith used his experiences as the son of a clergyman to write his most successful novel, a masterpiece of gentle irony, laced with common-sense philosophical reflections.

Dermot Healy *Sudden Times.* A rich tale of paranoia, innocence and the tragedy of the working-class Irish in England.

James Joyce *Portrait of the Artist as a Young Man*; *Ulysses.* A largely autobiographical tale of a claustrophobic religious education and social oppression, *Portrait* is Joyce's most accessible novel, while *Ulysses* is one of the greatest modernist works, a stylistically brilliant parody of Homer's *Odyssey* that roams over Dublin in a single day.

Deirdre Madden *Authenticity.* Evocative and ambitious novel, both a love story and a reflection on being an artist in contemporary society.

Patrick McCabe *The Butcher Boy.* Darkly humorous tale of rural Ireland that was nominated for the Booker Prize. The funny and inventive *Emerald Germs of Ireland* is a dark fairy-tale for adults.

Colum McCann *This Side of Brightness.* McCann's breakthrough novel, a multiracial story set in New York, about survival and redemption, and the rise and fall of America.

John McGahern *The Leavetaking.* Semi-autobiographical tale, in which a teacher at a Clontarf national school reviews his life on the day he expects to be sacked for marrying an American divorcée. One of McGahern's finest works is *Amongst Women*, which details the final years and recollections of a disillusioned former IRA soldier, who dominates the women of his family on a small farm in the west of Ireland. *That They May Face the Rising Sun*, McGahern's last novel, is a dark and elegiac narrative set in rural County Leitrim (published as *By the Lake* in the US).

Bernard MacLaverty *Cal.* The Belfast-born writer's best-known book, which tells of the tragic relationship between a young IRA man and his victim's wife. He's recently followed it up with *The Anatomy School*, an exuberantly funny story of male adolescence in 1960s Belfast.

Eoin McNamee *The Ultras.* Dark, claustrophobic tale centred on the disappearance of a captain in the British Army Special Forces, employing the film noir and postmodern stylistics found in McNamee's earlier works, *Resurrection Man*, about the Shankill Butchers, and *The Blue Tango*, about a real-life murder.

Brian Moore *The Lonely Passion of Judith Hearne.* Set in Moore's native Belfast, a moving tale of a lonely Catholic woman's descent into alcoholism and mental breakdown.

Christopher Nolan *Under the Eye of the Clock.* Powerful, largely autobiographical story of a severely disabled boy's struggles and joys.

Flann O'Brien *At Swim-Two-Birds.* Hilariously subversive reworking of *Buile Shuibhne*, the medieval saga of the mad King Sweeney, in which the characters try to take control of the story from their "author". *The Third Policeman* is a darkly absurdist vision of Purgatory. See also Myles na gCopaleen, opposite.

Joseph O'Connor *Star of the Sea.* Rich, tragic historical thriller set on a refugee ship bound for New York in 1847. *Redemption Falls.* A gripping and often graphic tale of the exigencies of life for immigrants, revolutionaries and ne'er-do-wells in the post–Civil War US, given solidity by

O'Connor's sure narrative hold and a multiplicity of contemporary cultural references.

Seán O'Reilly *Love and Sleep*. A bleak, distinctive novel set in Derry, blending hard-edged realism with vivid, dream-like qualities.

Keith Ridgway *The Long Falling*. Ridgway's often harrowing debut novel is both a love story and murder story, set in a Dublin that is dangerous and alienating. He followed it up with *The Parts*, a compelling and stylistically inventive mystery, also set in Dublin.

Laurence Sterne *The Life and Opinions of Tristram Shandy, Gentleman*. An eighteenth-century comic masterpiece, described as "the greatest shaggy-dog story in the English language".

Bram Stoker *Dracula*. Stoker penned his most famous novel as a psychological thriller, though it's taken on a life of its own since then…

Eamon Sweeney *The Photograph*. Witty and erudite novel that deals with the big issues of religion and politics, and their role in Irish culture.

Jonathan Swift *Gulliver's Travels; The Tale of a Tub and Other Stories*. Glorious satires by the Dean of St Patrick's Cathedral, Dublin (see p.103).

Colm Tóibín *The Master*. Moving, beautifully crafted novel, dealing with the sexually repressed life of Henry James.

William Trevor *The Story of Lucy Gault*. Nominated for the Booker Prize, a powerful tale beginning in rural Cork – where Trevor was born – during the troubles of 1921 and telling the story of the disasters that ensued for one family.

Oscar Wilde *The Picture of Dorian Gray*. Wilde developed similar Gothic themes to his acquaintance Bram Stoker's in this novel, an allusive exploration of "the enemy within".

Poetry

Samuel Beckett *Poems 1930–1989*. The most complete collection of Beckett's poetry, in both English and French (with his own translations), and including translations of major twentieth-century French poets such as Rimbaud and Eluard.

Eavan Boland *Collected Poems*. Ireland's leading female poet, also a central voice in American poetic circles, explores the boundaries of women's experiences.

Paul Durcan *Greetings to Our Friends in Brazil*. Best of the recent offerings from this accessible Dublin-born poet. Many of the poems centre on a priest who, far from being repressive and hypocritical as in his earlier works, is honourable and truly spiritual.

Michael Hartnett *Collected Poems*. A richly lyrical and rhythmical collection covering Hartnett's forty-year career, compiled by Gallery Press since his recent death.

Seamus Heaney *Opened Ground: Poems 1966–96* is a huge selection of Heaney's work, which was followed by a dazzling collection, *Electric Light*. *Finders Keepers* is an anthology of his energetic prose, consisting of essays and lectures written between 1971 and 2001.

Patrick Kavanagh *Collected Poems*. Ireland's best-loved poet is perhaps most famous for *The Great Hunger*, in which he attacked sexual repression in 1940s Ireland.

Thomas Kinsella *Collected Poems: 1956–2001*. The full variety of Kinsella's work is on display here, employing modernist and traditional elements, on subjects ranging from love to political satire, social commentary and metaphysical speculation.

Michael Longley *Gorse Fires*; *The Ghost Orchid*; *The Weather in Japan*. Three fine collections, which show Longley as a highly skilled poet with a strong moral voice.

Nuala Ní Dhomhnaill *The Astrakhan Cloak*; *The Water Horse*. Good introductions to her work, in Irish and English, with translations in the former by Paul Muldoon, in the latter by Medbh McGuckian and Eileán Ní Chuilleanáin.

William Butler Yeats *The Poems* (published as *The Collected Poems* in the US). Love, anger, meditation and disillusionment from W.B., one of the greatest figures of twentieth-century literature.

Gaelic literature and folklore

Ciaran Carson *The Midnight Court*. Vibrant rendering of Brian Merriman's bawdy, eighteenth-century Gaelic poem, *Cúirt an Mheán Oíche*.

Kevin Danaher *In Ireland Long Ago*. Vivid and detailed, the classic work on all aspects of Irish folk life.

Seamus Heaney *Sweeney Astray*. The Nobel laureate's version of *Buile Shuibhne*, the twelfth- or thirteenth-century tale of Sweeney's mad wanderings and healing.

Thomas Kinsella *The Táin*. The best translation of the *Táin Bó Cúailnge* (The Cattle Raid of Cooley), the heroic centrepiece of the Ulster Cycle.

Tomás Ó Criomhthain (aka Thomas O'Crohan) *An tOileánach* (The Islandman). Vivid insights into the cruelties of life on the Blasket Islands, available in an authoritative new edition by Seán Ó Coileáin.

Maurice O'Sullivan *Twenty Years A-Growing*. The story of O'Sullivan's youth and the traditional way of life on the Blasket Islands in the early twentieth century, in a style derived from folk tales.

History and politics

Jonathan Bardon *A History of Ulster*. A comprehensive account from early settlements to the Troubles.

Angela Bourke *The Burning of Bridget Cleary*. Impeccably researched account of nefarious goings-on in Tipperary in the 1890s, describing the sensational case of a young woman supposedly taken by the fairies, tortured and murdered, and the subsequent trial of her husband, father, aunt and four cousins.

Tim Pat Coogan *Ireland in the Twentieth Century*. An engrossing account of political and social developments, both North and South, by the former editor of the *Irish Press*, who has written many readable histories that are worth seeking out, notably *The IRA*, *1916: The Easter Rising* and biographies of Michael Collins and Éamon de Valera. His *Wherever Green is Worn: The Story of the Irish Diaspora* is a ground-breaking account of Irish emigration and the impact of the émigrés on culture throughout the world.

Richard English *Irish Freedom: A History of Nationalism in Ireland*. Lucid and fascinating scholarly dissection of Irish nationalism over the last three centuries.

Diarmaid Ferriter *The Transformation of Ireland 1900–2000*. Extensive and insightful account of the making of modern Ireland, combining politics, economics and social history.

Garret FitzGerald *Reflections on the Irish State*. The former Taoiseach offers perceptive insights and challenging theories on the big issues of Irish public life.

R.F. Foster *Modern Ireland 1600–1972*. The best history of the period, authoritative and comprehensive, though heavy going at times for the lay reader. *The Irish Story: Telling Tales and Making It Up in Ireland* is a provocative, witty deconstruction of myth-making and clichés in Ireland's telling of its own history.

Tom Garvin *Preventing the Future: Why Was Ireland So Poor for So Long?* Perhaps the most important socio-historical analysis of post-war Ireland, not least in terms of the "lost" decades of the 1950s and 1960s. Garvin offers not only an acute analysis of the rotten core of Irish social policy but a persuasive and often witty account of its impact upon future generations.

Robert Kee *The Green Flag*. Lucid and incisive account of nationalism from the Elizabethan Plantations to "ourselves alone" after Independence.

Conan Kennedy *Ancient Ireland: The User's Guide*. Extremely useful descriptions of Ireland's various types of megalithic field monuments, plus a fascinating account of the place of magic, ritual and mythology.

Declan Kiberd *Inventing Ireland*. Witty, insightful and thought-provoking re-reading of the literature of the modern nation.

Christine Kinealy *This Great Calamity: The Irish Famine*. Unravels fact from fiction through systematic analysis of primary source material related to the Great Famine.

Henry McDonald *Colours: Ireland from Bombs to Boom*. *The Observer*'s Ireland correspondent takes his Belfast upbringing during the time of the Troubles as a base for a sparkling comparison between Ireland past and present.

Susan McKay *Northern Protestants: An Unsettled People*. Utterly grim but absolutely essential account of the North's Protestant community and its disparate views, based on numerous interviews, simultaneously offering hope for the future and showing sheer desperation.

David McKittrick and David McVea *Making Sense of the Troubles*. Clear, dispassionate and authoritative crash-course on the conflict.

Ed Moloney *A Secret History of the IRA*. Authoritative account, with Gerry Adams as its sinisterly intriguing central character, of the struggle within the Republican movement over the last forty years.

George Morrison *The Irish Civil War*. A powerful collection of photographic images of the Civil War, accompanied by commentary by Tim Pat Coogan.

Breandán Ó hEithir *The Begrudger's Guide to Irish Politics*. Astonishingly funny, acerbic and still relevant account of the Republic's political history, written exclusively from the aspect of the begrudger.

Henry Patterson *Ireland Since 1939: The Persistence of Conflict*. At times iconoclastic, Patterson's account of an Ireland divided not only by boundaries, but by ideologies and class-related interests, breaks new ground and provides utterly stimulating reading.

Peter Taylor *Provos: The IRA and Sinn Féin* (published in the US as *Behind the Mask*); *Loyalists* and *Brits: The War against the IRA*. Accompaniments to three fascinating BBC TV series, shedding welcome light on the mind-sets and development of the three protagonists in Northern Ireland, including eye-opening interviews with leading participants.

Colm Tóibín and Diarmaid Ferriter *The Irish Famine: A Documentary*. Highly readable and thought-provoking analysis of the Great Famine, which takes an incisive look at both the complex issues surrounding the failure of the potato crop, and the inadequacy of previous historical accounts of the crisis.

John Waters *An Intelligent Person's Guide to Modern Ireland*. A controversial book, by the *Irish Times*' gadfly columnist, arguing that the Irish have lost their cohesiveness in the drive for a "perverse and lonely" prosperity.

Biography and memoirs

Christy Brown *My Left Foot*. Born with cerebral palsy, Brown painstakingly typed out this unsentimental autobiography, published in 1954 when he was 22, focusing on his upbringing in a huge Dublin family, dominated by the remarkable character and endurance of his mother.

Ruth Dudley Edwards *James Connolly*. A short, direct biography of the socialist leader, which gathers pace around the time of his relations with Larkin, the 1913 Lock-Out in Dublin and the 1916 Rising.

Richard Ellmann *James Joyce*; *Oscar Wilde*. Ellmann's wonderful biography of Joyce is a literary masterpiece in its own right. His work on Wilde was, unfortunately, unfinished when he died, but is still an excellent insight into the work of this often misunderstood writer.

Christopher Fitz-Simon *The Boys*. Frank and conscientious biography of the founders of Dublin's Gate Theatre, Micheál Mac Liammóir and his equally mysterious lifelong lover, Hilton Edwards.

R.F. Foster *W.B. Yeats: A Life – Volume I, The Apprentice Mage*; *Volume II, The Arch-poet*. A magisterial work, the first fully authorized biography, incisive, exhaustive and compellingly readable.

James Knowlson *Damned to Fame: The Life of Samuel Beckett*. Excellent biography by one of the world's pre-eminent Beckett experts.

Hugh Leonard *Home before Night*; *Out after Dark*. Beautifully written evocations by the noted playwright of, respectively, his childhood and his adolescence in south Dublin around the 1940s. At times moving, often hilarious.

Antoinette Quinn *Patrick Kavanagh: A Biography*. Astute and often gently paced account of the life and poetry of County Monaghan's favourite son.

Music

Helen Brennan *The Story of Irish Dance*. Not just a fascinating history of the development of traditional dancing in Ireland, but a (literally) step-by-step guide to some of the most popular set-dances.

Victoria Mary Clarke and Shane MacGowan *A Drink with Shane MacGowan*. Shane's long-time – now former – partner takes the singer and songwriter through his personal history and several large martinis on the way.

Colin Harper and Trevor Hodgett *Irish Folk, Trad & Blues: A Secret History*. Fascinating accounts of key figures in Ireland's recent musical history, from Van the Man to Altan.

Colin Irwin *In Search of the Craic*. Wittily written account of a quest to hear some of the best of Ireland's traditional music.

Christy Moore *One Voice*. Not just a scintillating account of Moore's own life through song, but a hard-hitting analysis of Ireland over the last thirty years.

Pádraigín Ní Uallacháin *A Hidden Ulster*. Mammoth and utterly engrossing account of the Irish song tradition, centred on the area known as Oriel (containing parts of Armagh, Monaghan and Louth).

Francis O'Neill *The Dance Music of Ireland*. Known as "O'Neill's 1001" or to some musicians simply as "the book", this compiles 1001 of the best-known traditional tunes.

Tommy Sands *The Songman*. Illuminating, droll and incisive autobiographical account by the singer and broadcaster of growing up in 1950s rural Down, being enticed by and rejecting the idea of the priesthood, and moving on to a musical career whose increasingly sharp-edged political tone saw him play a pivotal role in the peace process.

Fintan Vallely (ed) *The Companion to Irish Traditional Music*. Provides constant delight in its copious accounts of the music's form, style and qualities, and brief biographies of many key participants; required reading.

Fintan Vallely and Charlie Piggott *Blooming Meadows: The World of Irish Traditional Musicians*. The fascinating biographical snapshots of a broad range of singers and musicians are enhanced by evocative photographs of their subjects.

Geoff Wallis and Sue Wilson *The Rough Guide to Irish Music*. A quintessential account of the roots and current state of traditional music in Ireland, containing a comprehensive directory of more than four hundred singers, musicians and groups, and details of the best places to see them in action.

Miscellaneous

Aalen, Stout and Whelan (eds) *Atlas of the Irish Rural Landscape*. Fascinating, lucid exploration of the geography and history of the Irish landscape, beautifully illustrated with photographs and maps. The recent *Newgrange and the Bend of the Boyne*, by Geraldine Stout, is the first of several planned offshoots of the atlas.

Deirdre and Laurence Flanagan *Irish Place Names*. Exhaustive guide to the names of over three thousand towns, villages and physical features and their derivations.

Pete McCarthy *McCarthy's Bar*. Runaway bestseller by the late, former travel-show presenter and stand-up comedian. An extended crawl around the *McCarthy's* bars of Ireland provides occasion for insight and plenty of irresistible humour.

Patrick McKay *A Dictionary of Ulster Place-Names*. Not just a cornucopia of etymological derivations but a veritable treasure-trove of information about almost every single place in the province of Ulster.

Eric Newby *Round Ireland in Low Gear*. Enjoyable account by the doyen of travel writers of a leisurely cycle trip around the country.

Tim Robinson *Connemara*. Fascinating story of the Roundstone area, ranging over everything from geology to folklore, written in a deceptively plain, easy style.

Paul Sterry *Complete Irish Wildlife*. Useful spotter's guide to Ireland's flora and fauna, with over a thousand photographs illustrating every species described.

Guides

Kevin Corcoran *West Cork Walks*, *Kerry Walks* and *West of Ireland Walks* (Counties Clare, Galway and Mayo). Also **Paddy Dillon** *The Mournes Walks* and *The Complete Ulster Way Walks*. A series of detailed, easy-to-follow guides published by O'Brien, covering mostly circular day-walks, with lots of information about the wildlife and landscape.

Cycling in the Southwest of Ireland; **Cycling in the Southeast of Ireland**; **Cycling in the North of Ireland** Collins guides, fully mapped in colour, each covering 25 routes ranging from short rides suitable for families to regional tours.

Pat Liddy *Secret Dublin*; *Walking Dublin*. Two beautifully written walking guides to the city, replete with historical insights and up-to-date information.

Joss Lynam (ed) *Best Irish Walks*. Authoritative and informative guide to over 75 hill walks all around Ireland. Lynam's *Easy Walks near Dublin* and the more recent *Leisure Walks near Dublin* each cover around forty mostly circular walks of between half an hour and three hours on the city's doorstep, mainly in the Wicklow Mountains.

John and Sally McKenna *The Bridgestone Irish Food Guide*. Hundreds of detailed reviews of cafés, restaurants, pubs serving meals, specialist shops, wine merchants, and even the best Irish chippers. Also by the same authors are a guide for vegetarians and annual round-ups of Ireland's hundred best restaurants and places to stay.

Language

Language

Language

You're most likely to hear the distinctive sounds of spoken Irish if you travel in the **Gaeltacht** regions, designated areas of Irish-speakers (*Gaeilgeoirí*), the largest of which are in Kerry, Galway and Donegal. Here in summer, you're likely to come on crowds of teenagers from all over Ireland who are passing through the annual ritual of Irish college, learning the language by immersion and spending a few precious weeks away from their parents. If you're interested in having a go yourself, well-respected courses are run by Gael Linn, 35 Dame St, Dublin (ⓣ01/675 1200 or 670 4180, ⓦwww.gael-linn.ie), whether in Dublin over six weeks or in summer staying for a week in the Donegal Gaeltacht; and by the excellent Oideas Gael in Glencolmcille, Donegal (see p.517). Among language-learning materials, Gael Linn produces *Gaeilge agus Fáilte*, an up-to-date, easy-to-follow combination of book and two cassettes aimed at adult beginners. Also recommended is *Teach Yourself Irish*, by Diarmuid O Sé and Joseph Sheils, a recently revised and updated course, with two cassettes or CDs.

Some history

Irish is one of the Celtic languages, along with Welsh and Breton, and belongs in particular to the **Gaelic** branch, sometimes known as **Goidelic**, which also includes Scottish Gaelic. The Celts first arrived in Ireland probably in the seventh century BC, and their language and culture had become dominant by around 300 BC. **Primitive Irish**, the earliest form known to us, is found only in **ogham** inscriptions on stone monuments, dating from the fifth to seventh centuries AD. This highly unusual script consists of tally-like notches cut along the edge of standing stones, rather than conventional letters.

In the next linguistic phase, **Old Irish** (seventh to ninth centuries), the language changed quickly, as Christian monks, now writing in Latin script, adopted a more colloquial form of Irish; from this period comes a fine body of lyric poetry and the earliest version of the *Táin Bó Cúailnge* ("The Cattle Raid of Cooley"), the central saga of the Ulster Cycle. **Middle Irish** (eleventh to thirteenth centuries) was a phase of linguistic confusion and new grammatical forms, with the language going into a decline after the twelfth-century Anglo-Norman conquest. By the fourteenth century it had recovered, entering the period known as **Early Modern** or **Classical Modern Irish**. The use of the language was now governed by the **filí**, a class of professional scholars and poets, among whom the most respected might have the status of a bishop or minor king. Meanwhile, the Anglo-Norman settlers had mostly integrated with the native population, adopting Irish language and customs.

In the seventeenth and eighteenth centuries, however, with the Flight of the Earls, Cromwell's Act of Settlement and the penal laws, the structures of traditional society were comprehensively destroyed. At the beginning of the nineteenth century, just under half the population was purely Irish-speaking, mostly in poor rural areas. These were the very areas, however, that were decimated by the Great Famine of the 1840s and the mass emigration that followed. As early as 1851, the proportion of Irish speakers had declined to a quarter of the population, and by the end of the century it was down to one percent.

Despite the tragic decline of Irish in the nineteenth century, several organizations dedicated to reviving its use sprang up, most notably the **Gaelic League** (Conradh na Gaeilge), founded in 1893 by Douglas Hyde and others. The League ensured that, after Independence in 1921, Irish was constitutionally recognized as the first official language, and was compulsory in the school system and for entry to the Civil Service. Today, over 1.4 million – nearly forty percent of the Republic's population – can speak Irish to a certain degree, 86,000 of whom live in the **Gaeltacht** areas, in counties Donegal, Mayo, Galway, Kerry, Cork, Waterford and Meath. A recent decline in the actual use of Irish in the *Gaeltachtaí* can be detected, however: a 1980s survey of schoolchildren there showed that nearly half of them spoke only English at home, while just twenty percent of them spoke only Irish.

On the other hand, there's been a remarkable recent growth throughout the island, both North and South, in the number of **Gaelscoileanna**, schools in which every subject is taught in Irish and which are known for their high general standards of education. From just sixteen such schools in the Republic in 1974, the figure had risen to 174 by 2001. In **the North**, where the British government is committed to supporting Irish-medium education, the use of Irish has naturally been more politicized. However, about ten percent of the North's population can now speak Irish, and since the Good Friday Agreement of 1998 there's been an all-Ireland body to promote the language, Foras na Gaeilge (Ⓦwww.gaeilge.ie), with offices in Belfast and Dublin.

For over thirty years now, the **Irish-language radio station**, Raidió na Gaeltachta, which is known especially for its support for traditional music, has been broadcasting all over the country from its base in Connemara; it's now 24-hour, with studios in all the Gaeltacht regions. In 1996, it was joined in Connemara by a **national television station**, TG4 (Teilifís na Gaeilge Cathair), which, through its often progressive and upbeat programming, has done much to reinvigorate the language.

Basic pronunciation of Irish

Irish **pronunciation** is notoriously difficult for outsiders, bearing little resemblance to English pronunciation. A few basic, simplified pointers are given below. To make matters even more challenging, however, Ulster, Connacht and Munster have distinct dialects, with different pronunciations and, to a lesser extent, grammars.

Vowels

Note the acute accent, a *fada*, which is used to lengthen vowels.

a as in "bat", or like the "o" in "slot"
á as in "paw"
e as in "bet"
é as in "prey"
i as in "bit"
í as in "machine"
o as in "ton"
ó as in "bone"
u as in "book"
ú as in "rule"

Consonants

Irish distinguishes between slender consonants – when beside an "e" or "i" – and broad consonants – when beside an "a", "o" or "u". For many consonants the slender pronunciation is different from the broad one.

bh broad, **mh** broad – "w" or "v"
bh slender, **mh** slender – "v"
c – always hard, as in "cot"
ch – like Scottish "loch"
d broad – "th" as in "this"
d slender – sharp "d", almost a "j" as in "jelly"

dh broad, **gh** broad – "gh", like a voiced version of "ch" in "Bach"

dh slender, **gh** slender – "y" as in yes

fh is silent

g – always hard, as in "gift"

ph – as in "phone"

s broad – "s" as in "some"

s slender – "sh" as in "sugar"

sh, th – "h" as in "hat"

t broad – aspirated, with the tongue against the upper teeth, somewhere between the "t" in "toad" and the "th" in "thin"

t slender – as the "t" in "tin"

A few simple phrases

Dia duit	Hello (lit. "God be with you")
Dia is Muire duit	Hello (in reply, lit. "God and Mary be with you")
Ceád míle fáilte	Welcome (lit. "a hundred thousand welcomes")
Cad is ainm duit?	What is your name?
… is ainm dom	My name is…
Conas atá tú?	How are you?
Go maith	Well
Más é do thoil é	Please
Go raibh (míle) maith agat	Thank you (very much)
Ní thuigim	I don't understand
Slán leat	Goodbye (to the person staying)
Slán agat	Goodbye (to the person leaving)
Slán	Bye (more informal)

Signs and place names: some common Irish terms

an lár	city centre
árd	height
áth	ford
baile	town – often anglicized as "bally"
beag	small – "beg"
bóthar	road
bun	base
caiseal	stone ring fort – "cashel"
caisleán	castle
carn	cairn
carraig	rock – "carrick"
cathair	fort – "caher"
ceann	head, headland – "can" or "ken"
cill	church – "kill" or "keel"
cnoc	hill – "knock"
doire	oak wood – "derry" or "dereen"
dún	fort
eaglais	church
fir	men
geill slí	give way
gleann	valley – "glen"
go mall	slow down
gort	field
inis	island – "inish"
leithreas	toilet
leitir	hillside – "letter"
lios	ring fort – "lis"
loch	lake – "lough"
mná	women
mór	big – "more"
mullach	summit – "mullagh"
oileán	island – "illaun"
páirc	field – "park"
ráth	ring fort
rinn	point – "reen"
ros	headland – "ross"
sliabh	mountain – "slieve"
sráid	street
teach, tí	house, cottage
teampall	church
tír	country – "tyr"
tobar	well
trá	beach

Glossary

Ascendancy The Protestant aristocracy, whether descended from Anglo-Normans granted land in Ireland or plutocrat planters subsequently installed in the country from the late sixteenth century onwards. Often prefixed by the term "Anglo-Irish".

bawn Fortification around a castle enclosure or cattlefold.

big house Mansion built by the Ascendancy.

Blue Flag beach Beach granted European Blue Flag status on the grounds of cleanliness, lack of sea pollution, and safety for swimming.

bodhrán (pronounced "bore-run" or "bough-ron" depending on the region of Ireland) A shallow, hand-held goatskin-frame drum, played either with a wooden beater or the hand.

B Specials Auxiliary Northern Irish police force formed after Partition and disbanded in 1971.

cashel A stone ring fort.

céilí/ceilidh An evening of Irish traditional dancing usually accompanied by a band.

clochán An early Christian beehive-shaped hut constructed of stones fitted tightly together without the use of mortar.

craic/crack General term for a good time, usually accompanying drinking. "What's the crack?" means "What's going on?"

crannóg A Bronze Age artificial island in a lough, constructed to camouflage an otherwise vulnerable dwelling.

Dáil Literally means "meeting", but has come to stand for the lower house of the Republic's parliament.

Diamond A central area in a planned Irish town, sometimes actually diamond-shaped, with streets surrounding an open space where usually some form of memorial is erected.

dolmen Dating from around 2500–2000 BC, a burial chamber set below an often triangular placement of standing stones, surmounted by an impressively weighty capstone. Also called a portal tomb.

drumlin A small oval hummock resulting from Ice Age glacial retreat.

DUP The Democratic Unionist Party. A staunchly traditional right-wing Loyalist party, cofounded by Ian Paisley in 1971, opposed to any attempts at loosening Northern Ireland's ties with the United Kingdom.

esker/eskar A ridge of gravel and sand formed by a retreating glacier.

famine wall/famine road An enterprise of local landowners during the Great Famine of 1845–51 whereby starving tenants would be rewarded for work given them to build a wall or road rather than aid through hunger-relieving largesse.

Fenian A member of the nineteenth-century revolutionary organization that fought for an independent Ireland; often used as an anti-Catholic term of abuse by Northern Irish Loyalists.

Fianna Fáil Irish Republic political party that emerged from the Civil War, opposing the partitioning treaty, to become a major force under its long-time leader Éamon de Valera. Still largely conservative in aspect, it has retained governmental control for most of the last eighty years, despite being embroiled in a farrago of financial and political scandals in recent decades.

Fine Gael The Republic's long-term and long-suffering (usually) opposition party, whose origins go back to Michael Collins' support for the Independence Treaty (see p.702). Little distinguishes it from Fianna Fáil, though its social policies seem a little more liberal, and its membership is largely drawn from agricultural areas.

Fleadh Literally meaning a "festival", the term has become associated with the Irish traditional-music organization Comhaltas Ceoltóirí Éireann's music competitions in which musicians and singers compete at county and provincial levels before going on to the annual Fleadh Cheoil na Éireann ("Ireland's music festival"). This also includes the winners of the UK and US *fleadhanna* (the plural of "fleadh").

Gaeltacht Regions of Ireland where the Irish language is the predominant vernacular tongue, mainly in the country's west.

gallowglass An armed mercenary in medieval times (from the Irish for "foreign soldier").

Garda Siochána The police force of the Republic of Ireland.

High cross A tall stone cross in which normally the cross itself is surrounded by a circle. The earliest known Irish examples date from the seventh century and are often richly ornamented with biblical scenes.

IRA Irish Republican Army. Longstanding upholders of the Republican drive to restore a united 32-county Ireland, based largely in the North. Particularly from the late 1960s onwards, it embarked on an armed struggle to force the British to withdraw from Ireland, with major bombing campaigns in the UK and Northern Ireland. The IRA unreservedly renounced its military initiatives in late 2005.

lough A commonly used term for lake; also a narrow coastal bay.

Loyalist Hardline Northern Irish Protestant loyal to the British Crown, sometimes linked to paramilitary activity.

LVF Loyalist Volunteer Force. Paramilitary group based around Portadown and founded by Billy Wright.

Martello tower Circular coastal tower built for defence during the Napoleonic wars.

MLA Member of the (Northern Ireland) Local Assembly.

motte An early medieval fortification, much used by the Normans, consisting of a circular earthwork mound, flattened on top, on which would be sited a primitive form of castle.

Nationalists Those wishing to achieve a united Ireland, usually by peaceful means.

The North Politically neutral euphemism for Northern Ireland.

ogham Ancient twenty-letter alphabet used in both Celtic and Pictish inscriptions on standing stones, comprising parallel carved lines or notches.

Orange Hall A local building where members of the Orange Order meet.

Orange Order Loyalist Protestant organization founded in 1795. Subdivided into local lodges, it derives its name from William of Orange (see p.659) and annually celebrates his victory over Catholic James II at the 1690 Battle of the Boyne on July 12 with parades across Northern Ireland. The majority of Unionist politicians and many Presbyterian clergymen belong to the Order.

Palladian A style of architecture derived from the designs of the Italian Andrea Palladio (1508–1580), whose work incorporated a rigid adherence to mathematical proportions, first promulgated by the Roman architect Vitruvius. Among the most stunning examples of Palladian architecture in Ireland are Castletown (see p.164), Russborough House (see p.156) and Florence Court (see p.686).

partition The division of Ireland into the 26 counties of the Republic and six of the North created by the 1921 Government of Ireland Act.

passage grave The oldest form of megalithic tomb, dating from around 4000 BC, consisting of a rounded mound or cairn with a stone-lined passage leading from the perimeter to a central chamber.

plantation The process of colonization of Ireland by the English Crown by which land was confiscated from the indigenous people and given to English and Scottish Protestant settlers.

portal tomb see "dolmen".

PSNI The Police Service of Northern Ireland (see "RUC").

rath or ring fort The most common form of ancient monument found in Ireland, dating from between the late Neolithic period and early medieval times. Consists of a circular (sometimes oval or D-shaped) enclosure surrounded by an earthen bank rising from a defensive ditch. A roofed dwelling, of stone or timber, would be constructed within the enclosure.

The Real IRA Breakaway political faction which rejects the Northern Ireland political process and maintains the armed struggle.

Republicans Supporters of the ideals incorporated in the 1916 Proclamation of the Republic, the overthrow of British rule in Ireland and the promotion of Irish language and culture.

ring fort see "rath".

round tower Usually part of a monastic settlement, these lofty and slenderly tapering, circular stone towers range in height from around 20 to 35 metres and were often capped with a conical roof. The earliest examples of this uniquely Irish construction date from around the ninth century. The building would have had a variety of purposes, serving as a belfry, a lookout post and a place for storage of goods and valuables. The entrance was often set some 3–5m above ground level, allowing the means of access, a ladder, to be withdrawn inside the building in case of a Viking raid, some claim.

RUC Royal Ulster Constabulary. The Northern Ireland police force from 1921 until 2001, when it was replaced by the Police Service of Northern Ireland.

SDLP Social Democratic and Labour Party. A left-of-centre Northern Irish Nationalist party, currently led by Mark Durkan.

Sheila-na-gig A carved stone representation of a squatting woman, often displaying an over-large vulva; believed to avert death and prevent evil, they are similar to the carvings of Yoni found on Hindu temples. Many Irish churches once bore these carvings, particularly above doors or windows, but they were often removed during the Victorian era. Well-preserved examples are visible on White Island, Co. Fermanagh, in Boyle Abbey and on the ruined church at Kilnaboy, Co. Clare.

Sinn Féin ("We, Ourselves"). Republican political party opposed to the 1921 political treaty that played a major role in the subsequent civil war. From the late 1970s onwards, and, allegedly, closely linked to the IRA, it rose to electoral prominence among the North's Catholics and achieved significant success in the Republic. Since 1983 its leader has been Gerry Adams, one of the key figures in the gradual move towards peace in Northern Ireland.

The Six Counties Nationalist/Republican euphemism for Northern Ireland.

souterrain Prehistoric underground passage which offered sanctuary for those fleeing their enemies; in some mythical locations, seen as an entry to the otherworld.

sweathouse A small stone-constructed, low-roofed building in which a turf fire was lit. Once sufficient heat had been generated those suffering from aches and pains or a fever would enter and would stay long enough to generate a sufficient sweat before emerging to take a dip in the nearest cold stream. In other words, an early Irish version of the sauna.

Taoiseach Prime minister of the Republic of Ireland.

TD Teachta Dála. Member of the lower house of the Republic's parliament (see "Dáil").

townland An area of land, similar to a parish, but not necessarily a village.

Troubles Euphemism for the vicious years of infighting and, from the Republican standpoint, resistance to British armed occupation of Northern Ireland that began in the late 1960s.

turlough A lake with a limestone base that causes water to drain away during drier months of the year.

Twenty-six counties Somewhat begrudging Republican description of the Republic of Ireland.

UDA (Ulster Freedom Fighyers) and **UFF** (Ulster Defence Association). Northern Irish Loyalist paramilitary organizations, linked to each other, which now seem more concerned about controlling the Northern Ireland drugs trade.

Ulster One of Ireland's four provinces, comprising Northern Irish counties Antrim, Armagh, Derry, Down, Fermanagh and Tyrone, plus Cavan, Donegal and Monaghan in the Republic. Often erroneously used by Unionists and journalists as a synonym for Northern Ireland.

Unionists A term describing those (mainly Protestant) who wish to maintain Northern Ireland's union with the UK.

UUP Ulster Unionist Party. The dominant party in Northern Ireland from 1921 to 1972, retaining control of its government for the period's entirety. Though initially retaining ascendancy under David Trimble following the enactment of the Good Friday Agreement in 1998, its support subsequently dwindled. It is currently led by Sir Reg Empey.

Travel store

Kenya
Marrakesh **D**
Morocco
South Africa, Lesotho & Swaziland
Syria
Tanzania
Tunisia
West Africa
Zanzibar

Travel Specials
First-Time Africa
First-Time Around the World
First-Time Asia
First-Time Europe
First-Time Latin America
Travel Health
Travel Online
Travel Survival
Walks in London & SE England
Women Travel
World Party

Maps
Algarve
Amsterdam
Andalucia & Costa del Sol
Argentina
Athens
Australia
Barcelona
Berlin
Boston & Cambridge
Brittany
Brussels
California
Chicago
Chile
Corsica
Costa Rica & Panama
Crete
Croatia
Cuba
Cyprus
Czech Republic
Dominican Republic
Dubai & UAE
Dublin
Egypt
Florence & Siena
Florida
France
Frankfurt
Germany
Greece
Guatemala & Belize
Iceland
India
Ireland
Italy
Kenya & Northern Tanzania
Lisbon
London
Los Angeles
Madrid
Malaysia
Mallorca
Marrakesh
Mexico
Miami & Key West
Morocco
New England
New York City
New Zealand
Northern Spain
Paris
Peru
Portugal
Prague
Pyrenees & Andorra
Rome
San Francisco
Sicily
South Africa
South India
Spain & Portugal
Sri Lanka
Tenerife
Thailand
Toronto
Trinidad & Tobago
Tunisia
Turkey
Tuscany
Venice
Vietnam, Laos & Cambodia
Washington DC
Yucatán Peninsula

Dictionary Phrasebooks
Croatian
Czech
Dutch
Egyptian Arabic
French
German
Greek
Hindi & Urdu
Italian
Japanese
Latin American Spanish
Mandarin Chinese
Mexican Spanish
Polish
Portuguese
Russian
Spanish
Swahili
Thai
Turkish
Vietnamese

Computers
Blogging
eBay
iPhone
iPods, iTunes & music online
The Internet
Macs & OS X
MySpace
PCs and Windows
PlayStation Portable
Website Directory

Film & TV
American Independent Film
British Cult Comedy
Chick Flicks
Comedy Movies
Cult Movies
Film
Film Musicals
Film Noir
Gangster Movies
Horror Movies
Kids' Movies
Sci-Fi Movies
Westerns

Lifestyle
Babies
Ethical Living
Pregnancy & Birth
Running

Music Guides
The Beatles
Blues
Bob Dylan
Book of Playlists
Classical Music
Elvis
Frank Sinatra
Heavy Metal
Hip-Hop
Jazz
Led Zeppelin
Opera
Pink Floyd
Punk
Reggae
Rock
The Rolling Stones
Soul and R&B
Velvet Underground
World Music (2 vols)

Popular Culture
Books for Teenagers
Children's Books, 5-11
Conspiracy Theories
Crime Fiction
Cult Fiction
The Da Vinci Code
His Dark Materials
Lord of the Rings
Shakespeare
Superheroes
The Templars
Unexplained Phenomena

Science
The Brain
Climate Change
The Earth
Genes & Cloning
The Universe
Weather

Small print and Index

A Rough Guide to Rough Guides

Published in 1982, the first Rough Guide – to Greece – was a student scheme that became a publishing phenomenon. Mark Ellingham, a recent graduate in English from Bristol University, had been travelling in Greece the previous summer and couldn't find the right guidebook. With a small group of friends he wrote his own guide, combining a highly contemporary, journalistic style with a thoroughly practical approach to travellers' needs.

The immediate success of the book spawned a series that rapidly covered dozens of destinations. And, in addition to impecunious backpackers, Rough Guides soon acquired a much broader and older readership that relished the guides' wit and inquisitiveness as much as their enthusiastic, critical approach and value-for-money ethos.

These days, Rough Guides include recommendations from shoestring to luxury and cover more than 200 destinations around the globe, including almost every country in the Americas and Europe, more than half of Africa and most of Asia and Australasia. Our ever-growing team of authors and photographers is spread all over the world, particularly in Europe, the USA and Australia.

In the early 1990s, Rough Guides branched out of travel, with the publication of Rough Guides to World Music, Classical Music and the Internet. All three have become benchmark titles in their fields, spearheading the publication of a wide range of books under the Rough Guide name.

Including the travel series, Rough Guides now number more than 350 titles, covering: phrasebooks, waterproof maps, music guides from Opera to Heavy Metal, reference works as diverse as Conspiracy Theories and Shakespeare, and popular culture books from iPods to Poker. Rough Guides also produce a series of more than 120 World Music CDs in partnership with World Music Network.

Visit www.roughguides.com to see our latest publications.

Rough Guide travel images are available for commercial licensing at www.roughguidespictures.com.

Rough Guide credits

Text editor: Helena Smith
Layout: Ajay Verma
Cartography: Animesh Pathak
Picture editor: Sarah Cummins
Production: Rebecca Short
Proofreader: Diane Margolis
Cover design: Chloë Roberts
Editorial: **London** Ruth Blackmore, Alison Murchie, Karoline Densley, Andy Turner, Keith Drew, Edward Aves, Alice Park, Lucy White, Jo Kirby, James Smart, Natasha Foges, Róisín Cameron, Emma Traynor, Emma Gibbs, Kathryn Lane, Christina Valhouli, Monica Woods, Joe Staines, Peter Buckley, Matthew Milton, Tracy Hopkins, Ruth Tidball; **New York** Andrew Rosenberg, Steven Horak, AnneLise Sorensen, April Isaacs, Ella Steim, Anna Owens, Sean Mahoney; **Delhi** Madhavi Singh, Karen D'Souza
Design & Pictures: **London** Scott Stickland, Dan May, Diana Jarvis, Mark Thomas, Nicole Newman, Emily Taylor;
Delhi Umesh Aggarwal, Jessica Subramanian, Ankur Guha, Pradeep Thapliyal, Sachin Tanwar, Anita Singh, Nikhil Agarwal
Production: Vicky Baldwin
Cartography: London Maxine Repath, Ed Wright, Katie Lloyd-Jones; **Delhi** Jai Prakash Mishra, Rajesh Chhibber, Ashutosh Bharti, Rajesh Mishra, Jasbir Sandhu, Karobi Gogoi, Amod Singh, Alakananda Bhattacharya, Swati Handoo
Online: Narender Kumar, Rakesh Kumar, Amit Verma, Rahul Kumar, Ganesh Sharma, Debojit Borah, Saurabh Sati
Marketing & Publicity: **London** Liz Statham, Niki Hanmer, Louise Maher, Jess Carter, Vanessa Godden, Vivienne Watton, Anna Paynton, Rachel Sprackett; **New York** Geoff Colquitt, Megan Kennedy, Katy Ball; **Delhi** Ragini Govind
Manager India: Punita Singh
Reference Director: Andrew Lockett
Publishing Coordinator: Helen Phillips
Publishing Director: Martin Dunford
Commercial Manager: Gino Magnotta
Managing Director: John Duhigg

Publishing information

This 9th edition published April 2008 by
Rough Guides Ltd,
80 Strand, London WC2R 0RL
345 Hudson St, 4th Floor,
New York, NY 10014, USA
14 Local Shopping Centre, Panchsheel Park,
New Delhi 110017, India
Distributed by the Penguin Group
Penguin Books Ltd,
80 Strand, London WC2R 0RL
Penguin Group (USA)
375 Hudson Street, NY 10014, USA
Penguin Group (Australia)
250 Camberwell Road, Camberwell,
Victoria 3124, Australia
Penguin Books Canada Ltd,
10 Alcorn Avenue, Toronto, Ontario,
M4V 1E4 Canada
Penguin Group (NZ)
67 Apollo Drive, Mairangi Bay, Auckland 1310,
New Zealand

Cover concept by Peter Dyer.

Typeset in Bembo and Helvetica to an original design by Henry Iles.

Printed and bound in China.

776pp includes index

A catalogue record for this book is available from the British Library

ISBN: 978-1-85828-056-1

1 3 5 7 9 8 6 4 2

Help us update

We've gone to a lot of effort to ensure that the ninth edition of **The Rough Guide to Ireland** is accurate and up to date. However, things change – places get "discovered", opening hours are notoriously fickle, restaurants and rooms raise prices or lower standards. If you feel we've got it wrong or left something out, we'd like to know, and if you can remember the address, the price, the hours, the phone number, so much the better.

Please send your comments with the subject line "**Rough Guide Ireland Update**" to Ⓔmail@roughguides.com. We'll credit all contributions and send a copy of the next edition (or any other Rough Guide if you prefer) for the very best emails.

Have your questions answered and tell others about your trip at Ⓦcommunity.roughguides.com.

Acknowledgements

The authors would like to thank: Tourism Ireland; Dublin Tourism; Fáilte Ireland and other tourist offices across Ireland; Ireland's Blue Book; the Irish Hotels Federation and, especially, Joy Bradley; Seán Crosson for the literature section; and our editor, Helena Smith.

Paul would also like to thank: Emma Gorman; Sinéad Barden and Sam Johnston; the Cailìn Óir; Aran Island Ferries; Doolin Ferries; the Island Discovery; Frank Shalvey at the OPW; Mazz O'Flaherty at Dingle Record Shop; Anne and Agnes; Ursula Roncken; James McConnachie; Alexia, Andy, Sarah, John and Kate Grier; Will, Sarah, Eleanor and Ben Jacob; Jack Grassby; and Bill Gray.

Geoff would also like to thank the Northern Ireland Tourist Board; the IHH; the IHO; HINI; An Óige; PJ Curtis and Holly; Éamonn Jordan and Mireille Cambier; Seán McCloskey; the Charles Stewart; Finbar Boyle; Ronan Browne and family (especially the pink wasp); Joanie McDermott; Hugh Gallagher; Ian and Bríde Smith; Paul and Katherine at Tessie's; Bartley Brennan; Tony Hughes and the lads; Sheila Deegan; and Dermot the Plumber.

Readers' letters

Thanks to all the readers who have taken the time to write in with comments and suggestions (and apologies if we've inadvertently omitted or misspelt anyone's name):

Els Acke, Linda Auty, John Benson, Alison Bevan, Jill Bickerton, Katie Boon, Shane Cahill, Paul Carroll, Adrian Cosby, Barbara and David Cross, Jane Darke, Martin Dunne, George Flanders, Paul Foreman, D. L. French, Ronan Garvey, Mary Gleeson, Verity Gorry, Nicholas Groves, Peter Gumbrell, The Hickey family, Charlotte Hodkinson, Malcolm James, Michael and Elizabeth Johnson, Desmond Julian, Gill Kaye, Tom Kelley, W. J. C. Kitto, Sarah Lane, Clare Leon, Caroline Lynch, Christine Maddison, Louise Maher, James McConachie, Harry McKone, Heather Moat, Theresa Morrow, Gillian O'Driscoll, Catherine O'Grady-Powers, John and Joan O'Hare, Ronald Orton, Wouter Piesens, John Richards, Philip Ryan, Paul Schuller, Mike Spillane, Alan Sweeny, Marion Thomas, Pam Walker, Hannah Westland, Helen Wiffen and Patrick Worth

Photo credits

All photos © Rough Guides except the following:

Cover

Front image: Seascape, Inishowen Peninsula, Trawbreaga Bay © Ripani Massimo/ 4cornersimages
Back image: Kinsale, Cork © Alamy

Title page

Walker on the summit of Benchoona, Connemara © Gareth McCormack/Alamy

Introduction

Puffins on Skellig © Michael Gareth McCormack/ Alamy
Church painting © Alamy
Carved spiral and chevron motifs, Newgrange © David Lyons/Alamy
Cross © Axiom
Kilkenny pub door and sign © Peter Horree/ Alamy
Gaelic football © Getty

Things not to miss

01 Surfers © David Lyons/Alamy
05 Ulster Folk and Transport Museum © Ulster Folk and Transport Museum
06 Satellite tombs at Knowth © Martyn Vickery/ Alamy
07 Dun Aengus © Alamy
08 Or in the National Museum © INTERFOTO Pressebildagenteur/Alamy
10 Hill walkers © Alan Reevell /Alamy
13 Horn Head Co Donegal © Stephen Emerson/ Alamy
16 Connemara, fishing port © Robert Harding Picture Library/Alamy
17 Horse racing © Sportsfile
18 Italianate garden on Garinish Island © Alamy
22 Strangford Lough, Scrabo Tower © David Lyons/Alamy
23 Derry murals © Isifa Image Service s.r.o/Alamy
24 Killarney National Park, Upper Lake © BL Images LTD/Alamy
25 Festival, St Patrick's Day © Robert Harding Picture Library/Alamy
26 Bloomsday © Corbis
27 Horse riding on the beach © Barry Lewis/ Alamy
30 Walking © Gareth McCormack/Alamy
31 Skellig Michael Co Kerry © Robert Harding Picture Library/Alamy

Black and whites

p201 Ruins of Drumlane © Isifa Image Service s.r.o/Alamy
p216 Clonmacnois beside the River Shannon © Siegfried Kuttig/Alamy
p282 Fota House and Garden © Stephen Saks Photography/Alamy
p328 Beehive huts on Skellig Michael © Alamy
p417 Lynch's Castle © Leslie Garland Picture Library/Alamy
p521 John Doherty © Eamonn O'Doherty
p528 Mount Errigal, Donegal © Eye Ubiquitous/ Alamy
p515 Cliffs of Teelin © Daryl Webb/Alamy
p539 Beltany stone circle © Jon Sullivan
p550 The Laganside © J Orr/Alamy
p566 Botanic Gardens, Belfast © scenicireland .com/Alamy
p573 Crown bar, National Trust pub © Alamy
p597 Giants Causeway coast © David Lyons/ Alamy
p609 Derry Ireland cannon © David Lyons/Alamy
p673 Beaghmore stone circles, Co Tyrone © Alamy
p700 Éamon de Valera © Hulton-Deutsch Collection/Corbis
p715 Christy Moore © S.I.N/Corbis
p720 Oscar Wilde © Bettmann/Corbis

Colour inserts

Festivals

St Patrick's Day parade © Robert Harding/Jupiter Images
Boy with a hat. St Patrick's Day parade © J Orr/Alamy
Galway Arts Festival © Paul Lindsay/Alamy
Cork Jazz Festival © Andia.fr/Digital Rail Road
Puck Fair © Patrick Ward/Alamy
Raft racing © Irish Image collection

Food and drink

Oysters and Guinness © Corbis
Market in Cork © Chris Rout/Alamy
Traditional Irish stew © foodfolio/Alamy

Index

Map entries are in colour.

C

D

INDEX

INDEX

L

M

N

O

P

Q

R

S

T

U

V

W

Y